PSYCHOLOGY
THE SCIENCE OF BEHAVIOUR

'It is well written and really explains things. You could be confident that a student could come to grips intellectually with arguments on the basis of the text alone ... The Psychology in Action sections are of high quality and the overall level of analysis in the book is very high for an introductory textbook.'
Paddy O'Donnell, Glasgow University, Scotland.

'I would recommend the text, which I consider to be of a very high standard. The Controversies in Psychology feature seems to be an excellent idea. Questions such as "Is psychology common sense?" are most suitable for tutorial and seminar groups.'
Tony Shelton, The Centre for Applied Psychology, School of Human Sciences, Liverpool John Moores University, England.

'Well written, very up to date and giving a fine picture of what modern psychology is all about ... I was very impressed by this text and thoroughly enjoyed reading it.'
Dr Jimmie Thomson, Strathclyde University, Scotland.

'Written in a lively style that is clear, interesting and easy to read ... Suggested further reading is excellent.'
Professor Gillian Cohen, The Open University.

'The approach is refreshing ... The text is well written.'
Professor Paul Emmelkamp, Amsterdam University, The Netherlands.

'The chapters are well organised, written very clearly and contain up-to-date research evidence. The frequent references to European research are impressive and refreshing.'
Professor Aidan Moran, University College Dublin, Ireland.

'Well written ... should provide a good, interesting and comprehensive introduction to the field.'
Dr Trevor Harley, University of Dundee, Scotland.

PSYCHOLOGY
THE SCIENCE OF BEHAVIOUR

EUROPEAN ADAPTATION

NEIL R CARLSON
University of Massachusetts

WILLIAM BUSKIST
Auburn University

G NEIL MARTIN
Middlesex University

MICHAEL HOGG
University of Queensland

DOMINIC ABRAMS
University of Kent

ALLYN AND BACON

An imprint of **PEARSON EDUCATION**

Harlow, England · London · New York · Reading, Massachusetts · San Francisco · Toronto · Don Mills, Ontario · Sydney
Tokyo · Singapore · Hong Kong · Seoul · Taipei · Cape Town · Madrid · Mexico City · Amsterdam · Munich · Paris · Milan

To Paula, for being there when I couldn't be.
She was the force that through the green fuse drove this flower.

Pearson Education Limited

Edinburgh Gate
Harlow
Essex CM20 2JE
England

and Associated Companies around the world

Visit us on the World Wide Web at:
www.pearsoneduc.com

Original edition published by
Allyn and Bacon
Needham Heights
Massachusetts, USA
Copyright © 1997 by Prentice-Hall, Inc.

This edition first published by
Pearson Education Limited in Great Britain in 2000.

Authorised for sale only in Europe, The Middle East and Africa.

© Pearson Education Limited 2000

The right of Neil R Carlson, William Buskist and G Neil Martin
to be identified as authors of this work has been asserted by them
in accordance with the Copyright, Designs and Patents Act 1988.

ISBN 0 130 21228 8

British Library Cataloguing in Publication Data
A CIP catalogue record for this book can be obtained from the British Library.

10 9 8 7 6 5 4 3 2 1

Typeset by 42
Printed and bound by Rotolito Lombarda, Italy

Note: Every effort has been made to trace and acknowledge ownership of
copyright. The publishers will be pleased to hear from any copyright holders
whom it has not been possible to contact.

We are grateful to the National Library of Medicine,
Bethesda, MD, for the pictures on pp. 17, 18, 24 and 26,
and to the Archives of the History of American Psychology
for the picture on p. 20. Figure 12.5 is reproduced by courtesy of
J. Campos, B. Bertenthal and R. Kermoran.

CONTENTS

PREFACE

Imagine what brought you to pick up this book and read it. You might be an undergraduate on a psychology course and have spotted this book in your library or bookshop. Your tutor or friend might have recommended it to you. You might have been at a friend's house, become bored and begun leafing through this book lying on a table. You might have been attracted to the cover. You might even have liked the authors' other books so much you had to read this one as well.

This very simple exercise illustrates the essence of psychology – the scientific study of why and how humans (and animals) behave in the way that they do. Psychology is the science of behaviour and, being a science, it approaches the understanding of behaviour in a different way from that normally taken by the lay public. Everyone has an opinion on psychology and on what motivates people and what brings people to react and behave in the way that they do. Psychologists, however, attempt to understand behaviour through careful experimentation and empirical observation. They do this because they believe that this provides us with better, reliable information about behaviour and the causes of behaviour. This book introduces you to the scientific approach to understanding human behaviour and in each of the chapters it reviews the current state of knowledge about behaviour – from intelligence and emotion to child development and prejudice – based on sound scientific study.

Let us go back to the opening paragraph. The reason you are reading this book is probably because it is recommended on your psychology course or because you have spotted it in the library or bookshop and think that it will give you good value for money. As a student of psychology, you are studying the most fascinating and complex subject matter in science – human behaviour. You will study not just how individuals develop language, perceive visual images, reason, feel, respond to others and learn, but also the biological bases of these behaviours. You will learn about the various methods that psychologists adopt when studying behaviour and how people evolved to do the things that they do (although scientists do have disagreements over the best method of study to adopt – the one certain fact you will learn in psychology is that no finding is ever 'cut and dried', there is always discussion and controversy).

A well-known teacher of psychology has described the skills that students obtain after studying a degree in psychology. This is the list of those skills:

- Literacy
- Numeracy
- Computer literacy
- Research skills
- Information-finding skills
- Measurement skills
- Environmental awareness
- Interpersonal awareness
- Problem-solving skills
- Critical evaluation
- Perspectives
- Higher-order analysis
- Pragmatism

With skills like these, you might wonder why anyone should bother studying any other type of degree! Psychology is one of the most popular degree courses in Europe and in North America. The subject matter is intrinsically interesting and the methods of studying this subject matter allow students to develop what are called in management-speak, 'transferable skills' – skills such as operating a computer, writing laboratory reports, producing clear and evaluative written work, performing statistical operations, using computer software packages, designing projects, using statistical computer packages, presenting material to an audience ... all of these, in addition to understanding specific aspects of human behaviour such as how children learn to read, why we perceive in the way that we do, how the brain works, how we reason and so on.

This book is designed to give you a flavour of what modern psychology is about. It describes every major

xv

field of psychology and includes up-to-date information and clear evaluation of controversial findings, theories and models in psychology. The book is a new, thoroughly revised edition of Carlson and Buskist's *Psychology: The science of behavior*. This revision is different because it features a massive expansion in the material covered and an increase in the amount of up-to-date findings. The book also has several new features to help you understand the applications and controversies in psychology and to make you think more deeply about psychological issues and psychological research. These features are described below.

Controversies in psychological science (CiPS)

Each chapter contains at least one section which focuses on a controversy in psychological science. The best advice I was given by my tutor as an undergraduate was, 'question everything'. By this, he did not mean criticizing studies or theories for the sake of it. He meant that psychology was a live, constantly evolving science which, like all sciences, progresses by contradiction: somebody reports a finding; another refines this finding by showing that it applies only to certain contexts, people, conditions and so on. Most introductory texts can appear biblical: unquestionable towers of knowledge. But, although a great deal of fact is presented in this text, it also shows you how facts can be interpreted in different ways.

The CiPS sections are made up of three parts. The first part (the issue) outlines the controversy; the second part (the evidence) describes and evaluates the data that give rise to the controversy; finally, the third part (conclusion) briefly suggests what we can conclude from the evidence available. One aim of the CiPS is to engage you in critical thinking by presenting you with a controversial topic, theme or idea in psychology and take you through evidence for and against a topic, theme or idea. Some of these controversies are well known if ill understood (for example: Is intelligence racially determined? Can children's IQ be affected by vitamin intake? Can primates learn language?). Others are not so well known but cast some useful light on some aspect of psychology and behaviour (for example: Can music improve cognitive performance? Is psychology common sense? Is the diagnosis of mental disorder culture-free?). Such controversies should give you a flavour of the liveliness of debate surrounding some issues in psychology and could form the basis of discussion with your fellow students or with colleagues in tutorials or seminars.

Psychology in action (PiA)

Each chapter contains a section which gives an example of psychology in action. Research in psychology is aimed at exploring, defining and predicting the causes of behaviour. Some of it is also aimed at using such research in an applied, practical setting. The PiA sections review the evidence for the application of psychological principles to a 'real-life' issue (such as using CCTV to identify criminals, or believing in the paranormal or in astrology, or working as a forensic psychologist). Chapter 17 on mental disorders is almost a whole PiA section in itself because it describes the study and treatment of mental illness. These sections aim to show you how principles from psychology can be used to help us to understand why we behave in the way that we do.

What you should be able to do after reading the Chapter

At the beginning of each chapter there is a brief outline of what the chapter contains. There is a list of questions for you to think about before embarking on your reading and also a section on what you should be able to do after reading the chapter. This last section should provide you with a set of goals that you should try to achieve. These should be your learning objectives.

Questions to think about

In addition to the questions for you to think about which appear at the beginning of each chapter, there are further questions for you to think about featured at the end of each major section within each chapter. The 'Questions to think about' feature has been designed to help you ask questions about your knowledge of psychology and to probe what you have learned from the chapters. There are different forms of 'Questions to think about': some are straightforward and factual, others are more like essay or assignment questions designed to make you think more deeply about psychological issues and psychological evidence; still others expect you to generate your own ideas, suggestions and experiments about psychology. All of them, however, should provoke you into thinking about psychological issues and ideas.

Chapter reviews

At the end of each chapter there is a summary of the information that has gone before. The summary has been bullet-pointed to make it easier to read and understand.

Key terms and glossary

Each chapter ends with a list of key terms: important terms that you should learn because they are essential. These terms appear in bold when first introduced in the text and are defined when they appear. They have also been collected together and appear alphabetically, with definitions, in a glossary at the end of the book.

Suggestions for further reading and journals to consult

As an intelligent reader of an introductory textbook you will be hungry for more psychological knowledge after having tasted this starter. The suggestions for further reading are designed to satisfy your appetite. All the recommended readings come with comments from the adapting author and these comments should help you to decide on what further reading is best for you. Some of the reading is quite advanced; other readings are less demanding. You should try to consult at least a few of these per chapter because the further reading will lead you into more detailed description and discussion of psychological topics.

In addition to the further reading, I have added a list of journals for you to consult. About 90 per cent of the facts, theories and ideas that you read about in this book have been published in science journals and there are many different types of journal in psychology. This is where original research, theories and methods in psychology are published. If you want to go direct to the source of psychological research then journals are the place to go. You might find much of the material in them deeply unattractive, incomprehensible or abstruse. However, you will also find material that is original and new. Textbook authors are a little like journalists reporting the events and people that they think readers will be interested in. Of course, textbook authors have few of the failings of journalists but they can only give you a brief glimpse of the events that they report. The beauty of psychology is that you can consult the source yourself and the journals listed should help you do this.

Websites

Following the annotated suggested reading, I have included, for each chapter, the Internet addresses of some websites which I think are worth visiting. Some of these give you more information about the general or specific issues raised in the chapter (so some sites recommended for the chapter on perception, for example, give you general information about perception whereas others provide you with more information about the perception of faces, say); some provide you with online tutorials, or virtual libraries, or bibliographies.

All of these new features, together with the radical revision of the text to make it up-to-date and comprehensive should provide you with an effective learning tool. To familiarise yourself with these features and how they will benefit your study of this text, they are reproduced and described in the Guided tour which follows.

Guided tour

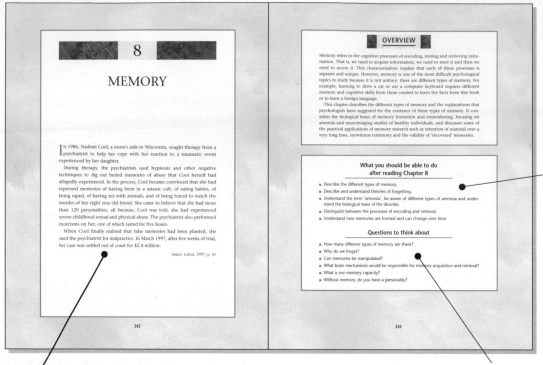

What you should be able to do after reading this chapter provides a set of goals that you should try to achieve by the end of the chapter.

Each chapter opens with a brief **vignette** which gives a flavour of the material in the chapter. This is followed by an **Overview** of the specific chapter.

The **Questions to think about** are things to think about before beginning to read the chapter.

Controversies in psychological science sections in each chapter give an idea of how one issue can be interpreted differently and hence the lively debate that surrounds certain issues.

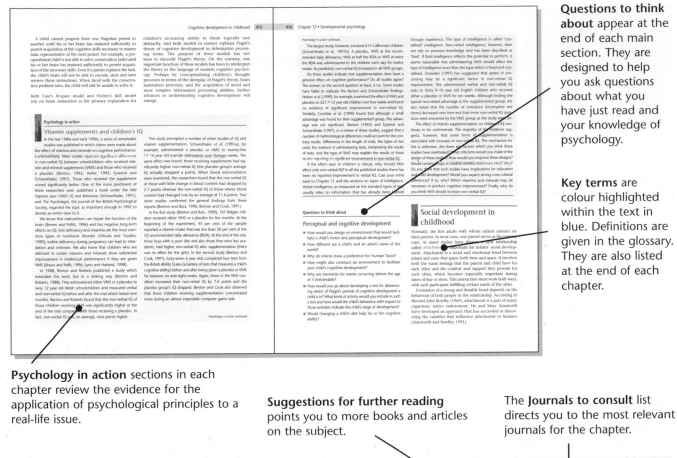

Questions to think about appear at the end of each main section. They are designed to help you ask questions about what you have just read and your knowledge of psychology.

Key terms are colour highlighted within the text in blue. Definitions are given in the glossary. They are also listed at the end of each chapter.

Psychology in action sections in each chapter review the evidence for the application of psychological principles to a real-life issue.

Suggestions for further reading points you to more books and articles on the subject.

The **Journals to consult** list directs you to the most relevant journals for the chapter.

Key terms are listed at the end of each chapter with page references to aid revision.

Chapter reviews at the end of each chapter enable you to review what you have covered.

A list of **Websites** at the end of each chapter points you to sites worth visiting for information about specific or general issues within the chapter.

The teaching/learning package

Lecturer's Resource Manual

Dr Nicky Brunswick of Middlesex University has developed an innovative *Lecturer's Resource Manual* to accompany the text, adapted from the *Instructor's Resource Manual* of *Psychology: The Science of Behavior* by Bill Buskist of Auburn University.

The *Manual* is designed to provide the tutor or lecturer with the tools to deliver the text material effectively and to provide students with a valuable learning experience. It includes:

- chapter overviews;
- chapter objectives with the reference to the relevant text pages;
- ten tutorial/seminar ideas per chapter;
- more than one hundred handouts to use for demonstrations;
- ten essay questions per chapter;
- ideas on relevant websites for each chapter and how they can be used for teaching.

CD-ROM

The *Lecturer's Resource Manual* is supported by a CD-ROM containing PowerPoint slides of the key figures from the text, and a test item file.

The test item file has also been prepared by Nicky Brunswick of Middlesex University. There are approximately 3,000 multiple-choice or true/false questions. The questions are divided into three levels of difficulty – easy, moderate and difficult.

Psychology Website

Address: www.booksites.net/carlson

The website for *Psychology* provides additional material to promote learning and thinking by students. Student quizzes allow the students to test themselves and on-line exercises promote their use of the Internet. Regular updates provide users with access to new research.

Lecturers will have access to the *Lecturer's Resource Manual* and PowerPoint slides.

I very much hope that you will learn a lot about psychology from this edition of *Psychology*. I also hope that you enjoy what you learn and that the book will take you to places you had not thought of exploring. This is the beauty of psychology. Opening one door will lead you to several others. If you like what you have read, then please do let me know. One of the joys of teaching and researching is obtaining feedback about the work that you produce. If you have any comment to make or suggestion for improvement, then please write to me at the School of Social Science, Middlesex University, Queensway, Enfield, London, EN3 4SF, UK, or email me at: n.martin@mdx.ac.uk.

You can visit my website at:
www.apx.mdx.ac.uk/www/psychology/sinfo/Nmartin.htm

G. Neil Martin
London, 1999

THE AUTHORS

Dr G. Neil Martin is the youngest principal lecturer in psychology at Middlesex University, where he has taught and undertaken research since 1994. He graduated with a first-class Master of Arts degree in psychology from the University of Aberdeen, Scotland, where he also won the annual Henry Prize for outstanding academic achievement in psychology. He completed his PhD on the psychophysiology of olfactory perception at the University of Warwick, where his thesis was examined by E.T. Rolls and John Annett.

He is the author of *Human Neuropsychology* (Prentice Hall Europe), the first European textbook on general human neuropsychology, and is associate editor of *The Psychologist*, the official journal of the British Psychological Society. He is a member of *The Psychologist* policy committee and the Committee of the British Psychophysiology Society. He was honorary secretary of the British Psychophysiology Society from 1996 to 1999 and was editor of the *British Psychophysiology Society Quarterly* during the same period.

He researches in the area of olfaction, psychophysiology, humour and perceptions about psychological research. His work on human olfaction was recently recognised by the Royal Society of Arts, Manufactures and Commerce when he was asked to address its Fellows. In 1998, he published the world's first systematic study of the effect of synthetic and real food aroma on human brain activity. He also works as a freelance journalist; his first article for a major national newspaper was entitled 'More than 20 things you needed to know about the nose'.

Dr Neil R. Carlson is Professor of Psychology at the University of Massachusetts. He studied as an undergraduate and postgraduate at the University of Illinois.

He wrote his first textbook, *Physiology of Behavior*, while on sabbatical leave at the University of Victoria in British Columbia. He was the first Allyn and Bacon author to submit a book manuscript on a computer disk. Now the publisher requires that manuscripts be submitted that way.

A few years ago he began to collaborate with Jay Alexander, an artist who works as a lab technician at the University of Massachusetts. They prepare all the artwork for Professor Carlson's books.

Dr William Buskist is Professor of Psychology at Auburn University, where he regularly teaches the introductory psychology and the teaching of psychology courses. He has directed Auburn's Psychology Research Laboratories. He also teaches seminars and workshops for undergraduates who are preparing for graduate study in psychology.

He graduated from Brigham Young University in 1981 with a PhD in experimental psychology. Although most of his research has been in the area of human social behaviour, particularly competitive behaviours, Dr Buskist's research now largely focuses on issues in the teaching of psychology.

Dr Michael Hogg is Professor of Social Psychology and Director of the Centre for Research on Group Processes at the University of Queensland, Brisbane. He obtained his BSc at Birmingham University in the UK and, in 1984, his PhD at Bristol University, also in the UK. He has held faculty teaching positions at Bristol University in the UK, at the University of Melbourne and the University of Queensland in Australia, and at Princeton University in the USA; and research positions at Macquarie University, Sydney, the University of California, Los Angeles, and University of California, Santa Cruz.

He serves on the editorial board of numerous journals, including *Journal of Personality and Social Psychology*, *Personality and Social Psychology Bulletin*, *European Review of Social Psychology*, *Group Dynamics*, *Asian Journal of Social Psychology* and, until recently, the *British Journal of Social Psychology*. With Dominic Abrams he is the founding editor of the journal *Group Processes and Intergroup Relations*.

Michael Hogg's research is on social cognition, group processes and intergroup relations, and he is particularly closely associated with the development of self-categorisation theory and the social identity perspective. He has published over 140 scientific books, and chapters and articles. His books include a scientific bestseller, *Social Identifications* (1988, with Dominic Abrams), and two introductory social psychology texts with Graham Vaughan which are now in their second edition, *Social Psychology* and *Introduction to Social Psychology* (1998).

Dr Dominic Abrams is Professor of Social Psychology and Director of the Centre for the Study of Group Processes at the University of Kent in the UK. He obtained his BSc at Manchester University in the UK and, in 1984, his PhD at the University of Kent. He has held faculty teaching positions at Bristol University and Dundee University before returning to Kent, and has been a visiting scholar at the University of Illinois Urbana-Champaign.

He has been Associate Editor of the *British Journal of Social Psychology*, and special issue editor on the *Journal and Community and Applied Social Psychology* and the *International Journal of Intercultural Relations*. With Michael Hogg he is the foundation editor of the journal *Group Processes and Intergroup Relations*.

Dominic Abrams's research concerns intergroup and intragroup processes, particularly prejudice, tolerance and social influence. He has worked extensively on social identity theory, self-categorisation and self-attention processes. He has published over one hundred scientific books, chapters and articles. His books with Michael Hogg include *Social Identifications* (1988), *Social Identity Theory* (1990), *Group Motivation* (1993) and *Social Identity and Social Cognition* (1999).

Dr Nicky Brunswick is Experimental Officer in Psychology at Middlesex University. She studied for her PhD in the psychophysiology of dyslexia at the University of Warwick and completed her postdoctoral training with Chris and Uta Frith at the Wellcome Department of Cognitive Neurology, Institute of Neurology, London. She researches in the areas of health psychology and dyslexia.

ACKNOWLEDGEMENTS

In the course of writing and revising this major introductory textbook, I have had the good fortune to call on the expertise and detailed knowledge of a number of people. These include colleagues who reviewed my proposal for a revision of this text, members of Prentice Hall Europe's Special Editorial Board for this edition of *Psychology: The science of behaviour*, and my colleagues at Middlesex University and elsewhere. Their comments and suggestions, plaudits and brickbats have helped make this revision a better one than it would have been without their advice.

My colleagues at Middlesex and elsewhere: Bahman Baluch, Vicki Bruce, Nicky Brunswick, Tracey Cockerton, Mark Coulson, Alison Dewey, Brian Evans, Fabia Franco, Peter Halligan, David Marks, Stephen Nunn, Kerry Sims, David Sladen, Steve Torrance, David Westley and Carla Willig.

I also extend thanks to my colleagues at my publishers: my editor, Tim Pitts, for his unfailing philosophical outlook and his boundless enthusiasm; development editor Sue Phillips, who read through all 17 chapters and half a million words; Susan Richards and Christina Wipf-Perry who started this large ball rolling; and Jane Powell and Liz Tarrant for keeping the ball rolling.

G. Neil Martin

REVIEWERS

The publishers would like to express their appreciation for the invaluable advice and encouragement they have received for this book from educators in Europe.

BRIEF CONTENTS

THE SCIENCE OF PSYCHOLOGY

It appears to be an almost universal belief that anyone is competent to discuss psychological problems, whether he or she has taken the trouble to study the subject or not and that while everybody's opinion is of equal value, that of the professional psychologist must be excluded at all costs because he might spoil the fun by producing some facts which would completely upset the speculation and the wonderful dream castles so laboriously constructed by the layman.

Source: Eysenck, 1957, p. 13.

OVERVIEW

To judge from the public interest in human thought and behaviour, you would not be wrong in assuming that there has never been a greater desire to understand why people think and behave in the way that they do. Human behaviour is probably the most fascinating subject matter a scientist can study; it can also be one of the most difficult. Psychology is the scientific study of the determinants of behaviour and cognition and the way in which such behaviour and thought can be influenced and changed.

Psychology is a relatively young science, having its experimental origins in the nineteenth century. It has, however, a long history, and different periods in this history have yielded different methods of studying behaviour. This chapter introduces you to the history of psychology and to some of the pioneers of the discipline. You will see how psychology has its early roots in ancient philosophy and how these origins gave rise to a more scientific approach to studying behaviour.

What you should be able to do after reading Chapter 1

- Define psychology and trace the history of the discipline.
- Be aware of the different methods of studying behaviour that have emerged in psychology.
- Describe the sub-areas of psychology.
- Describe and understand developments in the history of psychology such as structuralism, behaviourism and the cognitive revolution.
- Be wary of 'common-sense' answers to questions regarding psychological knowledge.

Questions to think about

- What types of behaviour do you think a psychologist studies?
- Are there any types of behaviour that a psychologist should not study?
- Can psychologists use data from animal experiments to draw meaningful conclusions about human behaviour?
- What do you think a 'scientific approach' means?
- How do you think the approach of a psychologist to studying his or her subject matter differs from that of an historian, a philosopher, a chemist or a biologist?
- Do you think that much of what we know from psychology is 'common sense'?

What is psychology?

If you asked this question of several people, you would receive several different answers. In fact, if you asked this question of several psychologists, you would still not receive complete agreement on the answer. Psychologists engage in research, teaching, counselling and psychotherapy; they advise industry and government about personnel matters, the design of products, advertising and marketing, and legislation; they devise and administer tests of personality, achievement and ability. And yet psychology is a relatively new discipline; the first modern scientific psychology laboratory was established in 1878 and the first person ever to call himself a psychologist was still alive in 1920. In some European universities the discipline of psychology was known as 'mental philosophy' even as late as the beginning of the twentieth century.

Psychologists study a wide variety of phenomena, including physiological processes within the nervous system, genetics, environmental events, personality characteristics, human development, mental abilities and social interactions. Because of this diversity, it is very rare for a person to be described simply as a psychologist; instead, a psychologist is defined by the sub-area in which he or she works. For example, an individual who measures and treats psychological disorders is called a clinical psychologist; one who studies child development is called a developmental psychologist; a person who explores the relationship between physiology and behaviour might call him or herself a neuropsychologist (if he or she studies the brain) or a biopsychologist/physiological psychologist/psychobiologist (if they study parts of the whole body). Modern psychology has so many branches that it is often impossible to demonstrate expertise in all of these areas. Consequently, and by necessity, psychologists have a highly detailed knowledge of sub-areas of the discipline.

Psychology defined

Psychology is the science of behaviour. The word psychology comes from two Greek words, *psukhe*, meaning 'breath' or 'soul', and *logos*, meaning 'word' or 'reason'. The modern meaning of *psycho-* is 'mind' and the modern meaning of *-logy* is 'science'; thus, the word 'psychology' literally means 'the science of the mind'. Early in the development of psychology, people conceived of the mind as an independent, free-floating spirit. Later, they described it as a characteristic of a functioning brain whose ultimate function was to control behaviour. Thus, the focus turned from the mind, which cannot be directly observed, to behaviour, which can. And because the brain is the organ that both contains the mind and controls behaviour, psychology very soon incorporated the study of the brain.

The study of physical events such as brain activity has made some psychologists question whether the word 'mind' has any meaning in the study of behaviour. Perhaps 'mind' is a metaphor for what the brain does; because it is a metaphor it should not be treated as if it actually existed. In the philosopher Gilbert Ryle's famous book *The Concept of Mind*, he describes this as the 'ghost in the machine' (Ryle, 1949). One might, for example, determine that a personality trait of extroversion exists and people will fall on different points along the introversion–extraversion dimension. But does this mean that this trait *really* exists? This is called the problem of reification in psychology: the assumption that your subject matter is concrete and actually exists in substance.

The approach adopted by modern psychology is scientific, that is, it adopts the principles and procedures of science to help answer the questions it asks. Psychologists adopt this approach because they believe that this is the most effective way of determining 'truth' and 'falsity'; the scientific method, they argue, incorporates fewer biases and greater rigour than do other methods. Of course, not all approaches in psychology have this rigorous scientific leaning: early theories of personality, for example, did not rely on the scientific method (and these are described in Chapter 14). Recent developments in the methodology of psychology have yielded methods that are not considered to be part of the scientific approach: qualitative approaches to human behaviour, for example, which are reviewed later in this chapter, are an example of this. You will learn more about the scientific approach (or, more accurately, these approaches) in Chapter 2.

For the moment, however, consider the value of this approach in psychology. Imagine that you were allowed to answer any psychological question that you might wish to ask: what is the effect of linguistic deprivation on language development, say, or the effect of personality on the stability of romantic relationships? How would you set about answering such questions? What approach do you think would be the best? And how would you ensure that the outcome of your experiment is determined only by those factors you studied and not by any others? These are the types of problem that psychologists face when they design and conduct studies. Sometimes, the results of scientific studies are denounced as 'common sense': that they were so obvious as to be not worth the bother setting up an experiment. This is a rather naive view because, as you will see throughout this book, psychological research frequently contradicts common-sense views. This issue forms the basis of the first of the 'Controversies in psychological science' which appear throughout the book. Before you go on, take the time to read this section (p. 6), and then resume your reading where you left off.

Explaining behaviour

The ultimate goals of research in psychology are to understand, predict and change human behaviour: to explain why people do what they do. Different kinds of psychologist are interested in different kinds of behaviour and different levels of explanation. Not all psychologists study humans; some conduct research using laboratory animals or study the behaviour of wild animals in their natural habitat. Research using animals has provided many insights into the factors that affect human behaviour, such as the effect of sensory deprivation on the development of the senses.

How do psychologists 'explain' behaviour? First, we must describe it accurately and comprehensively. We must become familiar with the things that people (or other animals) do. We must learn how to categorise and measure behaviour so that we can be sure that different psychologists in different places are observing the same phenomena. Next, we must discover the causes of the behaviour we observe – those events responsible for its occurrence. If we can discover the events that caused the behaviour to occur, we have 'explained' it. Events that cause other events (including behaviour) to occur are called causal events or determinants

For example, one psychologist might be interested in visual perception and another might be interested in romantic attraction. Even when they are interested in the same behaviour, different psychologists might study different levels of analysis. Some look inside the organism in a literal sense, seeking physiological causes, such as the activity of nerve cells or the secretions of glands. Others look inside the organism in a metaphorical sense, explaining behaviour in terms of hypothetical mental states, such as anger, fear, curiosity or love. Still others look only for events in the environment (including things that other people do) that cause behaviours to occur.

Established and emerging fields of psychology

Throughout this book you will encounter many types of psychologist and many types of psychology. As you have already seen, very few individuals call themselves psychologists, rather they describe themselves by their specialism such as cognitive psychologist, developmental psychologist, social psychologist and so on. Before we describe and define each branch of psychology, it is important to distinguish between three general terms: psychology, psychiatry and psychoanalysis. A psychologist normally holds a university degree in a behaviour-related discipline (such as psychology, zoology, cognitive science) and usually possesses a higher degree if he or she is teaching or is a researcher. This higher degree is called a doctorate (or PhD), the highest academic qualification obtainable, and is awarded after a period of producing original scientific research. Those not researching but working in applied settings such as hospitals or schools have other, different qualifications which enable them to practise in those environments.

Psychiatrists are physicians who have specialised in the causes and treatment of mental disorder. They are medically qualified (unlike psychologists who nonetheless do study medical problems and undertake biological research) and have the ability to prescribe medication (which psychologists do not). Much of the work done by psychologists in psychiatric settings is similar to that of the psychiatrist, however, such as implementing psychological interventions for patients with mental illness. Psychoanalysts are specific types of counsellor who attempt to understand mental disorder by reference to the workings of the unconscious. There is no formal academic qualification necessary to become a psychoanalyst and, as the definition implies, they deal with a limited range of behaviour.

Most research psychologists are employed by colleges or universities, by private organisations or by government. Research psychologists differ from one another in two principal ways: in the types of behaviour they investigate and in the causal events they analyse. That is, they explain different types of behaviour, and they explain them in terms of different types of cause. For example, two psychologists might both be interested in memory, but they might attempt to explain memory in terms of different causal events – one may focus on physiological events (such as the activation of the brain during memory retrieval) whereas the other may focus on environmental events (such as the effect of noise level on task performance). Professional societies such as the American Psychological Association and the British Psychological Society have numerous sub-divisions representing members with an interest in a specific aspect of psychology. This section outlines some of the major branches or sub-divisions of psychology. A summary of these can be found in Table 1.1

Physiological psychology is the study of the biological basis of behaviour (Carlson, 1995). It investigates the causal events in an organism's physiology, especially in the nervous system and its interaction with glands that secrete hormones. Physiological psychologists study almost all behavioural phenomena that can be observed in non-human animals, including learning, memory, sensory processes, emotional behaviour, motivation, sexual behaviour and sleep. The notion that all behaviour can be explained by biological processes is called biological reductionism

Psychophysiology is the measurement of people's physiological reactions, such as heart rate, blood pressure, electrical resistance of the skin, muscle tension, and electrical activity of the brain (Andreassi, 1996). These measurements provide an indication of a person's degree of arousal or relaxation. Most psychophysiologists investigate phenomena such as sensory and perceptual responses, sleep, stress, cognition and emotion.

Neuropsychology and neuroscience examine the relationship between certain parts of the nervous system (the brain and spinal cord) and behaviour (Martin, 1998a). Neuropsychology helps to shed light on the role of the

Controversies in psychological science

Is psychology common sense?

The issue

Consider the following questions:

1 Schizophrenics suffer from a split-personality. Is this:
   (a) true most of the time
   (b) true some of the time
   (c) true none of the time, or
   (d) true only when the schizophrenic is undergoing psychotherapy?

2 Under hypnosis, a person will, if asked by a hypnotist:
   (a) recall past life events with a high degree of accuracy
   (b) perform physical feats of strength not possible out of hypnosis
   (c) do (a) and (b), or
   (d) do neither (a) nor (b).

3 The learning principles applied to birds and fish also apply to:
   (a) humans
   (b) cockroaches
   (c) both (a) and (b), or
   (d) neither (a) nor (b).

4 Are physically attractive people:
   (a) more likely to be stable than physically unattractive persons
   (b) equal in psychological stability
   (c) likely to be less psychologically stable, or
   (d) likely to be much more unstable?

How well do you think that you did? In a study published in 1997, these four questions featured in the ten most difficult questions answered by first-year psychology undergraduates who completed a 38-item questionnaire about psychological knowledge (Martin *et al.*, 1997). In fact, when the responses from first- and final-year psychology, engineering, sociology, English and business studies students were analysed, the greatest proportion of questions that any one group accurately answered was 50 per cent. Perhaps not surprisingly, psychologists did significantly better than did the other students, with sociologists following close behind. Why should psychology (and other) students perform so badly on a test of psychological knowledge?

The answer lies in the fact that the questionnaire was not really a test of psychological knowledge. Instead, it was a questionnaire designed to establish whether different disciplines make common-sense mistakes when answering questions about psychological research. Common-sense mistakes are those committed when the obvious answer that a respondent selects is not, in fact, the correct one. Considerable debate in the social science and natural sciences has revolved around the issue of whether what we know about psychology is common sense. It has been argued that 'a great many of psychology's basic principles are self-evident' (Houston, 1983), and that 'much of what psychology textbooks purport to teach undergraduates about research findings in the area may already be known to them through common, informal experiences' (Barnett, 1986). Houston reports that although introductory psychology students answered 15 out of 21 questions about 'memory and learning' correctly, a collection of 50 individuals found in a city park on a Friday afternoon scored an average of 16.

The evidence

Is the common-sense view of psychological research justified? Not quite. Since the late 1970s, a number of studies have examined individuals' false beliefs about psychology, and students' beliefs in particular. These studies employed questionnaires which featured items very similar to those appearing at the beginning of this CiPS section (McCutcheon *et al.*, 1993; Furnham, 1993). One of the earliest of these tests, the Test of Common Beliefs (Vaughan, 1977) was a true-or-false questionnaire in which respondents would make judgements about items such as: 'memory can be likened to a storage chest in the brain into which we deposit material and from which we can withdraw later', 'personality tests reveal your basic motives, including those you may not be aware of', and 'blind people have unusually sensitive organs of touch'. Eighty-seven per cent, 85 per cent and 76 per cent, respectively, of first-year psychology students thought that these statements were true. Even though course materials directly contradicted some of these statements, the students still considered them to be true! True–false questionnaires, of course, can be criticized on methodological grounds. There is a tendency to observe 'response set', for example. This describes the way in which respondents reply 'yes' only or 'no' only. Findings from other tests with different formats (for example, multiple choice), however, suggest the same outcome occurs: respondents make consistently inaccurate common-sense mistakes when answering questions about psychological research.

Furnham (1992c, 1993), for example, has reported that only half of such 'common-sense' questions were answered correctly by 250 prospective psychology students and only 20 per cent of questions were answered correctly by half or more of a sample of 110 first-year psychology, fine arts, biochemistry and engineering students. Do these students' scores improve over time? One might expect some improvement, for example, from first to final year of a degree course in psychology. The evidence is mixed. Gardner and Dalsing (1986) found that the greater the number of courses taken by students, the fewer the misperceptions they held at the end of these courses. We have already seen that Vaughan found no effect of number of courses taken on degree of misperception held. In Martin *et al.*'s (1997) study, the experimenters compared first- and final-year students' scores across five disciplines and found only an effect for year: final-year students answered more questions correctly than did first-year students but there was no significant difference between first- and final-year psychology students. This suggests that misperceptions are slowly dispelled after students undergo the process of higher education and learning, but that studying specific disciplines does nothing to dispel these myths effectively. This is just one explanation. Can you think of any others?

Why, however, is the view of psychology as common sense common? One explanation may be tied to a concept called 'fantastical thinking'. This describes ways of reasoning about the world that violate known scientific principles (Woolley, 1997). For example, the belief that women can control breast cancer by positive thinking (Taylor, 1983), that walking under a ladder brings bad luck and that knocking wood brings good luck (Blum and Blum, 1974) violate known physical laws but people still believe in doing such things. People often draw erroneous conclusions about psychological knowledge because they rely on small sets of data, sometimes a very small set of data (such as a story in a newspaper or the behaviour of a friend). Take the relationship between a mental disorder such as schizophrenia and murders committed by schizophrenics, for example. Despite the small number of murders committed by schizophrenic patients, the few cases which do receive media attention suggest that schizophrenics are uncontrollable murderers who should be put out of harm's way. You will see from the chapter on abnormal psychology that such thinking is blatantly perverse: the majority of schizophrenic individuals will not cause harm to others. It is an example of what social psychologists call the 'underutilisation of base rate information' (Fiske and Taylor, 1991). This means that individual, vivid, single or a small number of examples are taken to represent the behaviour of an entire group. The base rate information (the actual incidence of behaviour in such groups in general), however, contradicts these single, vivid examples but is either ignored or dismissed. A similar process may be operating when people misperceive some aspects of psychology. Psychologists have discovered that two determinants of fantastical thinking are lack of information and an inability to explain behaviour. It seems likely that these factors could underpin misperceptions about psychology.

This said, do people who should know a bit about psychology – psychology students – feel that psychology is common sense and unscientific? Throughout a psychology degree, a student will be taught the principles of scientific investigation, experimentation, logical thinking and research methods and design, and rightly so because these are the tools of discovery in psychology. Psychology students, more than other students, should be aware of the scientific approach that psychology adopts. In Martin *et al.*'s (1997) study, participants on average did believe that psychology was not common sense (although their responses on the questionnaire suggested that they acted otherwise). Does this finding highlight a problem with studying such topics (think of what people say and what they actually do)?

Conclusion

As you work through your psychology course and through this book, discovering new and sometimes complicated ways of analysing and understanding human behaviour, you will realise that many of the beliefs and perceptions you had about certain aspects of psychology are false or only half right. This is not unexpected. You will find research that will surprise you and other research that will not surprise you but you will be intrigued by how psychologists obtained the results of such research. Of course, no science is truly infallible and there are different ways of approaching psychological problems. Psychology, however, attempts to adopt the best of scientific approaches to understanding potentially the most unmanageable of subject matter: behaviour. And, for those of you who were wondering, the answers to the questions at the top of the box are c, d, c, a.

Table 1.1 The branches of psychology

Branch	Subject of study
Physiological psychology	Biological basis of behaviour
Psychophysiology	Psychophysiological responses such as heart rate, galvanic skin response and brain electrical activity
Neuropsychology	Relationship between brain activity/structure and function
Comparative psychology	Behaviour of species in terms of evolution and adaptation
Ethology	Animal behaviour in natural environments
Sociobiology	Social behaviour in terms of biological inheritance and evolution
Behaviour genetics	Degree of influence of genetics and environment on psychological factors
Cognitive psychology	Mental processes and complex behaviour
Cognitive neuroscience	Brain's involvement in mental processes
Developmental psychology	Physical, cognitive, social and emotional development from birth to senescence
Social psychology	Individuals' and groups' behaviour
Individual differences	Temperament and characteristics of individuals and their effects on behaviour
Cross-cultural psychology	Impact of culture on behaviour
Cultural psychology	Variability of behaviour within cultures
Forensic and criminological psychology	Behaviour and mental processes in the context of crime and the law
Clinical psychology	Causes and treatment of mental disorder and problems of adjustment
Health psychology	Impact of lifestyle and stress on health and illness
Educational psychology	Social, cognitive and emotional development of children in the context of schooling
Consumer psychology	Motivation, perception and cognition in consumers
Organisational or occupational psychology	Behaviour of groups and individuals in the workplace
Ergonomics	Ways in which humans and machines work together
Sport and exercise psychology	The effects of psychological variables on sport and exercise performance and vice versa

central nervous system in movement, vision, hearing, tasting, smelling and touching as well as emotion, thinking, language and object recognition and perception. Neuropsychologists normally (but not always) study patients who have suffered brain damage as a result of disease or stroke or accident which disrupts functions such as language, object recognition, perception and so on. Clinical neuropsychology involves the identification and treatment of the behavioural consequences of nervous system disorders and injuries. Clinical neuropsychologists typically work in a hospital and collaborate closely with neurologists (physicians who specialise in diseases of the nervous system), although some teach or work in private practice.

Modern neuropsychology also relies on sophisticated brain imaging techniques such as positron emission tomography (PET) and magnetic resonance imaging (MRI) which allow researchers to monitor the activity and structure of the brains of healthy individuals while they perform some psychological task. This approach combines two approaches in psychology – neuroscience and cognitive psychology (which we will define below). Because of this, the area of study is sometimes described as cognitive neuroscience (Rugg, 1997; Gazzaniga, 1995) or behavioural neuroscience. We look at the work of behavioural neuroscientists in more detail in Chapter 4.

Comparative psychology is the study of the behaviour of members of a variety of species in an attempt to explain behaviour in terms of evolutionary adaptation to the environment. Comparative psychologists study behavioural phenomena similar to those studied by physiological psychologists. They are more likely than most other psychologists to study inherited behavioural patterns, such as courting and mating, predation and aggression, defensive behaviours, and parental behaviours. Closely tied to comparative psychology is **ethology**. Ethologists study the biological basis of behaviour by focusing on the evolution of development and function and usually make their observations based on studies of animal behaviour in natural conditions. Ethologists study topics such as instinct, social and sexual behaviour and co-operation. A sub-discipline of ethology is **sociobiology** which attempts to explain social behaviour in terms of biological inheritance and evolution. Ethology and sociobiology are described in more detail in Chapter 3.

Behaviour genetics is the branch of psychology that studies the role of genetics in behaviour (Plomin and DeFries, 1998). The genes we inherit from our parents include a blueprint for the construction of a human brain. Each blueprint is a little different, which means that no two brains are exactly alike. Therefore, no two people will act exactly alike, even in an identical situation. Behaviour geneticists study the role of genetics in behaviour by examining similarities in physical and behavioural characteristics of blood relatives, whose genes are more similar than those of unrelated individuals. They also perform breeding experiments with laboratory animals to see what aspects of behaviour can be transmitted to an animal's offspring. Of course, genetic differences are only one of the causes of individual differences. People have different experiences, too, and these experiences will affect their behaviour. Behavioural geneticists study the degree to which genetics are responsible for specific behaviours such as cognitive ability. We examine the work of behavioural geneticists in Chapter 3 (on the evolution of behaviour) and evaluate their contribution to the study of intelligence in Chapter 11 (on intelligence and thinking).

Cognitive psychology is the study of mental processes and complex behaviours such as perception, attention, learning and memory, verbal behaviour, concept formation, and problem solving (Eysenck and Keane, 1995). To cognitive psychologists, the events that cause behaviour consist of functions of the human brain that occur in response to environmental events. Their explanations involve characteristics of inferred mental processes, such as imagery, attention, and mechanisms of language. Most of them do not study physiological mechanisms, but recently, some have begun collaborating with neurologists and other professionals who utilise neuroimaging. A branch of cognitive psychology involves the modelling of human function using computer simulation or 'neural networks'.

This is called **cognitive science** and we briefly examine the contribution of such computer simulations to our understanding of a specific behaviour (reading) in Chapter 11 (Intelligence and thinking).

Developmental psychology is the study of physical, cognitive, emotional, and social development, especially of children (Berk, 1997). Some developmental psychologists study phenomena of adolescence or adulthood, in particular the effects of ageing. We describe and evaluate the work of developmental psychologists in detail in Chapter 12 (Developmental psychology). The development of children's language is described in Chapter 10, and the effects of ageing on cognitive performance are reviewed in Chapter 11.

Social psychology is the study of the effects of people on people. Social psychologists explore phenomena such as perception (of oneself as well as of others), cause-and-effect relations in human interactions, attitudes and opinions, interpersonal relationships, group dynamics, and emotional behaviours, including aggression and sexual behaviour (Hogg and Vaughan, 1998). Chapter 15 explores the issues and themes in social psychology.

Individual differences is the area of psychology which examines individual differences in temperament and patterns of behaviour. The primary focus of individual differences research is on how large groups can be further sub-divided into more meaningful groups. For example, instead of examining a group's response to the effect of mild alcohol intake on task performance, a psychologist might decide to examine differences between people who are extroverted, introverted or neurotic under these conditions. Some examples of individual differences studied by psychologists include personality, hand preference, sex and age.

Cross-cultural psychology is the study of the impact of culture on behaviour (Segall *et al.*, 1998). The ancestors of people of different racial and ethnic groups lived in different environments which presented them with different problems and opportunities for solving those problems. Different cultures have, therefore, developed different strategies for adapting to their environments. These strategies show themselves in laws, customs, myths, religious beliefs and ethical principles as well as in thinking, health beliefs and approaches to problem solving.

A similar – but different – term, **cultural psychology**, has been used to describe the study of variations within cultures (not necessarily across cultures). The assumption in cultural psychology is that cultures, and their processes and contents, are variable and not universal (Shweder and Sullivan, 1993; Miller, 1997).

Forensic or **criminological psychology** applies psychological knowledge to the understanding, prediction and nature of crime and behaviour related to crime (Davies, 1995). There is a distinction between criminological and forensic psychology. Forensic psychology refers to the use of material in a court of law. Criminological psychology refers to the application of psychological principles to the criminal justice system (Blackburn, 1996). The terms, however, are often used interchangeably. One example of the way in which criminological psychologists can apply their research to crime is in the study of eyewitness testimony. Eyewitness testimony is a highly unreliable source of information and psychologists have helped show how flawed this method of memory retrieval is and have suggested alternative methods of prompting witnesses' memory of crime. We examine some of these methods in Chapter 8 (Memory).

Criminological psychology is a relatively young branch of psychology. In the 'Psychology in action' section below, you will discover some of the ways in which psychologists can help the criminal justice system and encounter the potential applications of psychology to criminal detection. Many psychologists' work can help to solve or understand pressing human problems such as drug and alcohol abuse, stress, susceptibility to illness, mental disorder, developmental disorders, work inefficiency, witness memory, eyewitness testimony, crowd control and so on. This section focuses on one of these applications: the work of the criminological psychologist.

Psychology in action

Psychology in the witness box

In recent years, there has been a surge of interest in forensic or criminological psychology. Forensic psychology refers to a branch of psychology which involves the 'collection, examination and presentation of evidence for judicial purposes' (Haward, 1981; Blackburn, 1996). Forensic psychologists can be commissioned by courts to prepare reports on the fitness of a defendant to stand trial, on the general psychological state of the defendant, on aspects of psychological research (such as post-traumatic stress disorders), on the behaviour of children involved in custody disputes and so on. The British Psychological Society has its own division of criminological and legal psychology and an European Association for Psychology and Law was recently established (Blackburn, 1996). Several popular accounts of the forensic psychologist's work have been published (for example, Canter, 1994; Britton, 1997) and the work of such individuals has been made even more popular (although not portrayed more accurately) by television series such as *Cracker* and films such as *The Silence of the Lambs* which involve forensic psychologists in lead roles.

The application of psychology to law, however, is a very recent phenomenon. The first psychologist to give expert testimony in court was the German Albert Schrenk-Notzing in 1896. Schrenk-Notzing became involved in the trial of a Munich man accused of murdering three women (Bartol and

Bartol, 1987). His contribution focused on retroactive memory falsification – the confusion that arises between what witnesses say they saw and what actually happened. A little later, in the United States, the advice of Hugo Munsterberg, one of the pioneers in forensic psychology, was sought in two murder trials (Colman, 1995). Munsterberg published one of the earliest texts on the application of psychology to crime and the law, *On the Witness Stand: Essays in psychology and crime*, in 1908, and his work on the reaction time between rifle shots was cited in the case relating to the assassination of John F. Kennedy (Haward, 1979; Colman, 1995).

The psychologists most often consulted by lawyers are clinical and educational psychologists (Lloyd-Bostock, 1988; Gudjonsson, 1996a). Prison psychologists might also be consulted to assess offenders and give supporting evidence in court; occupational psychologists might be called on in cases involving personal injury or discrimination; academic psychologists might be asked to advise on specialised areas of psychology, such as factors which could influence face identification (Lloyd-Bostock, 1988); clinical neuropsychologists might be asked to determine whether a defendant is malingering, that is, feigning mental disorder or intellectual incompetence (Martin, 1998a).

Some of the types of questions asked of forensic psychologists in court include:

- Is the accused fit to stand?
- Is the accused's testimony genuine?
- Does the defendant suffer from severe learning difficulties?
- What are the long-term effects of alcohol abuse on a person's memory?
- How suggestible are child witnesses when interrogated by police?
- Is the defendant malingering?
- What factors might be responsible for a retracted confession?

Source: Adapted from Colman, 1995.

In a survey of psychologists who had engaged in court work, Gudjonsson (1996b) found that the majority of the issues addressed by forensic psychologists involved post-traumatic stress disorder, child care and factors affecting sentencing and mitigation. These issues and the types of evidence provided by psychologists are summarised in Table 1.2.

The type of information provided by psychologists can be very different from that provided by a forensic psychiatrist. Forensic psychiatrists have little training or expertise in administering psychological tests which assess personality, intelligence, aptitude and so on, and usually provide evidence based on a clinical interview. Psychiatrists are, therefore, more likely to offer an opinion rather than

Table 1.2 The types of issue addressed by psychologists when giving legal testimony and the type of evidence provided by forensic psychologists

	Percentage of reports produced
Types of issue addressed	
Post-traumatic stress disorder	55%
Other compensation	51%
Child care	47%
Sentencing	25%
Mitigation	24%
Fitness to plead/stand trial	14%
Reliability of witness statement	14%
Diminished responsibility	10%
Disputed confessions	9%
Types of evidence provided	
Interview with client	97%
Studying relevant documents	87%
Psychometric test results	85%
Interview with informants	79%
Behavioural assessment	64%
Other (e.g. reviewing audio/video material, conducting research reviews/ psychophysiological measurements)	20%

Source: based on the responses of 522 psychologists in the United Kingdom (Gudjonsson, 1996b). Psychological Evidence in Court. *The Psychologist*, May, 213–217. © The British Psychological Society.

objective data in court cases. Forensic psychologists have recourse to objective, standardised data provided by objective tests. Psychologists are, however, often asked to go beyond interpreting objective data and to provide an opinion on various criminal issues. Very few psychologists are happy to go beyond such objective, scientific data and have difficulty in giving clear-cut answers demanded by lawyers when they believe that no clear-cut answers are available (Beaumont, 1994; Colman, 1995).

Haward (1981) has suggested that the psychologist can play four roles in court proceedings. The *clinical role*, the most common one, involves interviewing clients and carrying out behavioural or psychological assessment. The *experimental role* involves the examination of behaviour through experimentation, not interview or assessment. *Actuarial roles* involve suggesting statistical probabilities about events and behaviour. Finally, *advisory roles* involve advising lawyers about the opposition's evidence such as the reliability and strength of the research it cites.

In the most serious of legal proceedings, criminal proceedings, psychologists may be involved at three stages: pre-trial, trial and sentencing (Gudjonsson, 1994; 1996a, b). At *pre-trial*, the defendant's fitness to plead, stand trial and be cross-examined is assessed. Gudjonsson, a forensic psychologist who has been actively involved in over 450 legal cases, gives an example of the forensic psychologist's input at this stage. He describes a case in which a middle-aged man was charged with laundering millions of pounds stolen in an armed robbery (Gudjonsson, 1994). According to psychiatric reports, the man suffered from depressive illness which would impair his ability to brief counsel and follow proceedings. Gudjonsson administered a series of psychological tests which showed that the accused had attention problems and was slow in cognitive processing. He was declared unfit to stand and was given treatment. Two years later, the man was reassessed, deemed fit to stand, tried and convicted.

Trial issues involve factors such as individuals' state of mind at the time of the event and whether the offence was intentional. Much of the empirical research in psychology could be applied at this stage and one of the most consistently well conducted and researched of legally relevant behaviour is witness memory and eyewitness identification (Faigman, 1995; Loftus, 1986), as we will see in Chapter 8. The final stage involves *sentencing* and here psychologists are less involved than are psychiatrists.

This unglamorous world of the forensic psychologist is far removed from that of Agent Starling and Dr Fitzgerald. Much of the public interest in forensic psychology has been aroused by the potential of such 'professionals' to provide insights into the criminal mind. One technique that has received much publicity is offender profiling, a technique that dates back to the 1950s (Brown, 1998). The purpose of offender profiling is to present a composite description of a perpetrator, based on biographical and behavioural cues, that can lead to the apprehension of that perpetrator. It can also be used to narrow the focus of an investigation (by specifying an area in which the perpetrator lives or to specify the perpetrator's sex or age) or to provide suggestions for interviewing suspects (McCann, 1992). By collating data and evaluating evidence, such techniques have led to arrest of serious criminals such as the British criminal, John Duffy, the perpetrator of murders which were localised around railways (Canter, 1989). However, even psychologists who have used – and pioneered – such techniques have suggested caution in using this technique. One leading forensic psychologist, David Canter, gives a vivid example of how such a technique can be misused. In his website article 'Profiling as poison', he describes a team of Northern European profilers who mistakenly assumed that because a murdered woman's face had been severely beaten, the offender knew her victim and was exacting some form of revenge (http:// www.liv.ac.uk/Investigative Psychology/invpub.htm). The murdered woman was a teacher and attention was quickly focused on those pupils who may have been ignored or spurned by the teacher. The murderer turned out to be a drug addict who killed the woman when she disturbed him burgling her house. This mistaken profiling receives some support from the empirical literature. For example, Pinizzotto and Finkel (1990) asked professional profilers, psychologists, detectives and students to draw up a profile of a sex attacker and a murderer (using real-life data where the perpetrator's identity was known). Although the profilers' report was richer in detail for both offences, the profilers' reports were more accurate than the other groups' only for the sex offence.

It is clear from the work currently undertaken by forensic psychologists that their contribution to the legal process can be quite valuable. The reliance on objective measures of assessment and on scientific data makes the testimony of psychologists more reliable than witnesses who have a more informal means of assessing data or individuals. Techniques such as offender profiling may assist in the apprehension of criminals but their reliability is far from clear.

Clinical psychology is the study of mental disorders and problems of adjustment (Lindsay and Powell, 1994). It is an applied branch of psychology because clinical psychologists do not work in the laboratory under well controlled experimental conditions but out in the field, applying the knowledge gained from practice and research. Most clinical psychologists are specially trained practitioners who attempt to assess and treat people's psychological problems. The remainder are scientists who investigate a wide variety of causal events, including genetic factors, physiological factors and environmental factors such as parental upbringing, interactions with siblings and other social stimuli. Clinical psychologists can work in private practice (on their own or as part of a joint practice), in hospitals and mental health clinics, as part of government

services, in work organisations, and sometimes as lecturers in colleges and universities. Chapter 17 (Abnormal psychology) describes some of the problems seen by clinical psychologists.

Health psychology is the study of the ways in which behaviour and lifestyle can affect health and illness (Sarafino, 1998). For example, smoking is associated with a number of illnesses and is a strong risk factor for death. Health psychologists help to devise strategies whereby smoking behaviour is reduced or eliminated; they also investigate those factors which are likely to make individuals start smoking and maintain this behaviour. Health psychologists are employed in a variety of settings including hospitals, government, universities and private practice. The work of health psychology is described in Chapter 16.

Educational psychology is another applied branch of psychology. Educational psychologists assess the behavioural problems of children at school and suggest ways in which these problems may be remedied. For example, the educational psychologist might identify a child's early inability to read (dyslexia) and suggest a means by which this may be overcome through special training. The educational psychologist might also deal with all aspects of school life including learning, social relations, testing, violence, substance abuse and neglect.

Consumer psychology is the study of the motivation, perception, learning, cognition, and purchasing behaviour of individuals in the marketplace and their use of products once they reach the home. Some consumer psychologists take a marketer's perspective, some take a consumer's perspective, and some adopt a more-or-less neutral perspective, especially if they work at a university.

Organisational or **occupational psychology** is one of the largest and oldest fields of applied psychology and involves the study of the ways in which individuals and groups perform and behave in the workplace (Buchanan and Huczynski, 1997). Early organisational psychologists concentrated on industrial work processes (such as the most efficient way to shovel coal), but organisational psychologists now spend more effort analysing modern plants and offices. They are involved in the administration and development of personality aptitude tests and can also be involved in stress management. Most are employed by large companies and organisations, but almost one-third are employed in universities.

Ergonomics or **human factors psychology** focuses mainly on the ways that people and machines work together (Shackel, 1996). They study machines ranging from cockpits to computers, from robots to CD players, from transportation vehicles for the disabled to telephones. If the machine is well designed, the task can be much easier, more enjoyable and safer. Ergonomists help designers and engineers to design better machines; because of this, the terms ergonomics and engineering psychology are sometimes used interchangeably (Stanton, 1996).

Sport and exercise psychology applies psychological principles to the applied setting of sport (Steinberg *et al.*, 1998). It also involves the study of the effects of sport and exercise on mood, cognition, well-being and physiology. We will examine one specific area of sport and exercise psychology in Chapter 16 when we look at the effect of exercise on health and mood.

Questions to think about

The science of psychology

- Before you had read the previous section, how would you have answered the question, 'What is psychology?' Would your answer be different now?

- Think about the experiment you were asked to consider at the beginning of the chapter. Now that you are familiar with the various branches of psychology, which branch would your experiment fall under? Would your experiment perhaps straddle two or more branches? If so, how would the approaches of each sub-area help you to set up your experiment?

- In what ways do you think that psychologists might help individuals and groups outside the 'laboratory'?

- Do you think that the knowledge learned from psychological research should have practical applications? If so, why? Can you think of examples of research where the practical application may not be clear but the research is valuable because we can learn more about the way in which people behave?

- Why do you think that people give 'common-sense' answers to questions about psychological research?

- In James Joyce's novel *Ulysses*, the author narrates twenty-four hours in the life of Leopold Bloom, an insurance clerk from Dublin. Looking at twenty-four hours in your life, in what ways could psychologists study your behaviour in that period? What sorts of behaviour do you think would be psychologically interesting to study in your life?

Psychology: the development of a science

Although philosophers and other thinkers have been concerned with psychological issues for a long time, the science of psychology is comparatively young and has its roots in Europe: it began in Germany in the late nineteenth century and we will trace its modern origins in a later section. In order to understand how this science came into being, however, it is useful to trace its roots back through philosophy and the natural sciences because these disciplines originally provided the methods we use to study human behaviour and took many centuries to develop. The next section gives an outline of the major philosophical schools of thought which set the stage for the emergence of the science of psychology in the late nineteenth century.

Philosophical roots of psychology

Animism

Each of us is conscious of our own existence. Furthermore, we are aware of this consciousness. Although we often find ourselves doing things that we had not planned to do (or had planned not to do), by and large we feel that we are in control of our behaviour. That is, we have the impression that our conscious mind controls our behaviour. We consider alternatives, make plans, and then act. We get our bodies moving; we engage in behaviour.

Consciousness is a private experience, and yet although we can experience only our own consciousness directly, we assume that our fellow human beings are also conscious, and, to at least some extent, we attribute consciousness to other animals as well. To the degree that our behaviours are similar, we tend to assume that our mental states, too, resemble one another. Earlier in human history, philosophers attributed a life-giving animus, or spirit, to anything that seemed to move or grow independently. Because they believed that the movements of their own bodies were controlled by their minds or spirits, they inferred that the sun, moon, wind, tides and other moving entities were similarly animated. This primitive philosophy is called animism (from the Latin *animare*, 'to quicken, enliven, endow with breath or soul'). Even gravity was explained in animistic terms: rocks fell to the ground because the spirits within them wanted to be reunited with Mother Earth.

Obviously, our interest in animism is historical. No educated person in our society believes that rocks fall because they 'want to'. Rather, we believe that they fall because of the existence of natural forces inherent in physical matter, even if we do not understand what these forces are. But note that different interpretations can be placed on the same events. Surely, we are just as prone to subjective interpretations of natural phenomena, albeit more sophisticated ones, as our ancestors were. In fact, when we try to explain why people do what they do, we tend to attribute at least some of their behaviour to the action of a motivating spirit – namely, a will. In our daily lives, this explanation of behaviour may often suit our needs. However, on a scientific level, we need to base our explanations on phenomena that can be observed and measured objectively. We cannot objectively and directly observe 'will'.

The best means we have to ensure objectivity is the scientific method, which is described in more detail in

Chapter 2. Psychology as a science must be based on the assumption that behaviour is strictly subject to physical laws, just as any other natural phenomenon is. The rules of scientific research impose discipline on humans whose natural inclinations might lead them to incorrect conclusions. It seemed natural for our ancestors to believe that rocks had spirits, just as it seems natural for people nowadays to believe that behaviour can be affected by a person's will. In contrast, the idea that feelings, emotions, imagination and other private experiences are the products of physical laws of nature did not come easily; it evolved through many centuries.

Dualism: René Descartes

Although the history of Western philosophy properly begins with the Ancient Greeks, we will begin here with René Descartes (1596–1650), a French philosopher and mathematician. Descartes has been called the father of modern philosophy and advocated a sober, impersonal investigation of natural phenomena using sensory experience and human reasoning. He assumed that the world was a purely mechanical entity that, having once been set in motion by God, ran its course without divine interference. Thus, to understand the world, one had only to understand how it was constructed. This stance challenged the established authority of the Church, which believed that the purpose of philosophy was to reconcile human experiences with the truth of God's revelations.

To Descartes, animals were mechanical devices; their behaviour was controlled by environmental stimuli. His view of the human body was much the same: it was a machine. Thus, Descartes was able to describe some movements as automatic and involuntary. For example, the application of a hot object to a finger would cause an almost immediate withdrawal of the arm away from the source of stimulation. Reactions like this did not require participation of the mind; they occurred automatically.

René Descartes (1596–1650)

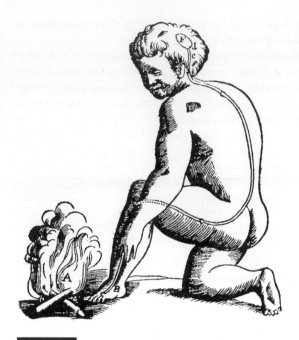

Figure 1.1

Descartes's diagram of a withdrawal reflex.

Descartes called these actions **reflexes** (from the Latin *reflectere*, 'to bend back upon itself'). A stimulus registered by the senses produces a reaction which is entirely physically and beyond voluntary control. There would be no intention or will to produce this physical reaction. Consider the well known reflex of sensing the heat of a flame, as seen in Figure 1.1.

The body recoils from flame in an involuntary way: we do not intentionally move away from the flame but our body reflexively puts in place a chain of muscle contractions which make us withdraw. The term 'reflex' is still in use today, but, of course, we explain the operation of a reflex differently.

What set humans apart from the rest of the world, according to Descartes, was their possession of a mind. The mind was a uniquely human attribute and was not subject to the laws of the universe. Thus, Descartes was a proponent of **dualism**, the belief that all reality can be divided into two distinct entities: mind and matter (this is often referred to as **Cartesian dualism**). He distinguished between 'extended things', or physical bodies, and 'thinking things', or minds. Physical bodies, he believed, do not think, and minds are not made of ordinary matter. Although Descartes was not the first to propose dualism, his thinking differed from that of his predecessors in one important way: he was the first to suggest that a link exists between the human mind and its purely physical housing. Although later philosophers pointed out that this theoretical link actually contradicted his belief in dualism, the proposal of an interaction between mind and matter, interactionism, was absolutely vital to the development of the science of psychology.

Descartes reasoned that mind and body were capable of interaction. From the time of Plato onwards, philosophers had argued that the mind and the body were different entities. They also suggested that the mind could influence the body but the body could not influence the mind, a little like a puppet and puppeteer with the mind pulling the strings of the body. Not all philosophers adopted this view, however. To some, such as Spinoza (1652–1677), both mental events (thinking) and physical events (such as occupying space) were characteristic of one and the same thing in the same way that an undulating line can be described as convex or concave – it cannot be described as exclusively one thing or another (this is called double-aspect theory).

Descartes hypothesised that this interaction between mind and body took place in the pineal body, a small organ situated on top of the brain stem, buried beneath the large cerebral hemispheres of the brain. When the mind decided to perform an action, it tilted the pineal body in a particular direction, causing fluid to flow from the brain into the proper set of nerves. This flow of fluid caused the appropriate muscles to inflate and move.

How did Descartes come up with this mechanical concept of the body's movements? Western Europe in the seventeenth century was the scene of great advances in the sciences. This was the century, for example, in which William Harvey discovered that blood circulated around the body. It was not just the practical application of science that impressed Europeans, however, it was the beauty, imagination and fun of it as well. Craftsmen constructed many elaborate mechanical toys and devices during this period. The young Descartes was greatly impressed by the moving statues in the Royal Gardens (Jaynes, 1970). These devices served as models for Descartes as he theorised about how the body worked. He conceived of the muscles as balloons. They became inflated when a fluid passed through the nerves that connected them to the brain and spinal cord, just as water flowed through pipes to activate the statues. This inflation was the basis of the muscular contraction that causes us to move.

This story illustrates one of the first examples of a technological device used to model and explain how the nervous system works. In science, a model is a relatively simple system that works on known principles and is able to do at least some of the things that a more complex system can do. For example, when scientists discovered that elements of the nervous system communicate by means of electrical impulses, researchers developed models of the brain based on telephone switchboards and, more recently, computers. Abstract models, which are completely mathematical in their properties, have also been developed. Clinical psychologists may interpret mental disorder according to a medical model which conceives of clinical mental disturbance as an illness.

Although Descartes's model of the human body was mechanical, it was controlled by the non-mechanical (in fact, non-physical) mind. Thus, humans were born with a special capability that made them greater than simply the sum of their physical parts. Their knowledge was more than merely a physical phenomenon.

Descartes's influence on the development of psychology was considerable. He proposed the revolutionary idea that the mind and the body were mutually interacting and suggested a method of studying 'the mind' which was based on reasoning and not metaphysical analysis. Descartes's notion of interactionism gave rise to two very influential but very different schools of thought in psychology at the end of the nineteenth and the beginning of the twentieth century: introspectionism and behaviourism. We consider these later in the chapter.

Empiricism: John Locke and David Hume

With the work of the English philosopher John Locke (1632–1704), the mechanisation of the whole world became complete. Locke did not exempt the mind from the mechanical laws of the material universe. Descartes's rationalism – pursuit of truth through reason – was replaced by empiricism – pursuit of truth through observation and experience (in Greek, *empeiria* means experience). A prevalent belief in the seventeenth century was that ideas were innately present in an infant's mind. Locke rejected this belief. Instead, he proposed that all knowledge must come through experience: it is empirically derived. His model of the mind was a tablet of soft clay, a *tabula rasa*, smooth at birth and ready to accept the writings of experience imprinted upon it.

Locke believed that our knowledge of complex experiences was nothing more than links between simple, primary sensations: simple ideas combined to form complex ones. This notion was developed further by the Scottish philosopher David Hume (1711–1776). In his book, *A Treatise of Human Nature* (1739), Hume argued that the study of human nature could best be undertaken through experience and observation. Hume's conception of the mind was slightly different from that of Locke. Whereas Locke wrote of ideas, Hume wrote of *perceptions* which were composed of *impressions* and *ideas*. Impressions were what we would consider sensations – seeing print on a paper or hearing a loud bang; ideas were the less vivid recollection of such sense experiences. Impressions, according to Hume were the most important perceptions because these were derived directly from observation. Any ideas based on content which was not derived empirically were not valuable and not trustworthy. Hume, therefore, espoused what is known as positivism – the school of thought which argues that all meaningful ideas can be reduced to observable material.

Perhaps Hume's greatest contribution to psychology was the doctrine of the association of ideas. In *An Inquiry*

Concerning Human Understanding, Hume argued that there were various types of connection or association between ideas. This, of course, was not itself a new idea. Aristotle has proposed the notion of an association of ideas: two stimuli if paired frequently enough would result in the presentation of one event stimulating thoughts of the other. Hume suggested three specific types of association: resemblance (when we look at someone's photograph, for example, this triggers off thoughts about that person), contiguity (thoughts of an object or event will trigger thoughts related to those objects and events) and cause and effect (the idea that actions have identifiable causes). These associations were the 'cement' that helped bind the universe, and all complex human experiences were based on simple ideas derived from impressions. The most important of these associations was cause and effect, and Hume developed this theme further by describing behaviour in terms of custom and habit. According to Hume, if one performs an act which produces an effect which makes a repetition of that act likely, this is a habit or custom. For example, think of a simple behaviour such as switching on a light. The fact that switching a light on will illuminate a room will result in your habitually throwing the switch if you need light. These notions of habit and causality became very important in the twentieth century with the development of behaviourism and the work of the Swiss developmental psychologist Jean Piaget (1896–1981).

Idealism: Bishop Berkeley

In contrast to the empiricists, the Irish bishop, philosopher, and mathematician George Berkeley (1685–1753) believed that our knowledge of events in the world did not come simply from direct experience. Instead, Berkeley (who gave his name to the famous American university in Los Angeles, California) argues that this knowledge is the result of inferences based on the accumulation of past experiences derived through the senses. In other words, we must learn how to perceive. For example, our visual perception of depth involves several elementary sensations, such as observing the relative movements of objects as we move our head and the convergence of our eyes (turning inward towards each other or away) as we focus on near or distant objects. Although our knowledge of visual depth seems to be immediate and direct, it is actually a secondary, complex response constructed from a number of simple elements. Our perceptions of the world can also involve integrating the activity of different sense organs, such as when we see, hear, feel and smell the same object. The aspect of Berkeley's philosophy which argues that all ideas come from the senses (*esse est percipi*) is called idealism.

As you can see, the philosophers Locke, Hume and Berkeley were grappling with the workings of the human mind and the way in which people acquire knowledge.

They were dealing with the concept of learning. Modern psychologists are still concerned with the issues that Berkeley raised. As philosophers, they were trying to fit a non-quantifiable variable – reason – into the equation.

With the work of the Scottish philosopher James Mill (1773–1836), the pendulum took its full swing from animism (physical matter animated by spirits) to materialism (mind composed entirely of matter). Materialism is the belief that reality can be known only through an understanding of the physical world, of which the mind is a part. Mill worked on the assumption that humans and animals were fundamentally the same. Both humans and animals were thoroughly physical in their make-up and were completely subject to the physical laws of the universe. He agreed in essence with Descartes's approach to understanding the human body but rejected the concept of an immaterial mind. Mind, to Mill, was as passive as the body. It responded to the environment in precisely the same way. The mind, no less than the body, was a machine.

Modern psychology: from the Leipzig laboratory to the cognitive revolution

Modern psychology, as we understand it today, began in Germany in the late nineteenth century with Wilhelm Wundt (1832–1920). Wundt was the first person to call himself a psychologist and he shared the conviction of other German scientists that all aspects of nature, including the human mind, could be studied scientifically. His book *Principles of Physiological Psychology* was the first textbook of psychology.

Wundt's approach was experimental in nature and his and his colleagues' work was conducted at the Leipzig laboratory. Over one hundred studies were conducted in the first twenty years of the laboratory's life. Initially, these were studies of the psychological and psychophysiological aspects of vision (seeing), audition (hearing) and somatosensation (feeling and touching). Later work focused on reaction time and the process involved in perceiving and then responding to a stimulus. Wundt also explored the nature of attention and emotional feeling as well as word association.

The fact that Germany was the birthplace of psychology had as much to do with social, political and economic influences as with the abilities of its scientists and scholars. The German university system was well established, and professors were highly respected members of society. The academic tradition in Germany emphasised a scientific approach to a large number of subject areas, such as history, phonetics, archaeology, aesthetics and literature. Thus, in contrast to French and British scholars, who adopted the more traditional, philosophical approach to the study of the human mind, German scholars were open to the possibility that the human mind could be studied scientifically. Experimental physiology, one of the most important roots of experimental psychology, was well established there. Eventually, Wundt's influence began to extend to other parts of Europe (especially, the UK) and to the USA.

Structuralism: Wilhelm Wundt

Wundt defined psychology as the 'science of immediate experience', and his approach was called structuralism, the first proper school of thought to emerge in the history of psychology. Its subject matter was the structure of the mind, built from the elements of consciousness, such as ideas and sensations. These elements could be constructed into a table of elements similar to a chemical table of elements. Structuralism's raw material was supplied by trained observers who described their own experiences. The observers were taught to engage in introspection (literally, 'looking within'), the use of which was governed by strict rules. Introspectionists observed stimuli and described their experiences. According to Boring (1953), observers participating in reaction time experiments had to produce approximately ten thousand introspective observations before their data were considered valid and themselves qualified introspectionists. Such introspection would be conducted under well controlled conditions so that the contents of consciousness could be carefully monitored and analysed. Wundt's aims were threefold: to analyse the content of conscious experience, to determine how the elements of consciousness are connected and to devise a law which would explain such connections. Wundt and his associates, Edward Tichener (1867–1927) and Gustav Fechner

Wilhelm Wundt (1832–1920)

(1801–1887), made inferences about the nature of mental processes by seeing how changes in the stimuli caused changes in the verbal reports of their trained observers.

Wundt was particularly interested in the problem that had intrigued George Berkeley: how did basic sensory information give rise to complex perceptions? His doctrine of apperception attempted to account for the fact that when we perceive, this perception is of a whole object and not separate elements of it. We see wholes, according to Wundt, because of the process of creative synthesis (or law of psychic resultants): a process which combines or synthesises elements to form a whole. Again, this process is very similar to a process in chemistry in which individual chemical elements when combined will form a new, wholly different entity. The whole would not be equivalent to the sum of its parts. Much of Wundt's work, however, aimed to break down and analyse the contents of the mind rather than determine how they are combined.

Wundt was an ambitious and prolific scientist who wrote many books and trained many other scientists in his laboratory. However, his method did not survive the test of time; structuralism died out in the early twentieth century. The major problem with his approach was the difficulty encountered by observers in reporting the raw data of sensation, data unmodified by experience. Although introspectionism aimed to establish well controlled experimental conditions which would lead to reliable introspective observations, there was often little agreement between observers about their introspections. The method has also been criticised for its reliance on retrospection; the recollection of an experience was frequently elicited some time after the experience itself had occurred and was, therefore, subject to error.

In addition, attention began to shift from study of the human mind to the study of human behaviour. Behaviourism provided a devastating and critical alternative to introspectionism. According to behaviourism's founding father, the American B. Watson, introspectionism was akin to superstition. More recently, psychologists have resumed the study of the human mind, but we now have better methods for studying it than were available to Wundt. Although structuralism has been supplanted, Wundt's contribution must be acknowledged. He was responsible for establishing psychology as a recognised, experimental science that was separate from philosophy. He used methods which involved observation and experimentation and trained a great number of psychologists, many of whom established their own schools and continued the evolution of the new discipline.

Memory: Herman Ebbinghaus

Most of the pioneers of psychology founded schools, groups of people having a common belief in a particular theory and methodology. In this context, the word school refers to a branch of a particular academic discipline, not a building or institution. Structuralism was a school of psychology. The exception to this trend was Hermann Ebbinghaus (1850–1909). In 1876, after receiving his PhD in philosophy but still unattached to an academic institution, Ebbinghaus came across a secondhand copy of a book by Gustav Fechner in which he described his mathematical approach to the measurement of human sensation. Intrigued by Fechner's research, Ebbinghaus decided to attempt to measure human memory: the processes of learning and forgetting.

Working alone, Ebbinghaus devised methods to measure memory and the speed with which forgetting occurred. He realised that he could not compare the learning and forgetting of two prose passages or two poems, because some passages would undoubtedly be easier to learn than others. Therefore, he devised a relatively uniform set of materials – nonsense syllables, such as 'juz', 'bul' and 'gof'. He printed the syllables on cards and read through a set of them, with the rate of presentation controlled by the ticking of a watch. After reading the set, he paused a fixed amount of time, then read the cards again. He recorded the number of times he had to read the cards to be able to recite them without error. He measured forgetting by trying to recite the nonsense syllables on a later occasion – minutes, hours or days later. The number of syllables he remembered was an index of the percentage of memory that had been retained.

Ebbinghaus's approach to memory was entirely empirical; he devised no theory of why learning occurs and was interested only in gathering facts through careful, systematic observation. However, despite the lack of theory, his work made important contributions to the development of the science of psychology. He introduced the principle of eliminating variable errors by making observations repeatedly on different occasions (using different lists each time) and calculating the average of these observations. Variable errors include errors caused by random differences in the subject's mood or alertness or by uncontrollable changes in the environment. He constructed graphs of the rate at which the memorised lists of nonsense syllables were forgotten, which provided a way to measure mental contents across time. As we see in Chapter 8, Ebbinghaus's research provided a model of systematic, rigorous experimental procedures that modern psychologists still emulate.

Functionalism: William James and James Angell

After structuralism, the next major trend in psychology was functionalism. This approach, which began in the USA, was in large part a protest against the structuralism of Wundt. Structuralists were interested in what they called the components of consciousness (ideas and sensations); functionalists were more interested in the process of conscious activity (perceiving and learning). Functionalism

William James (1842–1910)

grew from the new perspective on nature provided by Charles Darwin and his followers. Proponents of functionalism stressed the biological significance (the purpose, or function) of natural processes, including behaviours. The emphasis was on overt, observable behaviours, not on private mental events.

The most important psychologist to embrace functionalism was William James (1842–1910). As James said, 'My thinking is first, last, and always for the sake of my doing.' That is, thinking was not an end in itself; its function was to produce useful behaviours. Although James was a champion of experimental psychology, he did not appear to enjoy doing research, instead spending most of his time reading, thinking, teaching and writing during his tenure as professor of philosophy (later, professor of psychology) at Harvard University.

Unlike structuralism, functionalism was not supplanted; instead, its major tenets were absorbed by its successor, behaviourism. One of the last of the functionalists, James Angell (1869–1949), described its basic principles:

■ Functional psychology is the study of mental operations and not mental structures. For example, the mind remembers; it does not contain a memory. It is not enough to compile a catalogue of what the mind does; one must try to understand what the mind accomplishes by doing this.

■ Mental processes are not studied as isolated and independent events but as part of the biological activity of the organism. These processes are aspects of the organism's adaptation to the environment and are a product of its evolutionary history. For example, the fact that we are conscious implies that consciousness has adaptive value for our species.

■ Functional psychology studies the relation between the environment and the response of the organism to the environment. There is no meaningful distinction between mind and body, they are part of the same entity.

Evolution and heritability: Charles Darwin and Francis Galton

Charles Darwin (1809–1882) proposed the theory of evolution in his book, *On the Origin of Species by Means of Natural Selection*, published in 1859. His work, more than that of any other person, revolutionised biology. The concept of natural selection showed how the consequences of an animal's characteristics affect its ability to survive. Instead of simply identifying, describing and naming species, biologists began now to look at the adaptive significance of the ways in which species differed.

Darwin's theory suggested that behaviours, like other biological characteristics, could best be explained by understanding their role in the adaptation of an organism (a human or other animal) to its environment. Thus, behaviour has a biological context. Darwin assembled evidence that behaviours, like body parts, could be inherited. In *The Expression of the Emotions in Man and Animals*, published in 1872, he proposed that the facial gestures that animals make in expressing emotions were descended from movements that previously had other functions. New areas of exploration were opened for psychologists by the ideas that an evolutionary continuity existed among the various species of animals and that behaviours, like parts of the body, had evolutionary histories.

Darwin's notion of natural selection has had great impact on the way in which we view the genetic determinants of behaviour, as we will see in more detail in Chapter 3. One of the first psychologists to study the influence of genetics on human behaviour was Sir Francis Galton (1822–1911), Charles Darwin's first cousin. Galton was a polymath who made many other contributions to the field of science: he constructed the first weather maps of the British Isles, discovered and named the weather phenomenon we know as anticyclone, invented the term 'correlation' (which describes the statistical relationships between two variables or factors), developed the technique of fingerprinting, founded the discipline of psychometrics, which applies statistical principles to the measurement of individual differences and the construction of psychological tests, and established the Anthropometric Laboratory in London in 1884, the birthplace of intelligence testing.

Galton was interested in discovering whether people's physical features correlated with each other and whether such correlations occurred for psychological features such as sensory capacity, reaction time, intellect and eminence. In fact, Galton did find that features such as height, arm length and weight were highly and positively correlated and argued from this that if one part of the body's dimensions were known then one could construct the rest of the body to scale. Importantly, however, Galton was the first to provide statistical evidence for the heritability of psychological variables. In his study of eminent men, published in his book *Hereditary Genius* (Galton, 1869), Galton found that 31 per cent of illustrious men had eminent fathers and 48 per cent of these men had eminent sons. Of course, by today's standards, this study has many methodological shortcomings not least of which is the collection of data from eminent men only (to make a valid comparison, you might also need to look at non-eminent men and their offspring). There is also the argument that eminence may not have been inherited but had been determined by the environment in which these men were raised (these issues are discussed further in Chapter 11). However, Galton remains an important figure in the history of psychology. His greatest contribution is the establishment of the study of individual differences as a scientific enterprise.

Psychodynamic theory: Sigmund Freud

While psychology was developing as a fledgling science, Sigmund Freud (1856–1939) was formulating a theory of human behaviour that would greatly affect psychology and psychiatry and radically influence intellectuals of all kinds. Freud began his career as a neurologist, so his work was originally firmly rooted in biology. He soon became interested in behavioural and emotional problems and began formulating his psychodynamic theory of personality, which would evolve over his long career. Although his approach was based on observation of patients and not on scientific experiments, he remained convinced that the biological basis of his theory would eventually be established.

Freud and his theory are discussed in detail in Chapter 14 but is mentioned here to mark his place in the history of psychology. His theory of the mind included structures, but his structuralism was quite different from Wundt's. He devised his concepts of ego, superego, id, and other mental structures through talking with his patients, not through laboratory experiments. His hypothetical mental operations included many that were unconscious and hence not available to introspection. And unlike Wundt, Freud emphasised function; his mental structures served biological drives and instincts and reflected our animal nature.

Behaviourism: Edward Thorndike, Ivan Pavlov and John Watson

The next major trend in psychology, behaviourism, followed directly from functionalism. It went further in its rejection of the special nature of mental events, denying that unobservable and unverifiable mental events were properly the subject matter of psychology. Behaviourists believed that because psychology is the study of observable behaviours, mental events – which cannot be observed – are outside the realm of psychology. Behaviourism is thus the study of the relation between people's environments and their behaviour; what occurs within their heads is irrelevant.

One of the first behaviourists was Edward Thorndike (1874–1949), an American psychologist who studied the behaviour of animals. He noticed that some events, usually those that one would expect to be pleasant, seemed to 'stamp in' a response that had just occurred. Noxious events seemed to 'stamp out' the response, or make it less likely to occur. We now call these processes reinforcement and punishment, and they are described in more detail in Chapter 7. Thorndike defined the law of effect as follows:

> 'Any act which in a given situation produces satisfaction becomes associated with that situation, so that when the situation recurs the act is more likely than before to recur also. Conversely, any act which in a given situation produces discomfort becomes disassociated from that situation, so that when the situation recurs the act is less likely than before to recur.' (Thorndike, 1905, p. 203)

The law of effect is in the functionalist tradition. It observes that the consequences of a behaviour act back upon the organism, affecting the likelihood that the behaviour that just occurred will occur again. An organism does something, and the consequences of this action make that action more likely. This process is very similar to the principle of natural selection. Just as organisms that successfully adapt to their environments are more likely to survive and breed, behaviours that cause useful outcomes become more likely to recur.

Although Thorndike insisted that the subject matter of psychology was behaviour, his explanations contained mentalistic terms. For example, in his law of effect he spoke of 'satisfaction', which is certainly not a phenomenon that can be directly observed. Later behaviourists threw out terms like 'satisfaction' and 'discomfort' and replaced them with more objective terms that reflected the behaviour of the organism rather than any feelings it might have.

Another major figure in the development of the behaviourism was not a psychologist but a physiologist: Ivan Pavlov (1849–1936), a Russian who studied the physiology of digestion (for which he later received a Nobel Prize). In the course of studying the stimuli that produce salivation, he discovered that hungry dogs would salivate at the sight of the attendant who brought in their dishes of food. Pavlov found that a dog could be trained to salivate at completely arbitrary stimuli, such as the sound of a bell, if the stimulus was quickly followed by the delivery of a bit of food into the animal's mouth.

Pavlov's discovery had profound significance for psychology. He showed that through experience an animal could learn to make a response to a stimulus that had never caused this response before. This ability, in turn, might explain how organisms learn cause-and-effect relations in the environment. In contrast, Thorndike's law of effect suggested an explanation for the adaptability of an individual's behaviour to its particular environment. So, from

Ivan Pavlov (1849–1936) in his laboratory with some of his collaborators. His research revealed valuable, though unsought, information about the principles of learning. (UPI/Corbis-Bettmann)

Thorndike's and Pavlov's studies two important behavioural principles had been discovered.

Behaviourism as a formal school of psychology began with the publication of a book by John B. Watson (1878–1958), *Psychology from the Standpoint of a Behaviorist* (Watson, 1919). Watson was a professor of psychology at the Johns Hopkins University, a popular teacher and writer and was a very convincing advocate of behaviourism. Even after leaving Johns Hopkins and embarking on a highly successful career in advertising, he continued to lecture and write magazine articles about psychology.

According to Watson, psychology was a natural science whose domain was restricted to observable events: the behaviour of organisms. Watson's behaviourism can be best summed up by his definition published in an article entitled, 'Psychology as the behaviorist views it' (Watson, 1913):

> 'Psychology as the behaviorist views it is a purely objective experimental branch of natural science. Its theoretical goal is the prediction and control of behavior. Introspectionism forms no essential part of its methods, nor is the scientific value of its data dependent upon the readiness with which they lend themselves to interpretation in terms of consciousness. The behaviorist, in his efforts to get a unitary scheme of animal response, recognises no dividing line between man and brute.'

John B. Watson (1878–1958)

You can clearly glean from this quotation that Watson believed that the elements of consciousness studied by the structuralists were too subjective to lend themselves to scientific investigation. He defined psychology as the objective study of behaviour and the stimuli which produce such behaviour. The important feature of behaviourism was its reliance only on observable behaviour. Even thinking was reduced to a form of behaviour – talking to oneself. Watson described visually observable behaviour as 'explicit behaviour' and those behaviours which could not be directly observed but potentially observed as 'implicit behaviour'. For example, we cannot see the body's cells transmitting electrical signals but we can observe such behaviour by using the correct electrical recording equipment.

Another important feature, tied to observation, was that the brain had very little to do with what was directly observed. What was important to Watson was the concept of stimulus and response, an idea suggested by Descartes and explicitly described by Pavlov. Watson argued that given the correct stimuli, the organism could learn to behave (give responses) in a specific way (in the same way that Pavlov's dogs had 'learned' to associate the bell with the appearance of food). Watson, however, famously went further. In his book *Behaviourism*, he argued:

'Give me a dozen healthy infants, well-formed, and my own specified world to bring them up in and I'll guarantee to take any one at random and train him to become any type of specialist I might select – doctor, lawyer, artist, merchant-chief and, yes, even beggar-man and thief, regardless of his talents, penchants, tendencies, abilities, vocations and race of his ancestors.' (Watson, 1930)

Many of Watson's ideas, such as the notion that reflexes can be conditioned, have been incorporated into the mainstream of psychology, although the central tenet that all behaviour that is studied must be observable, has not. After Watson, a new form of behaviourism emerged which took Watson's ideas and developed them further. This new form became known as neobehaviourism or radical behaviourism

Radical behaviourism: Edward Tolman, Clark Leonard Hull and Burrhus Frederick Skinner

The period 1930–1960 saw a tremendous surge not only in the description of the ways in which organisms behaved but also in the explanations for why they behaved in the way they did. This surge was generated largely by the work of a group of American psychologists, Edward Tolman (1886–1959), Clark Leonard Hull (1884–1952) and B.F. Skinner (1904–1990). Each had a different view on how behaviour occurred but all used animal experiments and the procedures of learning experiments to support their theories. Hull, for example, proposed a highly detailed mathematical model of behaviour, based on his conditioning work with rats in his book *Principles of Behaviour* (Hull, 1943), which sought to explain almost all behaviour. The basic feature of Hull's model was that all human (and any organism's) behaviour evolves through interaction with the environment. However, this interaction occurs within a wider frame of reference – the biological adaptation of the organism to the environment. The variable intervening between environment and organism was drive – a bodily need arising from deprivation or desire or another motivational spur. Although one of the more widely cited psychologists of his day, Clark has not made a lasting impact on psychology largely because his extremely detailed mathematical analyses were based on few experiments, the results of which were generalised well beyond the scope of the experimental context.

Tolman suggested that it was important not only to observe the stimulus and response but to take into account intervening variables. To Tolman, these intervening variables were cognitions and demands, and Tolman's theory became known as purposive behaviourism, so-called because all behaviour was goal-directed and had a purpose. Tolman's work did not bequeath any major principles or laws, however, although interest in his work continues (Reid and Staddon, 1998).

The bequest of a major framework of thinking in psychology was left to B.F. Skinner (1904–1990), one of the most influential psychologists of the twentieth century. Skinner's work gave birth to the technology of teaching machines (which have since been replaced by computers), the use of behaviour modification in instruction of the mentally retarded, and the use of behaviour therapy to treat mental disorders.

Skinner's work focused on the idea of reinforcement and was based largely on observation of behaviour in pigeons. He found that a certain set of stimulus conditions (such as a box, hunger, food in sight) would emit certain behaviours (strutting, random pecking). If the animal behaved in a certain way to obtain food then the food became the

B.F. Skinner (1904–1990)

reinforcing stimulus or the reinforcer – a stimulus which increases the probability that behaviour will occur again. Using his observations of pigeons' behaviour, Skinner found that the pigeons could be trained to behave in a specific way when responding to specific signals from their environment. For example, the pigeon would learn that it would receive food only if it pecked a food-dispensing lever a certain number of times; instead of randomly pecking at this lever it would then peck only the number of times necessary.

This form of learning, instrumental or operant learning, was of three types. Positive reinforcement refers to pleasant reinforcers such as the attention or approval given to a child from a teacher. Punishment refers to a negative stimulus which is presented when a behaviour occurs (for example, a rat receiving an electric shock whenever it presses a lever). Negative reinforcement refers to a behaviour which reduces the likelihood of negative stimulation (for example, a rat pressing a lever to avoid electric shock).

Reinforcement could also occur according to scheduling. For example, fixed-interval reinforcement involved a reinforcer that was given only after a set time; fixed-ratio reinforcement involved a reinforcer that was given only after a predetermined number of responses. Examples of fixed-interval reinforcement include receiving a wage at the end of the week or a salary at the end of a month; an example of fixed-ratio reinforcement would be the delivery of payment after, say, a certain number of items had been produced in a factory or after a specific number of products had been sold. Chapter 7 takes up these ideas.

Unlike Tolman and Hull, however, Skinner did not propose any intervening variables. To him, the behaving person or pigeon or rat was an 'empty organism'. He argued that humans were machines which behaved in lawful and predictable ways and his system was almost entirely descriptive with little in the way of theory emerging from it. In addition to his scientific work, Skinner published a novel, *Walden Two*, in which he described the way in which radical behaviourism could operate (Skinner, 1948).

Psychologists, including modern behaviourists, have moved away from the strict behaviourism of Watson and Skinner; mental processes such as imagery and attention are again considered to be proper subject matter for scientific investigation. But Watson's emphasis on objectivity in psychological research remains. Even those modern psychologists who most vehemently protest against what they see as the narrowness of behaviourism use the same principles of objectivity to guide their research. As research scientists, they must uphold the principles of objectivity that evolved from empiricism to functionalism to behaviourism. A psychologist who studies private mental events realises that these events can only be studied indirectly, by means of behaviour – verbal reports of inner experiences. Psychologists realise that these reports are not pure reflections of these mental events; like other behaviours, these responses can be affected by many factors. But as much as possible, they strive to maintain an objective stance to ensure that their research findings will be valid and capable of being verified.

Genetic epistemology: Jean Piaget

While American approaches to psychology were dominated by the new behaviourism, a different approach to the study of cognitive function was being espoused in Europe. The Swiss psychologist Jean Piaget (1896–1980) became interested in the question of human knowledge and how we begin to acquire knowledge. He believed that answers to such questions could be obtained by empirical, scientific research and he would measure the development of the acquisition of knowledge in children by presenting them with intellectual tasks at various stages of their lives (in fact, Piaget had worked with Theophile Simon, the collaborator of the man who designed the first IQ test, Alfred Binet). Piaget termed his approach to psychology as genetic epistemology: the study of the origin of knowledge in child development. Apart from Piaget's focus on the acquisition of knowledge in groups of individuals, another difference between his European approach and that of his American counterparts was the lack of interest in the applied nature of research. Questions regarding the possibility of improving or accelerating children's learning did not interest Piaget, nor did it interest other European researchers (Leahey, 1997). Although his work made little impact on psychology at the time, the subsequent circulation of his work – with translations of his books – led to a considerable interest in his research (Smith, 1996), so much so, that few psychologists have dominated the study of child development in the way that Piaget has. Piaget's contribution to our understanding of child cognition is reviewed in Chapter 12.

Gestalt psychology: Max Wertheimer

The structuralism of Wilhelm Wundt was not the only German influence on the development of psychology. In 1911, a German psychologist, Max Wertheimer (1880–1943), bought a toy that presented a series of pictures in rapid succession. Each picture was slightly different from the one that preceded it, and the resulting impression was that of continuous motion, like a film. Wundt and his followers insisted that if we want to understand the nature of human consciousness we must analyse it – divide it into its individual elements. But Wertheimer and his colleagues realised that the perception of a motion picture was not that of a series of individual still pictures. Instead, viewers saw continuity in time and space. They saw objects that retained their identity as they moved from place to place. Asking people to study these pictures one at a time and to describe what they saw (the structuralist approach) would never explain the phenomenon of the motion picture.

Wertheimer and his colleagues attempted to discover the organisation of cognitive processes, not their elements. They called their approach Gestalt psychology. Gestalt is a German word that roughly translates into 'unified form' or 'overall shape'. Gestalt psychologists insisted that perceptions resulted from patterns of interactions among many elements – patterns that could exist across both space and time. For example, a simple melody consists of a pattern of different notes, played one at a time. If the melody is played in different keys, so that the individual notes are different, people can still recognise it. Clearly, they recognise the relations the notes have to each other, not just the notes themselves.

Although the Gestalt school of psychology no longer exists, its insistence that elements of an experience interact – that the whole is not simply the sum of its parts – has had a profound influence on the development of modern psychology. Gestalt psychology did not disappear because of some inherent fatal flaw in its philosophy or methodology. Instead, many of its approaches and ideas were incorporated into other areas of psychology. Gestalt psychology is discussed in more detail in Chapter 6.

Humanistic psychology

For many years, philosophers and other intellectuals have been concerned with what they see as the special nature of humanity – with freewill and spontaneity, with creativity and consciousness. As the science of psychology developed, these concerns received less attention because researchers could not agree on objective ways to study them. Humanistic psychology developed during the 1950s and 1960s as a reaction against both behaviourism and psychoanalysis. Although psychoanalysis certainly dealt with mental phenomena that could not be measured objectively, it saw people as products of their environment and of innate, unconscious forces. Humanistic psychologists insist that human nature goes beyond environmental influences, and that conscious processes, not unconscious ones, are what psychologists should study. In addition, they note that psychoanalysis seems preoccupied with disturbed people, ignoring positive phenomena such as happiness, satisfaction, love and kindness. Humanistic psychology is an approach to the study of human behaviour that emphasises human experience, choice and creativity, self-realisation and positive growth. The father of humanistic psychology, Abraham Maslow (1908–1970), wrote: 'What a man can be, he must be. He must be true to his own nature … [to a] desire to become more and more what one idiosyncratically is, to become everything that one is capable of becoming' (1970, p. 46).

Humanistic psychologists emphasise the positive sides of human nature and the potential we all share for personal growth. In general, humanistic psychologists do not believe that we will understand human consciousness and behaviour through scientific research. Thus, the humanistic approach has not had a significant influence on psychology as a science. Its greatest impact has been on the development of methods of psychotherapy based on a positive and optimistic view of human potential.

The cognitive revolution: beyond behaviourism

The emphasis on behaviourism restricted the subject matter of psychology to observable behaviours. For many years, concepts such as consciousness were considered to be outside the domain of psychology. As one psychologist put it, 'psychology, having first bargained away its soul and then gone out of its mind, seems now … to have lost all consciousness' (Burt, 1962, p. 229).

During the past three decades many psychologists have protested against the restrictions of behaviourism and have turned to the study of consciousness, feelings, imagery, and other private events. Much of cognitive psychology uses an approach called information processing – information received through the senses is 'processed' by various systems in the brain. Some systems store the information in the form of memory, and other systems control behaviour. Some systems operate automatically and unconsciously, while others are conscious and require effort on the part of the individual. Because the information-processing approach was first devised to describe the operations of complex physical systems such as computers, the modern model of the human brain is, for most cognitive psychologists, the computer. As you will learn in Chapter 7, another model (neural networks) is beginning to replace the computer.

Although cognitive psychologists now study mental structures and operations, they have not gone back to the introspective methods that structuralists such as Wundt employed. For example, several modern psychologists have studied the phenomenon of imagery. If you close your eyes and imagine what the open pages of this book look like, you are viewing a mental image of what you have previously seen. This image exists only within your brain, and it can be experienced by you and no one else. Another person has no way of knowing whether your images are like his or hers any more than that person knows whether the colour red looks the same to you as it does to him or her. The experience of imagery cannot be shared.

However, behaviours that are based upon images can be measured. For example, Kosslyn (1973) asked a group of people to memorise several drawings. Then, he asked them to imagine one of them, focusing their attention on a particular feature of the image. Next, he asked them a question about a detail of the image that was either 'near' the point they were focusing on or 'far' from it. For example, if they were picturing a boat, he might ask them to imagine that they were looking at its stern. Then he might ask them

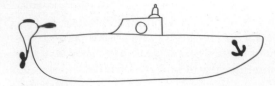

Figure 1.2

A drawing used in the imagery study by Kosslyn.

Source: Kosslyn, S.M., *Perception and Psychophysics*, 1973, 14, 90–94. Reprinted with permission.

whether the boat had a rudder at the stern, or whether a rope was fastened to its bow. Because the bow is at the opposite end of the boat, it should be located at the 'opposite end' of the image.

Kosslyn found that people could very quickly answer a question about a feature of the boat that was near the place they were focusing on, but they took longer to answer a question about a part that was farther away. It was as if they had to scan their mental image to get from one place to the other (see Figure 1.2).

The biological revolution

Biology has always been closely tied to psychology. René Descartes and his model of muscular physiology provides a good beginning for a discussion of the biological roots of psychology. Descartes's concept was based on an actual working model (the moving statue) whose movements seemed similar to those of human beings. Recognition of that similarity served as 'proof' of his theory; he did not have the means available to offer a scientific proof. But technological development soon made experimentation and manipulation possible. Truth need not only be reasoned, it could also be demonstrated and verified. Descartes's hydraulic model of muscular movement was shown to be incorrect by Luigi Galvani (1737–1798), an Italian physiologist who discovered that muscles could be made to contract by applying an electrical current directly to them or to the nerves that were attached to them. The muscles themselves contained the energy needed for them to contract. They did not have to be inflated by pressurised fluid.

The work of the German physiologist Johannes Müller (1801–1858) flags a definite transition from the somewhat sporadic, isolated instances of research into human physiology to the progressively more direct and precise exploration of the human body. Müller was a forceful advocate of applying experimental procedures to the study of physiology. He recommended that biologists should do more than observe and classify; they should remove or isolate animals' organs, test their responses to chemicals, and manipulate other conditions in order to see how the organism worked. His most important contribution to

Johannes Müller (1801–1858)

what would become the science of psychology was his doctrine of specific nerve energies. He noted that the basic message sent along all nerves was the same – an electrical impulse. And the impulse itself was the same, regardless of whether the message concerned was, for example, a visual perception or an auditory one. What, then, accounts for the brain's ability to distinguish different kinds of sensory information? That is, why do we see what our eyes detect, hear what our ears detect, and so on? After all, both the optic nerves and the auditory nerves send the same kind of message to the brain.

The answer is that the messages are sent over different channels. Because the optic nerves are attached to the eyes, the brain interprets impulses received from these nerves as visual sensations. You have probably already noticed that rubbing your eyes causes sensations of flashes of light. When you rub your eyes, the pressure against them stimulates visual receptors located inside. As a result of this stimulation, messages are sent through the optic nerves to the brain. The brain interprets these messages as sensations of light.

Müller's doctrine had important implications. If the brain recognises the nature of a particular sensory input by means of the particular nerve that brings the message, then perhaps the brain is similarly specialised, with different parts having different functions. In other words, if different nerves convey messages about different kinds of information, then those regions of the brain that receive these messages must have different functions. Müller's ideas have endured, forming the basis for investigations into the functions of the nervous system. For centuries, philosophers had identified thinking or consciousness as the distinguishing feature of the human mind and had concluded that the mind was located in the brain. Now the components of the nervous system were being identified and their means of operation were being explored.

Pierre Flourens (1774–1867), a French physiologist, provided experimental evidence for the implications of Müller's doctrine of specific nerve energies. He operated on animals, removing various parts of the nervous system. He found that the resulting effects depended on which parts were removed. He observed what the animal could no longer do and concluded that the missing capacity must have been the function of the part that he had removed. For example, if an animal could not move its leg after part of its brain was removed, then that region must normally control leg movements. This method of removal of part of the brain, called experimental ablation (from the Latin *ablatus*, 'carried away'), was soon adopted by neurologists, and it is still used by scientists today. Through experimental ablation, Flourens claimed to have discovered the regions of the brain that control heart rate and breathing, purposeful movements, and visual and auditory reflexes.

The first person to apply the logic of Flourens's method to humans was Paul Broca (1824–1880). In 1861, Broca, a French surgeon, performed an autopsy on the brain of a man who had suffered a stroke several years previously. The stroke (damage to the brain caused, in this case, by a blood clot) had caused the man to lose the ability to speak. The patient, who's real name was Leborgne, was called Tan because this was the only word he could utter. Broca discovered that the stroke had damaged part of the brain on the left side. He suggested that this region of the brain is a centre for speech (this part is now called Broca's area and we will learn more about this in Chapter 10).

Although subsequent research has found that speech is not controlled by a single 'centre' in the brain (and Marc Dax had reported similar findings earlier that century), the area that Broca identified is necessary for speech production. This finding was quickly followed up independently by Carl Wernicke who noted that damage to an adjacent part of the brain on the same side in his patient impaired speech comprehension and production. Studying the accidental effects of brain damage on function has allowed neuroscientists to predict which regions of the brain may be involved in specific functions. Psychologists can operate on the brains of laboratory animals, but obviously they cannot operate on the brains of humans. Instead, they must study the effects of brain damage that occurs from natural causes. You will find out more about this approach in Chapter 4 and in other chapters. One example of brain damage leading to speculation about the function a brain region performs is that of Phineas Gage. You can find further details about this patient in Chapter 13, but in short, Gage was a railroad construction supervisor who, in the mid-nineteenth century, had an accident at work. An iron rod shot through his face, through the front part of his brain and straight out of the top of his head. A reconstructed image of the trajectory of the rod through his skull can be seen in Figure 1.3.

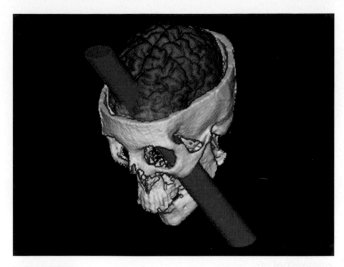

Figure 1.3

On a September afternoon in 1848, an unusual accident befell a young American railroad worker called Phineas Gage. An iron rod shot through his head as a result of an uncontrolled explosion at work. Almost 150 years later, Hannah Damasio and her colleagues at the University of Iowa took the medical reports of Gage's injury and plotted the course of the rod, using modern computer technology. One of the images showing the rod's trajectory is seen here.

Source: Damasio, H., Grabowski, T., Frank, R., Galaburda, A.M. and Damasio, A.R.: The return of Phineas Gage: Clues about the brain from a famous patient. *Science*, 264: 1102–1105, 1994. Department of Neurology, University of Iowa.

Whereas before the injury, Gage had been a hardworking and conscientious individual, after the injury, he became boorish, unpleasant and unreliable. The part of the brain damaged seemed to be that responsible for inhibiting inappropriate behaviour. We now know that patients with damage to this part of the brain have difficulty in inhibiting such behaviour and you will encounter such cases in Chapter 13.

In 1870, the German physiologists Gustav Fritsch and Eduard Hitzig introduced the use of electrical stimulation as a tool for mapping the functions of the brain. For example, Fritsch and Hitzig discovered that applying a small electrical shock to different parts of the cerebral cortex caused movements of different parts of the body. In fact, the body appeared to be 'mapped' on the surface of the brain, as seen in Figure 1.4.

Originally, this work was conducted on dogs on Frau Hitzig's dressing table (because they had no available laboratory space). Such humble conditions gave rise to the first experiment in localisation of function in the brain – the goal of neuropsychology.

A different and yet essentially physical approach to studying behaviour was also seen in the work of the German physicist and physiologist Hermann von Helmholtz (1821–1894) who did much to demonstrate that

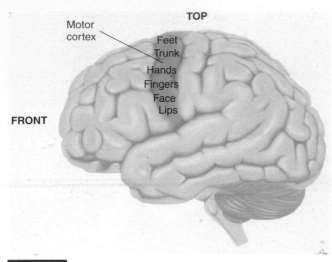

Hermann von Helmholtz (1821–1894)

mental phenomena could be explained by physiological means. This extremely productive scientist made contributions to both physics and physiology. He actively disassociated himself from natural philosophy, from which many assumptions about the nature of the mind had been derived. Müller, under whom Helmholtz had conducted his first research, believed that human organs were endowed with a vital immaterial force that co-ordinated physiological behaviour, a force that was not subject to experimental investigation. Helmholtz would allow no such assumptions about unproved (and unprovable) phenomena. He advocated a purely scientific approach, with conclusions based on objective investigation and precise measurement.

Until Helmholtz's time, scientists believed that the transmission of impulses through nerves was as fast as the speed of electricity in wires; under this assumption, transmission would be virtually instantaneous, considering the small distances that impulses have to travel within the human body. Helmholtz successfully measured the speed of the nerve impulse and found that it was only about 90 feet per second, which is considerably slower than the speed of electricity in wires. This finding suggested to later researchers that the nerve impulse is more complex than a simple electrical current passing through a wire, which is indeed true.

Helmholtz also attempted to measure the speed of a person's reaction to a physical stimulus, but he abandoned this attempt because there was too much variability from person to person. However, this variability interested scientists who followed him; they tried to explain the reason for individual differences in behaviour. Because both the velocity of nerve impulses and a person's reactions to stimuli could be measured, researchers theorised that mental events themselves could be the subject of scientific investigation. Possibly, if the proper techniques could be developed, one could investigate what went on within the human brain. Thus, Helmholtz's research was important in setting the stage for the science of psychology.

In Germany, a contemporary of von Helmholtz's, Ernst Weber (1795–1878), began work that led to the development of a method for measuring the magnitude of human sensations. Weber, an anatomist and physiologist, found that people's ability to tell the difference between two similar stimuli – such as the brightness of two lights, the heaviness of two objects, or the loudness of two tones – followed orderly laws. This regularity suggested to Weber and his followers that the study of perceptual phenomena could be as scientific as that of physics or biology. In Chapter 6 we consider the study of the relation between the physical characteristics of a stimulus and the perceptions they produce, a field called *psychophysics*, or the physics of the mind.

Cognitive neuroscience: the future of the biology of the 'mind'?

During the early and mid-twentieth century, the dominance of behaviourism led to a de-emphasis of biological factors in the study of behaviour. At the time, scientists had no way of studying what went on in the brain, but that did not prevent people from spinning elaborate theories of how the brain controlled behaviour. Behaviourists rejected such speculation. They acknowledged that the brain controlled behaviour, but because we could not see what was happening inside the brain, we should refrain from inventing physiological explanations that could not be verified.

Cognitive psychologists inherited from early behaviourists a suspicion of the value of biology in explaining behaviour. Thus, the cognitive revolution did not lead to a renewed interest in biology. But the extraordinary advances in neurobiology in the late twentieth century have revolutionised psychology. Neurobiologists (biolo-

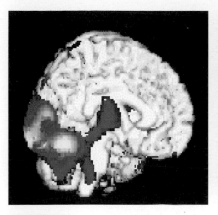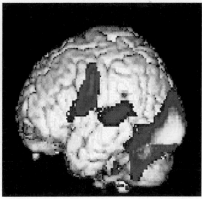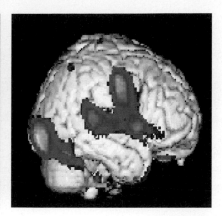

Figure 1.5

Areas of activation in the human brain while it engages in language tasks.

Source: Brunswick *et al.*, 1999. Reproduced with permission.

gists who study the nervous system) and scientists and engineers in allied fields have developed ways to study the brain that were unthinkable just a few decades ago. We can study fine details of nerve cells, discover their interconnections, analyse the chemicals they use to communicate with each other, produce drugs that block the action of these chemicals or mimic their effects.

More importantly, we can see the internal structure of a living human brain, and measure the activity of different parts of the brain – regions as small as a few cubic millimetres – while people are thinking, feeling, perceiving, comprehending and moving (Martin, 1998a; Frackowiak *et al.*, 1997), as seen in Figure 1.5.

This combination of cognitive psychology and neuroscience – cognitive neuroscience – may provide the best opportunity psychologists have for studying behaviour

and describing its causes. Currently, the endeavours in cognitive neuroscience are, because of the nature of the techniques used, directed towards studying basic, yet essential, behaviour such as reading, recognising emotion, remembering and speaking. In the future, there may be a means of observing the brain as it operates in 'real life', while encountering 'real-life' situations, events and problems. This approach holds much promise.

In this chapter, we have described and reviewed the major divisions of psychology and briefly outlined the history of the discipline. A survey of the history of psychology reveals a number of methodological approaches to the study of behaviour. In the next chapter, we will consider in more detail the ways in which psychologists study behaviour. You will also discover the dominant methodological approach to answering questions about psychology.

Questions to think about

The development of ideas in psychology

- In what way can the development of psychology as a science be seen as multi- and inter-disciplinary?

- It has been said that once questions have been answered in philosophy then there is no philosophy. Do you think that philosophy can still contribute to psychological questions or could psychology answer philosophical questions better than philosophy could?

- Does the 'mind' exist only as a metaphor? Do you think that it is useful to invoke the concept of 'mind' in modern psychology?

- What is Cartesian dualism? Can this form a part of modern psychological thinking?

- What are the essential features of structuralism and behaviourism? What would you consider to be the pros

and cons of introspectionism and behaviourism? Which would you consider to have been the best method of understanding behaviour at the beginning of the century?

- Why do you think that behaviourism was so popular?

- What is Darwin's theory of natural selection and why do you think psychologists consider this to be so important?

- Why is the study of individual differences important to psychology?

- Why was 'the cognitive revolution', a 'revolution'? What could cognitive psychologists study that their predecessors didn't or couldn't?

- Can we understand behaviour without reference to the workings of the brain and the rest of the body?

Key terms

psychology *p.4*
reification *p.4*
causal event/determinant *p.5*
psychiatry *p.5*
psychoanalysis *p.5*
physiological psychology *p.5*
biological reductionism *p.5*
psychophysiology *p.5*
neuropsychology/ neuroscience *p.5*
clinical neuropsychology *p.8*
cognitive neuroscience *p.8*
comparative psychology *p.9*
ethology *p.9*
sociobiology *p.9*

behaviour genetics *p.9*
cognitive psychology *p.9*
cognitive science *p.9*
developmental psychology *p.9*
social psychology *p.9*
individual differences *p.9*
cross-cultural psychology *p.9*
cultural psychology *p.9*
forensic/criminological psychology *p.9*
offender profiling *p.11*
clinical psychology *p.12*
health psychology *p.12*
educational psychology *p.12*
consumer psychology *p.12*
organisational/occupational psychology *p.12*

ergonomics/human factors psychology *p.12*
sport and exercise psychology *p.13*
animism *p.13*
reflexes *p.14*
dualism/Cartesian dualism *p.14*
interactionism *p.15*
double-aspect theory *p.15*
model *p.15*
empiricism *p.15*
positivism *p.15*
doctrine of the association of ideas *p.15*
idealism *p.16*
materialism *p.16*
experimental psychology *p.17*
structuralism *p.17*

introspection *p.17*
doctrine of apperception *p.17*
variable errors *p.18*
functionalism *p.18*
behaviourism *p.20*
law of effect *p.20*
neobehaviourism/radical behaviourism *p.21*
purposive behaviourism *p.21*
genetic epistemology *p.22*
Gestalt psychology *p.23*
humanistic psychologists *p.23*
information processing *p.23*
doctrine of specific nerve energies *p.24*
localisation of function *p.25*

CHAPTER REVIEW

What is psychology?

■ Psychology is the science of behaviour, and psychologists study a large variety of behaviours in humans and other animals.

■ Psychology has several major branches:

- Physiological psychologists study the biological basis of behaviour.
- Psychophysiologists study people's physiological reactions, such as changes in heart rate and muscle tension.
- Neuropsychologists study the relationship between Central Nervous System activity and structure and function.
- Comparative psychologists study the evolution of behaviour by comparing the behavioural capacities of various species of animals.
- Ethologists study the biological bases of behaviour through observation of animals in natural environments.

- Sociobiologists attempt to interpret human and animal behaviour in terms of evolution and biological inheritance.
- Behaviour geneticists study the degree of influence exerted by heredity and environment on behaviour.
- Cognitive psychologists study complex human behaviours such as cognition, memory and attention.
- Cognitive neuroscientists study the role of the brain in cognition.
- Developmental psychologists study the development of behaviour throughout the lifespan.
- Social psychologists study the effects of people on the behaviour of other people.
- Individual differences involves the study of the effects of specific characteristics or traits on behaviour.
- Cross-cultural psychologists study the impact of culture on behaviour.

- Forensic and criminological psychologists study the ways in which psychological knowledge can help in criminal and legal settings.
- Clinical psychologists study the causes and treatment of mental disorders and problems of adjustment.
- Health psychologists study the ways in which lifestyle and behaviour affect illness and health.
- Educational psychologists assess the cognitive, social and emotional development of children in the school environment.
- Consumer psychologists advise people who buy or sell goods and services.
- Organisational or occupational psychologists help organisations become more efficient and effective.
- Ergonomists help to design machines and workplace environments that enhance work performance.

The development of psychology as a science

- Psychology has its modern roots in the thinking of the French philosopher and mathematician René Descartes who argued that the mind and the body were two separate entities which interacted (dualism).
- The mid-nineteenth century gave rise to materialism and empiricism. Materialism maintained that the mind was made of matter; thus all natural phenomena, including human behaviour, could be explained in terms of physical entities: the interaction of matter and energy. Empiricism emphasised that all knowledge was acquired by means of sensory experience; no knowledge was innate. The concept of empiricism was developed by the philosophers John Locke and David Hume.

Modern psychology

- The first laboratory of experimental psychology was established in Leipzig in 1879 by Wilhelm Wundt.
- Wundt and his colleagues' work gave rise to structuralism: the idea that the mind was made up of components which could be broken apart and studied. The method of studying these components was introspection – the observation and recall of experience.
- At about the same time, Ebbinghaus contributed important methods for objectively measuring learning and forgetting.

- Darwin's ground-breaking theory of evolution, or theory of natural selection, argued that traits necessary for survival would be inherited and that only those adaptively useful traits would survive.
- Francis Galton founded the scientific study of individual differences in human behaviour and suggested that certain psychological characteristics could be inherited.
- Functionalism, which grew out of Darwin's theory of evolution, was concerned with the processes of consciousness such as perceiving and learning. Its major advocates were William James and James Angell.
- Functionalism gave rise to behaviourism, founded by John Watson, which still dominates the way we do research. The subject matter of behaviourism is observable behaviour; according to the behaviourists, mental events – because they were unobservable – should play no part in scientific psychology. Behaviourism developed a radical strain in the 1950s which viewed the organism's behaviour strictly in terms of stimulus and response.
- Humanistic psychology is concerned with the special nature of humanity and emphasises human experience, choice and creativity, and the potential for personal growth.
- The cognitive revolution arose from the belief that behaviourism's emphasis on observable behaviour missed some of the complexity of human cognition and behaviour. The cognitive revolution saw a rekindling of interest in phenomena such as memory, thinking, creativity, imagination and so on, and human behaviour was interpreted in terms of information processing.
- The biological revolution in psychology manifested itself in the increased interest of psychologists in all fields – not just physiological psychology – in the role of biological factors in behaviour. This has given rise to cognitive neuroscience in which the disciplines of neuropsychology and cognitive psychology have combined and used neuroimaging methods to create a greater understanding of the role of the brain in thinking, feeling and perceiving, specifically to localise function in the brain.

Suggestions for further reading

Leahey, T.H. (1997). *A History of Psychology* (5th edition). New Jersey: Prentice Hall International.

Schultz, D. and Schultz, S.E. (1987). *A History of Modern Psychology* (4th edition). New York: Academic Press.
Several books describe the history of psychology, including its philosophical and biological roots, and you may wish to read one of them and then expand your reading from there to learn more. The books by Leahey and Schultz are good introductions.

Furnham, A. (1996). *All in the Mind*. London: Whurr Publishers.

Valentine, E.R. (1992). *Conceptual Issues in Psychology* (2nd edition). London: Routledge.
Furnham's book is an excellent introduction to some of the controversial issues in psychology whereas Valentine's book provides a good, comprehensive review of all the major concepts and developments of thinking in psychology.

Cohen, D. (1985). *Psychologists on Psychology*. London: Routledge.

Fancher, R.E. (1996). *Pioneers of Psychology* (3rd edition). New York: W.W. Norton.

Kimble, G.A., Wertheimer, M. and White, C.L. (1991). *Portraits of Pioneers in Psychology*. Hillsdale, NJ: Lawrence Erlbaum Associates/American Psychological Association.
Cohen's book contains an excellent set of interviews with some of the leading psychologists of the time. Kimble et al. and Fancher's books contain biographical sketches of all the major scientists who have contributed to psychology and so provide a good potted introduction to the personalities (and themes, ideas and developments) in psychology.

Fuller, R., Walsh, P.N. and McGinley, P. (1997). *A Century of Psychology*. London: Routledge.

Solso, R.L. (1997). *Mind and Brain Sciences in the 21st century*. Cambridge, MA: MIT Press.
These two books – one a retrospective look at what psychology has achieved this century, the other a prognosticatory look at psychology's role in the next – comprise a collection of chapters written by some of the century's outstanding psychologists. Both are good books to read if you are interested in the leading researchers' assessment of psychology's past and their predictions of how psychology will develop in the future.

Journals to consult

American Psychologist
British Journal of Psychology
Current Directions in Psychological Science
Journal of Experimental Psychology
Philosophical Psychology
Psychological Bulletin
Psychological Review
Psychological Science
The Psychologist

Website addresses

http://www.sp.utoledo.edu/~mcaruso/prolynx.html
A massive collection of links to psychology and education-related websites.

http://www.utexas.edu:80/world/lecture/psy/
This is a link to the 'World Lecture Hall', a stunning collection of links (about 80) to on-line course material in psychology written by various teachers across the world. There is a link to almost every aspect of psychology.

http://www.tamiu.edu/coah/psy/directories.htm
A collection of psychological resources webpages.

http://www.tiac.net/users/fscpac1/
A site maintained by Harold Kiess of Framingham State College which has material on the history and ideas of psychology.

http://www.mtsu.edu/~studskl/
A study skills help page run by Middle Tennessee State University. Some useful links to help you with studying psychology.

2

THE WAYS AND MEANS
OF PSYCHOLOGY

Because of his long-lasting fame at the turn of the century many people know about 'Clever Hans', the mind-reading horse. People flocked to see the horse perform his amazing feats. If people gave the owner a question for Hans, he would look directly at the horse and repeat the question in what seemed like a normal tone of voice. Hans would then lift his hoof and tap out the answer. Thus, if asked, 'What is 2 + 2?', Hans would tap the ground four times. After Hans had been given the correct answer, the owner would reward the animal by patting it or give it food as a reward.

In 1904, several of the best-known scientists in Germany formed a 'commission' to study the animal. These distinguished scientists stated boldly that they could find no evidence that Hans was responding to external cues from his questioners and perhaps really could read minds.

However, the psychologist on the commission, clearly not satisfied, told one of his graduate students to look into the matter.

The student put blinkers on Hans so the animal could not watch the people who were asking him the questions. The horse's ability to respond correctly decreased significantly.

Clever Hans was, indeed, a 'genius of a horse' but was not a mind-reader. The animal was superb at reading 'body language' – cues that questioners almost always give to an animal. But these were so slight and so subtle that most people were completely unaware they were giving them. In this sense, the sceptics were right all along.

Furnham, 1996, *All in the mind: The essence of mind*, pp. 83–85

OVERVIEW

As scientists, psychologists believe that behaviour, like other natural phenomena, can be studied objectively. The scientific method permits psychologists to discover the nature, causes and predictors of behaviour. There are, of course, other methods and some of these are described in various parts of subsequent chapters. Here, we concentrate on the scientific approach. This approach has become the predominant method of investigation for a very practical reason: It works better than any other method we have discovered.

In this chapter you will learn how the scientific method is used in psychological research. What you learn here will help you understand how research into these topics is carried out and how research described in the rest of the book is conducted. It will also help you adopt a more inquisitive, critical approach to 'evidence' that you hear in everyday conversation.

What you should be able to do after reading Chapter 2

- Define and describe the scientific approach.
- Define concepts such as hypotheses, theories and variables.
- Have an awareness of the ethical principles adopted by psychologists.
- Describe quantitative and qualitative approaches to psychology.
- Have an awareness of how psychologists control variables.
- Understand concepts such as correlation.
- Describe measures of central tendency and dispersion.

Questions to think about

- What is the scientific method?
- Does following the steps of the scientific method guarantee that the results of a study will be important?
- Does the scientific method apply to all psychological research?
- How would you set up experiments to answer some of the questions you have about behaviour?
- Are there alternative approaches to studying human behaviour?

The process of discovery in psychology: the scientific method

The goal of psychological research is to discover, describe, explain and change the causes of behaviour. To do so we need to describe behaviours and the events that are responsible for their occurrence in a language that is both precise enough to be understood by others and general enough to apply to a wide variety of situations. As we saw in Chapter 1, this language takes the form of explanations, which are general statements about the events that cause phenomena to occur. The nature of these general statements will become clear as we see how psychologists use the scientific method.

There are three major types of scientific research. Naturalistic observations – observations of people or animals in their natural environment – are the least formal and are constrained by the fewest rules. Naturalistic observations provide the foundations of the biological and social sciences. For example, as we will see in more detail in Chapter 3, Charles Darwin's observation and classification of animals, plants and fossils during his voyage around the world provided him with the raw material for his theory of evolution. Correlational studies are observational in nature, but they involve more formal measurement – of environmental events, of individuals' physical and social characteristics, and of their behaviour. Researchers examine the relations between these measurements in an attempt to discover the causes of the observed behaviours. Experiments go beyond mere measurement. A psychologist performing an experiment makes things happen and observes the results. As we will see, only an experiment can positively identify cause-and-effect relations.

The scientific method consists of a set of rules that dictate the general procedure a scientist must follow in his or her research. These rules are not arbitrary; as we will see, they are based on logic. The following five steps summarise the rules of the scientific method that apply to experiments, the most rigorous form of scientific research. As we will see later, many of these rules also apply to observational studies. Some new terms introduced here without definition will be described in detail later in this chapter.

Stages in experimentation

1 *Identify the problem and formulate hypothetical cause-and-effect relations among variables.* This step involves identifying variables (particular behaviours and particular environmental and physiological events) and describing the relations among them in general terms. Consider the hypothesis that positive mood increases risk-taking

(a) *Source*: Photograph by Vanessa Sherry.

(b) *Source*: Photograph by Vanessa Sherry.

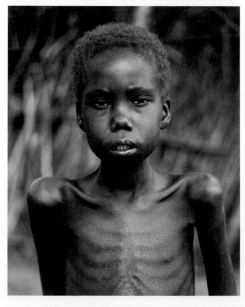

(c) *Source*: Courtesy of Telegraph Colour Library.

Psychologists study the nature of romantic attraction (a); interpersonal conflict (b); and responses to emotionally provocative stimuli (c), amongst many other behaviours.

behaviour. This statement describes a relation between two variables – mood and risk-taking – and states that an increase in one causes an increase in the other.

2 *Design the experiment.* Experiments involve the manipulation of independent variables and the observation of dependent variables. For example, if we wanted to test the hypothesis that positive mood (independent variable) increases risk-taking behaviour (dependent variable), each variable would have to be operationally defined. The independent variable must be controlled so that only it, and no other variable, is responsible for any changes in the dependent variable.

3 *Conduct the experiment.* The researcher must organise the material needed to perform the experiment, train the people who will conduct the research, recruit volunteers whose behaviour will be observed, and assign each of these volunteers to a treatment group or a control group. The experiment is performed and the observations are recorded.

4 *Evaluate the hypothesis by examining the data from the study.* Do the results support the hypothesis, or do they suggest that it is wrong? This step often involves special mathematical procedures used to determine whether an observed relation is statistically significant.

5 *Communicate the results.* (See next section, 'Communicating the results of scientific research'.)

Following these simple steps decreases the chances that we will be misled by our observations and come to incorrect conclusions from our research. The approach of formulating hypotheses and then setting up experiments to test them is sometimes known as hypothetico-deductive. As we saw in Chapter 1 and shall see in Chapter 11, people have a tendency to accept some types of evidence even though the rules of logic indicate that we should not. This tendency usually serves us well in our daily lives, but it can lead us to draw the wrong conclusions when we try to understand the true causes of natural phenomena, including our own behaviour.

Communicating the results of scientific research

Once psychologists have learned something about the causes of a behaviour from an experiment or observational study, they must tell others about their findings. When a piece of research is complete, it is written up and sent to an academic, peer-reviewed scientific journal. This means that the paper will be critically evaluated usually anonymously by two or three of the author's peers. The editor and reviewer will be individuals with expertise in the areas researched by the author and will be recognised authorities in their area.

The scientific method insists that scientists report the details of their research so that other investigators can repeat, or replicate, the study. Replication is one of the great strengths of science; it ensures that erroneous results and incorrect conclusions are weeded out. When scientists publish a study, they know that if the findings are important enough, their colleagues will try to replicate it (perhaps with some minor variations) to be sure that the results were not just a statistical fluke or the result of some unsuspected errors in the design or execution of the study.

The types of article that scientists will write fall broadly into four categories. There are empirical papers which report the conduct and results of an experiment. Most scientific journals publish papers of this kind (such as *Nature, Journal of Experimental Psychology, British Journal of Psychology, Psychological Science, European Psychologist*, etc.). All empirical articles follow the same general format. They begin with a title followed by the author/s' name/s and affiliation, an abstract briefly summarising the content of the article, an introduction section which reviews the literature pertaining to the topic reported and presents the author's hypotheses, a method section which gives comprehensive detail about the way in which the experiment was undertaken, a results section which reports the results of the experiment, a discussion section in which the results are discussed and explained, and a reference list which contains details of all the articles, books and chapters cited in the paper.

There are methodological papers which report a new technique, questionnaire, procedure or new piece of equipment for use in psychological research. There are theoretical papers which formulate a new theory arising from reviewed data. The journal *Psychological Review* devotes its pages to articles of this kind. Finally, there are review papers which synthesise a number of articles on a given topic. *Psychological Bulletin* publishes papers of this kind and is a good journal for keeping abreast of general topics in psychology.

In addition, researchers often present their findings at conferences or professional conventions. As a result, other psychologists will be able to incorporate these findings into their own thinking and hypothesising. Most good university libraries will stock the best of the journals which publish each of these types of paper. In addition to general journals (such as those listed above) there are numerous journals which publish in the sub-areas of psychology. Examples of these include the *European Journal of Social Psychology, Memory and Cognition, Journal of Applied Psychology, Neuropsychologia, Child Development, British Journal of Clinical Psychology, International Journal of Psychophysiology, Personality and Individual Differences, Health Psychology.*

Simply because a paper is published in a scientific journal, however, does not mean that the results and methods of that article are unquestionable or cannot be challenged. In experiments to examine whether the 'peer review' process works, researchers find large variation in what reviewers judge to be quality research – reviewers can normally agree on the really bad ones, but there is more disagreement about the average-to-good ones. Science progresses by contradiction, and new articles develop ideas generated by previous publications or take into account variables that the previous studies had not. Although there are checks in place to weed out 'bad' research, it is common to see a lot of it published. This is why you should adopt an inquisitive but informed approach when reading research papers: don't be afraid to question an aspect of procedure, analysis of logical thinking if you think it is wrong or misguided. You might be right.

Journals are intended primarily for other scientists. Journals, however, are also consulted by medical or science journalists who are interested in writing about innovative breakthroughs in psychological science in their newspapers and magazines. Conferences are also extensively reported by specialist reporters in the press (and television) and some psychological societies have effective press offices which publicise the papers that their conferences are presenting and advise their members on how best to present themselves and their data clearly (White *et al.*, 1993).

Identifying the problem: getting an idea for research

According to Bausell (1993), psychologists undertake research for a wide variety of reasons – some sensible, some impracticable. Some of these include:

- changing distasteful professional practice
- learning everything there is to know about a subject
- discrediting a theory that is archaic or wrong
- testing a theory to see if it is valid
- lending credence to the experimenter's own theory
- furthering a career by producing a seminal study
- furthering a career by obtaining a publication
- obtaining doctorate for professional gain
- becoming famous
- furthering scientific progress
- discovering something of intellectual interest.

Which of these do you think makes the best, most realistic goal? Although scientists may undertake study for some or all of these reasons, it is unlikely that they will become famous through their scientific work. Very few scientists attract the fame (and pay) of members from more alluring professions. There are millionaires in psychology, but more in pop music. Publishing a paper for personal gain is also a poor reason. Perhaps the two most important spurs to scientific research are the desires to further science and, more importantly, to discover something of intellectual interest. What do you need to become a good scientist? A great scientist certainly needs to be curious, hard working and dedicated – perhaps even obstinate and relentless. He or

she needs to be sceptical, open-minded and methodical. But above all, a successful scientist needs to have good ideas. Where do they come from?

Hypotheses

A hypothesis is the starting point of any study. It is an idea, phrased as a general statement, that a scientist wishes to test through scientific research. In the original Greek, *hypothesis* means 'suggestion', and the word still conveys the same meaning. When scientists form a hypothesis, they are simply suggesting that a relation exists among various phenomena (like the one that might exist between increased positive mood and increased risk-taking). Thus, a **hypothesis** is a tentative statement about a cause-and-effect relation between two or more events. Productive and creative scientists formulate new hypotheses by thinking about the implications of studies that they have performed or that have been performed by others.

At other times, however, researchers may not know exactly what they expect to find. Such research endeavours are called 'fishing expeditions'. In the same way that an angler may not know whether he or she will catch a trout or an old car seat, the researcher does not know whether he or she will find result X or result Y. An example of such research would be the measurement of people's attitudes towards a particular subject such as animal experimentation or alternative medicine. In such cases, an experimenter would not be able to make an accurate prediction based on hypothetico-deductive reasoning (unless, for example, he or she compared attitudes amongst two groups such as vegans vs meat-eaters or conventional medicine users vs homeopathic users).

Theories

A **theory**, a set of statements designed to explain a set of phenomena, is an elaborate form of hypothesis. In fact, a theory can be a way of organising a system of related hypotheses to explain some larger aspect of nature. A good theory fuels the creation of new hypotheses. More accurately, a good scientist, contemplating a good theory, thinks of more good hypotheses to test. For example, Albert Einstein's theory of relativity states that time, matter and energy are interdependent. Changes in any one will produce changes in the others. The hypotheses suggested by this theory revolutionised science; the field of nuclear physics rests largely on experiments arising from Einstein's theory.

A good theory is one that generates testable hypotheses – hypotheses that can potentially be supported or proved wrong by scientific research. Some theories are so general or so abstract that they do not produce testable hypotheses and hence cannot be subjected to scientific rigour. The framework for most psychological research is larger in scope than a hypothesis but smaller in scope than a full-fledged theory. For example, the frustration–aggression hypothesis suggests that people (or other animals) tend to become aggressive when they do not achieve a goal that they have been accustomed to achieving. This hypothesis makes a prediction that might fit many different situations. Indeed, many experiments have been performed to test this hypothesis under different conditions.

Even though the frameworks that most psychologists construct fall short of constituting theories, they serve a similar function by stimulating researchers to think about old problems in new ways and by showing how findings that did not appear to be related to each other can be explained by a single concept. One recent theory of emotional experience, for example, suggests that different types of activity in the left and right frontal brain are associated with positive and negative emotions and that this activity reflects a disposition to 'withdraw' or 'approach' (Davidson and Sutton, 1995). Such a theory can be used to test a number of hypotheses such as 'depressed individuals will show less left frontal brain activity'.

Quantitative research methods: designing an experiment

Although naturalistic observations enable a psychologist to classify behaviours into categories and provide hypothetical explanations for these behaviours, only an experiment can determine whether these explanations are correct. This approach is known as **quantitative research** because behaviours are reduced to quantities or can at least be seen as quantifiable. Personality or visuospatial ability may be quantified by a score on a questionnaire, for example, or the ability to react correctly and quickly on a reaction time task may be quantified by the number of correct decisions and the speed of responding.

There are various types of experiment we can design. We could conduct an experiment in which we looked at the effect of sleep deprivation on mental arithmetic ability; one group might be deprived of sleep for 24 hours, another for 36 hours and another would be allowed to sleep normally. This last group is called a **control group** because it is unaffected by the features of the experiment that we are interested in looking at and can, therefore, be used as a comparison group. The others are called **experimental groups**. Because the individuals in one group are not the same people as the ones in another group, the design of the experiment is called **independent groups** or **between groups**.

A slightly different experiment might involve the same people performing different levels of the same experiment. For example, we may be interested in finding out if people recognise real English words more quickly than they do pseudowords (words which follow the same rules of English but have no meaning) or non-words (words which do not follow the rules of English). This is called a lexical decision task. Here, every individual would respond to each type of word (but might be quicker responding to

some types of word than others). Because each individual is exposed to the same condition of the experiment (each type of word), the design is called **repeated measures** or **within-groups**.

There are advantages to using both types of design: independent groups and independent measures. For statistical reasons, it may be easier to obtain significant results by employing a repeated measures design because this approach eliminates the amount of variability that exists between data from different individuals. Because each participant acts as his or her control (that is, completes each condition in the experiment), there is less variability in the data (such as sex, age and personality differences or the ability to respond quickly to visual stimuli or the tendency to think better in the morning than in the afternoon). Independent groups designs are advantageous when one does not want to expose the same individuals to the same conditions. For example, if we wanted to compare the effect of fat, carbohydrate and protein intake on people's ability to react quickly to visual stimuli (because we hypothesised that certain foods made you drowsy), there would be disadvantages to having them all eat each different type of food (to begin with, if they were tested on different days, they may get better on the reaction time tasks because of practice; secondly, because different food is presented on each occasion, they may become suspicious). An independent groups design would help to eliminate these problems. Such designs are of great use in medicine and in the study of the efficacy of treatment for mental illness (as you will see in Chapter 17). A mentally ill group would take treatment A, another group treatment B, another group a placebo (we will come on to this later) and a final group would receive no treatment. If treatment A is successful, there should be a difference in outcome between this group and others in the study.

Another approach to studying behaviour might be to conduct an experiment under laboratory or naturalistic conditions. In a laboratory experiment, the experimenter has control over most of the variables that he or she thinks will affect the outcome of the experiment. For example, we could design an experiment in which the effect of ambient noise on work performance was measured. We could expose individuals to specific noises at specific noise levels at specific times while they completed specific tasks and questionnaires asking for details about mood. Alternatively, we could set up a **field experiment** in which participants would be observed under fairly 'natural' conditions. For example, we might compare the effects of different lighting conditions on individuals' mood and productivity in the workplace.

The important feature of naturalistic observations is that the observer remains in the background and does not interfere with the people (or animals) being observed. In some cases, psychologists do interfere with a situation in a natural setting. For example, Chapter 15 describes some experiments designed to discover what factors determine whether bystanders come to the aid of people who have been hurt or who are in some other sort of distress. An 'accident' is staged, and the behaviour of passers-by is surreptitiously observed. Although studies such as these take place outside the laboratory – at job sites or on the street – they are experiments, not naturalistic observations. Such experiments might be called quasi-field studies.

Variables

Variables are things that have a particular value but which can vary. Scientists either measure or manipulate the values of variables. Manipulate literally means 'to handle' (from *manus*, 'hand'). Psychologists use the word 'manipulate' to refer to setting the value of a variable for experimental purposes. The results of this manipulation determine whether the hypothesis is true or false. Direct manipulation of an independent variable, for example, would involve placing individuals into different treatment groups, such as drug A, drug B, a placebo and no drug. Indirect manipulation would involve differentiating individuals with different personality types. For example, we might be interested in whether individuals low, medium or high in trait anxiety (the degree of anxiety they habitually feel) selectively attend to anxiety-related stimuli (such as pictures of snakes, spiders, blood and so on).

Or we might look at the effect of positive mood on risk-taking. We would assemble four groups of volunteers to serve as participants. We manipulate mood by having participants watch a comedy film (which would put participants in a positive mood), an unpleasant film (which would put participants in a negative mood) or a neutral film (which would not be expected to influence participants' mood negatively or positively). We would have a fourth group which would watch no film (the control group). We would then examine the effect of this measure (mood) on risk-taking, such as the amount spent gambling at roulette.

This experiment examines the effect of one variable on another. The variable that we manipulate (mood) is called the independent variable. We could also have a second independent variable, such as the sex of the gambler (do men or women gamble more?). The variable that we measure (risk-taking) is the dependent variable. An easy way to keep the names of these variables straight is to remember that a hypothesis describes how the value of a dependent variable depends on the value of an independent variable. Our hypothesis proposes that increased gambling depends on the individual's level of mood. We can illustrate the relationship between these two variables, as seen in Figure 2.1.

Sometimes, we want to understand the causes of behaviour in more than one specific situation. Thus, the variables that hypotheses deal with are expressed in general terms. Independent and dependent variables are categories into which various behaviours are classified. For example, we would probably label all of the following behaviours as 'interpersonal aggression': hitting, kicking, throwing something at someone. Presumably, these behaviours would have very similar causes. A psychologist must know enough about a particular type of behaviour to be able to classify it correctly.

Although one of the first steps in psychological investigation involves naming and classifying behaviours, we must be careful to avoid committing the nominal fallacy or reification. The nominal fallacy refers to the erroneous belief that one has explained an event simply by naming it (*nomen* means 'name'). Classifying a behaviour does not explain it; classifying only prepares us to examine and discover events that cause a behaviour. For example, suppose that we see a man frown and shout at other people without provocation, criticise their work when really it is acceptable, and generally act unpleasantly towards everyone around him. Someone says, 'He's really angry today.' Does this statement explain his behaviour?

It does not; it only describes the behaviour. To say that he is angry suggests that an internal state is responsible for his behaviour – that anger is causing his behaviour. But all we have observed is his behaviour, not his internal state. Even if he is experiencing feelings of anger, these feelings still do not explain his behaviour. What we really need to know is what events made him act the way he did. Perhaps he has a painful toothache. Perhaps he had just learned that he was passed over for a promotion. Perhaps he had a terrible fight with his wife or girlfriend. Perhaps he had just read a book that advised him to be more assertive. Events like these are causes of both the behaviour and the feelings. Unless they are discovered, we cannot say that we have explained his behaviour. The task of a psychologist is to determine which of the many events that occurred before a particular behaviour caused that behaviour to happen.

Operational definitions

This translation of generalities into specific operations is called an operational definition: independent variables

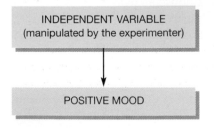

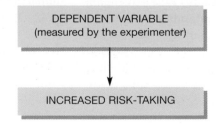

Figure 2.1

Independent and dependent variables described in the mood and risk-taking experiment.

and dependent variables are defined in terms of the operations an experimenter performs to set their values or to measure them. In our proposed experiment, the operational definition of the independent and dependent variables might be the following:

- Independent variable: Participants' mood was induced by watching positive, neutral or negative video films; a control group watched none of the films.
- Dependent variable: Participants' risk-taking behaviour was measured by monitoring the amount of money spent betting on the outcome of a roulette wheel when the probability of winning was high and when it was low.

Providing an operational definition of variables is a hallmark of well conducted research. If research is to be understood, evaluated and replicated by other people (step 5 of the scientific method), the investigator must provide others with a thorough and adequate description of the procedures used to manipulate the independent variable and to measure the dependent variable. For example, a complete definition of the dependent variable (risk-taking) would have to include a detailed description of the type of gambling task and how frequently the probability of winning was high or low.

There are many ways to translate a general concept into a set of operations. We might decide to adopt a different measure of mood, such as having participants complete an intelligence test and inform them that they did well or badly (regardless of how they actually performed). This might also be expected to increase or decrease mood. We might choose a different measure of risk-taking such as asking participants to make decisions about a hypothetical risky treatment for a disease that they have (hypothetically) developed. Which operational definition of mood and risk-taking do you think is correct? Is there only one correct definition in this case? What these questions address is the issue of validity.

Validity

The validity of an operational definition refers to how appropriate it is – how accurately it represents the variable whose value has been manipulated or measured. Sometimes the term 'ecological validity' is used: this refers to the degree to which the experimental context accurately presents that which the experimenter wants to reproduce. If you set up an experiment to monitor how much people laughed at a comedy, for example, and also measured their brain electrical activity and heart rate, which means attaching wires with electrodes to the head, fingers and chest, would this accurately represent the context in which a person would normally laugh at a comedy programme?

Given enough time, the validity of an operational definition will emerge (or so we hope). If different investigators define the variable in slightly different ways but their experiments yield similar results, we become more confident that the research is leading to an understanding of the phenomena we are studying.

The issue of validity is seen very clearly in what has become known as the Barnum effect – see the 'Psychology in action' section below.

Psychology in action

The Barnum effect

Consider the following evaluation of your personality (this evaluation is based on research which indicates that intelligent but sceptical readers are drawn to boxed off areas of textbooks).

You are the type of person who has a tendency to be critical of yourself. You have a great need for other people to like and admire you but you pride yourself on being an independent thinker and do not accept others' statements without satisfactory proof. You have a great deal of unused capacity which you have not turned to your advantage. While you have some personality weakness, you are generally able to compensate for them. You prefer a certain amount of change and variety and become dissatisfied when hemmed in by restrictions and limitations.

Does this description accurately reflect your own personality? It probably does. In fact, it probably applies to the majority of the population. These are universally valid statements which refer to nothing specific but only to general feelings and beliefs that could apply to almost everyone. The fact that most people believe that such vague personality descriptions are an accurate reflection of their own personality is called the Barnum effect (Meehl, 1956). The phenomenon is named after Phineas T. Barnum, the great American circus showman, who declared that there was a 'sucker born every minute' and that his entertainments provided 'a little something for everybody'. The Barnum effect is seen clearly when individuals accept as correct 'generalized, vague, bogus descriptions of themselves which have high base-rate occurrence in the general population' (Furnham and Schofield, 1987). You can try the exercise above on your friends. It is almost guaranteed that they will agree with the evaluation and consider it to be an uncannily accurate reflection of their personality.

The phenomenon has a long history in psychology and a less honourable one amongst proponents of pseudo-science and pseudo-therapy. Any clairvoyant or fortune-teller will make cunning use of the Barnum effect to dupe credulous punters. This is not surprising: people have been found to be more accepting of generalised feedback than actual, factual feedback (Merrens and Richards, 1970). A study of 68 personnel managers in the 1950s highlights the way in

Psychology in action continued

Psychology in action continued

(a) Fortune-tellers make good use of the Barnum effect.

Source: Photograph by Vanessa Sherry.

which we can accept the most vague statements about our personality as reflecting reality. Stagner (1958) administered personality tests to these managers and gave them thirteen bogus statements that were assumed to represent actual feedback about their personality from the tests. The statements are listed in Table 2.1. See how many you agree with.

(b) The circus showman, P.T. Barnum, who gave his name to the Barnum effect.

Source: Courtesy of Popperfoto.

Table 2.1   The Barnum effect I: personnel managers' reactions to their 'personality analysis'

	Judgements as to accuracy of item (% choosing)				
	Amazingly accurate	*Rather good*	*About half and half*	*More wrong than right*	*Almost entirely wrong*
You have a great need for other people to like and admire you	39	46	13	1	1
You have a tendency to be critical of yourself	46	36	15	3	0
You have a great deal of unused capacity which you have not turned to your advantage	37	36	18	1	4
While you have some personality weaknesses, you are generally able to compensate for them	34	55	9	0	0
Your sexual adjustment has presented problems for you	15	16	16	33	19
Disciplined and self-controlled outside, you tend to be worrisome and insecure inside	40	21	22	10	4
At times you have serious doubts as to whether you have made the right decision or done the right thing	27	31	19	18	4
You prefer a certain amount of change and variety and become dissatisfied when hemmed in by restrictions and limitations	63	28	7	1	1
You pride yourself as an independent thinker and do not accept others' statements without satisfactory proof	49	31	12	4	4
You have found it unwise to be too frank in revealing yourself to others	31	37	22	6	4

Table 2.1   *(continued)*

	Judgements as to accuracy of item (% choosing)				
	Amazingly accurate	Rather good	About half and half	More wrong than right	Almost entirely wrong
At times you are extroverted, affable, sociable, while at other times you are introverted, wary and reserved	43	25	18	9	5
Some of your aspirations tend to be pretty unrealistic	12	16	22	43	7
Security is one of your major goals in life	40	31	15	9	5

Source: Furnham, A. (1994). The Barnum effect in medicine. In *Complementary Therapies in Medicine*, 2, 1–4. Reprinted by permission of Churchill Livingstone, London, UK.

When asked to rate how strongly the participants agreed with these statements, almost all indicated that they believed them to some extent and one-third regarded their profile as a 'good' reflection of their character. For some statements such as 'you prefer a certain amount of change and variety...' and 'while you have some personality weaknesses...', over 80 per cent of participants expressed agreement with them.

In an ingenious spin on the Barnum phenomenon, Furnham (1994) set up an experiment in which undergraduates gave samples of their hair to an experimenter. A week later the participants were given a 'trichological analysis' – twenty-four bland statements regarding their health based on the hair sample – that was totally bogus. However, when the students rated these statements for accuracy, most rated them as highly accurate (see Table 2.2 for a list of the statements).

Table 2.2   The Barnum effect II: how respondents reacted to feedback from the medical Barnum

		% accuracy (0–100)	% giving maximum accurate scores
1	Your diet, while adequate, would benefit from an increase in fresh fruit and vegetables	65.6	19.1
2	You are probably hairier than most other people of your sex and age	44.9	4.3
3	Not all your measurements are symmetrical (e.g. your hands, feet, breasts are not exactly the same size/cup)	55.6	2.1
4	Your sex drive is very variable	56.3	4.3
5	There is evidence of a tendency to arthritis in your family	47.7	12.8
6	You are prone to feel the cold more than other people	58.0	19.1
7	Your skin texture changes under stress	54.4	10.6
8	You are prone to occasional patterns of sleeplessness	62.6	25.5
9	Your metabolic rate is at the 40th percentile (just below average for your age and sex)	50.1	4.2
10	You sometimes feel very tired for no reason	64.7	23.4
11	You can get depressed for no apparent reason	58.7	14.9
12	You are occasionally aware that your breath smells for no reason	44.9	2.1

Psychology in action continued

Psychology in action continued

Table 2.2   *(continued)*

		% accuracy (0–100)	% giving maximum accurate scores
13	Your nose bleeds occasionally	34.9	8.5
14	You are more prone to tooth decay than others	42.8	10.6
15	Your appetite varies extensively	63.5	23.4
16	You have a tendency to put weight on easily	44.6	8.5
17	You sometimes experience symptoms of anxiety (e.g. tension headaches, indigestion)	65.9	23.4
18	There are no major heredity defects in your family	75.6	34.0
19	Your bowel movements are not always regular	51.3	8.5
20	Your cardiovascular efficiency is average for your age and sex	67.7	14.9
21	You experience frequent changes in your urine colour	41.3	4.3
22	You occasionally get a craving for certain food	66.5	25.5
23	Your body fat distribution is not perfectly normal	56.8	12.8
24	You frequently get indigestion	43.7	4.3

Source: Furnham, A. (1994). The Barnum effect in medicine. In *Complementary Therapies in Medicine*, 2, 1–4. Reprinted by permission of Churchill Livingstone, London, UK.

What does research on the Barnum effect tell us? First, it shows us that most individuals are inclined to accept bland feedback about themselves. Secondly, it shows us that the validity of a test involves more than intuitively 'knowing' that a test measures something. Most individuals – unless they knew about the Barnum effect – would have regarded the statements at the beginning of this section as true and might have accepted the statement that intelligent but sceptical readers are drawn to boxed off areas of textbooks. This statement, of course, is nonsense (in any case, we regard all readers of this book as highly intelligent and sceptical). Thirdly, and perhaps most importantly, the Barnum effect shows us that we should always adopt a sceptical and questioning approach to statements made about human behaviour – even to this last statement.

Control of independent variables

A scientist performs an experiment by manipulating the value of the independent variable and then observing whether this change affects the dependent variable. If an effect is seen, the scientist can conclude that there is a cause-and-effect relation between the variables. That is, changes in the value of the independent variable cause changes in the value of the dependent variable.

In designing an experiment, the experimenter must manipulate the value of the independent variable and only the independent variable. For example, if we want to determine whether noise has an effect on people's reading speed, we must choose our source of noise carefully. If we use the sound from a television set to supply the noise and find that it slows people's reading speed, we cannot conclude that the effect was caused purely by noise. We might have selected an interesting programme, thus distracting the participants' attention from the material they were reading. If we want to do this experiment properly, we should use noise that is neutral and not a source of interest by itself, for example, noise like the 'sssh' sound that is heard when an FM radio is tuned between stations.

In this example, we intended to test the effects of an independent variable (noise) on a dependent variable (reading speed). By using a television to provide the noise, we were inadvertently testing the effects of other variables besides noise on reading speed. We introduced unwanted variables in addition to the independent variable.

One of the meanings of the word 'confound' is to fail to distinguish. If an experimenter inadvertently introduces one or more unwanted independent variables, he or she cannot distinguish the effects of any one of them on the dependent variable. That is, the effects of the variables will be confounded and this is called the confounding of variables. It is often difficult to be sure that independent variables are not confounded. We must be certain that when we manipulate the independent variable that that variable only, and no other variable, is affected.

One method of addressing confounding variables is called counterbalancing which means to 'weigh evenly'. Imagine that an experimenter decided to investigate the effect of a memory-enhancing drug on people's ability to remember concrete and abstract nouns. An experiment is designed in which three groups of people – one taking the drug, another taking a harmless pill and a control group which takes nothing – complete a word recognition experiment. For all groups, the concrete words are presented in the first part of the experiment and the abstract words are presented in the second half. To the experimenter's surprise, although the drug group's performance is better than the others', all groups have more difficulty in remembering the abstract nouns. Does this finding mean that individuals find abstract nouns less memorable?

The answer is that, on the basis of the design of the experiment, we cannot know. Because the abstract words always appeared in the second half of the experiment, it is possible that the groups simply felt more tired towards the end of the experiment and that their fatigue influenced their recognition scores; they may even have become more bored towards the end of the experiment. Perhaps, having been used to memorising concrete nouns, the shift to a different type of word interfered with the individuals' memory strategy. One way of circumventing this confound is to present abstract and concrete nouns randomly: in this way concrete and abstract nouns have an equal probability of occurring at the beginning, middle and end of the experiment. But what if there was some reason for concrete and abstract nouns being presented together? A solution would be to counterbalance the presentation of the types of words so that some individuals received the abstract nouns first followed by the concrete nouns whereas others received the concrete nouns first. If the original results were attributable to tiredness or fatigue then the same decrease in recall should be seen in the second half of the experiment. If individuals continue to recall abstract nouns less frequently than concrete nouns, then the result is not due to the effects of the confounding variables of tiredness and fatigue.

Having carefully designed a study, we must then decide how best to conduct it. This brings us to step three of the scientific method: perform the experiment. We must decide what participants will be used, what instructions will be given, and what equipment and materials will be used. We must ensure that the data collected will be accurate.

Reliability

If the procedure described by an operational definition gives consistent results under consistent conditions, the procedure is said to have high reliability. For example, measurements of people's height and weight are extremely reliable. Measurements of their academic aptitude (by means of standard, commercial tests) are also reliable, but less so.

Achieving reliability is usually much easier than achieving validity. Reliability is mostly a result of care and diligence on the part of researchers in the planning and execution of their studies. Alert, careful experimenters can control most of the extraneous factors that might affect the reliability of their measurements. Conditions throughout the experiment should always be as consistent as possible. For example, the same instructions should be given to each person who participates in the experiment, all mechanical devices should be in good repair, and all assistants hired by the experimenter should be well trained in performing their tasks. Noise and other sources of distraction should be kept to a minimum.

Another issue that affects reliability is the degree of subjectivity involved in making a measurement. In our earlier experiment, our definition of mood was objective; even a non-expert could follow our procedure and obtain the same results. But researchers often attempt to study variables whose measurement is subjective, that is it requires practical judgement and expertise. For example, suppose that a psychologist wants to count the number of friendly interactions that a child makes with other children in a group. This measurement requires someone to watch the child and count the number of times a friendly interaction occurs. But it is difficult to be absolutely specific about what constitutes a friendly interaction and what does not. What if the child looks at another child and their gazes meet? One observer may say that the look conveyed interest in what the other child was doing and so should be scored as a friendly interaction. Another observer may disagree.

The solution in this case is, first, to try to specify as precisely as possible the criteria to be used for defining an interaction as friendly in order to make the measurement as objective as possible. Then, two or more people should watch the child's behaviour and score it independently, that is, neither person should be aware of the other person's ratings. If their ratings agree, we can say that the scoring system has high interrater reliability. If they disagree, interrater reliability is low, and there is no point in continuing the study. Instead, the rating system should be refined and the raters should be trained to apply it consistently. Any investigator who performs a study that requires some degree of skill and judgement in measuring the dependent variables must do what is necessary to produce high interrater reliability.

There are other ways in which a researcher can test the reliability of his or her data. For example, say that we wanted to examine whether an individual's responses on a personality questionnaire were reliable. One method of determining this might be to divide the questionnaire and compare the responses of the participant in each of the two sections of the questionnaire. If there is strong agreement between scores from each half, the questionnaire results are said to be reliable. This is called **split-half reliability** because the measure (the personality questionnaire) is split and responses to the two split parts compared.

But what if the questionnaire is too short for split-half reliability to be tested or the test measures many different factors (as an intelligence test does)? One way of testing reliability in such circumstances might be to administer the test at one session and then again at another session, some time apart. If the test is reliable, it should yield the same scores at the first as at the second session. This is called test–retest reliability. However, can you see a possible confound here? Imagine if you were to examine the test–retest reliability of an IQ test. The scores at the second session may actually be better because the participant has already undertaken the same test once. So, the test may be reliable but the data obtained from the test suggest that it is not. Can you think of a way of circumventing this problem? (Chapter 11 takes up this issue in more detail.)

Selecting participants

So far, we have dealt with what we, as researchers, would do – what hypothesis we would test, how we would design the experiment, and how we would obtain valid and reliable measurements. Now let us turn to the people who will participate in our experiment: our participants. How do we choose them? How do we assign them to the experimental or control group? These decisions must be carefully considered because just as independent variables can be confounded, so can variables that are inherent in participants whose behaviour is being observed.

Consider the following example. A lecturer wants to determine which of two teaching methods works best. She teaches two courses in introductory psychology, one that meets at 9.30 a.m. and another that meets at 4 p.m. She uses one teaching method for the morning class and another for the afternoon class. At the end of the term she finds that the final examination scores were higher for her morning class. She concludes that from now on she will use that particular teaching method for all of her classes. However, there is a problem. Think about what this might be before you read the next sentence.

The two groups of participants for the experiment are not equivalent. People who sign up for a class that meets at 9.30 a.m. are likely to differ in some ways from those who sign up for a 4 p.m. class. Some people prefer to get up early while others prefer to sleep late, so-called larks (as opposed to 'owls'). Perhaps the university sports department schedules some kinds of activity late in the afternoon, which means that students interested in participating in these activities will not be able to register for the 4 p.m. class. For many reasons, the students in the two classes will probably not be equivalent. Therefore, we cannot conclude that the differences in their final examination scores were caused solely by the differences in the teaching methods.

Participants must be carefully assigned to the various groups used in an experiment. The usual way to assign them is by **random assignment**. One way to accomplish random assignment is to list the names of the available participants and then to toss a coin for each one to determine the participant's assignment to one of two groups. More typically, the assignment is made by computer or by consulting a list of random numbers. We can expect people to have different abilities, personality traits and other characteristics that may affect the outcome of the experiment, but if people are randomly assigned to the experimental conditions, these differences should – according to the principle of random sampling – be equally distributed across the groups.

Researchers must remain alert to the problem of confounding subject variables even after they have designed an experiment and randomly assigned participants to the groups. Some problems will not emerge until the investigation is actually performed. Suppose that an experimenter was interested in learning whether anger decreases a person's ability to concentrate. The experimenter acts very rudely towards the participants in the experimental group, which presumably makes them angry, but treats the participants in the control group politely. After the rude or polite treatment, the participants watch a video screen that shows a constantly changing display of patterns of letters. Participants are instructed to press a button whenever a particular letter appears. This vigilance test is designed to reveal how carefully participants are paying attention to the letters.

The design of this experiment is sound. Assuming that the participants in the experimental group are really angry and that our test is a valid measure of concentration, we should be able to make conclusions about the effects of anger on concentration. However, the experiment, as performed under real conditions, may not work out the way it was designed. Suppose that some of our 'angry' participants simply walk away. All experimenters are required to tell participants that they are free to leave at any time (and the section on ethics later in this chapter will tell you why); some angry participants might well do so. If they do, we will now be comparing the behaviour of two groups of participants of somewhat different character – a group of people who are willing to submit to the experimenter's rude behaviour and a group of randomly selected people, some of whom would have left had they been subjected to the rude treatment. Now the experimental group and control group are no longer equivalent. Figure 2.2 illustrates this.

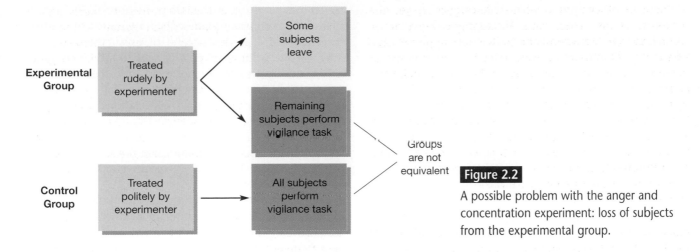

Figure 2.2

A possible problem with the anger and concentration experiment: loss of subjects from the experimental group.

The moral of this example is that an experimenter must continue to attend to the possibility of confounded variables even after the experiment is under way. The solution in this case? There probably is none. Because we cannot force participants to continue to participate, there is a strong possibility that some of them will leave. There is also the flip-side to this problem where participants will respond in an unnaturally positive way because this is what they believe the experimenter wants. For example, they may give answers on personality or other questionnaires that portrays them in the best light. This is called social desirability. As we will see in Chapter 15, the relationship between experimenter and participant is sometimes a very complex one. Some psychological variables are, by their very nature, difficult to investigate.

Participants' expectations

Participants in a psychology experiment are not simply passive participants whose behaviour is controlled solely by the independent variables manipulated by the experimenter. Participants who are participating in experiments know that they are being observed, and this knowledge is certain to affect their behaviour. In fact, some participants may try to outwit the experimenter by acting in a way that is opposite to what they think is expected. However, most participants will try to co-operate because they do not want to ruin the experiment for the investigator. They may even try to figure out what question is being asked so that they can act accordingly. Because the study is being run by a psychologist, some participants are unlikely to take what he or she says at face value and will look for motives hidden behind an apparently simple task. Actually, most experiments are not deceptive at all; they are what they appear to be.

'Deceptive' studies do not always succeed in fooling the participants. For example, suppose you are a participant in an experiment that was represented as being a learning study. On the table in front of you is an assortment of knives and pistols. The experimenter says, 'Oh, ignore them. Someone else left them here. They have nothing to do with this study.' Do you believe her? Probably not, and you will undoubtedly try to figure out how the presence of these weapons is supposed to affect your behaviour. You may suspect that the psychologist is trying to determine whether the presence of weapons will increase your hostility. With this suspicion in mind, you may (1) act naturally, so that you will not spoil the experiment; (2) act aggressively, to help the experimenter get the results you think she wants; or (3) act non-aggressively, to prove that you are immune to the effects of objects associated with violence. The results of this study may not show the effects of the presence of weapons on aggression but, rather, show the relative numbers of people who select strategy 1, 2 or 3 in response to the knowledge that they are being observed.

Experimenters must always remember that their participants do not merely react to the independent variable in a simple-minded way. As you will see in Chapter 15, these considerations are especially important in social psychology experiments. In some of these studies, the experimenter or the experimenter's assistants act out roles designed to provide a particular kind of social situation to which the participants are exposed. Obviously, the participants' interpretation of these situations affects their behaviour.

Single-blind experiments

A special problem is posed by experiments in which participants' behaviour might be affected by their knowledge of the independent variable. Two methods of circumventing this problem are single- and double-blind experiments. For example, suppose that we want to study the effects of a stimulant drug, such as amphetamine, on a person's ability to perform a task that requires fine manual dexterity. We will administer the drug to one group of participants and leave another group untreated. We will count how many times each subject can thread a needle in a ten-minute period (our operational definition of fine manual dexterity). We will then see whether taking the drug had any effect on the number of needle threadings.

But there is a problem in our design. For us to conclude that a cause-and-effect relation exists, the treatment of the two groups must be identical except for the single variable that is being manipulated. In this case the mere administration of a drug may have effects on behaviour, independent of its pharmacological effects. The behaviour of participants who know that they have just taken amphetamine is very likely to be affected by this knowledge as well as by the drug circulating in their bloodstream. To solve this problem, we should give pills to the members of both groups. People in one group will receive amphetamine, and those in the other group will receive an inert pill – a placebo, from the Latin placere, 'to please'. A physician sometimes gives a placebo to anxious patients to placate them. Participants will not be told which pill they receive. By using this improved experimental procedure, called a single-blind study, we can infer that any observed differences in needle-threading ability of the two groups were produced solely by the pharmacological effects of amphetamine.

Double-blind experiments

In a single-blind experiment, only the participants are kept ignorant of their assignment to a particular experimental group; the experimenter knows which treatment each subject receives. Now let us look at an example in which it is important to keep both the experimenter and the participants in the dark. Suppose we believe that if patients with mental disorders take a particular drug, they will be more willing to engage in conversation. The drug is given to some patients and a placebo is administered to others. We talk with all the patients afterwards and rate the quality of the conversation. But 'quality of conversation' is a difficult dependent variable to measure, and the rating is therefore likely to be subjective. The fact that the experimenters know which patients received the drug means that we may tend to give higher ratings to the quality of conversation with those patients. Of course, we would not intentionally cheat, but even honest people tend to perceive results in a way that favours their own preconceptions.

The solution to this problem is simple. Just as the patients should not know whether they are receiving a drug or a placebo, neither should the experimenter. That is, we should carry out a double-blind study. Someone else should administer the pill, or the experimenter should be given a set of identical-looking pills in coded containers so that both experimenter and patient are unaware of the nature of the contents. Now the ratings cannot be affected by any preconceived ideas the experimenter may have. The double-blind procedure does not apply only to experiments that use drugs as the independent variable. Suppose that the experiment just described attempted to evaluate the effects of a particular kind of psychotherapy, not a drug, on the willingness of a patient to talk. If the same person does both the psychotherapy and the rating, that person might tend to see the results in a light that is most favourable to his or her own expectations. In this case, then, one person should perform the psychotherapy and another person should evaluate the quality of conversation with the patients. The evaluator will not know whether a particular patient has just received psychotherapy or is a member of the control (untreated) group.

The expectations of experimenters can influence results in studies with laboratory animals as much as in studies with human participants. Rosenthal and Fode (1963) demonstrated the influence of expectations by having students train rats to learn the way through a maze. They told half the students that they had 'stupid' rats and the other half that they had 'smart' rats. In fact, there were no differences in the animals' abilities. However, an analysis of the results indicated that the 'smart' animals learned faster than the 'stupid' ones. The students' expectations clearly affected their rats' performances. Presumably, the students who had 'smart' rats took better care of them, which affected the animals' performances.

Correlational studies

To be sure that a cause-and-effect relation exists, we must perform an experiment in which we manipulate the independent variable and measure its effects on the dependent variable. But there are some variables, especially participant variables, that a psychologist cannot manipulate. For example, a person's sex, genetic history, income, social class, family environment and personality are obviously not under the psychologist's control. Nevertheless, these variables are important and interesting because they often affect people's behaviour. Because they cannot be manipulated, they cannot be investigated in an experiment. A different method must, therefore, be used to study them: a correlational study.

The basic principle of a correlational study is simple: in each member of a group of people we measure two or more variables as they are found to exist, and we determine whether the variables are related by using a statistical procedure called correlation. Correlational studies are often done to investigate the effects of personality variables on behaviour. For example, we may ask whether shyness is related to daydreaming. Our hypothesis is that shy people tend to daydream more than less shy people. We decide how to assess a person's shyness and the amount of daydreaming that he or she engages in each day, and we then take the measure of these two variables for a group of people. If shy people tend to daydream more (or less) than do people who are not shy, we can conclude that the variables are related.

Imagine that we do, in fact, find that shy people spend more time daydreaming. Such a finding tells us that the variables are related – we say they are correlated – but it does not permit us to make any conclusions about cause and effect. Shyness may have caused the daydreaming, or daydreaming may have caused the shyness, or perhaps some other variable that we did not measure caused both shyness and an increase in daydreaming. In other words, correlations do not necessarily indicate cause-and-effect relations.

A good illustration of this principle is provided by a correlational study that attempted to determine whether membership in the Boy Scouts would affect a person's subsequent participation in community affairs (Chapin, 1938). The investigator compared a group of men who had once been Boy Scouts with a group of men who had not. He found that the men who had been Boy Scouts tended to join more community affairs groups later in life. The investigator concluded that the experience of being a Boy Scout increased a person's tendency to join community organisations. However, this conclusion is not warranted. All we can say is that people who join the Boy Scouts in their youth tend to join community organisations later in life. It could be that people who, for one reason or another, are 'joiners' tend to join the Boy Scouts when they are young and community organisations when they are older. To determine cause and effect, we would have to perform an experiment. For example, we would make some boys join the Boy Scouts and prevent others from doing so, and then see how many organisations they voluntarily joined later in life. Because we cannot interfere in people's lives in such a way, we can never be certain that being a Boy Scout increases a person's tendency to join community organisations later.

The news media often report the results of correlational studies. We are led to believe that because two variables are correlated, one event causes another. But this conclusion may not be true. For example, a news magazine reported a study in which small companies that make heavy use of computers were found to have productivity-per-employee levels two and a half times greater than companies that did not. Can we conclude that the heavy use of computers is the cause of the increased productivity? No, we cannot; correlation does not prove causation. Is it likely that the two types of small company (those that make heavy use of computers and those that do not) are identical in all other ways? Probably not. For example, companies that make heavy use of computers can afford to do so, and they can probably afford to make other investments that might increase productivity. In addition, these companies may also have managers who are up-to-date in other respects, and having modern ideas about other aspects of running a company may also improve productivity. The use of computers may indeed increase productivity, but the information presented does not permit us to come to this conclusion.

Can anything be done to reduce some of the uncertainty inherent in correlational studies? The answer is yes. When attempting to study the effects of a variable that cannot be altered (such as sex, age, socio-economic status, or personality characteristics), we can use a procedure called matching. Rather than selecting participants randomly, we match the participants in each of the groups on all of the relevant variables except the one being studied. For instance, if we want to study the effects of shyness on daydreaming, we may gather two groups of participants, shy and non-shy. We select the participants in each group in such a way that the effects of other variables are minimised. We make sure that the average age, intelligence, income and personality characteristics (other than shyness) of the two groups are the same. If we find that, for example, the shy group is, on average, younger than the non-shy group, we will replace some of the people in the shy group with older shy people until the average age is the same.

If, after following this matching procedure, we find that shyness is still related to daydreaming, we can be more confident that the relation is one of cause and effect and that the differences between the two variables are not caused by a third variable. The limitation of the matching procedure is that we may not know all the variables that should be held constant. If, unknown to us, the two groups are not matched on an important variable, then the results will be misleading. In any case, even the matching procedure does not permit us to decide which variable is the cause and which is the effect; we still do not know whether shyness causes daydreaming or daydreaming causes shyness.

The strengths and limitations of correlational studies will become evident in subsequent chapters in this book. For example, almost all studies that attempt to discover the environmental factors that influence personality characteristics or the relation between these characteristics and people's behaviour are correlational.

Single-case studies

Not all investigations use groups of participants. Single-subject research investigates the behaviour of individuals, and for some phenomena this method is very effective. Single-subject research can involve either experiments or correlational studies. In single-subject research, individual participants can serve as their own controls. Suppose that we wanted to see whether a particular hormone affected a rat's level of activity. We would house a rat in a cage that contained a running wheel in which the animal could exercise. An electric counter connected to the wheel would keep track of how many revolutions the wheel made each day. We would record the animal's activity for several days and wait until this measure had stabilised. Once it had, we would start giving the rat an injection of a placebo each day. At first, the injections might affect the animal's activity level, but eventually the animal would become habituated to the injections. Next, we would start giving the rat injections of the hormone. We might try several different doses to see whether different concentrations of the hormone had different effects. Following each change in dose, we would wait until the animal's activity level had stabilised before moving on to the next dose. Finally, we would begin administering the placebo again.

Figure 2.3 shows some hypothetical results. We see the rat's habituation to the effects of a daily injection on days 1 through 6 and the effects of various doses of the hormone. We also see that the animal's activity level returns to normal soon after the injections contain no hormone. This return to the baseline level of activity assures us that the hormone has not had long-term effects on the animal's behaviour.

In another type of single-subject study, a **case study**, psychologists take advantage of events that have occurred outside their control. For example, a patient known as HJA was a businessman who had suffered a stroke and had consequently also sustained damage to specific regions of his brain. HJA's behaviour after the damage, however, was perceptually unusual. Although his ability to tell lines of different length apart and to tell whether lines were in the same or different positions was unimpaired, he would have difficulty in perceiving objects. Specifically, he would spend up to six hours making painstaking drawings and at the end of his endeavour be unable to name what he had drawn (Humphreys and Riddoch, 1987a, b). This is a form of agnosia, a specific deficit in the ability to perceive objects, and we consider this in more detail in Chapter 6. By conducting singe-case studies of patients like HJA in this way, psychologists can explore the consequences of unusual events or actions that the patient has suffered.

Single-case studies have contributed substantially to our knowledge of neuropsychology, the study of the relationship between the activity of the brain and its function, although this method has been criticised. For example, there is frequently no way of knowing for certain how an individual behaved before the accident, there is no control over the degree and type of injury, and there is the possibility that personal characteristics (such as medication use, sex, age, socio-economic status, IQ) could influence results (Shallice, 1988; Martin, 1998a).

Obviously, psychologists do not go about damaging the brains of patients to satisfy their scientific curiosity. Instead, they study patients whose brains have been damaged by accident or disease. We compare their performance before and after the brain damage occurred. Usually, we do not meet the patients until after the brain damage occurs, so we must compare their performance with our estimate of what it was previously. This is called a premorbid estimate and there are tests available which give quite sensitive measures of premorbid intellectual ability, for example the National Adult Reading Test, or NART (O'Carroll, 1995; Crawford, 1992). Examples from the NART can be seen in Table 2.3.

Case studies are also performed by clinical psychologists and other mental health professionals, who observe the behaviour of clients and listen to what they have to say about their lives. Clinicians often try to correlate events in the client's past with the client's present behaviour and personality. Studies like these are called **retrospective studies** ('backward looking'), and their validity depends heavily on the client's memory of past events. Because recollections are often faulty, one must be cautious about accepting the conclusions of retrospective studies whose results cannot be independently verified. And because these studies are correlational and not experimental, we cannot be sure that the events that occurred in the past were the causes of the client's present behaviour.

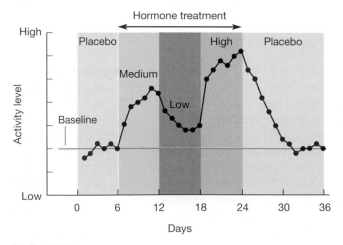

Figure 2.3

Results of a hypothetical single-subject experiment.

Table 2.3 Examples of 'easy' and 'difficult' items on the National Adult Reading Test

Easy	Difficult
CHORD	QUADRUPED
ACHE	DRACHM
DEPOT	SIDEREAL
AISLE	DEMESNE
DENY	BEATIFY
PSALM	CAMPANILE

Generalising from data

When we carry out an experiment or a correlational study, we probably assume that our participants are representative of the larger population. In fact, a representative group of participants is usually referred to as a sample of the larger population. If we study the behaviour of a group of 5 year old children, we want to make conclusions about 5 year olds in general. We want to be able to generalise our specific results to the population as a whole – to conclude that the results tell us something about human nature in general, not simply about our participants.

Many researchers recruit their participants from introductory courses in psychology because this is a very convenient way of obtaining subjects. The results of studies that use these students as participants can be generalised only to other groups of students who are similarly recruited. In the strictest sense, the results cannot be generalised to students in other courses, to adults in general, or even to all students enrolled in introductory psychology – after all, students who volunteer to serve as participants may be different from those who do not. Even if we used truly random samples of all age groups of adults in our area, we could not generalise the results to people who live in other geographical regions. If our ability to generalise is really so limited, is it worthwhile to do psychological research?

Well, we are not so strictly limited, of course. Most psychologists assume that a relation among variables that is observed in one group of humans will also be seen in other groups as long as the sample of participants is not especially unusual. For example, we may expect data obtained from prisoners to have less generality than data obtained from college students.

Application of psychological research

There is sometimes a distinction made in the sciences between applied and pure aspects of research. Pure research is research carried out for its own ends; the implications or consequences of such research are not known but it is designed simply to find out how something works or behaves (or does not). Applied research, on the other hand, is designed to have a practical application. Often in psychology (as, in fact, in most other sciences), this dichotomy is false. Pure research can often have surprising practical applications: it depends on how creative the scientist is in finding such applications. Throughout this book, you will find examples of research that seems to fall into these categories. When you do, reflect on what you have read and try to see the point of having conducted that piece of research. In the 'Psychology in action' sections in this book, you should be able to see how what appears to be fairly dry, academic, laboratory-based research tells us much about how we behave, 'outside' the laboratory.

Qualitative analysis

Although the majority of research undertaken in psychology is empirical and quantitative, in recent years the validity of this method has been challenged. This challenge has come from researchers who undertake a method of study called qualitative analysis. These researchers argue that traditional quantitative techniques do not allow psychologists to explore the richness of human experience, feeling, thought and social interaction. They suggest that this richness is better measured by paying close attention to the ways in which people use words, express feelings and arguments and by allowing individuals to explore ideas in discussion. Themes and ideas can then be interpreted from transcripts of these discussions. Qualitative analysis, therefore, is concerned with 'meanings, context and a holistic approach to material' (Hayes, 1997). This approach is called phenomenological because the experience, reactions and feelings of the individual are considered to be of paramount importance. Originally, qualitative analysis emerged as a new paradigm in the 1970s called ethogenics which sought to provide a better method of investigation in psychology (Harre and Secord, 1972). The new approach placed great emphasis on the use of language, especially the ways in which people accounted for their behaviour, thoughts and feelings: to understand real psychology meant analysing real talk (Foster and Parker, 1997).

The emphasis in the qualitative approach is not on quantifying data (in fact, this is actively discouraged) but in exploring the quality of data in depth. Some qualitative analysts have insisted that this form of analysis should not involve any numbers or counting at all (Strauss and Corbin, 1990), although this strict criterion is not often adhered to. Many qualitative analyses draw attention to concepts involving quantity such as frequency of utterances. Another important distinction between qualitative and quantitative analysis is that the former views the researcher as being central to the analysis and the process of data collection: he or she may participate in or facilitate discussion and will analyse the data obtained from his or her research. The interpretation of the data is also undertaken by the researcher/interviewer.

The data for qualitative analysis usually come from group discussions or interviews and there are various methods for conducting qualitative analysis. Some of these are outlined below. According to Miles and Huberman (1994), the format for conducting most qualitative analysis follows three stages:

1 collecting and reducing data

2 displaying data

3 drawing/verifying conclusions.

Structured and semi-structured interviews

Using the format of an interview to obtain information in psychology is not unusual. Many neuropsychological tests are administered by experimenters in an interview-type context. When such tests are administered, the researcher keeps to a strict 'script' in order to avoid influencing the performance of the respondent. In a sense, this is something like the format of a structured interview. The structured interview is conducted along predefined and predetermined lines with little scope for deviation from a script. The experimenter decides what he or she wants to explore, with little variation between interviews. Many structured interviews may comprise of an interviewer reading questions from a questionnaire and soliciting responses from an interviewee.

Sometimes, however, it may be interesting and informative to explore interviewees' responses more deeply while keeping to some overall plan or structure. Semi-structured interviews provide such a possibility. The semi-structured interview allows the establishment of rapport with the interviewee by placing less emphasis on the order of questions, where the interviewer is free to develop themes and issues raised by the interviewee and where open-ended questions are used. For example, whereas a structured interview might ask 'do you think that racism is caused by a, b, c or d?', a semi-structured interview might ask 'what do you think are the causes of racism?' It is suggested that funnelling is a useful approach to semi-structured interviews: the interviewer elicits a general opinion and then probes more specific issues relating to this general view.

The semi-structured interview has proved to be useful to some qualitative analysts. Others, however, would argue that even a semi-structured format is too restricting and that in order to elicit and understand genuine thoughts and feelings, you must allow discussion to occur freely. Such an approach is taken by discourse analysis.

Discourse analysis

Discourse analysis is a method which was developed in the mid-1980s to identify thoughts, feelings and themes from transcripts of data derived from conversations involving two or more individuals. Discourse analysis examines what people do with conversation and writing (Parker, 1992; Potter and Wetherell, 1995). Of course, the idea of conversational analysis was not new – sociologists had been using such techniques for some time – but discourse analysis was established with specific aims. It would attempt to look for contradictions in data and for contrasting ways of conversing about a topic (Foster and Parker, 1997). Discourses themselves are linguistic repertoires (Potter and Wetherell, 1987) which vary according to context. The most detailed analysis of discourses would examine the use of sound and verbal devices in conversation as well as mechanisms of persuasion and argument (Edwards and Potter, 1992).

Billig (1997) gives a comprehensive account of the rationale and the process involved in discourse analysis. Discourse analysis places importance on the use of language and what people mean when they express themselves verbally. Such speech acts could be complicated and would require careful analysis in order to discover what was meant. Discourse analysis does not assume that attitudes are stable; in fact, it assumes that 'giving views' is relatively unstable and that a person can give one view to one person and a contrary view to another: context, therefore, is important to the interpretation of attitude. A teenage girl's attitudes towards social issues might be expressed differently to a parent and to a member of her peer group, for example (Billig, 1997).

He also gives a typical example of a discourse analysis. In his book, *Talking of the Monarchy*, Billig (1992) interviewed 63 families from the East Midlands, England, about their attitudes towards the British royal family. All sessions were tape-recorded and samples included working- and middle-class families from urban and rural areas. Billig chose families because he wanted to explore the pattern of argument and thought in a group which could identify with the dynamics of a family and which could discuss issues in a relaxed context. The study accumulated over three thousand pages of transcription. In Table 2.4, Billig outlines the typical discourse analysis which could be performed on these transcripts.

Transcripts should be read and reread, the analyst should begin to develop 'hunches' or intuitive understanding and he or she should, after rereading, create index

---

Table 2.4 Suggested procedure for qualitative analysis

- Read background material about discursive psychology and topic of interest
- Decide on type of data to be studied
- Collect data
- Collect, listen to and transcribe tape-recordings
- Check the transcriptions against the tapes
- Read transcriptions
- Look for interesting features and develop 'intuitive hunches'
- Begin indexing themes and discursive features
- Write preliminary analysis, testing 'hunches' against data
- Draft and redraft analyses making note of counterexamples

Source: adapted from M. Billig (1997) Rhetorical and discursive analysis. In N. Hayes (ed.) *Doing Qualitative Analysis in Psychology*. © 1997. Reprinted by permission of Psychology Press Limited, Hove, UK.

Table 2.5 Extract from a transcription used for qualitative analysis

F: I can remember when Charles and Di got married I did an extra 4 hours that afternoon at work and I got 12 hours double time for that {D laughs} oh and a day off in lieu

I: So you made the most of it

F: Well certainly yeah I mean I'd got to work anyway I was on early shift and at that time we did 4 hours extra in the afternoon so it was my turn to do it so I made the extra 4 hours at double time you see as well and a day off because it was a bank holiday sort of thing that sticks out in my mind

D: Elaine er Elaine Paige sang at er Charles and Diana's wedding

S: Ssh (to baby)

F: I remember Charles and Di as regards Princess Anne's wedding and even Princess Margaret's wedding erm I mean there may be a vague recollection but I don't there's nothing that sticks in me mind to say Ah I know what happened when they got wed sort of thing you know and the same with Princess Alexandra er (.) I recall them getting wed you know er but as regards to anything that's [stuck in me mind

M: [It weren't her name's Kiki

    [Whatever her name is

D: [No Elaine [Elaine Paige

S: [No it wasn't

M: It weren't it was [Kik it weren't it were an opera singer

D: [No (.) Elaine Paige yeah Elaine Paige Kik Dee

        [isn't an opera singer

S: [It wasn't Elaine Paige it was

M: I didn't say Kiki Dee ...

D: You did ...

M: I didn't Kiki la er er ever such a foreign name

D: Elaine Paige sang in church

D: Daughter-in-law; F: Father; I: Interviewer; M: Mother; S: Son (husband of D)

categories of themes and major issues and of conversational details such as interruption or non-verbal agreement.

Table 2.5 is an extract from Billig's transcript. The discussion takes place between a mother and father (39 and 40 years old, respectively), their 22 year old son and their 21 year old daughter-in-law. Billig's analysis of this extract highlights the patterns of interaction between family members. We can also see the ebb and flow of argument during the discussion.

Grounded theory

Grounded theory was one of the earliest attempts at qualitative analysis and involves establishing a set of inductive strategies for the analysis of data (Glaser and Strauss, 1967;

Charmaz, 1990). Individual cases, incidents or experiences are analysed and theories are derived from such analysis (Charmaz, 1990). Unlike discourse analysis, grounded theory actively attempts to develop theory from information obtained from transcripts of conversations. Theorising is made possible by painstaking line-by-line coding of transcripts, by memo-taking and by constructing categories (themes/patterns) from responses. The theory is therefore grounded in what the respondents have had to say.

Objections to qualitative analysis

Qualitative analysis, although not widely used, has become a popular research tool in social and health psychology where analysis can be used to explore issues such as attitudes to death, racism, the monarchy, chronic illness and so on. Currently, qualitative analysis has had little impact outside these areas because of several perceived shortcomings. The most obvious, and difficult to reject, is that the process of qualitative analysis is subjective: the selection, analysis and interpretation of the material is made by the analyst. This introduces an element of bias into the study which could cloud an 'objective' analysis of the data. This argument is difficult to challenge effectively, although Hayes (1997) has suggested a 'half-way house' solution whereby a theory determined prior to the study may be used to guide later analysis. In this way, the study has a pre-stated focus and direction but it also allows for unpredicted insights.

Hammersley (1992) has identified several examples of the perceived differences between qualitative and quantitative analysis. For example, it is assumed that the types of data analysed by the two methods are totally different; the environments in which studies take place are different; one focuses on meaning (qualitative), the other on behaviour; quantitative methods adopt natural science as a model whereas qualitative analysis rejects it; one is inductive, the other deductive, one seeks patterns, the other seeks laws and so on. Hayes (1997) has given an excellent account of how this dichotomy may be more imagined than real. For example, she argues that qualitative researchers do sometimes use measures of quantity and that quantitative methods are often applied in naturalistic settings. Qualitative analysts do use conversational analysis to study behaviour as well as meaning. Furthermore, the rejection of the natural science model assumes that all of the natural sciences adopt the same experimental approach. Of course, they do not. Hayes, therefore, argues that the dichotomy between the two types of research methods is not as great as it would appear.

Questions to think about

How to conduct psychological research

- At the beginning of Chapter 1, you were asked to think about an experiment which you might like to conduct. Now that you know the five steps for conducting scientific research, how would your approach to carrying out your experiment alter?

- Imagine that you were a researcher who was interested in discovering whether people's cognitive ability declined with age. You take five groups of adults: 20–30 year olds, 31–40 year olds, 41–50 year olds, 51–60 year olds and the over 61 year olds. You administer a series of tests which measures a range of cognitive abilities such as verbal and visuospatial ability. You find that whereas most of the 61 and over group perform more poorly at most of the tests than do the other groups, they do better at some of the verbal tests such as vocabulary. What do you conclude from this study? If you conclude that verbal ability does not decline as rapidly as other abilities with age, you would be wrong. Can you think why? (The answer appears in Chapter 11.)

- Again, using the example above, what would be the theory and what would be the hypothesis in this experiment?

- In the same experiment, what would be the independent and dependent variables?

- Suppose that you were interested in studying the effects of sleep deprivation on learning ability. Which of these two variables would be the independent variable and which would be the dependent variable? How might you define these variables operationally?

- In what ways might an operational definition be reliable yet not valid? Valid yet not reliable?

- What are the advantages and disadvantages of laboratory and field studies? If you wanted to investigate the effect of alcohol and social interaction on aggressive behaviour how might you do this (1) in a laboratory and (2) in a naturalistic setting? Describe what your independent and dependent variables would be, how you would operationalise them and how you would overcome the influence of confounding variables.

- Should psychological research always have a practical outcome?

- An investigator is interested in discovering whether hunger makes you more attentive to food-related words. She sets up an experiment in which individuals have to decide whether words presented on a computer screen are printed in blue or red. There are food-related words and neutral words. She asks her participants to forgo breakfast and lunch and then has them perform the task. She finds that her participants make quicker colour decisions when the words are food-related. What is the design of this experiment? She argues that hunger does indeed make you more attentive to food-related words. But she is wrong. Can you see why?

- You read a study which shows that drug X has a significant effect on the improvement of mood in depressed individuals. Your friend – a depressive – takes a course of this drug but shows little sign of improvement. You conclude that the drug is ineffective in treating depression. Why would you be wrong in drawing this conclusion? Clue: Think about issues of generalisability and individual differences.

- In what ways does quantitative analysis differ from qualitative analysis? How would you apply each of these approaches to the study of people's attitudes towards animal experimentation?

Ethics

Because psychologists must study living participants, they must obey ethical rules as well as scientific rules. Great care is needed in the treatment of human participants because we can hurt people in very subtle ways. The rules that govern psychologists' conduct during experiments have been set by governments, institutions or professional societies and all psychologists engaged in research must abide by them.

Research with human participants

In Europe, North America and elsewhere, research undertaken by hospitals and universities will have been vetted by an ethics committee which decides on whether the proposed research meets the institution's ethical criteria regarding the welfare of human and animal participants in scientific research. Various professional societies such as the American Psychological Association (APA) and British Psychological Society (BPS) issue guidelines for the treatment of humans and animals participating in research. In some countries, data may also fall within the remit of a Data Protection Act which, in its most general form, allows an individual access to any information held electronically about him or her and, in research, allows the participant control over the use of such material.

The BPS lists a number of recommendations which its members should follow (British Psychological Society, 1991). These recommendations fall into the general categories of consent, deception, debriefing, withdrawal, confidentiality and protection of participants.

In general terms, a psychologist must treat participants with respect and must have taken all conceivable and practicable precautions to ensure that participants are not harmed. Threats to health, well-being, values and dignity should be eliminated.

Consent

An important part of any procedure designed to ensure the proper treatment of participants is informed consent. When possible, a psychologist should always inform the participant of the nature of the experiment and, having been told the detail of this research, the participant – if willing – will consent to take part. This represents informed consent. Of course, it is not always possible to secure informed consent because divulging all aspects of the experiment will influence the decisions, thoughts, feelings and behaviours of the participant. This is considered in more detail in the section on deception.

Usually, the potential participant reads a written statement prepared by the researcher. This discloses aspects of the research that might affect a person's willingness to participate in the study. The informed consent statement constitutes a contract between participant and researcher and is normally signed by both of them. Examples of these appear below.

If the individuals studied are children, then informed consent should be obtained from parents or guardians. Similarly, if participants are mentally ill, are unable to communicate or are mentally retarded, then a parent, healthcare worker or guardian should be informed and consent obtained from disinterested independent advisors.

Spider Phobia Study

Consent form

Please read the following information carefully and before you sign this form please ask questions you may have about the 'spider phobia study' and your participation in it.

I _____ fully understand the nature of the 'spider phobia study', that my participation is voluntary and that at any time I may terminate my participation without penalty. I am also aware that all my personal details and any information gathered about me will be kept confidential and will not be used for any purpose that is unrelated to the 'spider phobia study'.

Signed _____ Date _____ (participant)

Signed _____ Date _____ (experimenter)

Figure 2.4

(a) An example of a consent form used in research.

HIGHFLYER UNIVERSITY

DEPARTMENT OF PSYCHOLOGY

Psychology of Learning Experiment

I confirm that I give my full and informed consent to participate in the above experiment. I understand that the information I provide will remain anonymous and disguised so that I may not be identified. I therefore give my permission for the results of this study to be published.

(a) I understand that as part of this study I will be required to learn the works of Shakespeare.

(b) I have been informed that the general aim of the study is to investigate learning strategies.

(c) I have been informed that my general participation in this study will not involve unexpected discomforts or risks

(d) I have been informed that there are no disguised procedures in this experiment. The instructions can be taken at face value.

(e) I understand that the experimenter will answer any questions that I have regarding the study once I have participated

(f) I understand that I am free to withdraw from the study at any time without penalty.

Concerns about the study may be directed to the Chair of the Ethics Committee, School of Psychology, HighFlyer University.

Experimenter _____ Date _____

Participant _____ Date _____

Figure 2.4

(b) This second example of a consent form used in research is similar to that given by R.J. Sternberg (1988a).

If a researcher is undertaking observational research then the privacy and psychological well-being of the participant must be accounted for. Unless consent to being observed is obtained, participants should normally be observed only under conditions where they would expect to be observed by strangers.

Deception

Psychologists are advised never to withhold information or mislead participants if an individual is likely to be uneasy when eventually told the purpose of the experiment. Sometimes, however, withholding information or using misleading information is necessary for very good scientific reasons. When this occurs, it must be undertaken after obtaining the sound advice and approval of an ethics committee and colleagues.

Debriefing

When participants take part in an experiment, the experimenter is obliged to disclose to the participant the real and actual nature of the experiment and to answer any questions that the participant may ask about the experiment. This is called debriefing.

Withdrawal

If a participant feels that he or she has been unfairly misled or improperly treated, the participant has the absolute right to withdraw from the experiment. In fact, it should be made clear to all participants from the outset of the experiment that they are free to withdraw at any time. The participant has the right to withdraw consent following the experiment or debriefing and request that their data be discarded or destroyed, or both.

Confidentiality

Laws of the land notwithstanding, information and data provided by the participant in research are confidential. If data are published then those of individuals should not be identifiable, unless consent has been obtained.

Controversies in psychological science

Can research with animals help us to understand human behaviour?

The issue

Although most psychologists study the behaviour of humans, some study the behaviour of other animals. When we use another species of animal for our own purposes, we should be sure that what we are doing is both humane and worthwhile. Evidence suggests that whereas students regard the use of animals in medical testing as being warranted, they are less likely to agree that animals should be used in psychological experiments (Furnham and Heyes, 1993; Baluch and Kaur, 1995). Can animal research in psychology, therefore, be humane and worthwhile?

The evidence

Humane treatment is a matter of procedure. We know how to maintain laboratory animals in good health in comfortable, sanitary conditions. For experiments that involve surgery, we know how to administer anaesthetics and analgesics so that animals do not suffer. Most industrially developed societies have very strict regulations about the care of animals and require approval of the procedures that will be used in the experiments in which they participate. There is no excuse for mistreating animals in our care. In fact, the vast majority of laboratory animals are treated humanely because government departments ensure it.

Whether an experiment is worthwhile is more difficult to say. We use animals for many purposes. We eat their meat and their eggs and drink their milk; we turn their hides into leather; we extract insulin and other hormones from their organs to treat people with diseases; we train them to do useful work on farms or to entertain us. These are all forms of exploitation. Even having a pet is a form of exploitation: it is we – not they – who decide that they will live in our homes. The fact is, we have been using other animals throughout the history of our species.

Pet owning causes much more suffering among animals than scientific research does. As Miller (1983) notes, pet owners are not required to receive permission to house their pets from boards of experts that include veterinarians, nor are they subject to periodic inspections to be sure that their homes are clean and sanitary, that their pets have enough space to exercise properly, and that their diets are appropriate. Scientific researchers are. Miller also notes that fifty times more dogs and cats are killed by humane societies each year because they have been abandoned by their former owners than are used in scientific research.

The use of animals in research and teaching is a special target of animal rights activists. Nicholl and Russell (1990) examined twenty-one books written by activists and calculated the number of pages devoted to concern for different uses of animals. Next, they compared the relative concern the authors showed for these uses to the numbers of animals actually involved in each of these categories. The authors showed relatively little concern for animals used for food, hunting, or furs or for those killed in pounds. However, although only 0.3 per cent of the animals were used for research and education, 63.3 per cent of the pages are devoted to this use. In terms of pages per million animals used, the authors showed 665 times more concern for research and education than for food and 231 times more than for hunting. Even the use of animals for furs (which consumes two-thirds as many animals as research and education) attracted 41.9 times less attention per animal.

Conclusion

Our species is beset by medical, mental and behavioural problems, many of which can be solved only through research involving animals. In fact, research with laboratory animals has produced important discoveries about the possible causes or potential treatments of neurological and mental disorders, including Parkinson's disease, schizophrenia, manic–depressive illness, anxiety disorders, obsessive compulsive disorders, anorexia nervosa, obesity and drug addictions. Although much progress has been made, these problems are still with us and cause much human suffering. Unless we continue our research with laboratory animals, these problems will not be solved. Some people have suggested that instead of using laboratory animals in our research, we could use tissue cultures or computer simulations. Unfortunately, tissue cultures or computer simulations are not substitutes for living organisms. We have no way to study behavioural problems such as addictions in tissue cultures, nor can we program a computer to simulate the workings of an animal's nervous system. If we could, we would already have all the answers.

Protection of participants

Tied to the recommendations issued for consent and deception are those governing the protection of the participant, which are very similar. Psychologists have a primary responsibility to their participants to avoid harm (physical or mental) and if harm is identified, to remove it.

Understanding research results

In most of the examples cited so far, the behaviour of groups of participants was observed and measured. Once a study is finished, we need some way to compare these measurements. To do so, we use descriptive statistics

Descriptive statistics

Descriptive statistics, or summary statistics, are mathematical procedures that permit us to summarise sets of numbers. Using these procedures, we will calculate measures that summarise the performance of the participants in each group. Then we can compare these measures to see whether the groups of participants behaved differently (step 4 of the scientific method). We can also use these measures to describe the results of the experiment to others (step 5 of the scientific method). You are already familiar with some descriptive statistics. For example, you know how to calculate the average of a set of numbers; an average is a common measure of central tendency. You might be less familiar with measures of variability, which tell us how groups of numbers differ from one another, and with measures of relations, which tell us how closely related two sets of numbers are.

Measures of central tendency

When we say that the average weight of an adult male in Europe is 170 pounds or that the average density of population in Wales is 40 people per square mile, we are using a measure of central tendency, a statistic that represents many observations. There are several different measures of central tendency (summarised in Table 2.6), but the most common is the average, also called the mean. The mean of a set of observations is calculated by adding the individual values and dividing by the number of observations. The mean is the most frequently used measure of central tendency in reports of psychological experiments.

Although the mean is usually selected to measure central tendency, it is not the most precise measure, especially if a set of numbers contains a few especially high or low values. The most representative measure of central

Table 2.6   Measures of central tendency

Measure	Description
Mean	the sum of a group of values divided by their number
Median	the midpoint of a group of values arranged numerically
Mode	the most frequently occurring value in a set of values

tendency is the median. For this reason, we usually read 'median family income' rather than 'mean family income' in newspaper or magazine articles. To calculate the median of a set of numbers, we arrange them in numerical order and find the midpoint. For example, the median of the numbers 1, 2 and 6 is 2. The other measure of central tendency is the mode. The mode is the most frequently occurring value in a set of values.

To understand why the median is the best representative of a set of numbers that contains some extreme values, consider a small town of one hundred families. Ninety-nine of the families, all of whom work in the local textile factory, make between £15,000 and £20,000 per year. However, the income of one family is £2 million per year. This family consists of a popular novelist and her husband, who moved to the area because of its mild climate. The mean income for the town as a whole, considering the novelist as well as the mill workers, is £37,325 per year. In contrast, the median income for the town is £17,500 per year. Clearly, the median represents the typical family income of the town better than the mean does.

Why, then, would we ever bother to use the mean rather than the median? As we will see later in this chapter, the mean is used to calculate other important statistics and has special mathematical properties that often make it more useful than the median.

Measures of variability

Many experiments produce two sets of numbers, one consisting of the experimental group's scores and one of the control group's scores. If the mean scores of these two groups differ, the experimenter can conclude that the independent variable had an effect. However, the experimenter must decide whether the difference between the two groups is larger than what would probably occur by chance. To make this decision, the experimenter calculates a measure of variability – a statistic that describes the degree to which scores in a set of numbers differ from each other. The psychologist then uses this measure as a basis for comparing the means of the two groups.

Table 2.7 Two sets of numbers having the same mean and median but different ranges

	Sample A		Sample B
	8		0
	9		5
	10 ← Median		10 ← Median
	11		15
	12		20
Total:	50	Total:	50
Mean:	50/5 = 10	Mean:	50/5 = 10
Range:	12 – 8 = 4	Range:	20 – 0 = 20

Table 2.8 Calculation of the variance and standard deviation of two sets of numbers having the same mean

Sample A

Score	Difference between score and mean	Difference squared
8	10 – 8 = 2	4
9	10 – 9 = 1	1
10	10 – 10 = 0	0
11	11 – 10 = 1	1
12	12 – 10 = 2	4
Total: 50	Total:	10
Mean: 50/5 = 10	Mean (variance):	10/5 = 2
	Square root (standard deviation):	1.41

Sample B

Score	Difference between score and mean	Difference squared
0	10 – 0 = 10	100
5	10 – 5 = 5	25
10	10 – 10 = 0	0
15	15 – 10 = 5	25
20	20 – 10 = 10	100
Total: 50	Total:	250
Mean: 50/5 = 10	Mean (variance):	250/5 = 25
	Square root (standard deviation):	5

Two sets of numbers can have the same mean or median and still be very different. For example, the mean and median of both sets of numbers listed in Table 2.7 are the same, but the numbers are clearly different. The variability of the scores in set B is greater.

One way of stating the difference between the two sets of numbers is to say that the numbers in set A range from 8 to 12 and the numbers in set B range from 0 to 20. The range of a set of numbers is simply the largest number minus the smallest. Thus, the range of set A is 4 and the range of set B is 20.

The range is not used very often to describe the results of psychological experiments because another measure of variability – the standard deviation – has more useful mathematical properties. To calculate the standard deviation of a set of numbers, you first calculate the mean and then find the difference between each number and the mean. These difference scores are squared (that is, multiplied by themselves) and then summed. The mean of this total is called the variance; the standard deviation is the square root of the variance. The more different the numbers are from each other, the larger the standard deviation will be. This can be seen from the workings illustrated in Table 2.8.

Measurement of relations

In correlational studies, the investigator measures the degree to which two variables are related. For example, suppose that a psychologist has developed a new aptitude test and wants to sell the test to university admissions committees for screening applicants. Before the committees will consider buying the test, the psychologist must show that a person's score on the test is related to his or her subsequent success at university. To do so, the psychologist will give the test to a group of first-year undergraduates entering university and later obtain their average course grades. The psychologist will then measure the relation between test scores and grades.

Imagine that we give the test to ten students entering university and later obtain their average grades. We will have two scores for each person. We can examine the relation between these variables by plotting the scores on a

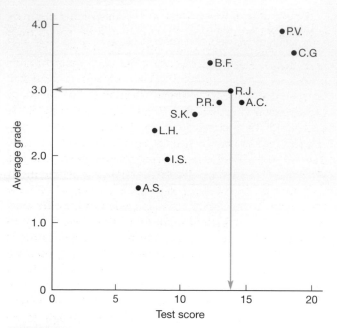

Figure 2.5

A scatterplot of the test scores and average grades of ten students. An example of graphing one data point (student R.J.) is shown.

graph. For example, student R.J. received a test score of 14 and earned an average grade of 3.0 (corresponding to a good class of degree). We can represent this student's score as a point on the graph shown in Figure 2.5.

The horizontal axis represents the test score, and the vertical axis represents the average grade. We put a point on the graph that corresponds to R.J.'s score on both of these measures.

We do this for each of the remaining students and then look at the graph, called a scatterplot, to determine whether the two variables are related. When we examine the scatterplot, we see that the points tend to be located along a diagonal line that runs from the lower left to the upper right, indicating that a rather strong relation exists between a student's test score and average grade, as seen in Figure 2.4. High scores are associated with good grades, low scores with poor grades.

Although scatterplots are useful, we need a more convenient way to communicate the results to others, so we calculate the correlation coefficient, a number that expresses the strength of a relation. Calculating this statistic for the two sets of scores gives a correlation of +0.9 between the two variables.

The size of a correlation coefficient can vary from 0 (no relation) to 1.0 (perfect relation). A perfect relation means that if we know the value of a person's score on one measure, then we can predict exactly what his or her score will be on the other. Thus, a correlation of +0.9 is very close to perfect; our hypothetical aptitude test is an excellent predictor of how well a student will do at university.

Correlations can be negative as well as positive. A negative correlation indicates that high values on one measure are associated with low values on the other and vice versa. An example of a negative correlation is the relation between people's mathematical ability and the amount of time it would take them to solve a series of math problems. People with the highest level of ability will take the least amount of time to solve the problems. For purposes of prediction a negative correlation is just as good as a positive one. A correlation of –0.9 is an almost perfect relation, but in this case high scores on one measure predict low scores on the other. Examples of scatterplots illustrating high and low correlations, both positive and negative, are shown in Figure 2.6.

If the points in a scatterplot fall along a line, the relation is said to be linear. But many relations are non-linear. For example, consider the relation between level of illumination and reading speed. Obviously, it is impossible to read in the dark. As the light level increases, people's reading

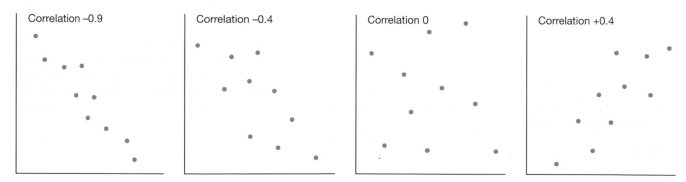

Figure 2.6

Scatterplots of variables having several different levels of correlation.

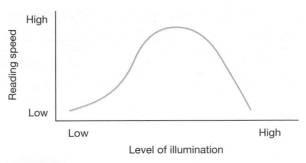

Figure 2.7

A non-linear relation. Results of a hypothetical experiment investigating the relation between level of illumination and reading speed. A correlation coefficient cannot adequately represent this kind of relation.

speed will increase, but once an adequate amount of light falls on a page, further increases in light will have no effect. Finally, the light becomes so bright and dazzling that people's reading speed will decline, as seen in Figure 2.7.

A correlation coefficient cannot accurately represent a non-linear relation such as this because the mathematics involved in calculating this measure assume that the relation is linear. Scientists who discover non-linear relations in their research usually present them in graphs or express them as non-linear mathematical formulae.

Inferential statistics: are the results significant?

When we perform an experiment, we select a sample of participants from a larger population. In doing so, we hope that the results will be similar to those we might have obtained had we used all members of the population in the experiment. We randomly assign the participants to groups in an unbiased manner, alter only the relevant independent variables, and measure the dependent variable using a valid and reliable method. After the experiment is completed, we must examine the results and decide whether a relation really exists between independent and dependent variables. That is, we must decide whether the results have statistical significance and are not simply due to chance. To do so, we will use inferential statistics. As we saw, descriptive statistics enable us to summarise our data. Inferential statistics enable us to determine whether the results are statistically significant.

For example, if we conduct an experiment and find that individuals low in self-esteem engage in fewer social interactions than do individuals with high self-esteem, how great does the difference between our two groups have to be before it is meaningful? How different is different? Suppose that we tested another two groups of people, both treated exactly the same way. Would the mean scores of the two groups be precisely the same? Well, no, because by chance, they would be at least slightly different. Imagine that we find that the mean score for the group that was subjected to a loss of self-esteem is lower than the mean score for the control group. How much lower would it have to be before we could correctly conclude that the difference between the groups was significant? The obvious way to determine whether two group means differ significantly is to look at the size of the difference. If it is large, then we can be fairly confident that the independent variable had a significant effect. If it is small, then the difference is probably due to chance. What we need are guidelines to help us to determine when a difference is large enough to be statistically significant. This can be done using inferential statistics.

Psychologists can calculate the mean and standard deviation for each group and consult a table that statisticians have already prepared for them. The table (which is based upon mathematical properties of the mean and standard deviation) will tell them how likely it is that their results could have been obtained by chance. In other words, the table tells them how likely it is that low self-esteem is not related to the number of social interactions. Note that the table tells them how likely it is that there will be *no* effect of our independent variable. This is known as the null hypothesis: there is no relationship between variable X and variable Y. The experimental hypothesis suggests that there is a difference between variable X and variable Y and will specify the direction of the difference (X will make Y increase, for example). If the likelihood of accepting the null hypothesis is low enough, psychologists will conclude that the results they obtained are statistically significant. Most psychologists consider a 5 per cent probability to be statistically significant but are much more comfortable with 1 per cent or less.

Statistical tests help us decide whether results are representative of the larger population but not whether they are important. In general usage, the word 'significant' does mean important, but statistical significance simply means that the results appear not to be caused by chance.

Questions to think about

Analysing data

- Can you think of some variables that you would expect to be positively or negatively correlated?

- An experimenter finds that there is a significant positive correlation between the amount of breakfast cereal consumed in the morning and performance on an IQ test. Is he or she right to conclude that eating breakfast makes you cleverer than those who don't?

- What does it mean to say that a study produced statistically significant results?

- Why might the results of a study be statistically significant but nevertheless unimportant?

- What if you had performed an experiment but found non-significant results? Does this mean that your experimental hypothesis is wrong? Can you think of alternative explanations for your negative results?

- In your opinion, should ethical rules be absolute or should they be flexible? Suppose that a researcher proposed to perform an experiment whose results could have important and beneficial consequences for society. However, the proposed study would violate ethical guidelines because it would involve a moderate degree of psychological discomfort for the participants. Should the researcher be given permission to perform the experiment? Should an exception be made because of the potential benefits to society?

- Why do you think some people apparently are more upset about using animals for research and teaching than for other purposes?

Key terms

scientific method *p.34*

naturalistic observations *p.34*

correlational studies *p.34*

experiments *p.34*

hypothetico-deductive *p.35*

replication *p.35*

hypothesis *p.36*

theory *p.36*

quantitative research *p.37*

control group *p.37*

experimental groups *p.37*

independent/between-groups design *p.37*

repeated measures/within-groups design *p.37*

field experiment *p.37*

variables *p.38*

independent variable *p.38*

dependent variable *p.38*

nominal fallacy *p.38*

operational definition *p.38*

validity *p.39*

Barnum effect *p.39*

confounding of variables *p.43*

counterbalancing *p.43*

reliability *p.43*

interrater reliability *p.43*

split-half reliability *p.44*

test–retest reliability *p.44*

random assignment *p.44*

social desirability *p.45*

placebo *p.46*

single-blind study *p.46*

double-blind study *p.46*

matching *p.47*

single-subject research *p.47*

case study *p.48*

retrospective studies *p.48*

sample *p.49*

generalise *p.49*

qualitative analysis *p.49*

structured interview *p.50*

semi-structured interview *p.50*

discourse analysis *p.50*

grounded theory *p.51*

informed consent *p.53*

debriefing *p.54*

confidential *p.54*

descriptive statistics *p.56*

measure of central tendency *p.56*

mean *p.56*

median *p.56*

mode *p.56*

measure of variability *p.56*

range *p.57*

variance *p.57*

standard deviation *p.57*

scatterplot *p.58*

correlation coefficient *p.58*

statistical significance *p.59*

inferential statistics *p.59*

CHAPTER REVIEW

The scientific method in psychology

- The scientific method allows us to determine the causes of natural phenomena. There are three basic forms of scientific research: naturalistic observations, experiments, and correlational studies.

- Hypotheses are statements or predictions made on the basis of naturalistic observations, previous experiments, or from formal theories.

- Psychologists might conduct experiments in which groups are independent of each other (the individuals in one group are not the same as those in the other; independent groups design) or experiments in which the same individuals take part in all conditions of the experiment (repeated measures design).

- An independent variable is an event, factor or action that is manipulated by the experimenter; the dependent variable is the quantity measured in an experiment (and is hypothesised to be influenced by the independent variable). To perform an experiment, a scientist alters the value of the independent variable and measures changes in the dependent variable.

- A psychologist must specify the particular operations that he or she will perform to manipulate the independent variable and to measure the dependent variable. Operational definitions are a necessary part of the procedure by which a hypothesis is tested; they also can eliminate confusion by giving concrete form to the hypothesis, making its meaning absolutely clear to other scientists.

- Validity is the degree to which an operational definition produces a particular value of an independent variable or measures the value of a dependent variable.

- Reliability refers to the consistency and precision of an operational definition. Researchers achieve high reliability by carefully controlling the conditions of their studies and by ensuring that procedures are followed correctly. Measurement involving subjectivity requires researchers to seek high interrater reliability.

- When designing an experiment, experimenters ensure that they control extraneous variables that may confound their results. If an extra variable is inadvertently manipulated and if this extra variable has an effect on the dependent variable, then the results of the experiment will be invalid. Confounding of subject variables can be caused by improperly assigning participants to groups or by treatments that cause some participants to leave the experiment.

- Most participants in psychological research try to guess what the experimenter is trying to accomplish, and their conclusions can affect their behaviour. If knowledge of the experimental condition could alter the participants' behaviour, the experiment should be conducted with a single-blind procedure (where the participant is unaware of the condition he or she is in). If that knowledge might also alter the experimenter's assessment of the participants' behaviour, a double-blind procedure should be used (where the participant and experimenter are unaware of the condition that the participant is in).

- Correlational studies involve assessing relations among variables that the researcher cannot readily manipulate, such as personality characteristics, age and sex. The investigator attempts to hold these variables constant by matching members in each of the groups on all relevant variables except for the one being studied. Correlational studies cannot determine which variable is the cause and which is the effect.

- Single-subject research consists of the detailed observation of individual participants under different conditions. Case studies involve careful observations of the behaviour of specific people, such as those with psychological or neurological disorders. Retrospective case studies ask participants to recall events from earlier in their lives.

- Researchers are almost never interested only in the particular participants they study; they want to be able to generalise their results to a larger population. The confidence that researchers can have in their generalisations depends on the nature of the variables being studied and on the composition of the sample group of participants.

- Qualitative analysis involves the examination of individuals' expression of ideas, thoughts and feelings and is usually based on transcripts of discussion between individuals or between the experimenter and an individual/individuals.

Ethics

- Because psychologists study living organisms, they must follow ethical principles in the treatment of their participants. Professional societies run by and for psychologists develop ethical guidelines that require informed consent, confidentiality, and a post-experiment debriefing.

- Participants may withdraw their consent to participate at any time before or during an experiment without any penalty. If deception is necessary, the experimenter must be certain that the participants will not be harmed psychologically or physically and that their dignity will be maintained. Committees review all psychological research before giving their consent for it to be carried out to assure that these guidelines are met.

- Research that involves the use of laboratory animals is also guided by ethical principles. It is incumbent on all scientists using these animals to see that they are housed comfortably and treated humanely, and laws have been enacted to ensure that they are. Such research has already produced many benefits to humankind and promises to continue to do so.

Analysing data

- Psychologists typically employ three kinds of descriptive statistics: measures of central tendency, variability and relations. The most common examples of these measures are the mean, the median, the standard deviation and the correlation coefficient.

- If psychologists test a hypothesis by comparing the scores of two groups of participants, they must have some way of determining whether the observed difference in the mean scores is larger than what would be expected by chance.

- Psychologists perform experiments by observing the performance of two or more groups of participants who have been exposed to different conditions, each representing different values of the independent variable. They then calculate the group means and standard deviations of the values of the dependent variable that were measured.

- Finally, they determine the statistical significance of the results. To do so, they plug means and standard deviations into a formula and consult a special table that statisticians have devised. The table indicates the likelihood of getting such results when the independent variable actually has no effect on the dependent variable. If the probability of obtaining these results by chance is sufficiently low, the psychologists will reject the possibility that the independent variable had no effect and decide in favour of the alternative – that it really did have an effect on the dependent variable.

Suggestions for further reading

There are many books about research methods, design and analysis available. Some of them you probably would not want to read – they are not the easiest books to read, nor are they the most coruscating texts you are likely to consult as a psychology student, but they serve a purpose in explaining how to do things. The best of research methods books, however, manage to engage you in the process of finding out how people behave. Some of these include the following:

Bausell, R.B. (1993). *Conducting Meaningful Experiments: 40 steps to becoming a scientist*. London: Routledge.
Bausell's short book is a very well written, straightforward account of what you need to know and to do in order to become a scientist. It is laid out in the form of principles (40 of them) which the author describes, explains and illustrates.

Coolican, H. (1994). *Research Methods and Statistics in Psychology* (2nd edition). London: Hodder & Stoughton.
Few books describe, with any ease, the nature of research methods and the principles and processes of statistical analysis, but Coolican's book is one that does. Highly readable and not too demanding for the beginner.

Foster, J.J. and Parker, I. (1995). *Carrying Out Investigations in Psychology*. Leicester: BPS Books.
Another text which approaches research methods from the psychologist's perspective and considers aspects of design not considered in more quantitative texts.

Hayes, N. (1997). *Doing Qualitative Analysis in Psychology*. Hove, UK: The Psychology Press.
An excellent introduction to this method of analysis. Most qualitative texts are unreadable and a lot of the material is heavy going. In this book, however, Hayes places each chapter (written by known qualitative researchers) in context and introduces each in a very comprehensive and comprehensible way.

Haworth, J. (1996). *Psychological Research: Innovative methods and statistics*. London: Routledge.
Like Foster and Parker's, this text covers unusual (or 'innovative') approaches to studying psychology. Not much on quantitative analysis but much on surveys and the approaches taken by sub-areas of psychology (such as the single-case study in psychology; hypnotic techniques in clinical/consciousness research).

Meltzoff, J. (1998). *Critical Thinking about Research: Psychology and related fields*. Washington, DC: American Psychological Association.
This is an extraordinary book because instead of analysing real research articles for quality, the author has composed several fictitious ones to highlight flaws in the ways in which studies are conducted, analysed and reported. The first half of the book is an excellent introduction to research methods; the second half consists of fictitious research articles and an critical analysis of each. Superb for helping you develop critical thinking skills.

Robson, C. (1993). *Real World Research*. Oxford: Blackwell.

Solso, R.L., Johnson, H.H. and Beal, M.K. (1998). *Experimental Psychology* (6th edition). Harlow: Longman.

Robson's excellent, well written book delivers a comprehensive account of how to conduct 'difficult' research (i.e. out of the laboratory). Solso et al.'s text provides a lot of very useful information about tracking down materials and writing up research as well as analysing some real, published research section by section.

Blum, D. (1994). *The Monkey Wars*. Oxford: Oxford University Press.
This is a well written, generally well balanced account of the use of animals (primarily primates) in science research.

Gale, A. (1995). Ethical issues in psychological research. In A.M. Coleman (ed.), *Psychological Research Methods and Statistics*. London: Longman.

Lindsay, G. (1996). Psychology as an ethical discipline and profession. *European Psychologist*, 1, 2, 79–88.
Gale's succinct chapter is a good introduction to ethics and psychological research. Lindsay's article considers the ethical basis for the development of 'ethical codes' in psychology (such as those adopted by the BPS, APA and EFPPA).

Journals to consult

Behaviour Research, Instruments and Design
British Journal of Mathematical and Statistical Psychology
Current Directions in Psychological Science
Educational Measurement and Assessment
Psychological Bulletin
Psychological Methods

Website address

http://www.mwsc.edu/~psych/research/psy302.html
This is a link to a large collection of interesting psychology journal articles put on the web. It doesn't give you the source of the article (where it was published) but the range of articles will show you how research in psychology is conducted and how it is written up. Some of the topics are unusual.

EVOLUTION, GENETICS AND BEHAVIOUR

In a psychology laboratory in Texas, a man is sitting in front of a television screen which shows an apparently live video link to a woman in another room. This woman will converse with him and will decide whether she chooses him or another man for a date. The woman asks the man a variety of questions about himself, how he enjoys spending his time, how he would approach someone that he finds attractive in a bar and so on. At the end of each question, the man's competitor – sitting in another laboratory and saying nothing – is shown on the monitor. The participant is then asked to explain why he should be the date of choice for this woman. At this point both the woman and the competing date can see and hear the participant but he cannot see them. After this, the man is asked a series of questions about how attractive he found the woman and how likely he was to go on a date with her.

Men with more symmetrical bodies displayed more direct, sexual, competitive tactics when trying to win their date. These men compared themselves directly with their competitor, used humour less, and did not claim to be likeable.

The researchers conclude that 'more symmetrical men do, in fact, have physical and personal attributes necessary to pull off direct competition tactics in initial heterosexual encounters' (Simpson *et al.*, 1999). They do this because they have the genetic viability needed to compete with other men and the relevant physical attributes needed to support a direct, confrontational approach. That is, they have an evolutionary advantage over other men.

OVERVIEW

The human race has existed, in various forms, for over 10 million years. This timespan has seen a tremendous change in our physical appearance, our biology and our behaviour. Our brains have developed, our societies have become more sophisticated, our intelligence has increased, our ability to communicate has improved, we have developed language systems. These processes illustrate the ways in which we have evolved.

This chapter describes the nature of these processes: how and why behaviour has evolved. Darwin's theory of evolution is probably one of the most profound and important theories in all science; it has influenced the way in which we think that the human race and other species have evolved; no other theory has come close to it in terms of explaining evolution. Recently, the principles of evolution have been used to explain a broad range of behaviours (D.M. Buss, 1995) and current research is exploring how the principles of evolution can be applied to understanding the development of mental illness (Baron-Cohen, 1997; Gilbert, 1998).

The sub-areas of psychology, sociobiology and evolutionary psychology, explicitly apply the principles of evolutionary theory to concepts such as mate selection, parenting, jealousy, altruism and deception. These applications are controversial and this chapter will evaluate the controversy and the reasons for it.

What you should be able to do after reading Chapter 3

- Describe Darwin's theory of evolution.
- Outline the principles of genetic inheritance.
- Evaluate the contribution of genetics to psychology.
- Describe and evaluate sociobiology and evolutionary psychology's contribution to our understanding of behaviour.

Questions to think about

- What do you think is meant by the term 'evolution of behaviour'?
- How do you think the process of evolution could explain modern behaviour such as romantic attraction, jealousy, language and marriage?
- Why do you think that we have become more intelligent and sophisticated than our ancestors?
- What do you understand by the terms 'genetics' and 'heredity'?
- Does culture or genetics have a greater influence on behaviour? Do they interact?

'From my early youth I have had the strongest desire to understand and explain whatever I observed, that is, to group all facts under some general laws. ... Therefore, my success as a man of science, whatever this may have amounted to, has been determined, as far as I can judge, by complex and diversified mental qualities and conditions. Of these, the most important have been – the love of science – unbounded patience in long reflecting over any subject – industry in observing and collecting facts – and a fair share of invention and common sense. With such moderate abilities as I possess, it is truly surprising that I should have influenced to a considerable extent the belief of scientific men on some important points.' (Darwin, 1887, pp. 67–71)

The development of evolutionary theory

These fairly humble words were written by a man who has influenced the course of scientific thought more than any other individual since Copernicus (who, in 1543, proposed that the sun, not the earth, was at the centre of the universe). Charles Darwin argued that, over time, organisms originate and become adapted to their environments by biological means. This concept is referred to as biological evolution – changes that take place in the genetic and physical characteristics of a population or group of organisms over time – and it stands as the primary explanation of the origin of life (Dawkins, 1986). Evolutionary theory seeks to explain why we have evolved in the way that we have. Why do birds have wings, giraffes have long necks, humans have bigger brains than other higher primates? How do changes in organic structure occur and how does this happen? The answers to questions such as these have important implications for the topics discussed in other chapters in this book: intelligence, personality, social interaction, the use of language, the perception and expression of emotion, sex, hunger, mental disorder and so on.

Although it has its roots in biology, Darwin's work transcends biology and has influenced other natural sciences, especially psychology. In the past two decades, some psychologists have become increasingly aware of the various ways that biology can influence behaviour. As you will see in this chapter, many behavioural differences among organisms, both within and across species, correspond to genetic and other biological differences. Understanding these differences and their evolution allows psychologists to understand behaviour in terms of its possible origins and adaptive significance – its effectiveness in aiding the organism to adapt to changing environmental conditions.

For example, gregariousness is the tendency to form groups or to be sociable; people tend to form social units. We live in families, have circles of friends, and join groups, such as churches, clubs or professional or recreational societies and political organisations. To understand the adaptive significance of gregariousness, we need to consider two questions. First, what events and conditions in a person's lifetime might contribute to an individual's gregariousness – what function does gregariousness serve in helping people adapt to the changing circumstances of life? Secondly, what events and conditions in the evolution of our species favoured gregariousness – what functions has gregariousness served in the history of humankind? These are important questions because a complete understanding of gregariousness, like any behaviour, requires that we understand both the past and present conditions that influence it.

In other words, psychologists might research how past environmental conditions favoured gregariousness over a more solitary existence as a means of organising human culture and how the immediate environment influenced day-to-day sociability. They are interested in understanding both ultimate causes (from the Latin *ultimatus*, 'to come to an end') of behaviour – events and conditions that, over successive generations, have slowly shaped the behaviour of our species – and proximate causes (from the Latin *proximus*, 'near'), namely immediate environmental variables that affect behaviour.

By understanding how adaptive behaviour developed through the long-term process of evolution, psychologists are able to gain a more thorough understanding of our ability to adjust to changes in our immediate environment (Skinner, 1987). To understand the present, we must understand the past – the history of the individual and the history of our species. We behave as we do because we are members of the human species – an ultimate cause – and because we have learned to act in special ways – a proximate cause. Both biology and environment contribute to our personal development.

A new field of psychology, evolutionary psychology (Tooby and Cosmides, 1989; D.M. Buss, 1995) investigates how an organism's evolutionary history contributes to the development of behaviour patterns and cognitive strategies related to reproduction and survival during its lifetime (Leger, 1991). Evolutionary psychology's contribution to our understanding of human behaviour will be assessed later in the chapter. First, however, we describe Darwin's theory of evolution. An understanding of this complex theory will help shed light on how behaviour has been interpreted, by some psychologists, in terms of evolution.

'In the beginning': the voyage of the *Beagle*

The story of how Charles Darwin developed his theory illustrates the mix of hard work, intellect and good fortune that often makes scientific discovery possible. In fact, Darwin's work is an excellent example of how observation and experimentation can lead to scientific breakthroughs.

After receiving a degree in theology from the University of Cambridge, England, in 1831, Darwin met a Captain

Charles Darwin (1809–1882)

Source: Northwind Photo Library

Robert Fitz Roy who was looking for someone to serve as an unpaid naturalist and travelling companion during a five-year voyage on board *HMS Beagle*. The *Beagle*'s mission was to explore and survey the coast of South America and to make longitudinal measurements worldwide.

During the voyage, Darwin observed the flora and fauna of South America, Australia, South Africa and the islands of the Pacific, South Atlantic and Indian Oceans. He collected creatures and objects of every sort: marine animals, reptiles, amphibians, land mammals, birds, insects, plants, rocks, minerals, fossils and seashells. These specimens, which were sent back to England at various stages of the trip, were later examined by naturalists from all over Europe.

Darwin did not form his theory of evolution while at sea. Although he was impressed by the tremendous amount of diversity among seemingly related animals, he believed in *creationism*, the view that all living things were designed by God and are non-evolving (Gould, 1985).

The Origin of Species

Upon his return home to England in 1836, Darwin continued to marvel at the many ways animals and plants adapt to their environments. He sifted through his collections, often discussing his findings and ideas with other scientists. He carefully reviewed the work of earlier naturalists who had developed their own theories on evolution. Darwin was not the first person to propose a theory of evolution, but he was the first to amass weighty evidence in its favour. He became interested in artificial selection, a procedure in which particular animals are mated to produce offspring who possess especially desirable characteristics. For example, if a farmer wished to develop cattle that

yielded the largest steaks, then he or she would examine the available breeding stock and permit only the 'beefiest' ones to reproduce. If this process is repeated over many generations of animals, the cattle should become beefier. In other words, in artificial selection people select which animals will breed and which will not based on specific, desirable characteristics of the animals.

As he pondered on whether there might be a natural process corresponding to the role humans play in artificial selection, Darwin's views on evolution began slowly to change. He believed 'that selection was the keystone of man's success in making useful races of animals and plants. But how selection could be applied to organisms living in a state of nature remained for some time a mystery to me' (Darwin, 1887, p. 53).

A year and a half later, on reading Malthus's *Population*, Darwin proposed that because the 'struggle for existence' continued in plants and animals, then favourable variations would be preserved and unfavourable ones would die out. The result of such 'selection' would be the development of new species (Darwin, 1887).

This proposal contains the idea of natural selection: within any given population, some members of a species will produce more offspring than will others. Any animal that possesses a characteristic that helps it to survive or adapt to changes in its environment is likely to live longer and to produce more offspring than are animals that do not have this characteristic.

Darwin was well aware of the significance of his discovery but did not publish his theory until twenty years later, taking great pains to develop a clear, coherent and accurate case for his theory.

Darwin might have been even slower in publishing his theory had it not been for an intriguing coincidence. In 1858, he received a manuscript from Alfred Russell Wallace, another naturalist, outlining a theory of natural selection identical to his own. If Darwin had published his theory at this time, it would look as if he had stolen the idea from Wallace; if he did not publish it, his twenty years of painstaking toil would be wasted. His colleagues suggested that he and Wallace make a joint presentation of their separate works before a learned society – the Linnean Society – so that each might lay equal claim to the theory of natural selection. This was done, and a year later Darwin published his 'abstract', which we know today as *The Origin of Species*. The book sold out on its first day of publication and has been selling steadily ever since.

Natural selection and evolution

Two concepts are central to Darwin's theory of evolution: adaptation and natural selection. Adaptation refers to the ability of generations of species to adapt effectively to changes in the environment. Natural selection refers to the process whereby some variations in species will be transferred from one generation to the next but others will not. The Oxford zoologist Richard Dawkins has likened the process of natural selection to a sieve because it leaves out what is unimportant (Dawkins, 1996).

Darwin's theory has four basic premises:

1 The world's animal and plant communities are dynamic, not static: they change over time with new forms originating and others becoming extinct.

2 The evolutionary process is gradual and continuous. New species arise through slow and steady environmental changes that gradually 'perfect' each species to its surroundings. When sudden and dramatic changes occur in the environment, a species' ability to adapt is usually challenged. Some species adapt and live, others become extinct.

3 All organisms descended from an original and common ancestor. Over time, the process of natural selection has created different species, each specifically adapted to its ecological niche.

4 Natural selection not only causes changes within populations during changing environmental conditions but also acts to maintain the status quo under relatively constant environmental conditions.

According to Jacob (1977), natural selection results from two characteristics of life. First, reproduction produces offspring that are slightly different from their parents. Secondly, interaction with a changing environment requires that living things adapt behaviourally to its vagaries, otherwise they will risk injury, illness or death. The interaction of these factors causes differential reproduction, and, ultimately, evolution. Evolution, in this sense, is a process that is strongly influenced by behavioural adaptations to changing environments (Buss *et al.*, 1998).

Natural selection

The essence of Malthus's essay, which Darwin was reading when the idea of natural selection first occurred to him, was that the earth's food supply grows more slowly than populations of living things. The resulting scarcity of food produces competition among animals, with the less fit individuals losing the struggle for life. For example, wolves who are agile are better able to capture prey than are slower packmates. Fast wolves will therefore tend to outlive and outreproduce slower wolves. If a wolf's tendency to run fast is a genetically controlled trait, it will be passed on to its offspring. These offspring will be more likely to catch prey and will therefore live longer and have more opportunities to reproduce.

The ability of an individual to produce offspring defines that individual's reproductive success – the number of viable offspring it produces relative to the number of viable offspring produced by other members of the same species. Contrary to popular interpretation, 'survival of the fittest' does not always mean survival of the most physically fit or of the strongest. The evolutionary 'bottom line' is not physical strength but reproductive success. Physical strength is only one factor that might contribute to such success. In humans, for example, good looks, charm and intelligence play an important role in an individual's ability to attract a mate and reproduce. What is more, natural selection is not 'intentional'. Giraffes did not grow long necks in order to eat leaves from trees but those with longer necks who were able to reach the leaves successfully reproduced while the others died out (Buss *et al.*, 1998).

Two aspects of natural selection – variation and competition – are the critical factors that determine whether any particular animal and its offspring will enjoy reproductive success.

Variation

Variation includes differences among members of a species such as physical characteristics (size, strength or physiology), and behavioural characteristics (intelligence or sociability). What factors are responsible for these sorts of variation?

First, an individual organism's genetic make-up, or its genotype, differs from that of all other individuals (except in the case of identical twins). As a result of these genetic differences, an individual organism's physical characteristics and behaviour, or its phenotype, also differs from that of every other individual.

Every individual's phenotype is produced by the interaction of its genotype with the environment. In essence, the genotype determines how much the environment can influence an organism's development and behaviour. For instance, identical twins have exactly the same genotype. If they are separated at birth and one twin has a better diet than the other, their phenotypes will be different: The better-fed twin is likely to be taller and stronger. However, regardless of diet neither twin will ever become extremely tall or very muscular if they do not possess the genes for tallness and muscularity. Likewise, neither twin will realise his or her full potential for tallness and muscularity if he or she does not eat a nutritional diet. In this example, both the genotype (the genes related to tallness and muscularity) and a favourable environment (a well balanced, nutritional diet) must be present for either twin to reach his or her full growth potential.

The interaction between genetic and environmental factors in determining a phenotype is made especially clear in the case of dermatographia, an inherited trait in which genetic factors permit the skin to react to surface pressure. Although this trait is genetic, without the environmental factor of pressure, the phenotype – the welting of the skin – will not be expressed.

Phenotypes and the genotypes responsible for them may or may not be selected, depending on the particular advantage they confer. Consider, for example, the thirteen species of finch that Darwin discovered in the Galapagos Islands, located off the west coast of South America. A striking physical difference among these birds is beak size. Some finches have a small, thin beak phenotype and others have a large, thick beak phenotype. Birds having small, thin beaks feed on small seeds covered by weak shells, and birds having large, thick beaks feed on large seeds covered by tough shells.

In a study that investigated the relationship between rainfall, food supply and finch population on one island, Grant (1986) discovered that the amount of rainfall and the size of the food supply directly affected the mortality of finches having certain kinds of beak. During droughts, small seeds became scarce. As a result, the finches having small, thin beaks died at a higher rate than finches having bigger, thicker beaks. During the next few years, the number of finches having bigger, thicker beaks increased – just as the principle of natural selection would predict. During times of plentiful rain, small seeds became abundant, and the number of finches having small, thin beaks became more plentiful in subsequent years.

Grant's study makes two important points. First, although evolution occurs over the long run, natural selection can produce important changes in the short run – in the space of only a few years. Secondly, phenotypic variation, in this case differences in beak size, can produce important selective advantages that affect survival. Imagine if all the finches had small, thin beaks: during the drought, most, if not all, of these finches might have died. None would be left to reproduce and these finches would have become extinct on this island. Fortunately, there was phenotypic variation in beak size among the finches, and because phenotypic variation is caused by genetic variation (different genotypes give rise to different phenotypes), some finches – those having large, thick beaks – had an advantage. Their food supply (the larger seeds) was relatively unaffected by the drought, enabling them to outsurvive and outreproduce the finches having small, thin beaks.

On the basis of this evidence, one might reasonably assume that all finches should have developed large, thick beaks. However, when rain is plentiful and small seeds are abundant, birds having small, thin beaks find it easier to feed. Under these environmental conditions, these birds have a phenotypic (and genotypic) advantage.

Competition

The second aspect of natural selection is competition. Individuals of a given species share a similar environment. Because of this, competition within a species for food, mates and territory is inevitable. Every fish captured and eaten by one bald eagle is a fish that cannot be captured and eaten by another bald eagle. If one bald eagle finds a suitable mate, then there is one fewer potential mate for other bald eagles and so on.

Competition also occurs between species when members of different species vie for similar ecological resources, such as food and territory. For example, yellow-headed blackbirds and red-winged blackbirds eat the same foods and occupy the same type of breeding territories; thus, they compete for these resources. Such competition does not involve competition for mates (yellow-headed blackbirds do not court red-winged blackbirds and vice versa). However, although these species do not compete for mates, their competition for other resources indirectly influences reproductive success because the ability to find and court a suitable mate depends on the ability to stake out and defend a territory having an adequate food supply. The probability of a yellow-headed blackbird finding a mate and successfully rearing a family depends not only on its success in competing against other yellow-headed blackbirds, but also on its success in competing against red-winged blackbirds.

Natural selection works because the members of any species have different phenotypes. Because these phenotypes are caused by different genotypes, successful individuals will pass on their genes to the next generation. Over time, competition for food and other resources will allow only the best-adapted phenotypes (and their corresponding genotypes) to survive, thereby producing evolutionary change. At least, this is what the theory would predict.

Natural selection in human evolution

Reconstruction of human evolution is a difficult job, something akin to assembling a giant jigsaw puzzle whose pieces have been scattered throughout the world. Some of the pieces may have been lost for ever; others have become damaged beyond recognition; and those few that are found force continual reinterpretation of how the other pieces might fit the puzzle. Some of our past will likely remain a mystery for ever. At best, all we can do is make an educated guess about the evolution and lifestyles of our ancestors.

Many biologists and natural historians of Darwin's time believed that natural selection applied to all animals, including humans. Others insisted that although natural selection applied to other animals, it did not apply to humans. However, through study of the fossil record and recent developments in genetic research, we now know that our species is related genetically to other mammals. The gorilla and the chimpanzee are our closest living relatives, and together we appear to have descended from a common ancestor.

Our dependence on information from fossil remains and other archaeological artefacts is problematic. As Byrne (1995) has colourfully pointed out, much of what we conclude about our ancestors' behaviour from archaeological findings is speculative; some is sensible speculation but it is speculation none the less. There is no way of empirically or conclusively demonstrating that artefacts were used in the way in which we suggest or that they indicate a specific way of living or behaving. In this sense, paleoanthropology – the study of human behaviour using information from fossil remains – is more like detective work than scientific work. 'The reality is', Byrne argues, 'that we will never know with confidence the answers to many of the most important questions we would like to ask about what happened in the past five million years' (1995, p. 6).

With this caveat in mind, the general pattern of evolution is thought to occur something like this. Our evolution from a common ancestor appears to have begun in Africa about 2 million years ago (Clark, 1993); a map of the suspected sites for hominid evolution can be seen in Figure 3.1.

The earliest humans have been labelled *Homo habilis* (literally 'handy man'). *Homo habilis* was small (only about 1.3 metres tall and about 40 kilograms in weight), but was bipedal (able to walk upright on two feet). Compared with its predecessor – a species called Australopithecus – *Homo habilis* had a larger brain and more powerful hands. The strong hands were well suited to making simple stone tools; hence the name 'handy man'. A natural selection interpretation of such adaptively significant traits would argue that these early humans adapted to the environment in terms of creating shelter against the elements, catching and preparing food, and making weapons for self-defence.

Homo habilis was succeeded, about 400,000 years later, by *Homo erectus* ('upright man'). *Homo erectus* had a much larger brain and stood more erect than *Homo habilis* and had a more complex lifestyle. *Homo erectus* was the first of our ancestors to establish regular base camps, which probably served as centres for social activities, including the preparation and eating of food. We cannot be absolutely sure that these interpretations are the correct ones, however (Byrne, 1995). *Homo erectus* created more efficient and stronger tools than did *Homo habilis*, successfully hunted big game, and discovered and used fire. Fire enabled these early humans to cook food, remain warm in cold weather and protect themselves from predators. *Homo erectus*'s use of fire, coupled with its apparent social nature and its ability to hunt and/or scavenge big game, permitted it to explore and settle new environments, including Europe, Asia and other parts of Africa.

The earliest known *Homo sapiens* ('intelligent man') appears to have arisen about 500,000 years ago. The best known of the early *Homo sapiens*, *Homo sapiens neanderthalensis*, lived throughout Europe and Central Asia between approximately 300,000 and 35,000 years ago. Neanderthals constructed small huts from bones and animal skins and sometimes burned bones as fuel. They were skilled big game hunters, tool makers and clothiers, and they had cultural rituals for burying their dead. In one Neanderthal burial site unearthed in France, a small boy was found positioned on his left side with a small pillow of flints under his head and an axe positioned by his right hand. Similar Neanderthal burial sites have been discovered, suggesting that these humans possessed cultural traditions not previously found in the prehistoric record.

Informed speculation suggests that Neanderthals and modern humans (*Homo sapiens sapiens*) overlapped each other, although the origin of *Homo sapiens sapiens* is unclear. It seems to have arisen between 200,000 and 100,000 years ago. What is clear, though, is that the *Homo sapiens sapiens* line has survived to flourish in all parts of the world, despite the presence of hostile climate, terrain and predators. Figure 3.2 charts the suspected development of *Homo sapiens sapiens*.

The apparent success of the human species in adapting to a variety of ecological niches stems from the fact that

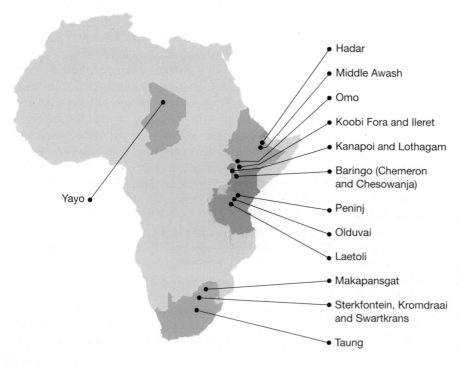

- Hadar
- Middle Awash
- Omo
- Koobi Fora and Ileret
- Kanapoi and Lothagam
- Baringo (Chemeron and Chesowanja)
- Peninj
- Olduvai
- Laetoli
- Makapansgat
- Sterkfontein, Kromdraai and Swartkrans
- Taung
- Yayo

Figure 3.1

A map of Africa indicating those areas thought to reveal the origins of hominid evolution.

Source: Reproduced with permission from Eccles, J.C., *Evolution of the Brain*. London: Routledge, 1989.

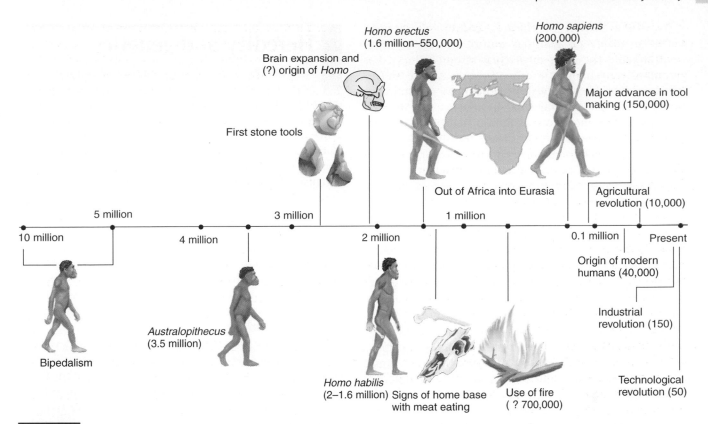

Figure 3.2

Major milestones in human evolution. The ability to walk upright freed the hands for tool use and other manipulative skills. Increased brain size accompanied increased intelligence. These two adaptations combined probably contributed significantly to all other major adaptations in human evolution.

Source: Adapted from Lewin, R., *Human Evolution: An illustrated introduction.* Cambridge, MA: Blackwell Scientific Publications, Inc., 1984.

natural selection has favoured two important human characteristics: bipedalism, the ability to move about the environment on two feet, and encephalisation, increased brain size. The ability to walk upright, which appears to have evolved in our early hominid ancestors over 4 million years ago (Boaz, 1993; Ruff *et al.*, 1997), not only allowed greater mobility, but also freed the hands for grabbing, holding and throwing objects. The ability to grasp objects, in combination with an expanding capacity for learning and remembering new skills provided by a larger brain, led to advances in tool making, food gathering, hunting and escaping predators (Eccles, 1989).

As the brain became larger, more of its volume – especially the front part of the brain which is the most recently evolved – appeared to become devoted to thinking, reasoning, decision making and other complex cognitive, 'higher' functions. We will return to the role of this part of the brain in thinking in Chapter 11.

Another important ability that emerged from encephalisation was planning – the capacity to anticipate future events and to take into account the effects that those events might have on an individual or group of individuals. Such planning might have involved the organisation of hunts, the institution of social customs and events (such as weddings and funerals), and the planting and harvesting of crops. Over time, the interaction of bipedalism and encephalisation permitted humans to exploit new environments and establish well organised communities.

Advances in tool making and hunting, combined with the use of fire for cooking, protection and warmth, were adaptive: they helped humans to live longer. The increased lifespan of humans may have aided the gradual accumulation of wisdom as the older members of early human communities began to share their knowledge with younger members through language. Although the fossil record cannot tell us when language first developed, we assume that those who were able to communicate with others through language had a distinct advantage over those who could not.

Language originated and subsequently evolved because of its immensely adaptive significance (Pinker, 1994). As Skinner (1986) noted, language not only provided a simple means of warning others of danger, but also provided a means of communicating important information to others, such as the location of a good hunting spot or instructions on how to craft a tool. Perhaps the most important advantage conferred by language was its ability to reinforce the already strong social tendencies of early humans. Language is the foundation upon which all human cultures are built.

As the evolution of cultures continued, humans gained an increasing ability to control and modify their environment. The same intellectual resourcefulness that permitted early humans to discover and use fire and to invent useful tools prompted the agricultural revolution of 10,000 years ago, the Industrial Revolution of 150 years ago, and the technological revolution that began only 50 years ago with the invention of the transistor, the integrated circuit and the computer. **Cultural evolution**, or the adaptive changes of cultures in response to changes in the environment over time, is possible only because humans have been genetically endowed with a capacity for learning and language. As cultural anthropologist Marvin Harris (1991) has noted, our capacity for learning has evolved because (1) it leads to 'a more flexible and rapid method of achieving reproductive success', and (2) it allows entire groups of people to 'adjust or take advantage of novel opportunities in a single generation without having to wait for the appearance and spread of genetic mutations' (p. 27). For example, advances in medicine have allowed us to control life-threatening diseases such as polio, smallpox, malaria, tetanus, typhoid fever and diphtheria. It would take hundreds of thousands of years, maybe even millions, to evolve immunities to these diseases.

Questions to think about

Darwin's theory of evolution

- In what ways are psychology and biology related disciplines?
- How does understanding biological aspects of behaviour contribute to our understanding of psychological aspects of behaviour?
- How do ultimate and proximate causes of behaviour influence a human behaviour such as eating?
- Is the human species no longer evolving via natural selection? What argument can you suggest to support this suggestion?
- How might the course of human evolution have been different had natural selection not favoured encephalisation?
- What are the implications of the theory of evolution for psychology?
- Is the theory of evolution the best theory we have for explaining the development of species?
- Can you hold religious beliefs and still agree with the tenets of the theory of evolution?
- In what way is paleoanthropology 'detective work' rather than a 'science'?

Heredity and genetics

Darwin's work unveiled the process of natural selection and created new frontiers for exploration and experimentation. One of the most important of these frontiers is **genetics**, the study of 'the structure and function of genes and the way in which genes are passed from one generation to the next' (Russell, 1992, p. 2). Genetics, then, also involves the study of how the genetic make-up of an organism influences its physical and behavioural characteristics. Related to genetics are the principles of **heredity**, the sum of the traits and tendencies inherited from a person's parents and other biological ancestors. Although Darwin had built a strong case for natural selection, he could not explain a key tenet of his theory – inheritance. He knew that individual differences occurred within a given species and that those differences were subject to natural selection. But he did not know how adaptations were passed from parent to offspring.

Six years after *The Origin of Species* was published, Gregor Mendel, an Austrian monk who conducted experimental cross-breeding studies with pea plants, uncovered the basic principles of heredity. Mendel demonstrated conclusively how height, flower colour, seed shape and other traits of pea plants could be transmitted from one generation to the next. His work has since been applied to studying heredity in thousands of plants and animals.

The basic principles of genetics

Genes are segments of genetic material called **DNA (deoxyribonucleic acid)** – strands of sugar and phosphate that are connected by nucleotide molecules of adenine, thymine, guanine and cytosine. Each pairs up with another but guanine always pairs with cytosine and adenine with thymine. These pairs form steps in a spiral staircase called a double helix. That is, the DNA is configured like a twisted ladder: the sugar and phosphate form the sides and the four nucleotides form the rungs. You can see this in Figure 3.3.

The particular sequence of these nucleotide molecules directs the synthesis of protein molecules that regulate the biological and physical development of the body and its organs. Some protein molecules regulate cell development and others regulate the chemical interactions that occur within cells. Three billion pairs of these proteins form our genetic code (Plomin, 1997).

Protein synthesis

Genes can only influence our development and behaviour through protein synthesis. Proteins are strings of amino acids arranged in a chain. Each sequence of nucleotides (adenine, thymine, guanine and cytosine) specifies a develop physiological structures and for behaviour – how those structures might function in response to environmental stimulation.

Strictly speaking, however, there are no genes for behaviour, only for the physical structures and physiological processes that are related to behaviour. For example, when we refer to a gene for schizophrenia (a mental disorder characterised by irrational thinking, delusions, hallucinations and perceptual distortions), we are really referring to a gene that contains instructions for synthesising particular proteins, which, in turn, are responsible for the development of specific physiological processes that are sensitive to certain stressful environmental conditions (we may even be wrong in specifying just one gene – there may be more than one). The influence of genetics on mental disorders is discussed in more detail in Chapter 17.

Genes also direct the synthesis of enzymes, proteins which govern the processes that occur within every cell in the body, and thus control each cell's structure and function. As we will see later, a faulty gene may contain instructions for synthesis of faulty enzymes, which produces serious physiological and behavioural problems.

Chromosomes and meiosis

Genes are located on chromosomes, the rod-like structures made of DNA found in the nucleus of every cell. In essence, genes are particular regions of chromosomes that contain the recipes for particular proteins. Each set of chromosomes contains a different sequence of genes. We inherit 23 individual chromosomes from each of our parents, giving us 23 pairs – 46 individual chromosomes – in most cells of the body. One pair of chromosomes, the sex chromosomes, contains the instructions for the development of male or female sex characteristics – those characteristics that distinguish males from females.

Sexual reproduction involves the union of a sperm, which carries genetic instructions from the male, with an ovum (egg), which carries genetic instructions from the female. Sperms and ova differ from the other bodily cells in at least two important ways. First, new bodily cells are created by simple division of existing cells. Secondly, all 23 pairs of chromosomes divide in two, making copies of themselves. The copies pull apart, and the cell splits into two cells, each having a complete set of 23 pairs of chromosomes. Sperms and ova are formed by a special form of cell division called meiosis. The 23 pairs of chromosomes break apart into two groups, with one member of each pair joining one of the groups. The cell splits into two cells, each of which contains 23 individual chromosomes. The assignment of the members of each pair of chromosomes to a particular group is a random process; thus, a single individual can produce 2^{23} (8,388,608) different ova or sperms.

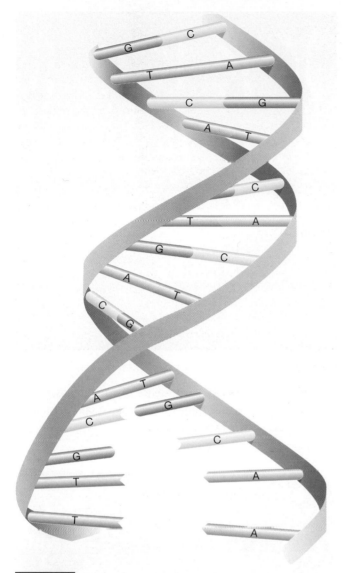

Figure 3.3

The structure and composition of DNA. DNA resembles a twisted ladder whose sides are composed of molecules of sugar and phosphate and whose rungs are made of combinations of four nucleotide bases: adenine (A), thymine (T), guanine (G) and cytosine (C). Genes are segments of DNA that direct the synthesis of proteins and enzymes according to the particular sequences of nucleotide bases that they contain. In essence, genes serve as 'recipes' for the synthesis of these proteins and enzymes, which regulate the cellular and other physiological processes of the body, including those responsible for behaviour.

Source: Based on Watson J.D., *Molecular Biology of the Gene.* Menlo Park, CA: Benjamin, 1976.

particular amino acid. In a sense, genes are 'recipes' consisting of different nucleotide sequences. In this case, the recipe is for combining the proteins necessary to create and

Although brothers and sisters may resemble each other, they are not exact copies. Because the union of a particular sperm with an ovum is apparently random, a couple can produce 8,388,608 × 8,388,608, or 70,368,774,177,664 different children. Only identical twins are genetically identical. Identical twins occur when a fertilised ovum divides, giving rise to two identical individuals. Fraternal twins are no more similar than any two siblings. They occur when a woman produces two ova, both of which are fertilised (by different sperms).

Sex is determined by the twenty-third pair of chromosomes: the sex chromosomes. There are two different kinds of sex chromosomes, X chromosomes and Y chromosomes. Females have a pair of X chromosomes (XX); males have one of each type (XY). Because women's cells contain only X chromosomes, each of their ova contains a single X chromosome (along with 22 other single chromosomes). Because men's cells contain both an X chromosome and a Y chromosome, half of the sperm they produce contain an X chromosome and half contain a Y chromosome. Thus, the sex of a couple's offspring depends on which type of sperm fertilises the ovum. A Y-bearing sperm produces a boy, and an X-bearing sperm produces a girl. Figure 3.4a. illustrates this process. Figure 3.4b shows the human chromosomes and Figure 3.4c a sperm fertilising an ovum.

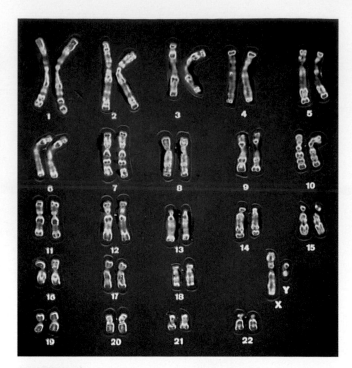

Figure 3.4

(b) Human chromosomes: the presence of a Y chromosome indicates that this sample came from a male. A sample from a female would include two X chromosomes.

Source: CNRI/Science Photo Library/Photo Researchers Inc.

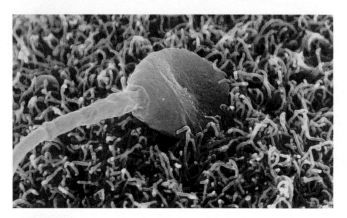

Figure 3.4

(c) Fertilisation – a human sperm penetrating an egg.

Source: David Phillips/Photo Researchers Inc.

Dominant and recessive alleles

Each pair of chromosomes contains pairs of genes: one gene in each pair is contributed by each parent. Individual genes in each pair can be identical or different. Alternative forms of genes are called **alleles** (from the Greek *allos*, 'other'). Consider eye colour, for example. The pigment found in the iris of the eye is produced by a particular gene. If parents each contribute the same allele for eye colour to

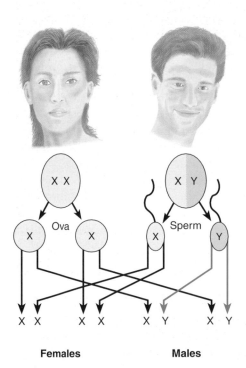

Figure 3.4

(a) Determination of sex: the sex of human offspring depends on whether the sperm that fertilises the ovum carries an X or a Y chromosome.

their child, the gene combination is called homozygous (from the Greek *homo*, 'same', and *zygon*, 'yolk'). However, if the parents contribute different alleles, the gene combination is said to be heterozygous (from the Greek *hetero*, 'different'). Heterozygous gene combinations produce phenotypes controlled by the **dominant allele** – the allele that has a more powerful influence on the expression of the trait. The allele for brown eyes is dominant. When a child inherits the allele for brown eye colour from one parent and the allele for blue eye colour from the other parent, the child will have brown eyes. Brown eyes is said to be a dominant trait. The blue eye colour controlled by the **recessive allele** – the allele that has a weaker effect on the expression of a trait – is not expressed. Only if both of a child's alleles for eye colour are of the blue type will the child have blue eyes. Thus, having blue eyes is said to be a recessive trait. Inheritance of two alleles for brown eyes will, of course, result in brown eyes. You can see this in Figure 3.5.

Other eye colours, such as hazel or black, are produced by the effects of other genes, which influence the dominant brown allele to code for more (black) or less (hazel) pigment in the iris.

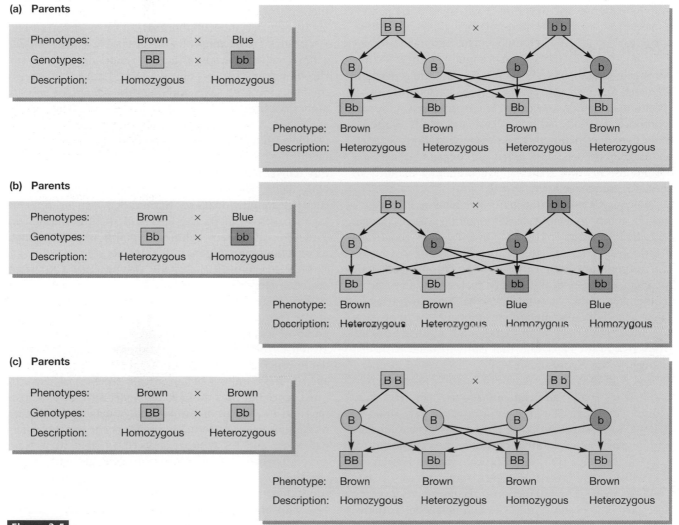

Figure 3.5

Patterns of inheritance for eye colour. (a) If one parent is homozygous for the dominant eye colour (BB), and the other parent is homozygous for the recessive eye colour (bb), then all their children will be heterozygous for eye colour (Bb) and will have brown eyes. (b) If one parent is heterozygous (Bb), and the other parent is homozygous recessive (bb), then their children will have a 50 per cent chance of being heterozygous (brown eyes) and a 50 per cent chance of being homozygous recessive (blue eyes). (c) If one parent is homozygous dominant (BB), and the other parent is heterozygous (Bb), then their children will have a 50 per cent chance of being homozygous for the dominant eye colour (BB) and will have brown eyes, and a 50 per cent chance of being heterozygous (Bb) for the trait and will have brown eyes.

Source: Adapted from Klug, W.S. and Cummings, M.R., *Concepts of Genetics* (2nd edition). Glenview, IL: Scott, Foresman, 1986. © 1986 Scott, Foresman and Co. Reprinted by permission of Addison Wesley Educational Publishers Inc.

It is important to remember that the genetic contributions to our personal development and behaviour are extremely complex. One reason for this complexity is that protein synthesis is often under polygenic control, that is, it is influenced by many pairs of genes, not just a single pair. The inheritance of behaviour is even more complicated, because different environments influence the expression of polygenic traits. Consider, for example, the ability to run. Running speed for any individual is the joint product of genetic factors that produce proteins for muscle, bone, blood, oxygen metabolism and motor co-ordination (to name but a few) and environmental factors such as exercise patterns, age, nutrition, accidents and so on.

Genetic diversity

No two individuals, except identical twins, are genetically identical. Such genetic diversity is a characteristic of all species that reproduce sexually. Some organisms, however, reproduce asexually such as yeast and fungi. Nurseries often reproduce plants and trees through grafting, which is an asexual process. But when we examine the world around us, we find that the overwhelming majority of species reproduce sexually. Why?

One answer is that sexual reproduction increases a species' ability to adapt to environmental changes. Sexual reproduction leads to genetic diversity, and genetically diverse species have a better chance of adapting to a changing environment. When the environment changes, some members of a genetically diverse species may have genes that enable them to survive in the new environment. These genes manufacture proteins that give rise to physical structures, physiological processes, and, ultimately, adaptively significant behaviour that can withstand particular changes in the environment.

This reasoning explains why so many insects, such as cockroaches, have survived our species' best efforts to exterminate them. The lifespan of insects is very short, so that even in a short period of time, many generations are born and die. When we attempt to alter their environment, as we do when we apply an insecticide to their habitat, we may kill many of them. However, some survive because they had the right combination of genes (and hence, the necessary physiological processes and behaviour patterns) to resist the toxic effects of the poison. The survivors then reproduce. Our reaction is to attempt to develop a new poison to which this generation of insects is not resistant. The result is sort of an evolutionary 'arms race' in which both insects and humans produce newer and more powerful adaptations in response to each other (Dawkins, 1986).

Influences of sex on heredity

An individual's sex plays a crucial role in influencing the expression of certain traits. A good example is haemophilia, an increased tendency to bleed seriously from even minor injuries. The blood of people who do not have haemophilia will begin to clot in the first few minutes after they sustain a cut. In contrast, the blood of people who have haemophilia may not do so for thirty minutes or even several hours. Haemophilia is caused by a recessive gene on the X chromosome that fails to produce a protein necessary for normal blood clotting. Because females have two X chromosomes, they can carry an allele for haemophilia but still have normal blood clotting if the other allele is normal. Males, however, have only a single X chromosome, which they receive from their mothers. If the gene for blood clotting carried on this chromosome is faulty, they develop haemophilia.

The gene for haemophilia is an example of a sex-linked gene, so named because this gene resides only on the sex chromosomes. There are also sex-related genes that express themselves in both sexes, although the phenotype appears more frequently in one sex than in the other. These genes are called sex-influenced genes. For example, pattern baldness (thin hair across the top of the head) develops in men if they inherit either or both alleles for baldness, but this trait is not seen in women, even when they inherit both alleles. The expression of pattern baldness is influenced by an individual's sex hormones, which are different for men and women. The effects of these hormones on expression of pattern baldness explains why it is much more common among men than women.

A recent, controversial study suggests that sex-related chromosomes may be responsible for social cognition in humans (Skuse et al., 1997). David Skuse and his colleagues at the Institute of Child Health in London examined a group of females between 6 and 25 years old who had Turner's syndrome. Turner's syndrome is a genetic disorder in which all or part of one X chromosome in females is absent. These individuals are within the normal range of intelligence but they do have problems with social adjustment. In 70 per cent of Turner's individuals, the remaining X chromosome is maternal in origin; in the rest it is paternal. Skuse and his group examined whether there were any differences between those individuals with an X chromosome that was maternal or parental in origin. Fifty-five individuals with a maternally derived X chromosome (45, Xm) and 25 individuals with a paternally derived X chromosome (45, Xp) were studied. The researchers asked teachers, parents and Turner's individuals themselves to complete a series of cognitive and social measures. One of these, a scale measuring social cognition, was completed only by the parents. This scale is summarised in Table 3.1.

The researchers found that those with the maternally derived chromosome were less well adjusted than the 45, Xp individuals. The 45, Xm individuals were also less skilled in verbal ability and in reasoning, two functions which are essential to social cognition. The authors of the

Table 3.1 Scale measuring social cognition

Complete the following section by circling 0 if the statement is not at all true of your child, 1 if it is quite true or sometimes true of your child, and 2 if it is very or often true of your child.

Lacking an awareness of other people's feelings	0	1	2
Does not realise when others are upset or angry	0	1	2
Is oblivious to the effect of his/her behaviour on other members of the family	0	1	2
Behaviour often disrupts normal family life	0	1	2
Very demanding of people's time	0	1	2
Difficult to reason with when upset	0	1	2
Does not seem to understand social skills: e.g. interrupts conversations	0	1	2
Does not pick up on body language	0	1	2
Unaware of acceptable social behaviour	0	1	2
Unknowingly offends people with behaviour	0	1	2
Does not respond to commands	0	1	2
Has difficulty following commands unless they are carefully worded	0	1	2

study suggest that these results indicate a genetic locus for social cognition. They also suggest that because the social cognition chromosome is derived from the father, this might explain why certain 46, XY males (whose X chromosome is derived from the mother) are more susceptible to developmental disorders such as autism (a disorder of social communication, language and emotion) than are 46, XX females. We examine developmental disorders such as autism in more detail in Chapter 12.

Mutations and chromosomal aberrations

Changes in genetic material are caused by mutations or chromosomal aberrations. Mutations are accidental alterations in the DNA code within a single gene. Mutations are the original source of genetic diversity. Although most mutations have harmful effects, some may produce characteristics that are beneficial in certain environments. Mutations can be either spontaneous, occurring naturally, or the result of human-made factors such as high-energy radiation.

Haemophilia provides one of the most famous examples of mutation. Although haemophilia has appeared many times in human history, no other case of haemophilia has had as far-reaching effects as the spontaneous mutation that was passed among the royal families of nineteenth-century Europe. Through genealogical analysis, researchers have discovered that this particular mutant gene arose with Queen Victoria (1819–1901). She was the first in her family line to bear affected children – two female carriers and an afflicted son. The tradition that dictates that nobility marry only other nobility caused the mutant gene to spread rapidly throughout the royal families, as you can see from Figure 3.6.

The second type of genetic change, chromosomal aberration, involves either changes in parts of chromosomes or a change in the total number of chromosomes. An example of a disorder caused by a chromosomal aberration – in this case, a partial deletion of the genetic material in chromosome 5 – is the cri-du-chat syndrome. Infants who have this syndrome have gastrointestinal and cardiac problems, are severely mentally retarded, and make crying sounds resembling a cat's mewing (hence its name, 'cry of the cat'). In general, the syndrome's severity appears to be directly related to the amount of genetic material that is missing. Psychologists and developmental disability specialists have discovered that early special education training permits many individuals having this syndrome to learn self-care and communication skills. This fact highlights an important point about genetics and behaviour: even behaviour that has a genetic basis can often be modified to some extent through training or experience.

Genetic disorders

Many genes decrease an organism's viability – its ability to survive. These 'killer genes' are actually quite common. On average, each of us has two to four of them. Fortunately, these lethal genes are usually recessive, and there are so many different types that most couples do not carry the same ones. When a child inherits the dominant healthy gene from one parent and the recessive lethal gene from the other, the destructive effects of the lethal gene are not expressed.

A few lethal genetic disorders are caused by a dominant gene, however. Different dominant lethal genes express themselves at different times in the lifespan. A foetus may die and be spontaneously aborted before a woman even realises that she is pregnant, a baby may be stillborn, or the lethal genes may not be expressed until adulthood.

There are many human genetic disorders. Those described below are some of the more common ones that impair mental functioning and behaviour and so are of special interest to psychologists.

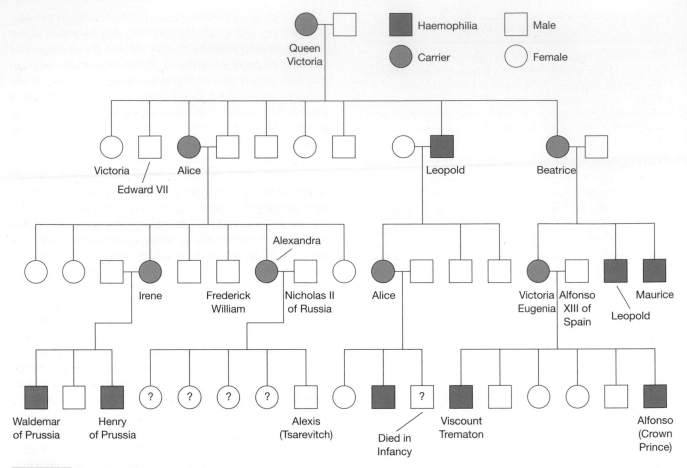

Figure 3.6

Genealogical analysis of the inheritance of haemophilia among European royal families. The gene for this disorder most likely originated with Queen Victoria of England. She was the first woman in the English royal family to bear an afflicted son or a carrier daughter. Circles represent females; squares represent males.

Source: Adapted from Winchester, A.M., *Genetics: A survey of the principles of heredity*. Boston: Houghton-Mifflin, 1972.

Down syndrome

Down syndrome is caused by a chromosomal aberration consisting of an extra twenty-first chromosome (Simonoff *et al.*, 1996). People having Down syndrome are generally short, have broad skulls and round faces, and show impaired physical, psychomotor, and cognitive development. It occurs in around 1 in 1,000 births (DeGrouchy and Turleau, 1990) and about 15 per cent of children born with this condition die before their first birthday, usually from heart and respiratory complications. The frequency of Down syndrome increases with the age of the mother: about 40 per cent of all Down syndrome children are born to women over forty. To a lesser extent, the age of the father also increases the chances of Down syndrome. Although people having Down syndrome are mentally retarded, special educational training permits many of them to hold jobs involving simple tasks. Despite the

fact that Down syndrome is caused by a chromosomal aberration, it is not a hereditary disorder.

Huntington's chorea

Huntington's chorea is a disorder of movement involving involuntary dance-like (choreiform), jerky movement (Martin, 1998a). It does not emerge until the afflicted person is between 30 and 40 years old and is caused by a dominant lethal gene on the arm of chromosome 4 that results in degeneration in certain parts of the brain. Before the onset of this disease, an individual may be healthy in every respect. After onset, however, the individual experiences slow but progressive mental and physical deterioration, including loss of co-ordination and motor ability. Death generally occurs five to fifteen years after onset. Because the age of onset for Huntington's chorea is long after sexual maturity, this lethal gene can be passed from parent to child before the parent even knows that he or she has the gene. Although the disease is rare (the prevalence is 2–7 individuals per 1,000), because it is autosomal dominant, the child of a parent with Huntington's chorea has a 50 per cent chance of developing the disease. If the gene is present in the carrier, it will be expressed. There are genetic tests which help identify those individuals who carry the gene but this may present a horrible dilemma: if a person takes the test and is found not to carry the gene, then all well and good. If, however, the person is identified as a carrier, then this person will develop the disease and die from it because there is currently no cure.

Phenylketonuria

Individuals having **phenylketonuria (PKU)** are homozygous for a recessive gene on chromosome 12 responsible for synthesis of a faulty enzyme. This renders them unable to break down phenylalanine, an amino acid found in many foods. As a result, blood levels of phenylalanine increase, causing severe brain damage and mental retardation. The disorder was originally reported by a Norwegian dentist who noticed that his two retarded children had a peculiar odour. This odour aggravated his asthma so badly that he could not stay in the same room as them (Plomin, 1997). Folling, the physician who examined the children, found excess amounts of phenylpyruvic acid in their urine because of disturbed phenylalanine metabolism.

PKU is one of the many diseases for which infants are routinely tested before they leave the hospital. It occurs in 1 in 10,000 infants and accounts for 1 per cent of all institutionalised retarded children. Infants diagnosed as having PKU are placed on a low-phenylalanine diet shortly after birth. If this diet is carefully followed, brain development will be normal. This demonstrates that a genetic influence can be modified or modulated by the environment.

Fragile X

Fragile X is the most important cause of mental retardation after Down syndrome and is the most common inherited cause of mental retardation (Simonoff et al., 1996). It affects twice as many boys as girls (Kahkonen et al., 1987) and is so-called because the X chromosome is fragile and easily broken. Children with fragile X tend to have large foreheads, prominent jaws and brow and protruding ears.

Genetic testing

Couples having a family history of genetic disorders often seek **genetic counselling**, the process of determining the likelihood that a couple may produce a child having a genetic disorder. Individuals who suspect that they may have a genetic disorder may also seek such counselling.

The first step in genetic counselling is generally a pedigree analysis of the family or families involved. This analysis identifies any family history of genetic disorders and provides an estimate of the likelihood that a genetic disorder is present. If a family history of genetic disorders is discovered, the genetic counsellor discusses the probability of the couple having a child who has a disorder. In the case of an individual, the counsellor may recommend screening for the disorder.

In the case of prospective parents who have a family history of a genetic disorder, the counsellor will generally recommend further analysis, this time to detect if either or both persons is a carrier for the gene causing the disorder. Carrier detection is a biochemical procedure in which people can be tested for the presence of particular proteins or enzymes produced by the genes in question. If high levels of one of these substances is found, the person may be a carrier. Carrier detection is also accomplished through DNA probes that detect whether the gene in question is normal or defective. The use of DNA probes is a relatively recent development in genetic counselling, and probes have not yet been developed for all genetic disorders.

Once the genetic counsellor informs the couple of the likelihood of producing a child who has a genetic disorder, the couple must then make the difficult decision of whether to have children. For example, a couple having a strong family history of PKU is likely to have a child who has PKU. However, the couple may decide to have a child anyway, knowing that PKU is treatable and that many people who have PKU lead happy, healthy and productive lives so long as they control their diets.

In instances in which the woman is already pregnant, the foetus can be tested for genetic disorders. In fact, such testing is often recommended for pregnant women over 35 or for those whose family pedigrees reveal a genetic problem. The most common prenatal detection method is amniocentesis, which involves removal and examination of foetal cells found in the amniotic fluid surrounding the foetus, usually during the sixteenth week of pregnancy. The chromosomes in the foetal cells are examined for incomplete, missing or extra chromosomes. In addition, amniocentesis allows parents to know the sex of their unborn child, which may be relevant in the case of sex-linked disorders.

It appears as if lay understanding of genetic disorders and genetic testing extends to child disorders but not to adult disorders (Henderson and Maguire, 1998). There is also evidence to suggest that most lay people are unaware of the treatments available for genetic disorders. Given the inherited component of genetic disorders, and anxieties about what can be done about the illness, genetic counselling and giving information about disorders may help patients to come to terms with their illness. However, the picture is not this clear, as the 'Psychology in action' section below points out.

Psychology in action

The psychological consequences of genetic counselling

Genetic testing of susceptibility to disease has brought with it many remarkable psychological benefits, certainty and relief following a negative outcome being two of the more obvious. Positive outcomes appear to present an entirely different picture and one which may not be beneficial. Many anecdotal sources suggest that knowing the positive outcome of a genetic test for disease is associated with a decline in self-esteem and psychological well-being. There may also be health impairments that are unrelated to the disease.

Tibben and his colleagues from the Netherlands (Tibben *et al.*, 1997) recently examined levels of psychological distress in carriers and non-carriers of Huntington's chorea at four testing points: before knowing the results, one week after, six months after and three years after. They found that although helplessness increased in carriers and decreased in non-carriers at one week, the difference disappeared after six months. Those carriers with children reported greater distress than those without and the partners of non-carriers were less distressed than those of carriers at three years. A study by Codori and her colleagues from Johns Hopkins University (Codori *et al.*, 1997) suggests a similar response but one which may be mediated by individual differences in approaches to coping with the illness. Codori *et al.* examined levels of hopelessness and depressive symptoms in patients tested positive for Huntington's disease and those tested negative four times in the year following the results of genetic testing. They found that those who were least well adjusted were likely to have been positively diagnosed, were married with no children and were closer to their estimated age of onset. These data suggest possible risk factors for undesirable psychological response to disclosure.

Differences between men and women in the ways that they respond to the results of genetic testing have also been reported. Marteau and colleagues from the United Medical and Dental School in London examined the impact of disclosure on those carrying the cystic fibrosis gene mutation (Marteau *et al.*, 1997). They found that women were more likely than men to be more relieved when told they were non-carriers but were also more likely to be less relieved than men when informed that they were carriers. The authors suggest that such a difference may be attributable to sex differences in coming to terms with, assessing or coping with the threat of illness.

These studies highlight a number of important questions in the area of genetic testing: which individual differences are risk factors for the anxiety and distress experienced following a positive test? Does the degree of distress change depending on the type of disease diagnosed? What are the long-term consequences of knowing the results of genetic testing? Studies such as those above present a fairly coherent beginning to finding answers to such questions.

Heredity and behaviour genetics

Each of us is born into a different environment and each of us possesses a unique combination of genetic instructions. As a result, we differ from one another. Consider your fellow undergraduates, for example. They come in different sizes and shapes, they vary in personality and intelligence, and they possess unequal artistic and athletic abilities. To what extent are these sorts of differences attributable to heredity or to the environment? If all your classmates had been reared in identical environments, any differences between them would necessarily be due to genetics. Conversely, if all your classmates had come from the same fertilised egg but were subsequently raised in different environments, any differences in their personal characteristics would necessarily be due only to the environment.

Heritability is a statistical term that refers to the amount of variability in a trait in a given population that is due to genetic differences among the individuals in that population. Heritability is sometimes confused with inheritance, the tendency of a given trait to be passed from parent to individual offspring. But heritability does not apply to individuals, it pertains only to the variation of a trait in a specific population. The more that a trait in a given population is influenced by genetic factors, the greater its heritability. The scientific study of heritability – of the effects of genetic influences on behaviour – is called behaviour genetics. As noted by one of this field's most prolific researchers, Robert Plomin (1990, 1997), behaviour genetics is intimately involved with providing an explanation of why people differ. As we will see below, behaviour geneticists attempt to account for the roles that both heredity and the environment play in individual differences in a wide variety of physical and mental abilities. The contribution of behaviour genetics to our understanding of the determinants of intelligence are considered in more detail in Chapter 11.

Studying genetic influences

Although farmers and animal breeders had experimented with artificial selection for thousands of years, only within the past 150 years has the relation between heredity and behaviour been formally studied in the laboratory. Mendel's careful analysis of genetic influences on specific characteristics gave us the first good clue that traits were actually heritable. As we saw in Chapter 1, Galton (1869) stimulated further interest in this field with his studies showing that intelligence tends to run in families: if parents are intelligent then, in general, so are their children. The search for genetic bases of behaviour has been active ever since. In fact, the search to understand the relative contributions of heredity and environment to human behaviour is among the most heavily researched areas in psychology.

Artificial selection in animals

Any heritable trait can be selected in a breeding programme. The heritability of many traits in animals, such as aggression, docility, preference for alcohol, running speed, and mating behaviours, can be studied by means of artificial selection.

Consider, for example, Robert Tryon's (1940) study of maze learning in rats. Tryon wished to determine whether genetic variables influenced learning. He began his study with a large sample of genetically diverse rats. He trained them to learn a maze and recorded the number of errors each rat made in the process. He then selected two groups of rats – those that learned the fastest (bright) and those that learned the slowest (dull). He mated 'bright' rats with other 'bright' rats and 'dull' rats with other 'dull' rats. To ensure that the rats were not somehow learning the maze from their mothers, he 'adopted out' some of the pups: some of the bright pups were reared by dull mothers and some of the dull pups were reared by bright mothers. He found that parenting made little difference in his results, so this factor can be discounted.

Tryon continued this sequence of having rats learn the maze and selectively breeding the best with the best (bright) and the worst with the worst (dull) over many generations. Soon, the maze performance of each group was completely different, as you can see from Figure 3.7. He concluded that maze learning in rats could be manipulated through artificial selection.

Later studies showed that Tryon's results were limited by the standard laboratory cage environment in which rats lived when they were not running the maze. For example, Cooper and Zubek (1958) demonstrated that differences in maze ability were virtually eliminated when bright and dull strains of rats were reared in either enriched environments designed to stimulate learning (cages containing geometric objects, such as tunnels, ramps and blocks) or impoverished environments designed to inhibit learning (cages containing only food and water dishes). However, Cooper and Zubek's rats who were reared in the standard laboratory cage performed similarly to Tryon's rats: the bright rats outperformed the dull rats. Thus, changing the environmental conditions in which the rats lived had an important result – reducing the effects of genetic differences between the bright and dull rats. This finding makes good sense when you consider the fact that genes are not expressed in the absence of an environment.

Tryon's research demonstrated that over successive generations a trait can be made to become more or less likely in a given population, but we do not know precisely why. We do not know whether genes related to learning or genes related to other traits were selected. Tryon's rats may have been neither especially bright nor especially dull. Perhaps each of these strains differed in its capacity to be motivated by the food reward that awaited it at the end of the maze.

Can gene manipulation ever occur in humans? Recent experiments involving the cloning of sheep illustrate the power of molecular genetics in radically altering Nature's forms. Gene mapping may help us to understand how specific DNA sequences can influence physiological processes that affect behaviour, emotion, remembering and thinking and play a crucial role in identifying specific genes involved in psychological disorders (Plomin and DeFries, 1998). Some of these issues are discussed in the chapters on memory, intelligence and mental disorders (Chapters 8, 11 and 17).

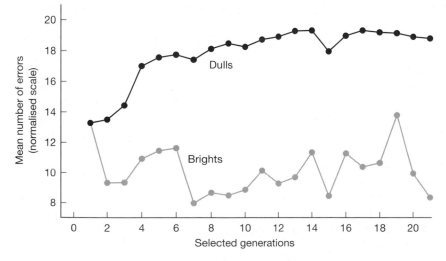

Figure 3.7

Results from Tryon's 1940 artificial breeding research of rats' ability to learn a maze. Within a few generations, differences in the rats' ability to negotiate the maze became distinct.

Source: Adapted from Tryon, R.C., Genetic differences in maze-learning ability in rats. *Yearbook of the National Society for the Study of Education*, 1940, 39, 111–119.

Is alcoholism a genetic defect?

The issue

There is a strong probability that you know an alcoholic – someone who is addicted to alcohol. If you do, then you know from first-hand experience the kinds of physical, personal, and social costs often associated with this disorder: increased risk of being injured in an accident; liver damage; loss of employment; marital problems, estrangement from family members, friends, and co-workers and so on. Cross-cultural research has shown that alcoholism is no respecter of geographic boundaries – it is prevalent in most countries in which alcohol is consumed (Helzer and Canino, 1992).

Because alcohol is available to most adults and because alcoholism is such a serious problem, psychologists and other scientists have long searched for causes of this disorder. Although the search is still under way, many researchers believe that genetic factors play an important role in alcoholism. Some of the early genetic theories of alcoholism suggested that the underproduction of genetically transmitted enzymes led to the individual's inability to utilise certain nutrients such as vitamins. As a result, individuals had a cellular need for certain nutrients which could only be obtained via alcohol. Little empirical research supports the theory (Heather and Robertson, 1997). Recent evidence suggests, however, that there may be some form of genetic influence on addiction to alcohol. This evidence comes from three lines of research: twin studies, adoption studies and artificial breeding studies of animals (Begleiter and Kissin, 1995).

The evidence

Twin studies

Twin studies have consistently shown that concordance rates for alcohol use and for alcoholism are higher for MZ twins than for DZ twins. For example, in a study of nearly 4,000 Australian twins, Heath *et al.* (1989) found that compared with DZ twins, MZ twins were more similar in their frequency of drinking and in the amount of alcohol consumed while drinking. Pickens *et al.* (1991), in a study of American twins and their genetic risk for alcoholism, found statistically significant differences in concordance rates for males: they found 76 per cent for MZ twins and 61 per cent for

DZ twins. Concordance rates for females were much lower and not statistically significant: the researchers found 36 per cent for MZ twins and 25 per cent for DZ twins. The results of a related study by McGue (1992) support these findings: concordance rates for males (77 per cent for MZ twins and 54 per cent for DZ twins) were higher than those for females (39 per cent for MZ twins and 42 per cent for DZ twins). The results of these two studies suggest that males are more likely than females to have a genetic predisposition for alcoholism.

About 25 per cent of the male relatives of alcoholics are also alcoholics. This number is five times as large as that for males in the general population (Cotton, 1979; Plomin, 1990). But these numbers raise an important question: if genetics are involved in alcoholism, why aren't more of the male relatives of alcoholics themselves alcoholics – shouldn't all of them abuse alcohol? The answer is no.

Remember that genes are expressed in an environment. Different environments affect genes in different ways. A person who has the gene (or set of genes) for alcoholism will not become an alcoholic if he or she does not first consume alcohol – the environmental factor of alcohol must be present. Thus, a person may have this gene and have parents who are alcoholics, but if he or she never consumes alcohol, there is no chance that he or she will become an alcoholic. In Plomin's (1990) words, 'it is unlikely that genes drive us to drink'.

Clearly, environmental factors must also play a crucial role in the development of alcoholism. But there is another important factor which we have overlooked. Alcoholism is a heterogeneous disorder, that is, it is associated with other behavioural problems as well as excess drinking. It also has 'co-morbidity' with other disorders which means that it is likely to appear with other behavioural problems. One of the most common disorders accompanying alcoholism is personality disorder, a psychopathological condition where the individual expresses severe antisocial behaviour. Co-morbidity has been found between personality disorder and alcoholism in community and clinical samples (Morgenstern *et al.*, 1997). There is also a high incidence of neuroticism in alcoholics compared with non-alcoholics. Are the genetic influences in alcoholism, therefore, not alcohol related but perhaps personality related?

Adoption studies

Adoption studies of alcoholism monitor children separated from their biological parents at birth or shortly thereafter. These children bear no genetic relation to their adoptive parents or siblings. In an adoption study conducted in Sweden involving nearly one thousand males, Cloninger and his colleagues (1981) reported that sons of alcoholic biological parents were more likely to become alcoholics than were sons of non-alcoholic biological parents, even when they were reared by non-alcoholic adoptive parents. A study of Swedish females found similar results (Bohman *et al.*, 1981). Cloninger (1987) had also shown that the drinking patterns of male and female alcoholics tended to differ. Whereas male alcoholics may become either steady (drinking daily or almost every day) or binge (sprees of heavy drinking followed by periods of non-drinking) drinkers, female alcoholics tend to become binge drinkers.

Artificial selection studies

Artificial selection studies using rats as subjects also suggest a genetic basis for alcoholism. In these studies, specific strains of rats are bred for their preference for alcohol. One strain, called the P (preference for alcohol) line, voluntarily drinks alcohol, prefers drinking alcohol to other liquids, shows increased blood-alcohol levels while drinking, will make specific responses to obtain alcohol in an experimental setting, develops a tolerance for alcohol, and develops a physical dependency on alcohol (that is, they show signs of withdrawal when alcohol is no longer available). In contrast, the NP (no preference for alcohol) strain shows none of these characteristics (Lumeng *et al.*, 1995). Examination of the brains of these two strains of rats shows distinct differences in the chemical composition of specific brain regions, suggesting that specific brain mechanisms are related to susceptibility to alcoholism. This finding supports the possible role of genes in alcoholism.

Given that there seems to be evidence to suggest a genetic role in alcoholism, in what form does the gene express itself? It has been suggested that the genetic code for the neurotransmitter receptor, D2, is responsible (Noble *et al.*, 1991). As we saw earlier in the chapter, genes have two versions or alleles. In humans, the alleles for the D2 receptor are A1 and A2. Some individuals have one copy of each, others have two A1 alleles or two A2 alleles. Noble *et al.* found that when they compared the postmortem brains of alcoholics and non-alcoholics, 69 per cent of the alcoholics had the A1 allele but only 20 per cent of the non-alcoholics did, a finding replicated in a sample of living participants. In addition, the postmortem brains with the A1 allele also had fewer D2 receptors (Blum *et al.*, 1990). Given that the D2 receptor serves the neurotransmitter dopamine, a chemical involved in mood alteration (amongst other behaviours), perhaps the affected individuals need greater stimulation of the few receptor sites that they have. Although, the results of these studies are dramatic, subsequent experiments have produced mixed findings (Heather and Robertson, 1997).

Conclusion

The three lines of research reviewed above are convergent, that is, twin studies, adoption studies and artificial breeding studies each independently suggest that there is a genetic basis for alcoholism. Convergent evidence is important in science because it shows that when a relationship between two variables is examined from different approaches, the conclusions are still the same. We are thus more likely to believe that a relationship between heredity and alcoholism really exists.

Questions to think about

Heredity and genetics

- How would you explain the fact that your brother has blue eyes but your sister has brown eyes?
- In scientific terms, what does it mean to say that there is a gene for shyness or for homosexuality or for social cognition?
- How might the gene related to the development of athletic ability interact with environmental variables to produce a specific phenotype (for example, a specific level of athletic ability in a specific individual)?

- How would you design a study to assess the genetic basis of human aggression? Could you use more than one approach to gathering this information, and if so, what would these other approaches entail?

- Do you think that there are any limits to the extent to which we can localise psychological traits to specific chromosomes?

Twin studies

There are two barriers to studying the effects of heredity on behavioural traits in humans. First, ethical considerations prevent psychologists and geneticists from manipulating people's genetic history or restricting the type of environment in which they are reared. For example, we cannot artificially breed people to learn the extent to which shyness, extroversion or any other personality characteristics are inherited or deprive the offspring of intelligent people of a good education to see if their intelligence will be affected. Secondly, in most cases, the enormous variability in human environments effectively masks any correlation that might exist between genetics and trait expression.

Psychologists have been able to circumvent these barriers by taking advantage of an important quirk of nature – multiple births. Recall that identical twins, also called monozygotic (MZ) twins, arise from a single fertilised ovum, called a zygote, that splits into two genetically identical cells. Fraternal, or dizygotic (DZ), twins develop from the separate fertilisation of two ova. DZ twins are no more alike genetically than any two siblings. Because MZ twins are genetically identical, they should be more similar to one another in terms of their psychological characteristics (such as personality or intelligence) than either DZ twins or non-twin siblings (*see* Figure 3.8).

Concordance research, which examines the degree of similarity in traits expressed between twins, supports this rationale (Plomin *et al.*, 1994b). Twins are concordant for a trait if both of them express it or if neither does, and they are discordant if only one expresses it. If concordance rates (which can range from 0 to 100 per cent) of any given trait are substantially higher for MZ twins than for DZ twins, heredity is likely involved in the expression of that trait.

Table 3.2 compares concordance values between MZ and DZ twins for several traits.

When we observe a trait exhibiting a high concordance for MZ twins but a low one for DZ twins, we can conclude that the trait may be strongly affected by genetics. This is especially true for a trait such as blood type, which has a heritability of 100 per cent. If the concordance rates are similar, the effect of heredity is low. For example, consider the characteristic of religious beliefs. In this case, a high concordance value (that is, both twins having similar beliefs) probably reflects the fact that they acquired their beliefs from their parents. In fact, the concordance rate for religious beliefs of DZ twins is generally just as high as that of MZ twins (Loehlin and Nichols, 1976). Thus, religious beliefs are not inherited.

Twin studies have been used to study a wide range of psychological phenomena. This research has shown that genetic factors affect cognitive abilities such as language ability, mathematical ability and vocabulary skills; personality traits such as extroversion (the tendency to be outgoing) and emotional stability; personality development; and the occurrence of psychological disorders such as schizophrenia and mental retardation (Bouchard and Propping, 1993). Further evidence for genetic influences on trait expression comes from extensive analyses of twin studies of heredity and intelligence (Bouchard, 1997; Petrill *et al.*, 1998) which are discussed in Chapter 11.

Figure 3.8

Monozygotic twins.

Source: Courtesy of Telegraph Colour Library.

Table 3.2   Comparison of concordance rates between monozygotic (MZ) and dizygotic (DZ) twins for various traits

	Concordance %	
Trait	*MZ*	*DZ*
Blood types	100	66
Eye colour	99	28
Mental retardation	97	37
Measles	95	87
Idiopathic epilepsy	72	15
Schizophrenia	69	10
Diabetes	65	18
Identical allergy	59	5
Tuberculosis	57	23

Source: Klug and Cummings, 1986

Sociobiology

Sociobiology is the study of the genetic bases of social behaviour. It represents the synthesis of research findings regarding social behaviour from many other fields of science, including those from evolutionary psychology, anthropology and behaviour genetics. Evolutionary psychology and behaviour genetics are broader fields than sociobiology in the sense that both are concerned with other phenomena, such as intelligence and cognition, in addition to social behaviour. Sociobiologists are especially interested in understanding the evolutionary roots of our modern-day social actions. More often than not, sociobiologists study the evolutionary bases of social behaviour in non-human animals and then extrapolate from those species to humans (Barash, 1982). Sociobiology represents an interface between the biological sciences and psychology. However, not all psychologists are convinced of the sociobiologists' claims, arguing that sociobiology is too simplistic and that its emphasis on genetics inadequately explains the complexities of human behaviour.

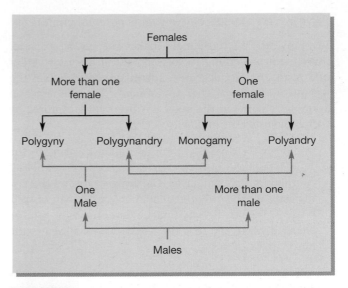

Figure 3.9

Reproductive strategies. Different numbers of males mating with different numbers of females yields the four reproductive strategies of monogamy, polygyny, polyandry and polygynandry.

Reproductive strategies and the biological basis of parenting

Perhaps the most important social behaviours related to the survival of a species are those related to reproduction and parenting. A focal point of sociobiological research and theory has been understanding more about the different kinds of social organisation that result from particular **reproductive strategies** – systems of mating and rearing offspring.

We assume that most Western sexual relationships are monogamous: the mating of one female and one male. If mating is successful, the individuals share in the raising of the child or children. But **monogamy** is just one of several reproductive strategies sexual creatures employ in mating and rearing of offspring (Barash, 1982). Three other major classes of reproductive strategy are also possible:

- **Polygyny**: one male mates with more than one female
- **Polyandry**: one female mates with more than one male
- **Polygynandry**: several females mate with several males

Figure 3.9 illustrates the combinations of partners that give rise to these classes.

According to Trivers (1972), these four reproductive strategies evolved because of important sex differences in the resources that parents invest in conceiving and rearing their offspring. **Parental investment** is the time, physical effort and risks to life involved in procreation and in the feeding, nurturing and protecting of offspring. According to sociobiologists, parental investment is a critical factor in mate selection. An individual who is willing and able to make a greater investment is generally more sought after as a mate and is often more selective or discriminating when selecting a mate (Trivers, 1972). Given that a human female will gestate for nine months, she should be highly selective about choosing a mate. On the basis of Trivers's theory it is possible to predict that women will express an (evolved) preference for men who have high status and will divorce those who do not contribute the expected resources or who divert them to other women and children (D.M. Buss, 1995).

In some species, competition for mates leads to **sexual selection** – selection for traits specific to sex, such as body size or particular patterns of behaviour. For example, in some animals, such as buffalo, females select mates based on the male's ability to survive the skirmishes of the rutting (mating) season. In general, the larger and more aggressive males win these battles and gain access to more females and enjoy greater reproductive success.

Polygyny is by far the most common reproductive strategy among humans. Eighty-four per cent of human societies practice polygyny or allow men who are either wealthy or powerful to practice it (Badcock, 1991). Monogamy is the next most popular reproductive strategy, with about 15 per cent of all human cultures practising it. Polyandry and polygynandry are both rare: combined, these two reproductive strategies dominate in fewer than 1 per cent of all human cultures.

Polygyny: high female and low male parental investment

In many species, the female makes the greater parental investment. According to sociobiological theory, whether one is an ova producer or a sperm producer defines the nature of one's parental investment. The fundamental asymmetry between the sexes has been aptly captured by sociobiologists Daly and Wilson (1978):

> 'Although each parent contributes almost equally to the genetic resources of the new creature they create, not all contributions are equitable. The female provides the raw materials for the early differentiation and growth of their progeny. Here at the very fundament of sexuality, is love's labour divided, and it is the female who contributes the most.' (p. 48)

Among most mammals (including humans), the costs associated with reproduction are higher for females than for males. First, females have fewer opportunities than males to reproduce. Generally, females produce only one ovum or a few ova periodically, whereas males produce vast quantities of sperm over substantially shorter time intervals. Secondly, females carry the fertilised ovum in their bodies during a long gestation period, continuously diverting a major portion of their own metabolic resources to nourish the rapidly growing foetus. Females also assume all the risks that accompany pregnancy and childbirth, including physical discomfort and possible death. The male's contributions to reproduction are, at a minimum, the sperm and the time needed for intercourse. Thirdly, after the offspring is born, females may continue to devote some of their metabolic resources to the infant by nursing it. Just as important, they usually devote more time and physical energy than males to caring for the newborn.

In addition, a female can only bear a certain number of offspring in a lifetime, regardless of the number of males with whom she mates. In contrast, a male is limited in his reproductive success only by the number of females he can impregnate. For example, consider the differences between females and males in our species. If a woman became pregnant once a year for ten years, she would have ten children – only a fraction of the number of children that a man is capable of fathering over the same interval. If a man impregnated a different woman every month for ten years, he would have fathered 120 children. This example is hardly an exaggeration. According to the *Guinness Book of World Records*, the largest number of live births to one woman is 69 (she had several multiple births). In contrast, King Ismail of Morocco is reported to have fathered 1,056 children.

In many polygynous species, intense competition for the opportunity to mate occurs among males. The competition almost always involves some sort of physical confrontation: that is, males fight among themselves for the opportunity to mate. Usually, the larger, stronger and more aggressive male wins, which means that only he will mate with the available females in the vicinity. If one of the smaller, weaker males attempts to mate with a female, he is generally chased away by the victorious male.

Because females in polygynous species invest so heavily in their offspring, they are – according to sociobiologists – usually highly selective of their mates, choosing to mate only with those males who possess specific attributes, such as physical size, strength and aggressiveness. Such selectivity makes adaptive sense for both her and her progeny. After all, bearing the offspring of the victor means that her male offspring will tend to possess the same adaptively significant attributes as their father and thus be more likely to win their own quests for mating privileges. And, as a result, genes for large size, increased strength and aggressiveness will continue to have greater representation in future generations than will genes for less adaptive attributes. The theory also works the other way – the male will select a female that he considers attractive and healthy and would, therefore, be a fit mother for a child. This interpretation, however, rests on the assumption that mate selection is governed by the perceived ability to reproduce successfully. In essence, it is, like the assumptions made about the evolution of our ancestors, speculative. This view does not explain why some couples decide to forgo the opportunity of having children. Physical attraction is also heavily culture-bound.

For example, in the developed world, the preference is for women with a low waist-to-hip ratio (WHR); this WHR is achieved because more fat is deposited on the buttocks and hips than the waist (this, in turn, is because females have higher levels of oestrogen than testosterone) (Singh, 1995). Those with more apple-shaped figures (i.e., with a high WHR) suffer more from a variety of illnesses. This apparent universal preference for women with low WHR would seem to bolster the sociobiologist's argument that mates are selected for their health and fitness. However, it appears that such preferences are not universal. A recent study by Yu and Shepard (1998) compared the female preferences of American men and men from the Matsigenka people in south-east Peru. The Matsigenka's culture is basically agrarian: they engage in slash and burn agriculture and supplement this food gathering with game and fruit gathered using traditional tools. Only scientists and official visitors are allowed to visit the village. The men had lived in the village since birth and would not, therefore, have been exposed to Western civilisation (no television, film, newspapers and so on). The authors found that there was a significant difference in the female preference of the American and Peruvian men; whereas the Western sample predictably preferred those females with low WHR, the Matsigenka men preferred overweight females and those with high WHR, rating these as the most attractive, healthy and most likely to be chosen as spouse. The authors repeated the experiment on two additional groups which lived outside the Matsigenka's village and had been exposed to more Western influences. Here, the findings were mixed. One group showed the same pattern whereas the other gave comparable ratings to the Americans. These findings cannot be explained in terms of individuals selecting the fittest, most convincing-looking baby-producing machines. The non-Westernised group regarded a high WHR as healthier than a low WHR; the opposite effect was seen in the American group. The study demonstrates that the decisions behind mate-selection may be culture-bound.

Monogamy: shared, but not always equal, parental investment

Monogamy has evolved in those species whose environments have favoured the contributions of both parents to the survival and reproductive success of their offspring. In other words, under some conditions, two individuals sharing parental duties enjoy more reproductive success than does one individual who must do it all alone.

Although both parents in monogamous species share offspring-rearing duties, each parent may not make an equal contribution towards that end. Like females in polygynous species, females in monogamous species generally have greater parental investment in the offspring, for many of the same reasons: the limited opportunity for mating relative to that for males, pregnancy and its accompanying risks, providing milk to the newborns, and the time and energy spent in caring for them. As a result, very few monogamous species, including our own, are exclusively monogamous. In fact, there is a strong tendency in most monogamous species towards patterns of reproductive behaviour and parental investment that resemble those of polygynous species.

For example, in monogamous species, females tend to be more careful than males in selecting a mate, and males tend to be more sexually promiscuous than females (Badcock, 1991). In our own species, men tend to engage in premarital sexual intercourse more often than do females (Kinsey *et al.*, 1948, 1953; Hunt, 1974), although this gap appears to be decreasing. Men also tend to have more premarital and extramarital sexual partners (Symons, 1979).

Reproductive success today may not be thought of in terms merely of the number of children we have (although among some religious subcultures this is still an important measure of success), but in terms of how well individuals raise healthy, happy and well adjusted children. Although most people have the biological capacity to produce a large number of children, many do not have the psychological or financial wherewithal to do so. Some people fear that a large family will reduce the amount of money they can make and will therefore lower their quality of life. Others see a large family as an impediment to obtaining other career goals and life aspirations. And still others simply have no desire to have any children at all.

Polyandry: high male and low female parental investment

Polyandry is a rare reproductive strategy among humans and non-existent in other mammals. It is more prevalent among species that lay eggs. Once the eggs are laid, then either the male or the female may take care of them, although in many instances, the male makes the greater investment of time and effort.

An example of polyandry in humans is found among some of the people who live in remote Himalayan villages. These people are extremely poor and live in a harsh environment, which makes their primary livelihood, farming, difficult. In order to prevent the dissolution of family farms through marriage, families that have more than one son limit the number of marriages to only one per generation – several brothers may share the same wife. A female tends to marry more than one man (most often brothers) to guarantee that she will be adequately supported. In other words, the male's primary investment – the farm, which is the source of food and some income for the family – is guarded jealously through polyandry.

Polygynandry: group parental investment

Many primates, such as chimpanzees, live in colonies in which few or no barriers are placed on which female mates with which male. In other words, the colonies are promiscuous – during periods of mating, intercourse is frequent and indiscriminate. What is the advantage of such a reproductive strategy?

The primary advantage seems to be the co-operation of males and females in the colony with respect to rearing offspring. Because the males in the colony are not sure which offspring belong to them, it is in their best interest to help rear and protect all the offspring and defend their mothers. The unity in the colony and the lack of aggression among the males contributes directly to the general welfare of all colony members. Females and males have access to many mates, and the offspring are well cared for.

However, a form of monogamy called a consortship is sometimes observed in polygynandrous species. For instance, a particular male chimpanzee may ward off other male suitors from a particular female, resulting in an exclusive sexual union. If successful, he is guaranteed the certainty of which offspring are his, albeit at some cost. There is a chance that he could be seriously injured in protecting his mate from other males, and therefore he becomes less useful as a parental investor in his offspring or those of the colony.

Incestuous relationships: a universal taboo

Different reproductive strategies have evolved because the environmental conditions under which various species have evolved are different. But the environments are not so different among species that each species requires its own unique reproductive strategy. Courtship rituals may vary across species, but these rituals still conform to one of the four reproductive strategies discussed above.

All reproductive strategies seem to have one element in common: avoidance of incest. Incest is the mating of kin who share many of the same genes. Avoidance of incest appears to have evolved for a very good reason: closely related relatives are likely to share the same recessive genes that cause genetic disorders. Thus, animals that avoid incestuous matings have an evolutionary advantage over those that do not; they produce healthier offspring who themselves are more likely to live to sexual maturity and produce offspring of their own.

All human cultures have taboos against incest. A taboo is a societal rule prohibiting the members of a given culture from engaging in specific behaviours – in this case, mating with a genetically related individual. Taboos are products of cultural evolution and are socially transmitted through language from one generation to the next.

Incest taboos are probably of secondary importance, serving to reinforce the natural aversion we have towards incest or mating with non-relatives with whom we were raised. For example, in one study (Shepher, 1983), the elders actually encouraged the children of the kibbutz to marry so that the children would not end up living far from home. Despite the absence of a taboo and the encouragement of the elders none of the children married each other.

The biological basis of altruism

Reproductive and parenting behaviours are not the only social behaviours studied by sociobiologists. A particularly interesting and important social behaviour that is central to sociobiological theory is altruism, the unselfish concern of one individual for the welfare of another. We consider the social importance of altruism again in Chapter 16. Examples of altruistic behaviour abound in our culture, and in their most extreme form are represented when one person risks his or her life to save the life of another. Examples of altruism are common throughout the animal kingdom. The honey bee, for example, sacrifices its life on behalf of its hivemates by stinging an intruder. Here, the altruist's chances of survival and reproductive success are lowered while that of the other individuals are raised.

Kin selection

Sociobiologists seek out ultimate causes, especially the consequences of natural selection, to explain altruism. They assert that natural selection has favoured the evolution of organisms that show altruistic tendencies. However, there is an important problem here. On the surface, altruism poses an enigma to evolutionary theory. Recall that according to natural selection only phenotypes that enhance one's reproductive success are favoured. How could altruistic behaviour have evolved given that, by definition, it is less adaptive than selfish or competitive behaviour?

The geneticist William D. Hamilton (1964, 1970) suggested an answer to this question in a series of mathematical papers. Hamilton's ideas stemmed from examining natural selection from the perspective of the gene instead of from the perspective of the whole, living organism. He argued that natural selection does not favour mere reproductive success but rather inclusive fitness, or the reproductive success of those individuals who share many of the same genes. Altruistic acts are generally aimed at close relatives such as parents, siblings, grandparents and grandchildren. The closer the family relation is, the more likely the genetic similarity among the individuals involved. Such biological favouritism towards relatives is called kin selection (Maynard Smith, 1964).

The message here is clear: under the proper circumstances, individuals behave altruistically towards others with whom they share a genetic history, with the willingness to do so decreasing as the relative becomes more distant. In this view, altruism is not necessarily a conscious act but rather an act driven by a biological prompt that has been favoured by natural selection. Natural selection would favour this kind of altruism simply because organisms who share genes also help each other to survive.

Parenting is a special case of kin selection and an important contributor to one's survival and reproductive success. In the short run, parents' altruistic actions promote the continued survival of their offspring. In the long run, these actions increase the likelihood that the offspring, too, will become parents and that their genes will survive in successive generations. Such cycles continue according to biological schedule, generation after generation. In the words of sociobiologist, David Barash (1982),

> 'It is obvious why genes for parenting have been selected: all living things are the offspring of parents who themselves were [the offspring of] parents! It is a guaranteed, unbroken line stretching back into time. [Genes] that inclined their bearers to be less successful parents left fewer copies of themselves than did those [genes] that were more successful.' (pp. 69–70)

What is at stake is not the survival of individual organisms but the survival of the genes carried by those organisms. Genes allow organisms to maximise their inclusive fitness through altruistic behaviour directed at other organisms sharing the same genes (Dawkins, 1986). You carry copies of genes that have been in your family line for thousands of years. When the opportunity presents itself, you will most likely carry on the tradition – reproducing and thus projecting your biological endowment into yet another generation. But you did not reach sexual maturity on your own; the concern for your welfare by your parents, brothers, sisters, grandparents and perhaps an aunt or uncle has contributed to your chances of being reproductively successful. Genes not projected into the next generation simply disappear.

Sociobiologists have marshalled evidence from steprelations' behaviour to support the idea of inclusive fitness. It has been reported, for example, that a disproportionate number of children in stepfamilies suffer injuries, especially assault (Daly and Wilson, 1988). Baby and child battering is more common in stepfamilies and the incidence of child abuse is generally higher in those families (Daly and Wilson, 1996). This evidence, the sociobiologists argue, supports the notion than non-genetic relatives are not disposed to invest resources in offspring that are genetically unrelated. There are problems with the inclusive fitness theory, however, and these are discussed in the 'Controversies in psychological science' section below.

Reciprocal altruism

Kin selection explains altruism towards relatives, but what about altruism directed towards non-relatives? According to Trivers (1971), this kind of altruism, called reciprocal altruism, is the expression of a crude biological version of the golden rule.

Reciprocal altruism exists because humans (and other organisms) can function more effectively if they work together. Human groups are hierarchical and co-operative (D.M. Buss, 1995) whether at the level of the family, canoe club or workplace. There is also evidence that kindness, dependability, emotional stability and intelligence (all traits one would associate with altruism) are the most valued personality characteristics in potential mates (D.M. Buss, 1995). Co-operation between groups is a fundamental survival strategy (Brewer and Caporael, 1990), and is seen in many higher primates (Byrne, 1995). For example, in order to win a mate from a dominant male savannah baboon, a male will engage the help of another baboon who will distract the dominant male and enter into a fight with him. This leaves the other, non-dominant male free to mate with the female. The altruism is reciprocal because the favour will be reciprocated by the successfully paired male in the future (Haufstater, cited in Byrne, 1995). Another primate example where reciprocal altruism can be seen is in food sharing.

An illustration of the way in which reciprocal altruism can work is provided by the Prisoner's Dilemma (Axelrod and Hamilton, 1981). The Prisoner's Dilemma is a scenario in which individuals are allowed to co-operate or not co-operate. Two suspects are imprisoned separately and are asked to consider being silent (to co-operate) or sing (to defect). If both prisoners co-operate then they both get lighter sentences; but if one sings then the prisoner gets off more lightly. If the game is played once, defection is the best strategy; however, if the game is played repeatedly then staying silent might be the best option because the other player can return the favour or punish the defection. Nowak and Sigmund (1998) have suggested that co-operation can still be established even if there were no chance for the co-operation to be reciprocated. The reason for this is that an individual seen to be co-operative or having a reputation for being co-operative will be more likely to experience reciprocal behaviour from others in future. In short, helping will be rewarded by someone who acknowledges your good reputation.

The Prisoner's Dilemma may not be the most effective test of co-operation because it allows only co-operation or defection. In real life, however, co-operation is not an all-or-nothing behaviour. Some individuals may invest slightly less in co-operation, some slightly more, but they may all co-operate in some form. Imagine two individuals giving to charity: one gives £10, the other gives £100. Both are co-operating (being altruistic) but one is more altruistic than another (one may be able to afford the £100 but the other is making a financial sacrifice by donating £10). Because of this variation in altruism, Roberts and Sheratt (1998) have suggested a 'raise the stakes' model of altruistic behaviour. This model argues that individuals would offer a small amount at the first meeting and if this amount is reciprocated, then more will be offered at the next opportunity. This model suggests that behaviour cannot be effectively exploited and so co-operation would be enhanced.

Questions to think about

Sociobiology and evolutionary psychology

- What are the main differences between the sociobiological and evolutionary psychology approaches to understanding behaviour?

- It has been suggested that evolutionary psychology currently offers the biggest, most wide-ranging theory of behaviour. Why do you think this is and do you think this is true?

- What are the limitations of sociobiology and evolutionary psychology?

- Do we have a selfish gene? Do you think that we have evolved to be altruistic?

- Does the incidence of child abuse in stepfamilies support sociobiological interpretations of altruism?

- Are political objections to sociobiology scientifically acceptable ones? Do you think that psychologists should be sensitive to political objections to their findings or theories?

- How would an evolutionary psychologist explain sexual jealousy?

Controversies in psychological science

Sociobiology vs evolutionary psychology – which best explains human behaviour?

The issue

We have seen in this chapter that sociobiology attempts to explain social behaviour by reference to natural selection and genetic inheritance. Evolutionary psychology, however, takes a broader, less hardline approach. Evolutionary psychologists 'develop hypotheses about the psychological mechanisms that have evolved in humans to solve the particular adaptive problems that humans have faced under ancestral conditions' (D.M. Buss, 1995, p. 4). Some of the adaptive problems which evolutionary psychologists see as having evolutionary solutions are listed in Table 3.3.

Sociobiology has been at the centre of a fierce scientific controversy ever since E.O. Wilson published *Sociobiology: The new synthesis* in 1975, the official birth date of this discipline. Although Wilson's work, which is based chiefly on studies of non-human animal behaviour, has generated an enormous outpouring of scientific research, it has also roused a number of serious charges (Montagu, 1980). Wilson's *On Human Nature* (1978), which extended sociobiological theory to human affairs, ignited even more criticism. Most of the criticism focuses on the extension of the theory to human behaviour. Two issues which have caused greatest controversy are inclusive fitness and the mechanisms of adaptation.

The evidence

Inclusive fitness theory (Hamilton, 1964) argues that reproduction and natural selection occur because species' survival success is measured through the production of offspring. Those characteristics which help promote the transmission of genes (either directly or indirectly) will be naturally selected, akin to Dawkins's sieve mentioned at the beginning of the chapter. Evolutionary psychologists agree with this, up to a point. However, sociobiologists

see humans as 'fitness maximisers', or 'fitness strivers' (Alexander, 1979), constantly applying the mechanisms for maximising inclusive fitness. The evolutionary psychologists call this the 'sociobiological fallacy' (D.M. Buss, 1991, 1995) because it confuses the theory of origins of mechanisms with the theory of the nature of mechanisms. As Buss argues, if humans were 'fitness maximising blobs', why are men not queuing up at sperm banks to donate their sperm? Why do some couples forgo reproduction? We have developed a preference for fatty foods but this is known to be detrimental to us. More to the point, we can look at individuals or their behaviour and easily find maximising fitness reasons for this behaviour. The inclusive fitness theory, therefore, cannot account for natural selection and, because of its breadth (one can interpret almost any behaviour in terms of maximising fitness), is virtually limitless in its application.

Instead of seeing humans as fitness maximisers, evolutionary psychologists see humans as 'adaptation executors' or 'mechanism activators' (Tooby and Cosmides, 1990). That is, humans apply evolved solutions to adaptive problems (D.M. Buss, 1995). These solutions are domain-specific. That is, the types of solution one would need to reach to select a mate are different from those one needs to obtain food or to parent children. Adaptive problems are large, complex and varied; the success of individuals in solving these problems depends on sex, species, age, context and individual circumstances (Buss *et al.*, 1998). Sociobiology, however, seems to ignore this psychological level of interpretation and goes from evolution straight to patterns of social organisation.

The most intense criticism of sociobiology is political, not scientific. Opponents argue that sociobiology sanctions the superiority of one group over another, be it a race, a gender, or a political organisation. After all, they argue, if one group of individuals is genetically superior to another, then there are 'natural' grounds for justifying the 'survival of the fittest' and one group's unethical and immoral domination of another. An example is Hitler's quest for world domination in the name of Aryan superiority. Sociobiologists flatly deny such allegations and argue that it is the critics and not they who have confused the term 'natural' with the terms 'good' and 'superior'.

Sociobiologists contend that they study the biological bases of social behaviour only to understand it further, not to find justification for particular cultural practices and customs. Wilson has stated that 'the purpose of sociobiology is not to make crude comparisons between animal species or between animals and men. ... Its purpose is to develop general laws of the evolution and biology of social behaviour, which might then be extended in a disinterested manner to the study of human beings' (Wilson, in Barash, 1982, pp. xiv–xv).

Conclusion

Given the broad-sweep nature of sociobiological theory, it is not surprising that the theory fails to account adequately for natural selection. Although kin selection and familial altruism could be interpreted as supporting the inclusive fitness theory, it is true that one could explain away a lot of behaviour by describing it as maximising fitness. Evolutionary psychology takes a less strident view and argues that the best way to understand psychological mechanisms is to articulate their functions; these functions were designed by natural selection to solve specific adaptive problems.

Table 3.3   Some of the psychological mechanisms which evolutionary psychologists believe have evolved to enable us to perform specific functions

	Psychological mechanism	Function
1	Fear of snakes	Avoid poison
2	Superior female spatial-location memory	Increase success at foraging/gathering
3	Male sexual jealousy	Increase paternity certainty
4	Preference for foods rich in fats and sugar	Increase calorific intake
5	Female mate preference for economic resources	Provision for children
6	Male mate preferences for youth, attractiveness, and waist-to-hip ratio	Select mates of high fertility
7	Landscape preferences for savanna-like environments	Motivate individuals to select habitats that provide resources and offer protection
8	Natural language	Communication/manipulation
9	Cheater-detection procedure	Prevent being exploited in social contacts
10	Male desire for sexual variety	Motivate access to more sexual partners

Source: D.M. Buss (1995). Evolutionary psychology: A new paradigm for psychological disease. In *Psychological Inquiry*, 6(1), 1–30. Copyright © Laurence Erlbaum Associates, Inc. 1995. Reproduced with permission.

Key terms

biological evolution *p.66*
adaptive significance *p.66*
ultimate causes *p.66*
proximate causes *p.66*
evolutionary psychology *p.66*
adaptation *p.67*
natural selection *p.67*
reproductive success *p.68*
genotype *p.68*
phenotype *p.68*
competition *p.69*
paleoanthropology *p.70*
bipedalism *p.71*
encephalisation *p.71*
cultural evolution *p.72*

genetics *p.72*
heredity *p.72*
genes *p.72*
DNA *p.72*
enzymes *p.73*
chromosomes *p.73*
sex chromosomes *p.73*
meiosis *p.73*
alleles *p.74*
dominant allele *p.75*
recessive allele *p.75*
sex-linked gene *p.76*
sex-influenced genes *p.76*
Turner's syndrome *p.76*
mutations *p.77*

chromosomal aberrations *p.77*
cri-du-chat syndrome *p.77*
genetic disorders *p.77*
Down syndrome *p.78*
Huntington's chorea *p.78*
phenylketonuria (PKU) *p.79*
fragile X *p.79*
genetic counselling *p.79*
heritability *p.80*
behaviour genetics *p.80*
monozygotic (MZ) twins *p.84*
dizygotic (DZ) twins *p.84*

concordance research *p.84*
sociobiology *p.85*
reproductive strategies *p.85*
monogamy *p.85*
polygyny *p.85*
polyandry *p.85*
polygynandry *p.85*
parental investment *p.85*
sexual selection *p.85*
incest *p.88*
taboo *p.88*
altruism *p.88*
inclusive fitness *p.88*
kin selection *p.88*
reciprocal altruism *p.89*

CHAPTER REVIEW

Natural selection and evolution

■ Understanding behaviour requires that psychologists learn more about both proximate causes of behaviour – how animals adapt to environmental changes through learning – and ultimate causes of behaviour – historical events and conditions in the evolution of a species that have shaped its behaviour. Evolutionary psychology is a relatively new sub-field of psychology that is devoted to the study of how evolution and genetic variables influence adaptive behaviour.

■ Darwin's voyage on the *Beagle* and his subsequent thinking and research in artificial selection led him to develop the idea of biological evolution, which explains how genetic and physical changes occur in groups of animals over time.

■ The primary element of biological evolution is natural selection: the tendency of some members of a species to produce more offspring than other members do. Members of a species vary genetically, such that some possess specific traits to a greater or lesser extent than other individuals do. If any of these traits gives an animal a competitive advantage over other members of the species – for example, a better ability to escape predators, find food or attract mates – then

that animal is also more likely to have greater reproductive success. Its offspring will then carry its genes into future generations.

■ Two important adaptations during the course of human evolution are bipedalism, the ability to walk upright, and encephalisation, an increase in brain size. The combination of these two factors allowed early humans to explore and settle new environments and led to advances in tool making, hunting, food gathering and self-defence.

■ Encephalisation appears to have been associated with language development and cultural evolution. The study of the evolution of our species suggests the nature of the circumstances under which adaptive behaviour first emerged and those circumstances that have been important for its continued expression to the present time.

Heredity and genetics

■ The instructions for the synthesis of protein molecules, which oversee the development of the body and all of its processes, are contained in genes. Genes are found on chromosomes, which consist of DNA and are found in every cell.

- We inherit 23 individual chromosomes, each of which contains thousands of genes, from each parent. This means that our genetic blueprint represents a recombination of the genetic instructions that our parents inherited from their parents.

- Such recombination makes for tremendous genetic diversity. Genetically diverse species have a better chance of adapting to a changing environment than do genetically non-diverse species because some members of the species may have genes that enable them to survive in a new environment.

- The expression of a gene depends on several factors, including its interaction with other genes (polygenic traits), the sex of the individual carrying the particular gene, and the environmental conditions under which that individual lives. Changes in genetic material caused by mutations or chromosomal aberrations lead to changes in the expression of a particular gene. For example, haemophilia, an increased tendency to bleed from even minor injuries, is the result of a mutation, and Down syndrome, which involves impaired mental, physical and psychomotor development, is the result of a chromosomal aberration.

- Behaviour genetics is the study of how genes influence behaviour. Psychologists and other scientists use artificial selection studies of animals, twin studies, and adoption studies to investigate the possible relationship between genes and behaviour in humans.

Sociobiology

- The discovery of the genetic basis for social behaviour is the primary goal of sociobiology. Sociobiologists have been especially interested in studying social behaviour related to reproduction and the rearing of offspring.

- Different reproductive strategies are believed to have evolved because of sex differences in the resources that parents invest in procreative and childrearing activities. These resources include the time, physical efforts and risks to life involved in procreation and in the feeding, nurturing and protecting of offspring.

- Polygynous and monogamous strategies tend to require greater female investment, polyandrous strategies tend to require greater male investment, and polygynandrous strategies tend to require investment on the part of members of a large group, such as a colony of chimpanzees. Despite these differences, all reproductive strategies entail avoidance of incest, either through migration or the recognition of closely related genetic kin or those individuals with whom one was raised. All human cultures have taboos about incest.

- Altruism is difficult to explain by appealing to natural selection. Altruistic behaviour generally involves one organism risking its life either for others with whom it shares some genes (kin selection) or who are likely to be in the position of later returning the favour (reciprocal altruism).

- Sociobiology has been criticised on the grounds that natural selection is no longer a factor in human evolution, that research on animal social behaviour is not relevant to understanding human social behaviour, that environmental factors play a greater role in shaping human behaviour than genetic factors, and that sociobiology is simply a way to justify the superiority of one group over another. Sociobiologists reply that natural selection has shaped and continues to shape the evolution of culture, that findings from animal research can be generalised to humans, that genes and environment interact to determine behaviour, and, finally, that sociobiology is an attempt to understand human behaviour, not to justify it.

Suggestions for further reading

Darwin, C. (1859). *The Origin of Species by means of Natural Selection*. London: Murray.

Dawkins, R. (1986). *The Blind Watchmaker*. London: Penguin.

Dawkins, R. (1989). *The Selfish Gene*. London: Penguin.

Dennett, D.C. (1995). *Darwin's Dangerous Idea*. London: Penguin.

Gould, S.J. (1980). *The Panda's Thumb: More reflections in natural history*. New York: W.W. Norton.

Gould, S.J. (1993). *Eight Little Piggies*. New York: W.W. Norton.
The best introduction to Darwin's work is his own writing and a good start is The Origin of Species. *Modern-day Darwinists (and anti-Darwinists) have been partly responsible for the explosion in popular interest in science books. Three of these are Dennett, Dawkins and Gould. Daniel Dennett gives a stout defence of Darwin and the theory of evolution, arguing that no other theory can account for the evolution of species. Others, such as Gould, beg to differ. Dawkins's books also take up the Darwinist torch and present evidence and ideas in a very accessible way.*

Eccles, J.C. (1989). *Evolution of the Brain: Creation of the self*. London: Routledge.
The late John Eccles's book provides a good grounding in the evolution of the brain.

Science, 281 (1998), special section on 'The evolution of sex'.
A large chunk of this volume of Science *considers why sex has evolved in the ways that it has. A lot of the material relates to the insect and other non-human worlds, but there are some interesting general articles on the role of sex in evolution.*

Plomin, R. (1990). *Nature and Nurture: An introduction to behavioural genetics*. Pacific Grove, CA: Brooks/Cole.

Plomin, R. and Rutter, M. (1998). Child development, molecular genetics and what to do with genes once they are found. *Child Development*, 69, 4, 1223–1242.

Rose, S., Kamin, L.J. and Lewontin, R.C. (1984). *Not in our Genes: Biology, ideology and human nature*. London: Penguin.

Turkheimer, E. (1998). Heritability and biological explanation. *Psychological Review*, 105, 4, 782–791.

These items give a useful introduction to behavioural genetics (and objections to behavioural genetics). Plomin's book introduces the basic features of behavioural genetics whereas Rose et al.'s book – now, with the development of new genetic marker techniques, a little dated – is a polemic on the futility of finding genetic causes for psychological variables. See which one you think makes best sense. Plomin and Rutter's article is a good, if advanced, guide to how genes are studied and how these can be linked with traits. Turkheimer's article takes a more theoretical approach to evaluating the claims made for the biology and heritability of behaviour.

Baron-Cohen, S. (1997). *The Maladapted Mind: Classic readings in evolutionary psychopathology*. Hove, UK: The Psychology Press.

Buss, D.M. (1995). Evolutionary psychology: a new paradigm for psychological science. *Psychological Inquiry*, 6, 1, 1–30.

Buss, D.M., Haselton, M.G., Shackelford, T.K., Bleske, A.L. and Wakefield, J.C. (1998). Adaptations, exaptations and spandrels. *American Psychologist*, 53, 5, 533–548.

Nesse, R.M. and Williams, G.C. (1998). Evolution and the origins of disease. *Scientific American*, November, 58–65.

Wilson, E.O. (1975). *Sociobiology: The new synthesis*. Cambridge, MA: Harvard University Press.

Special issue of *The British Journal of Medical Psychology*, 1998.

These selected readings are a good introduction to sociobiology and evolutionary psychology. Baron-Cohen's book and the special issue of the BJMP introduce different perspectives on the role of evolution in mental disorder and illness. Donald Buss is a highly active researcher and thinker in evolutionary psychology; his two articles are very good reviews of the limits and frontiers of this controversial sub-area.

Wilson's book is a classic in this area and the article by Nesse and Williams is an excellent, easy-to-read review of how disease has evolved and how we have evolved to cope with and combat it.

Byrne, R. (1995). *The Thinking Ape: Evolutionary origins of intelligence*. Oxford: Oxford University Press.

Richard Byrne's excellent little book is a provocative and detailed account of the evolution of intelligence from the perspective of evolutionary psychology.

Journals to consult

American Psychologist
Behavior Genetics
Child Development
Developmental Psychology
Ethology and Sociobiology
Journal of Evolutionary Psychology
Journal of Personality and Social Psychology
Human Nature, Motivation and Emotion
Nature
Personality and Individual Differences
Science

Website addresses

http://pespmcl.vub.ac.be/EVOMEMLI.html

Contains a large collection of links to evolution-related topics. Links are broken down into four categories: Evolutionary philosophy and theory, Biological evolution and the history of evolution, Evolutionary psychology, and Sociobiology and memetics.

http://www.tamiu.edu/coa/psy/biologicalbasis.htm

Under the 'Evolution' link on this page, you will find an on-line primer of molecular genetics, written by researchers involved in the Human Genome project.

4

PSYCHOBIOLOGY AND NEUROSCIENCE

Aman walks into a restaurant and sits down at a table. He orders his main course but becomes quite agitated by a person staring at him from the opposite side of the table. He orders a bottle of wine, trying to ignore the offensive stare of the person opposite. He is part-way through his meal when he decides that he has had enough of the intrusive diner and summons the waiter. The man asks the waiter to request that the gentleman sitting opposite him refrain from staring at him while he is eating. The waiter looks at him in a rather surprised fashion. He informs the diner that there is no one sitting opposite him. The diner is staring at his own reflection. Unknown to the waiter, the diner has damage to the back of his brain on the right-hand side.

In a quiet, dimly-lit psychology laboratory, a participant sits in a comfortable chair and looks at a television monitor. Attached to the participant's head is a set of electrodes which monitors the electrical activity of the person's brain. The individual sits there for a while looking at a point in the centre of the screen. The television flickers to life and a video tape is shown of some puppies playing; after a short break, this tape is followed by another, this time of a limb amputation. The viewer's brain seems to respond in an unusually specific way. The left side of the participant's brain at the front becomes more active during the puppy video; the right side at the front becomes more active when watching the amputation.

OVERVIEW

Every behaviour we engage in, from thinking to moving to seeing to preferring one type of food to another, is the result of the operation of one body organ and its interaction with other parts of the body and the environment – the brain. Psychobiology is the study of the role of physiological system in regulating, maintaining and executing behaviour. Neuroscience studies the role of the brain and its connected structures (parts of the central nervous system) in behaviour.

This chapter describes some of the main functions and structures of the nervous system. The brain communicates via electrical impulses and this process is described in some detail. We understand the function of the brain by using various techniques and methods: some of these involve studying the effects of naturally or accidentally occurring brain damage on behaviour (such as the offended diner's); others involve studying the activity of the healthy brain as it performs some function (such as watching pleasant and unpleasant video tapes); still others involve selectively damaging the brain of an animal and observing its effects on a specific function. The final part of the chapter considers the effects of drugs on the brain and how these drugs can alter behaviour.

What you should be able to do after reading Chapter 4

- Describe and understand the nervous system and its components.
- Describe and understand the functions of these components.
- Understand neurotransmission and how brain cells communicate.
- Describe the lobes of the brain.
- Understand the function of these lobes.
- Have an awareness of the effects of drugs on behaviour and the neurophysiological basis of these effects.

Questions to think about

- Are two human brains exactly alike?
- Do psychological functions such as language, memory or visual perception reside in specific parts of the brain?
- What do you think scientists mean by 'nature vs nurture'? Is this concept a sensible one?
- How can we measure the brain and body's responses to external and internal stimuli?
- Is any chemical that has an effect on our body and brain 'a drug'?
- Why do certain drugs have different effects on our behaviour?

Psychobiology and neuroscience

In Chapter 1, you saw that psychology is a discipline with many sub-divisions. Sometimes, these sub-divisions are further subdivided into other, more specific areas of study. Psychologists who study the role of physiology in behaviour, for example, may be interested only in specific behaviours, organisms and techniques. Consequently, psychologists who specialise in researching the role of the brain and body in behaviour are known by different names.

Psychobiology is the study of the role of physiology and anatomy in the regulation and execution of behaviour (such as the role of hormones in sexual reproduction, the effect of glucose deprivation on hunger or the relationship between hormone secretion and stress). Neuroscientists study similar processes but limit themselves to studying certain parts of the body – the brain and spinal cord. Together these parts are known as the central nervous system (CNS), so-called because not only do they occupy the central position of the body but they are also the most important part of the nervous system for maintaining and producing behaviour. Neuroscientists study the CNS of any organism that possesses one. Neuropsychologists study the relationship between the brain and its function. A goal of neuropsychology is localisation of function – the idea that parts of the brain perform specific functions. Although much of the research in neuropsychology derives from the effects of brain damage on behaviour, neuropsychologists also study psychological function in healthy individuals by using modern brain mapping techniques (described later on). Psychophysiologists, as we saw in Chapter 1, study physiological processes such as heart rate, hormone secretion, brain electrical activity and skin conductance and the conditions in which changes to these processes arise.

The nervous system: the brain and its components

The brain looks like a lump of porridge and has the consistency of blancmange. This organ, weighing an average 1,400 grams in an adult human, is the most important part of the body (it was not always so – Aristotle, for example, believed that the heart was more important to behaviour). It contains an estimated 10 to 100 billion nerve cells and about as many supporting cells, which take care of important support and 'housekeeping' functions. The brain contains many different types of nerve cell which differ in shape, size and the kinds of chemicals they produce.

Although nerve cells of the brain are organised in modules – clusters of nerve cells that communicate with each other – individual modules do not stand alone. They are connected to other neural circuits, receiving information from some of them, processing this information and sending the results on to other modules. In his famous book *The Modularity of Mind*, Jerry Fodor (Fodor, 1983) argues that particular modules have particular functions – just as the transistors, resistors and capacitors in a computer chip do – and are relatively independent of each other. Although this idea – modularity – is still controversial, the evidence broadly supports some degree of modularity in the brain. The aim of psychobiology and neuroscience is to understand how individual nerve cells work, how they connect with each other to form modules, and just what these modules do.

The central nervous system

The brain has two primary functions: the control of behaviour and the regulation of the body's physiological processes. The brain cannot act alone – it needs to receive information from the body's sense receptors and it must be connected with the muscles and glands of the body if it is to affect behaviour and physiological processes. The nervous system consists of two divisions. The brain and the spinal cord, as we have seen, make up the central nervous system. The spinal cord is a long, thin collection of nerve cells attached to the base of the brain and running the length of the spinal column. The spinal cord contains circuits of nerve cells that control some simple reflexes, such as automatically pulling away from a painfully hot object. The central nervous system communicates with the rest of the body through the nerves – bundles of fibres that transmit information in and out of the central nervous system. The nerves, which are attached to the spinal cord and to the base of the brain, make up the peripheral nervous system which is illustrated in Figure 4.1.

The human brain has three major parts: the brain stem, the cerebellum and the cerebral hemispheres. Figure 4.2 shows photographs of the side (A), bottom (B), back (C) and top (D) of the human cerebral hemispheres. The lower part of the cerebellum and brain stem projects beneath the cerebral hemisphere (see the bottom of Figure 4.2A); the upper part is normally hidden. If the human brain is removed from the skull, it looks as if it has a handle or stem. The brain stem is one of the most primitive regions of the brain, and its functions are correspondingly basic – primarily control of physiological functions and automatic behaviours such as swallowing and breathing (Brodal, 1992). The brains of some animals, such as amphibians, consist primarily of a brain stem and a simple cerebellum.

The two cerebral hemispheres constitute the largest, and most recently developed, part of the human brain. The cerebellum, attached to the back of the brain stem, looks like a miniature version of the cerebral hemispheres. Its primary function is to control and co-ordinate movements. You can see this structure (labelled 1) in Figure 4.2 (C).

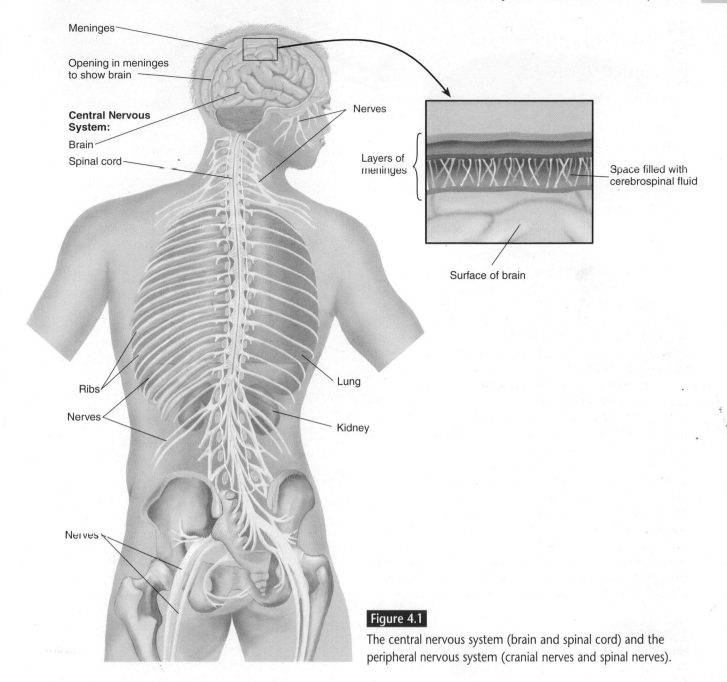

Meninges

Opening in meninges
to show brain

**Central Nervous
System:**

Brain

Spinal cord

Nerves

Layers of
meninges

Space filled with
cerebrospinal fluid

Surface of brain

Ribs

Nerves

Lung

Nerves

Kidney

Nerves

Figure 4.1

The central nervous system (brain and spinal cord) and the
peripheral nervous system (cranial nerves and spinal nerves).

Because the central nervous system is vital to an organism's survival, it is exceptionally well protected. The brain is encased in the skull and the spinal cord runs through the middle of a column of hollow bones known as vertebrae. Both the brain and the spinal cord are enclosed by a three-layered set of membranes called the meninges (meninges is the plural of *meninx*, the Greek word for 'membrane'; meningitis is an inflammation of the meninges). The brain and spinal cord do not come into direct contact with the bones of the skull and vertebrae. Instead, they float in a clear liquid called cerebrospinal fluid (CSF). This liquid fills the space between two of the meninges, thus providing a liquid cushion surrounding the brain and spinal cord and protecting them from being bruised by the bones that encase them.

The surface of the cerebral hemispheres is covered by the cerebral cortex (the word cortex means 'bark' or 'rind'). The cerebral cortex consists of a thin layer of tissue approximately 3 millimetres thick. It is often referred to as grey matter because of its appearance. It contains billions of nerve cells and is the structure where perceptions take place, memories are stored and plans are formulated and executed. The nerve cells in the cerebral cortex are connected to other parts of the brain by a layer of nerve fibres

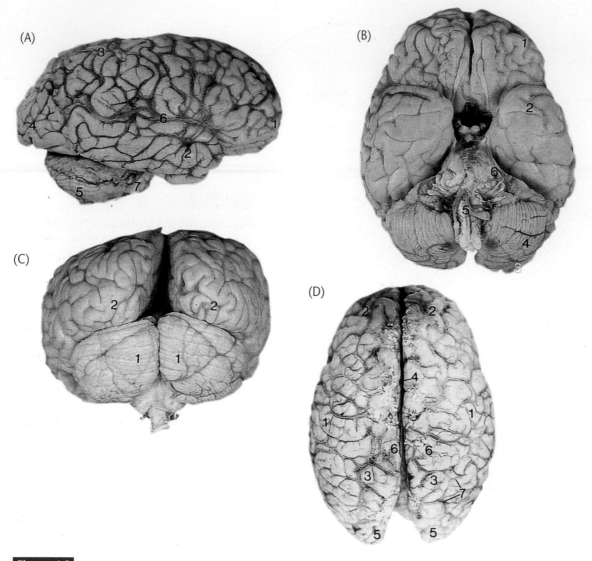

Figure 4.2

The external features of the brain from four angles: (A) the side, (B) bottom, (C) posterior and (D) top.

Source: Reprinted from England, M.A. and Wakely, J. (1991) *A Colour Atlas of the Brain and Spinal Cord*, pp. 39. Aylesbury: Wolfe. Copyright © 1991, by permission of the publisher Mosby.

called the white matter because of the shiny white appearance of the substance that coats and insulates them. Figure 4.3 shows a slice of the brain. As you can see, the grey matter and white matter are distinctly different.

The human cerebral cortex is wrinkled in appearance; it is full of bulges separated by grooves. The bulges are called gyri (singular 'gyrus'), and the large grooves are called fissures. Fissures and gyri expand the amount of surface area of the cortex and greatly increase the number of nerve cells it can contain. Animals with the largest and most complex brains, including humans and the higher primates, have the most wrinkled brains and, thus, the largest cerebral cortices.

The peripheral nervous system

The peripheral nervous system consists of the nerves that connect the central nervous system with sense organs, muscles and glands. Nerves carry both incoming and outgoing information. The sense organs detect changes in the environment and send signals through the nerves to the CNS. The brain sends signals through the nerves to the muscles (causing behaviour) and the glands (producing adjustments in internal physiological processes).

Nerves are bundles of many thousands of individual fibres, all wrapped in a tough, protective membrane. Under

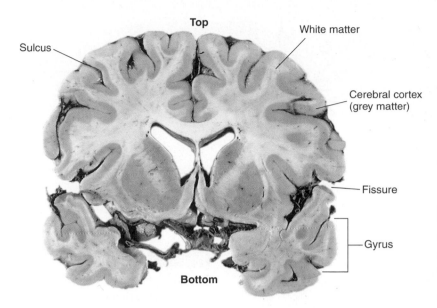

Top
White matter
Sulcus
Cerebral cortex
(grey matter)
Fissure
Gyrus
Bottom

Figure 4.3

A photograph of a slice of a human brain showing fissures and gyri and the layer of cerebral cortex that follows these convolutions.

Source: Harvard Medical School/Betty G. Martindale.

a microscope, nerves look something like telephone cables, with their bundles of wires, as you can see from Figure 4.4. Nerve fibres transmit messages through the nerve, from a sense organ to the brain or from the brain to a muscle or gland.

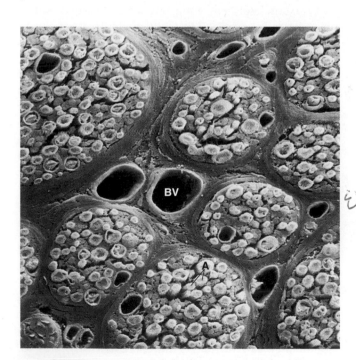

BV

A

Figure 4.4

Nerves. A nerve consists of a sheath of tissue that encases a bundle of individual nerve fibres (also known as axons). BV = blood vessel; A = individual axons.

As we saw earlier, some nerves are attached to the spinal cord and others are attached directly to the brain. The spinal nerves, attached to the spinal cord, serve all of the body below the neck, conveying sensory information from the body and carrying messages to muscles and glands. The twelve pairs of cranial nerves, attached to the brain, serve primarily muscles and sense receptors in the neck and head. For example, when you taste food, the sensory information gets from your tongue to your brain through one set of cranial nerves. Other sets of cranial nerves bring sensory information to the brain from the eyes, ears and nose. When you chew food, the command to chew reaches your jaw muscles through another set of cranial nerves. Still other cranial nerves control the eye muscles, the tongue, the neck muscles and the muscles we use for speech.

Cells of the nervous system

Neurons, or nerve cells, are the elements of the nervous system that bring sensory information to the brain, store memories, reach decisions and control the activity of the muscles. They are assisted in their task by another kind of cell: the glia. Glia (or glial cells) get their name from the Greek word for glue. At one time, scientists thought that glia simply held neurons – the important elements of the nervous system – in place. They do not, however, literally stick neurons together but they do provide important physical support to neurons as well as providing other forms of mechanical support. During development of the brain, some types of glial cells form long fibres that guide developing neurons from their place of birth to their final resting place. Other types of glia manufacture chemicals that neurons need to perform their tasks and absorb chemicals that might impair neurons' functioning. Others form protective insulating sheaths around nerve fibres. Still

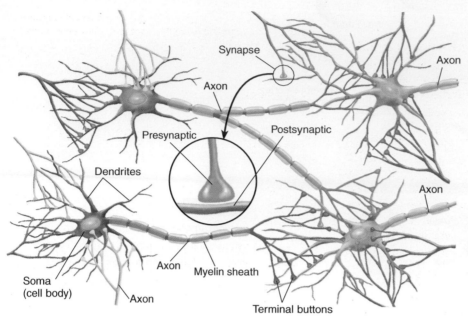

Synapse

Axon

Axon

Presynaptic

Postsynaptic

Dendrites

Axon

Axon

Soma
(cell body)

Axon

Myelin sheath

Terminal buttons

Figure 4.5

The principal parts of a neuron and its connections with other neurons (synapses).

others serve as the brain's immune system, protecting it from invading micro-organisms that might infect it.

The four principal parts of a neuron are shown in Figure 4.5.

- The soma, or cell body, is the largest part of the neuron and contains the mechanisms that control the metabolism and maintenance of the cell. The soma also receives messages from other neurons.

- The dendrites, the tree-like growths attached to the soma, function principally to receive messages from other neurons (dendron means 'tree'). They transmit the information they receive down their 'trunks' to the soma.

- The nerve fibre, or axon, carries messages away from the soma towards the cells with which the neuron communicates. These messages, called action potentials, consist of brief changes in the electrical charge of the axon. For convenience, an action potential is usually referred to as the firing of an axon.

- The terminal buttons are located at the ends of the 'twigs' that branch off the ends of axons. Terminal buttons secrete a chemical called a transmitter substance whenever an action potential travels down the axon, i.e. whenever the axon fires. These chemicals are called neurotransmitters. The transmitter substance affects the activity of the other cells with which the neuron communicates. Thus, the message is conveyed chemically from one neuron to another. Most drugs that affect the nervous system and hence alter a person's behaviour do so by affecting the chemical transmission of messages between cells.

Myelination

Many axons, especially long ones, are insulated with a substance called myelin. The white matter located beneath the cerebral cortex gets its colour from the myelin sheaths around the axons that travel through these areas. Myelin, which is part protein, part fat, is produced by special cells that individually wrap themselves around segments of the axon, leaving small bare patches of the axon between them. The principal function of myelin is to insulate axons from each other and thus to prevent the scrambling of messages. It also increases the speed of the action potential.

The symptoms of a particular neurological disease prove just how important the myelin sheath is. In some cases, people's immune systems go awry and begin to attack parts of their own bodies. One of these disorders is called multiple sclerosis, because an autopsy of the brain and spinal cord will show numerous patches of hardened, damaged tissue (*skleros* is Greek for 'hard'). The immune systems of people who have multiple sclerosis attack a protein in the myelin sheath of axons in the central nervous system, stripping it away. Although most of the axons survive this assault, they can no longer function normally, and so, depending on where the damage occurs, people who have multiple sclerosis suffer from various sensory and motor impairments.

There is also evidence to suggest that the central nervous system becomes fully mature when myelination is complete; speed of information processing in children, for example, seems to mirror the cortical development and ongoing myelination (Travis, 1998).

The action potential

The message carried by the axon – the action potential – involves an electrical current, but it does not travel down the axon the way electricity travels through a wire. Electricity travels through a wire at hundreds of millions of metres per second. The axon transmits information at a much slower rate – less than 100 metres per second.

The membrane of an axon is electrically charged. When the axon is resting (that is, when no action potential is occurring), the outside is charged at +70 millivolts (thousandths of a volt) with respect to the inside. An action potential is an abrupt, short-lived reversal in the electrical charge of an axon. This temporary reversal begins at the end of the axon that attaches to the soma and is transmitted to the end that divides into small branches capped with terminal buttons.

The electrical charge of the axon occurs because of an unequal distribution of positively and negatively charged particles inside the axon and in the fluid that surrounds it. These particles, called ions, are produced when various substances – including ordinary table salt – are dissolved in water. Normally, ions cannot penetrate the membrane that surrounds axons. However, the axonal membrane contains special submicroscopic proteins that serve as ion channels or ion transporters. Ion channels can open or close; when they are open, a particular ion can enter or leave the axon. Ion transporters work like pumps. They use the energy resources of the cell to transport particular ions into or out of the axon, as seen in Figure 4.6.

The outside of the membrane is positively charged (and the inside is negatively charged) because the axon contains more negatively charged ions and fewer positively charged ions. When an axon is resting, its ion channels are closed, so ions cannot move into or out of the axon. An action potential is caused by the opening of some ion channels in the membrane at the end of the axon nearest the soma. The opening of these ion channels permits positively charged sodium ions to enter, which reverses the membrane potential at that location. This reversal causes nearby ion channels to open, which produces another reversal at that point. The process continues all the way to the terminal buttons located at the other end of the axon.

Note that an action potential is a brief reversal of the membrane's electrical charge. As soon as the charge reverses, the ion channels close and another set of ion channels opens for a short time, letting positively charged potassium ions out of the axon. This outflow of positive ions restores the normal electrical charge. Thus, an action potential resembles the 'Mexican wave' that football fans often make in a stadium during a game. People in one part of the stadium stand up, raise their arms over their heads, and sit down again. People seated next to them see that a wave is starting, so they do the same – and the wave travels around the stadium. Everyone remains at the same

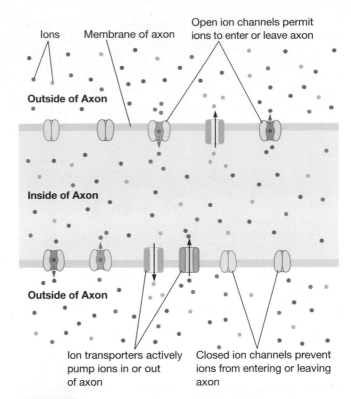

Figure 4.6

Ion channels and ion transporters. These structures regulate the number of ions found inside and outside the axon. An unequal distribution of positively and negatively charged ions is responsible for the axon's electrical charge.

place, but the effect is that of something circling in the stands around the playing field. Similarly, electricity does not really travel down the length of an axon. Instead, the entry of positive ions in one location reverses the charge at that point and causes ion channels in the adjacent region to open, and so on, as seen in Figure 4.7. The ion transporters pump sodium ions out of the axon and pump potassium ions back in, restoring the normal balance.

Synapses

Neurons communicate with other cells by means of synapses. A synapse is the conjunction of a terminal button of one neuron and the membrane of another cell – neuron, muscle cell or gland cell. The terminal button belongs to the presynaptic neuron – the neuron that sends the message. When terminal buttons become active, they release a chemical called a transmitter substance. The neuron that receives the message (detects the transmitter substance) is called the postsynaptic neuron. A neuron receives messages from many terminal buttons, and in turn its terminal buttons form synapses with many other neurons. The drawing in Figure 4.5 is much simplified; thousands of terminal buttons can form synapses with a single neuron.

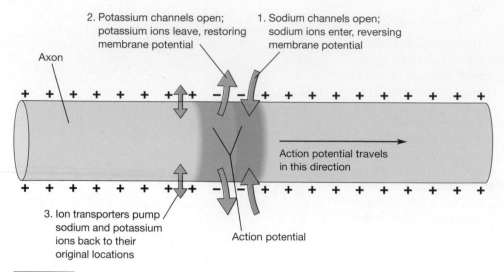

2. Potassium channels open; potassium ions leave, restoring membrane potential

1. Sodium channels open; sodium ions enter, reversing membrane potential

Axon

Action potential travels in this direction

3. Ion transporters pump sodium and potassium ions back to their original locations

Action potential

Figure 4.7

Movement of sodium and potassium ions during the action potential. Sodium ions are represented by orange arrows, potassium ions by green arrows.

Figure 4.8 illustrates the relation between a motor neuron and a muscle. A *motor neuron* is one that forms synapses with a muscle and controls its contractions. When the axon of a motor neuron fires, all the muscle fibres with which it forms synapses will contract with a brief twitch. A muscle consists of thousands of individual muscle fibres. It is controlled by a large number of motor neurons, each of which forms synapses with different groups of muscle fibres. The strength of a muscular contraction, then, depends on the rate of firing of the axons that control it. If they fire at a high rate, the muscle contracts forcefully; if they fire at a low rate, the muscle contracts weakly.

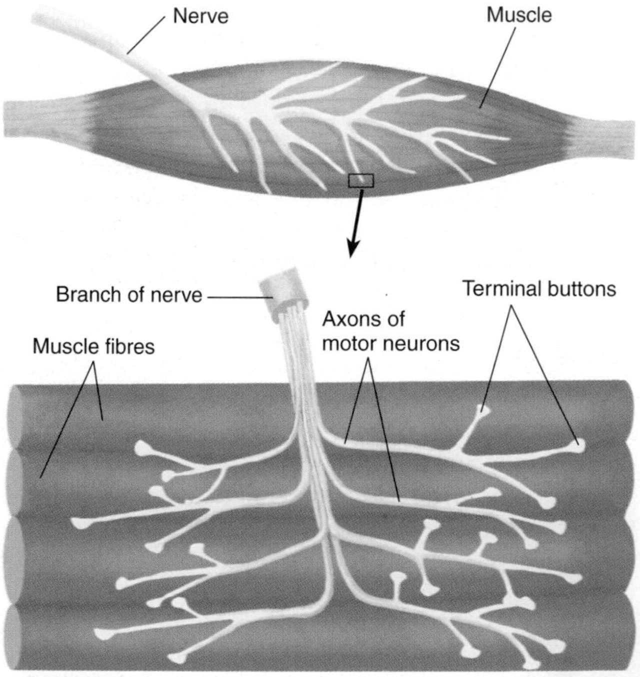

Excitation and inhibition

There are basically two types of synapse: excitatory synapses and inhibitory synapses. Excitatory synapses do just what their name implies. When the axon fires, the terminal buttons release a transmitter substance that excites the postsynaptic neurons with which they form synapses. The effect of this excitation is to make it more likely that the axons of the postsynaptic neurons will fire. Inhibitory synapses do just the opposite. When they are activated, they lower the likelihood that the axons of the postsynaptic neurons will fire.

The rate at which a particular axon fires is determined by the activity of the synapses on the dendrites and soma of the cell. If the excitatory synapses are the more active, the axon will fire at a high rate. If the inhibitory synapses are the more active, the axon will fire at a low rate or perhaps not at all, as seen in Figure 4.9.

How do molecules of transmitter substance exert their excitatory or inhibitory effect on the postsynaptic neuron? When an action potential reaches a terminal button, it causes the terminal button to release a small amount of transmitter substance into the synaptic cleft, a fluid-filled space between the terminal button and the membrane of the postsynaptic neuron. The transmitter substance causes reactions in the postsynaptic neuron that either excite or inhibit it. These reactions are triggered by special

Nerve

Muscle

Branch of nerve

Terminal buttons

Axons of motor neurons

Muscle fibres

Figure 4.8

Synapses between terminal buttons of the axon of a motor neuron and a muscle.

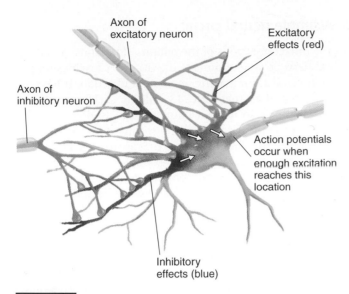

Axon of
excitatory neuron

Excitatory
effects (red)

Axon of
inhibitory neuron

Action potentials
occur when
enough excitation
reaches this
location

Inhibitory
effects (blue)

Figure 4.9

Interaction between the effects of excitatory and inhibitory synapses. The rate of firing of the axon of the neuron is controlled by these two factors.

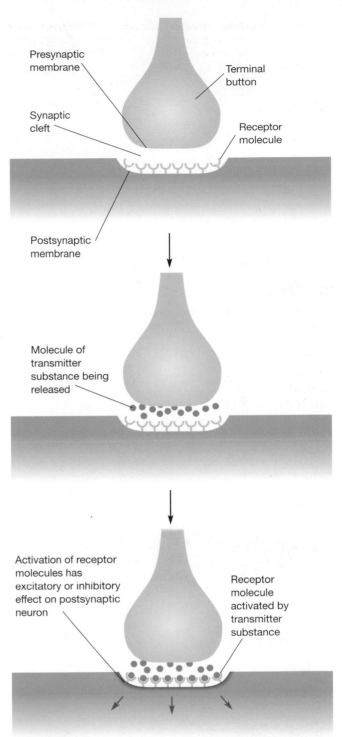

Presynaptic
membrane

Terminal
button

Synaptic
cleft

Receptor
molecule

Postsynaptic
membrane

Molecule of
transmitter
substance being
released

Activation of receptor
molecules has
excitatory or inhibitory
effect on postsynaptic
neuron

Receptor
molecule
activated by
transmitter
substance

Figure 4.10

The release of a transmitter substance from a terminal button. *Top*: Before the arrival of an action potential. *Middle*: Just after the arrival of an action potential. Molecules of transmitter substance have been released. *Bottom*: Activation of receptor molecules. The molecules of transmitter substance diffuse across the synaptic cleft and some of them activate receptor molecules in the postsynaptic membrane.

submicroscopic protein molecules embedded in the post-synaptic membrane called **receptor molecules** (see Figure 4.10).

A molecule of a transmitter substance attaches to a receptor molecule the way a key fits in a lock. After their release from a terminal button, molecules of transmitter substance find their way to the receptor molecules, attach to them and activate them. Once they are activated, the receptor molecules produce excitatory or inhibitory effects on the postsynaptic neuron. They do so by opening ion channels. The ion channels found at excitatory synapses permit sodium ions to enter the neuron; those found at inhibitory synapses permit potassium ions to leave it (see Figure 4.11).

The excitation or inhibition produced by a synapse is short-lived; the effects soon pass away, usually in a fraction of a second. At most synapses, the effects are terminated by a process called **reuptake**. The transmitter substance is released by the terminal button and is quickly taken up again. It, therefore, has only a short time to stimulate the postsynaptic receptor molecules, as you can see from Figure 4.12. The rate at which the terminal button takes back the transmitter substance determines how prolonged the effects of the chemical on the postsynaptic neuron will be. The faster the transmitter substance is taken back, the shorter its effects will be on the postsynaptic neuron. As we will see, some drugs affect the nervous system by slowing down the rate of reuptake, thus prolonging the effects of the transmitter substance.

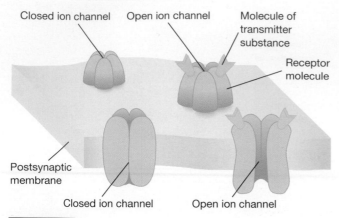

Figure 4.11

Detailed view of receptor molecules in the postsynaptic neuron. When activated by molecules of a transmitter substance, the receptor molecules allow sodium ions to enter the postsynaptic neuron, causing excitation, or allow potassium ions to leave, causing inhibition.

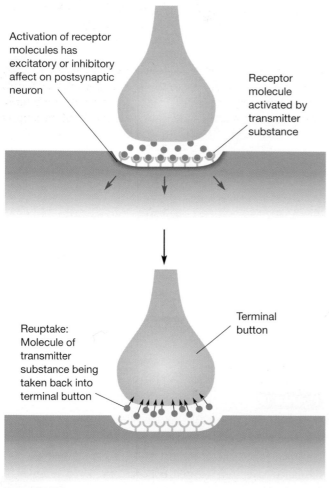

Figure 4.12

Reuptake of molecules of transmitter substance.

A simple neural circuit

The interconnections of the billions of neurons in our central nervous system provide us with the capacities for perception, decision making, memory and action. It has been estimated that there are 13 trillion such connections. Although we do not yet know enough to draw a 'neural wiring diagram' for such complex functions, we can do so for some of the simpler reflexes that are triggered by certain kinds of sensory stimuli. For example, when your finger touches a painfully hot object, your hand withdraws. When your eye is touched, your eyes close and your head draws back. When a baby's cheek is touched, it turns its mouth towards the object, and if the object is of the appropriate size and texture, the baby begins to suck. All these activities occur quickly, without thought.

A simple withdrawal reflex, which is triggered by a noxious stimulus (such as contact with a hot object), requires three types of neuron. **Sensory neurons** detect the noxious stimulus and convey this information to the spinal cord. **Interneurons**, located entirely within the brain or spinal cord, receive the sensory information and in turn stimulate the motor neurons that cause the appropriate muscle to contract, as seen in Figure 4.13.

The sequence is simple and straightforward. A noxious stimulus applied to the skin produces a burst of action potentials in the sensory neurons. Their axons fire, and their terminal buttons, located within the spinal cord, release an excitatory transmitter substance. The chemical stimulates the interneurons and causes them to fire. The interneurons excite the motor neurons, and these neurons cause the muscle to contract.

The next example adds a bit of complexity to the circuit. Imagine that you have removed a hot casserole dish from the oven. As you move over to the table to put it down, the heat begins to penetrate the rather thin ovengloves you are using. The pain caused by the hot dish triggers a withdrawal reflex that tends to make you drop it. And yet you manage to keep hold of it long enough to get to the table and put it down. What prevented your withdrawal reflex from making you drop the dish on the floor?

As we saw earlier, the activity of a neuron depends on the relative activity of the excitatory and inhibitory synapses on it. The pain from the hot casserole dish increases the activity of excitatory synapses on the motor neurons, which tends to cause the hand to open. However, this excitation is counteracted by inhibition from another source – the brain. The brain contains neural circuits that recognise what a disaster it would be if you dropped the casserole dish on the floor. These neural circuits send information to the spinal cord that prevents the withdrawal reflex from making you drop the dish. Figure 4.14 shows how this information reaches the spinal cord. As you can see, an axon from a neuron in the brain reaches the spinal cord, where it forms a synapse with an inhibitory

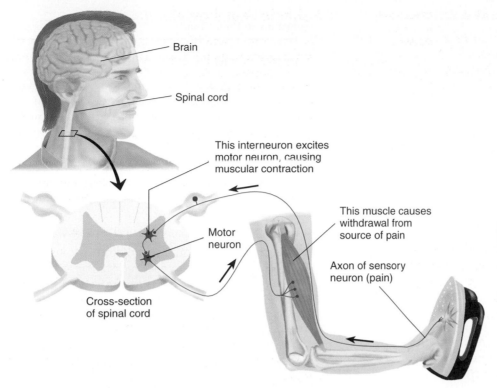

Figure 4.13

Schematic representation of the elements of a withdrawal reflex. Although this figure shows just one sensory neuron, one interneuron and one motor neuron, in reality many thousands of each type of neuron are involved.

interneuron. When the neuron in the brain becomes active, it excites this inhibitory interneuron. The interneuron releases an inhibitory transmitter substance, which decreases the rate of firing of the motor neuron, preventing your hand from opening. This circuit provides an example

of a contest between two competing tendencies: to drop the casserole dish and to hold onto it. Complex decisions about behaviour are made within the brain by much more complicated circuits of neurons, but the basic principles remain the same.

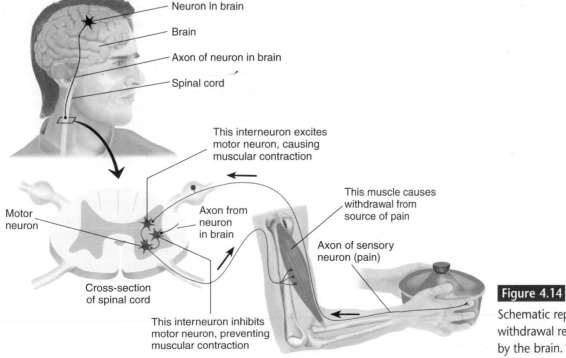

Figure 4.14

Schematic representation of a withdrawal reflex being inhibited by the brain.

Neuromodulators: action at a distance

Terminal buttons excite or inhibit postsynaptic neurons by releasing transmitter substances. These chemicals travel a very short distance and affect receptor molecules located on a small patch of the postsynaptic membrane. But some neurons release chemicals that get into the general circulation of the brain and stimulate receptor molecules on many thousands of neurons, some located a considerable distance away. The chemicals these neurons release are called neuromodulators, because they modulate the activity of the neurons they affect.

We can think of neuromodulators as the brain's own 'drugs'. Because these chemicals diffuse widely in the brain, they can activate or inhibit many different circuits of neurons, thus exerting several behavioural and physiological effects. These effects act together to help achieve a particular goal.

The best-known neuromodulator is a category of chemicals called endorphins, or opioids ('opium-like substances'). Opioids are neuromodulators that stimulate special receptor molecules (opioid receptors) located on neurons in several parts of the brain. Their behavioural effects include decreased sensitivity to pain and a tendency to persist in ongoing behaviour. Opioids are released while an animal is engaging in important species-typical behaviours, such as mating or fighting. The behavioural effects of opioids ensure that a mating animal or an animal fighting to defend itself is less likely to be deterred by pain; thus, conception is more likely to occur and a defence is more likely to be successful.

Many years ago, people discovered that eating or smoking the sap of the opium poppy decreased their sensitivity to pain, so they began using it for this purpose. They also discovered that the sap produced pleasurable effects: people who took it enjoyed the experience and wanted to take more. In recent times, chemists have discovered that the sap of the opium poppy contains a class of chemicals called opiates. They also learned how to extract and concentrate them and to produce synthetic versions with even greater potency. In the mid-1970s, neurobiologists learned that opiates produce their effect by stimulating special opioid receptor molecules located on neurons in the brain (Pert *et al.*, 1974). Soon after that, they discovered the brain's opioids (Terenius and Wahlström, 1975). Thus, opiates mimic the effects of a special category of neuromodulators that the brain uses to regulate some types of species-typical behaviours.

The brain produces other neuromodulators. Some help organise the body's response to stress, while others reduce anxiety and promote sleep. Some promote eating, while others help end a meal.

Questions to think about

The brain and its activity

- The idea that the brain controls our perceptions, thoughts and feelings was not always clear to our ancestors. Why do you think that thinkers such as Aristotle imbued the heart with more importance for behaviour? Why do we talk of making decisions 'from the heart'?

- Neuroscience is full of metaphors to describe neurophysiological processes. Why is the telephone line or copper wire metaphor inappropriate for describing the action potential?

- What are neuromodulators and how do they work?

- Opioids are useful neuromodulators because they encourage an animal to continue fighting or mating. Can you think of other behaviours that might be influenced by neuromodulators? Can you think of mental or behavioural problems that might be caused if too much or too little of these neuromodulators were secreted?

- Can we reduce all behaviour to the activity of certain cells being in a certain state (philosophers call this identity theory)? If so, why? If not, why not?

Techniques in psychobiology and neuroscience

Until relatively recently, most of our knowledge of the functions of the nervous system was obtained through research using laboratory animals. This research produced important discoveries about the causes and treatments of neurological and mental disorders, many of which are discussed in this book. It led to the development of drugs and surgical techniques that help people with neurological disorders such as Parkinson's disease and mental disorders such as schizophrenia, depression and obsessive compulsive disorders. As we saw in Chapter 2, all research using live animals must follow strict regulations designed to protect the animals' health and well-being.

Physiological psychologists now have at their disposal a range of research methods to study the function of the brain and body that would have been impossible to imagine just a few decades ago. We have ways to identify neurons that contain particular chemicals. We have ways to take photographs of particular ions entering neurons when the appropriate ion channels open. We have ways to inactivate individual genes to see what happens to behaviour when they no longer function. We can also witness the activity of the brain as it behaves, through the technique of neuroimaging.

Lesioning

The earliest research method of physiological psychology – and one that is still the most commonly used – involves correlating a behavioural deficit with damage to a specific part of the nervous system. This method can be used in one of two ways. For example, a neuropsychologist may examine the effects of brain damage on function, such as the effect of damage to the front part of the brain on the ability to create and adhere to plans (Shallice, 1988; Code *et al.*, 1996). As you saw in Chapter 1, to describe this as a method or technique is perhaps inaccurate because it implies that scientists go about damaging their patients' brains which is, of course, nonsense. It is an approach to the understanding of brain function. The second way does allow the investigator to produce an experimental brain lesion, an injury to a particular part of the brain, but only in an animal's brain. Of course, neurosurgeons do lesion parts of the brain to alleviate some forms of suffering. One recent, successful treatment for the movement disorder Parkinson's disease, for example, involves lesioning a small structure deep within the brain. But this is directed lesioning; it is not experimental. Neurosurgeons know the outcome of such lesioning. When an animal's brain is experimentally lesioned, the investigator then studies the effects of the lesion on the animal's behaviour. If particular behaviours are disrupted, the reasoning suggests, the damaged part of the brain must be involved in those behaviours.

Some lesioning techniques are used in both experimental and neurosurgical work. For example, to reach the region the experimenter or surgeon needs to lesion, he or she uses a device called a stereotaxic apparatus to insert a fine wire (called an electrode) into a particular location in the brain, as Figures 4.15 and 4.16 show. The term 'stereotaxic' refers to the ability to manipulate an object in three-dimensional space. The researcher passes an electrical current through the electrode, which produces heat that destroys a small portion of the brain around the tip of the electrode. After a few days, the animal recovers from the operation, and the researcher can assess its behaviour.

A stereotaxic apparatus can also be used to insert wires for recording the electrical activity of neurons in particular regions of the brain. But an electrode placed in an animal's brain can also be used to lead electrical current into the brain as well as out of it. If an electrical connector on the animal's skull is attached to an electrical stimulator, current can be sent to a portion of the animal's brain. This current activates neurons located near the tip of the electrode. The experimenter can then see how this artificial stimulation affects the animal's behaviour.

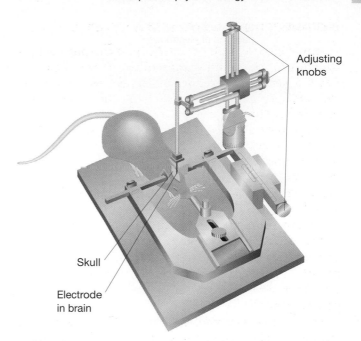

Figure 4.15

A stereotaxic apparatus, used to insert a wire into a specific portion of an animal's brain.

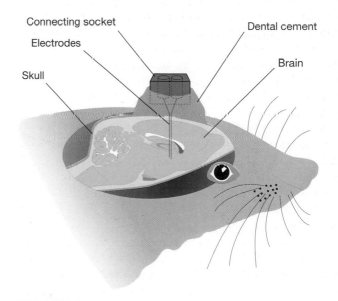

Figure 4.16

A permanently attached set of electrodes in an animal's brain and a connecting socket cemented to the skull.

Neurosurgeons sometimes use stereotaxic apparatus to operate on humans. For example, as we mentioned briefly above, destruction of a particular region near the centre of the cerebral hemispheres can alleviate the tremors

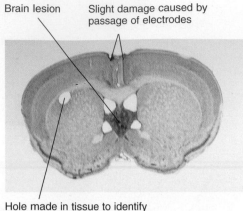

Brain lesion   Slight damage caused by
passage of electrodes

Hole made in tissue to identify
left and right sides of brain

Figure 4.17

A thin slice of a mouse brain stained with a dye that shows the location of cell bodies. The arrow indicates the location of a lesion made with a stereotaxic apparatus.

(trembling) that occur in some cases of Parkinson's disease (Samuel *et al.*, 1998; Krack *et al.*, 1998). Neurosurgeons can also insert electrodes into the human brain and record the electrical activity of particular regions to try to find locations that might be responsible for triggering epileptic seizures.

After a brain lesion has been made, or after an electrode has been placed in an animal's brain and its behaviour has been observed, the researcher must verify the location of the lesion or electrode. To do so, he or she humanely kills the animal with an overdose of an anaesthetic, removes the brain, and uses special histological procedures to slice the brain, dye the cells and fibre tracts, and examine the slices under a microscope (Rose, 1992). The prefix *histo-* refers to body tissue. Figure 4.17 is a photograph of a slice of a mouse's brain showing the location of a lesion made with a stereotaxic apparatus.

Psychophysiology

Although psychobiologists can record the electrical activity of the brain from deep inside the structure in animals and humans, such a technique is invasive. That is, the technique invades some part of the body, in this case the brain. However, there is a way of studying functions by using a technique called **electroencephalography (EEG)** which measures the brain's electrical activity non-invasively. Researchers called psychophysiologists can do this by placing electrodes outside the body, on the skin, at specified positions. If the skin is the scalp of the head, they can record the activity of groups of millions of neurons underneath the electrode (Andreassi, 1996; Martin, 1998a).

The number of electrodes used in brain research tends to be at the discretion of the experimenter. Some use two or three, others use a lot more (over one hundred in some cases). Figure 4.18 shows the position of nineteen electrodes as they would appear on the scalp. These electrodes are positioned in a specific way (according to

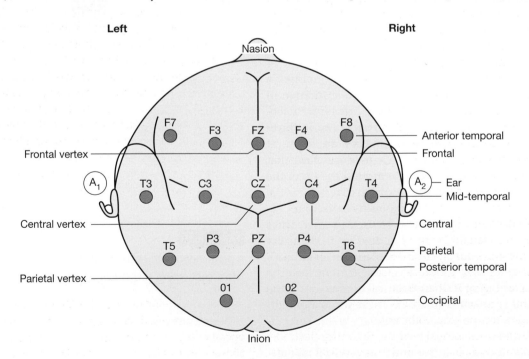

Figure 4.18

An example of the spread of electrodes on the scalp during EEG recording in humans. The number of electrodes used can be as few as 3 as many as 164.

international guidelines) so that researchers who record activity from these electrodes will be recording from consistent positions. This allows us to compare the EEG results across individuals, groups of individuals, research groups and international laboratories.

EEG activity is seen in the form of a line-tracing or electroencephalogram (EEG or 'brainwave') although some modern EEG recording machines allow the conversion of EEG data into 'brainmaps' – these are two-dimensional representations of the EEG activity. They can be coloured or in greyscale which means that areas of high and low activity can be represented by darker or lighter colours. There are different types of EEG and these are thought to represent different psychological states. Some large, slow EEG waves, for example, are characteristic of deep sleep; one type of activity, called alpha, is the resting adult EEG; when we are engaged in thinking or making rapid movements, alpha activity changes to another type of activity (Andreassi, 1996). In Chapter 9 (Consciousness), we will look at the different types of EEG brain activity that occurs during sleep because this behaviour is associated with quite marked changes in the EEG.

One benefit of the EEG technique is that, as well as being non-invasive, it provides a measure of the brain's activity in real time, as it happens. We can, therefore, match the presentation of a stimulus or a task with the brain activity associated with it. In this way, we can measure how the brain responds while it is engaged in tasks such as deciding whether two figures rotated in three-dimensional space are the same or different (Williams *et al.*, 1995) or watching pleasant or unpleasant visual stimuli (Davidson, 1992) or smelling food odour (Martin, 1998b) or recognising faces and words (Burgess and Gruzelier, 1997).

Sometimes, however, this electrical signal can be messy or noisy: it is difficult to distinguish the brain's normal background activity and the activity produced by perceiving or responding to a stimulus. To overcome this, psychophysiologists have devised the technique of averaging signals across trials. They can do this by recording event-related potentials or ERPs (these are sometimes also called *evoked potentials*). These are electrical signals recorded to a repeatedly presented stimulus (or set of stimuli). Each EEG response to a stimulus is added and averaged to produce one clearer signal or evoked potential. The potentials are event-related because they are related to a specific event that is external or internal to the individual such as decision making (internal stimulus) or perceiving a flash of light (external stimulus). The point of averaging is to make the effect of a stimulus on the EEG clearer; background noise is reduced and the effect of the stimulus becomes more obvious.

Some ERPs measure sensory responses to stimuli (this is called the N100, so-called because it appears 100 milliseconds after the onset of a stimulus), others are thought to be associated with more cognitive functions such as understanding words or being able to distinguish one type of

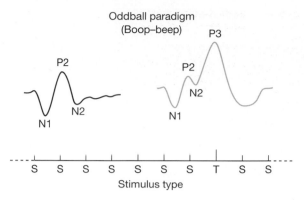

Figure 4.19

Two types of evoked potential (EP), a measure of the brain's electrical activity. When a participant is asked to undertake a task such as detecting the number of low tones in a series of high and low tones (where there are always fewer low tones), the EPs illustrated here are found. The waves on the right show the brain's response to the high tones (the common ones); the N100 sensory and P200 components can be clearly seen. However, when the participant has to make a decision (discriminating between high and low tones) a late wave – the P300 – appears in response to the low tones (the rarer ones). This wave is thought to reflect the brain's decision-making processes.

visual or auditory stimulus from another. These ERPs occur later, at around 300 or 400 milliseconds after stimulus onset, perhaps reflecting the time the brain takes to undertake these cognitive operations (Polich and Kok, 1995). The early and late ERPs are illustrated in Figure 4.19.

ERPs have been used to investigate a number of psychological functions such as decision making, sentence comprehension, recognition memory, visual, tactile and auditory perception. They are not as good as other techniques at localising activity to a specific brain area but they are good at measuring responses to stimuli in real time. The absence of an evoked potential indicates an impairment in function or a failure to attend to stimuli. Figure 4.20 shows the difference between ERPs evoked by a decision-making task in healthy volunteers and individuals with dementia. Note the reduction in the amplitude (size) of the wave in the demented group.

Neuroimaging techniques

The development of several different diagnostic machines which can be used to investigate the brain's structure and activity has revolutionised neuropsychological research (Posner and Raichle, 1994; Frackowiak *et al.*, 1997). These sophisticated techniques, more than any of the others, have provided neuroscientists with the opportunity of measuring how the whole, living, healthy brain functions.

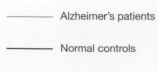

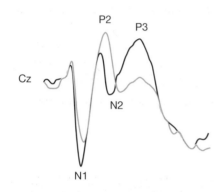

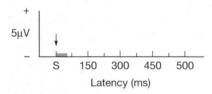

Figure 4.20

Examples of EPs measured in healthy individuals and those with Alzheimer's disease. Note how the amplitude (height) of the wave, especially the P300, is lower than that seen in healthy individuals.

They are called **neuroimaging** techniques because they allow us to visualise and obtain images of brain function and structure. These techniques include CT, PET, MRI and fMRI.

Computerised tomography (CT)

Computerised tomography is a technique used to display the structure of the brain (*tomos*, meaning 'cut', describes the CT scanner's ability to produce a picture that looks like a slice of the brain). The scanner sends a narrow beam of X-rays through a person's head (see Figure 4.21). The beam is moved around the patient's head, and a computer calculates the amount of radiation that passes through it at various points along each angle. The result is a two-dimensional image of a 'slice' of the person's head, parallel to the top of the skull.

Using the CT scanner, an investigator can determine the approximate location of a brain lesion in a living patient. Knowing the results of behavioural testing and the location of the brain damage, the neuropsychologist can compare them and make inferences about the normal function of the damaged brain tissue. Figure 4.22 shows several CT scans of the brain of a patient with a lesion caused by a stroke. The scans are arranged from the bottom of the brain (scan 1) to the top (scan 6). You can easily see the lesion, a white spot, in the lower left corner of scan 5.

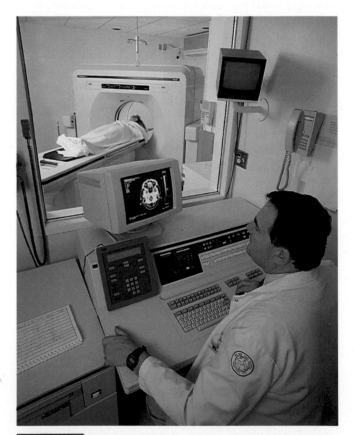

Figure 4.21

A patient being placed in a computerised tomography (CT) scanner.

Source: © Hank Morgan/Rainbow. Reproduced with permission.

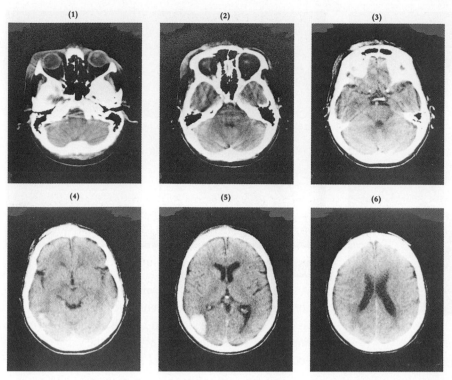

(1)   (2)   (3)

(4)   (5)   (6)

Figure 4.22

A set of CT scans from a patient with a brain lesion caused by a stroke (the white spot in the lower left corner of scan 5). Because left and right are traditionally reversed on CT scans, the brain lesion is actually in the *right* hemisphere.

Courtesy of Dr J. McA. Jones, Good Samaritan Hospital, Portland, Oregon.

Positron emission tomography (PET)

Positron emission tomography (PET) is an invasive measure of brain metabolism, glucose consumption and blood flow. The procedure for undergoing a PET scan goes something like this. A person is given a harmless dose of a radioactive substance (a form of glucose) which enters the brain (this is why the technique is invasive; the radioactive substance is injected into the participant's arm). The chemical accumulates in particular regions of the brain (the location depends on the specific chemical) but usually goes to active cells. PET measures brain activity by examining the amount of oxygen consumed by, or blood flow travelling to, neurons. The radioactive parts of the glucose emit positrons (hence positron emission) which are detected by a PET scanner, a large, doughnut shaped piece of equipment which accommodates the prostrate participant's head. This activity is then represented in the form of coloured maps such as those seen in Figure 4.23(c). Because of the radioactivity involved, only certain participants are allowed to take part in PET research. Premenopausal women and children, for example, cannot take part, which limits the use of PET when investigating how brain function develops during the early years.

It is difficult to overestimate the contribution of PET research to the study of brain function, however. PET has allowed researchers undertake investigations of the workings of the brain that were thought unrealisable thirty years ago. It is an expensive technique (the scanner's costs

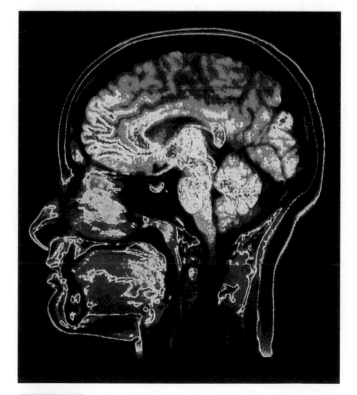

Figure 4.23

(a) A colour-enhanced sagittal MRI scan.

Source: Pinel, J., *Biopsychology* (3rd edition). Boston: Allyn and Bacon. Copyright © 1997 by Allyn and Bacon; reproduced with permission.

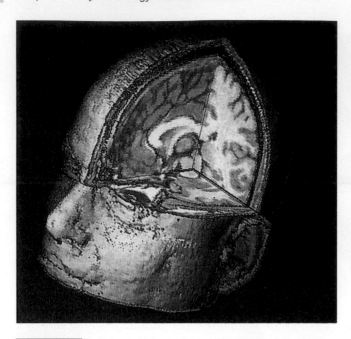

Figure 4.23

(b) A functional MRI scan providing a three-dimensional image of the brain.

Source: Courtesy of Bruce Forster, Radiology Department, and Robert Hare, Psychology Department, University of British Columbia. Research funded by the British Columbia Medical Services Foundation.

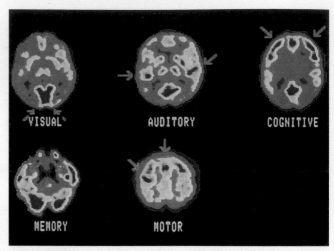

Figure 4.23

(c) A series of PET scans, each showing a horizontal section of the brain recorded during a different psychological activity. Areas of high activity are indicated by reds and yellows. For example, notice the high level of activity in the visual cortex of the occipital lobe when the subject scanned a visual display.

Source: Michael E. Phelps and John C. Mazziotta (1985) Positron Tomography: Human Brain Function and Biochemistry, *Science*, 228 (9701), 17 May, p. 804. Copyright 1985 by the AAAS. Reprinted by permission. Courtesy of Drs. Michael E. Phelps and John Mazziotta, UCLA School of Medicine.

run into millions) but a number of PET laboratories now exist around the world and the results from these laboratories have allowed us to see whether the technique shows a consistent pattern of findings. In later chapters, we will see how PET research has helped us to understand the neural basis of functions such as speech perception, speech comprehension, memory, reading, attention and many others. It has been used to localise the parts of the brain active during word and speech recognition (Petersen *et al.*, 1988; Karbe *et al.*, 1998; Zatorre *et al.*, 1992; Castro-Caldas *et al.*, 1998), face perception (Sergent *et al.*, 1992), language tasks performed by dyslexic individuals (Rumsey *et al.*, 1997; Brunswick *et al.*, 1999), object naming (Martin *et al.*, 1996), problem-solving (Baker *et al.*, 1996; Nagahama *et al.*, 1996) and remembering events (Fletcher *et al.*, 1998a,b) among others.

Magnetic resonance imaging (MRI)

Magnetic resonance imaging (MRI) is more expensive than the CT scanner, but it provides pictures of the structure of the brain in much greater detail. It does so with the use of magnetic fields and radio waves rather than with X-rays. When a magnetic field is passed over the head,

reverberations are produced by hydrogen molecules. These reverberations are picked up by the scanner which can convert the activity into a structural image. This image appears in a form like that seen in Figure 4.23(a).

It is also possible to use MRI in a functional capacity, that is to examine the brain's function as well as its structure (Frackowiak *et al.*, 1997); this is called functional magnetic resonance imaging (fMRI). An image using fMRI can be seen in Figure 4.23(b). Unlike PET, which is invasive (radioactively labelled substances are introduced into the body), MRI and fMRI are non-invasive which means that they can be used to investigate the development of function. fMRI and MRI have been used to investigate similar functions to those investigated using PET: language, attention, vision, memory and so on. Both PET and MRI can be used in combination. However, both PET and MRI, while having the advantage of good spatial resolution (you can see images and structure more precisely), have the disadvantage of poor temporal resolution, that is, it is difficult to match the psychological and neural event in time precisely. The reason for this is that in PET and MRI a number of scans are taken and these are averaged over time. In the case of PET, the images are taken slowly – the activity of the brain occurs too quickly for a neuroscientist to take an image of the brain responding as it undertakes a process in real time. Some have suggested that these techniques can and should be combined with ERPs (which have good temporal resolution but poor spatial resolution). An account of what it is like to undergo a PET and MRI scan can be found in Martin (1998a, Chapter 1).

Brain damage and neuropsychological assessment

Physiological psychologists know the approximate location of the brain lesions of their laboratory animals because they placed them there. In addition, they can confirm the precise location of the lesions by examining slices of the animals' brains under a microscope after behavioural testing is completed.

Study of the human brain is a different matter. Clinical neuropsychologists attempt to understand human brain functions by studying the behaviour of people whose brains have been damaged (Cipolotti and Warrington, 1995). Most human brain lesions are the result of natural causes, such as a stroke. A stroke (also known as a cerebrovascular accident, or CVA) occurs when a blood clot obstructs an artery in the brain or when a blood vessel in the brain bursts open. In the first case, the clot blocks the supply of oxygen and nutrients to a particular region and causes that region to die. In the second case, the blood that accumulates in the brain directly damages neural tissue, partly by exerting pressure on the tissue and partly through

its toxic effects on cells. The most common causes of strokes are high blood pressure and high levels of cholesterol in the blood. We consider these factors and their effect on health in Chapter 16 on health psychology.

In order to relate brain damage to behavioural changes, neuropsychologists must know just where the damage is. Until recently, the only way they could determine the location of the damage was to examine the brain after the patient died. To do so, they needed the family's permission. Often, the patient lived for many years, and some families would not grant permission to perform an autopsy.

However, the neuroimaging techniques described above have assisted in localising the area of damage. Further information about the extent of the damage can be obtained via a procedure called neuropsychological assessment. A large series of cognitive tests (called a test battery) or individual tests are administered by a clinician to determine the effect of the damage on intellectual functioning. These tests measure such abilities as short-term memory, the ability to memorise a series of digits which increases in size with each successive presentation, object assembly, vocabulary, mental rotation, locations of objects in space, verbal fluency (naming as many objects as possible beginning with a given letter), attention and concept formation amongst others (Martin, 1998a).

When testing is complete, psychologists can devise a programme of recovery for the patient. This is called rehabilitation and is described in the section below.

Psychology in action

Rehabilitation after brain damage

When individuals suffer brain damage either through cerebrovascular accident (CVA), surgical removal of a tumour, or head injury, there is normally a severe decline in cognitive ability. Recovery to premorbid levels of functioning (that is, pre-injury levels) are usually dependent on several factors such as the age of the patient, the size and extent of the lesion, the type of function disrupted, sex and hand preference of the patient, the patient's level of intelligence before the injury and the degree of social support available. One factor which may accelerate the process of recovery is neuropsychological rehabilitation.

According to McLellan (1991), rehabilitation is an 'active process whereby people who are disabled by injury or disease work together with professional staff, relatives and members of the wider community to achieve their optimum physical,

psychological, social and vocational well-being' (p. 785). This active process is important to recovery of function following brain damage (Van den Broek et al., 1995). Not only might the impairment disrupt the patient's day-to-day living but it might also affect the patient's ability to hold down a job.

There are various programmes of rehabilitation which have been found to be successful. Programmes have been introduced for reading disorders resulting from brain injury (acquired reading disorders) (Patterson, 1994), the inability to produce or understand speech (aphasia) (Berndt & Mitchum, 1995), an inability to attend or 'see' one half of the world (spatial neglect) (Robertson et al., 1993) and memory disorders (Wilson and Powell, 1994; Glisky, 1997).

Psychology in ac

An important consideration in initiating programmes of rehabilitation is the co-operation of the patient. Successful rehabilitation can only occur if the patient is fully involved and is willing to participate in the programme. Possl and von Cramon (1996), for example, asked 130 patients with mild to moderate brain injury to rate their satisfaction with their rehabilitation programmes. Around two-thirds of the sample were satisfied but the most severely handicapped were not. Despite the high satisfaction rate, 80 per cent desired a greater degree of success in future and 52 per cent had difficulty in accepting their deficits. Seventy-seven per cent indicated that their quality of life had been reduced following injury and 52 per cent were anxious about becoming reliant on others. These results indicate that patients invest a great deal of importance, time and optimism in the process of rehabilitation.

One type of rehabilitation programme is cognitive rehabilitation, a programme based on principles derived from cognitive psychology and neuropsychology (Parente and Stapleton, 1997). Ninety per cent of respondents in one US survey of rehabilitation programmes were offered some form of cognitive rehabilitation (Mazmanian *et al.*, 1991). In cognitive rehabilitation, the patient is encouraged to engage in two types of activity: (1) 'the reinforcing, strengthening or establishing of previously learned behaviour', and (2) the establishment of 'new patterns of cognitive activity or mechanisms to compensate' for the impairment (Bergquist and Malec, 1997). Cognitive rehabilitation is the dominant form of rehabilitation in neuropsychology and shows consistently successful results in the majority of cases of mild to severe brain injury (Ho and Bennett, 1997), even when administered in computerised form (Robertson, 1990).

A common form of impairment following brain injury is memory disorder. Specific problems include deficits in learning new material and in retaining other kinds of information (Wilson and Powell, 1994). According to Wilson (1991), it may be unrealistic to expect patients to reach their premorbid level of functioning with rehabilitation. She suggests, however, that modest improvements in specific types of behaviour dependent on memory might be facilitated by

rehabilitation. Glisky (1997) and Wilson and Powell (1994) provide a good review of these types of rehabilitation. Glisky (1997) points out that rehabilitation of memory focuses either on repairing damaged memory processes or on improving memory performance although the underlying memory ability is unalterable (this latter approach is a little like treating symptoms not causes in medicine).

Some techniques of rehabilitation used to improve memory include exercises and drills, use of external aids, use of mnemonic strategies, spaced retrieval and errorless learning. The use of exercises and drills encourages patients to engage in repeated behaviours until they become so natural that they do not need prompting. Evidence for the success of this approach is not strong. The use of external aids is much more effective – using notebooks, diaries, alarms and calendars can help the patient to recover some memory function (Wilson and Moffat, 1992). Although the use of these techniques requires considerable training, once learned they easily become part of the patient's everyday behaviour (Sohlberg and Mateer, 1989). The use of mnemonic strategies has met with limited success; it would seem as if these strategies rely on remaining memory ability. If damage to the brain is considerable, the capacity for using mnemonic strategies is reduced. There is also evidence to suggest that the patient does not use these strategies spontaneously. The techniques of spaced retrieval and errorless learning all rely on implicit memory, memory for events and objects that we are not aware of processing but can remember. In *spaced retrieval*, the patient is encouraged to rehearse items after given time intervals. This technique has been quite successful (Schacter *et al.*, 1985). Similarly, Baddeley and colleagues have argued that memory problems may be due to patients being unable to avoid early errors during learning (Baddeley, 1992a). When patients were trained to avoid making such errors, their function improved and they were able to acquire information such as names of acquaintances.

There is great scope for improvement in cognitive ability after brain damage. Although not successful for all patients (for a variety of reasons), judiciously administered programmes of rehabilitation can help the patient regain some of the ability lost through brain damage.

Controversies in psychological science

Does the environment affect brain development?

The issue

The nature–nurture controversy is one of the oldest in psychology. Normally, this controversy revolves around the origins of a particular behaviour, talent or personality trait. People ask, 'Is it caused by biological or social factors?' 'Is it innate or learned?' 'Is it a result of hereditary or cultural influences?' 'Should we look for an explanation in the brain or in the environment?' Almost always, biology, innateness, heredity and the brain are placed on the 'nature' side of the equation. Society, learning, culture and the environment are placed on the 'nurture' side. Rarely does anyone question whether these groups of items form a true dichotomy.

Most modern psychologists consider the nature–nurture issue to be a relic of the past. All behaviours, talents and personality traits are the products of both types of factor: biological and social, hereditary and cultural, physiological and environmental. The task of the modern psychologist is not to find out which one of these factors is more important but to discover the particular roles played by each of them and to determine the ways in which they interact.

The evidence

Studies using humans and laboratory animals show that interactions between hereditary and environmental factors – between nature and nurture – begin very early in life. Rosenzweig and his colleagues examined the effects of environmental stimulation on the development of the brain (see Rosenzweig, 1984, for a review) by dividing litters of rats and placing the animals into two kinds of environment: enriched and impoverished. The enriched environment contained items such as running wheels, ladders, slides and 'toys' that the animals could explore and manipulate. The experimenters changed these objects every day to maximise the animals' experiences and to ensure that they would learn as much as possible. The impoverished environments were plain cages in a dimly illuminated, quiet room.

Rosenzweig and his colleagues found that the brains of rats raised in the enriched environment had a thicker cerebral cortex, a better blood supply, more pro-

tein content and more acetylcholine, a transmitter substance that appears to play an important role in learning. Subsequent studies have found changes on a microscopic level as well. Greenough and Volkmar (1973) found that the neurons of rats raised in the enriched environment had larger and more complex dendritic trees. Turner and Greenough (1985) found that synapses in their cerebral cortices were larger and that more synapses were found on each of their neurons. Changes occur even in the adult brain. Sirevaag *et al.* (1988) found that when rats were placed in an enriched environment between the ages of 30 and 60 days (young adulthood), the capillaries in their visual cortices grew more branches and their surface areas increased, presumably to accommodate the growth that was stimulated by the experience.

Environmental stimulation does not begin at the time of birth. While in the uterus, foetuses feel the movements of their mothers' bodies and hear the sounds of their mothers' voices and sounds from the external environment that pass through the abdominal wall. This aspect of foetal behaviour is discussed more fully in Chapter 12.

What is the evidence from humans that environment is important for proper neuronal development? Obviously, scientists are constrained by what they can and cannot do. It is ethically impossible for a scientist to carry out an experiment in which one group of children is deprived of an enriched environment and another is not. Instead, psychologists have relied on so-called natural experiments. For example, rarely, individuals are discovered who have been deprived of exposure to language. One famous case is that of Genie, a 13 year old girl who had been severely abused by her parents and had severe language impairment (Rymer, 1993). Genie's father harnessed her to a potty, would beat her if she made a sound and covered her cot with a wire mesh. She was kept in a room at the back of the house and was exposed to little linguistic input. When she was spotted by Los Angeles social services (only by accident when her mother had visited their offices on another abuse-related matter), the social work supervisor thought that she was 6 years old and autistic (autism is a developmental disorder which

Continued overleaf

involves impaired language communication and social behaviour). In fact, she was 13 years and 9 months old and had a vocabulary of about twenty words. One theory suggested that there was a sensitive period for the development of language – between birth and puberty – (Lennenberg, 1967) and so Genie would have been an excellent, if terrible, test of this hypothesis. When studied by a young graduate student, Susan Curtiss (Curtiss, 1977), it was found that Genie had severely impaired language ability – she could hardly talk. Although remedial treatment programmes were put in place, Genie never recovered a normal level of language.

Other theories suggested that the early years were more important than the later ones for human development. In a natural experiment, Skeels (1966) had reported that children removed in orphanages and placed in mental institutions developed normal intelligence whereas those that stayed in orphanages did not. Recently, such marked effects of environment on cognitive development have been seen in a very real context. Sir Michael Rutter and his colleagues from the Institute of Psychiatry, London, examined the extent of 'developmental catch-up' in a group of 111

Romanian orphans adopted into English families within 24 months of being born (Rutter and English and Romanian Adoptees Study Team, 1998). Compared with a control group of 52 English adopted children, the orphans showed poorer attainment of the typical developmental milestones. At 4 years of age, however, the orphans had 'caught up' with their English counterparts.

Conclusion

Evidence from animal and human studies suggests that environment is important for the development of the central nervous system and intellectual development. Ethical considerations prevent us from having a clear picture of this relationship in humans because it is not possible to conduct experiments to test the hypothesis that an enriched environment has beneficial effects on development whereas an impoverished one has detrimental effects. Natural experiments, however, suggest that environment is influential in cases where the young individual has been exposed to an impoverished environment.

Questions to think about

Techniques in psychobiology and neuroscience

- There is a wide range of techniques for studying the neurophysiology of behaviour. If you wanted to investigate the neural basis of the ability to recognise fear in facial expressions, which technique would you use and why?

- What are the limitations of the use of animal lesion experiments in understanding the underlying physiology of behaviour?

- What are the principal advantages of PET methods over ERP methods and of ERP methods over PET methods?

- What do you think would be the advantages and disadvantages of combining methods?

- Are there any functions we could not study using neuro-imaging techniques?

Control of behaviour

The brain has two roles: controlling the movements of the muscles and regulating the physiological functions of the body. The first role looks outwards towards the environment and the second looks inwards. The outward-looking role includes several functions: perceiving events in the environment, learning about them, making plans, and acting. The inward-looking role requires the brain to measure and regulate internal characteristics such as body temperature, blood pressure and nutrient levels.

Organisation of the cerebral cortex

We become aware of events in our environment by means of the five major senses: vision, audition, olfaction (smell), gustation (taste) and the somatosenses ('body' senses: touch, pain and temperature). Three areas of the cerebral cortex receive information from the sensory organs. The primary visual cortex (V1), which receives visual information, is located at the back of the brain, on the inner surfaces of the cerebral hemispheres. The primary auditory cortex, which receives auditory information, is located on the inner surface of a deep fissure in the side of the brain. The primary somatosensory cortex, a vertical strip near the middle of the cerebral hemispheres, receives information from the body senses. Different regions of the primary somatosensory cortex receive information from different regions of the body. In addition, the base of the somatosensory cortex receives information concerning taste.

Primary sensory and motor cortex

The three regions of primary sensory cortex in each hemisphere receive information from the opposite side of the body. Thus, the primary somatosensory cortex of the left hemisphere learns what the right hand is holding, the left primary visual cortex learns what is happening towards the person's right, and so on. The connections between the sensory organs and the cerebral cortex are said to be contralateral (contra 'opposite', lateral 'side').

The region of the cerebral cortex most directly involved in the control of movement is the primary motor cortex (MI), located just in front of the primary somatosensory cortex. Neurons in different parts of the primary motor cortex are connected to muscles in different parts of the body. The connections, like those of the sensory regions of the cerebral cortex, are contralateral; the left primary motor cortex controls the right side of the body and vice versa. Thus, for example, damage to the left primary motor cortex will result in paralysis in the contralateral hand and sometimes in the left hand (Haaland and Harrington, 1989). Recently, a more complex picture of these motor connections has arisen. For example, neuroimaging studies suggest that the right MI is significantly active during contralateral hand movement but that the left MI is active during ipsilateral (the same side) hand movement (Kim et al.,

1993). The hand which one predominantly uses (and this usually means to write with) appears to be related to the side of the brain that is involved in speech production, and in Chapter 10 (Language) we look at this further relationship between handedness and language.

Association cortex

The regions of primary sensory and motor cortex occupy only a small part of the cerebral cortex. The rest of the cerebral cortex accomplishes what is done between sensation and action: perceiving, learning and remembering, planning, and acting. These processes take place in the association areas of the cerebral cortex. The central fissure provides an important dividing line between the anterior (front) part of the cerebral cortex and the posterior (back) regions. The anterior region is involved in movement-related activities, such as planning and executing behaviours. The posterior part is involved in perceiving and learning.

The cerebral cortex is divided into four areas, or lobes, named after the bones of the skull that cover them: the frontal lobe, parietal lobe, temporal lobe and occipital lobe. The brain contains two of each lobe, one in each hemisphere. The frontal lobe (the 'front') includes everything in front of the central fissure. The parietal lobe (the 'wall') is located on the side of the cerebral hemisphere, just behind the central fissure, behind the frontal lobe. The temporal lobe (the 'temple') juts forward from the base of the brain, beneath the frontal and parietal lobes. The occipital lobe (ob 'in back of', caput 'head') lies at the very back of the brain, behind the parietal and temporal lobes. The lobes and association regions of the brain can be seen in Figure 4.24.

Each primary sensory area of the cerebral cortex sends information to adjacent regions, called the sensory association cortex. Circuits of neurons in the sensory association

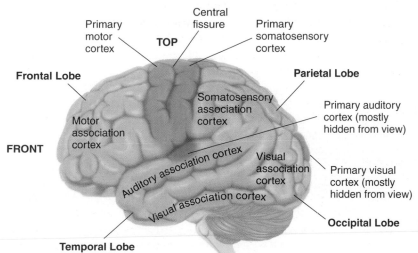

Figure 4.24

The four lobes of the cerebral cortex and the locations of the association cortex.

cortex analyse the information received from the primary sensory cortex; perception takes place there, and memories are stored there. The regions of the sensory association cortex located closest to the primary sensory areas receive information from only one sensory system. For example, the region closest to the primary visual cortex analyses visual information and stores visual memories. Regions of the sensory association cortex located far from the primary sensory areas receive information from more than one sensory system; thus, they are involved in several kinds of perception and memory. These regions make it possible to integrate information from more than one sensory system. For example, we can learn the connection between the sight of a particular face and the sound of a particular voice.

Just as regions of the sensory association cortex of the posterior part of the brain are involved in perceiving and remembering, the frontal association cortex is involved in the planning and execution of movements. The anterior part of the frontal lobe – known as the prefrontal cortex – contains the motor association cortex. The motor association cortex controls the primary motor cortex; thus, it directly controls behaviour. Obviously, we behave in response to events happening in the world around us. Therefore, the sensory association cortex of the posterior part of the brain sends information about the environment to the motor association cortex (prefrontal cortex), which translates the information into plans and actions (see Figure 4.25).

Lateralisation of function

Although the two cerebral hemispheres co-operate with each other, they do not perform identical functions. Some functions show evidence of lateralisation, that is, they are located primarily on one side of the brain (this is also called functional hemispheric asymmetry). It is commonly suggested that the left hemisphere participates in the analysis of information (making it good at recognising series of events) whereas the right hemisphere is good at putting items together (making it good at 'holistic' activities). This distinction may, however, be too simplistic (Davidson and Hugdahl, 1995). The left hemisphere does appear to be significantly more involved in aspects of language processing such as speech production and comprehension and the appreciation of the sounds in speech than is the right hemisphere.

However, as we will see in more detail in Chapter 10, the right hemisphere is better than the left hemisphere at comprehending metaphors and may undertake the linguistic duties of the left hemisphere when the left is damaged (Hugdahl, 1996). The right hemisphere also appears to be superior to the left at recognising faces, perceiving emotion and mentally rotating three-dimensional images in space. In the following chapters you will read about these and other examples of function that are lateralised in the brain; you will see that lateralisation of function does not occur in the whole of one hemisphere but in specific parts of it.

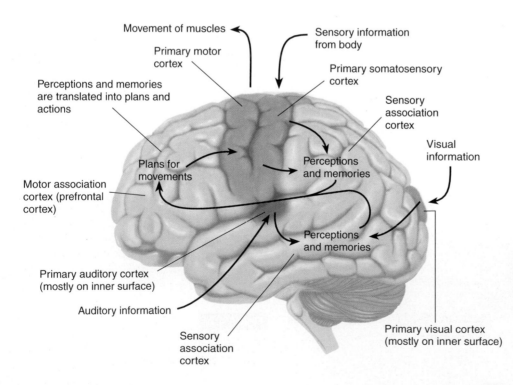

Figure 4.25

(a) The relation between the association cortex and the regions of primary sensory and motor cortex. Arrows refer to the flow of information.

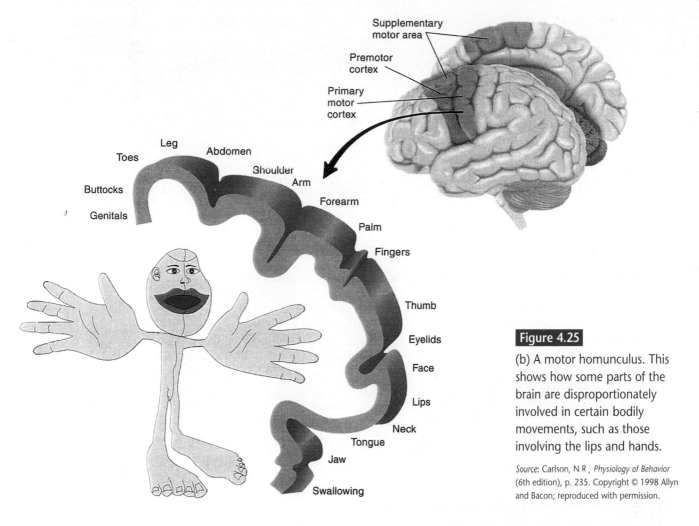

Figure 4.25

(b) A motor homunculus. This shows how some parts of the brain are disproportionately involved in certain bodily movements, such as those involving the lips and hands.

Source: Carlson, N R , *Physiology of Behavior* (6th edition), p. 235. Copyright © 1998 Allyn and Bacon; reproduced with permission.

The two cerebral hemispheres are connected by the corpus callosum, a large band of axons (Hoptman and Davidson, 1994), as seen in Figures 4.26(a) and (b). In fact, it is the brain's largest collection of connective fibre. The corpus callosum connects corresponding parts of the left and right hemispheres: the left and right temporal lobes are connected, the left and right parietal lobes are connected, and so on. Because of the corpus callosum, each region of the association cortex knows what is happening in the corresponding region of the opposite side of the brain. Some people have the corpus callosum surgically cut in order to alleviate the symptoms of epilepsy. So-called split-brain patients are interesting to psychologists because their two hemispheres do not appear to be able to communicate. We discuss the effects of split-brain surgery in more detail in Chapter 9 (Consciousness).

Vision: the occipital lobe

The primary business of the occipital lobe – and the lower part of the temporal lobe – is seeing. Total damage to the primary visual cortex, located in the inner surface of the posterior occipital lobe, produces cortical blindness (to distinguish it from other forms of blindness such as congenital blindness). Because the visual field is 'mapped' onto the surface of the primary visual cortex, a small lesion in the primary visual cortex produces a 'hole' in a specific part of the field of vision.

The visual association cortex is located in the rest of the occipital lobe and in the lower portion of the temporal lobe. Damage to the visual association cortex will not cause blindness. In fact, visual acuity may be very good; the person may be able to see small objects and may even be able to read. However, the person will not be able to recognise objects by sight. For example, when looking at a drawing of a clock, the person may say that he or she sees a circle, two short lines forming an angle in the centre of a circle, and some dots spaced along the inside of the circle, but will not be able to recognise what the picture shows. On the other hand, if the person is handed a real clock, he or she will immediately recognise it by touch. This fact tells us that the person has not simply forgotten what clocks are. Similarly, the person may fail to recognise his or her spouse by sight but will be able to do so from the sound of the spouse's voice. This deficit in visual perception is called visual agnosia (*a*- 'without', *gnosis* 'knowledge') and we will return to it in Chapter 6.

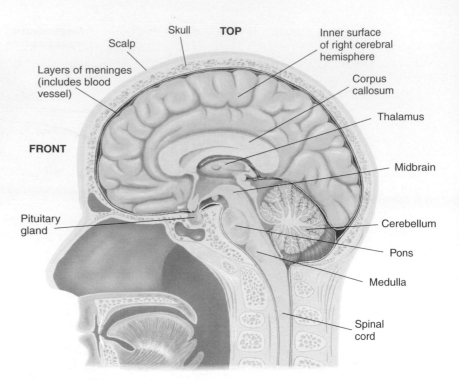

Figure 4.26

(a) A view of the brain that has been sliced through the midline. The corpus callosum unites the cerebral cortex of the two hemispheres.

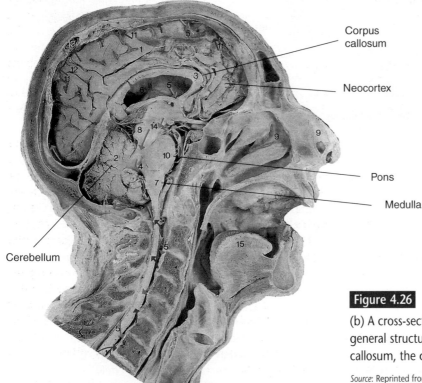

Figure 4.26

(b) A cross-section of a human head. You can clearly see the general structures of the brain: the neocortex, the corpus callosum, the cerebellum, the pons and the medulla.

Source: Reprinted from England, M.A. and Wakely, J. (1991) *A Colour Atlas of the Brain and Spinal Cord*, p. 76. Copyright © 1991, by permission of the publisher Mosby.

Audition: the temporal lobe

The temporal lobe contains both the primary auditory cortex and the auditory association cortex. The primary auditory cortex is hidden from view on the inner surface of the upper temporal lobe. The auditory association cortex is located on the lateral surface of the upper temporal lobe.

Damage to the primary auditory cortex leads to hearing losses, while damage to the auditory association cortex produces more complex deficits. Damage to the left auditory association cortex causes severe language deficits. People with such damage are no longer able to comprehend speech, presumably because they have lost the circuits of neurons that decode speech sounds. However, the deficit is more severe than that. They also lose the ability to produce meaningful speech; their speech becomes a jumble of words. Language deficits produced by brain damage are described in more detail in Chapter 10.

Damage to the right auditory association cortex does not seriously affect speech perception or production, but it does affect the ability to recognise non-speech sounds, including patterns of tones and rhythms. The damage can also impair the ability to perceive the location of sounds in the environment. As we will see later, the right hemisphere is very important in the perception of space. The contribution of the right temporal lobe to this function is to participate in perceiving the placement of sounds.

Somatosensation and spatial perception: the parietal lobe

The primary sensory function of the parietal lobe is perception of the body. However, the association cortex of the parietal lobe is involved in much more than somatosensation. Damage to a particular region of the association cortex of the left parietal lobe can disrupt the ability to read or write without causing serious impairment in the ability to talk and understand the speech of other people. Damage to another part of the parietal lobe impairs a person's ability to draw. When the left parietal lobe is damaged, the primary deficit seems to be in the person's ability to make precise hand movements; their drawing looks shaky and sloppy. In contrast, the primary deficit produced by damage to the right parietal lobe is perceptual. The person can analyse a picture into its parts but has trouble integrating these parts into a consistent whole. Thus, he or she has difficulty drawing a coherent picture. We will look at disorders such as these in Chapter 6 (Perception).

Most neuropsychologists believe that the left parietal lobe plays an important role in our ability to keep track of the location of the moving parts of our own body, whereas the right parietal lobe helps us to keep track of the space around us. People with right parietal lobe damage usually have difficulty with spatial tasks, such as reading a map. People with left parietal lobe damage usually have difficulty identifying parts of their own bodies by name. For example, when asked to point to their elbows, they may actually point to their shoulders. People with damage to the left parietal lobe also often have difficulty performing arithmetic calculations. This deficit is probably related to other spatial functions of the parietal lobe. Damage to the parietal lobes makes it impossible for people to keep the imaginary numbers in place and remember what they are.

The **posterior part of the parietal cortex (PPC)** may also be specialised for storing representations of motor actions (Milner, 1998). Snyder *et al.* (1997) found that some neurons in the PPC of two adult macaque monkeys were active before and during visually guided arm movements whereas others were active during eye movements. However, rather than directing attention to objects in space, the PPC is responsible for the intention to move. There may be visual neurons in the PPC which are responsible for visually guided movement (Sakata *et al.*, 1997).

Planning and moving: the frontal lobe

Because it contains the motor cortex, the principal function of the frontal lobe is to mediate motor activity (Passingham, 1995). However, it is also involved in planning, changing strategies, being aware of oneself, evaluating emotionally related stimuli and performing a variety of spontaneous behaviours. We consider the function of the frontal lobe in detail in Chapters 11 (Intelligence and thinking) and 13 (Motivation and emotion).

Damage to the primary motor cortex produces a very specific effect: paralysis of the side of the body opposite to the brain damage. If a portion of the region is damaged, then only the corresponding parts of the body will be paralysed (Passingham, 1995). However, damage to the prefrontal cortex produces more complex behavioural deficits. For example, the person with frontal lobe damage will react to events in the environment but show deficits in initiating behaviour. When a person with damage to the prefrontal cortex is asked to say or write as many words as possible or is asked to describe as many uses for an object as possible, he or she will have great difficulty coming up with more than a few, even though he or she has no problem understanding words or identifying objects by name (Eslinger and Grattan, 1993).

People with damage to the frontal lobe also tend to have difficulty changing strategies. If given a task to solve, they may solve it readily. However, they will fail to abandon the strategy and learn a new one if the problem is changed. The Wisconsin Card Sorting Task, for example, presents patients with packs of cards on which are printed symbols of different shape, colour or number. The experimenter decides on a sorting criterion (shape, for example) and the patient has to detect which criterion it is by sorting the cards into piles, receiving feedback from the experimenter. When the criterion unexpectedly shifts, some patients are unable to detect this shift and carry on responding as if the previous criterion still applied. This is called **perseveration**. However, not all frontal lobe patients will exhibit this behaviour (Anderson *et al.*, 1991).

People with damage to certain areas of the frontal lobe often have rather bland personalities. They seem indifferent to events that would normally be expected to affect them emotionally (Stuss *et al.*, 1992). For example, they may show no signs of distress at the death of a close relative. They have little insight into their own problems and are uncritical of their performance on various tasks (Brazzelli *et al.*, 1994; Stuss *et al.*, 1992; Cicerone and Tanenbaum, 1997; Hornak *et al.*, 1996). The most famous case study of frontal lobe damage resulting in shifts in emotional and social behaviour is that of Phineas Gage, a man we will return to in Chapter 13.

In terms of daily living, the most important consequences of damage to the frontal lobe are probably lack of foresight and difficulty in planning. A person with frontal lobe damage might perform fairly well on a test of intelligence but be unable to hold a job (Eslinger and Damasio, 1985). Sequencing – the organisation of material in logical, correct or learned order – is grossly impaired in frontal patients (Sirigu *et al.*, 1995). Often, when given tasks that tap everyday activities (such as undertaking an errand), patients with frontal lobe damage perform poorly (Shallice and Burgess, 1991).

Patients with damage to different regions of the frontal lobe exhibit different symptoms. For example, patients with damage to the orbitofrontal cortex (the tip of the frontal lobes) tend to exhibit impairment in social behaviour, personality and emotional expression but have relatively intact intellect. Eslinger and Damasio's (1985) patient, EVR, is a case in point. EVR, an ex-accountant who had a frontal lobe tumour surgically removed, has superior intellect but an impaired ability to plan and organise his daily life. He performs at normal levels on tests designed to tap perseveration (such as the Wisconsin Card Sorting Task) and he has superior IQ. However, his ability to maintain close relationships and a job and his ability to plan and organise his life was grossly impaired.

As you saw in Chapter 1, Paul Broca discovered that damage to a region of the left frontal lobe disrupts speech. This region, which we now call Broca's area, lies just in front of the 'face' region of the primary motor cortex, as you can see from Figure 4.27. Thus, Broca's area controls the muscles used for talking. Circuits of neurons located in Broca's area appear to contain the memories of the sequences of muscular movements that are needed to pronounce words, a topic we return to in Chapter 10.

Surgical treatment of seizure disorders

The neural circuits in the brain must maintain a close balance between excitation and inhibition. If there is too much inhibition, the brain cannot do its work. If there is too much excitation, neural activity gets out of control and causes a seizure disorder (otherwise known as epilepsy). During a seizure, the neurons in the brain fire wildly and uncontrollably, disrupting normal brain functions. Most seizure disorders can be controlled by drugs, but occasionally neurosurgeons must perform an operation known as seizure surgery.

Most seizure disorders are caused by the presence of one or more seizure foci in the brain – regions of scar tissue that irritate the brain tissue surrounding them. From time to time, excitation spreads throughout the brain, causing a seizure. Seizure surgery involves removing the abnormal brain tissue that contains a seizure focus. One of the pioneers of seizure surgery, the late Wilder Penfield, developed the operation, which has provided us with some interesting information about the functions of the human brain (Penfield and Jasper, 1954). The patient's head is first shaved. Then, with the patient under local anaesthesia, the surgeon cuts the scalp and saws through the skull so that a piece of bone can be removed and the brain itself exposed. The patient is conscious throughout the entire procedure.

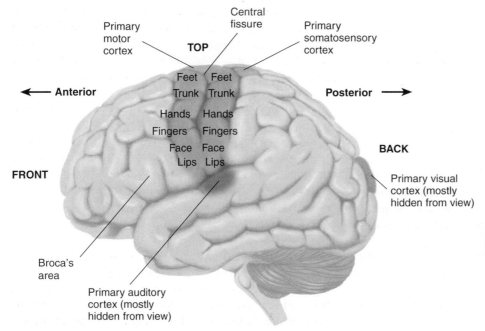

Figure 4.27

Broca's area, located just in front of the face region of the primary motor cortex. This region is involved in the control of speech.

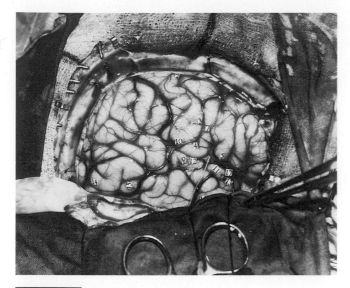

Figure 4.28

The appearance of the cortical surface of a conscious patient whose brain has been stimulated. The points of stimulation are indicated by the numbered tags placed there by the surgeon.

Source: Case M.M., in Wilder Penfield, *The Mystery of the Mind: A Critical Study of Consciousness and the Human Brain*, with Discussions by William Feindel, Charles Hendel and Charles Symonds. Copyright © 1975 by Princeton University Press, Figure 4, p. 24 reprinted by permission of Princeton University Press.

When removing the damaged part of the brain, the surgeon wants to cut away all the abnormal tissue – including the seizure focus – while sparing healthy neural tissue that performs important functions, such as the comprehension and production of speech. For this reason, Penfield first stimulated parts of the brain to determine what functions they performed so he could decide which regions he could safely remove. Penfield touched the tip of a metal electrode to various parts of the brain (as seen in Figure 4.28) and observed the effects of stimulation on the patient's behaviour.

For example, stimulation of one part of the brain produced movement, and stimulation of another part produced sensations of sounds. Stimulation of parts of the brain involved in verbal communication stopped the patient's ongoing speech and disrupted the ability to understand what the surgeon and his associates were saying. Penfield placed a sterile, numbered piece of paper on each point he stimulated. He then photographed the exposed brain with its numbered locations before removing the slips of paper and proceeding with the surgery. After the operation, he could compare his notes about the patient's behaviour with the photograph of the patient's brain showing the locations of the points of stimulation. A more recent description is given by Calvin and Ojemann (1994) in their book *Conversations with Neil's Brain*.

Questions to think about

The cerebral lobes and their function

- What effect do you think that hand preference has on the organisation of the brain?
- Do you think that your sex affects your brain's organisation and your ability to perform certain cognitive tasks?
- Do the lobes of the brain perform specific functions? What evidence is there for and against this hypothesis?
- The frontal lobe comprises about one-third of the entire cortex. Is it, therefore, the most important cerebral lobe?
- Explain why a brain lesion that impairs a person's speech often also affects movements of the right side of the body.
- You see a cream cake that you want to eat. You reach out for it. Which brain regions would be involved in this process?

Control of internal functions and automatic behaviour

The cortex consists of only the outer three millimetres of the surface of the cerebral hemispheres. There are other structures such as the brain stem, the cerebellum and the interior of the cerebral hemispheres which are important to the regulation of behaviour. The cerebellum helps the cerebral hemispheres to control movement and to initiate some automatic movements, such as postural adjustment, on its own. The brain stem and much of the interior of the cerebral hemispheres are involved in homeostasis and control of species-typical behaviours. Homeostasis (from the root words *homoios* 'similar', and *stasis* 'standstill') refers to maintaining a proper balance of physiological variables such as temperature, concentration of fluids, and the amount of nutrients stored within the body. Species-typical behaviours are the more-or-less automatic behaviours exhibited by most members of a species that are important to survival, such as eating, drinking, fighting, courting, mating and caring for offspring.

The brain stem

The brain stem contains three structures: the medulla, the pons, and the midbrain. Figure 4.29 shows a view of the left side of the brain. The brain has been rotated slightly so that we can see some of the front of the brain stem, and the cerebral hemispheres are shown lightly so that the details

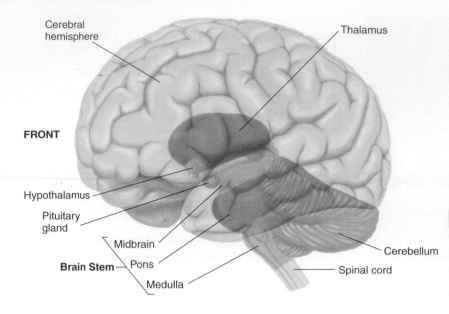

Cerebral
hemisphere

Thalamus

FRONT

Hypothalamus

Pituitary
gland

Midbrain

Cerebellum

Brain Stem — Pons

Spinal cord

Medulla

Figure 4.29

The divisions of the brain stem: the medulla, the pons and the midbrain. The thalamus, hypothalamus and pituitary gland are attached to the end of the brain stem.

of the brain stem can be seen. We also see the thalamus, the hypothalamus and the pituitary gland.

The brain stem contains circuits of neurons that control functions vital to the survival of the organism in particular and of the species in general. For example, circuits of neurons in the **medulla**, the part of the brain stem closest to the spinal cord, control heart rate, blood pressure, rate of respiration, and – especially in simpler animals – crawling or swimming motions. Circuits of neurons in the **pons**, the part of the brain just above the medulla, control some of the stages of sleep, and circuits of neurons in the **midbrain** control movements used in fighting and sexual behaviour and decrease sensitivity to pain while engaged in these activities.

The cerebellum

The cerebellum plays an important role in the control of movement. It receives sensory information, especially about the position of body parts, so it knows what the parts of the body are doing. It also receives information from the cortex of the frontal lobes, so it knows what movements the frontal lobes intend to accomplish. The cerebellum is basically a computer that compares the location of the body parts with the intended movements and assists the frontal lobes in executing these movements. Without the cerebellum, the frontal lobes would produce jerky, unco-ordinated, inaccurate movements – which is exactly what happens when a person's cerebellum is damaged. Besides helping the frontal lobes to accomplish their tasks, the cerebellum monitors information regarding posture and balance, to keep us from falling down when we stand or walk, and produces eye movements that compensate for changes in the position of the head.

Recently, some studies have suggested that the cerebellum may also play a role in people's cognitive abilities and emotional expression (Schmahmann and Sherman, 1998). Verbal fluency and performance on problem-solving tasks is impaired in patients whose cerebellum has been destroyed (Grafman *et al.*, 1992; Appollonio *et al.*, 1993). Cerebellar damage can interfere with people's ability to speak, but the deficit seems to involve control of the speech muscles rather than the cognitive abilities involved in language (Kingma *et al.*, 1994; Pollack *et al.*, 1995). It is possible that the varied deficits seen with cerebellar damage the result of disruption of pathways in the cerebellum which link with other parts of the brain such as the prefrontal and posterior parietal cortex and the limbic system (Schmahmann and Sherman, 1998).

Subcortical structures

The thalamus

If you stripped away the cerebral cortex and the white matter that lies under it, you would find a collection of brain structures. These are called subcortical brain structures. One of the most important is the **thalamus**, located in the heart of the cerebral hemispheres (*thalamos* is Greek for 'inner chamber'). The thalamus is divided into two parts, one in each cerebral hemisphere. Each part looks rather like a football, with the long axis oriented from front to back.

The thalamus performs two basic functions. The first – and most primitive – is similar to that of the cerebral cortex. Parts of the thalamus receive sensory information, other parts integrate the information, and still other parts assist in the control of movements through their influence on circuits of neurons in the brain stem. However, the second role of the thalamus – that of a relay station for the cortex – is even more important. As the cerebral hemispheres evolved, the cerebral cortex grew in size and its significance for behavioural functions increased. The thalamus took on the function of receiving sensory information from the sensory organs, performing some simple analyses, and passing the results on to the primary sensory cortex. Thus, all sensory information (except for olfaction, which is the most primitive of all sensory systems) is sent to the thalamus before it reaches the cerebral cortex.

The hypothalamus

Hypo- means 'less than' or 'beneath', and as its name suggests, the hypothalamus is located below the thalamus, at the base of the brain. The hypothalamus is a small region, consisting of less than 1 cubic centimetre of tissue (smaller than a grape). Its relative importance far exceeds its relative size.

The hypothalamus, like the brain stem, participates in homeostasis and species-typical behaviours. It receives sensory information, including information from receptors inside the organs of the body; thus, it is informed about changes in the organism's physiological status. It also contains specialised sensors that monitor various characteristics of the blood that flows through the brain, such as temperature, nutrient content and amount of dissolved salts. In turn, the hypothalamus controls the **pituitary gland**, an endocrine gland attached by a stalk to the base of the hypothalamus.

Hormones are chemicals produced by endocrine glands (from the Greek *endo-* 'within', and *krinein* 'to secrete'). **Endocrine glands** secrete hormones into the blood supply, which carries them to all parts of the body. Hormones are similar to transmitter substances or neuromodulators, except that they act over much longer distances. Like transmitter substances and neuromodulators, they produce their effects by stimulating receptor molecules. These receptor molecules are located on (or in) particular cells. The presence of a hormone causes physiological reactions in these cells, which are known as **target cells**. Almost every cell of the body contains hormone receptors of one kind or other. This includes neurons; hormones that affect behaviour do so by altering the activity of particular groups of neurons in the brain. For example, the sex hormones have important effects on behaviour and are discussed in later chapters.

The pituitary gland has been called the 'master gland' because the hormones it secretes act on target cells in other endocrine glands; thus, the pituitary gland controls the activity of other endocrine glands. By controlling the pituitary gland, the hypothalamus controls the entire endocrine system. Figure 4.30 shows some of the endocrine glands and the functions they regulate.

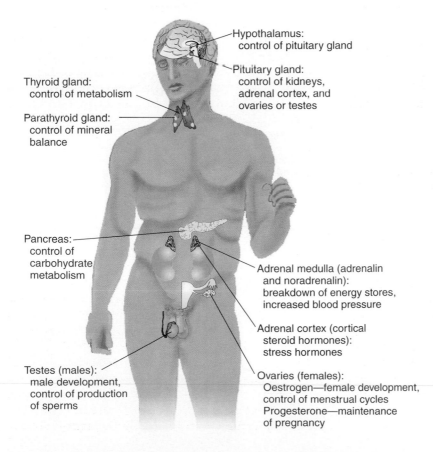

Thyroid gland: control of metabolism

Parathyroid gland: control of mineral balance

Pancreas: control of carbohydrate metabolism

Testes (males): male development, control of production of sperms

Hypothalamus: control of pituitary gland

Pituitary gland: control of kidneys, adrenal cortex, and ovaries or testes

Adrenal medulla (adrenalin and noradrenalin): breakdown of energy stores, increased blood pressure

Adrenal cortex (cortical steroid hormones): stress hormones

Ovaries (females): Oestrogen—female development, control of menstrual cycles Progesterone—maintenance of pregnancy

Figure 4.30

The location and primary functions of the principal endocrine glands.

The hypothalamus also controls much of the activity of the autonomic nervous system (ANS), which consists of nerves that control the functions of the glands and internal organs. The nerves of the autonomic nervous system control activities such as sweating, shedding tears, salivating, secreting digestive juices, changing the size of blood vessels (which alters blood pressure) and secreting some hormones. The autonomic nervous system has two branches. The sympathetic branch directs activities that involve the expenditure of energy. For example, activity of the sympathetic branch can increase the flow of blood to the muscles when we are about to fight someone or run away from a dangerous situation. The parasympathetic branch controls quiet activities, such as digestion of food. Activity of the parasympathetic branch stimulates the secretion of digestive enzymes and increases the flow of blood to the digestive system, as seen in Figure 4.31.

Psychophysiologists can monitor the activity of the autonomic nervous system and its relation to psychological phenomena such as emotion. For example, when a person is angry, heart rate and blood pressure rise. The lie detector (described in Chapter 13) works by recording emotional responses controlled by the autonomic nervous system.

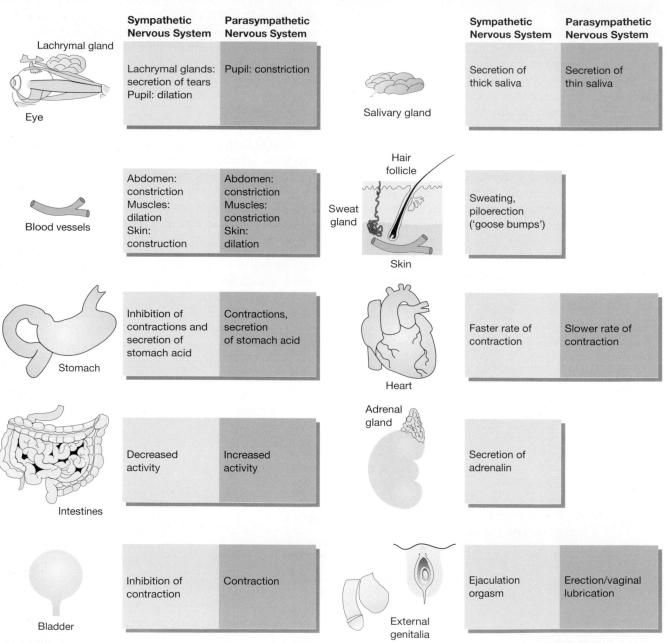

Figure 4.31

The autonomic nervous system and the organs it controls.

The homeostatic functions of the hypothalamus can involve either internal physiological changes or behaviour. For example, the hypothalamus is involved in the control of body temperature. It can directly lower body temperature by causing sweating to occur, or it can raise it by causing shivering to occur. If these measures are inadequate, it can send messages to the cerebral cortex that will cause the person to engage in a learned behaviour, such as turning on an air conditioner or putting another log on the fire. Damage to the hypothalamus can cause impaired regulation of body temperature, changes in food intake, sterility and stunting of growth.

The limbic system

The limbic system, a set of structures located in the cerebral hemispheres, plays an important role in learning and in the expression of emotion. Originally, this area was termed rhinencephalon (or 'smell brain') because the areas within it were thought to be involved primarily in the sense of smell.

The limbic system consists of several regions of the limbic cortex – the cerebral cortex located around the edge of the cerebral hemispheres where they join with the brain stem (*limbus* means 'border'; hence the term 'limbic system'). Besides the limbic cortex, the most important components of the limbic system are the amygdala and the hippocampus. The amygdala and the hippocampus get their names from their shapes; amygdala means 'almond' and hippocampus means 'sea horse'.

Figure 4.32 shows a view of the limbic cortex, located on the inner surface of the cerebral hemisphere. The left hippocampus and amygdala, located in the middle of the temporal lobe, are shown projecting out into the place where the missing left hemisphere would be. We can also see the right hippocampus and amygdala, 'ghosted in'.

Damage to the amygdala, a cluster of neurons located deep in the temporal lobe, affects emotional behaviour, especially negative emotions such as those caused by painful, threatening or stressful events (Adolphs *et al.*, 1995, 1999; Morris *et al.*, 1996). In addition, the amygdala controls physiological reactions that help provide energy for short-term activities such as fighting or fleeing (LeDoux, 1996). However, if these reactions are prolonged, they can lead to stress-related illnesses. If an animal's amygdala is destroyed, the animal no longer reacts emotionally to events that normally produce stress and anxiety. We might think that an animal would be better off if it did not become 'stressed out' by unpleasant or threatening situations. However, research has shown that animals with damaged amygdalas cannot survive in the wild. The animals fail to compete successfully for food and other resources, and often act in ways that provoke attacks by other animals. The role of the amygdala in emotion and stress is returned to in Chapters 13 and 16.

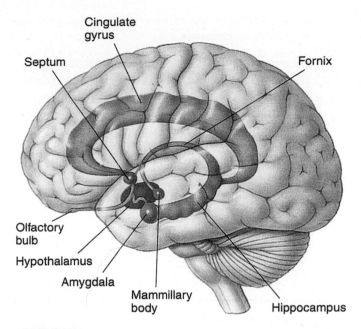

Figure 4.32

Schematic drawing illustrating the structures of the limbic system.

Source: Pinel, J., *Biopsychology* (3rd edition). Boston: Allyn and Bacon. Copyright © 1997 by Allyn and Bacon; reproduced with permission.

The hippocampus (or hippocampal formation), a collection of structures located just behind the amygdala, plays an important role in memory. People with lesions of the hippocampus lose the ability to learn anything new (Milner *et al.*, 1968; Keane *et al.*, 1995). For them, 'yesterday' is always the time before their brain damage occurred; everything after that slips away, just as the memory of dreams often slips away from a person soon after awakening. The hippocampus is also responsible for navigating one's way in the environment (Maguire *et al.*, 1997, 1998) and we will look at its role in memory and amnesia again in Chapter 8.

Questions to think about

Subcortical structures

- The cerebellum is one of the largest parts of the brain and contains billions of neurons. What does this fact suggest about the complexity of the task of co-ordinating movements of the body?

- The cerebellum is involved in cognition, movement co-ordination and emotion. The amygdala is involved in

Questions to think about (continued overleaf)

the recognition and expression of fear. Does this suggest that no subcortical structure performs just one function?

■ The subcortex is one of the oldest parts of the brain. Is there any relationship between this fact and the functions that the structures of this system performs?

■ Damage to different parts of the corpus callosum tends to disrupt different functions. Why do you think this is so?

■ If a patient's brain is electrically stimulated and the patient spontaneously recalls a memory, why can we not say that the stimulated area is the region in the brain responsible for memory?

Drugs and behaviour

Communication between neurons involves the release of transmitter substances. Neurons release many different kinds of transmitter substance, and various drugs can affect the production or release of one or more of these chemicals. Drugs can also mimic the effects of transmitter substances on receptor molecules, block these effects, or interfere with the reuptake of a transmitter substance once it is released. Via these mechanisms, a drug can alter the perceptions, thoughts, and behaviours controlled by particular transmitter substances.

Stimulating or inhibiting the release of transmitter substances

Some drugs stimulate certain terminal buttons to release their transmitter substance continuously, even when the axon is not firing. Other drugs prevent certain terminal buttons from releasing their transmitter substance when the axon fires. The effects of most of these drugs are more-or-less specific to one transmitter substance. Because different classes of neuron release different transmitter substances, these drugs affect only a selected set of neurons. An example of a stimulating drug is the venom of the black widow spider, which causes the release of a transmitter substance called acetylcholine, as illustrated by Figure 4.33. In contrast, botulinum toxin, a poison that is sometimes present in improperly canned food, prevents the release of acetylcholine. An adult will almost certainly survive the bite of a black widow spider; the symptoms are severe abdominal cramps. However, an extremely small amount of botulinum toxin – less than a millionth of a gram – is fatal. The victim becomes paralysed and suffocates to death.

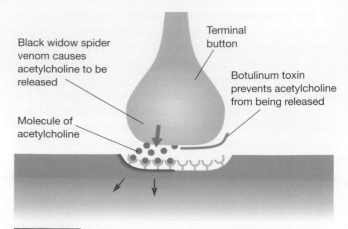

Figure 4.33

Drugs that affect the release of a neurotransmitter, acetylcholine. Black widow spider venom causes acetylcholine to be released. Botulinum toxin prevents the release of acetylcholine from the terminal buttons.

Stimulating or blocking postsynaptic receptor molecules

Transmitter substances produce their effects by stimulating postsynaptic receptor molecules, which excite or inhibit postsynaptic neurons by opening ion channels and permitting ions to enter or leave the neurons. Some drugs duplicate the effects of particular transmitter substances by directly stimulating particular kinds of receptor molecules. If we use the lock-and-key analogy to describe the effects of a transmitter substance on a receptor molecule, then a drug that stimulates receptor molecules works like a master key, turning the receptor molecules on even when the transmitter substance is not present. For example, nicotine stimulates acetylcholine receptors located on neurons in certain regions of the brain (see Figure 4.34). In low doses, this stimulation has a pleasurable (and addictive) excitatory effect; in high doses, it can cause convulsions and death.

Some drugs block receptor molecules, making them inaccessible to the transmitter substance and thus inhibiting synaptic transmission. A drug that blocks receptor molecules 'plugs up' the lock so that the key will no longer fit into it. For example, a poison called curare was discovered by South American Indians, who use it on the darts of their blowguns. This drug blocks the acetylcholine receptors that are located on muscle fibres. The curare prevents synaptic transmission in muscles. The paralysed victim is unable to breathe and consequently suffocates.

Some medically useful chemicals work by blocking receptor molecules. For example, antipsychotic drugs alleviate the symptoms of schizophrenia, a serious mental disorder, by blocking receptor molecules in the brain that

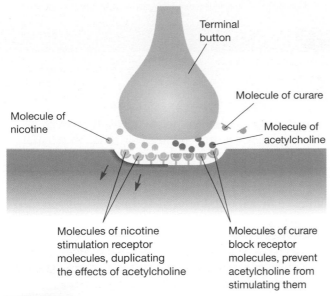

Molecule of
nicotine

Terminal
button

Molecule of curare

Molecule of
acetylcholine

Molecules of nicotine
stimulation receptor
molecules, duplicating
the effects of acetylcholine

Molecules of curare
block receptor
molecules, prevent
acetylcholine from
stimulating them

Figure 4.34

Drugs that interact with receptor molecules in the postsynaptic
membrane. Nicotine directly stimulates the receptor molecules.
Curare blocks receptor molecules and thus prevents
acetylcholine from activating them.

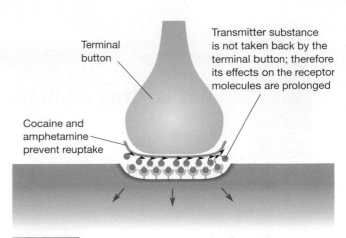

Terminal
button

Transmitter substance
is not taken back by the
terminal button; therefore
its effects on the receptor
molecules are prolonged

Cocaine and
amphetamine
prevent reuptake

Figure 4.35

Drugs that block reuptake. Cocaine and amphetamine block
the reuptake of certain transmitter substances, thus prolonging
their effects on the receptor molecules in the postsynaptic
membrane.

are normally stimulated by a transmitter substance called
dopamine. This fact has led some investigators to suggest
that the symptoms of schizophrenia may be caused by malfunctions of neurons that release dopamine. We discuss
antipsychotic drugs later in this chapter and in Chapter 17.

Inhibiting reuptake

The effects of most transmitter substances are kept brief by
the process of reuptake. Molecules of the transmitter substance are released by a terminal button, they stimulate the
receptor molecules in the postsynaptic membrane for a
fraction of a second, and then they are pumped back into
the terminal button. Some drugs inhibit the process of
reuptake so that molecules of the transmitter substance
continue to stimulate the postsynaptic receptor molecules
for a long time. Therefore, inhibition of reuptake increases
the effect of the transmitter substance. The excitatory
effects of cocaine and amphetamine are produced by their
ability to inhibit the reuptake of certain transmitter substances, including dopamine (see Figure 4.35).

Sedatives

Some drugs depress behaviour, causing relaxation, sedation, or even loss of consciousness. These are called **anti-
anxiety** or **anxiolytic drugs**. In most cases, the depression

is caused by stimulation of a class of receptor molecules
that is normally activated by neuromodulators produced
by the brain. **Barbiturates** depress the brain's activity by
stimulating a particular category of neuromodulator receptors. In low doses, barbiturates have a calming effect. In
progressively higher doses, they produce difficulty in walking and talking, unconsciousness, coma and death.
Barbiturates are abused by people who want to achieve the
relaxing, calming effect of the drugs, especially to counteract the anxiety and irritability that can be produced by
stimulants. They are occasionally prescribed as medication
for sleep, but they are a very poor choice for this purpose
because they suppress dreaming and produce a particularly
unrefreshing sleep. In addition, a dose of a barbiturate sufficient to induce sleep is not that much lower than a fatal
dose. Ideally, the therapeutic dose of a drug is much lower
than a fatal dose.

Many anti-anxiety drugs are members of a family known
as the **benzodiazepines**, which include the well-known
tranquilliser Valium (diazepam). These drugs, too, stimulate some sort of neuromodulator receptors located on neurons in various parts of the brain, including the amygdala.
The benzodiazepines are very effective in reducing anxiety
and are sometimes used to treat people who are afflicted by
periodic attacks of severe anxiety. In addition, some benzodiazepines serve as sleep medications. These behavioural
effects suggest that they mimic the effects of neuromodulators involved in the regulation of mood and the control
of sleep.

By far the most commonly used depressant drug is ethyl
alcohol, the active ingredient in alcoholic beverages. This
drug has effects similar to those of the barbiturates: Larger
and larger doses of alcohol reduce anxiety, disrupt motor

Controversies in psychological science

What is 'drug addiction'?

The issue

Some drugs have very potent reinforcing effects, which lead some people to abuse them or even to become addicted to them. Many people (psychologists, health professionals and lay people) believe that 'true' addiction is caused by the unpleasant physiological effects that occur when an addict tries to stop taking the drug. For example, Eddy *et al.* (1965) defined physical dependence as 'an adaptive state that manifests itself by intense physical disturbances when the administration of a drug is suspended' (p. 723). In contrast, they defined psychic dependence as a condition in which a drug produces 'a feeling of satisfaction and a psychic drive that requires periodic or continuous administration of the drug to produce pleasure or to avoid discomfort' (p. 723). Most people regard the latter as less important than the former. But, as we shall see, the reverse is true.

The evidence

For many years, heroin addiction has been considered as the prototype for all drug addictions. People who habitually take heroin (or other opiates) become physically dependent on the drug; that is, they show tolerance and withdrawal symptoms. Tolerance is the decreased sensitivity to a drug that comes from its continued use; the drug user must take larger and larger amounts of the drug in order for it to be effective. Once a person has taken an opiate regularly enough to develop tolerance, that person will suffer withdrawal symptoms if he or she stops taking the drug. Withdrawal symptoms are primarily the opposite of the effects of the drug itself. For example, heroin produces euphoria; withdrawal from it produces dysphoria – a feeling of anxious misery (euphoria and dysphoria mean 'easy to bear' and 'hard to bear', respectively). Heroin produces constipation; withdrawal from it produces nausea, cramping and diarrhoea. Heroin produces relaxation; withdrawal from it produces agitation.

Most investigators believe that the withdrawal symptoms are produced by the body's attempt to compensate for the unusual condition of heroin intoxication. That is, most systems of the body, including those controlled by the brain, are regulated so that they stay at an optimal value. When a drug artificially changes these systems for a prolonged time, homeostatic mechanisms begin to produce the opposite reaction, which partially compensates for the disturbance from the optimal value. These compensatory mechanisms account for the fact that more and more heroin must be taken in order to achieve the effects that were produced when the person first started taking the drug. They also account for the symptoms of withdrawal: when the person stops taking the drug, the compensatory mechanisms make themselves felt, unopposed by the action of the drug.

co-ordination and then cause unconsciousness, coma and finally death. The effects of alcohol and barbiturates are additive: a moderate dose of alcohol plus a moderate dose of barbiturates can be fatal.

The primary effect of alcohol appears to be similar to that of the benzodiazepines: it stimulates some type of neuromodulator receptor. Suzdak *et al.* (1986) discovered a drug that reverses alcohol intoxication, presumably by blocking some type of neuromodulator receptor. Although the behavioural effects of alcohol may be mediated by neuromodulator receptors, alcohol has other, potentially fatal effects on all cells of the body. Alcohol destabilises the membrane of cells, interfering with their functions. Thus, a person who takes some of the antialcohol drug could go on to drink himself or herself to death without becoming drunk in the process.

Stimulants

Several categories of drugs stimulate the central nervous system and thus activate behaviour. Because of the effects some of these drugs have on the neural circuits involved in reinforcement (reward), they tend to be abused. Two very popular stimulant drugs, amphetamine and cocaine, have almost identical effects: they inhibit the reuptake of dopamine and thus strengthen the effectiveness of synapses that use this transmitter substance. As we shall see in Chapter 13, reinforcing stimuli – such as food for a hungry animal, water for a thirsty one, or sexual contact for a sexually aroused one – exert their behavioural effects largely by increasing the activity of a circuit of dopamine-secreting neurons. Thus, amphetamine and cocaine mimic the effects of reinforcing stim-

Heroin addiction has provided such a striking example of drug dependence that some authorities have concluded that 'real' addiction does not occur unless a drug causes tolerance and withdrawal. Withdrawal symptoms make it difficult for a person to stop taking heroin – they help keep the person hooked. But withdrawal symptoms do not explain why a person becomes a heroin addict in the first place; that fact is explained by the drug's reinforcing effect. Certainly, people do not start taking heroin so that they will become physically dependent on it and feel miserable when they go without it. Instead, they begin taking it because it makes them feel good.

Even though the withdrawal effects of heroin make it difficult to stop taking the drug, these effects alone are not sufficient to keep most people hooked. In fact, when the cost of the habit gets too high, some addicts who stop taking heroin experience 'cold turkey'. Doing so is not as painful as most people believe; withdrawal symptoms have been described as similar to a bad case of influenza – unpleasant, but survivable. After a week or two, when their nervous systems adapt to the absence of the drug, these addicts recommence their habit, which now costs less to sustain. If their only reason for taking the drug was to avoid unpleasant withdrawal symptoms, they would be incapable of following this strategy. The reason that people take – and continue to take – drugs such as heroin is that the drugs give them a pleasurable 'rush'; in other words, the drugs have a reinforcing effect on their behaviour.

There are two other lines of evidence that contradict the assertion that drug addiction is caused by physical dependence. First, some very potent drugs, including cocaine, do not produce physical dependency. That is, people who take the drug do not show tolerance; and if they stop, they do not show any withdrawal symptoms. As a result, experts believed for many years that cocaine was a relatively innocuous drug, not in the same league as heroin. Obviously, they were wrong; cocaine is even more addictive than heroin. As a matter of fact, laboratory animals who can press a lever and give themselves injections of cocaine are more likely to die than are those who can give themselves injections of heroin. Secondly, some drugs produce physical dependence (tolerance and withdrawal symptoms) but are not abused (Jaffe, 1985). The reason they are not abused is that they do not have reinforcing effects on behaviour – they are just not any fun to take.

Conclusion

The most important lesson we can learn from the misguided distinction between 'physiological' and 'psychological' addiction is that we should never underestimate the importance of psychological factors. Given that behaviour is controlled by circuits of neurons in the brain, even psychological factors involve physiological mechanisms. People often pay more attention to physiological symptoms than psychological ones – they consider them more real. But behavioural research indicates that an exclusive preoccupation with physiology can hinder our understanding of the causes of addiction.

uli. Free-base cocaine (crack) is particularly addictive. The drug has an immediate effect on the reuptake of dopamine and produces such a profound feeling of euphoria and pleasure that the person wants to repeat the experience again and again.

Cocaine and amphetamine, if taken in large enough doses for a few days, can produce the symptoms of paranoid schizophrenia – a serious mental disorder described in Chapter 17 (Abnormal psychology). Heavy users of these drugs suffer from hallucinations and their thoughts become confused and difficult to control. They may come to believe that they are being attacked or plotted against. In fact, an experienced clinician cannot distinguish the drug-induced symptoms from those that occur in people who really have the psychosis. This fact has suggested to some investigators that schizophrenia may be caused by overactivity of dopamine-secreting synapses; this hypothesis is discussed in more detail in Chapter 17.

Opiate drugs have both excitatory and inhibitory effects on behaviour. All of these effects occur because these drugs mimic the effects of the body's own opioid neuromodulators: they stimulate opioid receptors located on neurons in various parts of the brain. The inhibitory effects include analgesia (reduced sensitivity to pain), hypothermia (lowering of body temperature), and sedation. The pain reduction is accomplished by neurons in the midbrain, the hypothermia by neurons in the hypothalamus, and the sedation by neurons in the medulla. A fatal overdose of an opiate kills its victim by inhibiting the activity of circuits of neurons in the medulla that control breathing, heart rate and blood pressure. But it is the excitatory effects of opiates that induce people to abuse them. Some opioid receptors are located on dopamine-secreting neurons involved in reinforcement (reward). When a person takes an opiate such as heroin, the activity of these neurons produces feelings of euphoria and pleasure, similar to those produced by cocaine or amphetamine. These excitatory effects, and not the inhibitory ones, are responsible for addiction.

Drugs and altered states of consciousness

Throughout history, people have enjoyed changing their consciousness now and then by taking drugs, fasting, meditating or chanting. Even children enjoy spinning around and making themselves dizzy – presumably for the same reasons. Chemicals found in several different plants produce profound changes in consciousness. Behaviourally, these changes are difficult to specify. Large doses of drugs such as marijuana or LSD tend to sedate laboratory animals, but the animals give no sign of having their consciousness altered. Only humans can describe the consciousness-altering effects of the drugs.

Drugs can affect consciousness in several different ways. We have the clearest understanding of one category of drugs: those that affect synapses that use a transmitter substance called serotonin. Serotonin plays an important role in the control of dreaming. Normally, we dream only when we are asleep, in a particular stage called REM sleep (because of the rapid eye movements that occur then). During the rest of the day, circuits of serotonin-secreting neurons inhibit the mechanisms responsible for dreaming, thus preventing them from becoming active. Drugs such as LSD, psilocybin, and DMT suppress the activity of serotonin-secreting neurons, permitting dream mechanisms to become active. As a result, hallucinations occur. These hallucinations are often interesting and even awe-inspiring, but sometimes produce intense fear and anxiety.

Not all hallucinogenic drugs interfere with serotonin-secreting synapses. Cocaine and amphetamine, which affect dopamine-secreting synapses, also produce hallucinations. However, the hallucinations produced by cocaine and amphetamine take some time to develop, and they are primarily auditory. LSD-induced hallucinations take place immediately and are primarily visual, as dreams are. The two types of hallucination undoubtedly occur for different reasons.

Tetrahydrocannabinol (THC), the active ingredient in marijuana, exerts its behavioural effects by stimulating THC receptors – specific neuromodulator receptors present in particular regions of the brain. THC produces analgesia and sedation, stimulates appetite, reduces nausea caused by drugs used to treat cancer, relieves asthma attacks, decreases pressure within the eyes in patients with glaucoma, and reduces the symptoms of certain motor disorders. On the other hand, THC interferes with concentration and memory, alters visual and auditory perception, and distorts perceptions of the passage of time (Howlett, 1990).

Devane et al. (1992) discovered that the brain produces a neuromodulator that activates the THC receptor: a fatlike substance that they named anandamide, from the Sanskrit word ananda, meaning 'bliss'. We do not yet know how it is released or what physiological functions it performs, but now that the THC receptor has been identified and the natural neuromodulator has been found, researchers also hope to find drugs that have the therapeutic effects of THC but not its adverse effects on cognition.

Questions to think about

Drugs and the brain

- If you were in charge of the research department of a pharmaceutical company, what new behaviourally active drugs would you seek? Analgesics? Anti-anxiety drugs? Anti-aggressive drugs? Memory-enhancing drugs?

- Should behaviourally active drugs be taken only by people with illnesses such as schizophrenia, depression or obsessive compulsive disorder, or should we try to find drugs that help people who want to improve their intellectual performance or social adjustment or simply to feel happier?

- If a person needs a drug in order to function normally, how can he or she be said to be abusing it?

- Will Self, the British novelist, is a heroin addict whose fiction is dark, dangerous, satirical and paronomasic. Do you think there is a causal link between drug-taking and creative ability?

- One of the world's leading diagnostic manuals for mental disorders now refers to substance 'dependency' and not 'addiction'. Why do you think this is?

- Do you think there is such a thing as an addictive personality?

- Can cravings, such as that for chocolate, be best explained by biochemistry or learned preferences?

Key terms

CHAPTER REVIEW

The brain and its components

- The brain has two major functions: to control behaviour and to regulate the body's physiological processes.

- The central nervous system (CNS) consists of the spinal cord and the three major divisions of the brain: the brain stem, the cerebellum, and the cerebral hemispheres. The cerebral cortex, which covers the cerebral hemispheres, is wrinkled by fissures and gyri.

- The brain communicates with the rest of the body through the peripheral nervous system, which includes the spinal nerves and cranial nerves.

- The basic element of the nervous system is the neuron. Neurons are assisted in their tasks by glia, which provide physical support, aid in the development of the nervous system, provide neurons with chemicals they need, remove unwanted chemicals, provide myelin sheaths for axons, and protect neurons from infection.

- One neuron communicates with another (or with muscle or gland cells) by means of synapses. A synapse is the junction of the terminal button of the presynaptic neuron with the membrane of the postsynaptic neuron.

- Synaptic communication is chemical; when an action potential travels down an axon, it causes a transmitter substance to be released by the terminal buttons.

- An action potential consists of a brief change in the electrical charge of the axon, produced by a brief entry of positively charged sodium ions into the axon followed by a brief exit of positively charged potassium ions. Ions enter the axon through ion channels, and ion transporters eventually restore the proper concentrations of ions inside and outside the cell.

- Molecules of the transmitter substance released by terminal buttons either excite or inhibit the firing of the postsynaptic neuron. The combined effects of excitatory and inhibitory synapses on a particular neuron determine the rate of firing of that neuron.

- Neuromodulators resemble transmitter substances but travel further and are dispersed more widely. They are released by terminal buttons and modulate the activity of many neurons. The best-known neuromodulators are the opioids, which are released when an animal is engaged in essential, meaningful behaviour. The opiates, extracted from the sap of the opium poppy or produced in a laboratory, stimulate the brain's opioid receptors.

Techniques for studying the brain

- Various techniques are available for neuroscientists to investigate brain function. These include experimental lesion, observing the effects of natural or accidental brain damage, recording the electrical activity of the brain or observing its structure or metabolic activity.

- Neuropsychologists study the effects of brain damage on people's behaviour, correlating their behavioural deficits with the location of their lesions. The assessment of cognitive impairment after brain injury is called neuropsychological assessment.

- Neuropsychological rehabilitation refers to a programme of remediation that helps the patient regain some of the function lost through brain injury.

- Sophisticated methods of observing brain structure and activity in healthy individuals include computerised tomography (CT), positron emission tomography (PET) and magnetic resonance imaging (MRI).

- CT allows us to view the brain's structure; PET permits researchers to study the neural activity of specific regions of the living human brain. MRI provides clearer images of the brain's structure than does CT; functional MRI provides information about brain activity. Neuropsychologists can also measure the brain's electrical activity using EEG and event-related potential (ERP).

- Normal development of the brain – which was generally assumed to be programmed solely by hereditary factors – is also affected by the environment.

Control of behaviour

- Anatomically, the cerebral cortex is divided into four lobes: frontal, parietal, occipital and temporal. Functionally, the cerebral cortex is organised into five major regions: the three regions of the primary sensory cortex (visual, auditory, and somatosensory), the primary motor cortex and the association cortex.

- The association cortex consists of sensory regions that are responsible for perceiving and learning and the motor regions that are responsible for planning and acting.

- Visual stimulation is transmitted from the eyes to the brain through the optic nerves, one of the pairs of cranial nerves. The information is sent to the primary visual cortex in the occipital lobe.

- The motor association cortex in the frontal lobe is responsible for planning activity; the primary motor cortex is responsible for initiating movement.

- Somatosensory information is transmitted from the skin to the spinal cord by means of a spinal nerve. It is then sent up through the spinal cord and is relayed to the primary somatosensory cortex.

- Lateralisation refers to whether a function is localised in the left or right hemisphere. The right and left hemispheres are involved with somewhat different functions.

- The left hemisphere appears to be concerned mostly with analysis – such as the processes involved in speech comprehension and production and reading. The right hemisphere appears to be concerned mostly with synthesis – with putting together a perception of the general form and shape of things from smaller elements that are present at the same time.

- The two cerebral hemispheres are connected by a large bundle of axons called the corpus callosum which allows the hemispheres to transfer information to one another.

- The frontal lobe is concerned with motor functions, planning strategies for action, and problem-solving.

A region of the left frontal cortex (Broca's area) is specialised for the control of speech.

- Somatosensory information is processed by the parietal lobe, visual information by the occipital and lower temporal lobes, and auditory information by the upper temporal lobe. Other functions of these lobes are related to these perceptual processes; for example, the parietal lobes are concerned with perception of space as well as knowledge about the body.

Control of internal functions and automatic behaviour

- The more primitive parts of the brain control homeostasis and species-typical behaviours. The brain stem, which consists of the medulla, the pons and the midbrain, contains neural circuits that control vital physiological functions and produce automatic movements such as those used in locomotion, fighting and sexual behaviour.

- The cerebellum assists the cerebral cortex in carrying out movements; it co-ordinates the control of muscles, resulting in smooth movements. It also regulates postural adjustments and appears to play some role in cognition and emotion.

- The thalamus participates in the control of movements and relays sensory information to the cerebral cortex.

- The hypothalamus receives sensory information from sense receptors elsewhere in the body and also contains its own specialised receptors, such as those used to monitor body temperature. It controls the pituitary gland, which, in turn, controls most of the endocrine glands of the body, and it also controls the internal organs through the autonomic nervous system.

- Hormones, secreted by endocrine glands, are chemicals that act on hormone receptors in target cells and produce physiological reactions in these cells. The hypothalamus can control homeostatic processes directly and automatically through its control of the pituitary gland and the autonomic nervous system, or it can cause neural circuits in the cerebral cortex to execute more complex, learned behaviour.

- The amygdala and the hippocampus, both located within the temporal lobe, specifically within the limbic system. The amygdala is involved in emotional behaviour.

- The hippocampus is involved in learning and memory; people with damage to this structure can recall old memories but are unable to learn anything new.

Drugs and behaviour

- Many chemicals found in nature have behavioural effects, and many more have been synthesised in the laboratory.

- Drugs can facilitate or interfere with synaptic activity. Facilitators include drugs that cause the release of a transmitter substance (such as the venom of the black widow spider); drugs that directly stimulate postsynaptic receptor molecules, thus duplicating the effects of the transmitter substance itself (such as nicotine); and drugs that inhibit the reuptake of a transmitter substance (such as amphetamine and cocaine).

- Drugs that interfere with synaptic activity include those that inhibit the release of a transmitter substance (such as botulinum toxin) and those that block receptor molecules (such as curare).

- There are several major categories of drugs that affect behaviour. Alcohol, barbiturates, and tranquillisers depress the activity of the brain by stimulating various types of receptor molecule.

- Amphetamine and cocaine stimulate the brain primarily by retarding the reuptake of dopamine. The opiates duplicate the effects of the brain's opioids, decreasing sensitivity to pain and producing intensely enjoyable feelings of euphoria and pleasure. LSD, psilocybin and related drugs inhibit the activity of synapses that use serotonin.

- The hallucinogenic effects of these drugs may be related to dreaming, which is controlled by circuits of serotonin-secreting neurons.

- The physiological effects of marijuana are produced by a compound called THC which stimulates receptors that are normally activated by a natural neuromodulator called anandamide.

- Psychotherapeutic drugs include those that reduce the symptoms of schizophrenia and those that relieve depression. Antischizophrenic drugs block dopamine receptors, and antidepressant drugs generally facilitate the action of serotonin.

- Opiates produce tolerance and withdrawal symptoms, which make their habitual use increasingly expensive and make quitting more difficult.

- The primary reason for addiction is the reinforcing effect, not the unpleasant symptoms produced when an addict tries to quit. Tolerance appears to be produced by homeostatic mechanisms that counteract the effects of the drug.

Suggestions for further reading

Carlson, N.R. (1995). *Foundations of Physiological Psychology* (3rd edition). Boston: Allyn & Bacon.

Martin, G.N. (1998). *Human Neuropsychology*. Hemel Hempstead: Prentice Hall Europe.
These two texts are good, comprehensive introductions to the physiology of behaviour (Carlson) and the relationship between human brain activity, structure and function (Martin).

Hugdahl, K. (1996). Brain laterality – beyond the basics. *European Psychologist*, 1, 3, 206–220.

Springer, S.P. and Deutsch, G. (1998). *Left Brain, Right Brain* (5th edition). New York: W.H. Freeman.
These two publications provide an excellent basic (despite the first's title) account of lateralisation of function.

Brodal, P. (1992). *The Central Nervous System*. Oxford: Oxford University Press.

England, M.A. and Wakeley, J. (1991). *A Colour Atlas of the Brain and Spinal Cord*. Aylesbury: Wolfe.

Kandel, E.R., Schwartz, J.H. and Jessell, T.M. (1995). *Essentials of Neural Science and Behaviour*. Upper Saddle River, NJ: Prentice Hall, Inc.
A number of books covers the neuroanatomy and neurophysiology of the brain. These three books cover most of these two topics and do it well. England and Wakeley's atlas is an excellent colour introduction to the CNS, with splendid illustrations of the brain's structures at the regional and cellular level. Brodal's book is a classic in the field and is a good, but tough-going, tour of the CNS. Kandel, Schwartz and Jessell is another well known text which gives an exhaustive account of the neurophysiology of behaviour.

Andreassi, J.L. (1996). *Psychophysiology* (3rd edition). Hillsdale, NJ: Lawrence Erlbaum Associates.

Cabeza, R. and Nyberg, L. (1997). Imaging cognition: an empirical review of PET studies with normal subjects. *Journal of Cognitive Neuroscience*, 9, 1, 1–26.

Calvin, W.H. and Ojemann, G.A. (1994). *Conversations with Neil's Brain*. New York: Addison-Wesley.

Gazzaniga, M.S., Ivry, R.B. and Mangun, G.R. (1998). *Cognitive Neuroscience: The biology of mind*. London: W.W. Norton.

Posner, M. and Raichle, M. (1994). *Images of Mind*. New York: Scientific American Library.

Rugg, M.D. (1997). *Cognitive Neuroscience*. Hove, UK: The Psychology Press.
These six books provide a thorough introduction to some of the techniques described in this chapter. Andreassi's book is the most well known general introduction to psychophysiology. Posner and Raichle's book, written by two pioneers in the field of neuroimaging, is a very accessible account of the applications of modern imaging techniques to understanding brain function. The Cabeza and Nyberg article gives a more critical account of the contribution of PET studies to neuropsychology. Rugg's book is a collection of chapters by well known researchers in their respective fields: they give a good overview of the areas of study found in cognitive neuroscience, as does Gazzaniga et al.'s text. Calvin and Ojemann's book is a colourful account of brain electrical stimulation studies.

Julien, R.M.A. (1997). *A Primer of Drug Action* (8th edition). San Francisco: W.H. Freeman.
This is an excellent introduction to drugs and the biochemistry of drug use.

Journals to consult

Brain
Brain and Cognition
Brain and Language
British Journal of Clinical Psychology
Cerebral Cortex
Cognitive Neuropsychology
Cortex
Journal of Cognitive Neuroscience
International Journal of Neuroscience
International Journal of Psychophysiology
Nature
Neuroimage
Neuropsychologia
Neuropsychological Rehabilitation
Neuropsychology
Psychobiology
Psychophysiology
Trends in Neuroscience

Website addresses

http://www.tamiu.edu/coa/psy/biologicalbasis.htm
A massive, excellent collection of links to psychobiology/neuroscience sites. Categories of links include: general resources, the nervous system, researching the brain, left-right brain, the endochrine system, genetics, animal behaviour and evolution. It has a collection of brain atlases and quizzes.

http://www.neuropsychologycentral.com
A link to 'Neuropsychology Central' an excellent collection of neuroscience links.

http://www.rci.rutgers.edu/~lwh/drugs/
A link to an on-line book, Drugs, brains and behaviour, *by Robin Timmons and Leonard Hamilton.*

5

SENSATION

I was glad Michael had invited me to dinner. I had long preferred the company of creative people over that of stuffy medical types.

I sat nearby while he whisked the sauce he had made for the roast chickens.

'Oh dear,' he said, slurping a spoonful, 'there aren't enough points on the chicken.'

'Aren't enough what?' I asked.

He froze and turned red, betraying a realisation that his first impression had been as awkward as that of a debutante falling down the stairs.

'Oh, you're going to think I'm crazy,' he stammered, slopping the spoon down. 'Sometimes I blurt these things out,' he whispered, leaning towards me. 'You're a neurologist, maybe it will make sense to you. I know it sounds crazy, but I have this thing, see, where I taste by shape.' He looked away. 'How can I explain?' he asked himself.

'Flavours have shapes,' he started, frowning into the depths of the roasting pan. 'I wanted the taste of this chicken to be a pointed shape, but it came out round ... Well, I mean, it's nearly spherical,' he emphasised, trying to keep the volume down. 'I can't serve this if it doesn't have points.'

Source: Cytowic, 1993, p. 4

Our thoughts and feelings, decisions and actions are made possible by our senses. Our senses of vision, hearing, taste, smell and touch allow us to do what we take for granted – behave.

This chapter describes the five senses and the physiological mechanisms behind them. It also consider whether these mechanisms are similar in principle or whether each sense operates in a unique way.

What you should be able to do after reading Chapter 5

- Be aware of the difference between sensation and perception.
- Describe the processes involved in sensation, such as transduction and sensory coding.
- Describe each of the sense organs and how they function.
- Be aware of different aspects of the same sense (such as light and colour sensation in vision).
- Think of reasons why such senses have evolved.

Questions to think about

- Why have we evolved five senses? Are there more?
- Do the different senses operate along similar lines, using similar mechanisms?
- Is the importance of a sense reflected in the amount of brain capacity needed to support it?
- Why are some animals more reliant on some senses than others?
- Are there some stimuli that we sense, even though we are not consciously aware of sensing them?

Sensation and behaviour

Behaviour does not exist in a vacuum, nor do our thoughts and emotions. Our actions are provoked, informed, and guided by events that occur in our environment, and we think about – and have feelings about – what is happening there. Our senses are the means by which we experience the world; everything we learn is detected by sense organs and transmitted to our brains by sensory nerves. Without sensory input, a human brain would be utterly useless; it would learn nothing, think no thoughts, have no experiences and control no behaviours.

Vision, to most people, is the most important sense modality. Through it we recognise family and friends, see their facial expressions and gestures, learn to read, perceive objects that are beyond our reach, and find our way around our environment. It provides us with information about the size, shape, colour and movement of objects nearby and at a distance. Through vision, we receive some of our most powerful aesthetic experiences, in the form of art and other beautiful images – experiences rivalled only by the hearing of music that we appreciate.

The other senses also contribute to the richness of experience. Because of the role that speech plays in human culture, audition is important for social behaviour and communication. Audition and vision provides information about distant events, as does the sense of smell, which can tell us about sources of aromatic molecules before we can see or hear that source (think of detecting the smell of smoke before you see the smoke or see or hear the fire). The other senses deal with immediate and proximal events such as the taste of our favourite food or the touch of a loved one. The body senses are closely tied to our own movements. When we feel an object, the experience is active, not passive; we move our hands over it to determine its shape, texture and temperature. And information from specialised organs in the inner ear and from receptors in the muscles and joints is actually produced by our own movements. This information helps us to maintain our balance as we engage in our everyday activities.

Sensory processing

Experience is traditionally divided into two classes: sensation and perception. Most psychologists define sensation as the detection of simple properties of stimuli, such as brightness, colour, warmth and sweetness. Perception is the detection of objects (both animate and inanimate), their locations, their movements and their backgrounds. According to these definitions, seeing the colour red is a sensation, but seeing a red apple is a perception. Similarly, seeing a movement is a sensation, but seeing a cricket ball coming towards us and realising that

we will have to move to the left to catch it is a perception. Psychologists used to believe that perceptions depended heavily on learning whereas pure sensations involved innate, 'prewired' physiological mechanisms. However, neither behavioural nor physiological research has been able to establish a clear boundary between 'simple' sensations and 'complex' perceptions. Research indicates that experience is essential to the development of some of the most elementary features of sensory systems (Blakemore and Mitchell, 1973).

According to tradition, we have five senses: vision (seeing), audition (hearing), gustation (tasting), olfaction (smelling) and somatosensation (touching). In fact, we have several more. The somatosensory system, for example, includes separate components that are able to detect touch, warmth, coolness, vibration, physical damage (pain), head tilt, head movement, limb movement, muscular contraction and various events occurring within our bodies (Kandel *et al.*, 1995). Whether we choose to call each of these components 'senses' is a matter of terminology.

Transduction

The brain, floating in cerebrospinal fluid and swaddled in its protective sheath of meninges and sheltered in the thick skull, is isolated from the world around us. The only sense receptors that the brain possesses detect such things as temperature and salt concentration of the blood, and these receptors cannot inform it about what is going on outside. Useful actions require information about the external world, and such information is gathered by the sense organs located outside the brain.

Sense organs detect the presence of environmental stimuli provided by light, sound, odour, taste or mechanical contact. This information is transmitted to the brain through neural impulses – action potentials carried by the axons in sensory nerves. The task of the sense organs is to transmit signals to the brain that are coded in such a way as to faithfully represent the events that have occurred in the environment. The task of the brain is to analyse this information and reconstruct what has occurred.

Transduction (literally, 'leading across') is the process by which the sense organs convert energy from environmental events into neural activity. Each sense organ responds to a particular form of energy given off by an environmental stimulus and translates that energy into neural firing to which the brain can respond. The means of transduction are as diverse as the kinds of stimuli we can perceive. In most senses, specialised neurons called receptor cells release chemical transmitter substances that stimulate other neurons, thus altering the rate of firing of their axons. In the somatosenses ('body senses'), dendrites of neurons respond directly to physical stimuli without the intervention of specialised receptor cells. However, some of

Table 5.1 The types of transduction accomplished by the sense organs

Location of sense organ	Environmental stimuli	Energy transduced
Eye	Light	Radiant energy
Ear	Sound	Mechanical energy
Vestibular system	Tilt and rotation of head	Mechanical energy
Tongue	Taste	Recognition of molecular shape
Nose	Odour	Recognition of molecular shape
Skin, internal organs	Touch Temperature Vibration Pain	Mechanical energy Thermal energy Mechanical energy Chemical reaction
Muscle	Stretch	Mechanical energy

these neurons do have specialised endings that enable them to respond to particular kinds of sensory information. Table 5.1 summarises the types of transduction accomplished by our sense organs.

Sensory coding

As we saw in Chapter 4, nerves are bundles of axons, each of which can do no more than transmit action potentials. These action potentials are fixed in size and duration; they cannot be altered. Thus, different stimuli cannot be translated into different types of action potential. Yet we can detect an enormous number of different stimuli with each of our sense organs. For example, we are capable of discriminating among approximately 7.5 million different colours. We can also recognise touches to different parts of the body, and we can further discriminate the degree of pressure involved and the sharpness or bluntness, softness or hardness, and the temperature of the object touching us. We can detect over 10,000 different odours. If action potentials cannot be altered, how do the sense organs tell the brain that a red apple or a yellow lemon has been seen or that the right hand is holding a small, cold object or a large, warm one? The answer is that the information from the sense organs must be coded in the activity of axons carrying information from the sense organs to the brain.

A code is a system of symbols or signals representing information. Spoken English, written French, semaphore signals, magnetic fields on a recording tape, and the electrical zeros and ones in the memory of a computer are all examples of codes. As long as we know the rules of a code, we can convert a message from one medium to another without losing any information. Although we do not know the precise rules by which the sensory systems transmit information to the brain, we do know that they take two general forms: anatomical coding and temporal coding.

Anatomical coding

Since the early 1800s, when Johannes Müller formulated his doctrine of specific nerve energies (discussed in Chapter 1), we have known that the brain learns what is happening through the activity of specific sets of neurons. Sensory organs located in different places in the body send their information to the brain through different nerves. Because the brain has no direct information about the physical energy impinging on a given sense organ, it uses anatomical coding to interpret the location and type of sensory stimulus according to which incoming nerve fibres are active. For example, if you rub your eyes, you will mechanically stimulate the light-sensitive receptors located there. This stimulation produces action potentials in the axons of the nerves that connect the eyes with the brain (the optic nerves). The visual system of the brain has no way of knowing that the light-sensitive receptors of the eyes have been activated by an unnatural stimulus. As a result, the brain acts as if the neural activity in the optic nerves was produced by light – so you see stars and flashes. Experiments performed during surgery have shown that artificial stimulation of the nerves that convey taste produces a sensation of taste, electrical stimulation of the auditory nerve produces a sensation of a buzzing noise, and so forth (Calvin and Ojemann, 1994).

Forms of anatomical coding distinguish not only between the sense modalities themselves, but also between stimuli of the same sense modality. Sensory coding for the body surface is anatomical: different nerve fibres serve different parts of the skin. Thus, we can easily discriminate a touch on the arm from a touch on the knee. As we saw in Chapter 4, the primary somatosensory cortex contains a neural 'map' of the skin. Receptors in the skin in different parts of the body send information to different parts of the primary somatosensory cortex. Similarly, the primary visual cortex maintains a map of the visual field.

Temporal coding

Temporal coding is the coding of information in terms of time. The simplest form of temporal code is rate. By firing at a faster or slower rate according to the intensity of a stimulus, an axon can communicate quantitative information to the brain. For example, a light touch to the skin can be encoded by a low rate of firing, and a more forceful touch by a high rate. Thus, the firing of a particular set of neurons (an anatomical code) tells where the body is being touched; the rate at which these neurons fire (a temporal code) tells how intense that touch is. As far as we know, all sensory systems use rate of firing to encode the intensity of stimulation.

Psychophysics

In Chapter 1, we saw that nineteenth-century Europe was the birthplace of psychophysics, the systematic study of the relation between the physical characteristics of stimuli and the sensations they produce (the 'physics of the mind'). To study perceptual phenomena, scientists had to find reliable ways to measure people's sensations. Two of these methods are the just-noticeable difference and the procedures of signal detection theory.

The principle of the just-noticeable difference

Ernst Weber (1795–1878), a German anatomist and physiologist, investigated the ability of humans to discriminate between various stimuli. He measured the just-noticeable difference (jnd) – the smallest change in the magnitude of a stimulus that a person can detect. He discovered a principle that held true for all sensory systems: the jnd is directly related to the magnitude of that stimulus. For example, when he presented subjects with two metal objects and asked them to say whether they differed in weight, the subjects reported that the two weights felt the same unless they differed by a factor of 1 in 40. That is, a person could just barely distinguish a 40 gram weight from a 41 gram weight, an 80 gram weight from an 82 gram weight, or a 400 gram weight from a 410 gram weight. Psychologically, the difference between a 40 gram weight and a 41 gram weight is equivalent to the difference between an 80 gram weight and an 82 gram weight: 1 jnd. Different senses had different ratios. For example, the ratio for detecting differences in the brightness of white light is approximately 1 in 60. These ratios are called Weber fractions.

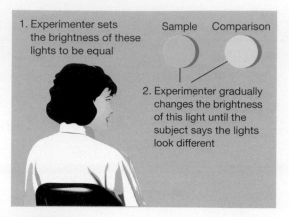

Figure 5.1

The method for determining a just-noticeable difference.

Gustav Fechner (1801–1887), another German physiologist, used Weber's concept of the just-noticeable difference to measure people's sensations. Assuming that the jnd was the basic unit of a sensory experience, he measured the absolute magnitude of a sensation in jnds. Imagine that we want to measure the strength of a person's sensation of light of a particular intensity. We seat the subject in a darkened room facing two disks of frosted glass, each having a light bulb behind it; the brightness of the light bulb is adjustable. One of the disks serves as the sample stimulus, the other as the comparison stimulus, as seen in Figure 5.1.

We start with the sample stimulus and the comparison stimulus turned off completely and increase the brightness of the comparison stimulus until our subject can just detect a difference. That value is 1 jnd. Then we set the sample stimulus to that intensity (1 jnd) and again increase the brightness of the comparison stimulus just until our subject can again tell them apart. The new value of the comparison stimulus is 2 jnds. We continue making these measurements until our stimuli are as bright as we can make them or until they become uncomfortably bright for our subject. Finally, we construct a graph indicating the strength of a sensation of brightness (in jnds) in relation to the intensity of a stimulus. See Figure 5.2.

Signal detection theory

Psychophysical methods rely heavily on the concept of a threshold, the line between not perceiving and perceiving. The just-noticeable difference can also be called a difference threshold, the minimum detectable difference between two stimuli. An absolute threshold is the minimum value of a stimulus that can be detected, that is, discriminated from no stimulus at all. Thus, the first comparison in the experiment just described – using a dark disk as the sample stimulus – measured an absolute threshold. The subsequent comparisons measured difference thresholds.

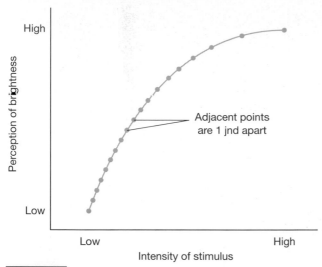

Figure 5.2

A hypothetical range of perceived brightness (in jnds) as a function of intensity.

Even early psychophysicists realised that a threshold was not an absolutely fixed value. When an experimenter flashes a very dim light, a subject may report seeing it on some trials but not on others. By convention, the threshold is the point at which a subject detects the stimulus 50 per cent of the time. This definition is necessary because of the inherent variability of the activity in the nervous system. Even when they are not being stimulated, neurons are never absolutely still; they continue to fire. If a very weak

Figure 5.3

According to signal detection theory, we must discriminate between the signal, conveying information, and noise, contributed by background stimuli and random activity of our own nervous systems.

stimulus occurs when neurons in the visual system happen to be quiet, the brain is likely to detect it. But if the neurons happen to be firing, the effects of the stimulus are likely to be lost in the 'noise'. Work such as that involved in air traffic control illustrates this point, as seen in Figure 5.3. The worker must select only the most relevant information from a background of competing information.

An alternative method of measuring a person's sensitivity to changes in physical stimuli takes account of random changes in the nervous system (Green and Swets, 1974). According to **signal detection theory**, every stimulus event requires discrimination between signal (stimulus) and noise (consisting of both background stimuli and random activity of the nervous system).

An example of this might involve an individual seated in a quiet room, facing a small warning light. The experimenter informs the individual that when the light flashes, he or she hears a faint tone one second later. The person's task is to say 'yes' or 'no' after each flash of the warning light, according to whether or not he or she hears the tone. At first, the task is easy: some flashes are followed by an easily heard tone; others are followed by silence. As the experiment progresses, however, the tone gets fainter and fainter, until it is so soft that the individual has doubts about how to respond. The light flashes but did the individual really hear a tone or was it just imagined?

Response bias – the tendency to say yes or no when unsure of detecting a stimulus – can have an effect. According to the terminology of signal detection theory, *hits* are saying 'yes' when the stimulus is presented; *misses* are saying 'no' when it is presented; *correct rejections* are saying 'no' when the stimulus is not presented; and *false alarms* are saying 'yes' when the stimulus is not presented. Hits and correct rejections are correct responses; misses and false alarms are incorrect responses. Figure 5.4 shows the relationship between these responses. If a person wants to ensure that he or she is correct when they say 'yes' (because they would feel foolish saying they have heard something that is not there), the response bias is to err in favour of making hits and avoiding false alarms, even at the risk of making misses. Alternatively, a response bias might be to err in favour of detecting all stimuli, even at the risk of making false alarms.

This response bias can seriously affect an investigator's estimate of the threshold of detection. A conservative person will appear to have a higher threshold than will someone who does not want to let a tone go by without saying 'yes'. Therefore, signal detection theorists have developed a method of assessing people's sensitivity, regardless of their initial response bias. They deliberately manipulate the response biases and observe the results of these manipulations on the people's judgements.

Imagine, for example, that you are a participant in an experiment and the experimenter promises you a sum of money every time you make a hit (correctly report hearing a tone), with no penalty for false alarms. You would

Judgement

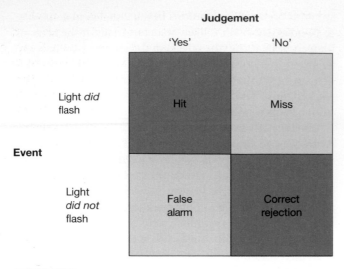

Figure 5.4

Four possibilities in judging the presence or absence of a stimulus.

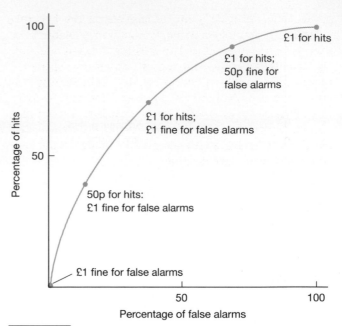

Figure 5.5

A receiver operating characteristic (ROC) curve. The percentage of hits and false alarms in judging the presence of a stimulus under several payoff conditions.

undoubtedly tend to say 'yes' on every trial, even if you were not sure you had heard the tone; after all, you have nothing to lose and everything to gain. In contrast, imagine that the experimenter announced that she would fine you the same amount of money every time you made a false alarm and would give you nothing for making hits. You would undoubtedly say 'no' every time, because you would have everything to lose and nothing to gain: you would be extremely conservative in your judgements.

Now consider your response bias under a number of intermediate conditions. If you receive money for every hit but are also fined half that amount for every miss, you will say 'yes' whenever you are reasonably sure you heard the tone. If you receive a sum of money for every hit but are fined twice as much for each false alarm, you will be more conservative. But if you are sure you heard the tone, you will say 'yes'.

The graph in Figure 5.5 is a **receiver operating characteristic curve (ROC curve)**, named for its original use in research at the Bell Laboratories to measure the intelligibility of speech transmitted through a telephone system. The curve shows performance when the sound is difficult to detect. If the sound were louder, so that you rarely doubted whether you heard it, you would make almost every possible hit and very few false alarms. The few misses you made would be under the low-payoff condition, when you wanted to be absolutely certain you heard the tone. The few false alarms would occur when guessing did not matter because the fine for being wrong was low or non-existent. The difference between the two curves seen in Figure 5.6 demonstrates that the louder tone is easier to detect. Detectability is measured by the relative distances of the curves from a 45-degree line.

The signal detection method is the best way to determine an individual's sensitivity to the occurrence of a particular stimulus. Note that the concept of threshold is not used. Instead, a stimulus is more or less detectable. The person decides whether a stimulus occurred, and the

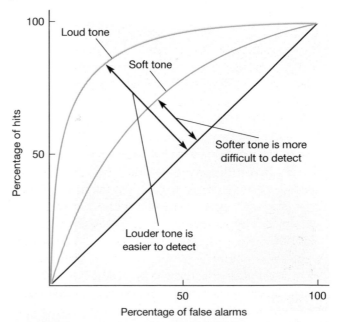

Figure 5.6

Two ROC curves, obtained by presenting a more discriminable stimulus (orange curve) and a less discriminable stimulus (blue curve).

consequences of making hits or false alarms can bias this decision: for example, missing the sound of an alarm clock may be more important than missing a telephone call. Signal detection theory emphasises that sensory experience involves factors other than the activity of the sensory systems, such as motivation and prior experience. Sensitivity to a signal can be influenced by these factors. The fact that you know that you will either be rewarded or financially penalised for making false alarms will influence the care with which you make decisions.

You can see signal detection theory applied in a number of important ways. For example, a radiologist who takes an X-ray has to discriminate between shadows on an X-ray image that indicate disease – the signal – and those that just show differences in the anatomy of the patient – the noise (Parasuraman, 1985). Response bias can occur if the radiologist knows whether the patient has a past history of disease or not. The likelihood of detecting a tumour increases or decreases, respectively.

Psychology in action

Does subliminal perception exist?

According to the seller of one subliminal self-help audio cassette, *Building Self-confidence*, the message provided by the tape reaches the subconscious mind, which is the seat of all memories, knowledge and emotions. The unconscious mind has a powerful influence on conscious actions, thoughts, feelings, habits and behaviours, and actually controls and guides your life. If you want to make real, lasting changes and improvements in any area of your life, you must reach the subconscious mind where the changes begin (Druckman and Bjork, 1991, p. 107).

According to the manufacturer, the tape contains a voice making positive statements such as: 'I am a secure person. I believe in myself more and more every day, and my confidence naturally rises to the surface in every situation.' The voice is inaudible, masked by the sound of sea surf. To profit from these messages, says a notice on the card insert, 'Simply play the tapes while you work, play, drive, read, exercise, relax, watch TV, or even as you sleep. No concentration is required for the tapes to be effective' (Druckman and Bjork, 1991, pp. 107–108). Do such tapes work?

The manufacturer's evidence is clear: testimonials from satisfied customers prove their efficacy. If a person is convinced that he or she received help from a subliminal tape, however, can we conclude that the system really works? The answer is no. At least three phenomena can account for the fact that some customers will say that they are satisfied. First, simply making a purchase indicates a commitment to self-improvement. In fact, some people with emotional or behavioural problems show improvements in their feelings and behaviour as soon as they register for psychotherapy – even before the therapy actually begins (Rachman and Wilson, 1980). Secondly, social psychologists learned long ago that once people have expended some effort towards reaching a goal, they tend to justify their effort by perceiving positive results. Finally, if a person expects an effect to occur, he or she is easily convinced that it really did.

The effect of expectation is demonstrated by a study carried out to follow up a famous hoax. In 1957, an advertising expert claimed that he had inserted subliminal visual messages in a showing of *Picnic*, a popular film. The messages, which said 'Eat Popcorn' and 'Drink Coke', supposedly caused people to rush to the refreshment stand and purchase these items. As you can imagine, this event received much attention and publicity. Several years later, the advertising expert revealed that he had invented the episode in an attempt to get some favourable publicity for his firm (Weir, 1984).

In 1958, long before the advertising expert admitted his hoax, the Canadian Broadcasting Corporation commissioned a study to determine whether a subliminal message could really work (Pratkanis *et al.*, 1990). At the beginning of a television show, an announcer described the alleged 'Popcorn' study and told the viewers that a test of subliminal persuasion would follow, with an unspecified message appearing on the screen. In fact, the message was 'Phone now'. According to the telephone company, no increase in the rate of phone calls occurred. But many viewers wrote to the television network to say that they had felt compelled to do something, such as eat or drink. Obviously, the specific message to 'Phone now' did not get across to the viewers, but the expectation that they should feel some sort of compulsion made many of them report that they did.

Is there any objective, scientific evidence that subliminal perception can occur? The answer is yes but the information transmitted by this means is very scanty. Subliminal literally means 'below threshold', after the Latin *limen*, 'threshold'. The term subliminal perception refers to the behavioural effect of a stimulus that falls below the threshold of conscious detection. That is, although the person denies having detected a stimulus, the stimulus has a measurable effect on

Psychology in action continued

Psychology in action continued

his or her behaviour. But the effects are subtle, and special procedures are required to demonstrate them. For example, if the word 'nurse' is first flashed on a screen, it becomes easier for the viewer to recognise a related word, such as 'doctor', but not an unrelated word, such as 'chair'. This phenomenon, called semantic priming, occurs even when the priming stimulus ('nurse') is presented so rapidly that the subjects deny having seen it, meaning that it can occur subliminally (Marcel, 1983).

Results such as these simply indicate that perception is a complex process – that when a stimulus is too weak to give rise to a conscious perception, it may still be strong enough to leave some traces in the brain that affect people's perception of other stimuli. And this effect has a threshold of its own; if a word is presented too briefly, it has no effect at all on the perception of other words. The phenomenon is a real one that involves the sense receptors and normal physiological processes.

Psychologists have examined very few of the many thousands of different subliminal self-help tapes that are available, but those they have examined seem to be ineffective. Some, according to Merikle (1988), contain stimuli that are simply too weak for the human ear to detect under any conditions. Others, when subjected to spectrographic analysis (which detects the presence of 'voiceprints' in the soundtrack) were found to contain no message at all.

Perhaps this fact explains the results of the experiment by Pratkanis *et al.* (1990). The experimenters recruited volunteers to listen to either a subliminal tape designed to improve memory or one designed to improve self-esteem. After the subjects listened to the tapes for five weeks, the experimenters asked them whether their memories or self-esteem had improved. About half of the subjects said that they had – but none of the objective tests of memory or self-esteem administered by the experimenters showed any effect. Besides, the experimenters had switched tapes for half of the subjects: some of those who thought they had received a memory tape actually received a self-esteem tape and vice versa. The switch made no difference at all in the satisfaction ratings. Thus, a person's satisfaction is no indication that subliminal perception has really taken place.

Only one conclusion seems possible: if you have been thinking about purchasing subliminal self-help tapes, save your money – unless you think you will be content with a placebo effect caused by commitment to change, a need to justify your efforts and expectation of good results. The type of perception possible when stimuli are delivered beneath threshold does not allow deep processing or remembering; people might have a vague idea of the type of stimulus they were presented with. We return to the ideas of conscious and unconscious learning again in Chapters 8 (Memory) and 9 (Consciousness).

Questions to think about

Sensation

- If you were to conduct a hypothetical survey on the importance of the senses, most people would probably not be prepared to live without the sense of sight but would be happy to lose the sense of smell. Why do you think that this is?

- Is there a sixth sense? How would you test the claims made for the existence of one?

- If you see a red apple and your friend sees a red apple, how do you know that you are both 'seeing red'?

- There is a quasi-experiment reported in the literature of factory workers complaining about the weight of large boxes that they had to shift. Carrying these heavy boxes made their backs ache. All the boxes were black. The supervisor, for reasons that you can imagine, decided to replace the black boxes with lighter-coloured ones. When the workers returned to the factory after the week-end and had to move the new boxes, they remarked on how lighter they were than the black boxes even though the new boxes weighed the same as the old boxes. Why?

Vision

The visual system allows us to do many activities that we take for granted: in a quick glance we can recognise what there is to see – people, objects and landscapes – in depth and full colour. Because of the dominance of visual information in our lives, it is perhaps not surprising that vision is our dominant sense.

Light

The eye is sensitive to light. Light consists of radiant energy similar to radio waves. As the radiant energy is transmitted from its source, it oscillates. For example, the antenna that broadcasts the programmes of your favourite FM station may transmit radio waves that oscillate at 88.5 MHz (megahertz, or million times per second). Because radiant energy travels at 297,600 km per second, the waves transmitted by this antenna are approximately 3.3 m apart (297,600 km divided by 88.5 million equals approximately 3.3 m). Thus, the wavelength of the signal from the station – the distance between the waves of radiant energy – is 3.3 metres. (See Figure 5.7.)

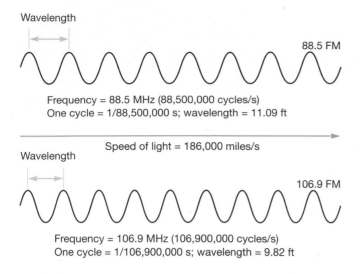

Wavelength

88.5 FM

Frequency = 88.5 MHz (88,500,000 cycles/s)
One cycle = 1/88,500,000 s; wavelength = 11.09 ft

Speed of light = 186,000 miles/s

Wavelength

106.9 FM

Frequency = 106.9 MHz (106,900,000 cycles/s)
One cycle = 1/106,900,000 s; wavelength = 9.82 ft

Figure 5.7

Wavelength versus vibration. Because the speed of light is constant, faster vibrations produce shorter wavelengths.

The wavelength of visible light is much shorter, ranging from 380 to 760 nanometers (a nanometer, nm, is one-billionth of a metre). When viewed by a human eye, different wavelengths of visible light have different colours: for instance, 380 nm light looks violet and 760 nm light looks red.

All other radiant energy is invisible to our eyes. Ultraviolet radiation, X-rays and gamma rays have shorter wavelengths than visible light has, whereas infrared radiation, radar and radio waves have longer wavelengths. The entire range of wavelengths is known as the electromagnetic spectrum; the part our eyes can detect – the part we see as light – is referred to as the visible spectrum, as seen in Figure 5.8.

The definition of the visible spectrum is based on the human visual system. Some other species of animals would define the visible spectrum differently. Bees, for example, can see ultraviolet radiation that is invisible to us. Some plants have taken advantage of this fact and produce flowers that contain dyes that reflect ultraviolet radiation, presenting patterns that attract bees to them. Some snakes (notably, pit vipers such as the rattlesnake) have special organs that detect infrared radiation. This ability enables them to find their prey in the dark by detecting the heat emitted by small mammals in the form of infrared radiation.

The eye and its functions

The eyes are important and delicate sense organs – and they are well protected. Each eye is housed in a bony socket and can be covered by the eyelid to keep dust and dirt out. The eyelids are edged by eyelashes, which help keep foreign matter from falling into the open eye. The eyebrows prevent sweat on the forehead from dripping into the eyes. Reflex mechanisms provide additional protection: the sudden approach of an object towards the face or a touch on the surface of the eye causes automatic eyelid closure and withdrawal of the head.

Figure 5.9 shows a cross section of a human eye. The transparent cornea forms a bulge at the front of the eye and admits light. The rest of the eye is coated by a tough white membrane called the sclera (from the Greek *skleros*, 'hard'). The iris consists of two bands of muscle that control the amount of light admitted into the eye. The brain controls these muscles and thus regulates the size of the pupil, constricting it in bright light and dilating it in dim light. The space immediately behind the cornea is filled with aqueous humour, which simply means 'watery fluid'. This fluid is constantly produced by tissue behind the cornea that filters the fluid from the blood. In place of blood vessels, the aqueous humour nourishes the cornea and other portions of the front of the eye; this fluid must circulate and be renewed. If aqueous humour is produced too quickly or if the passage that returns it to the blood becomes blocked, the pressure within the eye can increase and cause damage to vision – a disorder known as

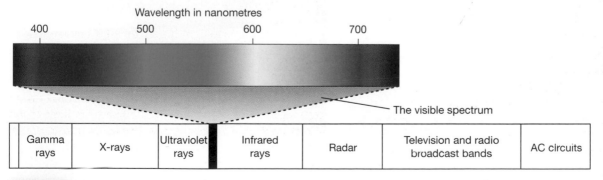

Wavelength in nanometres

400   500   600   700

The visible spectrum

Gamma rays	X-rays	Ultraviolet rays	Infrared rays	Radar	Television and radio broadcast bands	AC circuits

Figure 5.8

The electromagnetic spectrum.

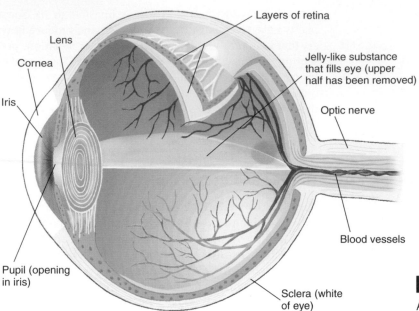

Layers of retina

Lens

Cornea

Jelly-like substance
that fills eye (upper
half has been removed)

Iris

Optic nerve

Pupil (opening
in iris)

Blood vessels

Sclera (white
of eye)

Figure 5.9

A cross-section of the human eye.

glaucoma. Because of its transparency, the cornea must be nourished in this unusual manner. Our vision would be less clear if we had a set of blood vessels across the front of our eyes.

The curvature of the cornea and of the **lens**, which lies immediately behind the iris, causes images to be focused on the inner surface of the back of the eye. Although this image is upside-down and reversed from left to right, the brain interprets this information appropriately. The shape of the cornea is fixed, but the lens is flexible; a special set of muscles can alter its shape so that the eye can obtain focused images of either nearby or distant objects. This change in the shape of the lens to adjust for distance is called **accommodation**.

Normally, the length of the eye matches the refractive power of the cornea and the lens so that the image of the visual scene is sharply focused on the retina. However, for some people these two factors are not matched, and the image on the retina is therefore out of focus. There is a problem with sensing objects at various distances: some have difficulty in focusing on objects in the distance; others have difficulty in focusing on near objects. These people need an extra lens in front of their eyes (in the form of spectacles or contact lenses) to correct the discrepancy and bring the image into focus. People whose eyes are too long (front to back) are said to be nearsighted; they need a concave lens to correct the focus. The image on the right of Figure 5.10 shows what a nearsighted person would see.

Figure 5.10

To a nearsighted person, distant objects are blurry and out of focus.

Source: © Tony Stone Images. Reproduced with permission.

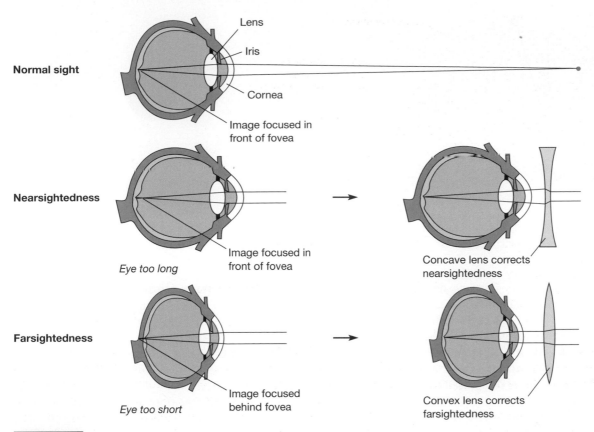

Figure 5.11

Lenses used to correct nearsightedness and farsightedness.

People whose eyes are too short are said to be farsighted; they need a convex lens. As people get older, not only does the cornea of the eye begin to yellow and the sensitivity of the rods to decline (Sturr *et al.*, 1997), but the lenses of their eyes also become less flexible and it becomes difficult for them to focus on objects close to them. These people need reading glasses with convex lenses (or bifocals, if they already wear glasses). See Figure 5.11.

The retina, which lines the inner surface of the back of the eye, performs the sensory functions of the eye. Embedded in the retina are over 130 million photoreceptors – specialised neurons that transduce light into neural activity. The information from the photoreceptors is transmitted to neurons that send axons towards one point at the back of the eye – the optic disk. All axons leave the eye at this point and join the optic nerve, which travels to the brain. See Figure 5.12.

Because there are no photoreceptors directly in front of the optic disk, this portion of the retina is blind. If you have not located your own blind spot, try the demonstration shown in Figure 5.13.

Before the seventeenth century, scientists thought that the lens sensed the presence of light. Johannes Kepler (1571–1630), the astronomer who discovered the true shape of the planets' orbits around the sun, is credited with the suggestion that the retina, not the lens, contained the receptive tissue of the eye. It remained for Christoph Scheiner (another German astronomer) to demonstrate in

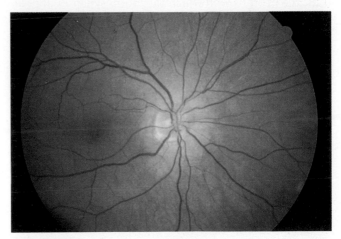

Figure 5.12

A view of the back of the eye. The photograph shows the retina, the optic disk and blood vessels.

Source: Courtesy of Douglas G. Mollerstuen, New England Medical Center.

Optic disk
(Blind spot)   Fovea

Figure 5.13

A test for the blind spot. With the left eye closed, look at the + with your right eye and move the page back and forth, towards and away from yourself. At about 20 centimetres, the coloured circle disappears from your vision because its image falls on your blind spot.

1625 that the lens is simply a focusing device. Scheiner obtained an ox's eye from a slaughterhouse. After carefully peeling the sclera away from the back of the eye, he was able to see an upside-down image of the world through the thin, translucent membrane that remained. As an astronomer, he was familiar with the fact that convex glass lenses could cast images, so he recognised the function of the lens of the eye.

Figure 5.14 shows a cross-section of the retina. The retina has three principal layers. Light passes successively through the ganglion cell layer (front), the bipolar cell layer (middle) and the photoreceptor layer (back). Early anatomists were surprised to find the photoreceptors in the deepest layer of the retina. As you might expect, the cells that are located above the photoreceptors are transparent.

Photoreceptors respond to light and pass the information on by means of a transmitter substance to the bipolar cells, the neurons with which they form synapses. **Bipolar cells** transmit this information to the **ganglion cells**,

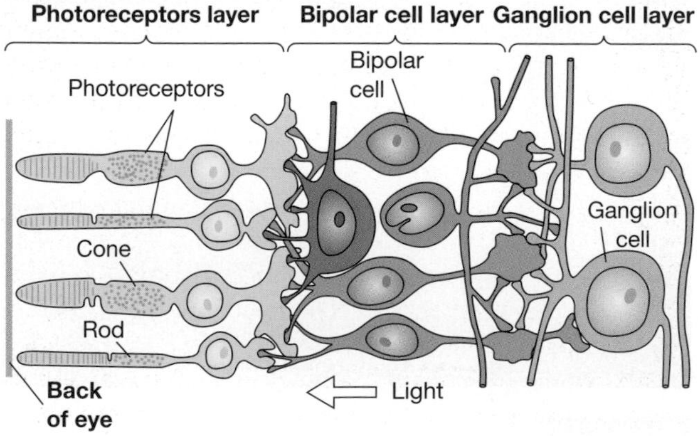

neurons whose axons travel across the retina and through the optic nerves. Thus, visual information passes through a three-cell chain to the brain: photoreceptor–bipolar; cell–ganglion; and cell–brain.

A single photoreceptor responds only to light that reaches its immediate vicinity, but a ganglion cell can receive information from many different photoreceptors. The retina also contains neurons that interconnect both adjacent photoreceptors and adjacent ganglion cells. The existence of this neural circuitry indicates that some kinds of information processing are performed in the retina.

The human retina contains two general types of photoreceptors: 125 million rods and 6 million cones, so called because of their shapes. **Rods** function mainly in dim light; they are very sensitive to light. **Cones** function when the level of illumination is bright enough to see things clearly. They are also responsible for colour vision. The **fovea**, a small pit in the back of the retina approximately 1 millimetre in diameter, contains only cones and is responsible for our finest, most detailed vision. When we look at a point in our visual field, we move our eyes so that the image of that point falls directly on the cone-packed fovea.

Farther away from the fovea, the number of cones decreases and the number of rods increases. Up to one hundred rods may converge on a single ganglion cell. A ganglion cell that receives information from so many rods is sensitive to very low levels of light. Rods are therefore responsible for our sensitivity to very dim light, but they provide poor acuity.

Transduction of light by photoreceptors

Although light-sensitive sensory organs have evolved independently in a wide variety of animals – from insects to fish to mammals – the chemistry is essentially the same in all species: a molecule derived from vitamin A is the central ingredient in the transduction of the energy of light into neural activity (carrots are said to be good for vision

Photoreceptors layer   Bipolar cell layer Ganglion cell layer

Photoreceptors

Bipolar
cell

Cone

Ganglion
cell

Rod

**Back
of eye**   ⬅ Light

Figure 5.14

The cells of the retina.

Source: Redrawn by permission of the Royal Society and the authors from Dowling, J.E. and Boycott, B.B., *Proceedings of the Royal Society* (London), 1966, Series B, 166, 80–111.

because they contain a substance that the body easily converts to vitamin A). In the absence of light, this molecule is attached to another molecule, a protein. The two molecules together form a photopigment. The photoreceptors of the human eye contain four kinds of photopigment (one for rods and three for cones), but their basic mechanism is the same. When a photon (a particle of light) strikes a photopigment, the photopigment splits apart into its two constituent molecules. This event starts the process of transduction. The splitting of the photopigment causes a series of chemical reactions that stimulate the photoreceptor and cause it to send a message to the bipolar cell with which it forms a synapse. The bipolar cell sends a message to the ganglion cell, which then sends one on to the brain, as seen in Figure 5.15.

Intact photopigments have a characteristic colour. Rhodopsin, the photopigment of rods, is pink (*rhodon* means 'rose' in Greek). However, once the photopigments are split apart by the action of light, they lose their colour – they become bleached. Franz Boll discovered this phenomenon in 1876 when he removed an eye from an animal and pointed it towards a window that opened out onto a brightly lit scene. He then examined the retina under dim light and found that the image of the scene was still there. The retina was pink where little light had fallen and pale where the image had been bright. It was Boll's discovery that led investigators to suspect that a chemical reaction was responsible for the transduction of light into neural activity.

After light has caused a molecule of photopigment to split and become bleached, energy from the photoreceptor's metabolism causes the two molecules to recombine. The photopigment is then ready to be bleached by light again. Each photoreceptor contains many thousands of molecules of photopigment. The number of intact, unbleached molecules of photopigment in a given cell depends on the relative rates at which they are being split by light and being put back together by the cell's energy. The brighter the light, the more bleached photopigment there is.

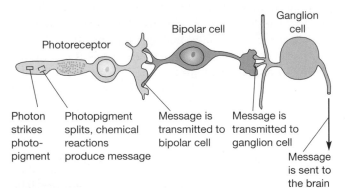

Figure 5.15

Transduction of light into neural activity. A photon strikes a photoreceptor and causes the photopigment to split apart. This event initiates the transmission of information to the brain.

Adaptation to light and dark

Think, for a moment, about how difficult it can be to find a seat in a darkened cinema. Another example: if you have just come in from the bright sun, your eyes do not respond well to the low level of illumination. However, after a few minutes, you can see rather well – your eyes have adapted to the dark. This phenomenon is called dark adaptation.

In order for light to be detected, photons must split molecules of rhodopsin or one of the other photopigments. When high levels of illumination strike the retina, the rate of regeneration of rhodopsin falls behind the rate of the bleaching process. With only a small percentage of the rhodopsin molecules intact, the rods are not very sensitive to light. If you enter a dark room after being in a brightly lit room or in sunlight, there are too few intact rhodopsin molecules for your eyes to respond immediately to dim light. The probability that a photon will strike an intact molecule of rhodopsin is very low. However, after a while, the regeneration of rhodopsin overcomes the bleaching effects of the light energy. The rods become full of unbleached rhodopsin, and a photon passing through a rod is likely to find a target. The eye has become dark adapted.

Eye movements

Our eyes are never completely at rest, even when our gaze is fixed on a particular place called the fixation point. Our eyes make fast, aimless, jittering movements, similar to the fine tremors our hands and fingers make when we try to keep them still. They also make occasional slow movements away from the target they are fixed on, which are terminated by quick movements that bring the image of the fixation point back to the fovea.

Although the small, jerky movements that the eyes make when at rest are random, they appear to serve a useful function. Riggs *et al.* (1953) devised a way to project stabilised images on the retina – images that remain in the same location on the retina. They mounted a small mirror in a contact lens worn by the participant and bounced a beam of light off it. They then projected the image onto a white screen in front of the participant, bounced it off several more mirrors, and finally directed it towards the participant's eye, as illustrated by Figure 5.16.

The path of the light was arranged so that the image on the screen moved in perfect synchrony with the eye movements. If the eye moved, so did the image; thus, the image that the experimenters projected always fell on precisely the same part of the retina despite the subject's eye movements. Under these conditions, details of visual stimuli began to disappear. At first, the image was clear, but then a 'fog' drifted over the subject's field of view, obscuring the image. After a while, some images could not be seen at all. All of this occurred within seconds.

These results suggest that elements of the visual system are not responsive to an unchanging stimulus. The pho-

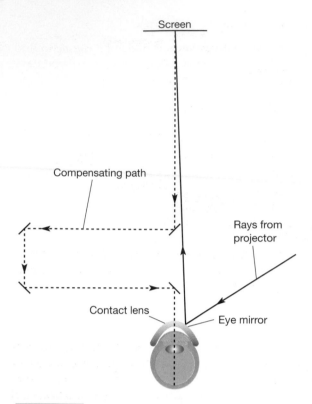

Screen

Compensating path

Rays from projector

Contact lens

Eye mirror

Figure 5.16

A procedure for stabilising an image on the retina.

Source: Riggs, L.A., Ratliff, F., Cornsweet, J.C. and Cornsweet, T.N., *Journal of the Optical Society of America*, 1953, 43, 495–501. Reprinted with permission.

toreceptors or the ganglion cells, or perhaps both, apparently cease to respond to a constant stimulus. The small, involuntary movements of our eyes keep the image moving and thus keep the visual system responsive to the details of the scene before us. Without these involuntary movements, our vision would become blurry soon after we fixed our gaze on a single point and our eyes became still.

The eyes also make three types of 'purposive' movement: conjugate movements, saccadic movements and pursuit movements. **Conjugate movements** are co-operative movements that keep both eyes fixed on the same target – or, more precisely, that keep the image of the target object on corresponding parts of the two retinas. If you hold up a finger in front of your face, look at it, and then bring your finger closer to your face, your eyes will make conjugate movements towards your nose. If you then look at an object on the other side of the room, your eyes will rotate outward, and you will see two separate blurry images of your finger. As you will learn in Chapter 6, conjugate eye movements assist in depth perception – in the perception of distance.

When you scan the scene in front of you, your gaze travels from point to point as you examine important or interesting features. As you do so, your eyes make jerky **saccadic movements** – you shift your gaze abruptly from one point to another. For example, when you read a line in

this book, your eyes stop several times, moving very quickly between each stop. You cannot consciously control the speed of movement between stops; during each saccade the eyes move as fast as they can.

Much of the time, the scene in front of us contains moving objects: objects blown by the wind, cars, aeroplanes, animals, other people. When we concentrate on one of these objects, we fix our gaze on it and track its movements with our eyes. These tracking movements, which follow the object we are watching, are called **pursuit movements**.

Colour vision

Light consists of radiant energy having wavelengths between 380 and 760 nm. Light of different wavelengths gives rise to sensations of different colours. How can we tell the difference between different wavelengths of light?

Experiments have shown that there are three types of cone in the human eye, each containing a different type of photopigment. Each type of photopigment is most sensitive to light of a particular wavelength. That is, light of a particular wavelength most readily causes a particular photopigment to split. Thus, different types of cone are stimulated by different wavelengths of light. Information from the three types of cone enables us to perceive colours.

Wavelength is related to colour, but the terms are not synonymous. For example, the spectral colours (the colours we see in a rainbow, which contains the entire spectrum of visible radiant energy) do not include all the colours that we can see, such as brown, pink, and the metallic colours silver and gold. The fact that not all colours are found in the spectrum means that differences in wavelength alone do not account for the differences in the colours we can perceive.

The dimensions of colour

Most colours can be described in terms of three physical dimensions: wavelength, intensity, and purity. Three perceptual dimensions – hue, brightness and saturation – corresponding to these physical dimensions describe what we see. The **hue** of most colours is determined by wavelength; for example, light having a wavelength of 540 nm is perceived as green. A colour's **brightness** is determined by the intensity, or amount of energy, of the light that is being perceived, all other factors being equal. A colour of maximum brightness dazzles us with a lot of light. A colour of minimum brightness is simply black. The third perceptual dimension of colour, **saturation**, is roughly equivalent to purity. A fully saturated colour consists of light of only one wavelength, for example pure red or pure blue. Desaturated colours look pastel or washed out. See Table 5.2 for a summary of the dimensions of colour.

Saturation is probably the most difficult dimension of colour to understand. White light consists of a mixture of all wavelengths of light. Although its components consist of light of all possible hues, we perceive it as being colour-

Table 5.2 Physical and perceptual dimensions of colour

Perceptual dimension	Physical dimension	Physical characteristics
Hue	Wavelength	Frequency of oscillation of light radiation
Brightness	Intensity	Amount of energy of light radiation
Saturation	Purity	Intensity of dominant wavelength relative to total radiant energy

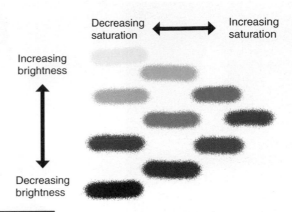

Figure 5.17

Hue, brightness and saturation. The colours shown have the same dominant wavelength (hue) but different saturation and brightness.

less. White light is completely desaturated; no single wavelength is dominant. If we begin with light of a single wavelength (a pure, completely saturated colour) and then mix in some white light, the result will be a less saturated colour. For example, when white light is added to red light (700 nm), the result is pink light. The dominant wavelength of 700 nm gives the colour a reddish hue, but the addition of white light to the mixture decreases the colour's saturation. In other words, pink is a less saturated version of red. Figure 5.17 illustrates how a colour having a particular dominant wavelength (hue) can vary in its brightness and saturation.

Colour mixing

Vision is a synthetic sensory modality. It synthesises (puts together) rather than analyses (takes apart). When two wavelengths of light are present, we see an intermediate colour rather than the two components. In contrast, the auditory system is analytical. If a high note and a low note are played together on a piano, we hear both notes instead of a single, intermediate tone. The addition of two or more lights of different wavelengths is called **colour mixing**. Colour mixing is an additive process and is very different from paint mixing. So are its results. If we pass a beam of white light through a prism, we break it into the spectrum of the different wavelengths it contains. If we recombine these colours by passing them through another prism, we obtain white light again (see Figure 5.18).

Colour mixing must not be confused with pigment mixing – what we do when we mix paints. An object has a particular colour because it contains pigments that absorb some wavelengths of light (converting them into heat) and reflect other wavelengths. For example, the chlorophyll found in the leaves of plants absorbs less green light than light of other wavelengths. When a leaf is illuminated by white light, it reflects a high proportion of green light and appears green to us.

When we mix paints, we are subtracting colours, not adding them. Mixing two paints yields a darker result. For example, adding blue paint to yellow paint yields green paint, which certainly looks darker than yellow. But mixing two beams of light of different wavelengths always yields a brighter colour. For example, when red and green light are shone together on a piece of white paper, we see yellow. In fact, we cannot tell a pure yellow light from a synthesised one made of the proper intensities of red and green light. To our eyes, both yellows appear identical.

To reconstitute white light, we do not even have to recombine all the wavelengths in the spectrum. If we shine a blue light, a green light and a red light together on a sheet of white paper and properly adjust their intensities,

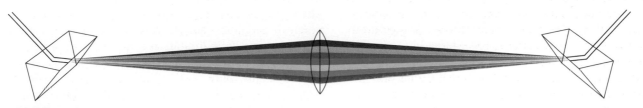

Figure 5.18

Colour mixing. White light can be split into a spectrum of colours with a prism and recombined through another prism.

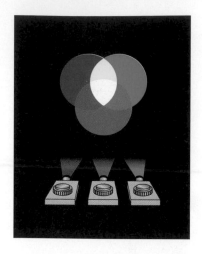

Figure 5.19

Additive colour mixing and paint mixing. When blue, red and green light of the proper intensity are all shone together, the result is white light. When red, blue and yellow paints are mixed together, the result is a dark grey.

the place where all three beams overlap will look perfectly white. A colour television or a computer display screen uses this system. When white appears on the screen, it actually consists of tiny dots of red, blue and green light (see Figure 5.19).

Colour coding in the retina

In 1802, Thomas Young, a British physicist and physician, noted that the human visual system can synthesise any colour from various amounts of almost any set of three colours of different wavelengths. Young proposed a trichromatic theory ('three colour' theory) of colour vision. He hypothesised that the eye contains three types of colour receptor, each sensitive to a different hue, and that the brain synthesises colours by combining the information received by each type of receptor. He suggested that these receptors were sensitive to three of the colours that people perceive as 'pure': blue, green and red. Young's suggestion was incorporated into a more elaborate theory of colour vision by Hermann von Helmholtz.

Experiments in recent years have shown that the cones in the human eye do contain three types of photopigment, each of which preferentially absorbs light of a particular wavelength: 420, 530 and 560 nm. Although these wavelengths actually correspond to blue-violet, green and yellow-green, most investigators refer to these receptors as blue, green and red cones. To simplify the discussion here, we will assume that the three types of cone respond to these three pure hues. Red and green cones are present in about equal proportions. There are far fewer blue cones.

Several scientists after Young and Helmholtz devised theories that took account of the fact that people also perceive yellow as a psychologically pure hue. Late in the nineteenth century, Ewald Hering, a German physiologist, noted that the four primary hues appeared to belong to pairs of opposing colours: red/green and yellow/blue. We

can imagine a bluish green or a yellowish green, or a bluish red or a yellowish red. However, we cannot imagine a greenish red or a yellowish blue. Hering originally suggested that we cannot imagine these blends because there are two types of photoreceptor, one kind responding to green and red and the other kind responding to yellow and blue.

Hering's hypothesis about the nature of photoreceptors was wrong, but his principle describes the characteristics of the information the retinal ganglion cells send to the brain. Two types of ganglion cell encode colour vision: red/green cells and yellow/blue cells. Both types of ganglion cell fire at a steady rate when they are not stimulated. If a spot of red light shines on the retina, excitation of the red cones causes the red/green ganglion cells to begin to fire at a high rate.

Conversely, if a spot of green light shines on the retina, excitation of the green cones causes the red/green ganglion cells to begin to fire at a slow rate. Thus, the brain learns about the presence of red or green light by the increased or decreased rate of firing of axons attached to red/green ganglion cells. Similarly, yellow/blue ganglion cells are excited by yellow light and inhibited by blue light. Because red and green light, and yellow and blue light, have opposite effects on the rate of axon firing, this coding scheme is called an opponent process.

Figures 5.20(a)–(c) provide a schematic explanation of the opponent-process coding that takes place in the retina. Stimulation of a red cone by red light excites the red/green ganglion cell, whereas stimulation of a green cone by green light inhibits the red/green ganglion cell (Figures 5.20(a) and (b)). If the photoreceptors are stimulated by yellow light, both the red and green cones are stimulated equally. Because of the neural circuitry between the photoreceptors and the ganglion cells, the result is that the yellow/blue ganglion cell is excited, signalling yellow (Figure 5.20(c)).

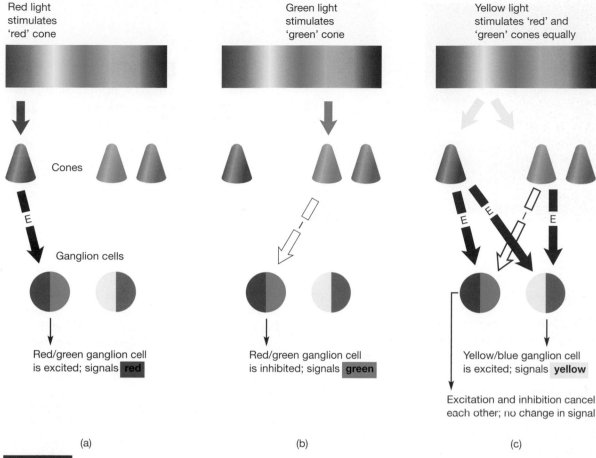

Figure 5.20

Colour coding in the retina. (a) Red light stimulating a 'red' cone, which causes excitation of a red/green ganglion cell. (b) Green light stimulating a 'green' cone, which causes inhibition of a red/green ganglion cell. (c) Yellow light stimulating 'red' and 'green' cones equally. The stimulation of 'red' and 'green' cones causes excitation of a yellow/blue ganglion cell. The arrows labelled E and I represent neural circuitry within the retina that translates excitation of a cone into excitation or inhibition of a ganglion cell, respectively. For clarity, only some of the circuits are shown.

The retina contains red/green and yellow/blue ganglion cells because of the nature of the connections between the cones, bipolar cells and ganglion cells. The brain detects various colours by comparing the rates of firing of the axons in the optic nerve that signal red or green and yellow or blue. Now you can see why we cannot perceive a reddish green or a bluish yellow: an axon that signals red or green (or yellow or blue) can either increase or decrease its rate of firing. It cannot do both at the same time. A reddish green would have to be signalled by a ganglion cell firing slowly and rapidly at the same time, which is obviously impossible.

Negative after-images

Figure 5.21 demonstrates an interesting property of the visual system: the formation of a negative after-image. Stare at the cross in the centre of the image on the left for approximately thirty seconds. Then quickly look at the cross in the centre of the white rectangle to the right. You will have a fleeting experience of seeing the red and green colours of a radish – colours that are complementary, or opposite, to the ones on the left. Complementary items go together to make up a whole. In this context, complementary colours are those that make white (or shades of grey) when added together.

The most important cause of negative after-images is adaptation in the rate of firing of retinal ganglion cells. When ganglion cells are excited or inhibited for a prolonged period of time, they later show a rebound effect, firing faster or slower than normal. For example, the green of the radish in Figure 5.20 inhibits some red/green ganglion cells. When this region of the retina is then stimulated with the neutral-coloured light reflected off the white rectangle, the red/green ganglion cells – no longer inhibited by the green light – fire faster than normal. Thus, we see a red after-image of the radish.

Defects in colour vision

Approximately one in twenty men has some form of defective colour vision. These defects are sometimes called colour blindness, but this term should probably be reserved for the very few people who cannot see any colour at all. Men and boys are affected more than women and girls because many of the genes for producing photopigments are located on the X chromosome. Because males have only one X chromosome (females have two), a defective gene there will always be expressed.

There are many different types of defective colour vision. Two of the three described here involve the red/green system. People with these defects confuse red and green. Their primary colour sensations are yellow and blue; red and green both look yellowish. Figure 5.22 shows one of the figures from a commonly used test for defective colour vision. A person who confuses red and green will not be able to see the '5'.

The most common defect, called **protanopia** (literally, 'first-colour defect'), appears to result from a lack of the photopigment for red cones. The fact that people with protanopia have relatively normal acuity suggests that they have red cones but that these cones are filled with green photopigment (Boynton, 1979). If red cones were missing, almost half of the cones would be gone from the retina, and vision would be less acute. To a protanope, red looks much darker than green. The second form of red/green defect, called **deuteranopia** ('second-colour defect'), appears to result from the opposite kind of substitution: green cones are filled with red photopigment. Around 8 per cent of European men and 0.5 per cent of European women have the inherited colour defect, Daltonism (protanopia and deuteranopia) (Fletcher and Voke, 1985) and there is evidence of other culture-related differences in colour vision impairment although whether such differences are due to cultural or physiological differences is unclear (Davies *et al.*, 1998). The topic of colour perception and the use of colour terms across cultures is discussed in more detail in the next chapter. The third form of colour defect, called **tritanopia** ('third-colour defect'), involves the blue cones and is much rarer: it affects fewer than 1 in 10,000 people.

Tritanopes see the world in greens and reds; to them, a clear blue sky is a bright green, and yellow looks pink. The faulty gene that causes tritanopia is not carried on a sex chromosome, therefore it is equally common in males and females. This defect appears to involve loss of blue cones, but because there are far fewer of these than of red and green cones to begin with, investigators have not yet determined whether the cones are missing or are filled with one of the other photopigments.

There are some individuals who seem to be able to sense colours when hearing words (and there are others who find that tastes elicit sensations of shapes). This is an example of synaesthesia and is taken up in the 'Controversies in psychological science' section below.

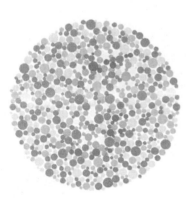

Figure 5.22

A figure commonly used to test for defective colour vision. People with red/green colour blindness will fail to see the 5.

Source: Courtesy of American Optical Corporation.

Controversies in psychological science

Can some people genuinely experience words as colours?

The issue

Imagine that you lived in a world in which words or smells evoked colours, and tastes evoked shapes, not just temporarily and not just metaphorically but in reality. This phenomenon is called synaesthesia (from the Greek *syn*, meaning 'union' and *aisthesis* meaning 'sensation'): a sensation in one modality produces an inexorable sensation in another (Harrison and Baron-Cohen, 1996). It affects about 1 in 100,000 and cases of 'coloured hearing' were reported as early as the nineteenth century (Galton, 1883).

One example of a synaesthete, as individuals who exhibit synaesthesia are called, was presented at the beginning of the chapter. Michael Watson – the individual who appeared in the opening quote – was a lecturer in the School of Arts at the University of North Carolina who claimed to be able to taste shapes (his condition gave Richard Cytowic's book its name). But is his condition genuine? Is synaesthesia a real phenomenon?

The evidence

One problem in determining whether synaesthesia exists is that the evidence is derived from self-reports. That is, individuals report their own synaesthesia. The evidence is, therefore, subjective. Using a single-case study self-report method, Baron-Cohen *et al.* (1987) investigated the synaesthetic ability of a 78-year-old woman (EP) who claimed to see colours when she heard words. Baron-Cohen *et al.* refer to this phenomenon as 'chromatic-lexical synaesthesia'. EP reported that different words evoked different colours and that this association was unsuppressable. In a test of the reliability of EP's claims, the experimenters presented her with 103 randomly presented words and asked her to indicate which colours she sensed. She was then retested, without forewarning, 10 weeks later. The researchers found that EP's responses were 100 per cent consistent at 10 weeks; an IQ-matched control was only 17 per cent consistent at two weeks.

Of course, this is one individual and the ability she exhibited might be unique to her and not to others claiming synaesthetic ability. To investigate this further, Baron-Cohen *et al.* (1993) studied nine individuals who claimed to sense colours when hearing speech. In an extensive series of tests, the experimenters examined synaesthesia for meaningful words, words from semantic categories, the days of the week, first names, letters of the alphabet, emotionally neutral words, pronouns and prepositions and nonsense words. The participants were tested at two points, one year apart. The researchers found that identical responses were reported in 92.3 per cent of cases over one year; for a control

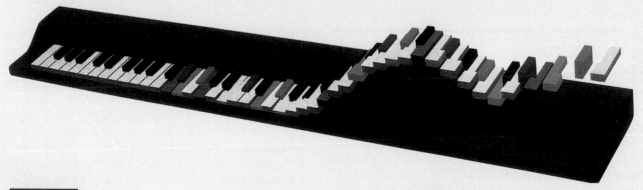

Figure 5.23

Some people claim to 'see' colours when they hear specific musical notes. The composer Liszt was one such person.

Source: Brash, S., Maranto, G., Murphy, W. and Walker, B. (1990) *How Things Work: The Brain*. Virginia: Time-Life Books. Copyright © 1990 by Time-Life Books.

Continued overleaf

group, the response rate was 37.6 per cent after only one week. Some colours were specifically elicited by vowels. For example, the same colours were consistently associated with 'i', 'o' and 'u' (88.9 per cent of the time).

These results across time are quite impressive. If synaesthesia is a genuine phenomenon, why should it happen? Baron-Cohen *et al.* suggest that because the brain contains regions responsible for colour sensation and another for language processing, two hypotheses are possible. One is that synaesthetes show a breakdown in modularity (recall from Chapter 4 that modularity refers to the notion that separate brain systems or 'modules' are responsible for specific functions). That is, there are links between the colour and language regions that have either disappeared or never even existed in non-synaesthetes. In synaesthetes, however, these links are intact. Alternatively, non-synaesthetes can inhibit the activity of these modules but this inhibition is dysfunctional in synaesthetes.

To examine these hypotheses, Paulesu *et al.* (1996) conducted a PET study of six synaesthete women who were asked to indicate which colours they sensed when hearing words and tones. A control group of non-synaesthete women also performed the same task under the same conditions. The experimenters found that synaesthesia was elicited by words but not by tones. The next step was to see whether the sensations elicited by the words activated the brain regions suggested by Baron-Cohen *et al.* While both synaesthetes and controls activated the perisylvian regions of the brain, the synaesthetes showed activation of other visual association areas including the posterior inferior temporal cortex (PITC) and the junction between the parietal and occipital cortex. Paulesu *et al.* (1996) draw attention to evidence indicating that the PITC is implicated in the integration of colour with shape when attending to visual features of objects that are referred to in verbal tasks. Activation was also found in the right prefrontal cortex, insula and superior temporal gyrus. However, no activation was observed in the major visual areas such as the primary visual cortex (V1) suggesting that it is possible to experience conscious visual perception without activating V1. This lack of V1 activation suggests to the researchers that synaesthesia involves an interaction between the areas of the brain responsible for higher visual function and the areas responsible for aspects of language processing.

Conclusion

Synaesthesia is a fascinating phenomenon but highlights one of the problems of studying sensation. The problem is as old as psychology and philosophy: how do we really know that the person is experiencing what he or she says she is experiencing. Baron-Cohen's studies suggest two ways of circumventing this problem: (1) look for consistency of responses in an experimental group over time and compare these with control responses, and (2) compare brain activation in these two groups, working under the assumption that synaesthesia activates different areas of the brain when compared with a resting state and with a non-synaesthete control group.

Audition

Vision involves the perception of objects in three dimensions, at a variety of distances, and with a multitude of colours and textures. These complex stimuli may occur at a single point in time or over an extended period. They may also involve an unchanging scene or a rapidly changing one. The other senses analyse much simpler stimuli (such as an odour or a taste) or depend on time and stimulus change for the development of a complex perception. For example, to perceive a solid object in three dimensions by means of touch, we must manipulate it – turn it over in our hands or move our hands over its surface. The stimulus must change over time for a fully-fledged perception of form to emerge. The same is true for audition: we hear nothing meaningful in an instant.

Most people consider the sense of hearing second in importance only to vision. In some ways it is more important. A blind person can converse and communicate with other people almost as well as a sighted person. Deafness is much more likely to produce social isolation. A deaf person cannot easily join in the conversation of a group of people who do not know sign language. Although our eyes can transmit much more information to the brain, our ears are used for some of our most important forms of social communication.

Sound

Sound consists of rhythmical pressure changes in air. As an object vibrates, it causes the air around it to move. When the object is in the phase of vibration in which it moves towards you, it compresses molecules of air; as it moves away, it pulls the molecules of air farther apart. As a pressure wave arrives at your ear, it bends your eardrum in. The following wave of negative pressure (when the molecules are pulled farther apart) causes your eardrum to bulge out.

Sound waves are measured in frequency units of cycles per second called **hertz (Hz)**. The human ear perceives vibrations between approximately 30 and 20,000 Hz. Sound waves can vary in intensity and frequency. These variations produce corresponding changes in sensations of loudness and pitch. Consider a loudspeaker, a device that contains a paper cone moved back and forth by a coil of wire located in a magnetic field. Alternations in the electrical current transmitted from an amplifier to this coil cause the coil (and the paper cone) to move back and forth. If the cone begins vibrating more rapidly, the pitch of the sound increases. If the vibrations become more intense (that is, if the cone moves in and out over a greater distance), the loudness of the sound increases. A third perceptual dimension, timbre, corresponds to the complexity of the sound vibration. See Figure 5.24.

The ear and its functions

When people refer to the ear, they usually mean what anatomists call the pinna – the flesh-covered cartilage attached to the side of the head (*pinna* means 'wing' in Latin). But the pinna performs only a small role in audition: it helps to funnel sound through the ear canal towards the middle and inner ear, where the business of hearing is done (see Figure 5.25).

The ear-drum is a thin, flexible membrane that vibrates back and forth in response to sound waves and passes these vibrations on to the receptor cells in the inner ear. The ear-drum is attached to the first of a set of three middle ear bones called the **ossicles** (literally, 'little bones'). The three ossicles are known as the hammer, the anvil and the stirrup because of their shapes. These bones act together, in lever fashion, to transmit the vibrations of the ear-drum to the fluid-filled structure of the inner ear that contains the receptive organ.

The bony structure that contains the receptive organ is called the **cochlea** (*kokhlos* means 'snail', which accurately

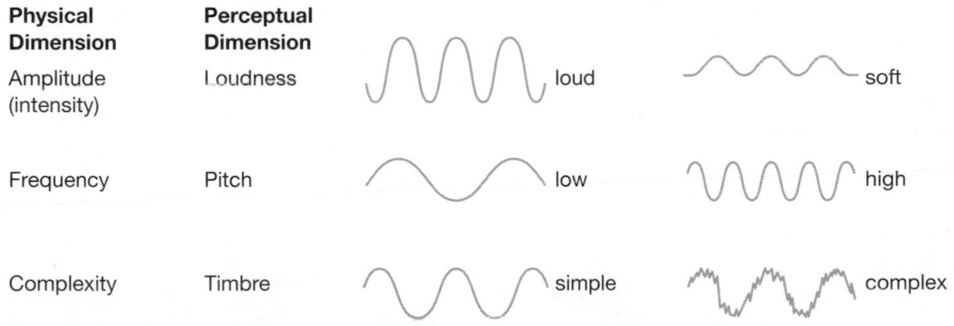

Physical Dimension	Perceptual Dimension				
Amplitude (intensity)	Loudness	∿	loud	∿	soft
Frequency	Pitch	∿	low	∿	high
Complexity	Timbre	∿	simple	∿	complex

Figure 5.24

The physical and perceptual dimensions of sound waves.

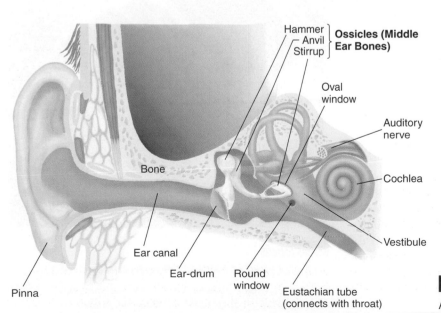

Figure 5.25

Anatomy of the auditory system.

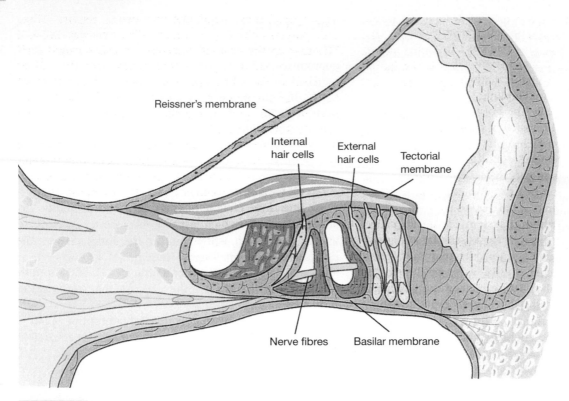

Reissner's membrane

Internal hair cells

External hair cells

Tectorial membrane

Nerve fibres

Basilar membrane

Figure 5.26

(a) A schematic image of the cochlea.

Source: Beatty, J., *Principles of Behavioral Neuroscience*. Madison: Wm C. Brown Communications, Inc. Copyright © 1995 by The McGraw-Hill Companies. Reproduced with permission of The McGraw-Hill Companies.

describes its shape). The cochlea is filled with a liquid. A bony chamber attached to the cochlea (the vestibule) contains two openings, the oval window and the round window. The last of the three ossicles (the stirrup) presses against a membrane behind an opening in the bone surrounding the cochlea called the oval window, thus transmitting sound waves into the liquid inside the cochlea, where it can reach the receptive organ for hearing. The cochlea is divided into two parts by the basilar membrane – a sheet of tissue that contains the auditory receptor cells. As the footplate of the stirrup presses back and forth against the membrane behind the oval window, pressure changes in the fluid above the basilar membrane cause the basilar membrane to vibrate back and forth. Because the basilar membrane varies in its width and flexibility, different frequencies of sound cause different parts of the basilar membrane to vibrate. High-frequency sounds cause the end near the oval window to vibrate, medium-frequency sounds cause the middle to vibrate, and low-frequency sounds cause the tip to vibrate. Figures 5.26(a) and (b) show a schematic drawing and the corresponding photographic image of the cochlea.

In order for the basilar membrane to vibrate freely, the fluid in the lower chamber of the cochlea must have

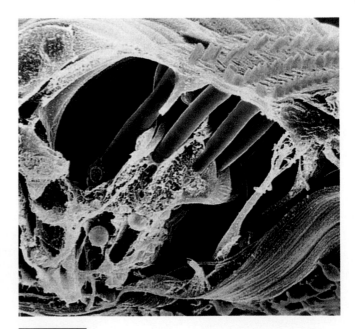

Figure 5.26

(b) A photographic image of the cochlea.

Source: Beatty, J., *Principles of Behavioral Neuroscience*. Madison: Wm C. Brown Communications, Inc. Copyright © 1995 The McGraw-Hill Companies.

somewhere to go. Free space is provided by the round window. When the basilar membrane flexes down, the displacement of the fluid causes the membrane behind the round window to bulge out. In turn, when the basilar membrane flexes up, the membrane behind the round window bulges in.

Some people suffer from a middle ear disease that causes bone to grow over the round window. Because their basilar membrane cannot easily flex back and forth, these people have a severe hearing loss. However, their hearing can be restored by a surgical procedure called fenestration ('window making') in which a tiny hole is drilled in the bone where the round window should be.

Sounds are detected by special neurons known as **auditory hair cells**, located on the basilar membrane. Auditory hair cells transduce mechanical energy caused by the flex-

ing of the basilar membrane into neural activity. These cells possess hairlike protrusions called **cilia** ('eyelashes'). The ends of the cilia are embedded in a fairly rigid shelf (the **tectorial membrane**) that hangs over the basilar membrane like a balcony. When sound vibrations cause the basilar membrane to flex back and forth, the cilia are stretched. This pull on the cilia is translated into neural activity (see Figure 5.27).

When a mechanical force is exerted on the cilia of the auditory hair cells, the electrical charge across their membrane is altered. The change in the electrical charge causes a transmitter substance to be released at a synapse between the auditory hair cell and the dendrite of a neuron of the auditory nerve. The release of the transmitter substance excites the neuron, which transmits messages through the auditory nerve to the brain.

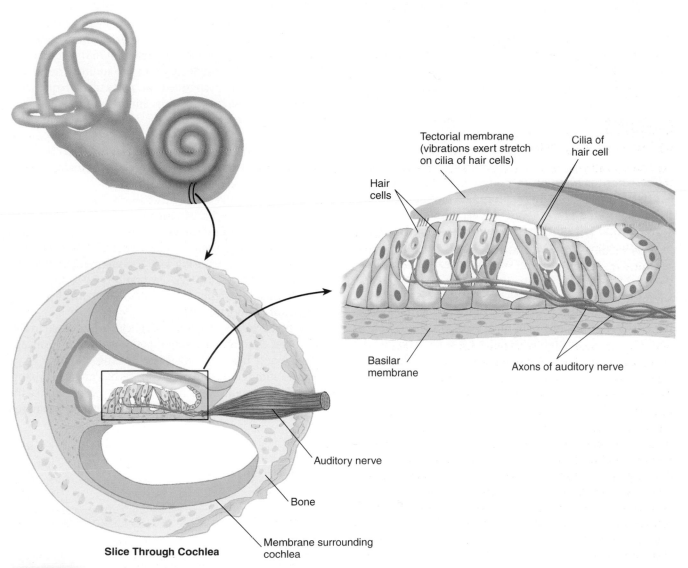

Slice Through Cochlea

Auditory nerve

Bone

Membrane surrounding cochlea

Tectorial membrane (vibrations exert stretch on cilia of hair cells)

Cilia of hair cell

Hair cells

Basilar membrane

Axons of auditory nerve

Figure 5.27

The transduction of sound vibrations in the auditory system.

Detecting and localising sounds in the environment

As we saw, sounds can differ in loudness, pitch and timbre. They also have sources; they come from particular locations. How does the ear distinguish these characteristics? The ear's ability to distinguish sounds by their timbre depends on its ability to distinguish loudness and pitch. Some common auditory stimuli and their loudness levels are presented in Figure 5.28.

Loudness and pitch

Scientists originally thought that the neurons of the auditory system represented pitch by firing in synchrony with the vibrations of the basilar membrane. However, they subsequently learned that axons cannot fire rapidly enough to represent the high frequencies that we can hear. A good, young ear can hear frequencies of more than 20,000 Hz, but axons cannot fire more than 1,000 times per second. Therefore, high-frequency sounds, at least, must be encoded in some other way.

As we saw, high-frequency and medium-frequency sounds cause different parts of the basilar membrane to vibrate. Thus, sounds of different frequencies stimulate different groups of auditory hair cells located along the basilar membrane. At least for high-frequency and medium-frequency sounds, therefore, the brain is informed of the pitch of a sound by the activity of different sets of axons from the auditory nerve. When medium-frequency sound waves reach the ear, the middle of the basilar membrane vibrates, and auditory hair cells located in this region are activated. In contrast, high-frequency sounds activate auditory hair cells located at the base of the basilar membrane, near the oval window.

Two kinds of evidence indicate that pitch is detected in this way. First, direct observation of the basilar membrane has shown that the region of maximum vibration depends on the frequency of the stimulating tone (von Békésy, 1960). Secondly, experiments have found that damage to specific regions of the basilar membrane causes loss of the ability to perceive specific frequencies. The discovery that some antibiotics damage hearing (for example, deafness is one of the possible side effects of an antibiotic used to treat tuberculosis) has helped auditory researchers to investigate the anatomical coding of pitch. Stebbins *et al.* (1969) administered an antibiotic to different groups of animals for varying times. Next, they tested the animals' ability to perceive tones of different frequencies. Afterwards, they removed the animals' cochleas and examined them. They found that the longer the animals were exposed to the antibiotic, the more of their hair cells were killed. Damage started at the end of the basilar membrane nearest the oval window and progressed towards the other end. The experimenters compared the various groups of animals and found that the hearing loss was proportional to the amount of damage to the hair cells. The loss began with the highest frequencies and progressed towards the lower frequencies. Thus, the hair cells nearest the oval window are responsible for detecting high-pitched sounds.

Although high-frequency and medium-frequency sounds are detected because they cause different regions of the basilar membrane to vibrate, low-frequency sounds are detected by a different method. Kiang (1965) recorded the electrical activity of single axons in the auditory nerve and found many that responded to particular frequencies. Presumably, these axons were stimulated by hair cells located on different regions of the basilar membrane. However, he did not find any axons that responded uniquely to particular frequencies lower than 200 Hz – and yet tones lower than 200 Hz are easily perceived. How, then, are the lower frequencies encoded?

The answer is this. Frequencies lower than 200 Hz cause the very tip of the basilar membrane to vibrate in synchrony with the sound waves. Neurons that are stimulated by hair cells located there are able to fire in synchrony with these vibrations, thus firing at the same frequency as the sound. The brain 'counts' these vibrations (so to speak) and thus detects low-frequency sounds. This process is an example of temporal coding.

The best evidence that low frequencies are detected in this way comes from an experiment performed many years ago by Miller and Taylor (1948). These investigators used white noise as a stimulus. White noise consists of a random mixture of all the perceptible frequencies of sound – it sounds like the 'sssh' heard when a television or FM radio is tuned between

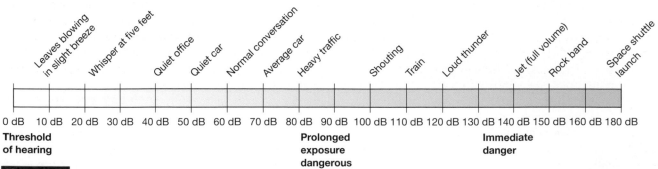

Figure 5.28

The average decibel level of some common (and uncommon) noises.

stations. White noise stimulates all regions of the basilar membrane because it contains all frequencies of sound.

Miller and Taylor presented participants with white noise that passed through a hole in a rotating disk. By spinning the disk at various speeds, the investigators could divide the noise into extremely brief pulsations, which could be presented at various time intervals. Thus, a 'pitch' was artificially created by setting the pulsation of the white noise at a certain speed. When the frequency of the pulsation was less than 250 Hz, the participants could accurately identify its pitch. However, above 250 Hz, the perception of pitch disappeared. Because the white noise stimulated all parts of the basilar membrane, the low-frequency sounds must have been detected by neurons that fired in synchrony with the pulsations. The medium-frequency and high-frequency sounds could not be differentiated by frequency of pulsation alone.

What about loudness? The axons of the cochlear nerve appear to inform the brain of the loudness of a stimulus by altering their rate of firing. More intense vibrations stimulate the auditory hair cells more intensely. This stimulation causes them to release more transmitter substance, which results in a higher rate of firing by the axons in the auditory nerve.

This explanation works for the axons involved in place coding of pitch; in this case, pitch is signalled by which neurons fire, and loudness is signalled by their rate of firing. However, the neurons that signal lower frequencies do so with their rate of firing. If they fire more frequently, they signal a higher pitch. Obviously, they cannot signal both loudness and pitch by the same means. Therefore, most investigators believe that the loudness of low-frequency sounds is signalled by the number of auditory hair cells that are active at a given time. A louder sound excites a larger number of hair cells.

Timbre

You can easily distinguish between the sounds of a violin and a clarinet, even if they are playing tones of the same pitch and loudness. So, clearly, pitch and loudness are not the only characteristics of a sound. Sounds can vary greatly in complexity. They can start suddenly or gradually increase in loudness, be short or long, and seem thin and reedy or full and vibrant. The enormous variety of sounds that we can distinguish is in large part owing to an important characteristic of sound called timbre.

The combining, or synthesis, of two or more simple tones, each consisting of a single frequency, can produce a complex tone. For example, an electronic synthesiser produces a mixture of sounds of different frequencies, each of which can be varied in amplitude (intensity). Thus, it can synthesise the complex sounds of a clarinet or violin or can assemble completely new sounds not produced by any other source. Conversely, complex sounds that have a regular sequence of waves can be reduced by means of analysis into several simple tones.

We can tell a clarinet from another instrument because each instrument produces sounds consisting of a unique set of simple tones called overtones. Their frequencies are multiples of the fundamental frequency, or the basic pitch of the sound. Timbre is the distinctive combination of overtones with the fundamental frequency. The fundamental frequency causes one part of the basilar membrane to flex, while each of the overtones causes another portion to flex. During a complex sound many different portions of the basilar membrane are flexing simultaneously. Thus, the ear analyses a complex sound. Information about the fundamental frequency and each of the overtones is sent to the brain through the auditory nerve, and the person hears a complex tone having a particular timbre. When you consider that we can listen to an orchestra and identify several instruments playing simultaneously, you can appreciate the complexity of the analysis performed by the auditory system.

Locating the source of a sound

When we hear an unexpected sound, we usually turn our heads quickly to face its source. Even newborn infants can make this response with reasonably good accuracy. And once our faces are oriented towards the source of the sound, we can detect changes in its location of as little as 1 degree. To do so, we make use of two qualities of sound: relative loudness and difference in arrival time.

Relative loudness is the most effective means of perceiving the location of high-frequency sounds. Acoustic energy, in the form of vibrations, does not actually pass through solid objects. Low-frequency sounds can easily make a large solid object such as a wall vibrate, setting the air on the other side in motion and producing a new sound across the barrier. But large solid objects cannot vibrate rapidly, so they effectively damp out high-frequency sounds. Thus, they cast a 'sound shadow', just as opaque objects cast a shadow in the sunlight. The head is one such large solid object, and it damps out high-frequency sounds so that they appear much louder to the ear nearer the source of the sound. Thus, if a source on your right produces a high-frequency sound, your right ear will receive more intense stimulation than your left ear will. The brain uses this difference to calculate the location of the source of the sound.

The second method involves detecting differences in the arrival time of sound pressure waves at each eardrum. This method works best for frequencies below approximately 3,000 Hz. A 1,000 Hz tone produces pressure waves approximately 0.3 m apart. Because the distance between a person's eardrums is somewhat less than half that, a source of 1,000 Hz sound located to one side of the head will cause one eardrum to be pushed in while the other eardrum is being pulled out. In contrast, if the source of the sound is directly in front of the listener, both eardrums will move in synchrony.

Researchers have found that when the source of a sound is located to the side of the head, axons in the right and left auditory nerves will fire at different times. The brain is able to detect this disparity, which causes the sound to be perceived as being off to one side. In fact, the brain can detect differences in firing times of a fraction of a millisecond (one-thousandth of a second). The easiest stimuli to locate are those that produce brief clicks, which cause brief bursts of neural activity. Apparently, it is easiest for the brain to compare the arrival times of single bursts of incoming information.

Deafness

Deafness profoundly affects a person's ability to communicate with others but hearing difficulties disappear in the company of other deaf people; it is only in the company of people who have normal hearing that deafness hinders a person's ability to communicate (Erting *et al.*, 1989; Sachs, 1989; Schein, 1989).

People who are postlingually deaf – people who become deaf late in life, after they have learned oral and written language – are unlikely to learn sign language. (In this context, lingual, from the word for 'tongue', refers to the acquisition of spoken language.) Some prelingually deaf people – people who are born deaf or who become deaf during infancy – never learn sign language, primarily because they are 'mainstreamed' in community schools or attend a school for the deaf that teaches oral communication.

A recent technological development, the cochlear implant, is an electronic device surgically implanted in the inner ear that can enable deaf people to hear. It is most useful for two groups: people who became deaf in adulthood and very young children. Putting a cochlear implant in a young child means that the child's early education will be committed to the oralist approach. Many deaf people, however, resent the implication that deafness is something that needs to be repaired, seeing themselves as different but not at all defective.

Questions to think about

Vision and audition

- A naturalist once noted that when a male bird stakes out his territory, he sings with a very sharp, staccato song that says, in effect, 'Here I am, and stay away!' In contrast, if a predator appears in the vicinity, many birds will emit alarm calls that consist of steady whistles that start and end slowly. Knowing what you do about the two means of localising sounds, why do these two types of call have different characteristics?
- Why do we have colour vision? Has the evolution of colour vision put us at an advantage over other species?
- If you had a child who was born deaf, would you send your child to a school that taught sign language or to one that emphasised speaking and lip-reading? Why? Now imagine that you are deaf (or, if you are deaf, that you are hearing). Would your answer change?

Gustation

We have two senses specialised for detecting chemicals in our environment: taste and smell. Together, they are referred to as the chemosenses and the process of sensing chemicals is called chemosensation. Taste, or gustation, is the simplest of the sense modalities. We can perceive four qualities of taste: sourness, sweetness, saltiness and bitterness. A fifth, umami, has been suggested and describes a savoury sensation (like monosodium glutamate). Taste is not the same as flavour; the flavour of a food includes its odour, texture, temperature, shape as well as its taste: these are called head factors and some of the most important are illustrated in Figure 5.29. You have probably noticed that the flavours of foods are diminished when you have a head cold. This loss of flavour occurs not because your taste buds are inoperative but because congestion with mucus makes it difficult for odour-laden air to reach your sense of smell receptors. Without their characteristic odours to serve as cues, onions taste much like apples (although apples do not make your eyes water).

Taste receptors and the sensory pathway

The tongue has a somewhat corrugated appearance, being marked by creases and bumps. The bumps are called papillae (from the Latin, meaning 'nipple'). Each papilla contains a number of taste buds (in some cases as many as 200). See Figure 5.30 for an illustration.

A taste bud is a small organ that contains a number of receptor cells, each of which is shaped rather like a segment of an orange. The cells have hairlike projections called microvilli that protrude through the pore of the taste bud into the saliva that coats the tongue and fills the trenches of the papillae. Molecules of chemicals dissolved in the

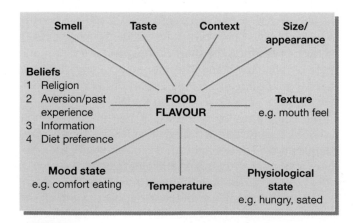

Figure 5.29

A list of factors influencing food flavour and the intention to ingest food.

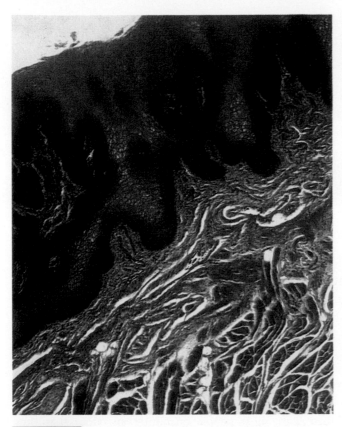

saliva stimulate the receptor cells, probably by interacting with special receptors on the microvilli that are similar to the postsynaptic receptors found on other neurons. The receptor cells form synapses with dendrites of neurons that send axons to the brain through three different cranial nerves. There are primary and secondary taste cortices in the brain, as Figure 5.31 illustrates (Rolls and Baylis, 1994); taste stimulation also activates areas of the subcortex such as the thalamus, insular cortex, anterior cingulate gyrus and lingual gyrus (Kinomura *et al.*, 1994).

The four qualities of taste

The surface of the tongue is differentially sensitive to taste. The tip is most sensitive to sweet and salty substances; the sides to sour substances; and the back of the tongue, the back of the throat, and the soft palate overhanging the back of the tongue to bitter substances (see Figure 5.32).

The physical properties of the molecules that we taste determine the nature of the taste sensations. Different molecules stimulate different types of receptor. For example, all substances that taste salty ionise (break into charged particles) when they dissolve. The most important salty substance is table salt – sodium chloride (NaCl). Other chlorides, such as lithium or potassium chloride, and some other salts, such as bromides or sulphates, are also salty in taste, but none tastes quite as salty as sodium chloride. This finding suggests that the specific function of salt-tasting receptors is to identify sodium chloride. Sodium plays a unique role in the regulation of our body fluid. If the body's store of sodium falls, we cannot retain water and

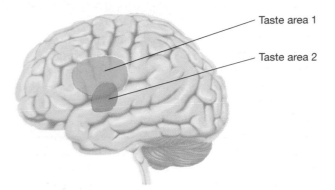

Taste area 1

Taste area 2

Figure 5.31

The brain seems to have two taste areas – a primary and a secondary taste area, located near the frontal lobe.

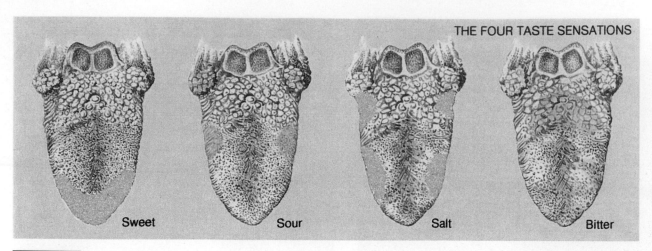

THE FOUR TASTE SENSATIONS

Sweet   Sour   Salt   Bitter

Figure 5.32

Different parts of the tongue allow the experience of different tastes.

Source: Whitfield, P. and Stoddart, M., *Pathways of Perception*. New York: Torstar Books. Copyright © 1985 by Torstar Books.

our blood volume will fall. The result can be heart failure. Loss of sodium stimulates a strong craving for the salty taste of sodium chloride.

Both bitter and sweet substances seem to consist of large, non-ionising molecules. Scientists cannot predict, merely on the basis of shape, whether a molecule will taste bitter or sweet (or neither). Some molecules (such as saccharin) stimulate both sweet and bitter receptors; they taste sweet at the front of the tongue and bitter at the back of the palate and throat. Most likely, the function of the bitterness receptor is to avoid ingesting poisons. Many plants produce alkaloids that serve to protect them against being eaten by insects or browsing animals. Some of these alkaloids are poisonous to humans, and most of them taste bitter. In contrast, the sweetness receptor enables us to recognise the sugar content of fruits and other nutritive plant foods. When sweet-loving animals gather and eat fruit, they tend to disperse the seeds and help propagate the plant; thus, the presence of sugar in the fruit is to the plant's advantage as well.

Most sour tastes are produced by acids, in particular, by the hydrogen ion (H+) contained in acid solutions. The sourness receptor probably serves as a warning device against substances that have undergone bacterial decomposition, most of which become acidic.

Olfaction

The sense of smell – olfaction – is one of the most interesting and puzzling of the sense modalities. It is unlike other sense modalities in two important ways. First, people have difficulty describing odours in words (Engen, 1987). Secondly, odours have a powerful ability to evoke old memories and feelings, even many years after an event, although they do not appear to be more effective than stimuli in other sensory modalities at doing this (Herz and Cupchik, 1992: Herz and Engen, 1996). At some time in their lives, most people encounter an odour that they recognise as having some childhood association, even though they cannot identify it. One of the most widely quoted examples of this is the French novelist, Marcel Proust, whose mammoth series of autobiographical adventures, *A la recherche du temps perdue*, was provoked by the odour of a madelein cake dipped in tea which transported him back to his childhood.

Olfaction, like audition, seems to be an analytical sense modality. That is, when we sniff air that contains a mixture of familiar odours, we can usually identify the individual components. The molecules do not blend together and produce a single odour the way lights of different wavelengths produce a single colour.

Other animals, such as dogs, have more sensitive olfactory systems than humans do because they have a great many more olfactory receptors (described below). The difference in sensitivity between our olfactory system and those of other mammals may be that other mammals put their noses where odours are the strongest – just above ground level. For example, watch a dog following an odour trail. The dog sniffs along the ground, where the odours of the passing animal will have clung. Even a bloodhound's nose would not be very useful if it were located five feet above the ground, as ours is. You can see how effective a hound's olfactory system is at tracking other animals, from Figure 5.33. However, we should not underrate our own. We can smell some substances at lower concentrations than can the most sensitive instruments (the human nose is actually more sensitive than a smoke detector).

Odours play a very important role in the lives of most mammals. Although we do not make use of olfaction in identifying one another, we do use it to avoid some dangers, such as food that has spoiled. In fact, the odour of rotting meat will trigger withdrawal – a useful response if some of the rotten meat has been swallowed. Other animals recognise friend and enemies by means of smell and use odours to attract mates and repel rivals. And the reproductive behaviour of laboratory mammals – and even the menstrual cycles of women – may be influenced by the odours emitted by other animals of the same species, a controversial topic taken up in the 'Controversies in psychological science' section below.

Anatomy of the olfactory system

Figure 5.34 shows the anatomy of the olfactory system. The olfactory system in humans is unique because it is the only sense whose receptors are directly exposed to the environment. These receptor cells lie in the olfactory mucosa, one inch square patches of mucous membrane located on the roof of the nasal sinuses, just under the base of the brain. The receptor cells have cilia that are embedded in the olfactory mucosa. They also have axons that pass through small holes in the bone above the olfactory mucosa and form synapses with neurons in the olfactory bulbs. The olfactory bulbs are stalk-like structures located at the base of the brain that contain neural circuits that perform the first analysis of olfactory information. There is evidence that the cortex also processes aspects of olfactory sensation and perception (Lorig, 1989; Martin, 1998b; Small et al., 1997).

Figure 5.33

A dog's sense of smell is vastly superior to that of humans.

Source: National Geographic, September 1986.

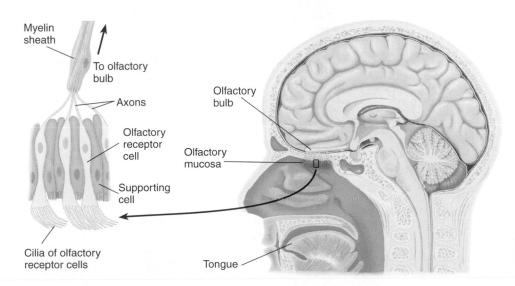

Myelin sheath

To olfactory bulb

Axons

Olfactory receptor cell

Supporting cell

Cilia of olfactory receptor cells

Olfactory bulb

Olfactory mucosa

Tongue

Figure 5.34

The olfactory system.

Controversies in psychological science

Do human pheromones exist?

The issue

Some species in the animal kingdom have a terrifically efficient sense of smell. Dogs have a remarkable ability to detect and discriminate between odours, hence their use in drug-sniffing operations. The odour of vaginal copulins can arouse male monkeys. Some odours affect the oestral cycle and sexual development of rodents. Some 'scents' are thought to produce stereotypical responses in a receiving organism without the scent being overtly detected. Such scents are called pheromones, chemicals secreted by the body which induce a stereotypical behavioural or physiological response. A well known example of a pheromone is androstenone (its full, chemical name is 5-alpha-16-androst-16-en-3-one), a steroid developed in the testes of pigs which has a musk-like odour and is secreted in the saliva of male pigs during mating.

The unusual feature of androstenone is that it can induce a sow to adopt the mating position when it is sprayed on her. Farmers and vets can even buy the chemical in aerosol form, *Boarmate*, so that the sow can be prepared for mating. (In fact, truffle hunters use sows to detect the delicacy because it contains androstenone). Pigs are not the only species to secrete androstenone. It is also present in men's sweat glands and in the urine of men and women, although at stronger concentrations in men (Brooksbank *et al.*, 1974).

The behaviour induced by androstenone in sows, together with the presence of the chemical in humans, has led some researchers to believe that a human pheromone effect exists (Cohn, 1994). Much of this work has focused on examining whether certain of the body's chemicals alter the length of the menstrual cycle and whether they increase sexual attractiveness in a person of the opposite sex.

The evidence

One of the earliest studies of the pheromone effect in humans was conducted by Martha McClintock in the 1970s (McClintock, 1971). She found that 17–22 year old women students who lived and slept in the same halls of residence reported menstrual synchrony. That is, their menstrual cycles began on or about the same time. The effect was unrelated to food intake, lifestyle pattern or stress. The result is difficult to explain because no mechanism that we know of can account for the finding. McClintock suggested that the mechanism might be pheromonal or mediated by an awareness of another's menstrual cycle. To explain the result, replications would be needed. If the effect was pheromonal then a controlled experiment in which menstrual cycles were deliberately manipulated would show this. This is what Russell *et al.* (1980) did.

They applied the sweaty secretions of a woman who had a history of 28 day cycles and experience of 'driving' (that is influencing) other women's cycles, on the upper lips of five women, three times a week for four months. Six individuals wore odourless alcohol (the control group). The mean difference in cycle onset for the experimental group was 3–9 days before the experiment; 3–4 days during driving. Controls' figures were

Figure 5.35

Farmers and veterinary surgeons sometimes spray 'Boarmate' on to a sow to get her to adopt the mating position ('Boarmate' contains a pheromone).

Source: National Geographic, September 1986.

8 days and 9.2 days respectively. A significant difference, therefore, was found between the experimental group's cycle onset and that of controls. However, there were some important limitations to the study. The experiment was not single- or double-blind which means (as you will recall from Chapter 2) that the experimenters knew which participant was in each condition and each participant knew the purpose of the experiment. The woman who provided the samples was also one of the experimenters.

In a similar experiment, Stern and McClintock (1998) examined whether such a pheromone could affect the length of ovulation. The experimenters took the odourless compounds from the armpits of women in the late (follicular) or ovulatory stages of their menstrual cycle and applied them to the top lips of 29 healthy young women aged between 20 and 35 years old. The length of the recipients' menstrual cycle was then measured. The experimenters found that women reported shorter cycles when receiving follicular compounds and longer cycles when receiving ovulatory compounds. There was a significant difference between the baseline cycle length and the cycle length reported when carriers 'wore' the compounds. Sixty-eight per cent of women responded to the compounds of both kinds. Does this suggest that 'pheromones' can modulate ovulation? Or are the effects limited to healthy young women? Would the same effect occur in women on various types of oral contraceptive? And are there alternative explanations, other than pheromonal ones, for the results?

Questions such of these crop up quite often in pheromone research in humans. They become even more pertinent when examining the results of studies investigating the effect of 'pheromones' on sexual attractiveness. One of the earliest reports suggested that men and women exposed to androstenol (a form of androstenone) rated photographs of women as sexier and more attractive than did a control group (Kirk-Smith et al., 1978). In this experiment, photographs of objects such as buildings were also rated. Oddly, these buildings were also described as 'less sensitive' in the presence of androstenol. This result, and others like it, suggests that the androstenol did not have sex-specific effects. More to the point, there was no control odour used in the experiment – participants could have made such ratings to any odour. Results since have not been particularly encouraging.

The majority of experiments, for example, have tended to expose subjects to volatile chemicals in contexts which are not generally appropriate. For example, participants have rated imaginary verbal descriptions of people (Cowley et al., 1977; Filsinger et al., 1984), pictures and slides of buildings, people and animals (Kirk-Smith and Booth, 1977; Kirk-Smith et al., 1978) or have indicated the number of sexual partners they have recently had (Filsinger and Monte, 1986). They have worn masks impregnated with an odour (Cowley et al., 1980), a necklace impregnated with the odour (Cowley and Brooksbank, 1991), worn the odour on the top lip (Benton, 1982), sat on a chair impregnated with the odour (Kirk-Smith and Booth, 1980), or used a doctored changing room cubicle (Gustavson et al., 1987). As you can see, none of these conditions reflects the behaviour and contexts normally seen when physical attraction might occur.

In the most ecologically valid experiment, Black and Biron (1982) required participants to interact with a confederate of the opposite sex who wore either androstenone or a control odour. The participant was later asked to rate the confederate for attractiveness. The experimenters found no effect of these chemicals on the rated attractiveness of the confederate.

Conclusion

Given the importance of vision to human beings and the apparent irrelevance of olfaction to most important social behaviour, it should not be surprising that odours do not produce the same reliable and strong effects in humans as they do in other animals. Vision is our dominant sense. There may also be another reason why pheromones 'don't work' in humans. There is evidence to suggest that the organ in the brain responsible for detecting and acting on these pheromones (the vomeronasal organ) may be absent in humans (Moran et al., 1995). If this organ is important for sensing pheromones then humans will have difficulty sensing pheromones. Meanwhile, however, the evidence suggests that if you want to attract a member of the opposite sex, a bottle of good perfume or cologne would be a better option than would exposing your armpits, or investing in a can of Boarmate.

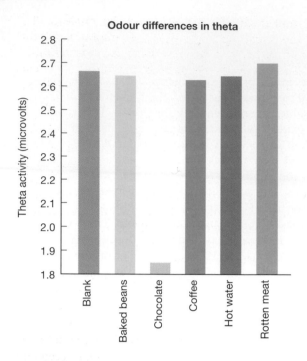

Odour differences in theta

Theta activity (microvolts)

Blank | Baked beans | Chocolate | Coffee | Hot water | Rotten meat

Figure 5.36

Differences in the amount of EEG theta activity seen when participants smell food odour. Notice the dramatic reduction in activity when they smell the odour of chocolate.

For example, Martin (1998b) recorded EEG from healthy individuals while they were exposed to a series of synthetic and real food odours. The odours included chocolate, spearmint, baked beans, strawberry, coffee and rotting pork. The results are presented in Figure 5.36. The odours of spearmint and chocolate (but primarily chocolate) were associated with significant reductions in one type of brain activity, theta (which we mentioned in Chapter 4 and will consider again in Chapter 9). This EEG waveband is associated with increases and decreases in attention and perhaps the change seen in Figure 5.36 in response to chocolate reflects this pleasant odour's ability to relax attention.

In a novel, neuroimaging experiment, Small *et al.* (1997) compared neural activation while people smelled, tasted or did both together (that is, perceived flavour). In some conditions, the odours and the tastes did not match. Using soy sauce, water, coffee, grapefruit and strawberry as stimuli, the experimenters found that when the odours and tastes were presented simultaneously, there was a decrease in activation at the primary taste cortex and the primary and secondary olfactory cortex. When tastes and smells did not match, increases in the amygdala were found. Perhaps this suggests a role for the amygdala in the processing of novel or unpleasant stimuli. (We return to the role of the amygdala in emotion in Chapter 13.)

The interaction between odour molecule and receptor appears to be similar to that of transmitter substance and postsynaptic receptor on a neuron. That is, when a molecule of an odorous substance fits a receptor molecule located on the cilia of a receptor cell, the cell becomes excited. This excitation is passed on to the brain by the axon of the receptor cell. Thus, similar mechanisms may detect the stimuli for taste and olfaction.

Unlike information from all other sensory modalities, olfactory information is not sent to the thalamus and then relayed to a specialised region of the cerebral cortex. Instead, olfactory information is sent directly to several regions of the limbic system, in particular to the amygdala and to the limbic cortex of the frontal lobe.

The dimensions of odour

We know that there are at least four qualities of taste and that a colour can be specified by hue, brightness and saturation. Recent research in molecular biology suggests that the olfactory system uses up to one thousand different

Questions to think about

Gustation and olfaction

- Bees and birds can taste sweet substances, but cats and alligators cannot. If, through the process of evolution, a species develops a greater range of foods, what do you think comes first, the food or the receptor?

- Would a species start eating something with a new taste (say, something sweet) and later develop the appropriate taste receptors, or do the taste receptors evolve first and then lead the animal to a new taste?

- Why do we prefer the taste of some types of food to others?

- Gustation and olfaction are two of the oldest senses. Why do you think this is?

- Why do you think that there are only four or five basic tastes but several thousand smells? Is it really possible to construct a classification system for odour? What are the problems with constructing one?

- Odours have a peculiar ability to evoke memories – a phenomenon vividly described by Marcel Proust in his novel *Remembrance of Things Past*. Why do you think that the memories evoked by odours are thought to be stronger and more emotional than those evoked by other sensory stimuli?

receptor molecules, located in the membrane of the receptor cells, to detect different categories of odours (Jones and Reed, 1989; Buck and Axel, 1991; Axel, 1995). Presumably, the presence of molecules of a substance with a particular odour produces a particular pattern of activity in the olfactory system. That is, the molecules will strongly stimulate some receptors, weakly stimulate others, and stimulate still others not at all. This pattern of stimulation is transmitted to the brain, where it is recognised as belonging to a particular odour. Researchers do not yet know exactly which molecules stimulate which receptors; nor do they know how the information from individual olfactory receptor cells is put together.

The somatosenses

The body senses, or somatosenses, include our ability to respond to touch, vibration, pain, warmth, coolness, limb position, muscle length and stretch, tilt of the head and changes in the speed of head rotation. The number of sense modalities represented in this list depends on one's definition of a sense modality. However, it does not really matter whether we say that we respond to warmth and coolness by means of one sense modality or two different ones; the important thing is to understand how our bodies are able to detect changes in temperature.

Many experiences require simultaneous stimulation of several different sense modalities. For example, taste and odour alone do not determine the flavour of spicy food; mild (or sometimes not-so-mild) stimulation of pain detectors in the mouth and throat gives Mexican food its special characteristic. Sensations such as tickle and itch are apparently mixtures of varying amounts of touch and pain. Similarly, our perception of the texture and three-dimensional shape of an object that we touch involves co-operation among our senses of pressure, muscle and joint sensitivity, and motor control (to manipulate the object). If we handle an object and find that it moves smoothly in our hand, we conclude that it is slippery. If, after handling this object, our fingers subsequently slide across each other without much resistance, we perceive a feeling of oiliness. If we sense vibrations when we move our fingers over an object, it is rough. And so on. If you close your eyes as you manipulate some soft and hard, warm and cold, and smooth and rough objects, you can make yourself aware of the separate sensations that interact and give rise to a complex perception.

The skin senses

The entire surface of the human body is innervated (supplied with nerve fibres) by the dendrites of neurons that transmit somatosensory information to the brain. Cranial nerves convey information from the face and front portion of the head (including the teeth and the inside of the mouth and throat); spinal nerves convey information from the rest of the body's surface. All somatosensory information is detected by the dendrites of neurons; the system uses no separate receptor cells. However, some of these dendrites have specialised endings that modify the way they transduce energy into neural activity.

Figure 5.37 shows the sensory receptors found in hairy skin and in smooth, hairless skin (such as skin on the palms of the hands or the soles of the feet). The most common type of skin sensory receptor is the free nerve ending, which resembles the fine roots of a plant. Free nerve endings infiltrate the middle layers of both smooth and hairy skin and surround the hair follicles in hairy skin. If you bend a single hair on your forearm, you will see how sensitive the free nerve endings are.

The largest of the special receptive endings, called the Pacinian corpuscle, is actually visible to the naked eye. Pacinian corpuscles are very sensitive to touch. When they are moved, their axons fire a brief burst of impulses. Pacinian corpuscles are thought to be the receptors that inform us about vibration. Other specialised receptors detect other sensory qualities, including warmth, coolness and pain.

Temperature

There is general agreement that different sensory endings produce the sensations of warmth and coolness. Detectors for coolness appear to be located closer to the surface of the skin. If you suddenly place your foot under a stream of rather hot water, you may feel a brief sensation of cold just before you perceive that the water is really hot. This sensation probably results from short-lived stimulation of the coolness detectors located in the upper layers of the skin.

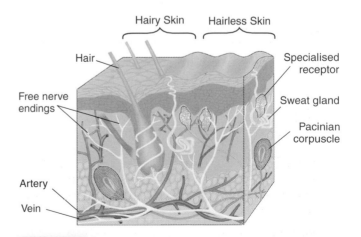

Figure 5.37

Sensory receptors in hairy skin (left) and in hairless skin (right).

Our temperature detectors respond best to changes in temperature. Within reasonable limits, the air temperature of our environment comes to feel 'normal'. Temporary changes in temperature are perceived as warmth or coolness. Thus, our temperature detectors adapt to the temperature of our environment. This adaptation can be easily demonstrated. If you place one hand in a pail of hot water and the other in a pail of cold water, the intensity of the sensations of heat and cold will decrease after a few minutes. If you then plunge both hands into a bucket of water that is at room temperature, it will feel hot to the cold-adapted hand and cold to the hot-adapted hand. It is mainly the change in temperature that is signalled to the brain. Of course, there are limits to the process of adaptation. Extreme heat or cold will continue to feel hot or cold, however long we experience it.

Pressure

Sensory psychologists speak of touch and pressure as two separate senses. They define touch as the sensation of very light contact of an object with the skin and pressure as the sensation produced by more forceful contact. Sensations of pressure occur only when the skin is actually moving, which means that the pressure detectors respond only while they are being bent. Just how the motion stimulates the neurons is not known. If you rest your forearm on a table and place a small weight on your skin, you will feel the pressure at first, but eventually you will feel nothing at all, if you keep your arm still. You fail to feel the pressure not because your brain 'ignores' incoming stimulation but because your sensory endings actually cease sending impulses to your brain. Studies that have measured the very slow, very minute movements of a weight sinking down into the skin have shown that sensations of pressure cease when the movements stop. With the addition of another weight on top of the first one, movement and sensations of pressure begin again (Nafe and Wagoner, 1941).

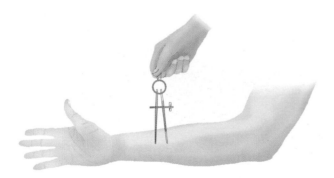

Figure 5.38

The method for determining the two-point discrimination threshold.

A person will feel a very heavy weight indefinitely, but the sensation is probably one of pain rather than pressure.

Sensitivity to subtle differences in touch and pressure varies widely across the surface of the body. The most sensitive regions are the lips and the fingertips. The most common measure of the tactile discrimination of a region of skin is the two-point discrimination threshold. To determine this measure, an experimenter touches a person with one or both legs of a pair of dividers and asks the person to say whether the sensation is coming from one or two points. The further apart the legs of the dividers must be before the person reports feeling two separate sensations, the lower the sensitivity of that region of skin, as seen in Figure 5.38.

Pain

Pain is a complex sensation involving not only intense sensory stimulation but also an emotional component. That is, a given sensory input to the brain might be interpreted as pain in one situation and as pleasure in another. For example, when people are sexually aroused, they become less sensitive to many forms of pain and may even find such intense stimulation pleasurable.

Physiological evidence suggests that the sensation of pain is quite different from the emotional reaction to pain. Opiates such as morphine diminish the sensation of pain by stimulating opioid receptors on neurons in the brain; these neurons block the transmission of pain information to the brain. In contrast, some tranquillisers (such as Valium) depress neural systems that are responsible for the emotional reaction to pain but do not diminish the intensity of the sensation. Thus, people who have received a drug like Valium will report that they feel the pain just as much as they did before but that it does not bother them much.

Evidence from surgical procedures also supports the distinction between sensation and emotion. Prefrontal lobotomy (a form of brain surgery), like the use of tranquillisers such as Valium, blocks the emotional component of pain but does not affect the primary sensation. Therefore, operations similar to prefrontal lobotomy (but much less drastic) are sometimes performed to treat people who suffer from chronic pain that cannot be alleviated by other means.

Many noxious stimuli elicit two kinds of pain – an immediate sharp, or 'bright', pain followed by a deep, dull, sometimes throbbing, pain. Some stimuli elicit only one of these two kinds of pain. For example, a pinprick will produce only the superficial 'bright' pain, whereas a hard blow from a blunt object to a large muscle will produce only the deep, dull pain. Different sets of axons mediate these two types of pain. Pain – or the fear of pain – is one of the most effective motivators of human behaviour. However, it also serves us well in the normal course of living. As unpleasant as pain is, we would have difficulty surviving without it. For example, pain tells us if we have sprained an ankle, broken a bone or have an inflamed appendix.

A particularly interesting form of pain sensation occurs after a limb has been amputated. After their limbs are gone, up to 70 per cent of amputees report that they feel as though their missing limbs still existed, and that they often hurt. This phenomenon is referred to as the phantom limb (Melzak, 1992). People who have phantom limbs report that the limbs feel very real, and they often say that if they try to reach out with their missing limbs, it feels as if they were responding. Sometimes, they perceive the limbs as sticking out, and they may feel compelled to avoid knocking them against the side of a door frame or sleeping in a position that would make the limbs come between them and the mattress. People have reported all sorts of sensations in phantom limbs, including pain, pressure, warmth, cold, wetness, itching, sweatiness and prickliness.

The classic explanation for phantom limbs has been activity of the sensory axons belonging to the amputated limbs. Presumably, this activity is interpreted by the nervous system as coming from the missing limbs. When nerves are cut and connections cannot be re-established between the proximal and distal portions, the cut ends of the proximal portions form nodules known as neuromas. The treatment for phantom pain has been to cut the nerves above these neuromas, to cut the bundles of nerve fibres that bring the information from these nerves into the spinal cord, or to make lesions in somatosensory pathways in the spinal cord, thalamus or cerebral cortex. Sometimes these procedures work for a while, but, unfortunately, the pain often returns.

Melzak suggests that the phantom limb sensation is inherent in the organisation of the parietal cortex. The parietal cortex is involved in our awareness of our own bodies. Indeed, people who have sensory neglect, caused by lesions of the right parietal lobe, have been known to push their own legs out of bed, believing that they actually belong to someone else. Melzak reports that some people who were born missing limbs nevertheless experience phantom limb sensations, which would suggest that our brains are genetically programmed to provide sensations for all four limbs even if we do not have them.

The internal senses

Sensory endings located in our internal organs, bones and joints, and muscles convey painful, neutral, and in some cases pleasurable sensory information. For example, the internal senses convey the pain of arthritis, the perception of the location of our limbs, and the pleasure of a warm drink descending to our stomachs.

Muscles contain special sensory endings. One class of receptors, located at the junction between muscles and the tendons that connect them to the bones, provides information about the amount of force the muscle is exerting.

These receptors protect the body by inhibiting muscular contractions when they become too forceful. During competition, some weightlifters have received injections of a local anaesthetic near the tendons of some muscles to eliminate this protective mechanism. As a result, they are able to lift even heavier weights. Unfortunately, if they use this tactic, some tendons may snap or some bones may break.

Another set of stretch detectors consists of spindle-shaped receptors distributed throughout the muscle. These receptors, appropriately called muscle spindles, inform the brain about changes in muscle length. People are not conscious of the specific information provided by the muscle spindles, but the brain uses the information from these receptors and from joint receptors to keep track of the location of parts of the body and to control muscular contractions.

The vestibular senses

What we call our 'sense of balance' in fact involves several senses, not just one. If we stand on one foot and then close our eyes, we immediately realise how important a role vision plays in balance. The vestibular apparatus of the inner ear provides only part of the sensory input that helps us remain upright.

The three semicircular canals, located in the inner ear and oriented at right angles to one another, detect changes in rotation of the head in any direction (see Figure 5.39). These canals contain a liquid. Rotation of the head makes the liquid flow, stimulating the receptor cells located in the canals.

Another set of inner ear organs, the vestibular sacs, contain crystals of calcium carbonate that are embedded in a gelatin-like substance attached to receptive hair cells. In one sac, the receptive tissue is on the wall; in the other, it is on the floor. When the head tilts, the weight of the calcium carbonate crystals shifts, producing different forces on the cilia of the hair cells. These forces change the activity of the hair cells, and the information is transmitted to the brain.

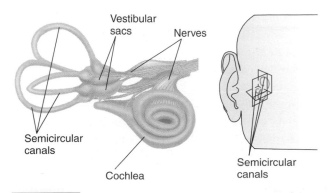

Figure 5.39

The three semicircular canals and two vestibular sacs located in the inner ear.

The vestibular sacs are very useful in maintaining an upright head position. They also participate in a reflex that enables us to see clearly even when the head is being jarred. When we walk, our eyes are jostled back and forth. The jarring of the head stimulates the vestibular sacs to cause reflex movements of the eyes that partially compensate for the head movements. People who lack this reflex because of localised brain damage must stop walking in order to see things clearly, for example to read a street sign.

Questions to think about

The somatosenses and other senses

- Our fingertips and our lips are the most sensitive parts of our bodies. It is easy to understand why our fingertips are so sensitive: we use them to explore objects by touch. But why are our lips so sensitive?

- Relatively large amounts of the primary somatosensory cortex are devoted to analysing information from the lips and fingers. Why do you think this is?

- Why can slow, repetitive vestibular stimulation (like that provided by a boat ride in stormy weather) cause nausea and vomiting? Can you think of any useful functions that this response might serve?

- Why do we experience different types of pain?

- When someone tickles you, you experience an odd sensation that does not occur when you tickle yourself. Why do you think this is?

Key terms

sensation *p.*142
perception *p.*142
transduction *p.*142
anatomical coding *p.*143
temporal coding *p.*144
psychophysics *p.*144
just-noticeable difference (jnd) *p.*144
Weber fractions *p.*144
threshold *p.*144
difference threshold *p.*144
absolute threshold *p.*144
signal detection theory *p.*145
response bias *p.*145
receiver operating characteristic curve (ROC curve) *p.*146
subliminal perception *p.*147
wavelength *p.*148
cornea *p.*149

sclera *p.*149
iris *p.*149
lens *p.*150
accommodation *p.*150
retina *p.*150
photoreceptors *p.*151
optic disk *p.*151
bipolar cells *p.*152
ganglion cells *p.*152
rods *p.*152
cones *p.*152
fovea *p.*152
photopigment *p.*153
rhodopsin *p.*153
dark adaptation *p.*153
fixation point *p.*153
conjugate movements *p.*154
saccadic movements *p.*154
pursuit movements *p.*154
hue *p.*154
brightness *p.*154
saturation *p.*154

colour mixing *p.*155
trichromatic theory *p.*156
opponent process *p.*156
negative after-image *p.*157
protanopia *p.*158
deuteranopia *p.*158
tritanopia *p.*158
synaesthesia *p.*159
synaesthete *p.*159
hertz (Hz) *p.*161
ossicles *p.*161
cochlea *p.*161
oval window *p.*162
basilar membrane *p.*162
round window *p.*163
auditory hair cells *p.*163
cilia *p.*163
tectorial membrane *p.*163
overtones *p.*165
fundamental frequency *p.*165
timbre *p.*165

chemosenses *p.*166
chemosensation *p.*166
gustation *p.*166
papillae *p.*166
taste bud *p.*166
olfaction *p.*168
olfactory mucosa *p.*169
olfactory bulbs *p.*169
pheromones *p.*170
androstenone *p.*170
menstrual synchrony *p.*170
somatosenses *p.*173
free nerve ending *p.*173
Pacinian corpuscle *p.*173
two-point discrimination threshold *p.*174
phantom limb *p.*175
muscle spindles *p.*175
vestibular apparatus *p.*175
semicircular canals *p.*175
vestibular sacs *p.*175

CHAPTER REVIEW

Sensory processing

- We experience the world through our senses. Our knowledge of the world stems from the accumulation of sensory experience and subsequent learning.

- All sensory experiences are the result of energy from events that is transduced into activity of receptors, which are specialised neurons. Transduction causes changes in the activity of axons of sensory nerves, and these changes in activity inform the sensory mechanisms of the brain about the environmental event. The information received from the receptors is transmitted to the brain by means of two coding schemes: anatomical coding and temporal coding.

- In nineteenth-century Germany, Weber devised the concept of the just-noticeable difference, and Fechner used the jnd to measure the magnitude of sensations. In the twentieth century, signal detection theory gave rise to methods that enabled psychologists to assess people's sensitivity to stimuli despite individual differences in response bias. The methods of psychophysics apply to all sensory modalities, including sight, smell, taste, hearing and touch.

- Subliminal perception can occur as long as the stimulus is not too weak, but the effects are subtle and are unlikely to produce useful changes in people's behaviour.

Vision

- The cornea and lens of the eyes cast an image of the scene on the retina, which contains photoreceptors: rods and cones. Cones gather visual information under illuminated conditions; rods work only when the light is very dim.

- The energy from the light that reaches cones is transduced into neural activity when photons strike molecules of photopigment, splitting them into their two constituents. This event causes the cones to send information through the bipolar cells to the ganglion cells. The axons of the ganglion cells travel through the optic nerves and form synapses with neurons in the brain.

- Vision requires the behaviour of looking, which consists of moving our eyes and head. Small, involuntary movements keep an image moving across the photoreceptors, thus preventing them from adapting to a constant stimulus.

- Saccadic eye movements are rapid ocular movements that are conjugate in nature; each eye is fixed on the same point.

- The focus of the lenses of the eyes are adjusted when looking from near to distant objects (and vice versa).

- When an image of the visual scene is cast upon the retina, each part of the image has a different colour, which can be specified in terms of its hue (dominant wavelength), brightness (intensity) and saturation (purity). Information about colour is encoded trichromatically by your cones; the red, green and blue cones respond in proportion to the amount of the appropriate wavelength contained in the light striking them. This information is transformed into an opponent-process coding, signalled by the firing rates of red/green and yellow/blue ganglion cells, and is transmitted to the brain.

- A man has around a one in twenty chance of having some defect in red/green colour vision. If this is the case, red or green cones contain the wrong photopigment. Male or female, chances of a blue/yellow confusion are slim because this is caused by the absence of functioning blue cones.

- Synaesthesia refers to the phenomenon of a stimulus in one modality provoking a sensation in another.

Audition

- The physical dimensions of sound – amplitude, frequency and complexity – can be translated into the perceptual dimensions of loudness, pitch and timbre for sounds ranging from 30 to 20,000 Hz.

- Sound pressure waves put the process in motion by setting up vibrations in the eardrum, which are passed on to the ossicles. Vibrations of the stirrup against the membrane behind the oval window create pressure changes in the fluid within the cochlea that cause the basilar membrane to flex back and forth. This vibration causes the auditory hair cells on the basilar membrane to move relative to the tectorial membrane. The resulting pull on the cilia of the hair cells stimulates them to secrete a transmitter substance that excites neurons of the auditory nerve. This process informs the brain of the presence of a sound.

- Two different methods of detection enable the brain to recognise the pitch of a sound. Different high-frequency and medium-frequency sounds are perceived when different parts of the basilar membrane vibrate in response to these frequencies. Low-frequency vibrations are detected when the tip of the basilar membrane vibrates in synchrony with the sound, which causes some axons in the auditory nerve to fire at the same frequency.

- Low-frequency sounds are located by differences in the arrival time of the sound waves in each ear. High-frequency sounds are located by differences in intensity caused by the 'sound shadow' cast by the head.

- The auditory system will analyse sounds of complex timbre into their constituent frequencies, each of which causes a particular part of the basilar membrane to vibrate. All these functions proceed automatically.

Gustation and olfaction

- Gustation and olfaction refer to the senses of taste and smell, respectively. Both are served by cells having receptors that respond selectively to various kinds of molecule.

- Taste buds have four kinds of receptor, responding to molecules that we perceive as sweet, salty, sour or bitter. To most organisms, sweet and moderately salty substances taste pleasant, whereas sour or bitter substances taste unpleasant.

- Sweetness and saltiness receptors permit us to detect nutritious foods and sodium chloride. Sourness and bitterness receptors help us avoid substances that might be poisonous.

- Olfactory information combines with information about taste to provide us with the flavour of a food present in our mouths. We can distinguish countless different odours and can recognise smells from childhood.

- Unlike visual stimuli, odours do not easily blend. The detection of different odours appears to be accomplished by up to one thousand different receptor molecules located in the membrane of the olfactory receptor cells.

- Pheromones are chemicals produced by the body which generate a stereotypical behavioural or physiological response without necessarily being detected. The evidence for human pheromones is weak, probably because humans lack the vomeronasal organ necessary to respond to such stimuli.

The somatosenses

- The somatosenses gather several different kinds of information from different parts of the body.

- The skin senses of temperature, touch and pressure, vibration, and pain inform us about the nature of objects that come in contact with our skin.

- Pacinian corpuscles in fingers can detect vibration caused by movement which helps us to determine the texture of surfaces.

- Temperature receptors detect hot and cold; free nerve endings can give rise to sensations of pain.

- Sensory receptors in muscles and joints inform the brain of the movement and location of arms and legs.

- The vestibular senses help an organism to keep balance.

Suggestions for further reading

Bruce, V., Green, P. and Georgeson, M. (1996). *Visual Perception: Physiology, psychology and ecology* (3rd edition). Hove, UK: Psychology Press.

Gregory, R.L. (1998). *Eye and Brain: The psychology of seeing* (5th edition). New York: Oxford University Press.

Zeki, S. (1993). *A Vision of the Brain*. Oxford: Blackwell.
These three texts provide an excellent introduction to visual perception. Bruce et al.'s book is a good, solid undergraduate textbook covering most aspects of vision. Gregory's and Zeki's books provide a neurophysiological account of vision: these are exemplary texts of their kind and you should try and consult these.

Gulick, W.L., Gescheider, G.A. and Frisina, R.D. (1989). *Hearing: Physiological acoustics, neural coding, and psychoacoustics*. New York: Oxford University Press.

Yost, W.A. (1994). *Fundamentals of Hearing: An introduction* (3rd edition). San Diego: Academic Press.
There are many excellent books on hearing. These two are recommended for their thoroughness and accuracy.

Schiffman, H.R. (1996). *Sensation and Perception: An integrated approach* (4th edition). Chichester: Wiley.
A good, solid consideration of the topics covered in this chapter.

Doty, R.L. (1995). *Handbook of Olfaction and Gustation*. New York: Dekker.
Doty's edited book covers a broad range of topics related to olfaction and gustation, with a particularly good introductory chapter.

Journals to consult

Chemical Senses
Journal of Experimental Psychology: Human Perception and Performance
Journal of Neuroscience
Nature
Neuroreport
Pain
Perception
Perception and Psychophysics
Quarterly Journal of Experimental Psychology
Science
Trends in Neurosciences
Vision Research

Website address

http://psych.hanover.edu/Krantz/sen_tut.html
A site that allows you to participate in interactive tutorials on sensation and perception.

6

PERCEPTION

In 1988, police raided the home of Cherry Groce, searching for her son, Michael, who was suspected of a robbery at a building society. A police officer shot Mrs Groce in the raid and the incident attracted considerable publicity. Subsequently, the son was apprehended and prosecuted for the robbery, a prosecution based entirely on the evidence of a CCTV (closed circuit television) image which showed a young black man, alleged to be Groce. One witness for the prosecution claimed that he was able to prove that the identities matched by comparing the precise numbers of pixels (the elements which make up a picture) separating key features of the face.

Now this was impressive technical stuff for a jury, until the defence called an expert in facial movement. Alf Linney, a medical physicist from University College London, pointed out that if any of his students had committed such elementary mistakes in face comparison and measurement (not correcting for viewpoint and resolution), they would certainly fail.

Michael Groce was acquitted.

Source: Bruce, 1998, p. 332

Perception of our environment entails attributing meaning to stimuli. Our senses provide us with the raw data about the components of stimuli; the process of perception allows us to understand what these stimuli are. The large, noisy, red object on the road is a collection of auditory and visual (and possibly, olfactory) sensory stimuli. This is what we sense. We perceive, however, that it is a moving bus.

This chapter outlines some of the important features and functions of perception including the processes responsible for the perception of form, movement and space. Sometimes, brain damage can result in an individual having intact sensation but impaired perception: the patient may be unable to identify objects, or neglect one half of space or be unable to identify familiar faces. This chapter considers the psychological mechanisms that allow us to perceive objects and faces and will describe the effect of brain damage on visual perception.

What you should be able to do
after reading Chapter 6

- Describe and understand the basis of form, motion and space perception.
- Describe the way in which the brain processes visual information.
- Describe and understand the way in which we recognise faces.
- Understand the consequences of brain damage on visual perception.

Questions to think about

- How do we assemble sensory cues from the environment and turn them into something meaningful?
- What is it about a face that makes it recognisable?
- How can we perceive a moving object as moving?
- How can we tell a moving car from a moving bus or train?
- Damage to which parts of the brain do you think would impair perception?
- If different parts of the brain are responsible for different aspects of perception, what does this say about the way in which the brain processes perceptual stimuli?

The nature of perception

Take a look around you – around the room or out the window. What do you see as you and your eyes move around? Shapes? Figures? Background? Shadows? Areas of light and dark? Your knowledge of the objects you see and their relative location is extensive, and you have a good idea of what they will feel like, even if you have not touched them. If the lighting suddenly changes (if lamps are turned on or off or if a cloud passes in front of the sun), the amount of light reflected by the objects in the scene changes too, but your perception of the objects remains the same – you see them as having the same shape, colour and texture as before. Similarly, you do not perceive an object as increasing in size as you approach it, even though the image it casts upon your retina does get larger. Form, movement and space are the essential elements of perception.

The brain receives fragments of information from approximately 1 million axons in each of the optic nerves. It combines and organises these fragments into the perception of a scene – objects having different forms, colours and textures, residing at different locations in three-dimensional space. Even when our bodies or our eyes move, exposing the photoreceptors to entirely new patterns of visual information, our perception of the scene before us does not change. We see a stable world, not a moving one, because the brain keeps track of our own movements and those of our eyes and compensates for the constantly changing patterns of neural firing that these movements cause.

Definition of perception

Perception is the process by which we recognise what is represented by the information provided by our sense organs. This process gives unity and coherence to this input. Perception is a rapid, automatic, unconscious process; it is not a deliberate one in which we puzzle out the meaning of what we see. We do not first see an object and then perceive it; we simply perceive the object. Occasionally we do see something ambiguous and must reflect about what it might be or gather further evidence to determine what it is, but this situation is more problem solving than perception. If we look at a scene carefully, we can describe the elementary sensations that are present, but we do not become aware of the elements before we perceive the objects and the background of which they are a part. Our awareness of the process of visual perception comes only after it is complete; we are presented with a finished product, not the details of the process.

The distinction between sensation and perception is not easy to make; in some respects, the distinction is arbitrary. Probably because of the importance we give to vision and because of the richness of the information provided by our visual system, psychologists make a more explicit distinction between visual sensation and perception than they do for any other sensory system.

Perception of form

When we look at the world, we do not see patches of colours and shades of brightness. We see things – cars, streets, people, desks, books, trees, dogs, chairs, walls, flowers, clouds, televisions. We see where each object is located, how large it is, and whether it is moving. We recognise familiar objects and also recognise when we see something we have never seen before. The visual system is able to perceive shapes, determine distances and detect movements; it tells us what something is, where it is located, and what it is doing.

Figure and ground

Most of what we see can be classified as either object or background. Objects are things having particular shapes and particular locations in space. Backgrounds are essentially formless and serve mostly to help us judge the location of objects we see in front of them. Psychologists use the terms **figure** and **ground** to label an object and its background, respectively. The classification of an item as a figure or as a part of the background is not an intrinsic property of the item. Rather, it depends on the behaviour

Figure 6.1

A drawing in which figure and ground can be reversed. You can see either two faces against a white background or a goblet against a dark background.

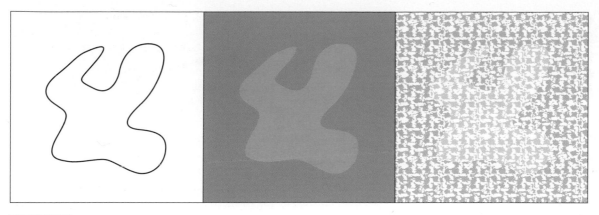

Figure 6.2

From perception and boundaries. We immediately perceive even an unfamiliar figure when its outline is closed.

of the observer. If you are watching some birds fly over-head, they are figures and the blue sky and the clouds behind them are part of the background. If, instead, you are watching the clouds move, then the birds become back-ground. If you are looking at a picture hanging on a wall, it is an object. Sometimes, we receive ambiguous clues about what is object and what is background. For example, do you think that Figure 6.1 illustrates two faces or a wine goblet?

What are the characteristics of the complex patterns of light – varying in brightness, saturation and hue – that give rise to perceptions of figures, of things? One of the most important aspects of form perception is the existence of a boundary. If the visual field contains a sharp and distinct change in brightness, colour or texture, we perceive an edge. If this edge forms a continuous boundary, we will probably perceive the space enclosed by the boundary as a figure, as Figure 6.2 illustrates.

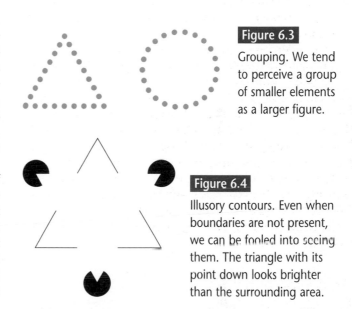

Figure 6.3

Grouping. We tend to perceive a group of smaller elements as a larger figure.

Figure 6.4

Illusory contours. Even when boundaries are not present, we can be fooled into seeing them. The triangle with its point down looks brighter than the surrounding area.

Organisation of elements: the principles of Gestalt

Most figures are defined by a boundary. But the presence of a boundary is not necessary for the perception of form. Figure 6.3 shows that when small elements are arranged in groups, we tend to perceive them as larger figures. Figure 6.4 demonstrates illusory contours – lines that do not exist. In this figure, the orientation of the pie-shaped objects and the three 45-degree segments make us perceive two trian-gles, one on top of the other. The one that looks like it is superimposed on the three black circles even appears to be brighter than the background.

As we saw in Chapter 1, earlier this century, a group of psychologists, Max Wertheimer (1880–1943), Wolfgang Kohler (1887–1967) and Kurt Koffka (1886–1941), devised a theory of perception called Gestalt psychology. Gestalt is the German word for 'form'. They maintained that the

task of perception was to recognise objects in the environ-ment according to the organisation of their elements. They argued that in perception the whole is more than the sum of its parts. Because of the characteristics of the visual sys-tem of the brain, visual perception cannot be understood simply by analysing the scene into its elements. Instead, what we see depends on the relations of these elements to one another (Wertheimer, 1912).

Elements of a visual scene can combine in various ways to produce different forms. Gestalt psychologists have observed that several principles of grouping can predict the combina-tion of these elements. The fact that our visual system groups and combines elements is useful because we can then perceive forms even if they are fuzzy and incom-plete. The real world presents us with objects partly obscured by other objects and with backgrounds that are the same colour as parts of the objects in front of them. The laws of grouping discovered by Gestalt psychologists describe the ability to distinguish a figure from its background.

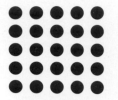
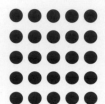

Figure 6.5

The Gestalt principle of proximity. Different spacing of the dots produces five vertical or five horizontal lines.

The **adjacency/proximity principle** states that elements that are closest together will be perceived as belonging together (Wertheimer, 1912). Figure 6.5 demonstrates this principle. The pattern on the left looks like five vertical columns because the dots are closer to their neighbours above and below them than to those located to the right and to the left. The pattern on the right looks like five horizontal rows.

The **similarity principle** states that elements that look similar will be perceived as part of the same form. We can easily see the diamond inside the square in Figure 6.6.

Good continuation is another Gestalt principle and refers to predictability or simplicity. For example, in Figure 6.7 it is simpler to perceive the line as following a smooth course than as suddenly making a sharp bend.

Often, one object partially hides another, but an incomplete image is perceived. The **law of closure** states that our visual system often supplies missing information and 'closes' the outline of an incomplete figure. For example, Figure 6.8 looks a bit like a triangle, but if you place a pencil on the page so that it covers the gaps, the figure undeniably looks like a triangle.

The final Gestalt principle of organisation relies on movement. The **principle of common fate** states that elements that move in the same direction will be perceived as belonging together and forming a figure. In the forest, an animal is camouflaged if its surface is covered with the same elements found in the background – spots of brown, tan and green – because its boundary is obscured. There is no basis for grouping the elements on the animal. As long as the animal is stationary, it remains well hidden. However, once it moves, the elements on its surface will move together, and the animal's form will quickly be perceived.

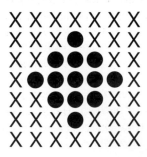

Figure 6.6

The Gestalt principle of similarity. Similar elements are perceived as belonging to the same form.

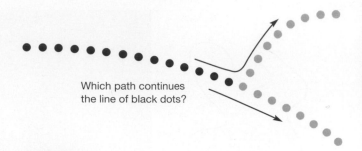

Which path continues the line of black dots?

Figure 6.7

The Gestalt principle of good continuation. It is easier to perceive a smooth continuation than an abrupt shift.

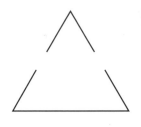

Figure 6.8

The Gestalt principle of closure. We tend to supply missing information to close a figure and separate it from its background. Lay a pencil across the gaps and see how strong the perception of a complete triangle becomes.

Models of pattern perception

Templates and prototypes

One explanation for our ability to recognise shapes of objects is that as we gain experience looking at things, we acquire templates, which are special kinds of visual memories stored by the visual system. A **template** is a type of pattern used to manufacture a series of objects (Selfridge and Neisser, 1960). When a particular pattern of visual stimulation is encountered, the visual system searches through its set of templates and compares each of them with the pattern provided by the stimulus. If it finds a match, it knows that the pattern is a familiar one. Connections between the appropriate template and memories in other parts of the brain could provide the name of the object and other information about it, such as its function, when it was seen before, and so forth.

The template model of pattern recognition has the virtue of simplicity. However, it is unlikely that it could actually work because the visual system would have to store an unreasonably large number of templates. Despite the fact that you may look at your hand and watch your fingers wiggling about, you continue to recognise the pattern as belonging to your hand. How many different templates would your visual memory have to contain just to recognise a hand? Figure 6.9 illustrates this problem using the letter A.

A more flexible model of pattern perception suggests that patterns of visual stimulation are compared with

Input   Template

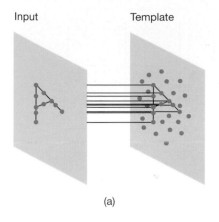

(a)

Input   Template

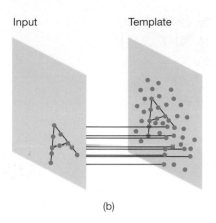

(b)

Input   Template

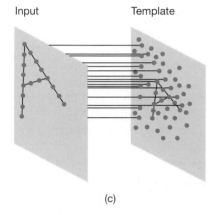

(c)

Input   Template

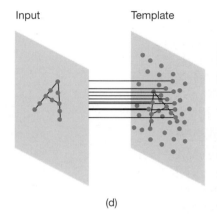

(d)

Figure 6.9

These four figures illustrate how template matching can fail. The position of the input may change (b), its size may change (c) or its orientation may change (d).

Source: Neisser, U., *Cognitive Psychology*. New York: Appleton-Century-Crofts, 1967.

prototypes rather than templates. **Prototypes** (Greek for 'original model') are idealised patterns of a particular shape; they resemble templates but are used in a much more flexible way. The visual system does not look for exact matches between the pattern being perceived and the memories of shapes of objects but accepts a degree of disparity; for instance, it accepts the various patterns produced when we look at a particular object from different viewpoints.

Most psychologists believe that pattern recognition by the visual system does involve prototypes, at least in some form. For example, you can undoubtedly identify maple trees, fir trees and palm trees when you see them. In nature, each tree looks different from all the others, but maples resemble other maples more than they resemble firs, and so on. A reasonable assumption is that your visual system has memories of the prototypical visual patterns that represent these objects. Recognising particular types of tree, then, is a matter of finding the best fit between stimulus and prototype.

The visual system of the brain may indeed contain generic prototypes that help us recognise objects we have never seen before: coffee cups, maple trees, human faces. But we do more than recognise categories of objects; we can recognise particular coffee cups, maple trees, or human faces. In fact, we can learn to recognise enormous numbers of objects. Think of how many different people you can

recognise by sight, how many buildings in your town you can recognise, how many pieces of furniture in your house and in your friends' houses you are familiar with – the list will be very long. Standing (1973) showed people 10,000 colour slides and found that they could recognise most of them weeks later, even though they had seen them just once.

Feature detection models

Some psychologists suggest that the visual system encodes images of familiar patterns in terms of **distinctive features** – collections of important physical features that specify particular items (Selfridge, 1959). For example, Figure 6.10 contains several examples of the letter N. Although the examples vary in size and style, recognising them is not problematic because your visual system contains a specification of the distinctive features that fit the criterion for an N: two parallel vertical lines connected by a diagonal line sloping downward from the top of the left one to the bottom of the right one.

An experiment by Neisser (1964) supports the hypothesis that perception involves analysis of distinctive features. Figure 6.11 shows one of the tasks he asked people to do. The figure shows two columns of letters. Scan through them until you find the letter Z, which occurs once in each column.

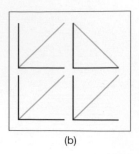

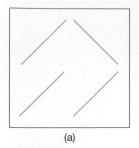

Figure 6.10

Distinctive features. We easily recognise all of these items as the letter N.

```
GDOROC      IVEMXW
COQUCD      XVIWME
DUCOQG      VEMIXW
GRUDQO      WEKMVI
OCDURQ      XIMVWE
DUCGRO      IVMWEX
ODUCQG      VWEMXI
CQOGRD      IMEWXV
DUZORQ      EXMZWI
UCGROD      IEMWVX
QCUDOG      EIVXWM
RQGUDO      WXEMIV
DRGOQC      MIWVXE
OQGDRU      IMEVXW
UGCODQ      IEMWVX
ODRUCQ      IMWVEX
UDQRGC      XWMVEI
ORGCUD      IWEVXM
```

Figure 6.11

A letter-search task. Look for the letter Z hidden in each column.

Source: Adapted from Neisser, J., *Scientific American*, 1964, 210, 94–102.

You probably found the letter in the left column much faster than you did the one in the right column. Why? The letters in the left column have few features in common with those found in the letter Z, so the Z stands out from the others. In contrast, the letters in the right column have many features in common with the target letter, and thus the Z is 'camouflaged'.

There are some phenomena that cannot easily be explained by the distinctive-features model. The model suggests that the perception of an object consists of analysis and synthesis; the visual system first identifies the component features of an object and then adds up the features to determine what the object is. We might expect, then, that more complex objects, having more distinctive features, would take longer to perceive. But often, the

Figure 6.12

Contextual cues. Perceiving a simple stimulus is facilitated by contextual cues. The line that does not match the other three is more easily recognised in (b).

addition of more features, in the form of contextual cues, speeds up the process of perception. Figure 6.12 contains two sets of four items. One item in each is different from the other three.

The patterns in both sets differ with respect to only one feature: the tilt of the diagonal line. But the addition of the horizontal and vertical lines in Figure 6.12(b) makes the perceptual task much easier. We see a triangle and three right angles bisected by a diagonal line; the triangle just pops out as being different. If we perceived individual features (such as the diagonal lines) before perceiving more complex figures (such as triangles and bisected right angles) that are composed of these features, then we should perceive simpler figures faster than we perceive more complex ones. The fact that we do not means that a perception is not simply an assembly of individual features.

The distinctive-features model appears to be a reasonable explanation for the perception of letters, but what about more natural stimuli, which we encounter in places other than the written page? Biederman (1987, 1990) suggests a model of pattern recognition that combines some aspects of prototypes and distinctive features. He suggests that the shapes of objects that we encounter can be constructed from a set of thirty-six different shapes that he refers to as **geons**. Figure 6.13 illustrates a few geons and some objects that can be constructed from them. Perhaps, Biederman suggests, the visual system recognises objects by identifying the particular sets and arrangements of geons that they contain.

Even if Biederman is correct that our ability to perceive categories of common objects involves recognition of geons, it seems unlikely that the geons are involved in perception of particular objects. For example, it is difficult to imagine how we could perceive faces of different people as assemblies of different sets of geons. The geon hypothesis appears to work best for the recognition of prototypes of generic categories: telephones or torches in general rather than the telephone on your desk or the torch a friend lent you.

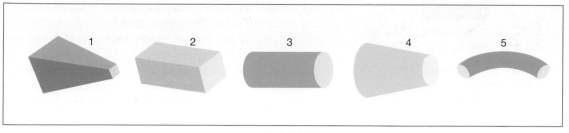

(a) Goono

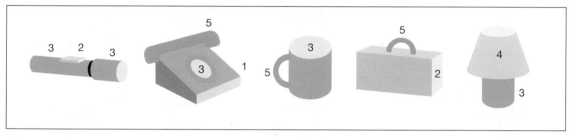

(b) Objects

Figure 6.13

Geons for perception. (a) Several different geons. (b) The combination of two or three geons (indicated by the numbers) into common three-dimensional objects.

Source: Adapted from Biederman, I., in *An Invitation to Cognitive Science. Vol. 2: Visual Cognition and Action*, edited by D.N. Osherson, S.M. Kosslyn and J. Hollerbach. Cambridge, MA: MIT Press, 1990.

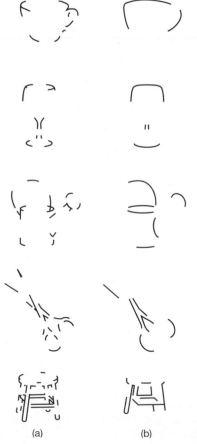

Figure 6.14

Incomplete figures. (a) With cusps and joints. (b) Without cusps and joints. Which set is easier to recognise?

Source: Adapted from Biederman, I., Higher-level vision. In *An Invitation to Cognitive Science. Vol. 2: Visual Cognition and Action*, edited by D.N. Osherson, S.M. Kosslyn and J. Hollerbach. Cambridge, MA: MIT Press, 1990.

(a)   (b)

Biederman points out that particular features of figures – cusps and joints formed by the ends of line segments – are of critical importance in recognising drawings of objects, presumably because the presence of these joints enables the viewer to recognise the constituent geons. Figure 6.14 shows two sets of degraded images of drawings of five common objects. One set, (a), shows the locations of cusps and joints; the other, (b), does not. Biederman (1990) found that people found the items with cusps and joints much easier to recognise.

Top-down processing: the role of context

We often perceive objects under conditions that are less than optimum; the object is in a shadow, camouflaged against a similar background or obscured by fog. Nevertheless, we usually manage to recognise the item correctly. We are often helped in our endeavour by the context in which we see the object. For example, look at Figure 6.15. What do you see? Can you tell what they are? Now look at Figure 6.16. With the elements put in context it is quite easy to see what they are.

Palmer (1975b) showed that even more general forms of context can aid in the perception of objects. He first showed his participants familiar scenes, such as a kitchen. Next, he used a tachistoscope to show them drawings of individual items and asked the participants to identify them. A **tachistoscope** can present visual stimuli very briefly so that they

Figure 6.15

Simple elements that are difficult to recognise without a context.

Figure 6.16

An example of top-down processing. The context facilitates our recognition of the items shown in Figure 6.15.

Source: Adapted from Palmer, S.E., in *Explorations in Cognition*, edited by D.A. Norman, D.E. Rumelhart and the LNR Research Group, San Francisco: W.H. Freeman, 1975.

are very difficult to perceive. Sometimes, participants saw an object that was appropriate to the scene, such as a loaf of bread. At other times, they saw an inappropriate but similarly shaped object, such as a letterbox (see Figure 6.17).

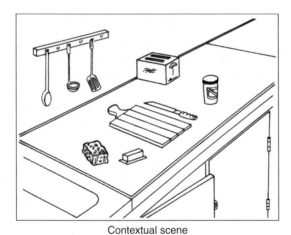

Contextual scene

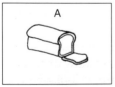 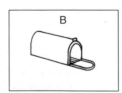

A   B

Target object (presented very briefly)

Figure 6.17

Stimuli from the experiment by Palmer (1975). After looking at the contextual scene, participants were shown one of the stimuli below it very briefly, by means of a tachistoscope.

Source: Palmer, S.E., *Memory and Cognition*, 1975, 3, 519–526. Reprinted by permission of the Psychonomic Society, Inc.

Palmer found that when the objects fitted the context that had been set by the scene, participants correctly identified about 84 per cent of them. But when they did not, performance fell to about 50 per cent. Performance was intermediate in the no-context control condition, under which subjects did not first see a scene. Thus, compared with the no-context control condition, an appropriate context facilitated recognition and an inappropriate one interfered with it.

The context effects demonstrated by experiments such as Palmer's are not simply examples of guessing games. That is, people do not think to themselves, 'Let's see, that shape could be either a letterbox or a loaf of bread. I saw a picture of a kitchen, so I suppose it's a loaf of bread.' The process is rapid, unconscious and automatic; thus, it belongs to the category of perception rather than to problem solving, which is much slower and more deliberate. Somehow, seeing a kitchen scene sensitises the neural circuits responsible for the perception of loaves of bread and other items we have previously seen in that context.

Psychologists distinguish between two categories of information-processing models of pattern recognition: bottom-up processing and top-down processing. In **bottom-up processing**, also called data-driven processing, the perception is constructed out of the elements – the bits and pieces – of the stimulus, beginning with the image that falls on the retina. The information is processed by successive levels of the visual system until the highest levels (the 'top' of the system) are reached, and the object is perceived. **Top-down processing** refers to the use of contextual information – to the use of the 'big picture'. Presumably, once the kitchen scene is perceived, information is sent from the 'top' of the system down through lower levels. This information excites neural circuits responsible for perceiving those objects normally found in kitchens and inhibits others. Then, when the subject sees a drawing of a loaf of bread, information starts coming up through the successive levels of the system and finds the appropriate circuits already warmed up, so to speak.

Haenny *et al.* (1988) obtained direct evidence that watching for a particular stimulus can, indeed, warm up neural circuits in the visual system. They trained monkeys to look at a pattern of lines oriented at a particular angle, to remember that pattern, and then to pick it out from a series of different patterns presented immediately afterwards. A correct response would be rewarded by a sip of fruit juice. While the animals were performing the task, the experimenters recorded the activity of individual neurons in the visual association cortex. They found that watching for a pattern of lines having a particular orientation affected the responsiveness of the neurons. For example, if the monkeys were watching for a pattern containing lines oriented at 45 degrees, neurons that detected lines of that orientation responded more vigorously than normal when that pattern was presented again. Haenny *et al.* found that

TAE CAT
RED
SPOT
EISH

Figure 6.18

Examples of combined top-down/bottom-up processing. The effect of context enables us to perceive the letters despite the missing or ambiguous features. Note that a given letter may be perceived in more than one way, depending on the letters surrounding it.

Source: Adapted from McClelland, J.J., Rumelhart, D.E. and Hinton G.E., in *Parallel Distributed Processing. Vol. 1: Foundations*, edited by D.E. Rumelhart, J.L. McClelland and the PDP Research Group. Copyright © 1986 the Massachusetts Institute of Technology; published by the MIT Press, Cambridge, MA.

this enhancement could even be produced by letting the monkeys feel the orientation of a pattern of grooves in a metal plate they could not see; when a subsequent visual pattern contained lines whose orientation matched that of the grooves, a larger neural response was seen.

In most cases, perception consists of a combination of top-down and bottom-up processing. Figure 6.18 shows several examples of objects that can be recognised only by a combination of both forms of processing. Our knowledge of the configurations of letters in words provides us with the contexts that permit us to organise the flow of information from the bottom up.

Direct perception: Gibson's affordances

In the chapter so far, we have considered some of the mechanisms that underlie visual perception. But is this perception a response or a process? That is, is visual perception an active or passive process? We saw in an earlier section that context is important for visual perception. The psychologist J.J. Gibson took this notion a step further. Over a period of 35 years, Gibson proposed a theory of perception which argued that perception was direct and did not depend on cognitive processes to bring together fragmented data (Gibson, 1950, 1966, 1979). Because of this, it is considered a direct theory of perception. Originally, Gibson was interested in distinguishing between unsuccessful and successful World War II pilots. Some of the unsuccessful pilots were unable to land accurately and seemed unable to appreciate distance. However, Gibson found that even when these pilots were given training in depth perception – which may have remedied the problem – the pilots continued to have difficulty.

According to Gibson, 'perceiving is an act, not a response; an act of attention, not a triggered impression; an achievement, not a reflex' (Gibson, 1979). Gibson's view of perception was that classical optical science ignored the complexity of real events. For example, it would focus on the effects of trivial, basic or simple stimuli on perceptual response. Gibson abandoned the depth/space perception view of the world and, instead, suggested that our perception of surfaces was more important. Surfaces comprised ground (which we discussed earlier) and texture elements in surfaces that would be attached or detached. Attached features would include bumps and indentations in the surface, such as rocks or trees; detached features would include items such as animals (which are detached from the surface).

Given the complex world in which we live, we must be able to perceive not just simple stimuli but stimuli which mean something more to us. We must decide whether an object is throwable or graspable, whether a surface can be sat upon and so on. We ask ourselves what can this object furnish us with, what does it afford us (Gibson, 1982). These are the meanings that the environment has and Gibson called them **affordances**. Thus, Gibson highlighted the ecological nature of perception: we do not simply perceive simple stimuli but these stimuli mean something more in a wider, more complex context. This was a radical departure in visual perception because it implied that the perception of object meaning is direct. Perception involves determining whether something is capable of being sat upon or is throwable.

However, the theory is not without its problems. Costall (1995), for example, suggests that some affordances may not be able to afford. Consider this example. Imagine the ground covered in frost and a frozen lake. According to Gibson, the ground afforded walking. However, although the frosty ground does, the frozen lake does not. Similarly, although we might agree with Gibson that some surfaces are graspable or supporting we might disagree quite reasonably with the notion that surfaces are edible, for example, that they afford eating. Our decision that something is edible appears to rely on more than direct perception of surfaces.

Face perception

Although object perception is important to us, the perception of specific categories of stimuli may be even more important. One such category is 'faces'. How do we perceive and recognise faces? What makes a face distinctive? What features do we remember about a face? Being able to recognise and identify faces is one of the most important social functions human beings can perform (Bruce, 1994). This helps us form relationships with people, can help us spot faces in a crowd and provides us with non-verbal cues as to what a person is thinking or feeling (the role of emotion in facial expression is returned to in Chapter 13).

Psychologists in the nineteenth century were interested in what makes a face attractive and constructed composites – averages of several different images – to produce a face which they believed was attractive (Galton, 1878; Stoddard, 1886). Recent work by psychologists has outlined a clearer picture of what makes an attractive face; it has also helped to indicate which features of the face best allow us to remember a face or which make a face distinctive.

In terms of facial features, people indicate that the eyes seem to be more important than the mouth and both are more important than the nose in being able to distinguish between people's faces (Bruce et al., 1993). Individuals can recognise others' faces on the basis of these features even when hairstyle, make-up and facial hair are removed or minimised. A three-dimensional image of a face – such as that seen in three-quarter profile – is better recognised than is a full-frontal photograph. Figure 6.19 shows examples of these.

Sex of the face

Perhaps the most obvious basis on which we distinguish one face from another (apart from race; Doty, 1998) is sex: whether the face is male or female. We can usually discriminate between faces more quickly on the basis of sex than familiarity (Bruce et al., 1987). Some psychologists have investigated the features that make a face distinctively male or female. Enlow (1982) and Moss et al. (1987), for example, have suggested that men tend to have larger noses and nasopharynxes, more prominent brows, a more sloping forehead and more deeply set eyes than do women. Shepherd (1989) noted that women had fuller cheeks and less facial hair (including eyebrows). Women are also thought to have smaller noses, a more depressed bridge of the nose, a shorter upper lip, and larger eyes with darker shadows, especially young women (Liggett, 1974).

A series of experiments by Vicki Bruce and her colleagues at the University of Stirling has highlighted other sex differences in facial features. In one study, the eyes, mouth and nose in the photographs of men and women were covered with tape and participants were asked to determine the sex of the face as the time taken to make a decision was measured (Roberts and Bruce, 1988). Participants took longer to make discriminations when those features were covered than when uncovered and took longer to make discriminations when the eyes, mouth and nose were covered, respectively.

When features were presented in isolation, eyes were the most reliable indicator of sex and the nose was the least reliable. With hair concealed, 96 per cent of participants were able to distinguish between faces based on sex (Burton et al., 1993). When individual facial features or pairs of features (such as brow and eyes, nose and mouth) were presented to participants, the features which afforded the best opportunity to make sex discriminations were, in this order: brow and eyes, brow alone, eyes alone, whole jaw, chin, nose and mouth, and mouth alone (Brown and

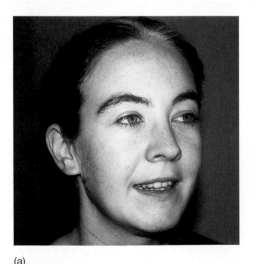

(a)   (b)

Figure 6.19

A three-dimensional image of a face is better recognised in (a) three-quarter profile than (b) as a full-frontal photograph.

Source: Photograph by Vanessa Sherry.

Perrett, 1993). Brown and Perrett's findings suggest that all facial features carry some information about sex (except the nose). Furthermore, these results, like those of Roberts and Bruce (1988), suggest that it is difficult to find even one or two features which absolutely distinguish between men's and women's faces. Some features, however, provide better clues than others.

Distinctiveness and attractiveness

Each of us finds different faces attractive: some of us find faces friendlier than others, some meaner and others more sexually alluring. Although individual differences exist at this, what seems like, subjective level, studies have shown that some features of the face are generally regarded as more attractive than others. To begin, the distinctiveness of the face – defined as the deviation from the norm – is unrelated to attractiveness (Bruce *et al.*, 1994). Secondly, Galton had hypothesised that averageness was attractiveness. That is, the more average looking the face, the more attractive it was likely to be. This hypothesis was tested and challenged by Perrett *et al.* (1994) who compared the attractiveness ratings for average, attractive and highly attractive Caucasian female faces.

Using special computer technology, Perrett *et al.* constructed an average composite of photographs of sixty female faces. The fifteen faces rated as most attractive from the original sixty were then averaged. Finally, the attractiveness of this average was enhanced by 50 per cent to provide a 'highly attractive' composite. Composites similar to those used in the experiment can be seen in Figure 6.20.

Caucasian raters found the 'attractive' composite more attractive than the average composite and the highly attractive composite more attractive than the 'attractive' composite, thus disconfirming Galton's hypothesis. Furthermore, when similar composites were made of Japanese women, the same results were obtained: both Caucasian and Japanese raters found the enhanced composite more attractive. What distinguished an average face from an attractive one?

Analysis of the composites showed that the more attractive faces had higher cheek bones, a thinner jaw and larger eyes relative to the size of the face. There was also a shorter distance between mouth and chin and between nose and mouth in the attractive faces.

Theories of face perception

The mechanisms that allow us to perceive faces are considered to be different from those that allow us to perceive objects; face perception has been thought of as 'special' (Farah *et al.*, 1998). Face perception involves a number of operations. We can perceive general characteristics such as the colour, sex and age of a face; we can perceive whether

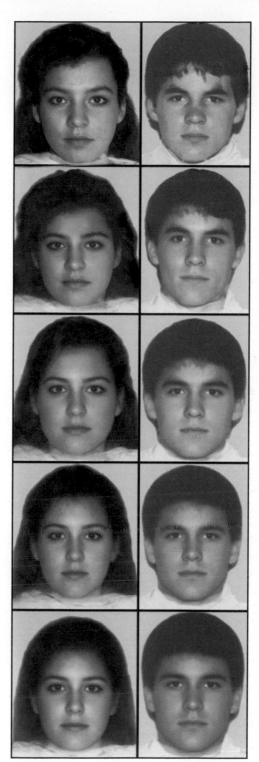

Figure 6.20

Faces similar to those used in Perrett *et al.*'s (1994) experiment. The faces are 'morphed' from averagely attractive (top two faces) to very attractive (bottom two faces). Most people rate the last two faces as most attractive.

Source: Young, A.W. and Bruce, V. (1998). Pictures at an exhibition: The science of the face. *The Psychologist*, 11(3), 120–125.

a face expresses anger, sadness or joy; we can distinguish familiar from unfamiliar faces. What model of face processing can account for these operations?

Bruce and Young (1986) have suggested that face processing is made up of these three functions: perception of facial expression, perception of familiar faces and perception of unfamiliar faces. Why does the model dissociate these functions? Bruce and Young reviewed extensive evidence which suggested that each of these functions is dependent on different cognitive abilities. Evidence from neuropsychology also supports such a model.

Some patients with right hemisphere damage, as we will see later in the chapter, can perceive and correctly identify facial expressions and the sex and age of faces but cannot identify faces (Tranel *et al.*, 1988). In a now classic study, Young *et al.* (1993) studied face perception in ex-servicemen who had sustained missile wounds to the posterior left and right hemispheres. They administered a series of face perception tests which included tests of familiar face identification, matching unfamiliar faces and facial expression identification. The experimenters found that one patient was poor at identifying familiar faces only, another was selectively poor at matching unfamiliar faces and a group of men was impaired at analysing facial expressions. A PET study by Sergent *et al.* (1992) in which healthy individuals performed similar tasks also showed a difference between the three different operations in terms of the regional brain activity they activated. The results from these studies strongly support Bruce and Young's model and provide a neuropsychological basis for the dissociations it suggests.

However, as we will see in Chapter 13, individuals with damage to the amygdala may be unable either to express fear or recognise fear in the facial expressions of others; other individuals with Huntington's chorea are poor at identifying facial expression of disgust. This suggests that the 'analysis of facial expression' may be too broad an operation. On the basis of this evidence, it is reasonable to hypothesise that different regions in the brain mediate responses to different kinds of facial expression of emotion and not of emotional expression in general.

Questions to think about

Form and models of perception

- Explore your environment a little and look for examples of figure and ground. Can you change your focus of attention and make items previously seen as figures become part of the background and vice versa? Can you find some examples of how Gestalt principles of grouping help you perceive particular objects?

- How many unique objects do you think you can recognise? How many more do you think you will learn to recognise during the years ahead of you? Think of the efficiency of the coding of this information in the computer contained in your head.

- What principles do you use when you try to assemble the pieces of a complex jigsaw? Can you relate these principles to the concepts of templates, prototypes and distinctive features?

- People who want to appear thinner are often advised to wear clothes having vertical stripes, while those who want to appear heavier are advised to wear clothes having horizontal stripes. Can you think of an explanation for such advice?

- What do you find attractive in an attractive face? Do your preferences match those found in experimental studies? Do you think that some facial features we find attractive are so subtle that we cannot consciously detect them?

- What distinguishes a man's from a woman's face and why do you think this is so? What do you think distinguishes an old face from a young face? How would you set up an experiment to answer this question?

Perception of space and motion

In addition to being able to perceive the forms of objects in our environment, we are able to judge quite accurately their relative location in space and their movements. Perceiving where things are and perceiving what they are doing are obviously important functions of the visual system (Jeannerod, 1997; Decety *et al.*, 1997).

Depth perception

Depth perception requires that we perceive the distance of objects in the environment from us and from each other. We do so by means of two kinds of cues: binocular ('two-eye') and monocular ('one-eye'). Binocular cues arise from the fact that the visual fields of both eyes overlap. Only animals that have eyes on the front of the head (such as primates, cats and some birds) can obtain binocular cues. Animals that have eyes on the sides of their heads (such as rabbits and fish) can obtain only monocular cues.

One monocular cue involves movement and thus must be experienced in the natural environment or in a motion picture. The other monocular cues can be represented in a drawing or a photograph. Most of these cues were originally discovered by artists and only later studied by psychologists (Zeki, 1998). Figure 6.21 shows the ten most important sources of depth cues.

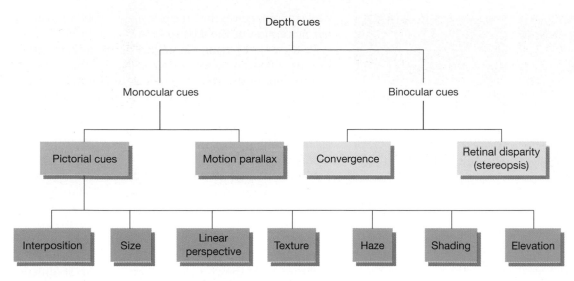

Figure 6.21

The principal monocular and binocular depth cues.

Source: Adapted from Matlin, M.W. and Foley, H.J., *Sensation and Perception* (3rd edition). Boston: Allyn & Bacon, 1992.

Binocular cues

Convergence provides an important cue about distance. The eyes make conjugate movements so that both look at (converge on) the same point of the visual scene. If an object is very close to your face, your eyes are turned inwards. If it is farther away, they look more nearly straight ahead. Thus, the eyes can be used like range finders. The brain controls the extraocular muscles, so it knows the angle between them, which is related to the distance between the object and the eyes. Convergence is most important for perceiving the distance of objects located close to us, especially those we can reach with our hands (see Figure 6.22).

Another important factor in the perception of distance is the information provided by **retinal disparity** ('unlikeness' or 'dissimilarity'). Hold up a finger of one hand at arm's length and then hold up a finger of the other hand midway between your nose and the distant finger. If you look at one of the fingers, you will see a double image of the other one.

Whenever your eyes are pointed towards a particular point, the images of objects at different distances will fall on different portions of the retina in each eye. The amount of disparity produced by the images of an object on the two retinas provides an important clue about its distance from us.

The perception of depth resulting from retinal disparity is called **stereopsis**. A stereoscope is a device that shows two slightly different pictures, one to each eye. The pictures are taken by a camera equipped with two lenses, located a few inches apart, just as our eyes are. When you look through a stereoscope, you see a three-dimensional image. An experiment by Julesz (1965) demonstrated that retinal disparity is what produces the effect of depth. Using a computer, he produced two displays of randomly positioned dots in which the location of some dots differed slightly. If some of the dots in one of the displays were displaced slightly to the right or the left, the two displays gave the impression of depth when viewed through a stereoscope.

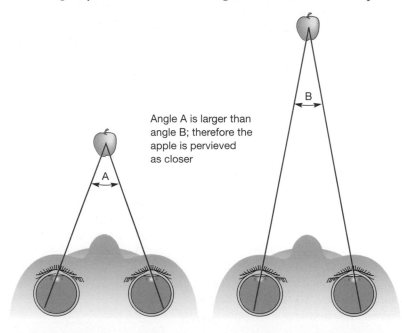

Angle A is larger than angle B; therefore the apple is pervieved as closer

Figure 6.22

Convergence. When the eyes converge on a nearby object, the angle between them is greater than when they converge on a distant object. The brain uses this information in perceiving the distance of an object.

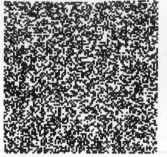

Figure 6.23

A pair of random-dot stereograms.

Figure 6.23 shows a pair of these random-dot stereograms. If you look at them very carefully, you will see that some of the dots near the centre have been moved slightly to the left. Some people can look at these figures without using a stereoscope and see depth. If you want to try this, hold the book at arm's length and look at the space between the figures. Now pretend you are looking 'through' the book, into the distance. Each image will become double, since your eyes are no longer converged properly. If you keep looking, you might make two of these images fuse into one, located right in the middle. Eventually, you might see a small square in the centre of the image, raised above the background.

Monocular cues

One of the most important sources of information about the relative distance of objects is interposition (meaning 'placed between'). If one object is placed between us and another object so that the closer object partially obscures our view of the more distant one, we can immediately perceive which object is closer to us.

Obviously, interposition works best when we are familiar with the objects and know what their shapes should look like. Just as the Gestalt law of good continuation plays

a role in form perception, the principle of good form affects our perception of the relative location of objects: We perceive the object having the simpler border as being closer. Figure 6.24(a) can be seen either as two rectangles, located one in front of the other (Figure 6.24(b)), or as a rectangle nestled against an L-shaped object (Figure 6.24(c)). Because we tend to perceive an ambiguous drawing according to the principle of good form, we are more likely to perceive Figure 6.24(a) as two simple shapes – rectangles – one partly hiding the other.

Another important monocular distance cue is provided by our familiarity with the sizes of objects. For example, if a car casts a very small image on our retinas, we will perceive it as being far away. Knowing how large cars are, our visual system can automatically compute the approximate distance from the size of the retinal image.

Figure 6.25 shows two columns located at different distances. The drawing shows linear perspective: the tendency for parallel lines that recede from us to appear to converge at a single point. Because of perspective, we perceive the columns as being the same size even though they produce retinal images of different sizes. We also perceive the segments of the wall between the columns as rectangular, even though the image they cast on the retina does not contain any right angles.

Texture, especially the texture of the ground, provides another cue we use to perceive the distance of objects sitting on the ground. A coarser texture looks closer, and a finer texture looks more distant. The earth's atmosphere, which always contains a certain amount of haze, can also supply cues about the relative distance of objects or parts of the landscape. Parts of the landscape that are farther away become less distinct because of haze in the air. Thus, haze provides a monocular distance cue (see Figure 6.26).

The patterns of light and shadow in a scene – its shading – can provide us with cues about the three-dimensional shapes of objects. Although the cues that shading provides do not usually tell us much about the absolute distances of objects from us, they can tell us which parts of objects are closer and which are further away. Figure 6.27 illustrates the power of this phenomenon. Some of the circles look as

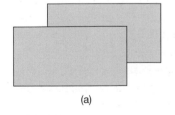 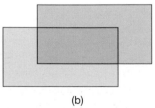 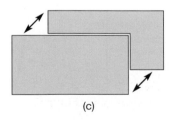

(a)   (b)   (c)

Figure 6.24

Use of the principle of good form in the perception of depth. The two objects shown in (a) could be two identical rectangles, one in front of the other, as shown in (b) or a rectangle and an L-shaped object, as shown in (c). The principle of good form states that we will see the ambiguous object in its simplest (best) form – in this case a rectangle. As a result, the shape to the right is perceived as being partly hidden and thus further away from us.

Figure 6.25

Principle of perspective. Perspective gives the appearance of distance and makes the two columns look similar in size.

Figure 6.26

Cues from atmospheric haze. Variation in detail, owing to haze, produces an appearance of distance.

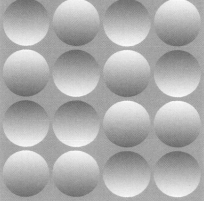

Figure 6.27

Depth cues supplied by shading. If the tops of the circles are dark, they look like depressions. If the bottoms are dark, they appear as bumps.

if they bulge out towards us; others look as if they were hollowed out (dimpled). The only difference is the direction of the shading. Our visual system appears to interpret such stimuli as if they were illuminated from above. Thus, the top of a convex (bulging) object will be light and the bottom will be in shadow. If you turn the book upside down, the bulges and dimples will reverse.

These features are important to practical aspects of our lives, an example of which appears in the 'Psychology in action section'.

Psychology in action

CCTV and face perception

Imagine that you are spending your Saturday afternoon in a busy shopping centre. Browsing in a store, you spot a particularly attractive shirt that you want and go to the counter. When you place the shirt and your wallet on the counter, you feel someone nudge you from behind. Before you have a chance to remonstrate, you notice that your wallet has disappeared and that a person whose face you partly see is running out of the store. Fortunately, the police manage to apprehend a suspect and the store detective informs you that he has video surveillance footage of a man who might be the suspect. He does not have your wallet but the image on the surveillance camera looks like the suspect. How accurately would you be able to match the suspect to the image on the video screen?

The extract at the opening of this chapter indicates how careful one has to be when making such decisions. Recall from that narrative that Michael Groce had been arrested for a robbery on the basis of evidence from surveillance camera footage which showed a man similar to him. The prosecution's case was so scientifically unsound that Groce was acquitted.

Closed-circuit television (CCTV) has become a useful and increasingly used tool in the prevention of crime. Many city centres and shopping malls are dotted with such cameras, sometimes covertly, sometimes in full view. The increasing use of CCTV has led to an increase in the reliance on CCTV evidence in prosecutions. Bruce (1998) has pointed out that CCTV footage is usually variable in quality with camera angles and lighting conditions producing an unclear image of the top or back of the head.

To examine whether such conditions could affect accuracy of eyewitnessing, Bruce and her colleagues set up a series of experiments in which such conditions were manipulated and the effects of these manipulations on the

Psychology in action continued overleaf

Psychology in action continued

accuracy of face recognition were measured. In one study, lighting conditions in which faces were observed were changed as was the viewpoint of the face (Hill and Bruce, 1996). The experimenters found that changing the lighting conditions reduced performance in a task which required individuals to match the face they had seen with a photograph. Changing the viewpoint also impaired recognition accuracy but changing both lighting and viewpoint did not make performance any worse.

Which conditions produced the best recognition performance? Matching faces (and even recognising familiar surfaces) was more accurate when lighting was from above. Why? One explanation is that light from above provides more information by casting fewer shadows. Hill and Bruce suggest that lighting a face from the bottom reverses the brightness of facial areas such as the eye sockets and nostrils. In fact, lighting of this sort makes the face look like a negative. This study highlights an important point about face perception (and about the erroneous testimony described at the opening of the chapter). Our recognition of faces is not simply based on 'edge' information, that is, on contour. The shape of the face (viewpoint) and shading are crucial in enabling us to make accurate recognition judgements.

Is recognition improved if the face is moving? After all, a moving image might give more information about shading, shape and contour than would a static one. Current evidence is mixed. Some researchers have reported that a moving image is more advantageous to accurate recognition than is a static one (Pike *et al.*, 1997; Knight and Johnston, 1997). Others have found little improvement in recognition when moving and static images are compared (Christie and Bruce, 1998).

Are there any other factors which psychologists could emphasise as important to the process of recognition of faces seen on CCTV? One factor could be familiarity (Bruce, 1998). It is possible that CCTV image recognition would be better if the person is already known. If familiarity is a factor, could this expedite recognition or could it lead to false identification?

New surveillance techniques such as CCTV offer great hope for improving crime prevention and detection. Because such techniques are new, however, those who use them would be wise to treat the evidence they provide with great care. The work of Bruce and her colleagues indicates how CCTV could enhance the recognition of a suspect's face but the research also shows how CCTV can lead to identifications that are not accurate.

Distance and location

When we are able to see the horizon, we perceive objects near it as being distant and those above or below it as being nearer to us. Thus, **elevation** provides an important monocular depth cue. For example, cloud B and triangle B in Figure 6.28 appear further away from us than do cloud A and triangle A.

So far, all the monocular distance cues discussed have been those that can be rendered in a drawing or captured by a camera. However, another important source of distance information depends on our own movement. Try the following demonstrations. If you focus your eyes on an object close to you and move your head from side to side, your image of the scene moves back and forth behind the nearer object. If you focus your eyes on the background while moving your head from side to side, the image of the nearer object passes back and forth across the background. Head and body movements cause the images from the scene before us to change; the closer the object, the more it changes relative to the background. The information contained in this relative movement helps us to perceive distance.

Figure 6.29 illustrates the kinds of cue supplied when we move with respect to features in the environment. The top part of the figure shows three objects at different distances from the observer: a man, a house and a tree. The lower

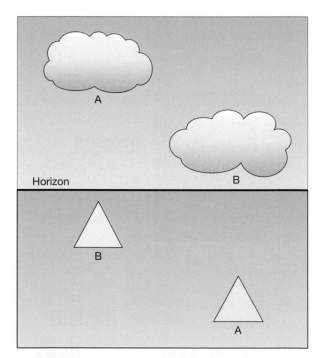

Figure 6.28

Depth cues supplied by elevation. The objects nearest the horizontal line appear furthest away from us.

Source: Adapted from Matlin, M.W. and Foley, H.J., *Sensation and Perception* (3rd edition). Boston: Allyn & Bacon, 1992.

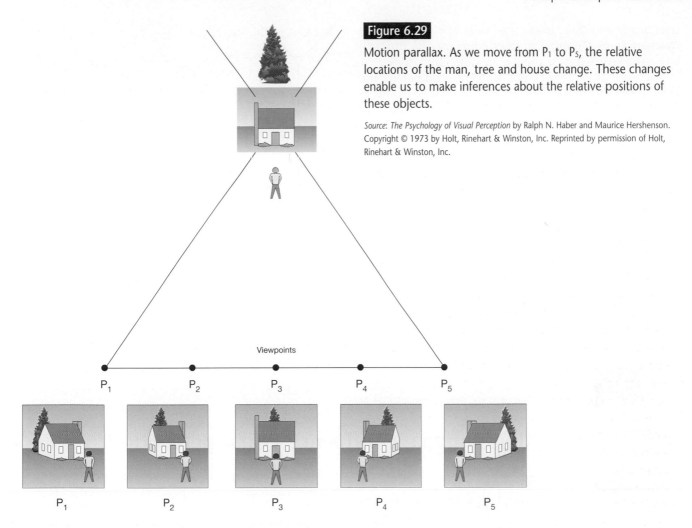

Figure 6.29

Motion parallax. As we move from P₁ to P₅, the relative locations of the man, tree and house change. These changes enable us to make inferences about the relative positions of these objects.

Source: *The Psychology of Visual Perception* by Ralph N. Haber and Maurice Hershenson. Copyright © 1973 by Holt, Rinehart & Winston, Inc. Reprinted by permission of Holt, Rinehart & Winston, Inc.

part shows the views that the observer will see from five different places (P1–P5). The changes in the relative locations of the objects provide cues concerning their distance from the observer. The phenomenon is known as **motion parallax** (parallax comes from a Greek word meaning 'change').

Cross-cultural variation in visual perception

From birth onwards, we explore our environment with our eyes. The patterns of light and dark, colour and movement, produce changes in the visual system of the brain. There is evidence, however, that perception is not absolute, that it varies across cultures. Ecological variables such as those associated with geography, cultural codes and education influence perception.

The visual stimulation we receive, particularly during infancy, affects the development of our visual system. If the environment lacks certain features – certain visual patterns – then an organism might fail to recognise the significance of these features if it encounters them later in life (Blakemore and Mitchell, 1973). But this is not the only type of environment that can influence perception.

There may also be differences in the cultural codes found in pictorial representations (Russell *et al.*, 1997). Although artists have learned to represent all the monocular depth cues (except for those produced by movement) in their paintings, not all cues are represented in the traditional art of all cultures. For example, many cultures do not use linear perspective. Does the absence of particular cues in the art of a particular culture mean that people from this culture will not recognise them when they see them in paintings from another culture?

It is quite rare for a member of one culture to be totally unable to recognise a depiction as a depiction (Russell *et al.*, 1997). However, Deregowski *et al.* (1972) found that when the Me'en tribe of Ethiopia, a culture unfamiliar with pictures, were shown a series of pictures from a children's colouring book, they would smell them, listen to the pages while flexing them, examined their texture but would ignore the actual pictures. They did recognise depictions of indigenous animals, suggesting that the familiarity of a pictorial depiction is important for recognition within cultures. Familiar objects are sometimes depicted in an exaggerated way. Aboriginal depictions of the crocodile, for example, are distorted: the trunk is seen from above and the head and tail from the side (Dziurawiec and Deregowski, 1992), although this finding may be attributable to the fact that such animals are difficult to draw.

There are other geographical influences on perception. People who live in 'carpentered worlds', that is, worlds in which buildings are built from long, straight pieces of material that normally join each other in right angles, are more likely to be subject to the Müller–Lyer illusion. This illusion is shown in Figure 6.30. Look at the two vertical lines and decide which is longer. Actually, the lines are of equal length.

Segall *et al.* (1966) presented the Müller–Lyer illusion (and several others) to groups of subjects from Western and non-Western cultures. Most investigators believe that the Müller–Lyer illusion is a result of our experience with the angles formed by the intersection of walls, ceilings and floors (Redding and Hawley, 1993). The angled lines can be seen as examples of linear perspective (see Figure 6.31). In fact, Segall and his colleagues did find that people from

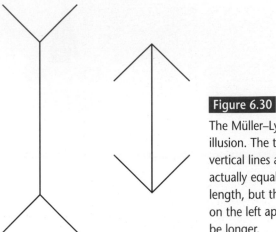

Figure 6.30

The Müller–Lyer illusion. The two vertical lines are actually equal in length, but the one on the left appears to be longer.

'carpentered' cultures were more susceptible to this illusion: experience with straight lines forming right angles appeared to affect people's perception.

Controversies in psychological science

How does language influence visual perception?

The issue

The effects on perception of another cultural code – language – has received much attention from psychologists for a good reason. Words for shades of light and colour seem to be more limited in some cultures than others. The Inuit, for example, have more than one name for various shades of snow, whereas Africans have different words for different shades of sand, presumably because these features form a crucial part of the culture's environment. There are also difference in the number of colour-words that different cultures use. This has important implications for our understanding of the cross-cultural generalisability of colour perception which we discussed in Chapter 5. For example, do all cultures use all the primary and secondary colour terms? Does the word 'blue' mean the same across cultures? Do cultures have different words for various shades of blue? If so, why?

The evidence

In the mid-nineteenth century, the British statesman William Gladstone noted that the writings of the ancient Greeks did not contain words for brown or blue. Perhaps the ancient Greeks did not perceive these colours. Magnus (1880) investigated this hypothesis by gathering both linguistic and perceptual data. He sent questionnaires and colour chips to Western residents of European colonies and asked them to test the abilities of the native people to distinguish among the various colours. He assumed that language would reflect perceptual ability. If a language did not contain words to distinguish between certain colours, then the people who belonged to that culture would not be able to distinguish these colours perceptually.

Magnus was surprised to discover very few cultural differences in people's ability to perceive various colours. Linguistic differences did not appear to reflect perceptual differences. The issue emerged again in the mid-twentieth century with the principle of linguistic relativity. Briefly stated, this principle asserts that language used by the members of a particular culture is related to these people's thoughts and perceptions. The best-known proponent of this principle, Benjamin Whorf, stated that 'the background linguistic system … of each language is not merely a reproducing instrument for voicing ideas but rather is itself a shaper of ideas, the program and guide for the individual's mental activity, for his analysis of impressions, for his synthesis of his mental stock-of-trade' (Whorf, 1956, p. 212). This became known as the Sapir–Whorf hypothesis – the idea that language can determine thought (Kay and Kempton, 1984).

Figure 6.31

The impact of culture on the Müller–Lyer illusion. People from 'non-carpentered' cultures that lack rectangular corners are less likely to be susceptible to this illusion. Although the two vertical lines are actually the same height, the one on the right looks shorter.

Proponents of linguistic relativity suggested that colour names were cultural conventions – that members of a given culture could divide the countless combinations of hue, saturation and brightness (defined in Chapter 5) that we call colours into any number of different categories (Kay *et al.*, 1997). Each category was assigned a name, and when members of that culture looked out at the world, they perceived each of the colours they saw as belonging to one of these categories.

Two anthropologists, Berlin and Kay, examined this hypothesis in a linguistic study of a wide range of languages. They found the following eleven primary colour terms: black, white, red, yellow, green, blue, brown, purple, pink, orange and grey (Berlin and Kay, 1969; Kay, 1975; Kay *et al.*, 1991). The authors referred to these as focal colours. Not all languages used all eleven (as English does). In fact, some languages used only two: black and white (Heider, 1972). Others, such as Russian, had two words for blue.

If a language contained words for three primary colours, these colours were black, white and red. If it contained words for six primary colours, these were black, white, red, yellow, green and blue. Berlin and Kay suggested that basic colour terms would be named more quickly than non-basic colour terms, that basic terms would be more salient, that is, they would be elicited first if you asked people to name colours spontaneously, and that basic terms would be more common in written communications such as texts. In fact, people do respond more quickly to basic than they do non-basic colour terms across a range of languages; when asked to write down a list of as many colour words in five minutes as possible and draw a line under the last words written, every minute, basic terms invariably appear at the beginning of the list (Corbett and Davies, 1997). Similarly, Heider (1971) found that both children and adults found it easier to remember a colour chip of a focal colour (such as red or blue) than one of a non-focal colour (such as turquoise or peach).

In a famous cross-cultural study, Heider (1972) studied members of the Dani culture of New Guinea. The language of the Dani people has only two basic colour terms: mili ('black') and mola ('white'). Heider assembled two sets of colour chips, one containing focal colours and the other containing non-focal colours. She taught her participants arbitrary names that she made up for the colours. Even though the participants had no words in their language for any of the colours, the group learning names for focal colours learned the names faster and remembered them better.

Conclusion

Colour is a difficult topic to study cross-culturally. The evidence suggests, however, that although there are cultural variations in the number of colour words used, there seems to be cross-cultural agreement on the colours considered as 'basic'.

Constancies of visual perception

An important characteristic of the visual environment is that it is almost always changing as we move, as objects move, and as lighting conditions change. However, despite the changing nature of the image the visual environment casts on our retinas, our perceptions remain remarkably constant.

Brightness constancy

People can judge the whiteness or greyness of an object very well, even if the level of illumination changes. If you look at a sheet of white paper either in bright sunlight or in shade, you will perceive it as being white, although the intensity of its image on your retina will vary. If you look at a sheet of grey paper in sunlight, it may in fact reflect more light to your eye than will a white paper located in the shade, but you will still see the white paper as white and the grey paper as grey. This phenomenon is known as **brightness constancy**.

Katz (1935) demonstrated brightness constancy by constructing a vertical barrier and positioning a light source so that a shadow was cast to the right of the barrier. In the shadow, he placed a grey square card on a white background. In the lighted area on the left of the barrier, he placed a number of shades of grey and asked participants to choose one that matched the grey square in the shadow (see Figure 6.32).

His participants matched the greys not in terms of the light that the cards actually reflected but in terms of the light they would have reflected had both been viewed under the same level of illumination. In other words, the participants compensated for the dimness of the shadow.

The match was not perfect, but it was much closer than it would have been if perception of brightness had been made solely on the basis of the amount of light that fell on the retina. The perception of white and grey, then, is not a matter of absolutes; rather, the colours are perceived relative to the surrounding environment.

Form constancy

When we approach an object or when it approaches us, we do not perceive it as getting larger. Even though the image of the object on the retina gets larger, we perceive this change as being due to a decrease in the distance between ourselves and the object. Our perception of the object's size remains relatively constant.

The unchanging perception of an object's size and shape when it moves relative to us is called **form constancy**. Psychologists also refer to size constancy, but size is simply one aspect of form. In the nineteenth century, Hermann von Helmholtz suggested that form constancy was achieved by **unconscious inference** – a mental computation of which we are unaware. We know the size and shape of a familiar object. Therefore, if the image it casts upon our retina is small, we perceive it as being far away; if the image is large, we perceive it as being close. In either case, we perceive the object itself as being the same size.

Form constancy also works for rotation. The drawing of Figure 6.33(a) could be either a trapezoid or a rectangle rotated away from us. However, the extra cues clearly identify the drawing in Figure 6.33(b) as a window, and experience tells us that windows are rectangular rather than trapezoidal; thus, we perceive it as rectangular. Obviously, this effect will not be seen in members of cultures that do not have buildings fitted with rectangular windows (or seen by people unfamiliar with the object).

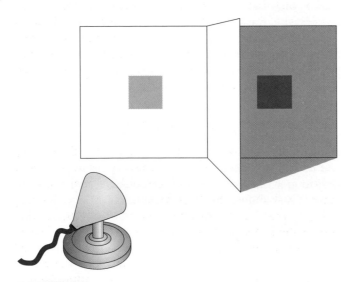

Figure 6.32

Brightness constancy as demonstrated by the experiment by Katz (1935).

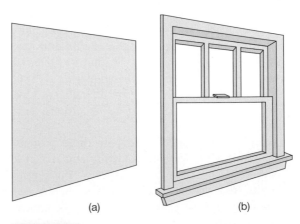

(a)   (b)

Figure 6.33

Form constancy. (a) This figure can be perceived as a trapezoid. (b) Because we recognise this figure as a window, we perceive its shape as rectangular.

Figure 6.34

Effect of perceived distance. Although both letterboxes are exactly the same size, the upper one looks larger because of the depth cues (perspective and texture) that surround it. If you turn the book upside-down and look at the picture, thus disrupting the depth cues, the letterboxes look the same size.

The process just described works for familiar objects. However, we often see unfamiliar objects whose size we do not already know. If we are to perceive the size and shape of unfamiliar objects accurately, we must know something about their distance from us. An object that produces a large retinal image is perceived as big if it is far away and small if it is close. Figure 6.34. illustrates this phenomenon. Although the two letterboxes are exactly the same size, the one that appears to be further away looks larger. If you turn the book upside-down and look at the figure again, the appearance of depth is greatly diminished, and the two letterboxes appear to be approximately the same size.

Perception of motion

Detection of movement is one of the most primitive aspects of visual perception (Milner and Goodale, 1995). This ability is seen even in animals whose visual systems do not obtain detailed images of the environment. Of course, our visual system can detect more than the mere presence of movement. We can see what is moving in our environment and can detect the direction in which it is moving.

Adaptation and long-term modification

One of the most important characteristics of all sensory systems is that they show adaptation and rebound effects. For example, when you stare at a spot of colour, the adaptation of neurons in your visual system will produce a negative after-image if you shift your gaze to a neutral background; and if you put your hand in some hot water, warm water will feel cool to that hand immediately afterwards.

Motion, like other kinds of stimuli, can give rise to adaptation and after-effects. Tootell *et al.* (1995) presented participants with a display showing a series of concentric rings moving outwards, like the ripples in a pond. When the rings suddenly stopped moving, participants had the impression of the opposite movement – that the rings were moving inwards. During this time, the experimenters scanned the participants' brains to measure their metabolic activity. The scans showed increased activity in the motion-sensitive region of the visual association cortex, which lasted as long as the illusion did. Thus, the neural circuits that give rise to this illusion appear to be located in the same region that responds to actual moving stimuli.

A study by Ball and Sekuler (1982) suggests that even the long-term characteristics of the system that detects movement can be modified by experience. The experimenters trained people to detect extremely small movements. Each participant sat in front of a display screen. A series of dots appeared, scattered across the screen, and either all moved an extremely small distance or all remained stationary. The dots always moved in the same direction, but the direction was different for each person in the experiment. After several sessions, the experimenters assessed the participants' sensitivity to detecting movements of the dots. They found that each person was especially good at detecting movement only in the direction in which he or she had been trained; the training did not increase their detection of movements in other directions. The effect was still present when the participants were tested again ten weeks later.

The fact that the participants learned to detect a small movement in a particular direction, and not small movements in general, shows that particular aspects of their visual systems were modified by experience. Did they acquire new sets of feature detectors, or were parallel networks of neurons modified in some way?

Interpretation of a moving retinal image

As you read this book, your eyes are continuously moving. Naturally, the eye movements cause the image on your retina to move. You can also cause the retinal image to move by holding the book close to your face, looking straight ahead, and moving it back and forth. In the first case, when you were reading normally, you perceived the book as being still. In the second case, you perceived it as moving. Why does your brain interpret the movement differently in these two cases? Try another demonstration. Pick a letter on this page, stare at it, and then move the book around, following the letter with your eyes. This time you will perceive the book as moving, even though the image on your retina remains stable. Thus, perception of movement requires co-ordination between movements of the image on the retina and those of the eyes.

Obviously, the visual system must know about eye movements in order to compensate for them in interpreting the significance of moving images on the retina. Another simple demonstration suggests the source of this information. Close your left eye and look slightly down and to the left. Gently press your finger against the outer corner of the upper eyelid of your right eye and make your right eye move a bit. The scene before you appears to be moving, even though you know better. This sensation of movement occurs because your finger – not your eye muscles – moved your eye. When your eye moves normally, perceptual mechanisms in your brain compensate for this movement. Even though the image on the retina moves, you perceive the environment as being stationary. However, if the image moves because the object itself moves or because you push your eye with your finger, you perceive movement (see Figure 6.35).

In general, if two objects of different size are seen moving relative to each other, the smaller one is perceived as moving and the larger one as standing still. We perceive people at a distance moving against a stable background and flies moving against an unmoving wall. Thus, when an experimenter moves a frame that encloses a stationary dot, we tend to see the dot move, not the frame. This phenomenon is also encountered when we perceive the moon racing behind the clouds, even though we know that the clouds, not the moon, are moving.

Perception of movement can even help us perceive three-dimensional forms. Johansson (1973) demonstrated just how much information we can derive from movement. He dressed actors in black and attached small lights to several points on their bodies, such as their wrists, elbows, shoulders, hips, knees and feet. He made movies of the actors in a darkened room while they were performing various behaviours, such as walking, running, jumping, limping, doing push-ups, and dancing with a partner who was also equipped with lights. Even though observers who watched the films could only see a pattern of moving lights against a dark background, they could readily perceive the pattern as belonging to a moving human and could identify the behaviour the actor was performing. Subsequent studies (Kozlowski and Cutting, 1977; Barclay *et al.*, 1978) showed that people could even tell, with reasonable accuracy, the sex of the actor wearing the lights. The cues appeared to be supplied by the relative amounts of movement of the shoulders and hips as the person walked.

Combining information from successive fixations

As Chapter 5 showed, when examining a scene, our eyes do not roam slowly around; rather, they make rapid steplike movements called saccades. After each saccade, the eyes rest for a while, gathering information before moving again. These stops are called fixations. The visual system combines the information from each fixation and perceives objects too large or too detailed to see in a single glance. Obviously, in doing so, it must keep track of the locations of each of the fixations.

Figure 6.36(a) illustrates an impossible object. That is, an artist can draw lines that, at first glance, represent a three-dimensional object. However, careful inspection shows that the object cannot possibly exist. But the drawing in Figure 6.36(b) creates a very different impression; it does not look at all like a unified three-dimensional object. The difference in the two impressions is that the details of the larger figure cannot be gathered in a single glance. Apparently, when we look from one end of the figure to the other, the information we gather from the first fixation is slightly modified to conform to the image of the second one. Of course, the two images do not exactly match, as a careful inspection shows.

Clearly, what we see during one fixation affects what we see in another. If two visual stimuli are presented, one after the other, the second stimulus could sometimes erase the image of the first. That is, under the appropriate conditions, the subject would fail to perceive the image that came first. This phenomenon is known as **backward masking** (Werner, 1935).

Normally, backward masking can be demonstrated only in the laboratory, where the shape and intensity of the stimuli and the time interval between them can be carefully controlled. Breitmeyer (1980) suggests that the

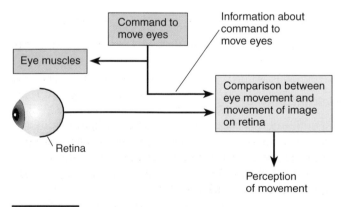

Figure 6.35

A schematic representation of the brain mechanisms responsible for the interpretation of a moving retinal image. This system must compensate for eye movements.

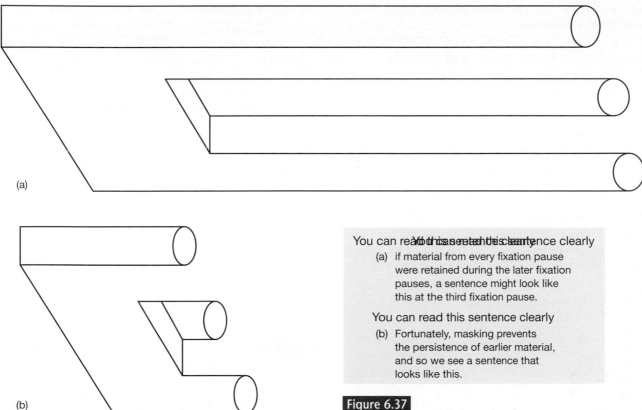

(a)

(b)

You can read this sentence clearly

(a) if material from every fixation pause were retained during the later fixation pauses, a sentence might look like this at the third fixation pause.

You can read this sentence clearly

(b) Fortunately, masking prevents the persistence of earlier material, and so we see a sentence that looks like this.

Figure 6.36

(a) An impossible figure. Only after carefully studying the figure do we see that it cannot be a drawing of a real three-dimensional object. (b) An unconvincing impossible figure. When the legs are short enough so that the entire figure can be perceived during a single fixation, the figure does not look paradoxical.

Figure 6.37

The role of backward masking. If each saccade did not erase the remaining image from the previous fixation, we probably would not be able to read.

Source: Margaret W. Matlin, *Sensation and Perception* (2nd edition). Copyright © 1988 by Allyn & Bacon. Reproduced with permission.

explanation for this phenomenon lies in the nature of the saccadic movements made by the eyes when gathering information about the visual environment. For example, consider the saccadic movements that your eyes make as you read a line of text in this book. You do not stop and look at each letter or even at each word; instead, you make several fixations on each line. During each one, your visual system gathers information and begins decoding the letters and words. Your eyes move on, and you perceive more words. Breitmeyer suggests that each saccade erases the image remaining from the previous fixation, leaving only the information that has been analysed by the visual system. Figure 6.37 illustrates what might happen if this erasure did not occur.

Perception of movement in the absence of motion

If you sit in a darkened room and watch two small lights that are alternately turned on and off, your perception will be that of a single light moving back and forth between two different locations. You will not see the light turn off at one position and then turn on at the second position. If the distance and timing are just right, the light will appear to stay on at all times, quickly moving between the positions. This response is known as the phi phenomenon. Theatre marquees, 'moving' neon signs and some computer animations make use of it.

This characteristic of the visual system accounts for the fact that we perceive the images in cinema films, video tapes and television as continuous rather than separate. The images actually jump from place to place, but we see smooth movement.

Questions to think about

Perception of form, space and motion

- Why do you think that artists often hold their thumbs in front of them while looking at the scene they are painting?

- Recent evidence suggests that painters place the eye of the subject in the centre of a portrait (Tyler, 1998). Why would they do this?

- You have undoubtedly tried to see the hidden three-dimensional images in the 'magic eye' pictures that became popular several years ago. What phenomenon described in this section accounts for the existence of these images? Why do you think that some people are able to see these 'hidden' images and others are not?

- When we ride in a car and can see the sun or moon through a side window, why does it look as if these objects are following us?

- When we see an approaching bus, train or taxi, we are perceiving form, space and motion. In what way do you think the brain makes the best sense of organising all of these data? Does it process all of them in the same way together? Or do you think that different parts of the system process the different aspects of information in parallel?

- What are the problems that psychologists face in conducting cross-cultural studies of visual perception? What methods of presenting material do you think would work best in such experiments?

Brain mechanisms of visual perception

Although the eyes contain the photoreceptors that detect areas of different brightnesses and colours, perception takes place in the brain. As we saw in Chapters 4 and 5, the optic nerves send visual information to the thalamus, which relays the information to the primary visual cortex (PVC), located in the occipital lobe at the back of the brain. In turn, neurons in the primary visual cortex send visual information to two successive levels of the visual association cortex. The first level, located in the occipital lobe, surrounds the primary visual cortex. The second level is divided into two parts, one in the middle of the parietal lobe and one in the lower part of the temporal lobe. Figure 6.38 illustrates these regions.

Visual perception by the brain is often described as a hierarchy of information processing. According to this scheme, circuits of neurons analyse particular aspects of

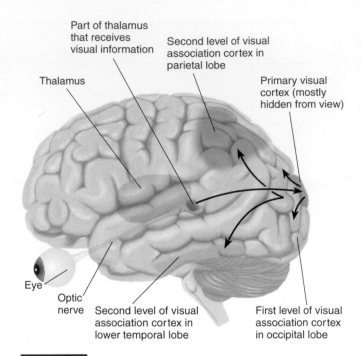

Figure 6.38

The visual system of the brain. Arrows represent the flow of visual information. Sensory information from the eye is transmitted through the optic nerve to the thalamus, and from there it is relayed to the primary visual cortex. The results of the analysis performed there are sent to the visual association cortex of the occipital lobe (first level) and then on to that of the temporal lobe and parietal lobe (second level). At each stage, additional analysis takes place.

visual information and send the results of their analysis on to another circuit, which performs further analysis. At each step in the process, successively more complex features are analysed. Eventually, the process leads to the perception of the scene and of all the objects in it. The higher levels of the perceptual process interact with memories: the viewer recognises familiar objects and learns the appearance of new, unfamiliar ones.

The primary visual cortex

Our knowledge about the characteristics of the earliest stages of visual analysis has come from investigations of the activity of individual neurons in the thalamus and primary visual cortex. For example, David Hubel and Torsten Wiesel have inserted microelectrodes – extremely fine wires having microscopically sharp points – into various regions of the visual system of cats and monkeys to detect the action potentials produced by individual neurons (Hubel and Wiesel, 1977, 1979). The signals detected by the microelectrodes are electronically amplified and sent to a recording device so that they can be studied later.

After positioning a microelectrode close to a neuron, Hubel and Wiesel presented various stimuli on a large screen in front of the anaesthetised animal. The anaesthesia makes the animal unconscious but does not prevent neurons in the visual system from responding. The researchers moved a stimulus around on the screen until they located the point where it had the largest effect on the electrical activity of the neuron. Next, they presented stimuli of various shapes to learn which ones produced the greatest response from the neuron.

From their experiments, Hubel and Wiesel (1977, 1979) concluded that the geography of the visual field is retained in the primary visual cortex. That is, the surface of the retina is 'mapped' on the surface of the primary visual cortex. However, this map on the brain is distorted, with the largest amount of area given to the centre of the visual field. The map is actually like a mosaic. Each piece of the mosaic (usually called a module) consists of a block of tissue, approximately 0.5 × 0.7 mm in size and containing approximately 150,000 neurons.

All of the neurons within a module receive information from the same small region of the retina. The primary visual cortex contains approximately 2,500 of these modules. Because each module in the visual cortex receives information from a small region of the retina, that means that it receives information from a small region of the visual field – the scene that the eye is viewing. If you looked at the scene before you through a straw, you would see the amount of information received by an individual module. Hubel and Wiesel found that neural circuits within each module analysed various characteristics of their own particular part of the visual field, that is of their receptive field. Some circuits detected the presence of lines passing through the region and signalled the orientation of these lines (that is, the angle they made with respect to the horizon). Other circuits detected the thickness of these lines. Others detected movement and its direction. Still others detected colours.

Figure 6.39 shows a recording of the responses of an orientation-sensitive neuron in the primary visual cortex. This neuron is located in a cluster of neurons that receive information from a small portion of the visual field. That is, the neuron has a small receptive field. The neuron responds when a line oriented at 50 degrees to the vertical is placed in this location – especially when the line is moving through the receptive field. This response is specific to that orientation; the neuron responds very little when a line having a 70 degree or 30 degree orientation is passed through the receptive field. Other neurons in this cluster share the same receptive field but respond to lines of different orientations. Thus, the orientation of lines that pass through this receptive field is signalled by an increased rate of firing of particular neurons in the cluster.

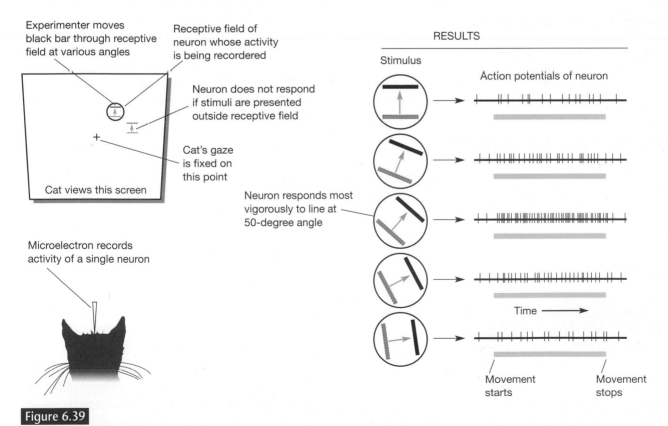

Figure 6.39

Responses of a single neuron to lines of particular orientations that are passed through its receptive field.

Because each module in the primary visual cortex receives information about only a restricted area of the visual field, the information must be combined somehow for perception to take place. This combination takes place in the visual association cortex.

The visual association cortex

The first level of the visual association cortex, which surrounds the primary visual cortex, contains several subdivisions, each of which contains a map of the visual scene. Each subdivision receives information from different types of neural circuit within the modules of the primary visual cortex. One subdivision receives information about the orientation and widths of lines and edges and is involved in perception of shapes. Another subdivision receives information about movement and keeps track of the relative movements of objects (and may help compensate for movements of the eyes as we scan the scene in front of us). Yet another subdivision receives information concerning colour (Zeki, 1993; Milner, 1998). You can see these subdivisions in Figure 6.40.

The two regions of the second level of the visual association cortex put together the information gathered and processed by the various subregions of the first level. Information about shape, movement and colour are combined in the visual association cortex in the lower part of the temporal lobe. Three-dimensional form perception takes place here. The visual association cortex in the parietal lobe is responsible for perception of the location of objects. It integrates information from the first level of the visual association cortex with information from the motor system and the body senses about movements of the eyes, head and body.

Researchers have studied the anatomy and functions of the visual association cortex in laboratory animals. Neuroimaging studies have also been used to locate comparable subregions in humans. For example, when a person looks at a display containing irregular patches of different colours, one region of the visual association cortex becomes active. When a person looks at a display of moving black-and-white squares, another region becomes active (see Figure 6.41). Presumably, these areas are involved in the analysis of colour and movement, respectively.

Brain damage and visual perception

Research with laboratory animals and data from individuals with brain damage have shown that certain areas of the visual cortex, the lingual and fusiform gyri, are important for discriminating between colours (Damasio *et al.*, 1980; Davidoff, 1997). Damage to this area causes achromatopsia, a form of colour blindness in which the world is seen in shades of grey, as Figure 6.42 shows.

Neuroimaging studies also suggest that these areas are active in healthy individuals during a simple task where participants perceive colours (McKeefry and Zeki, 1997). McKeefry and Zeki suggest that there is an area or areas outside the primary visual cortex – V4, in the ventral occipitotemporal cortex – which mediates colour perception.

Damage to different parts of the visual system resulting in different types of impairment in visual perception suggests that some visual system pathways carry one type of information whereas others carry different types of information. Schneider (1969), for example, had proposed that there were two major visual system pathways: a geniculostriate pathway which was responsible for identifying

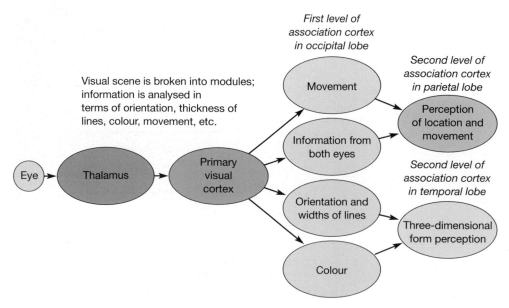

Figure 6.40

Schematic diagram of the types of analysis performed on visual information in the primary visual cortex and the various regions of the visual association cortex.

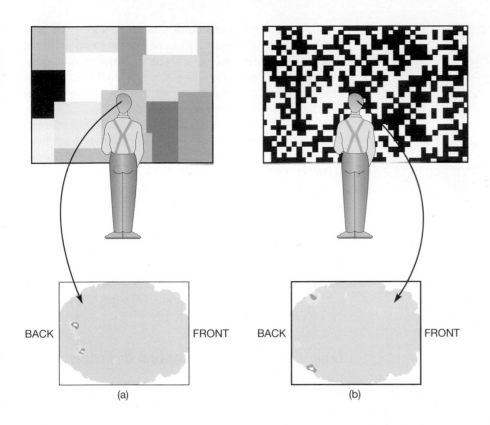

Figure 6.41

PET scans of the human brain showing regions of increased metabolic activity (indicating increased neural activity) when the subjects looked at multicoloured patterns (a) and moving black and white rectangles (b).

Source: Adapted from Zeki, S., *La Recherche*, 1991, 21, 712–721.

stimuli and discriminating between patterns, and a retino-tectal pathway which was responsible for locating objects in space. Schneider's theory has since been modified, although the idea that different brain regions are responsible for the perception of an object's qualities and its location is valid.

Ungerleider and Mishkin (1982), for example, have suggested that different parts of the brain are involved in object identification and object location: the appreciation of an object's qualities is the role of the inferior temporal cortex; the ability to locate an object is the role of the posterior parietal cortex. Primates with posterior parietal cortex lesions make consistent errors in accurately reaching out for or grasping objects although their ability to discriminate between objects is intact. Similar damage in humans also results in difficulties performing visuospatial tasks such as estimating length and distance (von Cramon and Kerkoff, 1993; Jeannerod *et al.*, 1994). Recall from Chapter 4 that the parietal cortex plays an important role in visually guiding movement and in grasping or manipulating objects (Sakata *et al.*, 1997).

Importantly, Ungerleider and Mishkin distinguished between a ventral and dorsal pathway or stream which projected from the primary visual cortex to these areas. Thus, although originating in the PVC, the two pathways were independent and projected to different areas of the brain (to the temporal and posterior parietal cortices, respectively).

Goodale and Milner (1992; Milner and Goodale, 1995) have developed this theory further. What is important,

they argue, is not 'what' and 'where' but 'what' and 'how'. In Ungerleider and Mishkin's model, the ventral stream processes the 'what' component of visual perception (identification of an object) whereas the dorsal stream processes the 'where' component (the spatial location of an object). Goodale and Milner's research has focused on the 'what' and 'how' areas. The brain regions representing these streams can be seen in Figure 6.43.

Figure 6.42

A photograph illustrating the way the world would look to a person who had achromatopsia in the right visual field, caused by damage on the left side of the brain to the region of the visual association cortex shown in Figure 6.41(a).

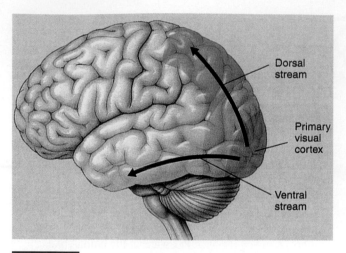

The two visual routes (ventral and dorsal) and their pathway from the visual cortex.

Source: Pinel, J., *Biopsychology* (3rd edition). Boston: Allyn and Bacon. Copyright © 1997 by Allyn and Bacon.

Goodale and Milner have made an extensive study of DF, a woman with substantial bilateral damage to the occipital cortex (but sparing the PVC) resulting from carbon monoxide poisoning (Goodale and Milner, 1992; Milner and Goodale, 1995). DF is unable to discriminate between geometric shapes and is unable to recognise or identify objects, despite having no language or visual sensory impairment (Milner *et al.*, 1991). That is, she exhibits visual form agnosia (agnosia is described in more detail in the next section). DF is able to respond to objects. For example, she can place her hand into a slot of varying orientations or grasp blocks (Goodale *et al.*, 1991). However, when she is asked to estimate the orientation of the slot or the width of the box by verbally reporting or by gesturing, she is unable to do so. Why?

Goodale and Milner (Milner and Goodale, 1995; Milner, 1998) suggest that DF is using the intact visuomotor processing system in the parietal cortex to perform the grasping and orientation tasks. The guidance of motor behaviour relies on a primitive dorsal stream in the parietal cortex and this has been spared. This is why the execution of DF's motor behaviour is accurate. When asked to indicate which of two boxes is a rectangle and which is a square, she can respond correctly when holding the boxes but less correctly when making a verbal response (Murphy *et al.*, 1996). These experimenters noticed that DF would make partial movements towards one of the boxes before correcting herself. When these initial reaches were analysed, they showed the same level of accuracy as if she had verbally reported which box was which. Did DF monitor the size of her anticipatory grip before making a decision?

There is evidence that DF does indeed self-monitor. For example, when asked to look at a series of lines of varying orientation and then copy them on a separate piece of paper, DF would outline the line in the air before making a

copy. When asked not to do this, her copies were still relatively accurate. An examination of DF's strategy indicated that she found the task easier if she imagined herself drawing the line. When, therefore, she was asked to copy the line immediately (thereby preventing rehearsal from taking place) she failed (Dijkerman and Milner, 1997). DF must have generated a motor image of the lines to allow her to accomplish this task, a behaviour which would have been made possible by intact functioning of frontal and parietal cortex regions.

On the basis of DF's behaviour, research from neuroimaging studies of motor movement and vision, and animal lesions to parietal and occipital areas, Milner and Goodale (1995) propose that the dorsal stream sends information about object characteristics and orientation that is related to movement from the primary visual cortex to the parietal cortex. Damage to the ventral stream, which projects to the inferior temporal cortex, is what is responsible for DF's inability to access perceptual information.

Brain damage and perceptual disorders

When the brain is damaged and visual perception is impaired, the patient is said to exhibit a **perceptual disorder**. There are several perceptual disorders and each is associated with damage to different parts of the visual system. It is important to note that these disorders are strictly perceptual, that is, there is no underlying impairment in sensation (patients still retain visual acuity and the ability to tell light from dark and so on). The basic visual sensory system itself is, therefore, unimpaired. Three of the most important perceptual disorders are blindsight, agnosia and spatial neglect. Each is important in its own way because they demonstrate how brain damage can affect different aspects of visual perception.

Blindsight

When the primary visual cortex is damaged, a person becomes blind in some portion of the visual field. Some individuals, however, can lose substantial areas of the PVC and yet show evidence of perceiving objects despite being 'cortically blind'. This phenomenon is called **blindsight** (Weiskrantz, 1986, 1997) because although patients are unable to see properties of objects, patients are aware of other aspects such as movement of objects. (There are equivalent phenomena in the auditory and somatosensory systems called deaf hearing and blindtouch.) The earliest case was reported at the beginning of the century (Riddoch, 1917). Riddoch was an army medical officer who had made a study of soldiers whose primary visual cortex had been damaged by gunshot wounds. Although none of the patients could directly describe objects placed in front of them (neither shape, form nor colour), they were conscious of the movement of the objects, despite the movement being 'vague and shadowy'. This suggested to

Riddoch that some residual visual ability in the PVC remained which allowed the perception of object motion but no other aspect of visual perception.

Since Riddoch's study, several other cases of blindsight have been reported, notably Larry Weiskrantz's famous patient, DB (Weiskrantz, 1986). DB had undergone surgery for a brain tumour, which necessitated removal of the area of the visual cortex in the right occipital lobe. This surgery resulted in a scotoma – an area of complete blindness in the visual field. DB could indicate whether a stick was horizontal or vertical, could point to the location of an object when instructed, and could detect whether an object was present or absent. Other tasks presented greater difficulty: DB could not distinguish a triangle from a cross or a curved triangle from a normal one. The most intriguing feature of DB's behaviour, however, was a lack of awareness of the stimuli presented. According to DB, he 'couldn't see anything' when test stimuli were seen. Why could DB, and patients like DB, make perceptual decisions despite being unaware of visual stimuli?

One hypothesis suggests that blindsight patients have degraded normal vision. The normal vision is degraded because some of the visual areas remain but are clearly not working at an optimal level. So, the residual visual cortex is capable of providing a primitive perceptual service to its user. However, evidence from animals studies in which the striate cortex is completely removed suggests that this hypothesis is not correct because these animals exhibit blindsight (Stoerig and Cowey, 1997).

A more plausible alternative is that there are areas outside the PVC which allow perception to take place in the absence of awareness. For example, neuroimaging studies show that when the brain activity of blindsight patients is measured, areas outside V1/PVC are activated (Barbur et al., 1993; Zeki and ffytche, 1998). In fact, Zeki and ffytche propose that the processes of awareness and visual discrimination are independent but closely coupled in normal individuals. The result of damage to the PVC is to uncouple these functions; this can lead to awareness without discrimination (AWD) and discrimination without awareness (DWA). Activity in a visual association area called V5 has been found to be greater during DWA than AWD; this area may, therefore, mediate the functions seen in blindsight patients.

Visual agnosia

Patients with posterior lesions to the left or right hemisphere sometimes have considerable difficulty in recognising objects, despite having intact sensory systems. We saw an example of this in an earlier section when we discussed the perceptual impairments seen in patient, DF. This disorder is called agnosia (literally, 'without knowledge'), a term coined by Sigmund Freud. Agnosia can occur in any sense (tactile agnosia refers to the inability to recognise object by touch, for example) but visual agnosia is the most common type (Farah, 1990; Farah and Ratcliff, 1994).

The existence of specific types of agnosia is a controversial topic in perception and neuropsychology. A distinction is usually made between two types of visual agnosia: associative and apperceptive. Apperceptive agnosia is the inability to recognise objects whereas associative agnosia is the inability to make meaningful associations to objects that are visually presented. Some neuropsychologists have argued that the boundaries between these two types are 'fuzzy' (DeRenzi and Lucchelli, 1993) and other subtypes of visual agnosia have been suggested (Humphreys and Riddoch, 1987a). Apperceptive agnosics have a severe impairment in the ability to copy drawings, as patient DF did. Associative agnosics, conversely, can copy accurately but are unable to identify their drawings. For example, Humphreys and Riddoch's patient, HJA, spent six hours completing an accurate drawing but was unable to identify it when he had finished.

A more category-specific form of agnosia is prosopagnosia. Some individuals with damage to specific areas of the posterior right hemisphere (and sometimes left and right hemispheres) show an impairment in the ability to recognise familiar faces. This condition is known as prosopagnosia ('loss of knowledge for faces'). Some patients are unable to recognise famous faces (Warrington and James, 1967) or familiar people such as spouses (DeRenzi, 1986).

There has been considerable debate concerning the specificity of visual object agnosia, that is, whether some patients are unable to recognise some categories of object but not others (Newcombe et al., 1994). The commonest dissociation is seen between living and non-living things. Generally, it has been found that recognition of living objects (such as animals) is less accurate in agnosic patients than is recognition of non-living objects (Warrington and Shallice, 1984; Silveri et al., 1997). To determine whether different brain regions were responsible for this dissociation, Martin et al. (1996) conducted a PET study of healthy individuals' brain activity as the subjects named pictures of tools or animals. Both categories of words were associated with activation in the visual cortex and Broca's area (because the participants saw and spoke) but some areas were activated by the naming of animals (left occipital region) and others by the naming of tools (right premotor regions).

Some psychologists, however, have argued that these studies do not show differences between the categories of object but between the ways in which these two different types of stimulus are presented. Parkin and Stewart (1993), for example, have suggested that it is more difficult to recognise drawings of animate than inanimate objects. An inanimate object such as a cup, is a lot less detailed than an animate object, such as a fly. The dissociation seen in agnosic patients, therefore, may be due to the complexity and/or familiarity of the perceived stimulus. Stewart et al. (1992) have suggested that when these artifacts are controlled for, these dissociations disappear. However, the issue continues to be controversial. Sheridan and

Humphreys (1993), for example, have shown that patients show such dissociations even under well controlled conditions.

Spatial neglect

Patients with lesions in the right parietotemporal cortex sometimes have difficulty in perceiving objects to their left (Vallar, 1998). In fact, in 80 per cent of patients with right hemisphere stroke, patients are unable to attend automatically to any stimuli in left space (Halligan and Marshall, 1994). This is called spatial neglect (or unilateral spatial hemineglect) and occurs on the side of the body that is contralateral to the side of the brain damage (the regions damaged can be seen in Figure 6.44). Neglect for the left side is more common than right neglect (which would be caused by damage to the left hemisphere).

Patients exhibiting spatial neglect behave as if half of the world does not exist. They may forget to attend to their clothing on the left-hand side, neglect food on the left side of the plate or ignore the left-hand side of their newspaper (Halligan and Cockburn, 1993; Halligan and Marshall, 1994).

Spatial neglect patients show a characteristic pattern of behaviour on visuospatial tests. For example, if they are required to bisect lines of varying length, they will err to the right. If they are presented with an array of stimuli (such as small lines) and asked to mark off as many as possible, they mark off those on the right-hand side but fail to mark off those on the left, as seen in Figure 6.45.

Similarly, neglect patients, when asked to draw (or mentally image a scene) fail to draw or report details from the left side of the object or image (Halligan and Marshall, 1994; Guariglia *et al.*, 1993). Sometimes, patients will transfer details from the left to the right-hand side, as seen in Figure 6.46. This is called allesthesia or allochiria (Meador *et al.*, 1991).

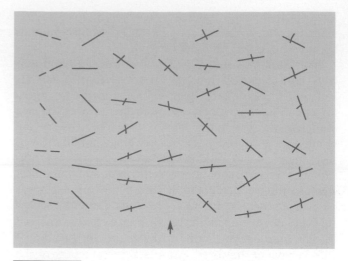

Figure 6.45

The line cancellation task. Spatial neglect patients consistently neglect one side of the display (in this example, the left side).

Halligan and Marshall (1997) have recently reported a case study of a 75 year old artist and sculptor who had suffered a right hemisphere stroke. Six months after the stroke, his drawings were poorer and less elaborate than they were before the stroke. His family also noted that he seemed to concentrate on the right-hand side of the drawings. In fact, on all the standard tests of neglect, he showed impairment. Figures 6.47(a), (b) and (c) show examples of the patient's sculptures before and 3–4 months after the stroke.

The examples shown in Figure 6.47 illustrate the profound consequences that brain damage can have on perceptual behaviour, not just in terms of behavioural impairment but in terms of disruption to a patient's life and work.

The reasons for spatial neglect are unclear (see Halligan and Marshall, 1994 and Mozer *et al.*, 1997, for a detailed consideration of the reasons for, and models of, neglect).

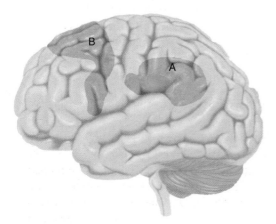

Figure 6.44

The areas of the brain damaged in spatial neglect patients. Most patients have damage to region A; some can have damage to region B.

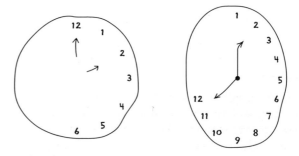

Figure 6.46

The famous clock drawing task at which spatial neglect patients are impaired. Patients either neglect the numerals on the left side completely or bunch them up on the right.

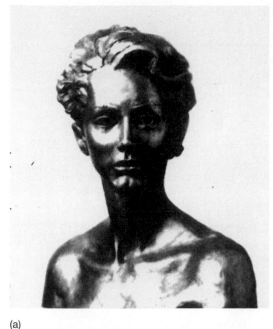

(a)

(b)

(c)

Figure 6.47

These show the effects of brain damage on the work of a sculptor. (a) A sculpture made before the injury. (b) Another sculpture made after the injury. (c) A drawing made by the same artist after injury.

Source: Halligan, P. and Marshall, J. (1997) The art of visual neglect, *The Lancet*, 350, July, pp. 139–40. © by The Lancet Limited 1997.

Questions to think about

The brain and perceptual disorders

- What are the consequences of visual cortex and association visual cortex damage? Which do you think is worse?

- How have the results of neuropsychological case studies helped us to understand the way in which the visual system processes different types of information?

- DF often found mentally imaging motor movements helpful in being able to copy geometrical shapes or estimating the size of shapes. To what extent do you think that motor imagery could help in other types of perceptual disorder such as spatial neglect?

- Spatial neglect patients seem to have a problem in automatically attending the left half of space. Can you think of any way in which this could be remedied? How would you set up an experiment to test your solution?

- Imagine that you could not identify people or recognise your car by sight. Or imagine that you could not recognise common objects but could read. How could you arrange your behaviour so that you would function at a high level of independence?

- What neural mechanism could account for the phenomenon of blindsight? Do all patients with V1 damage show blindsight?

Key terms

figure *p.182*

ground *p.182*

Gestalt psychology *p.183*

adjacency/proximity principle *p.184*

similarity principle *p.184*

good continuation *p.184*

law of closure *p.184*

principle of common fate *p.184*

template *p.184*

prototypes *p.184*

distinctive features *p.185*

geons *p.186*

tachistoscope *p.187*

bottom-up processing *p.188*

top-down processing *p.188*

affordances *p.189*

convergence *p.193*

retinal disparity *p.193*

stereopsis *p.193*

interposition *p.194*

linear perspective *p.194*

texture *p.194*

haze *p.194*

shading *p.194*

elevation *p.196*

motion parallax *p.197*

linguistic relativity *p.198*

Sapir–Whorf hypothesis *p.198*

brightness constancy *p.200*

form constancy *p.200*

unconscious inference *p.200*

backward masking *p.202*

phi phenomenon *p.203*

receptive field *p.205*

achromatopsia *p.206*

perceptual disorder *p.208*

blindsight *p.208*

apperceptive agnosia *p.209*

associative agnosia *p.209*

prosopagnosia *p.209*

spatial neglect *p.210*

allesthesia/allochiria *p.210*

CHAPTER REVIEW

Perception of form

- Perception of form requires recognition of figure and ground. The Gestalt organisational laws of proximity, similarity, good continuation and common fate describe some of the ways in which we distinguish figure from ground even when the outlines of the figures are not explicitly bounded by lines.

- Psychologists have advanced two major hypotheses about the mechanism of pattern perception, or visual recognition of particular shapes. The first hypothesis suggests that our brain contains templates of all the shapes we can perceive. We compare a particular pattern of visual input with these templates until we find a fit. The second hypothesis suggests that our brain contains prototypes, which are more flexible than simple templates. Some psychologists believe that prototypes are collections of distinctive features (such as the two parallel lines and the connecting diagonal of the letter N).

- Perception involves both bottom-up and top-down processing. Our perceptions are influenced not only by the details of the particular stimuli we see, but also by their relations to each other and our expectations. Thus, we may perceive a shape either as a loaf of bread in the kitchen or as a letterbox alongside a country road.

- We can usually distinguish male and female faces on the basis of eyes, mouth and nose but rarely on the basis of single features alone.

- Lighting, form and contour significantly influence our ability to recognise faces correctly.

Perception of space and motion

- Because the size and shape of a retinal image vary with the location of an object relative to the eye, accurate form perception requires depth perception – perception of the locations of objects in space.

- Depth perception comes from binocular cues (from convergence and retinal disparity) and monocular cues (from interposition, size, linear perspective, texture, haze shading, elevation and the effects of head and body movements).

- Culture can affect visual perceptions. The Sapir–Whorf hypothesis suggests that language can strongly affect the way we perceive the world although there is not much research to support it. It is possible that experience with some environmental features, such as particular geographical features or buildings composed of straight lines and right angles, has some influence on the way people perceive the world.

- We perceive the brightness of an object relative to that of objects around it; thus, objects retain a constant brightness under a variety of conditions of illumination. In addition, our perception of the relative distance of objects helps us maintain form constancy.

- Because our bodies may well be moving while we are visually following some activity in the outside world, the visual system has to make further compensations. It keeps track of the commands to the eye muscles and compensates for the direction in which the eyes are pointing.

- Movement is perceived when objects move relative to one another. In particular, a smaller object is likely to be perceived as moving across a larger one. Movement is also perceived when our eyes follow a moving object, even though its image remains on the same part of the retina.

- Movement supplies important cues about an object's three-dimensional shape.

- Because a complex scene, covering a large area, cannot be seen in a single glance, the visual system must combine information from successive fixations. The phenomenon of backward masking suggests that the image received from the previous fixation is erased immediately after a saccade so that blurring does not occur.

- The phi phenomenon describes our tendency to see an instantaneous disappearance of an object and its reappearance somewhere else as movement of that object. Because of the phi phenomenon, we perceive television shows and movies as representations of reality, not as a series of disconnected images.

The brain and perceptual disorders

- Visual information proceeds from the retina to the thalamus, and then to the primary visual cortex (PVC). The primary visual cortex is organised into modules, each of which receives information from a small region of the retina.

- Neural circuits within each module analyse specific information from their part of the visual field, including the orientation and width of lines, colour and movement.

- The different types of information analysed by the neural circuits in the modules of the primary visual cortex are sent to separate maps of the visual field in the first level of the visual association cortex. The information from these maps is combined in the second level of the visual association cortex: form perception in the base of the temporal lobe and spatial perception in the parietal lobe.

- The brain seems to contain visual systems which process (1) features of objects and (2) the space indication of objects. The first, the ventral stream, projects from the primary visual cortex to the inferior temporal cortex; the second, the dorsal stream projects from the PVC to the posterior parietal cortex.

- Visual agnosia is the inability to perceive objects accurately (apperceptive agnosia) or assign meaning to visually presented objects (associative agnosia). Prosopagnosia is the inability to identify familiar faces and results from bilateral or unilateral posterior brain damage.

- The agnosic deficits seen in patient DF may be due to an intact dorsal steam but an impaired ventral stream.

- Blindsight refers to the ability to perform perceptual tasks despite a lack of awareness of the perceived stimuli; it is normally associated with damage outside the primary visual cortex.

- Spatial neglect is the inability to attend to stimuli in one half of space. Patients usually neglect the left-hand side as a result of right parietotemporal cortex damage (that is, the deficit is contralesional – occurs on the opposite side to the brain damage).

Suggestions for further reading

Bruce, V, Green, P. and Georgeson, M. (1996). *Visual Perception* (3rd edition). Hove, UK: The Psychology Press.

Gordon, I.E. (1997). *Theories of Visual Perception* (2nd edition). Chichester: Wiley.

Zeki, S. (1993). *A Vision of the Brain*. Oxford: Blackwell.
The Bruce et al. text gives a good introduction to the visual system. Gordon's book is a little heavy going but covers all the major theories of visual perception. Zeki's book is a splendid example of a leading researcher explaining the results of his and others' work.

Bruce, V. (1998). Fleeting images of shade: identifying people caught on video. *The Psychologist*, 7, 331–337.

Bruce, V. and Young, A.W. (1998). *In the Eye of the Beholder: The science of face perception*. Oxford: Oxford University Press.
The perceptual importance of the face is discussed in Bruce's very lucid article and Bruce and Young's well illustrated book.

Davidoff, J. (1997). The neuropsychology of colour. In C.L. Hardin and Maffi, L. (eds), *Color Categories in Thought and Language*. Cambridge: Cambridge University Press.

Milner, A.D. (1998). Streams of consciousness: visual awareness and the brain. *Trends in Cognitive Science*, 2, 1, 25–30.

Milner, A.D. and Goodale, M.A. (1995). *The Visual Brain in Action*. Oxford: Oxford University Press.

Tanaka, K. (1997). Mechanisms of visual object recognition: monkey and human studies. *Current Opinion in Neurobiology*, 7, 523–529.

Thier, P. and Karnath, H-O. (1997). *Parietal Lobe Contributions to Orientation in 3D Space*. Berlin: Springer-Verlag.
This selection of readings covers various aspects of visual processing. Davidoff's chapter provides a general introduction to colour perception while the Milner article and Milner and Goodale book are good explorations of the components of the visual system when it is damaged. Similarly, Tanaka, and Thier and Harnath outline some of

the behavioural and neurophysiological aspects of object recognition and visual perception.

Farah, M.J. and Radcliff, G. (1994). *The Neuropsychology of High-level Vision.* Hove, UK: The Psychology Press.

Halligan, P.W. and Marshall, J.C. (1994). *Spatial Neglect: Position papers on theory and practice.* London: Macmillan.

Martin, G.N. (1998). *Human Neuropsychology.* Harlow: Prentice Hall Europe.

Weiskrantz, L. (1997). *Consciousness Lost and Found: A neuropsychological exploration.* Oxford: Oxford University Press. *Farah and Radcliff, Halligan and Marshall, and Weiskrantz give an excellent description of visual agnosia, spatial neglect and blindsight, respectively. Martin also provides coverage of these and other perceptual disorders as well as describing the neuroanatomy of the visual system.*

Journals to consult

British Journal of Psychology
Cortex
Journal of Experimental Psychology: Human Perception and Performance
Neuropsychologia
Neuropsychology
Perception
Perception and Psychophysics
Perceptual and Motor Skills
Psychological Science
Quarterly Journal of Experimental Psychology
Trends in Cognitive Science
Vision Research
Visual Neuroscience

Website addresses

http://cns-web.bu.edu/pub/laliden/WWW/Visionary/Visionary.html
 An on-line dictionary of terms used in visual perception.

http://www.yorku.ca/eye
 An on-line textbook called The joy of visual perception, *written by Peter Kaiser at York University.*

http://www.illusionworks.com
 A link to lots of perceptual illusions. It also has introductory and advanced-level explanations of the illusions.

http://www.trochim.human.cornell.edu/gallery/young/emotion.htm
 An excellent, well-illustrated site listing all major theorists and researchers in the field of facial analysis (e.g. Duchenne, Bruce, Ekman, Perrett).

7

LEARNING AND BEHAVIOUR

In a busy supermarket, the managers and staff, as part of a psychology experiment, decide to do something unusual to their wine shelves. They decide to play either French accordion music or German Bierkeller music at the German and French sections of the wine display. National flags also accompany the displays and consumers who decide to buy from the shelves are quizzed about their wine-buying.

When the results are analysed, the experimenters find that more French than German wine was bought when French music was played whereas more German wine was bought when German music was played. None of the customers, however, expressed an absolute preference for either French or German wine.

Our behaviour is governed by the degree to which we learn: from walking and talking to success at school, college and university. We learn linguistic skills such as reading and speaking our own and foreign languages; we learn practical skills such as driving a car, operating a computer keyboard, riding a bike or fusing a plug; we learn how not to behave (we know that it is wrong to commit murder or cause another person bodily harm).

This chapter considers three kinds of learning: habituation, classical conditioning and operant conditioning. All three involve cause-and-effect relations between behaviour and the environment. We learn which stimuli are trivial and which are important, and we learn to make adaptive responses and to avoid maladaptive ones. We learn to recognise those conditions under which a particular response is useful and those under which a different response is more appropriate. The types of learning described in this chapter serve as the building blocks for more complex behaviours, such as problem solving and thinking, which we consider in later chapters.

What you should be able to do after reading Chapter 7

- Describe habituation, classical conditioning and operant learning.
- Understand the principles of classical conditioning.
- Understand the principles of operant conditioning.
- Describe and explain conditioned aversions.
- Describe the nature of insight.
- Apply the principles of learning theory to behaviour.

Questions to think about

- Do different aspects of learning have different underlying principles? Is learning to ride a bike governed by different principles from those used for learning to find your way around college or university?
- Does all learning have to be intentional? Can you learn something without knowing it or without wanting to learn it?
- Is learning a process that depends on innate ability, the ability to adopt successful learning strategies or both?
- What factors do you think enhance and promote the process of learning?

The purpose of learning

Behaviours that produce favourable consequences are repeated and become habits, but those that produce unfavourable consequences tend not to recur (Ouellette and Wood, 1998). In other words, we learn from experience. Learning is an adaptive process in which the tendency to perform a particular behaviour is changed by experience. As conditions change, we learn new behaviours and eliminate old ones.

Learning, however, cannot be observed directly; it can only be inferred from changes in behaviour. But not all changes in behaviour are caused by learning. For example, your performance on an examination or the skill with which you operate a car can be affected by your physical or mental condition, such as fatigue, fearfulness or distraction. Moreover, learning may occur without noticeable changes in observable behaviour taking place. In some cases, learning is not apparent – at least, not right away – from our observable behaviour. In other cases, we may never have the opportunity to demonstrate what we have learned. For example, although you may have received training in how to conduct an orthogonally-rotated factor analysis in your computer's statistics package, you may never need to demonstrate the results of your learning again. In still other cases, you may not be sufficiently motivated to demonstrate something you have learned. For example, a tutor might pose a question in a seminar but although you know the answer, you do not say anything because you get nervous when speaking in front of others.

Learning takes place within the nervous system. Experience alters the structure and chemistry of the brain, and these changes affect the individual's subsequent behaviour. Performance is the behavioural change (or new behaviour) produced by this internal change.

Habituation

Many events may cause us to react automatically. For example, a sudden, unexpected noise causes an orienting response: we become alert and turn our heads towards the source of the sound. However, if the noise occurs repeatedly, we gradually cease to respond to it; we eventually ignore it. Habituation, learning not to respond to an unimportant event that occurs repeatedly, is the simplest form of learning. As we will see in Chapter 12 (Developmental psychology), even infants a few months old show evidence of habituation.

From an evolutionary perspective, habituation makes adaptive sense. If a once-novel stimulus occurs again and again without any important result, the stimulus has no significance to the organism. Obviously, responding to a stimulus of no importance wastes time and energy.

The simplest form of habituation is temporary, and is known as short-term habituation. Imagine entering a new room in an inhabited house. It is likely that you will perceive the distinctive odour of the room. Eventually, however, you begin not to notice the odour; you will have become habituated. If you return to the same house the next day, however, you will perceive that distinctive smell again but if you stay in the room for long enough, you will again become habituated.

Animals that have more complex nervous systems are capable of long-term habituation. For example, a hunting dog may be frightened the first few times it hears the sound of a shotgun, but it soon learns not to respond to the blast. This habituation carries across from day to day and even from one hunting season to the next. Likewise, your behaviour has habituated to stimuli that you have probably not thought about for a long time. When people move to new houses or apartments, they often complain about being kept awake by unfamiliar noises, but after a while they no longer notice them.

Classical conditioning

Unlike habituation, classical conditioning involves learning about the conditions that predict that a significant event will occur. We acquire much of our behaviour through classical conditioning. For example, if you are hungry and smell a favourite food cooking, your mouth is likely to water. If you see someone with whom you have recently had a serious argument, you are likely to experience again some of the emotional reactions that occurred during the encounter. If you hear a song that you used to listen to with a loved one, you are likely to experience a feeling of nostalgia. If you listen to a piece of music that can be distinctly identified by nation, then people will buy more of that nation's wine (as we saw in the opening of the chapter). How does such classical conditioning take place?

Imagine that you have an uninflated balloon directly before you. Someone starts inflating the balloon with a pump; the balloon gets larger and larger. What are you likely to do? You will probably grimace and squint your eyes as you realise that the balloon is about to burst in your face.

Now consider how a person learns to flinch defensively at the sight of a tightly stretched balloon. Suppose that we inflate a balloon in front of a young boy who has never seen one before. The boy will turn his eyes towards the enlarging balloon, but he will not flinch. When the balloon explodes, the noise and the blast of air will cause a defensive startle reaction: he will squint, grimace, raise his shoulders and suddenly move his arms towards his body. A bursting balloon is an important stimulus, one that causes an automatic, unlearned defensive reaction.

We will probably not have to repeat the experience many times for the boy to learn to react the way we all do –

flinching defensively before the balloon actually bursts. A previously neutral stimulus (the overinflated balloon), followed by an important stimulus (the explosion that occurs when the balloon bursts), can now trigger the defensive flinching response by itself. The defensive flinching response has been classically conditioned to the sight of an overinflated balloon. Two stimuli have become associated with each other.

Pavlov's serendipitous discovery

In December 1904, the Russian physiologist Ivan Pavlov was awarded the Nobel Prize in physiology and medicine for his work on the digestive system. Invited to Stockholm to accept the award and to deliver an acceptance speech, the 55 year old Pavlov did not speak of his pioneering work on digestion (Babkin, 1949). Instead, his address, entitled 'The first sure steps along the path of a new investigation', focused on his more recent work involving conditional reflexes or 'involuntary' responses. Pavlov's new line of research was to take him far from the research for which he was awarded the Nobel Prize, and today he is remembered more for his work in psychology than in physiology. But it was while studying the digestive system that Pavlov stumbled on the phenomenon that was to make a lasting impact on psychology (Windholz, 1997).

Pavlov's chief ambition as a physiologist was to discover the neural mechanisms controlling glandular secretions during digestion. He measured the secretions during the course of a meal by inserting a small tube in a duct in an animal's mouth and collected drops of saliva as they were secreted by the salivary gland. During each of the test sessions, he placed dry food powder inside the dog's mouth and then collected the saliva. All went well until the dogs became experienced subjects. After several testing sessions, the dogs began salivating before being fed, usually as soon as they saw the laboratory assistant enter the room with the food powder. What Pavlov discovered was a form of learning in which one stimulus predicts the occurrence of another. In this case, the appearance of the laboratory assistant predicted the appearance of food.

Rather than ignoring this phenomenon or treating it as a confounding variable that needed to be controlled, Pavlov designed experiments to discover exactly why the dogs were salivating before being given the opportunity to eat. He suspected that salivation might be triggered by stimuli that were initially unrelated to eating. Somehow, these neutral stimuli came to control what is normally a natural reflexive behaviour. After all, dogs do not naturally salivate when they see laboratory assistants.

To do so, he placed an inexperienced dog in a harness and occasionally gave it small amounts of food powder. Before placing the food powder in the dog's mouth, Pavlov sounded a bell, a buzzer or some other auditory stimulus. At first, the dog showed only a startle response to the sound, perking its ears and turning its head towards the sound. The dog salivated only when the food powder was placed in its mouth. But after only a dozen or so pairings of the bell and food powder, the dog began to salivate when the bell rang. Placing the food powder in the dog's mouth was no longer necessary to elicit salivation; the sound by itself was sufficient. Pavlov showed that a neutral stimulus can elicit a response similar to the original reflex when the stimulus predicts the occurrence of a significant stimulus (in this case, food powder).

This type of learning is called classical or Pavlovian conditioning. Pavlov demonstrated that conditioning occurred only when the food powder followed the bell within a short time. If there was a long delay between the sound and the food powder or if the sound followed the food powder, the animal never learned to salivate when it heard the sound. Thus, the sequence and timing of events are important factors in classical conditioning. Classical conditioning provides us with a way to learn cause-and-effect relations between environmental events. We are able to learn about the stimuli that warn us that an important event is about to occur. Obviously, warning stimuli must occur prior to the event about which we are being warned.

Figure 7.1 shows the basic classical conditioning procedure – the special conditions that must exist for an organism to respond to a previously neutral stimulus.

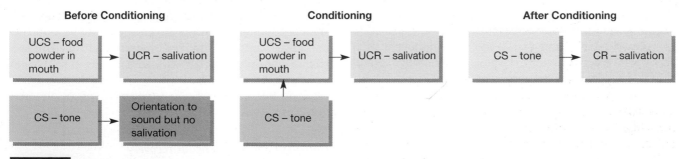

Figure 7.1

Basic components of the classical conditioning procedure. Prior to conditioning, the UCS but not the CS, elicits a response (the UCR). During conditioning, the CS is presented in conjunction with the CS. Once the conditioning is completed, the CS alone elicits a response (the CR).

A stimulus, such as food, that naturally elicits reflexive behaviour, such as salivation, is called an unconditional stimulus (UCS). The reflexive behaviour itself is called the unconditional response (UCR). If, for a certain dog, a bell signals food, then the bell may also come to elicit salivation through classical conditioning. Another dog may hear the sound of an electric can opener just before it is fed, in which case that sound will come to elicit salivation. A neutral stimulus paired with the unconditional stimulus that eventually elicits a response is called a conditional stimulus (CS). The behaviour elicited by a conditional stimulus is called a conditional response (CR). In the case of Pavlov's dogs, food powder was the UCS: it elicited the UCR, salivation.

At first, when Pavlov presented the sound of the bell or buzzer, the dogs did not salivate; the sound was merely a neutral stimulus, not a CS. However, with repeated pairings of the sound and the food powder, the sound became a CS, reliably eliciting the CR – salivation.

The biological significance of classical conditioning

Salivation is an innate behaviour and is adaptive because it facilitates digestion. Through natural selection, the neural circuitry that underlies salivation has become part of the genetic endowment of many species. Pavlov's experiments demonstrated that an innate reflexive behaviour, such as salivation, can be elicited by novel stimuli. Thus, a response that is naturally under the control of appropriate environmental stimuli, such as salivation caused by the presence of food in the mouth, can also come to be controlled by other kinds of stimuli.

Classical conditioning accomplishes two functions. First, the ability to learn to recognise stimuli that predict the occurrence of an important event allows the learner to make the appropriate response faster and perhaps more effectively. For example, hearing the buzz of a wasp near your head may make you duck and allow you to avoid being stung. Seeing a rival increases an animal's heart rate and the flow of blood to its muscles, makes it assume a threatening posture, and causes the release of hormones that prepare it for vigorous exercise.

The second function of classical conditioning is even more significant. Through classical conditioning, stimuli that were previously unimportant acquire some of the properties of the important stimuli with which they have been associated and thus become able to modify behaviour. A neutral stimulus becomes desirable when it is associated with a desirable stimulus or it becomes undesirable when it is associated with an undesirable one. In a sense, the stimulus takes on symbolic value. For example, we respond differently to the sight of a stack of money and to a stack of paper napkins. The reason for the special reaction to money is that money has, in the past, been associated with desirable commodities, such as food, clothing, cars, electrical equipment and so on.

Basic principles of classical conditioning

Classical conditioning involves several learning principles including acquisition, extinction, spontaneous recovery, stimulus generalisation and discrimination.

Acquisition

In laboratory experiments, a single pairing of the CS with the UCS is not usually sufficient for learning to take place. Only with repeated CS–UCS pairings does conditional responding gradually appear. The learning phase of classical conditioning, during which the CS gradually increases in frequency or strength, is called acquisition. The left side of Figure 7.2 shows a learning curve that illustrates the course of acquisition of a conditional eyeblink response in two human participants.

In this study (Trapold and Spence, 1960), a tone (CS) was paired with a puff of air into the eye (UCS). The puff of air caused the participants' eyes to blink automatically (UCR). Conditioning was measured as the percentage of trials in which conditional eyeblinks (CR) occurred. Note that at the beginning of the experiment, the tone elicited very few CRs. During the first fifty trials, the percentage of CRs increased rapidly but finally stabilised.

Two factors that influence the strength of the CR are the intensity of the UCS and the timing of the CS and UCS. The intensity of the UCS can determine how quickly the CR will be acquired: more intense UCSs usually produce more rapid learning. For example, rats will learn a conditioned fear response faster if they receive higher levels of a painful stimulus (Annau and Kamin, 1961). Classical conditioning of a salivary response in dogs occurs faster when the animals are given larger amounts of food (Wagner *et al.*, 1964). Generally speaking, the more intense the UCS, the stronger the CR.

The second factor affecting the acquisition of the CR is the timing of the CS and UCS. Classical conditioning occurs fastest when the CS occurs shortly before the UCS and both stimuli end at the same time. In his experiments on salivary conditioning, Pavlov found that one-half second was the optimal delay between the onset of the CS and the onset of the UCS. With shorter or longer delays between the CS and UCS, conditioning generally was slower and weaker (see Figure 7.3).

Extinction and spontaneous recovery

Once a classically conditioned response has been acquired, what happens to that response if the CS continues to be presented but is no longer followed by the UCS? This procedure, called extinction, eventually eliminates the CR.

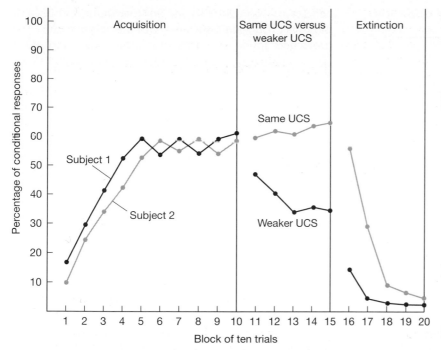

Figure 7.2

Acquisition and extinction of a conditional response. The left panel shows the learning curve for acquisition of an eyeblink response by two people. The middle panel shows a decrease in the percentage of CRs (eyeblinks) elicited by the CS (tone) when the intensity of the UCS (puff of air) was reduced. The right panel shows the extinction curves produced when the CS (tone) was no longer followed by the UCS (puff of air).

Source: Adapted from Trapold, M.A. and Spence, K.W., Performance changes in eyelid conditioning as related to the motivational and reinforcing properties of the UCS, *Journal of Experimental Psychology*, 1960, 59, 212.

Returning to our classically conditioned eyeblink response, suppose that after we reduce the intensity of the UCS, we stop presenting the UCS (the puff of air). However, we do continue to present the CS (the tone). The third panel of Figure 7.2 shows the results of our extinction procedure. CRs become less frequent, and eventually they cease altogether. Note that extinction occurs more rapidly for participant 1, which indicates that extinction is affected by the UCS intensity. Thus, once CRs are formed, they do not necessarily remain a part of an organism's behaviour.

It is important to realise that extinction occurs only when the CS occurs but the UCS does not. For example, the eyeblink response will extinguish only if the tone is presented without the puff of air. If neither stimulus is presented, extinction will not occur. In other words, the subject must learn that the CS no longer predicts the occurrence of the UCS – and that cannot happen if neither stimulus is presented.

Once a CR has been extinguished, it may not disappear from the organism's behaviour permanently. Pavlov demonstrated that after responding had been extinguished, the CR would often suddenly reappear the next time the dog was placed in the experimental apparatus. Pavlov referred to the CR's reappearance after a 'time out' period as **spontaneous recovery**. He also found that if he began presenting the CS and the UCS together again, the animals would acquire the conditional response very rapidly – much faster than they did in the first place.

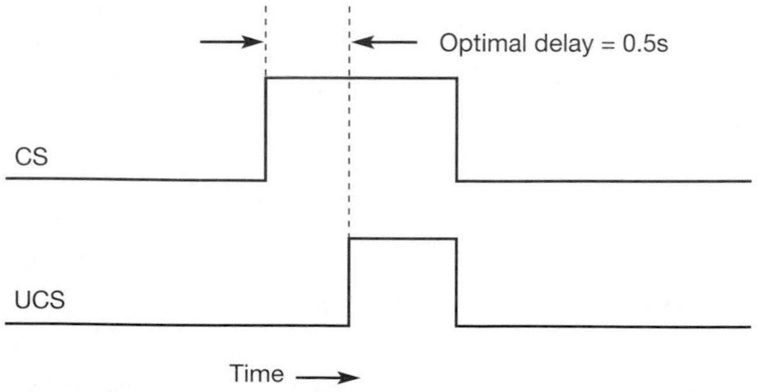

Stimulus generalisation and discrimination

No two stimuli are exactly alike. Once a response has been conditioned to a CS, similar stimuli will also elicit that response. The more closely the other stimuli resemble the CS, the more likely they will elicit the CR. For example, Pavlov discovered that once a dog learned to salivate when it heard a bell, it would salivate when it heard a bell having a different tone or when it heard a buzzer. This phenomenon is called **generalisation**: a response produced by a particular CS will also occur when a similar CS is presented. Of course, there are limits to generalisation. A dog that learns to salivate when it hears a bell will probably not salivate when it hears a door close in the hallway.

In addition, an organism can be taught to distinguish between similar but different stimuli – a phenomenon called **discrimination**. Discrimination training is accomplished by using two different CSs during training. One CS

Figure 7.3

The timing of the CS and UCS in classical conditioning. The CS precedes the UCS by a brief interval of time, and both stimuli end simultaneously.

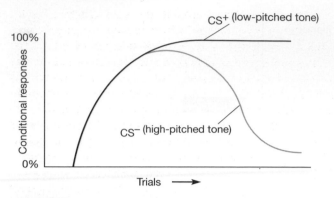

Figure 7.4

Behaviour produced through discrimination training. The CS⁺ is always followed by the UCS (a puff of air directed towards the eye); the CS⁻ is always presented without the UCS.

is always followed by the UCS; the other CS is never followed by the UCS. For example, suppose that we regularly direct a puff of air at an animal's eye during each trial in which a low-pitched tone (CS⁺) is sounded, but on trials in which a high-pitched tone (CS⁻) is sounded, we present no air puff. At first, increased amounts of blinking will occur in response to both stimuli (generalisation). Gradually, however, fewer and fewer blinks will occur after the CS⁻ but they will continue to be elicited by the CS⁺ (see Figure 7.4). Discrimination, then, involves learning the difference between two or more stimuli. An animal learns that differences among stimuli are important – it learns when to respond to one stimulus and when not to respond to a different stimulus.

Conditional emotional responses

Many stimuli are able to arouse emotional responses, such as feelings of disgust, contempt, fear, anger, sadness, tenderness, longing or sexual desire. Many of these stimuli, such as a place, a phrase, a song or someone's voice and face, originally had no special significance. But because these stimuli were paired with other stimuli that elicited strong emotional reactions, they came, through classical conditioning, to take on emotional significance.

If you read or hear words such as 'enemy', 'ugly', 'bitter' or 'failure', you are likely to experience at least a weak negative emotional response. In contrast, the words gift, win, happy and beauty may elicit positive responses. These words had no effect on you before you learned what they meant. They took on their power through being paired with pleasant or unpleasant events or perhaps with descriptions of such events.

Staats and Staats (1957) found that if people read neutral nonsense words such as 'yof' or 'laj' while hearing positive or negative words, they later said that they liked those that

had been associated with the positive words and disliked those that had been associated with the negative ones. The researchers found that this procedure could even affect people's ratings of the pleasantness of names such as Tom or Bill or nationalities such as Italian or Swedish (Staats and Staats, 1958). Berkowitz (1964) found that when people had received unpleasant electrical shocks while in the company of another person, they later acted in a hostile manner towards that person. Thus, classical conditioning may play a role in the development of ethnic prejudices and personal dislikes (and, of course, of positive reactions as well). We are often not aware of the reason for our emotional reactions, we simply feel them and conclude that there is something 'nice' or something 'nasty' about the stimulus (or the person).

Phobias

Many people are troubled by behaviours that they wish they could stop or by thoughts and fears that bother them. Phobias are unreasonable fears of specific objects or situations, such as spiders, cars or enclosed spaces, and we will look at phobias in more detail in Chapter 17. Presumably, at some time early in life, the person having the phobia was exposed to the now-feared object in conjunction with a stimulus that elicited pain or fear. For example, being stuck in a hot, overcrowded lift with a group of frightened and sweating fellow passengers might be expected to lead to a fear of lifts or perhaps even to produce a fully fledged phobia.

Classical conditioning can occur even without direct experience with the conditional and unconditional stimuli. For example, a child of a parent who has a snake phobia can develop the same fear simply by observing signs of fear in his or her parent. The child need not be attacked or menaced by a snake. In addition, people can develop phobias vicariously – by hearing about or reading stories that vividly describe unpleasant episodes. The imaginary episode that we picture as we hear or read a story (UCS) can provide imaginary stimuli (CSs) that lead to real conditional emotional responses (CRs).

The case of 'Little' Albert

A famous example of an experimentally induced learned phobia is that of Little Albert. In Chapter 1 we came across the work and ideas of John Watson. To Watson, behaviour had to be observable in order to be measured. He was excited by Pavlov's finding that dogs could be conditioned to respond in a specific way to a previously neutral stimulus. He and Rosalie Rayner set up the first experiment in which fear was experimentally conditioned in a human being (Watson and Rayner, 1920).

At the age of nine months, a healthy infant called Albert B was shown to have no fear of live animals such as rats and rabbits (Albert is forever known in textbooks as Little Albert). When a steel bar was unexpectedly struck by a claw hammer, however, he became distressed and frightened. Watson and Rayner attempted to condition fear of a previously unfeared object (a white rat) in Little Albert by pairing it with a feared stimulus (the noise of the hammer hitting the bar). They paired the rat with the noise seven times in two sessions, one week apart. When the rat was presented on its own, Albert became distressed and avoided the rat. Five days later, Albert was exposed to a number of other objects such as familiar wooden blocks, a rabbit, a dog, a sealskin coat, white cotton, the heads of Watson and two assistants and a Santa Claus mask. Albert showed a fear response to the rabbit, the dog and the sealskin coat. The initial conditioned response had generalised to some objects but not others.

Watson and Rayner's experiment is famous for two reasons. The first is the successful attempt at experimentally conditioning fear in a human being; the second is the number of inaccuracies reported in articles and textbooks describing the experiment (Harris, 1979). These include inaccurate information about Albert's age, the conditioned stimulus and the list of objects that Albert was believed to be frightened of after conditioning (the list includes fur pelt, a man's beard, a cat, a puppy, a glove, Albert's aunt and a teddy bear). These inaccuracies teach a very valuable lesson and that is the wisdom of consulting original sources of information. Because the study of Albert is part of psychology's history, details become distorted when information is passed down from textbook to textbook (this view of memory as being the reconstruction of events is discussed in Chapter 8).

Fetishes

Fetishes, unusual sexual attachments to objects such as articles of clothing, also develop through classical conditioning. These attachments probably occur because of a prior association of a stimulus that most people find neutral with sexual stimuli. One possible scenario is that of a teenage boy looking at sexually arousing pictures of women wearing high-heeled shoes. His arousal may become conditioned to the shoes worn by the women, and the boy may subsequently become a shoe fetishist. Of course, fetishism cannot be that simple; there must be other factors operating too. Some people are undoubtedly more susceptible than others to developing fetishes. Women, for example, very rarely develop them. Nevertheless, the process by which the attachment occurs most likely involves classical conditioning.

In a rather unusual study of fetishes, Rachman and Hodgson (1968) conditioned a sexual response to an object popular among fetishists, women's knee-length boots. Their subjects, young single males, were first shown a colour slide of the boots, then a slide of an attractive, naked woman. Sexual arousal was measured by a device called a plethysmograph, which measures changes in an object's size. In this case, the plethysmograph was attached to the men's penises to make an accurate record of the size of their erections. The pairing of the boots as a conditional stimulus and the pictures of naked women as unconditional stimuli resulted in classical conditioning: the subjects' penises enlarged in response to the slide of the boots alone. The subjects' responses also generalised to colour slides of shoes. Repeated presentation of the boots alone (without the naked women) eventually led to decreases in the males' sexual arousal, that is the conditioned response was extinguished.

What is learned in classical conditioning?

Research shows that for classical conditioning to occur, the CS must be a reliable predictor of the UCS (Rescorla, 1991). Imagine yourself as the subject in a classical conditioning demonstration involving a tone as the CS, a puff of air into your left eye as the UCS and an eyeblink as the CR. Your psychology lecturer asks you to come to the front of the class and seats you in a comfortable chair.

Occasionally, a tone sounds for a second or two, and then a brief but strong puff of air hits your eye. The puff of air makes you blink. Soon you begin to blink during the tone, before the puff occurs. Now consider all the other stimuli in the seminar room – your tutor explaining the demonstration to the group, your colleagues' questions, squeaks from students moving in their chairs, and so on. Why don't any of these sounds become CSs? Why do you blink only during the tone? After all, some of these stimuli occur at the same time as the puff of air. The answer is that among the stimuli present during the demonstration, only the tone reliably predicts the puff of air. All the other stimuli are poor forecasters of the UCS. The neutral stimulus becomes a CS only when the following conditions are satisfied:

1 The CS must regularly occur prior to the presentation of the UCS.
2 The CS does not regularly occur when the UCS is absent.

Consider another example. The smell of food is more likely to elicit feelings of anticipation and excitement about supper if you are hungry than is the smell of your mother's cologne because the smell of the food is the best predictor of a meal about to be served. Similarly, the sound of footsteps behind you as you are walking is more apt to make you afraid than the sound of a car passing by or the wind blowing in the trees because the footsteps are better predictors of being mugged or threatened with danger.

It also appears that conditioned responses are more common to novel than familiar stimuli. Pavlov had observed that a novel CS was more successfully paired with an UCS than was a familiar one. This phenomenon is known as latent inhibition (Lubow, 1989) and because familiar stimuli are associated less successfully with conditioning than are novel ones, this effect is called the CS pre-exposure effect (because participants will have already been pre-exposed to the CS). Similarly, when an organism is presented with the UCS (which may be novel) before it is used as an UCS in the experiment proper, the link between CS and UCS is weaker. This is called the UCS pre-exposure effect (Randich and LoLordo, 1979). Why does latent inhibition occur? No one quite knows for sure, but one explanation is related to the degree of exposure to the stimulus. A familiar CS is familiar to individuals by being in the environment; because the CS is part of the environment of context then the CS becomes merged into the context of the conditioning. To use a description from signal detection theory which you learned about in Chapter 5, the signal-to-noise ratio is weak – the CS sends a weak signal because it cannot be distinguished from the context very well.

Questions to think about

Classical conditioning

■ Can you think of a personal situation in which an orienting response might not habituate?

■ Do you think it would take longer for a response to habituate to a stimulus associated with danger (for example, the lights and sounds signalling that a train is approaching) or to a stimulus associated with a non-dangerous situation, such as the hourly chiming of a grandfather clock?

■ Think of a recent event in which you became emotionally excited. Can you describe the situation in terms of the elements of the classical conditioning paradigm? Can all emotional responses be explained by classical conditioning?

■ Under what set of conditions might the emotion you just described be generalised to other situations? Under what set of conditions would this emotion not be generalised to other situations?

■ If unpleasant thoughts and feelings such as fear and phobia can be conditioned, do you think they can be extinguished using similar classical conditioning principles?

■ Our responses to harrowing news items such as reports of famine and war are frequently described as being numbed and that we have become desensitised. How can the principles of classical conditioning explain this 'desensitisation'?

Operant conditioning

Habituation and classical conditioning teach us about stimuli in the environment: we learn to ignore unimportant stimuli, and we learn about those that predict the occurrence of important ones. These forms of learning deal with relations between one stimulus and another. In contrast, operant conditioning tells about the relations between environmental stimuli and our own behaviour; it is also called instrumental learning. The term 'operant' refers to the fact that an organism learns through responding – through operating on the environment. The principle behind operant conditioning is already familiar to you: when a particular action has good consequences, the action will tend to be repeated; when a particular action has bad consequences, the action will tend not to be repeated.

The law of effect

Operant conditioning was first discovered in the basement of a house in Cambridge, Massachusetts, by a 24 year old man who would later become one of this century's most influential educational psychologists, Edward L. Thorndike. Thorndike placed a hungry cat inside a 'puzzle box'. The animal could escape and eat some food only after it operated a latch that opened the door. At first, the cat engaged in random behaviour: meowing, scratching, hissing, pacing and so on. Eventually, the cat would accidentally activate the latch and open the door. On successive trials, the animal's behaviour would become more and more efficient until it was operating the latch without hesitation. Thorndike called this process 'learning by trial and accidental success'.

Thorndike explained that the cat learned to make the correct response because only the correct response was followed by a favourable outcome: escape from the box and the opportunity to eat some food. The occurrence of the favourable outcome strengthens the response that produced it. Thorndike called this relation between a response and its consequences the law of effect.

The impact of Thorndike's discovery of the law of effect on the early development of scientific psychology would be difficult to overstate. It affected research in the study of learning in one very important way: it stimulated an enormous number of experimental studies aimed at understanding behaviour–environment interactions, a line of research that is known today as behaviour analysis. Nowhere was this effect more evident than in the work of B.F. Skinner.

Skinner and operant behaviour

Although Thorndike discovered the law of effect, Harvard psychologist Burrhus Frederic Skinner championed the laboratory study of the law of effect and advocated the

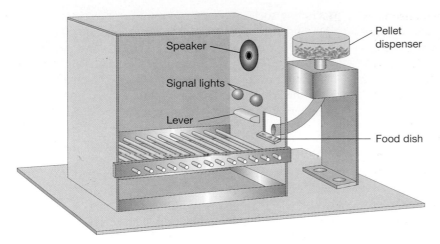

Speaker

Signal lights

Lever

Pellet dispenser

Food dish

Figure 7.5

An operant chamber. (This operant chamber is used for lever pressing by rats.)

application of behaviour analysis and its methods to solving human problems (Skinner, 1953, 1971; Mazur, 1994). He devised objective methods for studying behaviour, invented apparatus and methods for observing it, and created his own philosophy for interpreting it (Bolles, 1979). Moreover, he wrote several books for the general public, including a novel, *Walden Two*, that showed how his discoveries might be used for improving society (Skinner, 1948).

One of Skinner's most important inventions was the operant chamber (or Skinner box), an apparatus in which an animal's behaviour can be easily observed, manipulated, and automatically recorded (as seen in Figure 7.5).

For example, an operant chamber used for rats is constructed so that a particular behaviour, such as pressing on a lever, will occasionally cause a pellet of food to be delivered. An operant chamber used for pigeons is built so that a peck at a plastic disk on the front wall will occasionally open a drawer that contains some grain. Behaviour analysts who study human behaviour use special devices suitable to the unique characteristics of their human subjects (Baron *et al.*, 1991). In this case, instead of giving their participants some food, they give them points (as in a video game) or points exchangeable for money.

Behaviour analysts manipulate environmental events to determine their effects on response rate, the number of responses emitted during a given amount of time. Events that increase response rate are said to strengthen responding; events that decrease response rate weaken responding. To measure response rate, Skinner devised the cumulative recorder, a device that records each response as it occurs in time.

The invention of the operant chamber and the cumulative recorder represent clear advances over Thorndike's research methods because subjects can (1) emit responses more freely over a greater time period, and (2) be studied for longer periods of time without interference produced by the experimenter handling or otherwise interacting

with them between trials. Under highly controlled conditions such as these, behaviour analysts have been able to discover a wide range of important behavioural principles.

The three-term contingency

Behaviour does not occur in a vacuum. Sometimes a response will have certain consequences; sometimes it will not. Our daily behaviour is guided by many different kinds of discriminative stimuli – stimuli that indicate that behaviour will have certain consequences and thus sets the occasion for responding. For example, consider answering the telephone. The phone rings, you pick it up and say 'hello' into the receiver. Most of the time, someone on the other end of the line begins to speak. Have you ever picked up a telephone when it was not ringing and said, 'hello'? Doing so would be absurd, because there would be no one on the other end of the line with whom to speak. We answer the phone (make a response) only when the phone rings (the preceding event) because, in the past, someone with whom we enjoy talking has been at the other end of the line (the following event). Skinner referred formally to the relationship among these three items – the preceding event, the response and the following event – as the three-term contingency (see Figure 7.6).

The preceding event – the discriminative stimulus – sets the occasion for responding because, in the past, when that stimulus occurred, the response was followed by certain consequences. If the phone rings, we are likely to answer it because we have learned that doing so has particular (and generally favourable) consequences. The response we make – in this case, picking up the phone and saying 'hello' when the phone rings – is called an operant behaviour. The following event – the voice on the other end of the line – is the consequence of the operant behaviour.

Operant behaviour, therefore, occurs in the presence of discriminative stimuli and is followed by certain consequences. These consequences are contingent upon

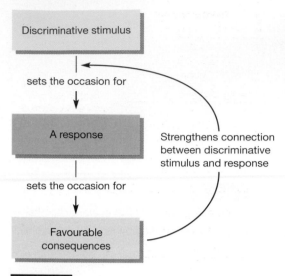

Figure 7.6

The three-term contingency.

behaviour, that is they are produced by that behaviour. In the presence of discriminative stimuli, a consequence will occur if and only if an operant behaviour occurs. In the absence of a discriminative stimulus, the operant behaviour will have no effect. Once an operant behaviour is established, it tends to persist whenever the discriminative stimulus occurs, even if other aspects of the environment change (Nevin, 1988; Mace *et al.*, 1990). Of course, motivational factors can affect a response. For example, you might not bother to answer the telephone if you are doing something you do not want to interrupt.

Reinforcement, punishment and extinction

Behaviour analysts study behaviour–environment interactions by manipulating the relations among components of the three-term contingency. Of the three elements, the consequence is the most frequently manipulated variable. In general, operant behaviours can be followed by five different kinds of consequence: positive reinforcement, negative reinforcement, punishment, response cost and extinction. These consequences are always defined in terms of their effect on responding.

Positive reinforcement

Positive reinforcement refers to an increase in the frequency of a response that is regularly and reliably followed by an appetitive stimulus. An appetitive stimulus is any stimulus that an organism seeks out. If an appetitive stimulus follows a response and increases the frequency of that response, we call it a positive reinforcer. For example, the opportunity to eat some food can reinforce a hungry pigeon's pecking of a plastic disk. Money or other rewards

(including social rewards) can reinforce a person's behaviour. Suppose that you visit a new restaurant and really enjoy your meal. You are likely to visit the restaurant several more times because you like the food. This example illustrates positive reinforcement. Your enjoyment of the food (the appetitive stimulus) reinforces your going to the restaurant and ordering dinner (the response).

Negative reinforcement

Negative reinforcement refers to an increase in the frequency of a response that is regularly and reliably followed by the termination of an aversive stimulus. An aversive stimulus is unpleasant or painful. If an aversive stimulus is terminated (ends or is turned off) as soon as a response occurs and thus increases the frequency of that response, we call it a negative reinforcer. For example, after you have walked barefoot across a stretch of hot pavement, the termination of the painful burning sensation negatively reinforces your response of sticking your feet into a puddle of cool water.

It is important to remember that both positive and negative reinforcement increase the likelihood that a given response will occur again. However, positive reinforcement involves the occurrence of an appetitive stimulus, whereas negative reinforcement involves the termination of an aversive stimulus. Negative reinforcement is thus not the same as punishment.

Punishment

Punishment refers to a decrease in the frequency of a response that is regularly and reliably followed by an aversive stimulus. If an aversive stimulus follows a response and decreases the frequency of that response, we call it a punisher. For example, receiving a painful bite would punish the response of sticking your finger into a parrot's cage. People often attempt to punish the behaviour of their children or pets by scolding them.

Although punishment is effective in reducing or suppressing undesirable behaviour in the short term, it can also produce several negative side effects: unrestrained use of physical force (for example, child abuse) may cause serious bodily injury. Punishment often induces fear, hostility and other undesirable emotions in people receiving punishment. It may result in retaliation against the punisher. Through punishment, organisms learn only which response not to make. Punishment does not teach the organism desirable responses.

Reinforcement and punishment are most effective in maintaining or changing behaviour when a stimulus immediately follows the behaviour. It may occur to you that many organisms, particularly humans, can tolerate a long delay between their work and the reward that they receive for it. This ability appears to contradict the principle that reinforcement must occur immediately. However, the apparent contradiction can be explained by a phenomenon called conditioned reinforcement.

Why is immediacy of reinforcement or punishment essential for learning? The answer is found by examining the function of operant conditioning: learning about the consequences of our own behaviour. Normally, causes and effects are closely related in time; you do something, and something immediately happens, good or bad. The consequences of our action teach us whether to repeat that action. Events that follow a response by a long delay were probably not caused by that response.

It is important not to confuse punishment with negative reinforcement. Punishment causes a behaviour to decrease, whereas negative reinforcement causes a behaviour to increase.

Response cost

Response cost refers to a decrease in the frequency of a response that is regularly and reliably followed by the termination of an appetitive stimulus. Response cost is a form of punishment. For example, suppose that you are enjoying a conversation with an attractive person that you have just met. You make a disparaging remark about a political party. Your new friend's smile suddenly disappears. You quickly change the topic and never bring it up again. The behaviour (disparaging remark) is followed by the removal of an appetitive stimulus (your new friend's smile). The removal of the smile punishes the disparaging remark.

Response cost is often referred to as time-out from positive reinforcement (or simply time-out) when it is used to remove a person physically from an activity that is reinforcing to that person.

As we have just seen, there are four types of operant conditioning – two kinds of reinforcement and two kinds of punishment – caused by the occurrence or termination of appetitive or aversive stimuli. Another way to change behaviour through operant conditioning is extinction, which involves no consequence at all. See Figure 7.7.

Extinction

Extinction is a decrease in the frequency of a previously reinforced response because it is no longer followed by a reinforcer. Behaviour that is no longer reinforced decreases in frequency: it is said to extinguish. For example, a rat whose lever pressing was reinforced previously with food will eventually stop pressing the lever when food is no longer delivered. People soon learn to stop dropping money into vending machines that don't work. A young boy will stop telling his favourite 'knock-knock' joke if no one laughs at it any more.

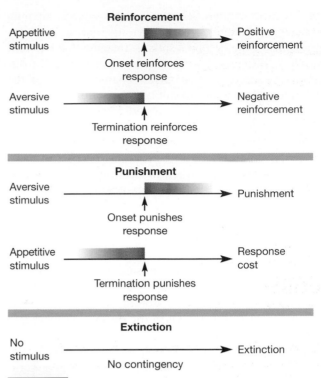

Figure 7.7

Reinforcement, punishment and extinction produced by the onset, termination or omission of appetitive or aversive stimuli. The upward-pointing arrows indicate the occurrence of a response.

Extinction is not the same as forgetting. Forgetting takes place when a behaviour is not rehearsed (or a person does not think about a particular memory) for a long time. Extinction takes place when an organism makes a response that is no longer reinforced. If the organism does not have an opportunity to make that response, it will not extinguish. For example, if you go out of town for a few weeks, you will not forget how to operate the vending machine where you often buy a bar of chocolate. However, if you put money in the machine and do not receive anything in return, your response will extinguish.

Other operant procedures and phenomena

The basic principles of reinforcement, punishment and extinction described above are used in other operant procedures to teach an organism a new response, to teach it when or when not to respond, or to teach it how to respond in a particular way.

Shaping

Most behaviour is acquired through an organism's interaction with reinforcing and punishing events in its environment. In fact, Skinner developed a technique, called shaping, to teach new behaviours to his subjects. Shaping involves reinforcing any behaviour that successively approximates the desired response. Imagine that we want to train a rat to press a lever when a red light is lit (the discriminative stimulus) in an operant chamber. Although the rat has used its paws to manipulate many things during its lifetime, it has never before pressed a lever in an operant chamber. And when it is first placed in the chamber, it is not likely to press the lever even once on its own.

The lever on the wall of the chamber is attached to an electrical switch that is wired to electronic control equipment or a computer. A mechanical dispenser can automatically drop moulded pellets of food, about the size of a very small pea, into a dish in the chamber. Thus, the delivery of a food pellet can be made dependent on the rat's pressing the lever.

Before we can shape lever pressing, we must make the rat hungry. We do so by letting the animal eat only once a day. When that time comes around, we know that it is hungry. We place the animal in the operant chamber and then train it to eat the food pellets as they are dispensed from the pellet dispenser. As each pellet is delivered, the dispenser makes a clicking sound. This sound is important. No matter where the rat is in the operant chamber, it can hear the sound, which indicates that the food pellet has been dispensed. Once the rat is hungry and has learned where to obtain food, we are ready to shape the desired response. We make the operation of the pellet dispenser contingent on the rat's behaviour. We start by giving the rat a food pellet for just facing in the direction of the lever. Next, we wait until the rat makes a move towards the lever. Finally, we give the rat a piece of food only if it actually touches the lever. Soon, our rat performs like Thorndike's cats: it makes the same response again and again.

Shaping is a formal training procedure, but something like it also occurs in the world outside the laboratory. A teacher praises poorly formed letters produced by a child who is just beginning to print. As time goes on, only more accurately drawn letters bring approval. The method of successive approximations can also be self-administered. Consider the acquisition of skills through trial and error. To begin with, you must be able to recognise the target behaviour – the behaviour displayed by a person having the appropriate skill. Your first attempts produce behaviours that vaguely resemble those of a skilled performer, and you are satisfied by the results of these attempts. In other words, the stimuli that are produced by your behaviour serve as reinforcers for that behaviour. As your skill develops, you become less satisfied with crude approximations to the final behaviour; you are satisfied only when your behaviour improves so that it more closely resembles the target behaviour. Your own criteria change as you become more skilled. Skills such as learning to draw a picture, catching a ball, or making a bed are all behaviours that are acquired through shaping. After all, when a child learns these skills, he or she first learns behaviours that only approximate the final level of skill that he or she will eventually obtain. This process is perfectly analogous to the use of changing criteria in training an animal to perform a complex behaviour.

Intermittent reinforcement

So far, we have considered situations in which a reinforcing stimulus is presented after each response (or, in the case of extinction, not at all). But usually, not every response is reinforced. Sometimes a kind word is ignored; sometimes it is appreciated. Not every fishing trip is rewarded with a catch, but some are, and that is enough to keep a person trying.

The term intermittent reinforcement refers to situations in which not every occurrence of a response is reinforced. The relation between responding and reinforcement usually follows one of two patterns: each response has a certain probability of being reinforced, or responses are reinforced after particular intervals of time have elapsed. Probability-based patterns require a variable number of responses for each reinforcer. Consider the performance of an archer shooting arrows at a target. Suppose that the archer hits the bull's-eye one-fifth of the time. On average, he will have to make five responses for every reinforcement (hitting the bull's-eye); the ratio of responding to reinforcement is five to one. The number of reinforcers the archer receives is directly proportional to the number of responses he makes. If he shoots more arrows (that is, if his rate of responding increases), he will receive more reinforcers, assuming that he does not get tired or careless.

Behaviour analysts refer to this pattern of intermittent reinforcement as a ratio schedule of reinforcement. In the laboratory, the apparatus controlling the operant chamber may be programmed to deliver a reinforcer after every fifth response (a ratio of five to one), after every tenth, after every two hundredth, or after any desired number. If the ratio is constant – for example if a reinforcer is programmed to be delivered following every tenth response – the animal will respond rapidly, receive the reinforcer, pause a little while, and then begin responding again. This type of ratio schedule is called a fixed-ratio schedule (specifically, a fixed-ratio 10 schedule).

If the ratio is variable, averaging a particular number of responses but varying from trial to trial, the animal will respond at a steady, rapid pace. For example, we might program a reinforcer to be delivered, on average, after every fifty responses. This type of ratio schedule is called a variable-ratio schedule (specifically, a variable-ratio 50 schedule). A slot machine is sometimes programmed to deliver money on a variable-ratio schedule of reinforcement. Variable in this instance means that the person cannot predict how many responses will be needed for the next payoff.

The second type of pattern of reinforcement involves time. A response is reinforced, but only after a particular time interval has elapsed. Imagine that you wanted to know what the weather was going to be like because your friends are due to visit but the weather where they are is quite snowy. In order to keep abreast of the weather, you listen to the half-hourly bulletin on your local radio station. This pattern of intermittent reinforcement is called an interval schedule of reinforcement. After various intervals of time, a response will be reinforced. If the time intervals are fixed, the animal will stop responding after each reinforcement. It learns that responses made immediately after reinforcement are never reinforced. Then it will begin responding a little while before the next reinforcer is available. This type of interval schedule is called a fixed-interval schedule.

If the time intervals are variable, an animal will respond at a slow, steady rate. That way, it will not waste energy on useless responses, but it will not miss any opportunities for reinforcement either. This type of interval schedule is called a variable-interval schedule. In a variable-interval sixty-second schedule of reinforcement, a reinforcer would be delivered immediately following the first response after different time intervals had elapsed. The interval might be thirty seconds at one time, and ninety seconds at another, but, on the average, it will be sixty seconds. An animal whose behaviour is reinforced by this schedule would learn not to pause immediately after a reinforcer was delivered. Instead, it would steadily respond throughout the interval, regardless of the length of the interval.

Resistance to extinction and intermittent reinforcement

A response that has been reinforced intermittently is more resistant to extinction. The more responses an organism has had to make for each reinforcement, the longer it will respond during extinction. Continuous reinforcement (that is, reinforcement after every response) is very different from extinction. The very first non-reinforced response signals that conditions have changed. In contrast, intermittent reinforcement and extinction are more similar. An organism whose behaviour has been reinforced intermittently has had a lot of experience making non-reinforced responses. The animal cannot readily detect the fact that responses are no longer being reinforced – that the contingencies have changed. Therefore, the behaviour extinguishes more slowly.

Generalisation and discrimination

In classical conditioning, generalisation means that stimuli resembling the CS also elicit the CR. In operant conditioning, generalisation means that stimuli resembling a discriminative stimulus also serve as discriminative stimuli for a particular response.

In operant conditioning, as in classical conditioning, generalisation can be reduced through discrimination training. In classical conditioning, discrimination means that CRs occur only in response to certain CSs and not to other, similar stimuli. In operant conditioning, discrimination means that responding occurs only when a particular discriminative stimulus is present – one that was present while responding was reinforced in the past. Responding does not occur when discriminative stimuli associated with extinction or punishment are present.

Obviously, recognising certain kinds of similarities between different categories of stimuli is a very important task in our everyday lives. When we encounter a problem to solve – for example, diagnosing a puzzling disease or improving a manufactured product – we attempt to discover elements of the situation that are similar to those we have seen in other situations and try to apply the strategies that have been successful in the past. That is, we try to generalise old solutions to new problems.

Discriminative stimuli can exert powerful control over responding because of their association with the consequences of such responding. In or out of the laboratory, we learn to behave appropriately to environmental conditions. For example, we usually talk about different things with different people. We learn that some friends do not care for sports, so we do not talk about this topic with them because we will receive few reinforcers (such as nods or smiles). Instead, we discuss topics that have interested them in the past.

Conditioned reinforcement and punishment

We have studied reinforcement mainly in terms of primary reinforcers and primary punishers. Primary reinforcers are biologically significant appetitive stimuli, such as food when one is hungry. Primary punishers are biologically significant aversive stimuli, such as those that produce pain. Behaviour can also be reinforced with a wide variety of other stimuli: money, a smile, a hug, kind words, a pat on the back, or prizes and awards. These stimuli, called conditioned (or secondary) reinforcers, acquire their reinforcing properties through association with primary reinforcers. Because it can be exchanged for so many different kinds of primary reinforcers in our society, money is the most common conditioned reinforcer among humans. That money is a conditioned reinforcer can be demonstrated by asking yourself whether you would continue to work if you could no longer exchange money for food, drink, shelter and other items.

Similarly, conditioned punishers acquire their punishing effects through association with aversive events. For example, the sight of a flashing light on top of a police car serves as a conditioned punisher to a person who is driving too fast because such a sight precedes an unpleasant set of stimuli: a lecture by a police officer and a speeding ticket.

A stimulus becomes a conditioned reinforcer or punisher by means of classical conditioning. That is, if a neutral stimulus occurs regularly just before an appetitive or aversive stimulus, then the neutral stimulus itself becomes an appetitive or aversive stimulus. The primary reinforcer or punisher serves as the UCS because it produces the UCR – good or bad feelings. After classical conditioning takes place, these good or bad feelings are produced by the CS – the conditioned reinforcer or punisher. Once that happens, the stimulus can reinforce or punish behaviours by itself. Thus, operant conditioning often involves aspects of classical conditioning.

Conditioned reinforcement and punishment are very important. They permit an organism's behaviour to be affected by stimuli that are not biologically important in themselves but that are regularly associated with the onset or termination of biologically important stimuli. Indeed, stimuli can even become conditioned reinforcers or punishers by being associated with other conditioned reinforcers or punishers. The speeding ticket is just such an example. If an organism's behaviour could be controlled only by primary reinforcers and punishers, its behaviour would not be very flexible. The organism would never learn to perform behaviours that had only long-range benefits. Instead, its behaviour would be controlled on a moment-to-moment basis by a very limited set of stimuli. Conditioned reinforcers and punishers, such as money, grades, smiles and frowns, allow for behaviour to be altered by a wide variety of contingencies.

Questions to think about

Operant conditioning

- The law of effect is often cited as a universal principle of behaviour. Can you think of an example in which the law of effect is not applicable to behaviour?

- Suppose that you run into a friend while walking along the street. You stop and talk to each other for a few minutes. How would you explain your interactions with your friend in terms of the three-term contingency?

- Reflect for a moment on the activities in which you have engaged so far today. How would the principles of positive reinforcement, negative reinforcement, punishment, response cost and extinction have operated to influence you.

- How would you shape your psychology lecturer's behaviour so that he or she stands only at the far left side of the lecture theatre while speaking?

- Many people have had the embarrassing experience of mistaking a stranger for a friend. For example, you may catch a glimpse of your 'friend' walking down the other side of the street, call out her name and wave rather excitedly only to discover as you look more closely that the person is not who you thought she was. How would you explain this event using the learning principles discussed in this section?

- Schedules of reinforcement are important because they show us that different reinforcement contingencies affect the pattern and rate of responding. Think about your own behaviour. How would you perform in subjects in which your grades were determined by a midterm and a final exam, or by weekly quizzes, or by unannounced quizzes that occur at variable intervals? What kind of schedule of reinforcement is a salesperson on while waiting on potential customers? Some people work at a slow, steady rate, but others work furiously after long periods of inactivity. Can it be that in the past their work habits were shaped by different schedules of reinforcement?

Conditioning of complex behaviours

The previous sections considered rather simple examples of reinforced behaviours. But people and many other animals are able to learn very complex behaviours. Consider the behaviour of a young girl learning to print letters. She sits at her school desk, producing long rows of letters. What kinds of reinforcing stimuli maintain her behaviour? Why is she devoting her time to a task that involves so much effort?

The answer is that her behaviour produces stimuli – printed letters – which serve as conditioned reinforcers. In previous class sessions, the teacher demonstrated how to print the letters and praised the girl for printing them herself. The act of printing was reinforced, and the printed letters that this act produces come to serve as conditioned reinforcers. The child prints a letter, sees that it looks close to the way it should, and her efforts are reinforced by the sight of the letter. Doing something correctly or making progress towards that goal can provide an effective reinforcer.

This fact is often overlooked by people who take a limited view of the process of reinforcement, thinking that it has to resemble the delivery of a small piece of food to an animal being taught a trick. Some people even say that because reinforcers are rarely delivered to humans immediately after they perform a behaviour, operant conditioning must not play a major role in human learning. This assertion misses the point that, especially for humans, reinforcers can be very subtle events.

Aversive control of behaviour

Your own experience has probably taught you that punishment can be as effective as positive reinforcement in changing behaviour. Aversive control of behaviour is common in our society, from fines given to speeding motorists to the prison sentences given to criminals. Aversive control of behaviour is common for two main reasons. First, it can be highly effective in inducing behaviour change, producing nearly immediate results. A person given a fine for jumping a red light is likely, at least for a short while, to heed the sign's message. The very effectiveness of punishment as a means of behaviour change can serve as an immediate reinforcer for the person doing the punishing.

Secondly, society cannot always control the positive reinforcers that shape and maintain the behaviour of its members. However, it can and does control aversive stimuli that may be used to punish misconduct. For example, suppose that a young person's peers encourage antisocial behaviours such as theft. Society has no control over reinforcers provided by the peer group, but it can control stimuli to punish the antisocial behaviours, such as fines and imprisonment.

How punishing stimuli work

How does a punishing stimulus suppress behaviour? Punishment, like reinforcement, usually involves a discriminative stimulus. A child's shouting is usually punished in the classroom but not outdoors during recess. A dog chases a porcupine, gets stuck with quills, and never chases one again. However, it continues to chase the neighbour's cat.

Most aversive stimuli elicit some sort of protective or defensive response, such as cringing, freezing, hiding or running away. The response depends on the species of animal and, of course, on the situation. If you slap your dog for a misdeed, the dog will cower down and slink away, looking clearly 'apologetic', because you are in a position of dominance. However, if the dog is struck by a stranger, it may very well react by attacking the person. Both types of behaviour are known as species-specific defence reactions (Bolles, 1970).

Escape and avoidance

Negative reinforcement teaches organisms to make responses that terminate aversive stimuli. These responses can make a stimulus cease or the organism can simply run away. In either case, psychologists call the behaviour an escape response: the organism endures the effects of the aversive stimulus until its behaviour terminates the stimulus. In some cases, the animal can do more than escape the aversive stimulus; it can learn to do something to prevent it occurring. This type of behaviour is known as an avoidance response.

Avoidance responses usually require some warning that the aversive stimulus is about to occur in order for the organism to be able to make the appropriate response soon enough. Imagine that you meet a man at a party who backs you against the wall and engages you in the most boring conversation you have ever had. In addition, his breath is so bad that you are afraid you will pass out. You finally manage to break away from him (an escape response). A few days later, you attend another party. You begin walking towards the buffet table and see the same man (discriminative stimulus) standing nearby. You decide that you will get some food later and turn away to talk with some friends at the other end of the room (an avoidance response).

As we saw earlier, phobias can be considered to be conditioned emotional responses – fears that are acquired through classical conditioning. But unlike most classically-conditioned responses, phobias are especially resistant to extinction. If we classically condition an eyeblink response in a rabbit and then repeatedly present the CS alone, without the UCS (puff of air), the response will extinguish. However, if a person has a phobia for cockroaches, the phobia will not extinguish easily even if he or she encounters cockroaches and nothing bad happens. Why does the response persist?

Most psychologists believe that the answer lies in a subtle interaction between operant and classical conditioning. The sight of a cockroach makes a person having a cockroach phobia feel frightened, that is, he or she experiences an unpleasant conditional emotional response. The person runs out of the room, leaving the cockroach behind and reducing the unpleasant feelings of fear. This reduction in an aversive stimulus reinforces the avoidance response and perpetuates the phobia.

Conditioning of flavour aversions

You have probably eaten foods that made you sick and now avoid them on the basis of their flavour alone. The association of a substance's flavour with illness, which is often caused by eating that substance, leads to conditioned flavour-aversion learning.

The study of flavour-aversion learning is important not only because it is a real-life experience, but also because it has taught psychologists about unique relations that may exist between certain CSs and certain UCSs. Just as punishment is a result of classical conditioning where a species-typical defensive response becomes classically conditioned to a discriminative stimulus, conditioned flavour aversions are acquired in the same way. The flavour is followed by an unconditional stimulus (sickness) that elicits the unpleasant responses of the autonomic nervous system, such as cramping and retching. Then, when the animal encounters the flavour again, the experience triggers unpleasant internal reactions that cause the animal to stop eating the food.

Many learning researchers once believed that nearly any CS could be paired with nearly any UCS to produce nearly any CR. However, in a now classic experiment, Garcia and Koelling (1966) showed that animals are more prepared to learn some types of relation among stimuli than others.

In the first phase of their experiment, Garcia and Koelling (1966) permitted rats to drink saccharine-flavoured water from a tube. Each lick from the tube produced three CSs: taste, noise and bright lights. This phase ensured that rats were equally familiar with each of the CSs. In the next phase, the rats were divided into four groups, each experiencing either 'bright-noisy' water or 'tasty' water. Each CS was paired with illness or electric shock.

After several trials, the experimenters measured the amount of saccharine-flavoured water the rats consumed. They found that the rats learned the association between flavour and illness but not between flavour and pain produced by electric shock. Likewise, the rats learned the association between the 'bright-noisy water' and shock-induced pain but not between the 'bright-noisy water' and illness. The results make sense; after all, the animal has to taste the flavour that makes it ill, not hear it, and in the world outside the laboratory, a particular flavour does not usually indicate that you are about to receive an electric shock.

This experiment draws two important conclusions: (1) rats can learn about associations between internal sensations (being sick) and novel tastes, and (2) the interval between the two stimuli can be very long. These facts suggest that the brain mechanisms responsible for a conditioned flavour aversion are different from the ones that mediate an aversion caused by stimuli applied to the outside of the body (such as a painful foot shock). It appears that conditioned flavour aversions serve to protect animals from poisonous foods by enabling them to learn to avoid eating them. Because few naturally occurring poisons cause sickness immediately, neural mechanisms that mediate conditioned flavour aversions must be capable of learning the association between events that are separated in time. Most other cause-and-effect relations involve events that occur close in time; hence the neural mechanisms that mediate an organism's ability to learn about them operate under different time constraints.

Some animals have eating habits quite different from those of rats; they eat foods that they cannot taste or smell. For example, some birds eat seeds that are encased in a tasteless husk. They do not have teeth, so they cannot break open the husk and taste the seed. Thus, they cannot use odour or taste as a cue to avoid a poison. However, Wilcoxon *et al.* (1971) found that quail (a species of seed-eating birds) can form a conditioned aversion to the sight of food that earlier made them sick. People can also acquire conditioned flavour aversions. A friend of mine often took trips on aeroplanes with her parents when she was a child. Unfortunately, she usually got airsick. Just before takeoff,

her mother would give her some spearmint-flavoured chewing gum to help relieve the pressure on her eardrums that would occur when the plane ascended. Yes, she developed a conditioned flavour aversion to spearmint gum. In fact, the odour of the gum still makes her feel nauseated.

Conditioned flavour aversions, like most learning situations, involve both classical and operant conditioning. From one point of view, we can say that the aversive stimuli produced by the poison punish the behaviour of eating a particular food. That is, the flavour serves as a discriminative stimulus for a punishment contingency (operant conditioning). However, it also serves as a conditioned stimulus for a classical conditioning situation: the flavour is followed by an unconditional stimulus (the poison) that elicits unpleasant responses of the autonomic nervous system, such as cramping and retching. Then, when the animal encounters the flavour at a later date, it experiences unpleasant reactions that cause it to leave the source of the stimulus and avoid the food.

Psychology in action

Flavour aversions

Because conditioned flavour aversions can occur when particular flavours are followed by feelings of nausea, even several hours later, this phenomenon has several implications for situations outside the laboratory. An unfortunate side effect of chemotherapy or radiation therapy for cancer is nausea. Besides killing the rapidly dividing cells of malignant tumours, both chemotherapy and radiation kill the rapidly dividing cells that line the digestive system and thus cause nausea and vomiting.

Knowing what we know about conditioned flavour aversions, we might predict that chemotherapy or radiation therapy would cause a conditioned aversion to the foods a patient ate during the previous meal. Bernstein (1978) showed that this prediction is correct. She gave ice cream to some cancer patients who were about to receive a session of chemotherapy and found that several months later, 75 per cent of these patients refused to eat ice cream of the same flavour. In contrast, control subjects who did not taste it before their chemotherapy said that they liked it very much. Only one trial was necessary to develop the conditioned flavour aversion. Even when patients have a clear understanding that the drugs are responsible for their aversion and that the food is really wholesome, they still cannot bring themselves to eat it (Bernstein, 1991). Thus, a conditioned food aversion is not a result of cognitive processes such as reasoning or expectation.

Psychology in action continued

Questionnaires and interviews reveal that cancer patients develop aversions to the foods that they normally eat even if their treatment sessions occur several hours after the previous meal (Bernstein *et al.*, 1982; Mattes *et al.*, 1987). When patients receive many treatment sessions, they are likely to develop aversions to a wide variety of foods. Because a treatment that produces nausea may cause the development of a conditioned flavour aversion to the last thing a person has eaten, Broberg and Bernstein (1987) attempted to attach the aversion to a flavour other than one that patients encounter in their normal diets. The experimenters had cancer patients eat a coconut or root beer Lifesaver (a sweet) after the last meal before a chemotherapy session, hoping that the unique flavour would serve as a scapegoat, thus preventing a conditioned aversion to patients' normal foods. The procedure worked; the patients were much less likely to show an aversion to the food eaten during the last meal before the treatment.

Conditioned flavour aversions can also have useful applications. For example, psychologists have applied conditioned aversions to wildlife control. In regions where coyotes have been attacking sheep, they have left chunks of dog food laced with an emetic drug wrapped in pieces of fresh sheepskin. The coyotes eat the bait, become sick and develop a conditioned aversion to the smell and taste of sheep (Gustavson and Gustavson, 1985). These methods can help protect endangered species as well as livestock. Mongooses have been introduced into some islands in the Caribbean, where they menace the indigenous population of sea turtles. Nicolaus and Nellis (1987) found that a conditioned aversion to turtle eggs could be established in mongooses by feeding them eggs into which an emetic drug had been injected.

Evidence suggests that for some species, conditioned flavour aversions can become cultural traditions. Gustavson and Gustavson (1985) reported that after adult coyotes had developed a conditioned aversion to a particular food, their offspring, too, avoided that food. Apparently, the young coyotes learned from their mothers what food was fit to eat. However, Nicolaus *et al.* (1982) found that adult racoons having a conditioned aversion to chickens did not teach their offspring to avoid chickens. In fact, after seeing the young racoons kill and eat chickens, the adults overcame their aversion and began preying on chickens again.

Applications of operant conditioning to human behaviour

Instructional control

Human behaviour is influenced not only by reinforcement but also by the interactions of reinforcement with rules, that is, verbal descriptions of the relation between behaviour and reinforcement. In fact, much of our everyday behaviour involves following rules of one sort or another. Cooking from a recipe, following directions to a friend's house, and obeying the speed limit are common examples. Because rules have the potential to influence our behaviour in almost any situation, behaviour analysts are interested in learning more about how rules and reinforcement interact.

One way to investigate this interaction is to give subjects rules that are false, that is, rules that are inaccurate descriptions of the behaviour required for reinforcement (Galizio, 1979; Baron and Galizio, 1983). In such experiments, people may behave in accordance with either the rule or the reinforcement requirement. For example, in one study (Buskist and Miller, 1986), one group of college students was told that the schedule in effect was a fixed-interval 15 second (FI 15) schedule, when in fact, it was a fixed-interval 30 second (FI 30) schedule. Recall that in a fixed-interval schedule, a response will be reinforced only after a certain amount of time has passed since the last reinforcement. Another group was told the truth about the schedule.

At first, the misinformed students responded according to the instructions, making one response about every 15 seconds. However, because the rule directly contradicted the actual reinforcement schedule, they soon learned to respond about once every 30 seconds. The students abandoned the rule they had been given by the experimenter in favour of the actual reinforcement contingency. The group of students who were told the truth responded accordingly.

A third group of students, also exposed to the FI 30 second schedule, was told that the schedule in effect was a FI 60 second schedule. The rule given to these students was ambiguous, but it was not exactly false. If the students made a response every 60 seconds, they would receive a reinforcer every time. These students could have received a reinforcer every 30 seconds, but they never learned to do so. The point is that rules can be influential in controlling behaviour not only when they are true, but also when they are ambiguous. The problem, of course, is that ambiguous instructions often lead to inefficient behaviour, as they did in this case.

Other researchers have shown that people sometimes generate their own rules about the consequences of their behaviour (Lowe, 1979). Lowe argues that our ability to verbally describe the consequences of our behaviour explains why humans often respond differently from other animals when placed under similar reinforcement contingencies (Lowe *et al.*, 1983). When exposed to FI schedules, animals do not respond immediately after each reinforcement. As time passes, though, responding gradually increases until the next reinforcer is delivered. Humans, on the other hand, tend to follow one of two strategies: responding very slowly or responding very rapidly. Those people who respond slowly often describe the schedule as interval-based and they respond accordingly. Those who respond rapidly usually describe the schedule as ratio-based – which it is not – and they respond accordingly. Thus, the language one uses may indeed exert some control over one's own behaviour. The extent to which language and other behaviours interact is the subject of ongoing experimental and theoretical work (Hayes, 1989; Cerruti, 1990).

Stimulus equivalence

Stimulus equivalence refers to the emergence of novel behaviour without direct reinforcement of that behaviour (Fields, 1993; Fields *et al.*, 1995). Imagine that you were asked to learn the relationship among a group of symbols: A, B and C. Suppose further that after training without reinforcement, you discovered that A = B and A = C. How then would you respond to the following question: does B = C? You would probably reason that if A = B and A = C, then B, too, is equal to C. But notice that you were never trained or received any direct reinforcement for learning that B = C. Rather, the equivalent relationship between B and C emerged from your previous learning; hence, the term 'stimulus equivalence'.

Stimulus equivalence is an important area of research because it represents one way we learn to use and understand symbols, such as language. For example, let A represent a picture of a dog, B represent the spoken word 'dog', and C represent the printed word 'dog'. Suppose that we teach a child to point to the picture of the dog (A) and say the word 'dog' (B). In this case, the child learns that A = B and B = A. Next, suppose that we teach the child to point to the picture of the dog (A) when he sees the printed word 'dog' (C). The child learns that A = C and that C = A. What we are really interested in, though, is whether the child will have learned that the spoken word 'dog' (B) is equivalent to, or means the same thing as, the printed word 'dog' (C).

This is precisely what children learn under these circumstances, even though the equivalent relationship, B = C, has not been directly trained (Sidman and Tailby, 1982). Rather, it emerged as a consequence of the child's learning history. Understanding how stimulus equivalence develops is likely to lead to a better understanding of language development.

Drug use and abuse

Soon after Skinner outlined the principles of operant behaviour, others were quick to apply them to the study of drug action and drug taking (Thompson and Schuster, 1968). In fact, Skinner's three-term contingency is now partly the basis of an entirely separate discipline of pharmacology known as behavioural pharmacology, the study of how drugs influence behaviour. In this field, the terms 'discriminative stimuli', 'responding' and 'consequences' translate into drugs as discriminative stimuli, the direct effects of drugs on behaviour, and the reinforcing effects of drugs, respectively. Perhaps the most interesting discovery in behavioural pharmacology is the finding that most psychoactive drugs function as reinforcers in both humans and animals.

When administered as a consequence of responding, these drugs will induce and maintain high rates of responding (Griffiths *et al.*, 1980). There is a very high correlation between drugs that will maintain animal responding in experimental settings and those that are abused by humans (Griffiths *et al.*, 1980). Cocaine, for example, maintains very high rates of responding and drug consumption, to the point that food and water consumption decreases to life-threatening levels. Unlimited access to cocaine in rhesus monkeys can lead, in some cases, to death. These findings have allowed psychologists to study the abuse potential of newly available drugs in order to predict their likelihood of becoming drugs of abuse. The realisation that drugs are reinforcers has, in turn, led behaviour pharmacologists to treat cocaine dependence in people successfully by scheduling reinforcement for non-drug-taking behaviour (Higgins *et al.*, 1994).

Just as the telephone ringing can serve as a discriminative stimulus for you answering it, the stimulus effects of drugs can also exert control over human behaviours that are reinforced by non-drug stimuli. People become more sociable under the influence of alcohol not only because the drug reduces their inhibitions, but also because people have some successful social interactions while under the drug's effects. These interactions reinforce their sociability. In fact, many laboratory studies have shown that certain drugs actually increase social responding and social reinforcement (Higgins *et al.*, 1989).

Observation and imitation

Normally, we learn about the consequences of our own behaviour or about stimuli that directly affect us. We can also learn by a less direct method: observing the behaviour of others.

Evidence suggests that imitation does seem to be an innate tendency. Many species of birds must learn to sing the song of their species; if they are raised apart from other birds of their species, they will never sing or they will sing a peculiar song that bears little resemblance to that of normally raised birds (Marler, 1961). However, if they hear the normal song played over a loudspeaker, they will sing it properly when they become adults. They have learned the song, but clearly there were no external reinforcement contingencies; nothing in the environment reinforced their singing of the song.

Classically conditioned behaviours, as well as operantly conditioned behaviours, can be acquired through observation. For example, suppose that a young girl sees her mother show signs of fear whenever she encounters a dog. The girl herself will likely develop a fear of dogs, even if she never sees another one. In fact, Bandura and Menlove (1968) reported that children who were afraid of animals – in this case, dogs – were likely to have a parent who feared dogs, but they usually could not remember having had unpleasant direct experiences with them. As we will see in Chapter 13, we tend to imitate, and feel, the emotional responses of people we observe.

Under normal circumstances, learning by observation may not require external reinforcement. In fact, there is strong evidence that imitating the behaviour of other organisms may be reinforcing in itself. However, in some cases in which the ability to imitate is absent, it can be learned through reinforcement. For example, Baer *et al.* (1967) studied three severely retarded children who had never been seen to imitate the behaviour of other people. When the experimenters first tried to induce the children to do what they themselves did, such as clap their hands, the children were unresponsive. Next, the experimenters tried to induce and reinforce imitative behaviour in the children. An experimenter would look at a child, say 'do this,' and perform a behaviour. If the child made a similar response, the child was immediately praised and given a piece of food. At first, the children were physically guided to make the response. If the behaviour to be imitated was clapping, the experimenter would clap his or her hands, hold the child's hands and clap them together, and then praise the child and give him or her some food.

The procedure worked. The children learned to imitate the experimenters' behaviours. More importantly, however, the children had not simply learned to mimic a specific set of responses. They had acquired the general tendency to imitate. When the researchers performed new behaviours and said 'do this,' the children would imitate them.

Obviously, teaching retarded children is much more effective when the children pay attention to their teachers and imitate their behaviours when requested to do so. This experiment indicates that imitation, as a general tendency, is subject to reinforcement (and presumably to punishment, as well). An organism can learn more than simply making a certain response to a certain stimulus; it can learn a strategy that can be applied to many different situations. Social learning theory emphasises the importance of learning through observation and we return to this topic in Chapter 14. We will also discuss the role of imitation in language acquisition by children in Chapter 10.

Questions to think about

Principles of learning

■ Skinner might argue that many of the laws that govern behaviour in our culture are based more on aversive control of behaviour (punishment, response cost, negative reinforcement) than on positive reinforcement. What evidence can you cite for or against this view?

■ Negative reinforcement is often a difficult concept to grasp. Can you think of any personal examples in which your behaviour has been negatively reinforced? Can you identify the stimuli in these examples that serve as the negative reinforcers and can you state which aspects of your behaviour were influenced by these stimuli?

■ Do you like whisky, curry, chilli, black coffee or cold custard (or all five)? Some people have an aversion to these types of food. Can you think of reasons why?

■ What important behaviours have you learned, wholly or partially, from first observing them being performed by others? Would you have been able to learn these behaviours as well or as quickly had you not first had the opportunity to see them being performed by someone else?

■ Is imitation a sound basis on which to develop learning?

■ Have you ever had moments of 'insight'? Can you explain these moments with reference to any of the learning principles you have read about in this chapter?

■ Despite the fact that very few of them will win the jackpot, millions of people across the world pay money to participate in national or state lotteries. What learning principle could explain this type of behaviour (think in terms of reinforcement, or lack of it)?

Controversies in psychological science

What is insight?

The issue

Many problems we have to solve in our daily lives require us to make responses that we have never made before and that we have never seen anyone else make, either. We often think about a problem, looking at the elements and trying to imagine various solutions. We try various responses in our heads, but none seems to work. Suddenly, we think of a new approach: maybe this one will work. We try it, and it does. We say that we have solved the problem through insight (Sternberg and Davidson, 1996).

But what is insight? Some people see it as almost a magical process: a sudden flash of inspiration, a bolt from the blue, an answer coming from nowhere. At the simplest level, it is a form of understanding that changes a person's perception of a problem and its solution (Dominowski and Dallob, 1996). Most people regard insight as a particularly human ability – or, at least, as an ability that belongs to our species and, perhaps, some of the higher primates. Some psychologists, however, regard the term as fairly meaningless.

The evidence

During the early part of this century, the German psychologist Wolfgang Köhler studied the problem-solving behaviours of chimpanzees. In one famous example (Köhler, 1927), he hung some bananas from the ceiling

of an animal's cage, just high enough to be out of reach. The cage also contained a large box. Sultan, one of the chimps, first tried to jump up to reach the bananas, then paced around the cage, stopped in front of the box, pushed it towards the bananas, climbed onto the box, retrieved and ate the fruit. Later, when the bananas were suspended even higher, he stacked up several boxes, and on one occasion when no boxes were present, he grabbed Köhler by the hand, led him over to the bananas and climbed on top of him. Figure 7.8 illustrates Sultan's attempt at solving the problem.

Köhler believed that the insightful problem-solving behaviour shown by the chimpanzees was different from the behaviour of Thorndike's cats as they learned to escape the puzzle boxes. The cats clearly showed trial-and-error behaviour, coming upon the solution by accident. The escape from the box served as a reinforcing stimulus, and eventually the animals learned to operate the latch efficiently. But the behaviour of the chimpanzees seemed very different. They suddenly came upon a solution, often after looking at the situation (and, presumably, thinking about it). Köhler saw no accidental trial-and-error behaviour. The problem used in Kohler's experiment is an example of an object-use problem. Another type of problem, a spatial insight problem (Dominowski and Dallob, 1996) is seen in Figure 7.9. This is the nine dot problem in which you have to connect all the dots using four straight lines

Figure 7.8

Insightful behaviour by a chimpanzee in an experiment similar to one performed by Köhler. The chimpanzee piles boxes on top of each other to reach the bananas hanging overhead.

Source: © Superstock UK. Reprinted with permission.

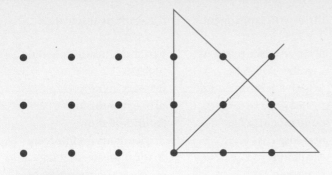

Figure 7.9

The nine dot problem. The challenge is to connect all nine dots using four straight lines without retracing any lines and without lifting your pen. The solution is seen in the figure on the right.

Source: Dominowski, R.L. and Dallob, P. (1996) Insight and problem solving. In Sternberg, R. and Davidson, J. (eds) *The Nature of Insight*. Published by the MIT Press, Cambridge, MA. Reproduced with permission.

and without lifting your pen from the page or retracing any of the lines.

More recent work suggests that insight may be less mysterious than it appears. Insight may actually be based on combinations of behaviours initially learned through trial and error. In one study (Epstein *et al.*, 1984), the experimenters used operant procedures (with food as the reinforcer) to teach a pigeon two behaviours: (1) to push a box towards a target (a green spot placed at various locations on the floor), and (2) to climb onto a box and peck at a miniature model of a banana which was suspended overhead. Once these behaviours had been learned, the experimenters confronted the pigeon with a situation in which the box was in one part of the chamber and the banana was in another.

'At first, the bird appeared to be confused: it stretched toward the banana, turned back and forth from the banana to the box, and so on. Then, rather suddenly, it began to push the box toward the banana, sighting the banana and readjusting the path of the box as it pushed. Finally, it stopped pushing when the box was near the banana, climbed onto the box, and pecked the banana.' (Epstein, 1985, p. 132)

The pigeon acted much the way that Sultan did. In a subsequent experiment, Epstein (1987) taught a pigeon to (1) peck at a model of a banana, (2) climb onto a box,

(3) open a door, and (4) push a box towards a target. When the pigeon was confronted with a banana hanging above its head and a box behind a door, it combined all four behaviours: it opened the door, pushed the box out and moved it under the banana, climbed the box and pecked the banana.

Insightful behaviour generally involves combining and adapting behaviours in a new context. We know from the experiments by Epstein and his colleagues that pigeons will show insightful behaviour only after they have learned the individual behaviours that must go together to solve a problem. For example, only if pigeons have learned to push a box towards a goal will they move it under a model banana hanging from the top of the cage. It is not enough to have learned to push a box; they must have learned to push it towards a goal. Presumably, the chimpanzees' experience with moving boxes around and climbing on them was necessary for them to solve the hanging banana problem.

Conclusion

In Chapter 2, we noted the concept of nominal fallacy – we tend to think that we have explained a phenomenon simply by naming it. Simply labelling behaviour as insightful does not help us to understand it. If we do not know what behaviours an animal has already learned, a novel and complex sequence of behaviours that solves a problem seems to come from nowhere. To understand the necessary conditions for insight to occur, we need to know more than what is happening during the current situation; we also need to know what kinds of learning experiences the animal has had.

The scientist's challenge is to dissect even the most complex behaviours and try to understand their causes. Perhaps chimpanzees, like humans, are capable of solving problems by using some sort of mental imagery, testing possible solutions in their heads before actually trying them. But neither humans nor chimpanzees will be able to think about objects they have never seen or imagine themselves performing behaviours they have never performed or seen others perform. Naturally, humans, chimpanzees and pigeons will be able to perform different kinds of behaviours and perceive different kinds of relations in their environments, because of their different habitats and because of differences in the complexities of their brains. But the raw material for problem solving – including the thinking that may accompany some forms of insightful behaviour – must come from previous experience. That, of course, is what this chapter has been all about.

Key terms

CHAPTER REVIEW

Habituation and classical conditioning

- Habituation screens out stimuli that experience has shown to be unimportant. This form of learning allows organisms to respond to more important stimuli, such as those related to survival and reproduction.

- Classical conditioning occurs when a neutral stimulus occurs just before an unconditional stimulus (UCS) – one that automatically elicits a behaviour. The response that an organism makes in response to the unconditional stimulus (the UCR) is already a natural part of its behaviour; what the organism learns to do is to make it in response to a new stimulus (the conditional stimulus, or CS). When the response is made to the CS, it is called the conditional response, or CR.

- The relationship between the conditional stimulus and unconditional stimulus determines the nature of the conditional response. Acquisition of the conditional response is influenced by the intensity of the unconditional stimulus and the delay between the conditional stimulus and unconditional stimulus.

- Extinction occurs when the conditional stimulus is still presented but is no longer followed by the unconditional stimulus; the conditional response may show spontaneous recovery later, even after a delay.

- Generalisation occurs when stimuli similar to the conditional stimulus used in training elicit the conditional response.

- Discrimination involves training the organism to make a conditional response only after a particular conditional stimulus occurs.

- Through classical conditioning, stimuli that were previously neutral with respect to an organism's behaviour can be made to become important.

- Classical conditioning can also establish various classes of stimuli as objects of fear (phobia) or of sexual attraction (fetishes). For classical conditioning to occur, the conditional stimulus must not only occur immediately before the unconditional stimulus, but it must also reliably predict the occurrence of the unconditional stimulus.

Operant conditioning

- The law of effect specifies a relation between behaviour and its consequences. If a stimulus that follows a response makes that response become more likely, we say that the response was reinforced. If the stimulus makes the response become less likely, we say that it was punished. The reinforcing or punishing stimulus must follow the behaviour almost immediately if it is to be effective.

- The process of operant conditioning helps adapt an organism's behaviour to its environment. Skinner described the relation between behaviour and environmental events as a three-term contingency: in the presence of discriminative stimuli, a consequence will occur if and only if an operant response occurs.

- A reinforcer is an appetitive stimulus that follows an operant response and causes that response to occur more frequently in the future.

- A punisher is an aversive stimulus that follows an operant response and causes it to occur less frequently in the future.

- If an aversive stimulus is terminated after a response occurs, the response is reinforced through a process called negative reinforcement. The termination of an appetitive stimulus can punish a response through a process called response cost.

- Extinction occurs when operant responses are emitted but not reinforced, which makes sense because organisms must be able to adapt their behaviour to changing environments.

- Complex responses, which are unlikely to occur spontaneously, can be shaped by the method of successive approximations.

- Various types of schedule of reinforcement have different effects on the rate and pattern of responding. When a response is reinforced intermittently, it is more resistant to extinction, probably because an intermittent reinforcement schedule resembles extinction more than a continuous reinforcement schedule does.

- Discrimination involves the detection of essential differences between stimuli or situations so that responding occurs only when appropriate. Generalisation is another necessary component of all forms of learning because no two stimuli, and no two responses, are precisely the same. Thus, generalisation embodies the ability to apply what is learned from one experience to similar experiences.

- The major difference between classical conditioning and operant conditioning is in the nature of the contingencies: classical conditioning involves a contingency between stimuli (CS and UCS), whereas operant conditioning involves a contingency between the organism's behaviour and an appetitive or aversive stimulus. The two types of conditioning complement each other. The pairings of neutral stimuli with appetitive and aversive stimuli (classical conditioning) determine which stimuli become conditioned reinforcers and punishers.

Conditioning of complex behaviours

- Much behaviour is under the control of aversive contingencies, which specify particular behaviours that are instrumental in either escaping or avoiding aversive stimuli.

- In conditioned flavour aversions, there is a delay between tasting a poison and getting sick; the rule that a reinforcing or punishing stimulus must immediately follow the response cannot, therefore, apply. Organisms are able to learn the association between flavour and illness over a long interval.

- The effects of reinforcing and punishing stimuli on behaviour can be complex and subtle. We are able to acquire both operantly and classically conditioned responses through observation and imitation.

- In addition, we can learn to modify and combine responses learned in other contexts to solve new problems. This is referred to as insight.

- Cognitive psychologists and behaviour analysts disagree about the determinants of behaviour. Behaviour analysts argue that behaviour is governed by external causes, such as discriminative stimuli and environmentally based reinforcers and punishers; cognitive psychologists maintain that behaviour is controlled by internal causes, such as thoughts, images, feelings, and perceptions.

Suggestions for further reading

Baldwin, J.D. and Baldwin, J.I. (1998). *Behavior Principles in Everyday Life* (3rd edition). Upper Saddle River, NJ: Prentice-Hall.

Barker, L.M. (1997). *Learning and Behaviour* (2nd edition). Upper Saddle River, NJ: Simon & Schuster.

Mazur, J.E. (1994). *Learning and Behaviour*. Upper Saddle River, NJ: Prentice-Hall.

Tarpy, R. (1997). *Contemporary Learning Theory and Research*. Maidenhead: McGraw-Hill.
These four texts provide a good, comprehensive account of the psychology of learning. Barker's book, in particular, is a very well written text with many interesting examples to illustrate the principles described. Baldwin and Baldwin do a similar thing (but with less well referenced examples) – see whether you think the examples they use explain learning or simply illustrate it.

Harris, B. (1979). Whatever happened to Little Albert? *American Psychologist*, 34, 2, 151–160.

Watson, J.B. and Rayner, R. (1920). Conditioned emotional reactions. *Journal of Experimental Psychology*, 3, 1–14.
Watson and Rayner's original article on conditioned human fear is a classic of its kind – the first scientific study of conditioning of fear in a human being. Apart from its historical interest, it is also useful to read in order to avoid the mistakes highlighted in Harris's incisive review.

Journals to consult

Behaviour Research and Therapy
British Journal of Psychology
Cognition
Journal of Applied Behaviour Analysis
Journal of Applied Psychology
Journal of Experimental Psychology: Learning, Memory and Cognition
Psychological Review
Psychological Science
Quarterly Journal of Experimental Psychology

Website address

http://www.guru.edu/~tip/theories.html
This is a link to 'Theory Into Practice Database', a good collection of theories of learning links.

8

MEMORY

In 1986, Nadean Cool, a nurse's aide in Wisconsin, sought therapy from a psychiatrist to help her cope with her reaction to a traumatic event experienced by her daughter.

During therapy, the psychiatrists used hypnosis and other negative techniques to dig out buried memories of abuse that Cool herself had allegedly experienced. In the process, Cool became convinced that she had repressed memories of having been in a satanic cult, of eating babies, of being raped, of having sex with animals, and of being forced to watch the murder of her eight year old friend. She came to believe that she had more than 120 personalities, all because, Cool was told, she had experienced severe childhood sexual and physical abuse. The psychiatrist also performed exorcisms on her, one of which lasted for five hours.

When Cool finally realised that false memories had been planted, she sued the psychiatrist for malpractice. In March 1997, after five weeks of trial, her case was settled out of court for $2.4 million.

Source: Loftus, 1997, p. 41

OVERVIEW

Memory refers to the cognitive processes of encoding, storing and retrieving information. That is, we need to acquire information, we need to store it and then we need to access it. This characterisation implies that each of these processes is separate and unique. However, memory is one of the most difficult psychological topics to study because it is not unitary: there are different types of memory. For example, learning to drive a car or use a computer keyboard requires different memory and cognitive skills from those needed to learn the facts from this book or to learn a foreign language.

This chapter describes the different types of memory and the explanations that psychologists have suggested for the existence of these types of memory. It considers the biological bases of memory formation and remembering, focusing on amnesia and neuroimaging studies of healthy individuals, and discusses some of the practical applications of memory research such as retention of material over a very long time, eyewitness testimony and the validity of 'recovered' memories.

What you should be able to do after reading Chapter 8

- Describe the different types of memory.
- Describe and understand theories of forgetting.
- Understand the term 'amnesia', be aware of different types of amnesia and understand the biological basis of the disorder.
- Distinguish between the processes of encoding and retrieval.
- Understand how memories are formed and can change over time.

Questions to think about

- How many different types of memory are there?
- Why do we forget?
- Can memories be manipulated?
- What brain mechanisms would be responsible for memory acquisition and retrieval?
- What is our memory capacity?
- Without memory, do you have a personality?

Memory: an introduction

Memory is the process of encoding, storing and retrieving information. **Encoding** refers to the active process of putting stimulus information into a form that can be used by our memory system. **Storage** refers to the process of maintaining information in memory. **Retrieval** refers to the active processes of locating and using information stored in memory.

When psychologists refer to the structure of memory, they are referring to two approaches to understanding memory – a literal one and a metaphorical one (Howard, 1995; Rose, 1992). Literally, memory may reflect the physiological changes that occur in the brain when an organism learns. Metaphorically, memory is viewed as a store or a process made up of systems and subsystems. These divisions may not necessarily have neurological meaning but they are useful metaphorical short-hand for describing aspects of memory. They are a way of explaining aspects of memory.

Types of memory

Research suggests that we possess at least three forms of memory: sensory memory, short-term memory (which incorporates working memory) and long-term memory (Baddeley, 1996). **Sensory memory** is memory in which representations of the physical features of a stimulus are stored for a very brief time, perhaps for a second or less. This form of memory is difficult to distinguish from the act of perception. The information contained in sensory memory represents the original stimulus fairly accurately and contains all or most of the information that has just been perceived. For example, sensory memory contains a brief image of a sight we have just seen or a fleeting echo of a sound we have just heard. Normally, we are not aware of sensory memory; no analysis seems to be performed on the information while it remains in this form. The function of sensory memory appears to be to hold information long enough for it to be transferred to the next form of memory, short-term memory.

Short-term memory refers to immediate memory for stimuli that have just been perceived. Its capacity is limited in terms of the number of items that it can store and of its duration. For example, most people who look at the set of numbers

1 4 9 2 3 0 7

close their eyes and recite them back, will have no trouble remembering them. If they are asked to do the same with the following set they might have a little more trouble:

7 2 5 2 3 9 1 6 5 8 4

Very few people can repeat eleven numbers. Even with practice, it is difficult to recite more than seven to nine independent pieces of information that you have seen only once. Short-term memory, therefore, has definite limits. However, there are ways to organise new information so that we can remember more than seven to nine items, but in such cases the items can no longer be considered independent.

We could have repeatedly recited the eleven numbers above until we had memorised them (rehearsal) and placed them in long-term memory. **Long-term memory** refers to information that is represented on a permanent or near-permanent basis. Unlike short-term memory, long-term memory has no known limits and, as its name suggests, is relatively durable. If we stop thinking about something we have just perceived (that is, something contained in short-term memory), we may not remember the information later. However, information in long-term memory need not be continuously rehearsed. We can stop thinking about it until we need the information at a future time.

Some cognitive psychologists argue that no real distinction exists between short-term and long-term memory; instead, they see them as different phases of a continuous process. These psychologists object to the conception of memory as a series of separate units with information flowing from one to the next, as seen in Figure 8.1. Memory may be more complex than this model would have us believe.

Sensory memory

Under most circumstances, we are not aware of sensory memory. Information we have just perceived remains in sensory memory just long enough to be transferred to short-term memory. In order for us to become aware of sensory memory, information must be presented very briefly so that we can perceive its after-effects. Although we probably have a sensory memory for each sense modality, research efforts so far have focused on the two most important forms: iconic (visual) and echoic (auditory) memory.

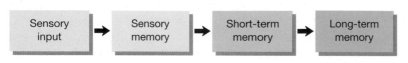

Figure 8.1

The information-processing model of human memory.

Iconic memory

Visual sensory memory, called iconic memory (icon means 'image'), is a form of sensory memory that briefly holds a visual representation of a scene that has just been perceived. To study this form of memory, Sperling (1960) presented visual stimuli to people by means of a tachistoscope, apparatus for presenting visual stimuli for extremely brief durations. Sperling flashed a set of nine letters on the screen for 50 milliseconds (ms). He then asked people to recall as many letters as they could, a method known as the whole-report procedure. On average, they could remember only four or five letters, but they insisted that they could see more. However, the image of the letters faded too fast for people to identify them all.

To determine whether the capacity of iconic memory accounted for this limitation, Sperling used a partial-report procedure. He asked people to name the letters in only one of the three horizontal rows. Depending on whether a high, middle or low tone was sounded, they were to report the letters in the top, middle or bottom line (see Figure 8.2). When the participants were warned beforehand to which line they should attend, they had no difficulty naming all three letters correctly. But then Sperling sounded the tone after he flashed the letters on the screen. The participants had to select the line from the mental image they still had: they had to retrieve the information from iconic memory. With brief delays, they recalled the requested line of letters with perfect accuracy. For example, after seeing all nine letters flashed on the screen, they would hear the high tone, direct their attention to the top line of letters in their iconic memory, and 'read them off'. These results indicated that their iconic memory contained an image of all nine letters.

Sperling also varied the delay between flashing the nine letters on the screen and sounding the high, medium or low tone. If the delay was longer than 1 second, people could report only around 50 per cent of the letters. This result indicated that the image of the visual stimulus fades quickly from iconic memory. It also explains why participants who were asked to report all nine letters failed to

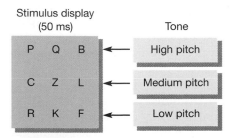

Stimulus display (50 ms)	Tone
P Q B	High pitch
C Z L	Medium pitch
R K F	Low pitch

Figure 8.2

The critical features of Sperling's iconic memory study.

Source: Adapted from Sperling, G., The information available in brief visual presentations, *Psychological Monographs*, 1960, 74, 1–29.

report more than four or five. They had to scan their iconic memory, identify each letter and store each letter in short-term memory. This process took time, and during this time the image of the letters was fading. Although their iconic memory originally contained all nine letters, there was time to recognise and report only four or five before the mental image disappeared.

Echoic memory

Auditory sensory memory, called echoic memory, is a form of sensory memory for sounds that have just been perceived. It is necessary for comprehending many sounds, particularly those that constitute speech. When we hear a word pronounced, we hear individual sounds, one at a time. We cannot identify the word until we have heard all the sounds, so acoustical information must be stored temporarily until all the sounds have been received. For example, if someone says 'mallet', we may think of a kind of hammer; but if someone says 'malice', we will think of something entirely different. The first syllable we hear – *mal* – has no meaning by itself in English, so we do not identify it as a word. However, once the last syllable is uttered, we can put the two syllables together and recognise the word. At this point, the word enters short-term memory. Echoic memory holds a representation of the initial sounds until the entire word has been heard; it seems to hold information for about four seconds (Darwin *et al.*, 1972).

Short-term memory

Short-term memory has a limited capacity, and most of the information that enters it is subsequently forgotten. Information in sensory memory enters short-term memory, where it may be rehearsed for a while. The rehearsal process keeps the information in short-term memory long enough for it to be transferred into long-term memory. After that, a person can stop thinking about the information; it can be recalled later, when it is needed.

This simple story is actually inaccurate. First of all, information does not simply 'enter short-term memory'. For example, most people who read the letters like these:

P X L M R

and put them in short-term memory, have a number of strategies for achieving this. Some would have repeated the letters to themselves or would have whispered or moved their lips. We can say the names of these letters because many years ago we learned them. But that knowledge is stored in long-term memory. Thus, when we see some letters, we retrieve information about their names from long-term memory, and then we hear ourselves rehearsing those names (out loud or silently). The five letters above contain

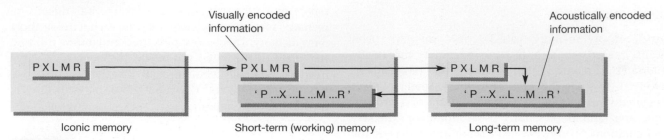

Figure 8.3

Relations between iconic memory, short-term memory and long-term memory. Letters are read, transformed into their acoustic equivalents and rehearsed as 'sounds' in the head. Information can enter short-term memory from both iconic memory and long-term memory. Visual information enters short-term memory from iconic memory, but what is already known about that information (such as names of letters) is moved from long-term memory to short-term memory.

only visual information, their names came from long-term memory, which means that the information put into short-term memory actually came from long-term memory.

To illustrate this, try the following experiment. Study the symbols below, then look away from the book, and try to keep them in short-term memory.

ζ ∩ ∂ ∍ ℘

This task is extremely difficult because few people will have learned the names of these symbols. Because of this, there is no way of recording them in short-term memory. Figure 8.3 may, therefore, be a better description of the memory process than is Figure 8.1.

Information can enter short-term memory from two directions: from sensory memory or from long-term memory. When we are asked to multiply 7 by 19, information about the request enters our short-term memory from our sensory memory. Actually performing the task, though, requires that we retrieve some information from long-term memory. What does 'multiply' mean? What is a 7 and a 19? At the moment of the request, such information is not being furnished through our senses; it is available only from long-term memory. However, that information is not recalled directly from long-term memory. It is first moved into short-term memory and then enters conscious awareness.

Working memory

The fact that short-term memory contains both new information and information retrieved from long-term memory has led some psychologists to prefer the term 'working memory' (Baddeley and Hitch, 1974; Baddeley, 1986, 1992b). Working memory acts on material we have just perceived and allows us to manipulate this in the short-term. It allows us to keep a new telephone number 'alive' in memory long enough to dial it or allows us to perform that multiplication task mentioned in the paragraph above. In short, it represents our ability to remember what we have just perceived and to think about it in terms of what we already

know (Baddeley, 1986; Logie, 1996). We use it to remember what a person says at the beginning of a sentence until we finally hear the end. We use it to remember whether any cars are coming up the street after looking left and then right. We use it to think about what we already know and to come to conclusions on the basis of this knowledge. According to Baddeley, working memory is a short-term memory system that allows us to retain and process information concurrently. It allows us to retain material for current use and not just for transport into long-term memory.

Working memory was a model devised in the 1970s and later developed extensively by Baddeley. He regarded this short-term memory as having three components which allowed us to store temporarily verbal material and visuospatial material, and to co-ordinate the storage of this material. The component which stores verbal material was originally called the articulatory loop although this term has been superseded by the term phonological loop (Baddeley and Logie, 1992). The component that allows storage of visuospatial material is called the visuospatial scratchpad and the co-ordinating system is called the central executive. The working memory 'system' is illustrated in Figure 8.4 and is described next.

Phonological working memory

When we see a printed word, we say it, out loud or silently. If it is said to ourselves, circuits of neurons that control articulation are activated. Information concerning this activity is communicated within the brain to circuits of neurons in the auditory system, and the word is 'heard'. Information is then transmitted back to the articulatory system, where the word is silently repeated. The loop continues until the person's attention turns to something else or until it is replaced with new information.

This articulatory or phonological loop allows the retention of verbal phonetic information (so it acts as a phonological store) and operates like the loop of an audio tape (hence, the name). Lists of long words are remembered

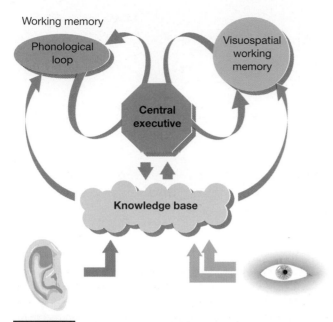

Figure 8.4

Logie's (1995) schematic drawing of the components of working memory.

Source: Adapted from Robert Logie, *Visual Spatial Working Memory*, p. 127, © 1995. Reprinted by permission of Psychology Press Limited, Hove, UK.

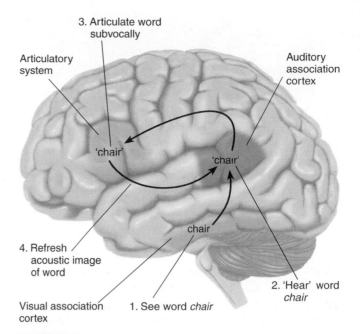

Figure 8.5

The articulatory loop. A hypothetical explanation of phonological working memory.

more poorly than lists of short words, for example, because there is less room on the loop for lists of long words (so the words 'encyclopaedia', 'constellation' and 'antediluvian' would be more difficult to recall than would the words 'clock', 'parrot' and 'daisy'). However, because the loop also allows the rehearsal of information by subvocal articulation (such as subvocally rehearsing a telephone number), the loss of information from the phonological store can be avoided. According to Baddeley *et al.* (1975), the capacity of the phonologial loop is determined by how much material the participant can rehearse in two seconds. (Figure 8.5 illustrates how the phonological loop is represented in the brain.)

However, the operation of the loop can be defective under certain circumstances. For example, Salame and Baddeley (1982) found that irrelevant speech played in the background while participants learned visually presented words interfered with the recall of these words, but the length of the words to-be-remembered had no significant effect on recall. The closer the irrelevant speech was to the to-be-remembered words, however, the greater the interference, suggesting that there was some interference in learning words while attending to the sound (or phonology) of similar ones. Similar interference had been found when participants in Baddeley's very early experiments were required to recall either words that were phonologically similar (man, mad, mat, map) or dissimilar (bus, clock, spoon, fish). Recall was poorer for the phonologically

similar words. Although the original conception of the loop suggested that only irrelevant speech could disrupt rehearsal, there is evidence that non-speech related material can have the same effect. For example, as we shall see in the section on selective attention in the next chapter, even background noise can disrupt recall of verbal and arithmetical material (Banbury and Berry, 1998).

Phonological working memory is an important feature of many cognitive operations: rehearsing telephone numbers, addresses and text from a page are some of the most obvious ones. It also seems to be an important component of reading, especially of learning to read. As we shall see in Chapter 10, phonological working memory is important for the successful development of reading ability in children (Gathercole and Baddeley, 1990; Gathercole *et al.*, 1992).

Visuospatial working memory

The material we keep in working memory need not be phonetic or phonological in nature. Much of the information we receive from the visual system is non-verbal. We recognise objects, perceive their locations and find our way around the environment. We can look at objects, close our eyes and then sketch or describe them. We can do the same with things we saw in the past. We seem to possess a working memory that contains visual information either obtained from the immediate environment by means of the sense organs or retrieved from long-term memory. This is called the visuospatial scratchpad.

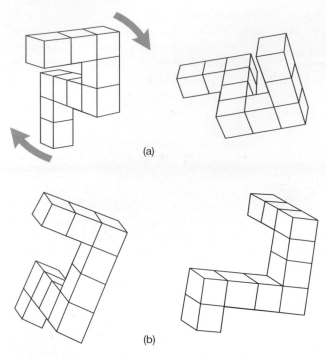

Figure 8.6

The mental rotation task. (a) The shape on the right is identical to the one on the left but rotated 80 degrees clockwise. (b) The two shapes are different.

Source: Adapted from Shepard, R.N. and Metzler, J., Mental rotation of three-dimensional objects, *Science*, 1971, 171, 701–703. Copyright © 1971 by the American Association for the Advancement of Science 1971.

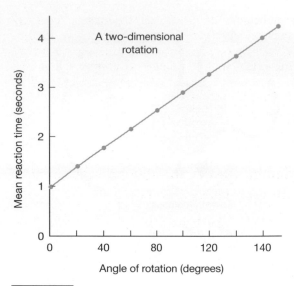

Figure 8.7

The results from the mental rotation task study. Mean reaction time is shown as a function of angle of rotation.

Source: Adapted from Shepard, R.N. and Metzler, J., Mental rotation of three-dimensional objects, *Science*, 1971, 171, 701–703. Copyright © 1971 by the American Association for the Advancement of Science 1971.

Logie (1995) has suggested that the visuospatial scratchpad can be further subdivided into other components. He suggests that there exists a passive visual store and another component which involves memory for movements and visuospatial rehearsal. The link between the visuospatial scratchpad and movement imagery seems to be supported by experiments in which the generation and retention of spatial images is impaired when the participants simultaneously either tap a set of keys on a table or move their arm to track a moving target (Logie *et al.*, 1990).

An example of the ability to manipulate visual information in working memory comes from Shepard and Metzler (1971). They presented people with pairs of drawings that could be perceived as three-dimensional constructions made of cubes. The participant's task was to see whether the shape on the right was identical to the one on the left; some were, and some were not. Even when the shapes were identical, the one on the right was sometimes drawn as if it had been rotated. For example, in Figure 8.6(a) the shape on the right has been rotated clockwise 80 degrees, but in Figure 8.6(b) the two shapes are different.

Shepard and Metzler found that people were accurate in judging whether the pairs of shapes were the same or different but took longer to decide when the right-hand shape was rotated. They reported that they formed an image of one of the drawings in their heads and rotated it until it was aligned the same way as the other one. If their rotated image coincided with the drawing, they recognised them as having the same shape. If they did not, they recognised them as being different. The data supported what the participants said – the more the shape was rotated, the longer it took for people to rotate the image of one of the shapes in working memory and compare it with the other one (see Figure 8.7).

The central executive

The elements of working memory – phonological loop and the visuospatial scratchpad – do not work independently. Information in working memory has to be regulated and supervised. Such regulation occurs via what Baddeley (1986) calls the central executive subsystem. This central executive not only allocates mental resources to working memory tasks but also supervises the updating of what is in working memory. Baddeley has compared the central executive with the supervisory attentional system (SAS) developed by Norman and Shallice (1986). This system was proposed to explain the behaviour of patients with frontal lobe impairment. These patients, as we shall see in Chapters 11 and 13, have difficulty in regulating their behaviour: they lack spontaneity, are poor at planning and are unable to change inappropriate behaviour. The SAS is responsible for the conscious attentional control needed to regulate behaviour. This overall executive control over regulation of behaviour is similar to that proposed for the central executive component of working memory. Interestingly, recent fMRI studies have shown that prefrontal brain activity is associated with the performance of tasks very similar to those performed in working memory tasks (Cohen *et al.*, 1997; Courtney *et al.*, 1997; Casey *et al.*, 1998).

Retention in short-term/working memory: primacy and recency effects

When individuals are asked to listen to a long list of words spoken one at a time and then write down as many as they can remember (a free-recall task), most participants will remember the words at the beginning and the end of the list and forget the words in between. The tendency to remember the words at the beginning of the list is called the primacy effect; the tendency to remember words at the end of the list is called the recency effect. Two factors may account for these effects.

The primacy effect appears to be due to the fact that words earlier in a list have the opportunity to be rehearsed more than do words in the other parts of a list. This makes good sense – the first words get rehearsed more because, at the experiment's outset, these are the only words available to rehearse. The rehearsal permits them to be stored in long-term memory. As more and more words on the list are presented, short-term memory becomes fuller so that words that appear later in the list have more competition for rehearsal time. Because the first words on the list are rehearsed the most, they are remembered better.

As Atkinson and Shiffrin (1968) point out, because the words at the end of the list were the last to be heard, they are still available in short-term memory. Thus, when you are asked to write the words on the list, the last few words are still available in short-term memory even though they did not undergo as much rehearsal as words at the beginning of the list.

The primacy and recency effects are important because they demonstrate that memory is not a random process. Information is not just plucked from the environment and stored away randomly in the brain. Instead, the processing of information is much more orderly; it follows predictable patterns and is dependent on the contributions of rehearsal and short-term memory.

The limits of working memory

How long does information remain in short-term or working memory? The answer may lie in a classic study by Lloyd and Margaret Peterson (Peterson and Peterson, 1959). The experimenters presented participants with a stimulus composed of three consonants, such as JRG. With

rehearsal, the participants easily recalled it thirty seconds later. The Petersons then made the task more challenging: they prevented participants from rehearsing. After they presented the participants with JRG, they asked them to count backwards by three from a three-digit number they gave them immediately after they had presented the set of consonants. For example, they might present participants with JRG, then say, '397'. The participants would count out loud, '397 ... 394 ... 391 ... 388 ... 385', and so on until the experimenters signalled them to recall the consonants. The accuracy of recall was determined by the length of the interval between presentation of the consonants and when recall was requested (see Figure 8.8). When rehearsal was disrupted by backward counting – which prevented individuals from rehearsing information in short-term memory – the consonants remained accessible in memory for only a few seconds. After a 15–18 second delay between the presentation of the consonants and the recall signal, recall dropped to near zero.

What, then, is the capacity of short-term memory? Miller (1956), in a famous article entitled 'The magical number seven, plus or minus two', demonstrated that people could retain, on the average, about seven pieces of information in their short-term memories: seven numbers, seven letters, seven words or seven tones of a particular pitch. If we can remember and think about only seven pieces of information at a time, how can we manage to write novels, design buildings or even carry on simple conversations? The answer comes in a particular form of encoding of information that Miller called chunking, a

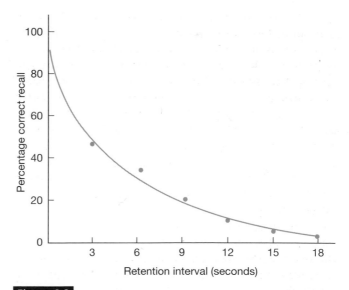

Figure 8.8

Limits of recall from working memory. Percentage correct recall of the stimulus as a function of the duration of the distractor task used in the study by Peterson and Peterson.

Source: Adapted from Peterson, L.M. and Peterson, J.M., Short-term retention of individual verbal items. *Journal of Experimental Psychology*, 1959, 58, 193–198.

process by which information is simplified by rules which make it easily remembered once the rules are learned.

A simple demonstration illustrates this phenomenon. Read the ten numbers printed below and see whether you have any trouble remembering them.

1 3 5 7 9 2 4 6 8 0

These numbers are easy to retain in short-term memory because we can remember a rule instead of ten independent numbers. In this case, the rule concerns odd and even numbers. The actual limit of short-term memory is seven chunks, not necessarily seven individual items. Thus, the total amount of information we can store in short-term memory depends on the particular rules we use to organise it.

In life outside the laboratory we are rarely required to remember a series of numbers. The rules that organise our short-term memories are much more complex than those that describe odd and even numbers. The principles of chunking can apply to more realistic learning situations. If we look at the following words:

along got the was door crept locked slowly he until passage the he to which

and try to remember them, the task is difficult; there is too much information to store in short-term memory. If we repeat the process for the following group of words:

He slowly crept along the passage until he got to the door, which was locked.

we would be much more successful. Once the same fifteen words are arranged in a sequence that makes sense, they are not difficult to store in short-term memory.

In a strict sense, the capacity of short-term memory for verbal material is not measured by the number of letters, syllables or words it can retain. Instead, the limit depends on how much meaning the information has: this is working memory and long-term memory working together. The first set of words above merely contains fifteen different words. Because few people can immediately recite back more than five to nine independent items, we are not surprised to find that we cannot store fifteen jumbled words in short-term memory. However, when the items are related, we can store many more of them. We do not have to string fifteen words together in a meaningless fashion. Instead, we can let the image of a man creeping down a passage towards a locked door organise the new information. Thus, we can read or hear a sentence such as the one above, understand what the sentence means, and remember that meaning.

Loss of information from short-term memory

The essence of short-term memory is its transience; hence, its name. Information enters from sensory memory and from long-term memory, is rehearsed, thought about,

modified and then leaves. Some of the information controls ongoing behaviour and some of it causes changes in long-term memory, but ultimately, it is lost from short-term memory. What causes it to leave? The simplest possibility is that it decays, it fades away. Rehearsal allows us to refresh information indefinitely, thus preventing the decay from eliminating the information.

However, the most important cause appears to be displacement. Once short-term memory has reached its capacity, either additional information will have to be ignored or some information already in short-term memory will have to be displaced to make room for the new information.

One of the best examples of displacement of information in short-term memory comes from an experiment conducted by Waugh and Norman (1965). The people in this study heard lists of sixteen digits. The last digit, accompanied by a tone, was called the probe digit. When people heard it, they had to think back to the previous occurrence of the same digit and tell the experimenter the digit that followed that one.

Look at the sequence of numbers listed below. The last one, a 9, was accompanied by a tone, which told the person that it was the probe. If you examine the list, you will see that the earlier occurrence of a 9 was followed by a 4. Thus, the target, or correct, response was 4.

2 6 7 5 1 3 7 2 6 3 9 4 5 8 1 9

Notice that the 4 is separated from the second 9 by three numbers (5, 8 and 1). Waugh and Norman presented many different lists in which the location of the correct response

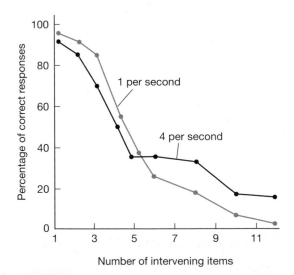

Figure 8.9

Displacement of information in short-term memory. The graph shows the percentage of correct responses as a function of intervening items presented at two different rates of time.

Source: Adapted from Waugh, N.C. and Norman, D.A., Primary memory, *Psychological Review*, 1965, 72, 89–104.

varied. The distance between the target and the probe ranged from one to twelve items.

The study had two conditions. In one, the lists were presented rapidly, at four digits per second. In the other, they were presented slowly, at only one digit per second. The reason for this manipulation was to determine whether any effects they observed were caused by the mere passage of time rather than by displacement. They found that the more items that came between the target and the probe, the less likely it was that the target would be remembered. The critical variable seemed to be the number of items between the target and the probe, not the time that had elapsed (see Figure 8.9).

The results indicate that new information displaces old information in short-term memory. But at the longest delays (six or more intervening items), subjects performed more poorly when the items were presented slowly. Perhaps information in short-term memory does decay, but the effect is much less important than displacement.

Questions to think about

Sensory and working memory

- In what ways can the systems of memory be described as metaphors? That is, when we refer to short-term memory and long-term memory are we actually referring to real things?

- Does the existence of echoic or sensory memory provide an explanation for subliminal perception?

- In what ways is short-term memory different from working memory? Are they different?

- How many tasks can you think of that involve working memory?

- Would finding different neural substrates for different memory systems confirm that these memory systems are independent?

- Why do we forget material in working/short-term memory so quickly?

Learning and encoding in long-term memory

Information that is present in short-term memory may or may not be available later. But once information has successfully made its way into long-term memory, it remains relatively stable. Memory involves both active and passive processes. Sometimes, we use deliberate strategies to remember something (encode the information into long-term memory), for example, rehearsing the lines of a poem or memorising famous dates for a history lesson. At other times, we simply observe and remember without any apparent effort, as when we tell a friend about an interesting experience we had. And memories can be formed even without our being aware of having learned something. What factors determine whether we can eventually remember an experience?

The consolidation hypothesis

The traditional view of memory is that it consists of a two-stage process (not counting sensory memory). Information enters short-term memory from the environment, where it is stored temporarily. If the material is rehearsed long enough, it is transferred into long-term memory. This transfer of information from short-term memory into long-term memory has been called consolidation (Hebb, 1949). Through rehearsal (for example, by means of the articulatory loop), the neural activity responding to sensory stimulation can be sustained; and if enough time passes, the activity causes structural changes in the brain. These structural changes are more-or-less permanent and solid (hence, the term 'consolidation'). They are responsible for long-term memory. This may be why individuals who have suffered severe concussion or have undergone a form of therapy called electroconvulsive therapy experience loss of memory: there has been no opportunity for memory to be rehearsed because the neural systems responsible for this have not been allowed to do their work.

The levels-of-processing hypothesis

The consolidation hypothesis makes several assertions about the learning process. It asserts that short-term memory and long-term memory are physiologically different and few investigators doubt that information that has just been perceived is stored in the brain in a different way from information that was perceived some time ago. However, some other features of the original consolidation hypothesis have been challenged. First, the hypothesis asserts that all information gets into long-term memory only after passing through short-term memory. Secondly, it asserts that the most important factor determining whether a particular piece of information reaches long-term memory is the amount of time it spends in short-term memory.

Craik and Lockhart (1972) have pointed out that the act of rehearsal may effectively keep information in short-term memory but does not necessarily result in the establishment of long-term memories. They suggested that people engage in two different types of rehearsal: maintenance rehearsal and elaborative rehearsal. Maintenance rehearsal is the rote repetition of verbal information – simply repeating an item over and over. This behaviour serves to maintain the information in short-term memory but does not necessarily result in lasting changes. In contrast, when people engage in elaborative rehearsal, they think about the information and relate it to what they already know. Elaborative rehearsal involves more than new information. It involves deeper processing: forming associations, attending to the meaning of the information, thinking about that information, and so on. Thus, we elaborate on new information by recollecting related information already in long-term memory. We are more likely to remember information for an examination by processing it deeply or meaningfully; simply rehearsing the material to be tested will not be effective.

The effectiveness of elaboration in remembering was nicely demonstrated in an experiment conducted by Craik and Tulving (1975). The investigators gave participants a set of cards, each containing a printed sentence including a missing word, denoted by a blank line, such as 'The _____ is torn.' After reading the sentence, the participants looked at a word flashed on a screen, then pressed a button as quickly as possible to signify whether the word fitted the sentence. In this example, dress will fit, but table will not. The sentences varied in complexity. Some were very simple:

She cooked the _____.
The _____ is torn.

Others were complex:

The great bird swooped down and carried off the struggling _____.
The old man hobbled across the room and picked up the valuable _____.

The sentences were written so that the same word could be used for either a simple or a complex sentence: 'She cooked the chicken' or 'The great bird swooped down and carried off the struggling chicken.' All participants saw a particular word once, in either a simple or a complex sentence.

The experimenters made no mention of a memory test, so there was no reason for the subjects to try to remember the words. However, after responding to the sentences, they were presented with them again and were asked to recall the words they had used. The experimenters found that the participants were twice as likely to remember a word if it had previously fitted into a sentence of medium or high complexity than if it had fitted into a simple one. These results suggest that a memory is more effectively established if the item is presented in a rich context – one that is likely to make us think about the item and imagine an action taking place.

Craik and Lockhart (1972) proposed a framework for understanding the process by which information enters long-term memory. They suggested that memory is a by-product of perceptual analysis. A central processor, analogous to the central processing unit of a computer, can analyse sensory information on several different levels. They conceived of the levels as being hierarchically arranged,

from shallow (superficial) to deep (complex). A person can control the level of analysis by paying attention to different features of the stimulus. If a person focuses on the superficial sensory characteristics of a stimulus, then these features will be stored in memory. If the person focuses on the meaning of a stimulus and the ways in which it relates to other things the person already knows, then these features will be stored in memory. For example, consider the word:

tree

This word is written in black type, the letters are lower case, the bottom of the stem of the letter 't' curves upwards to the right, and so on. Craik and Lockhart referred to these characteristics as surface features and to the analysis of these features as shallow processing. Maintenance rehearsal is an example of shallow processing. In contrast, consider the meaning of the word 'tree'. You can think about how trees differ from other plants, what varieties of trees you have seen, what kinds of foods and what kinds of wood they provide, and so on. These features refer to a word's meaning and are called semantic features. Their analysis is called deep processing. Elaborative rehearsal is an example of deep processing. According to Craik and Lockhart, deep processing generally leads to better retention than surface processing does.

Among the evidence reviewed by Craik and Lockhart to support their model were the results from a study conducted by Hyde and Jenkins (1969). These researchers

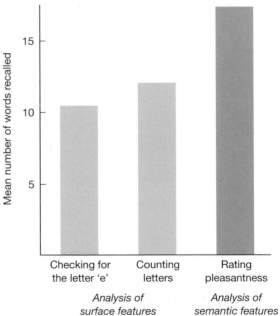

Figure 8.10

Shallow versus deep processing. Mean number of words recalled after performing tasks that required analysis of surface features or analysis of semantic features.

Source: Based on Craik, F.I.M. and Lockhart, R.S., Levels of processing: A framework for memory research. *Journal of Verbal Behavior*, 1972, 11, 671–684.

asked people to analyse lists of words. Some people were asked to analyse surface features – to count the letters in each word or to see whether the word contained the letter 'e'. Others were asked to analyse deeper features – to think about the word and decide how pleasant or unpleasant they found it to be. People who engaged in a deeper level of processing remembered more words, as Figure 8.10 shows.

Knowledge, encoding, and learning

As we gain more knowledge over time, our recall of that knowledge improves. However, simply possessing knowledge does not always facilitate recall: even the brightest people have problems remembering. What appears to be more important is what happens during the encoding of information, the process of getting material into memory. How we encode information is likely to affect our ability to remember it later.

Automatic versus effortful processing

Retrieval is enhanced by the extent to which we practise or rehearse information. Practising or rehearsing information, through either shallow or deep processing, is called effortful processing. As a student, you know that the more you concentrate on your studies, the more likely it becomes that you will do well in an exam. But your experience also tells you that you have stored information in memory that you had never rehearsed in the first place. Somehow, without any effort, information becomes encoded into your memory. This formation of memories of events and experiences with little or no attention or effort is called automatic processing.

Information that is automatically processed includes frequency (how many times have you read the word 'encode' today?), time (when did you experience your first kiss?), and place (where in the textbook is the graph of Sperling's data located?). Automatic processing helps us to learn things with relative ease, which makes life a lot less taxing than having continually to process information effortfully. Unfortunately, perhaps because of its complexity, most textbook learning is effortful, not automatic.

Encoding specificity

Encoding specificity refers to the principle that the way in which we encode information determines our ability to retrieve it later. For example, suppose that someone reads you a list of words that you are to recall later. The list contains the word 'beet', along with a number of terms related to music, such as 'melody', 'tune', and 'jazz'. When asked if the list contained the names of any vegetables, you may report that it did not. Because of the musical context, you encoded 'beet' as 'beat' and never thought of the tuberous vegetable while you were rehearsing the list (Flexser and Tulving, 1978). Many experiments have made the point

that meaningful elaboration during encoding is helpful and probably necessary for the formation of useful memories.

Criticisms of the levels-of-processing hypothesis

The concept of processing depth has been useful in guiding research efforts to understand how we learn and remember. However, the distinction between shallow and deep processing has never been rigorously defined. The difference between looking at the shape of the letters of a word and thinking about its meaning is clear, but most instances of encoding cannot be so neatly categorised. The term 'depth' seems to be a metaphor: it roughly describes the fact that information is more readily remembered when we think about it in relation to what we already know, but it is not exact and specific enough to satisfy most memory theorists.

Another problem with trying to understand exactly what is meant by expressions such as 'depth of processing' is that no matter what we may ask a person to do when we present a stimulus (for example, 'count the letters'), we have no way of knowing what else he or she may be doing that may aid recall of that item. In other words, researchers may not be able to control the depth to which a person processes information because they have no way of peering into his or her head and knowing exactly how the information is being manipulated. For each of us, our memory, its processes and its contents are private. Memory, like all cognitive processes, is not an observable phenomenon.

The use of mnemonics

When we can imagine information vividly and concretely, and when it fits into the context of what we already know, it is easy to remember later. Mnemonic systems (from the Greek *mnemon*, meaning 'mindful') – special techniques or strategies consciously used to improve memory – make use of information already stored in long-term memory to make memorisation an easier task.

Mnemonic systems do not simplify information but make it more elaborate. More information is stored, not less. However, the additional information makes the material easier to recall. Furthermore, mnemonic systems organise new information into a cohesive whole so that retrieval of part of the information ensures retrieval of the rest of it. These facts suggest that the ease or difficulty with which we learn new information depends not on how much we must learn but on how well it fits with what we already know. The better it fits, the easier it is to retrieve.

Method of loci

In Greece before the sixth century BC, few people knew how to write, and those who did had to use cumbersome clay tablets. Consequently, oratory skills and memory for long epic poems (running for several hours) were highly prized, and some people earned their livings by using them. Because people could not carry around several hundred pounds of clay tablets, they had to keep important information in their heads. To do so, the Greeks devised the method of loci, a mnemonic system in which items to be remembered are mentally associated with specific physical locations (the word *locus* means 'place').

To use the method of loci, would-be memory artists had to memorise the inside of a building. In Greece, they would wander through public buildings, stopping to study and memorise various locations and arranging them in order, usually starting with the door of the building. After memorising the locations, they could make the tour mentally, just as you could make a mental tour of your house to count the rooms. To learn a list of words, they would visualise each word in a particular location in the memorised building and picture the association as vividly as possible. For example, for the word 'love' they might imagine an embracing couple leaning against a particular column in a hall of the building. To recall the list, they would imagine each of the locations in sequence, 'see' each word, and say it. To store a speech, they would group the words into concepts and place a 'note' for each concept at a particular location in the sequence.

For example, if a person wanted to remember a short shopping list without writing it down and the list consists of five items: cheese, milk, eggs, soy sauce and lettuce, the person might first think of a familiar place, perhaps his or her house. Next, he or she would mentally walk through the house, visually placing different items from the list at locations – loci – in the house: a lump of cheese hanging from a coat rack, milk dripping from the kitchen tap, eggs lying in the hallway, a bottle of soy sauce on a dining chair, and a head of lettuce on the sofa (see Figure 8.11). Then, in the supermarket, the person mentally retraces his or her path through the house and notes what he or she has stored at the different loci.

Peg-word method

A similar technique, the peg-word method, involves the association of items to be remembered with a set of mental pegs that are already stored in memory (Miller *et al.*, 1960). As with the method of loci, the goal involves visually associating the new with the familiar. In the peg-word method, the familiar material is a set of 'mental pegs' that you already have in memory. One example is to take the numbers from one to ten and rhyme each number with a peg-word; for example, one is a bun, two is a shoe, three is a tree, four is a door, five is a hive, and so on. Returning to your grocery list, you might imagine the package of cheese in a hamburger bun, a shoe full of milk, eggs dangling from a tree, soy sauce on a door, and the lettuce on top of a bee hive (see Figure 8.12). In the supermarket, you review each peg word in order and recall the item associated with it. At first, this technique may seem silly, but there is ample research suggesting that it actually works (Marshark *et al.*, 1987).

Narrative stories

Another useful aid to memory is to place information into a narrative, in which items to be remembered are linked together by a story. Bower and Clark (1969) showed that

Cheese   Milk   Eggs   Soy sauce   Lettuce

SUPERMARKET

What do I need to get here?

Figure 8.11

The method of loci. Items to be remembered are visualised in specific, well known places.

Figure 8.12

The peg-word method. Items to be remembered are associated with nouns that rhyme with numbers.

even inexperienced people can use this method. The investigators asked people to try to learn twelve lists of ten concrete nouns each. They gave some of the people the following advice:

> 'A good way to learn the list of items is to make up a story relating the items to one another. Specifically, start with the first item and put it in a setting which will allow other items to be added to it. Then, add the other items to the story in the same order as the items appear. Make each story meaningful to yourself. Then, when you are asked to recall the items, you can simply go through your story and pull out the proper items in their correct order.' (Bower and Clark, 1969, p. 181)

Here is a typical narrative, described by one of the subjects (list words are italicised):

> 'A *lumberjack* darted out of the forest, *skated* around a *hedge* past a *colony* of *ducks*. He tripped on some *furniture*, tearing his *stocking* while hastening to the *pillow* where his *mistress* lay.'

People in the control group were merely asked to learn the lists and were given the same amount of time as the people in the 'narrative' group to study them. Both groups could remember a particular list equally well immediately afterwards. However, when all the lists had been learned, recall of all 120 words was far superior in the group that had constructed narrative stories.

Obviously, mnemonic systems have their limitations. They are useful for memorising information that can be reduced to a list of words, but not all information can easily be converted to such a form. For example, if you were preparing to take an examination on the information in this chapter, figuring out how to encode it into lists would probably take you more time than studying and learning it by more traditional methods.

Questions to think about

Encoding in long-term memory

- Imagine that a friend comes to you for advice about studying for a forthcoming psychology exam. Half of the exam involves multiple-choice questions about key terms and the other half involves essay questions about the principles of cognitive psychology. Based on what you now know about encoding and memory, what suggestions might you offer regarding how to prepare for the test?

- Do you think that information is best remembered if presented in parts or altogether? Can you think of examples to illustrate your answer?

- There are some individuals who seem to have a remarkable memory (being able to identify the day of a given date from the past, for example) but say that they have learned techniques for performing such memory feats. Based on what you know, what could explain this enhanced memory performance?

- Can anyone improve their long-term memory? If so, to what extent? And how would you set up an experiment to evaluate this?

The organisation of long-term memory

Consolidation is not a simple, passive process. Many investigators believe that long-term memory consists of more than a simple pool of information. Instead, it is organised – different kinds of information are encoded differently and stored in different ways.

Episodic and semantic memory

Long-term memory contains more than exact records of sensory information that has been perceived. It also contains information that has been transformed – organised in terms of meaning. For example, the type of information that is personally meaningful to us (such as what we had for breakfast this morning or what we were doing last night) appears to be different from the type of information that is based on general knowledge (such as knowing the capitals of the world or the order in which Shakespeare wrote his plays). These two types of memory have been termed episodic and semantic memory, respectively, and the distinction was originally made by Tulving (1972). Episodic memory (or autobiographical memory) provides us with a record of our life experiences. Events stored there are autobiographical. Semantic memory consists of conceptual information (general knowledge); it is a long-term store of data, facts and information. Our knowledge of what psychology is, how human sensory systems operate and how behaviour is affected by its consequences are now part of our semantic memory. Semantic memories can interact with episodic ones.

The distinction between episodic and semantic memory reflects the fact that we make different uses of things we have learned: we describe things that happened to us or talk about facts we have learned. Episodic memory and semantic memory may not be two different memory systems; they may simply be different kinds of information stored in the same system. Calling a particular memory 'semantic' may simply mean that we have forgotten some details about when we learned the information, not that it is part of a different system. In fact, Tulving (1983, 1984) revised his original views of the two systems, suggesting that episodic memory is a part of semantic memory, not a separate, independent system.

Explicit and implicit memory

Explicit memory refers to memory of which we are aware; we know that we have learned something, and we can talk about what we have learned to others. Recognition and recall of material in explicit memory require active recollection of material that has been studied (McBride and Dosher, 1997). For example, we might ask participants to recall freely as many words as they can after being presented with a long list of them, or to indicate which stimuli from an array of visual stimuli were previously seen. Under these conditions, participants are explicitly instructed to recall or to recognise.

Implicit memory, however, does not appear to rely on conscious awareness. Instead, it is memory for information that is incidentally or unintentionally learned (Reber, 1989; Cleermans, 1993). It is sometimes referred to as being synonymous with procedural memory, the memory for knowing *how* to do things (like ride a bike, operate a computer keyboard, play a musical instrument). There is some question, however, over whether implicit and procedural memory are truly synonymous. Procedural memory implies that some conscious effort has been made towards learning a skill such as riding a bike or playing a musical instrument; implicit memory would assume that skills were learned without such conscious effort, which seems highly unlikely. Also, there seems to be little procedural input to performing a stem-completion task (described below), which taps implicit memory. There continues to be debate about the number of memory systems, and whether these memory systems are separate or different forms of the same system.

The acquisition of specific behaviours and skills is probably the most important form of implicit memory. Driving a car, turning the pages of a book, playing a musical instrument, dancing, throwing and catching a ball, sliding a chair backwards as we get up from the dinner table – all these skills involve co-ordination of movements with sensory information received from the environment and from our own moving body parts. We do not need to be able to describe these activities in order to perform them. We may not be aware of all the movements involved while we are performing them. Implicit memory may have evolved earlier than explicit memory.

A good example of learning without awareness is provided by an experiment conducted by Graf and Mandler (1984). These investigators showed people a list of six-letter words and had some of them engage in a task that involved elaborative processing: they were to think about each word and to decide how much they liked it. Other people were given a task that involved processing superficial features: they were asked to look at the words and decide whether they contained particular letters. Later, their explicit and implicit memories for the words were assessed. In both cases the basic task was the same, but the instructions to the subjects were different. People were shown the first three letters of each word. For example, if one of the words had been 'define', they would have been shown a card on which was printed 'def' (this is called a word-stem completion task). Several different six-letter words besides define begin with the letters 'def', such as 'deface', 'defame', 'defeat', 'defect', 'defend', 'defied' and

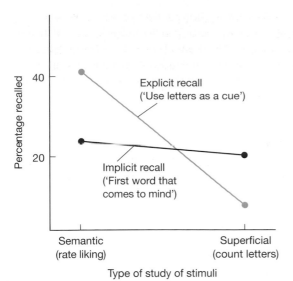

Figure 8.13

Explicit versus implicit memory. The graph shows the percentage of words recalled as a function of the type of study procedure. Deliberate processing improved performance of the explicit memory task but had little effect on the implicit memory task.

Source: Based on data from Graf, P. and Mandler, G., Activation makes words more accessible, but not necessarily more retrievable. *Journal of Verbal Learning and Verbal Behavior*, 1984, 23, 553–568.

'deform', so there are several possible responses. The experimenters assessed explicit memory by asking people to try to remember the words they had seen previously, using the first three letters as a hint. They assessed implicit memory by asking the people to say the first word that came to mind that started with the three letters on the card.

Deliberate processing (shallow or deep processing) had a striking effect on the explicit memory task but not on the implicit memory task. When people used the three letters as cues for deliberate retrieval, they were much more successful if they had thought about whether they liked the word than if they simply paid attention to the occurrence of particular letters. However, when people simply said the first word that came to mind, the way they had studied the words had little effect on the number of correct words that 'popped into their heads' (see Figure 8.13).

The biological basis of memory

Psychologists agree that long-term memory involves more or less permanent changes in the structure of the brain (Fuster, 1995; Horn, 1998). Much of what we know about the biology of human memory has been derived from studies of people who suffer from memory loss – amnesia – or from studies of animals in which amnesia is surgically induced to learn more about the specific brain mechanisms involved in memory (Parkin, 1996).

Amnesia

Damage to particular parts of the brain can permanently impair the ability to form new long-term memories. The inability to form new memories is called anterograde amnesia. The impairment in the ability to retrieve memories from before the brain injury is called retrograde amnesia. The brain damage can be caused by the effects of long-term alcoholism, severe malnutrition, stroke, head trauma or surgery (Parkin, 1996). In general, people with anterograde amnesia can still remember events that occurred prior to the damage. They can talk about things that happened before the onset of their amnesia, but they cannot remember what has happened since. They never learn the names of people they subsequently meet, even if they see them daily for years.

One of the most famous cases of anterograde amnesia is patient HM (Scoville and Milner, 1957; Milner, 1970; Corkin *et al.*, 1981). HM's case is interesting because his amnesia is both severe and relatively pure, being uncontaminated by other neuropsychological deficits. In 1953, when HM was twenty-seven, a neurosurgeon removed part of the temporal lobe on both sides of his brain. The surgery was performed to alleviate very severe epilepsy, which was not responding to drug treatment. The surgery cured the epilepsy, but it caused anterograde amnesia (this type of operation is no longer performed).

HM can carry on conversations and talk about general topics not related to recent events. He can also talk about his life prior to the surgery. However, he cannot talk about anything that has happened since 1953. He lives in an institution where he can be cared for and spends most of his time solving crossword puzzles and watching television. HM is aware that he has a memory problem. For example, here is his response to a researcher's question:

'Every day is alone in itself, whatever enjoyment I've had, and whatever sorrow I've had. … Right now, I'm wondering. Have I done or said anything amiss? You see, at this moment everything looks clear to me, but what happened just before? That's what worries me. It's like waking from a dream; I just don't remember. (Milner, 1970, p. 37)

Clearly, HM's problem lies in his ability to store new information in long-term memory, not in his short-term memory. His verbal short-term memory is normal; he can repeat seven numbers forwards and five numbers backwards, which is about average for the general population. At first, investigators concluded that the problem was in memory consolidation and that the part of the brain that was destroyed during surgery was essential for carrying out this process. But subsequent evidence suggests that the brain damage disrupts explicit memory without seriously damaging implicit memory.

Recently, however, psychologists have questioned whether HM has a pure memory deficit, that is, one that prevents the acquisition or consolidation of new information for explicit recall but leaves other cognitive abilities (such as the ability to produce and comprehend language) intact (Mackay *et al.*, 1998). They cite studies in which participants were asked to describe two meanings of visually presented ambiguous sentences (such as 'they talked about the problem with the mathematician') and these meanings were compared with those of HM. HM's descriptions were less clear and concise and more repetitive than controls'. Independent judges also rated HM's descriptions as less grammatical and comprehensible.

Other investigators have found that people with anterograde amnesia can learn to solve puzzles, perform visual discriminations, and make skilled movements that require hand–eye co-ordination (Squire, 1987). Clearly, their brains are still capable of undergoing the kinds of change that constitute long-term memory, but the people fail to remember having performed the tasks previously. For example, they may learn the task on one occasion. When, the next day, the experimenter brings them to the experimental apparatus and asks if they have ever seen it before, they say no. They have no explicit, episodic memory for having spent some time learning the task. But then they go on to perform the task well, clearly demonstrating the existence of implicit long-term memory.

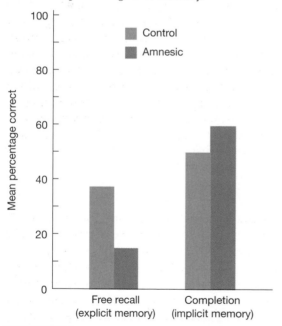

Figure 8.14

Explicit and implicit memory of amnesic patients and non-amnesic people. The performance of amnesic patients was impaired when they were instructed to try to recall the words they had previously seen but not when they were asked to say the first word that came into their minds.

Source: Adapted from Graf, P., Squire, L.R. and Mandler, G., The information that amnesic patients do not forget. *Journal of Experimental Psychology (Learning, Memory and Cognition)*, 1984, 10, 164–178.

Graf *et al.* (1984) showed lists of six-letter words to amnesic and non-amnesic people and asked them to rate how much they liked them. They then administered two types of memory test. In the explicit memory condition, they asked people to recall the words they had seen. In the implicit memory condition, they presented cards containing the first three letters of the words and asked people to say the first word that started with those letters that came into their minds. The amnesic people explicitly remembered fewer words than the non-amnesic people in the control group, but both groups performed well on the implicit memory task (see Figure 8.14).

The fact that amnesic patients can remember facts and describe experiences that occurred before the brain injury indicates that their ability to recall explicit memories acquired earlier is not severely disrupted. What parts of the brain are involved in the functions necessary for establishing new explicit memories? The most important part seems to be the hippocampus, a structure located deep within the temporal lobe that forms part of the limbic system.

The hippocampus

The hippocampus, like many structures of the brain, is not fully mature at birth. In fact, it is not until a child is 2–3 years old that most of these structures are fully developed. As a result, many cognitive activities, such as the formation of semantic memories, are not well developed until this age.

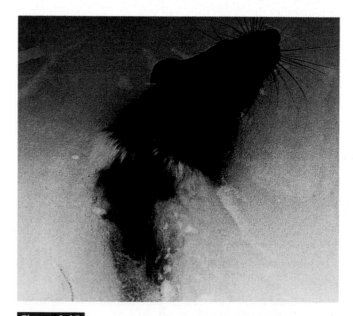

Figure 8.15

A rat immersed in milky water in Morris *et al.*'s 1982 experiment.

Source: Brash, S., Maranto, G., Murphy, W. and Walker, B. (1990) *How Things Work: The Brain*. Virginia: Time-Life Books. Copyright © 1990 by Time-Life Books.

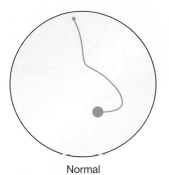

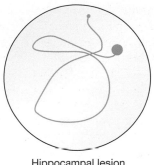

Normal   Neocortical lesion   Hippocampal lesion

Figure 8.16

The effects of damaging a rat's hippocampus on its ability to find a platform in opaque water after having initially been trained to locate the platform successfully.

Source: Morris, R.G.M. *et al.* (1982) Place navigation impaired in rats with hippocampal lesions. In *Nature*, 182, 297, 681–683. Reprinted with permission from *Nature*. Copyright 1982 Macmillan Magazines Limited.

One reason that few people remember events that occurred during infancy may be the immaturity of the hippocampus.

The hippocampus receives information from all association areas of the brain and sends information back to them. In addition, the hippocampus has two-way connections with many regions in the interior of the cerebral hemispheres. Thus, the hippocampal formation is in a position to 'know' – and to influence – what is going on in the rest of the brain (Gluck and Myers, 1995). Presumably, it uses this information to influence the establishment of explicit long-term memories.

The structure appears to be very important for navigating your way around the environment. To investigate this possibility, Morris *et al.* (1982) placed rats in a pool of milky water containing a platform just underneath the water. In order to avoid swimming constantly, the rats would have to find the platform which was hidden by the milky water (see Figure 8.15).

Eventually, through trial and error, the rats would find the platform. Then, the researchers performed a series of experimental ablations. One group of rats received lesions to the hippocampus, another received lesions to the cerebral cortex and another received no lesion. When the rats were then allowed into the pool, the pattern of behaviour seen in Figure 8.16 was observed. Notice how those rats with the hippocampus had extremely poor navigation compared with the cortex lesion and control group.

Evidence from neuroimaging

Much of our knowledge about the brain mechanisms which underlie memory has been derived from animal studies or from studies of individuals with brain injury, HM being one of the most famous case studies (in memory and in psychology). Recently, however, the development of neuroimaging and methods of analysing data from neuroimaging studies have provided evidence from healthy individuals suggesting that different regions of the brain are more involved than others in performing different types of memory task. As Horn (1998) asks, 'If memory consists of a mark made in the brain by a particular experience, where is the mark and what is its nature?'

Medial temporal lobe structures such as the hippocampus and the adjacent parahippocampal regions are important to memory performance. HM, as we have already seen, shows little short-term memory impairment but has problems in remembering items that were presented just a minute before. The hippocampus is also important for spatial orientation and awareness. Damage to this structure in animals causes severe impairments in their ability to navigate around their environment.

Spatial navigation

Recently, Maguire and her colleagues (Maguire *et al.*, 1997, 1998) examined the role of the hippocampus in memory for spatial relations in healthy individuals. In an unusual experiment, 11 London taxi drivers with 14 years' experience of driving participated in a positron emission tomography study in which they described the shortest legal route between two locations in London (Maguire *et al.*, 1997) – see Figure 8.17.

The taxi drivers were also asked to recall famous London landmarks (an examination of topographical memory). The activation during these tasks was compared with that during the recall of sequences from famous films. When the drivers described the route from one location to another, significant activation of the right hippocampus was found (but was not found with the landmark or film conditions), as Figure 8.18 illustrates.

This finding suggests that the right part of the hippocampus is important to retrieval of information which

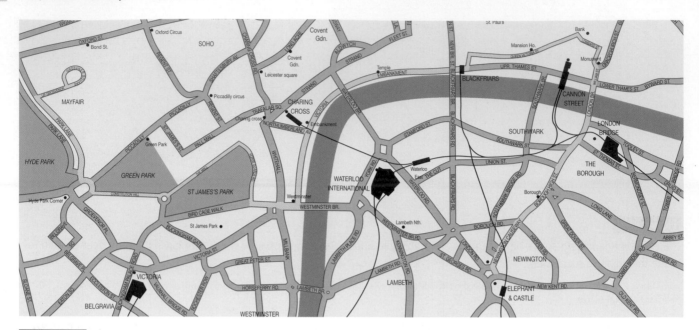

Figure 8.17

The route (in blue) that Maguire's taxi drivers had to describe.

Source: Maguire, E.A., Frackowiak, R.S.J. and Frith, C.D. (1997). Recalling routes around London: Activation of the right hippocampus in taxi drivers. *Journal of Neuroscience*, 17, 7103.
© Society for Neuroscience.

involves recall of movement in complex environments. In another PET experiment, individuals navigated their way around a familiar but complex virtual reality town (Maguire *et al.*, 1998). Activation of the right hippocampus was again associated with knowing accurately where places were located and navigating between them. The speed with which individuals navigated their environment was associated with right caudate nucleus activity. Also activated were the right inferior parietal and bilateral medial cortices, indicating that memory performance is not dependent solely on one structure.

Encoding and retrieval

Given that encoding and retrieval of information are two different cognitive tasks relating to the same function, you would expect these processes to have different underlying neural substrates. The frontal cortex is known to be involved in the operation of working memory (Goldman-Rakic, 1995; Courtney *et al.*, 1997) but may also be involved in learning and recall. Specifically, the left prefrontal cortex is activated during learning and encoding tasks whereas the right is activated by recall tasks (Tulving *et al.*, 1994; Nyberg *et al.*, 1996; Fletcher *et al.*, 1998a,b).

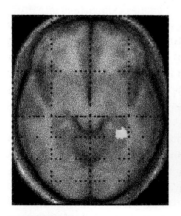
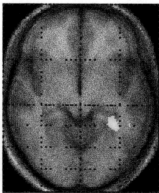
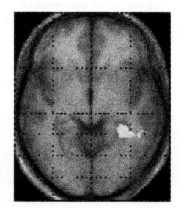

Figure 8.18

Areas of the brain activated by the recall of routes. Note the activation of the right hippocampus.

Source: Maguire, E.A., Frackowiak, R.S.J. and Frith, C.D. (1997). Recalling routes around London: Activation of the right hippocampus in taxi drivers. *Journal of Neuroscience*, 17, 7103.
© Society for Neuroscience.

The encoding and retrieval of both verbal or non-verbal material are associated with this lateralisation of brain activation in prefrontal regions (Shallice *et al.*, 1994; Haxby *et al.*, 1996). The role of the left prefrontal cortex has been thought to be related to the way in which we organise information. That is, encoding is dependent on our semantic memory, and the activation of the prefrontal cortex reflects the process whereby we group items on the basis of some characteristic or attribute (Gershberg and Shimamura, 1995). To test this hypothesis, Fletcher *et al.* (1998a) conducted a PET study in which participants listened to words that were either semantically organised or disorganised but had to be put into categories. As expected, the condition in which the list was already organised produced least amount of left prefrontal cortex activation whereas the task requiring the participant to generate an organisational structure resulted in greatest activation. A distractor task reduced activation during the organisation task but not during any other encoding task, suggesting that the organisational, executive role of the left prefrontal cortex can be disrupted.

Remembering

If encoding and retrieval are successful, would greater brain activation be seen during encoding for those stimuli that were successfully encoded or for all stimuli regardless of how well they were retrieved? There is evidence from EEG studies that a specific type of electrical activity, EEG theta, is greater during the encoding of successfully retrieved words than unsuccessfully retrieved ones (Klimesch, 1997). In a recent neuroimaging study, Brewer *et al.* (1998) examined differences in activation found in the parahippocampal gyrus and the right frontal area during the encoding of visual stimuli that had been subsequently remembered or forgotten. Individuals were asked to view a series of indoor or outdoor scenes and decide whether each scene depicted outdoors or indoors. Thirty minutes later, they were given a recognition test and asked to indicate whether they remembered the scene, thought the scene was familiar but not well remembered or was forgotten. Memory for the scenes was predicted by frontal and parahippocampal activation; greater activation was found for the remembered images.

A similar finding was reported by Wagner *et al.* (1998) but for verbal material. They found that the ability to remember verbal experiences accurately was predicted by activation of the left prefrontal and temporal cortices (including the parahippocampal and fusiform gyri). The activation of the left prefrontal cortex during successful encoding is similar to that reported by Fletcher *et al.* (1998b).

Together, these new recent findings suggest that certain parts of the cortex, especially the temporal and frontal cortex, and the subcortex (the hippocampal formation) play important roles in the encoding, retrieval and remem-

bering of material in healthy individuals. With animal and brain injury data, these findings can contribute to a better understanding of the way in which the brain allows us to acquire, remember and retrieve memories.

Questions to think about

The organisation of long-term memory

- Does it make sense to say that there are different types of memory for different kinds of information and that different kinds of information require different types of encoding? Can you propose alternative ways for thinking about how long-term memory might be organised (in contrast to the system we have described in this chapter)?

- Are long-term memories for smells, words and pictures organised differently?

- In the past two decades, many researchers have wondered whether non-human animals can think. Animals can remember and forget information. Does this mean that they can also think? What sort of evidence would you need to gather in order to be able to say that because animals possess memory, they also can think?

- To what extent is the type of brain activation seen during memory processing dependent on the sort of information we encode and the type of retrieval we undertake? Would you expect the brain to be activated differently during a free recall and a recognition task?

- What do the results of neuroimaging studies tell us about the localisation of memory in the brain?

Remembering

Remembering is an automatic process. The word 'automatic' means 'acting by itself'. But this definition implies that no special effort is involved. What is automatic is the retrieval of information from memory in response to the appropriate stimulus. What sometimes requires effort is the attempt to come up with the thoughts (the internal stimuli) that cause the information to be retrieved.

The retrieval of implicit memories is automatic: when the appropriate stimulus occurs, it automatically evokes the appropriate response. Explicit memories can be retrieved automatically. Whisper your name to yourself. How did you manage to remember what your name is? How did you retrieve the information needed to move your lips in the proper sequence? Those questions cannot be answered by introspection. The information just leaps out at us when the proper question is asked (or, more generally, when the appropriate stimulus is encountered).

Reading provides a particularly compelling example of the automatic nature of memory retrieval. When an experienced reader looks at a familiar word, the name of the word occurs immediately, and so does the meaning. In fact, it is difficult to look at a word and not think of its name. Figure 8.19 contains a list of words that can be used to demonstrate a phenomenon known as the Stroop effect (Stroop, 1935; MacLeod, 1992). Look at the words in Figure 8.19 and, as quickly as you can, say the names of the colours in which the words are printed; do not read the words themselves.

Most people cannot completely ignore the words and simply name the colours; the tendency to think of the words and pronounce them is difficult to resist. The Stroop effect indicates that even when we try to suppress a well practised memory, it tends to be retrieved automatically when the appropriate stimulus occurs.

But what about the fact that some memories seem to be difficult to recall? For most people, remembering information is effortless and smooth. It is something we do unconsciously and automatically – most of the time. Occasionally, though, our memory of a name or a place or something else fails. The experience is often frustrating because we know that the information is 'in there somewhere' but we just cannot seem to get it out. This phenomenon is known as the tip-of-the-tongue phenomenon. It was first studied carefully during the 1960s (Brown and McNeill, 1966), and since then, we have learned a great deal about it (Jones, 1989; A.S. Brown, 1991). It is a common, if not universal, experience; it can occur about once a week and increases with age; it often involves proper names and knowing the first letter of the word; and is solved during the experience about 50 per cent of the time.

The active search for stimuli that will evoke the appropriate memory, as exemplified in the tip-of-the-tongue phenomenon, has been called recollection (Baddeley, 1982). Recollection may be aided by contextual variables, including physical objects, suggestions, or other verbal stimuli. These contextual variables are called retrieval cues. The usefulness of these retrieval cues often depends on encoding specificity. The encoding specificity principle states that information can only be retained if it has been stored and the way in which it is retrieved depends on how it was stored. One famous example is that of encoding and retrieving material above and under water. Godden and Baddeley (1975) asked skilled scuba divers to learn lists of words either under water or on land. The divers' ability to recall the lists was later tested in either the same or a different environment. The variable of interest was where subjects learned the list: in or out of the water. When lists were learned underwater, they were recalled much better underwater than on land, and lists learned on land were recalled better on land than in the water. The context in which information is learned or processed, therefore, influences our ability to recollect that information.

How long does memory last?

In 1895, Hermann Ebbinghaus reported the results of the first experiment to determine memory duration. Using himself as a participant, Ebbinghaus memorised thirteen nonsense syllables such as 'dax', 'wuj', 'lep' and 'pib'. He then studied how long it took him to relearn the original list after intervals varying from a few minutes up to thirty-one days. Figure 8.20 shows what he found. Much of what

blue blue **blue green**
green **yellow** red
yellow yellow blue
red green yellow
yellow green **yellow**
yellow **red yellow**
green blue **yellow**
red blue green **green**
blue blue **green red**

The Stroop effect. Name the colour in which the words are printed as quickly as you can; you will find it difficult to ignore what the words say.

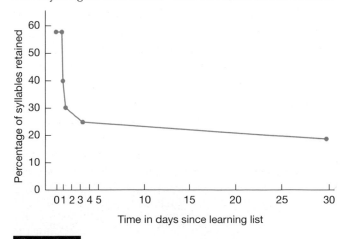

Figure 8.20

Ebbinghaus's (1885) forgetting curve.

Source: Adapted from Ebbinghaus, H., *Memory: A contribution to experimental psychology* (H.A. Ruger and C.E. Bussenius, trans.), 1885/1913, Teacher's College, Columbia University, New York.

he learned was forgotten very quickly – usually within a day or two. But even after thirty-one days, he could still recall some of the original information.

Ebbinghaus's research dealt with remembering nonsense syllables. What about remembering aspects of real life? For example, how long might you remember the important experiences of your childhood? Or the information in this book? This topic is taken up in the 'Psychology in action' section.

Psychology in action

How much of this book will you remember in twelve years' time?

As a student of psychology, you are currently studying a variety of psychological topics, from cognition and emotion to child development and biopsychology. You are also probably experiencing different ways of being assessed in these topics. You might be required to write an essay, to complete regular multiple choice questionnaires (MCQs) and will certainly sit exams in which one of these two forms of assessment will be used.

But how much of the material you revise for exams or coursework will you retain in, say one week, one month, one year or twelve years' time? And will the amount of information you retain depend on the type of course that you do? Will you retain more from research methods, cognitive psychology or physiological psychology courses?

In a well-known study, Bahrick and his colleagues (1975) investigated how much information about their classmates (such as faces or names), graduates would remember 25 years after graduation. Bahrick found that the ability to free-recall classmates' names and to generate a name from a photo declined over time. The longer the retention interval (or RI, the period between encoding and retrieval), the greater the decline. The correct recognition of faces and names and the matching of names to faces, however, was fairly robust. Ninety per cent of responses were correct over the first fifteen years of retention (although accuracy, again, declined when the RI became longer). Bahrick (1984a) also reported that retention for Spanish learned at school declined in the first six years after graduating, stabilised for the next 35 years and then declined thereafter (see Figure 8.21).

Bahrick argued that the period of stability from 6 to 35 years represents a 'permastore'; this was a store of knowledge that was resistant to forgetting and which must have been learned deeply. An alternative interpretation, however, was suggested by Neisser (1984). He suggested that individuals have a schematic representation of a 'knowledge domain', that is, specific knowledge is not stored in a permanent way, but ways of representing that knowledge allow the retrieval of information. On the basis of this view, conceptual knowledge should be better retained (and retrieved) than would, say, straightforward facts.

To test this hypothesis explicitly, Martin Conway and his colleagues from the University of Bristol and the Open University in England set up an ambitious experiment in which they measured students' retention of knowledge of cognitive psychology over twelve years (Conway et al., 1991). Over twelve years (between 1978 and 1989), the experimenters examined respondents' memory for the proper names of researchers, concepts and conceptual relations in cognitive psychology. They found that memory declined in the first 36 months, then stabilised, a finding that was not affected by age: both young and old showed the same pattern (Cohen et al., 1992). However, the recall and recognition of proper names declined more rapidly than did memory for concepts. Why? If you accept Neisser's position, conceptual information should be better retained because memory is organised in such a way as to facilitate the retention of this type of information. Cohen (1990) further suggests that proper names lack the semantic depth necessary for encoding concepts. Proper names do not need to be represented in abstract form and do not fall within a scheme of knowledge.

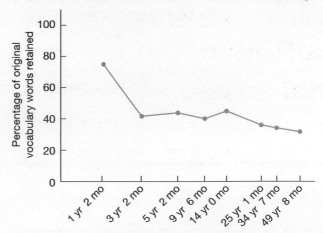

Figure 8.21

The forgetting curve for Spanish vocabulary.

Source: Adapted from Bahrick, H.P., Semantic memory content in permastore: Fifty years of Spanish learned in school. *Journal of Experimental Psychology (General)*, 1984, 113, 1–29.

Psychology in action continued

However, Bahrick (1992) suggested that the amount or distribution of practice in the Conway *et al.* study was not well controlled. Conway *et al.* (1992) re-analysed their data but this time, instead of using the composite mark of exam and coursework as they did in their earlier experiment, they separated these marks. From our understanding of the effects of massed and distributed practice, we might predict that coursework would be a better predictor of retention than would exam performance because the learning for the former is distributed across the term whereas learning for the exam is, arguably, massed (being crammed). In fact, this is exactly the pattern Conway *et al.* found and argued that examinations were not 'sensitive to the amount of knowledge acquired'.

However, is the grade a measure of how much material a student knows or a measure of how a student uses that material? Conway *et al.* argued that the exam may not measure the latter. It is also useful to think about how coursework and examination demands differ in other ways. Psychologically, the experience of sitting an end-of-term exam is stressful, a psychological factor that may not be in evidence when preparing coursework in cognitive psychology. In addition, although the assumption is implicit, there is no way of knowing whether those sitting the exam did, in fact, 'cram' and indulged in massed practice, because this was not measured. And what of different types of coursework assessment? Conway *et al.* point out that the coursework mark was itself a composite of different marks. What would we learn if we were able to examine performance across a range of different courses in psychology?

Using a different protocol, Conway *et al.* (1997) examined whether the type of course studied influenced the degree of knowledge retained. Importantly, they also sought to find out whether students themselves regarded the knowledge they learned as being 'known' or just 'remembered'. This distinction reflects the difference between deep and shallow processing. Would students carry on 'remembering' throughout the course or would they end up 'knowing'?

First-year British undergraduates completed multiple choice questionnaires after a series of introductory psychology, physiological psychology, cognitive psychology, and social and developmental psychology courses, two research

---

Table 8.1   Some typical MCQs used in Conway *et al.*'s study

Introduction to Psychology

In Pavlov's famous experiments, hungry dogs learned to salivate to the presence of a light. In these studies, what was the *unconditioned response* (UCR)?

(a) food   (b) the light   (c) salivation

Remember   Know   Familiar   Guess

Patients with neurological damage to Broca's area can no longer:

(a) produce fluent speech
(b) understand spoken language
(c) correctly perceive spoken words

Remember   Know   Familiar   Guess

Research Methods (Part I)

In a study of antidepressant drugs and memory, what is the group taking the drugs called?

(a) placebo   (b) control   (c) experimental

Remember   Know   Familiar   Guess

When a test measures what it claims to measure, it is:

(a) reliable   (b) valid   (c) sensitive

Remember   Know   Familiar   Guess

methods courses and a course of laboratory classes. There was also a delayed retest period for the research methods courses. Unlike previous experiments, this time Conway *et al.* asked respondents to indicate for each MCQ item whether they remembered the answer, knew it, thought it seemed familiar or just guessed. Examples of the MCQ items are presented in Table 8.1. If you have read all the chapters so far, you should be able to answer these.

Conway *et al.* found that there was a significant difference between the responses of good and poor students. The better students were characterised by more 'remember' responses for MCQs based on lecture courses. On the research methods courses, however, they were characterised as having 'known' more. According to the experimenters, this 'knowing' indicates a shift from remembering to knowing. They describe this as the remember-to-know shift (R-K shift) where there is a shift from shallow, episodic memory to deep, semantic memory. Why, then, did better students not 'know' more after their lecture courses? One reason is that the lecture courses contained more topics and that there was, therefore, greater variability in the types of knowledge domain to be learned (Conway *et al.*, 1997). Also, the research methods courses involved a strong degree of repetition (as research methods courses do) and problem solving is integral to the course: these factors might promote the R-K shift.

Does this R-K shift occur in other domains? Think about a novel that you read a few years ago, better still one that you studied for an English qualification at school. How much of this novel do you think you would remember today? Nicola Stanhope, Gillian Cohen and their colleagues examined this directly by looking at the long-term retention of a novel,

Charles Dickens's *Hard Times*, studied at university (Stanhope *et al.*, 1993). Stanhope *et al.* found that the free recall of names and character roles declined quickly in the first few months after study, with names being forgotten more quickly. Those events in the novel regarded as most important were more resistant to forgetting, again indicating that schematic knowledge (events) is retained more deeply and more accurately than is non-schematic knowledge (names).

What, therefore, can we conclude about long-term retention of knowledge learned during a degree? First, it appears that coursework may be a better predictor of retention than examination for cognitive psychology courses. However, it should be remembered that there are different types of coursework. Would an essay, a project or an MCQ be a better coursework predictor? Think about this for a moment. Which do you think would be the better predictor and why? Would any of the theories discussed in this section explain your conclusion? Secondly, non-schematic knowledge (such as the names of psychologists) declines more greatly than schematic knowledge (such as conceptual information). Thirdly, better students appear to remember more of non-research methods psychology lecture courses and know more from research methods courses. One reason for this is that there is a shift from remembering to knowing, from episodic to semantic memory.

Finally, in answer to the question posed in the title of this section, you'll probably remember the concepts in the book better than the names of psychologists (because these require a greater depth of processing) and you'll remember the more familiar names (because of repetition, and repetition promotes retention). See how you get on in twelve years' time.

Reconstruction: remembering as a creative process

Much of what we recall from long-term memory is not an accurate representation of what actually happened previously. It is a plausible account of what might have happened or even of what we think should have happened. An early experiment by Bartlett (1932) called attention to this fact. He had people read a story or essay or look at a picture. Then he asked them on several later occasions to retell the prose passage or draw the picture. Each time, the people 'remembered' the original a little differently. If the original story had contained peculiar and unexpected sequences of events, people tended to retell it in a more coherent and sensible fashion, as if their memories had been revised to make the information accord more closely with their own

conceptions of reality. Bartlett concluded that people remember only a few striking details of an experience and that during recall they reconstruct the missing portions in accordance with their own expectations.

Many studies have confirmed Bartlett's conclusions and have extended his findings to related phenomena. Experiments by Spiro (1977, 1980) illustrated that people will remember even a rather simple story in different ways, according to their own conceptions of reality. Two groups of people read a story about an engaged couple in which the man was opposed to having children. In one version, the woman was upset when she learned his opinion because she wanted to have children. In the other version, the woman also did not want to have children.

After reading the story, people were asked to fill out some forms. While collecting the forms, the experimenter either said nothing more about the story or 'casually mentioned' that the story was actually a true one and added one of two different endings: the couple got married and have been happy ever since, or the couple broke up and never saw each other again. Two days, three weeks or six weeks later, the participants were asked to recall the story they had read. If at least three weeks had elapsed, people who had heard an ending that contradicted the story tended to 'remember' information that resolved the conflict. For example, if they had read that the woman was upset to learn that the man did not want children but were later told that the couple was happily married, people were likely to 'recall' something that would have resolved the conflict, such as that the couple had decided to adopt a child rather than have one of their own. If people had read that the woman also did not want children but were later told that the couple broke up, then they were likely to 'remember' that there was a difficulty with one set of parents. In contrast, people who had heard an ending that was consistent with the story they had read did not remember any extra facts; they did not need them to make sense of the story. For example, if they had heard that the couple disagreed about having a child and later broke up, no new 'facts' had to be added.

When asking people to recall details from the story, Spiro also asked them to indicate how confident they were about the accuracy of particular details. He found that people were most confident about details that had actually not occurred but had been added to make more sense of the story. Thus, a person's confidence in the accuracy of a particular memory is not necessarily a good indication of whether the event actually occurred.

Recently, however, Wynn and Logie (1998) have suggested that the folk tale in Bartlett's study was poorly reproduced because it was written in an unusual style. Consequently, connections between parts of the story were difficult to make. To enhance the ecological validity of the stimulus material, Wynn and Logie quizzed undergraduates at two month intervals about an incident at the beginning of the academic year. The experimenters found that memories were resistant to change over time. However, although this study demonstrates that some memories (if distinctive) can be accurately recalled over time, it is not a direct replication of Bartlett's experiment. Furthermore, memories can be manipulated to the extent that false information introduced at recall can lead to this false information being incorporated into memory. This has important consequences for eyewitness identification.

Eyewitness testimony

On 4 October 1992, an El Al plane lost its engine after take-off from Amsterdam Schiphol Airport, returned to the airport but lost height and crashed into an eleven storey apartment building. Ten months later, Crombag *et al.*

(1996) questioned 193 individuals about the crash which was widely reported in the news but was not actually filmed. When individuals were asked if they saw the plane hit the building, 55 per cent said that they had (they had not been present at the time of the accident); 59 per cent said that the fire started immediately on impact. In a follow-up study, 68 per cent said they had seen the crash and 67 per cent of participants said that they saw the plane hit the building horizontally (in fact, it hit the building vertically).

This experiment and those of Elizabeth Loftus and her colleagues (Loftus, 1997) suggests that our recollections of events may not be infallible. Loftus, for example, has reported that the kinds of questions used to elicit information after an event has been experienced can have a major effect on what people remember. Loftus's research shows that even subtle changes in a question can affect people's recollections. For example, Loftus and Palmer (1974) showed people films of car accidents and asked them to estimate vehicles' speeds when they 'contacted/hit/bumped/collided/smashed' each other. People's estimates of the vehicles' speeds were directly related to the force of the impact suggested by the verb, such as 'hit', that appeared in the question (see Figure 8.22). That is, the more expressive and dramatic the verb, the greater the estimated speed.

In a similar experiment, when people were asked a week after viewing the film whether they saw any broken glass at the scene (there was none), people in the 'smashed' group were most likely to say yes. Thus, a leading question that encouraged them to remember the vehicles going faster also encouraged them to remember that they saw non-existent broken glass. The question appears to have modified the memory itself.

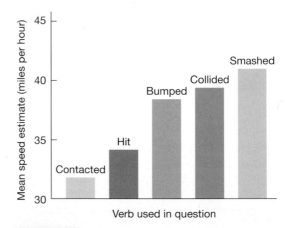

Figure 8.22

Leading questions and recall. Mean estimated speed of vehicles as recalled by people in the study of Loftus and Palmer (1974).

Source: Based on data from Loftus, E.F. and Palmer, J.C., Reconstruction of automobile destruction: An example of the interaction between language and memory. *Journal of Verbal Learning and Verbal Behavior*, 1974, 13, 585–589.

Another experiment indicated that even very subtle leading questions can affect people's recollections. Loftus and Zanni (1975) showed people short films of an accident involving several vehicles. Some people were asked, 'did you see a broken headlight?'; others were asked, 'did you see the broken headlight?' The particular question biased the people's responses: although the film did not show a broken headlight, twice as many people who heard the article 'the' said that they remembered seeing one.

These are not the only examples of the ways in which memories can be altered. Individuals can be misled into thinking that a 'stop' sign was a 'give way' sign (Loftus *et al.*, 1978) and that a bare-handed thief wore gloves (Zaragoza and Mitchell, 1996). Experiments such as these have important implications for eyewitness testimony in courts of law. Wells and Seelau (1995) illustrate this point with the following examples:

'In 1984, Frederick Rene Dange was identified from a set of photographs and served 10 years in a Californian prison for rape, kidnapping, robbery and murder he did not commit. Dange was released in 1994 after a DNA test proved his innocence. In 1980, James Newsome was convicted of murder on the basis of eyewitness evidence. Fifteen years later, he was released after his fingerprints were submitted to new computer technology that implicated someone else as the murderer.'

The fallibility of eyewitness testimony was highlighted by Rattner (1988) in a review of 205 cases of wrongful arrest. Rattner found that 52 per cent of these cases were associated with mistaken eyewitness testimony. Similar data have been reported more recently (Connors *et al.*, 1996)

Experiments like those of Loftus indicate that learning new information and recalling it later are active processes – information is not placed in a mental filing cabinet and picked up later. We organise and integrate information in terms of what we already know about life and have come to expect about particular experiences. Thus, when we recall the memory later, it may contain information that was not part of the original experience.

At first, this phenomenon may appear to be maladaptive because it means that eyewitness testimony cannot be regarded as infallible, even when a witness is trying to be truthful. However, it probably reflects the fact that information about an episode can be more efficiently stored by means of a few unique details. The portions of an episode that are common to other experiences, and hence resemble information already stored in long-term memory, need not be retained. If every detail of every experience had to be encoded uniquely in long-term memory, perhaps we would run out of storage space. Unfortunately, this process sometimes leads to instances of faulty remembering.

Accurate recall of information can have serious implications in situations outside the laboratory. Think of witnessing a crime, for example, and having to report evidence as testimony. How would you be able to prevent yourself from committing the reconstructive errors described above? Cognitive psychologists have recently applied the principles of cognitive psychology to an issue which has serious and direct real-life consequences, the police interview. This is discussed in the 'Psychology in action' section.

Another aspect of the fallibility of memory retrieval has been recently highlighted by cases of 'recovered' memories. These memories are (usually damaging) recollections allegedly repressed since childhood but have been uncovered during psychotherapy. The issues involved in this controversy together with an assessment of the evidence for and against recovered memories are discussed in the 'Controversies in psychological science' section below.

Psychology in action

The cognitive interview

Imagine that you are a witness to a violent crime. The crime itself is unexpected and quite frightening. You are asked by the police to provide a statement and are interviewed about what you saw. This interview could occur days or even weeks after the incident. How much of the information do you think you would be able to recall during the interview? And would the format of the interview enhance or impair your ability to recall detail and events?

These questions have been answered fairly recently by new developments in an area of research known as forensic or criminological psychology which, as we saw in Chapter 1, is the study of how psychological principles can be applied to crime (the event, the victim, the perpetrator and the law).

The reliability of witness testimony is clearly important to the victims and to the perpetrators of crime. Normally, law enforcement officers will quiz witnesses about the situational factors surrounding the event and ask questions about the atmosphere and the degree of stress they experienced. Witnesses will be asked to describe the incident and to answer specific questions about features of the crime (such as details of stolen goods, for example).

Psychology in action continued

Psychology in action continued

New research, however, suggests that there may be a better method of eliciting information from witnesses. This better method is called the cognitive interview. Originally conceived by Geiselman *et al.* (1984) and later refined (Fisher *et al.*, 1987), the cognitive interview utilises information about the way in which memory operates and applies it in the form of four retrieval techniques: (1) establishing the context in which the crime occurred, (2) retrieving details, however minor, (3) recalling events in a different order, and (4) changing perspective. Following the application of these techniques and the attainment of a fairly complete version of events, questions will then be asked about the suspect's physical appearance, objects, name, features of speech and so on. Thus, the cognitive interview relies on the principle of encoding specificity which we discussed earlier.

Compared with the standard interview format, the cognitive interview has been found to produce more correct information about persons and events with no significant increase in incorrect responses (Gwyer and Clifford, 1997). On average, there is an increase of 35 per cent more information from adults in cognitive interview compared with controls who were required to remember as much information as possible (Geiselman *et al.*, 1984, 1985). The technique has been used successfully in Europe, America and Australia (Fisher and Geiselman, 1992; Bekerian and Dennett, 1993).

The evidence indicates that the technique can certainly help adult witnesses recover more detail of the crime than would the standard interview. Could the technique be used just as well with child witnesses? It is commonly thought that children make poor witnesses because they are too suggestible and that their testimony can be changed either through slight pressure, memory failure or misleading suggestion (Flin, 1995; Qin *et al.*, 1997; Bruck and Ceci, 1995). Younger children are prone to give less complete testimonies than are older children (Kail, 1990). Would the cognitive interview, therefore, produce a more reliable statement from children than would a standard interview?

In one experiment, 7–12 year old children were shown a film of an off-licence robbery and were interviewed three days later (Geiselman and Padilla, 1988). The cognitive interview yielded significantly more correct information than did the standard interview. Similarly, Saywitz *et al.* (1992) questioned 7–11 year old children about an incident involving two children and a man. The cognitive interview yielded 21 per cent more correct information than did the standard interview with no significant increase in the number of incorrect answers. Other findings from studies of witnessing road traffic accidents have shown the same pattern of results (Chapman and Perry, 1995).

An interesting question is whether all four techniques need to be applied with child witnesses. This question was addressed by Hayes and Delamothe (1997) in an experiment which used only the 'context reinstatement' and 'retrieval of detail' parts of the cognitive interview. Evidence suggests that changing perspective is difficult for 7 year old children to do (Memon *et al.*, 1983; Bekerian and Dennett, 1993) and that the ability to organise events temporally increases with age (Farrar and Goodman, 1992). The two techniques chosen, therefore, might be more appropriate for young children.

The experimenters exposed a group of 5 and 7 year old children and a group of 9–11 year old children to a TV show in which children were trying to prevent smugglers from stealing artifacts from a Mediterranean island. When recall was tested three days later, those in the cognitive interview condition showed higher levels of accurate recall than did those in the standard condition. When children were given misleading suggestions, however, the type of interview had no effect on incorrect answers given which incorporated this misleading information. The researchers do caution that the experiment may not be a truly valid measure of the cognitive interview's reliability in children because the children watched a TV and were not directly involved in witnessing real-life crime and because the retention intervals and the interviews were also shorter than they would be if a real-life crime had been witnessed.

The evidence suggests, however, that the cognitive interview can be an effective tool in forensic psychology and illustrates one of the ways in which research from the psychology of memory can be applied to practical effect.

Remembering and interference

Although long-term memory is durable, it may also be susceptible to interference. The finding that some memories may interfere with the retrieval of others is well established. An early study by Jenkins and Dallenbach (1924) showed that people are less likely to remember information after an interval of wakefulness than after an interval of sleep, presumably because of new memories that are formed when one is awake (see Figure 8.23).

Subsequent research soon showed that there are two types of interference in retrieval. Sometimes we experience retroactive interference – when we try to retrieve information, other information, which we have learned more recently, interferes. You may have a hard time recalling your old telephone number because a new one has replaced it. When memories that interfere with retrieval are formed after the learning that is being tested, we experience retroactive interference.

At other times, retrieval is impaired by proactive interference, in which our ability to recall new information is reduced because of information we learned previously. Figure 8.24 illustrates the experimental procedure used to examine the effects of proactive interference.

In this procedure, the experimental group learns the words in both list A and list B. The control group learns only the words in list B. Both groups then experience a retention interval before they are asked to recall the words in list B. If the experimental group recalls fewer words in list B during the test than does the control group, proactive interference is said to have occurred.

As reasonable and intuitive as the principle of interference may be, it has not gone unchallenged. Researchers agree that interference can affect retrieval, but some argue that the kinds of recall task people are asked to perform in the laboratory are most likely to be affected by interference. In real life, such effects may not be so powerful. For example, meaningful prose, such as the kind found in novels, is resistant to interference.

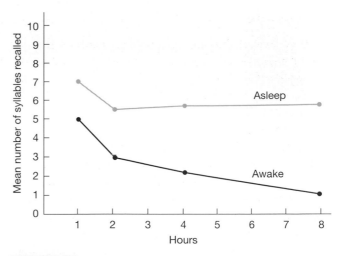

Figure 8.23

Interference in memory retrieval. The mean number of nonsense syllables recalled after sleeping or staying awake for varying intervals of time.

Source: Adapted from Jenkins, J.G. and Dallenbach, K.M., Oblivescence during sleep and waking. *American Journal of Psychology*, 1924, 35, 605–612.

Remembering and emotion

Research suggests that recall of memory is better when people's moods or emotional states match their emotional states when they originally learned the material. This phenomenon is called state-dependent memory. The experimental procedure used in tests of state-dependent memory usually requires manipulation of a person's mood by hypnosis (Bower, 1981), through drugs (Eich *et al.*, 1975), or by changing environmental contexts, as exemplified earlier in the study involving scuba divers who learned word lists either under water or on land (Godden and Baddeley, 1975). Next, the person is given a list of items to memorise. Later, when the person may or may not be experiencing the same mental or emotional state, he or she is asked to recall the items on the list.

Retroactive Interference

Group	Initial learning	Retention interval	Retention test
Experimental	Learn A	Learn B	Recall A
Control	Learn A		Recall A

Proactive Interference

Group	Initial learning		Retention interval	Retention test
Experimental	Learn A	Learn B		Recall B
Control		Learn B		Recall B

Figure 8.24

Retroactive and proactive interference illustrated.

Controversies in psychological science

Are 'recovered memories' genuine memories?

The issue

In recent years, one of the most controversial aspects of psychotherapy has been the claimed recovery of childhood memories by the client during therapy. These recovered memories are usually negative and the content includes reference to physical or sexual abuse, usually by a parent and most commonly by the client's father. These memories are thought to have been repressed because they occurred very early on in childhood and are accessible only by therapy and prompting during therapy. Many therapists with clients reporting recovered memories use different techniques to help the client to 'regress'. This idea is not new. Freud had argued that we repress thoughts and memories of events that are psychologically harmful to us and that such thoughts could be accessed only through psychotherapy (in Freud's case, psychoanalysis).

The current controversy, however, has revolved around the truthfulness or validity of these recovered memories. Are they genuinely repressed recollections of actual events, or are they events planted there by therapists? Are they distorted versions of actual memories? In short, are recovered memories real memories? Answers to such questions have very real practical consequences, especially for the accused. So great has the hostility towards such recovered memories become that two societies – one in Philadelphia founded in 1992, the other in the UK founded in 1993 – now exist which campaign against such 'false memories' and act as support groups for other 'falsely' accused individuals. The British Psychological Society became so concerned at the increased incidence of reported recovered memories that it set up a working party to determine the circumstances under which memories such as these might be true or might be false (Morton et al., 1995).

The evidence

Those individuals who report recovering memories seem to have fairly similar characteristics. Surveys reveal that the parent and the child (the adult accuser) are well educated and have high socioeconomic status (Wakefield and Underwager, 1992). A survey of the Philadelphia Society suggests that the accuser is normally female, in her thirties and attending therapy for psychological problems. The most common recovered memory is sexual abuse by the father. A similar demographic pattern has also been observed in societies from the UK (Gudjonsson, 1997) and New Zealand (Goodyear-Smith et al., 1997).

To further explore the nature of these memories and the characteristics of accused and accuser, Gudjonsson (1997) surveyed 282 members of the British False Memory Society. A number of findings in his study make interesting reading. Accusations were made predominantly towards the father, the most common recollections involved rape, sex, genital touching and oral sex, most of the accusers were female (87 per cent), most of the events were alleged to have occurred before the child's eighth birthday (71 per cent), most memories involved multiple episodes, most of the accusers indicated that the memory had been 'forgotten' and then recovered and most of the accusations were made during therapy (93 per cent). Around one-fifth of all accusations were reported to the police or to social services departments.

The conclusions of the survey should, as the author himself suggests, be treated with some caution because the study asked for information from the accused only and did not attempt to survey the accusers and did not include a control group of non-accused families. The results, however, are very similar to those reported in other national samples. Three main issues emerge from such work:

1 Are the memories true recollections or beliefs?
2 Are therapists responsible for provoking and encouraging false memories?
3 Can memories be manipulated so that details of some events can be changed or implanted in memory?

The memory/belief distinction is an interesting one and was suggested by Lindsay and Read (1994) to account for the nature of the recollections of some clients. Gudjonsson (1997) provides an account from a family about the accusations of their son. One mother claimed: 'Our son has no specific memories of any abuse. He believed he had "suppressed" these memories. He felt that the only explanation for his current feeling of depression must be the result of having been sexually abused by my husband when he was a child.' Again, it should be remembered that this view cannot be corroborated because we do not have the accuser's account. The belief in the events having occurred, however, is probably central to explaining how recovered memories may be false, and we shall come to this in a short while.

The responsibility of the therapists in such cases has also been questioned and the evidence has been reviewed by Critchlow (1998). A survey of experienced psychotherapists found that 70 per cent used some method of memory recovery such as hypnosis and guided imagery, with 58 per cent using two or more methods (Poole *et al.*, 1995). A significant correlation is found between the number of methods used and the percentage of women reporting memories of childhood sexual abuse. Intriguingly, if you compare the statistics from those individuals who have genuinely been sexually abused, some interesting discrepancies arise. Russell (1988) reports that of 930 cases of genuine sexual abuse, 54 per cent reported some form of sexual abuse before the age of eighteen; only 4.5 per cent, however, reported abuse by fathers or stepfathers. The incidence of accusations against fathers is substantially higher in recovered cases, which raises questions about the validity of recovered memory cases.

Can therapy or suggestion make an already vulnerable person think that they have experienced abuse when none has occurred? Given our knowledge about the impermanence of memory, yes. Loftus (1997) provides an extensive review of studies which indicate that even psychologically healthy individuals can be convinced that false aspects of their memories are actually true. Individuals may recall seeing a barn in a bucolic scene when, in fact, there was no such barn; they might recall seeing broken glass or witnessing a white car at a crime scene when there was no glass and only a blue car in the incident they recalled.

In a set of compelling experiments, Loftus and her colleagues (see Loftus, 1997 for a good review) showed how effectively memories could be altered after the event with the aid of false suggestion. In one study, individuals were presented with four childhood events recounted by siblings or other close family and were asked to describe these events. Only three were genuine; the fourth (a shopping trip where the individual got lost) was false. In a follow-up study, participants were asked to provide as much detail of the events as possi-

ble. Twenty-nine per cent reported remembering the false event at the time of the study, at follow-up this was still 25 per cent. A distinction between real and false memories which Loftus found was that the true events were recalled using more words; they were also clearer.

Kassin and Kiechel (1996) reported another memory manipulation experiment with a slight twist. They set up a study in which individuals were falsely accused of pressing the wrong computer key and damaging the computer. Although the accused initially denied the accusation, when the experimenter's confederate indicated seeing the accused press the key, a number of individuals signed a confession. This study suggests that the influence of others' recollections and views may also be important determinants of the development of false memories. One study also suggests that the more one imagines a childhood event, the greater the confidence one has in that event having occurred (Garry *et al.*, 1996). Perhaps this is one of the reasons why those who recover memories have such strong beliefs in such events having taken place.

The evidence from the memory literature is also supported by the views of some therapists. In a survey of 1,300 US registered psychotherapists, 300 doctoral clinicians and 300 chartered British clinical psychologists, 94 per cent agreed that it was possible for clients to develop illusory memories. Interestingly, most were confident that they could spot inaccurate memories in their own clients.

Conclusion

Current evidence suggests that the notion of repressed or recovered memories is still controversial. Although most of the evidence suggests that there is little scientific merit to claims for recovered memories, the area is hampered by poor methodology and a reliance on self-reports or reports at second – or third – hand.

State-dependent memory may be related to place-dependent memory (PDM), illustrated by the Godden and Baddeley experiment above. The demonstration of place-dependent memory depends on the event to be remembered, the nature of encoding and retrieval, the ease by which people can mentally reinstate themselves, and the retention interval (Wilhite, 1991; McDaniel *et al.*, 1989; Smith, 1979, 1988). Reinstatement is important to place-dependent memory and refers to the process whereby the individual is placed in the same environment or is experiencing the same mood as when they originally encoded or generated information.

Because all of the factors listed above are important to PDM, the evidence for the phenomenon is mixed. Perhaps this is so because the important factor is not how similar places look but how they feel to the individual (Eich, 1995); this is what Eich calls mood-dependent memory. Although replications in which positive effects in mood-dependent memory are rare (Bower and Mayer, 1989), Eich (1995) suggests that when participants in these experiments experience strong/stable moods and are responsible for generating memory cues, mood-dependent memory is robust.

In one experiment, participants were asked to generate specific memories for events from autobiographical memory in response to common words (Eich *et al.*, 1994). Two to three days later, participants were allowed to free recall the memories generated in the experiment. Eich *et al.* found that more events were recalled when the mood matched the mood at testing. In another set of experiments, Eich (1995) found that the transfer of information from one environment to another is better if these environments feel similar. However, changes in the environment are not important if the moods at acquisition and reinstatement are the same. There is also evidence to suggest that individuals with mood disorders have a greater ability to discriminate between old and new stimuli if their moods at exposure and testing match (Eich *et al.*, 1997).

Controversies in psychological science

The reliability of 'flashbulb' memories

The issue

In the early morning of Sunday, 31 August 1997, one of the authors was busy working on a scientific paper and listening intermittently to a late night radio discussion. The paper was being prepared for a psychophysiology conference in Scotland two days later; the radio discussion revolved around the role of mature students in higher education. Several speakers seemed to have opinions of varying intelligence and sense. At one point, however, the author's attention was distracted by the presenter's announcement that there had been a car accident in Paris. The Princess of Wales, and her companion Dodi Al Fayed, it was rumoured, had both been injured in the accident. Startled by such a novel and unexpected event, the author switched on the television to see if any other news was available. BBC News 24 had turned over its normal programming to reporting the crash. Within two hours, a band in red at the bottom of the screen flashed a message attributed to the Press Association. Diana, Princess of Wales, had been killed.

This recollection is an example of a 'flashbulb' memory. Flashbulb memories are recollections of events which are of personal or social importance, are novel, unexpected and vivid and have major long-term consequences. The assassinations of Martin Luther King and John F. Kennedy, for example, are thought to be events which trigger flashbulb memories. You will often hear people say that they knew exactly what they were doing when Kennedy was assassinated, in the same way that the author knew exactly what he was doing when the news of Diana's death was broadcast. The name 'flashbulb' memories was coined by Brown and Kulik (1977) to describe the vivid recollections from black and white respondents of the assassinations of Martin Luther King and JFK. According to Brown and Kulik, the memory has a ' "live" quality that is almost perceptual … like a photograph' (p. 74). Most Americans of the appropriate age will have a detailed recollection of what they were doing when JFK was assassinated (Winograd and Killinger, 1983).

Since Brown and Kulik's landmark paper was published, a small number of similar studies have examined the nature of flashbulb memories for other events. These events have included the death of the King of Belgium (Finkenauer *et al.*, 1998), the death of spectators at the Hillsborough football stadium, England (Wright, 1993; Wright *et al.*, 1998), the resignation of Margaret Thatcher as British prime minister (Conway *et al.*, 1994; Wright *et al.*, 1998), the Gulf War (Weaver, 1993), the assassination of Olaf Palme, the Norwegian prime minister (Christianson, 1989), the American Shuttle disaster (Bohannon, 1988) and the experience of being in an earthquake (Neisser *et al.*, 1996b).

Recently, however, there has been some debate on whether flashbulb memories are genuinely special. According to Brown and Kulik, flashbulb memories are of surprising or consequential events which are stored in the brain 'unchanged'; they also operate via a mechanism that is different from that which allows the formation of other types of memory. Wright (1993; Wright *et al.*, 1998), however, has conducted an extensive study of memories of the Hillsborough disaster and the resignation of Mrs Thatcher and suggests that flashbulb memories do not require a special mechanism. Furthermore, memories for these events may not even be vivid.

The evidence

At the Hillsborough football stadium, England, in 1989, 96 spectators were crushed to death during the Liverpool vs Nottingham Forest FA Cup semi-final. Wright (1993) asked 247 individuals at three periods after the event (two days, one month and five months) to estimate their emotional reaction to the event, the emotional and social importance of the event, their enthusiasm for football and the circumstances in which they heard of the disaster.

Does this evidence suggest that mood-dependent memory is genuinely robust? Smith (1995) and Eich (1995) himself suggest that mood-dependent memory effects may be explained by other factors. Smith, for example, suggests that active memories or pre-existing mood generated at the time of acquisition could have cued a representation of the initial context of the original event. Several factors, including mood, could explain the effects of context reinstatement in experiments like those discussed here.

Finally, one type of memory that is thought to be especially emotional – and as a result is more vivid and robustly retrieved – is the 'flashbulb memory'. This is discussed in the 'Controversies in psychological science' section.

The personal and social importance of the event increased over time. However, fewer details of the disaster were recalled at the third than at the first and second testing sessions. Wright also found evidence that memories were reconstructed over time and suggested that these memories were subject to systematic bias (as others had also suggested, for example McCloskey et al., 1988). Of course, if memories had to be reconstructed over time, the original memory was not vivid, certainly not as vivid as a photograph.

To examine the issues further, Wright and his colleagues (Wright et al., 1998) addressed three assumptions behind flashbulb memories: that they are 'collective' in nature (i.e. most of us will experience them when encountered by a surprising and important event); that the subjective characteristics of memories are reliable (would changing the order of questions in the study alter recollective ability, for example, especially if certain orders cued memories better?); and that flashbulb memories are actually vivid. The researchers looked at memories for the Hillsborough disaster and the resignation of Margaret Thatcher on 22 November 1990. An earlier study by Conway et al. (1994) had found a large number of memories classified as flashbulb memories in a group of British undergraduates. Eighty-six per cent of this sample gave consistent responses eleven months after the incident.

Wright et al. (1998) found that the memory for the resignation was more vivid than for Hillsborough but that the Hillsborough event was more important. The higher the social class of the respondent, the greater the interest in the Thatcher resignation. Twelve per cent of the sample had vivid recollections of the resignation whereas 9 per cent had vivid recollections of Hillsborough. This contrasts markedly with the 86 per cent reported by Conway et al. (1994). Were Conway and colleagues' university students more prone to flashbulb memories? A comparison of those in education and those not in the Wright et al. study showed no significant difference between the two groups. The 35–54 year olds also, however, gave the greatest number of responses. Perhaps age could have accounted for the difference, or even a lack of interest in football or politics.

What theory or theories can best account for the nature of these flashbulb memories? In a detailed report, Finkenauer et al. (1998) put the theories of Brown and Kulik, Conway et al. and their own (called the emotional-integrative model) to the test by examining responses to the death of the King of Belgium on 13 August 1993. The experimenters' own model suggests that the appraisal of the event as novel and important leads to surprise. Surprise and the importance of the event to the person determines the intensity of the emotion experienced. This reaction may be modified by personal characteristics.

Finkenauer et al. noted that all the theories agreed that surprise and consequentiality are necessary for flashbulb memories. The degree of consequentiality influenced the degree of completeness and explicitness of the memory. Rehearsal of the memory for the event (thinking and talking about it) is also important. However, although the photographic model suggested that importance and feeling state were important determinants of flashbulb memories, these factors did not predict flashbulb memories. Similarly, the Conway model, which suggests that surprise and emotional feeling are determinants of flashbulb memories, failed to show that these factors predicted such memories. What the experimenters' analysis suggested was that the appraisal of an event as novel causes surprise; this then leads to the formation of a flashbulb memory. Appraisal of an event as important together with attitude determines the intensity of the emotional response. This response has no direct effect on the formation of flashbulb memories. Instead, the data suggest that emotional state triggers rehearsal which strengthens memory.

Conclusion

The emotional-integrative model is a persuasive way of accounting for the factors necessary to determine a flashbulb memory. Because it is explicit, it is testable: that is, one can generate hypotheses from the model and test them empirically. The evidence at the moment, however, suggests that flashbulb memories may not be special. Events may be memorable but they may not be memorable for the reasons originally given by the authors of flashbulb memories.

Questions to think about

Remembering and forgetting

- The tip-of-the-tongue phenomenon has an olfactory analogue called tip-of-the-nose. Which types of stimuli do you think would be more likely to elicit the phenomenon – smells, words or faces? Why?

- Recall an event from your childhood and the activities and moods that surrounded that event. How much of the information that you recall about this event is accurate? How many of the details surrounding this event have you reconstructed?

- Based on your knowledge of place-dependent memory and context-reinstatement, would you expect to do better in an exam if you revised and sat an exam (a) at the same table, (b) in the same room or (c) in the same building? Would any of these work?

- Are there some events in your past that you remember as being more vivid and memorable than others? Would you describe them as flashbulb memories?

- You have seen how easy it is to alter people's memories after they have witnessed an event. How would you ensure that eyewitness testimony is accurate?

- Would you remember events better if you were in a happy or sad mood? Do you think your ability to complete intelligence tests would be affected by your mood? Would you expect a positive mood to enhance your test performance? (Chapter 13 will give you the answer to this one.)

- What seems to you to be the most convincing reason for forgetting?

Key terms

memory *p.244*
encoding *p.244*
storage *p.244*
retrieval *p.244*
sensory memory *p.244*
short-term memory *p.244*
long-term memory *p.244*
iconic memory *p.245*
echoic memory *p.245*
working memory *p.246*
articulatory/phonological loop *p.246*
visuospatial scratchpad *p.246*
central executive *p.246*

subvocal articulation *p.247*
supervisory attentional system (SAS) *p.248*
primacy effect *p.249*
recency effect *p.249*
chunking *p.249*
consolidation *p.251*
maintenance rehearsal *p.251*
elaborative rehearsal *p.252*
shallow processing *p.252*
deep processing *p.252*
effortful processing *p.253*
automatic processing *p.253*
encoding specificity *p.253*

mnemonic systems *p.253*
method of loci *p.254*
peg-word method *p.254*
narrative *p.254*
episodic/autobiographical memory *p.256*
semantic memory *p.256*
explicit memory *p.256*
implicit memory *p.256*
anterograde amnesia *p.257*
retrograde amnesia *p.257*
hippocampus *p.258*
tip-of-the-tongue phenomenon *p.262*
retrieval cues *p.262*

retention interval *p.263*
remember-to-know shift *p.265*
cognitive interview *p.268*
retroactive interference *p.269*
proactive interference *p.269*
state-dependent memory *p.269*
recovered memories *p.270*
place-dependent memory (PDM) *p.271*
flashbulb memories *p.272*

CHAPTER REVIEW

Sensory memory

- Memory is the process of encoding, storing and retrieving information. It exists in three forms: sensory, short-term/working and long-term. The characteristics of each differ, which suggests that they differ physiologically as well.

- Sensory memory provides temporary storage of information until the newly perceived information can be stored in short-term memory.

- Information in sensory memory lasts for only a short time. The partial-report procedure shows that when a visual stimulus is presented in a brief flash, all of the information is available for a short time (iconic memory). If the viewer's attention is directed to one line of information within a few hundred milliseconds of the flash, the information can be transferred into short-term memory. Echoic memory – sensory memory for sound – appears to operate similarly.

Short-term and working memory

- Short-term memory and working memory contains a representation of information that has just been perceived, such as a person's name or telephone number. Although the capacity of short-term memory is limited, we can rehearse the information as long as we choose, thus increasing the likelihood that we will remember it indefinitely.

- Information in short-term memory is encoded according to previously learned rules. Information in long-term memory determines the nature of the encoding.

- Because short-term memory contains information retrieved from long-term memory as well as newly perceived information, many researchers conceive of it as working memory – where thinking occurs.

- Working memory, however, appears to be different from short-term memory in that it allows the short-term manipulation as opposed to storage of material in memory.

- Working memory comprises a phonological loop – a store of phonetic, verbal information – a visuospatial scratchpad – a store of spatial information and memories for movement – and a central executive which supervises and updates the content of working memory.

- Short-term memory lasts for about twenty seconds and has a capacity of about seven items, give or take two. We often simplify large amounts of information by organising it into 'chunks' of information, which can then be more easily rehearsed and remembered.

- When presented with a list of items, we tend to remember the items at the beginning of the list (the primacy effect) and at the end of the list (the recency effect) better than items in the middle of the list.

- The primacy effect occurs presumably because we have a greater opportunity to rehearse items early in the list and thus store them in long-term memory. The recency effect occurs because we can retrieve items at the end of the list from short-term memory.

- The existence of acoustical errors (rather than visual ones) in the task of remembering visually presented letters suggests that information is represented phonologically in short-term memory. Phonological working memory is encoded acoustically as well.

- Loss of information from short-term memory appears to be primarily a result of displacement; new information pushes out old information. However, a small amount of simple decay may also occur.

Learning and encoding in long-term memory

- Long-term memory refers to the very long-term retention of information and appears to consist of physical changes in the brain – probably within the sensory and motor association cortex.

- Consolidation of memories is likely caused by rehearsal of information, which sustains particular neural activities and leads to permanent structural changes in the brain.

- Short-term memories probably involve neural activity (which can be prolonged by rehearsal), whereas long-term memories probably involve permanent structural changes.

- Elaboration is important to learning. Maintenance rehearsal, or simple rote repetition, is usually less effective than elaborative rehearsal, which involves deeper, more meaningful processing.

- Encoding of information to be stored in long-term memory may take place automatically or with effort. Automatic processing of information is usually related to the frequency, timing and place (location) of events. Textbook learning entails effortful processing, most likely because of its complexity.

- The principle of encoding specificity states that the material that is retrieved must have been stored and that the way in which material is stored depends on how the material is retrieved. The most durable and useful memories are encoded in ways that are meaningful.

- Some psychologists have argued that shallow processing is a less effective way of encoding information than is deep processing (levels of processing, therefore, determine the success of retrieval). Critics, however, point out that shallow processing sometimes produces very durable memories, and the distinction between shallow and deep has proved to be impossible to define explicitly.

- Mnemonic systems are strategies used to enhance memory and usually employ information that is already contained in long-term memory and visual imagery. These are useful for remembering lists of items but are less useful for more complex material, such as textbook information.

The organisation of long-term memory

- Episodic memory refers to memories of events and people that are personally meaningful to us; it is synonymous with autobiographical memory.

- Semantic memory refers to memory for knowledge and facts.

- Most psychologists believe that episodic and semantic memories are parts of different systems although this is controversial.

- Explicit memory refers to recollection of information that was deliberately encoded and retrieved; implicit memory refers to memory for information that is unintentionally learned.

- Much of what we have learned about the biological basis of memory comes from studies involving humans with brain damage, from laboratory studies in which animals undergo surgical procedures that produce amnesia, and from neuroimaging studies of memory in healthy individuals.

- Anterograde amnesia refers to an inability to learn new memories after brain injury; these individuals can learn to perform many tasks that do not require verbal rules, such as recognising fragmentary pictures. Retrograde amnesia refers to the inability to retrieve remote memories.

- Patient HM shows an inability to store new information in long-term memory as a result of damage to the temporal lobes in general and the hippocampus in particular.

- The hippocampus and frontal cortex are important for different types of memory. Neuroimaging studies show that navigating the environment from memory depends on the activity of the hippocampus whereas the left prefrontal cortex appears to be important for the encoding of material.

Remembering

- Remembering is an automatic process, although we may sometimes work hard at generating thoughts that will help this process along.

- Forgetting information occurs primarily in the first few years after it is learned and the rate of forgetting decreases slowly thereafter. Once we have learned something and retained it for a few years, the chances are that we will remember it for a long time afterwards.

- Recalling a memory of a complex event entails a process of reconstruction that uses old information.

- Our ability to recall information from episodic memory is influenced by retrieval cues, such as the questions people are asked in courts of law to establish how an event occurred. Sometimes, the reconstruction introduces new 'facts' that we perceive as memories of what we previously perceived.

- Recovered memories refer to recollections of allegedly repressed memories from childhood that can be elicited during psychotherapy; there is little evidence that these memories are genuine.

- Remembering is strongly influenced by contextual variables involving mood and emotion. Some evidence suggests that remembering is easier when an individual's mood during the attempt to recall information is the same as it was when that information was originally learned; this is called mood-dependent memory.

- We also tend to remember the circumstances that we were in when we first hear of a particularly emotional event such as the death of an internationally-famous person, a natural disaster, or an invasion of one country by another; these are called flashbulb memories.

- Sometimes recollecting one memory is made more difficult by the information contained in another memory, a phenomenon known as interference.

- In retroactive interference, information that we have recently learned interferes with our recollection of information learned earlier.

- In proactive interference, information that we learned a while ago interferes with information we have learned more recently.

- Although interference has been demonstrated in the laboratory, interference may not operate so obviously in real life. Prose and other forms of everyday language appear to be more resistant to interference than are the nonsense syllables that people who participate in memory experiments are often required to learn.

Suggestions for further reading

Rose, S. (1992). *The Making of Memory*. London: Bantam Press.

Schacter, D.L. (1996). *Searching for Memory: The brain, the mind and the past*. New York: Basic Books.
Rose and Schacter's books, written for a non-specialist audience, are engaging introductions to the study of animal and human memory.

Baddeley, A.D. (1996). *Human Memory: Theory and practice* (2nd edition). Hove, UK: The Psychology Press.

Groeger, J.A. (1997). *Memory and Remembering*. Harlow: Longman.

Parkin, A.J. (1993). *Memory: Phenomena, experiment and theory*. Oxford: Blackwell.

Shanks, D. (1997). *Human Memory: A reader*. London: Arnold.
The books by Baddeley, Groeger and Parkin are excellent, well written and comprehensive accounts of the psychology of memory, written by leading researchers in the field. Shanks's book is a collection of the most important papers published in the psychology of memory and is a handy sourcebook of information.

Eysenck, M.W. and Keane, M.T. (1995). *Cognitive Psychology: A student's handbook*. Hove, UK: The Psychology Press.

Gavin, H. (1998). *The Essence of Cognitive Psychology*. Harlow: Prentice Hall.
Both of these books – a modern classic and a recent, shorter addition to the literature – will give you a good overview of memory and other topics in cognitive psychology.

Richardson, J.T.E., Engle, R.W., Hasher, L., Logie, R.H., Stoltzfus, E.R. and Zacks, R.T. (1996). *Working Memory and Human Cognition*. Oxford: Oxford University Press.
This is a collection of chapters on various aspects of working memory. Compact and very useful for further reading on this type of memory.

Collins, A.F., Gathercole, S.E., Conway, M.A. and Morris, P.E. (1993) *Theories of Memory*. Hove, UK: The Psychology Press.

Conway, M.A., Gathercole, S.E. and Cornoldi, C. (1997). *Theories of Memory II*. Hove, UK: The Psychology Press.
For a detailed consideration of the theoretical explanations of memory, these two companion volumes are a useful introduction, although perhaps a little heavy going unless you are familiar with the rudiments discussed in the previously recommended texts.

Cohen, G. (1996). *Memory in the Real World* (2nd edition). Hove, UK: The Psychology Press.

Smyth, M.M., Collins, A.F., Morris, P.E. and Levy, P. (1994). *Cognition in Action* (2nd edition). Hove, UK: The Psychology Press.
Many of the scientific questions that psychologists attempt to answer have practical implications, deliberate or accidental. Cohen and Smyth et al.'s texts are tremendous reviews of the applications of memory research to real-life situations and problems. These are highly recommended for their ability to show how laboratory and field studies in psychology can interact successfully.

Gabrieli, J.D.E. (1998). Cognitive neuroscience of human memory. *Annual Review of Psychology*, 49, 87–115.

Parkin, A.J. (1996). *Memory and Amnesia: An introduction*. Oxford: Blackwell.

Parkin, A.J. (1997). *Case Studies in the Neuropsychology of Memory*. Hove, UK: The Psychology Press.
Memory disorders are frequently discussed in journal papers and there are many of these articles you can consult. However, two general texts to get you started, and lead you to more specific reading, are Parkin's. His Memory and Amnesia *is recommended as your first text: this is a thorough and readable review of the nature of amnesia.* Case Studies *provides a thoughtful and expansive collection of papers written about different kinds of memory disorder. Gabrieli's review takes a cognitive neuroscience perspective on declarative memory, skill learning and conditioning.*

Luria, A.R. (1968). *The Mind of a Mnemonist*. London: Penguin.

Wilding, J. and Valentine, E. (1997). *Superior Memory*. Hove, UK: The Psychology Press.
The use of mnemonics and the nature of superior memory ability are well reviewed in these two books. Luria's classic book is written by a pioneering neuroscientist and is based on an unusual case study of superior memory. Wilding and Valentine's book is a more up-to-date review of the nature and causes of superior memory.

Conway, M.A. (1997). *Recovered Memories and False Memories*. Oxford: Oxford University Press.

Loftus, E.F. (1997). Creating false memories. *Scientific American*, September, 50–55.

Wells, G.L. and Seelau, E.P. (1995). Eyewitness identification: psychological research and legal policy on line-ups. *Psychology, Public Policy and Law*, 1, 4, 765–791.
The study of false memories and malleability of memory in eyewitness identification are splendidly described in these three publications. Loftus's article is written for the general reader and gives an excellent review of most of her ground-breaking work on false memories. Conway's book is an edited collection of chapters dealing with various aspects of recovered memories. Wells and Seelau's article reviews and evaluates a wealth of research concerning the unreliability of eyewitness testimony (although predominantly from a North American legal perspective).

Journals to consult

Applied Cognitive Psychology
British Journal of Psychology
European Journal of Cognitive Psychology
Journal of Experimental Psychology
Journal of Memory and Language
Memory
Memory and Cognition
Psychological Science
Psychonomic Bulletin and Review
Quarterly Journal of Experimental Psychology

Website address

http://www.gemstate.net/susan/linksCogPsy.htm
An on-line guide to cognitive psychology websites.

9

CONSCIOUSNESS

Hypnotist denies show made man a schizophrenic

Paul McKenna, a stage hypnotist and television personality, denied that his show was responsible for turning a participant into a violent and aggressive schizophrenic.

The 34-year-old entertainer told a High Court judge that Christopher Gates had shown no signs that anything was amiss after leaving the stage following the show.

Mr Gates told the court that while in a trance lasting more than two hours during the show in March 1994, he was made to believe that he was, among other things, a ballet dancer, Mick Jagger, an interpreter for aliens from outer space and a contestant on the show *Blind Date*.

He claimed that all McKenna did to bring him out of hypnosis was utter the words 'wakey wakey'. He also said that, since the show, he had seen 'monsters' and heard the voices of Jesus and Moses.

McKenna said the 'dehypnosis' process in all his shows took three minutes. 'I ask them to go back in a trance, cast their minds back and remember some of the amusing and happy things we have done. I ask them to realise that all the hypnotic suggestions that were part of the show are now cleared by hypnotic suggestion. I say once again they are masters of their own destinies, their normal selves in every way.'

Source: *Daily Telegraph*, July 1998

OVERVIEW

What is consciousness and why are we conscious? How do we direct our consciousness from one event to another, paying attention to some stimuli and ignoring others? What do we know about the brain functions responsible for consciousness? What is hypnosis – can another person really take control of our own thoughts and behaviour? Why do we regularly undergo the profound alteration in consciousness called sleep?

This chapter is concerned with finding out the answers to these questions. It explores the nature of human consciousness: knowledge of our own existence, behaviour, perceptions and thoughts. Some psychologists argue that consciousness is beyond the scope of scientific investigation because its subject matter is too subjective. There are some aspects of consciousness that we can measure and study objectively, however, and these and other features of consciousness are described next.

What you should be able to do after reading Chapter 9

- Describe what psychologists and philosophers mean by consciousness.
- Understand the problems with studying consciousness.
- Be familiar with theories explaining consciousness.
- Understand the concept of selective and divided attention and give examples of it.
- Describe hypnosis and the reasons for hypnotically induced behaviour.
- Describe the behavioural and psychophysiological stages of sleep.
- Understand theories of why we sleep.
- Describe the symptoms of sleep disorders and their possible causes.

Questions to think about

- What is consciousness and how can we measure it?
- Is consciousness unitary?
- Where does consciousness come from?
- What is hypnosis and how does it work?
- How do we selectively attend to information in our environment?
- Why do we sleep?

'Consciousness poses the most baffling problems in the science of the mind. There is nothing that we know more intimately than conscious experience, but there is nothing that is harder to explain.'

(Chalmers, 1995)

Consciousness: an introduction

Why are we aware of ourselves, of our thoughts, our perceptions, our actions, our memories, and our feelings? Is some purpose served by our ability to realise that we exist, that events occur, that we are doing things, and that we have memories? According to James (1890), 'all people unhesitatingly believe that they feel themselves thinking. This belief is the most fundamental of all postulates of Psychology.'

Philosophers have puzzled over the questions raised above for centuries without finding a convincing answer (Block *et al.*, 1997). Psychologists, however, generally neglected the problem of consciousness for many years. Early behaviourists, as we saw in Chapter 1, denied that there was anything to explain and argued that the only subject matter for psychological investigation was behaviour, not consciousness. Several psychologists continue to believe that consciousness is a side effect of what we do – an epiphenomenon – that is not intrinsically interesting as a research question or a psychological topic. To illustrate psychology's lack of interest in this topic, consider the fate of one paper written by the influential neuropsychologist, Jeffrey Gray. Over two decades ago, Gray (1971) published a paper outlining what he regarded as the hard problems of consciousness. Gray (1998) noted that in the ten years since the publication of the article, he received just two requests for a copy of the paper!

Recent years, however, have seen a revival in the scientific study of consciousness, with philosophers, neuroscientists, mathematicians and psychologists contributing ideas and theories to this area (Pinker, 1997; Penrose, 1989, 1994; Crick, 1994; Gray, 1998; Dennett, 1991; Hameroff *et al.*, 1998). Consciousness, the bane of behaviourists, is now provoking new research and concepts from psychologists, particularly those who seek the neural basis of consciousness. Popular accounts of theories of consciousness such as Daniel Dennett's *Consciousness Explained* and Francis Crick's *The Astonishing Hypothesis* reflect a renewed interest in this topic and this chapter reviews current thinking and, more importantly, research findings in this complex area.

Philosophical approaches to consciousness

Historically, people have taken three philosophical positions about the nature of consciousness (Block *et al.*, 1997). The first, and earliest, position is that consciousness is not a natural phenomenon. That is, it is not subject to the laws of nature that all scientists attempt to discover: laws involving matter and purely physical forces. This position states that consciousness is something supernatural and miraculous, not to be understood by the human mind.

The second position is that consciousness is a natural phenomenon but also that, for various reasons, we cannot understand it. Consciousness exists because of the nature of the human brain, but just how this occurs is not known. We can never understand consciousness because our brains are simply not capable of doing so; it would take a more complex brain than ours to understand the biology of subjective awareness. An alternative but related view is that everything can be explained, including all aspects of the human brain, but that consciousness is a vague, poorly operationally defined term (Wilkes, 1988; McGinn, 1989).

The third position is that people are indeed conscious, that this consciousness is produced by the activity of the human brain, and that there is every reason for us to be optimistic about our ability to understand this phenomenon (Crick, 1994).

The meaning of 'consciousness'

Although the word 'consciousness' is a noun, 'consciousness' itself does not exist. What exist are humans having the ability to do something that we describe as 'being conscious'. So, then, what does it mean to be conscious? This has troubled philosophers and psychologists for many decades (Chalmers, 1998; Shanon, 1998). Allport (1988), for example, reported that, 'I find that I have no clear conception what people are talking about when they talk about consciousness or "phenomenal awareness", nor, for that matter, when they talk about its linguistic-conceptual Siamese twin, the conscious self.' Consciousness is a private experience, which cannot be shared directly. We experience our own consciousness but not that of others. We conclude that other people are conscious because they are like us and because they can tell us that they, too, are conscious. This, inevitably, has a subjective quality which makes consciousness difficult to study scientifically.

According to Chalmers (1995), consciousness investigators face easy problems and a hard problem. The easy problems include the ability to discriminate, categorise and react to stimuli, to integrate information by using a cognitive system, to report mental states and to access internal states, to control behaviour deliberately and to differentiate between wakefulness and sleep. All of these features are associated with consciousness but, according to Chalmers, they are the relatively easy topics of consciousness because they primarily involve the contents of consciousness; these features refer to functions or abilities. Understanding (or discovering) the neural correlates of consciousness is also an easy problem, according to Chalmers. A mental state is said to be conscious when this state can be verbally reportable or internally accessible; the organism is able to be conscious of some information, react to it and explain it. This is another easy problem. But this is only one side of the story. The hard problem lies in studying the experience of these mental events.

When we report these mental events we have an experience of reporting these mental events. Over and above this ability, we have the experience itself. There must be something 'that it is like' to be conscious (Nagel, 1974); there is a subjective quality about it and because of this, it poses a difficult problem. These conscious experiences are sometimes referred to as phenomenal consciousness or 'qualia'. In summary, the easy problems are understanding the functions and neurophysiology of consciousness; the hard problem is explaining why we have the experience of consciousness in the first place. The distinction between easy and hard problems is a controversial one and you yourself would probably challenge the notion that the understanding of the neural correlates of consciousness, for example, represents an easy problem. In the next section, we will consider some of the theories that have been proposed to account for the 'easy' and 'hard' aspects of consciousness.

Theories of consciousness
Neurobiological theories

Recent years have seen an increased interest from scientists in explaining the nature of consciousness neurobiologically (Rolls, 1997; Gray, 1998). In fact, Chalmers (1998) has listed over twenty proposed neural correlates of consciousness (NCC).

The essence of the neurobiological approach is that consciousness arises from the neural activity of the brain. Neurobiological approaches diverge, however, when they begin to specify which parts or elements of the brain give rise to the activity that is meant to represent consciousness. Neurobiological theories of consciousness derive their data from a number of sources such as those described in Chapter 4 – neuroimaging and brain damage – and other branches of natural science such as mathematics and quantum physics. Each type of study has yielded a different perspective on the NCC and some of the most important or influential of these theories are reviewed below.

Consciousness and brain damage

Brain damage can alter human consciousness. Patients with anterograde amnesia, for example, are unable to form new verbal memories but can learn some kinds of tasks. However, they remain unaware that they have learned something, even when their behaviour indicates that they have. The brain damage does not prevent all kinds of learning, but it does prevent conscious awareness of what has been learned.

As we saw in Chapter 6, there are individuals who, if they have damaged the posterior parts of their brain, show a lack of awareness of stimuli presented to their visual field. Brain damage which impairs the perception of visual stimuli also seems to impair the ability to be aware of perceiving these stimuli (Stoerig and Cowey, 1997). Individuals with blindsight have damage to the primary visual cortex and although they are able to perform some visual perception tasks, they report being unaware of the task stimuli that had been presented in their visual field. Remember from Chapter 6 that individuals with certain types of agnosia are unable to recognise objects or may be unable to ascribe meaning to such objects. Another form of agnosia is characterised by the inability to identify familiar faces by using facial cues alone. All of these disorders involve some lack of awareness and may help us to understand the regional contribution of the brain to conscious awareness.

Blindsight patients have damage to an area called V1, the primary visual cortex. This is the region in the brain to which information from the retina travels. Does the activity of V1 reflect conscious awareness of visual stimuli? Crick and Koch (1995) have proposed the controversial idea that it does not. They argue that it is not involved in conscious visual perception because V1 does not directly project to the frontal cortex (which integrates information from other parts of the cortex); the areas surrounding V1, however – the extrastriate cortex – do, and it is the activity of these areas which may reflect conscious processing, as seen in Figure 9.1. Crick and Koch (1995) admit that this is a subtle and speculative proposal and have not undertaken an empirical test of this hypothesis. It remains an intriguing hypothesis.

Another form of brain damage, this time a surgical procedure designed to eliminate the symptoms of intractable epilepsy, gives rise to what has become known as the **split brain** or **callosal syndrome** (Bogen, 1993). Individuals who suffer epilepsy which cannot be controlled by drugs, experience violent storms of neural activity which begin in one hemisphere and shift to the other via the corpus callosum, the large bundle of axons that connect one cerebral hemisphere to another. This causes an epileptic seizure. These seizures can occur many times each day, preventing the patient from leading a normal life. Neurosurgeons discovered that by severing the corpus callosum, thereby 'splitting' the brain, they could reduce the frequency of these seizures (Sperry *et al.*, 1969). This is illustrated in Figure 9.2.

Roger Sperry and Michael Gazzaniga and their associates (Gazzaniga, 1970, 1995, 1998; Gazzaniga *et al.*, 1996; Sperry, 1966) pioneered research into the psychological consequences of **split-brain surgery**. Sperry won the Nobel Prize in 1981 for his work on neurosurgery. Their work – initially with cats – demonstrated that the cerebral cortex of the left and right hemispheres normally exchange information via the corpus callosum. With one exception (described later),

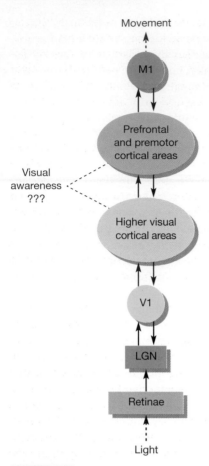

Figure 9.1

A schematic diagram of the brain areas involved in conscious visual awareness. LGN = lateral geniculate nucleus found in the thalamus; M1 is the primary motor cortex.

Source: Adapted with permission from *Nature* from Crick, F. and Koch, C. (1995). Are we aware of neural activity in the primary visual cortex?, *Nature*, 375, pp. 121–3. Copyright 1995 Macmillan Magazines Ltd.

each hemisphere receives sensory information from the opposite side of the body and controls muscular movements on that side, as we saw in Chapters 4 and 6. The corpus callosum permits these activities to be co-ordinated, so that each hemisphere 'knows' what is going on in the other hemisphere (Hoptman and Davidson, 1994; Banich, 1995).

When the two hemispheres are disconnected after split-brain surgery, they appear to operate independently; their sensory mechanisms, memories and motor systems no longer appear to exchange information. The effects of these disconnections are not obvious to a casual observer, for the simple reason that only one hemisphere – in most people, as we will see in the next chapter, the left – controls speech. The right hemisphere of an epileptic person with a split brain allows the patient to understand speech reasonably well, but it is poor at reading and spelling. Because

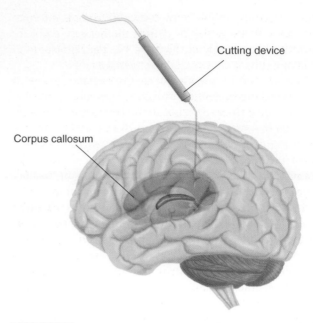

Figure 9.2

The split-brain operation. Holes are drilled in the top of the skull and a cutting device is introduced between the left and right cerebral hemispheres, severing the corpus callosum.

Broca's speech area is located in the left hemisphere, the right hemisphere is totally incapable of producing speech.

Given that only one side of the brain can 'talk about' what it is experiencing, a casual observer will not detect the independent operations of the right side of a split brain. Even the patient's left brain has to learn about the independent existence of the right brain. One of the first things that these patients say they notice after the operation is that their left hand seems to have a mind of its own. This is called **alien hand** ('la main étrangère'). For example, patients may find themselves putting down a book held in the left hand, even if they are reading it with great interest. At other times, they surprise themselves by making obscene gestures with the left hand. Because the right hemisphere controls the movements of the left hand, these unexpected movements puzzle the left hemisphere, the side of the brain that controls speech. One hypothesis suggests that the inhibition of actions organised elsewhere, but originating in the frontal cortex, is lost in split-brain patients hence the appearance of unusual, uninhibited behaviour in one hand. Another, different phenomenon is **intermanual conflict**. This refers to the apparently contradictory activity of the left and right hand; one might do up a set of buttons on a shirt, for example, while the other might undo them (Akelaitis, 1944/45).

If a patient with a split brain tries to use his or her right hand to arrange blocks to duplicate a geometrical design provided by the experimenter, the hand will hopelessly fumble around with the blocks. Often, the left hand (controlled by the right hemisphere) will brush the right hand aside and easily complete the task. It is as if the right hemisphere gets impatient with the clumsy ineptitude of the hand controlled by the left hemisphere.

The effects of cutting the corpus callosum suggest that consciousness depends on the ability of speech mechanisms in the left hemisphere to receive information from other regions of the brain. If such communication is interrupted, then some kinds of information can never reach consciousness.

Recently, a case study has been reported in which a patient demonstrated the behaviour that was typical of a split-brain patient but he had difficulty in matching colours and letters with the left hand when perceptual information was absent (Marangolo *et al.*, 1998). For example, the experimenters presented various stimuli, such as letters, objects and faces to the patient and asked him to match these objects with other objects. When all stimuli were in front of him, the patient was able to match the object correctly with both the left and the right hand. When the stimulus was removed, was referred to only verbally or had the same name but not same appearance as the matched stimulus (for example, capital vs lower case lettering), the patient committed more errors with the left hand, suggesting that the right hemisphere was unable to make such decisions without the assistance of the left hemisphere. In this patient, transfer of information could take place but the left side was unable to transmit what it knew to the right motor area.

There is still some controversy over whether split-brain patients are genuinely unable to perform the tasks that psychologists set them (see Martin, 1998a, for a review). For example, the degree to which split-brain patients can make decisions about stimuli presented to the left or right of their visual field may depend on the part of the corpus callosum damaged: normally, not all of the corpus callosum is damaged, only parts of it (Sergent, 1987, 1990, 1991). For example, two out of three patients when presented with circles in each hemifield could indicate which was bigger (Sergent, 1987). There are also other connections between the hemispheres, in addition to the corpus callosum. Some neuropsychologists, such as Sergent, have argued that split-brain patients who do not show the typical split-brain profile do so because of these intact channels of communication – there is still some way in which the hemispheres can transfer information (Seymour *et al.*, 1994).

An interesting exception to the crossed representation of sensory information in the human brain is the olfactory system. When a person sniffs a flower through the left nostril, only the left cerebral hemisphere receives a sensation of the odour. Thus, if the right nostril of a patient with a split brain is closed and the left nostril is open, the patient will accurately identify odours verbally. If the odour enters the right nostril, the patient will say that he or she smells nothing (Gordon and Sperry, 1969). But, in fact, the right brain has perceived the odour and can identify it, as seen in Figure 9.3.

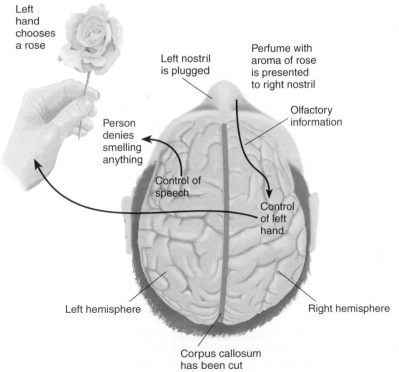

Left hand chooses a rose

Left nostril is plugged

Perfume with aroma of rose is presented to right nostril

Olfactory information

Person denies smelling anything

Control of speech

Control of left hand

Left hemisphere

Right hemisphere

Corpus callosum has been cut

Figure 9.3

Identification of an object by a person with a split brain in response to an olfactory stimulus.

This ability is demonstrated by an experiment in which the patient is told to reach for some objects hidden from view by a partition. If asked to use the left hand, with the left nostril closed, he or she will select the object that corresponds to the odour – a plastic flower for a floral odour, a toy fish for a fishy odour, a model tree for the odour of pine, and so forth. But if the left nostril is closed, the right hand fails this test, because it is connected to the left hemisphere, which did not smell the odour.

Crick's astonishing hypothesis

Other neurobiological models of consciousness specify more exact regions and neural elements which give rise to consciousness. Crick's theory (Crick, 1994), for example, suggests that consciousness is the result of the activity of collections of neurons called neural assemblies (this is the astonishing hypothesis). The behaviour of neurons is represented by 35–75 Hz oscillations in the cortex; these oscillations form the basis of consciousness and correlate with awareness in different sensory modalities. According to the theory, oscillation represents the way in which the information we process is bound. The concept of binding is important in consciousness; it refers to the process whereby separate pieces of information about a single entity are brought together and used for processing later (Chalmers, 1995).

Bringing together information about colour and shape to form an image of an object is an example of binding. When elements are bound together, Crick's theory argues, neural groups will oscillate in the same space and time. Such oscillations are the neural correlates of experience. While Crick's theory has received much attention and credit for specifically tying consciousness to specific brain activity, it has been criticised for not being able to explain the importance of these oscillations. If these oscillations give rise to conscious experience, why? Again, this is exactly Chalmers's hard problem, mentioned earlier.

Penrose and Hameroff's quantum model

Another neurobiological approach to consciousness focuses on the importance of chaos or non-linear dynamics in explaining consciousness. Much of Penrose's work is rooted in some quite complex physics and mathematics and we need not dwell on the detail here. In essence, Penrose (1989, 1994) argues that consciousness is a form of non-algorithmic processing which is important to conscious mathematical insight (Penrose himself is a famous mathematician). That is, consciousness is not an all-or-nothing, straightforward, linear process; instead, it is an uneven, non-linear process.

Penrose's model relies on an understanding of quantum physics and Penrose's excellent books in the further

reading suggestions will fill in the quantum physics blanks here. Quantum physics suggests that although events are observable and seem to follow a logical order, these events themselves are altered by being observed (this is called the Heisenberg Uncertainty Principle). In a revision of the original model, Hameroff and Penrose (1996) and Hameroff (1998) have suggested that consciousness takes place in the skeletal structure of neurons (called cytoskeleton), specifically in parts of the neuron called microtubules, as seen in Figure 9.4.

Hameroff is an anaesthetist and his ideas have been based on the processes involved in anaesthesia which induce loss of consciousness. For example, under general anaesthetic, individuals should not be able to move purposefully in response to a painful stimulus and should not be able to follow verbal commands (Franks and Lieb, 1998). The general process of anaesthesia is summarised in Table 9.1. There is some evidence that patients may be capable of remembering events/voices in the operating theatre during anaesthesia but this is quite controversial (Andrade, 1995).

In Hameroff's model, microtubules are essential to consciousness. The function of microtubules is to transport material inside the neuron and define the shape of the processes that they inhabit; they, therefore, serve an important neural function. The model suggests that quantum events occur in or around these microtubules and that these events give rise to our conscious experience. It suggests this for a number of reasons, not least the reason that microtubules are importance for the functioning of the

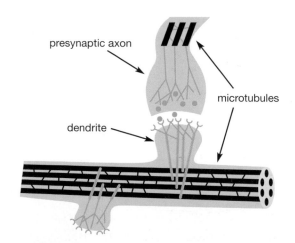

Figure 9.4

The black rods in the diagram represent microtubules. The green dots represent the neurotransmitter released by the presynaptic axon.

Source: From Hameroff, S.R. (1998). More neural than thou. In S.R. Hameroff, A.W. Kaszniak and A.C. Scott (eds) *Towards a science of consciousness II*. New York: Wiley.

Table 9.1 Stages of anaesthetic depth

Stage	Description
I	*Analgesia*. The patient is conscious but drowsy. The degree of analgesia (if any) depends on the anaesthetic.
II	*Excitement*. The patient loses consciousness and does not respond to a non-painful stimulus. The patient may move, talk incoherently, be hypotensive or have other respiratory or cardiovascular irregularities.
III	*Surgical anaesthesia*. Spontaneous movement ceases and ventilation becomes regular. As anaesthesia deepens, various reflexes are lost and the muscles relax.
IV	*Medullary depression*. Respiration and vasomotor control cease, leading to death.

Source: Rang *et al.*, 1995. *Pharmacology*. Churchill Livingstone. © Harcourt, Philadelphia.

neuron. However, this model could be criticised on the same grounds as Crick's in the way that it does not explain why such neural events should be associated with consciousness. In fact, Churchland (1998) has suggested that these microtubules might just as well be called pixie dust in the synapses – essence which magically gives rise to consciousness – although Hameroff (1998) has argued that the mechanism by which microtubules give rise to consciousness is detailed and not as vague as pixie dust. The model, because it is derived from data from anaesthesia, is a highly specific neural model of consciousness and, because of this, holds great promise.

Cognitive theories

Cognitive theories of consciousness, although recognising that consciousness arises from the activity of the brain, describe the way in which it occurs in more mentalistic, cognitive terms.

Baars's global workspace theory

The global workspace theory (Baars, 1988; Baars *et al.*, 1998) states that the contents of consciousness are contained in a central processor called a global workspace. This is used to mediate the activity of nonconscious processes. When such processes need to inform the rest of the system, they send information to the workspace which is a little like a blackboard used by the rest of the system (Baars *et al.*, 1998). The model can thus explain how different types of conscious information are available to us but it does not explain why this information in the global workspace is experienced; in other words it does not solve the 'hard' problem (Chalmers, 1995).

Dennett's multiple drafts

The philosopher and cognitive scientist Daniel Dennett had proposed a complex theory of consciousness that relies on the idea that consciousness is not an all-or-nothing phenomenon that occurs in exactly the same way whenever it is evoked. Dennett begins the rationale for his theory by debunking the mind–body interactionism proposed by Descartes. The notion of the Cartesian theatre where mind and body are interacting protagonists is untenable according to Dennett. Instead, he argues that consciousness is not a theatre but the activation of revised collections of sensory information called 'drafts'. Because sensory information is received in various forms and at various times, conscious experience is an updating, constantly revising process a little like an author's manuscript which is in a constant state of redrafting and revision. Conscious experiences, therefore, result from multiple drafts of sensory information which are assembled at particular points in time. You can see why the theory is complex. One criticism of Dennett's theory is that, although it seems to abolish the notion of the Cartesian theatre, he is replacing it with a large number of theatres.

Shanon's theory

Shanon (1990, 1998) has argued, like Dennett and Baars, that consciousness is not unitary. Unlike Dennett and Baars, however, he invokes three components which he regards as making up consciousness: sensed being, mental awareness and reflection. *Sensed being* distinguishes between animate and living and inanimate and dead; *mental awareness* refers to the idea that we are aware of thoughts that pass through our heads, that is, we are aware of the contents of consciousness; *reflection* refers to the idea that we are aware of our mental computations and that these 'mentations' can be the subject of future 'mentations'. According to Shanon, there are two types of reflection: *meta-observation* which reflects on the content of mental states, and *monitoring* or *control* which checks and evaluates thoughts; this control guides or governs our thinking process. According to Shanon, mental awareness is the core of consciousness whereas sensed being is a prerequisite and reflection is derived from it. How, however, would one go about testing Shanon's theory? This would be difficult because the components are vaguely and generally described. It is also open to the criticism that it is too descriptive and actually explains very little.

Consciousness and theories of consciousness

- What does it mean to be conscious?

- Do you think that other animals have consciousness? How would you define consciousness in other species?

- Some scientists suggest that conscious experience does and should lie outside the domain of scientific theory. Do you agree? Why?

- Is consciousness an epiphenomenon, as some have suggested, or a substantial phenomenon that we can study?

- If consciousness can be reduced to cells X being in state Y (this is called identity theory), what neurobiological theory reviewed in this chapter do you think would best account for the nature of consciousness?

- Chalmers (1998) has listed twenty possible neural correlates of consciousness. Can they all be right?

- When a stimulus is presented to the right hemisphere of a person with a split brain, the person (speaking with his or her left hemisphere) claims to be unaware of it. Thus, the left hemisphere is unaware of stimuli perceived only by the right hemisphere. Because the right hemisphere cannot talk to us, should we conclude that it lacks conscious self-awareness? If you think it is conscious, has the surgery produced two independent consciousnesses where only one previously existed?

- Are multiple drafts really multiple theatres?

- Is Chalmers (1995) right in describing the understanding of functions, neural correlates and abilities as the easy problems of consciousness, but the experience accompanying these processes as the difficult problem?

- Do we need consciousness to function? Think about your liver at this moment. Do you need to be aware of the way in which it works or even be aware of it working in order for it to do its job? What does your answer say about the importance of consciousness?

Selective attention

We do not become conscious of all the stimuli detected by our sensory organs. For example, if you are writing an essay or laboratory practical report while the radio is on in the background and you have to meet an urgent deadline, you probably are unaware of what song is actually playing on the radio, or of the noises outside your room, of the hum of the refrigerator. Attention is completely devoted to your work. The process that controls our awareness of particular categories of events in the environment is called selective attention.

As we saw in Chapter 8, sensory memory receives more information than it can transfer into short-term (working) memory. Sperling (1960) found that although people could remember only about four or five of the nine letters he flashed onto the screen if they tried to remember them all, they could direct their attention to any of the three lines of letters contained in sensory memory and identify them with perfect accuracy.

The process of selective attention determines which events we become conscious of. Attention may be controlled automatically, as when an intense stimulus (such as a loud sound) captures our attention; it may be controlled by instructions ('Pay attention to that one over there!'); or it may be controlled by the demands of the particular task we are performing. For example, when we are driving a car, we pay special attention to other cars, pedestrians, road signs and so on. Our attentional mechanisms serve to enhance our responsiveness to certain stimuli and to tune out irrelevant information.

Attention plays an important role in memory. By exerting control over the information that reaches short-term memory, it determines what information ultimately becomes stored in explicit long-term memory (the portion of long-term memory that we can talk about and can become conscious of, as we saw in Chapter 8). But the storage of information in implicit memory does not require conscious attention. Not all the information we do not pay attention to is lost.

Why does selective attention exist? Why do we not simply process all the information that is being gathered by our sensory receptors; we sometimes miss something important because our attention is occupied elsewhere. According to Broadbent (1958), the answer is that the brain mechanisms responsible for conscious processing of this information have a limited capacity. There is only so much information that these mechanisms can handle at one particular moment. Thus, we need some system to serve as a gatekeeper, controlling the flow of information to this system. The nature of this gatekeeper – selective attention – is the subject of ongoing research.

Dichotic listening

The first experiments to investigate the nature of attention scientifically took advantage of the fact that we have two ears. Cherry (1953) devised a test of selective attention called dichotic listening, a task that requires a person to listen to one of two messages presented simultaneously, one to each ear (dichotic means 'divided into two parts'). He placed headphones on his participants and presented recordings of different spoken messages to each ear, as illustrated by Figure 9.5.

He asked the participants to shadow the message presented to one ear – to repeat back as quickly but as accurately as possible what that voice was saying. Shadowing ensured that they would pay attention only to that message.

Figure 9.5

Dichotic listening and shadowing. A person listens to two different spoken messages simultaneously and continuously repeats back what one voice is saying.

The information that entered the unattended ear appeared to be lost. When questioned about what that ear had heard, participants responded that they had heard something, but they could not say what it was. Even if the voice presented to the unshadowed ear began to talk in a foreign language or read English backwards, participants do not notice the change (Wood and Cowan, 1995). Shadowing, however, is easier if the messages are physically different, that is, they are spoken by different sexes or one is louder than the other or one is speech and the other non-speech based.

Other evidence shows that selective attention is not achieved by simply closing a sensory channel. Some information, by its very nature, can break through into consciousness. For example, if a person's name is presented to the unattended ear, he or she will very likely hear it and remember it later (Moray, 1959). Or if the message presented to the unattended ear contains sexually explicit words, people tend to notice them immediately (Nielsen and Sarason, 1981). The fact that some types of information presented to the unattended ear can grab our attention indicates that even unattended information undergoes some verbal analysis. If the unattended information is 'filtered out' at some level, this filtration must not occur until after the sounds are identified as words.

Several studies have shown that information presented to the unattended ear can affect our behaviour even if we do not become conscious of the information. To put it another way, the information can produce implicit memories, memories of which we are unaware (Cleermans, 1993). Von Wright *et al.* (1975) showed that words previously presented along with an unpleasant electrical shock would produce an emotional reaction when the words were presented to the unattended ear. Even when the participant was not consciously attending to the voice, the information produced a non-verbal response – a classically conditioned emotional reaction. Thus, the unattended information could trigger the recall of an implicit memory.

McKay (1973) showed that information presented to the unattended ear can influence verbal processing even when the listener is not conscious of this information. In the attended ear, participants heard sentences such as:

They threw stones towards the bank yesterday.

While this sentence was being presented, the participants heard the word 'river' or 'money' in the unattended ear. Later, they were asked which of the following sentences they had heard:

They threw stones towards the side of the river yesterday.
They threw stones towards the savings and loan association yesterday.

Of course, the participants had heard neither of these sentences. McKay found that the participants' choices were determined by whether the word 'river' or 'money' was presented to the unattended ear. They did not specifically recall hearing the words presented to the unattended ear, but obviously these words had affected their perception of the meaning of the word 'bank'.

Treisman (1960) showed that people can follow a message that is being shadowed even if it switches from one ear to the other. Suppose a person is shadowing a message presented to the left ear, while the message to the right ear is unshadowed. In the example given in Figure 9.6, the person will probably say 'crept out of the swamp' and not 'crept out of flowers'. Apparently, the switch occurs when the message begins to make no sense. However, by the time the person realises that 'crept out of flowers' makes no sense, the rest of the message, 'the swamp', has already been presented to the right ear. Because the person is able to continue the message without missing any words, he or she must be able to retrieve some words from memory. Thus, even though an unshadowed message cannot be remembered later, it produces some trace that can be retrieved if attention is directed to it soon after the words are presented.

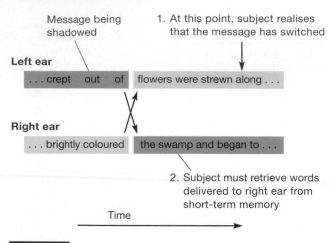

Figure 9.6

Shadowing a message that switches ears. When the message switches, the person must retrieve some words from memory that were heard by the unattended ear.

The cocktail-party phenomenon

Selective attention to auditory messages has practical significance outside the laboratory. For example, sometimes we have to sort out one message from several others without the benefit of such a distinct cue; we seldom hear one voice in one ear and another voice in the other. We might be trying to converse with one person while we are in a room with several other people who are carrying on their own conversations. We can usually sort out one voice from another – an example of the **cocktail-party phenomenon**.

In this case, we are trying to listen to the person opposite us and to ignore the cross-conversation of the people to our left and right. Our ears receive a jumble of sounds, but we are able to pick out the ones we want, stringing them together into a meaningful message and ignoring the rest. This task takes some effort; following one person's conversation in such circumstances is more difficult when what he or she is saying is not very interesting. If we overhear a few words of another conversation that seems more interesting, it is hard to strain out the cross-conversation.

Background noise

The opposite phenomenon – where we try to exclude (become less conscious of) auditory information – has great practical implications. Background noise, for example, is common in office environments and is a source of interference in open-plan offices (Klitzman and Stellman, 1989). Although there are very few controlled scientific experiments, existing studies report that background office noise is associated with stress, lack of concentration, low levels of performance and reduced employee efficiency (Loewen and Suedfeld, 1992; Sundstrom *et al.*, 1994).

Of course, we would not expect background noise to interfere with every type of behaviour. Music played in the background, for example, may even improve our performance (as we will see in Chapter 11). Are there specific auditory stimuli, therefore, that selectively impair the performance of specific tasks? Salame and Baddeley (1982), for example, have suggested that performance on a cognitive task can only be disrupted if the auditory stimulus doing the disruption is speech; others have suggested that stimuli other than speech can affect performance, giving rise to what has been termed the irrelevant speech effect (LeCompte *et al.*, 1997). The irrelevant speech effects suggests that any disruptive sound (delivered at conversational level) can impair memory for verbal material during serial (that is, when the material has to be recalled in a specific order) and free recall (Salame and Baddeley, 1990; Jones, 1995). An alternative to the speech effect is that the noise disrupting performance has to show variation from one part to the next (rather than being speech-like) before recall is disrupted. This is called the changing state hypothesis (Jones *et al.*, 1992). This theory would suggest that, in an office environment, performance would be disrupted by speech and office noise.

To test this hypothesis, Banbury and Berry (1998) exposed undergraduates to office noise with speech, office noise without speech, speech or no noise while they (1) memorised a prose passage describing martial arts instructions for the correct and incorrect way of stretching muscles, and (2) solved a variety of arithmetical problems (division and subtraction). Memory for the prose passage was measured shortly afterwards. The experimenters found that office noise with speech and speech alone had a detrimental effect on memory for the prose passage; individuals in the office noise without speech condition, however, did not perform significantly differently from the control group, suggesting that the speech component of the noise was important (as Salame and Baddeley suggested). All three noise conditions, however, were associated with deficits in arithmetic performance. The experimenters noted that individuals were exposed to a greater duration of noise during the arithmetic task. Before the irrelevant speech effect explanation could be ruled out, therefore, the experimenters suggested that length of exposure to noise needed to be extended in the prose recall condition. This they did by exposing individuals to office noise with speech, office noise without speech, meaningless speech or no noise during acquisition of the prose and during recall.

Extending the exposure period from five to nine minutes significantly and detrimentally affected memory performance when participants were exposed to office noise without speech and meaningless speech (duration did not affect performance in the office noise with speech condition). The greater impairment with greater exposure supported the results of other studies which showed that increasing the number of irrelevant background words presented during a primary task resulted in poorer memory performance (Bridges and Jones, 1996). This study, therefore, suggests that different categories of noise affect ongoing cognitive activity differently.

Models of selective attention

With all this evidence suggesting the robustness of selective attention, are we any closer to understanding how we selectively attend? In cognitive psychology, models of selective attention have been broadly divided into two: early selection models and late selection models. We consider the early selection models here.

Early selection models

The primary feature of early selection models (ESM) is that if items are not attended to, they are not selected for perceptual analysis and so play no further part in information processing. Late selection models, on the other hand, argue that all information is attended to and is only selected later on in the information processing chain, that is, after perceptual analysis of the stimuli. Most of the influential ESM models were developed in the 1950s and 1960s when organisational psychology was making large inroads into workforce behaviour. Psychologists such as Donald Broadbent were interested in how psychological principles could be applied to understanding real-life problems, such as operating air traffic control systems or navigating a plane, both of which require extraordinary attention and selective attention.

Broadbent proposed a model of attention which was popular at the time because it was testable and falsifiable. However, evidence has shown that features of the model were incorrect. Broadbent proposed a filter theory of attention which suggested that processing information was a little like the operation of a filtering system: a channel of communication would process information and transmit this information to other cognitive systems for analysis. Specifically, Broadbent suggested that this filter initially processes information from a 'sensory store' and transfers it to other cognitive systems. This was an all-or-nothing model: only selected material would pass through the filter system. This selected material would then make its way to a *limited capacity P(erceptual) system* which would identify the material.

The all-or-nothing feature of the model can certainly explain why material presented to the unattended ear in dichotic listening experiments is not processed. A series of experiments by Moray (1959), however, suggested that the basic feature of the model was wrong. Moray found that when participants were instructed to switch attention from one ear to another during the experiment, they were able to do this when the instruction was along the lines of, 'Robyn, switch ears.' According to the model, this channel

should have been blocked and should have remained unattended: the participant should have been attending exclusively to another channel. Another set of experiments also demonstrated that listeners could follow messages that were switched from one ear to the other. For example, a narrative would begin in one ear and be switched to the previously unattended ear (Treisman, 1960, 1964). Participants, contrary to the filter model, would switch attention to the unattended ear to follow the narrative.

Treisman proposed her own model of selective attention which was 'weaker' than that of Broadbent. She argued that selective attention is certainly an early information processing activity but that not only would attended messages get through to the system, but unattended material would also get through but in weakened, attenuated form. This is called the attenuation model (Treisman, 1960).

Visual information

Sperling's studies of sensory memory, discussed in Chapter 8, demonstrated the role of attention in selectively transferring visual information into verbal short-term memory (or, for our purposes, into consciousness). Other psychologists have studied this phenomenon in more detail. For example, Posner *et al.* (1980) had participants watch a computer-controlled video display screen as a small mark in the centre of the screen served as a fixation point for the participants' gaze. They were shown a warning stimulus near the fixation point followed by a target stimulus – a letter displayed to the left or the right of the fixation point. The warning stimulus consisted of either an arrow pointing right or left or simply a plus sign. The arrows served as cues to the participants to expect the letter to occur either to the right or to the left. The plus sign served as a neutral stimulus, containing no spatial information. The participants' task was to press a button as soon as they detected the letter.

Eighty per cent of the time, the arrow accurately pointed towards the location in which the letter would be presented. However, 20 per cent of the time, the arrow pointed away from the location in which it would occur. The advance warning clearly had an effect on the participants' response times: when they were correctly informed of the location of the letter, they responded faster. This is illustrated in the graph in Figure 9.7.

This study shows that selective attention can influence the detection of visual stimuli: If a stimulus occurs where we expect it, we perceive it more quickly; if it occurs where we do not expect it, we perceive it more slowly. Thus, people can follow instructions to direct their attention to particular locations in the visual field. Because gaze remained fixed on the centre of the screen in this study, this movement of attention was independent of eye movement. How does this focusing of attention work neurologically? The most likely explanation seems to be that neural circuits that detect a particular kind of stimulus are somehow

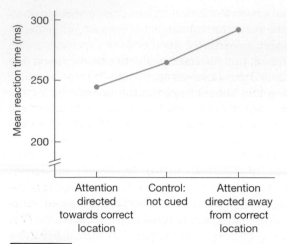

Figure 9.7

Location as a cue for selective attention. Mean reaction time in response to a letter displayed on a screen after subjects received a cue directing attention towards the location in which the letter appears was less than when no cue or an incorrect cue was received.

sensitised, so that they can more easily detect that stimulus. In this case, the mechanism of selective attention sensitised the neural circuits that detect visual stimuli in a particular region.

The second dimension of visual attention is the nature of the object being attended to (Vecera and Farah, 1994; Desimone and Duncan, 1995). Sometimes, two events happen in close proximity, but we can watch one of them while ignoring the other. For example, Neisser and Becklen (1975) showed participants a videotape that presented a situation similar to the one confronted by a person trying to listen to the voice of one person at a cocktail party. The videotape contained two different actions presented one on top of the other: a basketball game and a hand game in which people try to slap their opponents' hands which are resting on top of theirs. The participants could easily follow one scene and remember what had happened in it; however, they could not attend simultaneously to both scenes. The scenes are illustrated in Figure 9.8.

It is possible that the selective attention exercised by Neisser and Becklen's participants was controlled by eye movements as their gaze followed the actions of one of the games. However, Rock and Gutman (1981) found that people can pay attention to one of two shapes, even when the shapes overlap. They presented overlapping outlines of shapes of familiar objects and meaningless forms, drawn in different colours (red and green). They asked the participants to pay attention to only one of the colours. Afterwards, on a recognition test, they showed the participants all the forms they had seen. The participants recognised only those shapes that they had been instructed to pay attention to. Even when the non-attended figures

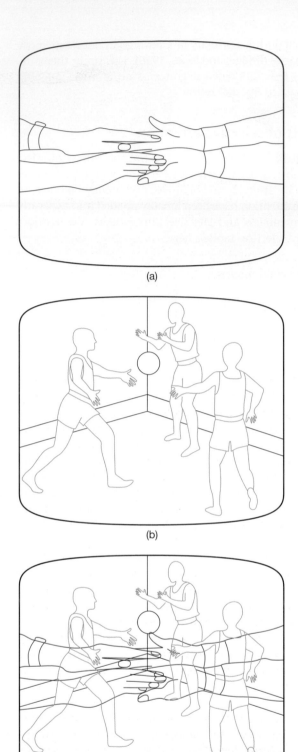

Figure 9.8

Drawings of the scenes from the videotapes in Neisser and Becklen's study. (a) The hand game. (b) The basketball game. (c) The two games superimposed.

Source: Neisser, U. and Becklen, R., *Cognitive Psychology*, 1975, 7, 480–494. Reprinted with permission of the Academic Press, Orlando, Florida.

Figure 9.9

Overlapping shapes. People were told to pay attention to only one colour. On a test later, they recognised only the shapes they had paid attention to previously.

Source: Rock, I. and Gutman, D., *Journal of Experimental Psychology (Human Perception and Performance)*, 1981, 7, 275–285. Copyright © 1981 by the American Psychological Association.

consisted of a familiar shape, they failed to recognise them. Some of the shapes used can be seen in Figure 9.9.

Divided attention

Although all people seem to attend selectively to stimuli in the environment, they also sometimes have to undertake tasks that are made up of multiple components. Imagine cooking a meal, for example. Monitoring your boiling pasta while chopping up peppers and warming up your bolognese sauce requires you to attend to several stimuli. When attention is split in this way it is called divided attention. Various models have sought to explain divided attention and how we can (or, more often, cannot) undertake many tasks all at once. Single-capacity models, for example, suggest that there is one pool of resources available to deal with perceptual and cognitive challenges (Kahneman, 1973). You can probably gather from this that the more tasks an individual undertakes, the less capacity will be left to undertake these tasks effectively because each task is competing for the same pool of resources.

Resources are, then, normally allocated to the most important task. Single-capacity model theorists have found some support for this proposition in experiments where individuals have to undertake two tasks simultaneously (this is called dual-task methodology). When this occurs, performance on both tasks diminishes. Results like these suggest that when the resources necessary to complete tasks exceed the available single capacity, then performance will deteriorate. However, not all evidence supports this view. The anecdotal example of preparing a meal is one subjective example. Experiments in which typists were asked to transcribe text and complete a shadowing task at the same time found the participants were able to do this effectively (Shaffer, 1975). Sometimes, two tasks can be performed as well as one can.

An alternative to the single resource models are the multiple resource models. These argue that, in fact, we have several resource pools to deal with various cognitive and perceptual processes. It is because of these various pools that we can divide our attention between tasks successfully. These models suggest that when two tasks compete for the same resource, this will result in an impairment in task performance. When tasks compete for different resource pools, then they should be performed successfully. A problem with the resource model, however, is operationally defining a resource and the types of task that would use the different 'resources'. There is no general agreement on what the different types of resources are.

A final explanation for divided attention concerns the processes involved in various tasks. For example, Johnston and Heinz (1978) suggest that selective and divided attention requires clearly requires some form of selection. They divide the type of selection required into early (selecting perceptual/sensory information) and late (selecting meaning). Their process model does not agree that there is one structure or system which allows attention. It argues that early selection uses less capacity than late selection. To test this hypothesis, they asked participants to undertake a dichotic listening task where the stimuli differed in terms of their physical features (perceptually) or in terms of their meaning (semantic). Concurrently, the participants undertook a reaction time task in which they had to press a button as soon as a light appeared. The experimenters found that although reaction time was slower when the participants listened to two messages, less capacity was required when the messages differed perceptually (such as the speaker's voice).

Brain mechanisms of selective attention

As we discussed earlier, one possible explanation for selective attention is that some components of the brain's sensory system are temporarily sensitised, which enhances their ability to detect particular categories of stimuli. For example, if a person were watching for changes in shapes, colours or movements (that is, if the person's attention were focused on one of these attributes), we might expect to see increased activity in the portions of the visual cortex devoted to the analysis of shapes, colours, or movements.

This result is exactly what Corbetta *et al.* (1991) found. These investigators had participants look at a computerised display containing thirty coloured rectangles, which could change in shape, colour or speed of movement. The participants were asked to say whether they detected a change. On some trials, the participants were told to pay attention only to one attribute: shape, colour or speed of movement. The stimuli were counterbalanced so that the same set of displays was presented during each condition. Thus, the only difference between the conditions was the type of stimulus change that the participants were watching for.

In a PET study of brain activity during game watching, the experimenters found that paying attention to shape, colour, or speed of movement caused activation of

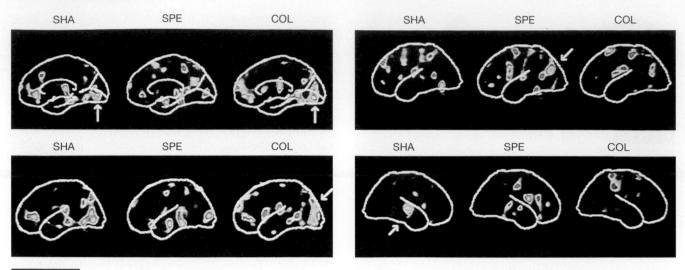

Figure 9.10

PET scans of visual selective attention. The arrows indicate regions of the brain that were activated the most. The three-letter abbreviations above each scan indicate the stimulus dimension to which the person was paying attention: SHA = shape; SPE = speed of movement; COL = colour.

Source: Corbetta, M., Miezen, F.M., Dobmeyer, S., Shulman, G.L. and Peterson, S.E., *Journal of Neuroscience*, 1991, 11, 2383–2402.

different regions of the visual association cortex. The locations corresponded almost precisely to the regions other studies have shown to be activated by shapes, colours or movements. Thus, selective attention towards different attributes of visual stimuli is accompanied by activation of the appropriate regions of the visual association cortex, as seen in Figure 9.10.

Furthermore, the left and right cerebral hemispheres appear to play different roles in attention. Focal attention (which involves attention to local cues) depends on the left hemisphere, whereas global attention (a holistic approach which takes in whole objects or scenes) is dependent on the right hemisphere (Fink *et al.*, 1996). This asymmetry of function may explain the symptoms seen in the perceptual disorder, spatial neglect, described in Chapter 6, in which brain-injured (usually right-hemisphere-damaged) patients are unable to report or respond to stimuli contralateral to the side of the brain injury.

Luck *et al.* (1993) obtained similar results to Corbetta *et al.* (1991) in a study using monkeys. They recorded the activity of single neurons in the visual association cortex. When a cue indicated that the monkey should be watching for a stimulus to be presented in a particular location, neurons that received input from the appropriate part of the visual field began firing more rapidly, even before the stimulus was presented. These neurons seemed to be 'primed' for detecting a stimulus in their part of the visual field.

The role of the brain in conscious awareness and its role in computation have led some psychologists to argue that the brain is a little like a computer. Furthermore, recent work in an area of research called neural networks suggests

that we can computer-simulate the way in which the brain works. These ideas form the basis of the 'Controversies in psychological science' section on pp. 293–5.

Control of consciousness

Every culture appears to have methods of altering consciousness, from the ingestion of coffee, tea, alcohol or tobacco to taking marijuana or cocaine. The urge to alter, expand, or even escape from one's consciousness does not require the use of drugs, however. There is some evidence that self-control may help to alter consciousness. The Ancient Hebrews and early Christians often fasted for many days, undoubtedly because of the effects that their altered metabolism had on their consciousnesses. In earlier times, there was also much more emphasis on ritualised chants and movements, such as those of the early Jewish Hasidim and Cabalists. In fact, the Christian Pentecostal sect and the Jewish Hasidic sects today practise dances and chanting that would not seem strange to thirteen-century mystics, and these rituals encourage the 'taking over' of one's consciousness.

The one function that all methods of changing consciousness have in common is an alteration in attention. The various exercises can be divided into those that withdraw attention from the stimuli around us and those that increase attention to events that have become so commonplace that we no longer notice them, including our own behaviours that have become automatic and relatively non-conscious. We refer to exercises in both categories as meditation. Forms of meditation have developed in almost every

Controversies in psychological science

Does the brain work like a computer?

The issue

In his editorial of an issue of the journal *Perception*, Gregory (1998) asked, 'is the brain a computer?' If a computer is anything that solves problems, then 'yes', says Gregory, 'the brain is a computer'. Similarly, if perception is problem solving (such as being able to perceive an object from poor amounts of sensory data), then the visual brain is also a computer.

Although cognitive psychology has a history that dates back to the early part of this century, most of its philosophy and methodology have developed during the past thirty years. During this time, the best-known physical device that performs functions similar to those of the human brain has been the general-purpose serial computer. Thus, it is the computer that provided (and still provides) much of the inspiration for the models of human brain function constructed by cognitive psychologists.

The evidence

To understand the thought processes that guide the development of models inspired by computers, we must understand something about how modern general-purpose computers work. They consist of four major parts.

- Input devices and output devices (or, collectively, I/O devices) permit us to communicate with the computer – to give it instructions or data and to learn the results of its computations.

- Memory permits information to be stored in the computer. This information can contain instructions or data we have given the computer or the intermediate steps and final results of its calculations.

- A central processor contains the electronic circuits necessary for the computer to perform its functions – to read the information received by the input devices and to store it in memory, to execute the steps specified by the instructions contained in its programs, and to display the results by means of the output devices.

Modern general-purpose computers can be programmed to store any kind of information that can be coded in numbers or words, can solve any logical problem that can be explicitly described, and can compute any mathematical equations that can be written. Therefore, in principle, at least, they can be programmed to do the things we do: perceive, remember, make deductions, solve problems. The power and flexibility of computers seem to make them an excellent basis for constructing models of mental processes. For example, psychologists, linguists and computer scientists have constructed computer-inspired models of visual pattern perception, speech comprehension, reading, control of movement, and memory (Rolls, 1997).

The construction of computer programs that simulate human mental functions is called artificial intelligence. Such an enterprise can help to clarify the nature of mental functions. For instance, to construct a program and simulate perception and classification of certain types of pattern, the investigator must specify precisely what the task of pattern perception requires. If the program fails to recognise the patterns, then the investigator knows that something is wrong with the model or with the way it has been implemented in the program. The investigator revises the model/program, tries again, and keeps working until it finally works (or until he or she gives up the task as being too ambitious). So far, no program is advanced enough to deal with more than a small fraction of the patterns a human can recognise.

Ideally, the task of discovering what steps are necessary in a computer program to simulate some human cognitive abilities tells the investigator the kinds of process the brain must perform. However, there is usually more than one way to accomplish a particular goal. Critics of artificial intelligence have pointed out that even if it is entirely possible to write a program that performs a task that the human brain performs – and comes up with exactly the same results – the computer may perform the task in an entirely different way. In fact, some say, given the way that computers work and what we know about the structure of the human brain, the computer program is guaranteed to work differently.

Serial computers work one step at a time and each step takes time. A complicated program will contain more steps and will take more time to execute. But we

Figure 9.11

Your brain can tell you that this is the Mona Lisa, but how quickly could a computer do this?

Source: Brash, S., Maranto, G., Murphy, W. and Walker, B. (1990) *How Things Work: The Brain*. Virginia: Time-Life Books. Copyright © 1990 by Time-Life Books.

about as quickly as we can a simple one. Look at Figure 9.11, for example.

We know that this is Leonardo Da Vinci's famous paining *La Giaconda* (the Mona Lisa): it is instantly recognisable to us. For a computer to achieve recognition, however, it would need to scan each line of numbers, match it with some sort of template and then identify the stimulus. For us, it takes about the same amount of time to recognise a friend's face as it does to identify a simple triangle. The same is not true at all for a serial computer. A computer must 'examine' the scene through an input device something like a television camera. Information about the brightness of each point of the picture must be converted into a number and stored in a memory location. Then the program examines each memory location, one at a time, and does calculations that determine the locations of lines, edges, textures and shapes. Finally, it tries to determine what these shapes represent. Recognising a face takes much longer than recognising a triangle.

If the brain were a serial device, its maximum speed would probably be around ten steps per second, considering the rate at which neurons can fire (Rumelhart *et al.*, 1986). This rate is extremely slow compared with modern serial computers. Obviously, when we perceive visual images, our brain does not act like a serial device.

Instead, the brain appears to be a parallel processor, in which many different modules (collections of circuits of neurons) work simultaneously at different tasks. A complex task is broken down into many smaller ones, and separate modules work on each of them. Because the brain consists of many billions of neurons, it can afford to devote different clusters of neurons to different tasks, as we saw in Chapters 4 and 6. With so many things happening at the same time, the task gets done quickly.

Recently, psychologists have begun to devise models of mental functions that are based, very loosely, on the way the brain seems to be constructed. These models are called neural networks, and the general approach is called connectionism. One area of psychology where

do some things extremely quickly that computers take a very long time to do. One of the best examples is visual perception. We can recognise a complex figure

culture. Zen Buddhism, Yoga, Sufism and Taoism are the best known and most influential in Eastern societies, where they first developed, but there is also a tradition of meditation and contemplation in the Western world, still carried on in Christian monasteries. Even the ritualised recitation of the Rosary and the clicking of the beads serve to focus a person's attention on the prayer he or she is chanting.

Techniques for withdrawing attention

The goal of most meditation exercises is to remove attention from all sensory stimuli – to think of absolutely nothing. The various techniques require that the meditator direct his or her attention to a single object (such as a specially prepared symbol), to a spoken or imagined word or neural networks have been applied is language, and we turn to this in the next chapter.

Computer simulation specialists have discovered that when they construct a network of simple elements interconnected in certain ways, the network does some surprising things. The elements have properties like those of neurons. They are connected to each other through junctions similar to synapses. Like synapses, these junctions can have either excitatory or inhibitory effects. When an element receives a critical amount of excitation, it sends a message to the elements with which it communicates, and so on. Some of the elements of a network have input lines that can receive signals from the 'outside', which could represent a sensory organ or the information received from another network. Other elements have output lines, which communicate with other networks or control muscles, producing behaviour. Thus, particular patterns of input can represent particular stimuli, and particular patterns of output can represent responses.

Investigators do not construct physical networks. Instead, they write computer programs that simulate them. The programs keep track of each element and the state of each of its inputs and outputs and calculate what would happen if a particular pattern of input is presented. Neural networks can be taught to 'recognise' particular stimuli. They are shown a particular stimulus, and their output is monitored. If the response on the output lines is incorrect, the network is given a signal indicating the correct response. This signal causes the strength of some of the junctions to be changed, just as learning is thought to alter the strength of synapses in the brain. After several trials, the network learns to make correct responses.

If the network uses a sufficiently large number of elements, it can be trained to recognise several different patterns, producing the correct response each time one of the patterns is shown to it. In addition, it will even recognise the patterns if they are altered slightly, or if only parts of the patterns are shown. Thus, neural networks can recognise not only particular patterns but also variations on that pattern. Thus, they act as if they had learned general prototypes, not specific templates. For example, it may learn that the letter A written in Times Roman font is the same as an A written in Palatino font.

Thus, visual perception consists of a series of analyses, beginning with simple features and progressing to more complex ones. Each level of analysis involves a different neural network. In the primary visual cortex the networks are small and local. Each one analyses simple features – such as orientation of lines and edges, colour and movement – within a restricted part of the visual field. In the subregions of the visual association cortex of the occipital lobes, larger networks process the information they receive from the primary visual cortex. For example, the region that receives information about orientation of lines and edges recognises shapes and patterns: squares, circles, dogs, cats, faces. Other networks of neurons in the visual association cortex of the temporal lobes put all the information together and perceive the entire, three-dimensional scene, with objects having particular shapes, colours and textures. The locations of the objects in the visual scene are determined by a network of neurons in the parietal lobes.

Conclusion

So what is the answer to the question 'does the brain work like a computer?' The answer seems to be that it does, but not like the most familiar kind of computer, which cognitive psychologists first used as a basis for constructing models of brain function. The brain appears to be a parallel processor made up of collections of neural networks. Neural networks attempts to simulate the functions of the brain have not met with considerable success (which is not surprising given the complexity of that organ). Most simulations have been of the very basic, perceptual kind. It is interesting to speculate that a strong artificial intelligence position on the nature of simulating brain function would effectively result in the creation of a conscious computer. How likely do you think this is?

phrase (such as a prayer or mantra), to a monotonous sound (such as the rushing of a waterfall), or to a repetitive movement, such as breathing or touching the tips of each of the four fingers with the thumb (West, 1996).

By concentrating on an object, a sound or a repetitive movement we can learn to ignore other stimuli. We achieve this kind of focus to some degree when we read a book intently or attempt to solve a problem. The difference is that the book or problem supplies a changing form of stimulation. Thoughts, words, images and ideas flow through our minds. In contrast, a person attempting to achieve a meditative trance selects an inherently static object of attention that leads to habituation. By concentrating on this unchanging source of information, continually bringing his or her attention back to it, the person achieves a state of utter concentration or nothing. Withdrawal of attention appears to have two primary goals: to reduce verbal control over non-verbal functions of the brain and to produce afterwards a 'rebound phenomenon' – a heightening of awareness and an increase in attention. The second goal is identical to that of consciousness-increasing exercises.

Questions to think about

Selective and divided attention

- Why do we find it difficult to perform two cognitively demanding tasks at the same time?

- Imagine that you were a person undertaking an extremely tedious and monotonous task (driving long distances, say, or working as an air traffic controller). Would exposure to a stimulus, such as a pleasant odour, help you to perform better or worse? Why?

- Do you work better with noise around you or in silence? Why do you think this is?

- What factors, apart from noise, could affect selective attention? Are some people immune to the effects of extraneous noise?

- Why do we feel that paying attention to something not very interesting takes some effort?

- If we concentrate for a long time, we become tired. Where does this tiredness take place? Do some circuits of neurons become 'weary'? Why do we not become tired when we are concentrating hard on something that interests us?

- Which model do you think best accounts for selective and divided attention? Why?

Hypnosis

Hypnosis is a process whereby verbal suggestions made by one individual can be acted on by another who would not normally and voluntarily perform those acts. Under hypnosis, a person can be induced to bark like a dog, act like a baby or tolerate being pierced with needles. Although these examples are interesting and amusing, hypnosis is important to psychology because it provides information about the nature of consciousness and has applications in the fields of medicine and psychotherapy, as discussed in the Psychology in action section on pp. 298–9.

Hypnosis, or mesmerism, was discovered by Franz Anton Mesmer (1734–1815), an Austrian physician. He found that when he passed magnets back and forth over people's bodies (in an attempt to restore their 'magnetic fluxes' and cure them of disease), they would often have convulsions and enter a trance-like state during which almost miraculous cures could be achieved. As Mesmer discovered later, the patients were not affected directly by the magnetism of the iron rods; they were responding to his undoubtedly persuasive and compelling personality. We now know that convulsions and trancelike states do not necessarily accompany hypnosis, and we also know that hypnosis does not cure physical illnesses. Mesmer's patients apparently had psychologically produced symptoms that were alleviated by suggestions made while they were hypnotised.

The induction of hypnosis

A person undergoing hypnosis can be alert, relaxed, tense, lying quietly or exercising vigorously. There is no need to move an object in front of someone's face or to say 'you are getting sleepy'; an enormous variety of techniques can be used to induce hypnosis in a susceptible person. The only essential feature seems to be the participant's understanding that he or she is to be hypnotised. Moss (1965) reported having sometimes simply said to a well practised subject, in a normal tone of voice, 'Please sit in that chair and go into hypnosis,' and the subject complied within a few seconds. Sometimes, this approach even worked on volunteers who had never been hypnotised before.

The induction process normally involves suggestions for sleep or relaxation, followed by a set of suggestions aimed to produce arm lowering or lifting, hand clasping ('you cannot separate your hands'), hallucinations and amnesia.

Characteristics of hypnosis

Hypnotised people are very suggestible; their behaviour will conform with what the hypnotist says, even to the extent that they may appear to misperceive reality (Wagstaff, 1996). Under hypnosis, people can be instructed to do things that they would not be expected to do under normal conditions, such as acting out imaginary scenes or pretending to be an animal. Hypnotised people can be convinced that an arm cannot move or is insensitive to pain, and they then act as if that is the case. They can also be persuaded to have positive or negative hallucinations – to see things that are not there or not to see objects that are there.

One of the most dramatic phenomena of hypnosis is posthypnotic suggestibility, in which a person is given instructions under hypnosis and follows those instructions after returning to a non-hypnotised state. For example, a hypnotist might tell a man that he will become unbearably thirsty when he sees the hypnotist look at her watch. She might also admonish him not to remember anything upon leaving the hypnotic state, so that posthypnotic amnesia is also achieved. After leaving the hypnotic state, the man acts normally and professes ignorance of what he perceived and did during hypnosis, perhaps even apologising for not having succumbed to hypnosis. The hypnotist later looks at her watch, and the man suddenly leaves the room to get a drink of water.

Studies indicate that when changes in perception are induced in hypnotised people, the changes occur not in the people's actual perceptions but in their verbal reports about their perceptions. For example, Miller *et al.* (1973) used the Ponzo illusion to test the effects of hypnotically induced blindness. This effect is produced by the presence of the slanted lines to the left and right of two horizontal ones; if these lines are not present, the horizontal lines appear to be the same length.

Through hypnotic suggestion, the experimenters made the slanted lines 'disappear'. But even though the participants reported that they could not see the slanted lines, they still perceived the upper line as being longer than the lower one. This result indicates that the visual system continues to process sensory information during hypnotically induced blindness; otherwise, the participants would have perceived the lines as being equal in length. The reported blindness appears to occur not because of altered activity in the visual system but because of altered activity in the verbal system (and in consciousness).

Theories of hypnosis

Most theories of hypnosis revolve around the question of whether hypnosis represents a different state of consciousness (Fellows, 1990; Lynn and Rhue, 1991). The *state hypothesis* of hypnosis suggests that this phenomenon is an example of an altered state of consciousness or a trance resulting from induction (Hilgard, 1986). Hilgard's neo-dissociation theory (Hilgard, 1978, 1991) suggests that we have multiple systems of control which are not all conscious at the same time. These systems are under the general, central control of an 'executive ego' which controls and motivates other systems. The theory suggests that when a person is under hypnosis, overall control is given up to the hypnotist who has access to various systems. Such a theory claims to find support from what is called the 'hidden observer' phenomenon. This is where the experimenter places a hand on the shoulder of the hypnotised individual and appears to be able to talk to a hidden part of the person's body (Knox *et al.*, 1974).

The *non-state hypothesis* of hypnosis argues that the process does not reflect altered states of consciousness but more mundane psychological functions such as imagination, relaxation, role-enactment, compliance, conformity, attention, attitudes and expectations (Coe and Sarbin, 1991; Wagstaff, 1991, 1996). Wagstaff (1996), for example, has argued that hypnosis may very well represent some altered state but the evidence suggests that hypnotic suggestion can be explained by what we already know about human behaviour and thought. Strategic role-enactment is common in psychological research, for example. The degree of role-taking depends on whether the participant is worried about giving up control or being manipulated. To experience a hand getting heavier, the individual can imagine a weight on his or her arm; to experience hypnotic 'amnesia', the individual can distract him or herself. Of course, state theorists would argue that such compliance or acting out is part of hypnotic behaviour that occurs without subjective experience (Spanos, 1991, 1992).

Barber (1979) suggests that at least some aspects of hypnosis are related to events that can happen every day and argues that hypnosis should not be viewed as a special state of consciousness, in the way that sleep is a state of consciousness that differs from waking; rather, the hypnotised person should be seen as acting out a social role. The phenomena of hypnosis are social behaviours, not manifestations of a special state of consciousness. Hypnotised people willingly join with the hypnotist in enacting a role expected of them. Some of the rules governing this role are supplied by the direct instructions of the hypnotist, others are indirectly implied by what the hypnotist says and does, and still others consist of expectations that the people already have about what hypnotised people do.

For example, Spanos (1992) induced negative hallucinations in participants who reported being unable to see the number eight (although it was visible before them). When these participants were told that 'real' hypnotisable individuals, unlike 'fakers', do see the number briefly at the beginning, almost all subjects confirmed that they had seen it. In a more amusing experiment, Barber *et al.* (1974) asked a group of 'hypnotised' participants whether they could hear the experimenter, to which they replied 'no'!

People's expectations about hypnosis do indeed play an important role in their behaviour while under hypnosis. In lectures to two sections of an introductory psychology class, Orne (1959) told one section (falsely) that one of the most prominent features of hypnosis was rigidity of the preferred (that is, dominant) hand. Later, he arranged a demonstration of hypnosis during a meeting of students from both sections. Several of the students who had heard that the dominant hand became rigid showed this phenomenon when hypnotised, but none of the students who had not heard this myth developed a rigid hand. Similarly, if people become willing to follow a hypnotist's suggestions, perhaps they do so because they believe that this suggested behaviour is what is supposed to happen. Perhaps people willingly follow a hypnotist's suggestion to do something silly (such as bark like a dog) because they know that hypnotised people are not responsible for their behaviour.

Psychology in action

Using hypnosis to reduce pain

Pain is the most unpleasant sensory experience humans can suffer. It can derive from many sources, although the commonest are illness and disease. Such pain is normally relieved by surgery or drugs (often the surgery itself causes pain and has to be relieved pharmacologically). There are instances, however, where surgical or pharmacological interventions in pain relief are not successful. Often, in such circumstances, patients turn to hypnotic analgesia as an alternative. Hypnotic analgesia refers to the ability to endure or eliminate surgical pain via hypnotic suggestion (Wagstaff, 1996). Does such analgesic intervention work?

Hypnosis can play a useful role in medicine, dentistry, and psychotherapy (Heap and Dryden, 1991). The analgesia – insensitivity to pain – produced by hypnosis is more effective than that produced by morphine, tranquillisers such as Valium, or acupuncture (Stern et al., 1977). Thus, it can be used to suppress the pain of childbirth or of having one's teeth drilled or to prevent gagging when a dentist is working in a patient's mouth. It is also useful in reducing the nausea caused by the drugs used in chemotherapy for cancer. However, because not all people can be hypnotised, and because the induction of hypnosis takes some time, few physicians or dentists use hypnosis to reduce pain; drugs are easier to administer.

Barber (1996, 1998) has reviewed evidence which suggests that hypnotic treatment for acute pain resulting from medical procedures (chemotherapy, surgery) or recurring pain, is effective. Of course, different types of condition produce different types of pain: some pains are constant, some intermittent. Osteoarthritis and trigeminal neuralgia, for example, produce almost constant pain whereas migraine and sickle cell disease and lower back pain caused by spinal nerve compression produce recurring pain.

Because pain in these conditions is constant or recurring any relief must also be constant and consistent and the duration of the effect must be sizeable (Barnier and McConkey, 1996). There are very few studies which have examined the effect of posthypnotic analgesia – the ability to relieve pain after hypnosis has taken place. Almost all studies of posthypnotic suggestion have been laboratory based. Usually, healthy individuals are asked to place an arm under ice-cold water (the cold-pressor test) or asked to withstand pressure on their limbs (muscle ischaemia). Both procedures do not cause damage although they are acutely painful.

While evidence suggests that pain can be reduced following hypnotic suggestion, the cognitive or physiological mechanisms underlying this reduction are not known. There are 'non-hypnotic' factors which could be involved in pain reduction. For example, non-specific coping strategies, pain relief through feeling numb or cold, the use of relaxation and pre-operative preparation to alleviate anxiety are all successful in reducing the degree of reported surgical pain (Barber et al., 1974; Chaves, 1989). There is also evidence from hypnotised individuals that they do not try to achieve pain reduction but that this comes effortlessly and automatically (Eastwood et al., 1998). Sometimes instructions to not think about a feared or anxiety-provoking stimulus can lead to increased thoughts about this stimulus (Wegner et al., 1987). Participants in an experiment where they deliberately attempted to suppress discomfort, perceived somatic sensations as more painful in a follow-up experiment (Cioffi and Holloway, 1993).

Compliance, role-enactment and other psychological process can also explain examples of antisocial or strange behaviour that individuals can apparently be hypnotised into doing. Hypnotists have induced individuals to expose themselves indecently, pick up dangerous snakes, steal, verbally attack others, put their hands in nitric acid, throw acid at the experimenter, deal heroin, mutilate the Bible and make homosexual approaches (Wagstaff, 1993; Orne and Evans, 1965). However, Orne and Evans (1965) reported that non-hypnotised individuals could also be instructed to perform these acts. What produces this apparent unusual behaviour is the need to want to help the hypnotist or thinking that the antics were safe or that someone else would take responsibility for them (Udolf, 1983).

The hypnotist, entertainer and erstwhile disk jockey Paul McKenna, for example, invokes such psychological mechanisms to explain the odd behaviour he can induce in members of the public during his stage show. There is no real, special trance-like state, only the ability of individuals to become more or less compliant, to be more or less willing to please the hypnotist. For this reason, amongst others, McKenna was acquitted of the charges described in the newspaper report at the beginning of this chapter.

These results have been explained in terms of the ironic processes theory (Wegner, 1989, 1994). According to this theory, the control of mental events is made possible by two processes working together. The operating process retrieves material that puts the organism in a desirable state; the maintaining process searches consciousness for any content that is inconsistent with the desired state. When cognitive tasks reduce the resources available, the effectiveness of the monitoring process increases in comparison with the operating process (Eastwood et al., 1998). Eastwood tested this hypothesis by requiring participants low and high in hypnotisability to report the degree of pain they were experiencing in a pain-induction task at regular intervals. The experimenters found that the frequency of pain reporting was associated with an increase in the level of experienced pain but that highly hypnotisable participants reported less pain.

The fact that only highly hypnotisable participants showed this effect explains why the published research has focused more on these individuals than those who are not particularly susceptible to hypnotic suggestion (Crawford, 1994). Why are highly susceptible individuals more likely to report reductions in pain? Some psychologists have suggested that these individuals can partition their attentional resources more effectively (Hilgard and Hilgard, 1994). Given that we know that certain parts of the brain are responsible for the allocation of attention resources, we might expect highly hypnotisable participants to show activation in these specific brain areas during hypnosis.

Crawford et al. (1993) have reported that highly susceptible individuals showed a bilateral increase in blood flow to the frontal cortex and somatosensory cortex during hypnotic analgesia and the experience of pain. The anterior part of the brain, especially the anterior cingulate cortex, is important for experiencing pain – PET and fMRI studies have shown this area to be active during pain perception, particularly perception of thermal pain (Davis et al., 1995). Studies of the brain's electrical activity have also implicated the frontal and temporal parts of the brain during hypnotically reduced pain perception (Crawford et al., 1998). According to Crawford et al. (1998), this evidence suggests that frontal region deals with the active allocation of attention, whereas the posterior parts are concerned with the spatiotemporal aspects of pain perception (such as where and when the pain is experienced).

This neural activation, of course, does not demonstrate that hypnotic suggestion placed participants in an altered state of consciousness or placed them in a trance. In fact, the findings have very plausible cognitive explanations. Wagstaff (1987) has suggested that many of the effects seen in hypnotic analgesia are the result of the same factors that result in other forms of hypnotism. These factors include social support, relaxation, covert modelling, placebo and social compliance. Belief in the efficacy of the hypnosis is also an important factor. Wagstaff and Royce (1994) found that although hypnotic suggestions for the alleviation of nail-biting was better than non-hypnotic suggestions, the best predictor of abstinence from nail-biting was belief in the efficacy of the procedure. There may, therefore, be a strong placebo effect seen in these studies.

Questions to think about

Hypnosis

- Some people prefer explanations that demystify puzzling phenomena such as hypnosis. Others resist such explanations; for them, an interesting phenomenon is spoiled by an explanation that places it in the realm of physics and biology. Why do you think that these individuals hold the opinions that they do?

- How would you convince a believer in altered states of consciousness that hypnosis can be explained by less exotic factors than altered states?

- Given that smoking is a problem behaviour that many people try to give up, why has hypnosis not helped every non-smoker who wants to give up, give up?

- Does the compliance seen in hypnotism devalue the concept of freewill or does it leave it intact?

- What makes a highly hypnotisable subject?

- How would you design an experiment to examine the effects of hypnotic analgesia on the pain induced by cancer and chemotherapy? How would you ensure that any effect was attributable to hypnosis?

Sleep

Sleep is not a state of unconsciousness. It is a state of altered consciousness. During sleep, we have dreams that can be just as vivid as waking experiences, and yet we forget most of them as soon as they are over. Our amnesia leads us to think, incorrectly, that we were unconscious while we were asleep. In fact, there are two distinct kinds of sleep – and thus, two states of altered consciousness. We spend approximately one-third of our lives sleeping, or trying to, although the reasons for why we sleep are not fully known.

The stages of sleep

Sleep is not uniform. We can sleep lightly or deeply; we can be restless or still; we can have vivid dreams, or our consciousness can be relatively blank. Researchers who have studied sleep have found that its stages usually follow an orderly, predictable sequence.

Most sleep research takes place in sleep laboratories. Because a person's sleep is affected by his or her surroundings, a sleep laboratory contains one or more small bedrooms, furnished and decorated to be as homelike and comfortable as possible. The most important apparatus of the sleep laboratory is the polygraph, a machine located in a separate room that records on paper the output of various devices that can be attached to the sleeper. For example, the polygraph can record the electrical activity of the brain through small metal disks pasted to the scalp, producing an electroencephalogram (EEG). It can record electrical signals from muscles, producing an electromyogram (EMG) or from the heart, producing an electrocardiogram (EKG). Or it can record eye movements through small metal disks attached to the skin around the eyes, producing an electro-oculogram (EOG). Other special transducers can detect respiration, sweating, skin or body temperature, and a variety of other physiological states (Andreassi, 1996).

The EEG record distinguishes between alert and relaxed wakefulness. When a person is alert, the tracing looks rather irregular, and the pens do not move very far up or down. The EEG shows high-frequency (15–30 Hz), low-amplitude electrical activity called beta activity. When a person is relaxed and perhaps somewhat drowsy, the record shows alpha activity, a medium-frequency (8–12 Hz), medium-amplitude rhythm.

When the individual relaxes and becomes drowsy, the EEG changes from beta activity to alpha activity. Figure 9.12 illustrates this and the subsequent stages of sleep.

The first stage of sleep (stage 1) is marked by the presence of some theta activity, EEG activity of 3.5–7.5 Hz.

Awake

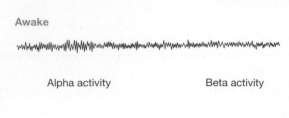

Alpha activity   Beta activity

Stage 1 sleep

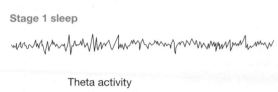

Theta activity

Stage 2 sleep

Stage 3 sleep

Seconds

0 1 2 3 4 5

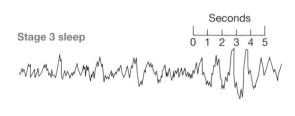

Delta activity

Stage 4 sleep

Delta activity

REM sleep

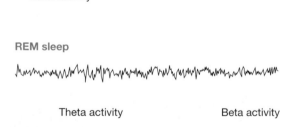

Theta activity   Beta activity

Figure 9.12

An EEG recording of the stages of sleep.

Source: Horne, J.A., *Why We Sleep: The functions of sleep in humans and other mammals*. Oxford: Oxford University Press, 1989. Copyright © 1988 Oxford University Press. By permission of Oxford University Press.

This stage is actually a transition between sleep and wakefulness; the EMG shows that muscles are still active, and the EOG indicates slow, gentle, rolling eye movements. The eyes slowly open and close from time to time. Soon, the person is fully asleep. As sleep progresses, it gets deeper and deeper, moving through stages 2, 3, and 4. The EEG gets progressively lower in frequency and higher in amplitude. Stage 4 consists mainly of delta activity, characterised by relatively high-amplitude waves occurring at less than 3.5 Hz. Our sleeper becomes less responsive to the environment, and it becomes more difficult to awaken him. Environmental stimuli that caused him to stir during stage 1 produce little or no reaction during stage 4. The sleep of stages 3 and 4 is called slow-wave sleep.

Stage 4 sleep is reached in less than an hour and continues for as much as a half hour. Then, suddenly, the EEG begins to indicate lighter levels of sleep, back through stages 3 and 2 to the activity characteristic of stage 1. The sleeper's heartbeat becomes irregular and his respiration alternates between shallow breaths and sudden gasps. The EOG shows that the person's eyes are darting rapidly back and forth, up and down. The EEG record looks like that of a person who is awake and active. Yet the sleeper is fast asleep. Although EMG is generally quiet, indicating muscular relaxation, the hands and feet twitch occasionally.

At this point, the subject is dreaming and has entered another stage of sleep, called rapid eye movement (REM) sleep. The first episode of REM sleep lasts about twenty to thirty minutes and is followed by approximately one hour of slow-wave sleep. As the night goes on, the episodes of REM sleep get longer and the episodes of slow-wave sleep get shorter, but the total cycle remains at approximately

REM sleep	Slow-wave sleep
Rapid EEG waves	Slow EEG waves
Muscular paralysis	Lack of muscular paralysis
Rapid eye movements	Slow or absent eye movements
Penile erection or vaginal secretion	Lack of genital activity
Dreams	

Table 9.2 Principal characteristics of REM sleep and slow-wave sleep

ninety minutes. A typical night's sleep consists of four or five of these cycles. Figure 9.13 shows a record of a person's stages of sleep; the coloured shading indicates REM sleep.

Although a person in REM sleep exhibits rapid eye movements and brief twitches of the hands and feet, the EMG shows that the facial muscles are still. In fact, physiological studies have shown that, aside from occasional twitching, a person actually becomes paralysed during REM sleep. Males are observed to have partial or full erections. In addition, women's vaginal secretions increase at this time. These genital changes are usually not associated with sexual arousal or dreams of a sexual nature. Table 9.2 lists the principal characteristics of REM sleep and slow-wave sleep.

Functions of sleep

Sleep is one of the few universal behaviours. All mammals, all birds and some cold-blooded vertebrates spend part of each day sleeping. Sleep is seen even in species that would seem to be better off without sleep. For example, the Indus dolphin (*Platanista indi*) which lives in the muddy waters of the Indus estuary in Pakistan (Pilleri, 1979). Over the ages, it has become blind, presumably because vision is not useful in the animal's environment (it has an excellent sonar system, which it uses to navigate and find prey). However, despite the dangers caused by sleeping, sleep has not disappeared. The Indus dolphin never stops swimming; doing so would result in injury, because of the dangerous currents and the vast quantities of debris carried by the river during the monsoon season. Pilleri captured two Indus dolphins and studied their habits. He found that they slept a total of seven hours a day, in very brief naps of four to sixty seconds each. If sleep did not perform an important function, we might expect that it, like vision, would have been eliminated in this species through the process of natural selection.

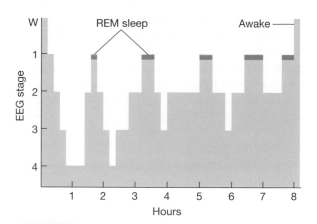

Figure 9.13

Typical progression of stages during a night's sleep. The dark blue shading indicates REM sleep.

Source: Hartmann, E., *The Biology of Dreaming*, 1967. Courtesy of Charles C. Thomas, Publisher, Springfield, Illinois.

The universal nature of sleep suggests that it performs some important functions (Hobson, 1988). One approach to discovering the functions of sleep is the deprivation study. Consider, for example, the function of eating. The effects of starvation are easy to detect: the person loses weight, becomes fatigued and will eventually die if he or she does not eat again. By analogy, it should be easy to discover why we sleep by seeing what happens to a person who goes without sleep.

Unfortunately, deprivation studies have not obtained persuasive evidence that sleep is needed to keep the body functioning normally. Horne (1978) reviewed over fifty experiments in which humans had been deprived of sleep. He reported that most of them found that sleep deprivation did not interfere with people's ability to perform physical exercise. In addition, they found no evidence of a physiological stress response to sleep deprivation. If people encounter stressful situations that cause illness or damage to various organ systems, changes can be seen in such physiological measures as blood levels of cortisol and epinephrine. Generally, these changes did not occur.

Although sleep deprivation does not seem to damage the body, and sleep does not seem to be necessary for athletic exercise, sleep may be required for normal brain functioning. Several studies suggest that sleep-deprived people are able to perform normally on most intellectual tasks, as long as the tasks are short. They perform more poorly on tasks that require a high level of cortical functioning after two days of sleep deprivation (Horne and Minard, 1985). In particular, they perform poorly on tasks that require them to be watchful, alert and vigilant.

During stage 4 sleep, the metabolic activity of the brain decreases to about 75 per cent of the waking level (Sakai *et al.*, 1979). Thus, stage 4 sleep appears to give the brain a chance to rest. In fact, people are unreactive to all but intense stimuli during slow-wave sleep and, if awakened, act groggy and confused, as if their cerebral cortex has been shut down and has not yet resumed its functioning. These observations suggest that during stage 4 sleep the brain is, indeed, resting.

Sleep deprivation studies of humans suggest that although the brain may need slow-wave sleep in order to recover from the day's activities, the rest of the body does not. Another way to determine whether sleep is needed for restoration of physiological functioning is to look at the effects of daytime activity on night-time sleep. If the function of sleep is to repair the effects of activity during waking hours, then we should expect that sleep and exercise are related. That is, we should sleep more after a day of vigorous exercise than after a day spent quietly at an office desk.

In fact, the relation between sleep and exercise is not very compelling. For example, Ryback and Lewis (1971) found no changes in slow-wave or REM sleep of healthy participants who spent six weeks resting in bed. If sleep repairs wear and tear, we would expect these people to sleep less. Adey *et al.* (1968) studied the sleep of completely immobile quadriplegics and paraplegics and found only a small decrease in slow-wave sleep as compared with uninjured people.

Although bodily exercise has little effect on sleep, mental exercise seems to increase the demand for slow-wave sleep. In an ingenious study, Horne and Minard (1985) found a way to increase mental activity without affecting physical activity and without causing stress. The investigators told volunteers to show up for an experiment in which they were supposed to take some tests designed to test reading skills. In fact, when the people turned up, they were told that the plans had been changed. They were invited for a day out, at the expense of the experimenters. They spent the day visiting an art exhibition, a shopping centre, a museum, an amusement park, a zoo and an interesting mansion. After a scenic drive through the countryside they watched a movie in a local cinema. They were driven from place to place and certainly did not become overheated by exercise. After the movie, they returned to the sleep laboratory. They said they were tired, and they readily fell asleep. Their sleep duration was normal and they awoke feeling refreshed. However, their slow-wave sleep, particularly stage 4 sleep, was increased.

Dreaming

A person who is awakened during REM sleep and asked whether anything was happening will almost always report a dream. The typical REM sleep dream resembles a play or movie – it has a narrative form. Conversely, reports of narrative, story-like dreams are rare among people awakened from slow-wave sleep. In general, mental activity during slow-wave sleep is more nearly static; it involves situations rather than stories and generally unpleasant ones. For example, a person awakened from slow-wave sleep might report a sensation of being crushed or suffocated.

Unless the sleep is heavily drugged, almost everyone has four or five bouts of REM sleep each night, with accompanying dreams. Yet if the dreamer does not happen to awaken while the dream is in progress, it is lost for ever. Some people who claimed not to have had a dream for many years slept in a sleep laboratory and found that, in fact, they did dream. They were able to remember their dreams because the investigator awakened them during REM sleep.

The reports of people awakened from REM and slow-wave sleep clearly show that people are conscious during sleep, even though they may not remember any of their experiences then. Lack of memory for an event does not mean that it never happened; it only means that there is no permanent record accessible to conscious thought during wakefulness. Thus, we can say that slow-wave sleep and REM sleep reflect two different states of consciousness.

Functions of dreams

There are two major approaches to the study of dreaming: a psychological analysis of the contents of dreams, and psychobiological research on the nature and functions of REM sleep.

Symbolism in dreams

Since ancient times, people have regarded dreams as important, using them to prophesy the future, decide whether to go to war, or to determine the guilt or innocence of a person accused of a crime. In this century, Sigmund Freud proposed a very influential theory about dreaming. He said that dreams arise out of inner conflicts between unconscious desires (primarily sexual ones) and prohibitions against acting out these desires, which we learn from society. According to Freud, although all dreams represent unfulfilled wishes, their contents are disguised and expressed symbolically. The latent content of the dream (from the Latin word for 'hidden') is transformed into the manifest content (the actual story-line or plot). Taken at face value, the manifest content is innocuous, but a knowledgeable psychoanalyst can supposedly recognise unconscious desires disguised as symbols in the dream. For example, climbing a set of stairs or shooting a gun might represent sexual intercourse. The problem with Freud's theory is that it is not disprovable; even if it is wrong, a psychoanalyst can always provide a plausible interpretation of a dream that reveals hidden conflicts disguised in obscure symbols.

Hall (1966), who agrees that symbols can be found in dreams, does not believe that they are usually hidden. For example, a person may plainly engage in sexual intercourse in one dream and have another dream that involves shooting a gun. Surely the 'real' meaning of shooting the gun need not be hidden from a dreamer who has undisguised dreams of sexual intercourse at other times or who has an uninhibited sex life during waking. Why should this person disguise sexual desires while dreaming? As Hall says, people use their own symbols, not those of anyone else. They represent what the dreamer thinks, and therefore, their meaning is usually not hidden from the dreamer.

Hobson (1988) proposed an explanation for dreaming that does not involve unconscious conflicts or desires. As we will see later, research using laboratory animals has shown that REM sleep occurs when a circuit of acetylcholine-secreting neurons in the pons becomes active, stimulating rapid eye movements, activation of the cerebral cortex and muscular paralysis. The activation of the visual system produces both eye movements and images. In fact, several experiments have found that the particular eye movements that a person makes during a dream correspond reasonably well with the content of a dream; that is, the eye movements are those that one would expect a person to make if the imaginary events were really occurring (Dement, 1974). The images evoked by the cortical activation often incorporate memories of episodes that have occurred recently or of things that a person has been thinking about lately. Presumably, the circuits responsible for these memories are more excitable because they have recently been active. Hobson suggests that although the activation of these brain mechanisms produces fragmentary images, our brains try to tie these images together and make sense of them by creating a more or less plausible story.

We still do not know whether the particular topics we dream about are somehow related to the functions that dreams serve or whether the purposes of REM sleep are fulfilled by the physiological changes in the brain regardless of the plots of our dreams. Given that we do not really know for sure why we dream, this uncertainty is not surprising. But the rapid progress being made in most fields of brain research suggests that we will have some answers in the not-too-distant future.

Effects of REM sleep deprivation

As we saw, total sleep deprivation impairs people's ability to perform tasks that require them to be alert and vigilant. What happens when only REM sleep is disrupted? People who are sleeping in a laboratory can be selectively deprived of REM sleep. An investigator awakens them whenever their polygraph records indicate that they have entered REM sleep. The investigator must also awaken control participants just as often at random intervals to eliminate any effects produced by being awakened several times.

If someone is deprived of REM sleep for several nights and is then allowed to sleep without interruption, the onset of REM sleep becomes more frequent. It is as if a need for REM sleep builds up, forcing the person into this state more often. When the person is no longer awakened during REM sleep, a rebound phenomenon is seen: the person engages in many more bouts of REM sleep than normal during the next night or two, as if catching up on something important that was missed.

Researchers have discovered that the effects of REM sleep deprivation are not very striking. In fact, medical journals contain reports of several patients who showed little or no REM sleep after sustaining damage to the brain stem (Lavie et al., 1984; Gironell et al., 1995). The lack of REM sleep did not appear to cause serious side effects. One of the patients, after receiving his injury, completed high school, attended law school and began practising law.

Several investigators have suggested that REM sleep may play a role in learning. For example, Greenberg and Pearlman (1974) suggest that REM sleep helps to integrate memories of events of the previous day – especially those dealing with emotionally related information – with existing memories. Crick and Mitchison (1983) suggest that

REM sleep helps flush irrelevant information from memory to prevent the storage of useless clutter. Many studies using laboratory animals have shown that deprivation of REM sleep does impair the ability to learn a complex task. However, although the animals learn the task more slowly, they still manage to learn it. Thus, REM sleep is not necessary for learning. If REM sleep does play a role in learning, it appears to be a subtle one, at least, in the adult. As we shall see next, REM sleep may be important for brain development.

Role of REM sleep in brain development

REM sleep begins early in development. Studies of human foetuses and infants born prematurely indicate that REM sleep begins to appear thirty weeks after conception and peaks at around forty weeks (Roffwarg et al., 1966; Petre-Quadens and De Lee, 1974; Inoue et al., 1986). REM sleep of foetuses was recorded harmlessly by using ultrasound to watch eye movements. Approximately 70 per cent of a newborn infant's sleep is REM sleep. By six months of age, this proportion has declined to approximately 30 per cent. By eight years of age, it has fallen to approximately 22 per cent. By late adulthood, it is less than 15 per cent.

Researchers have long been struck by the fact that the highest proportion of REM sleep is seen during the most active phase of brain development. Perhaps, then, REM sleep plays a role in this process. Of course, no one has experimented on infants by depriving them of REM sleep to see whether their brain development was impaired. But such studies have been carried out on laboratory animals. For example, Mirmiran (1995) described a series of studies he and his colleagues performed with infant rats. They injected the rats with drugs that suppressed REM sleep during the second and third weeks of life and found that the animals showed behavioural abnormalities as adults. In addition, their cerebral cortices and brain stems were smaller than those of control participants.

Of course, we cannot be sure that the effects of the drugs on brain development were caused by the REM sleep deprivation. The drugs may have had other effects beside REM sleep suppression that were responsible for these effects. However, Marks et al. (1995) deprived kittens of REM sleep without using drugs and found abnormalities in the development of the animals' visual systems. Thus, the hypothesis that REM sleep aids brain development seems to be reasonable and merits further study. Exactly what role REM sleep might play is still not known.

Brain mechanisms of sleep

If sleep is a behaviour, then some parts of the brain must be responsible for its occurrence. In fact, researchers have discovered several brain regions that have special roles in sleep and biological rhythms.

All living organisms show rhythmic changes in their physiological processes and behaviour. Some of these rhythms are simply responses to environmental changes. For example, the growth rate of plants is controlled by daily rhythms of light and darkness. In animals, some rhythms are controlled by internal 'clocks', located in the brain. Mammals have two biological clocks that play a role in sleep. One of these controls circadian rhythms – rhythms that oscillate once a day (circa 'about', dies 'day'). The second clock, which controls the cycles of slow-wave and REM sleep, oscillates several times a day.

The clock that controls circadian rhythms is located in a small pair of structures located at the bottom of the hypothalamus: the suprachiasmatic nuclei (SCN). The activity of neurons in the SCN oscillates once each day; the neurons are active during the day and inactive at night. These changes in activity control daily cycles of sleep and wakefulness. If people are placed in a windowless room with constant lighting, they will continue to show circadian rhythms, controlled by the oscillations of their suprachiasmatic nuclei. However, because this biological clock is not very accurate, people's circadian rhythms will eventually get out of synchrony with the day/night cycles outside the building. But within a few days after leaving the building, their rhythms will become resynchronised with those of the sun. This resynchronisation is accomplished by a direct connection between the eyes and the SCN. Each morning, when we see the light of the sun (or turn on the room lights), our biological clock resets and begins ticking off the next day.

The second biological clock in the mammalian brain runs considerably faster, and it runs continuously, unaffected by periods of light and darkness. In humans, this clock cycles with a ninety-minute period. The first suggestion that a ninety-minute cycle occurs throughout the day came from the observation that infants who are fed on demand show regular feeding patterns (Kleitman, 1961). Later studies found ninety minute cycles of rest and activity, including such activities as eating, drinking, smoking, heart rate, oxygen consumption, stomach motility, urine production and performance on various tasks that make demands on a person's ability to pay attention. Kleitman (1982) termed this phenomenon the basic rest–activity cycle (BRAC). During the night, the clock responsible for the BRAC controls the alternating periods of REM sleep and slow-wave sleep.

Studies using laboratory animals have found that the clock responsible for the BRAC is located somewhere in the pons. The pons also contains neural circuits that are responsible for REM sleep. The neurons that begin a period of REM sleep release acetylcholine. The release of this transmitter substance activates several other circuits of neurons. One of these circuits activates the cerebral cortex and causes dreaming. Another activates neurons in the midbrain and causes rapid eye movements. Yet another

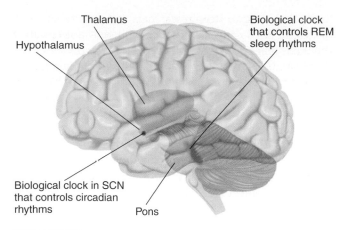

Thalamus

Hypothalamus

Biological clock that controls REM sleep rhythms

Biological clock in SCN that controls circadian rhythms

Pons

Figure 9.14

Two biological clocks in the human brain. The suprachiasmatic nucleus (SCN) of the hypothalamus is responsible for circadian rhythms. The clock in the pons is responsible for the basic rest–activity cycle (BRAC) and cycles of REM sleep and slow-wave sleep.

activates a set of inhibitory neurons that paralyses us and prevents us from acting out our dreams. The location of the two biological clocks is shown in Figure 9.14.

The first hint that REM sleep was turned on by acetyl-choline-secreting neurons came from the observation that overdoses of insecticides that excite such neurons also cause visual hallucinations, like those of dreaming. Subsequent research using laboratory animals confirmed this suspicion. These acetylcholine-secreting neurons (referred to as REM-ON neurons) are normally inhibited by neurons that secrete another transmitter substance, sero-tonin. Thus, drugs that decrease the activity of serotonin-secreting neurons will permit the REM-ON neurons to become active. LSD is one of these drugs, and this fact explains why people who take LSD experience visual hal-lucinations similar to the ones that occur during dreams. On the other hand, drugs that increase the activity of sero-tonin-secreting neurons will suppress REM sleep. All anti-depressant drugs have this effect, which suggests that excessive amounts of REM sleep may play a role in mood disorders.

What about the brain mechanisms responsible for slow-wave sleep? The most important brain region seems to be the **preoptic area**, located just in front of the hypothala-mus, at the base of the brain (this region is named after the fact that it is located anterior to the point where some axons in the optic nerves cross to the other side of the brain). If the preoptic area is destroyed, an animal will sleep much less (McGinty and Sterman, 1968; Szymusiak and McGinty, 1986). If it is electrically stimulated, an ani-mal will become drowsy and fall asleep (Sterman and Clemente, 1962a).

Sleep disorders

Sleep does not always go smoothly, and some of the brain mechanisms responsible for sleep can malfunction, causing medical problems that manifest themselves while a person is awake. Fortunately, some of the things that sleep researchers have learned can help people with sleep-associated disorders.

Insomnia

Insomnia is a problem that is said to affect at least 20 per cent of the population at some time (Raybin and Detre, 1969). There is no single definition of insomnia that can apply to all people. The amount of sleep that individuals require is quite variable. A short sleeper may feel fine with five hours of sleep; a long sleeper may still feel unrefreshed after ten hours. Insomnia must be defined in relation to a person's particular sleep needs.

Ironically, the most important cause of insomnia seems to be sleeping medication. Insomnia is not a disease that can be corrected with a medicine, in the way that diabetes can be treated with insulin. Insomnia is a symptom. If it is caused by pain or discomfort, the physical ailment that leads to the sleeplessness should be treated. If it is second-ary to personal problems or psychological disorders, these problems should be dealt with directly. Patients who receive sleeping medications develop a tolerance to them and suf-fer rebound symptoms if they are withdrawn (Weitzman, 1981). That is, the drugs lose their effectiveness, so the patient requests larger doses from the physician. If a patient attempts to sleep without his or her accustomed medication or even takes a smaller dose one night, he or she is likely to experience a withdrawal effect: a severe disturbance of sleep. The patient becomes convinced that the insomnia is even worse than before and turns to more medication for relief. This common syndrome is called drug dependency insomnia. Kales *et al.* (1979) found that withdrawal of some sleeping medications produced a rebound insomnia after the drugs were used for as few as three nights.

A common cause of insomnia, especially in older peo-ple, is **sleep apnoea** (apnoea means 'without breathing'): they cannot sleep and breathe at the same time. When they fall asleep, they stop breathing, the content of carbon dioxide in their blood builds up, and they awaken, gasping for air. After breathing deeply for a while, they go back to sleep and resume the cycle. Some people who suffer from sleep apnoea are blessed with a lack of memory for this periodic sleeping and awakening; others are aware of it and dread each night's sleep. Fortunately, some types of sleep apnoea in adults can be corrected by throat surgery.

Disorders associated with REM sleep

Two important characteristics of REM sleep are dreaming and paralysis. The paralysis results from a brain mechanism that prevents us from acting out our dreams. In fact, damage to specific regions of the pons of a cat's brain will produce just that result: the cat, obviously asleep, acts as if it were participating in a dream (Jouvet, 1972). It walks around stalking imaginary prey and responding defensively to imaginary predators.

This phenomenon can occur in humans, too. Several years ago, Schenck *et al.* (1986) reported the existence of an interesting syndrome: REM sleep behaviour disorder, the absence of the paralysis that normally occurs during REM sleep. Studies using laboratory animals have shown that the neural circuitry that controls the paralysis that accompanies REM sleep is located in the pons. In humans, REM sleep behaviour disorder seems to be produced by damage to this region (Culebras and Moore, 1989).

Dreams and muscular paralysis are fine when a person is lying in bed. But some people have periodic attacks of a sleep-related disorder called cataplexy (*kata-* 'down', *plessein* 'to strike'). They are struck down by paralysis while actively going about their business. They fall to the ground and lie there, paralysed but fully conscious. Attacks of cataplexy generally last less than a minute. The attacks are usually triggered by strong emotional states, such as anger, laughter or even lovemaking. People who have cataplectic attacks tend also to enter REM sleep as soon as they fall asleep, in contrast to the normal ninety-minute interval.

Cataplexy is a biological disorder, probably involving inherited abnormalities in the brain. In fact, researchers have even developed breeds of dogs that are subject to attacks of cataplexy so that they can study this disorder in the laboratory. As we saw, brain mechanisms responsible for REM sleep are normally inhibited by serotonin-secreting neurons. Cataplexy can be treated by drugs that increase the activity of these neurons, thus increasing the inhibition.

Disorders associated with slow-wave sleep

Several phenomena occur during the deepest phase (stage 4) of slow-wave sleep. These events include sleepwalking, sleeptalking, night terrors and enuresis.

Sleepwalking can be as simple as getting out of bed and right back in again or as complicated as walking out of a house and climbing into a car (sleepwalkers, apparently, do not try to drive). We know that sleepwalking is not the acting out of a dream because it occurs during stage 4 of slow-wave sleep, when the EEG shows high-amplitude slow waves and the person's mental state generally involves a static situation, not a narrative. Sleepwalkers are difficult to awaken; once awakened, they are often confused and disoriented. However, contrary to popular belief, it is perfectly safe to wake them up.

Sleepwalking is not a manifestation of some deep-seated emotional problem. Most sleepwalkers are children, who almost invariably outgrow this behaviour. The worst thing

to do, according to sleep researchers, is to try to get them treated for it. Of course, a house inhabited by a sleepwalker should be made as safe as possible, and the doors should be kept locked at night. Sleepwalking seems to run in families; Dement (1974) reports a family whose grown members were reunited for a holiday celebration. In the middle of the night they awoke to find that they had all gathered in the living room – during their sleep.

Sleeptalking sometimes occurs as part of a REM sleep dream, but it more usually occurs during other stages of sleep. Often, one can carry on a conversation with the sleeptalker, indicating that the person is very near the boundary between sleep and waking. During this state, sleeptalkers are sometimes very suggestible. So-called truth serums are used in an attempt to duplicate this condition, so that the person being questioned is not on guard against giving away secrets and is not functioning well enough to tell elaborate lies. Unfortunately for the interrogators, there are no foolproof, reliable truth serums.

Night terrors, like sleepwalking, occur most often in children. In this disorder, the child awakes, screaming with terror. When questioned, the child does not report a dream and often seems confused. Usually, the child falls asleep quickly without showing any after-effects and seldom remembers the event the next day. Night terrors are not the same as nightmares, which are simply frightening dreams from which one happens to awaken. Apparently, night terrors are caused by sudden awakenings from the depths of stage 4 sleep. The sudden, dramatic change in consciousness is a frightening experience for the child. The treatment for night terrors, like that for sleepwalking, is no treatment at all.

The final disorder of slow-wave sleep, enuresis, or bedwetting, is fairly common in young children. Most children outgrow it, just as they outgrow sleepwalking or night terrors. Emotional problems can trigger enuresis, but bedwetting does not itself indicate that a child is psychologically unwell. The problem with enuresis is that, unlike the other stage 4 phenomena, there are after-effects that must be cleaned up. Parents dislike having their sleep disturbed and get tired of frequently changing and laundering sheets. The resulting tension in family relationships can make the child feel anxious and guilty and can thus unnecessarily prolong the disorder.

Fortunately, a simple training method often cures enuresis. A moisture-sensitive device is placed under the bed sheet; when it gets wet, it causes a bell to ring. Because a child releases only a few drops of urine before the bladder begins to empty in earnest, the bell wakes the child in time to run to the bathroom. In about a week, most children learn to prevent their bladders from emptying and manage to wait until morning. Perhaps what they really learn is not to enter such a deep level of stage 4 sleep in which the mechanism that keeps the bladder from emptying seems to break down.

Questions to think about

Sleep and dreaming

- What is accomplished by dreaming?

- Some researchers believe that the subject matter of a dream does not matter – it is the REM sleep itself that is important. Others believe that the subject matter does count. Some researchers believe that if we remember a dream, the dream failed to accomplish all of its functions; others say that remembering is useful because it can give us some insights into our problems. What do you think of these controversies?

- Some people report that they are 'in control' of some of their dreams – that they feel as if they decide what comes next and are not simply swept along passively. Have you ever had this experience? And have you ever had a 'lucid dream', in which you were aware of the fact that you were dreaming?

- Until recently (in terms of the evolution of our species), our ancestors tended to go to sleep when the sun set and wake up when it rose. Once our ancestors learned how to control fire, they undoubtedly stayed up somewhat later, sitting in front of a fire. But it was only with the development of cheap, effective lighting that many members of our species adopted the habit of staying up late and waking several hours after sunrise. Considering that the neural mechanisms of sleep evolved long ago, do you think the changes in our daily rhythms affect any of our physical and intellectual abilities?

Key terms

split brain *p.281*
callosal syndrome *p.281*
split-brain surgery *p.281*
alien hand *p.282*
intermanual conflict *p.282*
cytoskeleton *p.284*
microtubules *p.284*
selective attention *p.286*
dichotic listening *p.286*
shadowing *p.286*
cocktail-party phenomenon *p.288*
divided attention *p.291*
dual-task methodology *p.291*

artificial intelligence *p.293*
parallel processor *p.294*
neural networks *p.294*
hypnosis *p.296*
mesmerism *p.296*
posthypnotic suggestibility *p.296*
posthypnotic amnesia *p.297*
'hidden observer' phenomenon *p.297*
hypnotic analgesia *p.298*
electroencephalogram (EEG) *p.300*

electromyogram (EMG) *p.300*
electrocardiogram (EKG) *p.300*
electro-oculogram (EOG) *p.300*
beta activity *p.300*
alpha activity *p.300*
theta activity *p.300*
delta activity *p.301*
slow-wave sleep *p.301*
rapid eye movement (REM) sleep *p.301*
circadian rhythms *p.304*

suprachiasmatic nuclei (SCN) *p.304*
basic rest–activity cycle (BRAC) *p.304*
preoptic area *p.305*
insomnia *p.305*
sleep apnoea *p.305*
REM sleep behaviour disorder *p.306*
cataplexy *p.306*
sleepwalking *p.306*
sleeptalking *p.306*
night terrors *p.306*
enuresis *p.306*

CHAPTER REVIEW

The nature of consciousness

- Consciousness refers to our awareness of our own perceptions, thoughts and feelings and our experience of these.

- Some psychologists and philosophers regard consciousness as a by-product of cognitive processing and believe it is outside the scope of scientific study because of its subjective nature.

- Several theories seek to explain the nature of consciousness. These fall mainly into two camps: the neurobiological and the cognitive.

- The neurobiological explanations (such as those of Crick and Penrose) suggest that consciousness occurs when cell assemblies behave together or is generated by specific parts of a neuron.

- Perceptual disorders (such as blindsight and visual agnosia) and other deficits following brain injury (such as those seen after the split-brain operation) help demonstrate the importance of various brain regions to conscious awareness.

Attention

- Because we cannot be conscious of all the events that take place in our environment, the process of selective attention determines which stimuli will be noticed and which will be ignored. The factors that control our attention include novelty, verbal instructions and our own assessment of the significance of what we are perceiving.

- The cocktail-party phenomenon is an example of selective attention: we are able to detect relevant information in an environment that contains irrelevant and relevant information.

- Noise (such as office noise and speech) in the working environment can significantly impair memory for prose and arithmetic performance; the longer the duration of the noise, the greater the deficit.

- Dichotic listening experiments show that what is received by the unattended ear is lost within a few seconds unless something causes us to take heed of it; after those few seconds we cannot say what that ear heard. Even unattended information can produce implicit (as opposed to explicit) memories, however.

- Studies using visually presented information indicate that attention can focus on location or on shape: we can pay attention to particular objects or to stimuli that occur in a particular place. When individuals pay attention to particular characteristics of visual stimuli, the activity of particular regions of the brain is enhanced.

- Techniques of meditation have been used since the beginning of history and include methods for increasing or decreasing attention to the external world. In meditative techniques, a person pays strict attention to a simple stimulus such as a visual pattern, a word or a monotonous, repetitive movement. As the response to the repeated stimulus habituates, the person is left with a relatively empty consciousness. The withdrawal of attention causes a rebound that leads the practitioner to look at his or her surroundings with revitalised awareness.

Hypnosis

- Hypnosis is a form of verbal control over a person's consciousness in which the hypnotist's suggestions affect some of the person's perceptions and behaviours.

- State theorists argue that consciousness during hypnosis is a mysterious, trancelike state. Non-state theorists argue that it can be explained by psychological factors such as compliance, role-enactment, imagination and willingness to please. Evidence suggests invoking the concepts of trance or altered states of consciousness is unnecessary.

- Barber asserts that being hypnotised is similar to participating vicariously in a narrative, which is something we do whenever we become engrossed in a novel, a movie, a drama or even the recounting of a friend's experience. When we are engrossed in this way, we experience genuine feelings of emotion, even though the situation is not 'real'.

- Although individuals under hypnosis appear to perform extraordinary, unusual or antisocial acts, non-hypnotic suggestion can result in the same behaviours being induced. People who would not normally perform antisocial or distasteful acts may do so because they (correctly) assume that the experimenter is responsible for what they do.

- Hypnosis has been shown to be useful in reducing pain, eliminating bad habits and helping people talk about painful thoughts and memories.

- The reasons for the efficacy of hypnotic analgesia have included highly hypnotisable participants' ability to partition attention and the role of the anterior brain regions in allocating attentional resources.

Sleep

- Sleep consists of several stages of slow-wave sleep, characterised by increasing amounts of delta activity in the EEG, and REM sleep. REM sleep is characterised by beta activity in the EEG, rapid eye movements, general paralysis (with twitching movements of the hands and feet), and dreaming.

- Sleep is a behaviour, not simply an altered state of consciousness.

- Although evidence suggests that sleep is not necessary for repairing the wear and tear caused by physical exercise, it may play an important role in providing an opportunity for the brain to rest.

- Although narrative dreams occur only during REM sleep, people often are conscious of static situations during slow-wave sleep. Freud suggested that dreams provided the opportunity for unconscious conflicts to express themselves through symbolism in dreams.

- Hobson suggested that dreams are the attempts of the brain to make sense of hallucinations produced by the activation of the cerebral cortex.

- The function of REM sleep in adults is uncertain, but it may be involved somehow in learning. Foetuses and infants engage in much more REM sleep than adults do, which suggests that REM sleep may play a role in brain development. Some experimental research supports this suggestion.

- The brain contains two biological clocks. One, located in the suprachiasmatic nucleus of the hypothalamus, controls circadian (daily) rhythms. This clock is reset when light strikes the retina in the morning. The second clock, located in the pons, controls the basic rest–activity cycle, which manifests itself in changes in activity during the day and alternating periods of slow-wave sleep and REM sleep during the night. A circuit of acetylcholine-secreting neurons in the pons, normally inhibited by serotonin-secreting neurons, turns on REM sleep. Slow-wave sleep is controlled by neurons in the preoptic area.

- Insomnia appears to be a symptom of a variety of physical and emotional disorders, not a disease. Although it is often treated by sleep medications, these drugs cause more sleep problems than they cure.

- Two neurological disorders involve mechanisms of REM sleep. REM sleep behaviour disorder occurs when brain damage prevents the paralysis that normally keeps us from acting out our dreams. Cataplectic attacks are just the opposite. They are caused by activation at inappropriate times of the mechanism that causes paralysis during REM sleep.

- Drugs that stimulate serotonin-secreting neurons are useful in treating cataplexy. The disorders of slow-wave sleep include sleepwalking, sleeptalking and night terrors.

- Sleepwalking and night terrors are primarily disorders of childhood. Sleeptalking is generally harmless so it probably should not even be considered a disorder.

Suggestions for further reading

Crick, F. (1994). *The Astonishing Hypothesis*. Harlow: Simon & Schuster.

Dennett, D.D. (1991). *Consciousness Explained*. London: Penguin.

Penrose, R. (1989). *The Emperor's New Mind*. Oxford: Oxford University Press.

Penrose, R. (1994). *Shadows of the Mind*. Oxford: Oxford University Press.

Penrose, R. (1997). *The Large, the Small and the Human Mind*. Cambridge: Cambridge University Press.

Pinker, S. (1997). *How the Mind Works*. New York: W.W. Norton.
The scientific interest in the topic of consciousness has resulted in a number of books written for the 'popular science' market. These five books written by a biologist, philosopher, mathematician and psychologist, respectively, are the best popular introductions to the study and nature of consciousness. Each proposes its own view of how consciousness works.

Block, N., Flanagan, O. and Guzeldere, G. (1997). *The Nature of Consciousness*. Cambridge, Mass.: MIT Press.

Hameroff, S.R., Kaszniak, A.W. and Scott, A.C. (1996). *Towards a Science of Consciousness*. Cambridge, Mass.: MIT Press.

Hameroff, S.R., Kaszniak, A.W. and Scott, A.C. (1998). *Towards a Science of Consciousness II*. Cambridge, Mass.: MIT Press.

Ito, M., Miyashita, Y. and Rolls, E.T. (1997). *Cognition, Computation and Consciousness*. Oxford: Oxford University Press.

Pickering, J. and Skinner, M. (1990). *From Sentience to Symbols: Readings on consciousness*. Hemel Hempstead: Harvester Wheatsheaf.

Shear, J. (1997). *Explaining Consciousness: The hard problem*. Cambridge, Mass.: MIT Press.

Weiskrantz, L. (1997). *Consciousness Lost and Found*. Oxford: Oxford University Press.
Consciousness is now well served by texts covering every aspect of its nature. The Shear and Block et al. books are texts edited by philosophers and examine the problems associated with the topic of consciousness and its study. The two Hameroff et al. books are also edited collections of papers given at the two recent Tucson 'Towards a science of consciousness' conferences. These are exciting, cutting-edge summaries of the current state of consciousness research and are easy to read. Ito et al.'s text is also useful because it contains a series of chapters, divided into three approaches of study, which examines the nature of consciousness in specific areas of psychology (such as vision, memory, awareness of the body, computational modelling and so on). This is another good, basic academic text. Pickering and Skinner's book is an excellent annotated anthology of writings on consciousness. Weiskrantz's book offers a more neuropsychological perspective on consciousness, drawing on the author's extensive research on patients with amnesia and blindsight.

Bundesen, C. and Shibyua, H. (1995). *Visual Selective Attention*. Hove, UK: The Psychology Press.

Pashler, H. (1997). *Attention*. Hove, UK: The Psychology Press.

Styles, E.A. (1997). *The Psychology of Attentional Behaviour*. Hove, UK: The Psychology Press.
These texts provide a good introduction to attention and selective attention.

Gazzaniga, M.S. (1998). The split brain revisited. *Scientific American*, July, 35–39.
Split-brain research has always occupied an exotic and unusual place in psychology. This presents some of the more recent developments in this area.

Wagstaff, G.F. (1996). Methodological issues in hypnosis. In J. Haworth (ed.), *Psychological Research*. London: Routledge.
There are few well researched, scientific books, chapters or papers on the nature of hypnosis, perhaps reflecting scientists' general scepticism. Graham Wagstaff is a psychologist who has examined hypnosis from a scientific perspective and summarises what we know and don't know about the psychological processes involved in hypnosis in this very accessible chapter.

Empson, J. (1993). *Sleep and Dreaming*. New York: Harvester Wheatsheaf.

Horne, J. (1988). *Why We Sleep: The functions of sleep in humans and other mammals*. Oxford: Oxford University Press.
These two books provide a good review of the activity which most of us spend one-third of our lives doing.

Journals to consult

Cognition and Consciousness
Imagination, Cognition and Personality
International Journal of Experimental and Clinical Hypnosis
Journal of Consciousness Studies
Journal of Experimental Psychology: Human Perception
Philosophical Psychology
Psyche (http:// psyche.cs.monash.edu.au/)
Trends in Cognitive Sciences

Website addresses

http://www.imprint.co.uk/jcs.html
This is a link to the Journal of Consciousness Studies. *You can look at the journal's table of contents, abstracts of articles and the full text of some articles (you have to subscribe to get full access). One such article is 'Sniffing the camembert: On the conceivability of zombies' by Allin Cottrell. You can find this at:*
http://www.imprint.co.uk/cottrell.html

http://psyche.cs.monash.edu.au/index.html
This is a link to the on-line consciousness journal Psyche.

http://www.newscientist.com/nsplus/insight/big3/conscious/day1a.html
A link to a series of the magazine New Scientist's *articles on consciousness.*

http://ai.miningco.com/mbody.htm?PID=2827&cors=home
A large collection of links to AI websites.

http://www.starlab.org/
A Belgian site which features its lab's work on Bits, Atoms, Neurons and Genes (BANG). There is an article on neurons here by Stuart Hameroff.

10

LANGUAGE

On November 7, 1970, the Los Angeles Times carried a headline that astonished most of its readers. 'Girl, 13', it read, 'prisoner since infancy, deputies charge; parents jailed'. The story went on to reveal that the girl's father had harnessed her to a potty in a room in the back of the family house since she was at least 20 months old. She slept in a crib which had wire mesh on its sides and which was also covered with wire mesh. Her father was intolerant of noise and would beat her whenever she made any sound. … The girl was four and a half feet tall and weighed four stone. She could not eat solid food and had nearly two complete sets of teeth. She was 13 years and 9 months old.

The most remarkable feature of the young girl's behaviour was her almost complete lack of language. She could not talk and had a vocabulary of about 20 words (she could understand concepts such as 'red', 'blue', 'green'). Her speech production was limited to 'nomore', 'stopit' and other negatives. Genie's malnourishment was remedied and the girl did not show evidence of brain damage. A year after she was discovered, Genie's language ability underwent marked improvement. Her ability to structure according to rules was the equivalent of a twenty year old's and her spatial ability placed her in the adult ability category. She could tell the difference between singular and plural words and positive and negative sentences and could understand some prepositions. Her speech was limited to one or two word sentences, however, eventually becoming very descriptive and concrete ('big rectangular pillow', 'very, very, very dark-green box'). The 'explosion' of language, normally expected after such dramatic improvements never materialised.

Source: Martin, 1998, pp. 395–396

OVERVIEW

Communication is probably one of the most important of all human behaviours. Our use of language can be private – we can think to ourselves in words or write diaries that are meant to be seen by no one but ourselves – but language evolved through social contacts among our early ancestors. Speaking and writing are clearly social behaviours: we learn these skills from other people and use them to communicate with them. An effective language system also abides by certain rules.

This chapter introduces an area of psychology called psycholinguistics and describes the basic elements of written and spoken language. It considers the ways in which speech is produced and words are recognised. It also reviews the effects of brain damage on language processing (in the form of language disorders) and compares and contrasts this information with data from neuroimaging studies.

What you should be able to do after reading Chapter 10

- Define psycholinguistics and describe the nature of spoken language.
- Explain various models of reading and hearing language.
- Describe various language disorders including the aphasias, the acquired dyslexias, developmental dyslexia and stuttering and indicate what these tell us about normal language processing.
- Understand the various neural mechanisms which underlie different aspects of language such as speech perception, reading and speech comprehension.

Questions to think about

- What is language?
- Why have humans evolved language?
- Can other primates learn language? Would this language approximate our own?
- What is the role of sound in understanding written and spoken language?
- What stages does language development go through?
- How do people learn to read?
- How do people learn to recognise words?
- What are the effects of brain damage on reading, writing and speaking?
- Do all humans have the same central mechanism for producing language although the languages themselves may be different?
- How are we able to comprehend language?

The use of language

In order to co-operate with others, we need to be able to communicate effectively. Language is the unique vehicle whereby humans communicate with each other. Although an exact definition is difficult to pin down (Harley, 1995), language can be characterised as a system of visual and/or vocal symbols which have meaning to the user and to the recipient. We can use language to speak, write and read and we can also use it to remember and to think. Language also enables us to consider very complex and abstract issues by encoding them in words and then manipulating the words according to specific rules. These rules are the subject of an area of study called linguistics.

Psycholinguistics: the study of language acquisition and meaning

The study of linguistics involves determining the 'rules' of language and the nature and meaning of written and spoken language. In contrast, psycholinguistics, a branch of psychology devoted to the study of verbal behaviour, examines the role of human cognition in language acquisition and comprehension: it is the integration of psychology and linguistics. Psycholinguists are interested in how we acquire language – how verbal behaviour develops – and how we learn to speak from our interactions with others. In short, they are interested in the interaction between the structure and processing of language.

Psycholinguistics is a relatively recent, distinct branch of psychology although psychologists have studied language since the discipline's early experimental days. Wundt, for example, is regarded as the father of psycholinguistics (in the same way that he might be described as the father of most of psychology's branches). Wundt's approach to studying the psychology of language postulated that there were external phenomena (speech production, for example) and internal phenomena (such as trains of thought). In common with other structuralists (as we saw in Chapter 1), he sought to discover the basic elements of speech and argued that the sentence was the most basic element of speech production and comprehension. Speech production involved the transformation of thought process in to sequences of speech segments; comprehension, on the other hand, was the reverse process. Wundt's view was not universally accepted. The linguist Hermann Paul, for example, argued that words, not sentences, were the building blocks of speech.

This essentially European debate became somewhat sterile during the 1920s and 1930s when the form of psychology championed by Wundt was usurped by behaviourism which, you will recall from Chapter 1, argued that psychology should concern itself only with observable behaviour. It was not until the 1950s that psychology began to take a renewed interest in the nature of language and, ironically, this interest was spurred by a linguist, Noam Chomsky. Chomsky's views of the nature of language are discussed later on in the chapter. This chapter reviews studies from psycholinguistics and cognitive psychology and introduces you to the ways in which we produce and comprehend speech.

Perception of speech

Speech involves the production of a series of sounds in a continuous stream, punctuated by pauses and modulated by stress and changes in pitch. Sentences are written as sets of words, with spaces between them. Speech, however, is a more flexible means of communication than is writing. The sentences we utter are a string of sounds, some of which are emphasised (stressed), some are quickly glided over. We can raise the pitch of our voice when uttering some words and lower it when speaking others. We maintain a regular rhythmic pattern of stress. We pause at appropriate times, for example between phrases, but we do not pause after pronouncing each word. Thus, speech does not come to us as a series of individual words; we must extract the words from a stream of speech.

Recognition of speech sounds

The human auditory system is responsible for performing the complex task of enabling us to recognise speech sounds. The sound system of speech is called phonology. These sounds vary according to the sounds that precede and follow them, the speaker's accent, and the stress placed on the syllables in which they occur. Phonemes are the elements of speech – the smallest units of sound that contribute to the meaning of a word. For example, the word 'pin' consists of three phonemes: /p/ + /i/ + /n/. It is important to note that phonemes are not the same as letters. The word 'ship', for example, has four letters but three phonemes: /sh/ + /i/ + /p/. Note that in linguistics phonemes are flanked by two forward-slanting lines to indicate that they are phonemes and not letters. The first step in recognising speech sounds, therefore, is the identification of phonemes.

Production of speech

The production of speech is the result of a co-ordinated set of muscles found in the face, mouth and throat. The muscles responsible for producing some common words are illustrated in Figure 10.1.

One detectable and distinctive phonetic feature is voice onset time, the delay between the initial sound of a voiced

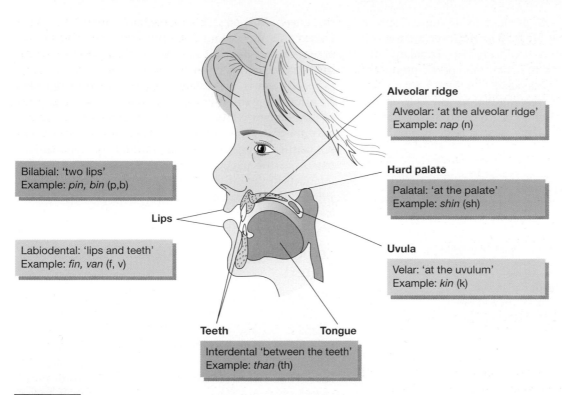

Bilabial: 'two lips'
Example: *pin, bin* (p,b)

Labiodental: 'lips and teeth'
Example: *fin, van* (f, v)

Lips

Alveolar ridge
Alveolar: 'at the alveolar ridge'
Example: *nap* (n)

Hard palate
Palatal: 'at the palate'
Example: *shin* (sh)

Uvula
Velar: 'at the uvulum'
Example: *kin* (k)

Teeth   Tongue
Interdental 'between the teeth'
Example: *than* (th)

Figure 10.1

The areas in the vocal tract where production of consonants takes place.

Source: Payne, D.G. and Wenger, M.J. (1998) *Cognitive Psychology*. New York: Houghton Mifflin.

consonant and the onset of vibration of the vocal cords. Voicing refers to the vibration of the vocal cords. The distinction between voiced and unvoiced consonants allows us to distinguish between /p/ (unvoiced) and /b/ (voiced), between /k/ (unvoiced) and /g/ (voiced), and between /t/ (unvoiced) and /d/ (voiced).

For example, although the difference between uttering 'pa' and 'ba' are subtle, they are discernible. Uttering 'pa' involves building up pressure in the mouth. When the lips are opened, a puff of air comes out. The 'ah' sound does not occur immediately, because the air pressure in the mouth and throat keeps air from leaving the lungs for a brief time. The vocal cords do not vibrate until air from the lungs passes through them. Uttering 'ba', however, does not involve the initial build-up of pressure. The vocal cords begin vibrating as soon as the lips open. The delay in voicing that occurs when uttering 'pa' is slight, only 0.06 seconds.

An experiment by Lisker and Abramson (1970) illustrates this point. They presented participants with a series of computer-generated sounds consisting of a puff followed by an 'ah'. The sounds varied only in one way: the amount of time between the puff and the 'ah'. When we speak, we make a puff for 'pa' but not for 'ba'. However, even though the computer always produced a puff, participants reported that they heard 'ba' when the delay was short and 'pa' when it was long. Participants discriminated between the phonemes /p/ and /b/ strictly according to the delay in

voicing. The experiment demonstrates that the auditory system is capable of detecting very subtle differences.

Although the fundamental unit of speech, logically and descriptively, is the phoneme, research suggests that psychologically the fundamental unit is larger. For example, the two syllables 'doo' and 'dee' each consist of two phonemes. When spoken, the same phoneme, /d/, is heard at the beginning. However, when Liberman *et al.* (1967) analysed the sounds of the syllables, they found that the beginning phonemes were not the same. In fact, they could not cut out a section of a tape recording of the two syllables that would sound like /d/.

These results suggest that the fundamental unit of speech consists of groups of phonemes, such as syllables. The perception of a phoneme is affected by the sounds that follow it (Ganong, 1980). Using a computer to synthesise a novel sound that fell between those of the phonemes /g/ and /k/, Ganong reported that when the sound was followed by 'ift', the participants heard the word 'gift', but when it was followed by 'iss', they heard 'kiss'. These results suggest that we recognise speech sounds in pieces larger than individual phonemes.

Errors in speech production

As you will see later in this chapter, some individuals with damage to a specific part of the brain have an inability to produce speech or will produce meaningless speech. Speech errors or slips of the tongue, however, are not confined to the brain-damaged (Dell *et al.*, 1997; Fromkin, 1988). Table 10.1 lists some of the common speech production errors made by normal individuals.

Some of these will be very familiar to you. One obvious error is where the beginnings of words are transposed. So, for example, instead of saying 'dear old queen', you might say 'queer old dean'. This is an example of a Spoonerism named after the Oxford don William A. Spooner who was noted for making such mistakes as saying 'noble tons of soil' instead of 'noble sons of the soil'.

Speech errors are interesting because although they are errors, they still follow the rules of grammar. For example, one might confuse nouns in a sentence ('would you pass me that cupboard from the pepper') but you would not confuse a noun with a verb ('would you cupboard the pass from the pepper'). Errors thus reflect what we had intended to say rather than what we want to say (Levelt, 1989). Somehow, an error occurs between conception and execution.

Table 10.1 Some common speech errors

1 Errors at phonemic segments
Consonant anticipation: a reading list/a leading list
Consonant deletion: speech error/peach error
Vowel exchange: fill the pool/fool the pill

2 Errors at phonetic features
Voicing reversal: big and fat/pig and vat
Nasality reversal: cedars of Lebanon/cedars of Lemadon

3 Errors at syllables
Syllable deletion: unanimity of opinion/unamity of opinion
Syllable reversal: Stockwell and Schacter/Schachwell and Stockter

4 Errors of stress (with the stressed syllable given in capital letters)
apples of the Origin/apples of the oRIgin
eCONomists: ecoNOMists, I mean, eCONomists

5 Errors of word selection
Word exchange: tend to turn out/turn to tend out
Word movement: I really must go/I must really go

6 Errors at morphemes
Inflection morpheme error: cow tracks/tracks cows
Derivational morpheme error: easily enough/easy enough

7 Errors at phases
A hummingbird was attracted by the red colour of the feeder/the red colour was attracted by a hummingbird of the feeder
My sister went to the Grand Canyon/the Grand Canyon went to my sister

8 Semantic and phonological word errors
Semantic substitution: too many irons in the fire/too many irons in the smoke
Phonological substitution: white Anglo-Saxon Protestant/white Anglo-Saxon Prostitute

9 Errors at morphologically complex words
Lexical selection error: it spread like wild fire/it spreads like wild flower
Exchange error: ministers in our church/churches in our minister

Source: adapted from Fromkin, 1993

Recognition of words: the importance of context

The perception of continuous speech involves different mechanisms from those used in the perception of isolated syllables. Because speech is full of hesitations, muffled sounds and sloppy pronunciations, many individual words can be hard to recognise out of context. For example, when Pollack and Pickett (1964) isolated individual words from a recording of normal conversations and played them back to other people, those people correctly identified the words only 47 per cent of the time. When they presented the same words in the context of the original conversation, the participants identified and understood almost 100 per cent of them. Miller *et al.* (1951) found that participants understood strings of words such as 'who brought some wet socks' in a noisy environment but failed to understand strings such as 'wet brought who socks some'. Similarly, one well known test of general intelligence, the National Adult Reading Test, involves reading aloud single, irregularly spelled English words. This task is performed better when the single words form part of a meaningful sentence than when presented singly (Conway and O'Carroll, 1997; Beardsall, 1998). These findings confirm that the context of speech provides important cues to aid our recognition of words.

Understanding the meaning of speech

The meaning of a sentence (or of a group of connected sentences that are telling a story) is conveyed by the words that are chosen, the order in which they are combined, the affixes that are attached to the beginnings or ends of the words, the pattern of rhythm and emphasis of the speaker, and knowledge about the world shared by the speaker and the listener.

Syntax

The understanding of speech entails following the 'rules' of language. Words must be familiar and combined in specific ways. For example, the sentence, 'The two boys looked at the heavy box' is comprehensible; but the sentence, 'Boys the two looking heavily the box at' is not. Only the first sentence follows the rules of English grammar.

All languages have a syntax, or grammar, which is a set of rules governing the ways in which words are used to form sentences. They all follow certain principles, which linguists call syntactical rules, for combining words to form phrases, clauses, or sentences (syntax, like synthesis, comes from the Greek *syntassein*, 'to put together'). Our understanding of syntax is automatic although learned. We are no more conscious of this process, for example, than a child is conscious of the laws of physics when he or she learns to ride a bicycle.

The automatic nature of syntactical analysis can be illustrated by experiments performed with artificial grammars. For example, Reber and Allen (1978) devised a set of (complex) rules for combining the letters M, V, R, T and X. For example, MRTXV and VXTTV were 'grammatical', but MXVTR and VMRTX were 'ungrammatical'. They asked participants to look at twenty 'grammatical' strings of letters, printed on index cards. The participants were told to 'pay the utmost attention to the letter strings' but were not instructed to do anything else. Later, the participants were presented with fifty different strings of letters, half of which were 'grammatical' and half of which were not. Some of the 'grammatical' strings were ones they had already seen, and some were new to them. The participants were asked to indicate whether the strings were 'grammatical'.

Although the participants did quite well – they correctly identified 81 per cent of the strings of letters – they could not express the rules verbally. The participants made statements like the following: 'The shapes of the items began to make sense.' 'Almost all my decisions are based on things looking either very right or very wrong. Sometimes for some reason things came out and glared at me saying, "bad, bad, bad", other times the letters just flowed together and I knew it was an OK item.'

This finding and others like it suggests that syntactic rules are learned implicitly (or not at all). Knowlton *et al.* (1991) found that patients with anterograde amnesia were able to learn an artificial grammar even though they had lost the ability to form explicit memories. In contrast, as Gabrieli *et al.* (1988) observed, such patients are unable to learn the meanings of new words. Thus, learning syntax and word meaning appears to involve different types of memory, and consequently, different brain mechanisms.

Word order

Word order is important in English. In the sentences 'The boy hit the ball' and 'The ball hit the boy', word order tells us who does what to whom. In English, the first noun of the sentence is the subject, the second noun is the object and the part in between is usually the verb. This structure

is referred to as S–V–O word order (for subject–verb–object) and around 75 per cent of the world's languages possess this sentence structure (Bernstein and Berko, 1993). Other languages, however, have different orders. Japanese, for example, uses the S–O–V order and both Welsh and Arabic use V–S–O. The assignation of words into meaningful categories (such as noun, verb, adjective and so on) is called parsing, and parsing involves being able to identify word classes.

Word class

Word class refers to the grammatical categories such as noun, pronoun, verb and adjective and words can be classified as function words or content words. Function words include determiners, quantifiers, prepositions and words in similar categories: 'a', 'the', 'to', 'some', 'and', 'but', 'when', and so on. Content words include nouns, verbs and most adjectives and adverbs: 'apple', 'rug', 'went', 'caught', 'heavy', 'mysterious', 'thoroughly', 'sadly'. Content words express meaning; function words express the relations between content words and thus are very important syntactical cues.

Affixes

Affixes are sounds that we add to the beginning (prefixes) or end (suffixes) of words to alter their grammatical function. For example, we add the suffix '-ed' to the end of a regular verb to indicate the past tense (drop/dropped); we add '-ing' to a verb to indicate its use as a noun (sing/singing as in 'we heard the choir sing' and 'the choir's singing was delightful'); and we add '-ly' to an adjective to indicate its use as an adverb (bright/brightly). We are quick to recognise the syntactical function of words with affixes like these. For example, Epstein (1961) presented people with word strings such as the following:

> *a vap koob desak the citar molent um glox nerf*
> *A vapy koob desaked the citar molently um glox nerfs*

The people could more easily remember the second string than the first, even though letters had been added to some of the words. Apparently, the addition of the affixes – 'y', '-ed' and '-ly' made the words seem more like a sentence and they thus became easier to categorise and recall.

Semantics

The meaning of a word – its semantics – provides important cues to the syntax of a sentence (semantics comes from the Greek *sema*, 'sign'). For example, consider the following set of words: 'Frank discovered a flea combing his beard'. The syntax of this sentence is ambiguous. It does not tell us whether Frank was combing Frank's beard, the flea was combing the flea's beard, or the flea was combing

Frank's beard. But our knowledge of the world and of the usual meanings of words tells us that Frank was doing the combing, because people, not fleas, have beards and combs.

Function words

Function words (such as 'the' , 'and', 'some') help us determine the syntax of a sentence; content words help us determine its meaning. For example, even with its function words removed, the following set of words still makes pretty good sense: 'man placed wooden ladder tree climbed picked apples'. You can probably fill in the function words yourself and get 'The man placed the wooden ladder against the tree, climbed it, and picked some apples.'

Prosody

Prosody is a syntactic cue which refers to the use of stress, rhythm and changes in pitch that accompany speech. Prosody can emphasise the syntax of a word or group of words or even serve as the primary source of syntactic information. For example, in several languages (including English), a declarative sentence can be turned into a question by means of prosody. Read the following sentences aloud to see how you would indicate to a listener which is a statement and which is a question.

> *You said that.*
> *You said that?*

We do this by intonation. In written communication, prosody is emphasised by punctuation marks. For example, a comma indicates a short pause, a full stop indicates a longer one along with a fall in the pitch of voice, and a question mark indicates an upturn in the pitch of voice near the end of the sentence. These devices serve as only partial substitutes for the real thing. Because writers cannot rely on the cues provided by prosody, they must be especially careful to see that the syntax of their sentences is conveyed by other cues: word order, word class, function words, affixes and word meaning.

The relationship between semantics and syntax

Sentences can be read or heard semantically in more than one way. Noam Chomsky (1957, 1965), a noted linguist, suggested that language can partly be explained by reference to sentence grammar. Although Chomsky's ideas underwent several revisions, the 1965 version of his theory suggests that there are three grammars. The first – generative grammar – represents the rules by which a speaker's ideas can be transformed into a final grammatical form. These transformed ideas or thoughts are called deep structures (the second grammar). The final output is the surface grammar or structure which is the end spoken product.

The deep structure represents the kernel of what the person intended to say. In order to utter a sentence, the brain must transform the deep structure into the appropriate surface structure: the particular form the sentence takes.

Most psychologists agree that the distinction between surface structure and deep structure is important (Tanenhaus, 1988; Bohannon, 1993; Hulit and Howard, 1993). Individuals with a language disorder known as conduction aphasia have difficulty repeating words and phrases, but they can understand them. The deep structure of other people's speech appears to be retained, but not its surface structure.

Knowledge of the world

Comprehension of speech also involves knowledge about the world and the particular situations encountered in it (Carpenter *et al.*, 1995). Schank and Abelson (1977) suggested that this knowledge is organised into scripts, which specify various kinds of events and interactions that people have witnessed or have learned about from others. Once a speaker has established which script is being referred to, the listener can fill in the details. For example, in order to understand what the speaker means in the following sentences:

> *I learned a lot about the clubs in town yesterday. Do you have an aspirin?*

we must be able to do more than simply understand the words and analyse the sentence structure (Hunt, 1985). We must know something about clubs; for example, that they serve alcohol and that 'learning about them' probably involves some drinking. We must also realise that imbibing these drinks can lead to a headache and that aspirin is a remedy for headaches.

Hunt notes that when we describe an event to someone else, not all the details are spelled out. For example:

> *Alison was hungry and so she went to a restaurant and ordered a pizza. When she had finished, she discovered that she had forgotten to take her purse with her. She was embarrassed.*

In this story we need to understand that after eating in a restaurant, you are expected to pay.

What is meaning?

Words refer to objects, actions, or relations in the world. Thus, the meaning of a word (its semantics) is defined by particular memories associated with it. For example, knowing the meaning of the word 'tree' means being able to imagine the physical characteristics of trees: what they look like, what the wind sounds like blowing through their leaves, what the bark feels like, and so on. It also means knowing facts about trees: about their roots, buds, flowers, nuts, wood and the chlorophyll in their leaves. These memories are not stored in the primary speech areas but in other parts of the brain, especially regions of the association cortex. Different categories of memories may be stored in particular regions of the brain, but they are linked, so that hearing the word 'tree' activates all of them.

To hear a familiar word and understand its meaning involves first recognising the sequence of sounds that constitute the word. We must, therefore, have some form of memory store which contains the auditory representations of words. This store forms part of our auditory word recognition system. When we find the auditory entry for the word in our mental lexicon (lexicon means 'dictionary'), we must be able to access semantic information about this word. The region of the brain responsible for the auditory comprehension of words must somehow communicate with another region (or regions) which allows us to ascribe meaning to what we have just heard.

Is there a universal language?

Or, put less controversially, are there some features of language that are shared by most, if not all, languages? The answer seems to be yes. For example, all languages have nouns and words to represent states of action or states of being because we all need a way of referring to objects, people and events. Hockett (1960a,b) has suggested that all languages share thirteen features. These are listed in Table 10.2. Are there others that you think could be added to the list?

Reading

Speech first developed as a means of communication between two or more people facing each other, or at least within earshot of each other. The invention of writing, which made it possible for people to communicate across both space and time, was an important turning point in civilisation. The first system of writing appears to have been developed around 4000 BC in Sumeria (the location of present-day Iran and Iraq), apparently in response to the need to keep records of ownership and of business transactions. The earliest forms of writing were stylised drawings of real objects (pictographs), but most cultures soon developed symbols based on sounds. For example, Egyptian hieroglyphic writing used some symbols as pictographs but used others phonetically, to spell out people's names or words that denoted concepts not easily pictured (Ellis, 1992).

With the notable exception of Chinese (and other Asian writing systems based on Chinese), most modern languages use alphabetic writing systems in which a small number of symbols represent (more-or-less) the sounds used to pronounce words. For example, most European languages are represented by the Roman alphabet, originally developed to represent the sounds of Latin and subsequently adopted by tribes of people ruled or influenced by the Roman Empire. The Roman alphabet was adapted from the Greek alphabet, which in turn was adapted from the Phoenician alphabet. For example, the letter D has its

Table 10.2   The thirteen features that Hockett regards as common to all languages

Universal	Description
Arbitrariness	There is no inherent connection between symbols and the objects they refer to
Broadcast transmission	Messages are transmitted in all directions and can be received by any hearer
Cultural transmission	Language is acquired through exposure to culture
Discreteness	A distinct range of possible speech sounds exists in language
Duality of structure	A small set of phonemes can be combined and recombined into an infinitely large set of meanings
Interchangeability	Humans are both message perceivers and message producers
Productivity	Novel messages can be produced according to the rules of the language
Semanticity	Meaning is conveyed by the symbols of the language
Specialisation	Sounds of a language are specialised to convey meaning (as compared with non-language sounds)
Total feedback	The speaker of a language has auditory feedback that occurs at the same time that the listener receives the message
Transitoriness	Linguistic messages fade quickly
Vocal–auditory channel	Means of transmission of the language is vocal–auditory

origin in the Phoenician symbol 'daleth', which meant 'door'. At first, the symbol literally indicated a door, but it later came to represent the phoneme /d/. The Greeks adopted the symbol and its pronunciation but changed its name to delta. Finally, the Romans took it, altering its shape into the one we recognise in English today.

Scanning text

When we scan a scene, our eyes make rapid jumps called saccades. These same rapid movements occur during reading (a French ophthalmologist in the nineteenth century discovered saccadic eye movements while watching people read).

The study of eye movements is made possible by a device called an eye tracker. This device consists of an apparatus that holds a person's head in a fixed position and a special video camera that keeps track of the person's gaze by focusing on an eye and monitoring the position of the pupil. The person reads material presented by a computer on a video monitor.

Perception does not occur while the eyes are actually moving but during the brief fixations that occur between saccades. The average fixation has a duration of about 250 milliseconds (ms, 1/1000 of a second), but their duration can vary considerably. Figure 10.2 shows the pattern of fixations made by good and poor readers.

The ovals above the text indicate the location of the fixations (which occur just below the ovals, on the text itself), and the numbers indicate their duration (in milliseconds). The fixations of good readers were made in the forward direction; the poor readers looked back and examined previously read words several times (indicated by the arrows). In addition, the good reader took, on average, considerably less time to examine each word.

University students fixate on most words when they are asked to read text carefully enough to understand its meaning. They fixate on 80 per cent of the content words but on only 40 per cent of the function words such as 'the' and 'and' (Just and Carpenter, 1980). Function words are generally shorter than content words, but the difference is not only a matter of size. Readers are more likely to skip over short function words such as 'and' or 'the' than over short content words such as 'ant' or 'run' (Carpenter and Just, 1983). For example, read the following sentence:

I love Paris in the
the springtime

You may not have noticed that second 'the' at the beginning of the second line and would have read the sentence as normal; we seem to be able to glide over function words such as 'the' without it detrimentally affecting the way in which we perceive and understand meaning.

As sentences are read, they are usually analysed word by word (Rayner and Pollatsek, 1989). Some words contribute more to our understanding than do others, and some sentences cannot make sense until we reach the end (compare and contrast: 'The capital of Kenya is Nairobi'; 'Nairobi is the capital of Kenya'). The more unusual a word is, the longer a reader fixates on it. The word 'sable', for example, receives a longer fixation than the word 'table'. The word that follows an unusual word does not receive a longer-than-usual fixation, which indicates that the reader finishes processing the word before initiating the next saccade (Thibadeau *et al.*, 1982).

Readers also spend more time fixating on longer words. In fact, if word familiarity is held constant, the amount of time a word receives is proportional to its length

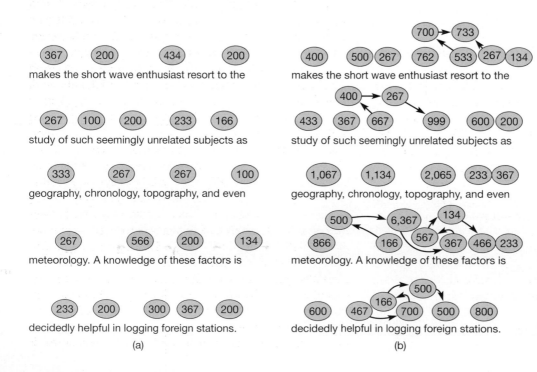

(a)   (b)

Figure 10.2

The pattern of fixations made by two readers. The ovals are placed above the locations of the fixations; the numbers within them indicate the durations of the fixations (in milliseconds). Arrows indicate backtracking to words already examined. (a) A good reader. (b) A poor reader.

Source: Marcel Adam Just and Patricia A. Carpenter, *The Psychology of Reading and Language Comprehension*. Copyright © 1987 by Allyn & Bacon. After Buswell (1937). Reproduced with permission.

(Carpenter and Just, 1983). In addition, Just *et al.* (1983) found that the amount of time that Chinese readers spent fixating on a Chinese character was proportional to the number of brush strokes used to make it. Because all Chinese characters are of approximately the same size, the increased fixation time appears to reflect the complexity of a word rather than the amount of space it occupies.

Phonetic and whole-word recognition

Most psychologists who study the reading process believe that readers have two basic ways of recognising words: phonetic and whole-word recognition. Phonetic reading involves the decoding of the sounds that letters or groups of letters make (in a similar way to which the units of speech are called phonemes, the units of written language are called graphemes). For example, the ability to pronounce nonsense words depends on our knowledge of the relation between letters and sounds in the English language. Such knowledge is used to 'sound the word out'. When we do this we apply grapheme–phoneme correspondence (GPC) rules: the rules which govern the ways in which we are able to translate written letters into the appropriate sounds. This is called whole-word reading: reading by recognising a word as a whole. But do we have to 'sound out' familiar, reasonably short words such as 'table' or 'grass'? Probably not. Familiar words are perceived as whole words. However, consider this list of words: 'knave', 'shave', 'slave', 'have'. How did you pronounce the last word? You probably pronounced it to rhyme with 'slave'. This example illustrates that although whole-word reading would seem to be intuitively correct, our pronunciation of words can depend on the context in which words are used.

The process of reading

A relatively inexperienced reader will have to sound out most words and, consequently, will read rather slowly. Experienced, practised readers will quickly recognise most of them as individual units. In other words, during reading, phonetic and whole-word reading are engaged in a race. If the word is familiar, the whole-word method will win. If the word is unfamiliar, the whole-word method will lose and the phonetic method will have enough time to complete.

Figure 10.3 illustrates some elements of the reading process and, for the sake of clarity and illustration, considers only reading and pronouncing single words, not understanding the meaning of text.

When we read a word, we must have some store of knowledge which allows us to identify words as words. In the same way that the auditory store was considered part of the auditory word recognition system, the visual store can be considered part of the visual word recognition system. But is our recognition of written words purely visual? Or can we read by 'ear'?

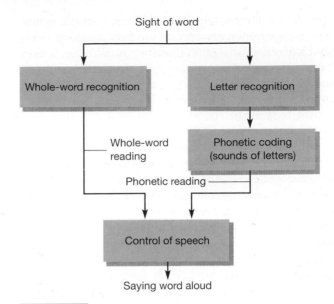

Figure 10.3

A simplified model of the reading process, showing whole-word and phonetic reading. The model considers only reading a single word aloud. Whole-word reading is used for most familiar words; phonetic reading is used for unfamiliar words and for non-words such as 'glab', 'trisk' or 'chint'.

Source: Brooks, L. (1977) pp. 146 and 147. Copyright © Lawrence Erlbaum Associates, Inc. 1977. Reprinted with permission.

To answer this question, Rubenstein *et al.* (1971) presented individuals with three types of non-word (strings of letters which make invalid English words): pseudowords, which conformed to the rules of English but had no meaning (for example GANK), non-words which were pronounceable but illegally spelled (for example MIRQ), and non-words which were unpronounceable and illegally spelled (for example HTTR). The participants had to decide whether these words, presented on a computer screen, were real English words or not (this is called a lexical decision task). The experimenters found that participants took longest to reject the pseudowords, followed by illegally spelled pronounceable words, followed by illegally spelled unpronounceable words. In a second experiment, Rubenstein *et al.* included a set of words called pseudohomophones; these are words which are legally spelled, are pronounceable, sound like real words but have no meaning (for example PHICKS, which sounds like 'fix'). They would, therefore, pass an auditory word recognition system, but not the visual word recognition system. As predicted, pseudohomophones took longest to reject, followed by pseudowords.

Rubenstein *et al.* suggested that visual information is translated into a phonological code, a sound-based representation of the word, using grapheme to phoneme conversion. This representation is then checked by the auditory word recognition system which decides whether the word sounds like a real word or not. Pseudowords would fail this test – they do not sound like real words. Pseudohomophones, however, would pass because they do sound like real words. They, therefore, need to be checked by the visual word recognition system in order to determine whether the word is real. The visual word recognition system checks the orthography of a word (the way in which it is spelled). The recognition of words, therefore, involves phonic mediation: the conversion of written language into a sound-based representation.

Phonic mediation, however, appears to be necessary only for the recognition of unfamiliar words (Ellis, 1992). When we see a familiar word, we normally recognise it as a whole and say it aloud. If we see an unfamiliar word or a pronounceable non-word, we must try to read it phonetically. We recognise each letter and then sound it out, based on our knowledge of how letters are sounded out (phonetics).

Whole-word recognition is not only faster than phonetic decoding, but also essential in a language (such as English) in which spelling is not completely phonetic. In the following pairs of words:

cow/blow   bone/one   post/cost   limb/climb

no single set of phonological rules can account for the pronunciation of both members of each pair (phonology refers to the relation between letters and the sounds they represent in a particular language). Yet all these words are familiar and easy to read. The ability to recognise words as wholes, therefore, may be necessary in order to read irregularly spelled words (although our 'have' example earlier on suggests how whole-word reading can fail).

Phonology, however, appears to be crucial for the development of language ability, as we will see later. Having good phonological skills appears to place children at an advantage linguistically. Gathercole and Baddeley (1990) found that 5 year old children with good phonological skills were better at remembering nonsense words than were those with poor phonological skills. This ability to repeat nonsense words appears to be a good predictor of later, successful vocabulary acquisition (Gathercole *et al.*, 1992). The role of phonology (and other processes) in learning to read is the topic of the 'Psychology in action' section below. There is much debate over the best way to teach children how to learn to read, and psychologists have discovered much that teachers can use in their instruction.

The dual-route model of reading

The dual-route model of reading model proposes that there are two, non-semantic routes that take the reader from spelling to sound (Coltheart, 1978; Morton and Patterson, 1980). The lexical route retrieves pronounced words from a lexicon (an internal word pool which contains items learned through experience, a little like a personalised dictionary). Because words are 'looked up' in this system, it is called the *addressed route*. The sublexical route is the system which converts letters into sounds, that

is, it applies the grapheme–phoneme correspondence rules. Because it assembles sounds from letters, it is called the *assembled route*. The lexical route would be able to identify all known words; the sublexical route would be able to identify non-words. There is some evidence for the dual-route model from individuals who present with certain types of reading difficulty (dyslexia). We look at this evidence in the section on dyslexia later in the chapter.

Are both routes activated simultaneously during reading? One view holds that both systems operate in parallel and are in some form of race, the winner being the system which produces the best pronunciation. A second view holds that the two processes are pooled until a match is made that would prompt articulation. No clear agreement on this process has been reached, although a great deal of excitement in cognitive psychology and psycholinguistics has been roused by the possibilities of connectionism, a form of computer modelling of human cognitive function, in solving this problem. This approach argues that there are no qualitatively different processes involved in recognising words and that there is no localised lexicon.

Connectionism takes as its starting point the view that the brain or our information processing system operates in a similar way to a computer and can, therefore, be modelled. Such a model should be capable of learning (as our brain is). This idea, of course, is not new. Rosenblatt (1962) had developed a parallel processing machine which was capable of simple learning. Modern, computer-based models of human computation, however, were pioneered by Seidenberg and McClelland (1989). Their parallel distributed processing (PDP) model did away with the notion of dual routes and instead posited one route only which was non-lexical. Their model is an example of a computational model of behaviour because it translates units of behavioural phenomena into computations. Seidenberg and McClelland's model was a three-layer neural network which sought to read regular, exception and non-words from spelling to sound. The three layers were: features, letters and words. Perception within each of these layers was argued to occur in parallel so that the system could analyse features while it identified letters and attempt to name the word a stimulus might represent (Zorzi *et al.*, 1998). An example of the type of network proposed by PDP can be seen in Figure 10.4.

The model, however, has run into some difficulty. It cannot read non-words, for example, and it cannot simulate a form of dyslexia called surface dyslexia, which is described later in the chapter (Besner *et al.*, 1990; Coltheart *et al.*, 1993). The PDP model has been replaced by that of Plaut and colleagues (Plaut and McClelland, 1993; Plaut *et al.*, 1996). This model seems to have met with some success in that it is at least capable of reading monosyllabic nonwords but does not appear to account for the flexibility of human language (see Zorzi *et al.*, 1998, for a review).

We will not say too much more about PDP and connectionism here. Although the PDP model and connectionism

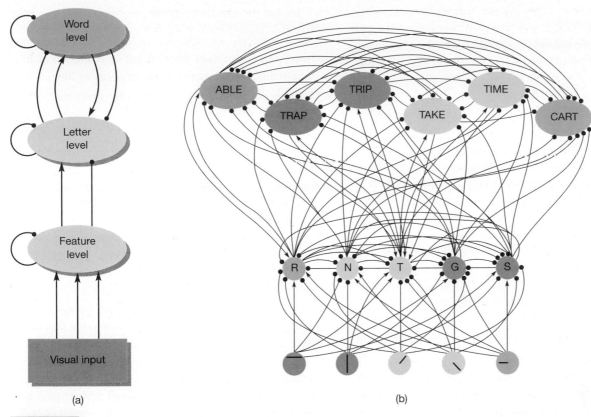

Figure 10.4

An example of the macrostructure (a) and microstructure (b) of McClelland and Rumelhart's activation model. The macrostructure illustrates the general organisation of the model. The microstructure shows how nodes within the model are connected. In these diagrams the arrows ending in points are excitatory connections, and the arrows ending in dots are inhibitory connections. The nodes at the bottom of (b) represent the physical features of words; the nodes at the next level represent the letters of words. Finally, the nodes at the top represent the actual words. You can see that there is an excitatory connection between the letter 'T' and the word 'TRIP' because the word contains this letter. However, there is an inhibitory connection between the letter 'N' and the word 'TRIP' because the word does not contain this letter.

Source: McClelland, J.L. and Rumelhart, D.E., *Psychological Review*, 1981, 88, 375–407. Copyright © 1981 by the American Psychological Association. Reprinted with permission.

are difficult concepts to grasp it is important to take note of them because there is great debate in psychology over the relevance and validity of connectionism in trying to explain the process of visual word recognition. If you are interested in this issue, then the items from the further reading list at the end of the chapter should furnish you with more information.

Psychology in action

How children learn to read

As literate adults, we usually have little difficulty with the process of reading. We come across the occasional unfamiliar word in our own language but, by and large, we can learn this word based on the rules of orthography and phonology that we implicitly know and the unfamiliar word becomes a newly learned word. These are rules that we know but have learned. Reading, however, is an artificial activity and must, therefore, be taught to us (usually at an early age). A beginning reader has much of his or her work cut out because he or she has no vocabulary and no set of rules. Are there any cognitive skills (such as an awareness of rhyme or having an effective short-term memory) that can help develop the child's vocabulary and skills? Does reading develop naturally or in stages? And how can we best teach children to read?

Psychology in action continued

Psychology in action continued

To begin with, reading requires adequate sight, so a child would need to be visually competent. Of course, blind children can be taught Braille but our concern here is with the development of visual word recognition and visual reading. The next important step is for the child to relate written letters or groups of letters to sounds. In some languages this is easier to do than it is in others. The rules needed to undertake this task are more complex in English, say, than in Finnish or Italian. Some of these rules will be simple – b corresponds to /b/. Others are not – the 'c' in 'car' and 'mince' is sounded differently, for example. These general rules are called spelling-to-pronunciation correspondence rules or, more accurately, grapheme–phoneme correspondence rules. The essential feature of these rules is that the child must break up words into segments and put them back together again to form a pronounceable whole. This breaking and putting together again are called segmentation and blending, respectively, and are two tasks the beginning reader has great difficulty in undertaking.

According to Oakhill and Garnham (1988), the child's reading process is dependent on the development of a number of skills. Whether these skills give rise to reading, are associated with reading or develop from reading is an interesting psychological question which many developmental psychologists and psycholinguists have attempted to answer. However, this debate need not concern us here. What will concern us are the skills associated with reading development. Oakhill and Garnham's list includes the following features/skills: *word consciousness, awareness of lower-level features, orthographic awareness, phonemic awareness* and *use of analogy*.

- *Word consciousness.* Word consciousness or lexical awareness refers to the ability to understand that speech and writing are composed of different, distinct elements called words. Of course, to us, as skilled readers, this is quite obvious. It is not, however, to a child who is learning to read and has not encountered such stimuli at any great length. Although it appears that young children have difficulties in indicating word boundaries (where one ends and another begins), children with strong lexical awareness tend to develop better reading ability (Ryan *et al.*, 1977).
- *Awareness of lower-level features.* A young child has a limited sight vocabulary and what it does have will have been learned through breaking down the elements of words into manageable, processable pieces. As suggested above, this is difficult for a young child to do. English, for example, although having an alphabet of 26 letters, has 45 phonemes. When Rozin *et al.* (1974) presented children

with two words such as 'mow' and 'motorcycle' and asked them – auditorily – which one was 'mow', the maximum correct response varied from 50 per cent for suburban nursery children to 10 per cent for inner-city children.

- *Orthographic awareness.* The ability to recognise that writing systems have sets of rules that must be followed is called orthographic awareness. For example, in English, we know that some sequences of letters are acceptable (for example 'able') but know that others are not ('kqxg').
- *Phonological awareness.* Perhaps the most important skill a child needs in order to develop adequate reading ability is the capacity to appreciate sound and be able to identify letters with sounds (this is sometimes called phonological awareness). To explore the contribution of phonological processing to reading, Bryant and Bradley (Bradley and Bryant, 1983; Bryant and Bradley, 1985) have administered a series of phonological tasks to children at various stages of learning to read. Such tasks include finding the odd one out from the following two sets of spoken words: sun, sea, sock, rag; weed, need, peel, deed. (Notice how these two examples rely on the respondent noting both the beginning and ending sounds of words.) Good performance at tasks such as these is a good predictor of later reading ability.
- *Use of analogy.* Sometimes, children will not use grapheme–phoneme correspondence rules to read a word because it looks like another word. For example, Marsh *et al.* (1977) asked children and adults to pronounce nonsense words such as 'tepherd'. This word, if pronounced according to GPC rules (with 'ph' pronounced as /f/) would be pronounced 'tefferd'. Children, however, pronounce it to rhyme with 'shepherd'. Adults do not. This is called children's use of analogy in reading.

The major ways in which children are taught to develop and use some or all of these skills are based on two systems: whole-word reading and phonics. Whole-word reading, as its name suggests, involves teaching the child to read whole words rather than analyse components of words and put them together to form whole words. This is sometimes called the look-and-say method because there is no room for segmentation of words. It is also called the meaning-based system because it encourages the child to think about the object the word represents. Words are usually displayed singly on cards and classrooms might have objects and pictures with word-labels attached to them. This means that the child begins to generate a pool of words which he or she will then be able to read in books after a sufficient number of words has been learned. Whole-word reading is easier for the child because it does not rely on segmentation. It also, as we have

Table 10.3 Two approaches to teaching of reading

Initial teaching alphabet	Diacritical marking system
wuns upon a ti-em a littl red hen livd in a barn with her fi-ev chicks.	Oncȩ upon ȧ timȩ Littlȩ Red Hen livȩd in ȧ barn with hȩr fivȩ chiȼks.

Source: Brooks, 1977, pp. 146–47. Copyright © Lawrence Erlbaum Associates, Inc. 1977. Reprinted with permission.

already mentioned, encourages the child to think about word meaning. One disadvantage of the system, however, is its inability to teach children how to decode new or unfamiliar words because no rule-based system is learned. If one considers that the average adult has a reading vocabulary of 50,000 words, the number of words a child would have to learn would be impracticable.

The alternative approach is called phonics. This rule-based system teaches the child correspondences between letters and sounds (that is, GPC rules, segmentation and blending). There are many forms of this teaching system and most teach the children letter-to-sound correspondences first before exposing them to actual words. The disadvantages of the system is that it cannot cope well with teaching the child irregular words and that 4–5 year old children find the segmentation of phonemes difficult.

Many other teaching-of-reading systems exist. For example, one approach, the Initial Teaching Alphabet, reforms the orthography of irregular words by transforming them into regular words. An example of this can be seen in the left-hand side of Table 10.3.

This, however, can have quite serious consequences for the child's spelling. Other approaches teach the child the letters of the alphabet first (success in which is a good predictor of reading ability). Another approach colour codes letters in words. For example, a letter written in a certain colour can only be pronounced in one way. Yet another approach places marks underneath certain letters to indicate how they should be pronounced (the technical name for this is the 'diacritical marking system'), as seen on the right-hand side of Table 10.3.

Is there a 'best' approach amid these myriad of approaches? As we have seen, although some of the well developed approaches have distinct advantages, all have certain disadvantages. However, one consistent predictor of later reading ability is successful phonological awareness. Pronunciation is also better if the phonetic aspects of speech are emphasised during the early stages of teaching. This may explain why developmental dyslexics often have good cognitive ability but have poor phonological processing skills, a topic we discuss in the section on language disorders below.

Understanding the meanings of words and sentences

The meanings of words are learned through experience. The meanings of content words involve memories of objects, actions and their characteristics; thus, the meanings of content words involve visual, auditory, somatosensory, olfactory and gustatory memories. These memories of the meanings of words are distributed throughout the brain. Our understanding of the meaning of the word 'apple', for example, involves memories of the sight of an apple, the way it feels in our hands, the crunching sound we hear when we bite into it, and the taste and odour we experience when we chew it. The understanding of the meanings of adjectives, such as the word 'heavy', involves memories of objects that are difficult or impossible to lift.

Abstract words are probably first understood as adjectives. Consider this example. An honest student is one who does not cheat on exams or plagiarise while writing papers,

an honest bank assistant does not steal money, and so on. The understanding of these words depends on our direct experience with such people or our vicarious experience with them through stories we read or hear about. By itself, the word 'honesty' is abstract; it does not refer to anything concrete.

The understanding of most function words is also abstract. For example, the word 'and' serves to link two or more things being discussed; the word 'or' indicates a choice; the word 'but' indicates that a contradiction will be expressed in the next clause. The meanings of such words are difficult to imagine or verbalise, rather like the rules of grammar. The meanings of prepositions, such as 'in', 'under' or 'through', are more concrete and are probably represented by images of objects in relation to each other.

A phenomenon known as semantic priming gives us some hints about the nature of activation of memories triggered by the perception of words and phrases. Semantic priming is a facilitating effect on the recognition of words having meanings related to a word encountered earlier. A particular word can be more easily read if the word preceding it is related in meaning. If an individual sees the word 'bread', he or she will be more likely to recognise a fuzzy image of the word 'butter' or an image that is presented very briefly by means of a tachistoscope (Johnston and Dark, 1986). Presumably, the brain contains circuits of neurons that serve as 'word detectors' involved in visual recognition of particular words (Morton, 1979; McClelland and Rumelhart, 1981). Reading the word 'bread' activates word detectors and other neural circuits involved in memories of the word's meaning. Apparently, this activation spreads to circuits denoting related concepts, such as butter. Thus, our memories must be linked according to our experience regarding the relations between specific concepts.

Context effects, an example of top-down processing, have been demonstrated through semantic priming. Zola (1984), for example, asked people to read sentences such as the following:

1 Cinemas must have adequate popcorn to serve their patrons.

2 Cinemas must have buttered popcorn to serve their patrons.

while he recorded their eye movements with an eye tracker.

Zola found that individuals fixated for a significantly shorter time on the word popcorn in the second sentence. Because the word 'adequate' is not normally associated with the word 'popcorn', individuals reading the first sentence were unprepared for this word. However, 'buttered' is commonly associated with popcorn, especially in the context of a cinema. The context of the sentence, therefore, activated the word detector for 'popcorn', making the recognition of the word easier.

Semantic priming studies have also shed some light on another aspect of the reading process, the development of a mental model. It has been suggested that when a person reads some text, he or she generates a mental model of what the text is describing (Johnson-Laird, 1983). If the text contains a narrative, for example, the reader will imagine the scenes and actions that are being recounted. These issues of semantic priming and semantic networks are taken up in Chapter 11.

Questions to think about

Speaking and reading

■ In what way do you think language differs from other communication systems such as traffic lights?

■ What different types of word make up a language system? Why do we have content and function words?

■ What are the principal differences between written and spoken sentences?

■ When President Kennedy addressed his German audience with the inclusive pronouncement, 'Ich bin ein Berliner', what he actually said (to a Germanic ear) was – 'I am a cream pastry.' It is easy to see why we make such mistakes in languages which are unfamiliar but why do you think that we make slips of the tongue in our native language?

■ What is the difference between a phoneme and a grapheme?

■ What do we mean by grapheme-to-phoneme conversion?

■ What model do you think best accounts for the development and teaching of reading? Can it account for reading in all languages?

■ What is the dual-route model of reading? How effective a model do you think it is?

■ If you were teaching a child to read, how would you start? What aspect of reading would you consider the most important to teach at the initial stages?

■ How does learning to speak differ from learning to read?

■ What are the arguments for and against 'reading by ear'?

Language acquisition by children

Perception of speech sounds by infants

Language development begins even before birth. Although the sounds that reach a foetus are somewhat muffled, speech sounds can still be heard. And some learning appears to take place prenatally (foetal learning is considered in more detail in Chapter 12). The voice that a foetus hears best and most often is obviously that of its mother. Consequently, a newborn infant prefers its mother's voice to that of others (DeCasper and Fifer, 1980). DeCasper and Spence (1986) even found that newborn infants preferred hearing their mothers reading a passage they had read aloud several times before their babies were born to hearing them read a passage they had never read before.

An infant's auditory system is well developed. Wertheimer (1961) found that newborns still in the delivery room can turn their heads towards the source of a sound. Babies two or three weeks of age can discriminate between the sound of a voice and other sounds. By the age of two months, babies can tell an angry voice from a pleasant one; an angry voice produces crying, whereas a pleasant one causes smiling and cooing.

One device used to determine what sounds a very young infant can perceive is the pacifier nipple, placed in the baby's mouth. The nipple is connected by a plastic tube to a pressure-sensitive switch that converts the infant's sucking movements into electrical signals. These signals can be used to turn on auditory stimuli. Each time the baby sucks, a particular sound is presented.

If the auditory stimulus is novel, the baby usually begins to suck at a high rate. If the stimulus remains the same, its novelty wears off (habituation occurs) and the rate of sucking decreases. With another new stimulus, the rate of sucking again suddenly increases, unless the baby cannot discriminate the difference. If the stimuli sound the same to the infant, the rate of sucking remains low after the change.

Using this technique, Eimas *et al.* (1971) found that one month old infants could tell the difference between the sounds of the consonants 'b' and 'p'. Like Lisker and Abramson (1970) in the study discussed earlier, they presented the sounds 'ba' and 'pa', synthesised by a computer. The infants, like the adult participants in the earlier study, discriminated between speech sounds having voice-onset times that differed by only 0.02 second. Even very early during postnatal development, the human auditory system is ready to make very fine discriminations. Table 10.4 lists some of the responses infants make to various types of speech sound.

The prespeech period and the first words

Kaplan and Kaplan (1970) have outlined the progression of early vocalisations in infants. The first sound that a baby makes is crying. As we will see in Chapter 12, this aversive stimulus serves a useful function. It is important in obtaining behaviours from the baby's carers. At about one month of age, infants start making other sounds, including one that is called cooing because of the prevalence of the 'ooing' sound. Often during this period, babies also make a series of sounds that resemble a half-hearted attempt to mimic the sound of crying.

At around six months, a baby's sounds begin to resemble those that occur in speech. Even though their babbling does not contain words – and does not appear to involve attempts to communicate verbally – the sounds that infants make, and the rhythm in which they are articulated, reflect the adult speech that babies hear. Mehler *et al.* (1988) found that 4 day old infants preferred to hear a voice speaking French, their parents' native language. And this ability to discriminate the sounds and rhythms of the language spoken around them manifested itself in the infants' own vocalisations very early. Boysson-Bardies *et al.* (1984) had adult French speakers listen to recordings of the babbling of children from various cultures. The adults could easily distinguish the babbling of 8 month old French infants from that of babies of different language backgrounds.

A study by Kuhl *et al.* (1992) provides further evidence of the effect of children's linguistic environment on their language development. Native speakers learn not to distinguish between slight variations of sounds present in their language. In fact, they do not even hear the differences between them. For example, Japanese contains a sound that comes midway between /l/ and /r/. Different native speakers pronounce the sound differently, but all pronunciations are recognised as examples of the same phoneme. When native speakers of Japanese learn English, they have great difficulty distinguishing the sounds /l/ and /r/; for example, 'right' and 'light' sound to them like the same word. Presumably, the speech sounds that a child hears alter the brain mechanisms responsible for analysing them so that minor variations are not even perceived. The question is, when does this alteration occur? Most researchers have supposed that it happens only after children begin to learn the meanings of words, which occurs at around 10–12 months of age.

Kuhl and her colleagues found, however, that this learning takes place much earlier. They studied 6 month old infants in the United States and Sweden. The infants were seated in their mothers' laps, where they watched an experimenter sitting nearby, playing with a silent toy. Every two seconds, a loudspeaker located to the infant's left presented the sound of a vowel. From time to time, the sound was altered. If the infant noticed the change and looked at the loudspeaker, the experimenter reinforced the response by

---

Table 10.4 Examples of responses infants make to various speech sounds

First age of occurrence	Response
Newborn	Is startled by a loud noise Turns head to look in the direction of sound Is calmed by the sound of a voice Prefers mother's voice to a stranger's Discriminates among many speech sounds
1–2 mo	Smiles when spoken to
3–7 mo	Responds differently to different intonations (e.g. friendly, angry)
8–12 mo	Responds to name Responds to 'no' Recognises phrases from games (e.g. 'Peekaboo', 'How big is baby?') Recognises words from routines (e.g. waves to 'bye-bye') Recognises some words

Source: Berko Gleason, 1993. Used by permission.

activating a toy bear that pounded on a miniature drum. Thus, the procedure provided a test of infants' ability to distinguish slight differences in vowel sounds.

The experimenters presented two different vowel sounds, one found in English but not in Swedish and the other found in Swedish but not in English. From time to time, they varied the sound slightly. The reactions of the Swedish infants and the American infants were strikingly different. Swedish infants noticed when the English vowel changed but not when the Swedish vowel changed; and American infants did the opposite. In other words, by the age of 6 months, the infants had learned not to pay attention to slight differences in speech sounds of their own language, but they were still able to distinguish slight differences in speech sounds they had never heard. Even though they were too young to understand the meaning of what they heard, the speech of people around them had affected the development of their perceptual mechanisms.

These results seem to support the native language recognition hypothesis – that infants have the ability to recognise words which belong to their native language (Moon *et al.*, 1993). Another hypothesis, the general language discrimination hypothesis, suggests that infants are capable of discriminating sentences from any two languages because they can extract sets of properties that these languages posses. The evidence above suggests that there is little support for this hypothesis. An alternative to these two hypotheses states that newborns are sensitive to prosody and can discriminate between languages on the basis of intonation and rhythm. This is called the rhythm-based language discrimination hypothesis (Nazzi *et al.*, 1998).

To test this hypothesis, Nazzi *et al.* (1998) compared the ability of 5 day old infants to discriminate between rhythmic and non-rhythmic sentences in various languages. They found that infants were able to discriminate between English and Japanese but not English and Dutch, thereby supporting the rhythm hypothesis. This suggests that infants may be more attuned to the rhythmic as opposed to the phonetic quality of speech.

Interestingly, there is now evidence to suggest that the ability to discriminate between phonetic sounds successfully may change with age. Stager and Werker (1997) have reported that 8 month old infants are capable of discriminating phonetic detail in a task in which 14 month old infants cannot. The researchers suggest that this represents a reorganisation in the infant's language processing capacity: it shifts from the processes needed to learn syllables to the process needed to learn words. This is advantageous to the infant as it grows and has to put names to objects, events and situations. Because these activities are computationally complex and involve a huge increase in input, the amount of detail that needs to be processed is, therefore, limited.

Infant communication

Even before infants learn to talk, they display clear intent to communicate. Most attempts at preverbal infant communication fall into three categories: rejection, request (for social interaction, for an object or for an action), and comment (Sachs, 1993). Rejection usually involves pushing the unwanted object away and using facial expression and characteristic vocalisations to indicate displeasure. A request for social interaction usually involves the use of gestures and vocalisations to attract the caregiver's attention. A request for an object usually involves reaching and pointing and particular vocalisations. A request for an action (such as the one described above) similarly involves particular sounds and movements. Finally, a comment usually involves pointing out an object or handing it to the carer, accompanied by some vocalisation.

Infants babble before they talk. They often engage in serious 'conversations' with their carers, taking turns 'talking' with them. Infants' voices are modulated, and the stream of sounds they make sound as though they are using a secret language (Menn and Stoel-Gammon, 1993). At about one year of age, a child begins to produce words. The first sounds children use to produce speech appear to be similar across all languages and cultures: the first vowel is usually the soft 'a' sound of father, and the first consonant is a stop consonant produced with the lips – 'p' or 'b'. Thus, the first word is often 'papa' or 'baba'. The next feature to be added is nasality, which converts the consonants 'p' or 'b' into 'm'. Thus, the next word is 'mama'. Mothers and fathers all over the world recognise these sounds as their children's attempts to address them.

The first sounds of a child's true speech contain the same phonemes that are found in the babbling sounds that the child is already making; thus, speech emerges from pre-speech sounds. During the course of learning words from their carers and from older children, infants often invent their own protowords, unique strings of phonemes that serve word-like functions. The infants use these protowords consistently in particular situations (Menn and Stoel-Gammon, 1993).

The development of speech sounds continues for many years. Some sequences are added very late. For example, the 'str' of string and the 'bl' of blink are difficult for young children to produce; they usually say 'tring' and 'link', omitting the first consonant. Most children recognise sounds in adult speech before they can produce them.

The two-word stage

At around 18–20 months of age, children start learning language by putting two words together, and their linguistic development takes a leap forward. It is at this stage that linguistic creativity begins.

As for first sounds, children's two-word utterances are remarkably consistent across all cultures. Children use words in the same way, regardless of the language their parents speak. Even deaf children who learn sign language from their parents put two words together in the same way as children who can hear (Bellugi and Klima, 1972). And deaf children whose parents do not know sign language invent their own signs and use them in orderly, 'rule-governed' ways (Goldin-Meadow and Feldman, 1977). Thus, the grammar of children's language at the two-word stage appears to be universal (Owens, 1992).

For many years, investigators described the speech of young children in terms of adult grammar, but researchers now recognise that children's speech simply follows different rules. Young children are incapable of forming complex sentences – partly because their vocabulary is small, partly because their short-term 'working' memory is limited (they cannot yet encode a long string of words), and partly because their cognitive development has not yet reached a stage at which they can learn complex rules of syntax (Locke, 1993).

How adults talk to children

When parents talk to children, they use only short, simple, well formed, repetitive sentences and phrases (Brown and Bellugi, 1964) called child-directed speech (Snow, 1986). Adults' speech to children is characterised by clear pronunciation, exaggerated intonations, careful distinctions between similar-sounding phonemes, relatively few abstract words and function words, and a tendency to isolate constituents that undoubtedly enables young children to recognise them as units of speech (deVilliers and deVilliers, 1978).

Another important characteristic of child-directed speech is that it tends to refer to tangible objects the child can see, to what the child is doing and to what is happening around the child (Snow et al., 1976). Words are paired with objects the child is familiar with, which is the easiest way to learn them. For example, carers make statements and ask questions about what things are called, what noises they make, what colour they are, what actions they are engaging in, who they belong to and where they are located. Their speech contains more content words, and fewer verbs, modifiers and functions words (Newport, 1975; Snow, 1977).

Adults – particularly carers, who have a continuing relationship with a child – tend to act as tutors when talking to children. For example, Snow and Goldfield (1982) found that as a mother and child repeatedly read a book over a period of thirteen months, the mother's speech became more and more complex, especially when they were discussing a picture that they looked at again and again.

Adults often expand children's speech by imitating it but putting it into more complex forms, which undoubtedly helps the child learn about syntactical structure (Brown and Bellugi, 1964):

Child: Baby highchair.
Adult: Baby is in the highchair.
Child: Eve lunch.
Adult: Eve is having lunch.
Child: Throw daddy.
Adult: Throw it to daddy.

People make allowances for the age of the child with whom they are talking. Mothers talk differently to 2 year olds than to 10 year olds (Snow, 1972a). Even 4 year old children talk differently to 2 year olds than they do to adults or other 4 year olds (Shatz and Gelman, 1973). It seems unlikely that these differentiated speech patterns are innately determined. Snow (1972a) compared the speech patterns of a mother talking to a child with her speech patterns when she only pretended to be talking to a child. The woman's speech when the child was absent was simpler than it would have been if addressed to an adult, but when the child was present, it was simpler still. Clearly, then, feedback from children is important.

The most important factor controlling adults' speech to children is the child's attentiveness. Both adults and children are very sensitive to whether another person is paying attention to them. As Snow (1986) notes, people do not talk at children, they talk with them. When a child looks interested, an adult continues with what he or she is doing. Signs of inattention in the child prompts an adult to advance or simplify the level of speech until the child's attention is regained. Stine and Bohannon (1983) found that when children give signs that they do not understand what an adult is saying, the adult adjusts his or her speech by simplifying it.

Infants also exert control over what their carers talk about. The topic of conversation usually involves what the infant is playing with or is guided by what the infant is gazing at (Bohannon, 1993). This practice means that infants hear speech that concerns what they are already paying attention to, which undoubtedly facilitates learning. In fact, Tomasello and Farrar (1986) found that infants of mothers who talked mostly about the objects of their infants' gazes uttered their first words earlier than other infants and also developed larger vocabularies early in life.

An experiment by Snow (1972b) showed that children pay more attention to a tape recording of speech directed to a child than to a recording of speech directed to an adult. Other researchers have found that children respond best to speech that is slightly more complex than their own (Shipley et al., 1969). Interacting with someone who has achieved slightly greater competence appears to be an optimum strategy for most learning. Thus, children modify adults' speech, keeping it at the optimal level of complexity.

Acquisition of adult rules of grammar

The first words that children use tend to be content words: these words are emphasised in adult speech and refer to objects and actions that children can directly observe

(Brown and Bellugi, 1964). As children develop past the two-word stage, they begin to learn and use more and more of the grammatical rules that adults use. The first form of sentence lengthening appears to be the expansion of object nouns into noun phrases (Bloom, 1970). For example, 'that ball' becomes 'that a big ball'. Next, verbs are used more frequently, articles are added, prepositional phrases are mastered and sentences become more complex. These results involve the use of *inflections* and function words. Table 10.5 shows the approximate order in which children acquire some of these inflections and function words.

It is more difficult for children to add an inflection or function word to their vocabulary than to add a new content word because the rules that govern the use of inflections or function words are more complex than those that govern the use of most content words. In addition, content words usually refer to concrete objects or activities. The rules that govern the use of inflections or function words are rarely made explicit. A parent seldom says, 'When you want to use the past tense, add "-ed" to the verb', nor would a young child understand such a pronouncement. Instead, children must listen to speech and figure out how to express such concepts as the past tense.

The most frequently used verbs in most languages are irregular. Forming the past tense of such verbs in English does not involve adding '-ed' (for example, go/went, throw/threw, buy/bought, see/saw). The past tense of such verbs must be learned individually. Because irregular verbs get more use than do regular ones, children learn them first, producing the past tense easily in sentences such as 'I came', 'I fell down', and 'she hit me'. Shortly after this period, they discover the regular past tense inflection and expand their vocabulary, producing sentences such as 'he dropped the ball'. But they also begin to say 'I comed', 'I falled down', and 'she hitted me'. Having learned a rule, they apply it to all verbs, including the irregular ones that they were previously using correctly. It takes children several years to learn to use the irregular past tense correctly again.

Acquisition of meaning

The simplest explanation of why children use and understand language is that they hear a word spoken at the same time that they see (or hear, or touch) the object to which the word refers. After several such pairings, they add a word to their vocabulary. In fact, children first learn the names of things with which they interact, or things that change (and thus attract their attention). For example, they are quick to learn words like 'biscuit' or 'blanket', but are slow to learn words like 'wall' or 'window' (Ross *et al.*, 1986; Pease *et al.*, 1993).

This quick learning of new, content words has been called **fast mapping** (Markman, 1989). The child is able to learn a word based on very few incidental exposures and is able to retain this word over long periods of time. There is some debate over whether fast mapping is specific to language or whether it is generated by other, cognitive processes. For example, if fast mapping is seen only for words then this would suggest that the process is language based; if fast mapping can extend to other domains, this suggests that the process is underpinned by general cognitive abilities (such as the ability to memorise). There is evidence to suggest that fast mapping may not be specific to word learning (Markson and Bloom, 1997).

In two experiments, Markson and Bloom (1997) taught 3–4 year old children and a group of university undergraduates to learn a word referring to an object ('kobi') and a fact about this object. In one experiment, participants were told that this was an object given to the experimenter by her uncle. The participants' ability to remember and identify the object was tested immediately after learning, one week after or one month after. Although the adults were better at remembering the object and object name than

Table 10.5   The approximate order in which children acquire inflections and function words

Item	Example
1 Present progressive: *ing*	He is *sitting* down.
2 Preposition: *in*	The mouse is *in* the box.
3 Preposition: *on*	The book is *on* the table.
4 Plural: *-s*	The *dogs* ran away.
5 Past irregular: e.g. *went*	The boy *went* home.
6 Possessive: *-'s*	The *girl's* dog is big.
7 Uncontractible copula *be*: e.g. *are, was*	*Are* they boys or girls? *Was* that a dog?
8 Articles: *the, a, an*	He has *a* book.
9 Past regular: *-ed*	He *jumped* the stream.
10 Third person regular: *-s*	She *runs* fast.
11 Third person irregular: e.g. *has, does*	*Does* the dog bark?
12 Uncontractible auxiliary *be*: e.g. *is, were*	*Is* he running? *Were* they at home?
13 Contractible copula *be*: e.g. *'s, -re*	That*'s* a spaniel. They*'re* pretty.
14 Contractible auxiliary *be*: e.g. *-'s, -'re*	He*'s* doing it. They*'re* running slowly.

Source: adapted from Clark and Clark, 1977. Copyright © Harcourt Brace Jovanovich 1977; reprinted by permission of the publisher.

were the children, all children performed comparably well when asked to retrieve the word, identify the object about which facts were presented and identifying the object given to the experimenter by her uncle. This study suggests, therefore, that fast mapping may not necessarily be specific to language processing but is made possible by learning and memory mechanisms that are not special to the language domain (Markson and Bloom, 1997).

Often, a child may commit what are called errors of overextension or underextension. If a child has learned to identify a ball but he or she says 'ball' when he sees an apple or an orange, or even the moon, we must conclude that he does not know the meaning of 'ball'. This type of error is called overextension – the use of a word to denote a larger class of items than is appropriate. If he uses the word to refer only to the small red plastic ball, his error is called an underextension – the use of a word to denote a smaller class of items than is appropriate. Table 10.6 lists some examples of children's overextensions while learning the meanings of new words.

Both overextensions and underextensions are normal; a single pairing of a word with the object does not provide enough information for accurate generalisation.

Carers often correct children's overextensions. The most effective type of instruction occurs when an adult provides the correct label and points out the features that distinguish the object from the one with which the child has confused it (Chapman *et al.*, 1986). For example, if a child calls a yo-yo a ball, the carer might say, 'That's a yo-yo. See? It goes up and down' (Pease *et al.*, 1993).

Many words, including function words, do not have physical referents. For example, prepositions such as 'on', 'in' and 'towards' express relations or directions, and a child needs many examples to learn how to use them appropriately. Pronouns are also difficult; for example, it takes a child some time to grasp the notion that 'I' means the speaker: 'I' means me when I say it, but 'I' means you when you say it. In fact, parents usually avoid personal pronouns in speaking with their children. Instead, they use sentences such as 'Does [baby's name] want another one?' (meaning 'Do you want another one?') and 'Daddy will help you' (meaning 'I will help you').

Abstract words such as 'apparently', 'necessity', 'thorough' and 'method' have no direct referents and must be defined in terms of other words. Therefore, children cannot learn their meanings until after they have learned many other words.

Bilingualism

Often, children are not exposed to one language but to many and learn to speak two or more languages. In such cases, individuals are said to be bilingual or multilingual. But what does being bilingual mean? A common factor which can be considered to be the core of bilingualism is that it represents the ability of the individual to meet the communication demands of the self or the individual's culture in two or more languages (Mohanty and Perregaux, 1997). Bilingualism has been described as simultaneous when two or more languages develop in childhood more or less simultaneously, spontaneously and naturally, and successive when a second (and third) language is learned after the first, such as learning a second language during puberty (Romaine, 1989).

Table 10.6 Some overextensions that children make while learning new words

Word	Original referent	Application
mooi	Moon	Cakes, round marks on windows, writing on windows and in books, round shapes in books, round postmarks, letter o
buti	ball	Toy, radish, stone sphere at park entrance
ticktock	watch	All clocks and watches, gas meter, firehose wound on spool, bath scale round dial
baw	ball	Apples, grapes, eggs, squash, bell clapper, anything round
mem	horse	Cow, calf, pig, moose, all four-legged animals
fly	fly	Specks of dirt, dust, all small insects, child's own toes, crumbs of bread, a toad
wau-wau	dog	All animals, toy dog, soft house slippers, picture of an old man dressed in furs

Source: adapted from Table 13.2 from *Psychology and Language: An Introduction to Psycholinguistics* by Herbert H. Clark and Eve V. Clark. Copyright © 1977 by Harcourt Brace Jovanovich, Inc.; reprinted by permission of the publisher. After E. Clark (1975).

Bilingualism and cognitive ability

Until relatively recently, it was thought that bilingualism was detrimental to cognitive performance. These early studies which compared Spanish–English bilinguals in America and English–Welsh bilinguals in Wales with monolinguals showed that being able to speak two languages from childhood had negative consequences for intellectual development. It now appears that such conclusions are incorrect and that these early studies did not take into account socioeconomic status, the degree of bilingualism or the skill in the second language (Lambert, 1977; Cummins, 1984). Studies since the 1960s have shown that, rather than impairing cognitive ability, bilingualism is beneficial to it (Perregaux, 1994). In a rare series of well-controlled studies, Mohanty (1982a,b, 1990) compared the cognitive performance of monolinguals with bilinguals in the Kand people of India. The samples came from the same culture and the experimenters ensured that monolinguals and bilinguals were matched for age, sex and socio-economic status. The bilinguals spoke Kui at home and Oriya outside the home environment. The bilinguals performed significantly better than the monolinguals on a series of cognitive and linguistic tasks. This superior performance in bilinguals was seen even in unschooled bilinguals (Mohanty and Das, 1987).

The precise effect of bilingualism on cognitive performance, however, is unclear. Some observers have suggested that the learning of a second language can have two effects: additive and subtractive. A second language has an additive effect when it adds to cognitive ability allowed by first language, that is it enriches the use of the second language; a second language has a subtractive effect when it replaces the first language. For example, a second language might interfere with the production of words in the first language (you are speaking in one language but you can only remember some words in the other).

Bilingualism is an interesting phenomenon for psychologists and linguists to study because it may help to determine whether there is an innate mechanism that allows these languages to develop or whether special non-innate mechanisms are needed to process a second language. All languages do not have the same structure or grammatical rules. English, for example, has a fixed word order; other languages have variable word orders with word endings marking grammatical relations within a sentence. Furthermore, word length also differs by language. The study of bilingualism may also tell us about the way in which the brain organises its capacity to produce and comprehend language during childhood and adulthood. Data from one functional magnetic resonance imaging study of individuals with various second languages, for example, had suggested that the second language acquired in adulthood (late bilingualism) activated different parts

of Broca's area than did the mother tongue (Kim *et al.*, 1997). These researchers concluded that a second language is processed somewhat differently from the native language and, as a result, the degree of regional brain activation differed. This conclusion was consistent with an earlier positron emission tomography study of Italian–English bilinguals in which the auditory processing of stories in the dominant language activated the temporal cortex and the tempo-parietal cortex more extensively than did similar processing in the second language (Perani *et al.*, 1996).

One reason for this finding, however, may have been that the second language was learned later and subjects were less competent in that language. Although the participants had a basic grasp of the second language, they were far from excellent. It was possible, therefore, that differences in brain activation were due to differences in language proficiency rather than in processing the languages themselves. In a subsequent experiment, Perani *et al.* (1998) examined the brain response of a group of Italian–English bilinguals who had learned the second language after the age of 10 years and a group of Spanish–Catalan bilinguals who acquired the second language before the age of two. When activation to tasks in both languages were compared, there was no significant difference in the language areas activated. This would suggest that the degree of proficiency in a second language may be the most important determinant of cortical activity.

The subtractive influence of a second language has been highlighted by results from digit span experiments. A digit span task is a test of short-term memory in which the individual is asked to recite a series of numbers from short-term memory after the experimenter has spoken them. Digit span reflects the largest number of digits a person can recall without error. Digit span in Chinese, for example, averages 9.9 (Hoosain, 1984); in Arabic it is 5.7 (Naveh-Benjamin and Ayres, 1986). Does this mean that Chinese people have a greater short-term memory than Arabs? It is possible, but you could not draw this conclusion based on digit span data because some words for digits are longer in some languages than others. Recall from Chapter 8 that working memory contains a phonological loop which determines our capacity to remember phonological information; the phonological store contains material that is speech-related but only stores it for a short period of time because of decay. Articulating (speaking out loud or quietly to oneself) allows the phonological store to be refreshed because we may subvocally rehearse items we wish to remember. However, if it takes us longer to articulate one word in one language than it does to articulate the same word in a different language, the longer word will not have as great an opportunity to get into the phonological store because items in it decay very quickly. Words requiring shorter articulation, therefore, place fewer demands on working memory. Languages with shorter articulation times should produce the longest digit spans.

Ellis and Hennelly (1980), for example, compared the digit span performance in English and Welsh of English–Welsh bilinguals. Digit span was shorter in Welsh – but because the Welsh words took longer to articulate than English ones. In a series of words, there would be significantly more syllables in Welsh and, therefore, longer articulation times. When articulation was suppressed, digit span differences between Welsh and English were eliminated.

But does articulation rate fully explain the difference in digit span? Da Costa Pinto (1991) found that articulation and digit span was faster in Portuguese than English even though the Portuguese words were longer. Suppressing articulation resulted in an even greater digit span for the Portuguese words. What Da Costa Pinto suggested was that articulation rate may be unimportant; what is important is familiarity with the language used. Such familiarity would result from massive practice in the mother tongue; digit span would be greater in the first language because this is the one that is practised the most (this is called mother tongue superiority). Chincotta and Underwood (1996) have suggested that the measures of language proficiency in the Ellis and Hennelly study were indirect and that the Welsh–English bilinguals were more dominant in English. These bilinguals even expressed a preference for English digits when speaking Welsh. This explanation is consistent with the findings of (and explanation provided by) Da Costa Pinto. However, it is made less likely by a study in which Spanish–English bilinguals, who expressed self-rated proficiency in Spanish, showed greater digit spans for English.

So, what could explain this and the other digit span findings? Naveh-Benjamin and Ayres (1986) have suggested that if bilinguals are equally fluent, then the language in which mathematics and science are taught will be the one which shows the largest digit span. Unfortunately, there are no consistent data to support this hypothesis. Chincotta and Underwood (1996) suggest that the English digit span superiority effect seen in the Welsh–English bilingual study may have been the result of schooling and the use of the language at home. They argue that digit span will be greater in the language used at home and at school. To test this hypothesis, they studied Finnish–Swedish bilingual undergraduates. There were four groups. Constant bilinguals were defined as those individuals whose mother tongue was the same as the language of schooling (so there were two groups of constant bilinguals, Finnish–Finnish and Swedish–Swedish). Compound bilinguals were defined as those individuals whose mother tongue differed from the language of schooling (so there were two groups: those whose mother tongue was Finnish but were taught in Swedish and those whose mother

tongue was Swedish but were taught in Finnish). The experimenters found that digit span performance was better for the language used during schooling. These results suggest that the language in which formal instruction occurs will lead to a better performance in that language compared with the second language. The cause of this superior performance is unknown: is it greater practice? Or does the use of the language of schooling result in better 'thinking skills' in that language (so it is not how much the language is used but what it is used for)?

Is there a language acquisition device?

According to Pinker (1984), 'In general, language acquisition is a stubbornly robust process; from what we can tell there is virtually no way to prevent it from happening, short of raising a child in a barrel.' The absence of barrels permitting, what shapes this linguistic learning process, and what motivates it?

There is vigorous controversy about why children learn to speak and, especially, why they learn to speak grammatically. Chomsky (1965) observed that the recorded speech of adults is not as correct as the dialogue we read in a novel or hear in a play; often it is ungrammatical, hesitating and full of unfinished sentences. In fact, he characterised everyday adult speech as 'defective' and 'degenerate'. If this speech is really what children hear when they learn to speak, it is amazing that they manage to acquire the rules of grammar.

The view that children learn regular rules from apparently haphazard samples of speech has led many linguists to conclude that the ability to learn language is innate. All a child has to do is to be in the company of speakers of a language. Linguists have proposed that a child's brain contains a language acquisition device which embodies rules of 'universal grammar'; because each language expresses these rules in slightly different ways, the child must learn the details, but the basics are already there in the brain (Chomsky, 1965; Lennenberg, 1967; McNeill, 1970).

The assertion that an innate language acquisition device guides children's acquisition of a language is part of a general theory about the cognitive structures responsible for language and its acquisitions (Pinker, 1990). The most important components are as follows:

1 Children who are learning a language make hypotheses about the grammatical rules they need to follow. These hypotheses are confirmed or disconfirmed by the speech that they hear.

2 An innate language acquisition device guides children's hypothesis formation. Because they have this device, there are certain types of hypothetical rule that they will never entertain and certain types of sentence that they will never utter.

3 The language acquisition device makes reinforcement unnecessary; the device provides the motivation for the child to learn a language.

4 There is a critical period for learning a language. The language acquisition device works best during childhood; after childhood, languages are difficult to learn and almost impossible to master.

Evaluation of the evidence for a language acquisition device

No investigator regards the first assertion – that children make and test hypotheses about grammatical rules – as tenable. Thus, we cannot simply ask children why they say what they do. Children's hypothesis testing is a convenient metaphor for the fact that their speech sometimes follows one rule or another.

A more important – and testable – assertion is that the hypothesis testing is guided by the language acquisition device. The most important piece of evidence in favour of this assertion is the discovery of language universals: characteristics that can be found in all languages that linguists have studied. Some of the more important language universals include the existence of noun phrases ('the quick brown fox …'); verb phrases ('…ate the chicken'); grammatical categories of words such as nouns and adjectives; and syntactical rules that permit the' expression of subject–verb–object relations ('John hit Andy'), plurality ('two birds'), and possession ('Rachel's pen').

However, the fact that all languages share certain characteristics does not mean that they are the products of innate brain mechanisms. For example, Hebb *et al.* (1973) observed that language universals may simply reflect realities of the world. When people deal with each other and with nature, their interactions often take the form of an agent acting on an object. Thus, the fact that all languages have ways of expressing these interactions is not surprising. Similarly, objects come in slightly different shapes, sizes and colours, so we can expect the need for ways (such as adjectives) to distinguish among them. It is not unreasonable to suppose that the same kinds of linguistic device have been independently invented at different times and in different places by different cultures. After all, archaeologists tell us that similar tools have been invented by different cultures all around the world. People need to cut, hammer, chisel, scrape and wedge things apart, and different cultures have invented similar devices to perform these tasks. We need not conclude that these inventions are products of a 'tool making device' located in the brain.

But even if some language universals are dictated by reality, others could indeed be the result of a language acquisition device. For example, consider the following sentences, adapted from Pinker (1990):

A1. Bill drove the car into the garage.
A2. Bill drove the car.
B1. Bill put the car into the garage.
B2. Bill put the car.

Someone (such as a child learning a language) who heard sentences A1 and A2 could reasonably infer that sentence B1 could be transformed into sentence B2. But the inference obviously is false; sentence B2 is ungrammatical. The linguistic rules that say that sentence A2 is acceptable but that sentence B2 is not are very complex; and their complexity is taken as evidence that they must be innate, not learned. Pinker (1990) concludes, 'The solution to the problem [that children do not utter sentence B2] must be that children's learning mechanisms ultimately do not allow them to make the generalisation' (p. 206).

This conclusion rests on the assumption that children use rules similar to the ones that linguists use. How, the reasoning goes, could a child master such complicated rules at such an early stage of cognitive development unless the rules were already wired into the brain? But perhaps the children are not following such complex rules. Perhaps they learn that when you say 'put' (something) you must always go on to say where you put something. Linguists do not like rules that deal with particular words, such as put (something) (somewhere); they prefer abstract and general rules that deal with categories: clauses, prepositions, noun phrases and the like. But children learn particular words and their meanings – why should they not also learn that certain words must be followed (or must never be followed) by certain others? Doing so is certainly simpler than learning the complex and subtle rules that linguists have devised. It would seem that both complex and simple rules (or innate or learned ones) could explain the fact that children do not utter sentence B2.

The third assertion is that language acquisition occurs without the need of reinforcement – or even of correction. Brown and Hanlon (1970) recorded dialogue between children and parents and found that adults generally did not show disapproval when the children's utterances were ungrammatical and approval when they were grammatical. Instead, approval appeared to be contingent on the truth or accuracy of the children's statements. If there is no differential reinforcement, how can we explain the fact that children eventually learn to speak grammatically?

It is undoubtedly true that adults rarely say, 'Good, you said that correctly', or, 'No, you said that wrongly'. However, adults do distinguish between grammatical and ungrammatical speech of children. A study by Bohannon and Stanowicz (1988) found that adults are likely to repeat children's grammatically correct sentences verbatim but to correct ungrammatical sentences. For example, if a child says, 'That be monkey', an adult would say, 'That is a monkey'. Adults were also more likely to ask for clarifications of ungrammatical sentences. Thus, adults do tend to provide the information children need to correct their faulty speech.

Chomsky's assertion about the defectiveness and degeneracy of adult speech is not strictly true, at least as far as it applies to what children hear. In fact, according to Newport *et al.* (1977), almost all the speech that a young child hears (at least, in industrialised English-speaking societies) is grammatically correct. If that is so, why should we hypothesise that a language acquisition device exists? Because, say some researchers, not all children are exposed to child-directed speech. 'In some societies people tacitly assume that children aren't worth speaking to and don't have anything to say that is worth listening to. Such children learn to speak by overhearing streams of adult-to-adult speech' (Pinker, 1990, p. 218).

Pinker's statement is very strong; it says that children in some cultures have no speech directed towards them until they have mastered the language. It implies that the children's mothers do not talk to them and ignores the fact that older children may not be quite so choosy about their conversational partners. To conclude that such an extreme statement is true would require extensive observation and documentation of child-rearing practices in other cultures. One of the strongest biological tendencies of our species is for a mother to cherish, play with and communicate with her offspring. If there really is a culture in which mothers do not do so, we need better documentation.

In fact, children do not learn a language that they simply overhear. Bonvillian *et al.* (1976) studied children of deaf parents whose only exposure to spoken language was through television or radio. This exposure was not enough, although the children could hear and did watch television and listen to the radio, they did not learn to speak English. It takes more than 'overhearing streams of adult-to-adult speech' to learn a language. The way that parents talk to their children is closely related to the children's language acquisition (Furrow *et al.*, 1979; Furrow and Nelson, 1986). Thus, the question is, just how much instruction (in the form of child-directed speech) do children need?

The fact that parents do not often reward their children's speech behaviours with praise or tangible reinforcers (such as sweets) does not prove that reinforcement plays no role in learning a language. We humans are social animals; our behaviour is strongly affected by the behaviour of others. It is readily apparent to anyone who has observed the behaviour of children that the attention of other people is extremely important to them. Children will perform a variety of behaviours that get other people to pay attention to them. They will make faces, play games and even misbehave in order to attract attention. And above all, they will talk.

The final assertion – that the language acquisition device works best during childhood – has received the most experimental support. For example, Newport and Supalla (1987) studied the ability of people who were deaf from birth to use sign language. They found that the earlier the training began, the better the person was able to communicate. Johnson and Newport (1989) also found that native Korean and Chinese speakers who moved to the United States learned English grammar better if they arrived during childhood. The advantage did not appear to be a result of differences in motivation to learn a second language. Such results are consistent with the hypothesis that something occurs within the brain after childhood that makes it more difficult to learn a language.

Conclusion

Observational studies such as these do not prove that a cause-and-effect relation exists between the variables in question. Johnson and Newport suggest that people's age (in particular, the age of their brain) affects their language-learning ability. But other variables are also correlated with age. For example, the Korean and Chinese speakers who moved to the United States as children spent several years in school; and perhaps the school environment is a particularly good place to learn a second language. In addition, adults are generally more willing to correct the grammatical errors made by children than those made by adolescents or other adults; thus, children may get more tutoring. It is certainly possible that the investigators are correct, but their results cannot be taken as proof that the brain contains an innate language acquisition device.

In one sense, a language acquisition device does exist. The human brain is a language acquisition device; without it, languages are not acquired. The real controversy is over the characteristics of this language acquisition device. Is it so specialised that it contains universal rules of grammar and provides innate motivation that makes reinforcement unnecessary?

The issue is made more interesting – if controversial – if we consider the ability of other higher primates to learn language. Other higher primates such as gorillas or chimpanzees do not naturally produce language although they have their own system of communication. Their vocal apparatus is different from that of humans so it would be unrealistic to assume that they would be able to articulate human language. However, these animals are the ones that are genetically closest to us; similar brain asymmetries, especially in those parts of the brain which are thought to mediate language, are seen in humans and apes. Would it be possible to teach primates human language? Do higher primates also possess an innate language acquisition device but need an environmental prompt for such a device to start working? These questions form the basis of the 'Controversies in psychological science' section.

Controversies in psychological science

Can other primates acquire language?

The issue

The members of most species can communicate with one another. Even insects communicate: a female moth that is ready to mate can release a chemical that will bring male moths from miles away; a dog can tell its owner that it wants to go for a walk by bringing its leash in its mouth and whining at the door. But until recently, humans were the only species that had languages – flexible systems that use symbols to express many meanings. Evidence suggests that other primates may also be able to learn and use symbols in the same linguistic way that humans do.

The evidence

In the 1960s, Beatrice and Roger Gardner of the University of Nevada began Project Washoe (Gardner and Gardner, 1969, 1978), a remarkably successful attempt to teach sign language to a female chimpanzee named Washoe. Previous attempts to teach chimps to learn and use human language focused on speech (Hayes, 1952). These attempts failed because, as we noted above, chimps lack the control of tongue, lips, palate and vocal cords that humans have and thus cannot produce the variety of complex sounds that characterise human speech.

Gardner and Gardner realised this limitation and decided to attempt to teach Washoe a manual language – one that makes use of hand movements. Chimps' hand and finger dexterity is excellent, so the only limitations in their ability would be cognitive ones. The manual language the Gardners chose was based on ASL, the American sign language used by deaf people. This is a true language, containing function words and content words and having regular grammatical rules.

Washoe was one year old when she began learning sign language; by the time she was four, she had a vocabulary of over one hundred and thirty signs. Like children, she used single signs at first; then, she began to produce two-word sentences such as 'Washoe sorry', 'gimme flower', 'more fruit', and 'Roger tickle'. Sometimes, she strung three or more words together, using the concept of agent and object: 'You tickle me'. She asked and answered questions, apologised, made assertions – in short, did the kinds of things that children would do while learning to talk. She showed overextensions and underextensions, just as human children do. Occasionally, she even made correct generalisations by herself. After learning the sign for the verb 'open' (as in open box, open cupboard), she used it to say open faucet, when requesting a drink. She made signs to herself when she was alone and used them to 'talk' to cats and dogs, just as children will do. Although it is difficult to compare her progress with that of human children (the fairest comparison would be with that of deaf children learning to sign), humans clearly learn language much more readily than Washoe did.

Inspired by Project Washoe's success, several other investigators have taught primate species to use sign language. For example, Patterson began to teach a gorilla (Patterson and Linden, 1981), and Miles (1983) began to teach an orang-utan. Washoe's training started relatively late in her life, and her trainers were not, at the beginning of the project, fluent in sign language. Other chimpanzees, raised from birth by humans who are native speakers of ASL, have begun to use signs when they are three months old (Gardner and Gardner, 1975).

Many psychologists and linguists have questioned whether the behaviour of these animals can really be classified as verbal behaviour. For example, Terrace et al. (1979) argue that the apes simply learned to imitate the gestures made by their trainers and that sequences of signs such as 'please milk please me like drink apple bottle' (produced by a young gorilla) are nothing like the sequences that human children produce. Others have challenged these criticisms (Fouts, 1983; Miles, 1983; Stokoe, 1983), blaming much of the controversy on the method Terrace and his colleagues used to train their chimpanzee.

Certainly, the verbal behaviour of apes cannot be the same as that of humans. If apes could learn to communicate linguistically as well as children can, then humans would not have been the only species to have developed language. The usefulness of these studies rests in what they can teach us about our own language and cognitive abilities. Through them, we may discover what abilities animals need to communicate as we do. They may also help us to understand the evolution of these capacities.

These studies have already provided some useful information. For example, Premack (1976) taught chimpanzees to 'read' and 'write' by arranging plastic tokens into 'sentences'. Each token represents an object, action or attribute such as colour or shape, much the way words do. His first trainee, Sarah, whom he acquired when she was one year old, learned to understand complex sentences such as 'Sarah insert banana in pail, apple in dish.' When she saw the disks arranged in this order, she obeyed the instructions.

Figure 10.5

Researcher Sue Savage-Rumbaugh taught her chimp, Kanzi, to communicate using a special keyboard.

Chimpanzees can, apparently, use symbols to represent real objects and can manipulate these symbols logically. These abilities are two of the most powerful features of language. For Premack's chimpanzees, a blue plastic triangle means 'apple'. If the chimpanzees are given a blue plastic triangle and asked to choose the appropriate symbols denoting its colour and shape, they choose the ones that signify 'red' and 'round', not 'blue' and 'triangular'. Thus, the blue triangle is not simply a token the animals can use to obtain apples; it represents an apple for them, just as the word apple represents it for us.

Even though humans are the only primates that can pronounce words, several other species can recognise them. Savage-Rumbaugh (1990; Savage-Rumbaugh *et al.*, 1998) taught Kanzi, a pygmy chimpanzee, to communicate with humans by pressing buttons that contained symbols for words, as seen in Figure 10.5.

Kanzi's human companions talked with him, and he learned to understand them. Although the structure of his vocal apparatus prevented him from responding vocally, he often tried to do so. During a three month period, Savage-Rumbaugh and her colleagues tested Kanzi with 310 sentences, such as 'Put a toothbrush in

Table 10.7   Semantic relations comprehended by Kanzi, a pygmy chimpanzee

Semantic relations	N	Examples (spoken)
Action-object	107	*'Would you please carry the straw?'* Kanzi looks over a number of objects on the table, selects the straw, and takes it to the next room.
Object-action	13	*'Would you like to ball chase?'* Kanzi looks around for a ball, finds one in his swimming pool, takes its out, comes over to the keyboard, and answers 'Chase'.
Object-location	8	*'Would you put the grapes in the swimming pool?'* Kanzi selects some grapes from among several foods and tosses them into the swimming pool.
Action-location	23	*'Let's chase to the A-frame.'* Kanzi is climbing in trees and has been ignoring things that are said to him. When he hears this he comes down rapidly and runs to the A-frame.
Action-object-location	36	*'I hid the surprise by my foot.'* Kanzi has been told that a surprise is around somewhere, and he is looking for it. When he is given this clue, he immediately approaches the speaker and lifts up her foot.
Object-action	9	*'Kanzi, the pine cone goes in your shirt.'* Kanzi picks up a pine cone and puts it in his shirt.
Action-location-object	8	*'Go the refrigerator and get out a tomato.'* Kanzi is playing in the water in the sink. When he hears this he stops, goes to the refrigerator, and gets a tomato.
Agent-action-object	7	*'Jeannine hid the pine needles in her shirt.'* Kanzi is busy making a nest of blankets, branches, and pine needles. When he hears this, he immediately walks over to Jeannine, lifts up her shirt, takes out the pine needles, and puts them in his nest.
Action-object-recipient	19	*'Kanzi, please carry the cooler to Penny.'* Kanzi grabs the cooler and carries it over to Penny.
Other – object-action-recipient; action-recipient-location; etc.	69	

Source: Savage-Rumbaugh, 1990. Reprinted by permission.

the lemonade.' Three hundred and two of these had never been heard by the chimpanzee before. Only situations in which Kanzi could not have been guided by non-verbal cues from the human companions were counted; often, Kanzi's back was to the speaker. He responded correctly 298 times. Table 10.7 presents specific examples of these sentences and the actions that Kanzi took.

One conclusion that has emerged from the studies of primates is that true verbal ability is a social behaviour. It builds on attempts at non-verbal communication in a social situation. The most successful attempts at teaching a language to other primates are those in which the animal and the trainer have established a close relationship in which they can successfully communicate non-verbally by means of facial expressions, movements and gestures. Apes and orang-utans clearly perceive people as other beings who can be loved, trusted or feared. Non-human primates (and humans, for that matter) learn a language best while interacting with others. Such interactions naturally lead to attempts at communication; and if signs (or spoken words) serve to make communication easier and more effective, they will most readily be learned.

One of the most interesting questions asked of researchers in this area is will animals who learn to communicate by means of signs will teach those signs to their offspring. The answer appears to be yes. Fouts *et al.* (1983) obtained a 10 month old infant chimpanzee, Loulis, whom they gave to Washoe to 'adopt'. Within eight days, the infant began to imitate Washoe's signs. To be certain that Loulis was learning the signs from Washoe and not from humans, the investigators used only the signs for who, what, want, which, where, sign and name in his presence. As Fouts (1983) reported:

'[A] sign, food [which he now uses], was ... actively taught by Washoe. On this occasion Washoe was observed to sign food repeatedly in an excited fashion when a human was getting her some food. Loulis was sitting next to her watching. Washoe stopped signing and took Loulis' hand in hers, molded it into the food sign configuration, and touched it to his mouth several times.' (pp. 71–72)

Questions to think about

The acquisition of language

- Can you think of any examples of child-directed speech that you may have overheard (or engaged in yourself while talking with a young child)? How would you feel if you were talking with a baby who suddenly lost interest in you? Would you be motivated to do something to regain the baby's attention? What would you do?

- When is the most appropriate time to learn a first and a second language?

- Do you think that a modified form of child-directed language could be developed as an effective way of tutoring adults who want to learn a second language?

- It has been said that only language separates us from other animals. Is this true?

- How can you account for the rapid development of language in children?

- Do you agree with Pinker's view that we cannot do very much to stop language developing in normal, healthy children? Do you think that a child's environment is irrelevant to the degree of language development? (We return to this question in more detail in the next chapter.)

The neuropsychology of language

The brain allows us to sense and perceive. The branch of psychology called neuropsychology, as we saw in Chapter 4, aims to localise not only these perceptual and sensory functions but also cognitive function. The most extensively studied cognitive function in neuropsychology is language, and our knowledge of the neuropsychology of language has come from two sources: studies of individuals with brain injury who show language impairment, and neuroimaging studies in which activation of the brain in healthy individuals is monitored while they are engaged in language processing. Data from these areas indicate that the mechanisms involved in perception, comprehension and production of speech are located in different areas of the cerebral cortex. This section begins with the meat and drink of neuropsychology: studies of brain injury and abnormal brain development.

Language disorders

Brain damage can result from a large number of factors and can cause a wide variety of impairments in cognitive function. Some of the most pronounced impairments are those related to language. Some language impairments result directly from brain injury, other do not but are likely to be the result of disorganised or abnormal brain activity or structure. The most common language disorders are called the aphasias. The key feature of the aphasias is the loss of language function; the patient is unable to produce or comprehend speech. Other important disorders of language are reading impairment (dyslexia) and stuttering and all three of these disorders are considered in the next sections.

Aphasia

Aphasia literally means 'total loss of language function' although patients with the disorder do not lose all language: they are able to perform some language tasks, for example, depending on the site of the brain injury. Because of this, the term dysphasia is sometimes used (*dys* – means 'partial loss of'). There are different types of aphasia, and the most common are summarised in Table 10.8. Two of the most common types are non-fluent (Broca's) aphasia and receptive (Wernicke's) aphasia. The areas of the brain which, when damaged, cause these aphasias can be seen in Figure 10.6.

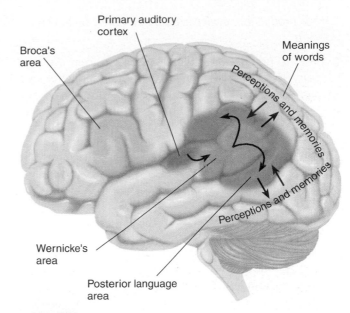

Figure 10.6

Words into thoughts and thoughts into words. The dictionary in the brain relates the sounds of words to their meanings and permits us to comprehend the meanings of words and translate our own thoughts into words. Black arrows represent comprehension of words; red arrows represent translation of thoughts or perceptions into words.

Table 10.8 Types of aphasia, their primary symptoms and the site of the associated brain lesion.

Type of aphasia	Primary symptoms	Brain lesion to
Sensory (Wernicke's) aphasia	General comprehension deficits, neologisms, word retrieval deficits, semantic paraphasias	Posterior perisylvian region: posterosuperior temporal, opercular supramarginal, angular and posterior insular gyri; planum temporale
Production (Broca's) aphasia	Speech production deficits, abnormal prosody, impaired syntactic comprehension	Posterior part of the inferior frontal and precentral convolutions of the left hemisphere
Conduction aphasia	Naming deficits and impaired ability to repeat non-meaningful single words and word strings	Arcuate fasciculus; posterior parietal and temporal regions: left auditory complex; insula; supramarginal gyrus
Deep dysphasia	Word repetition deficits: verbal (semantic) paraphasia	Temporal lobe, especially regions which mediate phonological processing
Transcortical sensory aphasia	Impaired comprehension, naming, reading and writing; semantic irrelevancies in speech	Temporoparieto-occipital junction of the left hemisphere
Transcortical motor aphasia	Transient mutism and telegrammatic, dysprosodic speech	Connection between Broca's area and the supplementary motor area; medial frontal lobe; regions anterolateral to the left hemisphere's frontal horn
Global aphasia	Generalised deficits in comprehension, repetition, naming and speech production	Left perisylvian region, white matter, basal ganglia and thalamus

Speech production: evidence from non-fluent (Broca's) aphasia

In order to produce meaningful communication, we need to convert perceptions, memories, and thoughts into speech. The neural mechanisms that control speech production appear to be located in the frontal lobes. Damage to a region of the motor association cortex in the left frontal lobe (Broca's area) disrupts the ability to speak: it causes non-fluent (Broca's) aphasia, a language disorder characterised by slow, laborious, non-fluent speech (it is also called expressive, production or motor aphasia; neuropsychology is a complicated business). When trying to talk with patients who have non-fluent aphasia, most people find it hard to resist supplying the words the patients are obviously groping for. But although these patients often mispronounce words, the ones they manage to produce are meaningful. They have something to say, but the damage to the frontal lobe makes it difficult for them to express these thoughts.

Here is a sample of speech from a man with Broca's aphasia, who is telling the examiner why he has come to the hospital. His words are meaningful but what he says is not grammatical. The dots indicate long pauses.

> 'Ah ... Monday ... ah Dad and Paul [patient's name] ... and Dad ... hospital. Two ... ah doctors ..., and ah ... thirty minutes ... and yes ... ah ... hospital. And, er Wednesday ... nine o'clock. And er Thursday, ten o' clock ... doctors. Two doctors ... and ah ... teeth. Yeah, ... fine.' (Goodglass, 1976, p. 278)

Lesions that produce non-fluent aphasia must be centred in the vicinity of Broca's area. However, damage restricted to the cortex of Broca's area does not appear to produce Broca's aphasia; the damage must extend to surrounding regions of the frontal lobe and to the underlying subcortical white matter (Damasio, 1989; Damasio *et al.*, 1996).

Wernicke (1874) suggested that Broca's area contains motor memories – in particular, memories of the sequences of muscular movements that are needed to articulate words. Talking involves rapid movements of the tongue, lips and jaw, and these movements must be co-ordinated with each other and with those of the vocal cords; thus, talking requires some very sophisticated motor control mechanisms. Because damage to the lower left frontal lobe (including Broca's area) disrupts the ability to articulate words, this region is the most likely candidate for the location of these 'programs'. The fact that this region is located just in front of the part of the primary motor cortex that controls the muscles used for speech certainly supports this conclusion.

In addition to their role in the production of words, neural circuits located in the lower left frontal lobe appear to perform some more complex functions. Damage to Broca's area often produces agrammatism: loss of the ability to produce or comprehend speech that employs complex syntactical rules. For example, people with non-fluent aphasia rarely use function words. In addition, they rarely use grammatical markers such as '-ed' or auxiliaries such as 'have' (as in 'I have gone'). A study by Saffran *et al.* (1980) illustrates this difficulty. The following quotations are from agrammatic patients attempting to describe pictures:

> 'Picture of a boy being hit in the head by a baseball
> The boy is catch ... the boy is hitch ... the boy is hit the ball.' (p. 229)

> 'Picture of a girl giving flowers to her teacher
> Girl ... wants to ... flowers ... flowers and wants to ... The woman ... wants to ... The girl wants to ... the flowers and the woman.' (p. 234)

In an ordinary conversation, non-fluent aphasics seem to understand everything that is said to them. They appear to be irritated and annoyed by their inability to express their thoughts well, and they often make gestures to supplement their scanty speech. The striking disparity between their speech and their comprehension often leads people to assume that their comprehension is normal. Their comprehension, however, is not normal. To test agrammatic people for speech comprehension, Schwartz *et al.* (1980) showed them a pair of drawings, read a sentence aloud and then asked them to point to the appropriate picture. The patients heard forty-eight sentences such as 'The clown applauds the dancer' and 'The robber is shot by the cop'. For the first sample sentence, one picture showed a clown applauding a dancer, and the other showed a dancer applauding a clown. On average, the brain-damaged people responded correctly to only 62 per cent of the pictures (responses at chance levels would be 50 per cent). In contrast, the performance of normal people is around 100 per cent.

The agrammatism that accompanies non-fluent aphasia appears to disrupt patients' ability to use grammatical information, including word order, to decode the meaning of a sentence. Thus, their deficit in comprehension parallels their deficit in production. If they heard a sentence such as 'The mosquito was swatted by the man', they would understand that it concerns a man and a mosquito and the action of swatting. Because of their knowledge of men and mosquitoes, they would have no trouble figuring out who is doing what to whom. But a sentence such as 'The cow was kicked by the horse' does not provide any extra cues; if the grammar is not understood, neither is the meaning of the sentence.

Other experiments have shown that people with non-fluent aphasia have difficulty carrying out a sequence of commands, such as 'pick up the red circle and touch the green square with it' (Boller and Dennis, 1979). This finding, along with the other symptoms described in this section, suggests that an important function of the left frontal lobe may be sequencing, both physically in terms of muscle movement (for example, the muscles of speech-producing words) and semantically in terms of sequencing actual words (for example, comprehending and producing grammatical speech). As we saw in the section on working memory in Chapter 8, the frontal cortex may be important in the correct sequencing of stimuli. This sequencing role of the frontal cortex is returned to in Chapter 11 (in relation to reasoning) and Chapter 13 (in relation to organising social and emotional behaviour).

Speech comprehension: evidence from receptive (Wernicke's) aphasia

Comprehension of speech obviously begins in the auditory system, which is needed to analyse sequences of sounds and to recognise them as words. Recognition is the first step in comprehension. As we saw earlier in this chapter, recognising a spoken word is a complex perceptual task that relies on memories of sequences of sounds. This task appears to be accomplished by neural circuits in the upper part of the left temporal lobe – a region that is known as Wernicke's area.

Brain damage in the left hemisphere that invades Wernicke's area as well as the surrounding region of the temporal and parietal lobes produces a disorder known as Wernicke's aphasia. The symptoms of receptive aphasia are poor speech comprehension and production of meaningless speech (Wernicke's aphasia is also known as sensory or receptive aphasia). Unlike non-fluent aphasia, speech in receptive aphasia is fluent and unlaboured; the person does not strain to articulate words and does not appear to be searching for them. The patient maintains a melodic line, with the voice rising and falling normally. When you listen to the speech of a person with receptive aphasia, it appears to be grammatical. That is, the person uses function words such as 'the' and 'but' and employs complex verb tenses and subordinate clauses. However, the person uses few content words, and the words that he or she strings together just do not make sense. In the extreme, speech deteriorates into a meaningless jumble often characterised by neologisms, illustrated by the following example from Kertesz (1981, p. 73):

Examiner: What kind of work did you do before you came into the hospital?
Patient: Never, now mista oyge I wanna tell you this happened when happened when he rent. His – his kell come down here and is – he got ren something. It happened. In thesse ropiers were with him for hi – is friend – like was. And it just happened so I don't know, he did not bring around anything. And he did not pay it. And he roden all o these arranjen from the pedis on from iss pescid. In these floors now and so. He hadn't had em round here.

A commonly used test of comprehension for receptive aphasia assesses the patient's ability to understand questions by pointing to objects on a table in front of them. For example, they are asked to 'point to the one with ink'. If they point to an object other than the pen, they have not understood the request. When tested this way, people with severe Wernicke's aphasia show poor comprehension.

Because Wernicke's area is a region of the auditory association cortex, and because a comprehension deficit is so prominent in receptive aphasia, this disorder has been characterised as a receptive aphasia. Wernicke suggested that the region that now bears his name is the location of memories of the sequences of sounds that constitute words. This hypothesis is reasonable; it suggests that the auditory association cortex of Wernicke's area recognises the sounds of words, just as the visual association cortex in the lower part of the temporal lobe recognises the sight of objects.

Wernicke's aphasia, like non-fluent aphasia, actually appears to consist of several deficits. The abilities that are disrupted include recognition of spoken words, comprehension of the meaning of words, and the ability to convert thoughts into words. Recognition is a perceptual task; comprehension involves retrieval of additional information from long-term memory. Damage to Wernicke's area produces a deficit in recognition; damage to the surrounding temporal and parietal cortex produces a deficit in production of meaningful speech and comprehension of the speech of others.

Brain damage that is restricted to Wernicke's area produces an interesting syndrome known as pure word deafness – a disorder of auditory word recognition, uncontaminated by other problems (Franklin *et al.*, 1994). Although people with pure word deafness are not deaf, they cannot understand speech. As one patient put it, 'I can hear you talking, I just can't understand what you're saying.' Another said, 'It's as if there were a bypass somewhere, and my ears were not connected to my voice' (Saffran *et al.*, 1976, p. 211). These patients can recognise non-speech sounds such as the barking of a dog, the sound of a doorbell, the chirping of a bird, and so on. Often, they can recognise the emotion expressed by the intonation of speech even though they cannot understand what is being said. More significantly, their own speech is excellent. They can often understand what other people are saying by reading their lips. They can also read and write, and, sometimes, they ask people to communicate with them in writing. Clearly, pure word deafness is not an inability to comprehend the meaning of words; if it were, people with this disorder would not be able to read people's lips or read words written on paper.

If the region around Wernicke's area is damaged, but Wernicke's area itself is spared, the person will exhibit all of the symptoms of receptive aphasia except a deficit in auditory word recognition. Damage to the region surrounding Wernicke's area (the posterior language areas) produces a disorder known as isolation aphasia, an inability to comprehend speech or to produce meaningful speech accompanied by the ability to repeat speech and learn new sequences of words. The difference between isolation aphasia and Wernicke's aphasia is that patients with isolation aphasia can repeat what other people say to them; thus, they obviously can recognise words. However, they cannot comprehend the meaning of what they hear and repeat; nor can they produce meaningful speech of their own. Apparently, the sounds of words are recognised by neural circuits in Wernicke's area, and this information is transmitted to Broca's area so that the words can be repeated. However, because the posterior language area is destroyed, the meaning of the words cannot be comprehended.

Damage to other regions of the brain can disrupt particular categories of meaning in speech. For example, damage to part of the association cortex of the left parietal lobe can produce an inability to name the body parts. This disorder is called autotopagnosia, or 'poor knowledge of one's own topography' (a better name would have been autotopanomia, 'poor naming of one's own topography'). People who can otherwise converse normally cannot reliably point to their elbows, knees or cheeks when asked to do so, and they cannot name body parts when the examiner points to them. However, they have no difficulty understanding the meaning of other words.

Specific language impairment

Some children have difficulties in producing or understanding spoken language, in the absence of known brain injury. The 3–4 per cent who exhibit this impairment are said to show specific language impairment. Grammar and phonology are the most affected aspects, but intelligence is within the normal range. When a 6 year old with adequate hearing but specific language impairment is asked to repeat the sentence, 'Goldilocks ran away from the three bears because she thought they might chase her', she says, 'Doedilot when away from berd. Them gonna chate her' (Bishop, 1997). A recent study suggests that one cause of these problems may be impaired auditory perception (Wright *et al.*, 1997). These researchers found that the children were impaired when perceiving tones that were brief but not tones that were long.

Some language impairments, however, seem to occur in the absence of such auditory impairment. These impairments arise from a child's inability to acquire the rules of language early (Gopnik, 1997). One example of such a language impairment is the inability to produce the past tense. For example, in the following statement,

'Everyday he walks eight miles. Yesterday he …'

some children would not be able to supply the past tense for 'walk' to complete the second sentence. These problems are seen in children who have normal auditory acuity and non-verbal and psychosocial skills, and, although they may have other difficulties such as dyslexia and depression, none of these factors has been reliably associated with these specific language impairments.

In a review and theoretical analysis of these impairments, Gopnik (1997) has suggested there may be a strong genetic influence on their development because they tend to cluster in families and seem to occur in families cross-culturally.

Such impairments have also been found in languages such as English, Japanese, Greek and French. An example of the types of test used to determine specific language

---

Table 10.9   The percentage of participants capable of marking novel words grammatically

Grammar	Language	Controls %	Impaired %
Past tense	English (in England)	95.4	38.0
	English (in Canada)	93.5	52.3
	Greek	87.1	20.0
	French	92.6	33.3
	Japanese	89.1	37.0
Plurals	English (in England)	95.7	57.0
	English (in Canada)	99.2	58.3
	Greek	79.8	42.1
Comparatives	English (in England)	74.0	21.0
Compounds	Japanese	80.5	20.2
	Greek	93.6	12.8
Diminutives	Greek	83.9	40.2

In each of these tests the subjects were given a context which required a grammatical rule to be applied to a novel word, for example 'This pencil is weff' would require the participant to supply 'This pencil is even . . . [weffer]'

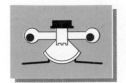
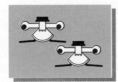

'This is a wug'   'These are...'

Figure 10.7

A task used to investigate a child's ability to understand grammar using novel words.

Source: Reprinted from *Trends in Cognitive Sciences*, 1(1), April, p. 7: M. Gopnik, Language deficits and genetic factors. Copyright 1997, with permission from Elsevier Science.

impairment is seen in Figure 10.7. Here, the participant is presented with a word they have never heard of (i.e., a non-word) and are given a grammatical rule to follow. The forms of impairment observed can be seen in Table 10.9.

Gopnik suggests that this specific impairment in the use of complex grammatical rules is universal, although critics have argued that auditory/articulation problems or general problems with cognition may be the source of the impairment rather than a genetic, neural component. For example, children may leave off the /d/ sound when transforming an English word into the past tense. However, the problem does not seem to be specific to /d/ sounds. In languages where the past tense is transformed in a different way, the same specific language impairments have been observed. English, for example, has about four regular-form verbs; Greek has sixty. The number of mistakes in making past tenses seen in each language is proportional to the number of regular verbs they use. More

to the point, as Gopnik notes, in French the final syllable is stressed so that it is not difficult to hear.

Dyslexia

The term **dyslexia** refers to a disorder involving impaired reading and it is one of the most common language disorders seen in children and adults. The incidence of the disorder lies between 5 and 17.5 per cent (Shaywitz, 1998). Although boys are thought to be affected more than girls, the evidence is unclear (Flynn and Rahbar, 1994). Many different types of dyslexia have been described but there are two broad categories: acquired dyslexia and developmental dyslexia. **Acquired dyslexia** describes a reading impairment resulting from brain injury in individuals with previously normal language. **Developmental dyslexia** refers to a difficulty in learning to read despite adequate intelligence and appropriate educational opportunity (Critchley, 1973). The types of dyslexia and their symptoms are described in Table 10.10.

Acquired dyslexia

The most important forms of dyslexia which result from brain injury are visual word form dyslexia, phonological dyslexia, surface dyslexia and deep dyslexia. Visual word form dyslexia describes an inability to recognise words immediately but gradually with the naming of each letter (Warrington and Shallice, 1980). Sometimes a patient might commit a letter naming mistake, pronouncing 'c,a,t ... cat' when the word to be read is 'mat'. The disorder is

Table 10.10 The dyslexias and the brain regions associated with them

Type of dyslexia	Primary symptoms	Brain regions implicated
Acquired dyslexia		
Visual word form dyslexia	Impaired sight reading; some decoding is possible	Disconnection between the angular gyrus of the dominant hemisphere and the visual input system
Phonological dyslexia	Deficits in reading pseudowords and non-words	Temporal lobe of the dominant hemisphere?
Surface dyslexia	Tendency to produce regularisation errors in the reading of irregular words	?
Deep dyslexia	Semantic substitutions, impaired reading of abstract words, inability to read non-words	Extensive damage to the dominant hemisphere
Developmental dyslexia	Impaired reading and spelling of words/non-words/pseudowords, poor phonological processing skills, sequencing and short-term memory, some visuoperceptual defects	Temporoparietal regions of the dominant hemisphere

thought to result from a disconnection between the region of the left hemisphere which mediates the recognition of word forms (Speedie *et al.*, 1982) and the visual input system. Reading ability may rely on the perceptual and visual skills of the right hemisphere.

Phonological dyslexia refers to an inability to read pseudowords and non-words and is relatively rare (although phonological deficits are also seen in developmental dyslexia, described below). Phonological dyslexia provides evidence that whole-word reading and phonological reading involve different brain mechanisms and provides some support for the dual-route model of reading outlined earlier in the chapter (see Figure 10.8). Phonetic reading, which is the only way we can read non-words or words we have not yet learned, entails some sort of letter-to-sound decoding. It also requires more than decoding of the sounds produced by single letters, because, for example, some sounds are transcribed as two-letter sequences (such as 'th' or 'sh') and the addition of the letter 'e' to the end of a word lengthens an internal vowel ('can' becomes 'cane').

Surface dyslexia is the inability to recognise and read words based on their physical characteristics. Individuals are able to apply the grapheme–phoneme correspondence rules, however (described earlier in the chapter), but have difficulties with irregular words (so, 'yacht' is pronounced as it reads and sounds).

Deep dyslexia refers to a severe inability to read; concrete words can sometimes be read but are commonly replaced by semantically related words. For example, a patient would read 'sleep' when the word is 'dream' (Coltheart *et al.*, 1980). Abstract words are rarely

pronounced accurately and neither are pronounceable non-words (indicating an inability to apply grapheme–phoneme correspondence rules).

Developmental dyslexia

The symptoms of developmental dyslexia resemble those of acquired dyslexias. Developmental dyslexia first manifests itself in childhood. It tends to occur in families, which suggests the presence of a genetic (and hence biological) component (Grigorenko *et al.*, 1997). Attempts have been made to categorise types of developmental dyslexia along the same lines as the acquired dyslexias. Such attempts usually distinguish between reading disorders which involve a deficit in 'sounding out' a word or in identifying words on the basis of visual form (Brunswick, 1998). Various names have been suggested for the two types such as dysphonetic vs dyseidetic (Fried *et al.*, 1981), phonological vs morphemic dyslexia (Temple and Marshall, 1983) and P (perceptual) and L (lingual) type (Bakker, 1992).

Although not all psychologists agree with such distinctions, a fairly constant factor in developmental dyslexia is poor awareness of the phonological features of sound, that is, poor phonological awareness (Stahl and Murray, 1994). The segmentation of words into sounds, being aware of alliteration, verbal repetition and verbal naming are all impaired in developmental dyslexia. For example, if children are asked to transpose the first sounds of the words 'mustard' and 'salad' (thereby producing 'sustard' and 'malad'), those with developmental dyslexia are unable to do this. Similarly, individuals with developmental dyslexia may be unable to perform phonological tasks such as indicating what is left when you take either the first or last sound away from a word such as 'mice'.

There also seems to be a deficit in the verbal or phonological memory of developmental dyslexics. For example, a number of studies has shown that these individuals have poorer memory span than good readers for letter strings, words in a sentence and strings of digits. The stimuli do not have to be printed, the deficit is purely language-based; memory for unfamiliar faces or abstract patterns is intact (Lieberman *et al.*, 1982). Is this poor phonological memory the cause of the reading disorder.

Some psychologists disagree, arguing that these impairments do not explain the persistent and severe nature of dyslexia (Hulme and Roodenrys, 1995). Reading is a complex task that requires phonology, memory and visual perception. Stein and his colleagues (Stein, 1991; Stein and Walsh, 1997), for example, have suggested that developmental dyslexics have poor visual direction sense, poor binocular convergence (which we discussed in Chapter 6) and visual fixation and have hypothesised that these impairments are implicated in the development of dyslexia.

Stein's hypothesis states that dyslexics are unable to process fast incoming sensory information adequately. The

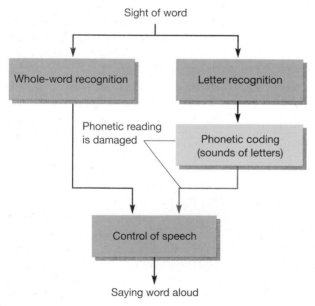

Figure 10.8

A hypothetical explanation of phonological dyslexia. Only whole-word reading remains.

magnocellular pathway of the visual system is responsible for the detection of orientation, movement, direction and depth perception (Dautrich, 1993) and is argued to be defective in dyslexics. Studies have shown that poor visual fixation, poor tracking from left to right and poor binocular convergence hinder the development of normal reading (Eden et al., 1994). In a functional magnetic resonance imaging study of developmental dyslexics' ability to process visual motion, Eden et al. (1996) found that moving stimuli (such as dots) failed to activate the cortical area that is projected to by the magnocellular pathway (area V5). In competent readers, this area was activated in both hemispheres during the task. Furthermore, the presentation of stationary patterns did not produce different patterns of brain activation in dyslexics and controls, suggesting that the dyslexic sample had difficulties specifically with attending to moving stimuli.

There may also be differences between controls and dyslexics at the structural, cellular level (Galaburda et al., 1985). These researchers found that a part of the thalamus projected to by the magnocellular pathway was disordered in five dyslexics; this region was 20 per cent smaller than that of a control group. A reduction in the number of cells in a similar area has also been reported by Rae et al. (1998). While it is too early to conclude for certain that this visual pathway is responsible for the impairments seen in dyslexia, the evidence suggests that some form of perceptual impairment related to vision may contribute to disordered reading.

Dyslexia and lateralisation

Geschwind and Behan (1984) proposed that there is an association between dyslexia, left handedness, and various immune disorders, such as thyroid and bowel diseases, diabetes and rheumatoid arthritis. They suggested that a genetic abnormality, as well as predisposing people to immune disorders, also affected the development of the left hemisphere of the brain. Although this hypothesis is interesting and has attracted a great deal of research interest, there is little evidence to support the predictions made by the model (Bryden et al., 1994).

Another neural model of developmental dyslexia suggests that dyslexics have delayed or reduced left hemisphere function or have no lateralised preference (Bishop, 1990; Galaburda et al., 1994). There is evidence that function and structure are more symmetrical in dyslexic samples, however. When good and poor readers respond to visual or auditory stimuli, brain electrical activity is symmetrical in dyslexics but typically left-based in controls (Cohen and Breslin, 1984; Brunswick and Rippon, 1994; Rippon and Brunswick, 1998).

A structure called the planum temporale found just above the primary auditory cortex is reported to be more symmetrical in dyslexics than in controls (Galaburda et al., 1994). That is, controls have a larger planum temporale in the left hemisphere than the right whereas dyslexics show a similarly-sized structure in both hemispheres. The planum temporale may be an important brain region because it is generally larger in the left hemisphere. Because of its prominence in the left hemisphere (where it is longer) and because it contains an area that is functionally the same as Wernicke's area, some researchers have suggested that this structure is important for language (see Beaton, 1997, for a very thorough discussion of this issue). This idea, however, is speculative (Galaburda, 1995). For example, the leftward asymmetry of the planum temporale may simply be nothing more than a physical feature of the brain; it simply happens to be larger on the left than the right. However, there do seem to be more anomalies in asymmetry in dyslexics than in normal-reading samples.

Stuttering

Stuttering is a disorder of the production of speech in which the individual involuntarily repeats sounds or syllables. The disorder is characterised by a breakdown in the control, timing or co-ordination of speech muscles (Braun et al., 1997). It affects approximately 4 per cent of children and 1 per cent of adults (Andrews et al., 1983).

There is very little relationship between the disorder and the content of language; it can even be eliminated when individuals practise their speech or utter slow, rhythmical speech (Jayoram, 1984). It occurs only during interpersonal communication and is made worse by stress and the complexity of the utterance. Speaking on the telephone and talking in front of an audience results in stuttering although it does not occur when the individual sings, speaks alone or to pets or to small children or when the speech is paced and the material overlearned (Braun et al., 1997).

Various theories have been suggested for the cause of the disorder. Some psychologists suggest that the problem is simply a motor one where there is a breakdown in the performance of the speech musculature. However, the fact that this breakdown only occurs under certain circumstances suggests that this may not be the sole cause. Another theory suggests that stutterers have problems perceiving auditory feedback from speech (Hall and Jerger, 1978). The errors and interruptions found in the speech of stutterers is the result of distortion from auditory feedback. If individuals are given external cues which allow them to pace speech, then stuttering is eliminated.

It is also possible that stutterers have incomplete or abnormal patterns of cerebral asymmetry. One theory suggests that there is greater right hemisphere activation in stutterers; the stuttering results either from the right hemisphere being in competition with the left or it may be overcompensating for the function of the left hemisphere. To test this hypothesis, Braun et al. (1997) conducted a PET study of adult stutterers who had developed the disorder in childhood. These individuals completed a series of speech and language tasks that either evoked or reduced stuttering. The experimenters found that left hemisphere activation was reduced during the formulation of language. When stuttered speech was produced, the anterior forebrain regions were activated but those areas responsible for the decomposition and perception of sensory information were silent. The results suggested to the experimenters that the left hemisphere was involved in the production of stuttered speech but that the right hemisphere was involved in the reduction of stuttering symptoms.

Similar results were reported by Fox *et al.* (1996). They also examined adult stutterers but asked them to either chorus read (with another voice) or read alone a section of prose. The experimenters found that there was an increase in right hemisphere activation during stuttered speech which did not normalise during fluent speech production. When fluency was induced, the overactivation in the motor areas was eliminated. Although the left auditory cortex was relatively inactive during stuttered reading, this underactivation was reversed when fluency was induced.

Word recognition and production: neuroimaging studies

Neuroimaging studies (using techniques such as positron emission tomography – PET – and functional magnetic resonance imaging – fMRI – which we described in Chapter 4)

have employed increasingly sophisticated designs in attempting to discover the neural basis of normal language processing (Brunswick, 1998; Price, 1997). These studies generally conclude that the left hemisphere participates in language-related tasks more actively than does the right hemisphere and that specific regions of the left hemisphere are involved in the different components of language such as production, comprehension, processing of sound, meaning, and so on.

Petersen *et al.* (1988) conducted the first PET investigation of language processing in healthy individuals. These researchers found that the left posterior temporal cortex (including the primary auditory cortex and Wernicke's area) was significantly more active during passive listening of words than during a control condition. Repeating the nouns activated the primary motor cortex and Broca's area. Petersen *et al.* (1990) later reported that the auditory association cortex is activated by the sounds of words but not by other sounds. You can see this difference in activation in Figure 10.9.

When people were asked to think of verbs that were appropriate to use with the nouns, even more intense activity was seen in Broca's area. Price *et al.* (1994) have also reported that greater activation in the left inferior and middle frontal cortices was found during performance of a lexical decision task whereas more temporal regions were activated during reading aloud and reading silently.

An important aspect of language analysis is, as we saw earlier in the chapter, phonological processing – the putting together of sounds to make meaningful words.

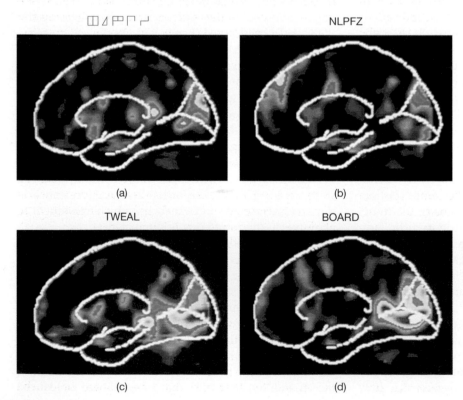

Figure 10.9

PET scans of the medial surface of the brains of people reading letter-like forms (a), strings of consonants (b), pronounceable non-words (c), and real words (d).

Source: Petersen, S.E., Fox, P.T., Snyder, A.Z. and Raichle, M.E., *Science*, 1990, 249, 1041–1044. Reprinted with permission.

Neuroimaging studies have found that when individuals discriminate between spoken words on the basis of phonetic structure, when they discriminate between consonants and when they make judgements about rhyme or engage in phonological memory tasks, activation in the left frontal cortex near Broca's area is found (Fiez *et al.*, 1995; Zatorre *et al.*, 1996; Paulesu *et al.*, 1996). Other studies report involvement of the temporal cortex and angular gyrus especially during tasks involving drawing analogies, repeating words and in reading words and pseudowords (Nobre *et al.*, 1994; Karbe *et al.*, 1998).

This evidence suggests that Broca's area and the frontal cortex are necessary for the phonetic manipulation of language but that the posterior temporal cortex is responsible for the perceptual analysis of speech (Zatorre *et al.*, 1996). However, the picture may be a little more complex. Binder *et al.* (1997) compared the analysis involved in the phonetic and semantic perception of aurally presented words with the analysis of non-linguistic stimuli such as tones. A large network of left-hemisphere regions was activated during the semantic analysis, including areas in the frontal, temporal and parietal cortex. Activation, therefore, was not limited to one specific region.

Damasio *et al.* (1996) in a comprehensive study of its kind, evaluated the effects of language processing in individuals with focal and stable brain lesions in both hemispheres, inside and outside the temporal regions. Damasio *et al.* hypothesised that there is no single mediating site for all words, but there are separate regions within a larger network that are activated by different kinds of word. There were three categories of words: persons, non-unique animals and non-unique tools, each of which should be processed by different parts of the frontal and temporal lobe. Although 97 individuals showed normal language, 30 did not; 29 of these had brain injury to the left hemisphere. While impaired retrieval of words was associated with temporal cortex damage, abnormal retrieval of animal words was found in patients with left interior temporal lobe damage and abnormal retrieval of tools was associated with posterolateral inferior temporal cortex damage.

Because we cannot infer normal function from brain damage, Damasio *et al.* conducted a second experiment in which healthy individuals performed the same language tasks while undergoing a PET scan. Although all words activated the left temporal cortex, specific categories were associated with activation of specific regions of the brain. Naming of tools activated the posterior, middle and inferior temporal gyri, for example, and animal naming activated other parts of the inferior temporal cortex. These results are similar to those of Martin *et al.* (1996), which showed that different categories of words appeared to activate different parts of the brain. A recent study has even suggested that silently naming the use of tools activates Broca's area and the left premotor and supplementary motor area (Grafton *et al.*, 1997). This suggests that even the naming of a tool's use can activate those parts of the brain that would be activated during the actual movement involved in using those tools.

Caveats and complications

Sex differences

There is evidence to suggest that men's and women's brains respond differently during language processing although this evidence is inconsistent (Frost *et al.*, 1999). In one fMRI study, for example, Shaywitz *et al.* (1995) found that left hemisphere (inferior frontal gyrus) activation was more pronounced in men whereas activation was more diffuse and bilateral in women. Pugh *et al.* (1997) reported greater activation in the left hemisphere in women during a phonological processing task. These sex differences do not necessarily mean that men's and women's brains are organised differently. It could be, for example, that the cognitive approaches of the sexes to these language tasks are different. Some tests do show quite defined sex differences, however, and the most consistent of these is discussed in Chapter 11.

Language and the right hemisphere

The right side of the brain is not neglected in language, even if the left hemisphere appears to receive the greatest share of attention (because it is the more involved of the two hemispheres). The right hemisphere takes on especial importance when the left hemisphere is damaged and may compensate for the language function lost after such damage. It is involved in the appreciation of metaphors (Bottini *et al.*, 1994) and in the processing of prosody and the affective tone of speech (Pell and Baum, 1997).

Individuals who are deaf but have learned sign language also appear to show activation in areas of the right hemisphere while signing. Neville *et al.* (1998) conducted an fMRI study of language in three groups of people: monolingual speakers of English who could hear; native deaf signers of American sign language (ASL); and bilingual users (of English and ASL) who could hear. Participants watched a videotape recording of a deaf signer producing sentences in ASL, and read English sentences presented on a computer monitor. The study found that although all groups activated the typical left hemisphere areas (Broca's and Wernicke's) when they processed English sentences, the native speakers of ASL also showed corresponding increases in the right hemisphere. Could the results have been attributable to the possibility that deafness had led to a reorganisation of the cortex in the deaf participants? This is unlikely because both the hearing and deaf participants who were fluent ASL signers showed the same right hemisphere activation. Paulesu and Mehler (1998) have suggested that this pattern of activity may, instead, reflect the possibility that the right hemisphere holds the grammar for sign language because it requires representations of both sides of the body. Because neuroimaging studies of sign language are relatively rare, this hypothesis has yet to be tested. However, it seems reasonable given the role of the right hemisphere in processing spatial relationships (such as interpreting movement in space).

Neuroimaging: validity and reliability

There has been some controversy recently over whether PET studies show consistent activation in specific regions during phonological processing (Poeppel, 1996). For example, Poeppel reviewed eight studies from six laboratories and found that no one region or set of regions was active during phonological processing in all of them. Demonet *et al.* (1996), however, point out that this is to be expected given that these studies were all different: the modality in which the stimulus was presented differed, the rate of stimulus presentation differed, the type of stimulus item used differed, the number of items differed and the short-term memory demands of tasks differed. Instead, Demonet *et al.* argue that phonological processing does not involve a unitary network; each study highlights a different aspect of phonological processing under different conditions.

Handedness: the right shift theory

Handedness refers to the degree to which individuals preferentially use one hand for certain activities (such as writing, unscrewing a jar, throwing a ball). It can also refer to the strength of hand skill. Handedness may be relevant to language because left- and right-handers may have speech localised in different hemispheres. According to one famous study by Rasmussen and Milner (1977), 96 per cent of right-handers and 70 per cent of left-handers in their study had left-hemisphere speech. Other, recent estimates place the figures at 95.3 per cent and 61.4 per cent (Segalowitz and Bryden, 1983). The implication of these figures is that a proportion of left-handers do not have left-hemisphere speech but may have right-hemisphere or bilateral speech (this is why most neuroimaging studies of language indicate that their participants were all right-handed; this reduces the likelihood of variability in brain asymmetry). Right-handers are called dextrals and right-handedness is referred to as dextrality. Left-handers are called sinistrals and left-handedness is referred to as sinistrality. You can quickly see from these terms, that left-handers have not been treated particularly fairly by language ('dextrous' means skilled; 'sinister' means menacing and evil; the French for left is *gauche* which can also mean clumsy). There is even a theory that left-handers die sooner that right-handers (you can find more on this controversy in Martin, 1998a).

One theory of handedness suggests that the distribution of differences between the skills of both hands is determined by a single gene (Annett, 1985). Individuals who possess the rs+ allele have their hand distribution shifted to the right; their left hemisphere becomes dominant for speech. Individuals with the rs++ gene show an even greater shift to the right hand (these individuals are called homozygotes) whereas those with the rs+− gene show a lesser degree of hand dominance (these individuals are called heterozygotes). Those without the rs+ allele (who express the rs− genotype) will show no overall bias in hand dominance.

This theory is called the right shift theory because it suggests that a single gene shifts dominance to one hand (this oversimplifies a complex theory but it is basically correct). Annett's theory is important because it suggests a relationship between hand skill and language (and even cognitive) ability. For example, Annett's theory predicts that heterozygotes (those with the rs+− allele) will be more advantaged on some skills than others and that homozygotes (those with the rs++ or the rs−− allele) and those with the rs+ gene absent, will be disadvantaged.

Annett and her colleagues (Annett and Manning, 1989; Annett, 1992) have shown that extreme left and right hand dominance in hand skill is associated with poorer reading ability than is intermediate hand skill. Annett (1993) also reported that children with intermediate hand skill were more likely to be selected for elite schools in the UK. Individuals with the least bias to dextrality perform better in terms of arithmetical ability and spatial skill (Annett and Manning, 1990; Annett, 1992).

However, research from other laboratories have not found unequivocal evidence for Annett's theory. For example, McManus *et al.* (1993) assessed the handedness and intellectual ability of medical students and examined differences between three degrees of right-handedness, from weak to strong preference. He found no evidence of cognitive advantage or disadvantage between weak, intermediate and strong right-handers. Similarly, Resch *et al.* (1997) administered a series of cognitive ability tests to 545 students whose hand preference they also measured. They found that although those at the left end of the handedness continuum showed the poorest spelling, non-verbal IQ and educational success, there was no difference between this group and an intermediate and right-handed group whereas Annett's theory might predict that strong right handers would also exhibit poorer language ability. Palmer and Corballis (1996) have also found no relationship between hand preference and reading ability in 11–13 year old children. Instead, reading ability was predicted by the *overall* level of hand skill rather than by the skill difference between hands.

Others have criticised Annett's model for other reasons. For example, Provins (1997) argues that handedness is a product of motor learning and environmental pressure. What is genetically determined, Provins argues, is not handedness but the motor capacity which could produce left and right hand preference, depending on the environment. Other critics such as Corballis (1997) have queried whether a single gene locus for handedness is reasonable: although the data would seem to fit a single-gene model, most genes have several loci, as we saw in Chapter 3 and will see again in Chapter 11 when we discuss the role of genetics in intelligence.

McManus (1985) has proposed that what is important is not *hand skill*, as Annett's model suggests, but hand preference. He proposes that a dextral allele (D) predisposes us towards right hand preference while a chance allele (C)

produces no directional bias. Individuals with the D allele (DD genotype) will develop a right hand preference whereas those with the C allele (CC genotype) are equally likely to show left or right hand preference. Both models have attracted interest from researchers investigating the relationship between handedness and cognitive/language ability. Neither has fully explained this relationship but provide an explanatory framework in which such relationships could operate.

Questions to think about

The neuropsychology of language and language disorders

- What are the principal characteristics of aphasia? Given that there are many aphasias, is using the term 'aphasia' very useful?

- Why are there different types of aphasia?

- Some educationalists have suggested that dyslexia is not a disorder and that reading problems should be viewed as lying on a continuum from very good reading ability to very poor reading ability. Do you agree? How would you set up an experiment to determine that dyslexic individuals were different from poor readers? Would you look for differences in the types of reading task that are impaired, in the degree of impairment, or both?

- What is the difference between acquired and developmental dyslexia?

- Is developmental dyslexia the result of delayed left hemisphere development, disorganised left-hemisphere

structures, visual processing impairments or all or none of these? Which neurobiological explanation do you think makes best sense?

- What can the study of dyslexia tell us about the way in which the brain learns to read?

- What do you think causes stuttering?

- What treatment would you suggest for stuttering? What would be the principles behind your treatment strategy?

- What regions of the brain are activated during language tasks presented in neuroimaging studies?

- Are different types of language processing associated with the activation of different brain regions? If so, why do you think this is?

- In what ways do your sex and handedness influence the way in which your brain processes language tasks?

Key terms

linguistics *p.314*
psycholinguistics *p.314*
phonemes *p.314*
voice onset time *p.314*
syntax *p.317*
function words *p.317*
content words *p.317*
affixes *p.317*
semantics *p.317*
prosody *p.318*
scripts *p.318*
mental lexicon *p.319*
fixations *p.320*
phonetic reading *p.321*

whole-word reading *p.321*
graphemes *p.321*
grapheme–phoneme
    correspondence (GPC)
    rules *p.321*
pseudowords *p.321*
pseudohomophones *p.321*
dual-route model of
    reading *p.322*
connectionism *p.322*
parallel distributed
    processing *p.322*
segmentation *p.324*
blending *p.324*

lexical awareness *p.324*
orthographic awareness
    p.324
phonological awareness
    p.324
semantic priming *p.325*
native language recognition
    hypothesis *p.328*
general language
    discrimination
    hypothesis *p.328*
protowords *p.328*
child-directed speech
    p.329

inflections *p.330*
fast mapping *p.330*
overextension *p.331*
underextension *p.331*
bilingualism *p.331*
language acquisition
    device *p.333*
aphasia *p.339*
non-fluent (Broca's)
    aphasia *p.340*
agrammatism *p.340*
Wernicke's area *p.341*
Wernicke's aphasia *p.341*
pure word deafness *p.341*

CHAPTER REVIEW

Speech and comprehension

- Language can be defined as an orderly system of communication that involves the understanding or interpretation of vocal or written symbols.

- Phonemes are the basic elements of speech but research has also shown that the primary unit of analysis is not individual phonemes but groups of phonemes, perhaps syllables.

- Recognition of words in continuous speech is far superior to the ability to recognise them when they have been isolated. We use contextual information in recognising what we hear.

- Meaning is a joint function of syntax and semantics. All users of a particular language observe syntactical rules that establish the relations of the words in a sentence to one another. These rules are not learned explicitly. People can learn to apply rules of an artificial grammar without being able to say just what these rules are.

- The most important features that we use to understand syntax are word order, word class, function words, affixes, word meanings and prosody. Content words refer to objects, actions and the characteristics of objects and actions, and thus can express meaning even in some sentences having ambiguous syntax.

- Chomsky has suggested that speech production entails the transformation of deep structure (ideas, thoughts) into surface structure (actual sentence).

- Speech comprehension requires more than an understanding of syntax and semantics: it also requires knowledge of the world. We must share some common knowledge about the world with a speaker if we are to understand what the speaker is referring to.

- Speech errors, although incorrect, follow syntactical rules; the errors lie in the content of the speech.

Reading

- Recognition of written words (reading) is a complex perceptual task which involves scanning text, perceiving and understanding symbols and sounding out these visual symbols.

- The eye-tracking device allows researchers to study people's eye movements and fixations and to learn from these behaviours some important facts about the nature of the reading process. For example, we analyse a sentence word by word as we read it, taking longer to move on from long words or unusual ones.

- Once a word has been perceived, recognition of its pronunciation and meaning takes place. Long or unfamiliar words are sounded out, that is, they are read phonologically by a process called phonic mediation.

- Short, familiar words are recognised as wholes. In fact, only whole-word reading will enable us to know how to pronounce words such as 'cow' and 'blow', or 'bone' and 'one', which have irregular spellings.

- The dual-route model of reading suggests that we have two routes for reading: one which does not rely on grapheme–phoneme correspondence rules and another which does.

Language acquisition

- Studies using the habituation of a baby's sucking response have shown that the human auditory system is capable of discriminating among speech sounds soon after birth.

- Human vocalisation begins with crying, then develops into cooing and babbling, and finally results in patterned speech. During the two-word stage, children begin to combine words creatively, saying things they have never heard.

- Child-directed speech is very different from that directed towards adults; it is simpler, clearer and generally refers to items and events in the present environment. As young children gain more experience with the world and with the speech of adults and older children, their vocabulary grows and they learn to use adult rules of grammar.

- Children seem to pay less attention to phonetic detail of language as they grow older, presumably because the process of acquiring vocabulary and understanding of objects and situations is computationally complex.

- Although the first verbs children learn tend to have irregular past tenses, once they learn the regular past tense rule (add '-ed'), they apply this rule even to irregular verbs they previously used correctly.

- A language acquisition device contains universal grammatical rules and motivates language acquisition. Although children's verbal performance can be described by complex rules, it is possible that simpler rules – which children could reasonably be expected to learn – can also be devised.

- Deliberate reinforcement is not necessary for language learning, but a controversy exists about just how important child-directed behaviour is.

- A critical period for language learning may exist, but the evidence is not yet conclusive.

- Bilingualism refers to competence in two or more languages that are used to communicate with significant others. Bilinguals seem to be more proficient in the language in which they are schooled.

- Studies of other primates suggest that apes can be taught at least some of the rudiments of language.

Aphasia

- The effects of brain damage suggest that memories of the sounds of words are located in Wernicke's area and that memories of the muscular movements needed to produce them are located in Broca's area.

- Wernicke's area is necessary for speech perception and Broca's area is necessary for its production.

- Wernicke's aphasia (caused by damage that extends beyond the boundaries of Wernicke's area) is characterised by fluent but meaningless speech that is lacking in content words but rich in function words.

- Broca's aphasia (caused by damage that extends beyond the boundaries of Broca's area) is characterised by non-fluent but meaningful speech that is lacking in function words but rich in content words.

- Damage restricted to Wernicke's area does not produce aphasia but produces pure word deafness, a deficit in speech comprehension unaccompanied by other language difficulties. Damage to the temporoparietal region surrounding Wernicke's area

produces isolation aphasia – loss of the ability to produce meaningful speech or to comprehend the speech of others but retention of the ability to repeat speech.

Dyslexia

- Dyslexia refers to an inability to read. There are two general types: acquired and developmental.

- Acquired dyslexia refers to reading disorder arising from brain injury and there are various types of dyslexia that result from brain injury such as deep dyslexia, phonological dyslexia and visual word form dyslexia. Although some regions of the brain are known to be involved in these disorders, their exact neural basis is unknown.

- Developmental dyslexia refers to a disorder of reading that occurs without brain injury and manifests itself in delayed reading development. Phonological processing (the ability to break down words into sounds and appreciate how they relate to each other) is severely impaired in developmental dyslexia.

- No one know the exact causes of developmental dyslexia. Theories include delayed or disorganised left hemisphere development, an impairment in the function of the magnocellular pathway, an inability to scan text efficiently and neuron degeneration in the temporal cortex.

- Stuttering is a disorder of speech production in which the individual involuntarily repeats sounds or syllables. There is evidence of greater right hemisphere activation during stuttering which some researchers have suggested reflects the hemisphere's attempt to reduce the stuttering produced by the left hemisphere.

Neuroimaging and language

- Neuroimaging studies of language production and comprehension suggest that no one brain region is involved in language processing. Instead, there is a complex mosaic of regions which contributes to language and which interacts in a way in which we only partially understand.

- Evidence suggests that Broca's area and the frontal cortex is necessary for the phonetic manipulation of speech but that the temporal cortex is necessary for the perceptual analysis of speech.

- The language areas of men and women are differently activated, with more bilateral activation in women; handedness also interact with the degree of language proficiency, but in slightly irregular ways.

Suggestions for further reading

Aitchison, J. (1998). *The Articulate Mammal* (4th edition). London: Routledge.

Gleitman, L.R. and Liberman, M. (1995). *Invitation to Cognitive Science: Language.* Cambridge, MA: MIT Press.

Harley, T.A. (1995). *The Psychology of Language.* Hove, UK: The Psychology Press.

Pinker, S. (1994). *The Language Instinct.* London: Penguin.
There are many books on language and specific aspects of language. These four books, however, approach language from a linguist's, a cognitive scientist's and two psychologists' point of view, respectively. All four are highly recommended.

Fletcher, P. (1998). *Child Language Acquisition.* London: Arnold.

Gleason, J.B. (1997). *The Development of Language* (4th edition). Boston: Allyn and Bacon.

Holtzman, M. (1997). *The Language of Children* (2nd edition). Oxford: Blackwell.

Jusczyk, P.W. (1997). *The Discovery of Spoken Language.* Cambridge, MA: MIT Press.
Language is the most important intellectual function we develop and the way in which we develop it so quickly is astonishing but not well understood. These four books give a comprehensive account of what we know about language acquisition and how it occurs.

Brent, M.R. (1997). *Computational Approaches to Language Acquisition.* Cambridge, MA: MIT Press.
This book is a little more specific in content. It gives an account of computational models of language, currently popular in language modelling research.

Underwood, G. and Batt, V. (1996). *Reading and Understanding.* Oxford: Blackwell.
This book gives a full account of the process of reading and reading development.

Blachman, B.A. (1997). *Foundations of Reading Acquisition and Dyslexia.* London: Lawrence Erlbaum Associates.

Brunswick, N. (1998). The neuropsychology of language and language disorders. In G.N. Martin, *Human Neuropsychology.* Harlow: Prentice Hall.

Thal, D.J. and Reilly, J.S. (1997). *Language Disorders.* London: Lawrence Erlbaum Associates.
Language disorders are the most common disorders studied by neuropsychologists, although not all of them are caused by brain injury. Blachman's book is a collection of state-of-the-art chapters by authorities in their respective fields. Brunswick's chapter is an excellent, up-to-date review of the neuropsychology of language. Thal and Reilly's book is a special edition of the journal Developmental Neuropsychology *and gives a more advanced account of language disorders. Consult this one once you have mastered the basics in Brunswick's chapter.*

Journals to consult

Brain and Language
British Journal of Developmental Psychology
British Journal of Psychology
Child Development
Cognition
Cognitive Neuropsychology
Developmental Psychology
Dyslexia
Journal of Child Language
Journal of Experimental Psychology: Learning, Memory and Cognition
Journal of Memory and Language
Language and Cognitive Processes
Nature
Neuroimage
Psycholinguistics
Psychological Review
Psychological Science
Quarterly Journal of Experimental Psychology
Reading and Writing: An Interdisciplinary Journal
Science
Trends in Cognitive Science

Website addresses

http://www.ccp.uchicago.edu/~alfr/Psych208/startup.html
A large collection of links to sites related to speech, neural nets, linguistics and cognitive neuroscience.

www.dialnsa.edu/schober/links.htm
A collection of psycholinguistics links. It includes a 'psychology of language' links page.

http://www.indiana.edu/~eric_rec/ieo/bibs/dyslexia.html
A collection of links to dyslexia-related sites.

11

INTELLIGENCE AND THINKING

In 1992, Arnold M. Ludwig of the University of Kentucky published an extensive biographical survey of 1005 famous 20th-century artists, writers and other professionals, some of whom had been in treatment for a mood disorder. He discovered that the artists and writers experienced two to three times the rate of psychosis, suicide attempts, mood disorders and substance abuse that comparably successful people in business, science and public life did. The poets in this sample had most often been manic or psychotic and hospitalized; they also proved to be some 18 times more likely to commit suicide than is the general public. In a comprehensive biographical study of 36 major British poets born between 1705 and 1805, Kay Jamison at Johns Hopkins University School of Medicine, found similarly elevated rates of psychosis and severe psychopathology. These poets were 30 times more likely to have had manic–depressive illness than were their contemporaries, at least 20 times more likely to have been committed to an asylum and some five times more likely to have taken their own life.

Alfred, Lord Tennyson, who experienced recurrent, debilitating depressions and probable hypomanic spells, often expressed fear that he might inherit the madness or 'taint of blood' in his family. His father, grandfather, two of his great-grandfathers as well as five of his seven brothers suffered from insanity, melancholia, uncontrollable rage or what is today known as manic–depressive illness.

Source: Jamison, 1997, pp. 46–48

OVERVIEW

What does it mean to behave intelligently? What does it mean to be intelligent? These questions have intrigued psychologists since the turn of the century. Much debate has focused on what intelligence is meant to represent and how it can be measured. The conclusions of such debate have frequently been controversial.

In this chapter, you will learn of some of the theories concerning the nature of intelligence and thinking that psychologists have proposed. The role of the environment and heredity in intelligence is assessed as are individual differences that can affect intelligence (such as race and sex). The second section of the chapter is devoted to thinking and reasoning. This also includes a discussion of creativity, the role of the brain in reasoning and the effects of ageing on cognitive ability.

What you should be able to do after reading Chapter 11

- Describe the ways in which intelligence has been defined.
- Understand the principles of intelligence testing.
- Evaluate the contribution of heredity and environment to intelligence.
- Be aware of and describe individual differences in intelligence.
- Define and give examples of inductive and deductive reasoning.
- Describe and understand the effects of ageing on cognitive ability.

Questions to think about

- What is intelligence?
- How can intelligence be measured?
- Is it useful to invoke a concept of intelligence?
- How do we reason?
- Are there different ways of reasoning?
- Why do we sometimes violate the 'the law' of logic?
- What is creativity? Can we measure creativity experimentally?
- What are the effects of ageing on functions such as language and remembering?

What is intelligence?

In general, if people do well academically or succeed at tasks that involve their heads rather than their hands, we consider them to be intelligent. If a politician makes a useful policy decision, we call it an intelligent decision. If an author writes an erudite book on an arcane subject, we might described him as having written an intelligent appraisal. But if asked to give a precise definition of intelligence, psychologists – in common with non-scientists – come slightly unstuck. Sternberg and Detterman (1986) asked a dozen theorists to provide definitions of intelligence and received a dozen different descriptions. Even according to one of psychology's historians, intelligence represents whatever intelligence tests measure (Boring, 1923).

In general, however, psychologists agree that the term intelligence describes a person's ability to learn and remember information, to recognise concepts and their relations, and to apply the information to their own behaviour in an adaptive way (Neisser *et al.*, 1996a). Where they diverge is in describing the nature of intelligence and how it works. For example, some psychologists argue that there is a general factor called intelligence but no different subtypes of intelligence; others argue intelligence is a series of abilities; yet others adopt a combinative approach arguing that there is general intelligence but there are also specific abilities. The number of these abilities depends on the theory one examines.

Theories of intelligence

Most theories of intelligence are based on the analysis of performance on tests which seek to measure specific abilities such as non-verbal and verbal intellectual competence. Much of the debate in the psychology of intelligence has focused on whether there is a single intelligence or there are multiple intelligences. Is our intellectual ability a unitary factor or is it made up of a number of different abilities? Are these abilities, if they do exist, completely separate from each other or are they related?

Intelligence tests yield a single number, usually called an IQ score, although this does not itself mean that intelligence is a single, general characteristic. Some investigators have suggested that certain intellectual abilities are completely independent of one another. For example, a person can be excellent at spatial reasoning but poor at solving verbal analogies. But psychologists disagree over whether specific abilities are totally independent or whether one general factor influences all abilities. The next sections consider some influential theories of intelligence.

Spearman's two-factor theory

Charles Spearman (1927) proposed that an individual's performance on a test of intellectual ability is determined by two factors: the *g factor*, which is a general factor, and the *s factor*, which is a factor specific to a particular test. Spearman did not call his *g* factor 'intelligence'; he considered the term too vague. He defined the *g* factor as comprising three 'qualitative principles of cognition': apprehension of experience, eduction of relations and eduction of correlates. A common task on tests of intellectual abilities – solving analogies – requires all three principles (Sternberg, 1985). For example, consider the following analogy:

LAWYER:CLIENT::DOCTOR: _____

This problem should be read as 'LAWYER is to CLIENT as DOCTOR is to _____ '.

Apprehension of experience refers to people's ability to perceive and understand what they experience; thus, reading and understanding each of the words in the analogy requires apprehension of experience. Eduction (not 'education') is the process of drawing or bringing out, that is making sense of, given facts. In this case, eduction of relations refers to the ability to perceive the relation between laywer and client; namely, that the lawyer works for and is paid by the client. Eduction of correlates refers to the ability to apply a rule inferred from one case to a similar case. Thus, the person whom a doctor works for and is ultimately paid by is obviously a patient. Because analogy problems require all three of Spearman's principles of cognition, he advocated their use in intelligence testing.

Empirical evidence for Spearman's two-factor theory comes from correlations among various tests of particular intellectual abilities. The governing logic is as follows. If we administer ten different tests of intellectual abilities to a group of people and each test measures a separate, independent ability, the scores these people make on any one test will be unrelated to their scores on any other; the correlations among the tests will be approximately zero. However, if the tests measure abilities that are simply different manifestations of a single trait, the scores will be related; the intercorrelations will be close to 1. In fact, the intercorrelations among a group of tests of intellectual abilities are neither zero nor 1. Instead, most of these tests are at least moderately correlated, so that a person who scores well on a vocabulary test also tends to score better than average on other tests, such as arithmetic or spatial reasoning. The correlations among various tests of intellectual ability usually range from 0.3 to 0.7, which means that they have between 9 per cent and 49 per cent of their variability in common (Ozer, 1985).

Spearman concluded that a general factor (*g*) accounted for the moderate correlations among different tests of ability. Thus, a person's score on a particular test depends on two things: the person's specific ability (*s*) on the particular test (such as spatial reasoning) and his or her level of the *g* factor, or general reasoning ability.

Evidence from factor analysis

Factor analysis is a statistical procedure developed by Spearman and Pearson that permits investigators to identify common factors among groups of tests. It is a form of data reduction in the sense that a large number of data can be reduced and explained by reference to two or three factors (Kline, 1993). In the case of intelligence tests, these common factors would be particular abilities that affect people's performance on more than one test. If a group of people take several different tests of intellectual ability and each person's scores on several of these tests correlate well with one another, the tests may (at least partly) be measuring the same factor. A factor analysis determines which sets of tests form groups. For example, Birren and Morrison (1961) administered the Wechsler Adult Intelligence Scale (WAIS, an intelligence test described in the next section) to 933 people. This test consists of eleven different subtests. Birren and Morrison calculated the correlations between subtests and then subjected these correlations to a factor analysis. Table 11.1 shows the results of the analysis.

The factor analysis revealed three factors, labelled A, B and C. The numbers in the three columns in the table are called factor loadings; they are somewhat like correlation coefficients in that they express the degree to which a particular test is related to a particular factor. For the various subtests on factor A, the largest factor loading is for vocabulary, followed by information, comprehension and

similarities. In the middle range are picture completion, arithmetic, picture arrangement and digit symbol. Digit span, object assembly and block design are the smallest. Verbal subtests make the most important contribution to factor A, so we might be tempted to call this factor verbal ability. But almost all tests make at least a moderate contribution, so perhaps this factor may reflect general intelligence. Digit span has a heavy loading on factor B (0.84), and arithmetic and digit symbol have moderate loadings. Factor B, therefore, is related to maintaining information in short-term memory and manipulating numbers. Factor C appears to be determined mainly by block design, object assembly, picture completion and picture arrangement, and might, therefore, represent the factor, spatial ability.

Although factor analysis can give hints about the nature of intelligence, it cannot provide definitive answers. The names given to factors are determined by the investigator and, although the names may appear to be quite appropriate, the process inevitably has a subjective element to it. There is also the danger of reification when conducting factor analysis. That is, the factors may wrongly be seen as concrete entities and not simply as labels used to describe a set of data as concisely and accurately as possible. Furthermore, factor analysis can never be more meaningful than the individual tests on which it is performed. To identify the relevant factors in human intelligence, one must include an extensive variety of tests in the factor analysis. The WAIS, for example, does not contain a test of musical ability. If it did, a factor analysis would undoubtedly yield an additional factor. Whether musical ability is a component of intelligence depends on how we decide to define intelligence; this question cannot be answered by a factor analysis.

Other psychologists have employed factor analysis to determine the nature of intelligence. Louis Thurstone (1938) study of students' performance on a battery of 56 tests extracted seven factors, which he labelled verbal comprehension, verbal fluency, number, spatial visualisation, memory, reasoning and perceptual speed. At first, Thurstone thought that his results contradicted Spearman's hypothesised g factor. However, Eysenck suggested a few years later that a second factor analysis could be performed on Thurstone's factors. If the analysis found one common factor, then Spearman's g factor would receive support. In other words, if Thurstone's seven factors themselves had a second-order factor in common, this factor might be conceived of as general intelligence.

Cattell performed a second-order factor analysis and found not one but two major factors. Horn and Cattell (1966) called these factors fluid intelligence (g_f) and crystallised intelligence (g_c). Fluid intelligence is reflected by performance on relatively culture-free tasks, such as those that measure the ability to see relations among objects or the ability to see patterns in a repeating series of items. Crystallised intelligence is defined by tasks that require people to have already acquired information, such as

Table 11.1   Three factors derived by factor analysis of scores on WAIS subtests

| Subtest | Factors | | |
	A	B	C
Information	0.70	0.18	0.25
Comprehension	0.63	0.12	0.24
Arithmetic	0.38	0.35	0.28
Similarities	0.57	0.12	0.27
Digit span	0.16	0.84	0.13
Vocabulary	0.84	0.16	0.18
Digit symbol	0.24	0.22	0.29
Picture completion	0.41	0.15	0.53
Block design	0.20	0.14	0.73
Picture arrangement	0.35	0.18	0.41
Object assembly	0.16	0.06	0.59

Source: adapted from Morrison, 1967

vocabulary and semantic information, and is therefore more culture-bound. Cattell regards fluid intelligence as closely related to a person's native capacity for intellectual performance; in other words, it represents a potential ability to learn and solve problems. In contrast, he regards crystallised intelligence as what a person has accomplished through the use of his or her fluid intelligence – what he or she has learned. Horn (1978) disagrees with Cattell by citing evidence suggesting that both factors are learned but are also based on heredity. He says that g_f is based on casual learning and g_c is based on cultural, school-type learning.

Figure 11.1 shows examples from five of the subtests that load heavily on fluid intelligence.

Tests that load heavily on the crystallised intelligence factor include word analogies and tests of vocabulary,

general information and use of language. According to Cattell, g_c depends on g_f. Fluid intelligence supplies the native ability, whereas experience with language and exposure to books, school and other learning opportunities develop crystallised intelligence. If two people have the same experiences, the one with the greater fluid intelligence will develop the greater crystallised intelligence. However, a person with a high fluid intelligence exposed to an intellectually impoverished environment will develop a poor or mediocre crystallised intelligence. Table 11.2 presents a summary of tests that load on g_f and g_c.

No two investigators agree about the nature of intelligence. However, most believe that a small number of common factors account for at least part of a person's performance on intellectual tasks.

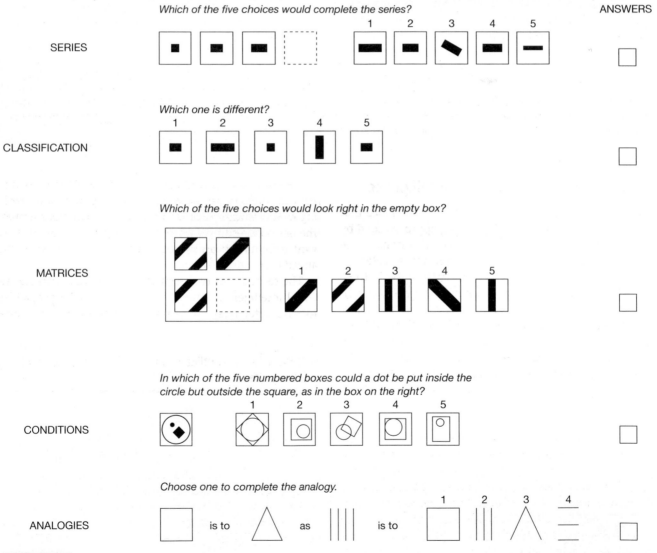

Figure 11.1

Five tests that correlate well with Cattell's g_f factor.

Source: First four tests taken from the *Culture–Fair Intelligence Test, Scale 2, Form A test booklet*. Copyright © 1949, 1960, 1977, by the Institute for Personality and Ability Testing, Inc. Reproduced by permission. Analogies test reproduced by permission of Raymond Cattell and of NFER/Nelson, Windsor, England.

Table 11.2 Summary of tests with large factor loadings on g_f or g_c

Test	Approximate factor loadings	
	g_f	g_c
Figural relations: Deduction of a relation when this is shown among common figures	0.57	0.01
Memory span: Reproduction of several numbers or letters presented briefly	0.50	0.00
Induction: Deduction of a correlate from relations shown in a series of letters, numbers, or figures, as in a letter series test	0.41	0.06
General reasoning: Solving problems of area, rate, finance, and the like, as in an arithmetic reasoning test	0.31	0.34
Semantic relations: Deduction of a relation when this is shown among words, as in an analogies test	0.37	0.43
Formal reasoning: Arriving at a conclusion in accordance with a formal reasoning process, as in a syllogistic reasoning test	0.31	0.41
Number facility: Quick and accurate use of arithmetical operations such as addition, subtraction, and multiplication	0.21	0.29
Experiential evaluation: Solving problems involving protocol and requiring diplomacy, as in a social relations test	0.08	0.43
Verbal comprehension: Advanced understanding of language, as measured in a vocabulary reading test	0.08	0.68

Source: adapted from Horn, 1968. Copyright © American Psychological Association 1968. Adapted by permission of the author.

Sternberg's triarchic theory of intelligence

Sternberg (1985) has devised a theory of intelligence that derives from the information-processing approach used by many cognitive psychologists. Sternberg's theory has three parts; he calls it a triarchic theory (meaning 'ruled by three'). The three parts of the theory deal with three aspects of intelligence: componential intelligence, experiential intelligence and contextual intelligence. Taken together, these three components go beyond the abilities measured by most common tests of intelligence. They include practical aspects of behaviour that enable a person to adapt successfully to his or her environment. Table 11.3 provides a summary of the key concepts of Sternberg's triarchic theory.

Componential intelligence consists of the mental mechanisms people use to plan and execute tasks. The components revealed by the factor analyses of verbal ability and deductive reasoning are facets of componential intelligence. Sternberg suggests that the components of intelligence serve three functions. Metacomponents (transcending components) are the processes by which people decide the nature of an intellectual problem, select a strategy for solving it, and allocate their resources. For example, good readers vary the amount of time they spend on a passage according to how much information they need to extract from it (Wagner and Sternberg, 1983). This decision is controlled by a metacomponent of intelligence.

Performance components are the processes actually used to perform the task, for example word recognition and working memory. Knowledge acquisition components are those the person uses to gain new knowledge by sifting out relevant information and integrating it with what he or she already knows.

The second part of Sternberg's theory deals with experiential intelligence. Experiential intelligence is the ability to deal effectively with novel situations and to solve

Table 11.3 An outline of Sternberg's triarchic theory of intelligence

Componential intelligence
Metacomponents (e.g. planning)
Performance components (e.g. lexical access)
Knowledge acquisition components (e.g. ability to acquire vocabulary words)

Experiential intelligence
Novel tasks
Automated tasks

Contextual intelligence
Adaptation (adapting to the environment)
Selection (finding a suitable environment)
Shaping (changing the environment)

automatically problems that have been previously encountered. According to Sternberg's theory, a person with good experiential intelligence is able to deal more effectively with novel situations than is a person with poor experiential intelligence. The person is better able to analyse the situation and to bring mental resources to bear on the problem, even if he or she has never encountered one like it before. After encountering a particular type of problem several times, the person with good experiential intelligence is also able to 'automate' the procedure so that similar problems can be solved without much thought, freeing mental resources for other work. A person who has to reason out the solution to a problem every time it occurs will be left behind by people who can give the answer quickly and automatically. Sternberg suggests that this distinction is closely related to the distinction between fluid and crystallised intelligence (Horn and Cattell, 1966). According to Sternberg, tasks that use fluid intelligence are those that demand novel approaches, whereas tasks that use crystallised intelligence are those that demand mental processes that have become automatic.

The third part of Sternberg's theory deals with contextual intelligence – intelligence reflecting the behaviours that were subject to natural selection in our evolutionary history. Contextual intelligence takes three forms: adaptation, selection and shaping. The first form, adaptation, consists of fitting oneself into one's environment by developing useful skills and behaviours. In different cultures, adaptation will take different forms. For example, knowing how to distinguish between poisonous and edible plants is an important skill for a member of a hunter-gatherer tribe. Knowing how to present oneself in a job interview is an important skill for a member of an industrialised society. The second form of contextual intelligence, selection, refers to the ability to find one's own niche in the environment. That is, individuals will decide on careers or activities which they both enjoy doing and do well.

The third form of contextual intelligence is shaping. Adapting to the environment or selecting a new one may not always be possible or profitable. In such cases, intelligent behaviour consists of shaping the environment itself. For example, a person whose talents are not appreciated by his or her employer may decide to start his or her own business.

Gardner's multiple intelligences theory

Gardner's theory of intelligence is based on a neuropsychological analysis of human abilities (Gardner, 1983). It argues that intelligence falls into seven categories: linguistic intelligence, musical intelligence, logical/mathematical intelligence, spatial intelligence, bodily/kinesthetic intelligence, and two types of personal intelligence. Bodily/kinesthetic intelligence includes the types of skill that athletes, typists, dancers or mime artists exhibit. Personal intelligence

includes awareness of one's own feelings (intrapersonal intelligence) and the ability to notice individual differences in other people and to respond appropriately to them – in other words, to be socially aware (interpersonal intelligence).

Three of Gardner's types of intelligence – verbal intelligence, logical/mathematical intelligence and spatial intelligence – are not unusual, having been identified previously by many other researchers. The other four are rather unusual. According to Gardner, all seven abilities are well represented in the brain, in that specific brain damage can impair some of them but leave others relatively intact. For example, people with damage to the left parietal lobe can show apraxia, an inability to perform sequences of voluntary skilled movements. In contrast, people with damage to the right parietal lobe develop the spatial neglect we described in Chapter 6. Individuals with frontal lobe damage, as we saw in Chapters 4 and will return to later in this chapter and in Chapter 13, have difficulty evaluating the significance of social situations and making decisions about social matters (the frontal lobes used to be regarded as the region of the brain responsible for intelligence). These examples illustrate bodily/kinesthetic intelligence and both intrapersonal and interpersonal intelligence.

Gardner's theory has the advantage of being based on neuropsychological reality. It also accommodates the views of intelligence held by some non-Western cultures. For example, he would recognise the ability of a member of the Puluwat culture of the Caroline Islands to navigate across the sea by the stars as an example of intelligence.

Sex differences

There is an interesting relationship between sex and intelligence. Whereas the proposition that differences in intelligence exist between men and women is controversial, there is now a great deal of evidence to suggest that males rate their own IQ more highly than do females (Beloff, 1992; Byrd and Stacey, 1993). These beliefs seem to be unrelated to actual cognitive performance because when IQ estimates are measured against performance, the performance of males is significantly lower than their IQ estimate whereas females' is also lower but not significantly so (Reilly and Mulhern, 1995).

A consistent finding is that participants of both sexes rate their fathers' IQ as being higher than their mothers' (Beloff, 1992; Furnham and Rawles, 1995). Not only are fathers rated as more intelligent than mothers, but boys are also rated as having a greater IQ than girls by their parents (Furnham and Gasson, 1998).

To determine whether such sex differences in estimates are global (general IQ) or specific (related to specific abilities), Furnham, Fong and Martin (1999) asked 400 participants from the UK, Hawaii and Singapore to estimate their own parents' and siblings' IQ score for each of Gardner's multiple intelligences, using the test described in Figure 11.2. There were no sex differences in the estimated intelligence of siblings and parents but men estimated their own mathematical, spatial and bodily/kinetic intelligence as well as their overall intelligence to be higher than did women.

These sex differences in the perception of relatives' intelligence perhaps underlie the sex differences seen in intellectual ability. There has been some controversy in psychology over whether men and women (and boys and girls) are better than each other on tests of cognitive abil-

ity. In fact, there do seem to be consistent sex differences in the performance of specific types of test (see below).

Are there consistent sex differences in cognitive ability?

Take a look at Figure 11.3. At the moment, the glass is empty but imagine that it is half full. Using a pencil, draw a line across the glass where you think the top of the water should be. Do that now before you read on.

How intelligent are you?

Intelligence tests attempt to measure intelligence. The average or mean score on these tests is 100. Most of the population (about 2/3 people) score between 85 and 115. Very bright people score around 130 and scores have been known to go over 145.

The following graph shows the typical distribution of scores.

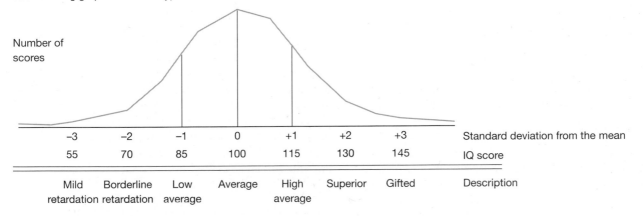

There are different types of intelligence. We want you to estimate your score on 7 basic types of intelligence. We want you to estimate the score of your mother, father and any brothers and sisters you may have.

	ESTIMATE						
	You	Father	Mother	Brother 1	Brother 2	Sister 1	Sister 2
1 *Verbal* or linguistic intelligence (the ability to use words)							
2 Logical or *mathematical* intelligence (the ability to reason logically, solve number problems)							
3 *Spatial* intelligence (the ability to find your way around the environment, and form mental images)							
4 *Musical* intelligence (the ability to perceive and create pitch and rhythm patterns)							
5 *Bodily/kinetic* intelligence (the ability to carry out motor movement, e.g. being a surgeon or a dancer)							
6 *Interpersonal* intelligence (the ability to understand other people)							
7 *Intrapersonal* intelligence (the ability to understand yourself and develop a sense of your own identity)							

Figure 11.2

Examples of a test used to examine individuals' perception of their own and their relatives' intelligence.

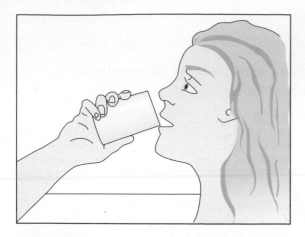

Figure 11.3

The Water Level Test. The glass is meant to be half full of water. The participant's task is to indicate where the top of the water should be.

Source: Reprinted with permission from Kalichman, S.C. (1989) The effects of sex and context on paper and pencil spatial task performance, *Journal of General Psychology*, 116, 133–9. Heldref Publishers, Washington, DC.

If you were a man, you probably drew the line horizontally across the glass; if you were a woman, you probably drew the line parallel to the direction in which the water glass is tipped. The correct line would be the horizontal one.

This phenomenon illustrates one of the most consistent sex differences in cognitive ability. The task is Piaget's Water Level Test and men tend to be better at it than women (Halpern, 1992). Other tests showing sex differences are summarised in Table 11.4.

Why should males tend to be better at this task? One explanation for the Water Level Test result is that men and boys are intrinsically superior at tests of spatial ability than are women and girls (we will come on to reasons why this should be a little later). Spatial ability refers to 'skills in representing, transforming, generating and recalling symbolic, nonlinguistic information' (Linn and Petersen, 1985). The test of spatial ability which shows the most consistent and reliable sex difference is mental rotation (Masters and Sanders, 1993). In this task, individuals are presented with three sets of cubes and have to match the target set with one of the other two. The task is not straightforward because the cubes have to be mentally rotated before a match can be made, as you saw in Chapter 8 (Figure 8.6).

The three-dimensional nature of the stimuli appears to be important. In one experiment the performance of 3 and 6 year old boys and girls were compared on a two-dimensional task (a jigsaw puzzle) or a three-dimensional task (constructing Lego). It was found that although there was no difference between boys and girls on the two-dimensional task, boys performed better than girls at the three-dimensional task (McGuiness and Morley, 1991).

One objection to the theory that males are intrinsically superior to females on tests of mental rotation is that the results are attributable to other causes. For example, because the task is timed, it has been argued that this is detrimental to women, who are more cautious when making decisions about rotation (Goldstein *et al.*, 1990). To test this hypothesis, Masters (1998) allowed male and female undergraduates either a short or unlimited time to perform a mental rotation task. She also used three different scoring procedures because previous studies had been criticised for basing their findings on using correct answers only (without looking at the number of incorrect responses too). Masters found that regardless of scoring procedure or time limit, men performed better than women.

Is this sex difference consistent across all spatial ability tests? The answer is no. In other types of visuospatial test, women tend to outperform men. For example, women have been found to be consistently superior to men at tests involving visual recognition. It has been suggested that this may be so because of women's superior linguistic ability (McGivern *et al.*, 1998). Women, for example, are better than men at tests involving verbal fluency, such as naming as many objects as possible beginning with a specific letter (Halpern, 1997), and boys tend to be diagnosed with reading and speech disorders more commonly than are girls (Flynn and Rahbar, 1994).

Performance on visual recognition tasks may be verbally mediated because objects and pictures are easier to name or could be named more effectively by women. Another possible explanation is that women are more compliant – they may pay more attention to test instructions and may spend more time studying test objects (Eagly, 1978). To test the compliance and linguistic mediation hypotheses, McGivern *et al.* (1998) set up two experiments where groups of men and women performed a recognition task involving abstract shapes and nameable objects. They found that women consistently outperformed the men on this task. They also found no effect of compliance.

Two important questions arise from these studies. Can sex differences be eliminated? And why do sex differences in specific cognitive abilities exist? An answer to the first question is provided by an interesting experiment reported by McLoy and Koonce (1988), cited in Halpern, 1992. They trained men and women on a standard simulated flight task and found that men were better at learning this task than were women. They also found that given sufficient training, women performed at about the same level as men; they simply needed more training to achieve this level of competence.

Why should men outperform women on spatial tasks? Halpern (1997) suggests that theories of sex differences in cognitive ability fall into three categories: evolutionary, psychosocial and biological.

Table 11.4 Cognitive tests and tasks that usually show sex differences

Type of test/task	Example
Tasks and tests on which women obtain higher average scores	
Tasks that require rapid access to and use of phonological, semantic and other information in long-term memory	Verbal fluency – phonological retrieval Synonym generation – meaning retrieval Associative memory Spellings and anagrams Mathematical calculations Memory for spatial locations
Knowledge areas	Foreign languages
Production and comprehension of complex prose	Reading comprehension Writing
Fine motor skills	Mirror tracing – novel, complex figures Pegboard tasks Matching and coding tasks
Perceptual speed	Multiple speeded tasks
Higher grades in school (all or most subjects)	
Speech articulation	Tongue twisters
Tasks and tests on which men obtain higher average scores	
Tasks that require transformations in visual working memory	Mental rotation Piaget Water Level Test
Tasks that involve moving objects	Dynamic spatiotemporal tasks
Motor tasks that involve aiming	Accuracy in throwing balls or darts
Knowledge areas	General knowledge Geographical knowledge Maths and science knowledge
Tests of fluid reasoning (especially in maths and science domain)	Proportional reasoning tasks Mechanical reasoning Verbal analogies Scientific reasoning

Source: adapted with permission from Halpern, 1997. Sex difference in intelligence. *American Psychologist*, 52, 10, 1091–1102. Copyright © 1977 by the American Psychological Association.

Evolutionary theories

The evolutionary point of view suggests that spatial superiority in men is a throwback to the evolution of men and women as hunters and gatherers (Eals and Silverman, 1994). This theory suggests that because men originally roamed and hunted (activities which rely on the manipulation of visuospatial features in the environment), and because women stayed 'at home' and gathered, it is not surprising that men are spatially superior. The greater visual recognition performance seen in women is meant to reflect women's evolutionary role as foragers (Tooby and DeVore, 1987). However, as we saw in Chapter 3, evolutionary theories such as these are so broad as to be untestable. As Halpern (1997) also notes, you can explain almost any finding by indicating how it would be advantageous to hunters and gatherers.

Psychosocial theories

Psychosocial theories suggest that sex differences are learned through experience or imitation. Children, it is argued, fulfil sex-role stereotypes: boys are encouraged to play with toys which involve visuospatial manipulation; girls are not. It has also been suggested that boys and girls receive different models, rewards and punishment. Interestingly, however, there seems to be little difference in the ways that parents socialise boys and girls (Lytton and Romney, 1991). That is, both boys and girls are brought up in similar ways with neither being reared in a 'masculine' or 'feminine' way. One researcher has suggested that peer interaction is more likely to lead to stereotypical sex-role behaviour than is parent–child interaction, although this idea is controversial (Harris, 1995).

Fairly strong evidence against a psychosocial explanation for sex differences in cognitive ability was cited by Halpern (1992). She noted that among individuals with high reasoning ability, right-handed men outperformed left-handed men on tests of spatial ability but were poorer than left-handed men at verbal tasks. Conversely, left-handed females were better at spatial tasks than were right-handers but the opposite pattern applied to verbal tasks. Any theory of psychosocial influence would have difficulty in explaining these findings: why should right- and left-handed boys and girls be socialised differently? It would also have difficulty in explaining why boys are more likely than girls to suffer from stuttering and reading disorders.

Biological theories

Biological theories suggest that sex differences in cognitive ability may be due to biological factors such as hormonal regulation and brain organisation. There is evidence that anatomical differences exist between the brains of boys and girls and men and women (Martin, 1998a). Witelson *et al.* (1995) reported that the number of neurons found in a structure thought to be important for language – the planum temporale (described in Chapter 10) – was 11 per cent greater in women than in men. A part of the tract of fibres that connects the two cerebral hemispheres (the corpus callosum) has also been found to be larger in women (Holloway *et al.*, 1993; Elster *et al.*, 1990). Some researchers have suggested that women's brains are more bilaterally organised. That is, whereas men rely predominantly on one or other hemisphere to perform a specific function, women use both (Jancke and Steinmetz, 1994). The processing of phonemes – the constituent sounds of words – is associated with greater activation in both hemispheres in women than men (Shaywitz *et al.*, 1995).

Apart from neuroanatomical differences, there may also be differences in the amount of, or sensitivity to, hormones (Collaer and Hines, 1995). Cognitive ability, for example, appears to fluctuate across the menstrual cycle (Hampson, 1990) and the amount of testosterone appears to correlate with spatial skill (Moffat and Hampson, 1996). In two interesting experiments, groups of individuals were given certain hormones for reasons other than enhancing cognitive ability. In one study, normal ageing men given testosterone to enhance their sex drive, showed increased visuospatial performance (Janowsky *et al.*, 1994). In another, transsexuals given testosterone as part of their preoperative sex change programme were found to show increased visuospatial ability and decreased verbal ability over a period of three months (Van Goozen *et al.*, 1995). As we saw in Chapter 10, one influential theory suggests that the degree of foetal testosterone influences the lateralisation of the brain; specifically it can affect the development of the left hemisphere (Geschwind and Galaburda, 1987). The evidence for this theory, however, is equivocal and mostly negative (Bryden *et al.*, 1994).

Although appealing and persuasive in explaining the mechanism of some cognitive abilities, biological theories cannot account for some of the findings in sex differences research. If, for example, spatial ability is 'hard-wired' in the brain, how can improvements in spatial ability be brought about by training? Is the capacity there but the strategy for using this capacity absent?

Sex differences in cognitive ability represents one of the more controversial areas of psychology because it involves two factors which always tend to arouse controversy: sex and intelligence. Evidence suggests that the only consistent and identifiable sex difference is in mental rotation ability. Here, men consistently outperform women and this has given rise to speculation that men have greater spatial ability than women. There are other differences such as superiority for verbal fluency and visual recognition in women and superiority for drawing verbal analogies in men (Halpern, 1992). The superior mental rotation performance in men is probably due to biological factors such as sensitivity to, or increases in, hormones. It may also be due to the ways in which the brains of men and women are organised: the function may be more lateralised in men than in women (Shaywitz *et al.*, 1995).

Questions to think about

Theories of intelligence

- Is intelligence best described by reference to a general factor, many specific factors or a combination of general and specific factors? Which of the models in this section do you think best defines the nature of intelligence?

- What are the advantages and disadvantages of factor analysis in intelligence research?

- How might these models be used to guide an individual's education? How could the principles of these theories be used to educate people more effectively?

- Men and women tend to estimate the various types of intelligence of their male and female relatives differently. Why do you think this is?

- Which theory gives the most convincing explanation of male superiority in visuospatial manipulation?

- Can intelligent behaviour be measured in the same way in all cultures? What problems would arise with such an approach?

Intelligence testing

Assessment of intellectual ability, or intelligence testing, is a controversial topic because of its importance in modern society. Unless people have special skills that suit them for a career in sports or entertainment, their economic success may depend heavily on formal education. Many employers use specialised aptitude tests to help them select among job candidates. Test scores correlate with school and university grades, the number of years in education and adult occupational status (Neisser *et al.*, 1996a). There are hundreds of tests of specific abilities, such as manual dexterity, spatial reasoning, vocabulary, mathematical aptitude, musical ability, creativity and memory. All these tests vary widely in reliability, validity and ease of administration.

Early intelligence tests

Intelligence testing has a long and chequered history. As early as 2200 BC, Chinese administrators tested civil servants (mandarins) periodically to be sure that their abilities qualified them for their job. In Western cultures, differences in social class were far more important than individual differences in ability until the Renaissance, when the modern concept of individualism came into being.

The term 'intelligence' is an old one, deriving from the Latin *intellectus* (meaning 'perception' or 'comprehension'). However, its use in the English language dates only from the late nineteenth century, when it was revived by the philosopher Herbert Spencer (1820–1903) and by the biologist/statistician Sir Francis Galton (1822–1911). Galton was the most important early investigator of individual differences in ability. He was strongly influenced by his cousin Charles Darwin, who stressed the importance of inherited differences in physical and behavioural traits related to a species' survival. Galton observed that there were family differences in ability and concluded that intellectual abilities were heritable. Having noted that people with low ability were poor at making sensory discriminations, he decided that tests involving such discriminations would provide valid measures of intelligence.

In 1884, Francis Galton established the Anthropometric Laboratory (meaning 'human-measuring') at the International Health Exhibition in London. His exhibit was so popular that afterwards his laboratory became part of the South Kensington Museum. He tested over nine thousand people on seventeen variables, including height and weight, muscular strength, and the ability to perform sensory discriminations. One task involved detecting small differences in the weights of objects of the same size and shape.

Galton made some important contributions to science and mathematics. His systematic evaluation of various large numbers of people and the methods of population statistics he developed served as models for the statistical tests now used in all branches of science. His observation that the distribution of most human traits closely resembles the normal curve (developed by the Belgian statistician Lambert Quételet, 1796–1874) is the foundation for many modern tests of statistical significance and can be seen in Figure 11.4.

Galton also outlined the logic of a measure he called correlation: the degree to which variability in one measure is related to variability in another. From this analysis, Karl Pearson derived the correlation coefficient (*r*) used today to assess the degree of statistical relation between variables. In addition, Galton developed the logic of twin studies and adoptive parent studies to assess the heritability of a human trait.

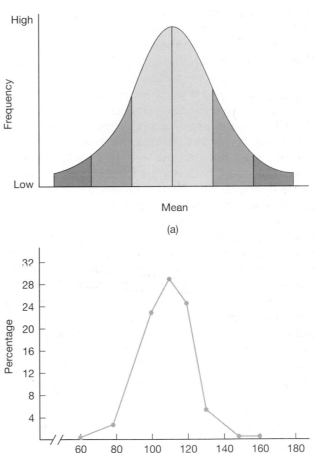

Figure 11.4

The normal curve and data from intelligence testing. (a) A mathematically derived normal curve. (b) A curve showing the distribution of IQ scores of 850 children 2^1/$_2$ years of age.

Source: Terman, L.M. and Merrill, M.A., *Stanford–Binet Intelligence Scale*. Boston: Houghton-Mifflin, 1960. Material cited pertains to the 1960 edition and not to the 4th edition, published in 1985. Reproduced by permission of the Riverside Publishing Company.

Modern intelligence tests

The Binet–Simon Scale

Alfred Binet (1857–1911), a French psychologist and a colleague (Binet and Henri, 1896) suggested that a group of simple sensory tests could not adequately determine a person's intelligence. They recommended measuring a variety of psychological abilities (such as imagery, attention, comprehension, imagination, judgements of visual space, and memory for various stimuli) that appeared to be more representative of the traits that distinguished people of high and low intelligence.

To identify children who were unable to profit from normal classroom instruction and needed special attention, Binet and Theodore Simon assembled a collection of tests, many of which had been developed by other investigators, and published the Binet–Simon Scale in 1905. The tests were arranged in order of difficulty, and the researchers obtained norms for each test. Norms are data concerning comparison groups that permit the score of an individual to be assessed relative to his or her peers. In this case, the norms consisted of distributions of scores obtained from children of various ages. Binet and Simon also provided a detailed description of the testing procedure, which was essential for obtaining reliable scores. Without a standardised procedure for administering a test, different testers can obtain different scores from the same child.

Binet revised the 1905 test in order to assess the intellectual abilities of both normal children and those with learning problems. The revised versions provided a procedure for estimating a child's mental age – the level of intellectual development that could be expected for an average child of a particular age. For example, if an 8 year old child scores as well as average 10 year old children, his or her mental age is 10 years. Binet did not develop the concept of IQ (intelligence quotient). Nor did he believe that the mental age derived from the test scores expressed a simple trait called 'intelligence'. Instead, he conceived of the overall score as the average of several different abilities.

The Stanford–Binet Scale

Lewis Terman of Stanford University translated and revised the Binet–Simon Scale in the United States. The revised group of tests, published in 1916, became known as the Stanford–Binet Scale. Revisions by Terman and Maud Merrill were published in 1937 and 1960. In 1985, an entirely new version was published. The Stanford–Binet Scale consists of various tasks grouped according to mental age. Simple tests include identifying parts of the body and remembering which of three small cardboard boxes contains a marble. Intermediate tests include tracing a simple maze with a pencil and repeating five digits orally. Advanced tests include explaining the difference between two abstract words that are close in meaning (such as fame and notoriety) and completing complex sentences.

The 1916 Stanford–Binet Scale contained a formula for computing the intelligence quotient (IQ), a measure devised by Stern (1914). The intelligence quotient (IQ) represents the idea that if test scores indicate that a child's mental age is equal to his or her chronological age (that is, calendar age), the child's intelligence is average; if the child's mental age is above or below his or her chronological age, the child is more or less intelligent than average. This relation is expressed as the quotient of mental age (MA) and chronological age (CA). The result is called the ratio IQ. The quotient is multiplied by 100 to eliminate fractions. For example, if a child's mental age is 10 and the child's chronological age is 8, then his or her IQ is (10 ÷ 8) × 100 = 125.

The 1960 version of the Stanford–Binet Scale replaced the ratio IQ with the deviation IQ. Instead of using the ratio of mental age to chronological age, the deviation IQ compares a child's score with those received by other children of the same chronological age (the deviation IQ was invented by David Wechsler, whose work is described in the next section). Suppose that a child's score is one standard deviation above the mean for his or her age. The standard deviation of the ratio IQ scores is 16 points, and the score assigned to the average IQ is 100 points. If a child's score is one standard deviation above the mean for his or her age, the child's deviation IQ score is 100 + 16 (the standard deviation) = 116. A child who scores one standard deviation below the mean receives a deviation IQ of 84 (100 – 16), as Figure 11.5 illustrates.

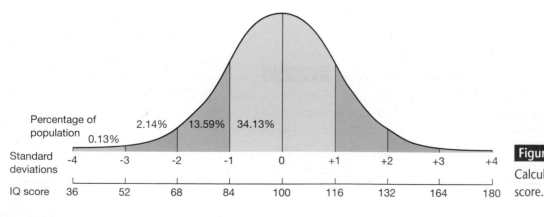

Figure 11.5

Calculating the deviation IQ score.

Wechsler Adult Intelligence Scale

When David Wechsler was chief psychologist at New York City's Bellevue Psychiatric Hospital he developed several popular tests of intelligence. The Wechsler–Bellevue Scale, published in 1939, was revised in 1942 for use in the armed forces and was superseded in 1955 by the Wechsler Adult Intelligence Scale (WAIS). This test was revised again in 1981 (the WAIS-R). The Wechsler Intelligence Scale for Children (WISC), first published in 1949 and revised in 1974 (the WISC-R), closely resembles the WAIS. Various versions of the WAIS-R have been devised for use with various populations (such as Irish, Scottish, Welsh and so on).

The WAIS-R consists of eleven subtests and is slightly more difficult than its predecessor. Around 20 per cent of the content has been updated. It is still divided into two categories – verbal and performance – which yield two scores: performance IQ and verbal IQ (the overall IQ is calculated from these two). An example of one of the performance scale tests can be seen in Figure 11.6.

Table 11.5 lists the subtests and a typical question or problem for each. The norms obtained for the WAIS-R permit the tester to calculate a deviation IQ score.

Figure 11.6

The block design subtest is part of both of Wechsler's Scales, the WISC-R for children and the WAIS-R for adults.

Source: © Bob Daemmrich/The Image Works. Reproduced with permission.

Table 11.5 WAIS-R subtests and typical questions or problems

Subtest	Typical question or problem
Verbal	
Information	'What is the capital of France?'
Digit span	'Repeat these numbers back to me: 46239.'
Vocabulary	'What does the word "conventional" mean?'
Arithmetic	'Imagine that you bought six postcards for thirteen pence each and gave the clerk a pound. How much change would you receive?' (Paper and pencil cannot be used.)
Comprehension	'Why are we tried by a jury of our peers?'
Similarities	'How are goldfish and canaries similar to each other?'
Performance	
Picture completion	The tester shows the subject a picture with a missing part (such as a mouse without its whiskers) and says, 'Tell me what's missing.'
Picture arrangement	The tester shows a series of cartoon pictures (without words) and instructs the subject to arrange them in the proper sequence.
Block design	The tester shows a picture and four or nine blocks divided diagonally into red and white sections, then instructs the subject to arrange the blocks so that they match the design in the picture.
Object assembly	The tester gives the subject pieces of cardboard cut like a jigsaw puzzle and instructs him or her to assemble it. (When properly assembled, the pieces form the shape of a common object.)
Digit symbol	The tester presents a set of ten designs paired with the ten numerals and instructs the subject to write the corresponding symbols beneath each of a long series of numerals.

The WAIS-R is the most widely administered adult intelligence test. An important advantage is that it tests verbal and performance abilities separately. Neuropsychologists often use it because people with brain damage tend to score very differently on the performance and verbal tests. In fact, it is so widely used that Lezak (1995) has called it the 'workhorse of neuropsychological assessment'. Comparisons of performance and verbal test scores suggest the presence of undiagnosed brain damage. Because people who have had few educational and cultural opportunities often do worse on the verbal tests than on the performance tests, the WAIS-R is useful in estimating what their score might have been had they been raised in a more favourable environment.

Reliability and validity of intelligence tests

The adequacy of a measure is represented by its reliability and validity (terms described in Chapter 2). In the case of intelligence testing, reliability is assessed by the correlation between the scores that people receive on the same measurement on two different occasions; perfect reliability is 1. High reliability is achieved by means of standardised test administration and objective scoring: all participants are exposed to the same situation during testing, and all score responses in the same way. The acceptable reliability of a modern test of intellectual ability should be at least 0.85. Validity is the correlation between test scores and the criterion – an independent measure of the variable that is being assessed.

However, most tests of intelligence correlate reasonably well with measures like success in school (between 0.40 and 0.75). Thus, because intellectual ability plays at least some role in academic success, IQ appears to have some validity.

Questions to think about

Intelligence testing

- Why were intelligence tests first developed? Did they succeed in this aim?

- What are the consequences of discovering your IQ?

- Is an IQ score truly reflective of a person's intelligence? Is it useful shorthand or overgeneralised nonsense?

- Test–retest reliability refers to the ability of a test to produce the same score in the same individual in two testing sessions separated by time. What difficulties could you foresee in investigating the test–retest reliability of the WAIS-R? (Remember that there is only one version of the WAIS-R.)

- What are the limitations of the WAIS-R in measuring the intellectual ability of an individual who has suffered brain damage? Remember that the WAIS-R produces norms on which individuals are compared.

The roles of heredity and environment

Abilities – intellectual, athletic, musical and artistic – appear to run in families. Why? Are the similarities owing to heredity, or are they solely the result of a common environment, which includes similar educational opportunities and exposure to people having similar kinds of interests?

According to Sternberg and Grigorenko (1997), we know three facts about the roles of heredity and environment in intelligence: (1) both contribute to intelligence, (2) heredity and environment interact in various ways, and (3) poor and enriched environments influence the development of intellectual ability regardless of heredity.

What these facts illustrate is that the typical nature–nurture debate in intelligence is no longer valid. Recall from Chapter 2 that the nature–nurture argument suggests that, in its most stark form, behaviour or function is determined solely by the environment or solely by genetics/ heredity. Psychologists have discovered that this argument is too simplistic. In fact, it is inaccurate. Almost all psychologists agree that intelligence has a hereditary (as well as environmental) component. The debate now focuses on the degree to which each contributes to intelligence and the ways in which they interact to influence intellectual development.

The meaning of heritability

When we ask how much influence heredity has on a given trait, we are usually asking what the heritability of the trait is. Heritability is a statistical measure that expresses the proportion of the observed variability in a trait that is a direct result of genetic variability. The value of this measure can vary from 0 to 1. The heritability of many physical traits in most cultures is very high; for example, eye colour is affected almost entirely by hereditary factors and little, if at all, by the environment. Thus, the heritability of eye colour is close to 1.

Heritability is a concept that many people misunderstand. It does not describe the extent to which the inherited genes are responsible for producing a particular trait; it measures the relative contributions of differences in genes and differences in environmental factors to the overall observed variability of the trait in a particular population. An example may make this distinction clear. Consider the heritability of hair colour in the Eskimo culture. Almost all young Eskimos have black hair, whereas older Eskimos have grey or white hair. Because all members of this population possess the same versions of the genes that determine hair colour, the genetic variability with respect to those genes is essentially zero. All the observed variability in hair colour in this population is explained by an environmental factor – age. Therefore, the heritability of hair colour in the Eskimo culture is zero.

As with hair colour, we infer the heritability of a person's intelligence from his or her observed performance. Thus, looking at a person's IQ score is equivalent to looking at the colour of a person's hair. By measuring the correlation between IQ score and various genetic and environmental factors, we can arrive at an estimate of heritability. Clearly, even if hereditary factors do influence intelligence, the heritability of this trait must be considerably less than 1 because so many environmental factors also influence intelligence. The branch of psychology called behaviour genetics, which we came across in Chapters 1 and 3, predicts the degree of parental influence via genetic and environmental transmission on the development of the child's intellectual development. The proportion of the variance associated with genetic differences among individuals is called h; the remaining variation which is associated with environmental influences is referred to as $1-h$ (Neisser et al., 1996a). The features which families share and have in common (such as choice of home) is sometimes referred to as c. H can be subdivided into two types: additive h, which refers to the amount of hereditary variance that is passed from parent to child, and non-additive h which refers to new, unique genetic expression in each generation. As children grow older h increases and c decreases (McGue et al., 1993b). In childhood the contribution of h and c to intelligence is similar; by adolescence h predicts about three-quarters of intellectual ability.

The heritability of a trait depends on the amount of variability of genetic factors in a given population. If there is little genetic variability, genetic factors will appear to be unimportant. Because the ancestors of people living in developed Western nations came from all over the world, genetic variability is likely to be much higher there than in an isolated tribe of people in a remote part of the world. Therefore, if a person's IQ score is at all affected by genetic factors, the measured heritability of IQ will be higher in, say, Western European culture than in an isolated tribe.

The relative importance of environmental factors in intelligence depends on the amount of environmental variability (EV) that occurs in the population. If environmental variability is low, then environmental factors will appear to be unimportant. In a society with a low variability in environmental factors relevant to intellectual development – one in which all children are raised in the same way by equally skilled and conscientious carers, all schools are equally good, all teachers have equally effective personalities and teaching skills, and no one is discriminated against – the effects of EV would be small and those of GV (genetic variability) would be large. In contrast, in a society in which only a few privileged people receive a good education, environmental factors would be responsible for much of the variability in intelligence: the effects of EV would be large relative to those of GV.

Although h an c give an indication of the degree of variance attributable to heredity and environment, they do not explain the mechanism by which intelligence is transmitted or developed (Neisser et al., 1996a).

Sources of environmental and genetic effects during development

Biological and environmental factors can affect intellectual abilities prenatally and postnatally. Newborn infants cannot be said to possess any substantial intellectual abilities; rather, they are more or less capable of developing these abilities during their lives. Therefore, prenatal influences can be said to affect a child's potential intelligence by affecting the development of the brain. Factors that impair brain development will necessarily also impair the child's potential intelligence.

As the axons of developing neurons grow, they thread their way through a tangle of other growing cells, responding to physical and chemical signals along the way. During this stage of prenatal development, differentiating cells can be misguided by false signals. For example, if a woman contracts German measles during early pregnancy, toxic chemicals produced by the virus may adversely affect the development of the foetus. Sometimes, these chemicals can misdirect the interconnections of brain cells and produce mental retardation. Thus, although development of a human organism is programmed genetically, environmental factors can affect development even before a person is born.

Harmful prenatal environmental factors include physical trauma injury to the mother (for example, in a car accident) and toxic effects. A developing foetus can be exposed to toxins from diseases contracted by the mother during pregnancy (such as German measles) or from other sources. A pregnant woman's intake of various drugs can have detrimental effects on foetal development. Alcohol, opiates, cocaine and the chemicals present in cigarettes are harmful to foetuses. One of the most common drug-induced abnormalities, foetal alcohol syndrome, is seen in many offspring of women who are chronic alcoholics. Children with foetal alcohol syndrome are much smaller than average, have characteristic facial abnormalities, and, more significantly, are mentally retarded. Figure 11.7 shows the face of a child with foetal alcohol syndrome as well as the faces of a normal rat foetus and of a rat foetus whose mother received alcohol during early pregnancy.

Development can also be harmed by genetic abnormalities. Some of these abnormalities cause brain damage and consequently produce mental retardation. The best-known example of these abnormalities is Down syndrome, which we considered in Chapter 3. Although Down syndrome is a genetic disorder, it is not hereditary; it results from imperfect division of the twenty-three pairs of chromosomes during the development of an ovum or (rarely) a sperm. Chapter 3 also described phenylketonuria (PKU), an inherited metabolic disorder that disrupts normal brain development. If left untreated, PKU can result in severe mental retardation.

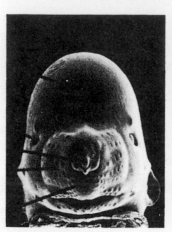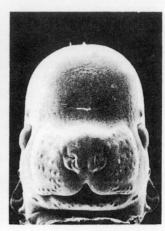

Narrow forehead

Short palpebral
fissures

Small nose

Long upper lip
with deficient
philtrum

Figure 11.7

A child with foetal alcohol syndrome, along with magnified views of a rat foetus whose mother received alcohol during pregnancy (*left*) and a normal rate foetus (*right*).

Photographs courtesy of Katherine K. Sulik.

From birth onwards, a child's brain continues to develop. Environmental factors can either promote or impede that development. Postnatal factors such as birth trauma, diseases that affect the brain, or toxic chemicals can prevent optimum development and thereby affect the child's potential intelligence. For example, encephalitis (inflammation of the brain), when contracted during childhood, can result in mental retardation, as can the ingestion of poisons such as mercury or lead.

Educational influences in the environment, including (but not limited to) schooling, enable a child to attain his or her potential intelligence. By contrast, a less than optimum environment prevents the fullest possible realisation of potential intelligence. Experience with mentally retarded people demonstrates this point. Known environmental causes account for only about 25 per cent of observed cases of mental retardation. In addition, people whose mental retardation has no obvious physical cause are likely to have close relatives who are also mentally retarded. These findings strongly suggest that many of the remaining 75 per cent of cases are hereditary. However, environmental causes (such as poor nutrition or the presence of environmental toxins) can produce brain damage in members of the same family; thus, not all cases of familial mental retardation are necessarily hereditary.

Results of heritability studies

Estimates of the degree to which heredity influences a person's intellectual ability come from several sources. As we saw in Chapter 3, the two most powerful methods are comparisons between identical and fraternal twins and comparisons between adoptive and biological relatives.

Identical and fraternal twins

Scarr and Weinberg (1978) compared some specific intellectual abilities of parents and their adopted and biological children and of children and their biological and adopted siblings. They administered four of the subtests of the Wechsler Adult Intelligence Scale: arithmetic, vocabulary, block design and picture arrangement. The correlations between biological relatives were considerably higher than those between adoptive relatives, indicating that genetic factors played a more significant role than shared environmental factors. In fact, with the exception of vocabulary, adopted children showed little resemblance to other members of their family.

These results suggest that a person's vocabulary is more sensitive to his or her home environment than are other specific intellectual abilities. Presumably, such factors as the availability of books, parental interests in reading, and the complexity of vocabulary used by the parents have a significant effect on the verbal skills of all members of the household, whether or not they are biologically related.

A more up-to-date and comprehensive survey of the differences between identical (monozygotic) and fraternal (dizygotic) twins on tests of spatial and verbal ability is illustrated in Figure 11.8, and is reported in Plomin and DeFries (1998).

The figure illustrates the differences between the intelligence of groups across the lifespan from childhood to old age. What is remarkable about these data is that, across the lifespan, the similarity between identical twins is significantly greater than that between fraternal twins. Compare these results with those seen in Table 11.6.

Table 11.6 summarises data from a number of published studies of biological and adoptive families and adolescent

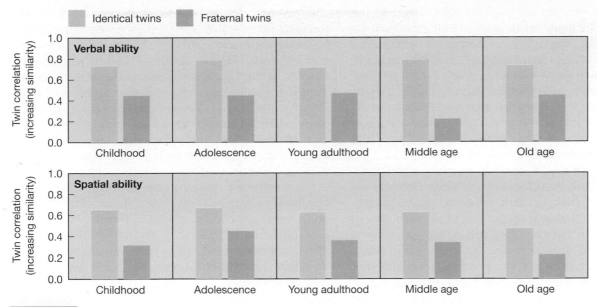

Figure 11.8

Differences between identical and fraternal twins on tests of spatial and verbal ability.

Source: Plomin, R. and DeFries, J.C. (1998) *Scientific American*, 287(5), May, pp. 40–7. Copyright © 1998 by Scientific American, Inc. All rights reserved.

and adult twins (Scarr, 1997). The table shows that although identical twins reared in the same home show a higher concordance rate than identical twins reared apart, these concordance rates are still higher (significantly so) than those of fraternal twins reared together.

Recent studies have indicated that not only are monozygotic children closer in intellectual ability than their fraternal counterparts but that this difference extends to old age. Petrill *et al.* (1998) studied the degree of heritability of general intelligence in monozygotic and dizygotic twins longitudinally during infancy and early childhood. The researchers found that h increases from zero at 14 months to 0.64 at 36 months and begins to exert a significant effect by 24 and 36 months. The influence of shared environment began to attenuate at 36 months. One reason for the pronounced influence of heredity at 36 months (and the attenuation of the influence of environment) may be the development of language, a function that is thought to be highly heritable.

The contribution of h to intelligence appears to increase from 0.3 in early childhood (Cherny *et al.*, 1994) to 0.8 in middle age (Finkel *et al.*, 1995). However, this influence

Table 11.6   Intelligence test correlations of siblings from five behaviour-genetic studies of biological and adoptive families and twins (adolescents and adults)

Genetic r	Relationship	Same home?	IQ correlation	Number of pairs
1.00	Same person tested twice	Yes	0.90	—
1.00	Identical twins	Yes	0.86	4,672
1.00	Identical twins	No	0.76	158
0.50	Fraternal twins	Yes	0.55	8,600
0.50	Fraternal twins	No	0.35	112
0.50	Biological siblings	Yes	0.47	26,473
0.50	Biological siblings	No	0.24	203
0.00	Adoptive siblings	Yes	0.02	385

Source: adapted with permission from Scarr, S. (1997). In R.J. Sternberg and E. Grigorenko (eds) *Intelligence, Heredity and Environments*. Copyright © 1997 Cambridge University Press, New York.

may extend to very old age (over 80 years of age). In the first study of its kind, Petrill *et al.* (1998) examined the influence of *h* in monozygotic and dizygotic twins greater than 80 years of age taken from the OctoTwin sample of the Swedish Twin Registry which contains details of 90 per cent of the twins born in Sweden. The mean age of the participants was 82.7 years and all were free from dementia and motor handicap. Petrill *et al.* (1998) found that there was a significant influence of *h* on ability, especially on memory performance.

At least half the total variance in IQ scores is accounted for by genetic variance (Chipuer *et al.*, 1990; Plomin *et al.*, 1997). The fact that, by most estimates, genetic factors account for approximately 50 per cent of the variability in IQ scores means that the other half of the variability is accounted for by environmental factors. However, when the data are taken from tables such as 11.6, contribution of the environment is less than 25 per cent. Some estimates, based on comparisons of parents and their offspring raised together or apart, suggest a value of only 4 per cent. Why are these figures so low?

Plomin (1988, 1990) suggests that estimates of the importance of environmental factors tend to be low because the environment in a given family is not identical for all its members. Some environmental variables within a family are shared by all members of the family, such as the number of books the family has, the examples set by the parents, the places the family visits on vacation, the noisiness or quietness of the home, and so on. But not all of the environmental factors that affect a person's development and behaviour are shared in this way. For example, no two children are treated identically, even by family members; differences in their appearances and personalities affect the way other people treat them. Different members of a family will probably have different friends and acquaintances, attend different classes in school, and, in general, be exposed to different influences. And once people leave home, their environments become even more different.

Estimates of the contribution of environmental variability to intelligence based on measurements made during childhood tend to be higher than similar estimates based on measurements made during adulthood. The reason for this difference may be that, during childhood, family members share a more similar environment, whereas during adulthood their environments become less similar. As Plomin (1997) notes, recent studies of genetically unrelated children (of a mean age of under 10 years) adopted and raised in the same families, suggest that up to 30 per cent of the variability in IQ scores is due to common environmental factors. However, when the comparison is made among young adults, the figure drops to less than 3 per cent. This can be seen in Figure 11.9, which summarises the correlations between children and their birth parents, adopted children and their birth parents, and adopted children and their adoptive parents for verbal and spatial ability from the time when the child was 3 years of age to

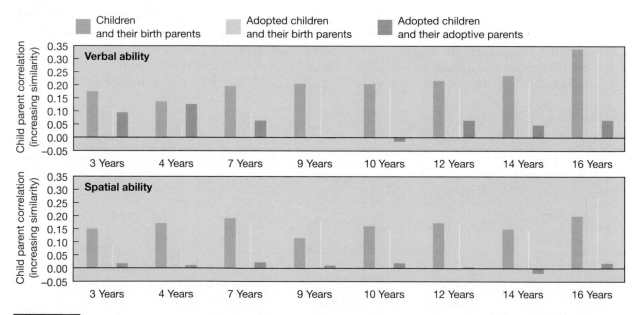

Figure 11.9

The Colorado Adoption Project monitored the spatial and verbal ability of (1) children and their birth parents; (2) adopted children and their birth parents; and (3) adopted children and their adoptive parents, from the child's third birthday to its sixteenth birthday. Notice how closely the adopted children's intelligence resembles that of their birth parents but that there is little resemblance between adopted children and their adopted parents.

Source: Plomin and DeFries (1998). *Scientific American,* 278, 5, 44. Reprinted with permission. Copyright © 1998 by Scientific American, Inc. All rights reserved.

adolescence (Plomin and DeFries, 1998). Adopted children appear to become more like their birth parents but do not become more like their adoptive parents, findings that were also reported in a study of the development of anti-social behaviour in twins (Pike *et al.*, 1996).

Thus, once children leave home and are exposed to different environmental variables, the effect of a common family environment almost disappears. What is left, in the case of related individuals, is their common genetic heritage.

If intelligence is inherited, how does inheritance occur?

Given that our DNA is what makes us what we are, the first and most obvious locus of any genetic cause would be our chromosomes (Plomin, 1997). The DNA contains sequences of information which are divided into sections by enzymes (called restriction enzymes). Sometimes these sequences are repeated. These enzymes act as markers which can be used to locate chromosomes and defects on chromosomes. Some genetic disorders of behaviour are single-gene disorders, that is, only one chromosome is affected (such as that seen in PKU, as we saw in Chapter 3). More complex behaviours, however, are likely to have multiple genetic loci called quantitative trait loci. The question, therefore, is whether intelligence is inherited through one gene or multiple genes.

Plomin and his colleagues have pioneered research in this, one of the most difficult areas in behaviour-genetics. Plomin *et al.* (1994a,b, 1995) have made an extensive study of DNA markers from Caucasian children of varying intelligence (from low IQ (less than 59) to high IQ (over 142) and have found small differences in intelligence between those with low and high IQ. Several of 100 identifiable DNA markers have been associated with intelligence, but no one marker has been consistently associated with it. A recent study has located a DNA marker for the gene on chromosome 6 which appears with greater frequency in a high IQ group (IQ > 136) than a control group (IQ = 103) (Chorney *et al.*, 1998). This is an exciting finding because it was replicated in a group with even higher IQ (over 160). The researchers caution, however, that the gene accounted for only a small portion of the genetic influence on intelligence and that many more genes may be implicated. Nonetheless, this new area of research may hold the key to identifying the genetic basis of intelligent behaviour.

Can low intelligence be improved?

Although the contributions of heredity and environment to intelligence seem to be consistent, there is some scope for improving IQ in those individuals who are low scorers. Such interventions studies, as they are called, aim to help the individual to develop the skills and abilities needed to function at an adequate intellectual level. The children in these studies more often than not come from families of low socioeconomic status and poor parental education. There are several of these projects and their efficacy has recently been evaluated (Perkins and Grotzer, 1997; Sternberg, 1997). Most of these interventions demonstrate some gains (Herrnstein *et al.*, 1986; Lipman *et al.*, 1980) with children attaining the intellectual status of controls.

Two such interventions include the Cognitive Acceleration Through Science Education programme (Adey and Shayer, 1994) and the Practical Intelligence for Schools Project (Sternberg and Wagner, 1986; W. Williams *et al.*, 1996). The former involves teaching children the pattern of thinking seen in science. In a two-year intervention study of 11–12 year old children, there was a significant increase in science achievement test scores at the end of the intervention. The latter helps the child to build coping strategies based on knowing the strengths, weaknesses and demands of a task and applying the appropriate steps and strategies to complete these tasks. Again, intervention improved the intellectual skill of children when measured on practical and academic measures of writing, homework and test taking. However, it is unclear whether these interventions make children think better or make them more intelligent.

Other factors have been thought to influence cognitive ability. Vitamins have been thought to increase non-verbal IQ in children, for example (this is discussed in the next chapter). Similar conclusions have been drawn about the effect of background music on cognitive performance, and the evidence for this is discussed in the next 'Psychology in action' section.

Psychology in action

Using music to influence cognition

Music exerts a potent effect on our mood. Some music we find soothing; other music we find noisily offensive. When we need relaxing, we listen to relaxing music; when we need arousing, we listen to something more stimulating; something louder and more up-tempo. What is more controversial, however, is the hypothesis that the type of music we listen to affects the way in which we think and work. Many of us will be familiar with the sound of background music at work or in shops. Would this background noise affect our cognitive performance without our directly knowing about it?

Psychology in action continued overleaf

Psychology in action continued

Adrian North and David Hargreaves at the University of Leicester, England, recently reviewed some of their own and others' studies which investigated the effects of different types of music on cognitive performance. They suggest that music can influence decision making, comprehension and consumer behaviour. However, the influence is not uniformly positive.

For example, Milliman (1982) reported that when a supermarket played slow music, customers walked around the store more slowly than when it played fast music. Similarly, Areni and Kim (1993) found that when an American wine store played either country music or classical music, people bought more expensive wine when classical music was played.

A more specific application of exposure to music on consumer decision making was described by North *et al.* (1997). The researchers set up an experiment in which four French and four German wines were displayed on a supermarket's wine shelves while either French accordion music or German Bierkeller music was played. National flags also accompanied the displays and consumers were asked to complete questionnaires distributed by the experimenters posing as customers. Forty-four individuals agreed to complete the questionnaire (54 per cent of those approached). The researchers found that more French than German wine was bought when French music was played whereas more German wine was bought when German music was played; none of the customers expressed an absolute preference for either nationality's wine so personal preference for German or French wine could not have been responsible for the results. North and colleagues suggest that the music triggered off thoughts about country-relevant material so that the French music prompted thoughts of France which in turn attracted individuals' attention to the French wine.

This evidence suggests that music can influence behaviour in real-life settings. There is also evidence to suggest that it can affect cognition in the laboratory. For example, the 'Mozart' effect describes the positive effect that listening to Mozart's Sonata for Two Pianos in D Major has on spatial IQ. Several experiments have shown that listening to this piece of music enhances spatial performance (Rauscher *et al.*, 1993, 1995; Rideout and Laubach, 1996). To examine whether this effect was attributable to this specific piece of music or to music like it, Rideout and colleagues compared spatial performance in individuals who either completed the task in silence or when listening to contemporary music with similar musical features (Rideout *et al.*, 1998). The experimenters found the Mozart effect: listening to the music produced enhanced spatial performance. The experimenters suggested that rapid tempo and fairly high melodic complexity were the two common features shared by the two pieces of music.

Is the complexity of the music important? Would more complex music have a detrimental effect on performance? After all, listening to music is not an entirely passive activity. Often, we attend to music even though it is in the background. North and Hargreaves (1996) found that music of moderate complexity made more people attend a stall set up to play various types of music as part of an experiment in a university cafeteria. Individuals in this condition were also more willing to complete questionnaires and rate the cafeteria more positively. In a more controlled experiment, Kiger (1989) found that comprehension of text was greatest when individuals listened to music that was 'low' in complexity than when 'high' or when the task was performed in silence. Arousing music has also been found to improve performance on maths tests (Mayfield and Moss, 1989).

Do all studies of the effect of music on behaviour produce positive results? Well, no. Other studies have found no effect of music on performance (Wolfe, 1983; Sogin, 1988). The Mozart effect, for example, was not replicated by Carstens *et al.* (1995) or Newman *et al.* (1995). The reason for such inconsistency may lie in the area of individual differences. Daoussis and McKelvie (1986), for example, have shown that whereas music does not affect extroverts' reading comprehension performance, it has a detrimental effect on the performance of introverts. The type of music played is also important. Minimalist or repetitive dance music, for example, appears to be ineffective in enhancing spatial performance (Stough *et al.*, 1994).

Given the importance of music to human beings, it should not surprise us to learn that it can influence our behaviour. Children often complete their homework with the radio or the CD player on; students often complete essays or lab reports, or revise for an exam with music in the background. Whether this background music affects our performance in these settings is unclear because no study has directly measured the effects of music in these contexts. As North and Hargreaves (1997) suggest, the results that studies have produced so far are mixed and a number of factors – especially individual differences – affect our responses to music. The studies to date, however, suggest that music may have a significant effect in altering behaviour in specific situations.

Giftedness

Although having a high IQ may seem less of an intellectual impediment than having a low IQ, gifted children encounter equally serious but different problems at school (Winner, 1997). Gifted children are frequently described as bored in classes of children of the same age (Gross, 1993) and there is little provision in most schools for the teaching of the very bright and able (Westberg *et al.*, 1993).

Gifted children have been found to be able to induce the rules of algebra at 4–5 years (Winner, 1996), memorise musical scores (Feldman and Goldsmith, 1991) and identify prime numbers (Winner, 1996). Are there specific features of the gifted child, apart from high IQ, which distinguishes him or her from a child of average intelligence? According to Davidson and Sternberg (1984), insight is a frequent characteristic of scholastic achievement; gifted children appear adept at selecting information and selectively encoding it. Similarly, gifted children may use the same memory strategies as other children but use them more effectively (Jackson and Butterfield, 1986). They also appear to think more independently and persistently than other children and require less structure in their work (Rogers, 1986).

Questions to think about

Heredity and environment

- Given that between 50 and 70 per cent of variation in IQ scores is determined by heredity, what capacity or function is inherited? We are not genetically programmed to acquire specific words, but we seem to be genetically programmed to develop language. Is this the only ability we inherit from our parents?

- How would you explain the development of a dull child from bright parents and a bright child from dull parents? Does this contradict what we know about behaviour genetics?

- Why does the amount of variance in IQ scores accounted for by heredity increase from childhood onwards?

- Do you suspect that intelligence is a single or multiple gene behaviour? Why?

- Given that racial group differences in IQ scores are consistent, even when the tests are culture-free, what could account for these differences?

Thinking

One of the most important components of intelligence is thinking: categorising, reasoning and solving problems. When we think, we perceive, classify, manipulate, and combine information. When we are finished, we know something we did not know before (although our 'knowledge' may be incorrect).

The purpose of thinking is, in general, to solve problems. These problems may be simple classifications (What is that, a bird or a bat?). They may involve decisions about courses of actions (Should I buy a new car or pay to fix the old one?) Or they may require the construction, testing and evaluation of complex plans of action (How am I going to manage to earn money to support my family, help raise our children and continue my education so that I can get out of this dead-end job – and still be able to enjoy life?). Much, but not all, of our thinking involves language. We certainly think to ourselves in words, but we also think in shapes and images. And some of the mental processes that affect our decisions and plans take place without our being conscious of them. Thus, we will have to consider non-verbal processes as well as verbal ones (Reber, 1992; Holyoak and Spellman, 1993).

Classifying

When we think, each object or event is not considered as a completely independent entity. Instead, we classify things – categorise them according to their characteristics. Then, when we have to solve a problem involving a particular object or situation, we can use information that we have already learned about similar objects or situations. To take a very simple example, when we enter someone's house for the first time, we recognise chairs, tables, sofas, lamps and other pieces of furniture even though we may have never seen these particular items before. Because we recognise these categories of objects, we know where to sit, how to increase the level of illumination, and so on.

Concepts are categories of objects, actions or states of being that share some attributes: cat, comet, team, destroying, playing, forgetting, happiness, truth, justice. Most thinking deals with the relations and interactions among concepts. For example, 'the hawk caught the sparrow' describes an interaction between two birds; 'studying for an examination is fun' describes an attribute of a particular action; and 'youth is a carefree time of life' describes an attribute of a state of being.

Concepts exist because the characteristics of objects have consequences for us. For example, angry dogs may hurt us, whereas friendly dogs may give us pleasure. Dangerous dogs tend to growl, bare their teeth and bite, whereas friendly dogs tend to prance around, wag their tails and solicit our attention. Thus, when we see a dog that growls and bares its teeth, we avoid it because it may bite us; but if we see one prancing around and wagging its tail, we may try to pat it. We have learned to avoid or approach dogs who display different sorts of behaviour through direct experience with dogs or through the vicarious experience of watching other people interact with them. The

Controversies in psychological science

Can race influence the development of intelligence?

The issue

Of all the controversies in psychological science discussed in this book, perhaps the most controversial is that of the contribution of race to intelligence. *The Bell Curve*, a book written by a psychologist and a sociologist (Herrnstein and Murray, 1994), provoked a furore among psychologists and in the media across the world. The book asserted that psychologists agree that a general intelligence factor exists; that IQ tests measure what most people think of as intelligence; that IQ is almost impossible to modify through education and special training; that IQ is genetically determined; and that racial differences in IQ are the result of heredity. Whereas the chapter has so far discussed the first four assertions, this section on controversies in psychological science addresses the last: whether race can influence IQ.

The evidence

Many studies have established the fact that there are racial differences in scores on various tests of intellectual abilities. For example, people who are identified as black generally score an average of 85 on IQ tests, whereas people who are identified as white score an average of 100 (Lynn, 1991; Jensen, 1985; Rushton, 1997). Although many blacks score better than many whites, on average

whites do better on these tests. A statement endorsed by 52 professors indicated that, on average, whites' average IQ score is 100, African Americans' is 85, American-Hispanics' is somewhere between whites and African Americans', and Asians' is above 100 (Mainstream Science, 1994, cited in Suzuki and Valencia (1997)). Lynn's (1996) study of 2,260 children between 6 and 17 years of age found that Asian children scored an average of 107 IQ points, white children an average of 103 and black children an average of 89. Interestingly, black infants are more advanced than their white counterparts in the first 15 months of life (Lynn, 1998).

The controversy lies not in the facts themselves but in what these facts mean. Some authors have argued that the racial differences in scores on the tests are caused by heredity (Lynn, 1993; Rushton, 1995, 1997). *The Bell Curve* highlighted other racial aspects of intelligence such as the failure of intervention programmes to improve the IQs of black children.

The assertions made in *The Bell Curve* have not gone unchallenged. In response to the book and issues surrounding intelligence, the American Psychological Association set up a taskforce to report on the current state of knowledge regarding the nature and determinants of intelligence (Neisser *et al.*, 1996a). The evidence we have reviewed so far in the chapter has helped to clarify some of the issues raised in *The Bell Curve*.

---

point is, we can learn the concepts of dangerous and friendly dogs from the behaviour of one set of dogs while we are young and respond appropriately to other dogs later in life. Our experiences with particular dogs generalise to others.

Formal and natural concepts

Formal concepts are defined by listing their essential characteristics, as a dictionary definition does. For example, dogs have four legs, a tail, fur and wet noses; are carnivores; can bark, growl, whine and howl; pant when they are hot; bear live young; and so on. Thus, a formal concept is a sort of category that has rules about membership and non-membership.

Psychologists have studied the nature of formally defined concepts, such as species of animals. Collins and Quillian (1969) suggested that such concepts are organised hierarchically in semantic memory. Each concept has asso-

ciated with it a set of characteristics. Consider the hierarchy of concepts relating to animals shown in Figure 11.10. At the top is the concept 'animal', with which are associated the characteristics common to all animals, such as 'has skin', 'can move around', 'eats', 'breathes' and so on. Linked to the concept 'animal' are groups of animals, such as birds, fish and mammals, along with their characteristics. These hierarchies are illustrated by Figure 11.10.

Collins and Quillian assumed that the characteristics common to all members of a group of related concepts (such as all birds) were attached to the general concept (in this case bird) rather than to all the members. Such an arrangement would produce an efficient and economical organisation of memory. For example, all birds have wings. Thus, we need not remember that a canary, a blue jay, a robin and an ostrich all have wings; we need only remember that each of these concepts belong to the category of bird and that birds have wings.

Some investigators have attempted to use statistical methods to remove the effects of environmental variables, such as socioeconomic status, that account for differences in performance between blacks and whites. However, these methods are controversial, and many statisticians question their validity. On the other hand, a study by Scarr and Weinberg (1976) provides unambiguous evidence that environmental factors can substantially increase the measured IQ of a black child. Scarr and Weinberg studied ninety-nine black children who were adopted into white families of higher-than-average educational and socioeconomic status. The expected average IQ of black children in the same area who were raised in black families was approximately 90. The average IQ of the adopted group was observed to be 105.

Other authors have flatly stated that there are no racial differences in biologically determined intellectual capacity. But this claim, like the one asserting that blacks are inherently less intelligent than whites, has not been determined scientifically. It is an example of what Jensen (1980) has called the egalitarian fallacy – the 'gratuitous assumption that all human populations are essentially identical in whatever trait or ability the test purports to measure' (p. 370). Although we know that blacks and whites have different environments and that a black child raised in an environment similar to that of a white child will receive a similar IQ score, the question of whether any racial hereditary differences exist has not been answered. When we point to group differences in races we are referring to general, average differences in intellectual performance; there are considerable within-group differences which may even be larger than between group differences (Suzuki and Valencia, 1997).

There is also a problem with what we mean by race. We can define race biologically by gene frequencies (Loehlin *et al.*, 1975) or we can define it as a social construct. For many people, race is whatever they believe it to mean; they themselves ascribe meaning to it (Omi and Winant, 1994). In this sense, the concept of race makes very little scientific sense.

Conclusion

Although the issue of race and intelligence as currently conceived does not appear to be meaningful, it would be scientifically interesting to study the effects of different environments on inherited intellectual capacity. The interesting and more valid questions concerning race are those addressed by social psychologists and anthropologists – questions concerning issues such as the prevalence of prejudice, ethnic identification and cohesiveness, fear of strangers (xenophobia), and the tendency to judge something (or someone) that is different as inferior.

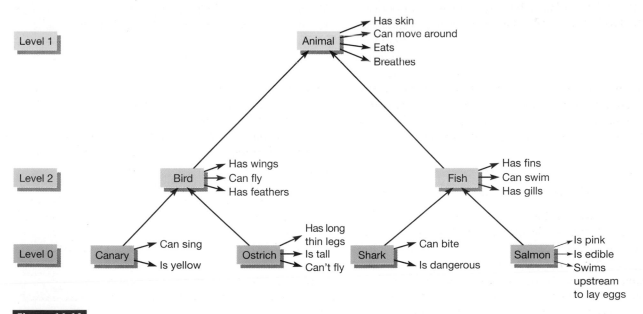

Figure 11.10

Collins and Quillian's model of the hierarchical organisation of concepts in semantic memory.

Source: Robert L. Solso, Cognitive Psychology (2nd edition). Copyright © 1988 by Allyn and Bacon. After Collins and Quillian, 1969. Reproduced with permission.

Collins and Quillian tested the validity of their model by asking people questions about the characteristics of various concepts. Consider the concept 'canary'. The investigators asked people to say true or false to statements such as 'A canary eats'. When the question dealt with characteristics that were specific to the concept (such as 'can sing', or 'is yellow'), the subjects responded quickly. If the question dealt with a characteristic that was common to a more general concept (such as 'has skin' or 'breathes'), the subjects took a longer time in answering. Presumably, when asked a question about a characteristic that applied to all birds or to all animals, the participants had to 'travel up the tree' from the entry for canary until they found the level that provided the answer. The further they had to go, the longer the process took.

The model above is attractive but it does not reflect realistically the way in which we classify concepts and their characteristics. For example, although people may conceive of objects in terms of a hierarchy, a particular person's hierarchy of animals need not resemble that compiled by a zoologist. For example, Rips *et al.* (1973) found that people said yes to 'A collie is an animal' faster than they did to 'A collie is a mammal'. According to Collins and Quillian's model, animal comes above mammal in the hierarchy, so the results should have been just the opposite.

Although some organisation undoubtedly exists between categories and subcategories, it appears not to be perfectly logical and systematic. For example, Roth and Mervis (1983) found that people judged Chablis to be a better example of wine than of drink, but they judged champagne to be a better example of drink than of wine. This inconsistency clearly reflects people's experience with the concepts. Chablis is obviously a wine: it is sold in bottles that resemble those used for other wines, it looks and tastes similar to other white wines, the word 'wine' is found on the label, and so on. By these standards, champagne appears to stand apart. A wine expert would categorise champagne as a particular type of wine. But the average person, not being particularly well acquainted with the fact that champagne is made of fermented grape juice, encounters champagne in the context of something to drink on a special occasion, something to launch ships with, and so on. Thus, its characteristics are perceived as being rather different from those of Chablis.

Rosch (1975; Mervis and Rosch, 1981) suggested that people do not look up the meanings of concepts in their heads in the way that they seek definitions in dictionaries. The concepts we use in everyday life are natural concepts, not formal ones discovered by experts who have examined characteristics we are not aware of. Natural concepts are based on our own perceptions and interactions with things in the world. For example, some things have wings, beaks and feathers, and they fly, build nests, lay eggs and make high-pitched noises. Other things are furry, have four legs and a tail, and run around on the ground. Formal concepts

consist of carefully defined sets of rules governing membership in a particular category; natural concepts are collections of memories of particular examples that share some similarities. Formal concepts are used primarily by experts (and by people studying to become experts), whereas natural concepts are used by ordinary people in their daily lives.

Rosch suggests that people's natural concepts consist of collections of memories of particular examples, called exemplars, that share some similarities. The boundaries between formal concepts are precise, whereas those between natural concepts are fuzzy – the distinction between a member and a non-member is not always clear. Thus, to a non-expert, not all members of a concept are equally good examples of that concept. A robin is a good example of bird; a penguin or ostrich is a poor one. We may acknowledge that a penguin is a bird because we have been taught that it is, but we often qualify the category membership by making statements such as 'strictly speaking, a penguin is a bird'. Exemplars represent the important characteristics of a category – characteristics that we can easily perceive or that we encounter when we interact with its members.

According to Rosch *et al.* (1976), natural concepts vary in their level of precision and detail. They are arranged in a hierarchy from very detailed to very general. When we think about concepts and talk about them, we usually deal with basic-level concepts – those that make important distinctions between different categories – but do not waste time and effort with those that do not matter. For example, chair and apple are basic-level concepts. Concepts that refer to collections of basic-level concepts, such as furniture and fruit, are called superordinate concepts. Concepts that refer to types of items within a basic-level category, such as deckchair and Granny Smith's, are called subordinate concepts. These can be seen in Figure 11.11.

The basic-level concept tends to be the one that people spontaneously name when they see a member of the

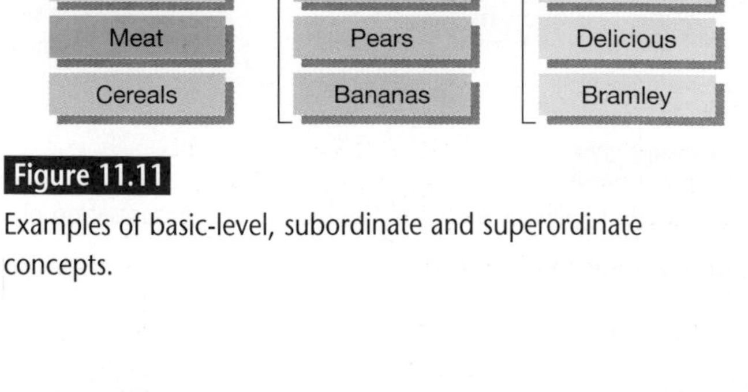

Level of Concept

Superordinate	Basic	Subordinate

Examples

Fruit	Oranges	Cox
Vegetables	Apples	Russett
Fish	Peaches	Granny Smith
Meat	Pears	Delicious
Cereals	Bananas	Bramley

Figure 11.11

Examples of basic-level, subordinate and superordinate concepts.

category. That is, all types of chair tend to be called 'chair', unless there is a special reason to use a more precise label. People tend to use basic-level concepts for a very good reason: cognitive economy. The use of subordinate concepts wastes time and effort on meaningless distinctions, and the use of superordinate concepts loses important information. Rosch *et al.* (1976) presented people with various concepts and gave them 90 seconds to list as many attributes as they could for each of them. The subjects supplied few attributes for superordinate concepts but were able to think of many for basic-level concepts. Subordinate concepts evoked no more responses than basic-level concepts did. Thus, because they deal with a large number of individual items and their characteristics, basic-level concepts represent the maximum information in the most efficient manner. When people think about basic-level concepts, they do not have to travel up or down a tree to find the attributes that belong to the concept. The attributes are directly attached to the exemplars that constitute each concept.

It is important to recognise that concepts can represent something more complex than simple exemplars or collections of attributes. Goldstone *et al.* (1991) showed participants groups of figures and asked them to indicate which were most similar to each other. When they showed the participants two triangles, two squares and two circles, the subjects said that the squares and triangles were most similar, presumably because both contained straight lines and angles. However, when they added a square to each of the pairs, the participants said that the two most similar groups were the triangles plus square and the circles plus square. The task is illustrated by Figure 11.12.

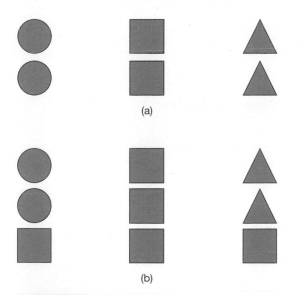

Figure 11.12

Concept formation. Subjects were asked which of the groups of shapes were most similar. (a) Three pairs of geometrical shapes. (b) The same shapes with the addition of squares.

The concept this time was 'two things and a square'. If the participants were simply counting attributes, then the addition of a square to the pairs should not have changed their decision. As this study shows very clearly, concepts can include relations among elements that cannot be described by counting attributes.

Concepts are the raw material of thinking; they are what we think about. But thinking itself involves the manipulation and combination of concepts. Such thinking can take several forms, but most the common forms are deductive reasoning and inductive reasoning.

Deductive reasoning

Deductive reasoning consists of inferring specific instances from general principles or rules. For example, the following two series of sentences express deductive reasoning:

> *John is taller than Phil.*
> *Sue is shorter than Phil.*
> *Therefore, John is taller than Sue.*

> *All mammals have fur.*
> *A bat is a mammal.*
> *Therefore, a bat has fur.*

Deductions consist of two or more statements from which a conclusion is drawn. The first group of sentences presented above involves the application of a simple mathematical principle. The second group presents a syllogism. The syllogism, a form of deductive logic invented by Aristotle, is often found in tests of intelligence. A syllogism is a logical construction that consists of a major premise (for example, 'all mammals have fur'), a minor premise ('a bat is a mammal'), and a conclusion ('a bat has fur'). The major and minor premises are assumed to be true. The problem is to decide whether the conclusion is true or false.

People differ widely in their ability to solve syllogisms. For example, many people would agree with the conclusion of the following syllogism:

> *All mammals have fur.*
> *A zilgid has fur.*
> *Therefore, a zilgid is a mammal.*

These people would be wrong; the conclusion is not warranted. The major premise says only that all mammals have fur. It leaves open the possibility that some animals that have fur are not mammals.

Cross-cultural differences in syllogistic reasoning

Several studies have suggested that illiterate, unschooled people in remote villages in various parts of the world are unable to solve syllogistic problems. Scribner (1977) visited two tribes of people in Liberia, West Africa, the Kpelle and the Vai, and found that tribespeople gave what Westerners would consider to be wrong answers. However, the people were not unable to reason logically but approached problems differently. For example, she presented the following problem to a Kpelle farmer. At first glance, the problem appears to be a reasonable one even for an illiterate, unschooled person because it refers to his own tribe and to an occupation he is familiar with.

All Kpelle men are rice farmers.
Mr Smith is not a rice farmer.
Is he a Kpelle man?

The man replied:

Participant: I don't know the man in person. I have not laid eyes on the man himself.

Experimenter: Just think about the statement.

Participant: If I know him in person, I can answer that question, but since I do not know him in person, I cannot answer that question.

Experimenter: Try and answer from your Kpelle sense.

Participant: If you know a person, if a question comes up about him you are able to answer. But if you do not know the person, if a question comes up about him it's hard for you to answer. (Scribner, 1977, p. 490)

The farmer's response did not show that he was unable to solve a problem in deductive logic. Instead, it indicated that as far as he was concerned, the question was unreasonable. In fact, his response contained an example of logical reasoning: 'If you know a person ... you are able to answer.'

Luria (1977) received a similar answer from an illiterate Uzbekistanian woman, who was asked the following:

In the far north all bears are white.
Novaya Zemyla is in the far north.
What colour are the bears there?

The woman replied, 'You should ask the people who have been there and seen them. We always speak of only what we see; we don't talk about what we haven't seen.'

Scribner found that illiterate people would sometimes reject the premises of her syllogism, replace them with what they knew to be true, and then solve the new problem, as they had defined it. For example, she presented the following problem to a Vai tribesperson.

All women who live in Monrovia are married.
Kemu is not married.
Does she live in Monrovia?

The answer was yes. The respondent said, 'Monrovia is not for any one kind of people, so Kemu came to live there.' The suggestion that only married women live in Monrovia was absurd, because the tribesperson knew otherwise. Thus, if Kemu wanted to live there, she could – and did.

Clearly, the intellectual ability of people in other cultures cannot be measured against Western standards. In the world of traditional tribal people, problems are solved by application of logical reasoning to facts gained through direct experience. Their deductive-reasoning ability is not necessarily inferior, it is simply different, pragmatic.

Mental models

Why are some people better than others at solving syllogisms? Johnson-Laird (1985) notes that syllogistic reasoning is much more highly correlated with spatial ability than with verbal ability. Spatial ability includes the ability to visualise shapes and to manipulate them mentally. Why should skill at logical reasoning be related to this ability? Johnson-Laird and his colleagues (Johnson-Laird and Byrne, 1991; Johnson-Laird *et al.*, 1992) suggest that people solve problems involving logical deduction by constructing **mental models**, mental constructions based on physical reality. For example, if you consider the following problem:

A is less than C
B is greater than C
Is B greater than A?

in order to compare A with B, you must remember the order of the three elements. One kind of mental model is an imaginary line going from small to large in which you mentally place each item on the line as you encounter it. Then, with all three elements in a row, you can answer the question. Figure 11.13 illustrates this.

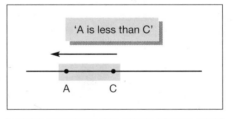

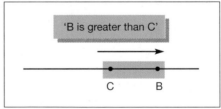

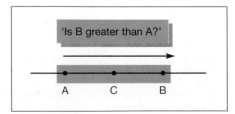

Figure 11.13

A mental model. Logical problems are often solved by imagining a physical representation of the facts.

In fact, when we solve problems concerning comparisons of a series of items, we tend to think about our own mental model that represents the information rather than about the particular facts given to us (Potts, 1972). For example, consider this passage:

Although the four craftsmen were brothers, they varied enormously in height. The electrician was the very tallest, and the plumber was shorter than him. The plumber was taller than the carpenter, who, in turn, was taller than the painter. (Just and Carpenter, 1987, p. 202)

After reading this passage, people can more easily answer questions about pairs of brothers who largely differ in height. For example, they are faster to answer the question 'who is taller, the electrician or the painter?' than the question 'who is taller, the plumber or the carpenter?' This finding is particularly important because the passage explicitly states that the plumber was taller than the carpenter, but one must infer that the electrician was taller than the painter. Just and Carpenter's study shows that the result of an inference can be more readily available than information explicitly given. How can this be? The most plausible explanation is that when people read the passage, they construct a mental model that represents the four brothers arranged in order of height. The painter is clearly the shortest and the electrician is clearly the tallest. Thus, a comparison between the extremes can be made very quickly.

Many creative scientists and engineers report that they use mental models to reason logically and solve practical and theoretical problems (Krueger, 1976). For example, the American physicist and Nobel laureate Richard Feynman said that he used rather bizarre mental models to keep track of characteristics of complex mathematical theorems to see whether they were logical and consistent. Here is how Feynman described his thought processes:

'When I'm trying to understand ... I keep making up examples. For instance, the mathematicians would come in with a ... theorem. As they're telling me the conditions of the theorem, I construct something that fits all the conditions. You know, you have a set [one ball] – disjoint [two balls]. Then the balls turn colours, grow hairs, or whatever, in my head as they [the mathematicians] put more conditions on. Finally, they state the theorem, which is some ... thing about the ball which isn't true for my hairy green ball thing, so I say "False!"' (Feynman, 1985, p. 70)

Such use of mental models by a talented and gifted scientist strengthens the conclusion that being able to convert abstract problems into tangible mental models is an important aspect of intelligent thinking.

Inductive reasoning

Deductive reasoning involves applying the rules of logic to infer specific instances from general principles or rules.

This type of reasoning works well when general principles or rules have already been worked out. **Inductive reasoning** is the opposite of deductive reasoning; it consists of inferring general principles or rules from specific facts. In one well known laboratory example of inductive reasoning, participants are shown cards that contain figures differing in several dimensions, such as shape, number and colour (Milner, 1964). On each trial, they are given two cards and asked to choose the one that represents a particular concept. After they choose a card, the experimenter indicates whether the decision is correct or not. The task is illustrated in Figure 11.14.

One trial is not enough to recognise the concept. If the first trial reveals that a card is correct, then the concept could be red, or four or triangle, or some combination of these, such as red triangle, four red shapes, or even four red triangles. Information gained from the second trial allows

Figure 11.14

A card sorting task. Participants are asked to sort cards according to a given criterion, such as colour or shape, that is unknown to them. After they have successfully determined this criterion, it is unexpectedly and unknowingly changed and the participant has to determine the new sorting criterion.

Source: Pinel, J., *Biopsychology* (3rd edition). Boston: Allyn and Bacon. Copyright © 1997 by Allyn and Bacon; reproduced by permission.

the subject to rule out some of these hypotheses – for example, shape does not matter, but colour and number do. The participant uses steps to solve the problem in much the same way as a scientist does: he or she forms a hypothesis on the basis of the available evidence and tests that hypothesis on subsequent trials. If it is proved false, it is abandoned, a new hypothesis consistent with what went before is constructed and this new hypothesis is tested.

Logical errors in inductive reasoning

Psychologists have identified several tendencies that interfere with people's ability to reason inductively. These include the failure to select the information they need to test a hypothesis, the failure to seek information that would be provided by a comparison group, and the disinclination to seek evidence that would indicate whether a hypothesis is false.

Failure to select relevant information

When reasoning inductively, people often fail to select the information they need to test a hypothesis. For example, consider the following task, from an experiment by Wason and Johnson-Laird (1972).

> *Your job is to determine which of the hidden parts of these cards you need to see in order to answer the following question decisively:*
>
> *For these cards is it true that if there is a vowel on one side there is an even number on the other side?*
>
> *You have only one opportunity to make this decision; you must not assume that you can inspect the cards one at a time. Name those cards which it is absolutely essential to see.*

The participants were shown four cards like those shown in Figure 11.15. Most people say that they would need to see card (a), and they are correct. If there was not an even number on the back of card (a), then the rule is not correct. However, many participants failed to realise that card (d) must also be inspected. True, there is no even number on this card, but what if there is a vowel on the other side?

If there is, then the rule is (again) proved wrong. Many subjects also wanted to see card (c), but there is no need to do so. The hypothesis says nothing about whether an even number can be on one side of the card without there being a vowel on the other side.

People have to be taught the rules of logic; they do not automatically apply them when trying to solve a problem. But under certain circumstances, most people do reason logically. For example, Griggs and Cox (1982) presented a slightly different version of this test. They asked people to decide which cards should be checked to see whether the following statement was true: 'If a person is drinking beer, she must be over age nineteen.' The cards represented people; their age was on one side and their drink (beer or Coke) was on the other. Which card(s) would you check? (See Figure 11.16.)

Most participants correctly chose cards (a) and (d). They knew that if someone were drinking beer, she must be old enough. Similarly, if someone were 16 years old, we must check to see what she was drinking. The subjects readily recognised the fact that we do not need to know the age of someone drinking Coke, and someone 22 years old can drink whatever beverage she prefers. This study shows that experiments using puzzles designed to test people's reasoning ability do not always assess their ability to apply a logical rule to a practical situation.

Failure to utilise a comparison group

Another tendency that interferes with people's ability to reason inductively is their failure to consider a comparison group. Imagine that you learn that 79 per cent of the people with a particular disease get well within a month after taking a new, experimental drug (Stich, 1990). Is the drug effective? The correct answer to this question is: we cannot conclude anything – we need more information. What we need to know is what happens to people with the disease if they do not take the drug. If we find that only 22 per cent of these people recover within a month, then we would conclude that the drug is effective; 79 per cent is much greater than 22 per cent. On the other hand, if we find that 98 per cent recover without taking the drug, then we would conclude that the drug is worse than useless – it

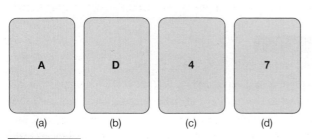

Figure 11.15

Cards used in a formal test of problem solving.

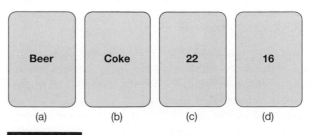

Figure 11.16

Cards used in a more realistic version of the problem solving test.

actually interferes with recovery. In other words, we need a control group. But most people are perfectly willing to conclude that, because 79 per cent seems like a high figure, the drug must work. Seeing the necessity for a control group does not come naturally; unless people are deliberately taught about control groups, they will not realise the need for them.

Failure to seek or use information that would be provided by a control group has been called ignoring base rate information. As several researchers have suggested, the problem here may be that we engage in two types of reasoning (Reber, 1992). One type of reasoning is deliberate and conscious and involves explicit memories of roles that we can describe verbally. The other type of reasoning is unconscious and uses information we have learned implicitly. Because the explicit and implicit memory systems involve at least some different brain mechanisms, information from one system cannot easily interact with information from the other system. In fact, if people are allowed to observe actual occurrences of certain events (that is, acquire the information about the base rate of occurrence automatically and implicitly), they do consider information about event frequency (Holyoak and Spellman, 1993).

Confirmation bias

Individuals may also show a disinclination to seek evidence that would indicate whether a hypothesis is false. Instead, people tend to seek evidence that might confirm their hypothesis; they exhibit the confirmation bias. For example, Wason (1968) presented people with the series of numbers 'two, four, six' and asked them to try to figure out the rule to which they conformed. The participant was to test his or her hypothesis by making up series of numbers and saying them to the experimenter, who would reply yes or no. Then, whenever the participant decided that enough information had been gathered, he or she could say what the hypothesis was. If the answer was correct, the problem was solved. If it was not, the participant was to think of a new hypothesis and test that one.

Several rules could explain the series 'two, four, six'. The rule could be 'even numbers', or 'each number is two more than the preceding one', or 'the middle number is the mean of the first and third number'. When people tested their hypotheses, they almost always did so by presenting several sets of numbers, all of which were consistent with their hypotheses. For example, if they thought that each number was two more than the preceding one, they might say 'ten, twelve, fourteen' or 'sixty-one, sixty-three, sixty-five'. Very few participants tried to test their hypotheses by choosing a set of numbers that did not conform to the rules, such as 'twelve, fifteen, twenty-two'. In fact, the series 'twelve, fifteen, twenty-two' does conform to the rule. The rule was so simple that few participants figured it out: each number must be larger than the preceding one.

The confirmation bias is very strong. Unless people are taught to do so, they tend not to think of possible non-examples of their hypotheses and to see whether they might be true – the way that scientists do. But in fact, evidence that disconfirms a hypothesis is conclusive, whereas evidence that confirms it is not.

The confirmation bias in inductive reasoning has a counterpart in deductive reasoning. For example, consider the following sentences (Johnson-Laird, 1985):

All the pilots are artists.
All the skiers are artists.
True or false: All the pilots are skiers.

Many people say 'true'. They test the truth of the conclusion by imagining a person who is a pilot and an artist and a skier – and that person complies with the rules. Therefore, they decide that the conclusion is true. But if they would try to disconfirm the conclusion – to look for an example that would fit the first two sentences but not the conclusion – they would easily find one. Could a person be a pilot but not a skier? Of course; the first two sentences say nothing to rule out that possibility. There are artist–pilots and there are artist–skiers, but nothing says that there must be artist–pilot–skiers.

The tendency to seek (and to pay more attention to) events that might confirm our beliefs is demonstrated by the way we have distorted the original meaning of the saying, 'the exception proves the rule'. Most people take this to mean that we can still consider a rule to be valid even if we encounter some exceptions. But that conclusion is illogical: if there is an exception, the rule is wrong. In fact, the original meaning of the phrase was, 'the exception tests the rule', which it does. The word 'prove' comes from the Latin *probare*, 'to test'.

Where in the brain does reasoning occur?

For most of our complex, intelligent behaviour a region in the front of the brain appears to be essential. Damage to the frontal lobes is associated with deficits in planning, with putting stimuli in the correct order, with behaving spontaneously and inhibiting incorrect responses (Adolphs *et al.*, 1996).

Antonio Damasio and colleagues' studies of patients with frontal lobe damage, for example, suggest that these individuals have great difficulty in making correct decisions (Damasio, 1995; Bechara *et al.*, 1996, 1997). Damasio suggests that the ability to make decisions leading to positive or potentially harmful consequences depends on the activation of somatic (that is, bodily) states. Damasio calls this the somatic marker hypothesis because such decisions involve automatic, endocrine and musculoskeletal routes. These routes mark events as important, but appear to be impaired in certain frontal lobe patients. For example, patients with damage to a specific area of the prefrontal cortex are unable to make decisions in real life despite having intact cognitive ability. When the decision can have a positive or negative outcome, the degree of physiological activity commonly seen in healthy individuals when they make such decisions is absent in these patients (Bechara *et al.*, 1997).

In one study, frontal lobe patients and healthy controls were taught to play a card game where they were told to make as much money as possible (Bechara *et al.*, 1997). There were four decks of cards and some had a high probability of delivering a large immediate monetary reward or a large delayed monetary loss or a low immediate monetary reward or a low delayed monetary loss. No participant was told which deck contained the greatest probability of obtaining these outcomes and, therefore, had to learn from experience, turning over cards and remembering the outcomes. They had hunches. When a decision involved a high degree of risk, for example (such as losing a large amount of money), a healthy individual would show a characteristic increase in physiological arousal; the frontal lobe patient, however, would not. The patients would show a characteristic response after they had lost or gained, as would controls, and all patients were aware that they had lost money.

If the frontal lobes are important for reasoning, then activation in these areas should be apparent when healthy individuals perform a reasoning task during neuroimaging. Goel *et al.* (1997, 1998) have recently reported two experiments in which they sought to test this hypothesis. In one experiment, they asked ten participants to undertake inductive and deductive reasoning tasks. These involved syllogistic reasoning tasks such as deciding whether the following logic was correct:

> *All carpenters are young*
> *All woodworkers are carpenters*
> *All woodworkers are young*

and

> *George was a woolly mammoth*
> *George ate pine cones*
> *All woolly mammoths ate pine cones*

The experimenters found that the frontal lobes were, indeed, involved. Significant increases in activation were reported in the left inferior and middle frontal gyri.

Duncan has suggested that the frontal lobes may not be necessarily involved in the operation of tasks requiring crystallised intelligence but are involved in the operation of tasks requiring fluid intelligence (Duncan, 1995; Duncan *et al.*, 1995). Three of the frontal lobe patients he studied had normal WAIS-R scores but reduced scores on a test of fluid intelligence. Scores on the fluid intelligence test were also lower than those of controls, suggesting that the frontal lobes are necessary for the fluid intelligence.

If the frontal cortex is important to reasoning, would more or less activation in this region be apparent in very bright individuals? An early PET study indicated that individuals with high IQ had lower metabolic rates than those with low IQ during problem solving (Haier *et al.*, 1988). When high and low IQ individuals were trained on a computer game, both groups' brain activity declined but the decline in the high IQ group was more rapid, suggesting that the highly intellectually able may need to use less of their neural machinery to think (Haier *et al.*, 1992).

The decline in activity, however, seems to be general, although some studies show that regional activation in high IQ individuals is specific but is non-specific in individuals with low IQ (Neubauer *et al.*, 1995). The less effort hypothesis also receives some support from EEG studies. High IQ individuals show consistently higher EEG alpha power (that is, less mental effort) during problem solving and preparation for problem solving than do low IQ individuals (Jausovec, 1996). The most pronounced differences between high and low IQ individuals during working memory and arithmetic tasks was found across the frontal regions (Jausovec, 1998).

Problem solving

The ultimate function of thinking is to solve problems. We are faced with an enormous variety of them in our daily lives: fixing a television set, planning a picnic, choosing a spouse, navigating across the ocean, solving a maths problem, tracking some game, designing a bridge, finding a job. The ability to solve problems is related to academic success, vocational success, and overall success in life, so trying to understand how we do so is an important undertaking.

The spatial metaphor

According to Holyoak (1990), a problem is a state of affairs in which we have a goal but do not have a clear understanding of how it can be attained. As he notes, when we talk about problems, we often use spatial metaphors to describe them (Lakoff and Turner, 1989). We think of the solving of a problem as finding a path to the solution. We may have to get around roadblocks that we encounter or backtrack when we hit a dead end. If we get lost, we may try to approach the problem from a different angle. If we have experience with particular types of problem, we may know some shortcuts.

In fact, Newell and Simon (1972) have used the spatial metaphor to characterise the problem solving process. At the beginning of a person's attempt to solve a problem, the initial state is different from the goal state – if it were not, there would be no problem. The person solving the problem has a number of operators available. Operators are actions that can be taken to change the current state of the problem; metaphorically, operators move the current state from one position to another. Not all people will be aware of the operators that are available. Knowledge of operators depends on education and experience. In addition, there may be various costs associated with different operators; some may be more difficult, expensive or time consuming than others. The problem space consists of all the possible states that can be achieved if all the possible operators are applied. A solution is a sequence of operators (a 'path') that moves from the initial state to the goal state.

Algorithms and heuristics

Some kinds of problem can be solved by following a sequence of operators known as an algorithm. Algorithms are procedures that consist of series of steps that, if followed in the correct sequence, will provide a solution. If you properly apply the steps of an algorithm (such as long division) to divide one number by another, you will obtain the correct answer. But many problems are not as straightforward as this. When there is no algorithm to follow, we must follow a heuristic to guide our search for a path to the solution. Heuristics (from the Greek *heuriskein*, 'to discover') are general rules that are useful in guiding our search for a path to the solution of a problem. Heuristics tell us what to pay attention to, what to ignore and what strategy to take.

Heuristic methods can be very specific, or they can be quite general, applying to large categories of problems. For example, management courses try to teach students problem solving methods they can use in a wide variety of contexts. Newell and Simon (1972) suggest a general heuristic method that can be used to solve any problem: means–ends analysis. The principle behind means–ends analysis is that a person should look for differences between the current state and the goal state and seek ways to reduce these differences. The steps of this method are as follows (Holyoak, 1990, p. 121):

1 Compare the current state to the goal state and identify differences between the two. If there are none, the problem is solved; otherwise, proceed.

2 Select an operator that would reduce one of the differences.

3 If the operator can be applied, do so; if not, set a new subgoal of reaching a state at which the operator could be applied. Means–ends analysis is then applied to this new subgoal until the operator can be applied or the attempt to use it is abandoned.

4 Return to step 1.

At all times, the person's activity is oriented towards reducing the distance between the current state and the goal state. If problems are encountered along the way (that is, if operators cannot be applied), then subgoals are created and means–ends analysis is applied to solving that problem, and so on until the goal is reached.

Of course, there may be more than one solution to a particular problem, and some solutions may be better than others. A good solution is one that uses the smallest number of actions while minimising the associated costs. The relative importance of cost and speed determines which solution is best. Intelligent problem solving involves more than trying out various actions (applying various operators) to see whether they bring you closer to the goal. It also involves planning. When we plan, we act vicariously, 'trying out' various actions in our heads. Obviously, planning requires that we know something about the consequences of the actions we are considering. Experts are better at planning than novices are. If we do not know the consequences of particular actions, we will be obliged to try each action (apply each operator) and see what happens. Planning is especially important when many possible operators are present, when they are costly or time consuming, or when they are irreversible. If we take an irreversible action that brings us to a dead end, we have failed to solve the problem.

Creative thinking

Creativity has almost as many definitions as intelligence. We recognise that the writing of a novel, the design of a sculpture and the construction of a painting are creative products but what does it mean to be creative? Feldhusen and Goh (1995) define creativity as a 'complex mix of motivational conditions, personality factors, environmental conditions, chance factors and end products'. Vernon (1989) suggests that creativity is a person's capacity to produce ideas, inventions, artistic objects, insight and products evaluated highly by experts. Torrance (1995) defines creativity as a set of abilities, skills, motivations and states linked to dealing with problems. Others define the components of creative thinking as involving a realisation that a problem exists, formulation of questions to clarify the problem, determining the causes of the problem, clarifying the desired goal or solution and selecting a way to achieve this goal (Feldhusen, 1993). Still others have suggested that creativity involves producing a recognised, important end-product, not rubbish.

All of these definitions seem to have a common feature – that creativity involves some form of end-product. However, this end-product need not be material. Albert (1990), for example, has suggested that creativity is expressed through decisions not products. There do, however, seem to be different degrees of creativity. The production of a novel, painting or sculpture are undoubtedly creative but solving inductive and deductive problems also involve a degree of creative thinking. The production of the latter, however, seems to require creativity plus talent. These are high-level creative behaviours as opposed to the basic creative behaviour involved in solving deductive reasoning puzzles.

Given that psychologists cannot measure high-level creativity directly in the laboratory – they cannot ask individuals to come into the laboratory and write full length novels, for example – they have devised other tests which tap the capacity to engage in creative thinking. The Torrance Tests of Creativity, for example, measure performance on a series of verbal and figural tasks such as naming as many objects beginning with a specific letter or creating as many designs using the same basic design (for example a circle). Torrance (1975) reports that performance on these tests predicts creative achievement, occupation and creative writing. Other tests include those by Wallach and Kogan (1965). These tests are verbal in nature and measure verbal fluency – the ability to devise many uses for objects and the ability to detect similarities between stimuli. Again, there is little evidence that performance on tests such as the Wallace and Kogan and the Torrance Tests – called tests of divergent thinking – predicts creativity (Brown, 1989).

Controversies in psychological science

Are creativity and psychopathology related?

The issue

According to Dryden, 'Great wits are sure to madness near allied, and thin partitions do their bounds divide.' As if providing direct evidence for Dryden's poetic analysis, Lady Caroline Lamb once famously described Lord Byron as mad, bad and dangerous to know. Although the link between badness, danger and creativity has not been the source of much research in psychology, the link between creativity and madness (or psychopathology) has. (Chapter 17 provides more detail on the various types of mental illness that fall under the category of psychopathology.) Anecdotal evidence suggests that two types of mental illness, manic–depression (alternating periods of elation and chronic sadness) and clinical depression exist preponderantly in novelists, poets, artists and performers. But what empirical evidence is there to link psychopathology and creativity? If there is a relationship, does creativity cause psychopathology or does psychopathology cause creativity? Is it possible to determine this?

The evidence

Kraeplin (1921) had originally described a disorder called manic–depressive insanity in which the manic aspect of the disorder would produce changes in thought that would increase creativity and thinking. A number of authors report that increases in creativity are common during the manic episodes of bipolar disorder (Sutherland, 1993; Jamison, 1989; Goodwin and Jamison, 1990). Jamison (1989), for example, found that creative individuals, especially poets, reported states of mania during creation although she did not specify the direction of the change in behaviour (whether the poetry caused the mania or vice versa). There was also a high incidence of suicide in poets.

Weisberg (1994), in studying the quantity and quality of the composer, Franz Schubert, who suffered what we would today call a bipolar disorder, found that although the quantity of the composer's work increased during manic episodes, the quality was not significantly improved.

In a famous study of the relationship between creativity and psychopathology, Ludwig (1994) compared 59 women writers from a Women Writers Conference at the University of Kentucky and 59 women from a housewives' association, medical centre and university women's club. Ludwig found that the writers were more likely to suffer from mood disorders, drug abuse, panic attacks, general anxiety and eating disorders. The results of this study complements that of writers attending an Iowa Writers' Workshop, 90 per cent of whom were men (Andreasen, 1987). The study found a greater incidence of mood disorder in this group than in the general population (80 per cent vs 30 per cent) and a greater incidence of bipolar disorder.

In two recent studies of creativity, Post (1994, 1996) extensively analysed the biographies of 291 world-famous creative men (visual artists, composers, creative writers, scientists, scholars and statesmen). He found that 90 per cent of the writers in his sample exhibited some traits which would be classified as a personality disorder according to mental disorder diagnostic manuals; only one scientist showed this profile (Henry Babbage, inventor of the first computer). In addition, 73.4 per cent of scientists exhibited unremarkable sexual behaviour whereas only 39 per cent of writers did. Depressive episodes occurred in 72 per cent of the writers. These data suggested to Post that, although the study was retrospective, a 'causal nexus' existed between creativity and psychopathology. In a subsequent study of 100 American and British writers (Post, 1996), there was a high prevalence of mood disorder, as seen in

Are there any features of the creative individual's personality that can predict creativity? Dacey (1989) has listed nine personality factors predictive of creativity and includes in this list flexibility, risk taking and tolerance of ambiguity. Other factors suggested by other psychologists include: cognitive complexity, perceptual openness, field independence, autonomy and self-esteem (Woodman and Schoenfeldt, 1989), and fluency, flexibility, curiosity and humour (Treffinger *et al.*, 1990). Other personality factors which have recently attracted a great deal of interest are psychopathological or psychotic personality characteristics. Are creative people more prone to mental disorder? Does the mental disorder predispose the individual to creative thinking? These questions are discussed in the 'Controversies in psychological science' section below.

Table 11.7   Mood disorders found in a sample of 100 writers

	N	Bipolar psychoses	Unipolar psychoses	Severely disabling depressions	Milder depressions	Brief reactions only	Depressive traits only	Cyclothymic traits only	Totals
Poets	35	2	1	4	11	4	5	1	28
Poets/novelists	41	2	1	8	13	2	7	0	33
Playwrights	24	1	0	4	8	4	3	1	21
Totals	**100**	**5**	**2**	**16**	**32**	**10**	**15**	**2**	**82**

Source: Post, 1996. Verbal creativity, depression and alcoholism. In *British Journal of Psychiatry*, 168, 545–555. Reproduced with permission of the Royal College of Psychiatrists.

Table 11.7. Poets showed the greatest degree of bipolar disorder although the incidence of depression, marital/sexual problems and alcoholism in poets was low.

If creativity and psychopathology are related, what creates this link? One personality trait which has been linked with creativity is psychoticism (Eysenck, 1995). Psychoticism refers to a cold, manipulative and indifferent personality style. A number of studies has shown that creative individuals score highly on tests of psychoticism (Fodor, 1994; Stavridou and Furnham, 1996). According to Kris (1952), creative people are able to shift between two modes of thinking called primary and secondary thinking. Primary thinking is artistic, free associative, analogical and relies on concrete rather than abstract concepts; secondary thinking is abstract and reality oriented. There seems to be no link between psychoticism and primary thinking, however (Martindale and Dailey, 1996). Similarly, Aguilar-Alonso (1996) found no difference between high and low psychoticism on a measure of verbal and drawing creativity. Rawlings (1985) has suggested that individuals high in psychoticism show the same impulsive, non-conforming processes that underlie creative think-ing ability. Perhaps what underlies creativity and psychoticism is disinhibition, the ability not to inhibit behaviour and thought.

Conclusion

Retrospective evidence suggests that there is a strong link between mental disorder and creativity. The problem with retrospective studies, however, is that we cannot empirically examine the personalities of creative individuals who are dead: we have to rely on books, anecdotes, personal reminiscences of creative individuals' relatives, friends or lovers. The findings of some recent empirical studies have been inconsistent. Some have shown a link between creativity and psychopathology but sometimes only for specific types of creative individual. Perhaps one problem in demonstrating this elusive link is that creativity is difficult to define absolutely. Modern studies employ creativity tests thought to tap specific forms of thinking but these may be far removed from the creativity seen in a visual artist, a poet or a novelist. While we can still describe creative individuals as bad or dangerous, their madness is still open to question.

Intelligence, thinking and ageing

Ageing and cognitive ability

As the body and the brain grow older, certain changes occur. The acuity of the senses may begin to decline, the ability to move quickly is reduced. On the cognitive level, there is also a decline in various functions such as the manipulation of information in working memory, retrieval of names, reaction time, declarative memory, information processing. Functions such as vocabulary, however, see some improvement with age (Woodruff-Pak, 1997). General IQ scores will peak at around 25 years of age and decline up to 65 years. After 65, the score drops rapidly (Woods, 1994). At the most severe end of cognitive decline, there is dementia – the gradual and relentless loss in intellectual function as the individual reaches the sixth decade of life and beyond. There may be great difficulty in separating the effects of normal ageing from the effects of dementia on cognitive ability (Alzheimer's disease, for example, can only be diagnosed with certainty postmortem when the brain can be examined). Recent data from a Canadian sample suggest that the degree of cognitive impairment that is not related to dementia is around 16.8 per cent (the usual prevalence of dementia is 8 per cent) (Graham *et al.*, 1997).

Our categorisation of individuals into age groups is fairly arbitrary. In most developed countries, the age of retirement is set at 65 (an age originally set by Otto von Bismark, the German chancellor from 1871 to 1890), although this does not mean that those people who are 65 or older are incapable of holding down a job or lack the cognitive and physical capacity to hold down such a job. The distribution of the elderly population in the Western world in 1950 was pyramid shaped, that is, there were fewer people reaching old and very old (over 80 years) age. It has been estimated that by 2030, this distribution will be pillar-shaped, with roughly equal numbers in the old and very old categories, as seen in Figure 11.17 (Quinn, 1996).

Improvements in health care, sanitation, crime prevention and nutrition are thought to be responsible for this increase in the number of years we are living. Psychologically, therefore, the more we learn about the effects of ageing – and in reversing its negative effects – the more important this information will become in countries where we are living longer.

What is ageing?

From a strict point of view, we age as soon as we emerge from the womb. We are born with all the neurons we will have in life and they begin dying as soon as we grow. There is a massive shedding of neurons and synapses during childhood; this continues to old age. Of course, this shedding does not leave us intellectually helpless. Although neurons are lost, new connections are formed between existing neurons (this is why, although neurons are lost, the brain

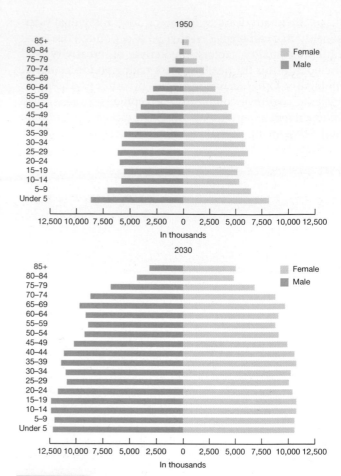

Figure 11.17

A graph illustrating the population of the United States in 1950 (top) and another estimating the population in 2030 (bottom).

Source: Quinn, J.F., Entitlements and the Federal budget. Copyright 1996 The National Academy on an Aging Society, a policy institute of The Gerontological Society of America. May 1996–1. Reproduced with permission.

increases in weight during childhood) and the existing neurons work more efficiently. It has been suggested that psychological ageing begins after maturity and that this is measured by behaviour that includes the ability to acquire, remember and retrieve words, people and events and the ability to process and manipulate information. This scientific study of the ageing process is called gerontology.

One problem with studying the ageing process, however, is the large variability between and within samples. For example, during a long period of study, older participants become susceptible to disease processes and illnesses which could directly affect the variables that gerontologists are interested in studying. This within-subject variation can also be seen in another capacity. If we take one age group, say the 50–60 year old, and compare it with another on some cognitive measure, we are defining a group of individuals by an age category but all individuals within this group may not show the same degree of ageing. For example, although the ability to remember strings of digits declines with age, some individuals perform badly, some stay the same and some actually get better (Holland and Rabbitt, 1991). Group variation becomes more of a problem when we look at data from cross-sectional studies.

Cross-sectional studies, you will remember from Chapter 2, compare independent groups on some measure. In ageing research, a cross-sectional design would involve assigning individuals to age categories such as 18–25, 26–35, 36–45, 46–55 and so on. These groups would then complete a series of tests of cognitive ability, and differences between groups would be examined. If a difference in memory was found between the younger groups and the older groups, however, we could not attribute this finding to ageing and cite ageing as a cause. Can you see why? (This question was posed in Chapter 2.) The reason is that we are not really looking at the effects of ageing but at the effect of age groups. We are not following one individual across all age ranges, but have sampled from several different age ranges. Because of this, our groups may differ on variables that we had not anticipated, such as improvement in nutrition and health care. When one group influences the results in this way, the study is said to show a cohort effect. The conclusion we can draw is that age groups differ from each other.

A different type of design looks at age change and this is called a longitudinal design. Here, individuals are assessed across the lifespan and each individual can act as his or her own control (we could combine the two designs as well and compare individuals within one age group which vary on another characteristic, such as occupation or education level). A problem here is that with repeated testing, the individual will become increasingly sophisticated with the measures employed. However, when longitudinal and cross-sectional measures are compared, the longitudinal assessments show least decline (Schaie, 1990). In addition to emphasising the importance of study design, this finding also suggests that age norms for test measures (that is, the average score and standard deviation for an age group) need to be regularly revised (Woods, 1994). There is considerable evidence that IQ scores have increased by 3 points a decade since 1940 (Flynn, 1987; Lynn, 1991). Because we are getting better at tests, or behaving more intelligently, we would need a new standard of comparison that reflects the current average range of ability.

Other factors in ageing research which are important are an awareness that older participants become tired more quickly (Furry and Baltes, 1973) and are more cautious in making decisions than are their younger counterparts (Birkhill and Schaie, 1975).

Memory

There is a gradual loss in performance for certain types of memory task with age. For example, older individuals have difficulty in retrieving names (Rabbitt *et al.*, 1995) and putting names to famous faces (Burke *et al.*, 1991). In the latter experiment, participants were allowed one minute in which to name famous faces. The number of correct responses increased with age as did the number of tip-of-the-tongue responses. When participants were allowed to try to remember the names on the tips of their tongues, 95 per cent of responses were accurate which suggests that the information had been stored but the retrieval of this information was difficult.

Age-related impairments have been reported for declarative memory, efficiency of processing information and metamemory (Woodruff-Pak, 1997). Metamemory refers to 'knowing about knowing'; this knowledge of skills that is necessary to complete a task may be absent in the elderly. For example, elderly individuals may not spend an appropriate amount of time on a task which requires time spent on it, such as the recall of digit names in serial order. When instructed to spent a certain length of time on this task, however, they recalled as many series of digits as younger participants with no impairment in accuracy.

Recent research on ageing and memory has focused on prospective memory, that is, remembering to perform an activity in the future (Maylor, 1996). This type of memory may be especially important to the elderly given that such monitoring is essential for taking medicine as particular times, for example (Park and Kidder, 1996; Einstein *et al.*, 1998). In experiments where a handkerchief or comb is borrowed by the experimenter at the beginning of a test session and/or hidden in a drawer and the individual has to remember to ask for the return of the item, there is an age-related decline in memory.

Studies of prospective memory can be either 'time based' or 'event based'. In time-based experiments, the participant engages in a task and has to inform the experimenter when a certain time has elapsed (Einstein *et al.*, 1995). This may be analogous to remembering to telephone someone in an hour's time (Maylor, 1996). In one study, Maylor (1990) asked 52–95 year olds to telephone her once a day for a week. Three-quarters of those who adopted a memory strategy or used external cues for remembering were more reliable at telephoning than were those who did not use such mnemonics. In event-based experiments, participants must make a response when a particular event occurs in a sequence of events. Although age-related impairments have been observed for time-based tasks, event-based tasks show mixed results.

Einstein *et al.* (1998), for example, gave a group of young (mean age 19.8 years) and old (mean age 70.73) individuals eleven tasks to complete. The participants were told that during each task they should press a key on a keyboard once, thereby encouraging habitual prospective memory. In a divided attention condition, some participants were also told that they would hear a series of digits and were asked to press a handheld counter when they heard two odd numbers. The young group performed the prospective memory task more effectively than did the old group and performance was worse in the divided attention condition, as expected. However, the impairment in the old group was made worse by divided attention. They omitted to make a response in 42 per cent of the first trials, and 12 per cent of the trials contained repetition errors. For trials occurring at the end of the experiment, 16 per cent contained omission errors whereas 42 per cent contained repetition errors.

During the experiment, participants were also presented with an external cue as a reminder that they should press the key. This cue resulted in the old group committing a greater number of omission errors, especially on later trials. One reason for this unexpected finding is that the old group came to rely on this (ineffective) external cue and not on an internal memory strategy. The poor performance on prospective memory tasks may be attributable to reduced or impaired functioning of the frontal lobes (we will see later that there is some frontal lobe impairment with ageing). Remember from the section on reasoning and the brain that the frontal lobes are especially important for planning; given that prospective memory involves a considerable degree of planning, and that frontal lobe function declines with age, perhaps these two factors are related.

Language

There are certain aspects of language processing that may not decline with age and may actually improve. One of the greatest gains is seen in vocabulary (Bayley and Oden, 1955; Jones, 1959; Rabbitt, 1993). However, older individuals have difficulty in retrieving or accessing these words and exhibit a greater number of tip-of-the-tongue responses than do young individuals during retrieval (Bowles and Poon, 1985).

According to LaRue (1992), the types of linguistic error made by elderly participants include: circumlocutions (giving inaccurate multi-word responses), nominalisations (describing functions not objects), perceptual errors (misidentifying stimuli) and semantic association errors (naming an object/feature associated with a target object). The elderly may also have difficulty in comprehending and initiating grammatically complex sentences (Kemper, 1992). Reasons for these – and other, memory impairments – are discussed below.

Why does cognitive ability decline?

The evidence discussed so far indicates that cognitive ability, especially certain types of memory, declines with age. But is this the case? Ritchie (1997), for example, distinguishes between behaviour that is ageing-related and age-related. Ageing-related processes are the result of ageing; age-related processes occur only at a specific age. Huntington's chorea, which we discussed in Chapter 3, is age – not ageing related, for example. Is the decline seen in the elderly, therefore, not the result of ageing but of other age-related illnesses? Some European longitudinal data suggests that ageing may not be a factor (Ritchie *et al.*, 1996; Leibovici *et al.*, 1996). These researchers found that when controlling for physical illness, depression and signs of dementia, participants' cognitive performance improved over three years. They suggest that the decline that is commonly reported is due to pathology not ageing per se.

Similarly, Salthouse (1992, 1993) has argued that the elderly perform more poorly at cognitive tasks because they become slower at performing them. If individual differences in speed are partialled out of these studies, then age-related differences disappear (Salthouse and Babcock, 1991). In fact, ageing could account for less than 1–2 per cent of the variance seen in such studies (Salthouse, 1993).

However, such an explanation could not account for the findings from prospective memory studies. Prospective memory tasks do not rely on speed but on retention of information for future use. It is possible that timed tasks impair the ability of the elderly. This was evident in experiments where participants could name famous faces if given enough time. Training also appears to be an important factor. In one study, older participants played video games for two hours a week for seven weeks or played no such games. Those who had played were faster at an experimental reaction time task than those who had not, and were also faster on several difficulty levels (Clark *et al.*, 1987). Another factor which can help to protect against certain types of cognitive impairment is education. In one Australian study of elderly blue collar workers and academics, degree of education was associated with stable crystallised intelligence but not other types of cognitive ability (Christensen *et al.*, 1997). A Dutch study has also shown that education was associated with a slower rate of memory decline (Schmand *et al.*, 1997). Another American study reported that the risk of developing dementia decreased by 17 per cent for each year of education (D.A. Evans *et al.*, 1997).

The environment of the individual also contributes to the stability or decline of cognition. Individuals with cognitive impairment were three times as likely to be living in community health care institutions (Graham *et al.*, 1997). Holland and Rabbitt (1991) found that when elderly participants were allowed ten minutes to recall autobiographical memories from each third of their lives, participants living in the community recalled significantly more memories from the recent than the remote period, in contrast to those in residential care who recalled more memories from the earliest period.

But why does such slowing occur in the first place? Why is memory performance one of the most consistently affected cognitive abilities? One suggestion is that cognitive decline is the result of changes in the central nervous system (Lowe and Rabbitt, 1997). In particular, researchers have focused on the hippocampus and the frontal cortex. There is a considerable loss in frontal lobe tissue over the course of the lifespan – around 17 per cent between the ages of 20 and 80 (Mittenberg *et al.*, 1989; West, 1996). One recent PET study compared the encoding and retrieval of word pairs in young (mean age 26) and old (70 and over) adults (Cabeza *et al.*, 1997). The young participants showed greater left prefrontal activation during encoding and right prefrontal activation during retrieval compared with the old sample. In fact, the old sample showed little frontal activation during encoding and more bilateral activation during retrieval. This pattern of activity suggested to the experimenters that the stimuli had been inefficiently processed or encoded. Other cognitive studies show that when material is learned thoroughly, then ageing has little effect on retrieval (Woodruff-Pak, 1997) although no neuro-imaging study has explored this yet.

At the neural level, one might expect gross changes in the language areas. This would explain the deficits seen on some language tasks. However, little change occurs in the language areas of the elderly. This has led some researchers to suggest that this ageing-related impairment is not due to ineffective language processing but to deficiencies in attention, perception, speed, memory and executive function (Glosser and Deser, 1992).

Dementia

Dementia refers to the gradual and relentless decline in cognitive ability and is characterised by impairment in short-term and long-term memory. There may also be confusion, change in personality and impaired abstract thinking and judgement. There are various types of dementia such as **dementia of the Alzheimer's type** (DAT, the commonest type), vascular dementia (the second commonest, caused by stroke), Pick's disease dementia and Lewy body dementia (both are characterised by neural abnormality). There are many causes of dementia: the most common is Alzheimer's disease. It is important to differentiate between Alzheimer's disease and DAT: the former is the disease, the latter is the psychological consequence of this illness.

Dementia of the Alzheimer's type

Alzheimer's disease is a degenerative disorder which occurs in approximately 45 per cent of demented patients in the United States (Cummings and Benson, 1992) and with an estimated prevalence of 3.75 million worldwide (Stuss and Levine, 1996). It has been estimated that between 5 and 10 per cent of individuals over 65 years of age will develop the disease (Rocca *et al.*, 1986; Ritchie, 1997). There is a genetic form of the disease which is autosomal dominant with the gene thought to be carried on chromosome 21 or 19 (or both). Evidence from Scandinavian studies suggests that the heritability of Alzheimer's disease is between 0.6 and 0.75 (Bergem *et al.*, 1997; Gatz *et al.*, 1997). The E4 allele also appears to be a risk factor in Alzheimer's disease and dementia arising from stroke (Farrer *et al.*, 1997; Slooter *et al.*, 1997).

The disease was named after Alois Alzheimer at the beginning of the century who reported the case of a 56 year old female patient who exhibited cognitive impairment as a result of abnormal brain formations. These formations are the characteristics of Alzheimer's disease and include (1) neurofibrillary tangles, abnormal proteins which are found in various parts of the patient's brain, especially the temporal, parietal and frontal cortices (Foster *et al.*, 1997), and (2) senile plaques, abnormal nerve cell processes which surround the protein and are found in the cortex. You can see these illustrated in Figures 11.18(a) and (b).

There is also neuron loss in Alzheimer's disease. The frontal and temporal gyri are thought to shrink by

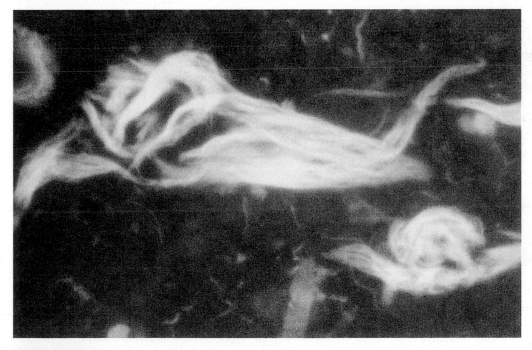

Source: Beatty, J. (1995). *Principles of Behavioral Neuroscience*. New York: Brown and Benchmark/William C. Brown Communications Inc. Copyright © 1995. Reproduced with permission of The McGraw-Hill Companies.

Figure 11.18

(a) One of the neurofibrillary tangles that characterises brain cell abnormality in Alzheimer's disease.

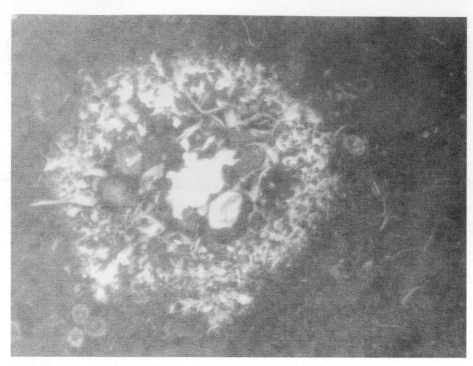

Figure 11.18

Images showing two of the characteristic neural features of Alzheimer's disease.
(b) The senile plaques seen in the nerve cell of a brain attacked by Alzheimer's disease.

Source: Beatty, J. (1995). *Principles of Behavioral Neuroscience*. New York: Brown and Benchmark/William C. Brown Communications Inc. Copyright © 1995. Reproduced with permission of The McGraw-Hill Companies.

approximately 20 per cent and there is cell loss in the hippocampus, amygdala and other subcortical areas such as the raphe nuclei and nucleus basalis of Meynert. Figure 11.19 shows how extensive this atrophy can be.

One difficulty in diagnosing Alzheimer's disease is that senile plaques are seen with normal ageing (tangles tend not to be) whereas tangles are seen in other types of dementia (Ritchie, 1997). Although the effects of ageing and dementia may be distinguished by the fact that abnormalities in the elderly affect the superficial cortex, they go much deeper in Alzheimer's disease. There are also biochemical abnormalities seen in Alzheimer's disease. In particular, there is significant loss of certain neurotransmitter pathways linking various brain structures, such as the cerebral cortex and the hippocampus, in Alzheimer's disease.

The major cognitive impairment in Alzheimer's disease is memory loss. Explicit memory is more seriously affected than implicit memory and both short- and long-term memory are impaired. Greene and Hodges (1996a,b), for example, found that patients with Alzheimer's disease performed poorly at naming, identifying and recognising famous faces from the present and past but also found that autobiographical memory declined less rapidly than did public memory (memory for events in public life). The cognitive decline seen in Alzheimer's patients is much more severe than that seen in disease-free individuals during normal ageing.

Is Alzheimer's disease reversible? At the moment, there is no cure for the disease. The drugs available help to combat various aspects of the dementia such as verbal and non-verbal memory (Thal, 1992). There is early research with animals which suggests that grafting new neural tissue to replace the defective, diseased tissue may be effective in reducing the symptoms of the disease (Sinden *et al.*, 1995). However, because the areas of the brain affected in Alzheimer's disease are many, this intervention may not be totally effective.

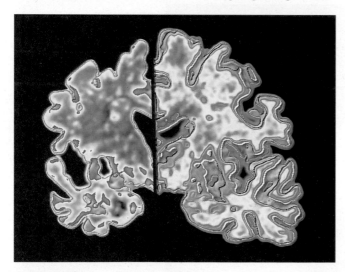

Figure 11.19

Alzheimer's disease. A computer-enhanced photograph of a slice through the brain of a person who died of Alzheimer's disease (left) and a normal brain (right). Note that the grooves (sulci and fissures) are especially wide in the Alzheimer's brain, indicating degeneration of the brain.

Source: Alfred Pasieka/Science Photo Library/Photo Researchers Inc.

Questions to think about

Thinking

- What are the principal differences between inductive and deductive reasoning?

- Which brain regions are most involved in problem solving? Why should these regions be involved?

- Given that not all creative individuals exhibit psychopathological characteristics, how strong is the link between creativity and mental disorder?

- Are the effects of ageing on cognitive ability selective?

- Is the intellectual decline that sometimes characterises normal ageing, relentless?

- What are the best methods of preventing cognitive decline that accompanies ageing?

Key terms

intelligence *p.*356
g factor *p.*356
s factor *p.*356
factor analysis *p.*357
triarchic theory *p.*359
componential intelligence *p.*359
experiential intelligence *p.*359
contextual intelligence *p.*360
Binet–Simon Scale *p.*366
norms *p.*366
mental age *p.*366

Stanford–Binet Scale *p.*366
intelligence quotient (IQ) *p.*366
ratio IQ *p.*366
deviation IQ *p.*366
Wechsler Adult Intelligence Scale (WAIS) *p.*367
Wechsler Intelligence Scale for Children (WISC) *p.*367
heritability *p.*368
h *p.*369
c *p.*369

foetal alcohol syndrome *p.*369
concepts *p.*375
formal concepts *p.*376
natural concepts *p.*378
exemplars *p.*378
basic-level concepts *p.*378
superordinate concepts *p.*378
subordinate concepts *p.*378
deductive reasoning *p.*379
mental models *p.*380
inductive reasoning *p.*381
confirmation bias *p.*383

somatic marker hypothesis *p.*383
algorithms *p.*385
heuristics *p.*385
means–ends analysis *p.*385
creativity *p.*385
psychoticism *p.*387
gerontology *p.*388
metamemory *p.*389
prospective memory *p.*389
dementia *p.*391
dementia of the Alzheimer's type *p.*391
Alzheimer's disease *p.*391

CHAPTER REVIEW

Theories of intelligence

- Although intelligence is often represented by a single score, IQ, modern investigators do not deny the existence of specific abilities. What is controversial is whether a general factor also exists.

- Factor analysis is a data reduction technique that attempts to explain a large amount of data with reference to one or two factors.

- Spearman argued that a general intelligence factor existed (which he called *g*) and demonstrated that people's scores on a variety of specific tests of ability were correlated. He also believed that specific factors (*s* factors) also existed.

- Thurstone performed a factor analysis on 56 individual tests that revealed the existence of seven factors, not a single *g* factor.

- Cattell's factor analysis on such data obtained two factors. The nature of the tests that loaded heavily on these two factors suggested the names fluid intelligence (*g*f) and crystallised intelligence (*g*c), with the former representing a person's native ability and the latter representing what a person learns.

- Sternberg's triarchic theory of intelligence attempts to integrate laboratory research using the information processing approach and an analysis of intelligent behaviour in the natural environment.

- According to Sternberg, we use componential intelligence to plan and execute tasks. We use experiential intelligence to apply past strategies to new problems. Finally, we use contextual intelligence to adapt to, select, or shape our environment.

- Gardner's multiple intelligences theory is based primarily on the types of skill that can be selectively lost through brain damage. His definition of intelligence includes many abilities that are commonly regarded as skills or talents.

- Like Sternberg's theory, Gardner's theory emphasises the significance of behaviours to the culture in which they occur.

- There are sex differences in ability and in the perception of ability. The most robust sex difference in ability concerns mental rotation; males are better at this than are females. The most consistent difference in perception is that men overestimate their own IQ and that both sexes rate their fathers and male children as having higher IQs that their mothers or female children.

Intelligence testing

- Although the earliest known instance of ability testing was carried out by the Ancient Chinese, modern intelligence testing dates from the efforts of Galton to measure individual differences.

- Galton made an important contribution to the field of measurement, but his tests of simple perceptual abilities were abandoned in favour of tests that attempt to assess more complex abilities, such as memory, logical reasoning and vocabulary.

- Binet developed a test that was designed to assess students' intellectual abilities in order to identify children with special educational needs.

- Although the test that superseded his, the Stanford–Binet Scale, provided for calculation of IQ, Binet believed that 'intelligence' was actually a composite of several specific abilities. For him, the concept of mental age was a convenience, not a biological reality.

- Wechsler's two intelligence tests, the WAIS-R for adults and the WISC-R for children, are the most widely used tests of intelligence. The WAIS-R has two scales: performance and verbal; each scale is made up of subscales.

- The reliability of modern intelligence tests is excellent, but assessing their validity is still difficult. Because no single criterion measure of intelligence exists, intelligence tests are validated by comparing the scores with measures of achievement, such as scholastic success.

- Intelligence tests can have both good and bad effects on the people who take them. The principal benefit is derived by identifying children with special needs (or special talents) who will profit from special programmes.

The roles of heredity and environment

- Variability in all physical traits is determined by a certain amount of genetic variability, environmental variability, and an interaction between genetic and environmental factors.

- The degree to which genetic variability is responsible for the observed variability of a particular trait in a particular population is called heritability or h.

- Heritability is not an indication of the degree to which the trait is determined by biological factors; rather, it reflects the relative proportions of genetic and environmental variability found in a particular population.

- Intellectual development is affected by many factors, both prenatal and postnatal. Potential intelligence can be permanently reduced during prenatal or postnatal development by injury, toxic chemicals, poor nutrition or disease.

- Twin studies and studies comparing biological and adoptive relatives indicate that both genetic and environmental factors affect intellectual ability, which is probably not surprising. These studies also point out that not all of a person's environment is shared by other members of the family; each person is an individual and is exposed to different environmental variables.

- The evidence suggests that biological children who are adopted are intellectually more like their biological parents; this finding applies across all age ranges.

- Although there are differences between races in terms of IQ score, it is unclear whether this is due to heredity. There are also problems in defining race.

- Music can affect thinking and decision making ability.

- The ingestion of food has variable effects on intellectual ability; breakfast seems to confer some cognitive advantage although results are mixed.

Thinking

- Formal concepts are defined as lists of essential characteristics of objects and events. In everyday life, we use natural concepts – collections of memories of particular examples, called exemplars.

- Concepts exist at the basic, subordinate and superordinate levels. We do most of our thinking about concepts at the basic level.

- Deductive reasoning consists of inferring specific instances from general principles.

- One of the most important skills in deductive reasoning is the ability to construct mental models that represent problems.

- Inductive reasoning involves inferring general principles from particular facts. This form of thinking involves generating and testing hypotheses.

- Without special training (such as learning the rules of the scientific method), people often ignore relevant information, ignore the necessity of control groups or show a confirmation bias – the tendency to look only for evidence that confirms one's hypothesis.

- Problem solving is best represented spatially: we follow a path in the problem space from the initial state to the goal state, using operators to get to each intermediate state. Sometimes a problem fits a particular mould and can be solved with an algorithm – a cut-and-dried set of operations.

- However, in most cases, a problem must be attacked by following a heuristic – a general rule that helps guide our search for a path to the solution of a problem. The most general heuristic is means–ends analysis, which involves taking steps that reduce the distance from the current state to the goal. If obstacles are encountered, subgoals are created and attempts are made to reach them.

- There is a general decline in cognitive ability after young adulthood; although various types of memory decline, the acquisition and retention of vocabulary remains intact.

- Prospective memory requires the individual to hold information in memory for later use; this is impaired in elderly individuals.

- Dementia is the gradual and insidious loss of cognitive function with age. The commonest form is dementia of the Alzheimer's type (DAT) and is caused by brain abnormalities involving excess protein deposits. The second commonest type (vascular dementia) results from stroke.

Suggestions for further reading

Neisser, U., Boodoo, G., Bouchard, T.J., Boykin, W.A., Brody, N., Ceci, S., Halpern, D.F. , Loehlin, J.C., Perloff, R., Sternberg, R.J. and Urbina, S. (1996). Intelligence: Knowns and unknowns. *American Psychologist*, 51, 2, 77–101.

Plomin, R. and DeFries, J.C. (1998). The genetics of cognitive abilities and disabilities. *Scientific American*, 287, 5, 40–47.

Plomin, R., DeFries, J.C., McClearn, G.E. and Rutter, M. (1997). *Behavioural Genetics* (3rd edition). New York: Freeman.

Sternberg, R.J. and Grigorenko, E. (1997). *Intelligence, Heredity and Environment*. New York: Cambridge University Press.
A good starting point for further reading in intelligence is Neisser et al.'s report on what we do and do not know about intelligence. Although later correspondence in American Psychologist *noted some omissions in the review, it is still a good, brief tour of various aspects of intelligence, including heredity, race, sex and intervention programmes. A follow-up text could be Sternberg and Grigorenko. This is a collection of (sometimes very detailed) chapters dealing with all aspects of environment, heredity and intelligence. Heredity is dealt with specifically in Plomin and DeFries's very good article in* Scientific American *and in greater depth in Plomin et al.'s book.*

Scientific American (1998). *Exploring Intelligence*. New York: Scientific American.
This is one of Scientific American's *special editions which features specialist scientists writing about issues of scientific interest. It is an excellent, popular-science account of almost every aspect of intelligence, from intelligence testing and 'smart' drugs to animal and computer intelligence.*

Halpern, D.F. (1997). Sex differences in intelligence. *American Psychologist*, 2, 10, 1091–1102.
For a good introduction to the complex area of sex differences in cognitive ability, Halpern's article is well recommended.

Garnham, A. and Oakhill, J. (1994). *Thinking and Reasoning*. Oxford: Blackwell.

Gilhooly, K. (1996). *Thinking: Directed, undirected and creative*. Oxford: Academic Press.

Newstead, S. and St B.T. Evans, J. (1995). *Perspectives on Thinking and Reasoning*. Hove, UK: The Psychology Press.
These three books provide a good coverage of all the major aspects of thinking.

Oakhill, J. and Garnham, A. (1996). *Mental Models in Cognitive Science*. Hove, UK: The Psychology Press.
Specific chapters in honour of Phillip Johnson-Laird make up this book which offers a distillation of current thinking on the role of mental models in thinking.

Eysenck, H.J. (1996). The measurement of creativity. In M.A. Boden (ed.), *Dimensions of Creativity*. Cambridge, MA: MIT Press.
Eysenck provides a highly readable account of the problems psychologists have faced in trying to study creativity.

Woodruff-Pak, D.S. (1997). *The Neuropsychology of Aging*. Oxford: Blackwell.
This is an excellent introduction to the effect of ageing on intelligence and thinking and has chapters devoted to each of the main cognitive functions.

Journals to consult

Aging and Psychology
Current Directions in Psychological Science
European Journal of Cognitive Psychology
European Psychologist
Intelligence
Journal of Experimental Psychology
Nature
Personality and Individual Differences
Psychological Science
Quarterly Journal of Experimental Psychology
Science
Thinking and Reasoning

Website addresses

http://www.scbe.on.ca/mit/mi.htm
A site focusing on Gardener's theory of multiple intelligences. Also has links to other intelligence sites.

http://www.skeptic.com/03.3.fm-sternberg-interview.html
An interview with Professor Robert Sternberg in which he discusses the impact of The Bell Curve *and the role of genetics/environment in intelligence.*

http://www.uwsp.edu/acad/educ/lwilson/LEARNING/index.htm
A collection of links to creative thinking websites, as well as links to major theories in intelligence.

12

DEVELOPMENTAL PSYCHOLOGY

As I watched five-year-old Keith in the waiting room of my office, I could see why his parents said he was having such a tough time in kindergarten. He hopped from chair to chair, swinging his arms and legs restlessly, and then began to fiddle with the light switches, turning the lights on and off again to everyone's annoyance – all the while talking non-stop. When his mother encouraged him to join a group of other children busy in the playroom, Keith butted into a game that was already in progress and took over, causing the other children to complain of his bossiness and drift away to other activities. Even when Keith had the toys to himself, he fidgeted aimlessly with them and seemed unable to entertain himself quietly.

Source: Barkley, 1998

OVERVIEW

Human development is a series of changes that occurs to each of us during our lives. We can see different parts of the cycle by looking at our grandparents, our parents, our friends, and our children. At one time, psychologists studied development from birth through childhood. But we have learned that developmental processes do not stop there. Growing older is a matter not only of ageing, but also of changing – personally, intellectually and socially.

Developmental psychology studies these changes. This chapter discusses how major psychological functions, such as perception, thinking, emotion, morality and socialisation, develop from birth onwards.

What you should be able to do after reading Chapter 12

- Describe the stages of psychological development from birth.
- Understand the nature of foetal development and learning.
- Understand the nature of infant perception, memory and cognition.
- Describe the psychological changes that occur during adolescence and adulthood and attempt to explain these.

Questions to think about

- How does a child learn to think and perceive?
- What are the most important psychological functions a child needs?
- How valid are categories such as 'adolescence' and 'infancy'?
- How does the child interpret the perceptual world?
- What are childhood disorders and what causes them?
- Do children have a 'theory of mind'?

Developmental psychology

Apart from conception, development is probably the most astonishing thing we do. From birth to around late adolescence, we develop from a fairly unsophisticated bundle of reflexes and crude cognition to a fantastically efficient organism that can use language, perceive depth, colour, shape and motion, walk, run and jump, drive a car, or parachute from a plane, become a novelist, mathematician or physicist. There is an impressively rapid development of sensory, perceptual, social and cognitive ability during infancy and childhood and this, together with the further development of these abilities in adolescence and adulthood, is the subject matter of developmental psychology.

Developmental psychologists study both the similarities and the differences among people as they develop and change over the course of their life. The major developmental periods are prenatal, infancy and childhood, adolescence, adulthood and old age, and the milestones of each stage are summarised in Table 12.1. The chapter begins with the earliest of these stages: prenatal development.

Prenatal development

The nine months between conception and birth is called the prenatal period. The length of a normal human pregnancy is 266 days, or 38 weeks. The prenatal period involves three developmental stages: the zygote, the embryo and the foetal stages.

Stages of prenatal development

Conception, or the union of the ovum (egg) and sperm, is the starting point for prenatal development. During the zygote stage, which lasts about two weeks, the zygote, or the cell that is formed at conception, divides many times and the internal organs begin to form. By the end of the first week, the zygote consists of about one hundred cells. Many of the cells are arranged in two layers, one for the skin, hair, nervous system and sensory organs, and the other for the digestive and respiratory systems and glands. Near the end of this stage, a third layer of cells appears, those that will eventually develop into the circulatory and excretory systems and muscles.

The second stage of prenatal development, the embryo stage, begins at about two weeks and ends about eight weeks after conception (see Figure 12.1).

During this stage, the zygote is transformed into an embryo and development occurs at an incredibly rapid pace. Within a month after conception, a heart has begun to beat, a tiny brain has started to function, and most of the major body structures are beginning to form. By the end of this stage, the major features that define the human body – the arms, hands, fingers, legs, toes, shoulders, head and eyes – are discernible. Behaviourally, the embryo can react reflexively to stimulation. For example, if the mouth is stimulated, the embryo moves its upper body and neck. This stage is also noteworthy because it is now that the embryo is most susceptible to chemicals that can cause birth defects, including drugs such as alcohol or toxins produced by diseases such as German measles. These substances are called teratogens (from the Greek *teras*, meaning 'monster').

Sexual development begins during the embryo stage. The determining factor for sex is the Y chromosome, which is contributed by the male parent at conception. If it is present, the embryo will become a male (XY); if it is not, it will become a female (XX). Early in prenatal development, the embryo develops a pair of gonads that will become either ovaries or testes (the word 'gonad' comes from the

Table 12.1 Phases of the lifespan

Phase	Approximate age	Highlights
1 Prenatal	Conception through birth	Rapid physical development of both nervous system and body
2 Infancy	Birth to 2 years	Motor development; attachment to primary caregiver
3 Childhood	1½ years to 12 years	Increasing ability to think logically and reason abstractly; refinement of motor skills; peer influences
4 Adolescence	13 years to about 20 years	Thinking and reasoning becomes more adultlike; identity crisis; continued peer influences
5 Adulthood	20 years to 65 years	Love, marriage, career; stability and then decrease in physical abilities
6 Old age	65 years to death	Reflection on life's work and accomplishments; physical health deteriorates; prepare for death; death

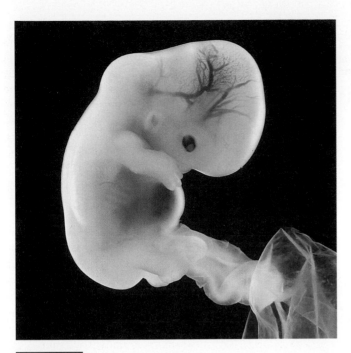

Figure 12.1

As this photograph of a 6-week old foetus illustrates, most of the major features that define the human body are present near the end of the embryonic stage of development (which starts at about 2 weeks and ends about 8 weeks after conception).

Source: © Tony Stone Images. Reproduced with permission.

Greek *gonos*, meaning 'procreation'). If a Y chromosome is present, a gene located on it causes the production of a chemical signal that makes the gonads develop into testes. Otherwise, the gonads become ovaries.

The development of the other sex organs is determined by the presence or absence of testes. If testes are present, they begin secreting a class of sex hormones known as androgens (*andros* in Greek means 'man'; *gennan* means 'to produce'). The most important androgen is testosterone. Androgens bring about the development of the male internal sex organs, the penis and the scrotum. Thus, these hormones are absolutely necessary for the development of a male. In contrast, the development of female sex organs (uterus, vagina and labia) occurs naturally, it does not need to be stimulated by a hormone. If the gonads completely fail to develop, the foetus becomes female, with normal female sex organs. Of course, lacking ovaries, such a person cannot produce ova. See Figure 12.2.

The final stage of prenatal development is the foetal stage, which lasts about seven months. It officially begins with the appearance of bone cells and ends with birth. At the end of the second month of pregnancy, the foetus is about 3 centimetres long and weighs about 28 grammes.

By the end of the third month, the development of major organs is completed and the bones and muscles are beginning to develop. The foetus is now 7–8 centimetres long and weighs about 90 grammes. The foetus may show some movement, especially kicking.

By the end of the fourth month, the foetus is about 18 centimetres long and weighs about 180 grammes. It is also now sleeping and waking regularly. Foetal movements also become strong enough to be felt by the mother, and the heartbeat is strong enough to be heard through a stethoscope. During the sixth month, the foetus grows to over 33 centimetres long and weighs almost 1 kilogram. The seventh month is a critical month because if the foetus is born prematurely at this point, it has a fair chance of surviving. However, foetuses mature at different rates, and some 7-month old foetuses may be mature enough to survive while others may not.

During the last two months of prenatal development, the foetus gains weight at the rate of about 0.2 kilograms per week. On average, the foetus is about 50 centimetres long and weighs about 2.8 kilograms at the end of this period. The foetus is now ready to be born.

Threats to normal prenatal development

Under normal conditions, the prenatal environment provides just the right supply of nutrients to the foetus. Probably the single most important factor in the foetus's development is the mother's diet: the food she eats is the foetus's only source of nutrition. If the mother is extremely malnourished, the foetus's nervous system develops abnormally, and it may be born mentally retarded.

In addition to poor diet, teratogens can also cause birth defects. Psychologists who study birth defects are very interested in how drugs affect the foetus, because taking drugs is a behaviour that is directly under the control of the mother. Certain antibiotics, especially when taken in large quantities over long periods, can produce foetal defects. For example, tetracycline, a common antibiotic, can cause irregularities in the bones and discoloration of the teeth. Certain tranquillisers may produce a cleft palate. Heroin and cocaine produce more dramatic effects. If a pregnant woman is addicted to heroin, her baby is likely to be born addicted. The baby will show withdrawal symptoms, such as hyperactivity, irritability and tremors. The symptoms make the baby harder to care for, which, in turn, makes attachment between mother and baby difficult.

A pregnant woman's cigarette smoking is another behaviour that can affect the foetus. The carbon monoxide contained in cigarette smoke reduces the supply of oxygen to the foetus. Reduced oxygen levels are particularly harmful to the foetus during the last half of pregnancy when the foetus is developing most rapidly and its demand for

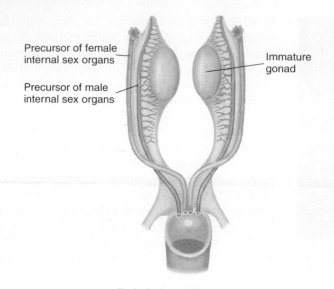

Early in Foetal Development

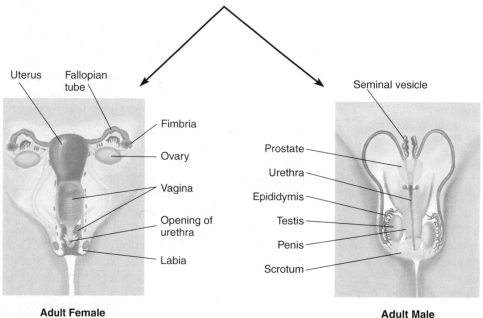

Adult Female

Adult Male

Figure 12.2

Differentiation and development of the sex organs.

oxygen is greatest. The main effects of mothers' smoking are increased rate of miscarriages, low birthweight babies and increased chance of premature birth.

Although a woman's regular use of any psychoactive drug during her pregnancy is likely to have harmful effects on the foetus, alcohol use during pregnancy has been most widely studied (Coles *et al.*, 1992). Collectively, these effects, including both pre – and postnatal growth deficits, deformations of the eyes and mouth, brain and central nervous system abnormalities, and heart deformation, are known as foetal alcohol syndrome (FAS). The likelihood of stunted growth is doubled if a woman drinks. Drinking as little as two ounces of alcohol a day early in pregnancy can produce some symptoms of FAS (Astley *et al.*, 1992). Even if children with FAS are reared in healthy environments with regular, nutritious meals, their physical and intellectual development still falls short of that of normal children (Hanson *et al.*, 1976).

Controversies in psychological science

Does foetal learning exist?

The issue

We assume that most development (cognitive, social and emotional) occurs from birth onwards. However, research suggests that learning could occur before then, in the womb. This is called foetal learning. The idea that the foetus can learn in the womb is controversial. It is clear that the foetus is active and that it is responsive to its external environment. The important question, however, is whether such activity is nothing but activity or represents meaningful behaviour which is characteristic of learning.

The evidence

One of the earliest studies of foetal behaviour was reported by Pieper in 1925. Using a very simple paradigm, he reported that when a hand was placed on the pregnant woman's abdomen and a car horn was sounded, foetal movement was detected 25–30 per cent of the time. Most of the research since has focused on the responsivity of the foetus to sensory stimulation (Kisilevsky and Low, 1998). For example, the foetus has been exposed to sound and vibration while bodily movement and foetal heart rate (FHR) were measured. Using these measures, responses to auditory stimuli have been elicited from 37–42 week old foetuses (Schmidt *et al.*, 1985) and FHR responses have been detected in foetuses as young as 29 weeks (Kisilevsky and Low, 1998; Kisilevsky, 1995). Movement has also been reported in 24–26 week old foetuses about 1–5 seconds after stimulus onset (Shahidullah and Hepper, 1993).

These findings suggest that the foetus is certainly active and may even respond to events outside the womb. The finding that body movement and FHR movement occur as a reaction to acoustic stimuli suggests that the foetus's auditory or vestibular system is working at a level that is better than rudimentary. Whether such activity represents meaningful behaviour, however, is questionable. Is the foetus responding to the acoustic stimuli because it is stimulated by the noise or is it simply showing a reflex action resulting, perhaps, from the vibration caused by the noise? In order to demonstrate that the behaviour is meaningful and that the foetus is capable or rudimentary cognition, we need to be able to demonstrate that other responses occur such as preference for specific stimuli or habituation to repeatedly presented stimuli (Kisilevsky and Low, 1998).

One source of evidence which suggests that foetuses are capable of discrimination (and, therefore, some form of elementary cognition) comes from studies of heart deceleration (or reduction). Deceleration of heart rate is thought to be a good measure of attention; a stimulus which impinges on the foetus's attentional radar is usually accompanied by a reduction in heart rate (Lecanuert *et al.*, 1992). Experiments have shown that such deceleration is seen in response to the discrimination of sound. For example, Lecanuert *et al.* (1989) found that heart rate decelerated when the stimulus exposed to the foetus changed from the word 'babi' to 'biba'. This evidence, then, suggests that the foetus is capable of discriminating between phonetic stimuli, at least as measured by heart rate.

Another measure which should demonstrate evidence of foetal learning is dishabituation – the renewed responding to a stimulus after a response has declined (Hepper, 1994). Habituation and dishabituation involve a degree of sensory discrimination because some stimuli will activate a response and others will not. How can such behaviours be measured postnatally?

One paradigm involves 'non-nutritive sucking', that is, measuring the degree of sucking a baby makes when it is exposed to an experimental and control stimulus – greater sucking is meant to indicate greater interest or attention. Using this technique, researchers have found that infants prefer the mother's voice and melodies exposed to the child when it was in the womb (DeCasper and Fifer, 1980), as well as stories told to it (DeCasper *et al.*, 1994).

Another aspect of learning that appears to occur in the womb is olfactory learning. This has been demonstrated by the finding that neonates are attracted to the odour of amniotic fluid (Schaal *et al.*, 1995). Given a choice between a breast covered in amniotic fluid and a control fluid, neonates chose to suckle on the nipple coated with amniotic fluid (Winberg and Porter, 1998). Even the mother's eating pattern can influence this 'learning'. Mothers who were garlic eaters gave birth to infants who recognised the odour of garlic (Hepper, 1995).

Conclusion

Does all of this evidence suggest that the foetus is capable of cognition? This depends on what we mean by cognition. If this means the ability to discriminate between

Continued overleaf

stimuli, then the neonates have demonstrated cognitive ability. They may be able to distinguish between the phonetic patterns in two stories, one of which was read to them when they were in the womb, but they clearly did not learn anything about the content or meaning of the story. Their learning was at a basic, perhaps even reflex, level. The auditory system may have sensed the phonetic nature of the story, but the neonate may not have been consciously aware of this sensation.

Whether exposure to specific stimuli (such as Shakespeare or Mozart) would help a foetus become more intelligent after birth is probably an even more controversial idea. There is no evidence for this at present and so any speculation as to a potential mechanism is exactly that – speculation. The evidence we have, however, seems to suggest that the foetus is not simply an inactive, non-behaving organism.

Questions to think about

Prenatal development

- What can influence the development of the foetus?

- What measures can the mother take to produce a healthy foetus?

- To what extent do you think can foetal learning be described as 'learning'?

- Would exposing a foetus to classical music or literary classics result in greater cognitive development when the child is born? Assuming that it did, how do you think this would work?

Physical and perceptual development in infancy and childhood

Babies are called infants until two years of age. A newborn human infant is a helpless creature, absolutely dependent on adult care. But recent research has shown that newborns interact proactively, not simply passively, with their carers. They quickly develop skills that shape the behaviour of the adults with whom they interact.

Motor development

At birth, the infant's most important movements are reflexes – automatic movements in response to specific stimuli. The most important reflexes are the rooting, sucking, and swallowing responses. If a baby's cheek is lightly touched, he or she will turn the head towards the direction of the touch (the rooting response). If the object makes contact with the baby's lips, the baby will open the mouth and begin sucking. When milk or any other liquid enters

the mouth, the baby will automatically make swallowing movements. These reflexes are important for the baby's survival and for an infant's social development.

Normal motor development follows a distinct pattern, which appears to be dictated by maturation of the muscles and the nervous system. Maturation refers to any relatively stable change in thought, behaviour or physical growth that is due to the ageing process and not to experience. Although individual children progress at different rates, their development follows the same basic maturational pattern (see Figure 12.3). Development of motor skills requires two ingredients: maturation of the child's nervous system and practice. Development of the nervous system is not complete at birth; considerable growth occurs during the first several months (Dekaban, 1970). In fact, some changes are still taking place in early adulthood.

Particular kinds of movement must await the development of the necessary neuromuscular systems. But motor development is not merely a matter of using these systems once they develop. Instead, physical development of the nervous system depends, to a large extent, on the baby's own movements while interacting with the environment. In turn, more complex movements depend on further development of the nervous system – different steps in motor development are both a cause of further development and an effect of previous development (Thelen, 1995).

Perceptual development

If we want to study how older children or adults perceive the world, we can simply ask them about their experiences. We can determine how large an object must be for them to see it or how loud a sound must be for them to hear it. But we cannot talk to infants and expect to get any answers; we must use their non-verbal behaviour as an indicator of what they can perceive.

Newborn infants indicate their taste preferences by facial expression and by choosing to swallow or not to swallow different liquids. When an infant is given a sweet liquid, the face relaxes in an expression rather like a smile;

Lifts head up
2 months

Rolls over
2½ months

Sits propped up
3 months

Sits without support
6 months

Stands holding on
6½ months

Walks holding on
9 months

Stands momentarily
10 months

Stands alone
11 months

Walks alone
12 months

Walks backwards
14 months

Walks up steps
14 months

Kicks ball
20 months

Figure 12.3

Milestones in a child's motor development.

Source: Adapted from Shirley, M.M., *The First Two Years. Vol. 2: Intellectual Development.* Minneapolis: University of Minnesota Press, 1933.

but when it is given a sour or bitter liquid, the face indicates displeasure. Newborn infants can even learn to recognise particular odours. Sullivan *et al.* (1991) presented one day old infants with a citrus odour and then gently stroked them. The next day, these infants (but not control infants) turned towards a cotton swab containing the odour that had been paired with the stroking.

Most investigations of the perceptual abilities of newborn infants have taken advantage of the fact that babies have good control of movements of their head, eyes, and mouth. We will look at the results of some of these studies next.

Perception of patterns

The visual perceptual abilities of infants can be studied by observing their eye movements as visual stimuli are shown to them. A harmless spot of infrared light, invisible to humans, is directed onto the baby's eyes. A special television camera, sensitive to infrared light, records the spot and superimposes it on an image of the display that the baby is looking at. The technique is precise enough to determine which parts of a stimulus the baby is scanning. For example, Salapatek (1975) reported that a one month old infant tends not to look at the inside of a figure. Instead, the

baby's gaze seems to be 'trapped' by the edges. By the age of two months, the baby scans across the border to investigate the interior of a figure. Before the age of two years, infants seem to be more concerned with the contours of visual stimuli and rarely attend to internal features. This is called the **externality effect** (Bushnell, 1979). One reason for the externality effect could be that the infant's visual system is developing and does not possess the acuity or contrast sensitivity (the ability to discriminate between degrees of shade) necessary to perceive complex stimuli.

The work by Salapatek and his colleagues suggests that at the age of one or two months, babies are probably not perceiving complete shapes; their scanning strategy is limited to fixations on a few parts of the object at which they are looking. However, by three months, babies show clear signs of pattern recognition. For example, they prefer to look at stimuli that resemble the human face over stimuli that do not (Rosser, 1994).

Face perception at birth

As we saw in Chapter 8, perceiving and recognising faces seems to rely on different perceptual mechanisms from those that allow us to recognise and perceive objects. One of the earliest examples of the infant's ability to discriminate between visual stimuli is face perception. At two years of age, infants show a preference for natural face arrangements (as opposed to face arrangements that have disorganised features), which suggests that they have become familiar with the human face (Fantz, 1961). There are two hypotheses regarding the way in which young infants perceive faces and other visual stimuli. The first, the *sensory hypothesis*, suggests that visual perception occurs in two stages (Kleiner, 1993). The first involves the infant comparing stimuli for contrast. If these stimuli are similar, then a second stage – the analysis of structure – takes place. This theory, therefore, suggests that if sensory characteristics are similar or identical, then preference for a stimulus will depend on the comparison of structure.

A competing hypothesis, the *structural hypothesis*, suggests that infants show a preference for face-like arrangements over non-face arrangements not because of the differences in the sensory properties of these stimuli but because infants have a specific device that contains information about the structural features of people's faces (Johnson and Morton, 1991). Johnson and Morton referred to this device which allows children to orient towards face-like stimuli as 'conspec'. Conspec is involved in perceiving the spatial relations between features of a face. For example, this device is responsible for perceiving that a cartoon face has elements in the right place to represent the mouth and eyes. Because conspec is a visual/perceptual device, it has a neural basis. This basis lies in the subcortex, specifically the superior colliculus, a structure which guides the infant's attention to visual patterns. Another process allows the infant to learn about faces because they are guided towards paying attention to them – this is called 'conlearn' and is thought to be a cortical function.

Current evidence is inconsistent regarding which hypothesis is correct, although the structural hypothesis has been successfully tested (Valenza *et al.*, 1996). Umilta and his colleagues presented healthy newborns with a variety of different face stimuli in a series of experiments designed to see whether the sensory properties of faces accounted for babies' orienting response or whether the arrangement of features in faces was the most important determinant of orienting (Umilta *et al.*, 1996; Simion *et al.*, 1998). In one experiment, when newborns were presented with two stimuli: one with facial features in correct arrangement, the other in a different order, the babies preferred to look at the correctly arranged stimulus (Umilta *et al.*, 1996). When similar face-like patterns were presented which differed only in their degree of sensory salience (blobs versus striped blobs), babies preferred to look at the striped blobs (see Figure 12.4(b) and (c)). The stimuli can be seen in Figure 12.4(a).

However, in a further experiment, the researchers observed that the babies also preferred stimuli whose sensory properties were pronounced. To test the structural

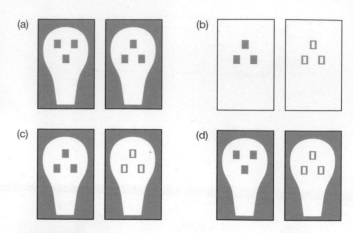

Figure 12.4

The stimuli used in Umilta *et al.*'s experiments: (a) the face- and non-face-like stimuli; (b) stimuli that are not placed in a face-like frame and where one stimulus is more sensorily stimulating (the one on the right); (c) the same stimuli placed in a face-like frame; (d) framed stimuli with face-like arrangement of features (left) or non-face-like arrangement of features (right) that is sensorily stimulating.

Source: Reproduced with permission from Umilta *et al.* (1996) Newborn's preference for faces, *European Psychologist*, 1(3), p. 202. Copyright 1996 by Hogrefe and Huber.

hypothesis in light of this finding, the researchers presented newborns with a face-like stimulus and a non-face-like stimulus which had optimal sensory properties but had features arranged in a different way. The structural hypothesis would state that babies would prefer the correctly-structured face to that which is incorrectly structured but sensorily more stimulating (see Figure 12.4(d)). In this experiment, newborns preferred to look at the face-like stimulus, thus supporting the structural explanation of babies' preference for faces.

Perception of space

The ability to perceive three-dimensional space comes at an early age. Gibson and Walk (1960) placed 6 month old babies on what they called a visual cliff – a platform containing a checkerboard pattern (see Figure 12.5). The platform adjoined a glass shelf mounted several feet over a floor that was also covered by the checkerboard pattern. Most babies who could crawl would not venture out onto the glass shelf. The infants acted as if they were afraid of falling.

As Chapter 6 showed, several different types of cue in the environment contribute to depth perception. One cue arises from the fact that each eye gets a slightly different view of the world (Poggio and Poggio, 1984). This form of depth perception, stereopsis ('solid appearance'), is the kind obtained from a stereoscope or a three-dimensional movie. The brain mechanisms necessary for stereopsis will not develop unless animals have experience of viewing objects with both eyes during a critical period early in life.

Figure 12.5

A visual cliff. The child does not cross the glass bridge.

The term critical period refers to the specific time during which certain experiences must occur if an organism is to develop normally. Many behavioural, perceptual and cognitive abilities are subject to critical periods. For example, as we shall see later in this chapter, if infants are not exposed to a stimulating environment and do not have the opportunity to interact with caregivers during the first two years of their life, their cognitive development will be retarded. As we saw in the previous chapter, if language is not learned before puberty, it is unlikely to be learned at all well. Human development is more than an unfolding of a genetically determined programme. It consists of a continuous interaction between physical maturation and environmental stimulation.

The critical period in the development of stereopsis has important implications for the development of normal vision. If an infant's eyes do not move together properly – if they both are directed towards the same place in the environment (that is, if the eyes are 'crossed') – the infant never develops stereoscopic vision, even if the eye movements are later corrected by surgery on the eye muscles. Banks *et al.* (1975) studied infants whose eye movement deficits were later corrected surgically. Their results show that the critical period ends sometime between 1 and 3 years of age. If surgery occurs before this time, stereoscopic vision will develop. If the surgery occurs later, it will not.

Cognitive development in childhood

As children grow, their nervous systems mature and they undergo new experiences. Perceptual and motor skills develop in complexity and competency. Children learn to recognise particular faces and voices, begin to talk and respond to the speech of others, and learn how to solve problems. Infants as young as 13 months are even able to form memories of specific events (Bauer, 1997). In short, their cognitive capacities develop.

Development of memory in infancy and childhood

Memory development in infancy

Memory is a difficult process to study in infants because they have yet to develop language and cannot give the sophisticated linguistic responses that older children can. It has been suggested that we have difficulty in retrieving memories from this period of our lives (before the age of 4 years) because our verbal ability and our memory structures are not yet sufficiently functional for us to be able to transfer material into long-term memory (Rubin, 1982; Eacott and Crawley, 1998). One year old infants, in particular, show rapid forgetting of material. The 'loss' of memory for events that occurs in infancy is called childhood or infantile amnesia.

Measures of memory in infancy

Because infants do not have sophisticated language, psychologists have studied memory in infants using other paradigms. These include novelty preference, paired-comparison, habituation, operant conditioning and deferred imitation paradigms. Many of these terms will be familiar to you from Chapter 7.

Usually when presented with two stimuli, one of which is familiar and the other novel, infants who are older than 8–10 weeks will look longer at the novel stimulus. This suggests that the infant is capable of being distracted by stimuli which it perceives as new. The perception of a stimulus as new implies that there is a memory of the old stimulus which is used as a comparison.

A version of this task, the paired-comparison task, involves exposing the infant to a stimulus and then, after a short while, presenting it with the pre-exposed stimulus and a novel one. Memory is measured by monitoring the length of time the infant gazes at the stimulus (Fantz, 1958). For successful recognition, the length between the initial presentation and the subsequent recognition task depends on the infant's age. Nine month old infants can recognise a stimulus successfully after a delay of between 90 and 160 seconds, whereas 6 month old infants require a much shorter interval.

Habituation paradigms involve the presentation of stimuli to infants repeatedly until they cease to make an orienting response to it; that is, they begin to ignore it because it does not seem to interest them. Attention tends to be paid to stimuli that are different from those that have been repeatedly presented. The longer the delay between the habituated stimulus and a novel stimulus, the more likely it is that the infant will produce a response to the habituated stimulus.

Operant conditioning makes use of the child's manipulation of mobiles. The child learns that if it moves its foot which is attached to the mobile, then the mobile moves and, therefore, catches its attention. The more vigorous the kicking, the greater the movement of the mobile (Rovee and Rovee, 1969). Technically, this paradigm is called the 'mobile conjugate reinforcement paradigm'. A version of this paradigm involves a period of not being able to move the mobile, then a period of being able to move the mobile (via a ribbon attached to the child's foot) followed by a period of not being able to move the mobile again (Sullivan *et al.*, 1979). This indicates whether the child has learned the association between moving its foot and the resulting effect on the mobile. See Figure 12.6.

Recognition memory using this technique seems to be poor. Young infants of 2–3 months, although able to detect small changes in the mobile, are unable to recognise the mobile one day after training if the mobile has more than one element that has changed (Rovee-Collier and Hayne, 1987). The older the infant, however, the longer the delay that can occur between presentations. For example, a 6 month old infant can discriminate between a novel and a familiar stimulus after a delay of two weeks; an infant of 3 months can discriminate after a delay of only three days (Borovsky and Rovee-Collier, 1990).

The deferred imitation paradigm involves exposing the child to an adult who is performing some actions with a set of novel stimuli. After a delay, the 9–18 month old infant is allowed to manipulate the objects used by the adult. Learning and memory is measured by the infant's ability to model its behaviour on the adult's (Meltzoff, 1988, 1995). If the toddler can understand instructions, it is given structured tasks, taken away, returned to the laboratory and asked to re-enact the activities it did earlier. Immediate recall results in quite accurate memory performance for novel actions (making a rattle) and familiar actions (putting a teddy to bed) (Bauer and Mandler, 1992; Mandler and McDonough, 1995). Over the course of devel-

opment from 1 to 2 years, the number of sequences of actions that the child can remember increases. At 20 months, for example, the child is able to remember three steps (Bauer and Dow, 1994); at 24 months, the child can act out five steps (Bauer and Travis, 1993), and at 30 months, the number of steps in the sequence can increase to eight. The finding that children can recall successively increasing series of steps with increasing age suggests that their memory capacity is increasing (or perhaps that their means of encoding is becoming more sophisticated and organised).

As age increases, so the delay between the initial and recall sessions can also increase without any detriment to performance. By 14 months, for example, children have been found to be able to demonstrate the use of a series of observed props after a delay of one week (Meltzoff, 1988).

By around 3 months, the infant shows awareness of changes in its environment; by 6 months, it is able to remember temporal orders of stimuli. At 8 months, it is able to recognise words spoken in a story that it heard a while before. For example, Jusczyk and Hohne (1997) exposed fifteen 8 month old infants to three children's stories for ten days. After two weeks, infants heard words that either occurred frequently in the stories or did not occur frequently. The infants listened significantly longer to the words that had been part of the stories.

This findings of this study suggest that because a delay of two weeks had passed between exposure and recognition, then the infant is already beginning to form long-term memories for words occurring in speech. This, of course, has implications for language development (as we saw in Chapter 10).

Memory in early childhood

Between the age of one to three years, the child develops the rudimentary language that allows him or her to communicate and to express an awareness of memory (Bauer,

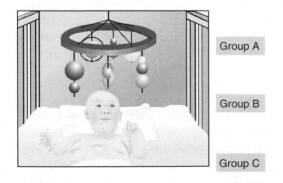

	First Condition	Later Condition
Group A	Head turning causes mobile to move. *Babies learn to move head.*	Head turning causes mobile to move. *Babies continue to move head.*
Group B	Mobile remains stationary	Head turning causes mobile to move. *Babies do not learn to move head.*
Group C	Mobile intermittently moves on its own.	Head turning causes mobile to move. *Babies do not learn to move head.*

Figure 12.6

The importance of a responsive environment.

Source: Based on Watson, J.S. and Ramey, C.T., Reactions to responsive contingent stimulation in early infancy. *Merrill–Palmer Quarterly*, 1972, 18, 219–227.

1997). This awareness of events that were experienced in the past is quite considerable. For example, a child of 3 years can recall a visit to McDonald's or report an event that occurred when he or she was two or, sometimes, even younger (Nelson, 1986; Fivush *et al.*, 1987). This evidence for children's ability to remember is based on the child's free recall of events. When the child is prompted by an adult, the memory performance is more impressive (Fivush, 1984; Bauer *et al.*, 1995). According to one study, 78 per cent of information from 3–5 year olds was prompted by adults' intervention and questions (Hamond and Fivush, 1991). If the child is asked to act out the event, as opposed to providing a verbal report of it, he or she is able to recall twice as much information.

At this age, children's memory can be tested in more sophisticated ways than those used for very young infants. For example, two of the most commonly used measures of memory in young children involve object hiding and retrieval and the acting out of observed events (which we also discussed in the section on memory in infancy). In the hidden object task, the child sees an object being hidden and after a delay is asked to retrieve it (DeLoache, 1984). In the observed actions task, the child is exposed to an adult performing a series of actions with props; either immediately after this, or after a delay (and, in both cases, without practice), the child is asked to act out this demonstration.

Children are able to perform such tasks, even at 1–2 years of age. Bauer and Dow (1994), for example, required 16 and 20 month old infants to demonstrate a series of seen actions after a delay of one week. At the time of the initial exposure, the action was putting a child's toy character to bed; at the retrieval session (one week later), the props had changed to a small dog and a plastic crib. Although the props were changed, the performance of the demonstration after a week's delay was not significantly different.

Why does the child's memory improve dramatically from one to four years of age?

Three factors which seem to account for the child's ability to recall information better with age are: the formation of memory-related structures, the development of language and the development of metamemory: the realisation that using memory strategies will help the child to think and behave. The relative contribution of each is unclear but we know that the brain develops until the age of adolescence (and some parts become mature after this). Myelination, for example – the process whereby the axons of the brain become insulated and allows them to transmit information to neurons more efficiently continues to adolescence – is correlated with speed of processing in children (Travis, 1998). The development of language means that a child has the capability to encode material verbally instead of via some other representation such as visual representation. By the age of 3, for example, the child begins initiating con-versation (Fivush *et al.*, 1987). Interestingly, it has been suggested that it is not the verbal encoding of material, per se, that causes improvement in memory but the verbal expression of memory. Thus, if a memory is verbally expressed, then this memory will be retained longer than if it had not been expressed (Nelson, 1993; Bauer and Wewerka, 1997).

It has also been suggested that the types of memory recalled from early and later infancy are dependent on whether the child is employing a narrative technique to give structure and give meaning to events. Autobiographical memory, for example, begins developing later in infancy and this form of memory relies on the structuring and organisation of events to make them meaningful. Perhaps one reason why we can remember events as adults from the age of 4 years onwards but not before then is because we did not have a narrative structure in place before the age of 4 to give material meaning and depth (Nelson, 1993). This is quite a controversial idea.

The work of Jean Piaget

The most influential student of child development has been Jean Piaget (1896–1980), a Swiss psychologist, who viewed cognitive development as a maturational process. Piaget formulated the most complete and detailed description of the process of cognitive development that we now have. His conclusions were based on his observations of the behaviour of children – first, of his own children at home and, later, of other children at his Centre of Genetic Epistemology in Geneva. He noticed that children of similar age tend to engage in similar behaviours and to make the same kinds of mistakes in problem solving. He concluded that these similarities are the result of a sequence of development that all normal children follow. Completion of each period, with its corresponding abilities, is the prerequisite for entering the next period.

According to Piaget, as children develop, they acquire cognitive structures – mental representations or rules that are used for understanding and dealing with the world and for thinking about and solving problems. The two principal types of cognitive structure are schemata and concepts. Schemata (schema is the singular form) are mental representations or sets of rules that define a particular category of behaviour – how the behaviour is executed and under what conditions. A child is said to have a 'grasping schema' when she is able to grasp a rattle in her hand. Once she has learned how to grasp a rattle, she can then use the same schema to grasp other objects. A child has acquired a 'picking up schema' when he is able to lift the rattle from a surface.

Piaget suggested that as a child acquires knowledge of the environment, he or she develops mental structures called concepts – rules that describe properties of environmental events and their relations to other concepts. For example, concepts about the existence of various objects include what the objects do, how they relate to other objects, and what happens when they are touched or manipulated. Thus, an infant's cognitive structure includes concepts of such things as rattles, balls, crib slats, hands and other people.

Infants acquire schemata and concepts by interacting with their environment. According to Piaget, two processes help a child to adapt to its environment: assimilation and accommodation. Assimilation is the process by which new information is modified to fit existing schemata. For example, when a child moves a wooden block along a surface while making the rumbling sound of an engine, he has assimilated the wooden block into his schema of a car. Accommodation is the process by which old schemata are changed by new experiences. Accommodation produces either new schemata or changes in existing ones. For example, suppose that a young girl's concept of animal has three categories: doggies, kitties and teddies. If she sees a picture of a deer and calls it a kitty, she has assimilated the new information into an existing concept. However, if she decides that a deer is a new kind of animal, she will accommodate her animal concept to include the new category. Now this concept consists of doggies, kitties, teddies and deer.

Piaget's four periods of cognitive development

Although development is a continuous process, the cognitive structures of children vary from age to age. We can make inferences about the rules that children of certain ages use to understand their environment and control their behaviour. Thus Piaget divided cognitive development into four periods: sensorimotor, preoperational, concrete operational and formal operational. What a child learns in one period enables him or her to progress to the next period. See Table 12.2 for a summary of these stages.

Table 12.2   The four periods of Piaget's theory of cognitive development

Period	Approximate age	Major features
Sensorimotor	Birth to 2 years	Object permanence; deferred imitation; rudimentary symbolic thinking
Preoperational	2 to 6 or 7 years	Increased ability to think symbolically and logically; egocentrism; cannot yet master conservation problems
Concrete operational	6 or 7 years to 11 years	Can master conservation problems; can understand categorisation; cannot think abstractly
Formal operational	11 years upwards	Can think abstractly and hypothetically

The sensorimotor period   The sensorimotor period, which lasts for approximately the first two years of life, is the first stage in Piaget's theory of cognitive development. It is marked by an orderly progression of increasingly complex cognitive development ranging from reflexes to symbolic thinking. During this period, cognition is closely tied to external stimulation. An important feature of the sensorimotor period is the development of object permanence, the idea that objects do not disappear when they are out of sight. Until about 6 months of age, children appear to lose all interest in an object that disappears from sight – the saying 'out of sight, out of mind' seems particularly appropriate. In addition, cognition consists entirely in behaviour: Thinking is doing.

At first, infants do not appear to have a concept for objects. They can look at visual stimuli and will turn their heads and eyes towards the source of a sound, but hiding an object elicits no particular response. At around 3 months, they become able to follow moving objects with their eyes. If an object disappears behind a barrier, infants will continue to stare at the place where the object has disappeared but will not search for it.

At around 5 months, infants can grasp and hold objects and gain experience with manipulating and observing them. They can also anticipate the future position of a moving object. If a moving object passes behind a screen, infants turn their eyes towards the far side of the screen, seeming to anticipate the reappearance of the object on the other side.

During the last half of the first year, infants develop much more complex concepts concerning the nature of physical objects. They grasp objects, turn them over and investigate their properties. By looking at an object from various angles, they learn that the object can change its visual shape and still be the same object. In addition, if an object is hidden, infants will actively search for it; their object concept now contains the rule of object permanence. For infants at this stage of development, a hidden object still exists. 'Out of sight' is no longer 'out of mind'.

By early in the second year, object permanence is well enough developed that infants will search for a hidden object in the last place they saw it hidden. However, at this stage, infants can only keep track of changes in the hiding place that they can see. For example, if an adult picks up an object, puts it under a cloth, drops the object while his or her hand is hidden, closes the hand again and removes it from the cloth, infants will look for the object in the adult's hand. When they do not find the object there, they look puzzled or upset and do not search for the object under the cloth (see Figure 12.7).

Near the end of the sensorimotor period, two other interesting developments occur. First, children develop the ability to imitate actions that they have seen others perform, a behaviour that Piaget called deferred imitation. This ability is due to their increasing ability to form mental representations of actions that they have observed. These representations may then be recalled at a later time

Object is in experimenter's hand.

Experimenter closes hand. . .

. . . puts hand under cloth. . .

. . . removes hand, leaving object under the cloth.

Infant looks in experimenter's hand.

Obviously upset, infant quits.

Figure 12.7

Object permanence. An infant will not realise that the object has been left under the cloth.

Source: Adapted from Bower, T.G.R., *Perception in Infancy* (2nd edition) San Francisco: W.H. Freeman, 1972.

to direct particular imitative actions and symbolic play, such as pretending to feed a doll or taking a stuffed animal for a walk. Secondly, as having an imagination shows, 2 year old children begin to think symbolically. They can use words to represent objects such as balls and animals. This is a critical developmental step because this skill is crucial to language development.

The preoperational period   Piaget's second period of cognitive development, the **preoperational period**, lasts from approximately age 2 to age 7 and involves the ability to think logically as well as symbolically. This period is characterised by rapid development of language ability and of the ability to represent things symbolically. The child arranges toys in new ways to represent other objects (for example, a row of blocks can represent a train), begins to classify and categorise objects, and starts learning to count and to manipulate numbers.

Piaget asserted that development of symbolism actually begins during the sensorimotor period, when a child starts imitating events in his or her environment. For example, a child might represent a horse by making galloping movements with the feet or a bicycle by making steering movements with the hands. Symbolic representations like these are called signifiers: the motor act represents (signifies) the concept because it resembles either the movements that

the object makes or the movements the child makes when interacting with the object.

Concepts can also be represented by words, which are symbols that have no physical resemblance to the concept; Piaget referred to such abstract symbols as signs. Signifiers are personal, derived from the child's own interactions with objects. Therefore, only the child and perhaps members of the immediate family will understand a child's signifiers. In contrast, signs are social conventions. They are understood by all members of a culture. A child who is able to use words to think about reality has made an important step in cognitive development.

Piaget's work demonstrated quite clearly that a child's representation of the world is different from that of an adult. For example, most adults realise that a volume of water remains constant when poured into a taller, narrower container, even though its level is now higher (see Figure 12.8). However, early in the preoperational period, children will fail to recognise this fact; they will say that the taller container contains more water. The ability to realise that an object retains mass, number or volume when it undergoes various transformations is called **conservation**; the transformed object conserves its original properties.

Piaget concluded that the abilities to perceive the conservation of number, mass, weight and volume are attributes of increasing cognitive development. His

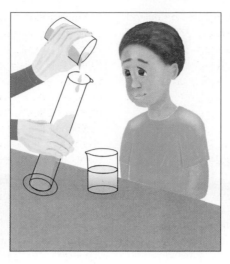

Figure 12.8

Conservation. Early in the preoperational period, a child does not have the ability to conserve a liquid quantity.

studies showed number to be conserved by age 6, whereas conservation of volume did not occur until age 11. Presumably, conservation of number comes first because children can verify the stability of number once they learn to count (see Figure 12.9).

Another important characteristic of the preoperational period is egocentrism, or a child's belief that others see the world in precisely the way he or she does. For example, a 3 year old child may run to a corner, turn his back to you and cover his eyes in an attempt to hide during a game of hide and seek, not realising that he is still in full view.

The period of concrete operations   Piaget's third stage of cognitive development, the period of concrete operations, spans approximately ages 7 to 11 and involves children's developing understanding of the conservation principle and other concepts such as categorisation. Its end marks the transition from childhood to adolescence. This period is characterised by the emergence of the ability to perform logical analysis, by an increased ability to empathise with the feelings and attitudes of others, and by an understanding of more complex cause-and-effect relations. The child becomes much more skilled at the use

Conservation of Mass   The experimenter presents two balls of clay.

The experimenter rolls one ball into a 'sausage' and asks the child whether they still contain the same amount of clay.

Conservation of Length   The experimenter presents two dowels.

The experimenter moves one dowel to the right and asks the child whether they are still the same length.

Conservation of Number   The experimenter presents two rows of counters

The experimenter moves one row of counters apart and asks the child whether each row still contains the same number.

Figure 12.9

Various tests of conservation.

Source: Adapted from *Of Children: An introduction to child development* (4th edition) by Guy R. Lefrancois. Copyright © 1983, 1980 by Wadsworth, Inc. Reprinted by permission of Wadsworth Publishing Company, Belmont, CA 94002.

of symbolic thought. For example, even before the period of concrete operations, children can arrange a series of objects in order of size and can compare any two objects and say which is larger. However, if they are shown that stick A is larger than stick B and that stick B is larger than stick C, they cannot infer that stick A is larger than stick C.

During the early part of this period, children become capable of making such inferences. However, although they can reason with respect to concrete objects, such as sticks that they have seen, they cannot do so with hypothetical objects. For example, they cannot solve the following problem: Judy is taller than Frank and Frank is taller than Carl. Who is taller, Judy or Carl? The ability to solve such problems awaits the next period of cognitive development.

The period of formal operations

During the period of formal operations, which begins at about age 11, children first become capable of abstract reasoning. They can now think and reason about hypothetical objects and events. They also begin to understand that under different conditions, their behaviour can have different consequences. Formal operational thinking is not 'culture free' – it is influenced by cultural variables, especially formal schooling (Piaget, 1972; Rogoff and Chavajay, 1995). Without exposure to the principles of scientific thinking, such as those taught at school, people do not develop formal operational thinking.

Although Piaget held that there are four periods of cognitive development, not all people reach the formal operational period, even as physically mature adults. In some cases, adults show formal operational thought only in their areas of expertise. Thus, a mechanic may be able to think abstractly while repairing an engine but not while solving maths or physics problems. A physicist may be able to reason abstractly when solving physics problems but not while reading poetry. However, once an individual reaches that level of thinking, he or she will always, except in the case of brain disease or injury, perform intellectually at that level.

Evaluation of Piaget's contributions

Piaget's theory has had an enormously positive impact, stimulating interest and research in developmental psychology (Halford, 1990; Beilin, 1990). However, not all of Piaget's conclusions have been accepted uncritically. One criticism levelled at Piaget is that he did not always define his terms operationally. Consequently, it is difficult for others to interpret the significance of his generalisations. Many of his studies lack the proper controls. Thus, much of his work is not experimental, which means that cause-and-effect relations among variables cannot be identified with certainty.

Subsequent evidence has suggested that a child's ability to conserve various physical attributes occurs earlier than Piaget had supposed. For example, Gelman (1972) found that when the appropriate task is used, even 3 year old children are able to demonstrate conservation of number. We must recognise that an estimate of a child's cognitive ability can be substantially affected by the testing method.

Piaget also appears to have underestimated the ability of young children to understand another person's point of view. In other words, they are less egocentric than he thought. For example, Flavell *et al.* (1981) found that even a 3 year old child realises that a person looking at the opposite side of a card to that which the child is examining will not see the same thing. Clearly, the child recognises the other person's point of view.

Despite the fact that Piaget's method of observation led him to underestimate some important abilities, his meticulous and detailed observations of child behaviour have been extremely important in the field of child development and have had a great influence on educational practice. His theoretical framework has provided a basis for more empirical studies and will undoubtedly continue to do so for many years.

Vygotsky's sociocultural theory of cognitive development

Piaget's theory of cognitive development focuses on children's interactions with the physical world – they form internal representations of the world based on their experiences with physical objects. Another theorist, Lev Vygotsky, agreed that experience with physical objects is an important factor in cognitive development, but he disagreed that this is the whole story. Instead, he argued that the culture in which one lives also plays a significant role in cognitive development (Vygotsky, 1987). Although Vygotsky's work was conducted during the 1920s and early 1930s (he died of tuberculosis in 1934), his writings have had a major impact on recent conceptualisations of cognitive development during childhood (Smith *et al.*, 1997). In this section, we briefly examine some of Vygotsky's ideas on how sociocultural variables influence cognitive development.

Vygotsky argued that children do not learn to think about the physical world in a vacuum. The cultural context – what they hear others say about the world and how they see others interact with physical aspects of the world – matters. Thus parents, teachers, friends and many others help children to acquire ideas about how the world works. We would expect, then, that children raised in non-stimulating environments devoid of stimulating interactions with others, with books, and, yes, with television would lag behind that of children raised in more stimulating environments. And this is exactly what has been found.

Controversies in psychological science

Does television viewing affect children's cognitive development?

The issue

A child's cognitive development is influenced by many factors, including parents' education and occupational status, number of siblings, social class of playmates, nature of the neighbourhood, availability of educational resources such as books in the home, opportunity for travel, and quality of schooling. A child from a privileged social milieu is much more likely to be exposed to situations that promote cognitive development. But almost all children in industrialised societies, even those in the poorest households, are exposed for several hours a day to a near universal factor – television.

The evidence

One of the best examples of the good television can do is demonstrated by *Sesame Street*, a programme that was devised to teach learning skills, such as counting, letter recognition and vocabulary, to children. Children who watch *Sesame Street* have better vocabularies, have better attitudes towards school, adapt better to the classroom, and have more positive attitudes towards children of other races (Bogatz and Ball, 1972). *Sesame Street* emphasises multiculturalism in its choice of characters and the activities and interests they display. Rice *et al.* (1990) studied a large sample of 3–5 year old children from a wide range of socioeconomic backgrounds and found that children of all backgrounds profited from watching *Sesame Street* – the advantages were not restricted to middle-class children.

On the other hand, many television programmes are full of violence, and watching them may well promote aggressiveness and impatience with non-violent resolution of disagreements in the children who watch such shows. In addition, commercial television affects consumer behaviour. Sponsors aim many of their commercial messages at children (McNeal, 1990). Furthermore, sponsors produce commercials that encourage children to demand that their parents purchase particular snack foods, toys and other items (Taras *et al.*, 1989). However, commercials related to the purchase and consumption of alcoholic beverages and those containing anti-drinking messages do not appear to influence children's expectancies about the positive or negative effects of alcohol (Lipsitz *et al.*, 1993), perhaps because they are not specifically aimed towards very young audiences. Nonetheless, we can ask ourselves whether sponsors are likely to find it in their interests to educate children to be informed consumers.

The second issue that people have raised about children and television regards the nature of the medium itself. Many people who have written about the potential effects of television as a medium on children's cognitive development have concluded that the medium is generally harmful. Anderson and Collins (1988) summarise some of the criticisms these people have made:

- Television has a mesmerising power over children's attention; this power is exerted by the movement, colour and visual changes typical of television.
- Children do not think about television programmes; that is, they do not engage in inferential and reflective thought while viewing television.
- Children get overstimulated by television. By some accounts, this leads to hyperactivity; by other accounts, this leads to passivity.
- Television viewing displaces valuable cognitive activities, especially reading and homework.
- Attention span is shortened, probably because of the rapid pace at which visual images are presented.
- Creativity and imagination are reduced; in general, the child becomes cognitively passive.
- Reading achievement is reduced.

In a review of their own research and of that of others, Anderson and Collins conclude that there is little evidence to support these criticisms. In fact, the evidence directly contradicts some of them. Let us examine four of the most important criticisms: that television mesmerises children, that it overstimulates them, that it displaces valuable cognitive activities, and that it reduces their reading achievement.

Studies of 2 year olds have shown that they view up to two hours of television per day (Hollenbeck, 1978), and studies of older children have shown that they may watch a little over three hours of television per day (Nielsen, 1990). Boys tend to view more television than do girls and, across all ages, children with low IQs from low income families watch more television than do other children (Huston *et al.*, 1989, 1990).

The most objective measures of the amount of time children spend watching television have been obtained by placing a time-lapse video camera and videotape machine in people's homes next to their television sets so that the viewers can be recorded. Anderson *et al.* (1985) used this method to measure television viewing by members of ninety-nine families in a New England city. They found that children watched television about sixteen hours per week.

According to Anderson and Collins (1988), while watching television, children are often engaged in other activities: they eat, play with toys, draw or colour pictures, read, play games, sleep, talk with others or do their homework. They often enter and leave the room while the television is on.

Some critics have said that television is addictive and mesmerising, that children who watch it have glazed eyes and are spaced out (Moody, 1980). Support for such terrible effects comes not from controlled experiments but from anecdotes and assertions of experts. In fact, studies that actually observe children who are watching television find no such effects. Children are rarely 'glued' to the television set. They look away from it between 100 and 200 times each hour (Anderson and Field, 1983). They rarely look at the screen for much more than one minute at a stretch. Their viewing behaviour is related to programme content: they tend to pay attention when they hear other children's voices, interesting sound effects and peculiar voices and when they see movement on the screen. They tend not to pay attention when they hear men's voices or see no signs of activity on the screen (Anderson and Lorch, 1983).

The selectivity shown by young viewers is certainly not consistent with the behaviour of someone who has been mesmerised. The fact that the soundtrack of a television programme has so much effect on children's looking behaviour suggests that children have learned to use auditory cues to help them decide whether to watch, especially when time sharing – alternating their attention between the television and another activity. If they hear certain kinds of sound, they turn their attention away from the alternative activity and look at the screen to see whether something interesting is happening.

Moody (1980) states that 'television is an intense kaleidoscope of moving light and sound. It can create extreme excitement in the brain and, after prolonged viewing, it can produce a "drugged state"' (p. 18). Anderson and Collins found no evidence to support such claims. And the fact that children look away from television so often suggests that if they found television too stimulating they would have an easy means for reducing potential overarousal – simply looking away from the screen. Certainly, an exciting programme can excite the viewer, but no evidence suggests that 'kaleidoscopic images' act like drugs on the brains of young children.

Perhaps television takes up time that would otherwise be spent on activities that would stimulate children's cognitive development (Singer and Singer, 1990). Some evidence with respect to this possibility comes from observations made before and after television was available in remote towns (Hornik, 1981). In fact, television viewing primarily displaced other entertainment activities, such as listening to the radio, reading comics, or going to the cinema. It had little effect on time spent reading or doing homework. As most parents undoubtedly know, many children do their homework in front of the television set, switching their attention back and forth between the screen and their studies. In general, children are more likely to use television as a backdrop for their homework than for reading (Patton *et al.*, 1983). Surprisingly, there is no evidence that the quality of the homework suffers.

The fact that children are less likely to watch television while doing homework that involves reading suggests that reading and viewing are at least somewhat incompatible. Indeed, one criticism of television – that it retards children's reading achievement – has received some support. Measurements of children's reading skills before and after television became available suggested that television viewing decreased the reading skills of young children (Corteen and Williams, 1986). However, the effects were slight and were not seen in older children. Perhaps, then, television viewing does interfere with reading achievement in young children.

Conclusion

Although children spend a considerable amount of time watching television, the negative effects of their viewing appear to be negligible. Children do not appear to become mesmerised or overstimulated by television. Nor does television viewing appear to detract significantly from other activities that would stimulate children's cognitive development or substantially reduce their reading achievement.

However, the possibility exists that television programmes could do more to stimulate children's cognitive development. Educational programmes and others that take into account children's developmental needs would seem to be especially conducive to the stimulation of children's imagination, creativity, language skills and prosocial behaviour.

Vygotsky further believed that children's use of speech also influences their cognitive development. Children up to about age 7 can often be observed talking to themselves. While drawing in a colouring book, a child may say, 'I'll colour her arms and face green and her trousers black.' Piaget would interpret such talk as being egocentric and non-social because it is directed at the self, because it may not make sense to a listener, and because its purpose is not to communicate information. Vygotsky's interpretation would be different. He would argue that the child's talk actually reflects the formulation of a plan that will serve as a guide to subsequent behaviour. According to Vygotsky, language is the basis for cognitive development, including the ability to remember, solve problems, make decisions and formulate plans.

After about the age of 7, children stop vocalising their thoughts and instead carry on what Vygotsky labelled inner speech. Inner speech represents the internalisation of words and the mental manipulation of them as symbols for objects in the environment. As children interact with their parents, teachers and peers, they learn new words to represent new objects. As the 'expertise' of the people they interact with increases, so does the children's cognitive skills. For example, Rogoff and her colleagues (1990) have shown that children become better problem-solvers if they practise solving problems with their parents or with more experienced children than if they practise the problems alone or with children of similar cognitive ability.

Thus, while Piaget argued for a purely maturational view of children's cognitive development, Vygotsky stressed the importance of sociocultural influences such as language and interactions with other people. As we have seen, research partially supports both theorists' ideas. Piaget's descriptions of the milestones involved in cognitive development have proved to be fairly accurate. However, Vygotsky's work has gone beyond Piaget's theory in explaining how cultural variables, especially language, influence cognitive development.

Developmental models of information processing in cognitive development

Both Piaget and Vygotsky saw cognitive development as a process of forming internal representations of the external world. Piaget focused on the development of schemata, the processes of assimilation and accommodation, and abstract reasoning. Vygotsky focused on the role of language in the development of problem-solving skills, decision making, and formulating plans. An alternative approach is to view cognitive development in terms of information processing, which involves the storage, encoding and retrieval of information. Two developmental models of information processing have emerged in recent years: Case's M-space model and Fischer's skill model.

Case's M-space model

According to Case (1985, 1992), cognitive development is a matter of a child becoming more efficient in using mental strategies. The heart of Case's model is mental space (M-space) – a hypothetical construct, similar to short-term or working memory, whose chief function is the processing of information from the external world. Expansion of M-space, or increases in a child's information processing capacity, is caused by a combination of three variables.

First, as the brain matures, so does its capacity to process greater amounts of information. Maturation of the brain, specifically the increasing number of networks of neural connections and increasing myelination of neurons, also enhances more efficient processing of information. Secondly, as children become more practised at using schemata, less demand is placed on cognitive resources, which can now be devoted to other, more complex cognitive tasks. For example, when children first learn to ride a bicycle, they must focus entirely on keeping their balance and steering the bike in a straight line. After they have acquired these skills, they no longer have to devote so much attention to steering the bike and not falling off. Now they can look around, talk to other bike riders and so on. Thirdly, schemata for different objects and events become integrated so that children now think in novel ways about these objects and events. The net result of such integration is the acquisition of central conceptual structures – networks of schemata that allow children to understand the relationships among the objects and events represented by schemata. As increasingly complex central conceptual structures are formed, children advance to higher levels of cognitive development, as represented in Piaget's stages. Each of the milestones in Piaget's theory, such as deferred imitation and conservation, requires increasing amounts of M-space.

Fischer's skill model

In Fischer's skill model, cognitive development involves the learning of skills, or the acquisition of competencies on particular tasks, such as those found in each of Piaget's developmental periods. Fischer emphasises the child's optimal level of skill performance, or the brain's maximal capacity for information processing. According to Fischer, as the brain matures, the child advances through stages of cognitive growth that parallel Piaget's periods of cognitive development (Fischer and Farrar, 1987; Fischer and Pipp, 1984). During each stage, the child's capacity to process information increases, as does the level of skill required for mastery of specific cognitive tasks, such as conservation tasks. As the child encounters different problems, new skills are acquired, practised and perfected. These skills become integrated, leading to increases in the child's ability to reason and think abstractly.

A child cannot progress from one Piagetian period to another until his or her brain has matured sufficiently to permit acquisition of the cognitive skills necessary to master tasks representative of the next period. For example, a pre-operational child is not able to solve conservation tasks until his or her brain has matured sufficiently to permit acquisition of the necessary skills. Even if a parent explains the task, the child's brain will not be able to encode, store and later retrieve those instructions. When faced with the conservation problem later, the child will still be unable to solve it.

Both Case's M-space model and Fischer's skill model rely on brain maturation as the primary explanation for children's increasing ability to think logically and abstractly. And both models in essence rephrase Piaget's theory of cognitive development in information processing terms. The purpose of these models has not been to discredit Piaget's theory. On the contrary, one important function of these models has been to reinterpret the theory in the language of modern cognitive psychology. Perhaps by conceptualising children's thought processes in terms of the interplay of Piaget's theory, brain maturation processes, and the acquisition of novel and more complex information processing abilities, further advances in understanding cognitive development will emerge.

Psychology in action

Vitamin supplements and children's IQ

In the late 1980s and early 1990s, a series of remarkable studies was published in which claims were made about the effect of vitamins and minerals on cognitive performance. Controversially, these studies reported significant differences in non-verbal IQ between schoolchildren who received vitamin and mineral supplements (VMS) and those who received a placebo (Benton, 1992; Haller, 1995; Eysenck and Schoenthaler, 1997). Those who received the supplement scored significantly better. One of the more prominent of these researchers even published a book under the title *Improve your Child's IQ and Behaviour* (Schoenthaler, 1991), and *The Psychologist*, the journal of the British Psychological Society, regarded the topic as important enough in 1992 to devote an entire issue to it.

We know that malnutrition can impair the function of the brain (Brown and Pollitt, 1996) and has negative long-term effects on IQ. Iron deficiency and anaemia are the most common types of nutritional disorder (Yehuda and Youdim, 1989); iodine deficiency during pregnancy can lead to retardation and cretinism. We also know that children who are deficient in certain vitamins and minerals show substantial improvement in intellectual performance if they are given VMS (Braun and Pollit, 1996; Lynn and Harland, 1998).

In 1988, Benton and Roberts published a study which extended this work, but in a striking way (Benton and Roberts, 1988). They administered either VMS or a placebo to sixty 12 year old Welsh schoolchildren and measured verbal and non-verbal IQ before and after the trial which lasted nine months. Benton and Roberts found that the non-verbal IQ of those children receiving VMS was significantly higher at the end of the trial compared with those receiving a placebo. In fact, non-verbal IQ was, on average, nine points higher.

This study prompted a number of other studies of IQ and vitamin supplementation. Schoenthaler *et al.* (1991a), for example, administered a placebo or VMS to twenty-five 13–16 year old juvenile delinquents over thirteen weeks. The same effect was found: those receiving supplements had significantly higher non-verbal IQ (the placebo group's average IQ actually dropped a point). When blood micronutrients were examined, the researchers found that the non-verbal IQ of those with little change in blood content had dropped by 2.7 points whereas the non-verbal IQ of those whose blood content had changed rose by an average of 11.6 points. Two other studies confirmed the general findings from these reports (Benton and Buts, 1990; Benton and Cook, 1991).

In the first study (Benton and Buts, 1990), 167 Belgian children received either VMS or a placebo for five months. At the beginning of the experiment, 45 per cent of the sample reported a vitamin intake that was less than 50 per cent of the US recommended daily allowance (RDA). At the end of the trial, those boys with a poor diet and also those that were less academic, had higher non-verbal IQ after supplementation (there was no effect for the girls). In the second study (Benton and Cook, 1991), forty-seven 6 year olds completed four tests from the British Ability Scales (a battery of tests that measures a child's cognitive ability) before and after being given a placebo or VMS for between six and eight weeks. Again, those in the VMS condition increased their non-verbal IQ by 7.6 points and the placebo group's IQ dropped. Benton and Cook also observed that those children receiving supplementation concentrated more during an almost impossible computer game task.

Psychology in action continued overleaf

Psychology in action continued

The largest study, however, involved 615 Californian children (Schoenthaler *et al.*, 1991b). A placebo, VMS at the recommended daily allowance, VMS at half the RDA or VMS at twice the RDA was administered to the children each day for twelve weeks. As predicted, non-verbal IQ increased in all VMS groups.

Do these studies indicate that supplementation does have a genuine effect on cognitive performance? Do all studies agree? The answer, to the second question at least, is no. Some studies have failed to replicate the Benton and Schoenthaler findings. Nelson *et al.* (1990), for example, examined the effect of VMS and placebo on 227 7–12 year old children over four weeks and found no evidence of significant improvement in non-verbal IQ. Similarly, Crombie *et al.* (1990) found that although a small advantage was found for their supplemented group, this advantage was not significant. Benton (1992) and Eysenck and Schoenthaler (1997), in a review of these studies, suggest that a number of methodological differences could account for the contrary results. Differences in the length of trials, the types of test used, the method of administering tests, interpreting the results of tests, and the type of VMS may explain the results of those studies reporting no significant improvement in non-verbal IQ.

If the effect seen in children is robust, why should VMS affect only non-verbal IQ? In all the published studies there has been no reported improvement in verbal IQ. Cast your mind back to Chapter 11 and the sections on types of intelligence. Verbal intelligence, as measured on the standard types of test, usually relies on information that has already been learned

through experience. This type of intelligence is called 'crystallised' intelligence. Non-verbal intelligence, however, does not rely on previous knowledge and has been described as 'fluid'. If fluid intelligence reflects the potential to perform, it seems reasonable that administering VMS should affect this type of intelligence more than the type which is fixed and crystallised. Snowden (1997) has suggested that speed of processing may be a significant factor in non-verbal IQ improvement. She administered verbal and non-verbal IQ tests to thirty 9–10 year old English children who received either a placebo or VMS for ten weeks. Although finding the typical non-verbal advantage in the supplemented group, she also noted that the number of omissions (incomplete test items) decreased over time and that more non-verbal IQ questions were answered by the VMS group as the study went on.

The effect of vitamin supplementation on children's IQ continues to be controversial. The majority of the evidence suggests, however, that some form of supplementation is associated with increases in non-verbal IQ. The mechanism for this is unknown. Are there any factors which you think these studies have overlooked? What criticisms would you make of the design of these studies? How would you improve these designs? Would certain groups of children benefit more from VMS? Why? Do you think that such studies have implications for education and child development? Would you expect strong cross-cultural differences? If so, why? Which vitamins and minerals may be necessary to produce cognitive improvement? Finally, why do you think VMS should increase non-verbal IQ?

Questions to think about

Perceptual and cognitive development

- How would you design an environment that would facilitate a child's motor and perceptual development?

- How different are a child's and an adult's views of the world?

- Why do infants show a preference for 'human' faces?

- How might you construct an environment to facilitate your child's cognitive development?

- Why are memories for events occurring before the age of 3 irretrievable?

- How would you go about developing a test for determining which of Piaget's periods of cognitive development a child is in? What kinds of activity would you include in such a test and how would the child's behaviour with respect to those activities indicate the child's stage of development?

- Would changing a child's diet help his or her cognitive ability?

Social development in childhood

Normally, the first adults with whom infants interact are their parents. In most cases, one parent serves as the primary carer. As many studies have shown, a close relationship called **attachment** is important for infants' social development. Attachment is a social and emotional bond between infant and carer that spans both time and space. It involves both the warm feelings that the parent and child have for each other and the comfort and support they provide for each other, which becomes especially important during times of fear or stress. This interaction must work both ways, with each participant fulfilling certain needs of the other.

Formation of a strong and durable bond depends on the behaviour of both people in the relationship. According to theorist John Bowlby (1969), attachment is a part of many organisms' native endowment. He and Mary Ainsworth have developed an approach that has succeeded in discovering the variables that influence attachment in humans (Ainsworth and Bowlby, 1991).

Infant attachment

Newborn infants rely completely on their parents (or other carers) to supply them with nourishment, keep them warm and clean, and protect them from harm. To most parents, the role of primary carer is much more than a duty; it is a source of joy and satisfaction. Nearly all parents anticipate the birth of their children with the expectation that they will love and cherish them. And when a child is born, most of them do exactly that. As time goes on, and as parent and child interact, they become strongly attached to each other. What factors cause this attachment to occur? Evidence suggests that human infants are innately able to produce special behaviours that shape and control the behaviour of their carers. As Bowlby (1969) noted, the most important of these behaviours are sucking, cuddling, looking, smiling and crying.

Sucking

A baby must be able to suck in order to obtain milk. But not all sucking is related to nourishment. Piaget (1952) noted that infants often suck on objects even when they are not hungry. Non-nutritive sucking appears to be an innate behavioural tendency in infants that serves to inhibit a baby's distress. In modern society, most mothers cover their breasts between feedings or feed with a bottle, so a baby's non-nutritive sucking must involve inanimate objects or the baby's own thumb. But in Uganda, mothers were observed to give their babies access to a breast when they were fussy, just as mothers in other cultures would give them a dummy (Ainsworth, 1967).

Cuddling

Infants of all species of primates have special reflexes that encourage front-to-front contact with their mothers. For example, a baby monkey clings to its mother's chest shortly after birth. This clinging leaves the mother free to use her hands and feet. Human infants are carried by their parents and do not hold on by themselves. However, infants do adjust their posture to mould themselves to the contours of the parent's body. This cuddling response plays an important role in reinforcing the behaviour of the carer. Some infants, perhaps because of hereditary factors or slight brain damage, do not make the cuddling response and remain rigid in the adult's arms. Adults who hold such infants tend to refer to them as being not very loveable (Ainsworth, 1973).

Harry Harlow (1974) conducted a series of experiments on infant monkeys and showed that clinging to a soft, cuddly form appears to be an innate response. Harlow and his colleagues isolated baby monkeys from their mothers immediately after birth and raised them alone in cages containing two mechanical surrogate mothers. One surrogate mother was made of bare wire mesh but contained a bottle that provided milk. The other surrogate was padded and covered with terry cloth but provided no nourishment.

The babies preferred to cling to the cuddly surrogate and went to the wire model only to eat. If they were frightened, they would rush to the cloth-covered model for comfort. These results suggest that close physical contact with a cuddly object is a biological need for a baby monkey, just as food and drink are. A baby monkey clings to and cuddles with its mother because the contact is innately reinforcing, not simply because she provides it with food.

Undoubtedly, physical contact with soft objects is also inherently reinforcing for human infants. The term 'security blanket' suggests that these objects are comforting during times of distress. Indeed, children are most likely to ask for their special blankets or stuffed animals before going to bed, when they are ill, or when they are in an unfamiliar situation.

Looking

For infants, looking serves as a signal to parents: even a very young infant seeks eye-to-eye contact with his or her parents. If a parent does not respond when eye contact is made, the baby usually shows signs of distress. Tronick et al. (1978) observed face-to-face interactions between mothers and their infants. When the mothers approached their babies, they typically smiled and began talking in a gentle, high-pitched voice. In return, infants smiled and stretched their arms and legs. The mothers poked and gently jiggled their babies, making faces at them. The babies responded with facial expressions, wiggles and noises of their own.

To determine whether the interaction was really two-sided, the experimenters had each mother approach her baby while keeping her face expressionless or mask-like. At first, the infant made the usual greetings, but when the mother did not respond, the infant turned away. From time to time, the infant looked at her again, giving a brief smile, but again turned away when the mother continued to stare without changing her expression. These interactions were recorded on videotape and were scored by raters who did not know the purpose of the experiment, so the results were not biased by the experimenters' expectations.

Each mother found it difficult to resist her baby's invitation to interact. In fact, some of the mothers broke down and smiled back. Most of the mothers who managed to hold out (for three minutes) later apologised to their babies, saying something like, 'I am real again. It's all right. You can trust me again. Come back to me' (Tronick et al., 1978, p. 110). This study clearly shows that the looking behaviour of an infant is an invitation for the mother to respond.

Smiling

By the time an infant is 5 weeks old, visual stimuli begin to dominate as elicitors for smiling. A face (especially a moving one) is a more reliable elicitor of a smile than a voice is;

even a moving mask will cause an infant to smile. At approximately 3 months of age, specific faces – those of people to whom the infant has become attached – will elicit smiles. The significance of these observations should be obvious. An infant's smile is very rewarding. Almost every parent reports that parenting becomes a real joy when the baby starts smiling as the parent approaches – the infant is now a 'person'.

Crying

For almost any adult, the sound of an infant's crying is intensely distressing or irritating. An infant usually cries only when he or she is hungry, cold or in pain (Wolff, 1969). In these situations, only the intervention of an adult can bring relief. The event that most effectively terminates crying is being picked up and cuddled, although unless the baby is fed and made more comfortable, he or she will soon begin crying again. Because picking up the baby stops the crying, the parent learns through negative reinforcement to pick up the infant when he or she cries. Thus, crying serves as a useful means for a cold, hungry or wet child to obtain assistance.

Wolff (1969) suggested that babies have different patterns of crying. Konner (1972), who was studying a hunter-gatherer tribe in Africa, found that a pain cry caused all the people in earshot to turn towards the infant and induced several of them to run towards the child. However, a hunger cry was responded to only by the child's carers. More recent evidence suggests that babies' cries do not fall into need-specific categories – there is no 'hunger cry', no different cry for pain, and so on. Instead, cries simply vary in intensity, according to the level of the infant's distress. However, the onset of crying provides important information. If a baby suddenly begins crying intensely, mothers are more likely to assume that the baby is afraid or in pain. If the cry begins more gradually, mothers suspect hunger, sleepiness or a need for a nappy change (Gustafson and Harris, 1990).

The nature and quality of attachment

For an infant, the world can be a frightening place. The presence of a primary caregiver provides a baby with considerable reassurance when he or she first becomes able to explore the environment. Although the unfamiliar environment produces fear, the caregiver provides a secure base that the infant can leave from time to time to see what the world is like.

Stranger anxiety and separation anxiety

Babies are born prepared to become attached to their primary caregiver, which in most cases is their mother. Attachment appears to be a behaviour pattern that is necessary for normal development (Ainsworth, 1973; Bowlby, 1973). However, although attachment appears to be an inherited disposition, infants do not have a natural inclination to become attached to any one specific adult. Rather, the person to whom the baby becomes attached is determined through learning; the individual who serves as the infant's primary caregiver (or, in Bowlby's terms, 'attachment figure') is usually the object of the attachment.

Attachment partially reveals itself in two specific forms of infant behaviour: stranger anxiety and separation anxiety. Stranger anxiety, which usually appears in infants between the ages of 6 and 12 months, consists of wariness and sometimes fearful responses, such as crying and clinging to their carers, that infants exhibit in the presence of strangers. Male strangers generate the most anxiety in infants. Child strangers generate the least anxiety, while female strangers generate an intermediate amount of anxiety (Skarin, 1977). Stranger anxiety can be reduced and even eliminated under certain conditions. For example, if the infant is in familiar surroundings with its mother, and the mother acts in a friendly manner towards the stranger, the infant is likely to be less anxious in the presence of the stranger than it would if the surroundings were unfamiliar or if the mother was unfriendly towards the stranger (Rheingold and Eckerman, 1973).

Separation anxiety is a set of fearful responses, such as crying, arousal and clinging to the carer, that an infant exhibits when the carer attempts to leave the infant. Separation anxiety differs from stranger anxiety in two ways: time of emergence and the conditions under which the fear responses occur. It first appears in infants when they are about 6 months old and generally peaks at about 15 months – a finding consistent among many cultures (Kagan *et al.*, 1978). Like stranger anxiety, separation anxiety can occur under different conditions with different degrees of intensity. For example, if an infant is used to being left in a certain environment, say a day-care centre, it may show little or no separation anxiety (Maccoby, 1980). The same holds true for situations in which the infant is left with a sibling or other familiar person (Bowlby, 1969). However, if the same infant is left in an unfamiliar setting, it will show signs of distress. Some infants show 'disorganised' attachment behaviour, that is, they show conflicting behaviour towards the carer. They may rush to the sound of an opening door when hearing the carer about to enter a room and then run away when the carer enters; they may also adopt a 'frozen' or still posture when the carer is in the room (Main and Solomon, 1990). A longitudinal study of disorganised attachment behaviour in 157 children (studied from 24 months to 19 years), found that disorganised behaviour was correlated with insensitive caring, living alone with the infant, neglect, physical and psychological neglect and an intrusive caring style (Carlson, 1998).

Ainsworth's Strange Situation

One measure of separation anxiety was devised by Ainsworth and her colleagues (Ainsworth *et al.*, 1978). They developed a test of attachment called the Strange Situation that consists of a series of eight episodes, during which the baby is exposed to various events that might cause some distress. The episodes involve the experimenter introducing the infant and the parent to a playroom and then leaving, the parent leaving and being reunited with the infant, or a stranger entering the playroom with and without the parent present. Each episode lasts for approximately three minutes. The Strange Situation test is based on the idea that if the attachment process has been successful, an infant should use its mother as a secure base from which to explore an unfamiliar environment. By noting the infant's reactions to the strange situation, researchers can evaluate the nature of the attachment.

The use of the Strange Situation test has led Ainsworth and her colleagues to identify three patterns of attachment. Secure attachment is the ideal pattern: infants show a distinct preference for their mothers over the stranger. Infants may cry when their carers leave, but they stop as soon as they return. Babies may also form two types of insecure attachment. Babies with resistant attachment show tension in their relations with their carers. Infants stay close to their mother before the mother leaves but show both approach and avoidance behaviours when the mother returns. Infants continue to cry for a while after their mother returns and may even push her away. Infants who display avoidant attachment generally do not cry when they are left alone. When their mother returns, the infants are likely to avoid or ignore them. These infants tend not to cling and cuddle when they are picked up.

Although infants' personalities certainly affect the nature of their interactions with their carers and hence the nature of their attachment, mothers' behaviour appears to be the most important factor in establishing a secure or insecure attachment (Ainsworth *et al.*, 1978; Isabella and Belsky, 1991). Mothers of securely attached infants tend to be those who respond promptly to their crying and who are adept at handling them and responding to their needs. The babies apparently learn that their mothers can be trusted to react sensitively and appropriately. Mothers who do not modulate their responses according to their infants' own behaviour – who appear insensitive to their infants' changing needs – are most likely to foster avoidant attachment. Mothers who are impatient with their infants and who seem more interested in their own activities than in interacting with their offspring tend to foster resistant attachment.

The nature of the attachment between infants and carers appears to be related to children's later social behaviour. For example, Waters *et al.* (1979) found that children who were securely attached at 15 months were among the most popular and the most sociable children in their nursery schools at 3^1/$_2$ years of age. In contrast, insecurely attached infants had difficulties with social adjustment later in childhood; they had poor social skills and tended to be hostile, impulsive and withdrawn (Erickson *et al.*, 1985).

Predictors of secure attachment

Recall that Ainsworth and her colleagues found that the insecure attachment features just described were strongly related to attachment security. What is unclear from Ainsworth's study, however, is which aspects of the mother–child interaction, if any, are predictive of a secure attachment style. Are all the features listed above necessary for secure attachment or only one? Some researchers suggest that maternal sensitivity is the greatest predictor (Goldsmith and Alansky, 1987); others show different factors.

One problem with studies of attachment is the variation in methodology. Sometimes, conclusions are drawn from a single observation or from multiple observations; the measures of attachment have ranged from asking parents about their attitudes to child care to observing the frequency of physical contact (Frodi *et al.*, 1985; Benn, 1986; Kerns and Barth, 1995). As a result, the determinants of attachment are unclear because different studies adopt different research designs.

In a meta-analysis of 66 attachment studies, De Wolff and Ijzendoorn (1997) found that there was a moderately strong relationship between maternal sensitivity, defined as the ability to respond appropriately and promptly to the signals of the infant, and attachment. However, they also found that other factors influenced attachment. These included the ability of the mother and child to behave synchronously, co-ordinated play, positive mood, stimulation and emotional support. In addition, the association between attachment and maternal behaviour was weaker in studies looking at families with clinical problems or in those of low socioeconomic status.

Questions to think about

Social development

- We know that attachment occurs in humans and other primates. Do you think it occurs in other species, especially other mammalian species, as well?
- What are the advantages of secure attachment?
- What are the disadvantages of poor attachment?
- Why is maternal sensitivity one of the primary predictors of secure attachment?
- Why should sociability and secure attachment be positively related?

Development of sex roles

Physical development as a male or a female is only one aspect of sexual development. Social development is also important. A person's sexual identity is one's private sense of being a male or female and consists primarily of the acceptance of membership in a particular group of people: males or females. Acceptance of this membership does not necessarily indicate acceptance of the sex roles or sex stereotypes that may accompany it. For example, a dedicated feminist may fight to change the role of women in her society but still clearly identify herself as a woman. Sex roles are cultural expectations about the ways in which men and women should think and behave. Closely related to them are sex stereotypes, beliefs about differences in the behaviours, abilities and personality traits of males and females. Society's sex stereotypes have an important influence on the behaviour of its members. In fact, many people unconsciously develop their sex identity and sex roles based on sex stereotypes they learned as children.

Berk (1994) notes that by 2 years of age children begin to perceive themselves as being a boy or a girl. In the process of learning what it means to be boys or girls, children associate, in a stereotypical manner, certain toys, games, attitudes and behaviours, such as being aggressive or compliant, with one sex or the other (Huston, 1983; Jacklin and Maccoby, 1983; Picariello *et al.*, 1990). For example, consider an experiment conducted by Montemayor (1974), who invited children between the ages of 6 and 8 years to play a game that involved tossing marbles into a clown's body. Some of the children were told that they were playing a 'girl's game', some were told it was a 'boy's game', and others were told nothing. Boys and girls both said that the game was more fun when it had been described as appropriate to their sex, and they even attained better scores when it was.

Where do children learn sex stereotypes? Although a child's peer group and teachers are important, parents play an especially important role in the development of sex stereotypes. For example, parents tend to encourage and reward their sons for playing with 'masculine' toys such as cars and trucks and objects such as baseballs and footballs (Fagot and Hagan, 1991). And parents tend to encourage and reward their daughters for engaging in 'feminine' activities that promote dependency, warmth and sensitivity, such as playing house or hosting a make-believe tea party (Dunn *et al.*, 1987; Lytton and Romney, 1991). Parents who do not encourage or reward these kinds of stereotypical activity tend to have children whose attitudes and behaviour reflect fewer sex stereotypes (Weisner and Wilson-Mitchell, 1990).

The nature of sex differences

The origin and nature of sex differences has been and is likely to continue to be a controversial topic in psychology (Eagly, 1995; Shibley Hyde and Plant, 1995). As you saw in Chapter 11, there are some reliable differences in cognitive ability between men and women, boys and girls, but these are few and far between. Part of the controversy stems from the way in which behaviour differences between men and women are measured and how large those differences seem to be.

Berk (1994) has reviewed recent research on sex differences and has concluded that the most reliable differences are the following. Girls show earlier verbal development, more effective expression and interpretation of emotional cues, and a higher tendency to comply with adults and peers. Boys show stronger spatial abilities, increased aggression, and greater tendency towards risk taking. Boys are also more likely to show developmental problems such as language disorders, behaviour problems or physical impairments. The reasons for such sex differences were discussed in Chapter 11.

Moral development

The word morality comes from a Latin word that means 'custom'. Moral behaviour is behaviour that conforms to a generally accepted set of rules, although whether these rules generally are accepted is quite controversial. With very few exceptions, by the time a person reaches adulthood, he or she has accepted a set of rules about personal and social behaviour. These rules vary in different cultures and may take the form of laws, taboos and even sorcery (Chasdi, 1994). How does a child acquire morality?

Piaget's theory of moral development

According to Piaget, the first stage of moral development (ages 5–10 years) is moral realism, which is characterised by egocentrism, or 'self-centredness', and blind adherence to rules.

Egocentric children can evaluate events only in terms of their personal consequences. Their behaviour is not guided by the effects it might have on someone else, because they are not capable of imagining themselves in the other person's place. Thus, young children do not consider whether an act is right or wrong but only whether it is likely to have good or bad consequences personally. Punishment is a bad consequence, and the fear of punishment is the only real moral force at this age. A young child also believes that rules come from parents (or other authority figures, such as older children or God) and that rules cannot be changed.

Older children and adults judge an act by the intentions of the actor as well as by the consequences of the act. A young child considers only an act's objective outcomes, not the subjective intent that lay behind the act. For example, Piaget told two stories, one about John, who accidentally broke fifteen cups, and Henry, who broke one cup while trying to do something that was forbidden to him. When a young child is asked which of the two children is the naughtiest, the child will say that John is, because he broke fifteen cups. He or she will not take into account the fact that the act was entirely accidental.

As children mature, they become less egocentric and more capable of empathy. Older children (older than age 7) can imagine how another person feels. This shift away from egocentrism means that children's behaviour may be guided not merely by the effects that acts have on themselves but also by the effects they have on others. At around 10 years of age, children enter Piaget's second stage of moral development, morality of co-operation, during which rules become more flexible as the child learns that many of them (such as those that govern games) are social conventions that may be altered by mutual consent.

Kohlberg's theory of moral development

Piaget's description of moral development has been considerably elaborated on by Lawrence Kohlberg (1927–1987). Kohlberg studied boys of between 10 and 17 years of age, and he studied the same boys over the course of several years. He presented the children with stories involving moral dilemmas. For example, one story described a man called Heinz whose wife was dying of a cancer that could only be treated by a medication discovered by a druggist living in the same town. The man could not afford the price demanded by the druggist, so the distraught man broke into the druggist's store and stole enough of the drug to save his wife's life. The boys were asked what Heinz should have done and why he should have done it. On the basis of his research, Kohlberg decided

that moral development consisted of three levels and seven stages (see Table 12.3). These stages are closely linked to children's cognitive development as outlined by Piaget.

The first two stages belong to the preconventional level, during which morality is externally defined. During stage 1, morality of punishment and obedience, children blindly obey authority and avoid punishment. When asked to decide what Heinz should do, children base their decisions on fears about being punished for letting one's wife die or for committing a crime. During stage 2, morality of naive instrumental hedonism, children's behaviour is guided egocentrically by the pleasantness or unpleasantness of its consequences to them. The moral choice is reduced to a weighing of the probable risks and benefits of stealing the drug.

The next two stages belong to the conventional level, which includes an understanding that the social system has an interest in people's behaviour. During stage 3, morality of maintaining good relations, children want to be regarded by people who know them as good, well behaved children. Moral decisions are based on perceived social pressure. Either Heinz should steal the drug because people would otherwise regard him as heartless, or he should not steal it because they would regard him as a criminal. During stage 4, morality of maintaining social order, laws and moral rules are perceived as instruments used to maintain social order and, as such, must be obeyed. Thus, both protecting a life and respecting people's property are seen as rules that help maintain social order.

Kohlberg also described a final level of moral development – the postconventional level, during which people realise that moral rules have some underlying principles that apply to all situations and societies. During stage 5,

Level and stage	Highlights
Preconventional level	
Stage 1: Morality of punishment and obedience	Avoidance of punishment
Stage 2: Morality of naive instrumental hedonism	Egocentric perspective; weighing of potential risks and benefits
Conventional level	
Stage 3: Morality of maintaining good relations	Morality based on approval from others
Stage 4: Morality of maintaining social order	Rules and laws define morality
Postconventional level	
Stage 5: Morality of social contracts	Obey societal rules for the common good, although individual rights sometimes outweigh laws
Stage 6: Morality of universal ethical principles	Societal laws and rules based on ethical values
Stage 7: Morality of cosmic orientation	Adoption of values that transcend societal norms

Table 12.3 Levels and stages of Kohlberg's theory of moral development

morality of social contracts, people recognise that rules are social contracts, that not all authority figures are infallible, and that individual rights can sometimes take precedence over laws. During stage 6, morality of universal ethical principles, people perceive rules and laws as being justified by abstract ethical values, such as the value of human life and the value of dignity. In stage 7, the morality of cosmic orientation, people adopt values that transcend societal norms. This stage represents the zenith of moral development. Kohlberg believed that not all people reach the post-conventional level of moral development.

Evaluation of Piaget's and Kohlberg's theories of moral development

Piaget's and Kohlberg's theories have greatly influenced research on moral development, but they have received some criticism. For example, Piaget's research indicated that children in the first stage (moral realism) respond to the magnitude of a transgression rather than to the intent behind it. But even adults respond to the magnitude of a transgression and rightly so. The theft of a few postage stamps by an office worker is not treated the same way as the embezzlement of thousands of pounds. In this sense, children's morality is quite adult-like.

Kohlberg's conclusions have also been challenged. For example, Sobesky (1983) found that changes in the wording of Heinz's dilemma would drastically change people's responses. If the possibility of imprisonment was underscored, people tended to make more responses belonging to the pre-conventional level. Many researchers agree with Rest (1979), who concluded that Kohlberg's 'stages' are not coherent entities but do describe a progression in the ability of children to consider more and more complex reasons for moral rules.

A different type of criticism was levelled by Gilligan (1977, 1982), who suggested that Kohlberg's theory is sex-biased. According to her, Kohlberg's studies seem to suggest that men (in general) adhered to universal ethical principles, whereas women (in general) preferred to base their moral judgements on the effects these judgements would have on the people involved. Men's judgements were based more on abstract ideas of justice, whereas women's judgements were based more on concrete considerations of caring and concern for relationships.

However, most researchers have not found that men's and women's moral judgements tend to be based on different types of values. For example, Donenberg and Hoffman (1988) found that boys and girls were equally likely to base their moral judgements on justice or caring and that the sex of the main character in the moral dilemma had no effect on their judgements. Walker (1989) tested 233 subjects ranging in ages from 5 to 63 years and found no reliable sex differences. Thus, the available evidence does not appear to support Gilligan's conclusion that such concern is related to a person's sex.

Questions to think about

Sex roles and moral development

- Do the social environments of boys and girls differ?
- Can assumed sex differences in behaviour be explained by socialisation or biology, or both? Why?
- Assuming that children are socialised differently, how would you rear a child without introducing the biases thought to be sex related? Would you want to rear a child in this way?
- How do Kohlberg's and Piaget's views of moral development differ?
- What are the obvious limitations of the database from which Piaget drew conclusions about moral development?
- The philosopher Sartre argued that mankind created morality for itself. By this he meant that what is moral for one person may not be moral to another. With this in mind, is it reasonable to assume that we can measure morality scientifically?
- Are the measures of morality in tests such as those of Kohlberg's more akin to tests of reasoning with emotion?
- Why do children derive pleasure from the misfortune of others?

Developmental disorders

A child can experience a number of cognitive and emotional obstacles that prevent him or her from developing normally. We saw in Chapters 3 and 10 that some children are born with disorders that are associated with mental retardation (such as Down syndrome) or they can develop reading disorders that seem unrelated to the opportunities that the child has for learning to read and are unrelated to any underlying brain damage (such as developmental dyslexia). If there is no underlying intellectual retardation or physical cause, cognitive and emotional disorders are sometimes described as specific developmental disorders or disorders of psychological development (Rispens and van Yperen, 1997).

In earlier chapters, we discussed some disorders of childhood in some detail. This section describes disorders we have not come across yet: autism, conduct disorder and Attention Deficit Hyperactivity Disorder, and disorders of emotional regulation.

Autism

Characteristics of autism

Autism is a developmental disorder characterised by three features: social abnormality, language abnormality, and stereotypical and repetitive patterns of behaviour (Frith, 1989; Happe, 1994; Bailey *et al.*, 1996), all of which can extend to adulthood (Gillberg, 1991). Autism was originally reported in 1943 by Leo Kanner in an article in which he described eleven cases of 'autistic disturbance of affective contact and … desire for preservation of sameness'. The symptoms he described form the core of the classification of autism today.

The social abnormality includes the child's inability to reciprocate in social interactions, to form or develop loving relationships and to interact spontaneously with others. Autistic children and adults have an impairment in the appreciation of social cues.

One characteristic feature of autism is the inability to look for emotion in the behaviour or expression of others; this may give autistic children an aloof and cold demeanour because they may be judged emotionally unresponsive. In an experiment in which autistic and control children were asked to sort pictures of individuals according to a category, autistic children would sort by appearance (hat) rather than emotion (Weeks and Hobson, 1987). The impairment in interpersonal communication, however, appears to be limited to interpersonal understanding – not all social communication is impaired (Mundy *et al.*, 1986; Sigman, 1995).

Language development in autism is severely delayed and about half of autistics do not develop useful language. In addition to this delay, there is evidence of deviant communication in the form of the idiosyncratic use of language, making up of new words (neologising) and engagement in little social chat. Rutter (1987) has argued that such poor communication skills arise from the autistic's impaired ability to use feedback. Other examples of deviant language use include a difficulty in maintaining a topic of conversation (Bailey *et al.*, 1996). There is also an impaired ability to play spontaneously with toys, possibly because autistics do not know what the toys mean. However, there is evidence that pretend play may not be totally absent in autistic children (Lewis and Boucher, 1988).

Stereotypical and repetitive behaviour includes an over-reliance on routines or rituals and an abnormal attachment to objects.

The development of autism

Autism develops in the first two years of a child's life and is four times as common in boys than girls (Gillberg and Coleman, 1992; Rapin, 1997). The prevalence of the disorder is 1 in 1,000 across most of the countries in which autism has been studied (Sugiyama *et al.*, 1992; Bryson *et al.*, 1988; Gillberg and Coleman, 1992). Autism may recede when the child develops language and uses it to communicate socially.

Early signs of the disorder include a failure to maintain eye-to-eye contact, to reach out to familiar persons

(Swettenham *et al.*, 1998) and to imitate (Klin *et al.*, 1992). There are checklists available which enable parents to determine whether their child is exhibiting autistic tendencies and such checklists include Baron-Cohen *et al.*'s (1992) Checklist for Autism in Toddlers (CHAT) which aims to identify those at risk of developing the disorder. Mental retardation is common in cases of autism and is estimated to occur in 75 per cent of cases (Rutter, 1979; Rapin, 1997). Whereas performance on some cognitive tasks is low (such as comprehension), performance on others is high (such as block design) (Venter *et al.*, 1992). Some autistics also exhibit exceptional abilities in specific domains such as reading, spelling, maths and music. When these abilities become extreme and highly remarkable, autistic individuals are called idiot savants although such exceptional abilities are not unique to autism (O'Connor and Hermelin, 1988).

Some researchers have also suggested that autism may be an inherited disorder because there is a high incidence of fragile X disorder in autistic children (Bailey *et al.*, 1996). Twin studies suggest a higher concordance rate in identical than fraternal twins (Bailey *et al.*, 1995; Steffenburg *et al.*, 1989). Currently, however, there is no evidence that autism is a simple inherited disorder and there is no clear-cut evidence for a genetic component (Rutter, 1994).

The outcome for autism is varied – some individuals develop little language whereas others are able to go on to full-time education, get married and start families (Rapin, 1997). The most important therapeutic intervention appears to involve intensive education aimed at changing the behavioural and communication problems. As such, most interventions are designed for use by parents and teachers who have greatest contact with the children. Medical interventions have also been developed but these appear to be more effective in improving attention than in eliminating all the characteristics of the disorder (Cohen and Volkmar, 1997).

Autism and theory of mind

In the late 1980s, a theme emerged in autism research which suggested that autistic children had impaired ability to make inferences about other people's mental states; that is, these children lacked, or had a defective, theory of mind (Leslie, 1987). According to this early model, in the second year of the child's development, it can pretend play and understand others' mental states, desires and beliefs. In autistic children, the mechanism which allows this is impaired. As a result, the lack of pretend play would also be accompanied, later on, by an inability to interpret others' mental states. This impairment did not occur in children with mental handicap or low IQ.

For example, Baron-Cohen *et al.* (1985) reported a study in which a child saw the unexpected transfer of an object from the location in which it was placed by the experimenter to a different location. The child's task was to predict where the experimenter would look for this object. Such tasks are now called 'theory of mind' tasks/tests of false belief. Four year old children could correctly indicate that the experimenter would look in the original location for the object; autistic children, however, could not and predicted that the experimenter would look in the new location. The children seemed unaware that the experimenter would not know about the transfer of the object – they could not imagine the task from the other person's perspective. Baron-Cohen (1995) later used the term 'mindblindness' to refer to such inabilities to understand the thoughts of others.

Russell and his colleagues hypothesised that similar deficits in theory of mind tasks would be expected in deaf children because deafness (as well as congenital blindness) could affect the child's social experience (Russell *et al.*, 1998). An earlier Australian study had found that 4–13 year old deaf children failed theory of mind tests habitually passed by 4 and 5 year old hearing children (Peterson and Siegal, 1995). Russell *et al.* administered a false belief task, similar to that used by Baron-Cohen, to deaf children between 4 and 16 years of age and matched hearing children. The deaf children performed significantly worse on the false belief tests than did hearing children, with the older deaf children performing better than the younger deaf children. From these findings, Russell *et al.* argue that there may be developmental delay in the ability to perform theory of mind tasks, hence the better performance of the older deaf children. This said, however, 40 per cent of the 13–16 year olds still failed the test, which demonstrates that the absence of a theory of mind is permanent in some deaf children.

Other theoretical approaches to autism

According to Karmiloff-Smith's theory of representational redescription (Karmiloff-Smith, 1988, 1992), the child is a scientist, exploring the environment and constructing and testing hypotheses. The child is seen as a theoretician who builds theories and explains events or stimuli that cannot be explained by simplifying them. To become an expert 'scientist' the child passes through a series of stages that involve the child constructing representations of stimuli around him or her. In the beginning, behaviour is externally driven and the child makes many mistakes before getting better. This process involves reconstructing or redescribing representations (hence, theory of *representational redescription*) as development occurs. This perspective on theory of mind, however, has been challenged (Gellaty, 1997). Gellaty argues that this theory sees the child as an isolated individual, not as part of a community; he also suggests that the concept of 'scientific thinking' which the child is thought to develop is too simplistic and assumes that all scientific thinking occurs in the same way.

There are other researchers, however, who argue that autistic children do not have an impaired theory of mind because there are some autistic individuals who can complete these tasks quite accurately (Happé, 1993, 1994). The major deficit in autistic children, according to Frith and her colleagues (Frith and Happé, 1994), is the inability to see situations and objects as wholes. Most of us see images and events as global images and events – we attend to the detail later. When you look at the television screen you do not attend to each individual detail of the image consciously (although your brain does do this) but you perceive a global image. The problem with autistics, according to this view, is that they process information piecemeal and not in the context in which it appears.

There appears to be some evidence for this hypothesis. In tests where participants have to find images within larger, more complex images, autistic children do very well (Shallice and Frith, 1983). Most normal participants have difficulty ignoring the large global image in which the 'hidden' image is embedded. Autistic children are also better than controls at discriminating among novel stimuli (but not familiar ones), indicating that they attend to specific features of stimuli (Plaisted *et al.*, 1998). Recently, Frith and Happé (1994) have developed their model and suggest that two cognitive systems may be impaired in autism: one which normally allows theory of mind and another which determines the way in which information is processed. This model has the benefit of accounting for the theory of mind deficits and the tendency of autistic individuals to segment information instead of perceiving it globally. However, the model does not explain why such impairment arose in the first place. One source of information suggests that this impairment may be neurological in nature.

Neuropsychology of autism

There are several neurobiological features of autism but few that are consistently reported. Increased head and/or brain size and a reduction or increase in different brain regions seem to be the most consistently observed deficits (Bailey *et al.*, 1993a). One study of American children has reported that 80 per cent of 8 year old autistic children had a head circumference above the mean for children of comparable sex and age (Stevenson *et al.*, 1997).

Other neural characteristics include reduced cerebellum (Courchesne *et al.*, 1987) and parietal lobe size (Courchesne *et al.*, 1993), and the appearance of small, densely-packed neurons in various subcortical structures such as the hippocampus and amygdala (Bauman and Kemper, 1994). None of these are consistently reported neurobiological features of autism, however.

A recent review of neuroimaging data concluded that a reduction in frontal lobe size and activation are some of the more consistent neuropsychological characteristics of the disorder (Deb and Thompson, 1998). Studies that have reported reductions in the neurotransmitter dopamine in the prefrontal cortex only (Ernst *et al.*, 1997) and decreased volume in the frontal lobes (Piven *et al.*, 1995) are more robust and are consistent with a theory of autism that attributes impaired planning and organisation to frontal lobe dysfunction (Hughes *et al.*, 1994). It is possible that the theory of mind deficit described in the section above could, for example, be accounted for by the inability to correct knowingly inaccurate responses and to plan and generate appropriate sequences, events and images (Stone *et al.*, 1998), behaviours that need the frontal lobes.

Autism: a case study

'A' seemed like a perfectly normal child until he reached six months of age. His mother began to notice 'bouts of odd behaviour': he did not place himself in the anticipatory position when he was about to be picked up, he kept himself still and was unresponsive to cuddling. By 12 months, he was clearly showing signs of behavioural disturbance: he would scream, shout, have tantrums, become hyperactive, sleep for only two to four hours and would obsessively attach himself to one play object. He showed an extreme dislike of being held.

Between 12 and 18 months, any behavioural progress stopped and his behaviour worsened. He became violent, destructive, would run around in circles, sat in boxes and hid behind piled up furniture, refused all food except that in a bottle, refused to wear clothes, chewed stones and paper and was indifferent to attention. He would play repetitively with the same toy and insisted on having two of everything.

Although he began speaking before 12 months, this language development stopped at 18 months and ceased for about two years. At three and a half years of age, speech resumed again. Despite having these language delays, his mother still considered him to be of above average intelligence and he appeared to have a very good memory for routes.

At 4 years and 8 months, 'A' joined school and was found to occupy the dull to normal range of intelligence. A travelling teacher found him to be destructive, hyperactive and show poor concentration and attention. The spinning and the ritualisation continued.

At this point, his mother decided to intervene proactively and tried to change his behaviour. She cleared the house of all breakable objects (to reduce his destructiveness) and spent more time with him up until eleven o'clock when he went to bed. She bought him clothes that he found attractive and talked to him constantly in order to try and encourage him to understand and produce speech. She would give running commentaries on everything she did to this end and she would read to 'A' whether he seemed interested in the book or text or not. Between

the age of 4 and 5 years, he was found to talk in numbers ('Look at that trick; that's a 23'); those things which appealed to him were 7, 8 and 9.

During school, language developed almost normally although his social behaviour was still considered to be distant. By the age of 14, he had a non-verbal IQ of 76 although on object assembly tasks he performed very well. At 17 years of age, he showed difficulty on tasks that involved forward planning. On maze-solving tasks, for example, he would stick to a set pattern of responses and was unable to correct his incorrect responses. Similarly, he was unable to abstract categories from sets of stimuli. His copying ability and his ability to read what he had copied was excellent.

A little later, he left home, got a job at a timber-mill, met a woman who already had a son, married her and had a son of his own.

This case study is a rather rare one in autism because it has a happy ending. Most outcomes are not as positive as this. Although A's intellectual ability is below average, he is considered to be a caring father and husband and leads a normal and happy life. Some aspects of his development, however, show the classic hallmarks of autism. His language ability was delayed in the first two years, he became inattentive and destructive during the same period and he would engage in ritualistic and obsessive behaviour. His eccentric behaviour (such as using numbers, hiding in boxes) also signified autism, and his inability to perform tasks that require executive function (such as the maze-solving task) is consistent with models of autism that suggest it involves an impairment in executive function. What was important in reducing and eliminating these behaviours, however, appeared to be the deliberate intervention of A's mother. Her constant attention to her son and her deliberate intention to expose her son to as much language as possible probably helped keep the disorder at bay. This exposure was important. This is why, as we saw in an earlier section, most remedial therapies focus intensively on solving communication and behavioural problems.

Source: Prior, 1992.

Asperger's syndrome

One disorder which has close links with autism is Asperger's syndrome. According to Asperger (1944), some individuals exhibit 'autistic psychopathy' that is reflected in poor social functioning and interpersonal communication; individuals usually have an obsessional and narrow range of interests. Because of these characteristics, some researchers have suggested that Asperger's is a milder form of autism (Schopler, 1996). There appears to be some support for this notion. When Asperger's original four cases were re-analysed, for example, they met current DSM-IV criteria for autistic disorder, not Asperger's (Miller and

Ozonoff, 1997). However, this finding could simply reflect the ways in which criteria for diagnosis have changed over the years. One way of determining the validity of a disorder would be to see if it was characterised by different features from those of related disorders.

For example, we saw in the section above that autistic individuals perform well on tasks that require them to assemble objects or to form a target abstract pattern from a set of blocks. If Asperger's syndrome is similar to autism, then we should see the same superior performance in both disorders. In a study comparing 120 Swedish individuals with Asperger's syndrome, autistic disorder or attention disorder on a range of tests from the WAIS-R, autistic individuals did better at the block design task and Asperger's individuals performed better at the verbal tasks and poorly at the object assembly task (Ehlers *et al.*, 1997). The result would suggest, therefore, that Asperger's can be distinguished from autism on the basis of spatial performance. However, whether this difference is meaningful is questionable. Abstract and portrait painters might be distinguished by some underlying characteristic, for example, but this does not negate the fact that they are both groups of artists using the same visuospatial and motor abilities. The fact that they differ on one dimension, does not make them totally different.

Conduct disorder/attention deficit hyperactivity disorder

Conduct disorder is a severe impairment in the ability of the child to inhibit its own behaviour and to inhibit antisocial and deviant behaviour (Nicol, 1998). It is related to a specific disorder termed attention deficit hyperactivity disorder (ADHD) whose main features are poor sustained attention, impulsiveness and hyperactivity (Barkley, 1997), as the example of Keith at the opening of the chapter illustrates.

There is evidence that ADHD runs in families, especially behaviourally disordered families (Faraone *et al.*, 1997), and that conduct disorder is six times more common in those children who had been sexually abused (Fergusson *et al.*, 1996; Herrenkohl *et al.*, 1997).

ADHD occurs in 3–7 per cent of the child population, with three times as many boys as girls exhibiting the disorder. Between 50 and 80 per cent of children with the disorder continue showing symptoms into adolescence; 30–50 per cent of affected adolescents show symptoms in adulthood. So, although the disorder recedes, it persists in a high percentage of affected cases. Because of the nature of the disorder, the problems associated with it can be cognitively damaging. ADHD has been associated with low academic achievement, school performance, suspension/expulsion from school, poor family and peer relationships, mental disorder and substance abuse (Barkley, 1997). Most of the 'treatment' approaches to the disorder involve some form of counselling, behaviour management and, sometimes, psychoactive medication.

It is unclear why ADHD appears; different authors have associated social and family problems with the disorder although determining cause and effect in these instances is difficult.

Disorder of emotional regulation

Disorders of emotional regulation refer to problems that the child has in operating at an emotionally normal level. They represent behavioural problems which impair the ability to undertake day-to-day activities (Zeanah *et al.*, 1997). For example, the child may be abnormally distressed, depressed, show sleep disturbance or feeding problems or exhibit anxiety.

The degree of attachment that the child demonstrates towards its caregiver is often used as a good index of these behaviours. Because the child has no sophisticated language, it is difficult to diagnose an emotional disorder in the first three years of life. A depressed person can express his or her depression verbally (and even suggest causes); this language facility is not available to infants. As a result, emotional disorder tend to be reported by parents who see their child behaving in a way that is out of the ordinary.

Sometimes, however, the child's emotional problems may be associated with those of the carer, especially the mother. Given that the mother makes the greatest investment in caring for the child during its early years, perhaps this is not unexpected. Depressed mothers, for example, have been shown to express more negative emotion, show less positive engagement with, and less sensitivity to the child's behaviour during interactions with the child (Lyons-Ruth *et al.*, 1990). If the mother is depressed for longer than three months after the birth of the child, the child can show developmental and growth delay (Field, 1992). Infants who interact with a nursery school teacher or non-depressed fathers have been found to show more positive and expressive behaviours than when interacting with their depressed mother (Pelaez-Noguera *et al.*, 1994).

Emotion, attachment and hemispheric asymmetry

As we will see in greater detail in the next chapter, one theory of emotional expression suggests that the front part of the brain regulates our experience of positive and negative emotions differently. The left frontal region is thought to be responsive to positive emotion and the right frontal region is thought to be more responsive to negative emotion. Negative emotion may also be associated with reduced activity in the left frontal cortex (Davidson and Sutton, 1995).

Studies of distressed infants have highlighted similar asymmetries. For example, Davidson and Fox (1989) measured EEGs from infants they characterised as criers and non-criers (criers were those who became distressed when separated from their mother). The criers were distinguished from the non-criers by greater right-sided frontal EEG activation. Dawson *et al.* (1997) reported that the infants of depressed mothers (as well as the mothers themselves) showed reduced left frontal EEG activity. These asymmetries have also been found in studies comparing 4 year old infants who are either happy and sociable or unhappy and unsociable. The sociable children showed greater left frontal activation (Fox *et al.*, 1995). What seems unclear in these studies, however, is the nature of cause and effect. Does the distress cause the EEG asymmetry or does the EEG asymmetry cause the distress? Does the asymmetry predispose the infant to distress? These are interesting and important questions. Because they have implications for theories of the nature of emotion and the neuropsychology of emotion, we discuss these in more detail in the next chapter.

The frontal lobes, as we saw in Chapters 4, 8 and 11, also are involved in executive functions such as regulating behaviour (planning, changing strategies, responding emotionally). A recent study by Claire Hughes and her colleagues at the Institute of Psychiatry in London, compared the performance of 3 or 4 year old children who were described as 'hard to manage', or not, on a range of theory of mind, emotional understanding and executive function (frontal lobe) tasks (Hughes *et al.*, 1998). They found that the disruptive children showed poorer understanding of emotion and less successful performance on the theory of mind tasks.

Questions to think about

Childhood disorders

- What are the main problems of studying psychopathology in children? How would you overcome these problems?
- What are the principal characteristics of autism? How would you try to eliminate these symptoms?
- What causes autism?
- What do psychologists mean by theory of mind? Do you think that autistic children lack a theory of mind?
- Is there a difference between conduct disorder and attention deficit hyperactivity disorder?
- What is the relationship between secure attachment and brain activity? Is this relationship causal? (If so, in what direction?)
- If regional brain activity can discriminate sociable from non-sociable children, what do you think would be the implications of this for child welfare and education?

Adolescence

After childhood comes adolescence, the threshold to adulthood (in Latin, *adolescere* means 'to grow up'). The transition between childhood and adulthood is as much social as it is biological. In some societies, people are considered to be adults as soon as they are sexually mature, at which time they may assume adult rights and responsibilities, including marriage. In most industrialised societies, where formal education often continues into the late teens and early twenties, adulthood officially comes several years later. The end of adolescence is difficult to judge because the line between adolescence and young adulthood is fuzzy: there are no distinct physical changes that mark this transition.

Physical development

Puberty (from the Latin *puber*, meaning 'adult'), the period during which a person's reproductive system matures, marks the beginning of the transition from childhood to adulthood. Many physical changes occur during this stage: people reach their ultimate height, develop increased muscle size and body hair, and become capable of reproduction. There is also a change in social roles. As a child, a person is dependent on parents, teachers and other adults. As an adolescent, he or she is expected to assume more responsibility. Relations with peers also suddenly change; members of one's own sex become potential rivals for the attention of members of the other sex.

Sexual maturation

The internal sex organs and genitalia do not change much for several years after birth, but they begin to develop again at puberty. When boys and girls reach about 11–14 years of age, their testes or ovaries secrete hormones that begin the process of sexual maturation. This activity of the gonads is initiated by the hypothalamus, the part of the brain to which the pituitary gland is attached. The hypothalamus instructs the pituitary gland to secrete hormones that stimulate the gonads to secrete sex hormones. These sex hormones act on various organs of the body and initiate the changes that accompany sexual maturation (see Figure 12.10).

The sex hormones secreted by the gonads cause growth and maturation of the external genitalia and of the gonads themselves. In addition, these hormones cause the maturation of ova and the production of sperm. All these developments are considered primary sex characteristics, because they are essential to the ability to reproduce. The sex hormones also stimulate the development of secondary sex characteristics, the physical changes that distinguish males from females. Before puberty, boys and girls look much the same, except, perhaps, for their hairstyles and clothing. At puberty, young men's testes begin to secrete

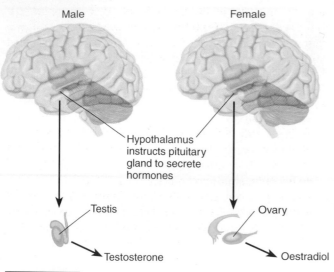

Male   Female

Hypothalamus instructs pituitary gland to secrete hormones

Testis   Ovary

Testosterone   Oestradiol

Figure 12.10

Sexual maturation. Puberty is initiated when the hypothalamus instructs the pituitary gland to secrete hormones that cause the gonads to secrete sex hormones.

testosterone; this hormone causes their muscles to develop, their facial hair to grow, and their voices to deepen. Young women's ovaries secrete oestradiol, the most important oestrogen, or female sex hormone. Oestradiol causes women's breasts to grow and their pelvis to widen, and it produces changes in the layer of fat beneath the skin and in the texture of the skin itself.

Development of the adult secondary sex characteristics takes several years, and not all characteristics develop at the same time. The process begins in girls at around age 11. The first visible change is the accumulation of fatty tissue around the nipples, followed shortly by the growth of pubic hair. The spurt of growth in height commences, and the uterus and vagina begin to enlarge. The first menstrual period begins at around age 13, just about the time the rate of growth in height begins to decline. In boys, sexual maturation begins slightly later. The first visible event is the growth of the testes and scrotum, followed by the appearance of pubic hair. A few months later, the penis begins to grow, and the spurt of growth in height starts. The larynx grows larger, which causes the voice to become lower. Sexual maturity – the ability to father a child – occurs at around age 15. The growth of facial hair usually occurs later; often a full beard does not grow until the late teens or early twenties.

In industrialised societies, the average age at the onset of puberty has been declining. For example, the average age at the onset of menstruation was between 14 and 15 years in 1900 but is between 12 and 13 years today. The most important reason for this decline is better childhood nutrition. It appears that this decline is levelling off in industrialised societies, but in many developing countries, the age of the onset of puberty is beginning to fall as these countries enjoy increasing prosperity.

Behavioural effects of puberty

The changes that accompany sexual maturation have a profound effect on young people's behaviour and self-concept. They become more sensitive about their appearance. Many girls worry about their weight and the size of their breasts and hips. Many boys worry about their height, the size of their genitals, their muscular development and the growth of their beards (Alsaker, 1996). In addition, most adolescents display a particular form of egocentrism that develops early in the stage of formal operations: self-consciousness. Some developmental psychologists believe that self-consciousness results from the difficulty in distinguishing their own self-perceptions from the views other people have of them.

Because the onset of puberty occurs at different times in different individuals, young adolescents can find themselves more or less mature than some of their friends, and this difference can have important social consequences. Early maturing boys feel more confident about themselves than do late maturing boys (Tobin-Richards *et al.*, 1983) and are also more satisfied with their looks and musculature (Cok, 1990). Early maturing girls, however, seem to exhibit greater depression and unhappiness, although the evidence for this is mixed (Alsaker, 1992). Early maturing girls do appear to have greater eating concerns (Brooks-Gun, 1988) and show greater variability in self-esteem.

Social development and peer relations

During adolescence, a person's behaviour and social roles change dramatically. Adolescence is not simply a continuation of childhood; it marks a real transition from the dependency of childhood to the relative independence of adulthood. Adolescence is also a period during which many people seek out new experiences and engage in reckless behaviour – behaviour that involves psychological, physical and legal risks for them as well as for others (Arnett, 1995).

Norm-breaking such as this is related to the adolescent's social network (Magnusson *et al.*, 1986). For example, early maturing girls have been found to have older female friends who engage in more adult behaviour (such as drinking and smoking). Such girls are also likely to regard themselves as more accepted by older girls, date more (Stattin and Magnusson, 1990) and are more sexually active (Meyer-Bahlburg *et al.*, 1989). The picture in boys is unclear; there is no such consistent pattern in the nature of their peer network or their behaviour.

Friendship in childhood appears to have greater long-term consequences than might first be apparent (Newcomb and Bagwell, 1995). For example, pre-adolescent friendship and peer rejection are significant predictors of adult adjustment. Poor peer relations are associated with later maladjustment and mental health problems (Parker *et al.*, 1995). In an extensive longitudinal study, Bagwell *et al.* (1998)

tracked 60 individuals from school age to twelve years after (when the mean age was 23 three months). These researchers found that lower levels of pre-adolescent peer rejection predicted overall adjustment. Those with friends reported higher self-esteem as adults whereas peer rejection and friendlessness was associated with mental disorder, especially depression. This evidence suggests that peer support and approval are important determinants of the adolescent's happiness and later adjustment. However, approval or rejection may not necessarily be causes of later adjustment or maladjustment. Perhaps these factors help to moderate maladjustment.

Sexuality

Sexual behaviour occurring during adolescence has increased in frequency during the past few decades, although studies do suggest that boys and girls spend more time thinking about the opposite sex than being with them (Richards *et al.*, 1998). Fifty years ago, approximately 20 per cent of the females and 40 per cent of the males in the United States said that they had engaged in sexual intercourse by age 20. Now these figures are approximately 50 per cent for both males and females (Brooks-Gunn and Furstenberg, 1989). These figures seem to have peaked in the late 1970s. Since then, they have declined slightly and expressions of guilt feelings about sexual behaviour have increased (Gerrard, 1986).

Relations with parents

As adolescents begin to define their new roles and to assert them, they almost inevitably come into conflict with their parents. Adolescents and their parents tend to have similar values and attitudes towards important issues (Youniss and Smollar, 1985). Unless serious problems occur, family conflicts tend to be provoked by relatively minor issues, such as messy rooms, loud music, clothes, curfews and household chores. These problems tend to begin around the time of puberty; if puberty occurs particularly early or late, so does the conflict (Paikoff and Brooks-Gunn, 1991).

Adolescence is said to be a time of turmoil, a period characterised by unhappiness, stress and confusion. Whereas a few adolescents are unhappy most of the time (and most are unhappy some of the time), studies have found that the vast majority of teenagers generally feel happy and self-confident (Offer and Sabshim, 1984; Peterson and Ebata, 1987). But mood states do seem to be more variable during the teenage years than during other times of life. Csikszentmihalyi and Larson (1984) randomly sampled the mood states of a group of teenage students. They gave them electronic beepers that sounded at random intervals that were, on average, two hours apart. Each time the beepers sounded, the students stopped what they were doing and filled out a questionnaire that asked what they were doing, how they felt, what they were thinking about,

and so on. The investigators found that the students' moods could swing from high to low and back again in the course of a few hours. The questionnaires also revealed conflicts between the participants and other family members. Although the subjects of the conflicts were usually trivial, they nevertheless concerned the teenagers deeply. As the authors noted,

> 'Asking a boy who has spent many days practising a song on the guitar "Why are you playing that trash?" might not mean much to the father, but it can be a great blow to the son. The so-called "growth pains" of adolescence are no less real just because their causes appear to be without much substance to adults. In fact, this is exactly what the conflict is all about: what is to be taken seriously?' (Csikszentmihalyi and Larson, 1984, p. 140)

The effects of parental conflict

The degree of parental conflict that a child is exposed to can have devastating consequences later in the child's life, especially in terms of the child's adjustment (Fincham, 1998). Although divorce may seem an obvious cause of problems for the child, evidence suggests that the negative effects seen after divorce are evident before separation occurs (Doherty and Needle, 1991). Parental conflict has been associated with poor academic performance, depression (Meyer *et al.*, 1993) and antisocial behaviour (Loeber and Dishion, 1983). Longitudinal studies suggest that high degrees of parental conflict at the age of 3 are associated with later adjustment problems in adulthood (Neighbors *et al.*, 1997). Although not all children will be affected detrimentally by parental conflict, this behaviour has consistently clear and negative effects on the child's immediate and future behaviour.

Questions to think about

Adolescence

- What distinguishes an adolescent from an adult?
- Why is adolescence seen as a troubled time for both children and adults?
- Do adolescents 'rebel'? If so, what are they rebelling against and why? Is rebellion a Western phenomenon?
- Why are the peer relations of early maturing girls more secure than those of early maturing boys?
- Puberty is associated with an increase in fat in girls and muscle in boys. Why do boys not become as concerned with their musculature as girls are with their weight?
- How do you think that divorcing parents should behave in order to protect the psychological health of their children?

Adulthood and old age

It is much easier to outline child or adolescent development than adult development; children and adolescents change faster, and the changes are closely related to age. Adult development is much more variable because physical changes in adults are more gradual. Mental and emotional changes during adulthood are more closely related to individual experience than to age. Some people achieve success and satisfaction with their careers, while some hate their jobs. Some marry and have happy family lives; others are happy to live without children, and others never adjust to the roles of spouse and parent. No single description of adult development will fit everyone.

Physical development

Muscular strength peaks during the late twenties or early thirties and then declines slowly thereafter as muscle tissue gradually deteriorates. By age 70, strength has declined by approximately 30 per cent in both men and women (Young et al., 1984). However, age has much less effect on endurance than on strength. Both laboratory tests and athletic records reveal that older people who remain physically fit show remarkably little decline in the ability to exercise for extended periods of time (Spirduso and MacRae, 1990).

Although it is easy to measure a decline in the sensory systems (such as vision, hearing and olfaction), older people often show very little functional change in these systems. Most of them learn to make adjustments for their sensory losses, using additional cues to help them decode sensory information. For example, people with a hearing loss can learn to attend more carefully to other people's gestures and lip movements; they can also profitably use their experience to infer what is said.

Functional changes with age are also minimal in highly developed skills. For example, Salthouse (1984, 1988) found that experienced older typists continued to perform as well as younger ones, despite the fact that they performed less well on standard laboratory tests of sensory and motor skills, including the types of skill that one would expect to be important in typing. The continuous practice they received enabled them to develop strategies to compensate for their physical decline. For example, they tended to read farther ahead in the text they were typing, which enabled them to plan in advance the patterns of finger movements they would have to make. However, as we saw in Chapter 11, the neurological diseases which can accompany ageing can have devastating intellectual and personal consequences.

Social development

Erikson argued that the adult years consist of three psychosocial stages: intimacy versus isolation, during which people succeed or fail in loving others; generativity versus stagnation, during which people either withdraw inwardly and focus on their problems or reach out to help others; and integrity versus despair, during which life is reviewed with either a sense of satisfaction or with despair.

Another attempt to understand stages of adult development is that of Levinson and his colleagues (Levinson et al., 1978). They interviewed forty men – business executives, blue collar workers, novelists and biologists – and analysed the biographies of famous men and examined stories of men's lives as portrayed in literature. They claimed to have discovered a pattern common to most men's lives. Instead of proceeding smoothly, their lives were characterised by several years of stability punctuated by crises. The crises were periods during which the men began to question their life structures: their occupations, their relations with their families, their religious beliefs and practices, their ethnic identities, and the ways they spent their leisure time. During times of transition – which caused considerable anxiety and turmoil – the men re-evaluated the choices they had made and eventually settled on new patterns that guided them through another period of stability. Periods of transition lasted around four or five years, whereas the intervening periods of stability lasted six or seven years.

For Levinson, the most important crises occur early in adulthood, when choices must be made about career and marriage, and at mid-life (during the early to mid-forties), when realities about one's life structure must finally be faced. Although Levinson did not invent the notion of the mid-life crisis, he certainly helped bring it to the attention of the general public and helped make the term a part of everyone's vocabulary. Levinson concluded that the mid-life crisis happened to all men. Men whose life structures do not yet meet their prior goals and expectations realise that the future will probably not bring the success that up until then has eluded them. Men who have succeeded begin to question whether the goals they had set for themselves were meaningful and worthwhile. All men, successful or not, also begin to confront the fact that they are getting older. They are starting to detect some signs of physical decline, and they are witnesses to the death of their parents or their parents' friends.

Several investigators have defined objective criteria for the presence of a mid-life crisis and have looked for its presence in representative samples of participants. For example, Costa and McCrae (1980) administered a Midlife Crisis Scale to a total of 548 men aged 35–79 years. The scale contained items asking whether the participants were experiencing any of the symptoms of a mid-life crisis, such as dissatisfaction with job and family, a sense of meaninglessness, or a feeling of turmoil. They found no evidence for a mid-life crisis. Some people did report some of the symptoms, but they were no more likely to occur during the early- to mid-forties than at any other age. A study of sixty women (Reinke et al., 1985) also found no evidence of a mid-life crisis. This finding does not mean that middle-aged people do not periodically contemplate or question the important issues in their lives; of course they do. But there appears to be no crisis – in the dramatic sense – to these reflective periods.

Adult development occurs against the backdrop of what many developmental psychologists consider to be the two most important aspects of life: love and work. For most of us, falling in love is more than just a compelling feeling of wanting to be with someone. It often brings with it major responsibilities, such as marriage and children. Work, too, is more than just a way to pass time. It involves setting and achieving goals related to income, status among peers and accomplishments outside the family.

Marriage and family

Generally speaking, mothers assume more responsibilities than fathers for the day-to-day care of children (Biernat and Wortman, 1991). As a result, they spend more time doing housework and less time talking to their husbands (Peskin, 1982), which can place strain on their marital happiness. However, if husband and wife can find time together in the evenings, and if the husband is able to share in the parenting and household chores, the stress of adapting to family life is lessened considerably (Daniels and Weingarten, 1982).

As children grow older and become more self-sufficient in caring for themselves, the day-to-day burdens of raising a family taper off and husbands and wives are able to spend more time with each other. However, adolescents pose new problems for their parents: they may question parental authority, and their burgeoning social agenda may put a wrinkle in their parents' personal and social calendars. For many parents, rearing adolescents, particularly during the time just prior to their leaving home, represents the low point of marital happiness (Cavanaugh, 1990).

Generally speaking, once a family's youngest child has left home, marital happiness increases and continues to do so through the remainder of the couple's life together. It was once thought that the 'empty nest' posed problems for the middle-aged couple, particularly for the mother, who was thought to define her role solely around her children. Although parents may miss daily contact with their children, they also feel happy (not to mention relieved) that a major responsibility of life – raising self-reliant children who become responsible members of society – has been completed successfully. Just as importantly, the parents now have time for each other and freedom to pursue their own interests. It may be true that an empty nest is a happy nest. Research tends to support this statement. In one study, only 6 per cent of empty nest couples reported that life prior to their last child leaving home was better than their empty nest experience. Over 50 per cent of the couples interviewed said that their lives were better now than before their children had left home (Deutscher, 1968; Neugarten, 1974).

Work

The task of raising a family is balanced with one or both parents having a career. In fact, events that occur in the workplace often affect the quality of home life. A promotion and a pay rise can mean that the family can now do things that they could not before. Working long hours to get that pay rise, however, can decrease the amount of time that a couple can spend together with their children.

With the dramatic increase in the number of women entering the workforce in the past twenty-five years, many psychologists have focused their research efforts on understanding dual-earner marriages – those in which both parents work full- or part-time. Compared to single-earner marriages, dual-earner families generally have a better standard of living in terms of material possessions and savings for their children's education and for retirement. Another important benefit accrues, especially to the wife: she is able to achieve recognition and independence outside the home (Crosby, 1991). Most husbands in dual-earner marriages support their wives' working. In addition, they find their wives more interesting, more essential and more helpful mates (Schaie and Willis, 1992).

But all is not bliss in dual-earner marriages. If both partners are working, who manages the household and takes care of the children? In most cases, the woman still does, which often means that she has two roles, one as mother and one as wage earner. Apparently, a husband's support of his wife's working does not always go as far as actually contributing at home. However, husbands who believe strongly in equality for women are likely to help out at home (Bird *et al.*, 1984).

Death

Death is the final event of life. It is a biological and social event – family and friends are emotionally affected by the death of a loved one. Although a death may claim a life at any time, most people die when they are old. One question that developmental psychologists have asked about death and dying among the elderly is, how do old people view the inevitability of their own death?

At one time or another, most of us contemplate our own death. Some of us may contemplate death more than others, but, to be sure, the thought of death crosses our minds at least occasionally. As you might expect, elderly people contemplate their death more often than do younger people. Generally speaking, they fear death less than their younger counterparts do (Kalish, 1976). Why? No one knows for sure, but a tentative explanation may be that older people have had more time to review the past and to plan for the future knowing that death is close at hand. Thus, they are able to prepare themselves psychologically (and financially) for death.

Contemplating and preparing for death, though, is not like knowing that you are actually dying. The changes in attitude that terminally ill people experience have been studied by Kübler-Ross (1969, 1981). After interviewing hundreds of dying people, she concluded that people undergo five distinct phases of psychologically coping with death. The first stage is denial. When terminally ill people learn of their condition, they generally try to deny it. Anger comes next – now they resent the certainty of death. In the third stage, bargaining, people attempt to negotiate their fate with God or others, pleading that their lives might be spared. While bargaining, they actually realise that they are, in fact, going to die. This leads to depression, the fourth stage, which is characterised by a sense of hopelessness and loss. The fifth and final stage, acceptance, is marked by a more peaceful resignation to the facts.

Kübler-Ross's work points up the psychological factors involved in dying and has provided an initial theory about how the dying come to grips with their fate. Her work, though, has not been accepted uncritically. Her research was not scientific – her method for interviewing people was not systematic, and her results are largely anecdotal. Moreover, of the five stages, denial is the only one that appears to be universal. Apparently, not all terminally ill people have the same psychological response to the fact that they are dying.

However, despite its flaws, Kübler-Ross's work is important because it has prompted an awareness, both scientific and public, of the plight of the terminally ill. The scientific response, as you might guess, has been to do more medical research in the hope of prolonging the life of people with cancer or other terminal illness. The public response has involved the attempt to provide support for the dying and their families through hospice services (Aiken, 1994). In the past, hospices were places where strangers and pilgrims could find rest and shelter. Today, hospices are special places that provide medical and psychological support for the dying and their families. In cases in which the dying person wishes to die at home, hospice volunteers work in that setting. The primary functions of hospice services are twofold: to provide relief from pain and to allow the person to die with dignity. No attempt is made to prolong life through technology if doing so would diminish the self-respect of the dying person and his or her family. To die with dignity is perhaps the best death possible – for together, the dying and his or her loved ones are able to experience, for the last time together, reverence for the life experience.

Questions to think about

Adulthood

- Are there ways of halting, or compensating for, the decline in physical ability? What are they?
- Is it valid to divide ages into middle and old age? Is creating homogeneous groups in this way scientifically useful?

- It has been argued that work gives life its structure. Do you agree? Why?
- What are your views on death? Have you thought about your own? Are you worried or indifferent? Why?
- Is marriage psychologically advisable?

Key terms

developmental psychology *p.398*

prenatal period *p.398*

zygote stage *p.398*

embryo stage *p.398*

teratogens *p.398*

androgens *p.399*

foetal stage *p.399*

foetal learning *p.401*

maturation *p.402*

externality effect *p.403*

critical period *p.405*

infantile amnesia *p.405*

deferred imitation paradigm *p.406*

cognitive structures *p.407*

schemata *p.407*

assimilation *p.408*

accommodation *p.408*

sensorimotor period *p.408*

object permanence *p.408*

deferred imitation *p.408*

preoperational period *p.409*

conservation *p.409*

egocentrism *p.410*

period of concrete operations *p.410*

period of formal operations *p.411*

mental space (M-space) *p.414*

optimal level of skill performance *p.414*

attachment *p.416*

stranger anxiety *p.418*

separation anxiety *p.418*

Strange Situation *p.419*

secure attachment *p.419*

resistant attachment *p.419*

avoidant attachment *p.419*

sexual identity *p.420*

sex roles *p.420*

sex stereotypes *p.420*

moral realism *p.420*

morality of co-operation *p.421*

preconventional level *p.421*

conventional level *p.421*

postconventional level *p.421*

autism *p.422*

idiot savants *p.423*

theory of mind *p.423*

Asperger's syndrome *p.425*

DSM-IV *p.425*

conduct disorder *p.426*

attention deficit hyperactivity disorder (ADHD) *p.426*

puberty *p.427*

CHAPTER REVIEW

Prenatal development

- The three stages of prenatal development span the time between conception and birth. In just nine months, the zygote grows from a single cell, void of human resemblance, into a fully developed foetus, complete with physical features that look much like yours and mine, except in miniature.

- Sex is determined by the sex chromosomes. Male sex organs are produced by the action of a gene on the Y chromosome that causes the gonads to develop into testes.

- The testes secrete androgens, which stimulate the development of male sex organs. If testes are not present, the foetus develops as a female.

- The most important factor in normal foetal development is the mother's nutrition.

- Normal foetal development can be disrupted by the presence of teratogens, which can cause mental retardation and physical deformities.

- One well-studied teratogen is alcohol, which, when consumed by a pregnant woman, may lead to foetal alcohol syndrome.

- There is evidence that the human foetus is capable of discriminating between sensory stimuli while in the womb, suggesting that it is capable of a rudimentary form of cognition.

Physical and perceptual development in infancy and childhood

- A newborn infant's first movements are actually reflexes that are crucial to its survival. For example, the rooting, sucking and swallowing reflexes are important in finding and consuming food.

- More sophisticated movements, such as crawling and standing, develop and are refined through natural maturation and practice.

- A newborn's senses appear to be at least partially functional at birth. However, normal development of the senses, like that of motor abilities, depends on experience.

- Genetically, an infant has the potential to develop motor and sensory abilities that coincide with the maturation of its nervous system. But in order for this potential to be realised, the infant's environment must supply the opportunity to test and practise these skills.

- If an infant is deprived of the opportunity to practise them during a critical period, these skills may fail to develop, which will affect his or her performance as an adult.

- Infants will prefer to gaze at an image that has the components of the face in the right places.

Cognitive development in childhood

- The first step in a child's cognitive development is learning that many events are contingent on his or her own behaviour. This understanding occurs gradually and is controlled by the development of the nervous system and by increasingly complex interactions with the environment.

- Piaget divided a child's cognitive development into four periods – a system that is widely, if not universally, accepted.

- The periods are determined by the joint influences of the child's experiences and the maturation of the child's nervous system.

- An infant's earliest cognitive abilities are closely tied to the external stimuli in the immediate environment; objects exist for the infant only when they are present (the sensorimotor period).

- Gradually, infants learn that objects exist even when hidden. The development of object permanence leads to the ability to represent things symbolically, which is a prerequisite for the use of language (pre-operational period).

- Next, the ability to perform logical analysis and to understand more complex cause-and-effect relations develops (period of concrete operations).

- Around the age of 11, a child develops more adultlike cognitive abilities – abilities that may allow the child to solve difficult problems by means of abstract reasoning (period of formal operations).

- Piaget's critics point out that, in some cases, his tests of cognitive development underestimate children's abilities. For example, if tested appropriately, it is evident that they conserve various properties earlier than he thought, and that their egocentrism is less pronounced than his tests indicated.

- Vygotsky's writings and the research they have stimulated have showed that the sociocultural context in which children are raised has a significant impact on their cognitive development.

- In particular, language appears to influence how children learn to think, solve problems, formulate plans, make decisions and contemplate ideas.

- Two information processing accounts of cognitive development have been developed recently. Case's M-space model argues that cognitive development proceeds according to expansion of mental space, or the brain's information processing capacity. M-space expands due to three causes: brain maturation, practice using schemata, and the integration of schemata for different objects and events.

- Fischer's skill model focuses on the relation between brain maturation and a child's ability to learn new cognitive skills specific to particular tasks, such as conservation. Maturation of the brain permits the child to acquire new cognitive skills necessary to solve increasingly complex tasks. Both of these models in essence reinterpret Piaget's theory in the language of information processing.

- The survey of the scientific literature by Anderson and Collins (1988) makes the medium of television look like less of a threat to children's cognitive development than many people believe.

- Studies that actually examine the viewing behaviour of children rather than speculate about harmful effects show us that children are not passive recipients of whatever the medium offers them. They watch what interests them and look away at other times, and they engage in a variety of other behaviours while sitting in front of the television set.

- Studies in psychonutrition have found significantly positive effects of vitamin supplementation on children's non-verbal IQ.

Social development in childhood

- Because babies are totally dependent on their parents, the development of attachment between parent and infant is crucial to the infant's survival.

- A baby has the innate ability to shape and reinforce the behaviour of the parent. To a large extent, the baby is the parent's teacher.

- In turn, parents reinforce the baby's behaviour, which facilitates the development of a durable attachment between them.

- Some of the behaviours that babies possess innately are sucking, cuddling, looking, smiling and crying. These behaviours promote parental responses and are instrumental in satisfying physiological needs.

- Infants are normally afraid of novel stimuli, but the presence of their carers provides a secure base from which they can explore new environments.

- Ainsworth's Strange Situation theory allows a researcher to determine the nature of the attachment between infant and caregiver. By using this test, several investigators have identified some of the variables – some involving infants and some involving mothers – that influence attachment.

- Maternal sensitivity (as measured by the mother's ability to respond positively to the baby's signals) appears to be the best predictor or secure attachment.

- Fathers, as well as mothers, can form close attachments with infants. Excellent child care by outsiders will not harm a child's social development, but less-than-excellent child care, especially if it begins in the child's first year of life, can adversely affect attachment.

- Development also involves the acquisition of social skills. Interaction with peers is probably the most important factor in social development among children and adolescents. However, a caregiver's style of parenting can also have strong effects on the social development of children and adolescents.

- Authoritative parents, compared to authoritarian and permissive parents, tend to rear competent, self-reliant and independent children. In addition, social development is also influenced by other aspects of the home environment, such as the presence or absence of either parent.

Development of sex roles

- Females tend to show earlier verbal development, are better at expressing emotion and interpreting emotional cues, and show more compliance with adults and peers.

- Males tend to have better spatial abilities, are more aggressive and tend to take more risks.

- Research has shown that both parents and peers tend to encourage children to behave in sex-appropriate ways – especially with regard to play activities and toys. However, scientific studies have revealed few other reliable differences in the ways that parents treat young boys and girls.

Moral development

- Piaget suggested that moral development consists of two principal stages: moral realism, characterised by egocentrism and blind adherence to rules, and morality of co-operation, characterised by empathy and a realisation that behaviour is judged by the effects it has on others.

- Kohlberg suggested that moral development consists of three levels, each divided into two stages. During the preconventional level, morality is based on the personal consequences of an act. During the conventional level, morality is based on the need to be well regarded and on sharing a common interest in social order. During the postconventional level, which is achieved by only a few people, morality becomes an abstract, philosophical virtue.

- Critics of Piaget and Kohlberg point out that the stages of moral development are, to a certain degree, products of the measuring instruments. Although it does not appear, as Gilligan originally suggested, that females follow different moral rules from males, her work has sensitised researchers to the importance of including both sexes in studies of human development. Subtle changes in the way that moral dilemmas are posed can produce very different answers.

Developmental disorders

- Cognitive, developmental and emotional problems that a child experiences have been described as specific developmental disorders.

- Autism is a childhood disorder in which the child shows abnormal patterns of social interaction (indifference and unwillingness to make eye or physical contact), delayed and/or idiosyncratic language and stereotypical and repetitive behaviour.

- Autism develops in the first two years of life and is four times more prevalent in boys than in girls; the outcome of the disorder is variable. Autistics appear to perform very well on block building and object assembly tasks although their IQ is generally low (there are also some autistic individuals with exceptional specific abilities but these are not unique to autism).

- An influential theory of autism suggests that autistic children lack a theory of mind: they are unable to imagine the thoughts, actions or feeling of others. Baron-Cohen's experiments have shown that when an autistic child sees an object removed from a location in which it was placed by the experimenter to a different location, and is asked where the experimenter will look for the object, autistic (but not age-matched controls) choose the second location.

- Others theories suggest that autistic children have an impairment of executive function or that they are unable to see wholes (instead of features); these theories are based on the finding that not all autistic children experience theory of mind difficulties. There seems to be a reduction in dopamine in the frontal regions of autistic children which may suggest an impairment in executive function.

- Asperger's disorder describes impaired interpersonal communication and social functioning but seems to differ from autism in also being characterised by individuals having a narrow and obsessional range of interests.

- Attention deficit hyperactivity disorder (ADHD) describes a failure of the child to inhibit its own anti-social and deviant behaviour; these children are impulsive, hyperactive and have a poor attention span.

- Evidence suggests that maternal depression is associated with poor social interaction with the child and poor sensitivity to the infant's behaviour; infants of depressed mothers are more expressive with care-givers than with the mother.

- Emotional distress may be predicted by decreased left frontal EEG activation and increased right frontal activation, although the direction of causality (distress causing EEG activity or EEG activity predisposing the child to distress) is unclear.

Adolescence

- Adolescence is the transitional stage between childhood and adulthood. Puberty is initiated by the hypothalamus, which causes the pituitary gland to secrete hormones that stimulate maturation of the reproductive system.

- Puberty marks a significant transition, both physically and socially. Early maturity appears to be socially beneficial to boys, because early maturers are more likely to be perceived as leaders. The effects of early maturity in girls is mixed; although their advanced physical development may help them acquire some prestige, early-maturing girls are more likely to engage in norm-breaking behaviour.

- The nature of friendship changes during adolescence. Girls seek out confidants rather than playmates, and boys join groups that provide mutual support in their quests to assert their independence. Insecure friendships at this time can lead to increased psychopathology later in life.

- Sexuality becomes important and many people engage in sexual intercourse in their teens.

- Although adolescence brings conflicts between parents and children, these conflicts tend to be centred on relatively minor issues. Most adolescents hold the same values and attitudes concerning important issues as their parents do. Mood swings during adolescence can be dramatic but, on the whole, teenagers report that they are generally happy and self-confident.

Adult development

- Up to the time of young adulthood, human development can reasonably be described as a series of stages: a regular sequence of changes that occurs in most members of our species. But development in adulthood is much more variable and few generalisations apply.

- Ageing brings with it a gradual deterioration in people's sensory capacities and changes in physical appearance that many people regard as unattractive. The effects of these changes can be minimised by vigorous participation in life's activities.

- Rather than undergoing sudden intellectual deterioration, older people are more likely to exhibit gradual changes, especially in abilities that require flexibility and in learning new behaviours.

- Intellectual abilities that depend heavily on crystallised intelligence – an accumulated body of knowledge – are much less likely to decline than are those based on fluid intelligence – the capacity for abstract reasoning.

- Erikson and Levinson have both proposed that people encounter a series of crises that serve as turning points in development. Erikson's stages span the entire lifecycle, from infancy to old age, whereas Levinson's stages concentrate on mid-life development.

- There appears to be no scientific evidence to support the idea that people experience a mid-life crisis.

- Marriages seem to be happiest just after the birth of children and after the children have left home. It appears to be unhappiest just before the children leave home – possibly owing to the emotional and time demands that adolescents place on their parents.

- Older people have less fear of death than younger people have, perhaps because they have had more time to contemplate and prepare for it.

- Kübler-Ross's interviews with terminally ill people have revealed that many of them seem to experience a five-stage process in facing the reality that they are, in fact, going to die. Although her research has been found to have some methodological flaws, it has drawn both scientific and public attention to the plight of the terminally ill and the necessity of caring for them properly.

Suggestions for further reading

Bee, H.L. (1996). *The Developing Child* (8th edition). New York: Addison Wesley Longman.

Berk, L.E. (1997). *Child Development* (4th edition). Boston: Allyn and Bacon.

Butterworth, G. and Harris, M. (1994). *Principles of Developmental Psychology*. Hove, UK: The Psychology Press.

Rosenblith, J.F. (1995). *In the Beginning: Development from conception to age two* (2nd edition). London: Sage.

Slater, A. and Muir, D. (1998). *The Blackwell Reader in Developmental Psychology*. Oxford: Blackwell.

Smith, P.K., Cowie, H. and Blades, M. (1997). *Understanding Children's Development*. Oxford: Blackwell.
There are dozens of books available on all aspects of development, making the choosing of the best text a little troublesome. The texts above are recommended as good introductory texts to general development. The Bee and Berk books, in particular, are recommended for further illumination. Slater and Muir's book is also useful because it reprints a collection of the most important articles published in developmental psychology. The books below are recommendations for more specific aspects of development.

Bremner, J.G. (1994). *Infancy* (2nd edition). Oxford: Blackwell.

Bremner, J.G., Slater, A. and Butterworth, G. (1997). *Infant Development*. Hove, UK: The Psychology Press.
Both of Bremner's books give a good outline of infant development.

Bee, H.L. (1997). *Lifespan Development* (2nd edition). New York: Addison Wesley Longman.

Berk, L.E. (1998). *Development Through the Lifespan*. Boston: Allyn and Bacon.

Hetherington, E.M. and Stanley-Hagan, M. (1999). The adjustment of children with divorced parents: A risk and resiliency perspective. *Journal of Child Psychology and Psychiatry*, 40, 1, 129–140.

Kimmel, D.C. (1995). *Adolescence*. Chichester: Wiley.

Turner, J.S. and Helms, D.B. (1994). *Contemporary Adulthood* (5th edition). London: Harcourt Brace.

Woods, R.T. (1998). *Psychological Problems of Ageing*. Chichester: Wiley.
The five books above give a readable account of the main phases of development after childhood. Hetherington and Stanley-Hagan's article is a state-of-the-art review of the effects of divorce on children.

Cowan, N. (1997). *The Development of Memory in Childhood*. Hove, UK: The Psychology Press.

Goswami, U. (1997). *Cognition in Children*. Hove, UK: The Psychology Press.

Karmiloff-Smith, A. (1992). *Beyond Modularity: A developmental perspective on cognitive science*. Cambridge, MA: MIT Press.
These excellent books provide an in-depth and fairly up-to-date account of what we know about the development of thinking and remembering in childhood.

Mitchell, P. (1996). *Introduction to Theory of Mind*. London: Arnold.

Yirmiya, N., Erel, O., Shaked, M. and Solomonica-Levi, D. (1998). *Meta-analyses comparing theory of mind abilities of individuals with autism, individuals with mental retardation, and normally developing individuals.* Psychological Bulletin, *124, 3, 283–307. These two items will give you a good background to theory of mind (and autism).*

Langford, P.E. (1995). *Approaches to the Development of Moral Reasoning.* Hove, UK: The Psychology Press. *This text will give you more detailed information about the child's moral reasoning ability.*

Smith, L. (1996). *Critical Readings on Piaget.* London: Routledge.

Smith, L., Dockrell, J. and Tomlinson, P. (1997). *Piaget, Vygotsky and Beyond.* London: Routledge. *Piaget and Vygotsky are very much alive in developmental thinking and these two books critically assess the contributions of these thinkers to developmental psychology.*

Durkin, K. (1995). *Developmental Social Psychology.* Oxford: Blackwell.

Schaffer, H.R. (1996). *Social Development.* Oxford: Blackwell. *The child's relations with others is examined in these two books – both are good examples of their genre.*

Gunter, B. and McAleer, J. (1997). *Children and Television* (2nd edition). London: Routledge. *This book is a well balanced review of the effects of television viewing on children's behaviour.*

Journals to consult

Autism
British Journal of Developmental Psychology
British Journal of Educational Psychology
Child Development
Developmental Neuropsychology
Developmental Psychology
Developmental Psychopathology
Developmental Review
Developmental Science
Journal of Adolescence
Journal of Child Psychology and Psychiatry
Journal of Educational Psychology
Journal of Experimental Child Psychology
Psychological Science

13

MOTIVATION AND EMOTION

On 13 September 1848, Phineas P. Gage, a 25 year old construction foreman for the Rutland and Burlington Railroad in New England, became a victim of a bizarre accident. In order to lay new rail tracks across Vermont, it was necessary to level the uneven terrain by controlled blasting. Among other tasks, Gage was in charge of the detonations, which involved drilling holes in the stone, partially filling the holes with explosive powder, covering the powder with sand, and using a fuse and a tamping iron to trigger an explosion into the rock. On the fateful day, a momentary distraction let Gage begin tamping directly over the powder before his assistant had a chance to cover it with sand. The result was a powerful explosion away from the rock and toward Gage. The fine-pointed, 3-cm thick, 109-cm-long tamping iron was hurled, rocket-like, through his face, skull, brain, and then into the sky. Gage was momentarily stunned but regained full consciousness immediately thereafter. He was able to talk and even walk with the help of his men. The iron landed many yards away.

Source: Damasio *et al.*, 1994, p. 1102

Our most basic 'drives' and 'instincts' are related to sex, aggression, eating, drinking or experiencing emotion (which may include all four). We all need food to provide us with energy to do the things we take for granted; most of us are attracted to the opposite sex for the good evolutionary reason that this allows our species to continue; we aggress because we are angry or because we are protective or because we are just being bullies. All of these behaviours are examples of motivated behaviours: we do them because we are motivated to do them.

This chapter discusses two important aspects of behaviour: motivation and emotion. The first half of the chapter considers what we know about the development of sexual, ingestive and aggressive behaviour. The second half reviews what we know about the nature of emotion, the existence of basic emotions and theories of emotion.

What you should be able to do after reading Chapter 13

- Define motivation.
- Describe and understand the processes involved in starting and stopping a meal.
- Describe and understand the process of sexual development and orientation.
- Evaluate the theories explaining aggression and describe the factors which lead to aggressive behaviour.
- Describe the ways in which psychologists have defined and studied emotion.
- Evaluate the 'fundamental emotion' debate.
- Outline the major theories of emotion and the biological basis of emotion.

Questions to think about

- What motivates us to eat, drink, aggress and have sex?
- What influences sexual preference and orientation?
- What causes eating disorders?
- How does aggressive behaviour manifest itself and what theories could account for it?
- How would you define emotion?
- Are there fundamental emotions? If so, how many?
- Can emotion best be explained by biology or cognition?

Motivation

Why do people behave differently? Why do some individuals eat particular foods whereas others eat different foods? Why do we eat in the first place? What makes us attracted to different sexual partners or any sexual partner? And why do we become aggressive?

Most of these questions can probably be answered by motivation. When commonly used, motivation refers to a driving force that moves us to a particular action. More formally, motivation is a general term for a group of phenomena that affect the nature of an individual's behaviour, the strength of the behaviour and the persistence of the behaviour.

Motivation includes two types of phenomenon. First, stimuli that were previously associated with pleasant or unpleasant events motivate approach or avoidance behaviours. For example, if something reminds you of an interesting person you met recently, you may try to meet that person again by consulting your address book and making a telephone call. Secondly, being deprived of a particular reinforcer increases an organism's preference for a particular behaviour. Besides obvious reinforcers such as food or water, this category includes more subtle ones. For example, after spending a lot of time performing routine tasks, we become motivated to go for a walk or meet with friends.

Motivation affects all categories of behaviour. This chapter considers three important categories of motivated behaviour: eating, sexual behaviour and aggression. Other types of motivation such as intention and being influenced by real or imaginary others will be discussed in Chapters 14 (Personality) and 15 (Social psychology).

Biological needs

Biological needs can be potent motivators. To survive, we need air, food, water, various vitamins and minerals, and protection from extremes in temperature. Complex organisms possess physiological mechanisms that detect deficits or imbalances associated with these needs and regulatory behaviours that bring physiological conditions back to normal. Examples of regulatory behaviours include eating, drinking, hunting, shivering, building a fire and putting on a warm coat. This process of detection and correction, which maintains physiological systems at their optimum value, is called homeostasis ('stable state'). Deficits or imbalances motivate us because they cause us to perform the appropriate regulatory behaviours.

A regulatory system has four essential features: the system variable (the characteristic to be regulated), a set point (the optimum value of the system variable), a detector that monitors the value of the system variable, and a correctional mechanism that restores the system variable to the set point. A simple example of such a regulatory system is a room where temperature is regulated by a thermostatically controlled heater. The system variable is the air temperature of the room, and the detector for this variable is a thermostat. The thermostat can be adjusted so that contacts of a switch will close when the temperature falls below a preset value (the set point). Closure of the contacts turns on the correctional mechanism – the coils of the heater. You can see this process illustrated in Figure 13.1.

If the room cools below the set point, the thermostat turns the heater on, which warms the room. The rise in room temperature causes the thermostat to turn the heater off. Because the activity of the correctional mechanism (heat production) feeds back to the thermostat and causes it to turn the heater off, this process is called negative feedback. Negative feedback is an essential characteristic of all regulatory systems.

The drive reduction hypothesis was the earliest attempt to explain the nature of motivation and reinforcement. This theory stated that biological needs, caused by deprivation of the necessities of life, are unpleasant. The physiological changes associated with, say, going without food for several hours produce an unpleasant state called hunger. Hunger serves as a drive, energising an organism's behaviour. The organism then engages in behaviours that in the past have obtained food. The act of eating reduces hunger, and this drive reduction is reinforcing, as seen in Figure 13.2.

Not all drives are based on homeostasis – on biological needs like the ones for food and water. The most obvious example is the drive associated with sexual behaviour. An individual can survive without sexual behaviour; but the sex drive is certainly motivating, and sexual contact is certainly reinforcing. Similarly, most organisms placed in a featureless environment will soon become motivated to seek something new; they will work at a task that gives them a view of the world outside.

The drive reduction hypothesis of reinforcement has fallen into disfavour for two primary reasons. The first is that drive is almost always impossible to measure. For example, suppose you obtain pleasure from watching a set of colour slides taken by a friend while on holiday.

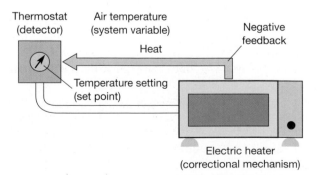

Figure 13.1

An example of a regulatory system.

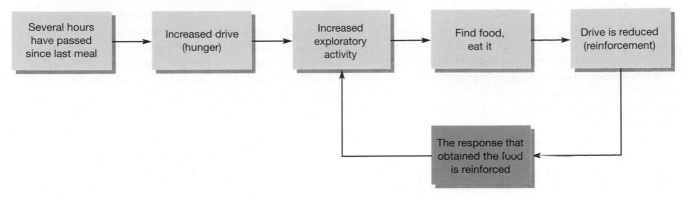

Figure 13.2

The drive reduction hypothesis of motivation and reinforcement.

According to the drive reduction hypothesis, your 'exploratory drive' or 'curiosity drive' is high, and looking at holiday slides reduces it, providing reinforcement. Or consider a woman who enjoys listening to music. What drive induces her to turn on her stereo system? What drive is reduced by this activity? There is no way to measure 'drive' in either of these examples and confirm that it actually exists; thus, the hypothesis cannot be tested experimentally.

The second problem is that if we examine our own behaviour, we find that most events we experience as reinforcing are also exciting, or drive increasing. The reason a rollercoaster ride is fun is certainly not because it reduces drive. The same is true for skiing, surfing or viewing a horror film. Likewise, an interesting, reinforcing conversation is one that is exciting, not one that puts you to sleep. And people who engage in prolonged foreplay and sexual intercourse do not view these activities as unpleasant because they are accompanied by such a high level of drive. In general, the experiences we really want to repeat (that is, the ones we find reinforcing) are those that increase, rather than decrease, our level of arousal.

Physiology of reinforcement

To understand the nature of reinforcement we must understand something about its physiological basis. Olds and Milner (1954) discovered quite by accident that electrical stimulation of parts of the brain can reinforce an animal's behaviour. For example, rats will repeatedly press a lever when the brain is electrically stimulated.

The neural circuits stimulated by this electricity are also responsible for the motivating effects of natural reinforcers such as food, water or sexual contact, and of drugs such as heroin, alcohol and cocaine. Almost all investigators believe that the electrical stimulation of the brain is reinforcing because it activates the same system that is activated by natural reinforcers and by drugs that people commonly abuse. The normal function of this system is to

strengthen the connections between the neurons that detect the discriminative stimulus (such as the sight of a lever) and the neurons that produce the operant response (such as a lever press). The electrical brain stimulation activates this system directly.

Researchers have discovered that an essential component of the reinforcement system consists of neurons that release dopamine as their transmitter substance. Thus, all reinforcing stimuli appear to trigger the release of dopamine in the brain.

Optimum-level theory

Although events that increase our level of arousal are often reinforcing, there are times when a person wants nothing more than some peace and quiet. In this case, avoidance of exciting stimuli motivates our behaviour. As we saw in Chapter 7, the removal (or avoidance) of an aversive stimulus produces negative reinforcement. In an attempt to find a common explanation for both positive and negative reinforcement, some psychologists have proposed the optimum-level hypothesis of reinforcement and punishment: when an individual's arousal level is too high, less stimulation is reinforcing; when it is too low, more stimulation is desired (Berlyne, 1966; Hebb, 1955). Berlyne hypothesised two forms of exploration: diversive exploration is a response to understimulation (boredom) that increases the diversity of the stimuli the organism tries to come in contact with; specific exploration is a response to overstimulation (usually because of a specific need, such as lack of food or water) that leads to the needed item, thereby decreasing the organism's drive level.

The hypothesis that organisms seek an optimum level of arousal is certainly plausible. Any kind of activity, even the most interesting and exciting one, eventually produces satiety; something that was once reinforcing becomes bothersome. Presumably, participation in an exciting behaviour gradually raises an organism's arousal above its optimum level. However, the logical problem that plagues the drive reduction hypothesis also applies to the opti-mum-level hypothesis. Because we cannot measure an organism's drive or arousal, we cannot say what its opti-mum level should be. Thus, the optimum-level hypothesis remains without much empirical support.

Effects of intermittent reinforcement

We saw in Chapter 7 that when an organism's behaviour is no longer reinforced, the behaviour eventually ceases, or extinguishes. If the behaviour was previously reinforced every time it occurred, extinction is very rapid. However, if it was previously reinforced only intermittently, the behav-iour persists for a long time. Intermittent reinforcement leads to perseverance, even when the behaviour is no longer reinforced.

Many human behaviours are reinforced on intermittent schedules that require the performance of long sequences of behaviours over long intervals of time. A person's previ-ous experience with various schedules of reinforcement probably affects how long and how hard the person will work between occasions of reinforcement. If all attempts at a particular endeavour are reinforced (or if none are), the person is unlikely to pursue a long and difficult project that includes the endeavour. If we knew more about a person's previous history with various schedules of reinforcement, we would probably know more about his or her ability to persevere when the going gets difficult (that is, when reinforcements become variable).

The role of conditioned reinforcement

Another phenomenon that affects the tendency to perse-vere is conditioned reinforcement. When stimuli are asso-ciated with reinforcers, they eventually acquire reinforcing properties of their own. For example, the sound of the food dispenser reinforces the behaviour of a rat being trained to press a lever.

Motivation is not merely a matter of wanting to do well and to work hard. It also involves the ability to be rein-forced by the immediate products of the work being done. If a person has regularly been exposed to particular stimuli in association with reinforcers, that person's behaviour can be reinforced by those stimuli. In addition, if the person has learned how to recognise self-produced stimuli as con-ditioned reinforcers, the performance of the behaviours that produce them will be 'self-reinforcing'.

Failure to persist: learned helplessness

A large body of evidence suggests that organisms can learn that they are powerless to affect their own destinies. Two social psychologists, Maier and Seligman (1976), reported a series of experiments demonstrating that animals can learn that their own behaviour has no effect on an environmental event. This result is exactly the opposite of what has been assumed to be the basis of learning. All the examples of learning and conditioning cited so far have been instances in which one event predicts the occurrence of another. Learned helplessness involves learning that an aversive event cannot be avoided or escaped.

Overmeier and Seligman (1967) conducted the basic experiment. They placed a dog in an apparatus in which it received electrical shocks that could not be avoided; noth-ing the animal did would prevent the shocks. Next, they placed the dog in another apparatus in which the animal received a series of trials in which a warning stimulus was followed by an electrical shock. In this case the animal could avoid the shocks simply by stepping over a small bar-rier to the other side of the apparatus. Dogs in the control group learned to step over the barrier and avoid the shock, but dogs that had previously received inescapable shocks in the other apparatus failed to learn. They just squatted in the corner and took the shock as if they had learned that it made no difference what they did. They had learned to be helpless.

Seligman (1975) has suggested that the phenomenon of learned helplessness has important implications for behav-iour. When people have experiences that lead to learned helplessness, they become depressed and their motiva-tional level decreases. The change in motivation occurs because the helplessness training lowers their expectation that trying to perform a task will bring success. Seligman also suggested that learned helplessness has the character-istics of a personality trait; that is, people who have had major experiences with insoluble tasks will not try hard to succeed in other types of task, including ones they could otherwise have solved.

Seligman's theory of learned helplessness has been chal-lenged by other investigators, who have explained the phe-nomenon in other ways. The issue is whether learning to be helpless in a particular situation generalises only to sim-ilar situations or to a wide variety of them. For example, McReynolds (1980) observed that when people experience a situation in which reinforcements are not contingent on their responding, their responding extinguishes. If the sit-uation then changes to one in which responding will be reinforced, the people will continue not to respond unless they perceive that the schedule of reinforcement has changed. The more similar the second situation is to the first, the more likely it is that the person will act helpless. This explanation describes the phenomenon of learned helplessness as a failure to discriminate between the condition under which responding is reinforced and the condition under which it is not. Further research will have to determine whether learned helplessness is, as Seligman asserts, a stable personality trait or whether it can be explained by the principles of instrumental conditioning. We will return to learned helplessness in Chapter 17.

What is motivation?

- What do we mean by motivation? Is it too vague a concept to be psychologically useful?

- What other behaviours, apart from those discussed so far, could be described as motivated? Are all behaviours motivated?

- People often talk about being driven or having drives. People sometimes also refer to others as having maternal instinct or refer to women as having feminine intuition. Do any of these phenomena have any scientific basis?

- What factors do you think influence a person to work successfully? Which of these are internal and which are external?

- What role does learning have in motivation?

- You sometimes hear people say that when they get knocked down (psychologically, not physically), they just get back up again. Others, however, stay down. What factors could account for the behaviours of these two groups of people?

Eating

Much of what an animal learns to do is motivated by the constant struggle to obtain food. The need to eat certainly shaped the evolutionary development of our own species. Simply put, motivation to eat is aroused when there is a deficit in the body's supply of stored nutrients, and it is satisfied by a meal that replenishes this supply. A person who exercises vigorously uses up the stored nutrients more rapidly and consequently must eat more food. Thus, the amount of food a person normally eats is regulated by physiological need. But what, exactly, causes a person to start eating, and what brings the meal to an end? These are simple questions, yet the answers are complex. There is no single physiological measure that can tell us reliably whether a person should be hungry; hunger is determined by a variety of conditions. So, instead of asking 'what is the cause of hunger?' we should ask, 'what are the causes?'

What starts a meal?

Cultural and social factors

Most of us in European societies eat three times a day. When the time for a meal comes, we get hungry and eat, consuming a relatively constant amount of food. The regular pattern of eating is not determined solely by biological need; it is at least partially determined by habit. If we miss a meal, we notice that our hunger does not continue to grow indefinitely. Instead, it subsides some time after the meal would normally have been eaten only to grow again just before the scheduled time of the next one. Hunger, then, can wax and wane according to a learned schedule.

Besides learning when to eat, we learn what to eat. Most of us would refuse to eat fresh clotted seal blood, but many Eskimos consider it a delicacy. What we accept as food depends on our culture. Our tastes are also shaped by habits acquired early in life.

Physiological factors

Cultural and social factors assuredly influence when and how much we eat. But everyone would also agree that the 'real' reason for eating must be related to the fact that the body needs nourishment: if all other factors were eliminated, eating would be determined by some internal physiological state. What are the internal factors that cause us to eat?

Many years ago, Cannon and Washburn (1912) suggested that hunger resulted from an empty stomach. The walls of an empty stomach rubbed against each other, producing what we commonly identify as hunger pangs. Cannon also suggested that thirst was produced by a dry mouth, because a loss of body fluid resulted in a decreased flow of saliva. Some sceptics called Cannon's explanation of hunger and thirst the 'spit and rumble theory'. However, removal of the stomach does not abolish hunger pangs. Inglefinger (1944) interviewed patients whose stomachs had been removed because of cancer or large ulcers; their oesophagi had been attached directly to their small intestines. Because they had no stomachs to catch and hold food, they had to eat small, frequent meals. Despite their lack of a stomach, these people reported the same feelings of hunger and satiety that they had experienced before the operation.

A more likely cause of hunger is depletion of the body's store of nutrients. The primary fuels for the cells of our body are glucose (a simple sugar) and fatty acids (chemicals produced when fat is broken down). If our digestive system contains food, these nutrients are absorbed into the blood and nourish our cells. But the digestive tract is sometimes empty; in fact, most of us wake up in the morning in that condition. So there has to be a reservoir that stores nutrients to keep the cells of the body nourished when the gut is empty. Indeed, there are two reservoirs, one short-term and the other long-term. The short-term reservoir stores carbohydrates, and the long-term reservoir stores fats.

The short-term reservoir is located in the cells of the muscles and the liver, and it is filled with a carbohydrate – a form of animal starch – called glycogen. When glucose is received from a meal, some of it is used for fuel and some is converted into glycogen and stored in the liver. Our long-term reservoir consists of adipose tissue (fat tissue), which is found beneath the skin and in various locations in the abdomen. Adipose tissue consists of cells capable of absorbing nutrients from the blood, converting them to triglycerides (fats), and storing them. They can expand in size enormously; in fact, the primary physical difference between an obese person and a person of normal weight is the size of their fat cells, which is determined by the amount of triglycerides that these cells contain.

The long-term fat reservoir is obviously what keeps us alive during a prolonged fast. Once the level of glycogen in our short-term carbohydrate reservoir gets low, fat cells start breaking down fats and releasing fatty acids and a carbohydrate called glycerol. The brain lives primarily on glucose, and the rest of the body lives on fatty acids. Glycerol is converted into glucose, so the brain continues to be nourished even after the short-term reservoir is depleted, as Figure 13.3 shows.

Because glucose is such an important fuel, Mayer (1955) proposed the glucostatic hypothesis of hunger. According to the glucostatic hypothesis, hunger occurs when the level of glucose in the blood becomes low, presumably after the glycogen in the body's short-term reservoir has been used up. Mayer theorised that this decrease in blood sugar is detected by glucose-sensitive neurons in the brain called glucostats (the term 'glucostat' is analogous to thermostat, but it refers to the measurement of glucose rather than temperature). Mayer suggested that these detectors activate neural circuits that make a person hungry, thus stimulating the correctional mechanism, eating.

Subsequent evidence suggests that there are two different types of nutrient detectors, which measure the blood level of the two primary nutrients, glucose and fatty acids (Friedman *et al.*, 1986, 1991). The glucose detectors appear to be located in the liver, but the location of the fatty acid detectors is not yet known (Ritter and Taylor, 1989; Ritter *et al.*, 1992). Both sets of detectors send information to the brain, and activity of neural circuits there stimulates hunger.

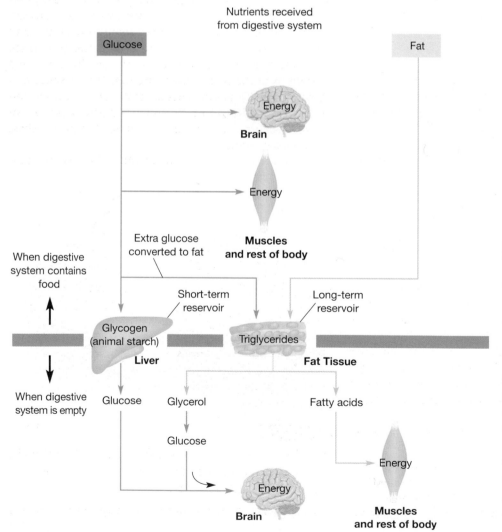

Figure 13.3

Overview of food metabolism. When the digestive system contains food, glucose nourishes the brain and muscles. Extra glucose is stored in the liver and converted to fat. When the digestive system is empty, glucose obtained from glycogen stored in the liver nourishes the brain until this short-term reservoir is used up. Fatty acids from fat tissue nourish the muscles, and glycerol is converted to glucose to nourish the brain.

What stops a meal?

Nutrient detectors sense the fact that the body's supplies of stored energy are getting low by measuring glucose and fatty acids in the blood. Through their connection with the brain these detectors are able to stimulate hunger. But what ends hunger? What brings a meal to its finish? Consider what happens when you eat. Your stomach fills with food, and the digestive process begins. However, about an hour passes before significant amounts of nutrients are absorbed from the intestines into the bloodstream. Therefore, the body's supply of fuel is not replenished until quite some time after the meal begins. If you were to continue to eat until the nutrients actually entered the bloodstream, your stomach would burst. Therefore, some other detectors must be responsible for stopping the meal.

Although evidence suggests that the primary cause of hunger is not an empty stomach, the primary cause of satiety (that is, the cessation of hunger caused by eating) seems to be a full stomach. Many studies have shown that satiety is caused by entry of a sufficient quantity of nourishing food into the stomach. Therefore, the stomach must contain detectors that sense the presence of food. We have known for a long time that hunger can be abolished by injecting food into an animal's stomach by means of a flexible tube. Even though the animal does not get to taste and smell the food, it will not subsequently eat. Davis and Campbell (1973) showed how precisely the stomach can measure its contents. The investigators allowed hungry rats to eat their fill and then removed some food from their stomachs. When they let the rats eat again, they ate almost exactly as much as had been taken out.

The stomach appears to contain detectors that inform the brain about the chemical nature of its contents as well as the quantity. The ability to detect the chemical nature of food that has entered the stomach is important, because eating should stop relatively soon if the food is very nutritious but should continue for a longer time if it is not. Deutsch et al. (1978) injected either milk or a dilute salt solution into hungry rats' stomachs and thirty minutes later allowed them to eat. The rats that had received injections of milk ate less than the ones that had received the salt solution. Because the rats could not taste what was put in their stomachs, the effect had to come from detectors there. The nature of these detectors is not known, but they must respond to some chemicals present in food. You can try an experiment of your own: drink two glasses of water when you are very hungry and see whether they satisfy your appetite.

Detectors that measure the amount and nutritive value of food in the stomach contribute only to short-term control of eating – the termination of a single meal. Long-term factors also control food intake. For example, when people eat especially nutritious food, they soon learn to eat less. When they begin to exercise more, and hence burn up

their store of nutrients faster, they soon start eating more. For a long time, investigators believed that fat tissue provided some chemical signal that could be detected by the brain. When too much fat began accumulating, more of this chemical was secreted, and the person began eating less. If the amount of body fat began to decrease, the level of the chemical fell and the person began eating more.

After many years of searching for such a chemical signal, researchers have finally succeeded in finding one. The discovery came after years of study with a strain of genetically obese mice. The ob mouse (as this strain is called) has a low metabolism, overeats and gets monstrously fat. It also develops diabetes in adulthood, just as many obese people do. Recently, researchers in several laboratories have discovered the cause of the obesity (Campfield et al., 1995; Halaas et al., 1995; Pelleymounter et al., 1995). A particular gene, called OB, normally produces a protein known as leptin (from the Greek word leptos, 'thin'). Leptin is normally secreted by fat cells that have absorbed a large amount of triglyceride. Because of a genetic mutation, the fat cells of ob mice are unable to secrete leptin.

Leptin has profound effects on metabolism and eating, acting as an anti-obesity hormone. If ob mice are given daily injections of leptin, their metabolic rate increases, their body temperature rises, they become more active and they eat less. As a result, their weight returns to normal. The treatment works even when the leptin is injected directly into the brain, indicating that the chemical acts directly on the neural circuits that control eating and metabolism. Figure 13.4 shows a photograph of an untreated ob mouse and an ob mouse that has received injections of leptin.

Maffei et al. (1995) found that leptin is found in humans

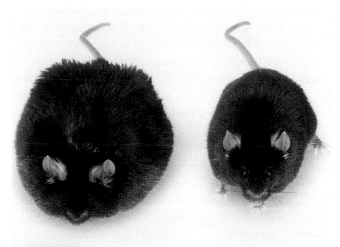

Figure 13.4

The effects of leptin on obesity in mice of the ob (obese) strain. The ob mouse on the left is untreated; the one on the right received daily injections of leptin.

and that the level of leptin in the blood is correlated with obesity; thus, this chemical signal appears to be present in our species as well as in mice. But if leptin is produced by human fat cells, why do some people nevertheless overeat and become obese? The section on obesity suggests a possible answer to this question.

Psychology in action

Sensory-specific satiety

Have you ever experienced the feeling when, after eating a big savoury meal, you could still manage to eat dessert? Or that you have had enough of eating peanuts but could quite happily contemplate eating a packet of crisps?

These experiences are examples of sensory-specific satiety (SSS) – the decrease in the pleasantness and consumption of specific food after eating it to satiety. The satiety is sensory-specific because individuals may become sated eating foods of specific tastes, shapes, sizes and textures but not foods of different taste, shape, size and texture (Rolls *et al.*, 1986). This phenomenon explains why, if we eat a meal composed of a variety of specific foods, we eat more of it because there is greater sensory stimulation available from a varied meal (say, a bowl of soup, sausages, egg and bacon, and chocolate mousse versus simply a big plate of sausages). SSS also has survival value because if we become bored with eating one food but not another, this increases the likelihood of a variety of foods being eaten. Much of the work on SSS has been conducted by Edmund and Barbra Rolls and their colleagues from the Universities of Oxford, England, and Pennsylvania State, USA. Before describing this work, it is important to distinguish between SSS and another phenomenon called negative alliesthesia (Cabanac, 1971). Negative alliesthesia refers to a decrease in the liking of food that results from internal, physiological signals and not the sensory properties of the food. The two phenomena seem quite alike but they are, in fact, different.

A common finding in SSS research is that if a food is eaten to satiety, then a second course of the same food will result in a reduction in intake of around 50 per cent (Rolls *et al.*, 1981). In Rolls's early experiment, all foods with the exception of roast beef produced sensory-specific satiety. In one experiment, participants ate either a four-course meal of sausages, bread and butter, chocolate dessert and bananas or ate only one of these foods to satiety. The researchers found that consumption was 60 per cent higher when foods were presented together than when presented singly, in one course (Rolls *et al.*, 1986). At a post-satiety tasting session, those foods presented singly were also rated as less pleasant than those eaten as part of a four-course meal (Rolls *et al.*, 1984). Even colour and shape can apparently influence the amount of food eaten. In Rolls's

experiments, when a variety of pasta shapes were presented for consumption, more was eaten than when only one pasta shape was presented; similarly a greater amount of food which varied in colour was consumed than when the food was of just one colour (Rolls *et al.*, 1982b). The effect of varying the shape and variety of food can be seen in Figures 13.5(a) and (b).

Recent research suggests that even the smell of eaten food is rated as less pleasant whereas the smell of unconsumed food remains unaffected. In an experiment where participants were asked to rate the pleasantness of the odours of banana, satsuma, fish paste, chicken and rose water before and after consuming bananas and chicken to satiety, the pleasantness of chicken and banana odours (but not other foods) significantly declined after satiety (Rolls and Rolls, 1997).

Why should this be? We have considered one possible hypothesis: that SSS allows us to enjoy and consume a greater variety of food and, therefore, represents a mechanism that enables us to consume a variety of nutrients. There is also evidence that certain regions of the brain may be responsible for our feeling of satiety. The hypothalamus, as we have already seen, is important to feeding. Neurons in this region in monkeys stop responding to the sight and taste of food when the food has been eaten to satiety (Rolls *et al.*, 1986). There may also be other mechanisms at work at other levels in the brain.

Critchley and Rolls (1996), for example, suggest that the primary and secondary taste cortices (found in the frontal part of the brain) mediate the sated response in different ways. The satiety produced by taste and smell is regulated by the secondary taste cortex, the part of the brain responsible for the hedonic (or pleasantness-related) effect of food. The primary taste cortex, however, allows us to identify the food. This is suggested by an experiment in which neurons in this area in monkeys responded either to the taste or the sight of food (unimodal neurons) or to both (bimodal neurons) (Rolls and Baylis, 1994). The primary taste cortex, therefore, appears to act as a convergence zone, where olfactory, gustatory and visual information come together to allow the food to be identified before messages are sent to the secondary taste cortex where the organism's emotional or hedonic response to the food is mediated.

Psychology in action continued

Psychology in action continued

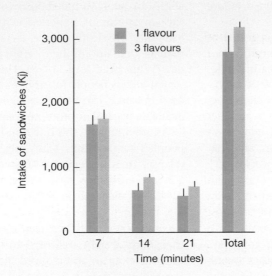

(a)

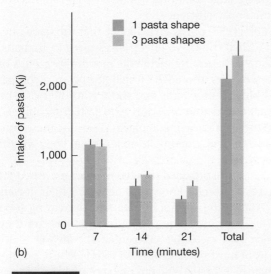

(b)

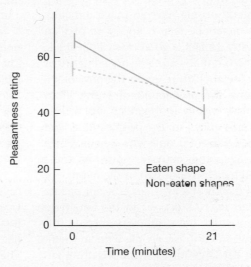

Figure 13.5

(a) The amount eaten of a one-flavoured and a three-flavoured meal. (b) The effect of varying the type of pasta shape on food intake and pleasantness ratings of the taste of the shapes. In both these examples, the sensory properties of the food influence intake and ratings of pleasantness.

Source: Reprinted from *Psychology and Behaviour*, 29. B.J. Rolls, E.T. Rolls and E.A. Rowe: How sensory properties of foods affect human feeding behaviour, 409–417. Copyright 1982 with permission from Elsevier Science.

Obesity

The mechanisms that control eating generally do an efficient job. However, some people do not control their eating habits and become too fat or too thin. Does what we have learned about the normal regulation of food intake help us to understand these disorders?

Obesity is extremely difficult to treat. The enormous financial success of diet books, fat farms and weight reduction programmes attests to the trouble that people have losing weight. Kramer *et al.* (1989) reported that four to five years after participating in a 15-week behavioural weight loss programme, fewer than 3 per cent of the participants managed to maintain the weight loss they had achieved during the programme. Even drastic means such as gastric and intestinal surgery (designed to limit the amount of food that the stomach can hold or to prevent food from being fully digested before it is eliminated) are not the answer. These procedures have risks of their own, often produce unpleasant side effects, and have a failure rate of at least 40 per cent (Kral, 1989).

Many psychological variables have been suggested as causes of obesity, including lack of impulse control, poor ability to delay gratification, and maladaptive eating styles (primarily eating too fast). However, in a review of the literature, Rodin *et al.* (1989) found that none of these suggestions has received empirical support. Rodin and her colleagues also found that unhappiness and depression seem to be the effects of obesity, not its causes, and that dieting behaviour seems to make the problem worse.

There is no single, all-inclusive explanation for obesity, but there are many partial ones. Habit plays an important role in the control of food intake. Early in life, when we are most active, we form our ideas about how much food constitutes a meal. Later in life, we become less active, but we do not always reduce our food intake accordingly. We fill our plates according to what we think is a proper-sized meal (or perhaps the plate is filled for us), and we eat everything, ignoring the satiety signals that might tell us to stop before the plate is empty.

One reason that many people have so much difficulty losing weight is that metabolic factors appear to play an important role in obesity. In fact, a good case can be made that obesity is most often not an eating disorder but rather a metabolic disorder. Metabolism refers to the physiological processes, including the production of energy from nutrients, that take place within an organism. Just as cars differ in their fuel efficiency, so do people. Rose and Williams (1961) studied pairs of people who were matched for weight, height, age, and activity. Some of these matched pairs differed by a factor of two in the number of calories they ate each day. People with an efficient metabolism have calories left over to deposit in the long-term nutrient reservoir; thus, they have difficulty keeping this reservoir from growing. In contrast, people with an inefficient metabolism can eat large meals without getting fat. Thus, whereas a fuel-efficient automobile is desirable, a fuel-efficient body runs the risk of becoming obese.

Differences in metabolism appear to have a hereditary basis. Griffiths and Payne (1976) found that the children of obese parents weighed more than other children even though they ate less. Stunkard *et al.* (1986) found that the body weight of a sample of people who had been adopted as infants was highly correlated with their biological parents but not with their adoptive parents. Thus, a person's weight (presumably closely related to his or her metabolic efficiency) is influenced by genetic factors.

Why are there genetic differences in metabolic efficiency? James and Trayhurn (1981) suggest that under some environmental conditions metabolic efficiency is advantageous. That is, in places where food is only intermittently available in sufficient quantities, being able to stay alive on small amounts of food and to store up extra nutrients in the form of fat when food becomes available for a while is a highly adaptive trait. Therefore, the variability in people's metabolisms may reflect the nature of the environment experienced by their ancestors. For example, physically active lactating women in Gambia manage to maintain their weight on only 1,500 calories per day (Whitehead *et al.*, 1978). This high level of efficiency, which allows people to survive in environments in which food is scarce, can be a disadvantage when food is readily available because it promotes obesity.

Another factor – this one non-hereditary – can influence people's metabolism. Many obese people diet and then relapse, thus undergoing large changes in body weight. Some investigators have suggested that starvation causes the body's metabolism to become more efficient. For example, Brownell *et al.* (1986) fed rats a diet that made them become obese and then restricted their food intake until their body weights returned to normal. Then they made the rats fat again and reduced their food intake again. The second time, the rats became fat much faster and lost their weight much more slowly. Clearly, the experience of gaining and losing large amounts of body weight altered the animals' metabolic efficiency.

Steen *et al.* (1988) obtained evidence that the same phenomenon (called the yo-yo effect) takes place in humans. They measured the resting metabolic rate in two groups of adolescent wrestlers: those who fasted just before a competition and binged afterwards and those who did not. The investigators found that wrestlers who fasted and binged developed more efficient metabolisms. Possibly, these people will have difficulty maintaining a normal body weight as they get older.

As we saw in the previous subsection, overnourished fat cells secrete a protein known as leptin, which lowers weight by increasing metabolic rate and decreasing food intake. Why, then, do some people become fat? Are they like ob mice, with defective OB genes? The answer is no. The fat cells of most obese people do secrete leptin, but the people nevertheless have efficient metabolisms and overeat (Maffei *et al.*, 1995). A recent discovery suggests a possible answer to this puzzle. As you saw in Chapter 4, hormones act on their target cells by stimulating receptor molecules located on these cells. Using the techniques of molecular genetics, Tartaglia *et al.* (1995) discovered the leptin receptor. In order for leptin to reduce weight, the brain must contain functioning leptin receptors. Perhaps, researchers speculate, some people have leptin receptors that do not respond normally to the presence of leptin in the blood. The overgrown fat cells of these people secrete high levels of leptin, but the effect the hormone produces in the brain is less intense than normal. Hence, people overeat.

Anorexia nervosa

Anorexia nervosa is an eating disorder characterised by a severe decrease in eating. The literal meaning of the word 'anorexia' suggests a loss of appetite, but people with this disorder generally do not lose their appetite (DSM-IV, 1994). Their limited intake of food occurs despite intense preoccupation with food, its preparation and with their own disorder (Hermans *et al.*, 1998). They may enjoy preparing meals for others to consume, collect recipes, and even hoard food that they do not eat. They have an intense fear of becoming obese, and this fear continues even if they become dangerously thin. There is a significant disturbance in the perception of body shape and size, with anorexics consistently overestimating body size and shape (Smeets *et al.*, 1997). Many exercise by cycling, running, or almost constant walking and pacing. The prevalence of the disorder is between 0.5 and 1 per cent (DSM-IV, 1994). A case study in anorexia, below, highlights some of the common features of the disorder.

Anorexia nervosa: a case study

Between the age of 29 and 34, Joan became ill. For a period of thirty days, she was hospitalised with a disorder that appeared to be controlling her life. Her weight had fallen to 38 kilos and she was suffering from anorexia nervosa.

A child of parents of average weight, Joan's childhood was quite normal and she was academically bright. When she was 14 years old, Joan was baby-sitting her 12 year old brother when a friend came to play. While she was indoors, her brother went outside. Unfortunately, he was run over by a motorist and was killed. From this time on her childhood became extraordinary: she felt excessive guilt for her brother's death and her parents imposed strict curfews and constantly monitored her movements, so concerned were they for the safety of their remaining child. At 19, she married and started her first job after passing a one-year business studies course. Although the marriage lasted for six years, within months it was in trouble. Joan did not love her husband and admitted that the marriage was an escape from her parents' home. Two years after the wedding, Joan gave birth to a son, Charlie, but she separated from her husband two years after the birth. The divorce and the tribulations of bringing up a child alone took its financial toll and Joan reluctantly moved back in with her parents after she was forced to sell her home.

Her parents cared for both her and her son and she began to feel more like her son's sister than his mother. Six months after moving in, she broke her leg in a car accident. Her weight dropped to 53 kilos (she weighed 88 kilos when carrying her child), although she was not deliberately dieting. At the age of 27, she met an alcoholic in one of the hospital's rehabilitation clinic and moved in with him. Again, the relationship floundered and she moved back in with her parents. At 29, she returned to the hospital for more surgery on her leg and began the diet which prompted her eating disorder.

At this stage, she weighted 55 kilos; within a year this had reduced to 44. Her daily food intake consisted of coffee with sweetener and fat-free milk and the occasional bit of fruit or bran. Food prepared by her parents was played with and hardly eaten. If she did eat, she would use laxatives to remove the food. Although she did not eat, she was ravenously hungry and sought out recipe books and thought about food constantly. She viewed any increase in weight as a sign that she was not perfect; although weighing less than 44 kilos at this point, she regarded herself as overweight.

The physical effects of the weight loss soon came – her periods stopped, her skin lost its elasticity, she had liver problems and she would get dizzy when standing up.

A year and a half after the onset of the disorder she moved out of her parents' house because of the unbearable nature of the interactions that took place. She now weighed 39 kilos and her son's diet became affected because there was little food in the house. Most of her own diet consisted of liquid; she was weak and many people commented on how thin she looked. To Joan, however, she was still overweight.

At the age of 32, she met Mike at a local church group meeting. At this time, she weighed about 44 kilos but this dropped again when she began dating Mike. Unlike her previous partners, Mike was sympathetic and urged her to seek medical attention. About a year since she first started seeing Mike, she was admitted to hospital for the removal of intestinal cysts. The surgeon noticed other complications and rearranged her entire bowel system. She now weighed 38 kilos. After two months, she returned to work and began her restrictive diet again. At this point, Mike and her friends demanded that she seek treatment, and this she did.

The treatment involved a 30 day stay hospital programme where Joan was required to consume 1,500 calories and three meals a day (the breakfast alone comprised her previous weekly intake). Privileges such as going on day trips were dependent on her fulfilling these eating requirements. Although this increase in eating behaviour was difficult, she received therapy sessions from staff who explored reasons for her restrictive eating, and as a result of the programme she gained 13 kilos. She experienced a period of remission a short while later and she asked to be taken back to the hospital. It was at this point that she realised the extent of her problem and what was required of her to change her problem behaviour. With the help of the hospital and the support of her partner, she eventually learned to control her weight without resorting to restrictive eating. Joan, however, could not exactly pinpoint what had occurred to make her change her behaviour.

Source: Oltmans *et al.*, 1995.

Bulimia nervosa

Another eating disorder, bulimia nervosa, is characterised by a loss of control of food intake. The term bulimia comes from the Greek *bous*, 'ox', and *limos*, 'hunger'. People with bulimia nervosa periodically gorge themselves with food, especially dessert or snack food, and especially in the afternoon or evening. These behaviours must occur at least twice a week for three months, for a diagnosis of bulimia nervosa to be made (DSM-IV, 1994). These binges are usually followed by self-induced vomiting or the use of laxatives, along with feelings of depression and guilt (Mawson, 1974; Halmi, 1978). This behaviour is called purging, although not all bulimics use this behaviour as a means of compensating for the binge eating. With this combination of bingeing and purging, the net nutrient intake (and consequently, the body weight) of bulimics can vary; Weltzin *et al.* (1991) report that 44 per cent of bulimics undereat, 37 per cent eat a normal amount, and 44 per cent overeat. Episodes of bulimia are seen in some patients with anorexia nervosa. Bulimics seem to be less concerned with food but are excessively preoccupied with body shape (Lovell *et al.*, 1997). The prevalence rate is a little higher than that for anorexia and ranges between 1 and 3 per cent (DSM-IV, 1994).

Aetiology of anorexia and bulimia nervosa

The fact that anorexia nervosa is seen primarily in young women has prompted biological, cognitive and sociocultural explanations, and there are many of them. There is good evidence, primarily from twin studies, that hereditary factors play a role in the development of anorexia (Russell and Treasure, 1989). The existence of hereditary factors suggests that abnormalities in physiological mechanisms may be involved. However, most psychologists believe that the emphasis our society places on slimness, especially in women, is largely responsible for this disorder. Others suggest that the excessive need to control eating (which is, in turn, caused by Western societies' preoccupation with shape and weight) is the characteristic feature (Fairburn *et al.*, 1999).

About one patient in thirty dies of the disorder. Many anorexics suffer from osteoporosis, and bone fractures are common. When the weight loss becomes severe enough, anorexic women cease menstruating (this is called amenorrhea). Two reports (Artmann *et al.*, 1985; Lankenau *et al.*, 1985) indicate that CT scans of anorexic patients show evidence of loss of brain tissue. Some of the lost tissue, but not all, apparently returns after recovery.

Another possible cause of anorexia and bulimia is that changes in a young woman's endocrine status alter her metabolism or the neural mechanisms involved in feeding. Indeed, the female sex hormones progesterone and oestradiol have been shown to affect food intake and body weight of laboratory animals through their interactions with receptors for these hormones located in various organs, including the brain and adipose tissue (Wade and Gray, 1979). However, no evidence yet shows that anorexia nervosa in humans is related to this phenomenon. Many studies have found evidence of metabolic differences between anorexics and people of normal weight. But because prolonged fasting and the use of laxatives have many effects, interpreting these differences is difficult (Halmi, 1978).

Questions to think about

Eating

- Why does hunger occur and why is it not a constant feeling?
- How is sensory-specific satiety different from alliesthesia?
- What do you think the advantages of sensory-specific satiety are? What are the disadvantages?
- What do you think is responsible for food 'cravings' such as that for chocolate?
- What distinguishes anorexia from bulimia nervosa?
- Do you think that most weight gain is avoidable? Why?
- Do you think that anorexia is caused entirely by social factors (such as the emphasis on thinness in our society) or do you think that biological factors (such as hormonal or biochemical changes) also play a role?
- Why do you think that anorexia and bulimia is not as common in men and boys as it is in women and girls?

Sexual behaviour

The motivation to engage in sexual behaviour can be very strong. However, sexual behaviour is not motivated by a physiological need, the way that eating is. Because we must perform certain behaviours in order to reproduce, the process of natural selection has ensured that our brains are constructed in such a way as to cause enough of us to mate with each other that the species will survive.

Effects of sex hormones on behaviour

Sex hormones, hormones secreted by the testes and ovaries, have effects on cells throughout the body. In general, these effects promote reproduction. For example, they cause the production of sperms, build up the lining of the uterus, trigger ovulation, and stimulate the production of milk. Sex hormones also affect nerve cells in the brain, thereby affecting behaviour, but they do not cause behaviours. Behaviours are responses to particular situations and are affected by people's experiences in the past. Sex hormones affect people's motivation to perform particular classes of reproductive behaviours. We therefore start our exploration of sexual behaviour with the motivational effects of sex hormones.

Effects of androgens

As we saw in Chapter 12, androgens such as testosterone are necessary for male sexual development. During prenatal development, the testes of male foetuses secrete testosterone, which causes the male sex organs to develop. This hormone also affects the development of the brain. The prenatal effects of sex hormones are called organisational effects because they alter the organisation of the sex organs and the brain. Studies using laboratory animals have shown that if the organisational effects of androgens on brain development are prevented, the animal later fails to exhibit male sexual behaviour. In addition, males cannot have an erection and engage in sexual intercourse unless testosterone is present in adulthood. These effects are called activational effects because the hormone activates sex organs and brain circuits that have already developed.

J.M. Davidson *et al.* (1979) performed a carefully controlled double-blind study of the activational effects of testosterone on the sexual behaviour of men whose testes failed to secrete normal amounts of androgens. The men were given monthly injections of a placebo or one of two different dosages of a long-lasting form of testosterone. When the men receiving testosterone were compared with the men in the control group, the effect of testosterone on total number of erections and attempts at intercourse during the month following the injection was found to be large and statistically significant, and the larger dosage produced more of an effect than did the smaller dosage. Thus, we may conclude that testosterone definitely affects male sexual performance.

If a man is castrated (has his testes removed, usually because of injury or disease), his sex drive will inevitably decline. Usually, he first loses the ability to ejaculate, and then he loses the ability to achieve an erection (Bermant and Davidson, 1974). But studies have shown that some men lose these abilities soon after castration, whereas others retain at least some level of sexual potency for many months. Injections or pills of testosterone quickly restore potency. Possibly, the amount of sexual experience prior to castration affects performance afterwards. Rosenblatt and Aronson (1958) found that male cats who had copulated frequently before castration were able to perform sexually for much longer periods of time after the surgery. Perhaps the same is true for men.

Testosterone affects sex drive, but it does not determine the object of sexual desire. A homosexual man who receives injections of testosterone will not suddenly become interested in women. If testosterone has any effect, it will be to increase his interest in sexual contact with other men.

Although evidence shows clearly that testosterone affects men's sexual performance, humans are uniquely emancipated from the biological effects of hormones in a special way. Not all human sexual activity requires an erect penis. A man does not need testosterone to be able to kiss and caress his partner or to engage in other non-coital activities. Men who have had to be castrated and who cannot receive injections of testosterone for medical reasons report continued sexual activity with their partners. For humans, sexual activity is not limited to coitus.

Androgens appear to activate sex drive in women as well as in men. Persky *et al.* (1978) studied the sexual activity of eleven married couples ranging in age from 21 to 31. The subjects kept daily records of their sexual feelings and behaviour, and the experimenters measured their blood levels of testosterone twice a week. Couples were more likely to engage in intercourse when the woman's testosterone level was at a peak. In addition, the women reported finding intercourse more gratifying during these times.

Effects of progesterone and oestrogen

In most species of mammals, the hormones oestradiol and progesterone have strong effects on female sexual behaviour. The levels of these two sex hormones fluctuate during the menstrual cycle of primates and the oestrus cycle of other female mammals. The difference between these two cycles is primarily that the lining of the primate uterus – but not that of other mammals – builds up during the first part of the cycle and sloughs off at the end. A female mammal of a non-primate species – for example, a laboratory rat – will receive the advances of a male only when the levels of oestradiol and progesterone in her blood are high. This condition occurs around the time of ovulation, when copulation is likely to make her become pregnant. During this time, the female will stand still while the male approaches her. If he attempts to mount her, she will arch her back and move her tail to the side, giving him access to her genitalia. In fact, an oestrus female rat often does not wait for the male to take the initiative; she engages in seductive behaviours such as hopping around and wiggling her ears. These behaviours usually induce sexual activity by the male (McClintock and Adler, 1978).

A female rat whose ovaries have been removed is normally non-receptive, even hostile, to the advances of an eager male. However, if she is given injections of oestradiol and progesterone to duplicate the hormonal condition of the receptive part of her oestrus cycle, she will receive the male or even pursue him. In contrast, women and other female primates are unique among mammals in their sexual activity: they are potentially willing to engage in sexual behaviour at any time during their reproductive cycles. Some investigators have suggested that this phenomenon made monogamous relationships possible; because the male can look forward to his mate's receptivity at any time during her menstrual cycle, he is less likely to look for other partners.

In higher primates (including our own species), the ability to mate is not controlled by oestradiol and progesterone. Most studies have reported that changes in the level of oestradiol and progesterone have only a minor effect on women's sexual interest (Adams *et al.*, 1978; Morris *et al.*, 1987). However, as Wallen (1990) points out, these studies have almost all involved married women who live with their husbands. In stable, monogamous relationships in which the partners are together on a daily basis, sexual activity can be instigated by either of them. Normally, a husband does not force his wife to have intercourse with him, but even if the woman is not physically interested in engaging in sexual activity at a particular moment, she may find that she wants to do so because of her affection for him. This fact poses an interesting question. If all of a woman's sexual encounters were initiated by her, without regard to her partner's desires, would we find that variations in oestradiol and progesterone across the menstrual cycle would affect her behaviour? Studies using monkeys suggest that this may be the case (Wallen *et al.*, 1986). And as Alexander *et al.* (1990) showed, women taking oral contraceptives (which prevent the normal cycles in secretion of ovarian hormones) were less likely to show fluctuations in sexual interest during the menstrual cycle.

Sexual orientation

When people reach puberty, the effects of sex hormones on their maturing bodies and on their brains increase their interest in sexual activity. As sexual interest increases, most people develop a special interest in members of the other sex – they develop a heterosexual orientation. Why does opposite-sex attraction occur? And why does same-sex attraction sometimes occur? As we shall see, research has not yet provided definite answers to these questions, but it has provided some hints.

Homosexual behaviour (engaging in sexual activity with members of the same sex; from the Greek *homos*, meaning 'the same') is seen in male and female animals of many different species. The widespread occurrence of homosexual behaviour means that we should not refer to it as unnatural. However, humans are apparently the only species in which some members regularly exhibit exclusive homosexuality. Other animals, if they are not exclusively heterosexual, are likely to be bisexual, engaging in sexual activity with members of both sexes. In contrast, the number of men and women who describe themselves as exclusively homosexual exceeds the number who describe themselves as bisexual.

Traditional theories of sexual orientation have stressed the importance of a person's early environment. Earlier in this century, most mental health professionals regarded homosexuality as a disorder, caused by a faulty home environment – for example, as the result of having been raised by an overprotective mother and an indifferent father. More recent research has refuted these conclusions. First, there is no evidence that homosexuality is a disorder. The adjustment problems that some homosexuals have occur because others may treat them differently. Therefore, even if we observe more neuroses in homosexuals than in heterosexuals, we cannot conclude that their maladjustment is directly related to their sexual orientation. In a society that was absolutely indifferent to a person's sexual orientation, homosexuals might be as well adjusted as heterosexuals. In fact, a large number of homosexuals are well adjusted and happy with themselves (Bell and Weinberg, 1978), suggesting that homosexuality is not necessarily associated with emotional difficulties.

As we saw, some studies suggested that homosexuality is an emotional disturbance caused by faulty child rearing. However, much of the data in these studies were gathered from people who went to a psychiatrist or clinical psychologist for help with emotional problems. Therefore, they were not necessarily typical of all homosexuals, and we cannot know whether their homosexuality was caused by an unhappy childhood, whether their unhappy childhood was caused by early manifestations of homosexual tendencies, or whether their emotional instability and homosexual orientation were purely coincidental.

An ambitious project reported by Bell *et al.* (1981) studied a large number of homosexual men and women, most of whom had not sought professional psychological assistance. The researchers obtained their subjects by placing advertisements in newspapers, approaching people in gay bars and bookstores, and asking homosexuals to recommend friends. The study took place in San Francisco, where homosexuals form a large part of the population.

The subjects were asked about their relationships with their parents, siblings and peers and about their feelings, gender identification and sexual activity. The results provided little or no support for traditional theories of homosexuality. The major conclusions of the study were:

1 Sexual orientation appears to be determined prior to adolescence and prior to homosexual or heterosexual activity. The most important single predictor of adult homosexuality was a self-report of homosexual feelings, which usually occurred three years before first genital homosexual activity. This finding suggests that homosexuality is a deep-seated tendency. It also tends to rule out the suggestion that seduction by an older person of the same sex plays an important role in the development of homosexuality.

2 Most homosexual men and women have engaged in some heterosexual experiences during childhood and adolescence, but in contrast to their heterosexual counterparts, they found these experiences unrewarding. This pattern is also consistent with the existence of a deep-seated predisposition prior to adulthood.

3 There is a strong relation between gender non-conformity in childhood and the development of homosexuality. Gender non-conformity is characterised by an aversion in boys to 'masculine' behaviours and in girls to 'feminine' behaviours.

As the researchers admit, the results of the study are consistent with the hypothesis that homosexuality is at least partly determined by biological factors. That is, biological variables may predispose a child to behaviour that is more typical of the other sex and eventually to sexual arousal by members of his or her own sex.

Is there evidence of what these biological causes of homosexuality may be? We can immediately rule out the suggestion that male homosexuals have insufficient levels of testosterone in their blood; well adjusted male homosexuals have normal levels of testosterone (Tourney, 1980).

A more likely cause of male homosexuality is the pattern of exposure of the developing brain to sex hormones. Some experiments suggest that if a female rat is subjected to stress during pregnancy, the pattern of secretion of sex hormones is altered, and the sexual development of the male offspring is affected (Ward, 1972; Anderson *et al.*, 1986). Three laboratories have studied the brains of deceased heterosexual and homosexual men and have found differences in the size of two different subregions of the hypothalamus and in a bundle of axons that connects the right and left temporal lobes (Swaab and Hofman, 1990; LeVay, 1991; Allen and Gorski, 1992). We cannot necessarily conclude that any of these regions is directly involved in people's sexual orientation, but the results do suggest that the brains may have been exposed to different patterns of hormones prenatally.

When the organisational effects of androgens are blocked in male laboratory animals, the animals fail to develop normal male sex behaviour. Nature has performed the equivalent experiment in humans (Money and Ehrhardt, 1972; Ris-Stalpers *et al.*, 1990). Some people are insensitive to androgens. They have androgen insensitivity syndrome, caused by a genetic mutation that prevents the formation of androgen receptors. Because the cells of the body cannot respond to the androgens, a genetic male with this syndrome develops female external genitalia instead of a penis and scrotum. The person does not develop ovaries or a uterus.

If an individual with this syndrome is raised as a girl, all is well. Normally, the testes (which remain in the abdomen) are removed because they often become cancerous. At the appropriate time, the person is given oestrogen pills to induce puberty. Subsequently, the individual will function sexually as a woman. Women with this syndrome report average sex drives, including normal frequency of orgasm in intercourse. Most marry and lead normal sex lives. Of course, lacking a uterus and ovaries, they cannot have children.

Although little research has been done on the origins of female homosexuality, Money *et al.* (1984) found that the incidence of homosexuality was several times higher than the national average in women who had been exposed to high levels of androgens prenatally. The cause of the exposure was an abnormality of the adrenal glands, which usually secrete very low levels of these hormones. Thus, sexual orientation in females may indeed be affected by biological factors.

There is also some evidence that genetics may play a role in sexual orientation. Twin studies take advantage of the fact that identical twins have identical genes, whereas the genetic similarity between fraternal twins is, on the average, 50 per cent. Bailey and Pillard (1991) studied pairs of male twins in which at least one member identified himself as homosexual. If both twins are homosexual, they are said to be concordant for this trait. If only one is homosexual, the twins are said to be discordant. Thus, if homosexuality has a genetic basis, the percentage of identical twins concordant for homosexuality should be higher than that for fraternal twins. And this is exactly what Bailey and Pillard found; the concordance rate was 52 per cent for identical twins and 22 per cent for fraternal twins. In a subsequent study, J.M. Bailey *et al.* (1993) found evidence that heredity plays a role in female homosexuality, too. The concordance rates for female identical and fraternal twins were 48 per cent and 16 per cent, respectively.

As we have seen, there is evidence that two biological factors – prenatal hormonal exposure and heredity – can affect a person's sexual orientation. These research findings certainly contradict the suggestion that a person's sexual orientation is a moral issue. It appears that homosexuals are no more responsible for their sexual orientation than heterosexuals are. Ernulf *et al.* (1989) found that people who believed that homosexuals were 'born that way' expressed more positive attitudes towards them than did people who believed that they 'chose to be' or 'learned to be' that way.

Questions to think about

Sexual behaviour

- Do our brains make men and women different or are sex differences largely socially determined?
- Do you think that there is such a thing as a sexual brain – one that determines our sexual orientation?
- What are the respective roles of hormones and environment in causing sexual behaviour?
- Why do other species' means of attracting a sexual partner seem more primitive than ours? Is it?

Aggressive behaviour

Aggression is a serious problem for humans: every day, we hear or read about incidents involving violence and cruelty, and undoubtedly, thousands more go unreported. Many factors probably influence a person's tendency to commit acts of aggression, including childhood experiences, peer group pressures, hormones and drugs, and malfunctions of the brain. Various aspects of aggressive behaviour have been studied by zoologists, physiological psychologists, sociologists, social psychologists, political scientists and psychologists who specialise in the learning process.

Ethological studies of aggression

The utility of species-typical behaviours such as sexual activity, parental behaviour, food gathering and nest construction is obvious; we can easily understand their value to survival. But violence and aggression are also seen in many species, including our own. If aggression is harmful, one would not expect it to be so prevalent in nature. Ethologists – zoologists who study the behaviour of animals in their natural environments – have analysed the causes of aggression and have shown that it, too, often has value for the survival of a species.

Intraspecific aggression

Intraspecific aggression involves an attack by one animal upon another member of its species. Ethologists have shown that intraspecific aggression has several biological advantages. First, it tends to disperse a population of animals, forcing some into new territories, where necessary environmental adaptations may increase the flexibility of the species. Second, when accompanied by rivalry among males for mating opportunities, intraspecific aggression tends to perpetuate the genes of the healthier, more vigorous animals.

Human cultures, however, are very different even from those of other species of primates. Perhaps intraspecific aggression has outlived its usefulness for humans and we would benefit by its elimination. Whatever the case may be, we must understand the causes of human aggression in order to eliminate it or direct it to more useful purposes.

Threat and appeasement

Ethologists have discovered a related set of behaviours in many species: ritualised threat gestures and appeasement gestures. Threat gestures enable an animal to communicate aggressive intent to another before engaging in actual violence. For example, if one dog intrudes on another's territory, the defender will growl and bare its teeth, raise the fur on its back (making it look larger to its opponent), and stare at the intruder. Almost always, the dog defending its territory will drive the intruder away. Threat gestures are particularly important in species whose members are able to kill each other (Lorenz, 1966; Eibl-Eibesfeld, 1980). For example, wolves often threaten each other with growls and bared teeth but rarely bite each other. Because an all-out battle between two wolves would probably end in the death of one and the serious wounding of the other, the tendency to perform ritualised displays rather than engage in overt aggression has an obvious advantage to the survival of the species.

Hormones and aggression

In birds and most mammals, androgens appear to exert a strong effect on aggressiveness. Do hormones also influence aggressive behaviour in humans? Men are generally more aggressive than women (Knight et al., 1996) although such differences are attenuated when factors such as provocation are considered (Bettencourt and Miller, 1996). The fact that a man's sexual behaviour depends on the presence of testosterone suggests that this hormone may also influence aggressive behaviour. Some cases of aggressiveness – especially sexual assault – have been treated with drugs that block androgen receptors and thus prevent androgens from exerting their normal effects (Brain, 1984, 1994; Heim and Hursch, 1979). The rationale is based on animal research that indicates that androgens promote both sexual behaviour and aggression in males. However, the efficacy of treatment with antiandrogens has yet to be established conclusively (Mazur and Booth, 1998).

Another way to determine whether androgens affect aggressiveness in humans is to examine the testosterone levels of people who exhibit varying levels of aggressive behaviour in the laboratory and outside the laboratory. Testosterone is secreted into the bloodstream sporadically and so changes in levels can be measured easily. Levels are greatest in the morning and lower in the afternoon (Dabbs, 1990). Clearly, in the laboratory it is unethical (and probably undesirable) to encourage aggression. Psychologists, therefore, have used measures that increase feelings of hostility rather than generate hostility itself and have reported a significant correlation between these measures and testosterone levels: increased testosterone levels were associated with increased feelings of hostility. Most studies, however, do report negative results, that is, no relationship between testosterone level and hostility (Mazur and Booth, 1998).

Outside the laboratory, the findings are slightly more promising. Dabbs et al. (1987), for example, measured the testosterone levels of 89 male prison inmates and found a significant correlation between these levels and (1) the violence of the crime, and (2) their fellow prisoners' ratings of their toughness. These effects were also found in female prison inmates. Dabbs et al. (1988) found that women prisoners who showed unprovoked violence and had several prior convictions also showed higher levels of testosterone. In a further study, Dabbs et al. (1991) reported that 17–18 year old criminals with high testosterone levels were more likely to have committed violent crimes and to have violated prison rules. The picture is not entirely uniform, however. Bain et al. (1987), for example, found no significant difference between the testosterone levels of those individuals charged with violent offences and those charged with property crime.

One problem with these findings is that they are correlational and a significant correlation, of course, does not mean causation. In an experimentally controlled study, researchers have noted that losing a tennis match or a wrestling competition, for example, causes a fall in blood levels of testosterone (Mazur and Lamb, 1980; Elias, 1981). In a very elaborate study, Jeffcoate *et al.* (1986) found that the blood levels of a group of five men confined on a boat for 14 days changed as they established a dominance-aggression ranking among themselves: the higher the rank, the higher the testosterone level was.

It seems unclear, however, what the increase in testosterone signifies. Such increases have been reported in individuals about to play a chess match, with greater increases found in winners than losers after the match (Mazur *et al.*, 1992). Increases have also been found in Brazilian supporters who saw their team on television win the 1994 World Cup against Italy; Italian viewers showed relatively lower levels (Fielden *et al.*, 1994, cited in Mazur and Booth, 1998).

Testosterone seems to have masculinising (androgenic) and anabolic (building protein tissue) effects. Some athletes take anabolic steroids in order to increase their muscle mass and strength and, supposedly, to increase their competitiveness. Anabolic steroids include natural androgens and synthetic hormones having androgenic effects. Several studies have found that anabolic steroids increase aggression. For example, Yates *et al.* (1992) found that male weightlifters who were taking anabolic steroids were more aggressive and hostile than those who were not. But, as the authors note, we cannot be certain that the steroid is responsible for the increased aggressiveness; it could simply be that the men who were already more competitive and aggressive were the ones who chose to take the steroids.

What could account for the relationship between testosterone and aggression? Mazur and Booth (1998) have recently proposed that a reciprocal relationship exists between these two factors. Specifically, high levels of testosterone encourages dominant behaviour which maintains high status. The model is reciprocal because testosterone and dominance are seen as reinforcing each other in contrast to the basal model which suggests that the individual has a static, basal level of testosterone which routinely predicts his behaviour. These authors suggest that reciprocal relationships can obviously only be observed across time and at different testing points. They point to a study in which testosterone levels in American Air Force veterans were low during marriage but increased during divorce as evidence for their model (Mazur and Michalek, 1998). The notion that testosterone is linked with dominance, however, continues to arouse controversy (see commentaries accompanying Mazur and Booth, 1998). Taken together, the findings reviewed in this section suggest (but still do not prove) that androgens play some role in stimulating aggression in humans.

Imitation and aggression

A large percentage of non-violent people may have been hit or punished at least once when they were children, with no obvious harm. But when parents habitually resort to aggression, their children are likely to do the same. In the extreme case of child abuse, parents who beat their children usually turn out to have been victims of child abuse themselves; this unfortunate trait seems to be passed along like an unwanted family heirloom (Parke and Collmer, 1975).

Another factor which is thought to influence aggression in children is exposure to violence on television, in films, video games and in comics. Does the continued observation of violence in the mass media lead children to choose aggressive means to solve their problems? Or are the television companies' representatives correct when they argue that children have no trouble separating fact from fantasy and that the mass media only give us what we want anyway?

Field studies suggest that long-term viewing of violence on television is associated with an increase in children's violent behaviour. For example, Lefkowitz *et al.* (1977) observed a correlation of 0.31 between boys' viewing of violence and their later behaviour. They reported that the greater the boys' preference for violent television at age 8, the greater their aggressiveness was both at that age and ten years later, at age 18. Girls were found to be much less aggressive, and no relation was observed between television viewing and violence.

Feshbach and Singer (1971) carried out a bold and interesting field study in an attempt to manipulate directly the amount of violence seen by boys on television, and thus to determine whether the viewing would affect their later aggressiveness. With the co-operation of directors of various private boarding schools and homes for neglected children, half the teenage boys were permitted to watch only violent television programmes, the other half only non-violent ones. Six months later, no effect was seen on the behaviour of the boys in the private schools. The boys in the homes for neglected children who had watched violent programmes tended to be slightly less aggressive than subjects who had watched the non-violent ones.

Two factors prevent us from concluding from this study that violent television programmes promote pacifism or at least have no effect. First, by the time people reach their teens, they may be too old to be affected by six months of television viewing; the critical period may come earlier. Secondly, some of the boys resented not being allowed to watch their favourite (in this case, violent) television programmes, and this resentment may have made them more aggressive.

As with many other complex social issues, we lack definitive evidence that television violence makes people more aggressive.

Questions to think about

Aggressive behaviour

■ It has been said that no species exhibits such high degrees of violence and aggression as humans. Why do humans aggress? What purpose, if any, should this behaviour serve?

■ Do you think that aggression is maladaptive in our increasingly technological world?

■ Do you think that there is a difference between aggressive and dominant behaviour?

■ How convincing do you find the evidence for a significant role for testosterone in aggressive behaviour?

■ Do you think that people are born with aggressive personalities? What evidence can you cite in support of your argument?

■ How compelling do you find the evidence for and against the hypothesis that watching violent television programmes causes violent behaviour in children and adults?

Emotion

Most psychologists who have studied emotion have focused on one or more of the following questions: What kinds of situations produce emotions? What kinds of feelings do people say they experience? What kinds of behaviours do people engage in? What physiological changes do people undergo in situations that produce strong emotions? What exactly is an emotion?

The word 'emotion' comes from Latin and means 'to move' or 'to stir up'. In general terms, emotion is used by psychologists to refer to a display of feelings that are evoked when important things happen to us. Emotions are relatively brief and occur in response to events having motivational relevance (or to their mental re-creation, as when we remember something embarrassing that we did in the past and experience the feelings of embarrassment again). Emotions are the consequence of events that motivate us. When we encounter reinforcing or punishing stimuli, stimuli that motivate us to act, we express and experience positive or negative emotions. The nature of the emotions depends on the nature of the stimuli and on our prior experience with them.

There are problems, however, associated with defining emotions. We have a multitude of ways of expressing what we think are emotional behaviours. Davitz (1970), for example, found 556 words and phrases that were emotion-related.

Some psychologists view emotion as being produced by reinforcing stimuli or by a set of interacting brain regions or by our awareness of bodily feelings. Given the disparate nature of these definitions, LeDoux (1995b) was right when he concluded that emotion had 'proved to be a slippery concept for both psychologists and neuroscientists'.

If the definition is unclear, then perhaps we can agree on examples of emotions and can describe a core set of basic, fundamental emotions. Yet, even here, the evidence is ambiguous. There are psychologists who have argued that a set of basic emotions exists (Ekman, 1973; Izard, 1977, 1992; Plutchik, 1980). The number of basic emotions has ranged from six or seven (Ekman, 1984, 1992) to eight (Plutchik, 1980) to ten (Izard, 1992). To Ekman, the basic emotions are sadness, joy (happiness), surprise, fear, anger, disgust and contempt (or fear), and these can be universally seen in facial expression (see Figure 13.6).

To Plutchik, the basic emotions are fear/terror, anger/rage, joy/ecstasy, sadness/grief, acceptance/trust, disgust/loathing, expectancy/anticipation and surprise/astonishment. There are other psychologists who have argued that because we have no satisfactory criteria on which to base any concept of 'basicness' then we cannot conclude that any emotions we care to list are basic ones (Ortony and Turner, 1990). Yet still others argue that the methods used to determine basic emotions are flawed and that the findings are not wholly conclusive (Russell, 1994; cf. Ekman, 1994). What, therefore, is the evidence for basic emotions?

Basic emotions

Charles Darwin (1872) suggested that human expressions of emotion have evolved from similar expressions in other animals. He said that emotional expressions are innate, unlearned responses consisting of a complex set of movements, principally of the facial muscles. Thus, a man's sneer and a wolf's snarl are biologically determined response patterns, both controlled by innate brain mechanisms, just as coughing and sneezing are. Some of these movements resemble the behaviours themselves and may have evolved from them. For example, a snarl shows one's teeth and can be seen as an anticipation of biting.

Darwin performed what was probably the first cross-cultural study of behaviour. He obtained evidence for his conclusion that emotional expressions were innate by observing his own children and by corresponding with people living in various isolated cultures around the world. He reasoned that if people all over the world, no matter how isolated, show the same facial expressions of emotion, these expressions must be inherited instead of learned. The logical argument goes like this. When groups of people are isolated for many years, they develop different languages. Thus, we can say that the words that people use are arbitrary; there is no biological basis for using particular words to represent particular concepts. However, if facial expressions are inherited, they should take approximately the same form in people from all cultures, despite their isolation from one another. And Darwin did, indeed, find that people in different cultures used the same patterns of movement of facial muscles to express a particular emotional state.

In 1967 and 1968, Ekman and Friesen reported a series of cross-cultural observations that validated those of

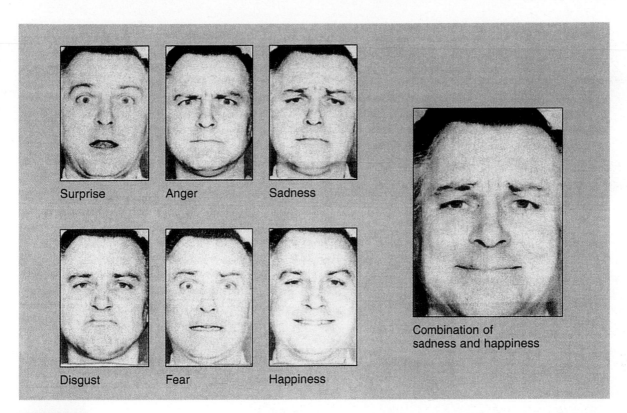

Surprise   Anger   Sadness

Disgust   Fear   Happiness

Combination of
sadness and happiness

Figure 13.6

The six basic emotions shown in facial expression, and a combination of two, as suggested by Ekman.

Source: Pinel, J., *Biopsychology* (3rd edition). Boston: Allyn and Bacon. Copyright © 1997 by Allyn and Bacon; reproduced by permission.

Darwin (Ekman, 1980). They visited an isolated tribe in a remote area of New Guinea – the South Fore tribe, a group of 319 adults and children who had never been exposed to Western culture. If they were able to identify accurately the emotional expressions of Westerners as well as they could identify those of members of their own tribe, and if their own facial expressions were the same as those of Westerners, then the researchers could conclude that these expressions were not culturally determined.

Because translations of single words from one language to another are not always accurate, Ekman and Friesen told little stories to describe an emotion instead of presenting a single word. They told the story to a subject, presented three photographs of Westerners depicting three different emotions, and asked the subject to choose the appropriate one. This they were able to do. In a second study, Ekman and Friesen asked Fore tribespeople to imagine how they would feel in situations that would produce various emotions, and the researchers videotaped their facial expressions. They showed photographs of the videotapes to American college students, who had no trouble identifying the emotions. Four of them are shown in Figure 13.7. The caption describes the story that was used to elicit each expression.

However, not all psychologists have agreed with Ekman's conclusions. While the finding that facial expres-

sions can be identified cross-culturally is robust, there is little agreement on what these findings mean. Zajonc (1985), for example, has suggested that facial expressions are epiphenomena – not important of themselves and, in fact, serving another purpose. Critics such as Fridlund (1992, 1994) have argued that all facial expressions are communicative and that to single out a group of emotional facial expressions ignores the fundamental social nature of facial expression. Expressions may not be emotional signals but social tools used for communication: we can communicate happiness or approval via a smile but this smile may not be generated by genuine emotion but by social cues or needs. This objection is difficult, in part, to counter because expressions may sometimes be used for non-emotional purposes. Smiling may indeed be an expression of joy, but it can also be an expression of sarcasm or even, in sinister contexts, threat. What critics suggest is that facial expressions do not reflect the emotion but the social signalling of the emotion; the two are different.

Other critics, such as Russell (1991, 1994), have even questioned whether the cross-cultural findings are robust. Russell has argued in some detail that the faults in the methodology in these experiments, particularly the method of presenting each emotion sequentially and asking respondents to choose from a list of alternative

(a)

(b)

(c)

(d)

Figure 13.7

Portraying emotions. Ekman and Friesen asked South Fore tribesmen to make faces (shown in the photographs) when they were told stories. (a) Your friend has come and you are happy. (b) Your child had died. (c) You are angry and about to fight. (d) You see a dead pig that has been lying there a long time.

Source: Ekman, P., *The Face of Man: Expressions of universal emotions in a New Guinea village*. New York: Garland STPM Press, 1980. Reprinted with permission.

descriptions the expression they have seen, make the conclusions of these studies uninterpretable.

Perhaps the evidence for universality is based on the wrong type of data collection; perhaps Russell has a valid point. If Ekman and Friesen's method is an invalid measure, what measure could demonstrate the existence of basic emotions?

The biology of emotion

Perhaps one way of determining whether an emotion is basic or not is by observing the neural machinery activated by these so-called basic emotions. If these emotions are distinct then it follows that different brain regions or pathways might mediate them. In animal research, much of the work on understanding the neural correlates of emotion has focused on fear because this emotion is easy to condition in the laboratory. Evidence from animal work and from studies of brain-damaged humans suggests that the amygdala is an important structure for the recognition and expression of fear. Other neuropsychological evidence suggests that other brain regions may also be involved in different types of emotion.

All emotional responses contain three components: behavioural, autonomic and hormonal. The behavioural component consists of muscular movements that are appropriate to the situation that elicits them. For example, a dog defending its territory against an intruder first adopts an aggressive posture, growls and shows its teeth. If the intruder does not leave, the defender runs towards it and attacks. Autonomic responses – that is, changes in the activity of the autonomic nervous system – facilitate these behaviours and provide quick mobilisation of energy for vigorous movement. As a consequence, the dog's heart rate increases, and changes in the size of blood vessels shunt the circulation of blood away from the digestive organs towards the muscles. Hormonal responses reinforce the autonomic responses. The hormones secreted by the adrenal glands further increase heart rate and blood flow to the muscles and also make more glucose available to them.

Emotional responses, like all other responses, can be modified by experience. For example, we can learn that a particular situation is dangerous or threatening. Once the learning has taken place, we will become frightened when we encounter that situation. This type of response, acquired through the process of classical conditioning, is called a conditioned emotional response.

A conditioned emotional response is produced by a neutral stimulus that has been paired with an emotion-producing stimulus. If an organism learns to make a specific response that avoids contact with the aversive stimulus (or at least minimises its painful effect), most of the non-specific 'emotional' responses will eventually disappear. That is, if the organism learns a successful coping response – a response that terminates, avoids, or minimises an aversive stimulus – the emotional responses will no longer occur.

The amygdala

The amygdala, located in the temporal lobe, just in front of the hippocampus, plays an important role in the expression of conditioned emotional responses. According to Aggelton and Mishkin (1986), it represents 'the sensory gateway to the emotions'. It serves as a focal point between sensory systems and the systems responsible for behavioural, autonomic, and hormonal components of conditioned emotional responses (Kapp *et al.*, 1982; LeDoux, 1995b). (The location of the amygdala can be seen in Chapter 4 in Figure 4.35.)

Many studies have found that damage to the amygdala disrupts the behavioural, autonomic and hormonal components of conditioned emotional responses. After this region has been destroyed, animals no longer show signs of fear when confronted with stimuli that have been paired with aversive events (LeDoux, 1995b, 1996). They also act more tamely when handled by humans, their blood levels of stress hormones are lower, and they are less likely to develop ulcers or other forms of stress-induced illnesses (Coover *et al.*, 1992; Davis, 1992; LeDoux, 1992). Conversely, when the amygdala is stimulated by means of electricity or by an injection of an excitatory drug, animals show physiological and behavioural signs of fear and agitation (Davis, 1992). In fact, long-term stimulation of the amygdala produces gastric ulcers (Henke, 1982). These observations suggest that the autonomic and hormonal components of emotional responses controlled by the amygdala are among those responsible for the harmful effects of long-term stress.

The role of the amygdala in human emotion

There is now considerable evidence to suggest that the effects seen in animals may be mirrored in humans. Two lines of research have converged to suggest a role for the amygdala in the recognition and expression of fear: brain lesioning and neuroimaging studies. For example, individuals with damage to the amygdala are unable to recognise fear in facial expression, are unable to draw a fearful expression (although they can draw other emotional expressions) and are impaired at recognising fear by sound (Calder *et al.*, 1996; Adolphs *et al.*, 1994, 1995, 1999; Scott *et al.*, 1997; Brooks *et al.*, 1998).

Neuroimaging data also suggest that the amygdala is relatively more involved than other brain regions during the perception of fear-related material. For example, Morris *et al.* (1996) reported that not only did activation increase in the left side of the amygdala when individuals were watching fearful facial expressions but also that this activation was greater when the facial expression was more intense. Other fMRI and PET studies have confirmed this activation in the amygdala during the perception of fear in facial expressions (Morris *et al.*, 1998) and in the perception of sad expressions, but not angry ones (Blair *et al.*, 1999).

The amygdala is not the only region to be involved in mediating human emotional response. Its specificity – it seems to respond primarily to negative or fear-related stimuli – suggests that other brain areas must be involved in regulating other types of emotion such as happiness or sadness. Although conditioned emotional responses can be elicited by very simple stimuli, our emotions are often reactions to very complex situations; those situations involving other people can be especially complex.

Perceiving the meaning of social situations is obviously more complex than perceiving individual stimuli, such as the expression of fear on people's faces; it involves experiences and memories, inferences and judgements. These skills are not localised in any one part of the cerebral cortex, although research does suggest that one region of the brain – the orbitofrontal cortex – appears to play a special role.

The orbitofrontal cortex

The orbitofrontal cortex is located at the base of the frontal lobes, as you can see from Figure 13.8. It covers the part of the brain just above the orbits – the bones that form the eye sockets – hence the term orbitofrontal. The orbitofrontal cortex receives information from the sensory system and from the regions of the frontal lobes that control behaviour. Thus, it knows what is going on in the environment and what plans are being made to respond to these events. It also communicates extensively with the limbic system, which is known to play an important role in emotional reactions. In particular, its connections with the amygdala permit it to affect the activity of the amygdala, which, as we saw, plays a critical role in certain emotional responses.

The fact that the orbitofrontal cortex plays an important role in emotional behaviour is shown by the effects of damage to this region. The first – and most famous – case comes from the mid-nineteenth century. Phineas Gage, the dynamite worker, described in the opening of this chapter,

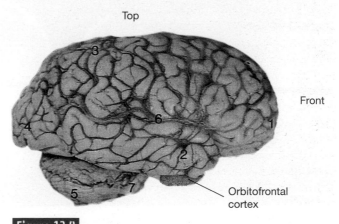

Figure 13.8

The orbitofrontal cortex.

Source: England, M.A. and Wakely, J. (1991) *A Colour Atlas of the Brain and Spinal Cord*. Aylesbury: Wolfe. Copyright © 1991, by permission of the publisher Mosby.

was using a steel rod to ram a charge of dynamite into a hole drilled in solid rock. The charge exploded and shot the rod into his cheek, through his brain and out the top of his head. He survived, but he was a different man. Before his injury, he was serious, industrious and energetic. Afterwards, he became childish, irresponsible, boorish and thoughtless of others (Harlow, 1848, 1868). He was unable to make or carry out plans, and his actions appeared to be capricious and whimsical. His accident largely destroyed the orbitofrontal cortex (Harlow, 1848; Damasio *et al.*, 1994). Figure 13.9 shows the plotted trajectory of the iron rod through Gage's head.

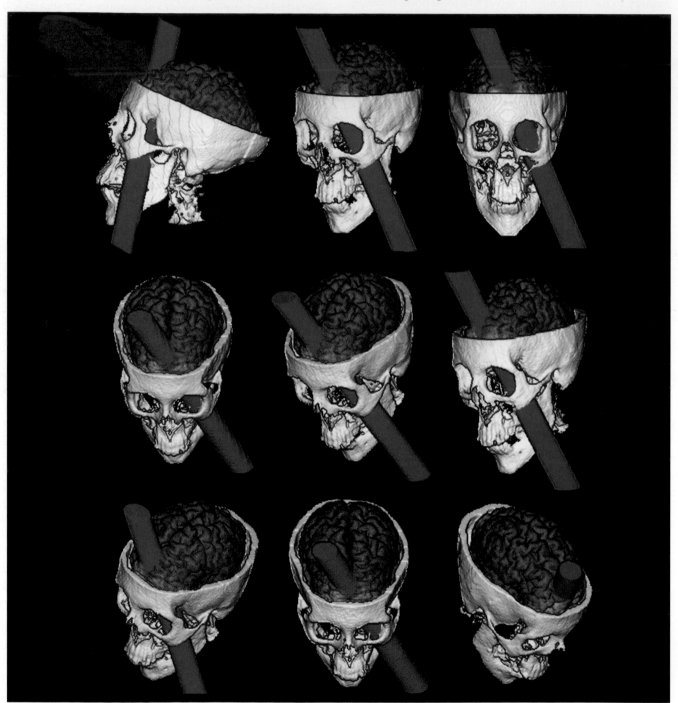

Figure 13.9

The trajectory of the iron bar through Phineas Gage's head.

Source: Damasio. H., Grabowski, T., Frank, R., Galaburda, A.M. and Damasio, A.R.: The return of Phineas Gage: Clues about the brain from a famous patient. *Science*, 246: 1102–1105, 1994. Department of Neurology and Image Analysis Facility, University of Iowa.

Over the succeeding years, physicians reported several cases similar to that of Phineas Gage. In general, damage to the orbitofrontal cortex reduced people's inhibitions and self-concern; they became indifferent to the consequences of their actions. A list of the behaviour thought to result from orbitofrontal cortex damage appears in Table 13.1.

The role of the orbitofrontal cortex

Given the large list of impairments in Table 13.1, what exactly is the role of the orbitofrontal cortex in emotion? One possibility is that it is involved in assessing the personal significance of what is currently happening to the individual (Prigatano, 1991). However, a person whose orbitofrontal cortex has been damaged by disease or accident is still able

Table 13.1 Some of the personality changes that can follow frontal lobe injury

Exaltation/depression

Decreased concern with social propriety

Apathy and indifference

Lack of judgement

Diminished reliability

Facetiousness

Childish behaviour

Anxiety

Social withdrawal

Irritability

Inertia

Lack of ambition

Indifference to opinions of others

Lack of restraint

Restlessness

Purposelessness

Slowness in thinking

Decreased self-concern

Impulsivity

Distractibility

Egocentricity

Source: adapted with permission from Stuss *et al.*, 1992. Copyright © 1992 by the American Psychological Association.

to assess accurately the significance of particular situations, but only in a theoretical sense. For example, Eslinger and Damasio (1985) found that their patient, EVR, who sustained bilateral damage of the orbitofrontal cortex displayed excellent social judgement. When he was given hypothetical situations that required him to make decisions about what the people involved should do – situations involving moral, ethical or practical dilemmas – he always gave sensible answers and justified them with carefully reasoned logic. However, his own life was a disaster.

EVR frittered away his life savings on investments that his family and friends pointed out were bound to fail. He lost one job after another because of his irresponsibility. He became unable to distinguish between trivial decisions and important ones, spending hours trying to decide where to have dinner but failing to use good judgement in situations that concerned his occupation and family life. As the authors noted, 'He had learned and used normal patterns of social behaviour before his brain lesion, and although he could recall such patterns when he was questioned about their applicability, real-life situations failed to evoke them' (p. 1737). Recall from the section on reasoning and the brain in Chapter 11, that Damasio proposed a somatic marker hypothesis of orbitofrontal cortex function. This suggests that our ability to make social and emotional decisions depends on our being able to make sense of somatic information that the body generates in response to specific events. If we are making a risky decision, this risk will be associated with a physiological response which will reflect our uncertainty about the decision we have made. In frontal lobe patients, Damasio argues, these connections between somatic states and an appreciation of them, are missing.

The type of behaviour seen in EVR is also seen in many patients with orbitofrontal cortex damage. Cicerone and Tanenbaum (1997), for example, have reported the case of a 38 year old woman with orbitofrontal damage who made good recovery from the injury but who showed disturbed social and emotional regulation. She appeared to have severe difficulty in integrating or appreciating subtle social and emotional cues. Hornak *et al.* (1996) have also reported twelve cases of ventral frontal lobe damage which was associated with an impairment at identifying facial and vocal emotional expression. Some of the comments made by orbitofrontal lobe patients on their disorder can help to illuminate the phenomenology of the social impairment – it shows us in very personal terms how the brain damage has affected that person's behaviour. Some of the comments made by Hornak *et al.*'s (1996) patients are highlighted in Table 13.2.

Specific emotional deficits

Intriguingly, a recent series of experiments has suggested that individuals suffering from Huntington's chorea, a genetically inherited disorder of movement characterised by jerky, dance-like movement, are disproportionately

Table 13.2   Some responses of frontal lobe patients after their injury

---

Case 2

'If I have something to say, I can't wait and have to say it straight away.'

Case 4

'Emotion, tears, that's all gone out of the window. If I saw someone cry I'd just laugh – people look really silly getting upset.'

'I'm much more aggressive and I feel less fear. I go fighting for no reason.'

'Since I've taken up body building, I tend to show off a bit.'

Case 5

Anger and irritability had increased; anxiety had decreased

Case 7

'I ain't scared of nobody. I'm not frightened of opening my mouth and speaking my mind. If I think someone's in the wrong, I'll tell them and not give a monkey's what they think of me.'

Case 8

'I'm not the woman he married; much more outspoken.'

Source: adapted from Hornak *et al.*, 1996

impaired at recognising the facial expression of disgust (Sprengelmeyer *et al.*, 1996; Phillips *et al.*, 1997, 1998). Similarly, Sprengelmeyer *et al.* (1997) have shown that individuals with a type of mental illness called obsessive-compulsive disorder (which we discuss in Chapter 17) show a selective deficit in the ability to recognise facial expressions of disgust. These specific impairments in emotion recognition suggest that there may be different pathways mediating the recognition of specific emotions. Further research should illuminate the nature of these pathways.

Left–right frontal asymmetry

Other evidence implicates the anterior cortex in emotion but in a different way. It has generally been thought that the right hemisphere was the dominant hemisphere for processing emotion. We now know, however, that this is far too crude a characterisation of a complex behaviour and function. While the right hemisphere is superior to the left at recognising and perceiving emotional stimuli – such as distinguishing neutral from emotional faces and distinguishing sentences that vary according to their emotional tone – the left hemisphere plays a more important role in the experience of emotion. This hypothesis has been suggested and tested most prolifically by Richard Davidson

and his colleagues at the University of Wisconsin (Davidson and Sutton, 1995; Tomarken *et al.*, 1990; Wheeler *et al.*, 1993). In Davidson's experiments participants are exposed to film clips designed to elicit specific emotions – positive and negative – as their EEG activity is recorded. Participants indicate when they are experiencing these positive and negative emotions during viewing.

Using such a paradigm – but employing only women participants – Davidson has found that left frontal activation in a specific EEG waveband (alpha) is associated with the experience of positive emotion, whereas increased relative right frontal activation and left frontal reduction in activation is associated with the experience of negative emotion (R. Davidson *et al.*, 1979; Wheeler *et al.*, 1993).

In one experiment, Ekman and his colleagues (1990) investigated the type of EEG activity associated with a genuine smile (the so-called Duchenne smile) and that associated with false smiles. The Duchenne smile is known as the genuine smile because it spontaneously activates the zygomatic muscles around the corners of the mouth and the orbicularis occuli muscles around the corners of the eyes, as you can see from Figure 13.10.

Ekman *et al.* found that the Duchenne smiles were associated with greater left-sided activation in temporal and parietal regions. On the basis of these and other studies, Davidson and others have suggested that the frontal asymmetry that occurs during the experience of emotion reflects motivational tendencies to withdraw or approach (Davidson, 1992; Ehrlichman, 1987). That is, pleasant stimuli should be approachable and, therefore, activates the left frontal region whereas unpleasant stimuli would be avoided or withdrawn from and would activate the right frontal region (and decrease activity in the left frontal region). Coupled with this motivational model is the idea that asymmetry predisposes individuals to react in a specific emotional way. Greater baseline right frontal activation, for example, may predict the intensity of response to negative stimuli but this activation is a necessary not sufficient condition for this response to occur (this is called the diathesis model).

A number of other studies has provided support for the asymmetry model (Biondi *et al.*, 1993; Schaffer *et al.*, 1983; Harmon-Jones and Allen, 1998). One unusual source of support comes from studies of muscle contraction. Bernard Schiff and his colleagues have found that when participants squeezed a ball with the left hand (thereby activating the negative, right hemisphere), they generated more negative stories to a neutral scene than when they contracted the right hand (Schiff and Lamon, 1994). Similar results were found when participants contracted either the left- or right-hand side of the face (Schiff and Lamon, 1989, 1994).

While some studies have supported the frontal asymmetry model, recent evidence has suggested that the type of asymmetry seen depends on the methods of analysis and EEG recording one uses (Hagemann *et al.*, 1998) although the criticism of these studies has not gone unchallenged (Davidson, 1998).

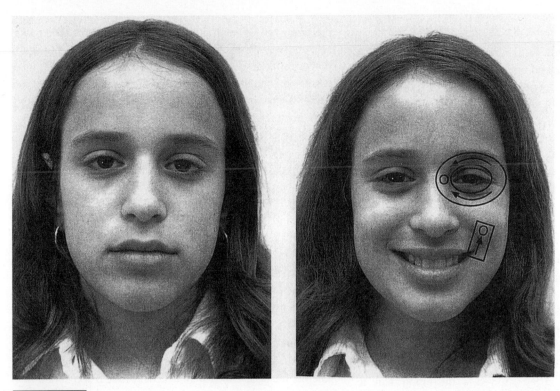

Figure 13.10

The Duchenne smile. The face on the right demonstrates activation of the orbicularis occuli (eye) and zygomatic (lip) movements seen when a person is expressing a genuine smile. The face on the left shows a neutral expression.

Source: Oatley, K. and Jenkins, M.M., *Understanding Emotion*, Oxford: Blackwell, 1996. Copyright © 1996 by Keith Oatley and Jennifer M. Jenkins.

Psychology in action

Using display rules

We all realise that other people can recognise our expressions of emotions. Consequently, we sometimes try to hide our true feelings, attempting to appear impassive or even to display an emotion different from what we feel. At other times, we may exaggerate our emotional response to make sure that others see how we feel. For example, if a friend tells us about a devastating experience, we make sure that our facial expression conveys sadness and sympathy. Researchers have studied all these phenomena.

Attempting to hide an emotion is called masking. An attempt to exaggerate or minimise the expression of an emotion is called modulation. And an attempt to express an emo-

tion we do not actually feel is called simulation. According to Ekman and Friesen (1975), the expression of emotions often follows culturally determined display rules – rules that prescribe under what situations we should or should not display signs of particular emotions. Although the patterns of muscular movements that accompany particular feelings are biologically determined, these movements can, to a certain extent, be controlled by display rules. See Figure 13.11.

Each culture has a particular set of display rules. For example, in Western culture, it is impolite for a winner to show too much pleasure and for a loser to show too much disappointment. The expression of these emotions is supposed to be

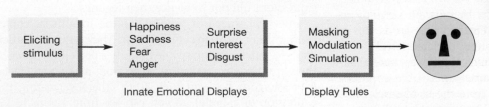

Innate Emotional Displays   Display Rules

Figure 13.11

Controlled facial displays. Innate emotional displays can be modified by display rules.

Source: Adapted from Ekman, P. and Friesen, W., *Semiotica*, 1969, 49–98.

Psychology in action continued

Psychology in action continued

modulated downwards. Also, in many cultures, it is unmanly to cry or to show fear and unfeminine to show anger.

Several studies have found that North American boys and girls differ in their facial expressions of emotion as they get older, presumably because they learn about their society's gender-specific display rules. Very young infants show no sex differences in facial expression (Field, 1982). However, by the time they are in nursery school, boys and girls begin to differ: girls are more likely to show facial expressions of emotion. Buck (1975, 1977) showed various types of colour slide to nursery-schoolchildren and unobtrusively videotaped their faces as they watched. Some slides were pleasant, some puzzling and some unpleasant. He showed the videotapes of the children to adults (university students) and asked them to try to guess the nature of the children's emotional expressions. Buck assumed that the accuracy of the ratings would indicate the degree of emotional expression. The adults could guess the girls' emotions more accurately than the boys'.

Ekman and his colleagues (Ekman *et al.*, 1972; Friesen, 1972) attempted to assess a different kind of culturally determined display rule. They showed a distressing film to Japanese and American college students, singly and in the presence of a visitor, who was described to the subjects as a scientist. Because the Japanese culture discourages public display of emotion, the researchers expected that the Japanese students would show fewer facial expressions of emotion when in public than when alone.

The researchers recorded the facial expressions of their participants with hidden cameras while the participants viewed a film showing a gruesome and bloody coming-of-age rite in a preliterate tribe. The results were as predicted. When the participants were alone, American and Japanese subjects showed the same facial expressions. When they were with another person, the Japanese participants were less likely to express negative emotions and more likely to mask these expressions with polite smiles. Thus, people from both cultures used the same facial expressions of emotion but were subject to different social display rules.

When people attempt to mask the expression of a strongly felt emotion, they are usually unable to do so completely. That is, there is some leakage, or subtle sign of the emotion (Ekman and Friesen, 1969). Ekman and Friesen (1974) investigated this phenomenon. They showed an unpleasant film of burns and amputations to female nursing students. After watching the film, the participants were interviewed by an experimenter, who asked them about the film. Some of the participants were asked to pretend to the interviewer that they had seen a pleasant film. The experimenters videotaped the participants during the interviews and showed these tapes to a separate group of raters, asking them to try to determine whether the people they were watching were being honest or deceptive. The raters were shown videotapes of the participants' faces or bodies. The results indicated that the raters could detect the deception better when they saw the subjects' bodies than when they saw their faces. Apparently, people are better at masking signs of emotion shown by their facial muscles than those shown by muscles in other parts of their body. Presumably, people recognise the attention paid to the face and learn to control their facial expressions better than they do the movements of the rest of the body.

Facial feedback hypothesis

The use of display rules suggests that we are capable of manipulating our facial expression to influence others. It has also been suggested that our own facial expressions can influence our own feelings. At the heart of the facial feedback hypothesis is that our awareness of facial expression influences the way in which we feel (Tourangeau and Ellsworth, 1979; Lanzetta *et al.*, 1976). If this is so, then manipulating a person's facial expression should result in the feeling of the expression-appropriate emotion. You cannot be angry with a smile on our face, for example. This idea has its origin in a remark by Darwin (1872) who had argued that 'the free expression by outward signs of an emotion intensifies it … the repression, as far as this is possible, of all outward signs softens our emotions.'

A test of the facial feedback hypothesis was undertaken by Laird (1974) who asked participants to view photographs while electrical activity from the face muscles was ostensibly recorded. The individuals were told that they would feel emotion-related muscle changes and, to counteract these changes, their muscles would be contracted or relaxed. In fact, the facial manipulation resulted in the participants expressing either a happy or angry face. As predicted, participants who then responded to specific photographs were angrier when exhibiting an angry expression and happier when exhibiting a happy face. However, a study by Tourangeau and Ellsworth (1979) cast doubt on these findings. They asked participants to exhibit either sad, fearful or neutral expressions while watching sad, anger-provoking and neutral films. Although the films themselves elicited the appropriate emotion, the facial expressions did not influence their feelings.

One final source of support for the hypothesis comes from a study by Strack *et al.* (1988). They required participants to watch cartoons while holding a pen either between their lips (thereby preventing them from making any facial expression) or between their teeth (thereby creating the expression of a smile), as you can see from Figure 13.12.

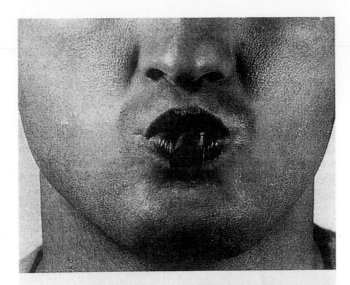

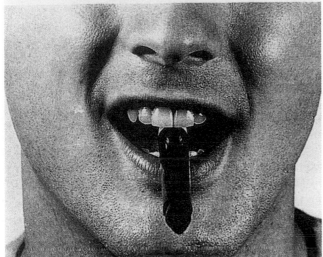

Figure 13.12

Illustrations of the conditions in Strack *et al.*'s experiment. Participants who watched cartoons while holding a pen between their lips in the 'sucking position' regarded them as less funny than did participants who held the pen between their teeth. In the 'lips' condition, the muscles involved in smiling were inhibited by the position of the pen.

Source: Strack, F., Stepper, S. and Martin, L.L., Inhibiting and facilitating conditions of the human smile. *Journal of Personality and Social Psychology*, 54, pp. 768–777. Copyright © Fritz Strack. Reproduced with permission.

Those who held the pen by their lips rated the cartoons as being less funny than did those who did not have their facial expression inhibited (i.e. held the pen between their teeth). The facial feedback hypothesis, therefore, seems to have garnered more support than not. What is controversial, and what is currently unclear, is why facial feedback provokes the emotions it does.

Theories of emotion

Theories of emotion have attempted to explain the nature of emotion from various perspectives. These perspectives can be broadly described as physiological, evolutionary and cognitive.

Physiological theories

The James–Lange theory

William James (1842–1910), an American psychologist, and Carl Lange (1834–1900), a Danish physiologist, independently suggested similar explanations for emotion, which most people refer to collectively as the James–Lange theory (James, 1884; Lange, 1887). Basically, the James–Lange theory states that emotion-producing situations elicit an appropriate set of physiological responses, such as trembling, sweating and increased heart rate. The situations also elicit behaviours, such as clenching of the fists or fighting. The brain receives sensory feedback from the muscles and from the organs that produce these responses, and it is this feedback that constitutes our feelings of emotion. As James put it:

> The bodily changes follow directly the perception of the exciting fact, and … our feelings of the same changes as they occur is the emotion. Common sense says we lose our fortune, are sorry, and weep; we meet a bear, are frightened, and run. … The hypothesis here to be defended says that this order of sequence is incorrect. … The more rational statement is that we feel sorry because we cry, angry because we strike, afraid because we tremble, and not that we cry, strike, or tremble because we are sorry, angry or fearful, as the case may be. (James, 1890, p. 449)

James suggested that our own emotional feelings are based on what we find ourselves doing and on the sensory feedback we receive from the activity of our muscles and internal organs. Where feelings of emotions are concerned, we are self-observers. Thus, patterns of emotional responses and expressions of emotions give rise to feelings of emotion. By this reasoning, feelings of emotions are simply by-products of emotional responses. The James–Lange model is illustrated in Figure 13.13.

James's and Lange's theory was not entirely correct, however. As Cannon (1927, 1931) pointed out:

1 separating the viscera from the central nervous system did not result in changes in emotional behaviour;

2 emotional and non-emotional states can be associated with the same physiological changes;

3 visceral changes are too slow to be able to reflect emotional changes; and

4 inducing visceral change that should result in emotional change usually does not produce these changes.

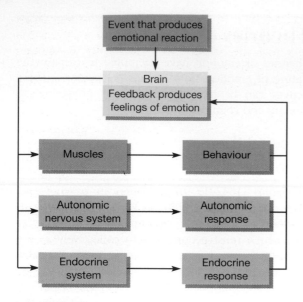

Figure 13.13

A diagrammatic representation of the James–Lange theory of emotion. An event in the environment triggers behavioural, autonomic and endocrine responses. Feedback from these responses produces feelings of emotions.

Schachter and Singer's model

Schachter (1964) proposed that feelings of emotions are determined jointly by perception of physiological responses and by cognitive assessment of a specific situation. Thus, to Schachter, emotion is cognition plus perception of physiological arousal. Both are necessary.

Schachter and Singer (1962) tested this hypothesis by inducing physiological arousal in groups of participants placed in various situations. All participants were told that they were part of an investigation on the effects of a vitamin called 'suproxin' on visual perception (no such vitamin exists). The investigators gave some participants injections of adrenalin, a hormone that stimulates a variety of autonomic nervous system effects associated with arousal, such as increased heart rate and blood pressure, irregular breathing, warming of the face, and mild trembling. Other participants received a control injection of a salt solution, which has no physiological effects.

Next, the researchers placed some participants in an anger-provoking situation in which they were treated rudely and subjected to obnoxious test questions such as, 'How many men, besides your father, has your mother slept with? (a) one, (b) two, (c) three, (d) four or more.' Others were treated politely and saw the antics of another 'participant' (a confederate who was hired by the experimenters) who acted silly and euphoric. The experimenters hoped that these two situations, together with the physiological reactions produced by the injections of adrenalin, would promote either negative or positive emotional states.

Finally, some participants were correctly informed that the injections they received would produce side effects such as trembling and a pounding heart. Others were told to expect irrelevant side effects or none at all. Schachter and Singer predicted that the participants who knew what side effects to expect would correctly attribute their physiological reactions to the drug and would not experience a change in emotion. Those who were misinformed would note their physiological arousal and conclude that they were feeling especially angry or happy, as the circumstance dictated. All participants reported their emotional states in a questionnaire.

The results were not as clear-cut as the experimenters had hoped. The adrenalin did not increase the intensity of the participants' emotional states. However, participants who expected to experience physiological arousal as a result of the injection reported much less of a change in their emotional states than did those who did not expect it, regardless of whether they had received the adrenalin or the placebo. These results suggest that we interpret the significance of our physiological reactions rather than simply experience them as emotions.

Nisbett and Schachter (1966) provided further evidence that participants could be fooled into attributing their own naturally occurring physiological responses to a drug and thus into feeling less 'emotional'. First, they gave all participants a placebo pill (one having no physiological effects). Half the participants were told that the pill would make their hearts pound, their breathing increase and their hands tremble; the other half (the control subjects) were told nothing about possible side effects. Then, the researchers strapped on electrodes and gave the participants electrical shocks. All participants presumably experienced pain and fear, and, consequently, their heart rates and breathing increased, they trembled, and so on. Yet the participants who perceived their reactions as drug-induced were able to tolerate stronger shocks than were the control subjects, and they reported less pain and fear. Thus, cognition can affect people's judgements about their own emotional states and even their tolerance of pain.

The precise nature of the interaction between cognition and physiological arousal has not been determined. For example, in the Nisbett and Schachter experiment, although the verbal instructions about effects of the placebo affected the participants' reactions to pain, it did not seem to do so through a logical, reasoned process. In fact, Nisbett and Wilson (1977) later reported that participants did not consciously attribute their increased tolerance of pain to the effects of the pill. When participants were asked whether they had thought about the pill while receiving the shocks or whether it had occurred to them that the pill was causing some physical effects, participants typically gave answers such as 'No, I was too worried about the shock' (Nisbett and Wilson, 1977, p. 237).

Evolutionary theories

Evolutionary theories of emotion view emotions as adaptive traits – they help the organism to adapt to the demands of the environment and thereby survive (Izard, 1977; Plutchik, 1984).

Plutchik's structural, psychoevolutionary theory of emotion

In common with other evolutionary theories of emotion, Plutchik's (1984) psychoevolutionary theory regards emotions as being important to adaptation and survival. However, he argues that in order to understand the nature emotions, they must be organised in a certain way. He argues, therefore, that emotions can be distinguished on the basis of intensity (anger is less intense than rage, for example), similarity (surprise may engage the same feelings as happiness), polarity (that is, opposites: grief is the opposite of joy), and whether they are primary or secondary (the secondary emotions derive from the primary ones).

Plutchik lists eight behavioural patterns, such as destruction, rejection and reproduction, which can be seen in all organisms; each of his primary emotions (described in an earlier section) is associated with these behavioural patterns.

Shaver's prototype theory

Shaver's et al.'s (1992) model of emotion also uses the notion that we react to the environment using a limited behavioural repertoire and argues that, like emotional facial expression, these repertoires should be universal. Furthermore, the assumption that emotions are universal suggests that they have a biological basis. Emotions are viewed as 'action tendencies' that arise from an appraisal of the environment. Because the similarities in environmental events are more common than dissimilarities, the theory argues, appraisals will be similar across cultures. Shaver and his colleagues suggest that such a view is supported by evidence from three countries – the USA, Italy and China – in which there was substantial overlap in the words that individuals listed as basic emotions.

Frijda's 'action tendencies'

Shaver adopted the concept of 'action tendencies' from Frijda's (1988) model which also views emotions as adaptive. There is a small number of these tendencies which represents the individual's readiness to respond to the environment in emotional ways. These tendencies mediate the individual's relationship with the environment and Frijda proposed ten of them.

Like Plutchik's model, Frijda's argues that emotions are adaptive in that they are used by individuals to solve problems posed by the environment. Unlike Plutchik's, it disagrees that the model can apply to any organism – it is specifically related to human behaviour. However, Frijda also argues that there is little difference between the action tendency and the emotion associated with it, emotion perhaps being the state of awareness of these action tendencies. He also suggests that these emotions (and tendencies) follow on from an individual's appraisal of the environment. That is, the individual first monitors the environment and appraises the threat or problem posed by this environment. Frijda and his colleagues (1989) have found that action tendencies and emotions can be predicted from individuals' appraisals of the environment.

This notion of appraisal is important to a number of models and theories of emotion. In general, such theories argue that emotion is dependent on the individual's appraisal of environmental events and situations. Schacter and Singer's model, although described as a physiological model, involved a strong appraisal component. Other models, however, include appraisal as a more explicit feature.

Cognitive theories

Lazarus's model

Lazarus's original model of emotion suggested that emotion arose from the individual's appraisal of the environment (Lazarus, 1966). Primary appraisal involved the initial evaluation of the environment – is it positive, negative or neutral; secondary appraisal involved the individual's evaluation of how best to cope with this environment and what options were available to facilitate this coping. Secondary appraisal was composed of two types: emotion-focused coping and problem-focused coping. Emotion-focused coping refers to the defence mechanisms that the individual might adopt, such as fleeing the situation or denying negative thoughts and feelings. Problem-centred coping is directed more at finding solutions to the problems posed by the environment when there are changes in the environment.

This original model, however, was devised to explain how people respond to stressors, factors which cause stress (and we will discuss this in more detail in Chapter 16). The later reformulation of the model (Lazarus, 1991) was designed to be a general theory of emotion which Lazarus called the 'cognitive–motivational–relational' theory of emotion. Primary appraisal now comprises the components: goal-relevance (is the environment related to the goal that the individual wants to pursue?), goal congruency/incongruency (is the goal possible or will it be prevented?) and ego-involvement (does the environment have consequences for the individual's self-esteem?). Secondary appraisal assesses the environment in terms of how the individual might cope with it and how such coping might affect future relations. Lazarus proposed that the appraisal of situations which might involve harm to the individual were innate; however, secondary appraisal could override the decisions derived from primary appraisal.

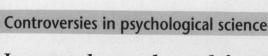

Controversies in psychological science

Is a good mood good for cognition?

The issue

Brewer's model of emotion is based in part on evidence which showed that individuals in a negative or a positive mood would recall material better if the material matched their mood. For example, individuals exposed to a malodour would recall more negative memories than they would if exposed to a pleasant odour. Similarly, they would recall more pleasant memories in the pleasant condition (Ehrlichman and Halpern, 1992). We saw in Chapter 8 that individuals who encode information in a pleasant environment will recall better if retrieval also occurs in the pleasant environment. What effects, therefore, does a person's emotional state have on that person's ability to perform cognitive operations?

The evidence

In a famous series of experiments, Isen and colleagues have demonstrated that being in a positive mood can have positive and negative consequences for behaviour. For example, in a laboratory-based study, Isen and Patrick (1983) reported that while positive mood led to undergraduates betting larger amounts in a gambling game than did controls, these bets were only large when the probability of winning was high. Isen *et al.* (1988) reasoned that either the positive mood predisposed people to believe that losing was likely or that thinking about negative events made them think that their positive mood might be lost. Isen and Geva (1987) found that those in a positive mood did indeed think about loss more than the controls did.

Positive mood has also been found to affect decisions made in more real-life (although still laboratory-based) risk situations. Individuals in a positive mood are more likely to choose a risky treatment for back pain than are those in a control group (Deldin and Levin, 1986).

These experiments, however, although showing the effects of positive mood on a behaviour that requires some decision making, do not measure the effect of positive mood on thinking and reasoning (i.e. cognition) directly.

In an investigation of the effect of induced positive mood on creative and executive thinking, Oaksford *et al.* (1996) tested two hypotheses. The facilitation hypothesis suggests that positive mood benefits creative thinking by facilitating it; the suppression hypothesis suggests that positive and negative moods take up resources that would normally be available for performing the cognitive task that the individual is presented with. Ellis *et al.* (1997), for example, found that negative mood was associated with impaired performance on a test in which participants looked for contradictions in a passage of text. The authors suggested that impairment occurred because intrusive and irrelevant thoughts impaired comprehension. Positive and negative mood should, therefore, also impair performance on reasoning and planning tasks, if a change in mood results in a reallocation of resources.

In an earlier experiment, Isen *et al.* (1987) had reported a beneficial effect of positive mood on a creative problem-solving task. The task was to support a lighted candle on a door using tacks, some matches in a matchbox and the candle (the solution, just in case you are not in a positive mood, is to tack the box to the door and place the candle lit with the matches, on top of the box). Those individuals who had watched some

---

Weiner's model

Weiner's model also utilises the concept of appraisal but is based on the notion that individuals make attributions to the environment and behaviour (Weiner, 1988). The environment provides the individual with a range of positive and negative stimuli which produce initial emotional reactions of pleasure and displeasure. These reactions are triggered automatically and are not emotional responses that rely on the individual's attributions such as experiencing depression because failure is attributed to poor ability and

general worthlessness. These emotions are fairly primitive and reflect conditioned emotional reactions.

The individual's account of how events in the environment were caused determines which positive and negative emotions are elicited. This attribution-dependent model suggests that these explanations depend on three factors: (1) whether the cause of the emotion is internal to the individual or external and caused by the environment; (2) whether the cause is stable or will change over time, and (3) whether the cause of the emotion is controllable or uncontrollable. Abramson *et al.* (1978) later added a fourth comedy were better at solving this problem than those exposed to a neutral or negative film or those exposed to no film.

Oaksford extended this study by having participants complete creative and reasoning tasks after watching either a comedy programme, a neutral, wildlife programme or a negative documentary about stress. The researchers found that although positive and negative mood impaired performance on a deductive reasoning task, the positive mood only was associated with poor performance on the Tower of London task which involves forward planning and reasoning. Some examples from the task can be seen in Figure 13.14.

Conclusion

The results of Oaksford's study provide some support for the suppression hypothesis in that a test requiring executive function (forward planning and sequencing of events) was disrupted by a positive mood. It also suggests that a positive mood may not always be beneficial to the performance of some cognitive tasks. The results of this and other research suggests that being in a good mood may not necessarily lead to better cognitive performance.

Initial position

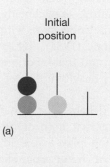

(a)

(1 move)   (2 moves)   (3 moves)   (4 moves)   Final position (5 moves)

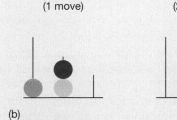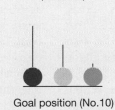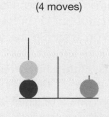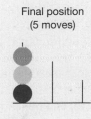

(b)   Goal position (No.10)

Figure 13.14

The Tower of London task. In (a) the participant is required to move the balls from the initial position to the target position in four moves; (b) shows how this is done.

dimension: whether the environment affected the individual's whole life (global change) or a specific part of it (specific change). According to this model, the attributions for success or failure will determine whether positive or negative emotions are experienced.

Other models

Other models of emotion assume that thoughts and feelings represent nodes in a network. Thus a node for a specific emotion triggers off activation of other related nodes.

Joy, for example, might trigger off nodes that recall past achievement or motivate the individual to achieve even greater success by generating creative plans for the future. Failure might trigger off nodes related to failure (such as feelings of self-worth and thoughts that previous successes may not have been deserved). This outline describes one model devised by Bower (1981; Bower and Cohen, 1982) which explained how mood-dependent memory occurred, that is, why we are more likely to recall happy events if we were happy at encoding and unhappy events if we were unhappy at encoding.

However, as we saw in Chapter 8, mood-dependent memory is not a particularly robust phenomenon and appears to be influenced by factors other than the encoding and retrieval conditions. Another problem is that in mood-dependent memory experiments it is unclear whether positive conditions increase accessibility to positive thoughts and feelings or reduce accessibility to negative ones. Bower (1987) later took account of this by arguing that the individual must realise that the material he or she learns is usefully related to the mood they are in. How this fits in with the network model, however, is unclear.

Other models such as those of Lang (1979, 1984) suggest that emotions may not be unitary phenomena but comprise three systems: verbal report, behaviour and physiology. This theory suggests that we can express emotion in one of these systems without experiencing it in another. For example, a depressed individual may show a positive disposition to those close around him (by verbal report) but his behaviour (withdrawal, quietness) and physiology suggest another emotion.

Two other models are also worthy of note. Leventhal and Scherer's (1987) model suggests that the emotion system is made up of three components. At the sensory motor level, individuals may respond to situations and events automatically. This automatic reaction is present from birth onwards. The schematic level is also an automatic level of processing but the automatic behaviour derives from learned associations. Finally, the conceptual level represents reactions that are not automatic but depend on the individual's memories about emotion, expectations, goals, plans and so on. The conceptual level places the event that causes the emotion in a long-term context, that is, how would it affect the individual's future behaviour? In addition to these levels, the model proposes that the stimuli giving rise to emotional reactions are evaluated along various dimensions including novelty, pleasantness, their relevance to goals and plans, the potential to cope with them and their compatibility with social norms and the individual's self-concept.

Finally, Oatley and Johnson-Laird's model (1987; Oatley, 1992) argues that because we often encounter environments in which multiple goals are possible, one of these goals must receive priority over the others. Emotion, according to the model, provides the means by which goals are prioritised. This is achieved by two mechanisms: one is primitive and has no symbolic significance (it is almost hormonal); the other is prepositional and symbolic (it has an internal structure and is more 'conscious' than the other mechanism). The model proposes five basic emotions: happiness, sadness, fear, anger and disgust, with other emotions derived from these. Complex emotions, the theory argues, are likely to involve only one of these emotions although others have suggested that one or two may be necessary

(Jones and Martin, 1992). All five of these emotions are related to the achievement of goals so that one type of emotion leads to the achievement of a goal whereas others are related to failure to achieve goals. However, it is difficult to reconcile these goals with certain emotions. Disgust, for example, as Power and Dalgleish (1997) have pointed out, is unlikely to violate only a 'gustatory goal' because disgust can be elicited by smells, sights and even sounds. In addition, why should the emotional reaction to a malodour be part of a goal – what would be the purpose?

Emotion without cognition?

Related to research on mood and cognition is a broader issue in emotion research. This is whether emotion can occur without cognition. Some psychologists, such as Lazarus (1984), believe that emotions are produced only by cognitive processes – by anticipating, experiencing, or imagining the outcomes of important interactions with the environment. Others, such as Zajonc (1984), insist that cognitive appraisal is not necessary and that emotions are automatic, species-typical responses heavily influenced by classical conditioning.

Although the two sides of the debate appear to have been drawn sharply, it seems clear that both automatic processes and conscious deliberation play a role in the expression and feelings of emotion. Some examples of emotions clearly involve cognitive processes. For instance, as we saw earlier in this chapter, a person can become angry after realising that someone's 'kind words' actually contained a subtle insult. This anger is a result of cognition. But sometimes, emotional reactions and their associated feelings seem to occur automatically. As we saw, through the process of classical conditioning, stimuli can evoke emotional reactions before we have time to realise what is happening. In some cases, we may be acting in a hostile and angry manner without realising what we are doing. If cognitive processes are responsible for our anger, they are certainly not conscious, deliberate ones.

One of the problems with this debate (as with many other debates) is that the opponents sometimes define the same terms in different ways. For example, not everyone agrees which operations of the brain should be regarded as cognitive and which should not. According to Lazarus, many cognitive processes are unconscious and relatively automatic. But if cognitive processes need not be conscious, how can we tell whether a given process is cognitive? And if we cannot tell, how can we hope to decide whether cognition is necessary for all emotions? If our definition of cognition is too general, we would have to conclude that all responses require cognition.

Questions to think about

Emotion

- What are the arguments for and against the proposition that there are basic emotions?

- Do facial expressions of emotion signal genuine emotion or something else?

- Why do you think that your face should exhibit signs of emotion?

- How would you distinguish between the various emotions? Are they discrete or do they fall along a continuum?

- How does emotional recognition and perception differ from emotional expression?

- Why does the amygdala seem particularly important for fear recognition?

- Some patients with frontal lobe damage are unable to inhibit making incorrect responses on some cognitive tasks (although others can). Do you think that this lack of inhibition may be related to the emotional changes seen after damage to the orbitofrontal cortex?

- What are the limitations of the approach–withdrawal model of emotion? Can you think of a stimulus that is both approachable and repelling?

- Do you consider evolutionary explanations of emotion to give an adequate explanation of the function of emotion?

- What is the difference between appraisal and attribution in relation to emotion?

- How can models of emotion account for the fact that we enjoy watching comedy programmes?

- If perception is cognition, is all emotion determined by cognition?

Key terms

motivation *p.*440

regulatory behaviours *p.*440

homeostasis *p.*440

system variable *p.*440

set point *p.*440

detector *p.*440

correctional mechanism *p.*440

negative feedback *p.*440

drive reduction hypothesis *p.*440

drive *p.*440

optimum-level hypothesis *p.*441

perseverance *p.*442

learned helplessness *p.*442

glucose *p.*443

glycogen *p.*443

glucostatic hypothesis *p.*444

glucostats *p.*444

leptin *p.*445

sensory-specific satiety *p.*446

negative alliesthesia *p.*446

anorexia nervosa *p.*448

bulimia nervosa *p.*449

organisational effects *p.*451

activational effects *p.*451

oestrus cycle *p.*451

androgen insensitivity syndrome *p.*453

intraspecific aggression *p.*454

threat gestures *p.*454

appeasement gestures *p.*454

emotion *p.*456

conditioned emotional response *p.*458

orbitofrontal cortex *p.*459

Duchenne smile *p.*462

diathesis model *p.*462

masking *p.*463

modulation *p.*463

simulation *p.*463

display rules *p.*463

leakage *p.*464

facial feedback hypothesis *p.*464

James–Lange theory *p.*465

primary appraisal *p.*467

secondary appraisal *p.*467

CHAPTER REVIEW

Motivation

- Motivation is a general term for a group of phenomena that affects the nature, strength, and persistence of an individual's behaviour. It includes a tendency to perform behaviours that bring an individual in contact with an appetitive stimulus or that move it away from an aversive one.

- One important category of motivated behaviours involves internal regulation – the maintenance of homeostasis. Regulatory systems include four features: a system variable (the variable that is regulated), a set point (the optimum value of the system variable), a detector to measure the system variable, and a correctional mechanism to change it.

- Formerly, psychologists believed that aversive drives were produced by deprivation and that reinforcement was a result of drive reduction. However, the fact that we cannot directly measure an individual's drive level makes it impossible to test this hypothesis.

- In addition, many reinforcers increase drive rather than reduce it. Thus, most psychologists doubt the validity of the drive reduction hypothesis of reinforcement.

- The discovery that electrical stimulation of parts of the brain could reinforce behaviour led to the study of the role of brain mechanisms involved in reinforcement. Apparently, all reinforcing stimuli (including addictive drugs) cause the release of dopamine in the brain.

- Because high levels of drive or arousal can be aversive, several investigators proposed the optimum-level theory of motivation and reinforcement. This theory suggests that organisms strive to attain optimum levels of arousal; thus, reinforcement and punishment are seen as two sides of the same coin.

- One problem, however, is that because drive cannot be directly measured, we cannot determine whether an individual's drive is above or below its optimum level.

- Perseverance is the tendency to continue performing a behaviour that is no longer being externally reinforced.

- Two factors appear to control perseverance. One is the organism's previous history with intermittent reinforcement. The second factor is its opportunity to develop behaviours that produce conditioned reinforcers, such as the satisfaction we derive when we complete the little steps that constitute a long and difficult task.

- Some experiences can diminish an organism's perseverance and its ability to cope with new situations. Learned helplessness involves learning that an aversive event cannot be avoided or escaped.

- Psychologists still dispute whether learned helplessness is specific to a particular situation or generalises to a wide variety of them. The phenomenon is of practical importance because it may be a factor in psychological disorders such as depression.

Eating

- Hunger is the feeling that precedes and accompanies an important regulatory behaviour: eating.

- Eating begins for both social and physiological reasons. Physiologically, the most important event appears to be the detection of a lowered supply of nutrients available in the blood.

- Detectors in the liver measure glucose level, and detectors elsewhere in the body measure the level of fatty acids. Both sets of detectors inform the brain of the need for food and arouse hunger.

- We stop eating for different reasons. Detectors responsible for satiety, which appear to be located in the walls of the stomach, monitor both the quality and the quantity of the food that has just been eaten.

- Long-term control of eating appears to be regulated by the chemical leptin, which is released by overnourished fat tissue and detected by cells in the brain. The effects of this chemical are to decrease meal size and increase metabolic rate, thus helping the body to burn up its supply of triglycerides.

- Sometimes, normal control mechanisms fail, and people gain too much weight. For any individual, genetic and environmental factors may interact to cause the person's weight to deviate from the norm.

- People differ genetically in the efficiency of their metabolisms and this efficiency can easily lead to obesity. Particular eating habits, especially those learned during infancy, can override the physiological signals that would otherwise produce satiety.

- Experiences such as repeated fasting and refeeding (the yo-yo effect) are often accompanied by overeating.

- Sensory-specific satiety refers to a reduction in the pleasantness of a food eaten to satiety while the pleasantness of others is relatively unaffected.

- People eat more of a four-course than of a one-course meal and more of a meal containing a variety of pasta shapes and colours than one containing one shape and one colour.

- The hedonic response to food after satiety is thought to be mediated by the secondary taste cortex; the primary taste cortex helps to identify the food.

- Anorexia nervosa is an eating disorder in which the individual is obsessed with food and weight but deliberately reduces her intake of food and avoids it.

- The prevalence of the disorder is between 0.5 and 1 per cent worldwide, and most anorexics are young women.

- Studies have found metabolic differences in anorexic patients, but we cannot determine whether these differences are the causes or the effects of the disorder.

- Bulimia nervosa is an eating disorder which involves a loss of control of food intake.

- Bulimic individuals will often binge and then use laxatives or vomiting to get rid of the consumed food. This abuse of the body has consequences for the normal functioning of the body.

Sexual behaviour

- Testosterone has two major effects on male sexual behaviour: organisational and activational.

- In the foetus, testosterone organises the development of male sex organs and of some neural circuits in the brain; in the adult, testosterone activates these structures and permits erection and ejaculation to occur.

- The sexual behaviour of female mammals with oestrus cycles depends on oestradiol and progesterone, but these hormones have only a minor effect on women's sexual behaviour. Women's sexual desire, like that of men, is much more dependent on androgens.

- The development of sexual orientation appears to have biological roots. A large-scale study of homosexuals failed to find evidence that child-rearing practices fostered homosexuality.

- Studies have identified three regions of the brain that are of different sizes in homosexual and heterosexual males. These results suggest that the brains of these two groups may have been exposed to different patterns of hormones early in life. In addition, twin studies indicate that homosexuality has a genetic component, as well.

Aggressive behaviour

- Ethological studies of other species suggest that aggression is a means of averting violence: threat gestures warn of an impending attack, and appeasement gestures propitiate the potential aggressor.

- In males of most animal species, androgens have both organisational and activational effects on aggressive behaviour.

- Testosterone appears to increase in a variety of situations and contexts. Increases have been found before chess-players play matches and in winners after matches; increased levels have been reported in prisoners convicted of violent crime and described by fellow inmates as being tough. These data are, however, correlational.

- Field studies on the effects of televised violence are not conclusive. Observational studies have revealed a modest relation between preference for violent television shows and boys' aggressiveness, but we cannot be sure that watching the violence causes the aggressiveness.

- An attempt to manipulate aggression by forcing children to watch violent or non-violent television programmes was inconclusive because many children resented their loss of choice.

Emotion

- Emotion refers to behaviours, physiological responses and feelings evoked by appetitive or aversive stimuli, although psychologists have defined emotion in various ways.

- Expressions of emotion communicate important information among people. An observational study of humans indicated that smiles appear to occur most often when someone is interacting socially with other people. This finding supports the social nature of emotional expression.

- Emotions are provoked by particular stimuli, and in humans these stimuli can involve cognitive processes as well as external events. For example, emotions can result from our judgements about complex social situations.

- Darwin believed that expression of emotion by facial gestures was innate and that muscular movements were inherited behavioural patterns.

- Ekman and his colleagues showed that members of the South Fore tribe recognised facial expressions of Westerners and made facial gestures that were clear to Westerners, suggesting that emotional expressions are innate behaviour patterns and universally found.

- There is controversy, however, over whether facial expressions reflect true emotions or whether they reflect the social communication of an emotion.

- A number of theorists have suggested that there is a group of basic emotions, although the exact number is controversial, as is the notion that there are basic emotions. The most widely accepted number of basic emotions is six or seven.

- Expressions of emotion are not always frank and honest indications of a person's emotional state. They can be masked, modulated or simulated according to culturally determined display rules.

- When a person attempts to mask his or her expression of emotion, some leakage occurs, particularly in movements of the body. Presumably, we learn to control our facial expressions better because we are aware of the attention that other people pay to these expressions.

- The amygdala organises behavioural, autonomic and hormonal responses to a variety of situations, including those that produce fear or anger.

- Destruction to parts of the amygdala prevents the recognition of fear in facial expressions and activation in the amygdala is seen in healthy individuals exposed to facial expressions of fear.

- The orbitofrontal cortex is also important to emotion and may be involved in the regulation of socially appropriate behaviour that involves complex decision making.

- People with damage to the orbitofrontal region are able to explain the implications of complex social situations but are unable to respond appropriately when put in these situations. Thus, this region appears to be necessary for translating judgements about the personal significance of events into appropriate actions and emotional responses.

- The affective asymmetry of emotion suggests that activation of the left frontal region may be involved in the experience of positive emotion whereas activation of the right frontal region is involved in the experience of negative emotion.

- James and Lange suggested that the physiological and behavioural reactions to emotion-producing situations were perceived by people as states of emotion and that emotional states were not the causes of these reactions.

- Although emotional states are sometimes produced by automatic, classically conditioned responses, some psychologists have suggested that the perception of our own emotional state is not determined solely by feedback from our behaviour and the organs controlled by the autonomic nervous system. It is also determined by cognitive assessment of the situation in which we find ourselves.

- Schachter and his colleagues found that information about the expected physiological effects of drugs (or placebos) influenced subjects' reports about their emotional state. In one study, subjects even tolerated more intense electrical shocks, apparently discounting their own fear.

- Appraisal theories suggest that emotion is experienced after the environment has been evaluated for threat, fear, joy or any other influential factor.

- Evolutionary theories argue that emotions are a means of adapting to change in the environment; these changes produce a restricted set of responses which are universal (hence, the emotions associated with them should also be universal).

- The debate over whether cognition is necessary for emotion continues. Ultimately, the argument rests on how one defines cognition.

Suggestions for further reading

Edwards, D.C. (1998). *Motivation and Emotion*. London: Sage.

Munro, D., Schumaker, J.F. and Carr, S.C. (1997). *Motivation and Culture*. London: Routledge.

Weiner, B. (1996). *Human Motivation*. London: Sage.
For an up-to-date introduction to current thinking on the psychology of motivation, these three texts are worth consulting.

Abraham, S. and Llewelyn-Jones, D. (1997). *Eating Disorders: The facts*. New York: Oxford University Press.

Capaldi, E.D. (1996). *Why We Eat What We Eat*. Washington, DC: American Psychological Association.
Both of these books cover different aspects of eating. Abraham and Llewelyn-Jones's book is a small but very readable review of what we know about the nature, causes and treatment of eating disorder. Capaldi's book is an edited collection of chapters on various aspects of eating and is worth reading for its variety.

LeVay, S. (1993). *The Sexual Brain*. Cambridge, MA: MIT Press.
The notion that our sexuality may be determined by our brains is thoroughly evaluated in this well presented book.

Heurmann, L.R. (1994). *Aggressive Behaviour: Current perspectives*. New York: Plenum Press.

Mazur, A. and Booth, A. (1998). Testosterone and dominance in men. *Behavioral and Brain Sciences*, 21, 353–397.
These two items provide a general and specific introduction to aspects of aggression. Heurmann's book is a collection of chapters covering various aspects of the nature and causes of aggression. Mazur and Booth's article reviews the effects of testosterone on dominance and aggression and is accompanied by comments from a number of other researchers.

Cornelius, R.R. (1996). *The Science of Emotion*. Upper Saddle River, NJ: Prentice Hall.

Ekman, P. and Davidson, R.J. (1995). *The Nature of Emotion*. New York: Oxford University Press.

Jenkins, J.M., Oatley, K. and Stein, N. (1998). *Human Emotions: A reader*. Oxford: Blackwell.

Oatley, K. and Jenkins, J.M. (1995). *Understanding Emotions*. Oxford: Blackwell.
Any of these four texts will give you a good, comprehensive and readable introduction to the psychology of emotion. Perhaps the most comprehensive and up-to-date is Oatley and Jenkins's; accompanying this book is Jenkins et al.'s reader which contains the most important articles published in the field of emotion.

Power, M. and Dalgleish, T. (1997). *Cognition and Emotion*. Hove, UK: The Psychology Press.

LeDoux, J. (1996). *The Emotional Brain*. Upper Saddle River, NJ: Simon & Schuster.
Two different perspectives on the same theme is provided by these books. LeDoux posits a powerful theory of emotion based on neurobiology whereas Power and Dalgleish review the cognitive aspects of emotion (and propose their own model of emotional processing).

Ekman, P. (1994). Strong evidence for universals in facial expressions: A reply to Russell's mistaken critique. *Psychological Bulletin*, 115, 2, 268–287.

Russell, J.A. (1994). Is there universal recognition of emotion from facial expression? A review of the cross-cultural studies. *Psychological Bulletin*, 115, 1, 102–141.
Finally, these two papers give you an idea of the cut-and-thrust nature of the debate that goes on in emotion (and psychology). Russell's detailed and massive critique of cross-cultural studies of emotion is countered by Ekman's equally critical reply.

Journals to consult

Appetite
British Journal of Clinical Psychology
Cognition and Emotion
International Journal of Eating Disorders
Journal of Abnormal Psychology
Journal of Consulting and Clinical Psychology
Journal of Personality and Social Psychology
Motivation and Emotion
Nature
Personality and Individual Differences
Physiology and Behaviour

14

PERSONALITY

Chidester *et al.* (1991) and Foushee and Helmreich (1988) studied the relation between a pilot's personality measures and the performance of his or her commercial airline flight crews. Given that breakdowns in team performance are the most common explanation of air transportation disasters, this research has important implications for the selection and training of airline pilots.

Pilots who were warm, friendly, self-confident and able to handle stress had crews who made the fewest, and the least significant, errors. In contrast, pilots who were arrogant, hostile, boastful, egotistical, dictatorial and passive–aggressive had crews who made the largest number of, and the most significant, errors. These findings are especially troubling because personality is not typically considered during the process of airline pilot selection.

Source: Phares and Chaplin, 1997, p. 578

What makes us individuals? What gives us a sense of identity, a sense of who we are? 'Personality' is used differently in psychology and in everyday conversation where we talk about people having effervescent personalities or having no personality. According to psychologists, personality is a tightly defined set of traits or responses to the environment that we can measure. Some have argued that personality comprises only a few essential characteristics and that we all differ according to the degree to which we exhibit or possess these characteristics.

In this chapter, we look at how psychologists have defined personality and consider all the major theories of personality from the psychodynamic perspective to the recent five-factor model of personality. The method of assessing personality will also be discussed.

What you should be able to do
after reading Chapter 14

- Describe and understand the methods used by psychologists to study personality.
- Describe and explain what is meant by trait theory and situationism.
- Describe and evaluate psychodynamic personality theory and humanistic approaches to personality.
- Describe and evaluate the trait theories of Cattell, Eysenck and Costa and Macrae.
- Evaluate the validity and reliability of personality tests.

Questions to think about

- What is personality?
- Can we measure personality scientifically? If so, how?
- If individuals possess personality characteristics, how do we explain people's behaviour when they act out of character?
- Does personality mean the same thing in every culture? Is personality a linguistic rather than behavioural phenomenon?

Towards a definition of personality

People have different styles of thinking, of relating to others, and of working, all of which reflect differences in personality – differences crucial to defining us as individuals. Common experience tells us that there is no one else just like us. There may even be significant differences in the personal characteristics of identical twins.

Such everyday observations provide a starting point for psychology's study of personality. But unlike such informal observations, psychology's approach to studying personality is considerably more calculated. For example, to many people, personality is nothing more than 'what makes people different from one another'. To psychologists, however, the concept is generally defined much more narrowly. Personality is a particular pattern of behaviour and thinking that prevails across time and situations and differentiates one person from another.

Psychologists do not draw inferences about personality from casual observations of people's behaviour. Rather, their assessment of personality is derived from results of special tests designed to identify particular personality characteristics. The goal of psychologists who study personality is to discover the causes of individual differences in behaviour.

This goal has led to two specific developments in the field of personality psychology: the development of theories that attempt to explain such individual differences and the development of methods by which individual patterns of behaviour can be studied and classified. Merely identifying and describing a personality characteristic is not the same as explaining it. However, identification is the first step on the way to explanation. What types of research effort are necessary to study personality? Some psychologists devote their efforts to the development of tests that can reliably measure differences in personality. Others try to determine the events – biological and environmental – that cause people to behave as they do. Thus, research on human personality requires two kinds of effort: identifying personality characteristics and determining the variables that produce and control them (Buss, 1995).

Trait theories of personality

As you will see in this chapter, the word 'personality' means different things to different people. The way in which personality is used by trait theorists is similar to the way in which we often think of personality in everyday life: a set of personal characteristics that determines the different ways we act and react in a variety of situations.

Personality types and traits

It has long been apparent that people differ in personality. The earliest known explanation for these individual differences is the humoral theory, proposed by the Greek physician Galen in the second century and based on then-common medical beliefs that had originated with the Ancient Greeks. The body was thought to contain four humours, or fluids: yellow bile, black bile, phlegm and blood. People were classified according to the disposition supposedly produced by the predominance of one of these humours in their systems. Choleric people, who had an excess of yellow bile, were bad tempered and irritable. Melancholic people, who had an excess of black bile, had gloomy and pessimistic temperaments. Phlegmatic people, whose bodies contained an excessive amount of phlegm, were sluggish, calm and unexcitable. Sanguine people had a preponderance of blood (sanguis), which made them cheerful and passionate. The four types of humour are illustrated in Figure 14.1.

Figure 14.1

Characteristics of the four humours, according to a medieval artist: (a) choleric – violent and aggressive temperament; (b) melancholic – gloomy and pessimistic temperament; (c) phlegmatic – sluggish, relaxed and dull temperament; and (d) sanguine – outgoing, passionate and fun-loving temperament.

Although later biological investigations discredited the humoral theory, the notion that people could be divided into different personality types – different categories into which personality characteristics can be assigned based on factors such as developmental experiences – persisted long afterwards. For example, Freud's theory, which maintains that people go through several stages of psychosexual development, predicts the existence of different types of people, each type having problems associated with one of these stages. We discuss some of these problems later in this chapter.

Personality types are useful in formulating hypotheses because when a theorist is thinking about personality variables, extreme cases are easily brought to mind. But after identifying and defining personality types, one must determine whether these types actually exist and whether knowing a person's personality type can lead to valid predictions about his or her behaviour in different situations.

Most modern investigators reject the idea that individuals can be assigned to discrete categories. Instead, they generally conceive of individual differences in personality as being in degree, not kind. Tooby and Cosmides (1990) also argue that the nature of human reproduction makes the evolution of specific personality types unlikely – fertilisation produces a reshuffling of the genes in each generation, making it highly unlikely that a single, unified set of genes related to personality type would be passed from one generation to the next.

Rather than classify people by categories, or types, many investigators prefer to measure the degree to which an individual expresses a particular personality trait. A personality trait is an enduring personal characteristic that reveals itself in a particular pattern of behaviour in different situations. A simple example illustrates the difference between types and traits. We could classify people into two different types: tall people and short people. Indeed, we use these terms in everyday language. But we all recognise that height is best conceived of as a trait – a dimension on which people differ along a wide range of values. If we measure the height of a large sample of people, we will find instances all along the distribution, from very short to very tall, as Figure 14.2 illustrates. It is not that people are only either tall or short (analogous to a personality type) but that people vary in the extent to which they are one or the other (analogous to a personality trait).

We assume that people tend to behave in particular ways: some are friendly, some are aggressive, some are lazy, some are timid, some are reckless. Trait theories of personality fit this common-sense view. However, personality traits are not simply patterns of behaviour: they are factors that underlie these patterns and are responsible for them. Once our personality traits are developed, they reside in our brains. This is not to say that the acquisition of personality traits is strictly biological and that learning is not involved, but if our personality traits are changed through

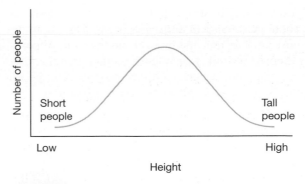

Figure 14.2

The distribution of height. We can measure people's heights, a trait, on a continuous scale. We can also look at the extremes and divide people into the categories of short and tall types.

learning, those changes must occur in our brains. In other words, we carry our personality traits around with us in our heads, or more exactly, in our brains.

Identification of personality traits

Trait theories of personality do not pretend to be all-encompassing explanations of behaviour – at least not yet. Instead, they are still at the stage of discovering, describing and naming the regular patterns of behaviour that people exhibit (Goldberg, 1993). In all science, categorisation must come before explanation; we must know what we are dealing with before we can go about providing explanations. The ultimate goal of the personality psychologist is to explain what determines people's behaviour – which is the ultimate goal of all branches of psychology.

Allport's search for traits

Gordon Allport (1897–1967), one of the first psychologists to search systematically for a basic core of personality traits, began his work by identifying all the words in an unabridged dictionary of the English language that described aspects of personality (Allport and Odbert, 1936). He found around 18,000 words, which he then further analysed for those that described only stable personality characteristics. He eliminated words that represented temporary states, such as 'flustered', or evaluations, such as 'admirable'. This still left him with over 4,000 words.

Allport was interested in learning how many traits are needed to describe personality and exactly what these traits may be. For example, many of those 4,000 words, such as 'shy' and 'bashful', are synonyms. Although each synonym presumably makes some sort of distinction about a trait, a group of synonyms together might be used to describe the same underlying trait. Many trait theorists believe that the most basic set of personality traits ranges from 3 to 16 traits.

Allport's research stimulated other psychologists to think about personality in terms of traits or dispositions. In fact, most modern trait theories can be traced to Allport's earlier theoretical work. Like Allport, modern trait theorists maintain that only when we know how to describe an individual's personality will we be able to explain it.

Cattell: sixteen personality factors

In Chapter 11 we considered the role of factor analysis in defining intelligence. Factor analysis identifies variables that tend to be correlated. To use factor analysis to study personality, researchers must observe the behaviour of a large number of people. Usually, the observations are limited to responses to questions on paper-and-pencil tests, but occasionally, investigators observe people's behaviour in semi-natural situations. Statistical procedures then permit investigators to determine which items a given person tends to answer in the same way; they can then infer the existence of common factors. For example, a shy person would tend to say no to statements such as 'I attend parties as frequently as I can' or 'When I enter a room full of people, I like to be noticed'. In contrast, outgoing people would tend to say yes to these statements.

To the degree that people possess orderly personality traits, they tend to answer certain clusters of questions in particular ways. Raymond Cattell (b. 1905) began his search for a relatively small number of basic personality traits with Allport and Odbert's (1936) list of adjectives. In addition, he collected data on people's personality characteristics from interviews, records describing their life histories, and from observing how people behave in particular situations. From this list, Cattell began to construct preliminary versions of a questionnaire called the 16PF. Then, using factor analysis, he analysed responses from thousands of people to whom the inventory had been administered. Eventually, he identified sixteen personality factors.

Cattell referred to these sixteen traits as source traits because, in his view, they are the cornerstones upon which personality is built: they are the primary factors underlying observable behaviour. He called groups of similar types of observable behaviour surface traits; he included such traits as kindness, honesty and friendliness because they are visible to others. They represent the surface of personality and spring forth from source traits, which lie deeper within the personality. Figure 14.3 illustrates a personality profile of a hypothetical individual rated on Cattell's sixteen factors. The factors are listed in order of importance, from top to bottom. Look at the ratings to see whether you think they would help you to predict the person's behaviour.

Eysenck: three factors

Hans Eysenck (1916–1997) also used factor analysis to devise his theory of personality (Eysenck, 1970; Eysenck and Eysenck, 1985). His research identified three important factors: extroversion, neuroticism and psychoticism. These factors are bipolar dimensions. Extroversion is the opposite of introversion, neuroticism is the opposite of emotional stability, and psychoticism is the opposite of self-control. **Extroversion** refers to an outgoing nature and a high level of activity; **introversion** refers to a nature that shuns crowds and prefers solitary activities. **Neuroticism** refers to a nature full of anxiety, worries and guilt; **emotional stability** refers to a nature that is relaxed and at peace with itself. **Psychoticism** refers to an aggressive, egocentric and antisocial nature; **self-control** refers to a kind and considerate nature, obedient of rules and laws. Eysenck's use of the term 'psychoticism' is different from its use by most clinical psychologists; his term refers to antisocial tendencies and not to a mental illness. A person at the extreme end of the distribution of psychoticism would receive the diagnosis of antisocial personality disorder.

Table 14.1 lists some questions that have high correlations or factor loadings on Eysenck's three factors. The best

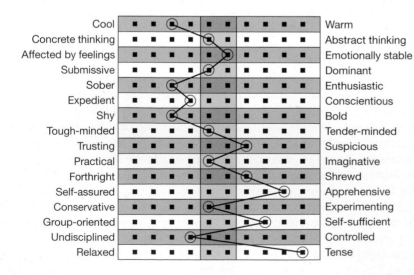

Figure 14.3

A hypothetical personality profile using Cattell's sixteen personality factors.

Source: *16PF* copyright © 1956, 1973, 1982, 1986 by the Institute of Personality and Ability Testing Inc. International copyright in all countries under the Berne Union, Buenos Aires, Bilateral and Universal Copyright Conventions. All property rights reserved by the IPAT Inc., PO Box 1188, Champaign, Illinois 61824-1188, USA. Adapted and reproduced by permission of NFER-NELSON Publishing Company Ltd, the sole publisher of *16PF* in the English language in the European Community. All rights reserved.

Table 14.1   Some items from Eysenck's tests of extroversion, neuroticism and psychoticism

Factor	Loading
Extroversion	
Do you like mixing with people?	0.70
Do you like plenty of bustle and excitement around you?	0.65
Are you rather lively?	0.63
Neuroticism	
Do you often feel fed-up?	0.67
Do you often feel lonely?	0.60
Does your mood often go up and down?	0.59
Psychoticism	
Do good manners and cleanliness matter much to you?	–0.55
Does it worry you if you know there are mistakes in your work?	–0.53
Do you like taking risks for fun?	0.51

Source: adapted from Eysenck, and Eysenck, 1985

way to understand the meaning of these traits is to read the questions and to imagine the kinds of people who would answer yes or no to each group. If a factor loading is preceded by a minus sign, it means that people who say no receive high scores on the trait; otherwise, high scores are obtained by those who answer yes.

According to Eysenck, the most important aspects of a person's temperament are determined by the combination of the three dimensions of extroversion, neuroticism and psychoticism – just as colours are produced by the combinations of the three dimensions of hue, saturation and brightness. Figure 14.4 illustrates the effects of various combinations of the first two of these dimensions – extroversion and neuroticism – and relates them to the four temperaments described by Galen.

More than most other trait theorists, Eysenck emphasises the biological nature of personality (Eysenck, 1991). For example, consider the introversion–extroversion dimension, which is biologically based, according to Eysenck, on an optimum arousal level of the brain. Eysenck believes that the functioning of a neural system located in the brain stem produces different levels of arousal of the cerebral cortex. Introverts have relatively high levels of cortical excitation, while extroverts have relatively low levels. Thus, in order to maintain the optimum arousal level, the extrovert requires more external stimulation than does the introvert. The extrovert seeks stimulation from external sources by interacting with others or by pursuing novel and highly stimulating experiences. The introvert avoids external stimulation in order to maintain his or her lower arousal level at an optimum state. Different states of arousal are hypothesised to lead to different values of the extroversion trait for different people.

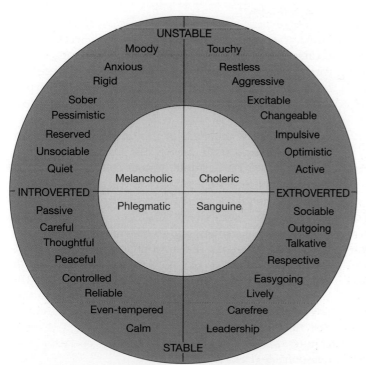

Figure 14.4

Eysenck's theory illustrated for two factors. According to Eysenck, the two dimensions of neuroticism (stable versus unstable) and introversion–extroversion combine to form a variety of personality characteristics. The four personality types based on the Greek theory of humours are shown in the centre.

Source: Eysenck, H.J., *The Inequality of Man*. London: Temple Smith, 1973. Reprinted with permission.

Eysenck's theory has received considerable support, especially from his own laboratory, which has been highly productive. Most trait theorists accept the existence of his three factors because they have emerged in factor analyses performed by many different researchers; these appear, in fact, to have the highest validity of all proposed personality factors (Kline, 1993).

The five-factor model

As we saw earlier, Allport attempted to discover personality traits through an analysis of the words we use to describe differences in personality. Languages reflect the observations of a culture; that is, people invent words to describe distinctions they notice. An analysis of such distinctions by Tupes and Christal (1961), replicated by Norman (1963), has led to the five-factor model (McCrae and Costa, 1985, 1987, 1990). The five-factor model proposes that personality is composed of five primary dimensions:

1 Neuroticism

2 Extroversion

3 Openness

4 Agreeableness

5 Conscientiousness

These factors are measured by the Neuroticism, Extroversion, and Openness Personality Inventory, or NEO-PI.

The NEO-PI consists of 181 items that potentially describe the person being evaluated, which can be the person answering the questions or someone he or she knows well (McCrae and Costa, 1990). Studies have shown that self-ratings agree well with ratings of spouses and other people who know a person well. The test items are brief sentences, such as 'I really like most people I meet' or (for ratings by someone else) 'She has a very active imagination'. The person taking the test rates the accuracy of each item on a scale of 1 to 5, from strong disagreement to strong agreement. The scores on each of the five factors consist of the sums of the answers to different sets of items.

McCrae *et al.* (1986) attempted to validate the five-factor model by performing a factor analysis on a list of adjectives contained in a test called the California Q-Set. This test consists of one-hundred brief descriptions (such as 'irritable', 'cheerful', 'arouses liking' and 'productive'). The items were provided by many psychologists and psychiatrists who found the words useful in describing people's personality characteristics. Thus, the words are not restricted to a particular theoretical orientation. McCrae and his colleagues found that factor analysis yielded the same five factors as the analysis based on everyday language: neuroticism, extroversion, openness, agreeableness and conscientiousness. The five-factor model is regarded by most personality psychologists as a fairly robust model of personality (Magai and McFadden, 1995).

Cross-cultural application of the Big Five

Any truly grand theory of personality must be able to encompass all cultures, countries and languages. If personality comprises three or five factors, which we all exhibit to a lesser or greater extent, then these factors should be exhibited or reported cross-culturally. If not, then the theory is culture-specific and describes only personality within a limited number of cultures.

One immediate problem in testing the universality of trait theories is that the way in which they are measured depends on language, and different cultures have slightly different words that they use to describe things. They also have words to represent events and objects that other cultures do not. Eskimos, for example, have tens of words to describe the quality of snow. Individuals in less Arctic climes would have no need for such a large vocabulary because snow appears only irregularly and does not impinge on their life in such a regular and intrusive way.

Translating tests (of personality and intelligence), therefore, must be a careful undertaking. Hambleton (1994) cites the following example taken from a psychological test:

Where is a bird with webbed feet most likely to live?

(a) in the mountains

(b) in the woods

(c) in the sea

(d) in the desert

When translated into Swedish, however, 'webbed feet' became 'swimming feet' which more or less suggests the correct answer but not quite. Translation problems can occur quite markedly with intelligence tests, if the psychologist is not careful (Van de Vijver and Hambleton, 1996).

In personality, problems in demonstrating universality lie in taxonomy. Do the same words mean the same thing across cultures? For example, various cultures have attributed different meanings to factor 5 (conscientiousness) in the Big Five model (Caprara and Perugini, 1994). Thus, this factor means something different to the Dutch, Hungarians and Italians, and to the Americans, Germans, Czechs and Poles. In a review of the evidence for the universality of a collection of basic personality traits, Boele de Raad, from the University of Groningen in The Netherlands, suggests that the best one can do is to find acceptable counterparts of the Big Five in all cultures; the first three factors of the model can be found in most cultures but the cross-cultural validity of factor 5 is questionable (DeRaad, 1998).

Heritability of personality traits

Several trait theorists, including Cattell and Eysenck, have asserted that a person's genetic history has a strong influence on his or her personality. Many studies have shown that some personality traits are strongly heritable (Emde *et al.*, 1992; McGue *et al.*, 1993b; Jang *et al.*, 1998).

As we saw in Chapter 3, the heritability of a trait can be assessed by comparing identical (monozygotic) with fraternal (dizygotic) twins, comparing twins raised together with twins raised apart, and comparing biological with adoptive relatives. Many studies have found that identical twins are more similar to each other than are fraternal twins on a variety of personality measures, which indicates that these characteristics are heritable (Loehlin, 1992).

Figure 14.5 shows the results of eleven studies using various tests of Eysenck's factors of extroversion, neuroticism and psychoticism (ENP) compiled by Zuckerman (1991). The results of each study are shown as data points connected by straight lines. Every study found that identical twins were more similar than fraternal twins on every measure. According to Zuckerman's calculations, the best estimates of the heritability of these three traits are extroversion (70 per cent), psychoticism (59 per cent) and neuroticism (48 per cent).

Similar data have been reported for the Big Five (see Table 14.2). Loehlin *et al.* (1998), for example, studied the degree of heritability of the Big Five personality traits in 490 monozygotic (MZ) twins and 317 dizygotic (DZ) twins. Correlations between MZ twins were consistently higher than those for the DZ twins.

The results of Big Five and ENP studies suggest that heredity is responsible for between 40 and 70 per cent of the variability in these three personality traits. Thus, it would appear that the remaining 30–60 per cent of the variability is caused by differences in environment. In other words, some family environments should tend to produce extroverts, others should tend to produce introverts, and so on. But research indicates that the matter is not so simple.

Zuckerman (1991) reviewed several studies that measured the correlation in personality traits of pairs of identical twins raised together and raised apart. If family environment has a significant effect on personality characteristics, then the twins raised together should be more similar than those raised apart. But they were not. Taken as a group, these studies found no differences, indicating that differences in family environment account for none of the variability of personality traits in the twins who were tested. Another approach, comparing the personality traits of parents with those of their adopted children, suggests that family environment may account for approximately 7 per cent of the variability (Scarr *et al.*, 1981). If 50–70 per cent of the variability in personality traits is caused by heredity and 0–7 per cent is caused by family environment, what is responsible for the remaining 23–50 per cent of the variability? The answer is, heredity and environment interact.

As we saw in Chapter 3, heredity and environment can interact. In fact, the major source of the interaction seems to be the effect that people's heredity has on their family environment (Plomin and Bergeman, 1991). That is, people's genetic endowment plays an important role in determining how family members interact with them.

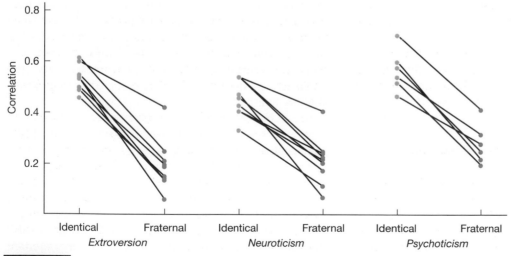

Figure 14.5

Correlations between members of pairs of identical and fraternal twins on tests of extroversion, neuroticism and psychoticism. Individual pairs of data points, connected by straight lines, come from different experiments.

Source: Based on data from Zuckerman, M., *Psychobiology of Personality*. Cambridge: Cambridge University Press, 1991.

Table 14.2   Monozygotic (MZ) and dizygotic (DZ) twin correlations for the Big Five scale scores

Factor	Ratings	
	MZ	DZ
Extroversion	0.47	0.01
Agreeableness	0.32	0.06
Conscientiousness	0.42	0.21
Neuroticism	0.43	0.17
Openness	0.39	0.19
Mean	**0.41**	**0.13**

Figure 14.6 shows the correlations between the ratings of various characteristics of the family environment made by pairs of identical and fraternal twins. The family characteristics that they rated included cohesion, expressiveness, conflict, achievement, culture, activity, organisation and control. The identical twins agreed on their ratings much more than the fraternal twins did; that is, identical twins were much more likely to have experienced similar family environments.

There are two possible explanations for these results: the family environments could have been more similar for

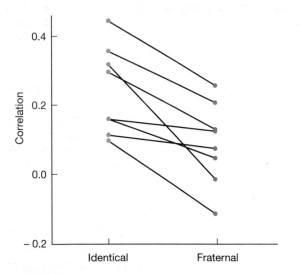

Figure 14.6

Correlations between members of pairs of twins on ratings of characteristics of their family environments. Individual pairs of data points represent ratings of cohesion, expressiveness, conflict, achievement, culture, activity, organisation, and control.

Source: Based on data from Plomin, R. and Bergemen, C.S., *Behavioral and Brain Sciences*, 1991, 14, 373–427.

identical twins than for fraternal twins, or the family environments could have really been the same in all cases but were simply perceived as different by the fraternal twins. Evidence suggests that the first possibility is correct, that is, the family environments really were more similar for identical twins (Loehlin, 1992). How can this be? One might think that each family has a certain environment and that everyone in the household comes under its influence.

Although there are aspects of a family that are shared by the entire household, the factors that play the largest role in shaping personality development appear to come from social interactions between an individual and other family members. These social interactions are different for different people. Because of hereditary differences, one child may be more sociable; this child will be the recipient of more social interaction. Another child may be abrasive and disagreeable; this child will be treated more coldly. In the case of identical twins, who have no hereditary differences, the amount of social interaction with each twin is likely to be similar.

Even physical attributes (which are largely hereditary) will affect a child's environment. A physically attractive child will receive more favourable attention than will an unattractive child. In fact, studies that examined videotaped interactions between mothers and their children confirm that heredity does have an important influence on the nature of these interactions (Plomin and Bergeman, 1991). Thus, although a child's environment plays an important part in his or her personality development, hereditary factors play a large role in determining the nature of this environment.

One caution about this interpretation is in order. Although the studies cited have been replicated in several cultures, none has investigated the effects of the full range of cultural differences in family lives. That is, when comparisons have been made between twins raised together and those raised apart, almost all have involved family environments within the same culture. It is possible that cultural differences in family environments could be even more important than the differences produced by a person's heredity; only cross-cultural studies will be able to test this possibility.

Are all personality traits a product, direct or indirect, of a person's heredity? The answer is no. Some personality characteristics show a strong effect of shared environment but almost no effect of genetics. For example, twin studies have found a strong influence of family environment, but not of heredity, on belief in God, involvement in religion, masculinity/femininity, attitudes towards racial integration, and intellectual interests (Loehlin and Nichols, 1976; Rose, 1988). Thus, people tend to learn some important social attitudes from their family environments.

Brain mechanisms in personality

There is no doubt that brain mechanisms are involved in personality traits. For example, brain damage can produce permanent changes in personality, and drugs that affect particular neurotransmitters can alter people's moods and anxiety levels. But what particular brain mechanisms are involved in personality, and what personality traits do they affect? Several psychologists have attempted to relate extroversion, neuroticism and psychoticism to underlying physiological mechanisms (Eysenck and Eysenck, 1985; Gray, 1987; Zuckerman, 1991).

Zuckerman (1991) suggests that the personality dimensions of extroversion, neuroticism and psychoticism are determined by the neural systems responsible for reinforcement, punishment and arousal. People who score high on extroversion are particularly sensitive to reinforcement – perhaps their neural reinforcement systems are especially active.

Infants who later become extroverts show higher activity levels, whereas adult extroverts show more reinforcement-seeking behaviour. Adult extroverts participate in more social activities and tend to shift from one type of activity to another. They are optimistic; they expect that their pursuits will result in reinforcing outcomes. However, unlike people who score high on psychoticism, they are sensitive to the effects of punishment and can learn to act prudently.

People who score high on neuroticism are anxious and fearful. If they also score high on psychoticism, they are hostile as well. These people are particularly sensitive to the punishing effects of aversive stimuli. Zuckerman therefore suggests that the personality dimension of neuroticism is controlled by the sensitivity of the neural system responsible for punishment, which appears to involve the amygdala. As we saw in Chapter 13, an important function of the amygdala is to organise the behavioural, autonomic and hormonal components of conditional emotional responses. If this system were oversensitive, a person would be expected to be especially fearful of situations in which he or she might encounter aversive stimuli. The amygdala is also involved in aggression. Thus, neurotics who also score high on psychoticism will tend to express their fear in the form of aggression.

People who score high on psychoticism have difficulty learning when not to do something. As Zuckerman suggests, they have a low sensitivity to punishment. They also have a high tolerance for arousal and excitation; in other words, we could say that their optimum level of arousal is abnormally high. As we saw in Chapter 13, some theorists hypothesise that people seek situations that provide an optimum level of arousal: too much or too little arousal is aversive. Therefore, a person with a high optimum level of arousal (a high tolerance for excitement) seeks out exciting situations and performs well in them. A neurotic would find these situations aversive, and his or her behaviour would become disorganised and inefficient. A person with a high tolerance for excitement makes a good warrior but does not fit in well in civilised society. Table 14.3 summarises Zuckerman's hypothetical explanations for the three major personality dimensions.

Table 14.3 Zuckerman's hypothetical biological characteristics that correspond to personality dimensions

Personality trait	Biological characteristics
Extroversion	High sensitivity to reinforcement
Neuroticism	High sensitivity to punishment
Psychoticism	Low sensitivity to punishment; high optimal level of arousal

Research using laboratory animals has provided support for Zuckerman's suggestions concerning neuroticism. A neurotic person avoids unfamiliar situations because he or she fears encountering aversive stimuli, whereas an emotionally stable person is likely to investigate the situation to see whether anything interesting will happen. The same is true for other species. For example, about 15 per cent of kittens avoid novel objects, and this tendency persists when they become adults; some cats are 'timid' whereas others are 'bold'. When a timid cat encounters a novel stimulus (such as a rat), the activity of the neural circuits in its amygdala responsible for defensive responses becomes more active (Adamec and Stark-Adamec, 1986).

Kagan et al. (1988) investigated the possibility that timidity in social situations (shyness) has a biological basis in humans. They noted that about 10–15 per cent of normal children between the ages of 2 and 3 become quiet, watchful and subdued when they encounter an unfamiliar situation. In other words, like the kittens, they are shy and cautious in approaching novel stimuli. Childhood shyness seems to be related to two personality dimensions: a low level of extraversion and a high level of neuroticism (Briggs, 1988).

Kagan and his colleagues selected two groups of 21-month-old and 31-month-old children according to their reactions to unfamiliar people and situations. The shy group consisted of children who showed signs of inhibition, such as clinging to their mothers or remaining close to them, remaining silent and failing to approach strangers or other novel stimuli. The non-shy group showed no such inhibition; these children approached the strangers and explored the novel environment. The children were similarly tested for shyness several more times, up to the age of 7½ years.

The investigators found shyness to be an enduring trait; children who were shy at the ages of 21 or 31 months continued to be shy at the age of 7½ years. In addition, the two groups of children showed differences in their physiological reactions to the test situation. Shy children were more likely to show increases in heart rate, their pupils tended to be more dilated, their urine contained more norepinephrine and their saliva contained more cortisol.

(Norepinephrine and cortisol are two hormones secreted during times of stress. Furthermore, their secretion in fearful situations is controlled by the amygdala.) Obviously, the shy children found the situation to be stressful, whereas the non-shy children did not.

This study suggests that the biological basis of an important personality characteristic during childhood – shyness – may be the excitability of neural circuits that control avoidance behaviours. Of course, the experimenters did not observe differences in the children's brains, so we cannot be sure about the nature of the brain differences between the two groups of children. Further research with both humans and laboratory animals may help us to understand the biological differences responsible for personality characteristics.

A recent Swedish PET study of Eysenck's typology found that no brain activation differentiated between high and low neurotics, but extroverts showed greater subcortical activity than did the introverts (Fischer *et al.*, 1997). Because this activity in the extroverts was found subcortically, Fischer *et al.* suggest that this area is involved in learning and motor behaviour that utilises dopamine. They argue that physiological differences between personality types, therefore, occur subcortically rather than cortically. This is an interesting hypothesis, although one might expect some form of subcortical involvement in personality given the complexity of the brain and the traits involved. Further research should help to clarify this role.

Questions to think about

Trait theories and the biological basis of personality

- Do you think that personality can be reduced to a few generic personality characteristics? Does it seem intuitively correct?

- Is it correct to answer such a question intuitively?

- What is the 'problem of reification' in personality research? (Chapter 2 defines this.)

- If you look at your own behaviour and personality, which theory do you think would best fit your own behaviour? Can the personalities of your friends and relatives be attributed to the traits suggested by these theories?

- Why do you think that trait theories suggest different numbers of traits? Why do they not agree?

- Should people who differ widely in personality type also show different patterns of brain activation? Why or why not?

- What would be the adaptive value of inheriting your parents' personality traits?

The social learning approach

Some psychologists, such as Cattell and Eysenck, are interested in the ways in which people differ with respect to their personality traits. Other psychologists are more interested in the ways in which a person's personality is affected by environmental and cognitive variables. These psychologists view personality and its development as a process in which behavioural, cognitive and environmental variables interact to produce a person's personality. Social learning theory embodies the idea that both the consequences of behaviour and an individual's beliefs about those consequences determine personality.

Social learning theory stems partially from Skinner's experimental analysis of behaviour. Although Skinner's work has influenced contemporary personality theory, he should not be mistaken for a personality theorist. He was definitely not one. For Skinner, behaviour is explained entirely in terms of its consequences. Behaviour is consistent from one situation to the next because it is maintained by similar kinds of consequences across those situations. Behaviour changes only when the consequences for behaving change. Skinner's ideas have attracted the attention of some personality researchers because they are experimentally based and provide testable hypotheses for predicting an individual's behaviour within and across situations. Social learning theorists have modified and applied Skinner's ideas to their own work. One such researcher is Albert Bandura (b. 1925), who blended Skinner's ideas with his own ideas about how cognitive factors may influence behaviour.

Expectancies and observational learning

Cognitive processing, including the individual's interpretation of the situation, is central to social learning theory (Bandura, 1973, 1986). An important aspect of cognition for Bandura and other social learning theorists is expectancy, the individual's belief that a specific consequence will follow a specific action. Expectancy refers to how someone perceives the contingencies of reinforcement for his or her own behaviour. If a person does something, it may be because he or she expects to be rewarded or punished. In different situations, expectancies may vary. For example, a child may learn that he can get what he wants from his younger sister by hitting her. However, on one occasion, his parents may catch him hitting his sister and punish him. His expectancy may now change: he may still get what he wants by behaving aggressively, but if he is caught, he'll be punished. This new expectancy may influence how he behaves towards his sister in the future (especially around his parents).

Expectancies also permit people to learn actions vicariously, that is, without those actions being directly reinforced. The vicarious nature of some learning experiences is obvious in children as they imitate the actions of others. A 3 year old who applies deodorant to herself does so not because this behaviour has been reinforced in the past, but rather because after watching her mother do it, she expects it would be 'fun' for her to do so too.

Vicarious learning is better known as observational learning, which is learning through observing the kinds of consequence that others (called models) experience as a result of their behaviour. Observational learning is a form of learning in which an expectancy about reinforcement is formed merely by observing another's behaviour and the consequences it produces. Your own experience is no doubt filled with examples of observational learning – learning to dance, to make a paper aeroplane, to write italic, and to engage in many other activities. The more complex the behaviour, the more times we must observe it being executed and practise what we have observed before we can learn it well. Learning to tie a shoelace requires more attention to detail than learning to roll a ball across the floor.

Reciprocal determinism and self-efficacy

Unlike many personality researchers, Bandura does not believe that either personal characteristics (traits) or the environment alone determines personality (Bandura, 1978). Rather, he argues for reciprocal determinism, the idea that behaviour, environmental variables and person variables, such as perception, interact to determine personality, as illustrated in Figure 14.7. We know that our actions can affect the environment. We also know that the environment can affect our behaviour. Likewise, our thoughts may affect the ways in which we behave to change the environment, and in turn, those changes can influence our thoughts. When our acts of kindness are met with kindness

in return, we perceive the environment as friendly and are apt to show kindness under other, similar circumstances. Likewise, when we are treated rudely, we perceive the environment as unfriendly (perhaps hostile) and will likely attempt to avoid or change similar environments in the future.

According to Bandura (1982), self-efficacy, or one's expectations of success in a given situation, is an important determinant of whether one will attempt to make changes in one's environment. Each day, we make many decisions based on our perceptions of the extent to which our actions will produce reinforcement. Our actions are based on our evaluation of our competency. Moreover, self-efficacy not only determines whether we will engage in a particular behaviour, it also determines the extent to which we will maintain that behaviour in the face of adversity. For example, if you believe that you are unqualified for a job even though you really desire it, you are apt not to apply for an interview for that job. However, if you are confident of your qualifications for the job, you will surely attempt the interview. Even if you are turned down for that job, you may interview for a similar position because you are sure of your abilities. Low self-efficacy can hamper both the frequency and the quality of behaviour–environment interactions, and high self-efficacy can facilitate both.

Related to self-efficacy is the extent to which an individual feels optimistic or pessimistic about his or her life's circumstances. Seligman and Schulman (1986) have found that people (in the case of their study, life insurance agents) who can find something positive in less-than-desirable circumstances are generally more successful than are people who view those circumstances negatively. It seems that otherwise cheerless circumstances stimulate optimists to seek creative means of 'putting the circumstances right'. Pessimists are more likely to throw up their arms in despair and to give up. Thus, if there is a solution to be found for a problem, the optimist has the better chance of finding it.

Person variables

Like Bandura, Walter Mischel (b. 1930) believes that much of one's personality is learned through interaction with the environment. Also like Bandura, Mischel emphasises the role of cognition in determining how one learns the relationship between one's behaviour and its consequences. In addition, though, Mischel argues that individual differences in cognition, or person variables as he calls them, account for differences in personality. Mischel (1984) proposed five person variables that figure significantly in social learning:

1 *Competencies*. We each have different skills, abilities and capacities. What we know and the kinds of behaviour that have been reinforced in the past influence the kinds of action in which we will likely engage in the future.

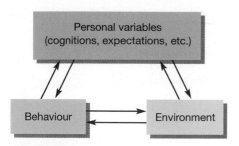

Figure 14.7

Patterns of interaction in reciprocal determinism. According to Bandura, behaviour, environment and personal variables, such as cognitions and expectations, interact to determine personality.

Controversies in psychological science

Do traits or situations best predict behaviour?

The issue

Social learning theorists stress the importance of the environment as an influence on behaviour and tend to place less emphasis on the role of personality traits. They argue that the situation often plays a strong role in determining behaviour. In contrast, trait theorists argue that personality traits are stable characteristics of individuals and that knowing something about these traits permits us to predict an individual's behaviour. Which of these views is correct? Is there a correct view?

The evidence

Mischel (1968, 1976) has suggested that stable personality traits do not exist – or if they do, they are of little importance. Situations, not traits, best predict behaviour. He asks us to consider two situations: a party to celebrate someone's winning a large sum of money and a funeral. People will be much more talkative, cheerful and outgoing at the party than at the funeral. How much will knowing a person's score on a test of introversion–extroversion enable you to predict whether he or she will be talkative and outgoing? In this case, knowing the situation has much more predictive value than knowing the test score.

Mischel cites several studies in support of his position. One of the first of these studies was performed over seventy years ago. Hartshorne and May (1928) designed a set of behavioural tests to measure the traits of honesty and self-control and administered them to over ten thousand students in elementary school and high school. The tests gave the children the opportunity to be dishonest – for example, to cheat on a test, lie about the amount of homework they had done, or keep money with which they had been entrusted. In all cases, the experimenters had access to what the children actually did, so they could determine whether the child acted honestly or dishonestly. They found that a child who acted honestly (or dishonestly) in one situation did not necessarily act the same way in a different situation. The average correlation of a child's honesty from situation to situation – the cross-situational consistency – was below 0.3. The authors concluded that 'honesty or dishonesty is not a unified character trait in children of the ages studied, but a series of specific responses to specific situations' (p. 243).

Mischel (1968) reviewed evidence from research performed after the Hartshorne and May study and found that most personal characteristics showed the same low cross-situational consistency of 0.3 or lower. He concluded that the concept of personality trait was not useful. People's behaviour was determined by the

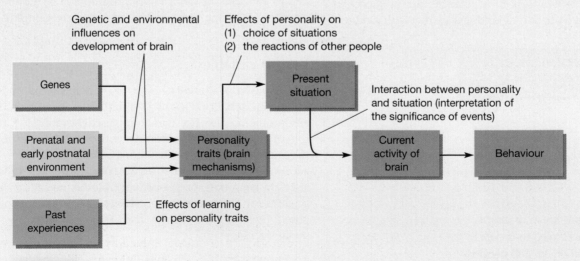

Figure 14.8

Personality traits and the interactions between traits and situations determine behaviour.

situations in which they found themselves, not by any intrinsic personality traits.

Other psychologists disagree with Mischel. For example, Epstein (1979) noted that personality traits are more stable than some of these measures had suggested. He noted that assessments of cross-situational consistency usually test a group of people on two occasions and correlate their behaviour in one situation with their behaviour in the other. He showed that repeated measurements across several days yielded much higher correlations. In a study of his own, a group of twenty-eight undergraduates kept daily records of their most pleasant and most unpleasant experiences for a month. For each experience, they recorded the emotions they felt, their impulses to action and their actual behaviour. The correlation between a person's emotions, impulses, or behaviour on any two days was rather low – of the order of 0.3. However, when he grouped measurements (that is, correlated the ratings obtained on odd-numbered days with those obtained on even-numbered days), the correlation rose dramatically – up to around 0.8.

Although Mischel is sceptical about the value of the concept of personality trait, he has acknowledged that particular personality traits may be important as predictors of behaviour (Mischel, 1977, 1979). He also points out that some situations by their very nature severely constrain a person's behaviour, whereas others permit a wide variety of responses. For example, red lights cause almost all motorists to stop their cars. In this case, knowing the particular situation (the colour of the traffic light) predicts behaviour better than knowing something about the personality characteristics of the drivers. Conversely, some situations are weak and have little control over people's behaviour. As Zuckerman (1991) points out, an amber light is such a situation; when drivers see an amber traffic light, some will stop if they possibly can and others will accelerate and rush through the junction. The difference between the two behaviours is likely determined by individual personality traits.

Personality and situations are usually conceived of as independent variables, but they are not always independent. In laboratory settings, experimenters assign people to various situations. Here, situation and personality are truly independent. However, as Bem and Allen (1974) pointed out, people in life outside the laboratory are able to exert some choice over the situations they enter. For instance, a party is a moderately powerful situation and tends to produce extroverted behaviours. Introverted people may stay away from parties to avoid situations that encourage behaviours with which they are not comfortable. Similarly, extroverts may avoid situations in which they are alone. The fact that people choose their own situations means that personality traits interact with situations. Emmons *et al.* (1986) found that people do, indeed, show consistent patterns in the types of situations they choose; and when circumstances force them to be in situations they do not normally choose, they feel uncomfortable.

Conclusion

Acknowledging the stability of personality over many situations and the interaction between personality and situations, most psychologists agree that the original question, 'Which is more important in determining a person's behaviour, the situation or personality traits?' has proved too simplistic. Some types of personality trait will prevail in most situations; some situations will dictate the behaviour of most people. But some interactions between situation and personality require the analysis of both variables. Figure 14.8 illustrates some of the important variables that control an individual's personality development.

2 *Encoding strategies and personal constructs.* We also differ in our ability to process information. The way we process information determines how we perceive different situations. One person may perceive going on a date as fun, and so look forward to it; another person may perceive going on a date as potentially boring, and so dread it.

3 *Expectancies.* On the basis of our past behaviour and our knowledge of current situations, we form expectancies about the effects of our behaviour on the environment.

Expecting our behaviour to affect the environment positively leads to one course of action; expecting our behaviour to affect it negatively leads to another.

4 *Subjective values.* The degree to which we value certain reinforcers over others influences our behaviour. We seek those outcomes that we value most.

5 *Self-regulatory systems and plans.* We monitor our progress towards achieving goals and subject ourselves to either

self-punishment or self-reinforcement, depending on our progress. We also modify and formulate plans regarding how we feel a goal can best be achieved.

Mischel's view is a dynamic one – people's thoughts and behaviours are undergoing constant change as they interact with the environment. New plans are made and old ones reformulated; people adjust their actions in accordance with their competencies, subjective values and expectancies of behaviour–environment interactions.

Locus of control

Other social learning theorists, such as Julian Rotter (b. 1916), have argued that the extent to which one perceives oneself to be in control of particular situations is also an important element of personality. Locus of control refers to whether one believes that the consequences of one's actions are controlled by internal, person variables or by external, environmental variables (Rotter, 1954, 1966). A person who expects to control his or her own fate – or, more technically, who perceives that rewards are dependent upon his or her own behaviour – has an internal locus of control. A person who sees his or her life as being controlled by external forces unaffected by his or her own behaviour has an external locus of control, as you can see from Figure 14.9.

Rotter developed the I–E Scale, which assesses the degree to which people perceive the consequences of their behaviour to be under the control of internal or external variables. The I–E Scale contains twenty-nine pairs of statements to which a person indicates his or her degree of agreement. A typical item on the scale might look something like this:

The grades that I achieve depend on my abilities and how hard I work to get them.

The grades that I achieve depend mostly on my teacher and his or her tests.

The scale is scored by counting the number of choices consistent with either the internal or the external locus of control orientation. Scores may range from 0 to 23, with lower scores indicative of greater internal locus of control. Of all the populations Rotter has assessed with the I–E Scale, the highest level of internal locus of control was obtained from a group of Peace Corps volunteers (Rotter, 1966).

Rotter's scale has been used in hundreds of studies of social behaviour in a wide variety of situations. Consider some of the findings obtained from research using the I–E Scale:

■ People having internal locus of control orientations will work harder to obtain a goal if they believe that they can control the outcome in a specific situation. Even when told that a goal could be obtained with their own skill and effort, those having external orientations tended not to try as hard as those having internal orientations (Davis and Phares, 1967).

■ People having internal orientations are also more likely to be aware of and to use good health practices. They are more apt to take preventive medicines, to exercise regularly and to quit smoking than are people having external orientations (Strickland, 1979). They are, however, also more likely to blame themselves when they fail, even when failure is not their fault (Phares, 1984).

Internal Locus of Control

Poor performance on test	Good performance on test
It's my own fault. I should have spent more time studying.	Great! I knew all that studying would pay off.

External Locus of Control

Poor performance on test	Good performance on test
These tests are just too hard. The questions are impossible.	Am I lucky or what? The teacher must have been really lenient.

Figure 14.9

Internal and external loci of control. People having internal loci of control perceive themselves as being able to determine the outcomes of the events in their lives. People having external loci of control perceive the events in their lives to be determined by environmental variables.

Questions to think about

Situationism

- Fred enjoys most sports and he enjoys most social activities such as drinking and partying. Sometimes, however, he prefers to spend some time by himself. Are we justified in arguing that Fred has a 'sociability' trait? Or does the situation determine his behaviour?

- Is the trait versus situationism argument a false one? Can the two not interact?

- Can you think of examples from your own day where your personality or behaviour might be better described by situationism than trait theory?

The psychodynamic approach

The work of Sigmund Freud has had a profound and lasting effect on twentieth-century society. Terms such as ego, libido, repression, rationalisation and fixation are as familiar to many Western laypeople as to clinicians. Before Freud formulated his theory, people believed that most behaviour was determined by rational, conscious processes. Freud was the first to claim that what we do is often irrational and that the reasons for our behaviour are seldom conscious. The mind, to Freud, was a battleground for the warring factions of instinct, reason and conscience; the term psychodynamic refers to this struggle.

The development of Freud's theory

Sigmund Freud (1856–1939) was a Viennese physician who acquired his early training in neurology in the laboratory of Ernst Wilhelm von Brücke, an eminent physiologist and neuroanatomist. Freud's work in the laboratory consisted mostly of careful anatomical observation rather than experimentation. Careful observation also characterised his later work with human behaviour; he made detailed observations of individual patients and attempted to draw inferences about the structure of the human psyche from these cases.

Freud left Vienna briefly and studied in Paris with Jean Martin Charcot, who was investigating the usefulness of hypnosis as a treatment for hysteria. Patients with hysteria often experience paralysis of some part of the body or loss of one of the senses, and no physiological cause can be detected. The fact that hypnosis could be used either to produce or to alleviate these symptoms suggested that they were of psychological origin. Charcot proposed

that hysterical symptoms were caused by some kind of psychological trauma. Freud was greatly impressed by Charcot's work and became even more interested in problems of the mind.

Freud returned home to Vienna, opened his medical practice and began an association with Josef Breuer, a prominent physician. Freud and Breuer together published a book called *Studies on Hysteria*, and one of the cases cited in it, that of Anna O., provided the evidence that led to some of the most important tenets of Freud's theory. Breuer had treated Anna O. twelve years before he and Freud published their book. She suffered from an incredible number of hysterical symptoms, including loss of speech, disturbances in vision, headaches, and paralysis and loss of feeling in her right arm. Under hypnosis, Anna was asked to think about the time when her symptoms had started. Each of her symptoms appeared to have begun just when she was unable to express a strongly felt emotion. While under hypnosis, she experienced these emotions again, and the experience gave her relief from her hysterical symptoms. It was as if the emotions had been bottled up, and reliving the original experiences uncorked them. This release of energy (which Breuer and Freud called catharsis) presumably eliminated the hysterical symptoms.

The case of Anna O. is one of the most frequently reported cases in the annals of psychotherapy. However, Breuer's original description appears to be inaccurate in some of its most important respects (Ellenberger, 1972). Apparently, the woman was not cured at all by Breuer's hypnosis and psychotherapy. Ellenberger discovered hospital records indicating that Anna O. continued to take morphine for the distress caused by the disorders Breuer had allegedly cured. Freud appears to have learned later that the cure was a fabrication, but this fact did not become generally known until recently. However, Breuer's failure to help Anna O. with her problems does not mean that we must reject psychoanalysis. Although Breuer's apparent success inspired Freud to examine the unconscious, Freud's theory of personality must stand or fall on its own merits when evaluated by modern evidence.

The case of Anna O., along with evidence obtained from his own clinical practice, led Freud to reason that human behaviour is motivated by instinctual drives, which, when activated, supply 'psychic energy'. This energy is aversive, because the nervous system seeks a state of quiet equilibrium. According to Freud, if something prevents the psychic energy caused by activation of a drive from being discharged, psychological disturbances will result.

Freud believed that instinctual drives were triggered by traumatic events in a person's life. During such an event, the individual is forced to hide strong emotion. Because it cannot be expressed normally, the emotion is expressed neurotically, that is, with excessive anxiety. The individual cannot recall the emotions or the events that produced it because they are embedded in the **unconscious**, the inaccessible part of the mind. Unconscious memories and emotions exert control over conscious thoughts and actions, causing the neurotic symptoms to linger and the emotions of the original traumatic event to stay secret.

Freud also believed that the mind actively prevents unconscious traumatic events from reaching conscious awareness. That is, the mind represses the memories of traumatic events, most of which are potentially anxiety-provoking, preventing their being consciously discovered. He used the idea of an iceberg as a metaphor to describe the mind. Only the tip is visible above water; the much larger and more important part of it is submerged. Likewise, the conscious mind hides a larger and more important part of the mind – the unconscious. To understand a person's personality, we must tap his or her unconscious.

Freud, then, argued that our personalities are determined by both conscious and unconscious powers, with the unconscious exerting considerable influence on the conscious. To understand how the unconscious exerts its control over conscious thought and action, we need to explore Freud's view of the structure of personality.

Structures of the mind: id, ego and superego

Freud was struck by the fact that psychological disturbances could stem from events that a person apparently could no longer consciously recall, although they could be revealed during hypnosis. This phenomenon led him to conclude that the mind consists of unconscious, preconscious and conscious elements. The unconscious includes mental events of which we are not aware, the conscious entails mental events of which we are aware, and the preconscious involves mental events that may become conscious through effort.

Freud divided the mind into three structures: the id, the ego and the superego. The operations of the **id** are completely unconscious. The id contains the **libido**, which is the primary source of instinctual motivation for all psychic forces; this force is insistent and is unresponsive to the demands of reality. The id obeys only one rule: to obtain immediate gratification in whatever form it may take – this is called the **pleasure principle**. If you are hungry, the id compels you to eat; if you are angry, the id prompts you to strike out or to seek revenge or to destroy something. Freud (1933) conceived of the id as

> the dark, inaccessible part of our personality. ... We approach the id with analogies: we call it a chaos, a cauldron full of seething excitations. ... It is filled with energy reaching it from the instincts, but it has no organisation, produces no collective will, but only a striving to bring about the satisfaction of the instinctual needs subject to the observance of the pleasure principle. (p. 65)

The **ego** is the self; it controls and integrates behaviour. It acts as a mediator, negotiating a compromise among the pressures of the id, the counterpressures of the superego and the demands of reality. The ego's functions of perception, cognition and memory perform this mediation. The ego is driven by the **reality principle**, the tendency to satisfy the id's demands realistically, which almost always involves compromising the demands of the id and superego. It involves the ability to delay gratification of a drive until an appropriate goal is located. To ward off the demands of the id when these demands cannot be gratified, the ego uses defence mechanisms (described later). Some of the functions of the ego are unconscious.

The **superego** is subdivided into the conscience and the ego-ideal. The **conscience** is the internalisation of the rules and restrictions of society. It determines which behaviours are permissible and punishes wrongdoing with feelings of guilt. The **ego-ideal** is the internalisation of what a person would like to be – his or her goals.

Freud believed the mind to be full of conflicts. A conflict might begin when one of the two primary drives, the sexual instinctual drive or the aggressive instinctual drive, is aroused. The id demands gratification of these drives but is often held in check by the superego's internalised prohibitions against the behaviours the drives tend to produce. Internalised prohibitions are rules of behaviour learned in childhood that protect the person from the guilt that he or she would feel if the instinctual drives were allowed to express themselves.

The result of the conflict is compromise formation, in which a compromise is reached between the demands of the id and the suppressive effects of the superego. According to Freud, phenomena such as dreams, artistic creations and slips of the tongue (we now call them Freudian slips) are examples of compromise formation.

In what many consider to be his greatest work, *The Interpretation of Dreams*, Freud wrote, 'The interpretation of dreams is the royal road to a knowledge of the unconscious activities of the mind' (Freud, 1900, p. 647). To Freud, dreams were motivated by repressed wishes and urges. By analysing dreams, Freud thought repressed wishes and memories could be rediscovered. For example, Freud believed that the **manifest content** of a dream – its actual storyline – is only a disguised version of its **latent content** – its hidden message, which is produced by the unconscious. The latent content might be an unexpressed wish related to the aggressive instinctual drive.

For example, a person may desire to hurt or injure another person, perhaps a co-worker with whom he or she is competing for a promotion. However, if the person acted out this scenario in a dream, he or she would experience guilt and anxiety. Therefore, the aggressive wishes of the unconscious are transformed into a more palatable form – the manifest content of the dream might be that the co-worker accepts a job offer from a different company, removing any competition for the promotion. The manifest content of this dream manages to express, at least partly, the latent content supplied by the unconscious.

In addition to analysing his patient's dreams, Freud also developed the technique of free association to probe the unconscious mind for clues of intrapsychic conflict. Free association is a method of analysis in which an individual is asked to relax, clear his or her mind of current thoughts and then report all thoughts, images, perceptions and feelings that come to mind. During free association, Freud looked for particular patterns in his patient's report that might reveal wishes, fears and worries that the patient's mind might be keeping hidden. For example, free association might reveal, among other things, the thought of beating someone up, an image of a knife, and perhaps a feeling of relief. Recognising a pattern in his patient's report, he may draw conclusions about the client's hidden desire to harm someone and about the reasons motivating both that desire and the relief experienced once the aggressive urge is satisfied.

Defence mechanisms

According to Freud, the ego contains defence mechanisms – mental systems that become active whenever uncon-scious instinctual drives of the id come into conflict with internalised prohibitions of the superego. The signal for the ego to utilise one of its defences is the state of anxiety produced by an intrapsychic conflict. This unpleasant con-dition motivates the ego to apply a defence mechanism and thus reduce the anxiety. The six important defence mechanisms are summarised in Table 14.4.

Repression

Repression is responsible for actively keeping threatening or anxiety-provoking memories from our conscious aware-ness. For example, a person may have witnessed a brutal murder but cannot recall it later because of the uncomfort-able emotions it would arouse. Freud believed that repres-sion was perhaps the most powerful of the defence mechanisms.

Reaction formation

Reaction formation involves replacing an anxiety-provoking idea with its opposite. An often-cited example of a reaction formation is that of a person who is aroused and fasci-nated by pornographic material but whose superego will not permit this enjoyment. He or she becomes a

Table 14.4   Freudian defence mechanisms

Defence mechanism	Description	Example
Repression	The mind's active attempt to prevent memories of traumatic experiences from reaching conscious awareness	Failure to remember the death of a loved one or other highly upsetting events that occurred earlier in your life
Reaction formation	Replacing an anxiety-provoking idea with its opposite	Having intense feelings of dislike for a person, but acting in a friendly manner towards him or her
Projection	Denial of one's unacceptable feelings and desire and finding them in others	Denying that you have negative feelings towards someone, but asserting that person to have negative feelings towards you
Sublimation	Channelling psychic energy from an unacceptable drive into a more acceptable one	Diverting energy from the sex drive to produce a work of art
Rationalisation	Creating an acceptable reason for a behaviour that is actually performed for a less acceptable reason	Asserting that you donate money to charities because you truly are a generous person when really you want the tax break for the donation
Conversion	The manifestation of a psychic conflict in terms of physical symptoms	A psychic conflict, perhaps aroused by a particular person, causes you to develop symptoms of deafness or blindness to avoid contact with him or her

militant crusader against pornography. Reaction formation can be a very useful defence mechanism in this situation, permitting acceptable interaction with the forbidden sexual object. The crusader against pornography often studies the salacious material to see just how vile it is so that he or she can better educate others about its harmful nature. Thus, enjoyment becomes possible without feelings of guilt.

Projection

Projection involves denial of one's own unacceptable desires and the discovery of evidence of these desires in the behaviour of other people. For example, a man who is experiencing a great deal of repressed hostility may perceive the world as being full of people who are hostile to him. In this way, he can blame someone else for any conflicts in which he engages.

Sublimation

Sublimation is the diversion of psychic energy from an unacceptable drive to an acceptable one. For example, a person may feel strong sexual desire but find its outlet unacceptable because of internalised prohibitions. Despite repression of the drive, its energy remains and finds another outlet, such as artistic or other creative activities. Freud considered sublimation to be an important factor in artistic and intellectual creativity. He believed that people have a fixed amount of drive available for motivating all activities, therefore surplus sexual instinctual drive that is not expended in its normal way can be used to increase a person's potential for creative achievement.

Rationalisation

Rationalisation is the process of inventing an acceptable reason for a behaviour that is really being performed for another, less acceptable reason. For example, a man who feels guilty about his real reasons for purchasing a pornographic magazine may say, 'I don't buy the magazine for the pictures. I buy it to read the interesting and enlightening articles it contains.'

Conversion

Conversion is the provision of an outlet for intrapsychic conflict in the form of a physical symptom. The conflict is transformed into blindness, deafness, paralysis or numbness. (This phenomenon has also been called hysteria, which should not be confused with the common use of the term to mean 'running around and shouting and generally acting out of control'.) For example, a person might develop blindness so that he or she will no longer be able to see a situation that arouses a strong, painful intrapsychic conflict. Anna O.'s problem would be described as a conversion reaction.

Freud's psychosexual theory of personality development

Freud believed that personality development involves passing through several psychosexual stages of development – stages that involve seeking pleasure from specific parts of the body called erogenous zones. As we will see, each stage of personality development involves deriving physical pleasure from a different erogenous zone. Freud used the term 'sexual' to refer to physical pleasures and the many ways an individual might seek to gratify an urge for such pleasure. He did not generally use the term to refer to orgasmic pleasure.

Freud's theory of personality development has been extremely influential because of its ability to explain personality disorders in terms of whole or partial fixation – arrested development owing to failure to pass through an earlier stage of development. Freud believed that a person becomes fixated at a particular stage of development when he or she becomes strongly attached to the erogenous zone involved in that stage. Although normal personality development involves passing successfully through all the psychosexual stages, Freud maintained that most people become more or less fixated at some point in their development.

Because newborn babies can do little more than suck and swallow, their sexual instinctual drive finds an outlet in these activities. Even as babies become able to engage in more complex behaviours, they continue to receive most of their sexual gratification orally. The early period of the oral stage of personality development is characterised by sucking and is passive. Later, as babies become more aggressive, they derive their pleasure from biting and chewing.

Fixation at the oral stage may result from early (or delayed) weaning from breast to bottle to cup. Someone whose personality is fixated at the early oral stage might be excessively passive. 'Biting' sarcasm or compulsive talking can represent fixation at the later, more aggressive phase of the oral stage. Other oral stage fixation activities include habits such as smoking and excessive eating.

The anal stage of personality development begins during the second year of life; now babies begin to enjoy emptying their bowels. During the early part of this stage, called the expressive period, babies enjoy expelling their faeces. Later, in the retentive period, they derive pleasure from retaining them. Improper toilet training can result in fixation at the anal stage. People fixated at the anal expressive period are characterised as destructive and cruel; anal retentives are seen as stingy and miserly.

At around age 3, a child discovers that it is pleasurable to play with his penis or her clitoris, and enters the phallic stage (phallus means 'penis', but Freud used the term bisexually in this context). Children also begin to discover the sex roles of their parents, and they unconsciously attach themselves to the parent of the opposite sex. A boy's attachment to his mother is called the Oedipus complex, after the Greek king of mythology who unknowingly married his mother after killing his father. For a time, Freud believed that a girl formed a similar attachment with her father, called the Electra complex, but he later rejected this concept. In Greek mythology, Electra, aided by her brother, killed her mother and her mother's lover to avenge her father's death.

In boys, the Oedipus complex normally becomes repressed by age 5, although the conflicts that occur during the phallic stage continue to affect their personalities throughout life. A boy's unconscious wish to take his father's place is suppressed by his fear that his father will castrate him as punishment. In fact, Freud believed that young boys regarded females as castrated males. The conflict is finally resolved when the boy begins to model his behaviour on that of his father so that he achieves identification with the father. Failure to resolve this conflict causes the boy to become fixated at this stage. The boy then becomes preoccupied with demonstrations of his manhood, continually acting 'macho'.

Girls supposedly experience fewer conflicts than boys do during the phallic stage. According to Freud, the chief reason for their transfer of love from their mothers (who provided primary gratification during early life) to their fathers is penis envy. A girl discovers that she and her mother lack this organ, so she becomes attached to her father, who has one. This attachment persists longer than the Oedipus complex, because the girl does not have to fear castration as revenge for usurping her mother's role. Freud believed that penis envy eventually becomes transformed into a need to bear children. The missing penis is replaced by a baby. A girl who becomes fixated during the phallic stage develops strong feelings of being inferior to men, which are expressed in seductive or otherwise flirtatious behaviour. For example, she may become attracted to older men ('father figures') and attempt to seduce them to demonstrate her power over them and thereby relieve her feelings of inferiority.

After the phallic stage comes a latency period of several years, during which the child's sexual instinctual drive is mostly submerged. Following this period, the onset of puberty, the child, now an adolescent, begins to form adult sexual attachments to age mates of the other sex. Because the sexual instinctual drive now finds its outlet in heterosexual genital contact, this stage is known as the genital stage.

Further development of Freud's theory: the neo-Freudians

Freud's theory created controversy in the Victorian era in which it was unveiled. Its emphasis on childhood sexuality and seething internal conflicts seemed preposterous and offensive. Yet, the theory's proposal that our thoughts and behaviour as adults stem from unconscious forces as well as from our early childhood experiences was revolutionary and these were recognised by many scholars as genuinely original ideas. Freud attracted a number of followers who studied his work closely but who did not accept it completely. Each of these people agreed with Freud's view on the dynamic forces operating within the psyche. Each of them disagreed with Freud, though, on how much importance to place on the role of unconscious sexual and aggressive instincts in shaping personality. Four psychodynamic theorists, Carl Jung, Alfred Adler, Karen Horney and Erik Erikson, have been particularly influential in elaborating psychodynamic theory.

Carl Jung: analytical psychology

Early in the twentieth century, several students of psychoanalysis met with Freud to further the development of psychoanalysis. One of these people was Carl Jung (1875–1961). Freud called Jung 'his adopted eldest son, his crown prince and successor' (Hall and Nordby, 1973, p. 23). However, Jung developed his own version of psychodynamic theory that de-emphasised the importance of sexuality. He also disagreed with his mentor on the structure of the unconscious. Unfortunately, Freud had little tolerance of others' opinions. After 1913, he and Jung never saw each other again. Jung continued to develop his theory after the split by drawing ideas from mythology, anthropology, history and religion, as well as from an active clinical practice in which he saw people with psychological disorders.

To Jung, libido was a positive creative force that propels people towards personal growth. He also believed that forces other than the id, ego and superego, such as the collective unconscious, form the core of personality. To Jung, the ego was totally conscious and contained the ideas, perceptions, emotions, thoughts and memories of which we are aware. One of Jung's more important contributions to psychodynamic theory was his idea of the collective unconscious, which contains memories and ideas inherited from our ancestors. Stored in the collective unconscious are archetypes, inherited and universal thought forms and patterns that allow us to notice particular aspects of our world (Carver and Scheier, 1992). From the dawn of our species, all humans have had roughly similar experiences with things such as mothers, evil, masculinity and femininity. Each one of these is represented by an archetype. For example, the shadow is the archetype containing basic instincts that allow us to recognise aspects of the world such as evil, sin and carnality. Archetypes are not stored images or ideas – we are not born with a picture of evil stored somewhere in our brain – but we are born with an inherited disposition to behave, perceive and think in certain ways.

Alfred Adler: striving for superiority

Like Jung, Alfred Adler (1870–1937) studied with Freud. Also like Jung, Adler felt that Freud overemphasised the role of sexuality in personality development. Adler argued that feelings of inferiority play the key role. Upon birth, we are dependent on others for survival. As we mature, we encounter people who are more gifted than we are in almost every aspect of life. The inferiority we feel may be social, intellectual, physical or athletic. These feelings create tension that motivates us to compensate for the deficiency. Emerging from this need to compensate is a striving for superiority, which Adler believed to be the major motivational force in life.

According to Adler (1939), striving for superiority is affected by another force, social interest, which is an innate desire to contribute to society. Social interest is not wholly instinctual though, because it can be influenced by experience. Although individuals have a need to seek personal superiority, they have a greater desire to sacrifice for causes that benefit society as a whole. Thus, while Freud believed that people act in their own self-interest, motivated by the id, Adler believed that people desire to help others, directed by social interest.

Karen Horney: The Flight of the Vagina

Karen Horney (pronounced 'horn-eye'; 1885–1952), like other Freudian dissenters, did not believe that sex and aggression are the primary themes of personality. She did agree with Freud, though, that anxiety is a basic problem that people must address and overcome.

According to Horney, individuals suffer from basic anxiety caused by insecurities in relationships. People often feel alone, helpless or uncomfortable in their interactions with others. For example, a person who begins a new job is often unsure of how to perform his or her duties, whom to ask for help, and how to approach his or her new co-workers. Horney theorised that to deal with basic anxiety, the individual has three options (Horney, 1950):

1 Moving towards others. Accept the situation and become dependent on others. This strategy may entail an exaggerated desire for approval or affection.

2 Moving against others. Resist the situation and become aggressive. This strategy may involve an exaggerated need for power, exploitation of others, recognition or achievement.

3 Moving away from others. Withdraw from others and become isolated. This strategy may involve an exaggerated need for self-sufficiency, privacy or independence.

Horney believed that these three strategies corresponded to three basic orientations with which people approach their life. These basic orientations reflect different personality characteristics. The self-effacing solution corresponds to the moving towards others strategy and involves the desire to be loved. The self-expansive solution corresponds to the moving against others strategy and involves the desire to master oneself. The resignation solution corresponds to the moving away strategy and involves striving to be independent of others.

Horney maintained that personality is a mixture of the three strategies and basic orientations. As the source of anxiety varies from one situation to the next, so may the strategy and basic orientation that is used to cope with it. Like Adler, Horney thought environmental variables influenced personality development. In her view, outlined in her book, *The Flight of the Vagina*, in order to understand personality one must consider not only psychodynamic forces within the mind, but also the environmental conditions to which those forces are reacting.

Erik Erikson: identity crisis

Erik Erikson (1902–1994) studied with Anna Freud, Sigmund Freud's daughter. He emphasised social aspects of personality development rather than biological factors. He also differed with Freud about the timing of personality development. For Freud, the most important development occurs during early childhood. Erikson emphasised the ongoing process of development throughout the lifespan. Erikson proposed that people's personality traits develop as a result of a series of crises they encounter in their social relations with other people. Because these crises continue throughout life, psychosocial development does not end when people become adults.

Erikson's theory of lifelong development has been very influential, and his term 'identity crisis' has become a familiar one. However, because his theory does not make many empirically testable predictions, it has received little empirical support.

Evaluation of psychodynamic theory and research

Freud's psychodynamic theory has had a profound effect on psychological theory, psychotherapy and literature. His writing, although nowadays regarded as sexist, is lively and stimulating, and his ideas have provided many people with food for thought. However, his theory has received little empirical support, mainly because he used concepts that are poorly defined and that cannot be observed directly. How is one to study the ego, the superego or the id? How can one prove (or disprove) that an artist's creativity is the result of a displaced aggressive or sexual instinctual drive? The writings of the neo-Freudians have had even less influence on modern research. Although the theories of Jung, Adler, Horney and Erikson have their followers, scientific research on personality has largely ignored them.

The emphasis by Freud and his followers on the potentially harmful effects of particular types of childhood environment has led some psychotherapists to conclude that their patients' maladjustments and mental disorders are, by and large, caused by their parents. Many parents have blamed themselves for their children's disorders and have suffered severe feelings of guilt. But many forms of mental disorders – particularly the most serious ones – are largely a result of heredity and are not affected much by family environment. Hence, the teachings of Freud and his followers have compounded the tragedy of mental illness by causing parents to be accused unjustly of poor parenting practices.

The one Freudian phenomenon that has undergone experimental testing is repression. This phenomenon is very important to Freud's theory because it is one of the primary ego defences and because it operates by pushing memories (or newly perceived stimuli) into the unconscious. Thus, experimental verification of repression would lend some support to Freud's notions of intrapsychic conflict and the existence of the unconscious.

The results of research on repression have not been conclusive. Typically, the researchers in repression experiments ask participants to learn some material associated with an unpleasant, ego-threatening situation, and they then compare their memory for the information with that of participants who learned the material under non-threatening conditions. If repression occurs, the threatened participants should remember less of the material than the non-threatened participants will. Some studies have reported positive results, but later experiments have shown that other, non-Freudian phenomena could explain them more easily (D'Zurilla, 1965). Perhaps the most important point here is that none of the experiments can really be said to have threatened the participants' egos, producing the level of anxiety that would lead to the activation of a defence mechanism. Any experimental procedure that did so would probably be unethical. Thus, it is difficult to test even the most specific prediction of Freud's theory. It is very hard, perhaps impossible, to prove that a person's behaviour and personality are products of unconscious conflicts.

Questions to think about

Psychodynamic theory

- Have you ever found yourself using any of the Freudian defence mechanisms discussed in this chapter? If so, under what circumstances do you tend to use them, and what unconscious conflict do you suppose you might be protecting yourself from?

- Do you possess any behaviours that may represent a fixation? If so, what are they and what fixations do they represent?

- Why do you think that the psychodynamic approach to personality is untestable?

- If a person admits to his or her sexual urges, psychoanalytic thinking would accept this as fitting the theory; if he or she denies them, they are repressing these urges and denying their existence. Can you see a problem here in scientifically accepting psychoanalytic explanations of personality?

The humanistic approach

The humanistic approach to the study of personality seeks to emphasise the positive, fulfilling elements of life. Humanistic psychologists are interested in nurturing personal growth, life satisfaction and positive human values. They believe that people are innately good and have an internal drive for self-actualisation – the realisation of one's true intellectual and emotional potential. The two most influential humanistic theorists have been Abraham Maslow and Carl Rogers.

Maslow and self-actualisation

For both Freud and Abraham Maslow (1908–1970), motivation is one of the central aspects of personality. However, where Freud saw strong instinctual urges generating tensions that could not be completely resolved, Maslow saw positive impulses that could be easily overwhelmed by the negative forces within one's culture. According to Maslow (1970), human motivation is based on a hierarchy of needs. Our motivation for different activities passes through several levels, with entrance to subsequent levels dependent on first satisfying needs in previous levels, as illustrated by Figure 14.10. If an individual's needs are not met, he or she cannot scale the hierarchy and so will fail to attain his or her true potential.

In Maslow's view, understanding personality requires understanding this hierarchy. Our most basic needs are physiological needs, including the need for food, water, oxygen, rest, and so on. Until these needs are met, we cannot be motivated by needs found in the next level (or any other level). If our physiological needs are met, we find ourselves motivated by safety needs, including the need for

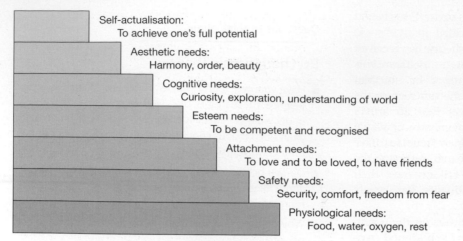

Self-actualisation:
To achieve one's full potential

Aesthetic needs:
Harmony, order, beauty

Cognitive needs:
Curiosity, exploration, understanding of world

Esteem needs:
To be competent and recognised

Attachment needs:
To love and to be loved, to have friends

Safety needs:
Security, comfort, freedom from fear

Physiological needs:
Food, water, oxygen, rest

Figure 14.10

Maslow's hierarchy of needs. According to Maslow, every person's goal is to become self-actualised. In order to achieve this goal, individuals must first satisfy several basic needs.

security and comfort, as well as for peace and freedom from fear. Once the basic survival and safety needs are met, we can become motivated by attachment needs, the need to love and to be loved, to have friends and to be a friend. Next, we seek to satisfy esteem needs – to be competent and recognised as such. You are probably beginning to get the picture: we are motivated to achieve needs higher in the hierarchy only after first satisfying lower needs. If we are able to lead a life in which we have been able to provide ourselves food and shelter and to surround ourselves with love, we are free to pursue self-actualisation.

Maslow based his theory partially on his own assumptions about human potential and partially on his case studies of historical figures whom he believed to be self-actualised, including Albert Einstein, Eleanor Roosevelt, Henry David Thoreau and Abraham Lincoln. Maslow examined the lives of each of these people in order to assess the common qualities that led each to become self-actualised. In general, he found that these individuals were very self-accepting of themselves and of their lives' circumstances, were focused on finding solutions to pressing cultural problems rather than to personal problems, were open to others' opinions and ideas, were spontaneous in their emotional reactions to events in their lives, had strong senses of privacy, autonomy, human values and appreciation of life, and had a few intimate friendships rather than many superficial ones.

Maslow (1964) believed that the innate drive for self-actualisation is not specific to any particular culture. He viewed it as being a fundamental part of human nature. In his words, 'Man has a higher and transcendent nature, and this is part of his essence ... his biological nature of a species which has evolved' (p. xvi).

Rogers and conditions of worth

Carl Rogers (1902–1987) also believed that people are motivated to grow psychologically, aspiring to higher levels of fulfilment as they progress towards self-actualisation (Rogers, 1961). Like Maslow, Rogers believed that people are inherently good and have an innate desire for becoming better. Rogers, though, did not view personality development in terms of satisfying a hierarchy of needs. Instead, he believed that personality development centres on one's self-concept, or one's opinion of oneself, and on the way one is treated by others.

Rogers argued that all people have a need for positive regard, or approval, warmth, love, respect and affection flowing from others. Young children, in particular, show this need when they seek approval for their actions from parents and siblings. In Rogers's view, children often want others to like them to the extent that gaining positive regard is a major focus of their lives. The key to developing a psychologically healthy personality, though, is to develop a positive self-concept or image of oneself. How does one do this? Rogers's answer is that we are happy if we feel that others are happy with us. Likewise, we are also unhappy with ourselves when others are disappointed in or unsatisfied with us.

Thus, our feelings towards ourselves depend to a large extent on what others think of us. As children, we learn that there exist certain conditions or criteria that must be met before others give us positive regard. Rogers called these criteria conditions of worth.

Positive regard is often conditional. For example, parents may act approvingly towards their young child when he helps in the kitchen or in the garden but not when he pinches his younger sister or tells a lie. The boy learns that what others think of him depends on his actions. Soon, too, he may come to view himself as others view him and his behaviour: 'People like me when I do something good and they don't like me when I do something bad.'

Although conditions of worth are a necessary part of the socialisation process, they can have negative effects on personality development if satisfying them becomes the individual's major ambition. As long as the individual focuses chiefly on seeking positive regard from others, he or she may ignore other aspects of life, especially those that lead to positive personality growth. In Rogers's view, then, conditions of worth may stand in the way of self-actualisation. An individual may devote her life to satisfying the expectations and demands of others in lieu of working towards realising her potential. In this sense, the need for positive regard may smother an individual's progress towards self-actualisation.

According to Rogers, the solution to this problem is unconditional positive regard, or love and acceptance that has no strings attached. In a family setting, this means that parents may establish rules and expect their children to obey them, unless doing so would compromise the children's feelings of worth and self-respect. For example, if a child misbehaves, the parents should focus on the child's behaviour and not the child. In this way, the child learns that her behaviour is wrong but that her parents still love her. Unconditional positive regard allows people to work towards realising their potential unfettered by what others think of them.

In developing his theory, Rogers used unstructured interviews in which the client, not the therapist, directed the course of the conversation. He believed that if the therapist provided an atmosphere of unconditional positive regard, a client would eventually reveal her true self, the kind of person she now is, as well as her ideal self, the kind of person that she would like to become. Rogers also gave the Q sort test to many of his clients. This test consists of a variety of cards, each of which contains a statement such as 'I am generally an optimistic person' or 'I am generally an intolerant person'. The client's task is to sort the cards into several piles that vary in degree from 'least like me' to 'most like me'. The client sorts the cards twice, first on the basis of his real self and next in terms of his ideal self. The difference between the arrangement of the cards in the piles is taken as an index of how close the client is to reaching his ideal self. Rogers's goal as a therapist was to facilitate the client's becoming his ideal self. Rogers's approach to therapy is discussed in more detail in Chapter 18.

Evaluation of the humanistic approach

The humanistic approach is impressive because of its emphasis on people seeking a healthy well-being. Indeed, the approach has wide appeal to those who seek an alternative to the more mechanistic and strictly biologically or environmentally determined views of human nature. However, critics point up two closely related problems with this approach.

First, many of the concepts used by humanistic psychologists are defined subjectively and so are difficult to test empirically. For example, how might we empirically examine the nature of self-actualisation? Few published studies have even attempted to answer this question. By now, you know the hallmark of a good theory – the amount of research it generates. On this count, the humanistic approach comes up short.

A second criticism of the humanistic approach is that it cannot account for the origins of personality. It is subject to the nominal fallacy; it describes personality, but it does not explain it. Humanistic psychologists believe that self-actualisation is an innate tendency, but there is no research that shows it to be so. Conditions of worth are said to hamper a child's quest for self-actualisation and thus to alter the course of personality development away from positive psychological growth. However, the humanistic approach provides no objective explanation of this process. Although the humanistic approach may offer a positive view of human nature and give apparent purpose to life, this view is largely unsubstantiated. Before moving on to the next section, take time to look at Table 14.5 which summarises the major theories of personality we have discussed so far.

Table 14.5 A summary of the major personality theories

Theory	Primary figures	Primary emphases	Primary strengths	Primary limitations
Trait	Allport, Cattell, Eysenck	An individual's traits determine personality	Focuses on stability of behaviour over long periods; attempts to measure traits objectively	Largely descriptive; ignores situational variables that may affect behaviour
Psychobiological	Eysenck, Zuckerman	The role of genetics and the brain and nervous system in personality development	Emphasis on the interaction of biology and environment in determining personality; rigorous empirical approach	Reliance on correlational methods in determining the role of genetics in personality
Social learning	Bandura, Mischel, Rotter	Personality is determined by both the consequences of behaviour and our perception of them	Focuses on direct study of behaviour and stresses rigorous experimentation	Ignores biological influences on personality development; often more descriptive than explanatory
Psychodynamic	Freud, Jung, Adler, Horney, Erikson	Unconscious psychic conflicts; repression of anxiety-provoking ideas and desires	The idea that behaviour may be influenced by forces outside conscious awareness	Basic concepts are not empirically testable
Humanistic	Maslow, Rogers	Stresses the positive aspects of human nature and how to become a better person	Useful in therapeutic settings	Contains vague and untestable concepts; primarily descriptive

Assessment of personality

Think for a moment of your best friend. What is he or she like? Outgoing? Impulsive? Thoughtful? Moody? You can easily respond yes or no to these alternatives because you have spent enough time with your friend to know him or her quite well. After all, one of the best ways to get to know people – what they are like and how they react in certain situations – is to spend time with them. Obviously, psychologists do not have the luxury of spending large amounts of time with people in order to learn about their personalities. Generally, they have only a short period to accomplish this goal. From this necessity, personality tests were first developed. The underlying assumption of any personality test is that personality characteristics can be measured. This final section of the chapter describes the two main types of personality test: objective tests and projective tests.

Objective tests of personality

Objective personality tests are similar in structure to classroom tests. Most contain multiple-choice and true/false items, although some allow the person taking the test to indicate the extent to which he or she agrees or disagrees with an item. The responses that subjects can make on objective tests are constrained by the test design. The questions asked are unambiguous, and explicit rules for scoring the subjects' responses can be specified in advance.

One of the oldest and most widely used objective tests of personality is the Minnesota Multiphasic Personality Inventory (MMPI), devised by Hathaway and McKinley in 1939. The original purpose for developing the test was to produce an objective, reliable method for identifying various personality traits that were related to a person's mental health. The developers believed that this test would be valuable in assessing people for a variety of purposes. For instance, it would provide a specific means of determining how effective psychotherapy was. Improvement in people's scores over the course of treatment would indicate that the treatment was successful.

In devising this test, Hathaway and McKinley wrote 504 true/false items and administered the test to several groups of people in mental institutions in Minnesota who had been diagnosed as having certain psychological disorders. These diagnoses had been arrived at through psychiatric interviews with the patients. Such interviews are expensive, so a simple paper-and-pencil test that accomplished the same result would be valuable. The control group consisted of relatives and friends of the patients, who were tested when they came to visit them. (Whether these people constituted the best possible group of normal participants is questionable.) The responses were analysed empirically, and the questions that correlated with various diagnostic labels were included in various scales. For example, if people who had been diagnosed as paranoid tended to say true to 'I believe I am being plotted against', this statement would become part of the paranoia scale.

The current revised version of the MMPI, the MMPI-2, has norms based on a sample of people that is much more representative ethnically and geographically than the original sample (Graham, 1990). It includes 550 questions, grouped into ten clinical scales and four validity scales. A particular item can be used on more than one scale. For example, both people who are depressed and those who are hypochondriacal tend to agree that they have gastrointestinal problems. The clinical scales include a number of diagnostic terms traditionally used to label psychiatric patients, such as hypochondriasis, depression or paranoia.

The four validity scales were devised to provide the tester with some assurance that subjects are answering questions reliably and accurately and that they can read the questions and pay attention to them. The '?' scale ('cannot say') is simply the number of questions not answered. A high score on this scale indicates either that the person finds some questions irrelevant or that the person is evading issues that he or she finds painful.

The L scale (lie) contains items such as 'I do not read every editorial in the newspaper every day' and 'My table manners are not quite as good at home as when I am out in company'. A person who disagrees with questions like these is almost certainly not telling the truth. A high score on the L scale suggests the need for caution in interpreting other scales and also reveals something about the participant's personality. In particular, people who score high on this scale tend to be rather naive; more sophisticated people realise that no one is perfect and do not try to make themselves appear to be so.

The F scale (frequency) consists of items that are answered one way by at least 90 per cent of the normal population. The usual responses are 'false' to items such as 'I can easily make other people afraid of me, and sometimes do it for the fun of it' and 'true' to items such as 'I am liked by most people who know me'. A high score on this scale indicates carelessness, poor reading ability or very unusual personality traits.

The K scale (defensiveness) was devised to identify people who are trying to hide their feelings to guard against internal conflicts that might cause them emotional distress. A person receives a high value on the K scale by answering 'false' to statements such as 'Criticism or scolding hurts me terribly' and 'At periods, my mind seems to work more slowly than usual'. People who score very low on this scale tend to be in need of help or to be unusually immune to criticism and social influences.

Some psychologists argue that validity scales are useless or even harmful in most testing situations. For example, consider the following item: 'Before voting, I thoroughly investigate the qualifications of all candidates'. According to Crowne and Marlowe (1964), anyone who answers yes to such a question has to be lying. But as McCrae and Costa (1990) note, people taking tests do not necessarily respond passively to each item, taking it at face value. Instead, their response is based on their interpretation of what they think the question means. They suggest that most people will say to themselves,

'"Surely these psychologists didn't mean to ask if I actually study the voting records of every single political candidate, from President to dogcatcher. No one does, so that would be a stupid question to ask. What they must have meant to ask was whether I am a concerned citizen who takes voting seriously. Since I am and I do, I guess I should answer yes".' (McCrae and Costa, 1990, p. 40)

There is evidence to support McCrae and Costa's suggestion. When psychologists calculate a person's score on the MMPI, they usually apply a correction factor derived from the validity scales. Several studies have shown that the application of the correction factors to the scores of normal subjects actually reduces the validity of these scores. McCrae and Costa suggest that when the MMPI is administered to normal subjects for research purposes, such corrections should not be made. However, validity scales may be useful in situations in which subjects may be motivated to lie (for example, when a personality test is used to screen job applicants) or in cases in which the test is being used clinically to evaluate the possibility of mental illness or personality disorder.

As well as being used in clinical assessment, the MMPI has been employed extensively in personality research, and a number of other tests, including the California Psychological Inventory and the Taylor Manifest Anxiety Scale, are based on it. However, the MMPI has its critics. As we saw earlier, the five-factor model of personality has received considerable support. Some of its advocates have noted that the MMPI misses some of the dimensions measured by the NEO-PI, which includes tests of neuroticism, extroversion, openness, agreeableness and conscientiousness (Johnson *et al.*, 1984). Thus, these factors will be missed by a clinician or researcher who relies only on the MMPI. For this reason, many researchers, especially those interested in the psychobiology of personality, no longer use the MMPI.

Projective tests of personality

Projective tests of personality are different in form from objective ones and are derived from psychodynamic theories of personality. Psychoanalytically oriented psychologists believe that behaviour is determined by unconscious processes more than by conscious ones. Thus, they believe that a test that asks straightforward questions is unlikely to tap the real roots of an individual's personality characteristics.

Projective tests are designed to be ambiguous so that the person's answers will be more revealing than simple agreement or disagreement with statements provided by objective tests. The assumption of projective tests is that an individual will 'project' his or her personality into the ambiguous situation and thus make responses that give clues to this personality. In addition, the ambiguity of the test makes it unlikely that subjects will have preconceived notions about which answers are socially desirable. Thus, it will be difficult for a subject to give biased answers in an attempt to look better (or worse) than he or she actually is.

The Rorschach Inkblot Test

One of the oldest projective tests of personality is the Rorschach Inkblot Test, published in 1921 by Hermann Rorschach, a Swiss psychiatrist. The Rorschach Inkblot Test consists of ten pictures of inkblots, originally made by spilling ink on a piece of paper that was subsequently folded in half, producing an image that is symmetrical in relation to the line of the fold. Five of the inkblots are black and white, and five are colour. The participant is shown each card and asked to describe what it looks like. Then the cards are shown again, and the participant is asked to point out the features he or she used to determine what was seen. The responses and the nature of the features the participant uses to make them are scored on several dimensions.

In the following example described by Pervin (1975), a person's response to a particular inkblot might be 'Two bears with their paws touching one another playing a game or could be they are fighting and the red is the blood from the fighting'. The classification of this response, also described by Pervin, would be: large detail of the blot was used, good form was used, movement was noted, colour was used in the response about blood, an animal was seen, and a popular response (two bears) was made. A possible interpretation of the response might be:

'Subject starts off with popular response and animals expressing playful, "childish" behaviour. Response is then given in terms of hostile act with accompanying inquiry. Pure colour response and blood content suggest he may have difficulty controlling his response to the environment. Is a playful, childlike exterior used by him to disguise hostile, destructive feelings that threaten to break out in his dealings with the environment?' (Pervin, 1975, p. 37)

Although the interpretation of people's responses to the Rorschach Inkblot Test was originally based on psychoanalytical theory, many investigators have used it in an empirical fashion. That is, a variety of different scoring methods have been devised, and the scores obtained by these methods have been correlated with clinical diagnoses, as investigators have done with people's scores on the MMPI. However, the validity of these scoring techniques and the validity of the test in general is questionable (Groth-Marnat, 1997).

The Thematic Apperception Test

Another popular projective test, the Thematic Apperception Test (TAT), was developed in 1938 by the American psychologists Henry Murray and C.D. Morgan to measure various psychological needs. People are shown a picture of a very ambiguous situation and are asked to tell a story about what is happening in the picture, explaining the situation, what led up to it, what the characters are thinking and saying, and what the final outcome will be. Presumably, the participants will 'project' themselves into the scene, and their stories will reflect their own needs. As you might imagine, scoring is difficult and requires a great deal of practice and skill. The tester attempts to infer the psychological needs expressed in the stories. Consider the responses of one woman to several TAT cards, along with a clinician's interpretation of these responses (Phares, 1979). The questions asked by the examiner are in parentheses.

> Card 3BM. Looks like a little boy crying for something he can't have. (Why is he crying?) Probably because he can't go somewhere. (How will it turn out?) Probably sit there and sob hisself to sleep. Card 3GF. Looks like her boyfriend might have let her down. She hurt his feelings. He's closed the door on her. (What did he say?) I don't know. Card 10. Looks like there's sorrow here. Grieving about something. (About what?) Looks like maybe one of the children's passed away.
>
> Interpretation: The TAT produced responses that were uniformly indicative of unhappiness, threat, misfortune, a lack of control over environmental forces. None of the test responses were indicative of satisfaction, happy endings, etc. ... In summary, the test results point to an individual who is anxious and, at the same time, depressed. (Phares, 1979, p. 273)

The pattern of responses in this case is quite consistent; few people would disagree with the conclusion that the woman is sad and depressed. However, not all people provide such clear-cut responses. As you might expect, interpreting differences in the stories of people who are relatively well adjusted is much more difficult. As a result, distinguishing among people with different but normal personality traits is hard.

One major problem with the TAT is in quantifying responses, such as the ones above. Often, responses are analysed qualitatively which makes assessing the reliability of the test difficult. Others have argued that subjecting the test to quantitative rigorous examination defeats the object of using the test which is to help guide a clinician's assessment of a patient's personality. However, even here, there are problems in that there is little agreement between clinicians regarding the assessment of the individual's responses on the TAT (Groth-Marnat, 1997).

Evaluation of projective tests

Most empirical studies have found that projective tests such as the Rorschach Inkblot Test and the TAT have poor reliability and little validity. For example, Eron (1950) found no differences between the scores of people who were in mental hospitals and college students. In a review of over three hundred studies, Lundy (1985) found that the validity of the TAT appears to be lower when it is administered by an authority figure, in a classroom setting or when it is represented as a test. Lundy (1988) suggests that in such situations, the participants are likely to realise that they are talking about themselves when they tell a story about the cards and may be careful about what they say.

Even if people taking the TAT are not on their guards, their scores are especially sensitive to their moods (Masling, 1960). So the scores they receive on one day are often very different from those they receive on another day. But a test of personality is supposed to measure enduring traits that persist over time and in a variety of situations. The TAT has also been criticised for potential sex bias, mostly because of male-dominated themes, such as power, ambition and status, used to score the test (Worchel et al., 1990).

The reliability and validity of the Rorschach Inkblot Test are also rather low. One study that used the most reliable scoring method found little or no correlation between subjects' scores on the Rorschach and their scores on six objective tests of personality (Greenwald, 1991).

If projective tests such as the Rorschach and the TAT have been found to be of low reliability and validity, why do many clinical psychologists and psychiatrists continue to use them? The primary reason seems to be tradition. The use of these tests has a long history and the rationale for the tests is consistent with psychodynamic explanations of personality. Many psychodynamic and clinical psychologists still argue that the tests are valuable for discovering and evaluating inner determinants of personality (Watkins, 1991).

Psychology in action

Do men's and women's personalities differ?

From a very early age, people in all cultures learn that boys and girls and men and women are different in at least two ways – physically and psychologically. The psychological differences often are more difficult to detect than the physical differences, but, nonetheless, males and females tend not only to perceive aspects of their environments differently, but also to behave differently under some circumstances.

People in all cultures hold certain beliefs, called stereotypes, about differences between males and females. A stereotype is

Psychology in action continued

a belief that people possess certain qualities because of their membership in a particular group, in this case, a sex. In general, stereotypes are more flattering about men than women: men are stereotyped to be more competent, independent, decisive and logical whereas women are stereotyped to be less competent, competitive, ambitious, independent and active (Broverman *et al.*, 1972; Pearson *et al.*, 1991). We will come back to stereotypes in more detail in the next chapter.

Thousands of psychological studies of sex differences do not confirm most of these stereotypes. In terms of personality, males and females are actually more alike than different. For instance, there seem to be few significant differences between the sexes in terms of the personality variables, such as introversion and extroversion, associated with intelligence (Snow and Weinstock, 1990), friendships (Jones, 1991), or perceived career success (Poole *et al.*, 1991).

Research has revealed some sex differences in personality characteristics related to social behaviour. One social behaviour that shows large sex differences is aggression. During play, young boys often display more aggression than do young girls (Fabes and Eisenberg, 1992). In a recent American longitudinal study of elementary and high school students, males where shown to be more aggressive than were females and patterns of aggression were found to be less stable for males than for females (Woodall and Matthews, 1993).

However, sex differences in aggression may vary in different cultures. In some cultures and subcultures, girls may join gangs that are involved in aggressive activities. For example, in Chihuahua, Mexico, a girl being initiated into a gang must fistfight a gang member (Bower, 1991). Girl gangs often join their 'brother' gangs in defending their turf against other male gangs. Girl gangs also fight other girl gangs, and such fights may involve knifefighting and rockthrowing as well as fistfighting.

Several other sex differences related to personality and social behaviour have recently been documented. Males tend to emerge as leaders when the group to which they belong needs to accomplish a specific task. Females tend to emerge as leaders when the groups to which they belong stress interpersonal relationships (Eagly and Karau, 1991). Females tend to be more empathetic and tend to offer assistance to others when the situation demands comforting others. Men are more likely to offer assistance when the situation demands physical aid (Eisenberg *et al.*, 1991). Likewise, females tend to be more empathetic and expressive in their relationships while males tend to be less intimate (Buss, 1995).

In a review of recent advances in behaviour genetic research related to personality, Rose (1995) concluded that heredity accounts for a large segment of the variability in personality traits among individuals and may also explain continuity and changes in personality over the lifespan.

Unfortunately, not much is known about how genes influence sex differences in personality and behaviour. The only thing we can say with any certainty is that personality differences between the sexes seem likely to have evolved as a direct result of the biological differences between males and females with respect to the division of labour required by sexual reproduction, as described in Chapter 3 (Loehlin, 1992; Tooby and Cosmides, 1990). For example, because of their greater physical and biological investment in reproduction, females may have developed tendencies to become more empathetic and interpersonally skilled. These traits would appear to be advantageous with respect to soliciting support from the father and others during pregnancy and childrearing (Buss, 1995). And because of their larger size and greater strength, males may have evolved tendencies towards hunting, fighting and protecting their families and social unit. In modern times, these behaviours may translate into aggression and leadership tendencies. Females still have strong tendencies to be empathetic and skilled interpersonal communicators, most likely because cultural evolution has favoured these behaviours.

While the genetic and evolutionary contributions to sex differences in personality remain matters of speculation, the cultural origins of such differences seem clearer and would appear to centre on the histories, environmental conditions, economic structures and survival needs of different cultures (Wade and Tavris, 1994). That is, the behavioural tendencies and personality traits of males and females vary from culture to culture, depending on the specific conditions under which members of each culture live.

For example, consider how males and females in three different New Guinea tribes are expected to act (Harris, 1991). Among the Arapesh, both men and women are expected to be co-operative and sympathetic, much as we expect the ideal Western mother to be. Among the Mundugumor, both men and women are expected to be fierce and aggressive, similar to what we might expect of the men in our culture whom we call 'macho'. Finally, among the Tchambuli, women shave their heads, are boisterous and provide food; the men tend to focus on art, their hairstyles, and gossiping about women.

As living conditions change, so does a culture's conception of the behaviours and personality traits appropriate to sex. For instance, as Wade and Tavris (1994) point out, the twentieth century has witnessed two unprecedented advances in technology, both of which have important implications for what most Western cultures consider to be sex-appropriate traits. First, because of advances in contraceptive technology, women may choose to limit the number of children they bear and make plans for when they bear them. Second, in today's job market, less emphasis is placed on physical skills and more on intellectual skills.

Questions to think about

Assessment of personality

- Would you be able to derive more information about personality from a trait inventory or a projective test? Why?

- Why might responses to inkblots be unreliable measures of personality?

- We often try to deny or ignore things we do not like or those we disagree with. Do you think that such factors would influence your ability to assess impartially trait or psychodynamic theories of personality?

- What kinds of personality differences between males and females have you noticed? Are these differences genuine or are they a product of the stereotypes you hold of the sexes? How do you know? Would your behaviour be an example of self-fulfilling prophecy – you behave towards them in a way that produces behaviour that confirms your hypothesis?

- Would having a knowledge of personality theory make you react with your friends and colleagues any differently?

Key terms

personality *p.478*
personality types *p.479*
personality trait *p.479*
extroversion *p.480*
introversion *p.480*
neuroticism *p.480*
emotional stability *p.480*
psychoticism *p.480*
self-control *p.480*
five-factor model *p.482*
social learning theory *p.486*
expectancy *p.486*
observational learning *p.487*
reciprocal determinism *p.487*
self-efficacy *p.487*

person variables *p.487*
locus of control *p.490*
psychodynamic *p.491*
unconscious *p.492*
id *p.492*
libido *p.492*
pleasure principle *p.492*
ego *p.492*
reality principle *p.492*
superego *p.492*
conscience *p.492*
ego-ideal *p.492*
manifest content *p.492*
latent content *p.492*
free association *p.493*
defence mechanisms *p.493*
repression *p.493*

reaction formation *p.493*
projection *p.494*
sublimation *p.494*
rationalisation *p.494*
conversion *p.494*
fixation *p.494*
oral stage *p.494*
anal stage *p.494*
phallic stage *p.495*
Oedipus complex *p.495*
Electra complex *p.495*
latency period *p.495*
genital stage *p.495*
collective unconscious *p.495*
archetypes *p.495*
striving for superiority *p.496*

basic orientations *p.496*
humanistic approach *p.497*
self-actualisation *p.497*
conditions of worth *p.498*
unconditional positive regard *p.499*
objective personality tests *p.500*
Minnesota Multiphasic Personality Inventory (MMPI) *p.500*
projective tests *p.501*
Rorschach Inkblot Test *p.501*
Thematic Apperception Test (TAT) *p.502*

CHAPTER REVIEW

Trait theories of personality

- We can conceive of personality characteristics as types or traits. The earliest theory of personality classified people into types according to their predominant humour, or body fluid. Today, most psychologists conceive of personality differences as being represented by degree, not kind.

- Personality traits are the factors that underlie patterns of behaviour. Presumably, these factors are biological

in nature, although they may be the products of learning as well as heredity.

- The search for core personality traits began with Allport, who studied how everyday words are used to describe personality characteristics. Although he never isolated a core set of traits, his work inspired others to continue the search for such traits.

- Several researchers developed their theories of personality through factor analysis, a statistical method of reducing a large amount of data to two or three single themes or ideas (called factors).

- Cattell's analyses indicated the existence of sixteen personality factors; Eysenck's research suggested that personality is determined by three dimensions: extroversion (versus introversion), neuroticism (versus emotional stability) and psychoticism (versus self-control).

- McCrae and Costa's five-factor model, based on an analysis of words used to describe people's behavioural traits, includes extroversion, neuroticism, agreeableness, openness and conscientiousness. There is strong cross-cultural agreement on the first three factors but not on the fifth.

Psychobiological approaches

- Studies of twins and adopted children indicate that personality factors, especially extroversion, neuroticism and psychoticism, are affected strongly by genetic factors. However, there is little evidence for an effect of common family environment, largely because an individual's environment is strongly affected by heredity factors, such as personality and physical attributes.

- Important personality traits are likely to be the products of neural systems responsible for reinforcement, punishment and arousal.

- Zuckerman believes that extroversion is caused by a sensitive reinforcement system, neuroticism is caused by a sensitive punishment system (which includes the amygdala), and psychoticism is caused by the combination of a deficient punishment system and an abnormally high optimum level of arousal.

- Few studies have directly tested the hypothesis that personality differences can be accounted for by biological differences. One experiment, however, indicates that childhood shyness is a relatively stable trait that can be seen in the way children react to strangers and strange situations. The differences between shy and non-shy children manifest themselves in physiological responses controlled by the amygdala that indicate the presence of stress.

The social learning approach

- Social learning theory blends Skinner's notion of reinforcement with cognitive concepts such as expectancy to explain social interaction and personality.

- According to Bandura, people learn the relation between their behaviour and its consequences by observing how others' behaviour is rewarded and punished. In this way, people learn to expect that certain consequences will follow certain behaviours.

- Bandura has also argued that personality is the result of reciprocal determinism – the interaction of behaviour, environment and person variables such as perception.

- The extent to which a person is likely to attempt to change his or her environment is related to self-efficacy, the expectation that he or she will be successful in producing the change. People with low self-efficacy tend not to try to alter their environments; the opposite is true for people with high self-efficacy.

- Mischel has argued that personality differences are due largely to person variables – individual differences in cognition. These variables include competencies, encoding strategies and personal constructs, expectancies, subjective values, and self-regulatory systems and plans.

- Rotter's research has shown that locus of control – the extent to which people believe that their behaviour is controlled by person variables or by environmental variables – is also an important determinant of personality.

- In the past, psychologists disagreed about the relative importance of situations and personality traits in determining a person's behaviour. It now appears that personality traits are correlated with behaviour, especially when multiple observations of particular behaviours are made.

- In addition, some situations (such as a funeral or a red traffic light) are more powerful than others, exerting more control on people's behaviour. Traits and situations interact: some people are affected more than others by a particular situation, and people tend to choose the types of situation in which they find themselves. People's personality traits directly affect situational variables.

The psychodynamic approach

- Freud believed that the mind is full of conflicts between the primitive urges of the id and the internalised prohibitions of the superego.

- According to Freud, these conflicts tend to be resolved through compromise formation and through ego defences such as repression, sublimation and reaction formation. His theory of psychosexual development, a progression through the oral, anal, phallic and genital stages, provided the basis for a theory of personality and personality disorders.

- Freud's followers, most notably Jung, Adler, Horney and Erikson, embraced different aspects of Freud's theory, disagreed with other aspects, and embellished still other aspects.

- Jung disagreed with Freud about the structure of the unconscious and the role of sexuality in personality development, and saw libido as a positive life force.

- Adler also disagreed with Freud on the importance of sexuality. Instead, Adler emphasised the need to compensate for our inferiority and our innate desire to help others as the major forces in personality development.

- Horney argued that personality is the result of the strategies and behaviours people use to cope with anxiety, which she believed is the fundamental problem that all people must overcome in the course of normal personality development.

- Erikson maintained that personality development is more a matter of psychosocial processes than of psychosexual processes. He viewed personality development as involving eight stages, each of which involves coping with a major conflict or crises. Resolution of the conflict allows the person to pass to the next stage; failure to resolve it inhibits normal personality development.

- Although Freud was a brilliant and insightful thinker, his theory has not been experimentally verified, primarily because most of his concepts are unobservable and, therefore, untestable. Even though many modern psychologists do not believe his psychodynamic theory to be correct, Freud made an important contribution to psychology with his realisation that not all causes of our behaviour are available to consciousness.

The humanistic approach

- The humanistic approach attempts to understand personality and its development by focusing on the positive side of human nature and people's attempts to reach their full potential: self-actualisation.

- Maslow argued that self-actualisation is achieved only after the satisfaction of several other important but lesser needs, for example, physiological, safety and attachment needs.

- Maslow's case study analysis of people whom he believed to be self-actualised revealed several common personality characteristics including self-acceptance, a focus on addressing cultural problems and not personal ones, spontaneity, preservation of privacy, an appreciation of life, and possession of a few very close friends.

- According to Rogers, the key to becoming self-actualised is developing a healthy self-concept. The primary roadblocks in this quest are conditions of worth – criteria that we must meet to win the positive regard of others. Rogers maintained that too often people value themselves only to the extent that they believe other people do. As a result, they spend their lives seeking the acceptance of others instead of striving to become self-actualised. Rogers proposed that only by treating others with unconditional positive regard could we help people to realise their true potential.

- Although the humanistic approach emphasises the positive dimensions of human experience and the potential that each of us has for personal growth, it has been criticised for being unscientific. Critics argue that its concepts are vague and untestable and that it is more descriptive than explanatory.

Assessment of personality

- Objective tests contain items that can be answered and scored objectively, such as true/false or multiple-choice questions.

- One of the most important objective personality tests is the Minnesota Multiphasic Personality Inventory (MMPI), which was empirically devised to discriminate among people who had been assigned various psychiatric diagnoses. It has since been used widely in research on personality.

- The MMPI's validity scales have been challenged by researchers who suggest that most people's responses can be taken at face value. More recently, researchers interested in personality have turned to tests not based on people with mental disorders, such as the NEO-PI.

- Projective tests, such as the Rorschach Inkblot Test and the Thematic Apperception Test, contain ambiguous items that elicit answers that presumably reveal aspects of participants' personalities. Because answers can vary widely, test administrators must receive special training to interpret them. Unfortunately, evidence suggests that the reliability and validity of such tests is not particularly high.

- The few sex differences which exist in personality seem to be related to social interaction. Although personality traits have been shown to have high heritability, cultural variables – living conditions related to a specific culture's traditions, economy, environmental conditions and survival needs – play a powerful role in shaping personality and behaviour.

- As these conditions change, so do the types of personality trait and behaviour necessary for survival during culture change. Thus, we should not be surprised when both males and females behave in ways that are contrary to the common stereotype.

Suggestions for further reading

Brody, N. and Ehrlichman, H. (1998). *Personality Psychology*. Harlow: Prentice Hall.

Buss, A. H. (1995). *Personality: Temperament, social behaviour and the self*. Boston: Allyn and Bacon.

Hall, C.S., Lindzey, G. and Campell, J. (1997). *Theories of Personality* (4th edition). Chichester: Wiley.

Monte, C.F. (1994). *Beneath the Mask* (5th edition). London: Harcourt Brace.

Pervin, L.A. and John, O.P. (1996). *Personality: Theories and research* (7th edition). Chichester: Wiley.

DeRaad, B. (1998). Five big, Big Five issues: Rationale, content, structure, status and cross-cultural assessment. *European Psychologist*, 3, 2, 113–124.

Eysenck, H. (1985). *Decline and Fall of the Freudian Empire*. London: Penguin Books.

Hampson, S.E. and Coleman, A. (1994). *Individual Differences in Personality*. Harlow: Longman.

Kline, P. (1994). *Personality: The psychometric view*. London: Routledge.

Each of these texts will introduce you to further topics of discussion in personality. Because, as you can imagine, the scope for study in personality is large, there is a large number of books that you can read. The Brody/Ehrlichman, Buss, Hall et al. and Pervin/John are good basic introductory books on personality. Monte's book is very detailed and Kline's book is a succinct account of psychometric approaches to personality, focusing largely on trait theories. Hampson and Coleman's book is an edited collection of chapters designed for undergraduates and looks at individual differences as well as personality. DeRaad's article looks at the development and cross-cultural applicability of the Big Five. Finally, Eysenck's book is an incisive analysis of psychoanalytic theory and psychoanalysis and an excellent example of a provocative, well written critique.

Journals to consult

British Journal of Psychiatry
British Journal of Psychology
European Journal of Personality
European Psychologist
International Journal of Psychology
Journal of Personality
Journal of Personality and Social Psychology
Journal of Research in Personality
Perceptual and Motor Skills
Personality and Individual Differences
Personality and Social Psychology Bulletin
Psychological Reports
Psychological Science

Website addresses

http://pmc.psych.nwu.edu/personality
The Personality Project at Northwestern University website. This excellent site has links to further reading, personality descriptions, related websites and much more.

http://galton.psych.nwu.edu/greatideas.html
The Great Ideas in Personality website provides an account of exactly that.

15

SOCIAL PSYCHOLOGY

Michael A. Hogg and Dominic Abrams

During the first 21 days of the World Cup soccer tournament 298 English supporters were arrested. Yet many described themselves as conventional law-abiding citizens, only there to enjoy the football.

On the day before England's match against Tunisia, 100 Tunisia supporters, including drummers and flag-waving youths, marched through the midst of a large group of England fans in Marseilles who were drinking. As the Tunisia fans turned to go back, some 200 England fans chased them up the street, both groups throwing missiles at one another. The riot police intervened with tear gas. Later, nearly 100 England fans and 200 Tunisia fans fought with one another, using chairs, belts, bottles and fists. The police eventually restored order. One café owner, Anastasia Philipine, was quoted as saying:

> 'Yesterday there were nice English people here who were brought up to be normal and I thought it went OK. Then, when they attacked, it was like a Western film and we were stuck in the middle like the Indians.'

A few days later, England and Argentina were due to play and tension was high. On the train from Lyon to Grenoble was Paul Birch from East London, a 43-year-old engineer, married with a 7-year-old son. Sitting opposite him was a French film stuntman, 33-year-old Eric Frachet. Frachet smiled at Birch, who perceived Frachet as an Argentinian fan who was mocking him. Birch stabbed and killed Frachet. He later wrote to Frachet's family hinting at the reasons for his actions. He claimed that to categorise him as a dangerous psychopath would be wrong. He had no previous criminal record and no medical history. He claimed that he had been chased over a period of three days by English right-wing Nazi hooligans, and had been:

> 'Set up ... trapped, chased and intimidated into killing Eric, but by the time of the murder I did not know where I was or what time of day it was ... [they] had done a good job on me.'

Sources: Daily Mail 29/1/99, Daily Telegraph 4/7/98, 23/6/98, 16/6/98

Social psychology is the study of human interaction. This includes how people think about and interact with individuals and groups, how groups think about and interact with one another, and how individuals and groups affect, and even form, their own thoughts and behaviours. This chapter examines how we process and store information about ourselves and about other people, how we form and maintain attitudes, how prejudice and discrimination develop (and how they can be reduced), how we construct 'norms' of behaviour, and how and why we conform to these norms. It concludes with a section which ranges from aggression, through interpersonal attraction to love.

What you should be able to do after reading Chapter 15

- Understand how we process, store and use information about ourselves and other people.
- Understand how attitudes are formed and changed, and how our attitudes are related to our behaviour.
- Understand why people are prejudiced and what we might be able to do to reduce prejudice.
- Describe the many ways in which we are influenced by groups and individuals – how norms arise, why people conform, why people obey orders, when people may help out in emergencies, why people behave differently in groups, and why groups may make poor or extreme decisions.
- Know some of the causes of aggression, attraction and loving.

Questions to think about

- If you try hard to suppress your prejudices, do you think they will gradually disappear?
- Are you more likely to change your attitude towards a boring activity if someone attractive or someone unattractive persuades you to engage in the activity?
- Will contact between racial groups reduce racial prejudice?
- If someone ordered you to do something that caused serious harm to another person, would you do it?
- Are men more aggressive than women?

Social psychology: an introduction

Most human activities are social. We spend most of our waking hours interacting with, thinking about, or being directly or indirectly influenced by other people. Our behaviour affects the way others act and, in turn, their behaviour affects our actions. The field of psychology that studies our social nature is called social psychology. It is, in the words of Gordon Allport (1968), the study of 'how the thoughts, feelings, and behaviour of individuals are influenced by the actual, imagined, or implied presence of others' (p. 3). In this chapter we explore the way in which people, as individuals or groups, affect one another. We examine the complex interplay of basic cognitive processes and structures that we use to process and store information, and the nature of human relations and interactions that occur in everyday life.

In a very real sense we are all social psychologists – just to get by in life we all need to develop an understanding of why people behave as they do, what causes particular behaviours, and what effect our behaviour has on others. These common-sense understandings are often quite accurate, but sometimes they are not. For example, we 'know' that, 'birds of a feather flock together' (similarity leads to attraction), but we also 'know' that, 'opposites attract'. Which is correct? Many of us may also think that friendship between people from different racial groups should reduce prejudice – but does it? How can we be sure? Under what circumstances is someone most likely to help someone in distress? To answer these questions, social psychologists use a wide range of scientific methods including laboratory experiments, field experiments, surveys, and observation of naturally occurring behaviour. They develop formal theories about human behaviour that, unlike common-sense theories, are carefully grounded in data from systematic and well controlled research. These theories sometimes confirm common-sense knowledge, but sometimes they do not, and many theories are actually about how people develop and use common-sense social psychological knowledge in the first place.

Social understanding: social cognition and social knowledge

At the heart of social behaviour is a person's ability to make sense of a social situation in order to know what to expect and what to do. The kind of explanations and interpretations available to people reflect the predominant social representations, cultural values and norms in society.

For example, Moscovici (1976) explored how Freudian concepts have become accepted and used in mass culture to account for individuals' behaviour. These social representations of the way people's minds work provide an evolving framework for making sense of the world, and they are formed through many means, such as mass communication, scientific and religious movements, and intergroup relationships (Moscovici, 1983).

Social representations have important consequences for the way we deal with one another. For example, whether the explanation for abnormal behaviour is conceived as having a moral, biological, religious, physical or social origin will determine how it is responded to by policymakers and the public (Jodelet, 1991). When the Yorkshire Ripper was convicted for multiple rapes and murders in England, he was deemed to be criminal rather than insane. Such distinctions are dependent more on society's current social representations of good and evil, sanity and insanity, than they are on objectively measurable criteria.

Given the existence of particular social representations, values and norms, social cognition processes affect the way we understand, use and respond to our social environment (Augoustinos and Walker, 1995). For example, Echebarria-Echabe et al. (1994) examined how smokers and non-smokers account for the causes of smoking. Two representations appeared to be common, one which emphasised the psychological weakness of people who fall prey to the attractions of tobacco, and another (defensive representation) which associated smoking with positive social factors and positive stereotypes of smokers. When the potential conflict between non-smokers and smokers was made more salient, smokers became significantly more likely to adhere to the defensive representation.

Our ability to interpret social situations involves a range of basic cognitive processes, including memory for people, places and events; concept formation skills; and, more fundamentally, sensory and perceptual abilities (Fiske and Taylor, 1991). A central, and over the past twenty years dominant, theme in social psychology is the development of our knowledge of these basic processes in understanding social cognition – how people attend to, perceive, interpret, store and respond to social information.

Forming and storing impressions of people

All of us form impressions of others: friends, neighbours, professors, Australians – virtually everyone we meet. We assign all sorts of characteristics to them. We may, for example, think of someone as friendly or hostile, helpful or selfish. A major task of social psychology is to understand how we form these impressions. In Solomon Asch's (1952) words, 'How do the perceptions, thoughts, and motives of one person become known to other persons?' (p. 143). To answer questions like this, psychologists study impression formation, the way in which we form impressions of others and attribute specific characteristics to them. As noted by Asch over four decades ago, our impressions of others are formed by more complex rules than just a simple sum of the characteristics that we use to describe people.

Central traits

Asch (1946) was able to show that when people form impressions of other people, some perceptual features seem to have more influence than others in the final impression. For example, your impression of someone may be swayed by whether people are intelligent or not, or whether people are musical or not. Kelly (1955) refers to these idiosyncratic views of what is most important in characterising people as personal constructs. Or, in one context, intelligence may be a more relevant dimension than musical ability (for example, evaluating someone as a member of a research team), whereas in another context the opposite may be true (evaluating someone as a band member). Asch called characteristics that are disproportionately influential in impression formation central traits. Central traits are very useful for organising and summarising large amounts of diverse information about a person you encounter.

To demonstrate this, Asch (1946) provided participants with a list of traits describing a hypothetical person. Some received a list that included the trait 'warm', whereas others received an identical list, except that the trait 'warm' was replaced by 'cold'. Participants given the list including 'warm' were more likely to see the person as generous, happy and altruistic. But not all traits seemed to be so important. When the words 'polite' and 'blunt' were substituted for 'warm' and 'cold', no differences were observed in participants' impressions. Our perception of others, then, seems to be based partially on central traits – which can vary from context to context, or from person to person.

The primacy effect

Another important influence on impression formation is called the primacy effect. Getting to know someone takes time and usually requires many interactions. Perhaps the first time you saw someone was at a party when he was loud and boisterous, having a good time with his friends. But later, you learn that he is a mathematics student with excellent grades who is actually generally reserved. What is your general impression of this person: loud and boisterous, or bright and shy? To determine whether first impressions might overpower later impressions, Asch (1946) presented one of the following lists of words to each of two groups of participants:

Intelligent, industrious, impulsive, critical, stubborn, envious

Envious, stubborn, critical, impulsive, industrious, intelligent

Notice that these lists contain the same words but in reverse order. After they saw the list, Asch asked the participants to describe the personality of the person having these characteristics. People who heard the first list evaluated the person much more favourably than people who heard the second list – a clear primacy effect.

Although more recent information can sometimes be influential (for example when there is a lot of information and we are distracted), the general rule is that first impressions have the most impact and are the most enduring.

Negativity bias and social judgeability

The impressions we form of people are also disproportionately influenced by negative information – although we like to think the best of people, bad impressions, once formed, are very difficult to change, whereas good impressions can easily change. One reason for this is that people are probably especially sensitive to negative information because it can signify potential harm or danger (Skowronski and Carlston, 1989).

We have seen that impression formation is influenced by the context in which people form impressions – the centrality, evaluative implications and order of presentation of information are all governed by the interactive context. So, it would not be a surprise to learn that sometimes there are social conventions and norms (sometimes even laws) that actually discourage us from forming impressions at all. For example, most of us would resist forming impressions based on race, gender or disability, particularly if we were serving on a job selection committee. People make an assessment of social judgeability, a perception of whether there is a legitimate and adequate basis for judging a specific person before forming an impression. Sometimes, merely believing one is in a position to make a judgement (but in reality lacking accurate or diagnostic evidence) can result in unwarranted evaluations of other people (Leyens *et al.*, 1992).

Schemas

A central theme of cognitive psychology is the concept of schema (schemata is the plural, though in social cognition we refer to 'schemas'), a mental framework or body of knowledge that organises and synthesises information about a person, place, or thing – in social cognition schemas also exist for events (for example, how to behave at restaurant) and social groups (for example, Algerians, the elderly). Schemas aid us in interpreting the world. The first time you visited your psychology tutor in his or her office, for example, there were probably few surprises. The schema that you have of 'tutor' guided your interactions with him or her. However, you would probably be surprised if you saw that your tutor's office was filled with bungy jumping trophies, autographed photos of heavy metal bands, or dead animals mounted on the walls as hunting trophies.

Such possessions are probably inconsistent with your impression of psychology tutors.

As an example of how schemas guide our interpretations, try to understand the following passage:

> 'The procedure is actually quite simple. First you arrange things into different groups. Of course, one pile may be sufficient depending on how much there is to do. ... It is important not to overdo things. That is, it is better to do too few things at once than too many. In the short run this may not seem important, but complications can easily arise. A mistake can be expensive as well. At first the whole procedure will seem complicated. Soon, however, it will become just another facet of life.' (Bransford and Johnson, 1972, p. 722)

Does this passage make sense to you? What if I tell you that the title of the passage is 'Washing clothes'? Now you can interpret the passage easily, for the sentences make perfect sense within the context of your schema for washing clothes. Not surprisingly, research has demonstrated that understanding is improved when people know the title of the passage before it is read (Bransford and Johnson, 1972).

Stereotypes

Schemas of social groups are particularly significant because they characterise large numbers of people in terms of a small number of properties that submerges the variety of differences that exist between people. Schemas of social groups are almost always shared among people in one group. For example, British people often believe that Americans are brash, the French think the British are cold, and so forth. Schemas of social groups are probably best described as stereotypes, and because they are closely associated with prejudice and discrimination we will return to them later in this chapter (Leyens et al., 1994).

According to Tajfel (1981), stereotypes are learned early in childhood through normal socialisation rather than direct experience. Research suggests that childrens' use of stereotypes and expression of negative attitudes towards outgroups peaks at around the age of 7 and then declines by 8 or 9 years of age. This may reflect cognitive developmental changes that affect the way children understand the meaning of categories and attributes, and changes in role-taking skills (Aboud, 1988). However, the content of stereotypes and the selection of groups to which they are applied have their origin in the history of relations between social groups. Stereotypes serve to justify that history, make people's experiences and anticipations meaningful, and, since images of another group (the outgroup) are generally less favourable than images of one's own group (the ingroup), provide a relatively positive evaluation of oneself. Once someone is categorised as a member of a particular group, the schema of that group (stereotype) influences the impression of that person. For example, if students believe that professors are pompous, boring and opinionated, then once you, as a student categorise someone as a professor you will automatically tend to assume that he or she is pompous, boring and opinionated, and that impression will influence the entire interaction.

Like other schemas, stereotypes are relatively automatically activated in particular contexts: however much we might like to avoid stereotyping it seems we have only limited conscious control over the process – see the discussion above of social judgeability (Bargh, 1989). In fact, according to Macrae et al. (1994), if we try too hard to suppress stereotypes we can actually strengthen the automatic link in our mind between the social group and its stereotype.

The self

We also have schemas about ourselves. If someone asked you who you are, how would you respond? You might tell them your name, that you are a student, and perhaps that you are also an athlete or have a part-time job. Alternatively, you could tell them about your family, your nationality, ethnicity or religion. There are many ways you could potentially describe yourself, all of which would reflect your self-concept – your knowledge, feelings, and ideas about yourself. In its totality, the self is a person's distinct individuality. At the core of the self-concept is the self-schema – a mental framework that represents and synthesises information about who you are. The self-schema, then, is a cognitive structure that organises the knowledge, feelings and ideas that constitute the self-concept.

The self-concept is dynamic; it changes with experience. Some researchers, such as Markus and Nurius (1986), argue that we should think of ourselves in terms of a working self-concept that changes as we have new experiences or receive feedback about our behaviour. That is, each of us has many potential selves that we might become depending on experience. Can you imagine the different twists and turns that your life might take and how your self-concept might be affected as a result? Can you imagine the circumstances that might lead you to change your major degree subject, drop out of university altogether, or get married or divorced, and how your self-concept might be affected? Consider how people who have experienced a traumatic life event (for example, the death of a family member or friend) responded when they were asked to describe their current and possible future selves (Porter et al., 1984). They all reported that they were worried, upset, depressed and lacked control over their lives. That is, everyone described similar current selves. Nonetheless, some people described different sorts of possible future selves. The people who had not yet recovered from the traumatic event predicted that they would be unhappy and lonely. The people in the recovered group predicted just the opposite: they saw themselves as being happy, self-confident and having many friends. Thus, thinking of ourselves only in terms of who we are at present does not accurately reflect the kind of person we might become.

Culture plays a powerful role in the formation of the self-concept, the perceptions one forms of others, and the extent to which others may influence the development of one's self-concept. For example, in Western cultures, parents may encourage their children to eat all their dinner by admonishing them to 'think about all the starving children in Africa and how lucky you are not to be in their situation', while in Japan, parents often urge their finicky children to 'think of the farmer who worked so hard to produce this rice for you; if you don't eat it he will feel bad, for his efforts will have been in vain' (Markus and Kitayama, 1991). Western cultures often emphasise the uniqueness of the individual and an appreciation of being different from others – these are individualistic cultures. In contrast, Japanese and other Eastern cultures often emphasise paying attention to others and the relatedness of the individual and others – these are collectivist cultures.

Markus and Kitayama (1991) have conceptualised two construals of the self that reflect such cultural differences (to construe something is to interpret it or explain its meaning). The independent construal emphasises the uniqueness of the self, its autonomy from others, and self-reliance. Although other people have an influence on a person's behaviour, a person's self-concept is largely defined independently of others. The interdependent construal emphasises the interconnectedness of people and the role that others play in developing an individual's self-concept. In the interdependent construal, what others think of the individual or do to the individual matters – the person is extremely sensitive to others and strives to form strong social bonds with them.

Markus and Kitayama's own research supports their model. For example, they have shown that students from India (a collectivist Eastern culture) judge the self to be more similar to others, whereas American students (members of an individualist culture) judge the self to be more dissimilar to others (Markus and Kitayama, 1991). Markus and Kitayama have also shown that Japanese students tend to associate positive feelings with interpersonal behaviours and tend not to associate such feelings with personal achievements. In contrast, American students tend to feel satisfaction in their accomplishments (Kitayama and Markus, 1992). In a similar vein, comparing workers' intentions to leave their organisations, Abrams et al. (1998) found that Japanese workers were influenced by the evaluations they expected from their friends, family and co-workers, whereas British workers were not.

This tendency for people to represent themselves more as separate individuals or more as part of a community of other people, may not only vary between individualist and collectivist cultures, but it may also vary within cultures from one context to another. Social identity theorists (for example, Hogg and Abrams, 1988) believe that one's self-concept comprises a large array of different identities that fall into two broad types: personal identities that derive from our close interpersonal relationships (such as friendships and romantic relationships) and our idiosyncratic characteristics (such as being humorous), and social identities that derive from the social groups to which we belong (ethnicity, gender, profession, age group and so on). Features of the immediate social context – situation, people, goals, activities and so forth – influence what aspect of the self-concept we experience and use to process information and plan action in that particular context. Social identities are uniquely associated with group behaviours, for example the stereotypes referred to above, but also other group behaviours such as conformity and discrimination that we discuss later in this chapter (Turner et al., 1987).

Attribution

As mentioned right at the start of this chapter, in some ways, we are all practising social psychologists (Jones, 1990). Each of us uses certain principles to construct theories about the nature and causes of other people's behaviour. We are confronted each day by many thousands of individual acts performed by other people. Some acts are important to us because they provide clues about people's personality characteristics, how they are likely to interact with us, and how they are perceiving us. If we had to pay careful attention to each of these acts – to classify them, to think about their significance, and to compare them with other observations – we would be immobilised in thought. Instead, we use schemas that often lead us to the correct conclusions. In doing so, we save time and cognitive effort.

However, as useful as these strategies may be, they sometimes lead us astray. We may unfairly categorise other people on the basis of superficial characteristics. We may uncritically adopt attitudes we were taught, to the detriment of other people and of ourselves. The process by which people infer the causes of other people's behaviour is called attribution (Hewstone, 1989).

Disposition versus situation

In deciding the causes of behaviour, the most important thing we need to know is whether the behaviour is a reflection of the person's disposition to behave in that way or a reflection of situational constraints that made him or her behave in that way, as we saw in Chapter 14. We need to assess the relative importance of situational and dispositional factors (Heider, 1958). Situational factors are stimuli in the environment. Dispositional factors are individual personality characteristics. One of the tasks of socialisation is to learn what behaviours are expected in various kinds of situation. Once we learn that in certain situations most people act in a specific way, we develop schemas for how we expect people to act in those situations. For example, when people are introduced, they are expected to look at each other, smile, say something like 'How do you do?' or 'It's nice to meet you', and perhaps offer to shake the other person's hand. If people act in conventional ways in given situations, we are not surprised. Their behaviour appears to be dictated by social custom – by the characteristics of the situation.

As we get to know other people, we also learn what to expect from them as individuals. We learn about their dispositions – the kinds of behaviour in which they tend to engage. We learn to characterise people as friendly, generous, suspicious, pessimistic or greedy by observing their behaviour in a variety of situations. Sometimes, we even make inferences from a single observation (Krull and Erickson, 1995). If someone's behaviour is very different from the way most people would act in a particular situation, we attribute his or her behaviour to internal or dispositional causes. For example, if we see a person refuse to hold a door open for someone in a wheelchair, we assign that person some negative dispositional characteristics.

Kelley's theory of attribution

Harold Kelley (1967) has suggested that we attribute the behaviour of other people to external (situational) or internal (dispositional) causes on the basis of consideration of three aspects of their behaviour: its consensus, its consistency and its distinctiveness (Kelley, 1967; Kelley and Michela, 1980).

Consensual behaviour – a behaviour shared by many people – is usually attributed to external causes. The behaviour is assumed to be demanded by the situation. For example, if someone asks an acquaintance for the loan of a coin to make a telephone call, we do not conclude that the person is especially generous if he or she complies. The request is reasonable and costs little; lending the money is a consensual behaviour. However, if a person has some change but refuses to lend it, we readily attribute dispositional factors such as stinginess or meanness to that person.

We also base our attributions on consistency – on whether a person's behaviour occurs reliably in the same situation. For example, if you meet someone for the first time and notice that she speaks slowly and without much expression, stands in a slouching posture, and sighs occasionally, you will probably conclude that she has a sad disposition. Now, suppose that after she has left, you mention to a friend that the young woman seems very passive. Your friend says, 'No, I know her well, and she's usually very cheerful.' With this new evidence about her behaviour you may reassess and wonder what happened to make her act so sad. If a person's pattern of behaviour is consistent, we attribute the behaviour to internal causes. Inconsistent behaviours lead us to seek external causes.

Finally, we base our attributions on distinctiveness – the extent to which a person performs a particular behaviour only in a particular situation. Behaviours that are distinctively associated with a particular situation are attributed to situational factors; those that occur in a variety of situations are attributed to dispositional factors. For example, suppose that a mother observes that her little boy is generally polite but also that whenever he plays with the child next door, he acts rudely towards her. She does not conclude that her son has a rude disposition; she probably concludes that the child next door has a bad influence on him. Because her child's rude behaviour occurs only under a distinctive circumstance (the presence of the child next door), she attributes it to external causes. Table 15.1 summarises Kelley's ideas about the factors that determine internal or external attributions.

Attributional biases

Finding out the causes of things is what science is all about. So it comes as no surprise that ordinary people in everyday circumstances are less accurate than scientists in attributing causes to behaviour. Attributional accuracy is compromised by the nature of human information processing and social cognition, but it is quite adequate for our everyday social interactional needs.

The fundamental attribution error

When attributing someone's behaviour to possible causes, an observer tends to overestimate the significance of dispositional factors and underestimate the significance of situational factors. This kind of bias is called the

Table 15.1   Kelley's theory of attribution

Principle	Attribution of external causality	Attribution of internal causality
Consensus	*High.* Person lends coin for telephone call, performing a socially acceptable behaviour	*Low.* Person refuses to lend coin and seems mean
Consistency	*Low.* Usually cheerful person acts sad and dejected; we wonder what event has caused the sadness	*High.* We meet a person who speaks slowly, slouches, and conclude that we have met a person who is sad by nature
Distinctiveness	*High.* A child is rude only when playing with a certain friend; we conclude that the friend is a bad influence	*Low.* A child acts impudently, says mean and nasty things to everyone he or she meets. We conclude that the child is rude

fundamental attribution error (Ross, 1977). For example, if we see a driver make a mistake, we are more likely to conclude that the driver is careless than to consider that external factors (for example, a crying baby in the back seat) may have temporarily distracted him.

The fundamental attribution error is remarkably potent (but see below). Even when evidence indicates otherwise, people seem to prefer dispositional explanations to situational ones. For example, consider a well known study by Jones and Harris (1967). Students read essays that other students had either freely chosen or been instructed to write in support of or in opposition to Fidel Castro. The students had to infer the writers' true attitude towards Castro. Where the writers had been free to choose, the students reasoned that those who wrote a pro-Castro essay were in favour of him, and those who wrote an anti-Castro essay were against him. Surprisingly, even when it was made quite clear that the writers had been instructed which essay to write, the students still believed that those who wrote a pro-Castro essay were in favour of him, and those who wrote an anti-Castro essay were against him. The students disregarded situational factors and made a dispositional attribution, thus committing the fundamental attribution error.

Actor–observer effect

In contrast, when trying to explain our own behaviour, we are much more likely to attribute it to characteristics of the situation than to our own disposition, a phenomenon called the actor–observer effect. In other words, we tend to see our own behaviour as relatively variable and strongly influenced by the situation, while we see the behaviour of others as more stable and due to personal dispositions. When we try to explain our own behaviour, we are not likely to make the fundamental attribution error (Sande *et al.*, 1988).

A study of college-age male–female couples demonstrates the actor–observer effect (Orvis *et al.*, 1976). Each partner was asked separately to describe disagreements in the relationship, such as arguments and criticism. Each partner was also asked to explain his or her attribution of the underlying causes of the disagreements. When describing his or her own behaviour, each person tended to refer to environmental circumstances, such as financial problems or not getting enough sleep. However, when describing their partners' behaviour, participants often referred to specific negative personality characteristics, such as selfishness or low commitment to the relationship.

Why do we tend to commit the fundamental attribution error when we observe the behaviour of others but not when we explain the causes of our own behaviour? Jones and Nisbett (1971) suggested two possible reasons. First, we have a different focus of attention when we view ourselves. When we ourselves are doing something, we see the world around us more clearly than we see our own behaviour. However, when we observe someone else doing something, we focus our attention on what is most salient and relevant: that person's behaviour, not the situation in which he or she is placed.

A second possible reason for these differences in attribution is that different types of information are available to us about our own behaviour and that of other people. We have more information about our own behaviour and we are thus more likely to realise that our own behaviour is often inconsistent. We also have a better notion of which stimuli we are attending to in a given situation. This difference in information leads us to conclude that the behaviour of other people is consistent and thus is a product of their personalities, whereas ours is affected by the situation in which we find ourselves.

Even though we may be aware of the difference in attributions that we make as actors or observers, this does not seem to prevent the actor–observer effect from happening. For example, Krueger *et al.* (1996) asked pairs of participants (one actor and one observer) to describe the actor on a series of trait adjectives and to rate the consistency of relevant behaviour. Participants then predicted one another's ratings. The actor–observer effect was obtained. Moreover, actors, but not observers, were aware that observers rated actors' behaviour as more consistent than actors themselves did.

The fundamental attribution error is also less 'fundamental' than was once thought. It is influenced by culture. As you might expect from our earlier comparison of individualist and collectivist cultures, it is more prevalent in the former than the latter types of society (Morris and Peng, 1994). People in individualist societies are more inclined to explain behaviour in terms of individual dispositions and freewill, whereas people in collectivist societies are more inclined to explain behaviour in terms of social obligations and situational constraints.

The fundamental attribution error is also influenced by more immediate social contexts and individual goals. For example, Schmid and Fiedler (1998) examined closing speeches made by trainee lawyers and university students acting as prosecutors or defending attorneys. Prosecutors tended to attribute internal causality to the defendants, whereas defence attorneys tried to support negative intentional attributions to the victim. When an audience of lay people was asked to judge the speeches, and recommend sentencing, its decisions reflected the attributions made in the speeches.

False consensus

Another attribution error is the tendency for someone to perceive his or her own behaviour as representative of a general consensus of how other people behave – an error called false consensus. For example, Sherman *et al.* (1984)

found that male school students who smoke believe that a majority of their peers do so too, whereas non-smokers believe that a majority do not smoke. Obviously, both groups cannot be correct.

One explanation for false consensus is that people tend to surround themselves with similar others and thus actually encounter a disproportionate number of people who behave like they do (Ross, 1977). Another possible explanation is that we dwell so much on our own behaviour that we are prevented from making the comparisons that might lead us to realise that others do not necessarily think or do as we do. A third possibility is that in order to have a stable perception of reality we need to believe that our perceptions, attitudes and behaviours are correct, and so we exaggerate the degree of consensual support we have. If a person believes the world is flat, then it helps them to believe this is really true if they can believe that lots of other people agree with them (Marks and Miller, 1987). However, recent research suggests that this social projection of one's own beliefs involves the inclusion of others in the same social category as oneself (Kreuger and Clement, 1997; Spears and Manstead, 1990), and it is increased when we are more self-attentive or self-conscious (Fenigstein and Abrams, 1993).

Self-serving biases

Some biases seem to be designed to protect or enhance our self-esteem or self-image (Hoorens, 1993). These are called self-serving biases. These may take a number of forms, and sometimes we may not even be aware of them. For example, people seem to feel more positive about letters of the alphabet that fall within their own names as compared with other letters (the 'name letter effect'). Hoorens and Nuttin (1993) examined the name letter effect among children and university students. Participants tended to think these letters appeared more frequently in other words relative to non-name letters. Moreover, because of their association with oneself, 'mere ownership' of the name letters was sufficient to make them more attractive.

Self-serving biases of this type also find expression in the attributions we make. For example, when we attempt to attribute causes to our own behaviour – to explain the reasons for our actions – we tend to attribute our accomplishments and successes to internal causes and our failures and mistakes to external causes. Suppose that you receive an outstanding score on a test. If you are like most people, you will feel the high score is well deserved. After all, you are an intelligent individual who studied hard for the test. Your attributions reflect internal causes for the test score: you are bright and a hard worker. Now suppose that you fail the test – now what sorts of attributions do you tend to make? Again, if you are like most people, you may blame your low score on the fact that it was a difficult, even 'unfair', test or on the lecturer for being so picky about the answers he or she counted as wrong. Your attributions in this case blame

external causes – the test's difficulty and the pickiness of your lecturer. One possible explanation for the self-serving bias is that people are motivated to protect and enhance their self-esteem (Brown and Rogers, 1991; Baron and Byrne, 1994). Simply put, we protect our self-esteem when we blame failure on the environment and we enhance it when we give ourselves credit for our successes.

However, people differ in their 'attributional style' – the extent to which they attribute their outcomes to stable and global causes (Metalsky et al., 1987). In general, people with a 'depressogenic' style are more likely to attribute their failures to these stable and global causes (for example, lack of ability that will affect performance in many ways), resulting in a sense of hopelessness and depression. On the other hand, there is some evidence that depressogenic attributional style is associated with very high levels of achievement among students, perhaps because such students actively seek to test the limits of their capability, and set very high standards for themselves (Houston, 1994).

This sort of bias can also occur at the group level, where it is called the ultimate attribution error. People tend to attribute ingroup failures and outgroup successes to external factors such as luck, and ingroup successes and outgroup failures internally to properties of the groups and their members (Pettigrew, 1979). This clearly makes the group you belong to, the ingroup, appear much more positive than the outgroup, and thus is a self-serving bias.

Another self-serving attributional phenomenon is the belief in a just world – the belief that people get what they deserve in life (Lerner, 1977). According to this idea, when misfortune or tragedy strikes, people tend to blame the victim instead of attributing the source of the problem to situational factors outside the victim's control. As a result, an innocent victim may be blamed for circumstances over which he or she had no control and any suffering is seen as being deserved. Common examples of this include the tendency to blame unemployed people, destitute people, rape victims and even victims of genocide for their plight. People may also be complacent about HIV infection because they overly attribute it to risky behaviour by homosexuals and thus not relevant to themselves (Ambrosio and Sheehan, 1991).

Although there is a sense in which the belief in a just world may reflect the fundamental attribution error, social psychologists believe it is also, and perhaps more importantly, a self-serving bias. By seeing people as bringing bad things upon themselves by being bad people we can reason that we are good, sensible people and thus these things will not happen to us. In this way the world appears more within our control and less fickle and unpredictable. An interesting twist, which is consistent with this idea is self-blame: people may sometimes blame themselves for their plight in order to avoid the frightening conclusion that the world is a completely unpredictable place where anything may happen irrespective of what you do (Miller and Porter, 1983). Belief in a just world also varies across cultures. In a study of people from twelve different countries, Furnham (1992b) discovered that the susceptibility to the belief in a just world attribution error was positively correlated with wealth and social status. That is, across many countries (which included countries from both Eastern and Western cultures), a person was more likely to commit this kind of attributional error if he or she was wealthy and had high social status.

Heuristic judgements and social inference

Social cognition refers to ways in which we make inferences about people, social inferences, and the world we live in, and then store these inferences as schemas that guide our perception and judgement. An important basis for social inference is to find causes for people's behaviour through attribution processes, however, as we have just seen, these processes are often not very accurate or reliable. Often we do not use attribution processes at all to make inferences about people, but instead use cognitive shortcuts or inferential rules called heuristics. Two of the most important heuristics that people use are representativeness and availability.

The representativeness heuristic

When we meet someone for the first time, we notice his or her clothes, hairstyle, posture, manner of speaking, hand gestures and many other characteristics. Based on our previous experience, we use this information to draw tentative conclusions about other characteristics that we cannot immediately discover. In doing so, we attempt to match the characteristics we can observe with schemas or stereotypes we have of different types or groups of people. If the person seems representative of one of these schemas, we conclude that he or she fits that particular category (Lupfer et al., 1990). In drawing this conclusion, we use the representativeness heuristic – we classify an object into the category to which it appears to be the most similar.

The representativeness heuristic is based on our ability to categorise information. We observe that some characteristics tend to go together (or we are taught that they do). When we observe some of these characteristics, we conclude that the others are also present. Most of the time this strategy works; we are able to predict people's behaviour fairly accurately. Tversky and Kahneman (1974) describe someone called Steve: he is 'very shy and withdrawn, invariably helpful, but with little interest in people, or in the world of reality. A meek and tidy soul, he has a need for order and structure, and a passion for detail'. Chances are you will infer that Steve is a librarian rather than a farmer, surgeon or trapeze artist – and you are probably quite likely to be correct. What we know about Steve seems to be quite representative of what we 'know' about librarians.

In relying on the representativeness heuristic we often engage in the base-rate fallacy – we overlook statistical information about the relative size of categories and therefore the probability that the person will belong to the category. If someone was described as being athletic and interested in surfing you are probably better off simply inferring she is Chinese than Australian (for every Australian there are 60 Chinese).

Learning to play the odds, so to speak, and so to avoid being misled by distinctive characteristics is particularly important in certain intellectual endeavours. For example, physicians who are experienced in making diagnoses of diseases teach their students to learn and make use of the probabilities of particular diseases and not to be fooled by especially distinctive symptoms. In fact, Zukier and Pepitone (1984) posed a problem to first-year medical students and to residents who had completed their clinical training. The inexperienced students were tricked by the base-rate fallacy but the residents played the odds, as they had been taught to do.

The availability heuristic

When people attempt to assess the importance or the frequency of an event, they tend to be guided by the ease with which examples of that event come to mind – by how available these examples are to the imagination. This mental shortcut is called the availability heuristic. In general, the things we are able to think of most easily are more important and occur more frequently than things that are difficult to imagine. Thus, the availability heuristic works well, most of the time.

Some events are so vivid that we can easily picture them happening. We can easily picture getting mugged while walking through the heart of a large city at night or being involved in an airplane crash, probably because such events are often reported in the news and because they are so frightening. Thus, people tend to overestimate the likelihood of such misfortunes happening to them. Tversky and Kahneman (1982) demonstrated the effect of availability by asking people to estimate whether English words starting with 'k' were more or less common than words with 'k' as the third letter (for example, 'kiss' versus 'lake'). Most people said that there were more words starting with 'k'. In fact, there are more than twice as many words with 'k' as their third letter as words with 'k' as their first, but because thinking of words that start with a particular letter is easier than thinking of words that contain the letter in another position, people are misled in their judgement.

Many variables can affect the availability of an event or a concept and thus increase its effect on our decision making. For example, having recently seen a particular type of event makes it easier for us to think of other examples of that event. This phenomenon is called priming. Many first-year psychology students demonstrate this phenomenon when, after learning the symptoms of various clinical disorders, they start 'discovering' these very symptoms in themselves.

Higgins *et al.* (1977) demonstrated the effects of priming on judging the personality characteristics of strangers. They had participants work on a task that introduced various descriptive adjectives. Next, the experimenters described an imaginary person, saying that he had performed such feats as climbing mountains and crossing the Atlantic in a yacht. Finally, they asked the participants to give their impressions of this person. Those participants who had previously been exposed to words such as adventurous reported favourable impressions, whereas those who had been exposed to words such as reckless reported unfavourable ones. The priming effect of the descriptive adjectives had biased their interpretation of the facts.

The availability heuristic also explains why personal encounters tend to have an especially strong effect on our decision making. For example, suppose that you have decided to purchase a new car. You have narrowed your choice down to two models, both available for about the same price. You read an article in a consumer magazine that summarises the experiences of thousands of people who have purchased these cars, and their testimony shows clearly that one of them has a much better repair record. You decide to purchase that model and mention the fact to a friend you happen to meet later that day. She says, 'Oh, no! Don't buy one of those! I bought one last year, and it has been nothing but trouble. I'd had it for only two weeks when it first broke down. I was in the middle of nowhere and had to walk five miles to the nearest phone. I got it towed to a garage, and they had to order a part from the manufacturer. I ended up staying in that town for two days before it was fixed. Since then, I've had trouble with the air conditioning and the transmission.' Would this experience affect your decision to buy that model of car?

Most people would take this personal encounter very seriously. Even though it consists of the experience of only one person, whereas the survey in the consumer magazine represents the experience of thousands of people, a vivid personal encounter is much more available and memorable than a set of statistics, and tends to have a disproportionate effect on our own behaviour (Borgida and Nisbett, 1977).

The cognitive accessibility of social information can also have dramatic effects on our behaviour and performance. Bargh *et al.* (1996) found that when participants had been primed with the stereotype of elderly people they walked away from the experiment more slowly than unprimed participants. Dijksterhuis *et al.* (in press) extended this research to explore the effects of making specific individuals salient. Participants were first asked to unscramble some sentences that contained within them words that describe the traits associated with the elderly stereotype. This primed the elderly stereotype by making the attributes of elderly people more accessible in participants' minds. Next, half the participants were asked to make judgements about a specific elderly person, Princess Julianna, the 89 year old Dutch Queen Mother. This made a specific 'exemplar'

accessible. Participants were then directed to the lifts at the end of the corridor where another experimenter was waiting. The time taken for them to reach this second experimenter was recorded. In contrast to Bargh *et al.*'s (1996) results, when Princess Julianna was primed, participants walked significantly faster than when the general stereotype of elderly people had been primed. These two studies illustrate that when general stereeteotypes are activated we may automatically adopt some of the stereotypical characteristics ourselves, but when images of specific extreme individuals are activated we automatically make a contrast between ourselves and the exemplar, making us react in opposition to the characteristics of the individual. For example, Dijksterhuis *et al.* (in press) also found that participants performed better on a test when the stereotype of professor had been primed than when the stereotype of supermodel had been primed. However, they performed worse on the test when the specific example of Einstein had been primed than when the specific example of Claudia Schiffer had been primed.

Questions to think about

Social cognition and social knowledge

- What factors do you feel have been most influential in the development of your self-concept? What sorts of experience do you think will influence continued development of your self-concept during your university career? How do you envision your working self-concept changing with these experiences?

- How much of our social behaviour do we engage in unconsciously, that is, without our awareness? What effect do you suppose being more conscious of our social interaction would have on that interaction? Might we be less prone to using heuristics incorrectly?

- Imagine yourself to be the first person on the scene of a motor accident in which several people have been injured badly. What factors – situational, dispositional, or some combination of them – would guide your behaviour?

- When you observe someone's behaviour, how do you know what caused that behaviour? How accurate and impartial do you think your inference might be? How might you minimise any biases and errors that do occur?

Attitudes and attitude change

The study of attitudes – relatively enduring sets of beliefs, feelings and intentions towards an object, person, event or symbol – is one of the most important fields of social psychology (Eagly and Chaiken, 1993; Pratkanis *et al.*, 1989). Some early definitions of social psychology actually defined social psychology as the study of attitudes.

The nature of attitudes

Many social psychologists believe that attitudes have three different components: affect, behavioural intention and cognition (see Figure 15.1). The affective component consists of the kinds of feeling that an attitude object (person, activity, object) arouses. The behavioural intentional component consists of an intention to act in a particular way with respect to a particular object. The cognitive component consists of a set of beliefs about an object. Social psychologists have studied all three aspects of attitudes, and we examine their findings in this section.

Affective components of attitudes

Affective components of attitudes can be very strong and pervasive. The bigot feels disgust in the presence of people

This family has a positive attitude towards one of these products if they believe it is nutritious and environmentally friendly (cognitive component), or they have a positive feeling about it (affective component) and if they intend to purchase it (behavioural intention component).

Source: Courtesy of Telegraph Colour Library.

from a certain religious, racial or ethnic group; the nature lover feels exhilaration from a pleasant walk through the woods. Like other emotional reactions, these feelings are strongly influenced by direct or vicarious classical conditioning (Rajecki, 1989).

Direct classical conditioning is straightforward. Imagine that you meet someone who seems to take delight in embarrassing you. She makes clever, sarcastic remarks that disparage your intelligence, looks and personality. Unfortunately, her remarks are so clever that your attempts to defend yourself make you appear even more foolish. After a few encounters with this person, the sight of her or the sound of her voice is likely to elicit feelings of dislike and fear. Your attitude towards her will be negative.

Vicarious classical conditioning undoubtedly plays a major role in transmitting parents' attitudes to their children. People are skilled at detecting even subtle signs of fear, hatred and other negative emotional states in other people, especially when they know the people well. Thus, children often vicariously experience their parents' prejudices and fears even if these feelings are unspoken. Children who see their parents recoil in disgust at the sight of members of some ethnic group are likely to feel the same emotion and thus, over time, develop the same attitude.

Simply being exposed repeatedly to an otherwise neutral object or issue over time may influence our attitude towards it, generally in a favourable direction. This attraction for the familiar is called the mere exposure effect. One of the first studies to demonstrate this effect used several neutral stimuli such as nonsense words, photographs of the faces of unknown people, and Chinese characters (Zajonc, 1968). The more the participants saw the stimuli, the more they liked the stimuli later. Stimuli that were seen only once were liked more than ones never seen before. Even when the stimuli were flashed so briefly that they could not be recognised, participants usually preferred a stimulus that had been previously presented to a novel one that they could recognise (Kunst-Wilson and Zajonc, 1980). The mere exposure effect probably reflects the human tendency to feel positive about things which do not pose a threat to us – our feelings towards a person, event or object will naturally improve if on repeated exposure we discover that no 'threat' is posed.

Cognitive components of attitudes

We acquire most beliefs about a particular attitude object quite directly: we hear or read a fact or opinion, or other people validate our expressed beliefs. However, we can often develop fairly nebulous likes and dislikes (affect) and then develop our beliefs subsequently, to justify our feelings. For example, you may feel you dislike Volvo cars, but really not have many beliefs about them. This affective orientation will guide the sorts of beliefs you subsequently hold about Volvos – you are more likely then to believe unfavourable than favourable things about Volvos. This illustrates an important point: although we can separate out different components of attitudes in order to describe them in a textbook, in reality they are inextricably linked.

We form and change our attitudes throughout our lives; however, children have an enormous task ahead of them. They, of course, come into the world with no attitudes, and so have very rapidly to learn attitudes in order to orient themselves to people, events and objects in their world. One way they do this is by simply imitating the behaviour of people who play an important role in their life. Children usually repeat opinions expressed by their parents. In Northern Ireland, many children label themselves as Catholic or Protestant long before they know the values for which these religious organisations stand. Often they ask their parents, 'Are we Catholics or Protestants?' without considering whether they might have any choice in the matter. The tendency to identify with the family unit (and, later with peer groups) provides a strong incentive to adopt the group's attitudes.

Attitudes and behaviour

Attitudes have a behavioural intention component – a motivation or expressed intention to behave in some way that is consistent with the affective and cognitive components of an attitude. For example, many people have negative attitudes towards smoking and express the intention not to smoke. However, we all know that the expressed intention to behave according to an attitude certainly does not guarantee that we actually behave in that way – people who intend not to smoke often smoke. Intentions and behaviour are not the same thing.

People do not always behave as their expressed attitudes and beliefs would lead us to expect. In a classic example, LaPiere (1934) drove through the United States with a Chinese couple. They stopped at over 250 restaurants and lodging places and were refused service only once. Several months after their trip, LaPiere wrote to the owners of the places they had visited and asked whether they would serve Chinese people. The response was overwhelmingly negative; 92 per cent of those who responded said that they would not. Clearly, their behaviour gave less evidence of racial bias than their expressed attitudes did. This study has been cited as evidence that attitudes do not always influence behaviour. Indeed, hundreds of studies of the relationship between attitudes and behaviour suggest that, on average, attitudes predict only about 2–3 per cent of behaviour (one way to think of this is that only 2 or 3 times out of 100 do people actually do what they say – perhaps we should not be quite so harsh on our politicians).

However, all is not lost. There are ways in which we can be much more accurate at predicting behaviour from attitudes. Attitude specificity is one important influence on the attitude–behaviour congruence. If you measure a person's general attitude towards a topic, you will be unlikely to be able to predict his or her behaviour. Behaviours, unlike attitudes, are specific events. However, as the attitude being measured becomes more specific, the person's behaviour becomes more predictable. For example, Weigel et al. (1974) measured people's attitudes towards a series of topics that increased in specificity from 'a pure environment' to 'the Sierra Club' (an American organisation that supports environmental causes). They used the participants' attitudes to predict whether they would volunteer for various activities to benefit the Sierra Club. A person's attitude towards environmentalism was a poor predictor of whether he or she would volunteer; his or her attitude towards the Sierra Club itself was a much better predictor (see Table 15.2). For example, a person might favour a pure environment but also dislike organised clubs or have little time to spare for meetings. This person would express a positive attitude towards a pure environment but would not join the club or volunteer for any activities to support it.

Reasoned action and planned behaviour

Probably the most systematic account of how attitudes and behaviour are related has been developed by Fishbein and Ajzen in their theories of reasoned action and of planned behaviour (see Ajzen, 1989). Someone's intention to behave in a certain way is strengthened if (1) she has a positive attitude towards the behaviour, (2) she believes many people that matter also have a favourable attitude towards the behaviour, (3) she believes she has the resources and opportunity to engage in the behaviour, and (4) the intention is very specific to one particular behaviour. For example, consider someone who loves going to Wagnerian operas, all of whose friends also love going to Wagnerian operas, and who has a ticket to go to *The Ring* which is on in his city tonight and who has nothing else to do tonight. If he expressed the strong intention of going to *The Ring* tonight, which he is likely to do, then you can probably pretty accurately predict that this is what he will do. In contrast, consider someone who loves going to Wagnerian

Table 15.2 Correlation between willingness to join or work for the Sierra Club and various measures of related attitudes

Attitude scale	Correlation
Importance of a pure environment	0.06
Pollution	0.32
Conservation	0.24
Attitude towards the Sierra Club	0.68

Source: based on Weigel et al., 1974

operas, but all of whose friends do not, and who has no ticket, or the opera is on in some remote city and he has no transport. He is unlikely to express a strong intention of going to *The Ring* tonight, and you are much less likely to know exactly what he will be doing.

D. Parker *et al.* (1995) surveyed almost six hundred drivers in the United Kingdom, and found that they could quite accurately predict whether those drivers would engage in specific reckless driving behaviours, for example cutting in, by measuring their attitudes towards the behaviour, the amount of support they perceived for this behaviour from their friends, and whether they had the resources and opportunity to behave in this way (for example, they had a car, they could get away with it, they had done it in the past and so knew what to do).

Attitudes may also influence behavioural intentions, and thus behaviour, more strongly if the attitude is accessible in memory (if you think about Volvos a lot, the chances are that you have a strong attitude and thus firm intentions) and if support for the attitude comes not so much from individuals but from a social group to which you belong and which matters to who you are (if owning a Volvo is *de rigeur* for 'people like you') then chances are you will own a Volvo.

We will return to another application of the theories of reasoned action and planned behaviour (this time to health-related behaviour) in the next chapter.

Attitude change and persuasion

People often attempt to persuade us to change our attitudes. Two aspects of the persuasion process have received special attention: the source of the message and the message itself.

A message tends to be more persuasive if its source is credible. Source credibility is high when the source is perceived as knowledgeable and is trusted to communicate this knowledge accurately. For example, in one study, people developed a more favourable attitude towards different types of medicine when the information appeared in the prestigious *New England Journal of Medicine* than when it appeared in a mass circulation tabloid (Hovland and Weiss, 1951).

Messages also seem to have more impact when the source is physically attractive. For example, physically attractive people are more likely than physically unattractive people to persuade others to sign a petition (Chaiken, 1979). Individuals who are asked to endorse products for advertisers are almost always physically attractive or appealing in other ways.

As you would expect, aspects of the message itself are important in determining its persuasive appeal. For example, is an argument that provides only one side of an issue more effective than one that presents both sides? The answer depends on the audience. If the audience either knows very little about the issue or already holds a strong position with respect to it, one-sided arguments tend to be

more effective. If the audience is well informed about the issue, however, a two-sided argument tends to be more persuasive (McAlister *et al.*, 1980).

How effective are scare tactics embedded in the message in changing someone's attitude? Some research suggests that frightening messages are very effective. Leventhal *et al.* (1967) found that people were more likely to stop smoking when the message was accompanied by a graphic video of surgery on a patient with lung cancer. Other research has shown that scare tactics may be effective in bringing about change, but only when combined with instructive information about how to change one's behaviour (Cialdini *et al.*, 1981). According to Janis (1967), a little bit of fear is good for motivation to change one's attitudes and behaviours, but too much fear can distract us from the message so that we are unable to conceive of ways to put the message into action.

Petty and Cacioppo (1986) have proposed the elaboration likelihood model to account for attitude change through persuasion (see Figure 15.2). According to this model, persuasion can take either a central or a peripheral route. The central route requires a person to think critically about the argument or arguments being presented, to weigh their relative strengths and weaknesses, and to elaborate on the relevant themes. At issue is the actual substance of the argument, not its emotional or superficial appeal. The peripheral route, on the other hand, refers to attempts at persuasion in which the change is associated with positive stimuli – a professional athlete, a millionaire, or an attractive model – that may actually have nothing to do with the substance of the argument. Selling products by associating them with attractive people or by implying that

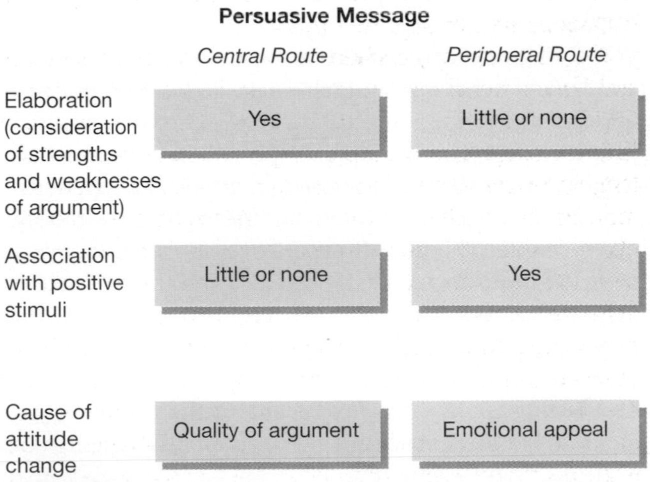

Persuasive Message

	Central Route	Peripheral Route
Elaboration (consideration of strengths and weaknesses of argument)	Yes	Little or none
Association with positive stimuli	Little or none	Yes
Cause of attitude change	Quality of argument	Emotional appeal

Figure 15.2

The elaboration likelihood model of attitude change. Persuasive messages may centre either on a substantive argument that requires an individual to think critically about the argument's strengths and weaknesses (the central route) or on a superficial argument that is associated with positive stimuli (the peripheral route).

buying the product will result in emotional, social or financial benefits are examples of the use of peripheral attitude change techniques.

Very closely related to Petty and Cacioppo's distinction between central and peripheral route processing, is Chaiken's distinction between systematic and heuristic processing (Bohner *et al.*, 1995). People can systematically consider all aspects of a message, or they can very superficially rely on simple heuristics such as thinking that longer arguments or arguments with more statistical facts and figures must be more true, or that all messages from politicians are lies. People are more likely to resort to heuristic processing if they have limited time to process the message or if they are in a good mood. So, to change attitudes towards consumer products it is quite effective to bombard people rapidly with advertisements that put them in a good mood and present statistical/scientific information from people dressed as scientists – this encourages heuristic processing and encourages the heuristic that messages backed by science must be true. One difference between the elaboration likelihood model and the heuristic/ systematic model is that whereas a message is processed either centrally *or* peripherally at any one time, it can be processed systematically *and* heuristically at the same time.

Cognitive dissonance

Although we usually regard our attitudes as causes of our behaviour, our behaviour also affects our attitudes. Two major theories attempt to explain the effects of behaviour on attitude formation. The oldest theory is cognitive dissonance theory, developed by Leon Festinger (1957). According to cognitive dissonance theory, when we perceive a discrepancy between our attitudes and behaviour, between our behaviour and self-image, or between one attitude and another, an unpleasant state of anxiety, or dissonance, results. For example, a person may successfully overcome a childhood racial prejudice but may experience unpleasant emotional arousal at the sight of a racially mixed couple. The person experiences a conflict between the belief in his own lack of prejudice and the evidence of prejudice from his behaviour. This conflict produces dissonance, which is an aversive state that people are motivated to reduce. A person can achieve dissonance reduction by (1) reducing the importance of one of the dissonant elements, (2) adding consonant elements, or (3) changing one of the dissonant elements.

Suppose that a student believes that he is very intelligent but he invariably receives poor grades in his courses. Because the obvious prediction is that intelligent people get good grades, the discrepancy causes the student to experience dissonance. To reduce this dissonance, he may decide that grades are not important and that intelligence is not very closely related to grades. He is using strategy 1, reducing the importance of one of the dissonant elements – the fact that

he received poor grades in his courses. Or he can dwell on the belief that his lecturers were unfair or that his job leaves him little time to study. In this case, he is using strategy 2, reducing dissonance by adding consonant elements – those factors that can account for his poor grades and hence explain the discrepancy between his perceived intelligence and grades. Finally, he can use strategy 3 to change one of the dissonant elements. He can either improve his grades or revise his opinion of his own intelligence.

Induced compliance

Most of us believe that although we can induce someone to do something, getting someone to change an attitude is much harder. However, Festinger's theory of cognitive dissonance and supporting experimental evidence indicate otherwise. Under the right conditions, when people are coerced into doing something or are paid to do something, the act of compliance – simply engaging in a particular behaviour at someone else's request – may cause a change in their underlying attitudes.

Cognitive dissonance theory predicts that dissonance occurs when a person's behaviour has undesirable outcomes for self-esteem; there is a conflict between the person's belief in his or her own worth and the fact that he or she has done something that damages this belief. The person will then seek to justify the behaviour. For example, a poorly paid vacuum cleaner sales representative is likely to convince himself that the shoddy merchandise he sells is actually good. Otherwise, he must question why he works for a company that pays him poorly and requires him to lie to prospective customers about the quality of the product in order to make a sale. Conversely, an executive of one of the commercial television networks may know that the programmes she produces are sleazy, mindless drivel, but she is so well paid that she does not feel bad about producing them. Her high salary justifies her job and probably also provides her with enough self-esteem that she has decided that the public gets what it deserves anyway.

Festinger and Carlsmith (1959) verified this observation by having participants perform very boring tasks, such as putting spools on a tray, tipping them off, putting them on the tray again, tipping them off again, and so on. After the participants had spent an hour on exercises like this, the experimenter asked each participant whether he or she would help out in the study by trying to convince the next person that the task was interesting and enjoyable. Some participants received one dollar for helping out; others received twenty dollars. Control participants were paid nothing. The experimenters predicted that participants who were paid only one dollar would perceive the task as being relatively interesting. They had been induced to lie to a 'fellow student' (actually, a confederate of the experimenters) for a paltry sum. Like the vacuum cleaner sales representative, they should convince themselves of the worth of the experiment to maintain their self-esteem. Poorly paid participants did in fact rate the task better than did those who were well paid (see Figure 15.3). Clearly, our actions have an effect on our attitudes. When faced with inconsistency between our behaviour and our attitudes, we often change our attitudes to suit our behaviour.

Arousal and attitude change

Festinger's theory hypothesises that dissonance reduction is motivated by an aversive drive. A study by Croyle and Cooper (1983) obtained physiological evidence to support this hypothesis. The experimenters chose as their participants Princeton University students who disagreed with the assertion 'Alcohol use should be totally banned from the Princeton campus and eating clubs'. Each participant was induced to write an essay containing strong and forceful arguments in favour of the assertion or in opposition to it. While the participants were writing the essay, the experimenters measured the electrical conductance of their skin, which is known to be a good indicator of the physiological arousal that accompanies stress. Some participants were simply told to write the essay. Other participants were told that their participation was completely voluntary and that they were free to leave at any time; they even signed a form emphasising the voluntary nature of the task. Of course, all participants felt social pressure to continue the study, and all of them did. Those who were simply told to write the essay should have felt less personal responsibility for what they wrote and would therefore be expected to experience less cognitive dissonance than those who believed that they had exercised free choice in deciding to participate.

Participants in the 'free choice' condition who had written essays contradicting their original opinion showed both a change in opinion and evidence of physiological arousal. Those participants who were simply told to write the essay or who wrote arguments that they had originally agreed with showed little sign of arousal or attitude change (see Figure 15.4).

Attitudes and expenditures

Festinger's theory of cognitive dissonance accounts for another relation between behaviour and attitudes: our tendency to value an item more if it costs us something. For example, some people buy extremely expensive brands of cosmetics even though the same ingredients are used in much cheaper brands. Following the same rationale, most animal shelters sell their stray animals to prospective pet owners, not only because the money helps defray their operating costs, but also because they assume that a purchased pet will be treated better than a free pet.

Aronson and Mills (1959) verified this phenomenon. The experimenters subjected female college students to varying degrees of embarrassment as a prerequisite for joining what was promised to be an interesting discussion about sexual behaviour. To produce slight embarrassment, they had the

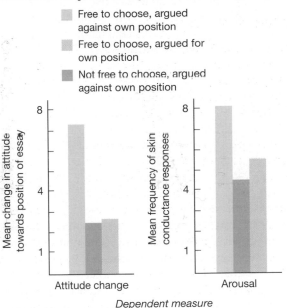

Figure 15.4

Physiological evidence for cognitive dissonance. Mean change in attitude towards the position advocated by the essay and mean frequency of skin conductance responses (a physiological index of arousal) in participants who argued for or against their own positions.

Source: Based on data from Croyle, R.T. and Cooper, J., Dissonance arousal: Physical evidence. *Journal of Personality and Social Psychology*, 1983, 45, 782–791.

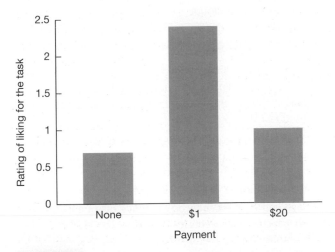

Figure 15.3

Effects of induced compliance. People who received $1 to lie about a boring task later indicated that they liked the task more than did people who had received $20.

Source: Based on data from Festinger, L. and Carlsmith, J.M., Cognitive consequences of forced compliance. *Journal of Abnormal and Social Psychology*, 1959, 58, pp. 203–210.

participants read aloud five sex-related words (such as prostitute, virgin and petting) to the experimenter, who was male. To produce more severe embarrassment, they had the women read aloud twelve obscene four-letter words and two sexually explicit passages of prose. The control group read nothing at all. The 'interesting group discussion' turned out to be a tape recording of a very dull conversation.

Festinger's theory predicts that the women who had to go through an embarrassing ordeal in order to join the group would experience some cognitive dissonance. They had suffered an ordeal in order to take part in an interesting discussion which turned out actually to be very dull. These negative and positive experiences are inconsistent and dissonance arousing, and should make them view the 'discussion' more favourably so that their effort would not be perceived as having been completely without value. The results were as predicted: the participants who had been embarrassed the most rated the discussion more favourably than did the control participants or those who had experienced only slight embarrassment. We value things at least partly by how much they cost us.

Self-perception

Daryl Bem (1972) proposed an alternative to the theory of cognitive dissonance. Drawing on attribution theory, which we discussed earlier in this chapter, he defined self-perception theory in the following way:

'Individuals come to "know" their own attitudes, emotions, and other internal states partially by inferring them from observations of their own overt behaviour and/or the circumstances in which this behaviour occurs. Thus, to the extent that internal cues are weak, ambiguous, or uninterpretable, the individual is functionally in the same position as an outside observer, an observer who must necessarily rely on those same external cues to infer the individual's inner states.' (p. 2)

Bem noted that an observer who attempts to make judgements about someone's attitudes, emotions, or other internal states must examine the person's behaviour for clues. For example, if you cannot ask someone why he or she is doing something, you must analyse the situation in which the behaviour occurs to try to determine the motivation. Bem suggested that people analyse their own internal states in a similar way, making attributions about the causes of their own behaviour.

You will recall the experiment by Festinger and Carlsmith (1959) in which students who were paid only $1 later rated a boring task as more interesting than did those who were paid $20. How does self-perception theory explain these results? Suppose that an observer watches a participant who has been paid $1 to deliver a convincing speech to another student about how interesting a task was. Because being paid such a small sum is not a sufficient reason for calling a dull

task interesting, the observer will probably conclude that the student actually enjoyed the task. Lacking good evidence for external causes, the observer will attribute the behaviour to a dispositional factor: interest in the task. Bem argued that the participant makes the same inference about himself or herself. Because the participant was not paid enough to tell a lie, he or she must have enjoyed the task. The principal advantage of self-perception theory is that it makes fewer assumptions than does dissonance theory; it does not postulate a motivating aversive-drive state.

But as Croyle and Cooper's (1983) experiment on essay writing showed, some conflict situations do produce arousal. Perhaps self-perception and cognitive dissonance occur under different conditions, producing attitude changes for different reasons. One factor which may determine whether dissonance or self-perception processes come into play involves the idea that attitudes have ranges of acceptable behaviour – for example, a pacifist might agree with using force to protect a helpless child from attack, but not with using force to react to a personal insult. According to Fazio *et al.* (1977) a pacifist who used force to protect a child might change his attitudes through self-perception (the behaviour falls within the latitude of acceptable behaviours), whereas a pacifist who struck out in retaliation for an insult would experience dissonance (the behaviour falls outside the latitude of acceptable behaviours). Using a slightly different logic, Cooper and Fazio (1984) suggest that when counterattitudinal behaviour has undesirable consequences we go through an attributional/self-perception process where we decide whether the behaviour was voluntary. If it was, then we experience dissonance.

Questions to think about

Attitudes and attitude change

- Attitudes have sometimes been described as 'predispositions to act'. What might this phrase mean? Do you believe this statement to be an accurate description of attitudes? Why or why not?

- What kinds of argument would be effective in persuading you to change your attitude towards a prominent political figure? How would you describe these arguments in psychological terms?

- Have you ever experienced cognitive dissonance? If so, what factors made you feel this way and how did you eventually reduce the dissonance?

- Based on social psychological knowledge about the relationship between attitudes and behaviour, what advice would you give to an organisation which wanted to combat waste (for example, excessive paper use, excessive power use)? Would you recommend changing employees' attitudes in order to change their behaviour?

Prejudice and intergroup behaviour

A prejudice is an attitude, generally negative, towards a social outgroup, and thus towards members of that group purely on the basis of their membership of that group. People have a remarkable ability to be prejudiced against almost any group you care to mention. Like other attitudes, prejudices have a cognitive component. In this case the cognitive component is, as discussed in the social cognition section of this chapter, a stereotype or schema – a set of interrelated (and shared) beliefs about members of the group that influences perception once we categorise someone as being a member of the group. Again, like other attitudes, there is no guarantee that prejudice will be expressed as behaviour – but when it is, that behaviour is called discrimination.

Stereotypical expectations can be used to exert control over others and to justify and maintain others in their present social standings (Fiske, 1993). For example, a male employer who holds a stereotype of women as followers rather than leaders effectively ensures that women in his business will not be promoted into management positions. In this case the stereotypical expectation, a negative attitude towards the abilities of women, has translated into discriminatory behaviour that has denied members of the outgroup, women, opportunities and advantages.

We tend to perceive members of our own ingroup more favourably than we perceive members of the outgroup. For example, Lee (1993) surveyed Chinese American and African American students concerning their perceptions of members of their own racial groups as well as their perceptions of the other racial group. Lee found that Chinese American students rated members of their own ingroup more favourably than they did members of the African American outgroup. Similarly, African American students rated members of their own ingroup more favourably than they did members of the Chinese American outgroup. It is easy to see how dividing the world into ingroups and outgroups – 'us and them' – could lead to prejudice, stereotyping and discrimination.

Although prejudice, stereotypes and discrimination are expressed by individuals, they are genuinely intergroup phenomena: individuals are prejudiced because they belong to groups that have developed certain relations with one another that are characterised by unequal status and advantage, and by conflict and hatred. At this level, prejudice is associated with ethnocentrism, which is the notion that one's own cultural, national, racial or religious group is superior to or more deserving than others. Conflict – international conflict, civil war or unrest, and gang violence – often results from particular ethnocentric beliefs and behaviours. Understanding prejudice, stereotyping and discrimination, then, are important aspects of understanding social interactions, especially conflict, across all levels of culture (Brown, 1995; Leyens et al., 1994).

Psychology in action

The social consequences of humour

Jokes and humour are a part of everyday life. However, humour can play both a negative and positive role in our psychological well-being and our perceptions of others. For example, Maio et al. (1997) explored the effects of telling jokes on joke tellers' stereotypes of disadvantaged groups. Canadian undergraduate students were asked to recite jokes about Newfoundlanders, a relatively disadvantaged group. Those who recited disparaging humour subsequently reported more negative stereotypes of Newfoundlanders than did those who recited non-disparaging humour.

Although we may find jokes amusing, our reaction is also determined by our own attitudes. For example, Monteith (1993) measured participants' attitudes towards gays and asked them to read jokes about gays, and to say how they would and should react to them. Among low prejudiced people, if they believed they should not be as amused as they actually were, feelings of compunction emerged and they tried to inhibit feelings of prejudice.

Another important issue is whether we are the target of the jokes or humour. LaFrance and Woodzicka (1998) assessed womens' reactions to sexist and non-sexist jokes. Women who heard the sexist jokes reported feeling less amused and more disgusted, angry, hostile, determined and surprised than women who heard the non-sexist jokes. They also displayed more eye rolling and touched their faces more often.

Hemmasi et al. (1994) examined how sexual humour is perceived in the workplace. They found that both men and women found jokes more amusing if they were disparaging to the opposite sex than if the jokes disparaged their own sex. Moreover, they considered sexist jokes towards women to be more offensive than sexist jokes towards men. Finally, when gender-related jokes were told by a superior they were more likely to be viewed as sexual harassment than when told by an equal status worker.

Psychology in action continued

Psychology in action continued

Ryan and Kanjorski (1998) asked college students to rate the funniness of ten sexist jokes. Male students who found the jokes funnier, had less negative attitudes towards rape, reported being more likely to force on a partner and higher levels of psychological, physical and sexual aggression. Females found the jokes to be less enjoyable, less acceptable and more offensive than the males did, but both sexes were equally likely to say they would tell the jokes.

Humour can also have positive effects on psychological well-being (Davidhizar and Bowen, 1992; Skevington and White, 1998). This is likely to be because humour can be a coping mechanism for the reduction of stress and tension, as well as a way of distancing oneself cognitively from threats or prob-

lems. For example, Houston *et al.* (1998) examined the impact of humour on very elderly people (mean age was 84) in residential care homes. They first measured aspects of psychological well-being such as anxiety, insomnia and depression. In half of the homes, during a 'social hour' each week for the subsequent four weeks, participants were brought together and presented with a comical singalong led by two female researchers. Participants in the remaining homes continued with their routine activities and social interaction. After the four week period, psychological well-being was measured again. For the people who had the humour intervention there was a significant reduction in levels of depression and anxiety, compared with people who had not had the intervention. We will return to the health benefits of humour in the next chapter.

The origins of prejudice

Unfortunately, prejudice seems to be an enduring characteristic of the human species. History has shown that even groups of people who have been oppressed go on to commit their own type of ethnocentric exploitation if they manage to overthrow their oppressors. Why is prejudice so prevalent and enduring?

The roots of prejudice in competition

Prejudice and affiliation are two sides of the same coin. That is, along with the tendency to identify with and feel close to members of our own group or clan goes the tendency to be suspicious of others. A classic experiment by Sherif *et al.* (1961) demonstrated just how easily intergroup mistrust and conflict can arise. The study took place at a remote summer camp in the United States. The participants, 11 year old boys, were assigned to one of two cabins, isolated from each other. During the first week, the boys in each cabin spent their time together as a group, fishing, hiking, swimming and otherwise enjoying themselves. The boys formed two cohesive groups, which they named the Rattlers and the Eagles. They became attached to their groups and identified strongly with them.

Next, the experimenters sowed the seeds of dissension. They set up a series of competition events between the two groups. The best team was to win a trophy for the group and individual prizes for its members. As the competition progressed, the boys began taunting and insulting each other. Then the Eagles burned the Rattlers' flag, and in retaliation, the Rattlers broke into the Eagles' cabin and scattered or stole their rivals' belongings. Although further physical conflict was prevented by the experimenters, the two groups continued to abuse each other verbally and seemed to have developed a genuine hatred for each other – stereotypes and prejudices developed and were expressed verbally and physically.

Finally, the experimenters arranged for the boys to work together in order to accomplish shared goals that both groups valued. The experimenters sabotaged the water supply for the camp and had the boys fix it; they had the boys repair a truck that had broken down; and they induced the boys to pool their money to rent a movie. After the boys worked on co-operative ventures, rather than competitive ones, the intergroup conflicts diminished.

The findings of this experiment suggest that when groups of people compete with each other, they tend to view their rivals negatively. Note that the boys at the summer camp were racially and ethnically mixed; the assignment to one cabin or the other was arbitrary. Thus, a particular boy could have been either a Rattler-hating Eagle or an Eagle-hating Rattler, depending on chance assignment.

The roots of prejudice in social categorisation

Although competitive goals and interaction between groups seem to encourage prejudice, there is substantial evidence that the mere existence of social categories or groups can be sufficient to provide the framework of prejudice and discrimination. Tajfel and his colleagues (Tajfel *et al.*, 1971) conducted an experiment in which school students were randomly assigned to groups (ostensibly on the basis of preferences for paintings by the artists Klee and Kandinsky, who were unknown to the students). The participants did not interact and did not know who was in their group or who in the other group. Neverthess they subsequently discriminated against the outgroup by repeatedly allocating less money to the outgroup than their own group (even though they personally did not benefit financially from this allocation). To explain this finding, Tajfel developed social identity theory, which proposed that people have a very strong tendency to categorise the social world into ingroup and outgroups in order to provide themselves with a social identity as a group member (Hogg and Abrams, 1988; Tajfel and Turner, 1986). Group membership as social identity furnishes people with a definition and evaluation of who they are; what they should believe, feel and do; and how they should interact with people. People like a clear sense of social identity and so they try to differentiate their group as distinctively as possible from relevant outgroups. They also tend to do this in ways which favour their own group over the outgroup because ingroup favouritism is self-favouritism.

The role of self-esteem in prejudice

Most social psychologists believe that competition is an important factor in the development of prejudice. The competition need not be for tangible goods; it can be motivated by a desire for social superiority, or, as in social identity theory, for a favourable self-definition based on social identity. As we have seen many times in this book, the concept of self-esteem helps to explain many different types of behaviour. The tendency to perceive one's own group as superior to that of others may be based on a need to enhance one's own self-esteem. If one's self-esteem has temporarily been depressed, then maybe it can be rectified by focusing on the perceived inferiority of an outgroup (Abrams and Hogg, 1988; Crocker and Luhtenan, 1990).

An experiment by Meindl and Lerner (1985) supports this conclusion. The experimenters exposed English-speaking Canadians to a situation designed to threaten their self-esteem. They asked the participants to walk across the room to get a chair. For members of the experimental group, the chair was rigged in such a way that a pile of index cards would be knocked over and scattered on the floor. In a situation like this, most people feel clumsy and foolish – and also a bit guilty about making trouble for the person who has to put the cards back in order. After this experience, the participants were asked to describe their attitudes towards French-speaking Canadians. Participants in the experimental group, who had toppled the cards, rated the 'others' more negatively than did those in the control group, who had not toppled the cards in retrieving the chair. Presumably, by viewing the French-speaking Canadians as members of a group inferior to their own, the participants partially compensated for the loss of their own self-esteem. Hunter *et al.* (1996) studied the intergroup relationship between Catholic and Protestant 16 year olds in Northern Ireland. Participants first completed some measures of self-esteem and then evaluated the two groups. Self-esteem was then measured again. Among those who expressed ingroup bias when they evaluated the groups (favouring their own group over the other), self-esteem was raised on dimensions such as honesty, academic ability and physical appearance.

More generally, according to social identity theory, groups which have lower social status in a particular society strive to improve their social identity and thus members' self-esteem. If group members believe that they can easily identify with the higher status group, then they do so as individuals. If, on the other hand, they feel that this is not possible then, as a group, they strive to improve the social evaluation of their group in quite creative ways, for example by trying to distract attention away from negative qualities. If a group feels that its inferior status is unfair and illegitimate then it can become very well organised and assertive in trying to change its objective status and thus the evaluation of its social identity. The Welsh language revival in Wales and the Basque revival in Spain are good examples of this. Dominant or high status groups typically react very negatively to threats to their privileged position – indeed this can be a circumstance when very extreme prejudices can be expressed.

The role of social cognition in prejudice

We have already seen one way in which social cognition is involved in prejudice: the mere categorisation of people into ingroup and outgroup seems to lay down the groundwork for possible prejudice. It may do this because it affects self-conception – it encourages people to view themselves as group members and think of themselves in terms of social identity, which can be considered a type of self-schema. Social categorisation causes people to view outgroup members in terms of stereotypes and to behave in ways that favour the ingroup and maintain the distinctiveness of ingroup identity.

Another cognitive process that is involved in stereotyping and prejudice is illusory correlation. Recall that the availability heuristic involves our assuming that distinctive, easily imagined items occur more frequently. This phenomenon probably explains why people overestimate the rate of violent crime (because an act of violence is a frightening, distinctive event) and overestimate the relative numbers of violent crimes committed by members of minority groups (because members of minority groups tend to be more conspicuous). This tendency is an example of an illusory correlation – the perception of an apparent relation between two distinct elements that does not actually exist or which is enormously exaggerated (Spears *et al.*, 1985).

Another fallacy that promotes stereotyping is the illusion of outgroup homogeneity. People tend to assume that members of other groups are much more similar than are members of their own group (Linville, 1982). This tendency is even seen between the sexes: men tend to perceive women as being more alike than men are, and women do the opposite (Park and Rothbart, 1982). The same is true for young and old people (Linville *et al.*, 1989). However, this effect can sometimes be reversed so that people think their own group is more homogeneous than the outgroup. Simon and Brown (1987) suggest that one situation in which this can happen is when the ingroup is a minority group in terms of status – and the reason for this is that solidarity and thus homogeneity may have a special value for minorities. Earlier in this section we described a study by Lee (1993) of Chinese American and African American students' perceptions of members of their own racial groups as well as their perceptions of the other racial group. In addition to the ethnocentrism findings reported earlier, Lee also found that each ingroup perceived its own members to be more similar to each other than members of the outgroup were to each other.

Self-fulfilling prophecies

A self-fulfilling prophecy is a stereotype that induces a person to act in a manner consistent with that stereotype. Such a tendency is especially insidious because the behaviour of the person who is the target of the stereotype then tends to confirm the stereotype.

One of the most memorable examples of the self-fulfilling prophecy was demonstrated in an experiment by Snyder *et al.* (1977). The experimenters had male participants carry on telephone conversations with female participants. Just before each conversation took place, the male participants were shown a photograph of the young woman to whom they were to talk. In fact, the pictures were not those of the partner but were photographs of attractive or unattractive women chosen by the experimenters. The conversations that took place were recorded, and the voices of the female participants were played to independent observers, who rated their impressions of the young women.

Based on the sound of the females' voices and what they said, the independent observers rated the women whose partners believed them to be attractive as being more friendly, likable and sociable. Obviously, the male participants talked differently to women they thought to be attractive or unattractive. Their words had either a positive or negative effect on the young women, which could be detected by the observers.

Hope for change

One of the primary reasons for prejudice is that prejudice can serve to justify exploitation of the outgroup by the ingroup. If the outgroup can be portrayed as 'stupid', 'dependent' and 'irresponsible', the ingroup can justify the exploitation of that outgroup as being in the outgroup's own best interest or at least conclude that its treatment of the outgroup is the best that the outgroup can reasonably expect. When ethnocentric practices lead to material advantages for the ingroup in the form of cheap labour or unequal sharing of resources, the injustices will tend to persist. Such situations are not easily altered by the discoveries of social psychologists.

However, many instances of personal prejudice are inadvertent. Many people are unaware of their stereotypes and preconceptions about members of other groups because, as we saw in the social cognition section of this chapter, stereotypes are automatically linked to categories. Although making people aware of their stereotypes can persuade people that their beliefs are unjustified, this can backfire if people then try too hard to suppress their stereotypes. As we saw in the social cognition section, stereotype suppression can rebound and strengthen the automaticity of stereotyping. The knack would seem to be to get people to have insight into their stereotypes – to understand them and see through them rather than merely to suppress them. The best solution is to teach people to become cognitively less lazy and to take the time to reflect about their biases. For example, Langer *et al.* (1985) gave a group of young children specific training in thinking about the problems of people with disabilities. They thought about such problems as the ways that a person with disabilities might drive a car and the reasons that a blind person might make a good newscaster. After this training, they were found to be more willing to go on a picnic with a person with disabilities than were children who did not receive the training. They were also more likely to see the specific consequences of particular disabilities rather than to view people with disabilities as 'less fit'. For example, they were likely to choose a blind child as a partner in a game of pin the tail on the donkey because they realised that the child would be likely to perform even better than a sighted child. Thus, at the individual level, people can learn to recognise their biases and to overcome their prejudices.

On a larger scale, a popular view about how to reduce prejudice is the contact hypothesis – if people from different races could just get to know one another through coming together to interact then prejudice would disappear (Allport, 1954). Although this idea has immediate appeal, and indeed it was part of the scientific justification for the racial desegregation of the American schooling system in the 1950s, it is rife with problems. For intergroup contact to work, people have to come together for prolonged equal-status, meaningful interaction that is pleasant and capable of changing stereotypes of entire groups not just attitudes towards the individuals with whom one interacts. Contact can often produce interracial friendships, but it rarely changes racial stereotypes. More often than not, contact can accentuate intergroup perceptions and further entrench stereotypes.

Nevertheless, contact between members of different groups may promote positive attitudes. It may foster good interpersonal relationships ('decategorisation' of group members; Brewer and Miller, 1984), or it may foster a sense of common membership in a superordinate ingroup ('recategorisation'; Gaertner *et al.*, 1993), or it may allow the recognition of positive features of other groups while preserving a sense of ingroup distinctiveness (mutual positive differentiation; Hewstone and Brown, 1986). Dovidio *et al.* (1997) asked sets of six participants to work first as two three-person groups. These groups then interacted and participants judged one another. Half of the participants were then encouraged to think of themselves as one larger (six-person) category. These recategorised participants were less likely to show evaluative preferences for their own subgroup, or to show a preference for disclosing information about themselves to and helping members of their own subgroup.

Prejudices are intergroup psychological mechanisms for protecting and enhancing our self-image and our material well-being. Not surprisingly, threats to racial or cultural identity are unlikely to reduce prejudice. Thus, nations that try to assimilate ethnic minorities threaten those minorities and cause them to react to protect themselves, which in turn threatens the dominant majority and fuels prejudice. One strategy that does seem to help is pluralism or multiculturalism – a social policy that recognises cultural diversity within the confines of a common national identity.

Questions to think about

Prejudice

- Think about a prejudice that you have. (It could be towards a place or a thing; it does not have to be directed towards a particular group of people.) What factors have caused this prejudice? To what extent are stereotypes involved in this prejudice?

- Think about the amount of contact you have with people who are ethnically different from yourself. Maybe you live in a diverse neighbourhood or have gone on hollday to countries which are ethnically quite different from your own. In what ways do you think this may have changed (or not changed) your images of other ethnic groups as a whole?

- If you were hired by an organisation to design and implement a strategy to reduce harmful ethnic prejudice among employees within the organisation, what would your strategy be?

- How different are the members of your family compared with those of another family that you know? Describe how the illusion of outgroup homogeneity may or may not apply in this instance.

Social influences and group processes

Human beings are unmistakably social creatures: a great deal of our life is spent in the company of others. By itself, this is not an especially profound observation, but it leads to some interesting implications, particularly for social psychologists. We do not merely occupy physical space with other people. We psychologically affiliate and form groups with each other. A **group** is a collection of individuals who have a shared definition of who they are and what they should think, feel and do. People in the same group generally have common interests and goals. Groups are very diverse in size, form and longevity – they include, ethnic groups, nations, organisations, departments, teams, clubs and even families. However, by the definition above, not all aggregations of people are groups in a psychological sense – a crowd of people shopping or some people standing at a bus stop are unlikely to be a group.

The emotions, cognitions and behaviours that define each of us as individuals are strongly influenced, often without our awareness, by those with whom we interact. This influence can be unintentional: other people may be equally unaware of how they are influencing us. At other times, this influence is intended to manipulate us in some way (Santos *et al.*, 1994). One of the most potent forms of influence is group influence where we conform to what we perceive to be group norms. In this section we consider the means by which we influence, and are influenced by, others.

Imitation

Probably the most powerful social influence on our behaviour and attitudes is the behaviour of other people. If we see people act in a particular way, we often tend to act in that way, too. Sometimes we observe that people are not performing a particular behaviour; if so, we, too, tend not to perform that behaviour.

Conformity

Most of us cherish our independence and like to think that we do what we do because we want to do it, not because others decree that we should – though, as we saw earlier in this chapter, this sort of belief is more prevalent in individualist societies; people in collectivist societies place greater emphasis on obligations and conforming to the group. In reality, none of us is immune to social influences, and most instances of conformity benefit us all. If we see someone whose face has been disfigured by an accident or disease, we do not stare at the person or comment about his or her appearance. If someone drops a valuable item, we do not try to pick it up and keep it for ourselves.

Many of the rules that govern our social behaviour are formally codified as laws that we are legally obligated to follow. However, many other rules that influence our behaviour are not formal laws but are, instead, unwritten agreements. These informal rules that define the expected and appropriate behaviour in specific situations are called social norms, or, when applied to members of a particular group, group norms. How we look at strangers, the way we talk to our friends or our supervisors at work, and the kind of food that we eat are all influenced by the norms of the society in which we live. Despite the fact that they do not develop from a conspicuous formal or legal process, norms are powerful sources of social influence.

A study by Sherif (1936) provided an empirical demonstration of how norms can arise out of social interaction, and then how these norms exert influence on behaviour. Sherif's study was based on a perceptual illusion, originally discovered by astronomers, called the autokinetic effect: a small stationary light, when projected in an otherwise completely darkened room, appears to move. The illusion is so strong that even if someone is aware of the effect, the apparent movement often persists.

Sherif first placed participants in the room individually and asked each of them how far the light was moving at different times. The answers were quite variable; one person might see the light move 6 cm on average, while another might see it move an average of 300 cm. Next, Sherif had groups of three people observe the light together and call out their judgements of movement one after the other. Finally, the participants would again observe the light individually. The most interesting result of the study was that when people made their judgements together they very rapidly converged on a narrow range that was pretty close to the average of their individual judgements, and their subsequent individual judgements also fell within this narrow range. The group had established what Sherif referred to as a collective frame of reference – a group norm. The changing of one's thoughts or behaviour to be similar to those of a social group – the internalisation of a group norm as a standard for one's own behaviour – is called conformity. Even when tested by themselves on a different day, the group members still conformed to this frame of reference.

Sherif's findings are not too surprising if we consider that the participants found themselves in an uncertain situation. It makes sense to use others' opinions or judgements as a frame of reference when you are not sure what is going on. But just how strongly do group norms influence individual behaviour when the situation is unambiguous – when we are certain that we perceive things as they really are? The answer to this question was provided in a series of elegant studies conducted by Asch (1951, 1952, 1955).

Asch asked several groups of seven to nine students to estimate the lengths of lines presented on a screen. A sample line was shown at the left, and the participants were to choose which of the three lines to the right matched it (see Figure 15.5). The participants gave their answers orally. In fact, there was only one true participant in each group; all the others were confederates of the experimenter. The seating was arranged so that the true participant answered last. Under some conditions, the confederates made incorrect responses. When they made incorrect responses on six of the twelve trials in an experiment, 76 per cent of the true

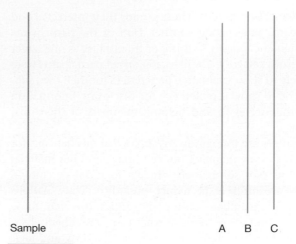

Sample   A   B   C

Figure 15.5

An example of the stimuli used by Asch (1951).

participants went along with the group on at least one trial. Under control conditions, when the confederates responded accurately, only 5 per cent of the participants made an error.

Group pressure did not affect the participants' perceptions; it affected their behaviour. That is, the participants went along with the group decision even though the choice still looked wrong to them – and even though the other people were complete strangers. When they were questioned later, they said that they had started doubting their own eyesight or had thought that perhaps they had misunderstood the instructions. The participants who did not conform felt uncomfortable about disagreeing with the other members of the group. The Asch effect shows how strong the tendency to conform can be. Faced with a simple, unambiguous task while in a group of strangers who showed no signs of disapproval when the participant disagreed with them, the vast majority of participants nevertheless ignored their own judgements and agreed with the obviously incorrect choice made by the other people.

There are at least three reasons why people conform (Turner, 1991). (1) People like to think their perceptions and attitudes are accurate and valid, so, if they are uncertain or find that others disagree with them they may think they are wrong and feel a need to change their perceptions and attitudes in line with those of other people. (2) People like to be liked and approved of by others and therefore do not like to stand out as different, particularly when in the presence of other people. (3) If people feel they belong with others – derive a sense of who they are, a social identity, from the group – then other people's behaviour becomes a self-defining norm that is internalised to regulate their own behaviour as a group member. Abrams *et al.* (1990) found that conformity in both the Sherif and the Asch paradigms was reduced when the source of influence was categorised as an outgroup, rather than an ingroup.

Minority influence

Individuals do not always conform to the majority. Sometimes a minority can change the attitudes of the majority. Indeed social change – from new trends and fashions to social movements and political revolutions – would not be possible if active minorities could not have influence (Moscovici, 1976). Because minorities have to combat a pervasive consensus that often has the support of a powerful elite, they need to adopt particular behavioural styles in order to be effective (Mugny, 1982). Minorities need to challenge the dominant consensus by providing an alternative viewpoint that is strongly consensual among minority members and has marked consistency across time. A consistent, but not rigid or inflexible, minority has what is called 'latent influence' that produces a conversion effect – majority members gradually think about the minority position but still conform to the majority position until suddenly, at a later point, they appear to be converted to the minority's position and switch their allegiance and change their behaviour.

Moscovici and Personnaz (1980) conducted an intriguing experiment in which participants called out the colour of a series of blue slides, which varied only in intensity, after they had heard a confederate, who had been described as either a member of the majority (82 per cent of people) or a member of a minority (18 per cent of people), describe the slide as green. Moscovici and Personnaz also had participants describe the chromatic after-image they saw when the slide had been removed (participants did not realise that the after-image of blue is yellow, and of green it is purple). Participants exposed to majority influence (the confederate who was a member of the majority) showed a tendency to call the blue slides green, but their after-image was unaffected – it remained yellow, indicating that although they may have complied with the majority they certainly had not changed what they actually saw. Participants exposed to minority influence, however, continued to call the slides blue, but remarkably their after-image had shifted towards purple, and the effect had become a little stronger when they were tested individually at a later stage. Although they had not changed their outward behaviour, there was a deeper, latent change in their perception as a consequence of minority influence.

Bystander intervention

People can often conform to false norms. For instance, you may be in a meeting where one person expresses a viewpoint that others do not publicly disagree with. You might assume therefore that everyone else agrees with that viewpoint – that it is a norm of the group – and therefore not publicly disagree with it yourself. In fact, unbeknown to you, everyone in the group may reason in the same way. This is an example of 'pluralistic ignorance' (Miller and McFarland, 1987) – everyone is ignorant of everyone else's true inclinations, perceptions and beliefs. One situation where pluralistic ignorance can have marked effects on behaviour is when a group of people witness an emergency and have to decide whether to offer help.

In 1964 in New York City, a woman named Kitty Genovese was chased and repeatedly stabbed by an assailant, who took thirty-five minutes to kill her. The woman's screams went unheeded by at least thirty-eight people who watched from their windows. No one tried to stop the attacker; no one even made a quick, anonymous telephone call to the police. When the bystanders were questioned later, they could not explain their inaction. 'I just don't know,' they said.

As you can imagine, people were appalled and shocked by the bystanders' response to the Genovese murder. Commentators said that the apparent indifference of the bystanders demonstrated that American society, especially in urban areas, had become cold and apathetic. Experiments performed by social psychologists suggest that this explanation is wrong – people in cities are not generally indifferent to the needs of other people. The fact that Kitty Genovese's attack went unreported is not remarkable because thirty-eight people were present; it is precisely because so many people were present that the attack was not reported.

Darley and Latané have studied the phenomenon of bystander intervention – the actions of people witnessing a situation in which someone appears to require assistance. Their experiments have shown that in such situations, the presence of other people who are doing nothing inhibits others from giving aid. For example, Darley and Latané (1968) staged an 'emergency' during a psychology experiment. Each participant took part in a discussion about personal problems associated with college life with one, two or five other people by means of an intercom. The experimenter explained that the participants would sit in individual rooms so that they would be anonymous and hence would be more likely to speak frankly. The experimenter would not listen in but would get their reactions later in a questionnaire. Actually, only one participant was present; the other voices were simply tape recordings. During the discussion, one of the people, who had previously said that he sometimes had seizures, apparently had one. His speech became incoherent and he stammered out a request for help.

Almost all participants left the room to help the victim when they were the only witness to the seizure. However, when there appeared to be other witnesses, the participants were much less likely to try to help. In addition, those who did try to help reacted more slowly if other people were thought to be present (see Figure 15.6).

Darley and Latané reported that the participants who did not respond were not indifferent to the plight of their fellow student. Indeed, when the experimenter entered the room, they usually appeared nervous and emotionally

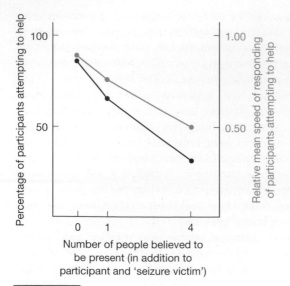

Figure 15.6

Bystander intervention. Percentage of participants attempting to help as a function of the number of other people the participants believed to be present.

Source: Based on data from Darley, J.M. and Latané, B., Bystander intervention in emergencies: Diffusion of responsibility. *Journal of Personality and Social Psychology*, 1968, 8, 377–383.

aroused, and they asked whether someone was helping the victim. The experimenters did not receive the impression that the participants had decided not to act; rather, they were still in conflict, trying to decide whether they should do something.

Thus, it seems that whether bystanders will intervene in a particular circumstance depends, at least in part, on how they perceive the situation. Latané and Darley (1970) have proposed a model describing a sequence of steps bystanders face when confronted with a potential emergency:

1 The event must come to their attention or be noticed.

2 They must assume some responsibility for helping the victim.

3 The possible courses of action must be considered and compared.

4 Finally, they must actually implement the chosen course of action.

Of course, this sequence takes place rapidly and without much awareness on the bystander's part, as is true of many situations to which we respond daily.

Unfortunately, at least from the perspective of the victim, obstacles may arise at any one stage in this decision making process that make it unlikely that a bystander will intervene. In many cases, the bystander who is aware that others are available to help may not feel any personal responsibility to do so, a phenomenon called **diffusion of responsibility**. This factor is considered to be responsible for the finding that help is less likely to be offered when there are several bystanders present. In addition, the bystander may not feel competent to intervene or may be fearful of doing so; consequently, no action is taken. Shotland and Heinold (1985) staged an accident in which a person seemed to be bleeding. Bystanders who had received training in first-aid were much more likely to come to the victim's aid, and they did so whether or not bystanders were present. Because they knew how to recognise an emergency and knew what to do, they were less likely to fear doing the wrong thing.

Social facilitation

As we just saw, the behaviour of other people has a powerful effect on our own behaviour. Studies have shown that even the mere presence of other people can affect a person's behaviour. Triplett (1897) published the first experimental study on **social facilitation** – the enhancement of a person's performance by the presence of other people. He had people perform simple tasks, such as turning the crank of a fishing reel. He found that his participants turned the crank faster and for a longer time if other people were present. Although many other studies found the same effect, some investigators reported just the opposite phenomenon: if the task was difficult and complex, the presence of an audience impaired the participants' performance. You yourself have probably noticed that you have difficulty performing certain tasks if someone is watching you.

Robert Zajonc (1965) has suggested an explanation for social facilitation. He claims that the presence of people who are watching a performer (or of people whom the performer perceives as watching) raises that person's arousal level. The increase in arousal has the effect of increasing the probability of performing dominant responses: responses that are best learned and most likely to occur in a particular situation. When the task is simple, the dominant response is generally the correct one (by definition an easy task is one which you get right all the time), so an audience improves performance. When the task is difficult the dominant response is generally not the correct one (by definition a difficult task is one which you get wrong all the time), so an audience impairs performance.

Subsequent experiments have supported Zajonc's explanation. For example, Martens (1969) tested the prediction that the presence of a group increases a person's level of arousal. While participants performed a complex motor task alone or in the presence of ten people, the experimenter determined physiological arousal by measuring the amount of sweat present on the participants' palms. The presence of an audience produced a clear-cut effect: the participants who performed in front of other people had sweatier palms.

Markus (1978) tested the effects of an audience on task performance. She had student participants get undressed and then dress up in either their own clothes (an easy task where the dominant response is to get it right) or in unfamiliar clothing involving a special lab coat and special shoes (a difficult task where the dominant response is to make mistakes). Some participants did this alone whereas others did this while being watched by someone. Relative to those who did the task alone, those who were being watched were faster on the easy task and slower on the difficult task – clear support for social facilitation.

One factor that affects an individual's arousal level and, in turn, social facilitation, is the person's perception of the audience. Sanna and Shotland (1990) found that participants who believed that an audience would evaluate them positively performed better when the audience was present. Those who anticipated a negative evaluation performed worse.

Social loafing

Working together on a task, rather than being merely watched by others or simply being in the presence of others, can have additional effects – the presence of a group sometimes results in a decrease in effort, or social loafing. Thus, a group is often less than the sum of its individual members. Many years ago, Ringelmann (cited by Dashiell, 1935) measured the effort that people made when pulling a rope in a mock tug-of-war contest against a device that measured the exerted force. Presumably, the force exerted by eight people pulling together in a simple task would be at least the sum of their individual efforts or even somewhat greater than the sum because of social facilitation. However, Ringelmann found that the total force exerted was only about half what would be predicted by the simple combination of individual efforts. The participants exerted less force when they worked in a group.

More recent studies have confirmed these results and have extended them to other behaviours. Several variables have been found to determine whether the presence of a group will produce social facilitation or social loafing. One of the most important of them is identifiability. Williams *et al.* (1981) asked participants to shout as loud as they could individually or in groups. Participants who were told that the equipment could measure only the total group effort shouted less loudly than those who were told that the equipment could measure individual efforts. The latter shouted just as loudly in groups as they did alone. These results suggest that a person's efforts in a group activity are affected by whether other people can observe his or her individual efforts. If they can, social facilitation is likely to occur; if they cannot, then social loafing is more likely.

Another variable that determines whether social facilitation or social loafing occurs is individual responsibility. If a person's efforts are duplicated by those of another person (and if his or her individual efforts are not identifiable), the person is likely to exert less than maximum effort. Harkins and Petty (1982) had participants work in groups of four on a task that required them to report whenever a dot appeared in a particular quadrant of a video screen. In one condition, each participant watched an individual quadrant and was solely responsible for detecting dots that appeared there. In the other condition, all four participants watched the same quadrant; thus, the responsibility for detecting dots was shared. Participants did not loaf when they were responsible for their own quadrants.

In a recent review of the social loafing literature, Karau and Williams (1995) noted that two variables – sex and culture – appear to moderate people's tendency to become social loafers. Although all people in different cultures are susceptible to social loafing, the effect is smaller for women than for men and for people living in Eastern cultures than for those living in Western cultures. Karau and Williams offer a reasonable explanation for this finding: both women and people living in Eastern cultures tend to be more group- or collectively oriented in their thinking and behaviour than do men and people living in Western cultures. That is, women and people living in Eastern cultures tend to place greater importance on participating in group activities, which partially buffers them from social loafing effects.

Reciprocity

Another very strong social influence is reciprocity, the tendency to repay favours others have done for us. When someone does something for us, we feel uncomfortable until the debt is discharged. For example, if people invite us to their house for dinner, we feel obliged to return the favour in the near future. And owing a social debt to someone we do not like is especially distasteful. Often people will suffer in silence rather than ask for help from someone they dislike. Reciprocity is pervasive – every culture is known to have some form of the 'golden rule' (Cialdini, 1993). It establishes a basic guideline for behaviour in a wide range of situations, and its emergence in evolutionary history is considered to be crucial to the development of social life.

Reciprocity does not require that the 'favour' be initially requested or even wanted. The debt of obligation can be so strong that reciprocity can be exploited by those who want us to comply with their requests when we would otherwise not do so. For example, people trying to sell something often try to capitalise on the reciprocity rule by giving the potential customer a free sample. Once the person has accepted the 'gift', the sales representative tries to get him or her to return the favour by making a purchase. If you have ever accepted a piece of food from a friendly person handing out samples in a supermarket, you realise how hard it is to walk away without purchasing something.

Experiments conducted by social psychologists have confirmed the strength of reciprocity in human interactions. For example, Regan (1971) enlisted the participation of university students in an experiment that supposedly involved art appreciation. During a break, some participants were treated to a soft drink by another 'participant' (a confederate) or by the experimenter; others received nothing. After the experiment, the confederate asked each participant to purchase some raffle tickets he was selling. Compliance with the request was measured by the number of tickets each participant bought (see Figure 15.7). The participants treated to a soft drink by the confederate purchased the most raffle tickets.

Commitment

Once people commit themselves by making a decision and acting on it, they are reluctant to renounce their commitment. For example, have you ever joined one side of an argument on an issue that you do not really care about only to find yourself vehemently defending a position that just a few minutes ago meant almost nothing to you? This phenomenon, which may reflect a cognitive dissonance process (see earlier in this chapter), was demonstrated in a clever study by Knox and Inkster (1968). The experimenters asked people at the betting windows of a racetrack how confident they were that their horse would win. They questioned half the people just before they had made their bets, the other half just afterwards. The people who had

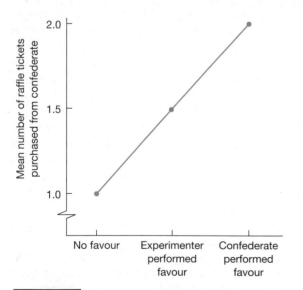

Figure 15.7

The strength of reciprocity. Mean number of raffle tickets purchased from a confederate when participants received a favour or no favour from the experimenter or confederate.

Source: Based on data from Regan, D.T., Effects of favor and liking on compliance. *Journal of Experimental Social Psychology*, 1971, 7, 627–639.

already made their bets were more confident than were those who had not yet paid. Their commitment increased the perceived value of their decision.

An experiment by Freedman and Fraser (1966) showed that commitment has a long-lasting effect on people's tendency to comply with requests. They sent a person posing as a volunteer worker to call on homeowners in a residential California neighbourhood and to ask them to perform a small task: to accept a 3 inch square sign saying 'Keep California Beautiful' or 'Be a Safe Driver' or to sign a petition supporting legislation favouring one of these goals. Almost everyone agreed. Two weeks later, the experimenters sent another person to ask these people whether they would be willing to have public service billboards erected in front of their houses. To give them an idea of precisely what was being requested, the 'volunteer worker' showed the homeowners a photograph of a house almost completely hidden by a huge, ugly, poorly lettered sign saying 'DRIVE CAREFULLY'. Over 55 per cent of the people agreed to this obnoxious request. In contrast, only 17 per cent of householders who had not been contacted previously (and asked to accept the smaller sign) agreed to have such a billboard placed on their property. Freedman and Fraser referred to their procedure as the foot-in-the-door technique.

Commitment increases people's compliance even when the reason for the original commitment is removed. For example, some of you may have had dealings with car sales agents. You are shown a beautiful car that you fall in love with and the agent commits you to purchasing the car which includes CD player, air conditioning, sunroof, electric windows and so forth, as well as all the various dealer costs. The agent now goes to get the paperwork ratified by her boss and comes back with the disappointing news that some of the 'extras' are not included. A rational choice would now be to decline to buy the car. However, because you are committed to your decision you are actually very likely still to purchase the car. This sales technique is called low-balling.

Commitment probably increases compliance for several reasons. First, the act of complying with a request in a particular category may change a person's self-image. Through the process of self-attribution, people who accept a small sign to support safe driving may come to regard themselves as public-spirited individuals – what sensible person is not for safe driving? Thus, when they hear the billboard request, they find it difficult to refuse. After all, they are public-spirited, so how can they say no? Saying no would imply that they did not have the courage of their convictions. Thus, this reason has at its root self-esteem; to maintain positive self-esteem, the person must say yes to the larger request.

Commitment may also increase compliance because the initial, smaller request changes people's perception of compliance in general. Evidence supporting this suggestion was provided by Rittle (1981). While sitting in a waiting room before taking part in an experiment, some adult participants were approached by an 8 year old child who was having trouble operating a vending machine. Later, while answering a series of questions designed to disguise the true nature of the experiment, they were asked to rate their perceptions of how unpleasant it might be to provide help to other people. After the participants had answered all the questions and the study was apparently over, the interviewer asked them whether they would volunteer between thirty minutes and four hours of their time to participate in a research project. Participants who had helped the child rated helping as less unpleasant and were more willing to participate in the research project than were people who had not helped the child (see Figure 15.8).

Attractive people

People tend to be influenced by requests or persuasive messages from attractive people. As we will see in a later section, physical good looks are one of the most important factors in determining whether we find someone likable.

Kulka and Kessler (1978) demonstrated the effect of good looks on people's behaviour in a controlled experiment. They staged mock trials of a negligence suit in which

someone was suing another person for damages. The participants served as jury members and decided how much money the plaintiffs should be awarded. Physically attractive plaintiffs received an average of $10,051, but physically unattractive plaintiffs received only $5,623. Justice is certainly not blind.

Why is attractiveness such a potent influence on people's behaviour? The most likely explanation involves classical conditioning and – again – self-esteem. Classical conditioning holds that when people have positive or negative reactions to some stimuli, they begin to have positive or negative reactions to other stimuli associated with those stimuli. Thus, as Cialdini (1993) notes, some people irrationally blame the weather forecaster for bad weather. Similarly, in ancient times, a messenger bringing news about a battle to the ruler of Persia was treated to a banquet if the news was good and beheaded if it was bad.

Advertisers regularly pay tribute to the effectiveness of association when they use attractive models and celebrities to endorse their products. For example, Smith and Engel (1968) showed two versions of an advertisement for a new car. One version included an attractive woman and the other did not. When the participants subsequently rated the car, those who saw the advertisement with the attractive woman rated the car as faster, more appealing, more expensive looking and better designed.

Besides making products or opinions more attractive by being associated with them, attractive people are better able to get others to comply with their requests. This phenomenon, like so many others, probably has self-esteem at its root. One of the reasons that people tend to comply with the requests of attractive people is that they want to be liked by attractive people; in their minds, being liked by attractive people makes them more desirable, too. People tend to emphasise their associations with attractive and important people. We have all encountered name-droppers who want us to think that they are part of a privileged circle of friends. This phenomenon is even demonstrated by fans of sports teams. Cialdini *et al.* (1976) found that university students were more likely to wear sweatshirts featuring the university name on Mondays after the football team had won a game than after the team had lost. Also, Wann and Dolan (1994) have shown that spectators identify with, and are biased in favour of, fellow spectators who support the same team as they do.

Although attractive people may influence our behaviour it is possible that they may only influence our underlying attitudes when we do not consider the underlying message carefully. You will recall from the section in this chapter on attitude change that, according to Petty and Cacioppo's (1986) elaboration likelihood model, people can process information either via a central or a peripheral route – attractive people may influence us via the peripheral route, and can thus be less influential if we adopt central route processing.

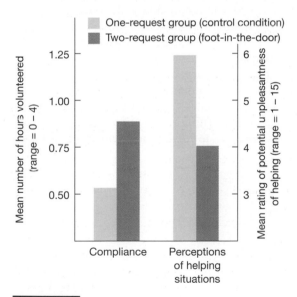

Figure 15.8

The effect of commitment on compliance and perceptions of the potential unpleasantness of helping situations. Mean number of hours volunteered (compliance) and mean rating of potential unpleasantness of volunteering for control participants and participants who first helped a child.

Source: Based on data from Rittle, R.H., Changes in helping behavior: Self versus situational perceptions as mediators of the foot-in-the-door technique. *Personality and Social Psychology Bulletin*, 1981, 7, 431–437.

Authority

People tend to comply with the requests of people in authority and to be swayed by their persuasive arguments, and such obedience is generally approved by society. For example, the Bible describes God's test of Abraham, who is ordered to sacrifice his beloved son Isaac. Just as he is about to plunge the knife, an angel tells him to stop; he has proved his obedience. Cohen and Davis (1981) cite a more recent, if less dramatic, example of unthinking obedience. A physician prescribed eardrops for a hospitalised patient with an ear infection. His order read 'place in R ear'. Unfortunately, he apparently did not put enough space between the abbreviation for right (R) and the word ear, because the nurse delivered the ear drops rectally. Neither she nor the patient thought to question such treatment for an earache.

A disturbing example of mindless obedience was obtained in a series of experiments performed by Milgram (1963), who advertised for participants in local newspapers in order to obtain as representative a sample as possible. The participants served as 'teachers' in what they were told was a learning experiment. A confederate (a middle-aged accountant) serving as the 'learner' was strapped into a chair 'to prevent excessive movements when he was shocked', and electrodes were attached to his wrist. The participants were told that 'although the shocks can be extremely painful, they cause no permanent tissue damage'.

The participant was then brought to a separate room housing an apparatus having dials, buttons and a series of switches that supposedly delivered shocks ranging from 15 to 450 volts. The participant was instructed to use this apparatus to deliver shocks, in increments of 15 volts for each 'mistake', to the learner in the other room. Beneath the switches were descriptive labels ranging from 'slight shock' to 'danger: severe shock'.

The learner gave his answers by pressing the appropriate lever on the table in front of him. Each time he made an incorrect response, the experimenter told the participant to throw another switch and give a larger shock. At the 300 volt level, the learner pounded on the wall and then stopped responding to questions. The experimenter told the participant to consider a 'no answer' as an incorrect answer. At the 315 volt level, the learner pounded on the wall again. If the participant hesitated in delivering a shock, the experimenter said, 'Please go on'. If this admonition was not enough, the experimenter said, 'The experiment requires that you continue', then, 'It is absolutely essential that you continue', and finally, 'You have no other choice; you must go on'. The factor of interest was how long the participants would continue to administer shocks to the hapless victim. A majority of participants gave the learner what they believed to be the 450 volt shock, despite the fact that he pounded on the wall twice and then stopped responding altogether (see Figure 15.9).

In a later experiment, when the confederate was placed in the same room as the participant and his struggling and apparent pain could be observed, 37.5 per cent of the participants obeyed the order to administer further shocks (Milgram, 1974). Thirty per cent were even willing to hold his hand against a metal plate to force him to receive the shock.

Milgram's experiments indicate that a significant percentage of people will blindly follow the orders of authority figures, no matter what the effects are on other people. Milgram had originally designed his experimental procedure to understand why ordinary people in Germany had participated in the murders of millions of innocent people during World War II. He had planned to perfect the technique in the United States and then travel to Germany to continue his studies. The results he obtained made it clear that he did not have to leave home. (However, as Lutsky

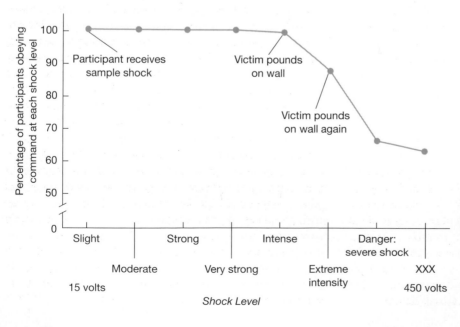

Figure 15.9

Data from one of Milgram's studies of obedience.

Source: Baron, R.A. and Byrne, D., *Social Psychology: Understanding human interaction* (8th edition). Boston: Allyn & Bacon, 1997. Reprinted with permission. After Milgram, 1963.

(1995) has pointed out, other factors, including voluntary actions on the part of many Germans, contributed to the atrocities committed by the Nazis during World War II.)

Most people find the results of Milgram's studies surprising. They cannot believe that for such a large proportion of people the social pressure to conform to the experimenter's orders is stronger than the participant's own desire not to hurt someone else. As Ross (1977) points out, this misperception is an example of the fundamental attribution error. People tend to underestimate the effectiveness of situational factors and to overestimate the effectiveness of dispositional ones. Clearly, the tendency to obey an authority figure is amazingly strong. However, one factor that can dramatically reduce it is social support for non-compliance. In one of his studies, Milgram had two confederates work with the participant. When the confederates were obedient so was the participant – obedience increased to 92.5 per cent. When the confederates were disobedient so was the participant – obedience dropped to 10 per cent.

Understandably, much of the attention given to Milgram's research focused on its considerable ethical implications (Elms, 1995). Many people, psychologists and non-psychologists alike, have attacked his research on the grounds that it involved deception and too much emotional strain on the participants. Indeed, Milgram's research helped prompt psychologists to strengthen ethical guidelines for conducting research with humans.

In his defence, however, it should be stressed that Milgram conducted an extensive debriefing at the end of each experimental session in which the true purpose of the experiment was explained to the participants. The participants were told that their behaviour was quite typical of the way most people responded to the situation posed by the experiment. In addition, the participants were later sent a detailed written report of the experimental procedure and a follow-up questionnaire asking them about their feelings regarding their participation. Eighty-four per cent of the participants said that they were glad to have participated in the experiment, and only 1.3 per cent indicated that they wished they had not participated.

An additional objection to Milgram's research is that people may have had to confront a disturbing aspect of their own behaviour – the self-realisation that they were capable of actions that they find reprehensible. Milgram replied that at least some of his participants considered their enhanced insight into their own behaviour to have been enough to justify their participation. Of course, Milgram could not guarantee that somebody, somewhere, who had participated in his research might be deeply troubled by his participation. And therein lies another moral dilemma: to what extent is knowledge about behaviour, in general, and insight about one's own behaviour, in particular, to be avoided in case some people think that others might find this knowledge disturbing? That is not an easy question to answer and one that psychologists must grapple with each time they perform research such as that conducted by Milgram.

Deindividuation and crowd behaviour

Blindly obeying the commands of an authority figure is not the only situation in which we might find ourselves behaving in less than admirable ways. Sometimes, just being part of a crowd can be sufficient to transform our otherwise civil behaviour into unruly, even violent acts. We have all seen media coverage of soccer riots, and of crowd aggression in, for example, Israel and Northern Ireland, and many of us may have been involved in protests or demonstrations that have turned ugly. We are also familiar with vivid literary accounts of the great riots and demonstration associated with the French and Russian Revolutions.

Many social psychologists explain these acts in terms of deindividuation, in which one loses one's sense of individuality and personal responsibility. In collective settings, people 'blend' into the crowd, achieving a sense of anonymity that causes them to assume less responsibility for their actions (Diener, 1980; Forsyth, 1990). Consider a study of empathy towards strangers conducted by Zimbardo (1970). In one condition, young women were easily identifiable: they wore name tags and were called by their names. In another condition, a different group of young women were not so easily identifiable: they wore large coats and hoods without name tags and were never referred to by their names. The two groups of women were given chances to administer electric shocks to a stranger, who was in actuality a confederate of Zimbardo's. The young women who were more-or-less unidentifiable gave nearly twice as many electric shocks to the stranger as did the young women whose identities were known. Thus, the amount of aggression Zimbardo observed in his participants was strongly correlated with the extent to which their identities were known, reinforcing the idea that antisocial behaviour observed in some groups is due to the loss of personal identity of its individual members.

People in crowds are not always antisocial, and crowds themselves are not always aggressive – witness the dismantling of the Berlin Wall in 1990, the last night of the proms, and numerous peaceful rock festivals. Deindividuation may not be an automatic consequence of crowds, or it may be a process that is less mechanically tied to antisocial behaviour. Taylor et al. (1994) actually characterise deindividuation as a process wherein one's personal identity – one's sense of self – is replaced by identification with the group's values and goals. This idea has been more fully explored in terms of social identity theory, which we discussed earlier in this chapter. Reicher (1987) suggests that crowds are events where people from the same group, and thus with a common social identity, come together to achieve a goal (which may or may not involve violence). The strong sense of common social identity ensures that people are highly attuned to the appropriate group norm, and thus conform tightly to it. There is no loss of identity or responsibility, no deindividuation, rather a change of identity.

Controversies in psychological science

Levels of explanation: the case of soccer 'hooliganism'

The issue

If you were asked to describe a kiss, there are many answers you could give. You could talk about neural transmitters and the biochemistry of the brain that sends messages to your lips. You could talk about the cognitive organisation of your thoughts that decides on giving a kiss and to whom. You could tell me about your past history of a relationship with someone that makes you like that person and want to kiss him or her. You could talk about the social conventions in your culture that encourage kissing in certain circumstances. All these answers are of course 'correct', but a biochemist would be disappointed with the last one, a sociologist with the first one, and a romantic with all of them. The level of explanation is wrong.

Social psychologists often argue about what is the appropriate level of explanation for social psychology. They worry about levels of explanation that are too low (for example, neurophysiology) or explanations that are too high (for example, sociology) and strive for a balance between cognitive processes and social conventions. This debate often focuses on how one should explain the behaviour of people in groups. Is group behaviour identical to individual behaviour but simply magnified because there are lots of people present? Is group behaviour identical to interpersonal behaviour, only magnified because there are lots of interpersonal links? Is group behaviour quite different from interpersonal behaviour because social interaction creates new properties (for example, norms) that were never there before but now influence behaviour.

Generally speaking, there are two camps in social psychology: those who believe that group behaviour is not qualitatively different from individual or interpersonal behaviour (we can call them 'individualists') and those who believe it is ('collectivists'). The debate mostly bubbles along in the background, but from time to time it seems to become a major preoccupation – the 1960s was one such occasion, when social psychology seemed to be deep in crisis (Elms, 1975). Critics felt the discipline was asking the wrong questions, providing inadequate explanations of trivial behaviours and using primitive methodologies. The resolution of the crisis had two contrasting prongs: social psychologists in the United States developed social cognition (discussed extensively in this chapter) in a drive for better methodology and better theory (Fiske and Taylor, 1991), and social psychologists in Europe developed what they

called a more social social psychology (Tajfel, 1984) in a drive for socially relevant research (for example, the study of prejudice and intergroup conflict) and theories that linked cognitive and social processes. Willem Doise uses the word 'articulation' to characterise these kinds of theory (Doise, 1986). One of these theories is Tajfel and Turner's social identity theory which we discuss at various points in this chapter. Minority influence research by Moscovici and Mugny (again discussed in this chapter) also grows from this European tradition, as does Moscovici's theory of social representations (Moscovici, 1983) which describes the way that groups collectively develop relatively simple explanations of complex events (for example, the economy, HIV infection, unemployment, immigration) that are internalised by their members as interpretive frameworks.

In reading this chapter, see if you recognise these different perspectives, or decide what you think about the appropriateness of the level of explanation offered by social psychology. The study of soccer 'hooliganism' is a good illustration.

The evidence

Since the early 1970s, European, but particularly British, soccer has become strongly associated with hooliganism. Soccer 'hooliganism' is quite clearly a group behaviour. It involves groups of people behaving in the same way. It is also a set of behaviours which is often associated in the popular mind with crowd behaviour, in particular the popular image of a riot or other violent and antisocial collective event. Popular hysteria tends to characterise soccer hooliganism in terms of the familiar stereotypical image of soccer fans on the rampage (Murphy *et al.*, 1990).

One individualistic level of analysis might focus on the fact that hooliganism is aggressive behaviour, and perhaps trace the behaviour back to personality traits that incline some people to be aggressive. From this perspective, soccer hooliganism arises because a soccer match acts like a beacon for aggressive people who need an outlet for their violent tendencies – a soccer match is simply a context that attracts aggressive people. Another individualistic explanation is that when people's goals are frustrated, people have an overwhelming urge to vent their frustration as aggression. People whose lives are frustrating may attend soccer matches because they see them as a context in which they can safely vent their frustration through aggression. It has also often been suggested that the very low scoring rate in soccer (in contrast, say, to basketball, rugby or cricket) may act as a powerful proximal frustration. But then why is it that the majority of soccer fans do not behave aggressively, and often the victors (less frustrated) are just as or even more aggressive than the losers?

None of these analyses approaches soccer hooliganism as a group behaviour. Deindividuation theories offer a more group-oriented analysis. A soccer match is a crowd context where people feel anonymous and unidentifiable (literally lost in the crowd); they lose their sense of individual identity and thus no longer feel constrained to act in socially acceptable ways. This perspective assumes that people are fundamentally antisocial and aggressive, and that the only reason people do not ordinarily act in this way is that they are usually identifiable in a society whose norms strongly proscribe such behaviour. Hooliganism is primitive unsocialised behaviour which lies deep in all our psyches, and which is released in crowd settings. Although recognising the group context of hooliganism, this analysis is also actually rather individualistic. The crowd releases individual aggressive instincts – and in fact any (non-group) context that makes one feel deindividuated may have the same effect (for example, darkness, or clothing which conceals who we are). One problem with this analysis is that it cannot easily explain why most people at soccer matches do not indulge in hooliganism. Perhaps they are not deindividuated – but why? Perhaps they are deindividuated, but deindividuation does not inevitably produce hooliganism – in which case alternative or additional processes must operate to produce hooliganism?

A different, more genuinely group-oriented analysis of soccer hooliganism is provided by Marsh *et al.* (1978). According to their analysis, violence by football fans is actually orchestrated far away from the stadium and long before a given match. What might appear to be a motley crowd of supporters on match day can actually consist of several distinct groups of fans with different status. By participating in ritualised aggression over a period of time, a faithful follower can be 'promoted' into a higher group and can continue to pursue a 'career structure'. Rival fans who follow their group's rules quite carefully can avoid real physical harm to themselves or others. For example, chasing the opposition after a match need not necessarily end in violence since part of the agreed code is not actually to catch anyone. Seen in this light, soccer hooliganism is a kind of staged production and is not the example of an uncontrollable mob sometimes depicted by the media. When real violence does take place it tends to be both unusual and attributable to particular individuals.

Soccer hooliganism can also be understood in more broadly societal terms. For example, Murphy *et al.* (1990) described how soccer arose in Britain as an essentially working class sport, and that by the 1950s working class values to do with masculine aggression had already become associated with the game. Attempts by the government (seen as middle class) to control this aspect of the sport can backfire because they merely enhance class solidarity and encourage increased violence that generalises beyond matches. This sort of explanation points towards an analysis in terms of intergroup relations and subcultural norms that prescribe and legitimate aggression. Fans derive a sense of who they are, a sense of identity, from being part of a group of supporters; some people, particularly those with few other valued sources of identity, identify more strongly than others. The attitudinal, dress and behavioural norms of the group are strongly adhered to, particularly in situations where the group is very salient, for example at, or around, a match when supporters of opposing teams are present in the stadium, in the streets and on public transport. The actual norms of the groups reflect the historical origins of the sport and the intrinsically competitive and masculine nature of the game. Soccer hooliganism is largely a display of controlled aggression and machismo that reflects strong identification with group norms (this sort of group-oriented analysis owes much to social identity theory).

Conclusion

Social psychologists worry about the appropriate level of analysis. This worry is particularly acute when they are dealing with group behaviour. Exclusively societal level analyses often have precious little psychology in them, whereas exclusively individualistic analyses tend to be unsatisfactory as they miss the collective nature of group behaviour. What is often sought is an analysis which incorporates many levels or, better still, is able to integrate or 'articulate' different levels.

A proper social psychological analysis of soccer hooliganism, for example, probably benefits from an integration of multiple levels of analysis. Identification with supporter groups that have evolved norms probably provides the main parameters of what goes on. This also explains the largely symbolic and ritualistic nature of much supporter behaviour. However, within these parameters, individual or group frustrations coupled with the highly emotional atmosphere of a match may occasionally tip the balance towards real aggression. In the mix, there may also be individuals who are simply aggressive, and who find the ferment of a match an ideal context in which to indulge in overt aggression.

Group decision making

The process by which members of a group reach a decision is different from the process involved in individual decision making if only because decisions in groups are usually preceded by discussion. However, discussing issues relevant to a decision does not always guarantee that the best decision will be made. Two examples of problems associated with group decision making are group polarisation and groupthink.

Group polarisation

In some group decision making situations, discussion of alternative choices leads to group decisions that are either riskier or more conservative than the group's initial position on the issue at hand. In general, if the initial position of group members is to make a risky decision, group discussion will lead to making an even riskier group decision. In contrast, if the initial position of group members is to make a conservative decision, group discussion will usually lead to an even more conservative decision. The tendency for a group decision to be more extreme than the mean of its members' positions, in the direction favoured by the mean, is called group polarisation.

One important consequence of group polarisation is attitude change. For example, suppose that you join a local environmental group because you have a desire to protect the environment. After attending several meetings and discussing environmental issues with other group members, you may find that your pro-environment attitude has become even stronger: You are more of an environmentalist than you thought you were. That group discussion can affect attitude change so powerfully has been documented in many psychology experiments. For example, Myers and Bishop (1970) found that the initial levels of racial prejudice voiced by groups was altered through group discussion. Discussion caused the group with an initially low level of prejudice to become even less prejudiced and discussion caused the group with an initially high level of prejudice to become even more prejudiced.

What causes group discussion to lead to polarization? Although several explanations have been offered, three seem the most plausible: those concerning informational and normative influence (Isenberg, 1986), and social identity processes (Turner *et al.*, 1989). Informational influence involves learning new information germane to the decision to be made. When you are in a group that is already slanted towards one decision, group discussion will bring to light new information that supports your position but that you have not heard before. This supportive novel information will strengthen commitment to your position – across the members of the group this will encourage the group to endorse a more extreme decision.

Normative influence involves comparison of one's individual views with that of the group. Just as we discussed in the earlier section of this chapter on conformity, people strive for social approval and do not like to stand out from the crowd. Discussion reveals what appears to be the socially desirable position to hold, and thus members of the group strive to be seen by the other members of the group to be adhering to the 'popular' position. In this way the group becomes more extreme and is able to endorse a more extreme decision.

Social identity processes involve people in the group constructing a group norm to define their membership in the group and then conforming to that norm. Polarisation occurs because the norm is polarised – the group is already extreme and thus in order to distinguish the group clearly from other groups or from people who are not in the group, group members perceive the norm to be more extreme than the mean group position.

Groupthink

Irving Janis has studied a related phenomenon that sometimes occurs in group decision making: groupthink, the tendency to avoid dissent in the attempt to achieve group consensus (Janis, 1972, 1982). Janis developed the notion of groupthink after studying the poor decision making that led President John F. Kennedy to order the ill-fated attempt to overthrow the Castro regime in Cuba in 1961. The decision to embark on the Bay of Pigs invasion was made by Kennedy and a small group of advisors. After studying the conditions that led to this decision as well as other important group decisions that altered the course of twentieth-century history (such as the Japanese attack on Pearl Harbor), Janis proposed his theory of groupthink.

The theory specifies the conditions necessary for groupthink as well as its symptoms and consequences (see Figure 15.10). The conditions that foster groupthink include a stressful situation in which the stakes are very high, a cohesive group of people who already tend to think alike and who are isolated from others who could offer criticism of the decision, and a strong group leader who makes his or her position well known to the group. In the Bay of Pigs example, the overthrow of one of America's arch-enemies was at stake, Kennedy's group of advisors were like-minded regarding the invasion and met in secret, and Kennedy was a forceful and charismatic leader who made his intentions to invade Cuba known to the group.

Janis also notes five symptoms of groupthink, all of which were present during the decision to invade Cuba. First, group members share the illusion that their decision is sound, moral and right – in a word, invulnerable. Second, dissent from the leader's views are discouraged, further supporting the illusion that the group's decision is the right one. Third, instead of assessing the strengths and weaknesses of the decision, group members rationalise their decision, looking only for reasons that support it. Fourth, group members are closed-minded – they are not willing to listen to alternative suggestions and ideas. And fifth, self-appointed 'mindguards' exist within the group who actively discourage dissent from the group norm.

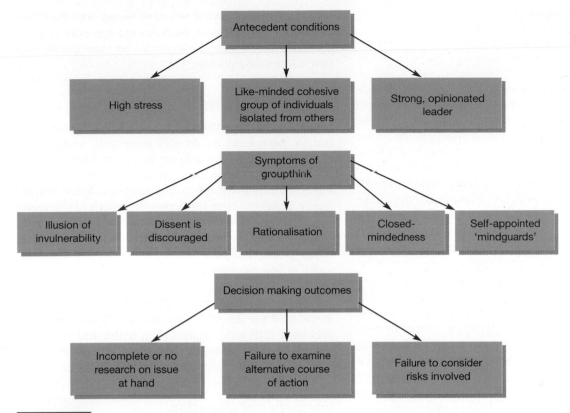

Figure 15.10

A summary of Janis's conception of groupthink.

Combined, these symptoms lead to flawed decision making. They contribute to several tendencies: to conduct only incomplete or no research on the issue about which a decision is being made; to fail to examine alternative courses of action specified by the decision, and finally, to fail to consider potential risks inherent in the decision.

Janis argues that groupthink may be avoided by taking several precautions. First, criticism by group members should be encouraged. Second, relevant input should be sought from appropriate people who are not members of the group. Third, the group should be broken down into subgroups in which different ideas and opinions are generated and developed. And fourth, the group leader should not overstate his or her position on the matter and should be on guard for rationalisation, closed-mindedness and illusions of invulnerability.

Questions to think about

Social influences and group processes

- How would social life be different if people tended not to conform to certain social norms? Think of an instance in which your behaviour conformed to a social norm. How might the outcome of this social interaction have been different had you not conformed?

- In lifesaving and first aid classes, people are taught to take control in emergency situations. For example, in a situation in which a person appears to be drowning, they assign onlookers specific responsibilities, such as calling emergency services or fetching rescue equipment. To what extent does taking control in this manner enhance bystander intervention? What effect might it have on the onlookers' tendency towards diffusion of responsibility?

- Suppose that you have been asked by your psychology lecturer to organise a small group of class members to prepare a presentation. As the leader of the group, what steps might you take to prevent the individual members of your group from becoming social loafers?

- How might the norm of reciprocity apply to social interactions on an international basis, for instance, negotiating trade agreements, peace treaties or cultural exchanges?

Aggression, attraction and loving

Social behaviour is extremely varied, perhaps no more evidently than in the contrast between aggression and love.

These are starkly different behaviours which may both, ironically, be fundamental to the survival of the species.

Aggression

As you saw in Chapter 13, human aggression is often considered to be an innate component of our biological inheritance – a behaviour which is a necessary part of the evolutionary process that ensures survival of the fittest (Lorenz, 1966). The ability to hurt others may well have these roots; however, social psychologists tend to be more interested in discovering environmental factors that encourage or inhibit aggression and in explaining the huge diversity of human aggression (Baron and Richardson, 1994).

There are many factors that can cause aggression. When important goals are frustrated people can feel angry and express this as aggression, particularly when there is an available target that can be aggressed against without fear of retaliation and the person who is frustrated has few other coping mechanisms available. According to social learning theory (Bandura, 1977), aggression can be learned by simply observing other people being reinforced for behaving aggressively. Aggression can also become more likely in a given situation if a person who has a tendency to respond aggressively is aroused, even if the arousal has nothing to do with anger (it could be arousal from a gym workout, a movie, a sexual encounter). People with a type-A personality, or elevated testosterone levels, are also more likely to be aggressive. Testosterone is the male hormone, and so males tend to be more aggressive than females; but the hormonal cause can be very difficult to dissociate from the fact that men are typically socialised to be more aggressive than are females. There is also evidence that disinhibition, caused perhaps by deindividuation which we described earlier in this chapter, can increase the probability of aggression.

There are many paths to aggression – not surprisingly, aggression is an enduring problem for society. Consider the following scenario. A man with a type-A personality and elevated testosterone is driving home in a hurry from the gym in traffic where people are successfully cutting in, and he is in a large car with dark windows and the CD on full blast. What do you think might happen if you were driving rather slowly in front of him, or took rather a long time to pull away from traffic lights?

Alcohol and aggression

Alcohol consumption is often associated with aggression. Research suggests that alcohol makes people more prone to social influence while at the same time less able to think through the consequences of their actions – together these facilitate aggression when people drink in groups in societies that glorify aggression (Bushman and Cooper, 1990). Causal links are complex – for example, perhaps aggressive people like to go drinking in groups, and they would be aggressive even if they had not been drinking. However, controlled studies have shown that people who have consumed alcohol are more likely to act aggressively when encouraged by a confederate to do so than people who have consumed a placebo.

Media violence and aggression

Many people believe that the mass media, particularly films and TV, have much to do with aggression, as we saw in Chapter 13. There is no denying that these media portray a great deal of aggression and in the majority of cases the aggression brings rewards to the aggressor. Social learning theory makes the clear prediction that much of the aggression in our society is caused by excessive violence on TV and in films. However, research is inconclusive about the causal links (Phillips, 1986) – perhaps aggressive people watch or pay more attention to media aggression, whereas non-aggressive people either do not watch media aggression or simply do not pay much attention to it. Similar arguments hold for the evidence that violent pornography is associated with more aggressive attitudes and behaviours towards women – perhaps misogynistic attitudes encourage men to view violent pornography rather than vice versa.

Interpersonal attraction

Many factors determine interpersonal attraction, or people's tendency to approach each other and evaluate each other positively. Some factors are characteristics of the individuals themselves; others are determined by the socially reinforcing aspects of the environment. Interpersonal attraction is an important aspect of more enduring and closer relationships, such as friendships; however, the bases of attraction can change as one moves through different stages of a relationship (Duck, 1992). Physical appearance and attitudinal similarity can be very important in the initial stages of a relationship, whereas deeper, personality similarities and complementarity of needs may become more important later on.

Positive evaluation

Humans like to be evaluated positively, to be held in high regard by other people. This tendency is expressed in interpersonal attraction. Consider the following study. Geller *et al.* (1974) had female university students individually join group discussions with two other women, confederates of the experimenter. During the discussion, the confederates either treated the participant normally or ignored her, showing a lack of interest in what she said and changing the subject whenever she spoke. The participants who were ignored found the conversations distressing; they felt very unhappy and even gave themselves poor ratings. Being ignored is a form of negative evaluation by other people, and it exerts a powerful effect.

Familiarity

We have learned that attractiveness plays an important role in social influence. Fortunately for the majority of us who are not especially beautiful or handsome, the variable of exposure also influences people's attitudes towards others. The more frequent the exposure, the more positive the attitude is – we have already mentioned this 'mere exposure' effect in the section of this chapter on attitudes.

In order for an attachment to form between people, they must meet each other. Festinger *et al.* (1950) found that the likelihood of friendships between people who lived in an apartment house was related to the distance between the apartments in which they lived; the closer the apartments, the more likely the friendship was. People were also unlikely to have friends who lived on a different floor unless their apartments were next to a stairway, where they would meet people going up or down the stairs.

Repetition generally increases our preference for a stimulus. This phenomenon applies to people as well. Even in the brief time it takes to participate in an experiment, familiarity affects interpersonal attraction. Saegert *et al.* (1973) had female university students participate in an experiment supposedly involving the sense of taste. Groups of two students (all were participants; no confederates this time) entered booths, where they tasted and rated various liquids. The movements of the participants from booth to booth were choreographed so that pairs of women were together from zero to ten times. Afterwards, the participants rated their attraction to each of the other people in the experiment. The amount of attraction the participants felt towards a given person was directly related to the number of interactions they had had: the more interactions, the more attracted they were (see Figure 15.11)

Similarity

Another factor that influences interpersonal attraction is similarity – similarity in looks, interests and attitudes. Couples tend to be similar in attractiveness. In fact, couples who are mismatched in this respect are the most likely to break up (White, 1980). Although we might think that people would seek the most attractive partners that they could find, people tend to fear rejection and ridicule. Men especially tend to be afraid of approaching attractive women for this reason (Bernstein *et al.*, 1983).

Couples (and groups of friends) also tend to hold similar opinions. Presumably, a person who shares our opinions is likely to approve of us when we express them. Also, having friends who have similar opinions guarantees that our opinions are likely to find a consensus; we will not often find ourselves in the unpleasant position of saying something that brings disapproval from other people.

Similarity of attitudes is not the only factor determining the strength of interpersonal attraction. Other kinds of similarity are also important, such as age, occupational

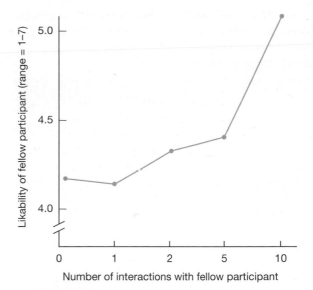

Figure 15.11

Familiarity, exposure, and attraction. The rated likability of a fellow participant as a function of number of interactions.

Source: Based on data from Saegert, S.C., Swap, W. and Zajonc, R.B., Exposure, context, and interpersonal attraction. *Journal of Personality and Social Psychology*, 1973, 25, 234–242.

status and ethnic background. Friends tend to have similar backgrounds as well as similar attitudes. However, as mentioned above, in longer-term relationships, need complementarity can become important – a relationship may endure and be more rewarding if the partners bring different qualities to it in order to satisfy each other's needs.

Physical appearance

We judge people by the characteristic that is supposed to be only skin deep – in general, we are more attracted to good-looking people than to unattractive people (Albright *et al.*, 1988). Social reinforcement provides a likely explanation for this phenomenon. Someone who is seen in the company of an attractive person and is obviously favoured by this person is likely to be well regarded by other people.

Walster *et al.* (1966) studied the effects of physical appearance at a dance at which university students were paired by a computer. Midway through the evening, the experimenters asked the participants to rate the attraction they felt towards their partners and to say whether they thought they would like to see them in the future. For both sexes, the only characteristic that correlated with attraction was physical appearance. Intelligence, grades and personality variables seemed to have no significant effect.

When people first meet someone who is good looking, they rate the person as probably holding attitudes similar to their own and tend to assume that he or she has a good personality, a successful marriage and high occupational status (Dion *et al.*, 1972). In fact, physically attractive people usually do possess many of these characteristics, probably because they receive favourable treatment from society (Hatfield and Sprecher, 1986).

However, among same-sex individuals, physical appearance may have its drawbacks, especially if members of the other sex are involved. For example, consider a study in which females were shown photos of the same woman dressed either casually or provocatively and either talking or not talking to a man in the presence of his female companion (Baenninger *et al.*, 1993). The female participants rated the 'other woman' in the photos more negatively when she was provocatively dressed than when she was casually dressed. Thus, we seem to take into account the particular circumstances under which we meet another person – his or her sex and the other people who may be present – when making judgements about that person and his or her attractiveness.

Loving

The relationships we have with others are generally marked by two different kinds of emotion: liking, a feeling of personal regard, intimacy and esteem for another person, and loving, a combination of liking and a deep sense of attachment to another person. Loving someone does not necessarily entail romance. You may have several close friends whom you love dearly yet have no desire to be involved with romantically.

Romantic love, also called passionate love, is an emotionally intense desire for sexual union with another person (Hatfield, 1988). Feeling romantic love generally involves experiencing five closely intertwined elements: a desire for intimacy with another, feeling passion for that person, being preoccupied with thoughts of that person, developing feelings of emotional dependence on that person, and feeling wonderful if that person feels romantic love towards you and dejected if not.

'Falling in love' and 'being in love' are common expressions that people use to describe their passionate desires for one another. Passionate love may occur at almost any time during the lifecycle, although people involved in long-term cohabitation or marriages seem to experience a qualitatively different kind of love. The partners may still make passionate love to one another, but passion is no longer the defining characteristic of the relationship. This kind of love is called companionate love and is characterised by a deep, enduring affection and caring for another. Companionate love is also marked by a mutual sense of commitment, or a strong desire to maintain the relationship. How passionate love develops into companionate love is at present an unanswered question, although odds are that the sort of intimacy that punctuates romantic love is still a major force in the relationship. An important feature of intimacy is self-disclosure, or the ability to share deeply private feelings and thoughts with another. Indeed, part of loving another is feeling comfortable sharing deeply personal aspects of yourself with that person.

Robert Sternberg (1988b) has developed a theory of how intimacy, passion and commitment may combine to produce liking and several different forms of love (see Table 15.3). According to this theory, liking involves only intimacy, infatuation involves only passion, and empty love involves only commitment. Combining any two of these elements produces still other kinds of love. Romantic love entails both intimacy and passion but no commitment. Companionate love entails both intimacy and commitment but no passion. Fatuous love (a kind of love marked by complacency in the relationship) entails both passion and commitment but no intimacy. The highest form of love, consummate love, contains all three elements.

Sternberg's theory is descriptive. It characterises different kinds of love, but it does not explain the origins of love. What function has love served in the evolution of our species? The answer can be summed up very succinctly: procreation and childrearing. Although love of any kind for another person is not a necessary requirement for sexual intercourse, a man and a woman who passionately love each other are more likely to have intercourse than are a man and a woman who do not. And if their union produces a child, then love serves another function – it increases the likelihood that both parents will share in the responsibilities of childrearing. Our capacity for loving, then, contributes in very practical ways to the continued existence of our species.

Table 15.3 Sternberg's theory of love

According to Sternberg, love is based on different combinations of intimacy, passion and commitment. These elements may combine to form eight different kinds of relationship.

	Intimacy	Passion	Commitment
Non-love			
Liking	*****		
Infatuated love		*****	
Empty love			*****
Romantic love	*****	*****	
Compassionate love	*****		*****
Fatuous love		*****	*****
Consummate love	*****	*****	*****

***** indicates that that element is present in the relationship; a blank space indicates that that element is absent or is present only in low quantities

Source: after Sternberg, 1986

Questions to think about

Aggression, attraction and loving

■ Are there individual differences in aggression, or do people differ in the way they express their aggression – some people are more physical and others are more verbal? How can one explain mass aggression?

■ To what kinds of persons are you most attracted? What factors, dispositional or situational, appear to be the most important in the relationships you have?

■ Is Sternberg's theory of love an accurate account of your own experience with different kinds of love? Are there kinds of love that you have experienced that are not included in his theory?

■ What is the link between media portrayal of violence and the level of violence we experience in our own society? Which causes which? On the basis of social psychological research on aggression, what would you recommend to policymakers who are thinking of stringent censoring of media violence?

Key terms

CHAPTER REVIEW

Social cognition and social knowledge

■ Impressions of people are strongly influenced by central traits, negative information, and information that one encounters first (primacy effect).

■ Our thoughts, feelings, perceptions and beliefs about the world are organised in mental frameworks, or schemas, which help us to manage and synthesise information about our social world.

■ Schemas about social groups that are widely shared within a group are stereotypes.

■ Schemas tend to be activated automatically once we have categorised a person, object or event.

■ Our self-concept is based on schemas that organise and synthesise personal knowledge and feelings we have about ourselves.

- There are cultural and situational differences in the extent to which self-schemas are based on being an individual or a member of a group.

- In making attributions about the causes of another person's behaviour, we consider the relative contributions of dispositional and situational factors.

- In making attributions about others' behaviour we tend to overestimate the role of dispositional factors and underestimate the role of situational factors (the fundamental attribution error). We do the opposite for our own behaviour.

- Attributions also tend to be self-serving. We attribute our own and our groups' good behaviours internally and bad behaviours externally. We also tend to think bad things happen to bad people and good things to good people.

- In making inferences about people, we tend to rely on cognitive shortcuts or heuristics, such as how available something is to memory, and how superficially representative something is of a category.

Attitudes and attitude change

- Attitudes have affective, cognitive and behavioural intention components and may be learned through mere exposure to the object of the attitude, classical conditioning processes and imitation.

- Attitudes are poor predictors of behaviour unless very specific attitudes and very specific behaviours are measured. Prediction is even better if attitudes towards behaviours are measured, and if normative support is strong and opportunity and resources to perform the behaviour are available.

- To understand explicit attempts to change a person's attitude, we must consider both the source of the intended persuasive message and the message itself.

- A message tends to be persuasive if its source is credible or attractive and if it is pitched correctly at its intended audience.

- There are at least two routes to persuasion. The central route involves careful consideration of the message, whereas the peripheral route involves superficial reliance on heuristics such as the attractiveness of the message source.

- Cognitive dissonance is an aversive state that occurs when our attitudes and behaviour are inconsistent. Resolution of dissonance often involves changing attitudes in line with behaviour.

- Our own observations of our behaviour and situation also influence attitude development.

Prejudice and intergroup behaviour

- Prejudice is an attitude, usually negative, towards a particular group. Its cognitive component is stereotypes, and its behavioural manifestation is discrimination.

- Prejudice and discrimination can develop out of competitive relations between social groups.

- The framework of prejudice and discrimination is also contained in the very fact of there exisiting different categories – ingroups and outgroups.

- Low self-esteem may encourage people to develop and express prejudices against easy targets.

- People derive a sense of who they are, a social identity, from the groups they belong to, and thus they are prepared to protect these groups against other groups and to strive to evaluate them more positively than other groups.

- Stereotypes may be further strengthened because people inflate the co-occurrence of negative behaviours and distinct groups, and also exaggerate the perceived homogeneity of outgroups.

- A self-fulfilling prophecy is a stereotype that constrains other people to act in ways that ultimately confirm the stereotype.

- Teaching people to think about members of other groups as individuals and to consider them in terms of their personal situations and characteristics can reduce prejudices and tendencies towards stereotyping.

- Although initially appealing, simply bringing different groups into contact with one another, so that they become familiar with one another, is not reliably effective in reducing prejudice.

Social influences and group processes

- Social interaction, particularly when people are uncertain or in need of social approval, produces group norms that subsequently regulate behaviour.

- People conform because they are unsure, in need of approval, or define themselves in terms of the norms and identity of a group.

- Misperception of norms can sometimes inhibit people from offering assistance in an emergency.

- Bystander intervention is facilitated if there are only few bystanders and if they feel they have the resources (time, ability etc.) to help.

- The presence of others enhances the performance of a well learned behaviour but interferes with the performance of complex or not well learned behaviour.

- When a group of people must collectively perform a task, the effort of any one individual is usually less than we would predict had the individual attempted the task alone – a behaviour known as social loafing.

- We tend to reciprocate favours that others do for us, honour commitments we make to others, respond positively to requests made of us by attractive people and authority figures, and identify with group values and goals. Unscrupulous persons often exploit these tendencies for their own gain.

- People in crowds can sometimes behave antisocially because they feel anonymous and not responsible for the consequences of their actions, that is, deindividuated.

- Collective events can also change people's identities so that they identify with the identity of the crowd and conform strongly to group norms.

- Effective group decision making can be hampered by elements of the discussion leading to the decision. This can cause groups to make very extreme decisions (polarisation) or very bad decisions (groupthink).

Aggression, attraction and loving

- Arousal, frustration, disinhibition and elevated testosterone levels are all factors which can lead to human aggression.

- People can also learn to be aggressive by witnessing other people being reinforced for aggressive behaviour.

- Alcohol and media violence may also contribute to aggression.

- We tend to be attracted to others who think positively of us, who are similar to us, who are physically attractive, and who live, work or play near us.

- Sternberg's theory of love describes how the elements of intimacy, passion and commitment are involved in the different kinds of love.

- From an evolutionary perspective, love plays an important role in reproduction and childrearing.

Suggestions for further reading

Gilbert, D.T., Fiske, S.T. and Lindzey, G. (eds) (1998). *The Handbook of Social Psychology* (4th edition). New York: McGraw-Hill.
This is the 'definitive' scientific overview of social psychology – with 1,984 pages and 37 chapters spread across two volumes, this book is extremely detailed and technical. Virtually everything you ever need to know about social psychology can be found somewhere in 'the handbook'.

Hogg, M.A. and Vaughan, G.M. (1998). *Social Psychology* (2nd edition). Harlow: Prentice Hall Europe.
This is a comprehensive and detailed 714 page introduction to social psychology which seamlessly integrates North American and European research. It is written specifically for European students of social psychology.

McGarty, C. and Haslam, A. (eds) (1997). *The Message of Social Psychology*. Oxford: Blackwell.
This edited collection provides an excellent overview of how many of the main researchers, in their own words, view social psychology and the contribution made by their work.

Manstead, A., Hewstone, M., Fiske, S.T., Hogg, M.A., Reis, H.T. and Semin, G.R. (eds) (1996). *The Blackwell Encyclopedia of Social Psychology*. Oxford: Blackwell.
This 694 page book contains approximately 350 entries by the world's leading social psychologists. If you are looking for a concise, brief and accessible description/definition of a topic, concept, theory, phenomenon or finding in social psychology, this is where you need to go.

Smith, P.B. and Bond, M.H. (1998). *Social Psychology Across Cultures* (2nd edition). Harlow: Prentice Hall Europe.
This 400 page survey of social psychology focuses on social psychological similarities and differences between cultures, and also on the psychological meaning of 'culture'.

Brown, R.J. (1988). *Group Processes: Dynamics within and between groups*. Oxford: Blackwell.

Cialdini, R.B. (1993). *Influence: Science and practice* (3rd edition). New York: HarperCollins.

Duck, S. (1992). *Human Relationships* (2nd edition). London: Sage.

Eagly, A.H. and Chaiken, S. (1993). *The Psychology of Attitudes*. San Diego, Calif.: Harcourt Brace Jovanovich.

Fiske, S.T. and Taylor, S.E. (1991). *Social Cognition* (2nd edition). New York: McGraw-Hill.

Hogg, M.A. and Abrams, D. (1988). *Social Identifications: A social psychology of intergroup relations and group processes*. London: Routledge.

Turner, J.C. (1991). *Social Influence*. Milton Keynes: Open University Press.
Although getting a little dated now, Brown's book is still a very solid and readable introduction to a wide range of topics in group processes and intergroup relations. Cialdini's book is written for a general audience. It provides a fascinating, well written and often humorous account of the ways people influence each other. Duck's text is an overview of research on close relationships and interpersonal aspects of human behaviour, from a leading scholar in the area. Attitude research has experienced a revival on the back of contemporary social

cognition – Eagly and Chaiken's book is already assuming the role of a new classic in the field. It is very scholarly and detailed. Although now almost ten years old, Fiske and Taylor's book is still probably the most detailed and complete overview of social cognition. Hogg and Abrams's book provides the most comprehensive account available of the social identity approach to intergroup relations and group processes. It shows how the different branches of research in Europe and North America led to quite distinct theories and methods for investigating these issues. Turner's text is a slim but scholarly introduction to social influence topics which takes a generally intergroup perspective, and covers both conformity and minority influence.

Journals to consult

British Journal of Social Psychology
European Journal of Social Psychology
Group Processes and Intergroup Relations
Journal of Experimental Social Psychology
Journal of Personality and Social Psychology
Journal of Social and Personal Relationships
Personality and Social Psychology Bulletin
Social Cognition

16

HEALTH PSYCHOLOGY

One September night in 1994, a mayday signal was sent from the *M/S Estonia*. It is thought that its high speed, a strong wind, and possibly a technical defect led to the ship's front bulkhead door breaking and masses of water rushing into the car decks. Within half an hour, the *Estonia* had sunk in the Northern Baltic Sea. Of the 996 people abroad, 859 perished. Two-thirds of those who were saved were men in the prime of life.

... the emergency psychology group in Finland gave [aid] to those who were affected by the disaster. Together with the Finnish Red Cross, this group is responsible for organising the emergency team in the event of a major disaster ... Psychologists spent a week in Tallin, where they organised several local crisis teams, training and counselling, and crisis interventions together with the Estonian Red Cross and the Ministry for Social Affairs and Health.

Source: Saari *et al.*, 1996, p. 135

We rely on our good health to be able to do many of the things described in this book: to sense, move, think, reason, create, feel and so on. Sometimes, our ways of behaving can influence the course of good health: whether we smoke or not, whether we have many sexual partners or none, engage in safe sex or not, take regular exercise or not, drink moderately or immoderately. Our personalities may mediate our reactions to external influences such as stressors, which may, in turn, affect our health.

This chapter introduces and describes a relatively new branch of psychology which investigates the relationship between health and behaviour – health psychology. The relevance of psychology to maintaining good health and preventing ill health is discussed, as is the concept of stress and its relation to personality.

What you should be able to do after reading Chapter 16

- Define health psychology.
- Describe the consequences of overeating, cigarette smoking, sexually transmitted disease, alcohol use and physical inactivity, and evaluate the strategies that have been employed to reduce these behaviours.
- Describe and understand the process of stress and its effects on the immune system.
- Define psychoneuroimmunology and understand its significance to health.
- Evaluate the role of personality and specific styles of behaving in the maintenance of health and ill health.

Questions to think about

- What is health psychology and how does it differ from abnormal psychology?
- What illnesses can psychology help prevent? How can it do this?
- What is the role of personality in the development of illness?
- What effect do stressors have on our health and the immune system?
- Can public health education campaigns change behaviour?

Health psychology: a definition

The particular behaviours that make up an individual's way of life have important consequences for that individual's quality of life. Whether a person smokes, drinks alcohol, eats specific foods, exercises, has regular health checks and is susceptible to stress can all have an impact on a person's health and beliefs about his or her health. Such beliefs and behaviour are at the core of what health psychology seeks to understand. Health psychology is the branch of psychology that applies psychological principles to the understanding of health and illness. Factors influencing health can be external (in the form of stressors, health promotion, advertising of health-impairing products) or internal (in the form of thoughts, beliefs, decision making and coping responses).

Health psychology is a relatively new branch of psychology and, as its subject matter suggests, has slight overlap with clinical psychology. Both health psychology and clinical psychology study stress and how people cope with it, but health psychology tends to concern itself with bodily illness whereas clinical psychology is primarily concerned with mental illness. (Clinical psychology is the subject of the next chapter.) Many of the theories and explanations for health-related behaviour and experience derive from work in cognitive and social psychology. Because of this fusion of psychologies and because of the subject matter of health psychology, the sub-area was not regarded as a distinct branch of the discipline until relatively recently.

Health and ill health

The starting point for all health psychologists is the definition of health and the determinants of health. A healthy lifestyle is one that can enhance an individual's physical and mental well-being; an unhealthy lifestyle is one that diminishes physical and psychological well-being. According to Whitehead (1995), the determinants of good health can be conceived of in the way suggested in Figure 16.1.

In this model, the individual is at the centre and possesses immutable characteristics which can influence health (such as age, sex, race, genetic make-up). Surrounding the individual are four interacting layers which represent external determinants of health. These include the individual's lifestyle, his or her social and community influences, living and working conditions and the general cultural and environmental conditions in which the individual lives.

Some specific examples of factors within each of these layers include nutrition, alcohol consumption, smoking, sexual behaviour and exercise. Health psychologists

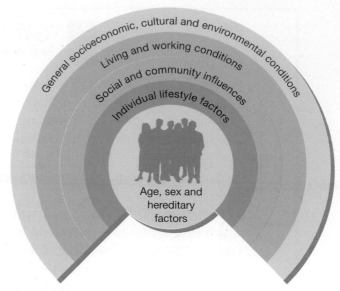

Figure 16.1

The types of factor which Whitehead suggests are contributors to health.

Source: Whitehead, M. (1995) Tackling health inequalities: All agenda for action, p. 23. In M. Benzenal, K. Judge and M. Whitehead (eds) *Tackling Inequalities in Health: An agenda for action*. London: King's Fund. Copyright © 1995 by King's Fund. Reprinted by permission.

attempt to understand the factors which influence health and, if these factors are detrimental to health, apply psychological techniques in order to promote good health and discourage unhealthy behaviour. They are also involved in psychological aspects of healthcare and in determining the effects of governmental health policy on behaviour. The following sections evaluate the role of specific behaviours – eating, exercising, smoking, drinking alcohol and having unprotected sex – in health and illness.

Nutrition

Over the past 150 years or so, our diet has changed considerably: it is higher in fat and lower in fibre, largely because processed foods, fast food and sweets are high in fat and low in fibre. Diets too high in saturated fats (those fats found in animal products and a few vegetable oils) and too low in fibre have been associated with specific health disorders, such as coronary heart disease (CHD), the narrowing of blood vessels that supply nutrients to the heart, and cancer, a malignant and intrusive tumour that destroys body organs and tissue (Cohen, 1987). CHD and cancer are two of the leading causes of death in Western nations (Light and Girdler, 1993).

The chief culprit in CHD is serum cholesterol, a chemical that occurs naturally in the bloodstream where it serves as a detoxifier. Cholesterol is also the source of lipid membranes of cells and steroid hormones. It is a vital substance and we would die without it. Cholesterol has two important forms: HDL (high-density lipoprotein) and

LDL (low-density lipoprotein). HDL is sometimes called 'good' cholesterol because high levels of it are inversely associated with CHD; it seems to play a protective role in the bloodstream. LDL is often called 'bad' cholesterol because high levels of it are associated with the formation of atherosclerotic plaques, which clog arteries. Fibre is an important dietary component because it helps to reduce LDL cholesterol levels (and aids digestion).

Cohen (1987) has shown that cultures having the highest death rates due to breast cancer are those in which large amounts of fats are consumed. People in countries such as the UK, The Netherlands, Canada and the United States have a relatively high fat intake and relatively high death rates due to breast cancer. In contrast, people in countries such as Japan and Thailand have both relatively low fat intake and relatively low death rates due to breast cancer. Figure 16.2 shows the relationship between mortality rates for breast cancer and estimated fat intake in over thirty countries.

There is evidence that specific lifestyles within these cultures can help to reduce the risk of cancer and other illnesses, and this is discussed in the section below. These data are correlational, however. They do not prove that high fat intake causes breast cancer, but they do suggest that such a possibility exists.

Physical fitness

People in developed countries lead increasingly sedentary lives; our work has changed (it is less physical) as have our leisure opportunities (we can watch more television, surf the internet and play computer games). Like high-fat, low-fibre diets, lack of exercise is correlated with increased risk of CHD (Peters *et al.*, 1983; Powell *et al.*, 1987). People who exercise regularly appear to accumulate less body fat and to be less vulnerable to the negative effects of stress than are people who do not exercise regularly (J.D. Brown, 1991).

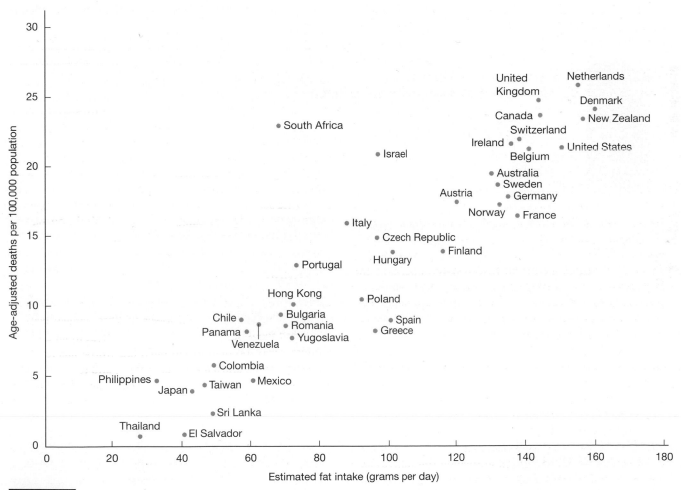

Figure 16.2

The correlation between diet and breast cancer. Nations whose citizens live on diets rich in fats face increased risk of death due to breast cancer.

Source: Adapted from Cohen, L.A., Diet and cancer. *Scientific American*, 1987, 42–48.

There is some evidence that regular exercisers are likely to live longer (Paffenbarger *et al.*, 1986). This evidence comes from a longitudinal study of the lifestyles of 17,000 Harvard University alumni. Between 1962 and 1978, 1,413 of the original 17,000 participants died, 45 per cent from CHD and 32 per cent from cancer. Significantly more of these deaths occurred in participants who had led sedentary lives. Those alumni who reported that they exercised the equivalent of thirty to thirty-five miles of running or walking per week faced half the risk of dying prematurely to that faced by those who reported exercising the equivalent of five or fewer miles per week. On average, those who exercised moderately (an equivalent of twenty miles running or walking per week) lived about two years longer than those who exercised less than the equivalent of five miles.

These results have recently been replicated in a sample of elderly individuals. The relationship between how much a cohort of elderly (61–81 years old) non-smoking men walked and the death rate in this cohort was monitored over a period of twelve years (Hakim *et al.*, 1998). Men who walked more than two miles a day lived signifi-

cantly longer than those who exercised less. Only 21.5 per cent of the two-mile walkers had died after twelve years whereas 43 per cent had died in the group that undertook less exercise. Cancer and CHD was also lower in the walkers: this effect occurred even when other factors (such as blood pressure, alcohol consumption, medical condition, cholesterol level) had been taken into account. However, diet was not considered. This suggests that healthy eating may have been responsible for the reduction in death rate. If a factor (such as walking or diet) can benefit health or make an individual less susceptible to illness or ill health, this factor is called a protective factor. In other words, this factor protects the individual from ill health.

Types of exercise

According to Cooper (1985), aerobic exercises such as running, walking, cycling, and swimming are superior to other forms of exercise for improving cardiovascular health. Aerobic exercises are those which expend considerable energy, increase blood flow and respiration and thereby

Controversies in psychological science

Can exercise improve mood?

The issue

Exercisers frequently report that they feel better after a good bout of vigorous exercise (the so-called feel-good effect). They feel an increase in positive mood and self-confidence that can sometimes translate into better work performance or cognitive ability. But is there scientific evidence for the positive effects of exercise on mood?

The evidence

Two recent reviews of the effects of exercise on factors such as anxiety, depression, self-esteem, personality and prosocial behaviour, have concluded that although exercise can have significant immediate effects on mood, these effects might be dependent on the types of exercise taken (Biddle, 1995; Scully *et al.*, 1998). Petruzello *et al.* (1997), for example, found that exercise had a positive effect on state anxiety (the anxiety felt at the time) but only after aerobic exercise. When trait anxiety was examined (the anxiety that individuals consistently feel, independently of their environment), a training programme lasting ten weeks reduced anxiety. Steinberg *et al.* (1997) have also recently reported

an increase in self-reported mood improvement after different types of aerobic exercise.

An analysis of a large number of studies investigating the effect of exercise on trait and state anxiety, has found a moderate effect of acute and chronic exercise on depression, with those requiring clinical treatment showed the greatest reduction in depression (North *et al.*, 1990). This effect has been found in clinical and non-clinical samples (Martinsen and Stephens, 1994; Mutrie and Biddle, 1995). In fact, exercise seems to be better than psychotherapy in alleviating negative mood, and exercise and psychotherapy seem to be better than exercise alone (Martinsen, 1995). Whether such increases in mood have a knock-on effect on self-concept (the individual's perception of him or herself) is unclear. Reviews of the literature suggest that exercise has a slight, positive effect on self-concept. Similar slight and mixed results have been found for prosocial and moral behaviour – the idea that sport builds 'character' (Shields and Bredemeier, 1995).

Other recent studies suggest similar effects of exercise on mood but in more specific contexts. Mondin *et al.* (1996), for example, examined the effects of exercise deprivation on the mood of ten volunteers who stimulate and strengthen the heart and lungs and increase the body's efficiency in using oxygen. Running at least two miles in less than twenty minutes four times a week (or any equivalent aerobic exercise) significantly increases cardio-vascular health (Cooper, 1985). One study showed that aerobic exercise had an additional benefit: reduced heart response to mental stress (Kubitz and Landers, 1993). Two groups of students who had not exercised for at least three months prior to the study were divided into two groups. One group rode an exercise bike three times a week for forty minutes for eight weeks; the other group did not perform any aerobic exercises. At the end of the eight-week period, both groups were given timed colour perception and maths tests. Participants in the aerobic exercise programme showed lower absolute heart rates in response to the tests than did the participants who did not exercise.

The effects of physical exercise on mood and even cognition have been the subject of research in another relatively new branch of psychology, sport and exercise psychology. Both the American Psychological Association and the British Psychology Society now have sections representing those psychologists who are interested in the psychological effects of sport and exercise. Sport and exercise psychology is concerned with studying those factors which can promote or impair the ability to engage in sporting activities and exercise (Steinberg et al., 1998). Much of the practical benefits of sport psychology can be seen in the effects of psychological techniques taught to sportsmen and women, such as the use of imagery in archers, martial artists, firearms users and other sports involving the use of guided movement. Psychological techniques are also used to help athletes and coaches maximise their performance in competition and in training (Milne and Common, 1998).

Sport and exercise psychologists also examine the effects of exercise in non-professionals. A link has been made between exercise and good mental health. For example, many exercisers indicate that they feel a 'high' after exercising. Perhaps such feelings interact with the actual physical exercise to protect health. The degree to which exercise can promote such positive behaviours, however, remains controversial. The evidence for the effect of exercise on mood is reviewed in the 'Controversies in psychological science' section below.

regularly exercised for 45 minutes a day, 6–7 days a week. The participants exercised for a day, took three days off and resumed exercise on the fifth day. Depriving participants of exercise was associated with an increase in self-reported mood disturbance, state anxiety, tension, depression, confusion and a decrease in vigour. These changes were reversed when exercise resumed. Of course, one could attribute these results to factors other than exercise. Perhaps the disturbance in these individuals' routine affected their performance.

Some studies, however, suggest that only certain types of exercise will effectively improve mood. In a comparison of participants' mood before and after aerobic dance exercise, soccer, tennis or bowling, Rudolph and Kim (1996) found that mood improved only after the aerobic exercise and soccer. Biddle's review (Biddle, 1995) suggests that intensity of exercise may be a factor in enhanced mood and perhaps this explains the result of this study. Another investigation of the effects of intense and non-intense running over long and short distances found that running at intense levels over short durations resulted in increased stress but running over long distances resulted in increased arousal (Kerr and Van den Wollenberg, 1997).

Perhaps, more controversially, it has also been suggested that exercise improves cognitive performance as well as mood: not only do exercisers feel better they also think more effectively (for example, Arcelin et al., 1998). However, a recent extensive review of the literature (a total of 134 studies) concluded that exercise and fitness had only a small effect on cognitive performance (Etnier et al., 1997). The largest effect was for chronic (as opposed to acute) bouts of exercise although the number of weeks or days of exercise was not related to improved cognitive performance. The reviewers suggest that a number of factors could explain the slight increase in cognitive performance, including pre-exercise differences in individuals' cognitive ability and interest in exercising. Participants who regularly exercise (say, in aerobics classes) may have a lifelong commitment to exercise; it may be this belief rather than the exercise which produced enhanced cognitive performance.

Conclusion

The studies reviewed here suggest that exercise can have a beneficial effect on mood by decreasing state anxiety and depression if the exercise is relatively acute and is of a specific type. Deprivation of exercise in those who habitually exercise may be detrimental to mood. Whether such exercise also results in better cognitive performance, however, is unclear. It is possible, but factors other than exercise may account for any improved performance.

Cigarette smoking

In the UK, the annual mortality rate that is attributable to smoking is 120,000, accounting for £400 million in hospital costs and 50 million lost working days (Health Education Authority, 1991). According to the Imperial Cancer Research Fund, the death rate is the equivalent of a jumbo jet crashing every day of the year and killing all the passengers. Worldwide, smoking causes 3 million deaths a year, and this is estimated to increase to 10 million by 2020 (Peto, 1994). The largest reduction in smoking has been found in the most well-off families (Marsh and McKay, 1994) and studies of specific cultural groups have associated a failure to quit with low income (Nevid *et al.*, 1996).

Smoking is associated with many problem behaviours such as a higher intake of fatty food (Shah *et al.*, 1993), lower fruit and vegetable intake, higher alcohol intake (Morabia and Wynder, 1990) and less physical activity. Current smokers have been found to consume more alcohol, meat, eggs and chips more frequently than former or non-smokers, although sweet consumption in those who have stopped smoking is higher (French *et al.*, 1996).

In addition to these health risks, people who use tobacco also face increased risks of cancer, bronchitis, emphysema, strokes and ulcers. Non-smokers who are exposed to air contaminated with cigarette smoke (second-hand smoke) also face increased risks of CHD and cancer. As a result of the negative effects of smoking, this behaviour is banned in many public places such as public transport, restaurants, cinemas, offices, hospitals, schools and so on.

Factors which promote the initiation and maintenance of smoking

What causes people, especially adolescents, to begin smoking? Psychologists know that both imitation and peer pressure contribute to the acquisition of the smoking habit (Lynskey *et al.*, 1998). For example, adolescents who have favourable impressions of a smoker are likely to imitate that person's actions. Cigarette manufacturers use this knowledge to advertise their products: they portray smoking as a glamorous, mature, independent, and sometimes rebellious behaviour. In a longitudinal study of 643 14–17 year olds and their smoking behaviour, the single best predictor of smoking was peers' smoking six months earlier; parental smoking also predicted smoking (Biglan *et al.*, 1995).

The news and entertainment media are powerful shapers of our opinions, beliefs and behaviours. Magazine advertisements generally portray cigarette smokers as young, healthy, attractive and exciting individuals, despite the reality. A recent survey of European women's magazines reported that only four of the highest selling weekly and monthly magazines refused tobacco advertising (Amos *et al.*, 1998). The annual death rate from smoking in women in Europe is estimated to be 214,000 (Peto, 1998),

and although around 20 per cent of women give up smoking when they are pregnant, they relapse after the birth of the child (Fingerhut *et al.*, 1990).

Some of the strategies which may prevent the recruitment of smokers could include price increases, limiting access to young people, developing non-smoking policies for schools, banning advertising and tobacco sponsorship of sporting (and any other public) event, and spending more on health education. A survey of 80 Australian smoking experts (from government, universities and professional and volunteer organisations) who had been asked to rate the smoking reduction strategies they considered to be most effective, reported that increased tobacco taxes would be the most effective strategy, followed by TV campaigning, having smoke-free areas and banning tobacco advertising (Paul and Sanson-Fisher, 1996). As we will see from the evidence below, and from the evidence from other areas of ill-health prevention, some of these strategies may be more effective than others.

Two recent ambitious American studies of adolescents' smoking habits show an interesting pattern of recruitment and cessation. Chassin *et al.* (1996) examined the history of smoking from adolescence to adulthood in a longitudinal study of 4,035 participants (with roughly equal numbers of men and women, with an average age of 29 at the end of the study). The authors reported an increase in the initiation of smoking from adolescence to adulthood, with a slight decrease in the participants' initiation in their mid-twenties and no initiation in adulthood. This finding suggests that smoking begins in adolescence and that the discouragement of smoking should target this age group. Those who did not quit were likely to have smoking parents and be less well educated than those who successfully quitted.

Rose *et al.* (1996) examined the specific predictors of successful quitting in a similarly ambitious study of 700 adolescents. They found that the likelihood of attempting to quit was associated with being female, attaining some college education, perceiving smoking as dangerous (both generally and personally), being married and occupying several social roles. However, the likelihood of successfully quitting was predicted by education, smoking less than one packet a day, perceiving oneself as being less likely to be smoking in a year, having fewer smoking friends, being employed and not living with children. Health beliefs about the dangers of smoking did not predict cessation. These predictors, of course, are correlational. None of these has been shown to cause quitting. However, they indicate the types of factor which can influence the degree of successful cessation. On the basis of such data, one might be able to focus smoking cessation programmes more effectively.

Smoking and physiology

Cigarette smoking, like other forms of drug use, is addictive: the nervous system may have developed a tolerance to the drug or become physically dependent on the drug. Tolerance simply means that the neurons in the central nervous system (CNS) respond progressively less to the presence of the drug; larger doses of the drug are required to produce the same CNS effects that smaller doses produced earlier. Physical dependence means that CNS neurons now require the presence of the drug to function normally. Without the drug in the CNS, the individual will experience withdrawal symptoms, or uncomfortable physical conditions, such as sweating, tremors and anxiety. In addition to tolerance and physical dependence, many drugs, including the nicotine in cigarette smoke, produce psychological dependence, a craving to use the drug for its pleasurable effects. In other words, obtaining and using the drug become focal points of an individual's life. An objective way of describing psychological dependence is to say that it involves behaviour that is acquired and maintained through positive reinforcement. A reinforcing drug is one that strengthens or maintains the behaviour that constitutes seeking, acquiring and using the drug.

The nicotine contained in cigarette smoke exerts powerful effects on the central nervous system and heart by stimulating postsynaptic receptors sensitive to the neurotransmitter acetylcholine. This stimulation produces temporary increases in heart rate and blood pressure, decreases in body temperature, changes in hormones released by the pituitary gland, and the release of adrenaline from the adrenal glands. In common with all reinforcers, natural and artificial, it also causes secretion of dopamine in the brain; the release of dopamine in the brain is reinforcing, so this effect contributes to the maintenance of cigarette smoking. Cigarette smoking may also be maintained by negative reinforcement. People who try to quit smoking usually suffer withdrawal symptoms, including headaches, insomnia, anxiety and irritability. These symptoms are relieved by smoking another cigarette. Such negative reinforcement appears to be extremely powerful. Over 60 per cent of all smokers have tried to quit smoking at least once, but have lit up again to escape the unpleasant withdrawal symptoms.

Nicotine alone cannot be blamed for the health risks posed by cigarette smoking. These risks are caused by the combination of nicotine with other toxic substances, such as the carbon monoxide and tars found in cigarette smoke. For example, while nicotine causes an increase in heart rate, the carbon monoxide in smoke deprives the heart of the oxygen needed to perform its work properly. The smoker's heart undergoes stress because it is working harder with fewer nutrients than normal. Over a period of years, this continued stress weakens the heart, making it more susceptible to disease than is the heart of a non-smoker.

Many smokers believe that they can diminish the health risks posed by their habit by switching to low-nicotine cigarettes. Unfortunately, this strategy is undermined by the fact that smokers develop a tolerance to nicotine and typically smoke more low-nicotine cigarettes to make up for the decreased nicotine content of their new brand.

Psychology in action

Smoking cessation

New treatment programmes for cigarette smokers have revolved around nicotine replacement. This replacement is normally undertaken via a nicotine gum or a transdermal patch, a plaster-like patch that allows nicotine to be absorbed through the skin. The patch was developed by a behavioural psychologist, Frank Etscorn. Over several months, the nicotine levels of the patches are reduced, and the individual is weaned from nicotine altogether. The success rate is mixed. A review of the effectiveness of nicotine gum and patches, suggests success rates of 11 per cent and 13 per cent for each therapy respectively (Law and Tang, 1995). These figures are comparable to the success of other treatment approaches.

Quitting smoking has both immediate and long-term positive effects, although quitting (and maintaining that quitting) is not easy for smokers. Table 16.1 shows the behavioural consequences of quitting.

Prevention programmes designed by health psychologists and health professionals are generally aimed at combating social factors such as imitation, peer pressure and influence from advertisements that can initially induce people to light up (Evans *et al.*, 1984). Situations in which quitters may lapse are those in which smoking cues and alcohol consumption are present (Schiffman, 1982). When smokers and quitters are tempted to smoke, they are usually feeling quite negative and restless, are exposed to smoking cues and are likely to be eating or drinking in company (Schiffman *et al.*, 1996).

Former drinkers are known to react more negatively to drinking images when they have given up drinking (Gibbons and Gerrard, 1995). Exposing smokers to positive images of smoking have been shown to predict their willingness or intention to smoke (Dinh *et al.*, 1995) whereas negative images predict successful abstinence from smoking (Gibbons and Eggleton, 1996). These findings suggest that altering the way in which one thinks about smoking can help stop the behaviour. For example, one Canadian anti-smoking

Psychology in action continued

Psychology in action continued

Table 16.1   The body's response to stopping cigarette smoking

Timescale	Response
Within 20 minutes of last puff	Blood pressure and pulse decrease to normal levels
	Body temperature of extremities increases to normal levels
Within 1 day	Risk of heart attacks decreases
Within 2 days	Nerve endings begin regenerating
	Taste and smell acuity increases
Within 3 days	Breathing becomes easier due to relaxing of bronchial tubes
	Lung capacity increases
From 2 weeks to 3 months	Blood circulation improves
	Walking and other exercises begin to seem easier
	Lung efficiency increases as much as 30 per cent
After 5 years	Risk of death due to lung cancer decreases by 47 per cent

Source: It's never too late to quit. *Living Well*, 1989, Vol. IX, No. 4. Kalamazoo, MI: Bob Hope International Heart Research Institute

programme, the Waterloo Smoking Prevention Project (Flay *et al.*, 1985), has been especially effective in reducing the number of young adolescents who experiment with smoking.

Students were first asked to seek out information about smoking and to think about their beliefs regarding smoking. Next, they were taught about the social pressures involved in smoking and were given explicit training in how to resist those pressures – for example, politely turning down a cigarette when one is offered. This training also included role playing such resistance strategies and asking each student to make a commitment regarding whether they would start smoking or not. The students were monitored five times over the next two years to see how many of them had experimented with smoking.

By the end of the two year period, fewer than 8 per cent of the students who had been involved in the prevention programme were experimenting with smoking. In contrast, almost 19 per cent of the students who had not gone through the programme had experimented with smoking. While these results are encouraging, the students were only monitored for two years. Long-term prevention programmes have shown that many participants begin experimenting with smoking later on, hinting that occasional 'booster' sessions may be necessary to maintain the effects of the initial training (Murray *et al.*, 1989).

Studies over longer time periods suggest that a large proportion of those patients with heart disease who were smokers quit smoking following a specially constructed smoking cessation programme. Only two long-term (more than 5 years) studies of intervention programmes for smokers diagnosed with heart disease have been published. One of these compared the rates of quitting over five years in 160 patients with coronary heart disease (Rosal *et al.*, 1998). The patients were randomly assigned to two groups: one received basic advice about stopping smoking; the other received a more intensive intervention programme which involved a 30 minute inpatient counselling session, an outpatient counselling visit and counselling by telephone. The group which received the intensive counselling maintained significantly higher quit rates over five years. Factors, apart from the intervention programme, which were associated with successful quitting included having twelve years of education, having the intention to quit and having high self-belief.

The psychological evidence suggests that a number of specific factors can trigger smoking: these include visual, social and physiological cues. Evidence from studies in which an attempt is made to stop smoking by engaging smokers in an intervention programme, shows that the studies' success rate is variable but that specially designed intervention programmes are more effective than doing nothing at all to stop smoking.

Alcohol use

Alcohol is probably the most widely used and abused substance that requires the consumer to be of a given age before it is sold or used. When psychologists refer to substance abuse, they mean that the substance is used in a way that poses a threat to the safety and well-being of the user, to another, or to both. Most people who use alcohol do not abuse it, and not all people who abuse alcohol are alcoholics. People who drive under the influence of alcohol pose a serious threat to both themselves and others, but they may not be alcoholics.

Alcoholism is an addiction to ethanol, the psychoactive agent in alcoholic drinks. A psychoactive substance is any substance that affects central nervous system functioning. Male alcoholics outnumber female alcoholics by a ratio of about four or five to one (Lauer, 1989). Table 16.2 describes some of the physical, psychological and social consequences of alcohol abuse. Abusing other drugs, such as cocaine or heroin, can produce similar effects.

Because neuronal activity of the brain becomes suppressed and reduces inhibitory controls on behaviour when moderate to heavy amounts of alcohol are consumed, individuals become more relaxed and more outgoing, show impaired motor co-ordination, and have difficulty thinking clearly. As more alcohol is consumed, neuronal activity in the brain is depressed further, producing distortions in perception, slurred speech, memory loss, impaired judgement and poor control of movement (Stritzke *et al.*, 1996). Unconsciousness and death may result from ingesting large amounts of alcohol over a relatively short period of time.

Table 16.2 **The negative physical, psychological and cultural consequences of alcohol abuse**

Physical
Cirrhosis of the liver, which results in death
Poor nutrition
Impaired sexual functioning
Psychological
Gradual deterioration of cognitive functioning
Increased feelings of anxiety and irritability
Aggressive behaviour
Cultural
Impaired social skills and interpersonal functioning
Divorce
Employee absenteeism and decreased productivity

Once ingested, alcohol is rapidly absorbed from the stomach and intestinal tract. Because alcohol is a small fat- and water-soluble molecule, it is quickly and evenly distributed throughout the body via the circulatory system. Blood alcohol levels are affected by body weight and muscularity. Generally speaking, an obese or muscular individual would have to consume more alcohol than a slender person to attain the same level of intoxication. In addition, regardless of body characteristics, blood levels of alcohol increase more slowly in people who drink on a full stomach than in those having little or no food in their stomach. Food in the stomach impairs absorption of substances through the gastrointestinal tract. Men appear to be heavier drinkers than women and, even accounting for total body weight, coping style and sensation-seeking, men still remain the heaviest consumers (Watten, 1997).

Inebriation is related to the manner in which alcohol is metabolised by the body. Unlike most other drugs, alcohol is metabolised by the liver at a constant rate, regardless of how much alcohol has been consumed. For example, in one hour, the body will metabolise the alcohol in 400 g of beer or 35 g of 80–100 per cent proof spirits. Hence, if a person consumes more than 400 g of beer or 35 g of spirits per hour, his or her blood alcohol level rises beyond that level caused by the first drink, and he or she may begin to become intoxicated. When blood alcohol levels reach 0.3–0.4 per cent, people lose consciousness, and at 0.5 per cent, neurons in the brain that control the respiratory and circulatory systems stop functioning, causing death. Driving under the influence of alcohol is defined in most countries as a blood alcohol level greater than 0.1 per cent.

Some recent evidence suggests that drinking moderate amounts of alcohol can serve as a protective factor against coronary heart disease. For example, drinking moderate to light amounts daily has been associated with a reduced risk of CHD (Thun *et al.*, 1997; Rehm *et al.*, 1997). Men suffering from myocardial infarction (a severe heart disease) but who consumed light to moderate amounts of alcohol (two to six drinks a week) showed a lower mortality rate than did those patients who abstained from alcohol (Muntwyler *et al.*, 1998). You can see this relationship in Figure 16.3.

However, these studies are correlational or epidemiological. That is, alcohol consumption is noted in retrospect and the mortality rates of those who drink a little or not at all, are compared: scientists do not directly manipulate the independent variable, alcohol consumption, by prescribing alcohol to one group and no alcohol to another.

Although moderate drinkers develop little or no tolerance to alcohol, people who regularly consume large quantities of alcohol usually develop a tolerance. Heavy drinkers often suffer delirium tremens – the DTs – a pattern of withdrawal symptoms that includes trembling, irritability, hallucinations, sleeplessness and confusion when they attempt to quit drinking. In many cases, alcoholics become so physically dependent on the drug that abrupt cessation

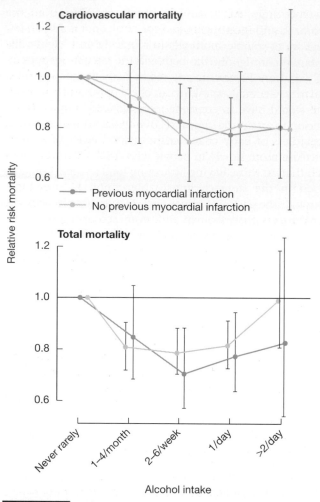

Figure 16.3

The association between alcohol intake and cardiovascular total mortality, with and without previous myocardial infarction.

Source: Muntmyler *et al.*, Mortality and light to moderate alcohol consumption after myocardial infarction. *The Lancet*, 352, 12 December 1998, p. 1884. © by The Lancet Ltd, 1998.

Table 16.3   The effects of mixing alcohol with other drugs

Drug	Example	Possible consequences of using simultaneously with alcohol
Narcotics	Codeine or Percodan	Increased suppression of CNS functions and possible death due to respiratory failure
Minor pain relievers	Aspirin or Tylenol	Stomach irritation and bleeding; increased likelihood of liver damage from acetaminophen
Antidepressants	Tofranil, Triavil	Increased suppression of CNS functions; drinking some red wines while using some kinds of antidepressants may produce extremely high blood pressure. May also lead to death due to respiratory failure
Antihistamines	Actifed	Increased drowsiness, making operation of motor vehicles and power equipment more dangerous
CNS stimulants	Caffeine, Dexedrine	Reverses some of the depressive effects of alcohol; however, they do not produce increases in sobriety if consumed while one is drunk
Antipsychotics	Thorazine	Impaired control of motor movements and possible death due to respiratory failure
Antianxiety drugs	Valium	Decreased arousal; impaired judgment, which can lead to accidents in the home or on the road

Source: based on Palfai and Jankiewicz, 1991, and data from the National Institute for Alcohol Abuse and Alcoholism Clearinghouse for Alcohol Information, 1982

of drinking produces convulsions and sometimes death. Consumption of alcohol and other drugs is also dangerous. Table 16.3 illustrates the consequences of mixing alcohol with various drugs.

Women who drink moderate to heavy quantities of alcohol during pregnancy risk giving birth to children who suffer from symptoms of foetal alcohol syndrome. Alcohol crosses the placental barrier and enters the foetal blood supply, where it retards the development of the foetus's nervous system. Foetal alcohol syndrome is characterised by decreased birth weight and physical malformations. It is the third leading cause of birth defects involving mental retardation, but it is also preventable: if a woman does not drink alcohol during her pregnancy, she will not give birth to a child with foetal alcohol syndrome.

The use of alcohol is prompted by the same factors that contribute to the initiation of smoking: imitation and peer pressure. Many young people see drinking as the thing to do because it seemingly represents maturity, independence and rebelliousness and because it is associated with having fun. For example, in their advertisements, brewers portray people using their products at the end of a hard day's work, at parties and celebrations.

Treatment programmes for drug abuse, including smoking and drinking, may take several forms. In some cases, aversion therapy is used; in others, less intrusive forms of therapy involving extensive counselling are used. In the latter case, the psychologist or therapist's general aim is to teach the individual the following:

1 To identify environmental cues or circumstances that may cause the addictive behaviour to occur or recur.

2 To learn to behave in ways that are incompatible with the undesired behaviour.

3 To have confidence that he or she can overcome the addiction.

4 To view setbacks in overcoming the addiction as temporary and to see them as learning experiences in which new coping skills can be acquired.

Prevention programmes for people with addictive behaviours are only moderately successful. For example, many alcohol management programmes have only a 30–50 per cent success rate (Marlatt *et al.*, 1986).

Sexually transmitted diseases (STD) and acquired immune deficiency syndrome (AIDS)

Sexual activity represents the most emotionally intense form of intimacy. Through casual sexual relationships, however, sexual activity may have severely negative consequences: it may result in contracting a sexually transmitted disease (STD). Individuals who contract an STD experience a loss of self-esteem and often they lose their ability to initiate or maintain sexual relationships. Table 16.4 lists the major types of STD, their symptoms and their treatment.

The most life-threatening illness that is transmitted sexually is acquired immune deficiency syndrome, or AIDS, which can also be transmitted through blood transfusions and the sharing of hypodermic needles among intravenous drug users. AIDS is the last stage of the illness triggered by the human immunodeficiency virus (HIV). AIDS has been reported in 163 countries.

According to the United Nations Joint Programme on AIDS (1996), the following data are available for the prevalence of AIDS.

Global total:	*21 million living with HIV/AIDS*
Sub-Sahara Africa:	*13.3 million*
	5 per cent of 15–49 year olds are HIV+
South and South-East Asia:	*4.7 million*
Latin America:	*1.3 million*
	(Brazil and Mexico account for 70 per cent of all cases)
North America, Western Europe:	*1.2 million*
Caribbean:	*250,000*
North Africa and Middle East:	*192,000*
East Asia/Pacific:	*50,000*
Eastern Europe and Central Asia:	*29,000*

Table 16.4   Four STDs, their causes, symptomology and treatment

STD	Cause	Symptoms	Treatment
Gonorrhoea	Gonococcus bacterium	Appear 3–5 days after sexual contact with afflicted person. In both sexes, discharges of pus. Urination accompanied by a burning sensation. In female, pelvic inflammatory disease. If untreated, fevers, headaches, backaches and abdominal pain develop	Penicillin or other antibiotics
Genital herpes	Herpes simplex type I and II virus	Small blisters around point of sexual contact. Blisters burst, causing pain. Symptoms recur every 1 to 2 weeks	No cure, but an ointment called acyclovir speeds the healing process if applied early in the first episode of the disease
Syphilis	Treponema pallidum bacterium	Chancre or lesion where bacteria first entered body. If untreated, the bacteria penetrate body tissue, including the brain. May result in death	Penicillin or other antibiotics
AIDS	Human immunodeficiency virus (HIV)	Destruction of body's immune system allowing diseases like cancer and pneumonia to infect the body	Still in experimental stages. Several drugs are currently being tested. So far, results are mixed – none is successful in curing AIDS, but some appear promising in lessening the symptoms

Other data from the same source suggest that:

- 28 million people have been infected with HIV, 2.4 million of whom are children
- 42 per cent of infected individuals are women
- 90 per cent live in developing countries
- 75–85 per cent of cases involve transmission through unprotected sex
- 70 per cent of infections are due to heterosexual transmission
- The majority of the newly infected are between 15 and 24 years old

Between 50 and 70 per cent of people infected with HIV will develop AIDS within 8–10 years (Moss and Baccetti, 1989). Changes in lifestyle, such as practising safe sex, can reduce one's risk of contracting an STD or AIDS. These practices include limiting the number of one's sexual partners, finding out the sexual history of partners before engaging in sexual relations, using a condom during sex, and abstinence from sexual intercourse. In the case of AIDS, these lifestyle changes must involve not only safe sex practices, but also behaviours that will prevent non-sexual transmission of the AIDS virus, such as refusal to share hypodermic needles.

Prevention programmes have been based on changing knowledge, attitudes, beliefs and practices (Janz and Becker, 1984; Sheeran and Abraham, 1996; Ajzen, 1985, 1991). One model, the theory of reasoned action, is based on principles from social and cognitive psychology (Ajzen, 1985, 1991; Conner and Sparks, 1996), as we saw in Chapter 15. According to the model, behaviour follows from an intention to act. These intentions are based on the individual's beliefs, attitudes and feelings. Attitudes, in turn, are based on beliefs about the evaluation of the consequences of behaviour. The model takes into account the possibility that an individual's attitude can be influenced by social factors and that others' perception of them can determine their intention to act. Thus, if we apply the model to AIDS: an individual will intend to act in a particular way (for example, using a condom) if he or she has a positive view of condoms and thinks that others would approve (Abraham et al., 1998).

Critics of the social cognitive models argue that the models do little to explain AIDS-related behaviour change and that intention to act does not explain behaviour change (Joffe, 1996, 1997; Fife-Shaw, 1997). Others, however, suggest that there is considerable evidence for the efficacy of the models (Abraham et al., 1998). Sheeran and Orbel et al. (1997) (cited in Abraham et al., 1998), for example, reported a positive correlation between behavioural intention and condom use. Abraham et al. (1998) also note that interventions based on theory are more effective than those based on information-giving (Kalichman et al., 1996). The most successful interventions are those which combine information-giving and the teaching of behavioural skills (Fisher and Fisher, 1992). A school curriculum intervention programme based on social cognitive models was significantly more effective in changing feelings and cognitions about HIV and safe sex than was standard Dutch sex education (Schaalma et al., 1996). At the beginning, 45 per cent reported inconsistent condom use; this had been reduced to 36 per cent by the end of the intervention.

Although prevention programmes have been partially successful in reducing high-risk sexual behaviours, they are least successful in situations in which a person's personal or cultural values prevent him or her from engaging in safe sex practices (Herdt and Lindenbaum, 1992). These values generally involve misperceptions of what practising safe sex means. Some men refuse to wear condoms because doing so would detract from their conception of what it means to be a man. Many people, especially young people, have the mistaken belief that they are invulnerable to any type of misfortune, including contracting an STD or AIDS.

Attitudes towards HIV and AIDS

Despite widespread media coverage of the AIDS epidemic throughout the world and instructional programmes designed to educate the general public about AIDS, it remains the most feared, stigmatised and publicly misunderstood contagious disease of our time (Rushing, 1995). When negative behaviour of this sort occurs, especially on a collective, widespread social basis, it is referred to as fear of contagion. Historical analyses of previous epidemics, such as the Black Death (bubonic plague) that struck Europe during the fourteenth century and the outbreak of cholera in Europe and the United States in the seventeenth century, have shown that fear of contagion is only likely to occur when four conditions are met: the disease must be deadly, it must appear suddenly, it must have no apparent explanation, and people must believe that many people are at risk of contracting it (Rushing, 1995).

The AIDS epidemic meets these four conditions. It is deadly and it appeared suddenly: the first cases of AIDS were reported in 1981, a year in which 295 diagnoses of AIDS were made worldwide and 126 people died from it. Only ten years later, in 1991, 41,871 new cases were reported and 31,381 people had died from AIDS. In the nine intervening years, 179,000 new cases were reported and 114,703 people died from it. AIDS still has no hard and fast explanation. We know that it is a virus, but we do not know how to kill it. Many people hold the false belief that AIDS is transmitted through casual contact (Bishop, 1991a,b).

It is relatively easy to explain fear of contagion during the periods of the bubonic plague and cholera. At that time, medical science was unsophisticated and lacked the technology needed to understand basic physiology. Fear of contagion in the time of AIDS is not so easily explained.

Bishop (1994) offers three possible explanations. First, some people may reason that just because no evidence currently exists that AIDS is spread through casual contact, it does not mean that such evidence may not be discovered. Medical experts tend to describe the transmission of AIDS through casual contact as being 'near impossible' or 'very unlikely', which leaves room for doubt in many people's minds.

Second, some people may mistake AIDS as having the same general characteristics of more typical contagious diseases such as chicken pox or influenza. People often use prototypes to represent concepts. Recall that a prototype represents the typical member of a class of things and that people organise information about other members in that class around the prototype. For example, if you think of influenza as a prototypical contagious disease, you may then apply the characteristics of this disease to other members of the same category, such as AIDS. Thus, because you know that influenza is a contagious disease spread by casual contact, you extend this same characteristic to AIDS and believe that it, too, is spread by casual contact.

Finally, the availability heuristic may also play a role in people's thinking about the transmission of AIDS. Recall from the discussion of the availability heuristic in Chapter 15 that when people attempt to assess the importance or the frequency of an event, they tend to be guided by the ease with which examples of that event come to mind. In the case of contagious diseases, AIDS has captured the world's attention.

Television, newspaper and radio reports involving AIDS have dominated coverage of medical, lifestyle and societal issues for the past fifteen years. Bishop and his colleagues (1992) have found a strong correlation between how many news reports on AIDS people have been exposed to and the number of lives they believe have been lost to AIDS.

Managing HIV and AIDS

Although psychologists and other health professionals have helped to develop programmes for the prevention of AIDS by devising interventions based on safe sex practices; these programmes are clearly too late for those with the HIV virus who may later develop AIDS. Psychology's contribution to the management of the virus has focused on the degree of support given to carriers, the reduction of risky sex following a positive diagnosis, and in helping maintain a regular drug regime for those infected.

For example, the standard drugs for treating the HIV virus are currently nucleoside analogue reverse transcriptase inhibitors (NARTIs) which interfere with the ability of the virus to produce DNA needed for cell replication (Perelson et al., 1996; Kelly et al., 1998). However, this drug is currently taken in combination with other drugs called protease inhibitors. Protease inhibitors reduce the viral load in patients, that is, they reduce the viral quantity in blood. The NARTIs attack the virus in its early stages, the protease inhibitors attempt to halt the maturation of cells that have already developed. The difficulty with such combination therapy, however, is that these drugs are taken at various dosages at various times of the day; some need refrigeration, some cannot be taken on a full stomach (whereas others must). Table 16.5 indicates the complexity of this drug regime.

Table 16.5 Typical regimens of protease inhibitor and nucleoside analogue inhibitor medications used in HIV combination therapy regimens

Variable	Typical dosage schedule	Temporal requirements
Protease inhibitors Ritonavir (Norvir)	Doses every 12 h	Taken with meals; must be kept in a cool, dry place
Indinavir sulphate (Crixivan)	Doses every 8 h	Taken on an empty stomach 1 h before or 2 h after meals; patients must also drink at least 48 oz of water each day
Nelfinavir mesylate (Viracept)	Doses every 8 h	
Nucleoside analogue reverse transcriptase inhibitors (NARTIs)		
Zidovudine (AZT)	Doses five times daily	
Didanosine	Doses twice daily	
Zalcitabine	Doses three times daily	
Stavudine	Doses twice daily	
Lamivudine	Doses twice daily	

Source: adapted from Kelly, J.A., Otto-Salaj, L.L., Sikkema, K.J., Pinkerton, S.D. and Bloom, R.R. (1998). Health Psychology, 17, 11, 310–319. Copyright © 1998 by the American Psychological Association. Reprinted with permission.

Even brief lapses in the drug regimen can cause an increase in viral load and replication of the HIV virus (it is also an expensive lapse; protease inhibitor therapy costs between £7,000 and £10,000). Some of the factors which can influence a successful adherence to the drug regime include a belief that the drugs are effective and beneficial (Geletko *et al.*, 1995) – this is sometimes difficult when the effect of the drugs are not seen for a considerable time – and personal involvement in decision making (Becker and Maiman, 1980), that is, the patient believes that the regimen is constructed for his or her condition and that he or she has responsibility for this regimen. The absence of negative affect and the availability of social support also enhance successful adherence (Freeman *et al.*, 1996).

Another problem associated with HIV infection is continued risky sexual and drug-use behaviour (Kelly and Kalichman, 1998). Between 30 and 35 per cent of HIV-infected individuals engage in unprotected sex and in unsafe needle-sharing drug practices, and a recent longitudinal study of women who were tested for HIV and given HIV counselling, showed no disengagement from high-risk sexual behaviour (Ickovics *et al.*, 1998). Two models have been formulated for the prediction of HIV-relevant risk behaviour. The information–motivation–behaviour model (Fisher and Fisher, 1992) argues that the factors which influence risk reduction are knowledge about AIDS risk reduction, a change in motivation and the presence of behavioural skills that can reduce risky practice. An alternative model, the Aids Risk Reduction Model (Catania *et al.*, 1990), suggests that a change in risky behaviour depends on the perception of the problem, a change in commitment and taking action. These factors can significantly influence the decision to use condoms (Kelly *et al.*, 1990).

With the seriousness of the illness being the most obvious and most pressing source of concern for carriers of the disease, the psychological effects of the disease have not been widely studied. There is insidious, cognitive impairment as the disease progresses (it is called a dementia, just as are the effects of Alzheimer's disease which we explored in Chapter 11) and this is well documented (Grant *et al.*, 1999). The social, personal consequences of the disease and its effects on mental health are less well understood. Studies reviewed by Emmelkamp (1996) suggest that individuals who have not accepted their homosexuality, who have received little or no social support and who have denied the effects of illness to themselves, are those most likely to develop severe psychological disturbances. In general, however, the degree of psychological distress is comparable to those of psychiatric outpatients or seronegative homosexuals. That is, after the initial shock of discovering their positive status, patients are not more depressed or anxious than are those who were diagnosed negative.

Alternatives to orthodox medicine

Most of the interventions we have discussed so far have been fairly orthodox in nature: science is applied to real-life health-related behaviour. Individuals believe in traditional or orthodox medicine because this has been seen as the best, most valid and most reliable treatment option. Another approach to treatment, however, does not rely on the methods of orthodox medicine. These approaches are called alternative or complementary. Some individuals decide to forgo orthodox medicine and choose complementary medicine. Why? Some possible reasons are discussed in the 'Controversies in psychological science' section on pp. 566–8.

Questions to think about

Health psychology and unhealthy behaviour

- In what way can health psychology be seen as a distinct branch of psychology?

- Which of the unhealthy behaviours described in this section do you think poses the greatest risk?

- Which do you think would be most responsive to psychological intervention?

- Why do only certain types of exercise improve mood?

- What characteristics distinguish the quitter from the smoker? Can these be used to determine a cessation programme for quitters?

- Why do smoking cessation programmes fail?

- Which strategies for preventing recruitment to smoking are likely to be effective? How important an effect do you think the prevention of cigarette advertising and sponsorships and the promotion of health education would have?

- HIV is almost 100 per cent preventable. Why, then, does the number of HIV cases worldwide continue to grow?

- How would you encourage the reduction in HIV-related risky behaviour?

- Why do people choose complementary medicine?

- If an unorthodox treatment approach works, why should we object to a person believing in it?

Stress and health

Stress is a pattern of physiological, behavioural, emotional and cognitive responses to real or imagined stimuli that are perceived as preventing a goal or endangering or otherwise threatening well-being. These stimuli are generally aversive and are called stressors. Stress is not a direct product of cultural evolution but is a product of natural selection. It is a behavioural adaptation that helped our ancestors to fight or flee from wild animals and enemies. Stress often helps us to confront or escape threatening situations (Linsky et al., 1995).

Stressors come in many forms. They may be catastrophic, such as floods and rape, or they may be relatively trivial, such as being stuck in traffic when you are late for an appointment. Stressors are not always bad. Some stressors, such as athletic competition, having to perform in front of an audience or sitting an exam, can affect behaviour in positive ways. However, when stress is extended over long periods, it can have negative effects on both a person's psychological health and a person's physical health (Selye, 1991).

The biological basis of stress

Physical response to stressors is governed by the autonomic nervous system, which is controlled by the hypothalamus. Stress is a biological response that is experienced as an emotion, although the form it takes varies depending on the nature of the stressor. In some situations we may feel frightened, and in others we may feel inspired or exhilarated.

When an individual senses a stressor, the hypothalamus sends signals to the autonomic nervous system and to the pituitary gland, both of which respond by stimulating body organs to change their normal activities:

- Heart rate increases, blood pressure rises, blood vessels constrict, blood sugar levels rise, and blood flow is directed away from extremities and towards major organs.
- Breathing becomes deeper and faster and air passages dilate, which permits more air to enter the lungs.
- Digestion stops and perspiration increases.
- The adrenal glands secrete adrenaline (epinephrine), which stimulates the heart and other organs.

It is easy to see why these changes are adaptive. They each prepare the body to deal with the stressor – collectively, these physiological responses produce a heightened psychological and physical state of alertness and readiness for action. Regardless of the nature of the stressor and whether we confront the stressor or run from it, the biological response is generally the same. Whether you find yourself in a dark alley confronted by a man with a knife or are facing your next psychology exam, the autonomic nervous system and the pituitary gland stimulate the body to respond to the stressor.

There are two cases in which such responses can be maladaptive. First, stress can produce anxiety, which may impair one's ability to perform a task. As you may have experienced yourself, anxiety can hinder performance in examinations, speaking in public, competition during sporting events, and remembering lines in a play.

The second case involves the effects of prolonged and severe stress. Many people's lifestyles place them in situations in which they are daily confronted with stressors. These lifestyles place these people at increased risk of illness.

Selye's general adaptation syndrome

Much of what we know about the effects of dealing with prolonged and severe stressors on the body stems from the work of Canadian endocrinologist Hans Selye. Through his work with laboratory animals, he found that chronic exposure to severe stressors produces a sequence of three physiological stages: alarm, resistance, and exhaustion, as illustrated by Figure 16.4. Selye (1956) referred to these stages collectively as the general adaptation syndrome (GAS).

The responses in the alarm stage involve arousal of the autonomic nervous system and occur when the organism is first confronted with a stressor. During this stage, the organism's resistance to the stressor temporarily drops below normal, and the organism may experience shock – impairment of normal physiological functioning. With continued exposure to the stressor, the organism enters the stage of resistance, during which its autonomic nervous system returns to normal functioning. Resistance to the stressor increases and eventually levels out at above normal levels. The stage of resistance, then, reflects the organism's

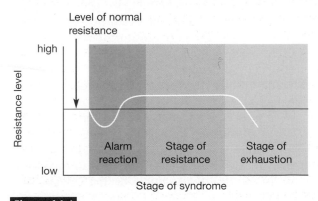

Figure 16.4

The general adaptation syndrome as proposed by Hans Selye.

Source: Selye, H., Stress without Distress. New York: Harper & Row, 1974. Reprinted by permission.

Controversies in psychological science

Why do people choose complementary medicine?

The issue

Complementary medicine refers to an alternative approach to the treatment of illness that is not based on orthodox, traditional medicine. The most common forms are acupuncture, herbalism, homeopathy, hypnosis and osteopathy; the most popular are acupuncture, chiropractice and osteopathy, accounting for 2 million consultations in the UK. Why is it that individuals chose complementary medicine? Are they disillusioned by orthodox medicine? Do they believe that complementary medicine should work better?

The evidence

According to one survey, complementary consultations in 1981 averaged 19,500 per 100,000 consultations in the UK – approximately 6 per cent of general practitioner consultations (Fulder and Munro, 1985). In the United States, visits to complementary therapists outnumber those to primary care doctors (Eisenberg *et al.*, 1993). In other parts of Europe, one-third to one-half of individuals are estimated to have used complementary medicine (Lewith and Aldridge, 1991; Sharma, 1992). A study of Danish hospital staff reported that 48 per cent of them had used complementary medicine, 23 per cent of them in the last three months (Raben *et al.*, 1993, cited in Norheim and Fonnebo, 1998). Eighty-eight per cent of new trainee GPs in the UK reported finding acupuncture useful (Reilly, 1983). A study of 1,135 Norwegian doctors found that 8 per cent of them had undergone acupuncture treatment, 38 per cent reported benefiting from the treatment and 53 per cent reported being willing to consult a complementary practitioner (Norheim and Fonnebo, 1998). Eighty-one per cent believed that acupuncture should be integrated into the national health care system.

What fuels beliefs such as these? A series of studies by Adrian Furnham and his colleagues has shed light on this issue. They looked at orthodox and complementary medicine users' beliefs about health and treatment of ill health. A study of individuals who consulted either a GP or a homeopath, for example, found that those seeking homeopathy were more critical and sceptical about the efficacy of orthodox medicine and were also more likely to report psychiatric

Table 16.6 Differences between the general practitioner (GP) and complementary medicine (CM) groups regarding whether illnesses are caused by physiological or psychological factors

	GP		CM	
	Mean	Standard deviation	Mean	Standard deviation
Angina	4.00	0.99	3.34	1.31
Arthritis	4.20	0.87	3.49	1.33
Asthma	3.15	1.27	2.51	1.20
Back tension	3.28	1.33	2.30	1.13
Blood pressure	3.11	1.10	2.82	1.17
Bronchitis	3.86	1.08	3.11	1.24
Cancer	3.81	1.07	3.00	1.13
Colds	3.93	0.95	3.14	1.34
Cystitis	4.27	0.90	3.11	1.47
Diabetes	4.14	0.92	3.36	1.20
Eczema	2.94	1.16	2.64	1.10
Gastric ulcers	2.22	0.99	2.11	1.06
Headaches	2.39	1.05	2.20	1.03
Haemorrhoids	4.28	0.88	3.71	1.27
Sleep disorders	1.89	0.88	1.98	1.08
Kidney disorders	4.17	0.91	3.34	1.20
Leukaemia	4.46	0.80	3.54	1.20
Menstrual problems	2.88	1.02	2.22	1.04
Migraine	3.28	0.94	1.96	0.99
Obesity	2.32	1.11	2.11	1.04
Pneumonia	4.31	0.83	3.69	1.24
Rheumatism	4.13	0.93	3.23	1.31

5 = physiological causes; 1 = psychological causes
Source: Furnham, A. and Kirkcaldy, B., 1996. Copyright © The British Psychological Society 1996.

complaints (Furnham and Smith, 1988). Neither group differed in terms of their beliefs in their susceptibility to illness. The dissatisfaction with orthodox medicine was also found in another study of patients from an outpatients department of a homeopathic hospital (Furnham and Bhagrath, 1993).

Do those who choose complementary medicine differ from those who do not? The critical approach to orthodox medicine by those who pursue complementary medicine is consistent. Users of complementary medicine have a greater knowledge of physiology and more 'self-aware' lifestyles than orthodox medicine users (Furnham and Forey, 1994). They seem to be highly educated and have a higher income (Sharma, 1992). A study of German users also found that complementary medicine patients were slightly older than their orthodox counterparts (Furnham and Kirkcaldy, 1996). However, the same self-aware lifestyle and critical approach to orthodox medicine was found. The percentage of ill-

nesses reported by these complementary medicine users was similar, although they expressed greater loyalty to their practitioner than did orthodox users. There was a great difference between the groups in terms of whether illnesses had 'physiological' or 'psychological' causes and these are listed in Table 16.6.

A number of reasons have been suggested for the increase in the number of people using complementary medicine. One is that the users' thinking represents a flight from science (Smith, 1983); another is that users have a credulous faith in the occult or paranormal (Baum, 1989). The overriding characteristic (and reason for using alternative approaches) in users appears to be a belief in the failure of orthodox medicine. But do all users of the different complementary therapies hold the same beliefs and views?

To answer this question, Vincent and Furnham (1996) studied users of acupuncture, osteopathy and homeopathy. All users reported that reasons for elect-

Table 16.7 Differences in the reasons given by three complementary medicine groups for selecting their treatment

	Acupuncture	Homeopathy	Osteopathy
1 Because the orthodox treatment I received had unpleasant side effects	4.29	3.80	4.60
2 Because I believe orthodox medicine is generally ineffective	3.25	3.30	4.00
3 Because my doctor did not understand my problem	3.80	3.80	4.44
4 Because my doctor did not give me enough time	3.64	4.15	4.42
5 Because I was persuaded to come by a friend or relative	3.62	4.34	4.31
6 Because it was easier to get an appointment with a complementary practitioner	3.16	3.62	4.33
7 Because I believe that complementary medicine enables me to take a more active part in maintaining my health	4.37	4.69	4.28
8 Because I value a form of therapy that involves actually touching me	3.20	3.97	3.58
9 Because I feel that complementary treatment is a more natural form of healing than orthodox medicine	3.81	4.45	3.88
10 Because complementary treatment is less expensive than orthodox private medicine	2.66	3.83	3.63
11 Because I am desperate and will try anything	3.42	4.59	4.01

5 = very important reason; 1 = not an important reason

Continued overleaf

ing complementary approaches included a belief in the treatment of the whole person, that it was more effective than orthodox medicine and that orthodox medicine was not effective. Very few differences existed between the groups, although those electing to use osteopathy were less concerned about the side effects of orthodox medicine whereas homeopathy users were more influenced by the ineffectiveness of orthodox medicine. Table 16.7 shows the items which elicited significantly different responses between groups.

Conclusion

Despite the overall effectiveness of orthodox medicine, some individuals' beliefs about health and treatment incline them to pursue alternative approaches. The principal reason for adopting these approaches is a dissatisfaction with orthodox medicine and a lack of belief in its effectiveness. It would be instructive to see whether these individuals' beliefs changed after using complementary medicine. If complementary medicine did not work effectively, would the client rationalise this ineffectiveness by arguing that the treatment still did more good than orthodox approaches?

The loyalty expressed by complementary users, and their self-awareness, perhaps suggests that any treatment which delivers care and attention in a focused and deliberate way might change an individual's perception of treatment. It is often difficult, in some countries, to see the doctor you want when you want; and even when this doctor is consulted, the time with him or her is limited because he or she has other patients to see. The fact that, in complementary medicine, the patient is allowed more time to develop a relationship with the practitioner might mean that the client is more positively predisposed to believe in the relative effectiveness of the therapy.

---

adaptation to environmental stressors. However, with continued exposure to the stressor, the organism enters the stage of exhaustion. During this stage, the organism loses its ability to adapt, and resistance plummets to below normal levels, leaving the organism susceptible to illness and even death.

The extent to which people can adapt varies across individuals and depends on how the stressor is perceived. Our emotional responses seem designed primarily to cope with short-term events. The physiological responses that accompany the negative emotions prepare us to threaten or fight rivals or to run away from dangerous situations. Walter Cannon coined the phrase **fight or flight response** to refer to the physiological reactions that prepare us for the strenuous efforts required by fighting or running away. Normally, once we have bluffed or fought with an adversary or run away from a dangerous situation, the threat is over and our physiological condition can return to normal. The fact that the physiological responses may have adverse long-term effects on our health is unimportant as long as the responses are brief. But when the threatening situations are continuous rather than episodic, they produce a more-or-less continuous stress response. This continued state of arousal can lead to coronary heart disease (CHD) and other physical problems.

Physiological mechanisms involved in stress

Emotions consist of behavioural, autonomic and hormonal responses. The latter two components – autonomic and hormonal responses – are the ones that can have adverse effects on health. Because threatening situations generally call for vigorous activity, the autonomic and hormonal responses that accompany them help to make the body's energy resources available. The sympathetic branch of the autonomic nervous system is active, and the adrenal glands secrete epinephrine, norepinephrine and steroid stress hormones.

Epinephrine (adrenaline) releases the stored form of glucose that is present in the muscles, thus providing energy for strenuous exercise. Along with norepinephrine (noradrenaline), it also increases blood flow to the muscles by increasing the output of the heart, which also increases blood pressure. Over the long term, these changes contribute to CHD. The other stress-related hormone is cortisol, a steroid secreted by the cortex of the adrenal gland. Cortisol is called a **glucocorticoid** because it has profound effects on glucose metabolism, effects similar to those of epinephrine. In addition, glucocorticoids help break down protein and convert it to glucose, help make fats available for energy, increase blood flow, and stimulate behavioural responsiveness, presumably by affecting the brain. They also have other physiological effects, some of which are only poorly understood. Almost every cell in the body contains glucocorticoid receptors, which means that few parts of the body are unaffected by these hormones. Figure 16.5 illustrates the effects of hormones on various body organs and their functions.

Selye (1976) suggested that most of the harmful effects of stress were produced by the prolonged secretion of glucocorticoids. Although the short-term effects of glucocorticoids are essential, the long-term effects are damaging. These effects include increased blood pressure, damage to muscle tissue, a particular form of diabetes, infertility, stunted growth, inhibition of the inflammatory responses and suppression of the immune system. High blood pressure can lead to heart attacks and stroke. Inhibition of growth in children subjected to prolonged stress prevents them from attaining their full height. Inhibition of the inflammatory response makes it more difficult for the body to heal itself after an injury, and suppression of the immune system makes an individual vulnerable to infections and (perhaps) cancer.

Several lines of research suggest that stress is related to ageing in at least two ways. First, older people, even when they are perfectly healthy, do not tolerate stress as well as younger people do (Shock, 1977). Second, stress may accelerate the ageing process (Selye and Tuchweber, 1976). Sapolsky and his colleagues have investigated one rather serious long-term effect of stress: brain damage. As you saw in Chapter 8, the hippocampal formation plays a crucial role in learning and memory. Evidence suggests that one of the causes of memory loss that occurs with ageing is degeneration of this brain structure. Research conducted on animals has shown that long-term exposure to glucocorticoids destroys neurons located in a particular zone of the hippocampal formation. The hormone appears to destroy the neurons by making them more susceptible to the normal wear and tear that accompanies the ageing process (Sapolsky, 1986; Sapolsky et al., 1986).

Cognitive appraisal and stress

Many of the harmful effects of long-term stress are caused by our own reactions – primarily the secretion of stress hormones. Some events that cause stress, such as prolonged exertion or extreme cold, cause damage directly. These stressors will affect everyone; their severity will depend on each person's physical capacity. Selye's model has been useful for understanding the biological components involved in stress, but it does not explain the role of psychological components in stress. The effects of other stressors, such as situations that cause fear or anxiety, depend on people's perceptions and emotional reactivity. That is, because of individual differences in temperament or experience with a particular situation, some people may find a situation stressful and others may not. In these cases, it is the perception that matters.

One of the most important variables that determines whether an aversive stimulus will cause a stress reaction is the degree to which the situation can be controlled. When an animal can learn a coping response that allows it to avoid contact with an aversive stimulus, its emotional response will disappear. Weiss (1968) found that rats that learned to minimise (but not completely avoid) shocks by making a response whenever they heard a warning tone developed fewer stomach ulcers than did rats that had no control over the shocks. The effect was not caused by the pain itself, because both groups of animals received exactly the same number of shocks. Thus, being able to exert some control over an aversive situation reduces an animal's stress. Humans react similarly. Situations that permit some control are less likely to produce signs of stress than are those in which other people (or machines) control the situation (Gatchel et al., 1989). Perhaps this phenomenon explains why some people like to have a magic charm or other 'security blanket' with them in stressful situations. Perhaps even the illusion of control can be reassuring.

Some psychologists argue that the psychological components in stress may influence the degree to which stressors arouse the autonomic nervous system. One such psychologist is Richard Lazarus, who argues that our

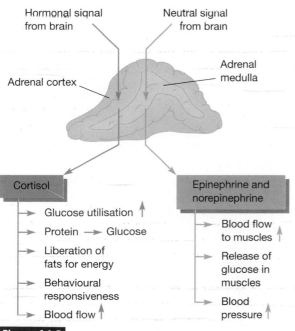

Figure 16.5

Control and the effects of secretion of epinephrine, norepinephrine and cortisol by the adrenal gland.

perception of the stressor does, to a large extent, determine the stress we experience (Lazarus and Folkman, 1984). According to Lazarus, an individual's stress levels are affected by his or her cognitive appraisal, or perception, of the stressful situation.

Cognitive appraisal is a two-stage process. In the first stage, we evaluate the threat: we attempt to judge the seriousness of the perceived threat posed by the stressor. If we decide that the threat is real, we pass to the second stage, during which we assess whether we have the resources necessary to cope adequately with the threat. The extent to which we believe both that the stressor is a serious one and that we do not have the resources necessary to deal with it determines the level of stress we will experience. The belief that we cannot deal effectively with a stressor perceived as being extremely dangerous leads to the highest levels of stress. Because different people may evaluate differently both the stressor and their ability to cope with it, they are likely to show different levels of stress when faced with the same stressor. We know from experience that this is true. For example, people vary tremendously in their reactions to snakes: a harmless grass snake will arouse intense fear in some people and none in others.

Selye's findings, then, do not apply to all people; there are individual differences in how people react to prolonged exposure to stress. Some people show little, if any, risk of becoming ill during or after chronic stress. Kobasa (1979) refers to these people as hardy individuals. In a study of how business executives coped with long-term stress, she found that some of her subjects became ill and some did not. She wanted to find out what caused this difference. Through detailed analyses of her subjects' responses to different psychological inventories, she found that the hardy subjects viewed the stressors in their lives as challenges and that they met these challenges head-on; they did not avoid them or become anxious about them. They also felt that they had control over the challenges (stressors).

In other words, Kobasa's findings support Lazarus's idea of the importance of cognitive appraisal in dealing with stress: how we initially assess the stressor, how we tackle it, and the extent to which we believe that we can control the stressor seem to influence whether we become at risk of illnesses related to being chronically stressed.

Stress and impaired health

Selye's research involved exposing laboratory animals to chronic and intense stressors under controlled laboratory conditions. In addition to showing that resistance to stressors appears to involve three stages, his results also showed that animals became seriously ill during the stage of exhaustion. Can prolonged exposure to severe stressors produce similar risks for humans? Many studies investigating the relationship of lifestyle to health have shown that the answer to this question is yes. Specifically, stressful lifestyles have been shown to be related to increased risk of impaired immune system functioning, ulcers, high blood pressure, cancer and CHD.

Ulcers

One of the commonest ulcers in the human body is peptic ulcer which is found in the stomach (the world's best-selling drug helps to combat ulcers). The cause of peptic ulcer is *Heliobacter pylori*, although, until this discovery, psychological stress was thought to be a principal precipitating factor. Since the discovery of this cause, interest in the psychological causes of ulcers has receded (Levenstein, 1998) although psychological stressors can influence the degree and course of ulcers. These stressors have been found to impair ulcer healing and to lead to an increase in the secretion of gastric acid. Patients with ulcers also seem to have experienced a greater number of life stressors compared with matched controls.

Psychoneuroimmunology

The most important causes of stress are elevated levels of glucocorticoids, epinephrine and norepinephrine. However, stress can also impair the function of the immune system, which protects us from assault by viruses, microbes, fungi and other types of parasite. Study of the interactions between the immune system and behaviour is called psychoneuroimmunology. Before discussing the effect of stressors on immune system functioning, it is useful to have an understanding of how the immune system works.

The immune system

The function of the immune system is to protect the body from infection. It is a network of organs and cells that protects the body from invading bacteria, viruses, and other foreign substances and is one of the most complex systems of the body. Because infectious organisms have developed devious tricks through the process of evolution, our immune system has evolved devious tricks of its own.

The immune system derives from white blood cells that develop in the bone marrow and in the thymus gland. Some of the cells roam through the blood or lymph glands and sinuses; others reside permanently in one place. The immune reaction occurs when the body is invaded by foreign organisms.

There are two types of specific immune reaction: chemically mediated and cell mediated. Chemically mediated immune reactions involve antibodies. All bacteria have unique proteins on their surfaces, called antigens. These proteins serve as the invaders' calling cards, identifying them to the immune system. Through exposure to the bacteria, the immune system learns to recognise these proteins. The result of this learning is the development of special lines of cells that produce specific **antibodies** – proteins that recognise antigens and help to kill the invading microorganism. One type of antibody is released into the circulation by **B lymphocytes**, which receive their name from the fact that they develop in bone marrow. These antibodies, called **immunoglobulins**, are chains of protein. Each of five different types of immunoglobulin is identical except for one end, which contains a unique receptor. A particular receptor binds with a particular antigen, just as a molecule of a hormone or a transmitter substance binds with its receptor. When the appropriate line of B lymphocytes detects the presence of an invading bacterium, the cells release their antibodies, which bind with the bacterial antigens. The antibodies either kill the invaders directly or attract other white blood cells which then destroy the invaders. This process is illustrated by Figure 16.6.

One class of antibody, **secretory immunoglobulin A (sIgA)** is secreted by and covers the mucosal surfaces such as those found in the respiratory and gastrointestinal tracts. Its role appears to be to provide protection against infection by creating a barrier to invading organisms (Kraehenbuhl and Neutra, 1992). Because this antibody can be measured from saliva, it has been one of the most widely researched of the antibodies (P. Evans *et al.*, 1997).

The other type of defence mounted by the immune system, **cell-mediated immune reactions,** is produced by **T lymphocytes**, which develop in the thymus gland. An example of T lymphocyte appears in Figure 16.7.

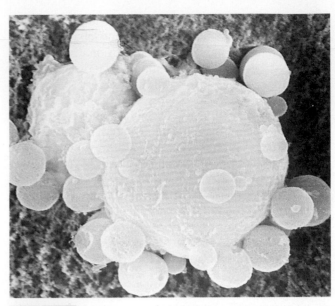

Figure 16.7

A T lymphocyte at work destroying tumour cells.

Source: Andrejs Liepins/Science Photo Library/Photo Researchers Inc.

T lymphocytes also produce antibodies, but the antibodies remain attached to the outside of the cell's membrane. T lymphocytes primarily defend the body against fungi, viruses and multicellular parasites. When antigens bind with their

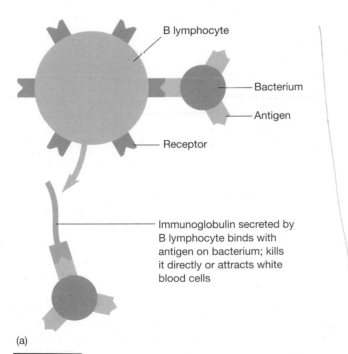

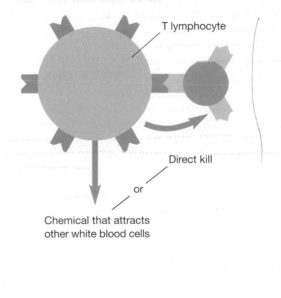

(a)   (b)

Figure 16.6

Immune reactions. (a) Chemically mediated reaction. The B lymphocyte detects an antigen on a bacterium and releases a specific immunoglobulin. (b) Cell-mediated reaction. The T lymphocyte detects an antigen on a bacterium and kills it directly or releases a chemical that attracts other white blood cells.

surface antibodies, the cells either kill the invaders directly or signal other white blood cells to come and kill them.

In addition to the immune reactions produced by lymphocytes, natural killer cells continuously prowl through tissue. When they encounter a cell that has been infected by a virus or that has become transformed into a cancer cell, they engulf and destroy it. Thus, natural killer cells constitute an important defence against viral infections and the development of malignant tumours. Although the immune system normally protects us, it can cause us harm, too. Allergic reactions occur when an antigen causes cells of the immune system to overreact, releasing a particular immunoglobulin that produces a localised inflammatory response. The chemicals released during this reaction can enter the general circulation and cause life-threatening complications. Allergic responses are harmful, and why they occur is unknown.

The immune system can do something else that harms the body – it can attack its own cells. Autoimmune diseases occur when the immune system becomes sensitised to a protein present in the body and attacks the tissue that contains this protein. Exactly what causes the protein to be targeted is not known. What is known is that autoimmune diseases often follow viral or bacterial infections. Presumably, in learning to recognise antigens that belong to the infectious agent, the immune system develops a line of cells that treat one of the body's own proteins as foreign. Some common autoimmune diseases include rheumatoid arthritis, diabetes, lupus and multiple sclerosis.

Neural control of the immune system

Stress can suppress the immune system, resulting in a greater likelihood of infectious diseases, and it can also aggravate autoimmune diseases. It may even affect the growth of cancers. What is the physiological explanation for these effects? One answer, and probably the most important one, is that stress increases the secretion of glucocorticoids, and these hormones directly suppress the activity of the immune system. All types of white blood cell have glucocorticoid receptors, and suppression of the immune system is presumably mediated by these receptors (Solomon, 1987).

Because the secretion of glucocorticoids is controlled by the brain, the brain is obviously responsible for the suppressing effect of these hormones on the immune system. For example, in a study of rats, Keller *et al.* (1983) found that the stress of inescapable shock decreased the number of lymphocytes found in the blood. This effect was abolished by removal of the adrenal gland. Thus, the decrease in lymphocytes appears to have been caused by the release of glucocorticoids triggered by the stress, as seen in Figure 16.8(a). However, the same authors found that removal of the adrenal glands did not abolish the effects of stress on another type of immune response: stimulation of lymphocytes by an antigen, as seen in Figure 16.8(b). Thus, not all the effects of stress on the immune system are mediated by glucocorticoids; there must be other mechanisms as well.

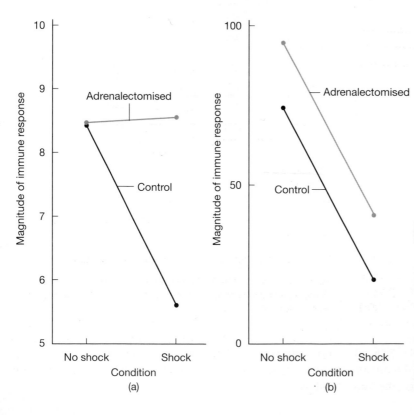

Figure 16.8

Effects of the removal of rats' adrenal glands on suppression of the immune system produced by inescapable shocks. (a) Number of white blood cells (lymphocytes) found in the blood. (b) Stimulation of lymphocyte production after exposure to an antigen.

Source: Based on data from Keller, S.E., Weiss, J.M., Schleifer, S.J., Miller, N.E. and Stein, M., Stress-induced suppression of immunity in adrenalectomized rats. *Science*, 1983, 221, 1301–1304.

These additional mechanisms may involve direct neural control. The bone marrow, the thymus gland and the lymph nodes all receive neural input. Although researchers have not yet obtained direct proof that this input modulates immune function, it would be surprising if it did not.

In addition, the immune system appears to be sensitive to chemicals produced by the nervous system. The best evidence comes from studies of the opioids produced by the brain. Shavit *et al.* (1984) found that inescapable intermittent shock produced both analgesia (decreased sensitivity to pain) and suppression of the production of natural killer cells. Both these effects seem to have been mediated by brain opioids, because both effects were abolished when the experimenters administered a drug that blocks opiate receptors. Shavit *et al.* (1986) found that natural killer cell activity could be suppressed by injecting morphine directly into the brain; thus, the effect of the opiates appears to take place in the brain. The mechanism by which the brain affects the natural killer cells is not yet known.

Stress and the immune system

The immune system does not appear to react to different types of stressor in the same way. Chronic stressors such as bereavement of a close friend or relative, caring for a relative with Alzheimer's disease and marital disharmony, tend to result in reduced immune system functioning (Kiecolt-Glaser *et al.*, 1993; Zisook *et al.*, 1994). Kiecolt-Glaser *et al.* (1995), for example, reported that wounds took longer to heal (in fact, nine days longer) in carers for individuals with Alzheimer's disease than in age – and income-matched 'stress-free' controls. Figures 16.9(a) and (b) show the relationship between caregiving and wound healing and wound size over the recovery period. Acute stress, however, does not appear to have the same effect. Acute stress appears actually to increase the number of natural killer cells (Delahanty *et al.*, 1996) and the levels of sIgA (Zeier *et al.*, 1996).

Evans *et al.* (1993) have reported that lower quality of life (such as experiencing more undesirable or fewer desirable experiences) is associated with lower levels of sIgA. However, undergraduates asked to present a piece of work orally in front of their colleagues, showed an increase in the levels of this antibody (Evans *et al.*, 1994). Levels of sIgA tend to decrease during examination periods (Jemmott and Magloire, 1988) which suggests that short- and long-term stressors have different effects on the immune system.

The immune system has recently been studied in experiments designed to examine the effects of laughter and humour on stress and coping with stress. The

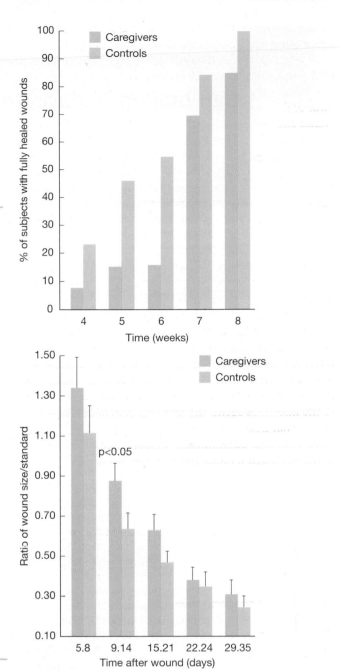

Figure 16.9

The progress of woundhealing in Alzheimer's disease.

(a) Percentage of caregivers and controls whose wounds had healed in time.

(b) Average wound size during first 5 weeks of study.

Source: Kiecolt-Glaser, J.K., Marucha, P.T., Malarkey, W.B., Mercado, A.M. and Glaser, R., Slowing of wound-healing by psychological stress. *The Lancet*, 346, 1194–96. © by The Lancet Limited 1995.

evidence for the role of humour and laughter in mediating the effects of the immune system is discussed in the 'Controversies in psychological science' section below.

Can humour reduce stress?

The issue

In 1979, Norman Cousin's published a rather unusual book called *The Anatomy of Illness*. It was unusual in that it described the way in which he used laughter to help him recover from a degenerative spinal condition. Since 1979, a number of popular and scientific accounts have suggested that using humour can help to combat stress and ill health. One contributor to the field has suggested that 'happy breathing, simulated smiles and transcendental breathing' can uplift spirits (Holden, 1993). 'Don your Super-Humour-Person cape', he exhorts, 'and save the world from the arch-villain over-seriousness.' While we can dismiss accounts like this as minor eccentricities of little psychological importance, more thoughtful researchers have examined whether humour does help us to cope with ill health and stress and provide immunity from these problems. These researchers have focused upon the effects of humour from several perspectives. Perhaps the most important of these are: producing humour, appreciating humour and using humour as a coping mechanism.

The evidence

Laughter is an intriguing behaviour: it can induce laughter in a passive listener, can enhance the enjoyment of comedy, despite people's claimed dislike of audience laughter (Martin and Gray, 1996) and provides vigorous muscle exercise. According to Hans Selye, laughter is a form of eustress: a positive, life-enhancing type of stress or pressure. In one experiment, twenty men and women endured pressure-induced discomfort after either having listened to a 20 minute laughter tape, a relaxation tape or a dull narrative (Cogan *et al.*, 1987). For both the laughter and relaxation conditions, discomfort thresholds were higher, that is, participants could endure greater stress.

Does this suggest that comedy is good for you? The picture is not altogether clear-cut. In a well controlled experiment where the effect of the appreciation of humour on stress reduction was examined, the experimenters found no relationship between appreciation and stress reduction (Martin and Lefcourt, 1983). They did, however, find a slight moderation of the stress when humour was *produced* by participants. Another study found that this moderating effect was significant for depression but not anxiety symptoms (Nezu *et al.*, 1988). This finding suggests that it may not necessarily be the blanket appreciation (watching, listening) of humour that is important but the way in which humour is used.

Rod Martin and Herbert Lefcourt and their colleagues from the University of Waterloo, Canada, have conducted a number of experiments in which they examined the relationship between a person's sense of humour, their use of humour as a coping mechanism and their response to stress. In a small number of detailed studies, the experimenters took measures of individuals' physical stress by sampling their salivary immunoglobin A concentrations (sIgA). In one study, 40 participants provided saliva samples, completed a Daily Hassles Scale (a measure of the degree of stress experienced daily) and a sense of humour questionnaire. The experimenters found a negative correlation between low scores on the sense of humour questionnaire and sIgA levels. A different experiment measured sIgA concentrations before and after the presentation of humorous stimuli and examined whether the presentation would interact with the participants' sense of humour (Lefcourt *et al.*, 1990). The researchers found that not only did saliva concentrations increase after presentation of humour but that those participants with the greatest sense of humour had larger concentrations of sIgA after exposure to an audio comedy tape.

More recently, Lefcourt *et al.* (1997) examined the relationship between pain endurance, coping and blood pressure in men and women. There is evidence to suggest that men and women do use humour in different ways. Men are reported to make more frequent attempts at humour, for example, and use it for more negative reasons than do women (Myers *et al.*, 1997). In Lefcourt *et al.*'s experiment, women who used coping humour a great deal exhibited lower systolic blood pressure than did low-scoring women. Men, on the other hand, showed the reverse pattern. On the basis of the participants' responses to the stressful tasks, the experimenters concluded that humour may moderate the effect of uncontrollable and passively experienced stress but that stressful problem solving tasks involving active participation are less susceptible to these moderating effects.

Conclusion

From what you have read so far, are you convinced that humour can help reduce the effect of stress? What influences your decision? Can you think of better ways of measuring the effects of sense of humour, or perceiving humour or generating humour, on stress reduction? Would you expect the effects of sense of humour on stress reduction to be long term? If so, why? If not, why not?

Finally, in an ingenious test of the hypothesis that laughter and humour help us combat the effects of stressful events, Rotton (1992) examined the death rates of comedians, literary humorists and non-humorous individuals by examining published biographical details. He found no significant difference between the lifespan of humorous entertainers and that of others.

Infectious diseases

A wide variety of stress-producing events in a person's life can increase the susceptibility to infectious diseases. For example, Glaser *et al.* (1987) found that medical students were more likely to contract acute infections – and to show evidence of suppression of the immune system – during final examinations than before. In addition, autoimmune diseases often get worse when a person is subjected to stress, as Feigenbaum *et al.* (1979) found for rheumatoid arthritis.

Stone *et al.* (1987) attempted to see whether stressful events in people's daily lives might predispose them to upper respiratory infection. If a person is exposed to a microorganism that might cause such a disease, the symptoms do not occur for several days; that is, there is an incubation period between exposure and signs of the actual illness. The authors therefore reasoned that if stressful events suppressed the immune system, one might expect to see a higher likelihood of respiratory infections several days after such stress. To test their hypothesis, they asked volunteers to keep a daily record of desirable and undesirable events in their lives over a twelve week period. The volunteers also kept a daily record of any discomfort or symptoms of illness.

The results were as predicted: during the 3–5 day period just before showing symptoms of an upper respiratory infection, people experienced an increased number of undesirable events and a decreased number of desirable events in their lives. Stone *et al.* (1987) suggest that the effect is caused by decreased production of a particular immunoglobulin that is present in the secretions of mucous membranes, including those in the nose, mouth, throat and lungs. This immunoglobulin serves as the first defence against infectious microorganisms that enter the nose or mouth. They found that this immunoglobulin (known as IgA) is associated with mood. When a subject is unhappy or depressed, IgA levels are lower than normal. The results suggest that the stress caused by undesirable events may, by suppressing the production of IgA, lead to a rise in the likelihood of upper respiratory infections.

However, this study did not manipulate exposure to the illness directly. In an extraordinary and well-controlled experiment, Cohen *et al.* (1998), exposed individuals to one of two common cold viruses, measured various personality and behavioural variables (such as sex, alcohol consumption, sleep pattern), and monitored which individuals developed a respiratory infection that led to the cold. Eighty-four per cent became infected but only 40 per cent developed a cold. Those who did were reported to have endured chronic life stressors for at least a month; those who had endured little stress or experienced the effect of stressors for less than a month did not, on average, develop the cold. Other factors which were positively related to developing a cold were smoking, less than three exercise sessions a week, poor sleep, drinking fewer than two alcoholic drinks a day, ingesting less than 85 mg of vitamin C and being introverted.

Bereavement

Bereavement, another source of stress, also suppresses the immune system. Cancer and other illnesses have been observed to occur at higher-than-average rates among people who are widowed. To investigate the possibility that bereavement suppresses the immune system, Schleifer *et al.* (1983) drew blood samples from fifteen men whose wives were dying of terminal breast cancer. Two blood samples were drawn, the first before the spouse's death and the second within two months afterwards. Both times, an agent that normally stimulates blood lymphocyte activity was mixed with the lymphocytes, and the resultant level of activity was measured. On average, the activity level of blood lymphocytes after the spouse's death was less than before her death, which meant that the bereaved spouses were more susceptible to illness. Taken together, the results of these studies (and many other similar studies) suggest a strong link between stress and weakening of the immune system.

Procrastination

Procrastination refers to the tendency to put off tasks and chores that could be done immediately. In the short term, you might think that this produces less stress because the individual is under less pressure to perform. In a study of procrastination among health psychology students, Tice and Baumeister (1997) noted the date on which students submitted coursework and took measures of procrastination from each. Not surprisingly, procrastinators submitted their coursework significantly later. They also received lower grades. However, and oddly, they also seemed to experience less stress than did non-procrastinators. In a term-long study, the researchers found that this was true, but only at the beginning of the term; at the end of the term their symptoms of stress were significantly greater than those of non-procrastinators, as seen in Figure 16.10. Readers should, perhaps, consider the implications of his study very, very carefully.

Personality

Friedman and Rosenman (1959) identified a behaviour pattern that appeared to be related to a person's susceptibility to CHD. Heart attacks occur when the blood vessels that serve the heart become blocked, whereas strokes involve the blood vessels in the brain. The two most important risk factors in CHD are high blood pressure and a high level of cholesterol in the blood. Friedman and Rosenman characterised the disease-prone type A pattern as one of excessive competitive drive, an intense disposition, impatience, hostility, fast movements and rapid speech. People with the type B pattern were less competitive, less hostile, more patient, easygoing and tolerant, and they moved and talked more slowly; they were also less likely to suffer from CHD. Friedman and Rosenman developed a questionnaire that distinguished between these two types of people. The test is rather interesting, because the person who

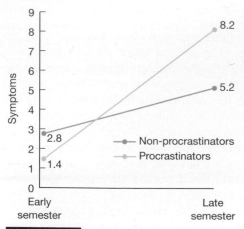

Figure 16.10

The number of symptoms reported by student procrastinators and non-procrastinators across a term on a health psychology course.

Source: Tice, D.M. and Baumeister, R.F. (1997) Longitudinal study of procrastination, performance, stress and health. In *Psychological Science*, 8(6), November, pp. 454–8.

administers it is not a passive participant. The interviewer asks questions in an abrupt, impatient manner, interrupting the subject if he or she takes too much time to answer a question. The point of such behaviour is to try to elicit type A behaviour from the subject.

Researchers have devoted much attention to the relation between type A personality and CHD. The Western Collaborative Group study (Rosenman *et al.*, 1975), which studied 3,154 healthy men for 8½ years, found that the type A behaviour pattern was associated with twice the rate of CHD relative to non-type-A behaviour patterns. Results such as these led an independent review panel to classify the type A behaviour pattern as a risk factor for CHD (Review Panel, 1981). However, since then, many contradictory results have been obtained. For example, one large study found that although people classified as type A were more likely to have heart attacks, the long-term survival rate after having a heart attack was higher for type A patients than for type B patients (Ragland and Brand, 1988). In this case, it would seem better to be type A, at least after having a non-fatal heart attack. Other studies have failed to find a difference in the likelihood of CHD in people with type A and type B personalities (Dimsdale, 1988). Recently, the personality characteristic of submissiveness has been correlated with lower rates of CHD in a group of Scottish individuals (Whiteman *et al.*, 1997). Submissiveness refers to a preference for staying in the background, letting others lead/dominate and lacking self-assurance and self-confidence. Submissiveness, however, is not type B behaviour because submissive people do not have the type B personality's sense of security.

Other characteristics which seem to be part of the type A personality are a greater need for control (Furnham, 1990), placing less value on avoiding problems and responsibilities (Smith and Brehm, 1981) and greater alertness and focus (Matthews and Brunson, 1979). Williams *et al.* (1980) suggested that one aspect of the type A personality – hostility – is of particular importance in CHD. Several studies carried out in the early to mid 1980s confirmed that hostility was an important risk factor for CHD, but more recent studies have not.

A focus of some recent research has been on the role of personality in causing motor accidents. A study of 108 drivers found that type A behaviour was associated with faster driving but not increased accidents (West *et al.*, 1993). A study of bus drivers in India and the United States (Evans *et al.*, 1987), however, found that type A behaviour was associated with high traffic accident rates per month, a finding that was replicated in Italian traffic policemen (Magnavita *et al.*, 1997).

Occupational stress

Occupational stress refers to the degree of stress experienced by members of different professions. This area of research is a popular one in organisational psychology and the Whitehall study of CHD in British civil servants is a good example of the type of work carried out in this area. This study has shown that the lower the grade of employment in the civil service, the higher the mortality rate from CHD. The Whitehall II Study followed a different cohort and investigated whether two factors might be associated with CHD-related mortality: high psychosocial pressure and low control over their environment (Marmot *et al.*, 1997).

Swedish studies suggest that sickness-related absenteeism from work is more common in blue-collar than white-collar workers (Steers and Rhodes, 1984). Several factors can influence the rate of sickness including the physical work environment, psychosocial factors, risk of unemployment, education level and absentee culture (Drago and Wooden, 1992). In an extensive study of absenteeism in 84,319 individuals in two counties in Sweden, Knutsson and Goine (1998) found that, for men, the professions showing highest degrees of absenteeism were shop assistants, repairmen and welders, whereas loggers and mechanics were absent for the fewest days. For women, the professions with the highest absenteeism rates were shop assistants, assistant nurses and secretaries (the lowest rates were for primary school teachers). Of course, these findings do not necessarily suggest that these professions are marked by acute stress (and, therefore, by high rates of absenteeism) although they might, but they suggest that some professions may be more susceptible to stressors.

Much of the applied work in occupational or organisational psychology has been directed towards helping people to cope with the stress generated by heavy workloads or excessive working hours (Warr, 1990; Buunk *et al.*, 1998). There appears to be a significant relationship between the number of hours worked and the degree of physical and mental ill health an employee experiences, but the extent of this relationship is unclear: most conclude that there is a significant relationship between these factors but that this relationship is not particularly strong (Sparks *et al.*, 1997). Recent studies from Japan, however, suggest that individuals who work in excess of 11 hours a day are more at risk of myocardial infarction than are those who work a moderate number (Sokejima and Kagamimori, 1998). In Japan, it is thought that long working hours can cause sudden fatal heart attacks, called 'karoshi' (Uehata, 1991; cited in Kageyama *et al.*, 1998). Kageyama *et al.*'s study of working commuters suggests that those with the longest commuting times and who work the most overtime, show greater variability in heart rate than do those who commute and work less.

Unemployment

Almost all of us have to earn a living: money allows us to do many of the things we want to do and employment gives structure and meaning to our lives. Unemployment, however, has been associated with an increase in ill health and psychological disturbance (Warr, 1987). One consequence of unemployment is increased isolation and loss of social context (Donovan and Oddy, 1982). A Danish study of employed and unemployed single mothers found that isolation led to depression (Beck-Jorgensen, 1991) and that lower self-esteem was characteristic of unemployment (Winefield and Tiggermann, 1994). A longitudinal study of 1,060 young people who were monitored over five years since their last term at school in northern Sweden found that unemployment was correlated significantly with increases in depressive symptoms, even when initial health was accounted for (Hammarstrom and Janlert, 1997).

In an innovative study of the ways in which the effects of unemployment could be reduced, Proudfoot and her colleagues (Proudfoot *et al.*, 1997) applied cognitive behaviour therapy (CBT) or a control programme to a group of long-term (more than 12 months) unemployed individuals. (Cognitive Behaviour Therapy is used to change maladaptic behaviour and thinking, and is discussed again, in more detail, in the next chapter.) The two treatment groups completed three one-hour sessions each week for seven weeks. A summary of the two conditions appears in Table 16.8.

Participants were questioned before, during and 3–4 months after completion of the treatments. General health and mental health were significantly better in the CBT group than in the control group. Although there were no differences in job-seeking ability, the CBT group were more successful in finding work four months after completion

(34 per cent of the CBT group found employment compared with 13 per cent of the control group). Figure 16.11 illustrates some of the effects of CBT on various behavioural measures.

Optimism

Optimism refers to a disposition to believe in positive outcomes. Evidence suggests that dispositional optimists (those who are characteristically optimistic) are more successful at coping with ill health (Stanton and Snider, 1993),

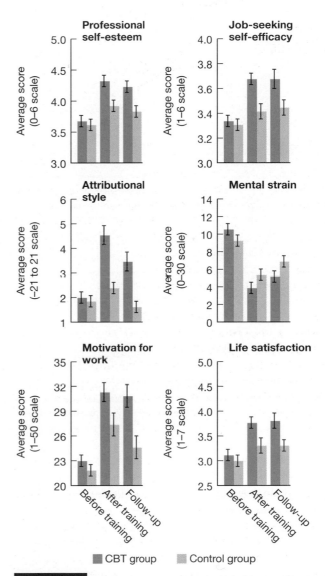

Figure 16.11

Mean scores before training, after training and at follow-up for cognitive behaviour therapy (CBT) and control unemployed groups.

Source: Proudfoot, J., Guest, D., Carson, J., Dunn, G. and Gray, J., Effect of cognitive-behavioural training on job-find among long-term unemployed people. *The Lancet*, 1997, 350, 12 July, pp. 96–100. © by The Lancet Ltd, 1997.

Table 16.8   Structure of the cognitive behaviour therapy (CBT) and control programmes used in Proudfoot *et al.*'s study

	CBT programme	Control programme
Structure	Seven 3 h seminars, one per week Assignments between seminars to assist experimentation with and application of strategies	Seven 3 h seminars, one per week Assignments between seminars to extend each topic
Content		
Seminar 1	Introduction to cognitive model	Concept of social support, health and unemployment
Seminar 2	Automatic thoughts, goal-settings, time management, task breakdown	Life satisfaction graphs, peaks and troughs, importance of people
Seminar 3	Thought-recording and common thinking errors, planning	Role-mapping, satisfying relationship, personal support networks
Seminar 4	Techniques to change unhelpful thinking	Social awareness, how to create a positive impression, rules of relationships
Seminar 5	Gaining access to deeper beliefs, dimensions of attributional thinking	Listening and conversation skills
Seminar 6	Specific applications to personal and work situations	People as resources, individual presentations
Seminar 7	Integration of strategies, action planning and relapse prevention	Goal-setting, course summary
Training process	Socratic questioning, group discussions, self-observations, experimentation, individual and group activities, homework assignments	Small group activities, group discussions, individual presentations
Session format	Review of previous seminar Discussion of homework assignments Introduction of seminar topic Individual or group activities Feedback and discussion Suggestion of weekly homework tasks Summary of session Survey of participants' response to session	Review of previous seminar Discussion of homework assignments Introduction of seminar topic Discussion Individual or group activities Feedback Outline of homework task Summary of session

Source: adapted from Proudfoot *et al.* 1997

are not as emotionally perturbed by stressors (Aspinwall and Taylor, 1992), can cope better with breast cancer surgery (Stanton and Snider, 1993), report better physical health (Scheier and Carver, 1992), have a better quality of life (Fitzgerald *et al.*, 1993) and show an increase in helper T cells and natural killer cells (Segerstrom *et al.*, 1998).

Is there a cancer-prone personality?

Many people, both professionals and lay people, believe that psychological factors play a role in determining whether people develop cancers or, if they do, whether the cancers can be 'beaten'. Some professionals have even suggested that having a 'cancer-prone personality' is a risk factor for the disease. Is there any truth in this?

The idea that personality is related to the development of cancer is not a new one. During the second century AD, Galen, the Greek anatomist and physician, concluded that melancholic women were more likely than optimistic women to develop cancer (Bastiaans, 1985). Physicians in more recent times have reported similar relations between cancer-proneness and personality, but it was not until the 1950s that investigators attempted to do systematic studies (Gil, 1989). Several studies (for example, LeShan and Worthington, 1956; Kissen, 1963) suggested that cancer-prone people had difficulty expressing emotions (especially anger and hostility) and had low self-esteem.

The concept of the **type C (cancer-prone) personality** was introduced in the 1980s (Morris, 1980; Eysenck, 1988). According to Temoshok *et al.* (1985), the type C pattern is shown by a person 'who is co-operative, unassertive, patient, who suppresses negative emotions (particularly anger), and who accepts/complies with external authorities' (p. 141). Temoshok and her colleagues conceive of the type C personality as the polar opposite of the type A pattern.

Investigators who believe in the existence of a cancer-prone personality assert that there is a direct physiological connection between personality characteristics and cancer. That is, the maladaptive coping styles of people with the type C personality cause physiological events that favour the development of cancer. For example, Temoshok (1987) suggests that the chronically blocked expressions of emotions in people with the type C personality cause the release of certain chemicals in the brain (neuropeptides) that disrupt the body's homeostatic mechanisms and impair the body's ability to defend itself against the growth of cancer cells.

Several studies have found a relation between personality variables and the presence or severity of cancer. For example, Temoshok et al. (1985) administered personality tests designed to measure type C personality characteristics to a group of patients who had been referred to a hospital for assessment and treatment of a malignant melanoma – a form of skin cancer that has a tendency to metastasise (spread to other parts of the body). They found that two personality variables were related to the thickness of the tumour: faith and non-verbal type C. People who scored high on faith agreed with statements such as 'I'm placing my faith in God' (or 'my doctor') and 'Prayer can work miracles'. People who scored high on non-verbal type C tended to be slow, lethargic, passive and sad. Presumably, the existence of these personality variables favoured the growth of the melanoma.

Most of the studies investigating the role of personality variables in cancer-proneness have assessed the personality characteristics of people who have already been identified as cancer patients. Some studies, like the one by Temoshok et al., have related the personality characteristics to severity of the disease; others have compared the personality variables of cancer patients with those of people without cancer. As we shall see in the next section, all such studies share some methodological problems. A more clear-cut approach is to administer personality tests to a large group of people and then follow them for several years, seeing who gets cancer and who does not. Grossarth-Maticek and his colleagues carried out an ambitious study on 1,353 residents of a small town in the former Yugoslavia (Grossarth-Maticek et al., 1985). They administered psychological tests and questionnaires about current health status and habits such as smoking and drinking in 1966 and then followed the subjects for ten years. Their results showed that people with type C personality characteristics were most likely to develop cancer, especially lung cancer.

Grossarth-Maticek and his colleagues began an even more ambitious follow-up study in 1974, when they administered personality tests to 19,000 residents of Heidelberg, Germany. The study is still under way, and so far only a few small samples of the original group have been examined. However, the results so far indicate that the test successfully identifies people who are likely to develop cancer (Grossarth-Maticek and Eysenck, 1990). Examples of the questions that tend to be answered yes by people who later develop cancer include 'I prefer to agree with others rather than assert my own views', 'I am unable to express my feelings and needs openly to other people' and 'I often feel inhibited when it comes to openly showing negative feelings such as hatred, aggression, or anger'.

According to Grossarth-Maticek, some personality types are predisposed to develop certain kinds of illness. He identified six of these.

> Type 1 – cancer prone
> Type 2 – CHD-prone
> Type 3 – psychopathy-prone
> Type 4 – health/autonomy driven
> Type 5 – depression and cancer-prone
> Type 6 – criminality and addiction-prone

Many of the studies that reported an association between personality variables and cancer can be criticised on methodological grounds. First, evidence from studies that test people who already have cancer cannot prove that personality variables play a role in the onset or progression of the disease. Physicians have known for a long time that malignancies can have physiological effects that alter people's emotions and personality, and these changes can occur even before the cancer is detected (Borysenko, 1982; Shakin and Holland, 1988). Thus, what may look like a cause of the disease may actually be an effect.

Evaluation

If a link exists between personality and cancer, we cannot be sure that cancer-proneness is a direct result of people's emotional reactions – that it is produced by suppression of the immune system, for instance. Instead, the effect could be caused by differences in people's behaviour. For example, people who are passive and who have faith that God or their doctors will take care of them might not take responsibility for their own health. Believing that someone else is responsible for their health, they might not bother to maintain a healthy lifestyle. They might not be alert for warning signs of cancer or might even disregard them until they become so blatant that they cannot be ignored. They might be less likely to comply with the treatments prescribed by their physicians; after all, it is the doctor's responsibility to take care of them, not their own.

What is more, when replications are conducted, results do not support the typology that Grossarth-Maticek suggests. Amelang et al. (1996), for example, found that although individuals with cancer and CHD had different personality profiles, they were not in the predicted direction. CHD patients exhibited types 1, 5 and 6 personality and cancer patients exhibited types 1 and 2. In fact, the researchers suggest that types 1 and 2 may be measuring the same personality variable.

Most investigators believe that if the immune system plays a role in the possible link between personality variables and cancer, it affects the growth of tumours, not their formation. Most of the studies using laboratory animals that have shown that stress can promote the growth of cancer have investigated tumours induced by viruses – and viruses do not appear to play a significant role in human tumours (Justice, 1985). Thus, this research may not be directly relevant to cancer in humans. The most important defence against the formation of tumours in humans appears to be carried out by mechanisms that help to repair damaged DNA, and no one has yet shown a connection between stress and these mechanisms.

The weight of the evidence suggests that personality variables, particularly those relevant to people's coping styles in dealing with unpleasant and stressful situations, can affect the development of cancer. What we do not know is whether these variables do so directly, by altering the activity of the immune system, or indirectly, by affecting people's health-related behaviour.

Questions to think about

Stress and health

- What personality characteristics are associated with relief from stress? Why?
- Why do acute and chronic stress have different effects on the immune system?
- Are there such factors as a cancer-prone or CHD-prone personality?
- What are the differences between type A and type B behaviours? Is such a dichotomy valid?
- Are all stressors experienced in the same way?
- Are successful coping style and dispositional optimism the same thing?
- Is all stress bad?
- Why are the effects of laughter and humour on stress so variable?

Coping with everyday stress

The degree to which we experience stress and the degree to which stress impairs our health depends to a large extent on our perception of the threat posed by the stressor. The number of potential stressors is very large.

Depending on the individual, almost any aspect of the environment can be perceived as a stressor.

Sources of stress

Stress can be induced by changes that threaten or otherwise complicate life. The death of a spouse, being promoted at work, changes in social activities, getting married, and sustaining a personal injury or illness are significant life changes that cause stress and disrupt everyday life (Holmes and Rahe, 1967). Some evidence has accumulated that suggests that if an individual experiences enough changes in lifestyle over a short time period, he or she is likely to develop a physical illness within the next two years (Rahe and Arthur, 1978). Other research suggests that not all people who encounter a series of significant stressors over a short period are at risk of illness (DePue and Monroe, 1986). Why? Once again, the answer lies in the way that people perceive stressors. Recall Lazarus's idea of cognitive appraisal: the amount of stress induced by a stimulus perceived to be a stressor is determined by how significant we believe its threat to be and whether we feel competent to cope with that threat.

Stressors do not have to be catastrophic or cause significant changes in lifestyle to induce stress. Often, the everyday hassles we experience are enough to leave us feeling stressed out. Locking our keys in the car, being late for an appointment, or having a disagreement with a friend are examples of stressful everyday events.

A common source of daily stress comes simply from making routine choices about what to do, how to do it or when to do it. Consider, for example, a choice between studying tonight for a test you have tomorrow or going to a party with some friends. You want to do both, but you can only do one (you are back into the classic self-control situation again – the choice between a small, short-term reward and a larger, long-term reward). Psychologists refer to this as an approach–approach conflict because the choice involves two desirable outcomes. Other choices involve approach–avoidance conflicts – one outcome is desirable and the other is not. For example, you live in Kent, want to visit Oslo and decide to travel by ship because you are afraid of flying. Still other choices involve avoidance–avoidance conflicts in which both outcomes are undesirable. For instance, choosing between having a root canal procedure or having a tooth extracted creates stress because you do not want to have either one of them, yet one needs to be done.

Several different tests have been developed to measure the severity of various stressors on people. Among the first measures to be developed was Holmes and Rahe's (1967) Social Readjustment Rating Scale (SRRS), which was devised on the assumption that any change in a person's life – for better or worse – is a stressor. The test asks people to rate the amount of change or adjustment caused by recent events in their life, such as getting married or divorced, getting a new job or being sacked, moving to a new location, and losing a loved one. Responses are given in terms of life-change units (LCUs) – how much change or adjustment is caused by specific events. Once a person completes the SRRS, the LCUs are summed, resulting in a single score. High scores indicate high levels of stress and low scores low levels of stress. People who get high scores have been shown to have more illness and adjustment problems than have people who get lower scores (Holmes and Rahe, 1967; Monroe *et al.*, 1992).

Another commonly used scale, the Daily Hassles and Uplifts Scale, measures daily events that are either troublesome (hassles) or pleasant (uplifts) (DeLongis *et al.*, 1988). This scale requires people to rate, at the end of each day, the extent to which an event, such as the weather, deadlines, family, or physical appearance, served as a hassle or uplift for them on that day. This scale may be completed daily over extended periods to provide a picture of how the routine events of everyday life create stress for people. Daily hassles yield a more accurate prediction of physical illness and adjustment problems than do daily uplifts (DeLongis *et al.*, 1988) and major life events (Garrett *et al.*, 1991).

Coping styles and strategies

So far, we have considered the negative effects of stress: its damaging effects on the body and mind. However, each of us can learn to control stress. We may not always be able to predict when and where we will encounter stressors or to control their intensity, but we can mitigate their damaging effects by adopting coping strategies that are consistent with our lifestyles. A coping strategy is simply a plan of action that we follow, either in anticipation of encountering a stressor or as a direct response to stress as it occurs, which is effective in reducing the level of stress we experience.

According to Lazarus and Folkman (1984; Folkman and Lazarus, 1991), there are two types of coping response: problem-focused and emotion-focused. Problem-focused coping is directed towards the source of the stress. For example, if the stress is job related, a person might try to change conditions at work or take courses to acquire skills that will enable him or her to obtain a different job. Emotion-focused coping is directed towards a person's own personal reaction to the stressor. For example, a person might try to relax and forget about the problem or find solace in the company of friends. Obviously, if the source of a stress-producing problem has a potential solution, problem-focused coping is the best strategy. If it does not, then emotion-focused coping is the only option.

We each have our own idiosyncratic ways of dealing with stress that can be categorised as being emotion-focused. In fact, health psychologists have shown several of these methods to be effective in controlling stress such as aerobic exercise, cognitive reappraisal, progressive relaxation training and social support.

Cognitive reappraisal

Aerobic exercise is not the coping strategy of choice for everyone. Some people find that simply altering their perception of the threat posed by stressors reduces stress. This coping strategy is called cognitive reappraisal (or cognitive restructuring) and is an extension of Lazarus and Folkman's idea of cognitive appraisal described in Chapter 13. The rationale underlying this strategy is easy to grasp: if our cognitive appraisal of a stressor is a determining factor in producing stress, then by reappraising that stressor as being less threatening, stress should be reduced. Sometimes, simply learning to substitute an incompatible response, such as replacing a negative statement with a positive one, is sufficient to reduce stress (Lazarus, 1971; Meichenbaum, 1977). For example, students who suffer from test anxiety perceive tests as extremely threatening. They may say to themselves, 'I am going to fail the exam tomorrow', or, 'That test is going to be far too hard'. To reappraise the stressor in this case would involve replacing these statements with ones such as 'I'm going to pass that test tomorrow' or 'Yes, the test will be difficult, but I'm ready for it'.

Cognitive reappraisal is an effective coping strategy because it is often a more realistic approach to interpreting the threat posed by stressors than is the original appraisal. We have good reason to appraise a charging bear as a real threat, but not a university examination. After all, we may not be able to deal with the bear, but we can always learn how to take tests and improve our study habits. An additional benefit of cognitive reappraisal is that it teaches the individual that he or she can take control of stressful situations.

Relaxation training

Another coping strategy is simply learning to relax when confronted with a stressor. Relaxing is based on the same principle as cognitive reappraisal: substitute an incompatible response for the stress reaction. One procedure for producing relaxation is the progressive relaxation technique. It involves three steps: (1) recognising your body's signals informing you that you are experiencing stress; (2) using those signals as a cue to begin relaxing, and (3) relaxing by focusing your attention on different groups of muscles, beginning with those in the head and neck and then those in the arms and legs. Imagine that when confronted by a stressor, for example an exam, you respond by tensing certain muscles: those in your hand and fingers that you use to hold your pen or pencil and those around your mouth that you use to clench your teeth. Once you become aware of these responses, you can use them as cues to relax the muscle groups involved.

Some have also suggested that the use of aromas can alleviate stress and anxiety; this is sometimes called aromatherapy. Aromatherapy is, in fact, a misnomer because there is usually more to actual aromatherapy than just the presentation of odour; clients normally receive massage as well. The evidence for a long-term, or even short-term, effect of odour on mental health is sparse; few studies have investigated this relationship scientifically and those that have done so have serious methodological or statistical flaws (see Martin, 1996, for a review).

Social support

Although all of us experience stress, the experience is a subjective and private matter. Nobody else can truly know what we feel. However, being confronted by a stressor and coping with stress are often social matters. We learn as children to seek others – parents, siblings and friends – when we need help. This is a pattern of coping that continues over the lifespan. Social support – the help that we receive from others in times of stress – is an important coping strategy for many people for two reasons. First, we can benefit from the experience of others in dealing with the same or similar stressors. Other people can show us how to cope, perhaps by teaching us how to reappraise the situation. Second, other people can provide encouragement and incentives to overcome the stressor when we may otherwise fail to cope with the stressful situation.

Stress inoculation training

According to psychologist Donald Meichenbaum, the best way to cope with stress is to take the offensive – to have a plan in mind for dealing with stressors before you are actually confronted by them. In other words, people should not wait until they are faced with a stressor to cope with it; instead, they should anticipate the kinds of stressor most likely to affect them and develop the most effective coping plan for dealing with specific stressors. Meichenbaum (1985), in fact, has devised a problem-focused coping method, called **stress inoculation training**, which focuses on helping people to develop coping skills that will decrease their susceptibility to the negative effects of stress. Stress inoculation training has been found to be effective in reducing stress levels among people working in a variety of settings, including nurses, teachers, police trainees (Bishop, 1994) and professional athletes (Cox, 1991).

In Meichenbaum's words, stress inoculation training

'is analogous to the concept of medical inoculation against biological diseases. … Analogous to medical inoculation, [stress inoculation training] is designed to build "psychological antibodies," or coping skills, and to enhance resistance through exposure to stimuli that are strong enough to arouse defenses without being so powerful as to overcome them.' (1985, p. 21)

Stress inoculation training usually occurs in a clinical setting involving a therapist and a client and takes place over three phases aimed at achieving seven goals, summarised in Table 16.9.

The first phase is called the conceptualisation phase and involves two basic goals. Goal 1 involves learning about the transactional nature of stress and coping. Stress and coping are strongly influenced by the interaction of cognitive and environmental variables. A person experiences stress to the extent that he or she appraises the stressor – an environmental variable – as taxing or overwhelming his or her ability to cope with it – a cognitive variable. In Meichenbaum's view, coping is any behavioural/cognitive attempt to overcome, eliminate or otherwise control the negative effects caused by the stressor (see also Lazarus and Folkman, 1984).

Goal 2 involves becoming better at realistically appraising stressful situations by taking stock of, or self-monitoring, patterns in maladaptive thinking, feeling and behaving. A person may keep a diary, or a 'stress log', to record stressful

Table 16.9 Summary of the phases and goals of Meichenbaum's stress inoculation training programme

Conceptualisation phase	
Goal 1:	Learning the transactional nature of stress and coping
Goal 2:	Learning to become better at realistically appraising stressful situations by learning self-monitoring skills with respect to negative or maladaptive thoughts, emotions and behaviours
Skills acquisition and rehearsal phase	
Goal 3:	Learning problem solving skills specific to the stressor
Goal 4:	Learning and rehearsing emotion-regulation and self-control skills
Goal 5:	Learning how to use maladaptive responses as cues to implement the new coping strategy
Application and follow-through phase	
Goal 6:	Learning to practise imagery rehearsal using progressively more difficult or stressful situations
Goal 7:	Learning to apply new coping skills to other, perhaps unexpected, stressors

Source: adapted from Meichenbaum, 1985

events, the conditions under which these events occur, and his or her reactions to these events.

The second phase is called the skills acquisition and rehearsal phase and involves goals 3–5. Goal 3 involves learning specific problem solving skills aimed at reducing stress. For example, a person may learn to identify and define a specific stressor and outline a plan for dealing with it in behavioural terms. The plan should include developing alternative ideas for dealing with the stressor and considering the possible consequences that correspond to each alternative. At this point, a person may find relaxation training and self-instructional training, in which he or she learns to make positive self-statements when confronted by a stressor, helpful.

Goal 4 involves learning and rehearsing emotion-regulation and self-control skills. These skills help people to remain calm and rational when confronted with a stressor. Goal 5 involves learning how to use maladaptive responses as a cue to invoke the new coping strategy. For example, when faced with a stressor, you may feel yourself getting tense. This feeling of tension is your cue to implement specific aspects of your inoculation training, which presumably would reduce your level of stress.

The third and final phase of Meichenbaum's programme is called the application and follow-through phase and comprises goals 6 and 7. Goal 6 involves imagery rehearsal, in which a person practises coping with the stressor by imagining being confronted by that stressor in progressively more difficult situations. The purpose of rehearsing the coping skills is to build confidence in one's ability to use the new coping strategy. Goal 7 involves learning to apply new coping abilities to both expected and unexpected stressors. This might be accomplished by imagining several situations in which you feel anxious, imagining implementing the coping strategy in response to the anxiety, and, finally, imagining feeling relieved as a result of coping with the stressor.

Stress is an inevitable consequence of environmental change. Both large changes, such as a natural disaster or changing jobs, and small changes, such as remembering that we have an exam tomorrow, contribute to the overall level of stress that we experience at any one time. Whether stress impairs our health depends on three variables: the extent to which we appraise the stressor as threatening, whether we engage in good health practices, and the extent to which we use coping strategies effectively. The combined effects of these variables on the relationship between stress and health are summarised in Figure 16.12.

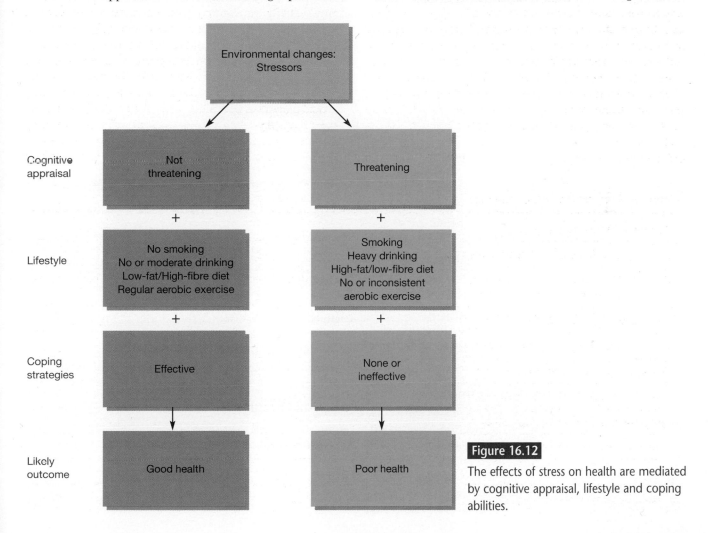

Figure 16.12

The effects of stress on health are mediated by cognitive appraisal, lifestyle and coping abilities.

Key terms

health psychology *p.*552

coronary heart disease (CHD) *p.*552

serum cholesterol *p.*552

protective factor *p.*554

aerobic exercises *p.*554

alcoholism *p.*559

foetal alcohol syndrome *p.*560

theory of reasoned action *p.*562

stress *p.*565

stressors *p.*565

general adaptation syndrome (GAS) *p.*565

complementary medicine *p.*566

fight or flight response *p.*568

glucocorticoid *p.*568

psychoneuroimmunology *p.*570

immune system *p.*570

antigens *p.*570

antibodies *p.*571

B lymphocytes *p.*571

immunoglobulins *p.*571

secretory immunoglobulin A (sIgA) *p.*571

T lymphocytes *p.*571

type A pattern *p.*575

type B pattern *p.*575

type C (cancer-prone) *p.*575

personality *p.*578

coping strategy *p.*581

problem-focused coping *p.*581

emotion-focused coping *p.*581

cognitive reappraisal *p.*581

progressive relaxation technique *p.*581

stress inoculation training *p.*582

CHAPTER REVIEW

Health psychology and unhealthy behaviour

- Health psychology applies psychological principles to the study of health and illness. It examines the effects of various psychological and physical factors on health and can also evaluate the effect of health policy and health education on behaviour.

- Behaviours which have implications for health psychology include smoking, eating, sexual behaviour, exercise and alcohol use.

- Protective factors are those which make the individual less susceptible to ill health.

- Evidence suggests that people who have high-fat, low-fibre diets tend to be more susceptible to coronary heart disease (CHD) and cancer than are people who have low-fat, high-fibre diets.

- Weight gain and increased low-density lipoprotein (LDL) cholesterol levels are both risk factors for CHD and cancer.

- A number of factors appears to influence the decision to begin smoking including peer pressure, low income and poor education; quitting smoking is made more difficult if the quitter possesses these characteristics; smoking is rarely initiated in adulthood and normally begins in adolescence.

- Smoking cessation programmes have met with limited success; a combination of nicotine replacement and psychological treatments appears to show the best outcome.

- Exercise appears to be effective in increasing positive mood and alleviating mild depression.

- The best precautionary measure against contracting any sexually transmitted disease (STD) is the practice of safe sex.

- Acquired immune deficiency syndrome (AIDS) refers to a disease resulting from infection by virus (HIV). There are 21 million people living in the world with AIDS; HIV can be contracted through unprotected homosexual and heterosexual sex, intravenous injection and transfusion of contaminated blood.

- Programmes aimed at preventing the spread of STDs and AIDS focus on teaching people the relationship between their behaviour and the likelihood of contracting one or more of these diseases and how to use safe sex strategies.

- Individuals with HIV must maintain a strict drug regimen; health psychology has helped to clarify the best predictors of adherence to this regimen.

- Fear of contagion is influenced by four factors: the disease must be deadly, it must appear suddenly, it must have no apparent explanation, and people must believe that many people are at risk of contracting it. Despite educational efforts to inform the public about AIDS, fear of contagion remains a serious problem.

Stress and health

- Stress is defined in terms of our physiological and psychological response to stimuli that either prevent us from obtaining a goal or endanger our well-being.

- Selye's model describes how prolonged exposure to stress leads to illness and sometimes death. The stress response, which Cannon called the fight or flight response, is useful as a short-term response to threatening stimuli but is harmful in the long term. This response includes increased activity of the sympathetic branch of the autonomic nervous system and increased secretion of epinephrine, norepinephrine and glucocorticoids by the adrenal gland.

- Although increased levels of epinephrine and norepinephrine can raise blood pressure, most of the harm to health comes from glucocorticoids.

- Prolonged exposure to high levels of these hormones can increase blood pressure, damage muscle tissue, lead to infertility, inhibit growth, inhibit the inflammatory response and suppress the immune system. It can also damage the hippocampus.

- Individual differences in personality variables can alter the effects of stressful situations. The most important variable is the nature of a person's coping response.

- Personality characteristics which may serve as protective factors against stress include submissiveness and optimism.

- Type A behaviour pattern refers to behaviour that is competitive, hostile, rapid and intense; some of these variables, especially hostility, may predict the likelihood of CHD, but the research findings are mixed.

- Psychoneuroimmunology is a new field of study that investigates the effects of psychological stressors on the immune system.

- The immune system consists of several types of white blood cell that produce chemically mediated and cell-mediated responses. The immune system can cause harm when it triggers an allergic reaction or when it attacks the body's own tissues in autoimmune diseases.

- The most important mechanism by which stress impairs immune function is increased blood levels of glucocorticoids. In addition, neural input to the bone marrow, lymph nodes and thymus gland may also play a role; and naturally occurring opioids appear to suppress the activity of internal killer cells.

- A wide variety of stressful situations, such as the death of a spouse or caring for a relative with Alzheimer's disease, has been shown to increase people's susceptibility to infectious diseases.

- Several investigators have suggested that a type C (cancer-prone) personality exists. Although the evidence is mixed, some careful, long-term studies suggest that cancerous tumours may develop faster in passive people who suppress the expression of negative emotions.

Coping with everyday stress

- Stress may stem from a wide variety of sources. Even positive events, such as the birth of a child or the marriage of a son or daughter can produce stress.

- Stress may lead to physical illness when a person undergoes several stressful events over a short period of time.

- The extent to which people become ill appears to depend on the extent to which they perceive a stressor as being a threat to their well-being and the extent to which they believe they can cope with that threat.

- Lazarus and Folkman have identified two types of coping. Problem-focused coping represents any attempt to reduce stress by attempting to change the event or situation producing the stress. Emotion-focused coping centres on changing one's personal reaction to the stressful event or situation. Emotion-focused coping may involve activities such as aerobic exercise, cognitive reappraisal, relaxation training and seeking social support.

- Meichenbaum's stress inoculation training programme is a problem-focused coping strategy that prepares people to cope with anticipated stressors. The programme involves three phases and seven goals. The first phase involves learning how to conceptualise the transactional nature of stress. The second phase entails learning coping skills specific to the stressors in their lives and practising or rehearsing these skills in hypothetical situations. The third phase involves preparing people to implement these coping skills in real-life situations. The seven goals of stress inoculation training focus on specific kinds of knowledge, behaviour, and coping strategies central to preparing people to anticipate, confront and reduce the threat posed by stressful situations.

Suggestions for further reading

Baum, A., Gatchel, R. and Krantz, D. (1997). *Introduction to Health Psychology* (3rd edition). Maidenhead: McGraw-Hill.

Pitts, M. and Phillips, K. (1998). *The Psychology of Health* (2nd edition). London: Routledge.

Sarafino, E.P. (1998). *Health Psychology: Biopsychosocial interactions* (3rd edition). Chichester: Wiley.

These three texts give an excellent, all-round, up-to-date review of the major areas of health psychology from a North American and European perspective.

Pitts, M. (1996). *The Psychology of Preventive Health*. London: Routledge.

Radley, A. (1994). *Making Sense of Illness*. London: Sage.
Both of these books discuss different general aspects of the psychology of health behaviour. Pitts's book is a good introduction to ill health prevention whereas Radley's is a critical account of the psychological and sociological significance of health.

Cohen, S., Frank, E., Doyle, W.J. *et al.* (1998). Types of stressors that increase susceptibility to the common cold in healthy adults. *Health Psychology*, 17, 3, 214–223.

Evans, P., Clow, A. and Hucklebridge, F. (1997). Stress and the immune system. *The Psychologist*, 303–307.

Rushing, W.A. (1995). *The AIDS Epidemic: Social dimensions of an infectious disease*. Boulder, CO: Westview Press.
These three recommendations provide different examples of interesting reading on three issues. The Evans et al. article is a good, gentle introductory-level review of stress and the immune system. Rushing's book considers the social and cultural significance of HIV and AIDS. Cohen et al.'s article is included because it is an example of one of the best treatments of an usually intractable topic in health psychology.

Journals to consult

British Journal of Health Psychology
British Journal of Medical Psychology
British Medical Journal
Health Psychology
International Journal of Behavioural Medicine
International Journal of Stress
Journal of Abnormal Psychology
Journal of Community and Applied Psychology
Journal of Health Psychology
Journal of Occupational Health Psychology
Journal of Occupational Medicine
Journal of Occupational and Organisational Psychology
Journal of Personality and Social Psychology
Journal of Social and Occupational Medicine
New England Journal of Medicine
Psychology, Health and Medicine
Psychosomatic Medicine
Social Science and Medicine
Stress Medicine
The Lancet
Work and Stress

ABNORMAL PSYCHOLOGY

Most people think that anorexia, bulimia and depression are all in the mind, according to a poll published for European Brain Day.

Very few people regard them as actual brain disorders.

The survey, carried out by Gallup, found that people tended to differentiate between conditions such as Alzheimer's and CJD, which are seen as caused by degeneration of the brain, and those illnesses which are perceived to have a psychological cause, such as anxiety, stress or alcohol or drug use.

Nearly two thirds of the 1,000 people questioned (61 per cent) thought anorexia and bulimia were all in the mind and that people bring these conditions on themselves.

Nearly everybody (92 per cent) thought they were curable.

Just under half (47 per cent) thought depression could be avoided and that it was all in the mind.

Source: *The Guardian*, May 1998

Abnormal psychology is the area of psychology which studies and treats mental disorder. Mental disorders are disorders of thought, feeling or behaviour and are characterised by behaviourally deviant features. Their causes may be genetic, environmental, cognitive or neurobiological.

Some of these disorders you will be familiar with – depression and anxiety, for example. Others will not be so familiar, such as paraphilia and conversion disorder. Although the symptoms described for each disorder may apply to healthy individuals who exhibit a 'bad mood' or who are under stress, these disorders represent a severe impairment in functioning. Clinical depression is not the same as the 'low' we sometimes feel in life, and generalised anxiety disorder does not represent the stress we feel before an exam or speaking in public.

This chapter describes all the major mental disorders and their treatment. The chapter is divided into three broad sections. The first deals with the classification of mental disorder, the second section describes the general approaches to the treatment of mental disorders and the third describes the major mental disorders, their possible causes and their treatment.

What you should be able to do after reading Chapter 17

- Explain the aim of classification of mental disorders and define mental abnormality.
- Describe the treatment approaches of clinicians to mental disorders.
- Describe all the major mental disorders.
- Understand the possible causal mechanisms for these disorders.
- Evaluate theories of mental disorder and the treatment of mental disorder.

Questions to think about

- What makes an abnormal behaviour abnormal?
- Which term makes the best sense: mental disorder or mental illness?
- Are there cross-cultural variations in the classification of mental disorders?
- Are some disorders more likely to have a biological basis than others?
- How effective is cognitive and pharmacological treatment of mental disorder?

CLASSIFICATION AND DIAGNOSIS OF MENTAL DISORDERS

The term 'mental disorder' refers to a clinical impairment characterised by abnormal thought, feeling or behaviour. Some mental disorders, especially the less severe ones, appear to be caused by environmental factors or by a person's perception of these factors, such as stress or unhealthy family interactions. In contrast, many of the more severe mental disorders appear to be caused by hereditary and other biological factors that disrupt normal thought processes or produce inappropriate emotional reactions. The descriptions of mental disorders in this chapter necessarily make distinctions that are not always easy to make in real life; the essential features of the more important mental disorders are simplified here for the sake of clarity. In addition, many of the cases that clinicians encounter are less clear-cut than the ones included here and are thus not so easily classified.

To understand, diagnose and treat psychological disorders, some sort of classification system is needed. The need for a comprehensive classification system of psychological disorders was first recognised by Emil Kraepelin (1856–1926), who provided his version in a textbook of psychiatry published in 1883. The classification most widely used today still retains a number of Kraepelin's original categories.

What is 'abnormal'?

Mental disorders are characterised by abnormal behaviour, thoughts and feelings. The term 'abnormal' literally refers to any departure from the norm. Thus, a short or tall person is 'abnormal' and so is someone who is especially intelligent or talented. Albert Einstein was 'abnormal', as were Oscar Wilde and Pablo Picasso. The term 'abnormal' is often used pejoratively – it is used to refer to characteristics that are disliked or feared – but this is not the way in which it is used when describing mental illness. The most important feature of a mental disorder, however, may not be whether a person's behaviour is abnormal – different from that of most other people – but whether it is maladaptive. Mental disorders cause distress or discomfort and often interfere with people's ability to lead useful, productive lives. They often make it impossible for people to hold jobs, raise families or relate to others socially.

Perspectives on the causes of mental disorders

What causes mental disorders? In general, they are caused by an interaction among hereditary, cognitive and environ-

mental factors. In some cases, the genetic component is strong and the person is likely to develop a mental disorder even in a very supportive environment. In other cases, the cognitive and environmental components are strong. A complete understanding of mental disorders requires that scientists investigate genetic, cognitive and environmental factors. Once genetic factors are identified, the scientist faces the task of determining the physiological effects of the relevant genes and the consequences of these effects on a person's susceptibility to a mental disorder. Understanding the cognitive factors involved in mental disorders requires identification of the origins of distorted perceptions and maladaptive thought patterns. And environmental factors encompass more than simply a person's family history or present social interactions; they also include the effects of prenatal health and nutrition, childhood diseases, and exposure to drugs and environmental toxins.

Different psychologists and other mental health professionals approach the study of mental disorders from different perspectives, each of which places more or less emphasis on these factors. The perspectives differ primarily in their explanation of the aetiology, or origin, of mental disorders. Some of these perspectives are described next.

The psychodynamic perspective

According to the psychodynamic perspective, which is based on Freud's early work described in Chapter 14, mental disorders originate in intrapsychic conflict produced by the three warring factions of the mind: the id, ego, and superego. For some people, the conflict becomes so severe that the mind's defence mechanisms are ineffective, resulting in mental disorders that may involve, among other symptoms, extreme anxiety, obsessive thoughts and compulsive behaviour, depression, distorted perceptions and patterns of thinking, and paralysis or blindness for which there is no physical cause.

As we saw in Chapter 14, the id, ego and superego are hypothetical constructs, they are not physical structures of the brain. But Freud and his followers often spoke as if these structures were real, at least in their functions. Even today, psychodynamic theorists and practitioners approach mental disorders by emphasising the role of intrapsychic conflict in creating psychological distress and maladaptive behaviour.

The medical perspective

The medical perspective has its origins in the work of the ancient Greek physician Hippocrates. Hippocrates formulated the idea that excesses in the four humours (black bile, yellow bile, blood and phlegm) led to emotional problems. Other physicians, Greek and Roman, extended Hippocrates's ideas and developed the concept of mental illness – illnesses of the mind. Eventually, specialised institutions or asylums were established where persons with mental disorders were confined. Early asylums were ill-run and the patients' problems were poorly understood and often mistreated. During the eighteenth and nineteenth centuries, massive reforms in the institutional care of people with mental disorders took place. The quality of the facilities and the amount of compassion for patients improved, and physicians, including neurosurgeons and psychiatrists, who were specifically trained in the medical treatment of mental disorders, were hired to care for these patients.

Today, the medical perspective is the dominant perspective in the treatment of mental disorders. Individuals with mental disorders are no longer confined to mental institutions. Instead, they are treated on an outpatient basis with drugs that are effective in abating the symptoms of mental disorders. Usually, only those people with very severe mental problems are institutionalised.

The medical model, as the medical perspective is properly called, is based on the idea that mental disorders are caused by specific abnormalities of the brain and nervous system and that, in principle, they should be approached the same way that physical illnesses are approached. As we shall see, several mental disorders, including schizophrenia, depression and bipolar disorder, are known to have specific biological causes and can be treated to some extent with drugs. We shall also see that genetics play a pivotal role in some of these disorders.

However, not all mental disorders can be traced so directly to physical causes. For that reason, other perspectives, which focus on the cognitive and environmental factors involved in mental disorders, have emerged.

The cognitive behavioural perspective

In contrast to the medical perspective, the cognitive behavioural perspective holds that mental disorders are learned maladaptive behaviour patterns that can best be understood by focusing on environmental factors and a person's perception of those factors. In this view, a mental disorder is not something that arises spontaneously within a person. Instead, it is caused by the person's interaction with his or her environment. For example, a person's excessive use of alcohol or other drugs may be negatively reinforced by the relief from tension or anxiety that often accompanies intoxication.

According to the cognitive behavioural perspective, it is not merely the environment that matters: what also counts is a person's ongoing subjective interpretation of the events taking place in his or her environment. Therapists operating from the cognitive behavioural perspective

therefore encourage their clients to replace or substitute maladaptive thoughts and behaviours with more adaptive ones (Emmelkamp, 1994).

The humanistic and sociocultural perspective

As we saw in Chapter 14, proponents of the humanistic perspective argue that proper personality development occurs when people experience unconditional positive regard. According to this view, mental disorders arise when people perceive that they must earn the positive regard of others. Cultural variables influence the nature and extent to which people interpret their own behaviours as normal or abnormal. What is considered perfectly normal in one culture may be considered abnormal in another. Moreover, mental disorders exist that appear to occur only in certain cultures – a phenomenon called culture-bound syndrome. These are discussed in the 'Controversies in psychological science' section below.

The diathesis–stress approach

None of the above perspectives is completely accurate in accounting for the origins of mental disorders. But elements of these perspectives may be combined to form a different, perhaps more comprehensive, perspective on mental disorders. The diathesis–stress model argues that the combination of a person's genetics and early learning experiences yields a predisposition (a diathesis) for a particular mental disorder. However, the mental disorder will develop only if that person is confronted with stressors that exceed his or her coping abilities. In other words, a person may be predisposed towards a mental disorder yet not develop it either because he or she has not encountered sufficient stressors to trigger its development or because he or she possesses the cognitive behavioural coping skills needed to limit the negative effects of the stressor.

Classification of disorders

Mental disorders can be classified in many ways, but the two systems most commonly used in the world are those presented in the American Psychiatric Association's *Diagnostic and Statistical Manual (of Mental Disorders) IV (DSM-IV)* and the World Health Organisation's International Classification of Diseases (ICD-10). DSM-IV was originally devised by American psychologists for the classification of mental disorders, whereas ICD-10 was devised as an international classification system for all diseases. These two are more alike than different, although differences do exist (Andrews *et al.*, 1999). Table 17.1 lists the classifications in DSM IV, with several subclassifications omitted for the sake of simplicity.

Controversies in psychological science

Is mental disorder culture-dependent?

The issue

The two manuals used by psychiatrists to diagnose mental disorder are the Diagnostic and Statistical Manual of Mental Disorders IV (DSM-IV; American Psychiatric Association, 1994) and *International Classification of Diseases 10* (ICD-10; World Health Organisation, 1992). Because these manuals are standard reference works for the diagnosis of mental illness, there is an implication that symptoms can be grouped together to form a disorder in any culture. DSM-IV, for example, lists 350 disorders which should apply across cultures. But is mental disorder culture-dependent? Are these diagnostic manuals too Western-based? Might a mental disorder in one culture be classed as normal behaviour in another?

The evidence

Some clinicians have argued that we cannot apply Western diagnostic criteria such as those in DSM to other cultures (Hinton and Kleinman, 1993). This cultural relativism argues that behaviour considered abnormal in one culture may be considered normal in another. In addition, a behaviour classed as one type of mental disorder in one culture may be classed as a different one in different culture. These two problems are generic in diagnosing mental illness across cultures. DSM-IV recognises the latter problem in its appendix which contains details of 25 culture-based syndromes. The authors responsible for DSM-IV and ICD-10 have also attempted to address the problem of cultural relativism by conducting extensive cross-cultural investigations on the generalisability of mental disorder diagnosis. How culture-bound, therefore, are mental disorders?

Tanaka-Matsumi and Draguns (1997) have reviewed a vast amount of research on cross-cultural studies of mental disorders including affective disorders, suicide, schizophrenia and anxiety disorders, and draw some instructive conclusions.

Depression, for example, appears to be a disorder which is common across most cultures. A World Health Organisation (WHO) study of depression in Switzerland, Canada, Japan and Iran (World Health Organisation, 1983) found that 76 per cent of individuals diagnosed as depressed exhibited symptoms of sadness, joylessness, anxiety, tension and lack of energy. Levels of guilt, however, showed large variation between cultures. Iran reported the lowest levels (22 per cent of respondents), followed by Japan (45 per cent),

Canada (58 per cent) and Switzerland (68 per cent). There was also within-culture variation. For example, the two Japanese cities studied (Nagasaki and Tokyo) showed different degrees of depression, with more core symptoms reported in Nagasaki.

A study of British and Turkish outpatients found that Turkish patients reported more somatic complaints (insomnia, hypochondria) whereas the British patients reported more psychological complaints such as guilt and pessimism (Ulusahin *et al.*, 1994). The prevalence of depression in Taiwan and Hong Kong is lower than in Western countries (Compton *et al.*, 1991), a finding which some have attributed to the greater degree of community and social support in Chinese culture (Tseng *et al.*, 1995).

Suicidal ideation (thoughts about suicide) and suicide are also symptoms of depression which show cultural variation. In a study of the suicide rates among 15 to 24 year olds in a large number of countries including Egypt, Jordan, Kuwait, Syria, the Scandinavian countries, Eastern Europe, Japan, Singapore and Sri Lanka, the Arabic states (Egypt, Jordan, etc.) had the lowest suicide rates whereas Scandinavia, eastern Europe and some Asian countries had the highest (Barraclough, 1988). The highest reported rates were for Sri Lanka (47 suicides per 100,000 of the population) and Hungary (38.6 per 100,000). The exact reasons for these high rates are unknown. Some have suggested that the weakening of family structure or religious values is responsible; others suggest that endemic group violence is responsible in Sri Lanka and a fear of failure is responsible in Hungary, but these are vague, general reasons which could apply to others countries (Jilek-Aal, 1988). Paris (1991) has also cautioned that suicide and suicide attempts fluctuate across space and time and that such fluctuation may not be detected in epidemiological surveys of suicide.

Schizophrenia has been subject to three major cross-cultural studies over 25 years in 20 research centres from 17 countries. The aim of such exhaustive research has been to collect data, standardise the instruments used for measuring schizophrenic symptoms and conduct follow-up assessments (Jablensky, 1989). If different countries have different ways of measuring schizophrenia, for example, then a higher or lower incidence of the disorder may not reflect actual incidence but differences in the ways in which schizophrenia is diagnosed. The 1979 study conducted by the World Health Organisation (1979) found that the prognosis (outcome) for schizophrenia was better in developing countries (Colombia, Nigeria, India) than in developed countries (USA, UK, Denmark). Schizophrenia was diagnosed as being more chronic in the most well educated people, but only in developing countries. Later studies indicated that the outcome for schizophrenia was worse in countries such as India.

One of the most comprehensive cross-cultural studies examined 1,379 schizophrenics in 12 centres from 10 countries: Denmark (Aarhus), India (Agra and Chandigarh), Columbia (Cali), Ireland (Dublin), Nigeria (Fbadai), Russia (Moscow), the UK (Nottingham), Japan (Nagasaki), the Czech Republic (Prague) and the USA (Honolulu, Hawaii and Rochester, New York). In each of the countries, the incidence rates were comparable (Jablensky et al., 1992).

A disorder which does present some cross-cultural problems is anxiety (Tseng et al., 1990). Here, there is great cultural variability in terms of the degree of generalised anxiety reported. Tseng et al. (1986) asked psychiatrists in Beijing, Tokyo and Honolulu to diagnose the mental disorder of Chinese patients recorded on videotape. The Beijing psychiatrists diagnosed the patients as exhibiting neurasthenia; the others diagnosed adjustment reaction. When Japanese and American psychiatrists were asked to diagnose patients with social phobia, the Japanese psychiatrists showed greater agreement in their diagnosis of Japanese social phobics than did their American counterparts (Tseng et al., 1990).

Results like these suggest that cultural variations exist in the diagnosis of some mental disorders. Perhaps because anxiety is a more vague syndrome than is depression or schizophrenia, it ought not to be surprising that great variation exists between cultures in diagnosing this disorder. When more specific anxiety disorders are examined, such as object phobia, some cross-cultural agreement occurs (Davey, 1992; Davey et al., 1998). In their

study of the nature of object phobia in Japanese, British, American, Scandinavian, Indian, Korean and Hong Kong individuals, Davey et al. (1998) reported that there was broad agreement on the stimuli considered phobia-related. This consistency suggests that, at least for some anxiety disorders, there is universality.

Slightly more problematic for diagnostic manuals such as DSM and ICD are culture-bound syndromes (Simons and Hughes, 1985). Although DSM-IV lists 25 of these, it does not provide any criteria for them. Anorexia, which is not explicitly defined as culture-bound in DSM-IV, seems to predominate in Western countries although there are reports of the disorder appearing in Asia (Lee, 1995). Three culture-bound syndromes are Koro, Taijin Kyofusho and Anthropophobia (Tanaka-Matsumi and Draguns, 1997). Koro is found in men in southern China or South-East Asia and refers to a belief that genitals are withdrawn into the abdomen and a fear of death provoked by a female ghost (Tseng et al., 1992). Taijin Kyofusho is a Japanese disorder similar to social phobia. However, individuals with this disorder have a specific fear of offending others by blushing, emitting offensive odours, staring inappropriately and presenting improper facial expressions (Tanaka-Matsumi, 1979). Anthropophobia seems to be the Chinese equivalent and involves the fear of being looked at.

Conclusion

It seems clear that although there is agreement between cultures about what constitutes a diagnosis for some mental disorders, there is clear variation for others. Anxiety, for example, seems to show the greatest variation, and depression and schizophrenia the least. Furthermore, there are some mental disorders which are culture-bound.

DSM-IV classification

The DSM-IV, perhaps the most widely used international classification system for mental disorders, is the latest version of a scheme that was devised to provide a reliable, universal set of diagnostic categories having criteria specified as explicitly as possible. The DSM-IV describes an individual's psychological condition using five different criteria, called axes. Individuals undergoing evaluation are assessed on each of the axes. Axis I contains information on major psychological disorders that require clinical attention, including disorders that may develop during childhood. Personality disorders are found on Axis II.

Diagnoses can be made that include both Axis I and Axis II disorders, and multiple diagnoses can occur on either axis alone. For example, major depression and alcohol dependence are both Axis I disorders, and both disorders may characterise one individual at any one period of time. A person's psychological condition may be due to several different psychological disorders described in the DSM-IV, just as one person may suffer simultaneously from several different physical disorders.

Axes III through V provide information about the life of the individual in addition to the basic classification provided by Axes I and II. Axis III is used to describe any physical disorders, such as skin rashes or heightened blood pressure, accompanying the psychological disorder. Axis IV

Table 17.1   Summary of the DSM-IV classification scheme for axes I and II

Axis I – Major clinical syndromes

Disorders usually first appearing in infancy, childhood or adolescence. Any deviation from normal development, including mental retardation, autism, attention deficit disorder with hyperactivity, excessive fears, speech problems and highly aggressive behaviour.

Delirium, dementia, amnestic and other cognitive disorders. Disorders due to deterioration of the brain because of ageing, disease (such as Alzheimer's disease, which was discussed in Chapter 11), or ingestion or exposure to drugs or toxic substances (such as lead).

Psychoactive substance abuse disorders. Psychological, social or physical problems related to abuse of alcohol or other drugs. (Psychoactive substance use and abuse was discussed in Chapters 3, 4 and 16 and is also discussed in this chapter.)

Schizophrenia and other psychotic disorders. A group of disorders marked by loss of contact with reality, illogical thought, inappropriate displays of emotion, bizarre perceptions and usually some form of hallucinations or delusions.

Mood disorders. Disorders involving extreme deviations from normal mood including severe depression (major depression), excessive elation (mania), or alternation between severe depression and excessive elation (bipolar disorder).

Anxiety disorders. Excessive fear of specific objects (phobia); repetitve, persistent thoughts accompanied by ritualistic-like behaviour that reduces anxiety (obsessive-compulsive behaviour); panic attacks; generalised and intense feelings of anxiety; and feelings of dread caused by experiencing traumatic events such as natural disasters or combat.

Somatoform disorders. Disorders involving pain, paralysis, or blindness for which no physical cause can be found. Excessive concern for one's health, as is typical in persons with hypochondriasis.

Factitious disorders. Fake mental disorders, such as Munchausen syndrome, in which the individual is frequently hospitalised because of his or her claims of illness.

Dissociative disorders. Loss of personal identity and changes in normal consciousness, including amnesia and multiple personality disorder, in which there exists two or more independently functioning personality systems.

Sexual and gender identity disorders. Disorders involving fetishes, sexual dysfunction (such as impotence or orgasmic dysfunctions), and problems of sexual identity (such as transsexualism).

Eating disorders. Disorders related to excessive concern about one's body weight, such as anorexia nervosa (self-starvation) and bulimia (alternating periods of eating large amounts of food and vomiting). (Eating disorders were discussed in Chapter 13.)

Sleep disorders. Disorders including severe insomnia, chronic sleepiness, sleep walking, narcolepsy (suddenly falling to sleep) and sleep apnoea. (Sleep disorders were discussed in Chapter 9.)

Impulse control disorders. Disorders involving compulsive behaviours such as stealing, fire setting or gambling.

Adjustment disorders. Disorders stemming from difficulties adjusting to significant life stressors, such as death of a loved one, loss of a job or financial difficulties, and family problems, including divorce. (Some adjustment disorders, as they pertain to difficulty in coping with life stressors, were discussed in Chapter 16.)

Axis II – Personality disorders

Personality disorders are long-term, maladaptive and rigid personality traits that impair normal functioning and involve psychological stress. Two examples are antisocial personality disorder (lack of empathy or care for others, lack of guilt for misdeeds, antisocial behaviour, and persistent lying, cheating and stealing) and narcissitic personality disorder (inflated sense of self-worth and importance and persistent seeking of attention).

specifies the severity of stress that the person has experienced (usually within the last year). This axis details the source of stress (for example, family or work) and indicates its severity and approximate duration. Axis V describes the person's overall level of psychological, social or occupational functioning. The purpose of Axis V is to estimate the extent to which a person's quality of life has been diminished by the disorder. Ratings are made on a 100-point global assessment of functioning (GAF) scale, with 100 representing the absence or near absence of impaired functioning, 50 representing serious problems in functioning,

and 10 representing impairment that may result in injury to the individual or to others.

The DSM-IV provides a systematic means of providing and evaluating a variety of personal and psychological information about any one specific individual. Alcohol dependence (Axis I) often leads to marital problems, which may also be partially associated with an antisocial personality disorder (Axis II). Marital problems may lead to a divorce and these problems and the divorce are themselves stressors (Axis IV) that may subsequently contribute to an episode of major depression (Axis I). Alcohol dependence may eventually lead to physical problems, such as cirrhosis of the liver (Axis III). These problems, now acting in concert, are likely to lead to an increased impairment in overall life functioning (Axis V) so that the individual has only a few friends, none of them close, and is unable to keep a job. The evaluation of this person might be summarised as follows:

Axis I: *Alcohol dependence*
Axis II: *Antisocial personality disorder*
Axis III: *Alcoholic cirrhosis of the liver*
Axis IV: *Severe – divorce, loss of job*
Axis V: *GAF evaluation = 30 (a very serious impairment of functioning)*

Some problems with DSM-IV classification

Although the DSM-IV is the most widely used classification system for mental disorders, it is not without its problems. Reflecting the fact that the DSM-IV has been strongly influenced by psychiatrists, the DSM-IV tends to be more consistent with the medical perspective on mental disorders. This means that diagnosis and treatment based on the DSM-IV emphasises biological factors, which, in turn, means that potential cognitive and environmental determinants may be overlooked.

Another potential problem with the DSM-IV (and perhaps with any classification scheme) is its questionable reliability. Reliability in this context means what it did in the context of psychological testing discussed in Chapter 2 – consistency across applications. If the DSM-IV was perfectly reliable, users would be able to diagnose each case in the same way. But evaluating psychological disorders is not so easy. Using the DSM-IV is not like using a recipe; it is more like navigating your way through an unfamiliar city using only a crude map. Using this map, you may or may not reach your ultimate destination. Mental disorders do not have distinct borders that allow a mental health professional to diagnose a disorder in a person with 100 per cent accuracy all of the time.

There will probably always be dangers in classifying mental disorders. No classification scheme is likely to be perfect, and no two people with the same diagnosis will behave in exactly the same way. Yet once people are labelled, they are likely to be perceived as having all the characteristics assumed to accompany that label; their behaviour will probably be perceived selectively and interpreted in terms of the diagnosis.

An experiment by Langer and Abelson (1974) illustrated how labelling can affect clinical judgements. A group of psychoanalysts were shown a videotape of a young man who was being interviewed. Half of the psychoanalysts were told that the man was a job applicant, while the other half were told that he was a patient. Although both groups of clinicians watched the same man exhibiting the same behaviour, those who were told that he was a patient rated him as being more disturbed, that is less well adjusted.

It is easy to lapse into the mistaken belief that, somehow or other, labelling disorders explains why people are like they are. Diagnosing a psychological disorder only describes the symptoms of the disorder; it does not explain its origins. To say that someone did something 'because he's schizophrenic' does not explain his behaviour at all. We need to be on guard against associating the names of disorders with people rather than with their symptoms. It is more appropriate to talk about 'someone who displays the characteristics of schizophrenia' than to say that 'he's a schizophrenic'.

The need for classification

Because labelling can have negative effects, some people, such as Thomas Szasz (1960, 1987), have suggested that we should abandon all attempts to classify and diagnose mental disorders. In fact, Szasz has argued that the concept of mental illness has done more harm than good because of the negative effects it has on those people who are said to be mentally ill. Szasz notes that labelling people as mentally ill places the responsibility for their care with the medical establishment, thereby relieving such people of responsibility for their mental states and for taking personal steps towards improvement.

However, proper classification has advantages for a patient. One advantage is that, with few exceptions, the recognition of a specific diagnostic category precedes the development of successful treatment for that disorder. Treatments for diseases such as diabetes, syphilis, tetanus and malaria were found only after the disorders could be reliably diagnosed. A patient may have a multitude of symptoms, but before the cause of the disorder (and hence its treatment) can be discovered, the primary symptoms must be identified. For example, Graves' disease is characterised by irritability, restlessness, confused and rapid thought processes, and, occasionally, delusions and hallucinations. Little was known about the endocrine system during the nineteenth century when Robert Graves identified the disease, but we now know that this syndrome results from oversecretion of thyroxine, a hormone produced by the thyroid gland. Treatment involves prescription of antithyroid drugs or surgical removal of the thyroid gland, followed by administration of appropriate doses of thyroxine. Graves's classification scheme for the symptoms was devised many years before the physiological basis of the disease could be understood. But once enough was known about the effects of thyroxine, physicians were able to treat Graves' disease and strike it off the roll of mental disorders.

On a less dramatic scale, different kinds of mental disorder have different causes, and they respond to different types of psychological treatment and drugs. If future research is to reveal more about causes and treatments of these disorders, we must be able to classify specific mental disorders reliably and accurately.

Another important reason for properly classifying mental disorders relates to their prognosis. Some disorders have good prognoses; the patients are likely to improve soon and are unlikely to have a recurrence of their problems. Other disorders have progressive courses; patients are less likely to recover from these disorders. In the first case, patients can obtain reassurance about their futures; in the second case, patients' families can obtain assistance in making realistic plans.

Questions to think about

Classification of mental disorders

- Consider the ways in which we divide behaviour into normal and abnormal. Does this division work?
- Is mental disorder better characterised as being one end of a continuum, the other being mentally stable and healthy?
- What does cross-cultural research say about the validity of the classification of mental disorders?
- What are the pros and cons of devising an international classification system for mental disorder?
- Thomas Szasz in his famous book *The Myth of Mental Illness*, argued that the term 'mental illness' was a misnomer. Why, and do you agree with him?

THE TREATMENT OF MENTAL DISORDERS

The evolution of interventions

Mental disorder and its treatment has a long history. In the past, people suffering from mental disorder have been regarded with awe or fear; others whom we would now probably classify as paranoid schizophrenics were seen as instruments through whom gods or spirits were speaking. More often, they were considered to be occupied by devils or evil spirits and were made to suffer accordingly. The earliest known attempts to treat mental disorders involved trephining, or drilling holes in a person's skull. Presumably, the opening was made to permit evil spirits to leave the victim's head. In prehistoric times, this procedure was performed with a sharp-edged stone; later civilisations, such as the Egyptians, refined the practice. Signs of healing at the edges of the holes in prehistoric skulls indicate that some people survived these operations. An example is seen in Figure 17.1.

Many painful practices were directed at people's presumed possession by evil spirits. Individuals were thought to be unwilling hosts for evil spirits were subjected to curses or insults designed to persuade the demons to leave. If this approach had no effect, exorcism was tried to make the person's body an unpleasant place for devils to reside. Other rituals included beatings, starving, near drowning and the drinking of foul-tasting concoctions. The delusional schemes of psychotics often include beliefs of personal guilt and unworthiness. In a society that accepted

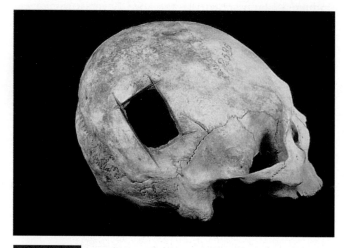

Figure 17.1

Among the earliest biological approaches to the treatment of mental disorders was the ancient practice of trephining, in which a hole was made in the skull to allow evil spirits to escape from the person's head.

Source: Loren McIntyre/Woodfin Camp & Associates Inc.

the notion that there were witches and devils, these people were ready to imagine themselves as evil. They confessed to unspeakable acts of sorcery and welcomed their own persecution and punishment.

Until the eighteenth century, many Europeans accepted the idea that devils and spirits were responsible for peculiar behaviours in some people. But a few people believed that these disorders reflected diseases and that they should be treated medically, with compassion for the victim. Johann Wier, a sixteenth-century physician, was among the first to challenge the practice of witchcraft. He argued that most people who were being tortured and burned for practising witchcraft in fact suffered from mental illness. The Church condemned his writings as heretical and banned them. However, even within the Church some people began to realise that the prevailing beliefs and practices were wrong.

As belief in witchcraft and demonology waned, the clergy, the medical authorities and the general public began to regard people with mental disorders as ill. Torture and persecution eventually ceased. However, the lives of mentally ill people did not necessarily become better. The unfortunate ones were consigned to various asylums established for the care of the mentally ill. Most of these mental institutions were inhumane. Patients were often kept in chains and sometimes wallowed in their own excrement. Those who displayed bizarre catatonic postures or who had fanciful delusions were exhibited to the public for a fee. Many of the treatments designed to cure mental patients were little better than the tortures that had previously been used to drive out evil spirits. Patients were tied up, doused in cold water, bled, made to vomit, spun violently in a rotating chair, and otherwise assaulted. See Figure 17.2.

Mistreatment of the mentally ill did not go unnoticed by humanitarians. A famous and effective early reformer was Philippe Pinel (1745–1826), a French physician. In 1793, Pinel was appointed director of La Bicêtre, a mental hospital in Paris. Pinel believed that most mental patients would respond well to kind treatment. As an experiment, he removed the chains from some of the patients, took them out of dungeons and allowed them to walk about the hospital grounds. The experiment was a remarkable success; an atmosphere of peace and quiet replaced the previous noise, stench and general aura of despair. Many patients were eventually discharged. Pinel's success at La Bicêtre was repeated when he was given charge of Salpêtrière Hospital. Some mentally ill people eventually recover – or at least get much better – without any treatment at all. But if a person was put in a mental institution that existed prior to Pinel's time, he or she had little chance to show improvement.

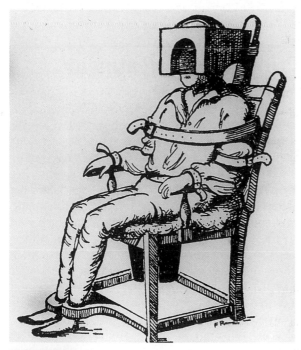

Figure 17.2

The 'tranquillising chair' devised by Benjamin Rush.

The development of modern treatment

The modern history of specific treatments for mental disorders probably began with Franz Anton Mesmer (1734–1815), an Austrian physician who practised in Paris in the late eighteenth and early nineteenth centuries. He devised a theory of 'magnetic fluxes' according to which he attempted to effect cures by manipulating iron rods and bottles of chemicals. In reality, he hypnotised his patients and thereby alleviated some of their symptoms. As a result, hypnosis was first known as mesmerism.

In 1815, there were approximately 2,000 individuals institutionalised in mental asylums in England. The number had increased one hundred years later when a hundred or so asylums in England and Wales housed an average of 1,000 patients. In America, at the same time, the number housed was between 1,500 and 3,000. Dr William Black, a nineteenth-century English physician kept a list of the causes of insanity of those individuals admitted to the Bethlem asylum, the largest madhouse in the UK at the time (it was also known as Bedlam). Figure 17.3 shows an example of one of these lists; it includes some unusual causes.

A French neurologist, Jean Martin Charcot (1825–1893), began his investigations of the therapeutic uses of hypnosis when one of his students hypnotised a woman and induced her to display the symptoms of a conversion reaction (hysteria). Charcot examined her and concluded that she was a hysterical patient. The student then woke the woman, and her symptoms vanished. Charcot had previously believed that hysteria had an organic basis, but this experience changed his opinion, and he began investigating its psychological causes.

Just before Freud began private practice, he studied with Charcot in Paris and observed the effects of hypnosis on hysteria. Freud's association with Charcot, and later with Breuer, started him on his life's study of the determinants of personality and the origins of mental illness. He created

Causes, both Moral and Physical, ascertained in 249 cases.

MORAL		PHYSICAL	
Domestic Grief, Affliction, and Disappointment	7	Intemperance and Debauchery	57
Unfaithfulness, Unkindness, or Intemperance of Wife	6	Bad Company	1
Loss of Situation and Dread of Poverty	7	Masturbation	5
Want of Employment, and sufferings therefrom	6	Fatigue and Over-exertion	3
Reverse of Fortune, Loss of Property, &c.	12	Over-study	6
Loss of Wife or Children	3	Injury to Head	14
Disappointed Affection	3	Disease of Brain	2
Unhappiness at Home	1	Delirium Tremens	1
Erroneous Views in Religion	3	Fever – Typhus, Yellow, Erysipelas, Small-pox	4
Sudden Shocks, Fright, &c.	29	Epilepsy	14
Jealousy	3	Paralysis	6
Pride	3	Chorea	2
Non-success in Business	1	Injury to Retina	1
Responsibility and over-anxiety	1	Disease of Lungs	3
Sudden Loss of Several Cows	1	_____ Liver	1
Regret for a Theft	1	Old Age	4
Suicide of a Brother	1	Congenital Deficiency	16
Over-excitement at the Great Exhibition	1		140
	89		

Hereditary Predisposition assigned 20

Figure 17.3

William Black's (1810) list of the causes of insanity.

the practice of psychoanalysis. Some modern psychiatrists and psychologists still use some of his therapeutic methods to treat their clients.

Current treatment: the eclectic approach

Most therapists adopt a general, eclectic approach to the treatment of mental disorders. The eclectic approach (from the Greek *eklegein*, to 'single out') involves the therapist using whatever methods he or she feels will work best for a particular client at a particular time. Such therapists are not strongly wed to particular theoretical orientations; instead, they seek the particular form of therapy that will best solve a particular client's problems. This often means combining aspects of several different treatment approaches according to a particular client's problem and personal circumstances. For example, Acierno *et al.* (1993) have shown that combinations of therapies are more effective in treating panic disorder than is any one alone.

Principles of treatment

Powell and Lindsay (1994) have listed a number of principles that underpin the treatment of mental disorder. They suggest that the client/patient be given realistic or achievable expectations regarding his or her conduct and outcome of the treatment, and that the progress of the treatment should be reinforced in order to make the effectiveness of the therapy clear to the patient (especially when the progress is slow or occurs imperceptibly to the patient). It is also important to give detailed feedback to the patient for the same reason. Eventually, with a treatment strategy in place, the patient should be encouraged or taught to transfer responsibility for the treatment from the therapist to him/herself in order to foster independence and to demonstrate that the treatment can work without the assistance of the therapist.

Treatment, however, is not a straightforward affair. There may be lack of compliance from the patient; he or she may not be that dedicated to some forms of treatment that rely on directly changing behaviour. There may also, for various reasons, be a lapse in the home practice of treatment. Patients may not remember the treatment advice given or may fail to remember when the treatment advice should be followed up at home.

Types of treatment
Psychoanalysis and psychodynamic therapy

Sigmund Freud is given credit for developing psychoanalysis which, as we saw in Chapter 14, is a form of therapy aimed at providing the client insight into his or her unconscious motivations and impulses. Freud's theory of personality suggests that unconscious conflicts based on the competing demands of the id (representing biological urges), the superego (representing the moral dictates of society), and the ego (representing reality) often lead to anxiety. The source of these conflicts, according to Freud, can usually be traced back to unacceptable, often sexually based, urges from early childhood: repressed impulses and feelings that lead to conscious anxiety. As Freud (1933) explained:

> 'One of the tasks of psychoanalysis ... is to lift the veil of amnesia which hides the earliest years of childhood and to bring to conscious memory the manifestations of early infantile sexual life which are contained in them.' (p. 26)

This veil is not easily lifted in the early stages of therapy because both the analyst and the client are unaware of the underlying conflicts. The repression of these conflicts is seldom complete, though, and they frequently intrude into consciousness in subtle ways. By encouraging the client to talk, the analyst tries to bring these conflicts into view. The obscurity of the conflicts requires the analyst to interpret them in order to uncover their true meaning and gradually weave together a complete picture of the unconscious.

The purpose of therapy is to create a setting in which clues about the origins of intrapsychic conflicts are most likely to be revealed by the client. These clues are revealed in clients' dreams, physical problems, memory (or failure to remember certain things), manner of speech, and cognitive and emotional reactions to therapy. Then, by exposing the client to these clues, he or she will gain insight into the problem.

The primary function of the psychoanalyst is to interpret the clues about the origins of intrapsychic conflict given by the client. Although clients may provide their own interpretations of these phenomena, Freud argued that people are biased observers of their own problems and thus their interpretations cannot be accurate. Instead, accurate interpretation is best accomplished by undergoing therapy with a specially trained therapist. Even today therapists who practise psychoanalysis (or one of its modern forms) emphasise interpretation as the basic means of uncovering the root causes of their clients' problems.

While the psychoanalyst's primary role is interpretation, the client's main job is to provide the psychoanalyst something to interpret: descriptions of his or her fears, anxieties, thoughts or repressed memories. This is not an easy task for the client to accomplish because the client unconsciously invokes one or more defence mechanisms, which, as you recall from Chapter 14, prevent anxiety-provoking memories and ideas from reaching conscious awareness. Together, the psychoanalyst and client work for insight into the client's problems.

The moment that insight is achieved, the veil of amnesia of which Freud spoke lifts and the client begins to understand the true nature of his or her problems. For some clients, insight is a sudden rush of profound understanding. For other clients, perhaps the majority who undergo long-term therapy, the feeling may be more one of quiet accomplishment, such as that which comes after a long struggle that finally ends with success.

Psychoanalytic techniques

Freud used free association to encourage the client to speak freely, without censoring possibly embarrassing or socially unacceptable thoughts. Freud achieved this goal in two ways. First, the client was encouraged to report any thoughts or images that came to mind, without worrying about their meaning. Second, Freud attempted to minimise any authoritative influence over the client's disclosures by eliminating eye contact. He usually sat in a chair at the head of a couch on which the client reclined.

Among the topics clients are encouraged to discuss are their dreams. Dream interpretation, the evaluation of the underlying meaning of dream content, is a hallmark of psychoanalysis (Freud, 1900). But even dream content is subject to some censoring, according to Freud, so that the analyst must be able to distinguish between the dream's manifest and latent content. Recall that the manifest content of a dream is the actual images and events that occur within the dream; latent content is the hidden meaning or significance of the dream. The manifest content masks the latent content because the latent content is anxiety-provoking and causes the person psychological discomfort. Thus, the analyst must be especially skilled in recognising the symbolic nature of dreams, for things are not always as they appear. For example, the client may relate the image of a growling, vicious dog chasing him or her down the street. The dog may actually symbolise an angry parent or spouse. The idea of a parent or spouse being angry and upset may be so painful to the client that it has been disguised within the dream. Bringing the client to an appreciation of the latent content of the dream is an important step towards insight and thus towards solving the client's psychological problems.

Insight is not achieved quickly, nor do clients always find it easy to disclose private aspects of their personal lives. In fact, there is something of a paradox involved in achieving insight, for the often painful or threatening knowledge resulting from insight is precisely what led to its repression in the first place. For example, a client may have to confront the reality of being abused as a child, or of being unloved, or of feeling peculiar, inferior or out of place. Although the client wishes to be cured, he or she does not look forward to the anxiety and apprehension that may result from recalling painful memories. The client often becomes defensive at some point during therapy, unconsciously attempting to halt further insight by censoring his or her true feelings: a process Freud called resistance.

A psychoanalyst may conclude that resistance is operating when the client tries to change the topic, begins to miss appointments for therapy, or suddenly forgets what he or she was about to say. The skilled therapist, who is not burdened by the client's resistance, recognises such diversions and redirects the discussion to the sensitive topics while minimising the pain of rediscovery.

Over a period of months or even years of therapy sessions taking place as often as several times a week, the client gradually becomes less inhibited, and the discussion begins to drift away from recent events to the more distant shores of early childhood. As the client relives aspects of childhood, he or she may begin to project powerful attitudes and emotions onto the therapist, a process called transference. The client may come to love or hate the therapist with the same intensity of the powerful emotions experienced in childhood towards parents or siblings.

Originally, Freud thought of transference as an impediment to therapy, a distraction from the real issues at hand. But he soon realised that the experience of transference was essential to the success of therapy (Erdelyi, 1985). Whereas free association uncovers many of the relevant events and facts of the client's life, transference provides the means for reliving significant early experiences. The therapist contributes to this experience by becoming a substitute for the real players in the client's life and so becomes a tool for illuminating the conflicts of the unconscious.

Freud reasoned that the analyst, being human too, could just as easily project his or her emotions onto the client, a process he called countertransference. Unlike transference, Freud believed countertransference to be unhealthy and undesirable. To be effective, the analyst must remain emotionally detached and objective in his or her appraisal of the client's disclosures. For this reason, he argued that the analyst, in order to understand his or her own unconscious conflicts, should undergo complete analysis with another therapist.

Although Freud was not the first to talk about the unconscious mind, he was the first to develop a significant theory of abnormal behaviour. He also developed an equally influential therapy designed to provide the client with insight into the unconscious motives that underlie behaviour. Psychoanalysis remains a force among contemporary therapeutic practices even a century after its founding, although its practice has undergone substantial modification.

Modern psychodynamic therapy

Psychoanalysis is now often referred to as psychodynamic therapy to reflect differences between modern psychoanalytic approaches and the original form of Freudian psychoanalysis. For example, although modern forms of psychodynamic therapies still focus on achieving insight into the unconscious, they tend to place less emphasis on sexual factors during development and more upon social and interpersonal experiences. Contemporary therapists also are more likely to address concerns and issues in the client's present life than to examine childhood experiences exclusively.

Modern psychodynamic therapists also view the ego as playing a more active role in influencing a person's thoughts and actions. Instead of viewing the ego as functioning merely to seek ways to satisfy the demands of the id and superego, they believe it to be a proactive component in one's overall psychological functioning. In other words, compared with Freud, modern psychodynamic therapists see the ego as having more control over the psyche. Thus, people receiving psychodynamic therapy are seen as being less constrained by the mind's unconscious forces than Freud thought them to be.

Although Freud considered analysis to be extremely involved and demanding, often requiring years to complete, today's therapists feel much can be gained by shortening the process, for example, by minimising the client's dependence on the therapist. Psychodynamic therapy, as presently practised, does not always take years to complete.

For example, one modern form of psychodynamic therapy, time-limited therapy, takes about twenty-five to thirty sessions with the therapist to complete (Strupp, 1993). The goal of time-limited therapy is to understand and improve the client's interpersonal skills through interpretation of transference processes. This therapy is based on Freud's belief that our early experiences with others influence the dynamics of our current relationships. Time-limited therapy focuses on the schemata that a client has about interpersonal relationships and attempts to modify those that are incorrect or that otherwise prevent the client from developing fulfilling relationships with others.

All forms of psychodynamic therapy share in common an interest in unconscious processes. There is an important corollary that attaches itself to this emphasis: behaviour or overt action is seldom important by itself. Rather, behaviour is important only to the extent that it serves as a manifestation of the real, underlying motive or conflict. As we will see a later section, not all therapists agree with this idea.

Evaluation

Evaluating the effectiveness of psychoanalysis or psycho-dynamic therapy is difficult because only a small proportion of people with mental disorders qualify for this method of treatment. To participate in this kind of therapy, a client must be intelligent, articulate and motivated enough to spend three or more hours a week working hard to uncover unconscious conflicts. In addition, he or she must be able to afford the therapist's fees, which are high. These qualifications rule out most psychotics, as well as people who lack the time or money to devote to such a long-term project. Furthermore, many people who enter this kind of therapy become dissatisfied with their progress and leave. In other cases, the therapist encourages a client to leave if he or she decides that the client is not co-operating fully. Thus, those who actually complete a course of therapy do not constitute a random sample, and we cannot conclude that this kind of therapy works just because a high percentage of this group is happy with the results. Those who have dropped out ought also to be counted.

Another problem in evaluating psychoanalysis and psy-chodynamic therapy is that therapists have a way to 'explain' their failures: They can blame them on the client (Eysenck, 1985). If the client appears to accept an insight into his or her behaviour but the behaviour does not change, the insight is said to be merely 'intellectual'. This escape clause makes the argument for the importance of insight completely circular and, therefore, illogical: if the client gets better, the improvement is due to insight; but if the client's behaviour remains unchanged, real (as opposed to 'intellectual') insight did not occur.

Humanistic therapies: client-centred therapy

In the 1940s, Carl Rogers (1902–1987) developed the first humanistic therapy, creating a major alternative to psy-choanalysis. The aim of humanistic therapy is to provide the client with a greater understanding of his or her unique potential for personal growth and self-actualisation. Humanistic therapies proceed from the assumption that people are good and have innate worth. Psychological problems reflect some type of blocking of one's potential for personal growth; humanistic therapy aims to realise this potential.

Rogers found the formalism of psychoanalysis too con-fining and its emphasis on intrapsychic conflict too pes-simistic (Tobin, 1991). His discontent led him to develop his own theory of personality, abnormal behaviour and therapy. His client-centred therapy is so named because of the respect given the client during therapy: the client decides what to talk about without direction or judgement from the therapist. The client takes ultimate responsibility for resolving his or her problems. The client, not a method or theory, is the focus of the therapy.

Rogers believed that the cause of many psychological problems can be traced to people's perceptions of them-selves as they actually are (their real selves) as differing from the people they would like to be (their ideal selves). Rogers called this discrepancy between the real and the ideal perceptions of the self incongruence. The goal of client-centred therapy is to reduce incongruence by foster-ing experiences that will make attainment of the ideal self possible.

Because the client's and not the therapist's thoughts direct the course of therapy, the therapist strives to make those thoughts, perceptions and feelings more noticeable to the client. This is frequently done through reflection, sensitive rephrasing or mirroring of the client's statements. For example:

Client: I get so frustrated at my parents. They just don't understand how I feel. They don't know what it's like to be me.

Therapist: You seem to be saying that the things that are important to you aren't very important to your parents. You'd like them now and then to see things from your perspective.

By reflecting the concerns of the client, the therapist demonstrates empathy, or the ability to perceive the world from another's viewpoint. The establishment of empathy is key in encouraging the client to deal with the incongruence between the real and the ideal selves.

For Rogers (1951), the 'worth and significance of the individual' is a basic ground-rule of therapy. This theme is represented in therapy through unconditional positive regard, in which the therapist tries to convey to the client that his or her worth as a human being is not dependent on anything he or she thinks, does or feels.

In client-centred therapy, the therapist totally and unconditionally accepts the client and approves of him or her as a person so that the client can come to understand that his or her feelings are worthwhile and important. Once the client begins to pay attention to these feelings, a self-healing process begins. For example, a client usually has difficulty at first expressing feelings verbally. The ther-apist tries to understand the feelings underlying the client's confused state and to help him or her put them into words. Through this process, the client learns to understand and heed his or her own drive towards self-actualisation. Consider the following example:

Alice: I was thinking about this business of standards. I somehow developed a sort of knack, I guess, of – well – habit – of trying to make people feel at ease around me, or to make things go along smoothly. ...

Counsellor: In other words, what you did was always in the direction of trying to keep things smooth and to make other people feel better and to smooth the situation.

A: Yes. I think that's what it was. Now the reason why I did it probably was – I mean, not that I was a good little Samaritan going around making other people happy, but that was probably the role that felt easiest for me to play. I'd been doing it around the home so much. I just didn't stand up for my own convictions, until I don't know whether I have any convictions to stand up for.

C: You feel that for a long time you've been playing the role of kind of smoothing out the frictions or differences or what not. …

A: M-hum.

C: Rather than having any opinion or reaction of your own in the situation. Is that it?

A: That's it. Or that I haven't been really honestly being myself, or actually knowing what my real self is, and that I've been just playing a sort of false role. Whatever role no one else was playing, and that needed to be played at the time, I'd try to fill it in. (Rogers, 1951, pp. 152–3)

As this example illustrates, in Rogers's view, the therapist should not manipulate events but should create conditions under which the client can make his or her own decisions independently.

Evaluation

Unlike many other clinicians, who prefer to rely on their own judgements concerning the effectiveness of their techniques, Rogers himself stimulated a considerable amount of research on the effectiveness of client-centred therapy. He recorded therapeutic sessions so that various techniques could be evaluated. One researcher, Truax (1966), obtained permission from Rogers (and his clients) to record some therapy sessions, and he classified the statements made by the clients into several categories. One of the categories included statements of improving mental health, such as 'I'm feeling better lately' or 'I don't feel as depressed as I used to'. After each of the patients' statements, Truax noted Rogers's reaction to see whether he gave a positive response. Typical positive responses were 'Oh, really? Tell me more' or 'Uh-huh. That's nice' or just a friendly 'Mm'. Truax found that of the eight categories of client statements, only those that indicated progress were regularly followed by a positive response from Rogers. Not surprisingly, during their therapy, the clients made more and more statements indicating progress.

This study attests to the power of social reinforcement and its occurrence in unexpected places. Rogers was an effective and conscientious psychotherapist, but he had not intended to single out and reinforce his clients' realistic expressions of progress in therapy. (Of course, he did not uncritically reinforce exaggerated or unrealistic positive statements.) This finding does not discredit client-centred therapy. Rogers simply adopted a very effective strategy for altering a person's behaviour. He used to refer to his therapy as non-directive; however, when he realised that he was reinforcing positive statements, he stopped referring to it as non-directive because it obviously was not.

Humanistic therapies: Gestalt therapy

The development of client-centred therapy owes much to its founder's disenchantment with classical psychoanalysis. For much the same reason, Fritz Perls (1893–1970), although trained in Freudian techniques, disengaged himself from orthodox psychoanalysis and founded Gestalt therapy (Perls, 1969). Gestalt therapy emphasises the unity of mind and body by teaching the client to 'get in touch' with bodily sensations and emotional feelings long hidden from awareness. Gestalt therapy, which bears no relation to the perception school of the same name which we described in Chapter 6, places exclusive emphasis upon present experience – not on the past – and the Gestalt therapist will often be quite confrontational, challenging the client to deal honestly with his or her emotions.

The therapist often uses the empty chair technique, in which the client imagines that he or she is talking to someone sitting in the chair beside him or her. For example, a woman may be asked to say the things that she had always wanted to say to her deceased father but did not while he was alive. The empty chair technique allows her to experience in the here and now the feelings and perceptions that she may have suppressed while her father was alive. It also allows her to express these feelings and to gain insight into how they have influenced her perception of herself and her world. This technique derives from Perls's belief that, for all of us, our memories, fears and feelings of guilt affect our relationships with others.

The Gestalt therapist also encourages the client to gain a better understanding of his or her feelings by talking to him or herself (to different parts of his or her personality) and to inanimate objects. Any attempt by the client to avoid the reality of his or her situation is challenged by the therapist, who constantly attempts to keep the client's attention focused on present problems and tries to guide the client towards an honest confrontation with these problems. Perls argued, 'In the safe emergency of the therapeutic situation, the neurotic discovers that the world does not fall to pieces if he or she gets angry, sexy, joyous, mournful'(1967, p. 331).

Evaluation

Like psychoanalysis and client-centred therapy, Gestalt therapy is inappropriate for serious problems such as psychoses. All three therapies are most effective for people who are motivated enough to want to change and who are intelligent enough to be able to gain some insight concerning their problems. Some of these problems include coping with everyday stressors as well as experiencing excessive anxiety and fear.

Behaviour and cognitive behaviour therapies

The fundamental assumption made by behaviour therapists is that people learn maladaptive or self-defeating behaviour in the same way that they learn adaptive behaviour. Undesirable behaviour, such as nail-biting or alcohol abuse, is the problem, not just a reflection of the problem. The methods that behaviour therapists use to induce behaviour change are extensions of classical and operant conditioning principles and work quite successfully.

Recall from Chapter 7 that, in classical conditioning, a previously neutral stimulus (ultimately the conditional stimulus, CS) comes to elicit the same response as a stimulus (unconditional stimulus, UCS) that naturally elicits that response because the CS reliably predicts the UCS. According to Joseph Wolpe (1958), one of the founders of behaviour therapy, many of our everyday fears and anxieties become associated with neutral stimuli through coincidence. Going to the dentist may evoke fear because the last time that you went you were not given enough anaesthetic and the drilling hurt. Although the dental surgery is usually not painful, you associate the dentists with pain because of your past experience. The next sections describe some of the more specific behavioural and cognitive behavioural approaches.

Systematic desensitisation

One behaviour therapy technique, developed by Wolpe, has been especially successful in eliminating some kinds of fears and phobias. This technique, called systematic desensitisation, is designed to remove the unpleasant emotional response produced by the feared object or situation and replace it with an incompatible one – relaxation.

The client is first trained to achieve complete relaxation. The essential task is to learn to respond quickly to suggestions to feel relaxed and peaceful so that these suggestions can elicit an immediate relaxation response. Next, client and therapist construct a hierarchy of anxiety-related stimuli.

Finally, the conditional stimuli (fear-eliciting situations) are paired with stimuli that elicit the learned relaxation response. For example, a person with a fear of spiders is instructed to relax and then to imagine hearing from a neighbour that she saw a spider in her garage. If the client reports no anxiety, he or she is instructed to move to the next item in the hierarchy and to imagine hearing a neighbour say that there is a tiny spider across the street; and so on. Whenever the client begins feeling anxious, he or she signals to the therapist with some predetermined gesture such as raising a finger. The therapist instructs the client to relax and, if necessary, describes a less threatening scene. The client is not permitted to feel severe anxiety at any time. Gradually, over a series of sessions (the average is eleven), the client is able to get through the entire list, vicariously experiencing even the most feared encounters.

Scientific evaluations of systematic desensitisation have been positive, and several experiments have found that all elements of the procedure are necessary for its success (Emmelkamp, 1994). For example, a person will not get rid of a phobia merely by participating in relaxation training or by constructing hierarchies of fear-producing situations. Only pairings of the anxiety-producing stimuli with instructions to relax will reduce the fear.

Whereas practitioners of systematic desensitisation are careful not to permit their clients to become too anxious, practitioners of a procedure called flooding attempt to rid their clients of their fears by arousing them intensely until their responses diminish through habituation and they learn that nothing bad happens. The therapist describes, as graphically as possible, the most frightening encounters possible with the object of a client's phobia. The client tries to imagine the encounter and to experience intense fear (thereby 'flooding' the client's mind with anxious thoughts). In some cases, the client actually encounters the object of his or her fear, in which case the treatment is called in vivo (live) implosion therapy. Of course, the client is protected from any adverse effects of the encounter (or the encounter is imaginary), so there are no dangerous consequences. Eventually, the fear response begins to subside, and the client learns that even the worst imaginable encounter can become tolerable. In a sense, the client learns not to fear his or her own anxiety attack, and avoidance responses begin to extinguish.

Aversion therapy

In aversion therapy, a negative reaction to a neutral stimulus is caused by pairing it with an aversive stimulus (UCS). Aversion therapy attempts to establish an unpleasant response (such as a feeling of fear or disgust) to the object that produces the undesired behaviour. For example, a person with a fetish for women's shoes might be given painful electrical shocks while viewing colour slides of women's shoes. Aversive therapy has also been used to treat drinking, smoking, transvestism, exhibitionism and overeating. This technique has been shown to be moderately effective (Marshall et al., 1991). However, because the method involves pain or nausea, the client's participation must be voluntary, and the method should be employed only if other approaches fail or are impractical.

The use of aversive methods raises ethical issues, particularly when the individual is so severely impaired that he or she is unable to give informed consent to a particular therapeutic procedure. Carr and Lovaas (1983) state that aversive methods involving stimuli such as electric shock should be used as the last resort. They should be used only when the patient's behaviour poses a serious threat to his or her own well-being and after the following methods have been employed unsuccessfully: reinforcing other behaviours, attempting to extinguish the maladaptive behaviours, temporarily removing the patient from the environment that reinforces the maladaptive behaviours (a method called time-out), and trying to arrange for the patient to perform behaviours that are incompatible with the maladaptive ones. In a method called covert sensitisation, instead of experiencing a punishing stimulus after performing a behaviour, the client imagines that he or she is performing an undesirable behaviour and then imagines receiving an aversive stimulus.

Behaviour modification

Behaviour modification, a general term describing therapy based on operant conditioning principles (which you will remember from Chapter 5), involves altering maladaptive behaviour by rearranging the contingencies between behaviour and its consequences. Increases in desirable behaviour can be brought about through either positive or negative reinforcement, and undesirable behaviour can be reduced through either extinction or punishment.

In its infancy, behaviour modification was applied chiefly to schizophrenic patients and the mentally retarded (Lindsley, 1956; Ayllon and Azrin, 1968; Neisworth and Madle, 1982). In the past three decades, however, use of operant principles has been extended to a wide array of behaviours and circumstances, for example weight management, anorexia nervosa, bed-wetting, smoking, and compliance with medical regimens (Kazdin, 1994).

Reinforcement of adaptive behaviours

Behavioural techniques are often used to alter the behaviour of mentally retarded or emotionally disturbed people with whom communication is difficult. Reinforcement can be a powerful method of behavioural change. If the therapist has established a warm relationship with the client, he or she can use ordinary social reinforcers, such as signs of approval (friendly smiles and nods of the head), to encourage positive behavioural change. As we saw in the section on client-centred therapy, even non-behavioural psychologists use reinforcement – deliberately or inadvertently – to produce behavioural change.

Token economies

The behaviour-analytic approach has been used on a large scale in mental institutions with generally good success. Residents are often asked to do chores to engage them in active participation in their environment. In some instances, other specific behaviours are also targeted as desirable and therapeutic, such as helping residents who have more severe problems. To promote these social behaviours, therapists have designed token economies. A list of tasks is compiled, and residents receive tokens as rewards for performing the tasks; later, they can exchange these tokens for snacks, other desired articles or various privileges. The tokens become conditioned reinforcers for desirable and appropriate behaviours. The amount of time spent performing the desirable behaviours was high when reinforcement contingencies were imposed and low when they were not.

Although token economies are based on a simple principle, they are very difficult to implement. A mental institution includes patients, caretakers, housekeeping staff and professional staff. If a token economy is to be effective, all staff members who deal with residents must learn how the system works; ideally, they should also understand and agree with its underlying principles. A token economy can easily be sabotaged by a few people who believe that the system is foolish, wrong or in some way threatening to themselves. If these obstacles can be overcome, token economies work very well.

Modelling

Humans (and many other animals) have the ability to learn without directly experiencing an event. People can imitate the behaviour of other people, watching what they do and, if the conditions are appropriate, performing the same behaviour. This capability provides the basis for the technique of modelling. Behaviour therapists have found that clients can make much better progress when they have access to a model providing examples of successful behaviours to imitate.

Social skills training

With social skills training, the client is taught to behave in a desirable and socially appropriate way. He or she might do this by engaging in assertiveness training which teaches the client to be more direct about his or her feelings (Oltmans and Emery, 1998). A part of assertiveness training might be role-playing in which the client is taught to act out or rehearse social skills by adopting the identity of another, socially skilled person.

Cognitive behavioural therapy

The first attempts at developing psychotherapies based on altering or manipulating cognitive processes emerged during the 1970s. These attempts were undertaken by behaviour therapists who suspected that maladaptive behaviour, or, for that matter, adaptive behaviour, could be due to more than only environmental variables. They began exploring how their clients' thoughts, perceptions, expectations and self-statements might interact with environmental factors in the development and maintenance of maladaptive behaviour.

The focus of cognitive behaviour therapy (CBT) is on changing the client's maladaptive thoughts, beliefs and perceptions. Like behaviour therapists – and unlike most insight psychotherapists – cognitive behaviour therapists are not particularly interested in events that occurred in the client's childhood. They are interested in the here and now and in altering the client's behaviour so that it becomes more functional. Although they employ many methods used by behaviour therapists, they believe that when behaviours change, they do so because of changes in cognitive processes.

There are many ways in which cognitive behavioural therapy can be applied to mental disorder. Attribution retraining, for example, involves retraining the client to alter his or her perception of causes of events or behaviour (attributions are perceived causes). One way in which this can be achieved is by requesting the client to adopt a more scientific approach to his or her beliefs. For example, it is common in depression for a depressed person to attribute causes for failure to him or herself but to attribute successes to others. Attribution retraining should encourage the client to change these 'faulty' attributions and make them more realistic. One form of CBT designed to treat depression requires the patient to assess whether their view of themselves and others is distorted based on a considered analysis of their lives. This approach based on the clinical work of Beck (1967, 1976; Beck and Emery, 1985) and is considered in the section on depression below.

Another CBT approach, rational-emotive therapy, was developed in the 1950s by Albert Ellis, a clinical psychologist, and is based on the belief that psychological problems are caused by how people think about upsetting events and situations. In contrast to the other forms of cognitive behaviour therapy, rational-emotive therapy did not grow out of the tradition of behaviour therapy. Ellis asserts that psychological problems are the result of faulty cognitions; therapy is therefore aimed at changing people's beliefs. Rational-emotive therapy is highly directive and confrontational. The therapist tells his or her clients what they are doing wrong and how they should change.

According to Ellis and his followers, emotions are the products of cognition. A significant activating event (A) is followed by a highly charged emotional consequence (C), but it is not correct to say that A has caused C. Rather, C is a result of the person's belief system (B). Therefore, inappropriate emotions (such as depression, guilt and anxiety) can be abolished only if a change occurs in the person's belief system. It is the task of the rational-emotive therapist to dispute the person's beliefs and to convince him or her that those beliefs are inappropriate. Ellis tries to show his clients that irrational beliefs are impossible to satisfy, that they make little logical sense, and that adhering to them creates needless anxiety, self-blame and self-doubt. The following are examples of the kinds of ideas that Ellis (1973) believes to be irrational:

'The idea that it is a necessity for an adult to be loved or approved by virtually every significant person in the community.

The idea that one should be thoroughly competent, adequate, and goal-oriented in all possible respects if one is to consider oneself as having worth.

The idea that human unhappiness is externally caused and that people have little or no ability to control their lives.

The idea that one's past is an all-important determinant of one's present behaviour.

The idea that there is invariably a right, precise, and perfect solution to human problems and that it is catastrophic if this perfect solution is not found.' (pp. 152–153)

In a review of research evaluating the effectiveness of rational-emotive therapy, Haaga and Davison (1989) concluded that the method has been shown to reduce general anxiety, test anxiety and unassertiveness. Rational-emotive therapy has appeal and potential usefulness for those who can enjoy and profit from intellectual teaching and argumentation. The people who are likely to benefit most from this form of therapy are those who are self-demanding and who feel guilty for not living up to their own standards of perfection. People with serious anxiety disorders or with severe thought disorders, such as schizophrenia and other psychoses, are unlikely to respond to an intellectual analysis of their problems.

Many therapists who adopt an eclectic approach use some of the techniques of rational-emotive therapy with some of their clients. In its advocacy of rationality and its eschewing of superstition, the therapy proposes a common-sense approach to living. However, many psychotherapists disagree with Ellis's denial of the importance of empathy in the relationship between therapist and client.

Evaluation

Psychotherapists of traditional orientations have criticised behaviour therapy for its focus on the symptoms of a psychological problem to the exclusion of its root causes. Some psychoanalysts even argue that treatment of just the symptoms is dangerous. In their view, the removal of one symptom of an intrapsychic conflict will simply produce another, perhaps more serious, symptom through a process called symptom substitution.

There is little evidence that symptom substitution occurs. It is true that many people's behavioural problems are caused by conditions that existed in the past, and often these problems become self-perpetuating. Behaviour therapy can, in many cases, eliminate the problem behaviour without delving into the past. For example, a child may, for one reason or another, begin wetting the bed. The nightly awakening irritates the parents, who must change the bed sheets and the child's pyjamas. The disturbance often disrupts family relationships. The child develops feelings of guilt and insecurity and wets the bed more often. Instead of analysing the sources of family conflict, a therapist who uses behaviour therapy would install a device in the child's bed that rings a bell when he or she begins to urinate. The child awakens and goes to the bathroom to urinate and soon ceases to wet the bed. The elimination of bed-wetting causes rapid improvement in the child's self-esteem and in the entire family relationship. Symptom substitution does not appear to occur (Baker, 1969).

Although cognitive behaviour therapists believe in the importance of unobservable constructs such as feelings, thoughts and perceptions, they do not believe that good therapeutic results can be achieved by focusing on cognitions alone. They, like their behaviour-analytic colleagues, insist that it is not enough to have their clients introspect and analyse their thought patterns. Instead, therapists must help clients to change their behaviour. Behavioural changes can cause cognitive changes. For example, when a client observes that he or she is now engaging in fewer maladaptive behaviours and more adaptive behaviours, the client's self-perceptions and self-esteem are bound to change as a result. Therapy is more effective when specific attention is paid to cognitions as well as to behaviours.

Other psychotherapies

Group therapy

Group psychotherapy, in which two or more clients meet simultaneously with a therapist to discuss problems, became common during World War II. The stresses of combat produced psychological problems in many members of the armed forces, and the demand for psychotherapists greatly exceeded the supply. What began as an economic necessity became an institution once the effectiveness of group treatment was recognised.

Because most psychological problems involve interactions with other people, treating these problems in a group setting may be worthwhile. Group therapy provides four advantages that are not found in individual therapy:

1 The group setting permits the therapist to observe and interpret actual interactions without having to rely on clients' descriptions, which may be selective or faulty.

2 A group can bring social pressure to bear on the behaviours of its members. If a person receives similar comments about his or her behaviour from all the members of a group, the message is often more convincing than if a psychotherapist delivers the same comments in a private session.

3 The process of seeing the causes of maladaptive behaviour in other people often helps a person to gain insight into his or her own problems. People can often can learn from the mistakes of others.

4 Knowing that other people have problems similar to one's own can bring comfort and relief. People discover that they are not alone.

The structure of group therapy sessions can vary widely. Some sessions are little more than lectures, in which the therapist presents information about a problem common to all members of the group, followed by discussion. For example, in a case involving a person with severe mental or physical illness, the therapist explains to family members the nature, treatment and possible outcomes of the disorder. Then the therapist answers questions and allows people to share their feelings about what the illness has done to their family. Other groups are simply efficient ways to treat several clients at the same time. Most types of group therapy involve interactions among the participants.

Family therapy and couples therapy

People are products of their environments, and the structure of a person's family is a crucial part of that environment. Consequently, helping an unhappy person frequently means also restructuring his or her relationship with other family members. In addition, problems in the relations between members of a couple – with or without children – can often lead to stress and unhappiness.

In family therapy, a therapist meets with (usually) all the members of a client's family and analyses the ways in which individuals interact. The therapist attempts to get family members to talk to each other instead of addressing all comments and questions to him or her. As much as possible, the family therapist tries to collect data about the interactions – how individuals sit in relation to each other, who interrupts whom, who looks at whom before speaking – in order to infer the nature of interrelationships within the family. For example, there may be barriers between certain family members; perhaps a father is unable to communicate with one of his children. Or two or more family members may be so dependent on each other that they cannot function independently; they constantly seek each other's approval and, through overdependence, make each other miserable.

After inferring the family structure, the therapist attempts to restructure it by replacing maladaptive interactions with more effective, functional ones. He or she suggests that perhaps all members of the family must change if the client is to make real improvement. The therapist gets family members to 'actualise' their transactional patterns – to act out their everyday relationships – so that the maladaptive interactions will show themselves. Restructuring techniques include forming temporary alliances between the therapist and one or more of the family members, increasing tension in order to trigger changes in unstable structures, assigning explicit tasks and homework to family members (for example, making them interact with other members), and providing general support, education and guidance. Sometimes, the therapist visits the family at home. For example, if a child in a family refuses to eat, the therapist will visit during mealtime in order to see the problem acted out as explicitly as possible.

Behaviour therapists have also applied their methods of analysis and treatment to families. This approach focuses on the social environment provided by the family and on the ways that family members reinforce or punish each other's behaviour. The strategy is to identify the maladaptive behaviours of the individuals and the ways these behaviours are inadvertently reinforced by the rest of the family. Then the therapist helps the family members find ways to increase positive exchanges and reinforce each other's adaptive behaviours. A careful analysis of the social dynamics of a family often reveals that changes need to be made not in the individual showing the most maladaptive behaviours but in the other members of the family.

All couples will find that they disagree on some important issues. These disagreements necessarily lead to conflicts. For example, they may have to decide whether to move to accommodate the career of one of the partners, they will have to decide how to spend their money, and they will have to decide how to allocate household chores. Their ability to resolve conflict is one of the most important factors that affects the quality and durability of their relationship (Schwartz and Schwartz, 1980).

When dealing with couples, therapists have learned that changes in the nature of the relations can have unforeseen consequences – and that they must be alert for these consequences. For example, LoPiccolo and Friedman (1985) describe treatment of a couple with a sexual problem. At first, the problem appeared to belong to the man.

'A couple with a marriage of twenty years duration sought treatment for the male's problem of total inability to have an erection. This had been a problem for over nineteen of their twenty years of marriage. Successful intercourse had only taken place in the first few months of the marriage. ... [The wife] reported that she greatly enjoyed sex and was extremely frustrated by her husband's inability to have an erection.'

The therapists used techniques developed by Masters and Johnson (1970) to treat the man's impotence, which succeeded splendidly. Within ten weeks the couple were able to have sexual intercourse regularly, and both had orgasms. However, even though the problem appeared to have been cured, and despite the physical gratification they received from their sexual relations, they soon stopped having them. In investigating this puzzling occurrence, the therapists discovered:

'that the husband had a great need to remain distant and aloof from his wife. He had great fears of being overwhelmed and controlled by her, and found closeness to be

very uncomfortable. ... For him, the inability to have an erection served to keep his wife distant from him, and to maintain his need for privacy, separateness, and autonomy in the relationship.' (LoPiccolo and Friedman, 1985, p. 465)

The therapists also found that the wife had reasons to avoid sexual contact. For one thing, she apparently had never resolved the antisexual teachings imparted to her as a child by her family. In addition,

'over the nineteen years of her husband being unable to attain an erection, she had come to have a very powerful position in the relationship. She very often reminded her husband that he owed her a lot because of her sexual frustration. Thus, she was essentially able to win all arguments with him, and to get him to do anything that she wanted.' (p. 465)

The therapists were able to address these issues and to help the couple resolve them. Eventually, the couple were able to alter the structure of their marriage and resumed their sexual relations.

This case illustrates the fact that a couple is not simply a collection of two individuals. Long-standing problems bring adjustments and adaptations (some of which may not be healthy). Even if the original problems are successfully resolved, the adjustments to these problems may persist and cause problems of their own.

Biological treatments

Psychopharmacological interventions in mental disorder are aimed at treating psychological problems by using chemical agents and is the most widely used form of biomedical therapy. Table 17.3 (p. 610) lists some of the more common drugs used to improve psychological functioning, their generic names and their more recognisable tradenames.

There are four classes of drugs used to treat mental disorders: antipsychotic drugs, antidepressant drugs, antimanic drugs and anti-anxiety drugs, and we discuss the application and effectiveness of these drugs in the sections describing mental disorders.

Some people with depression do not respond to antidepressant drugs, but a substantial percentage of these people improve after a few sessions of electro-convulsive therapy (ECT) in which electrodes are applied to a person's head and a brief surge of electrical current is passed through them. Because antidepressant medications are generally slow acting, taking ten days to two weeks for their therapeutic effects to begin, severe cases of depression are often treated with a brief course of ECT to reduce the symptoms right away. These people are then maintained on an antidepressant drug.

Controversies in psychological science

Does psychotherapy work?

The issue

Evaluation of therapies and therapists is an important issue. It has received much attention, but almost everyone who is involved agrees that too little is known about the efficacy of psychotherapeutic methods, partly because psychotherapeutic effectiveness is difficult to study (Vervaeke and Emmelkamp, 1998). The most well known psychotherapies, their goals and methods of intervention are summarised in Table 17.2. Given that there are at least 400 different types of therapy and over 150 classified mental disorders (Garfield and Bergin, 1994), achieving some consistency across studies would be difficult.

Several other factors make it extremely difficult to evaluate the effectiveness of a particular form of therapy or an individual therapist. One factor is the problem of measurement: there are no easily applied, commonly agreed criteria for mental health. Therefore, one usually cannot make valid before-and-after measurements. Most studies rely on ratings by the clients or the therapists to determine whether a therapy has succeeded.

Self-selection – the fact that clients choose whether to enter therapy, what type of therapy to engage in and how long to stay in therapy – makes it nearly impossible to establish either a stable sample population or a control group. That is, self-selection means that certain kinds of people are more likely than others to enter a particular therapy and stick with it, which produces a biased sample. Lack of a stable sample and of a control group makes it difficult to compare the effectiveness of various kinds of therapy. Many patients change therapists or leave therapy altogether. What conclusions can we make about the effectiveness of a therapy by looking only at the progress made by the clients who remain with it?

Table 17.2   Summary of the basic assumptions, goals and methods involved in traditional forms of psychotherapy

Type of therapy	Basic assumptions	Primary goals	Typical method of analysis or intervention
Psychoanalysis	Behaviour is motivated by intrapsychic conflict and biological urges	Discover the sources of conflict and resolve them through insight	Free association, dream interpretation, interpretation of transference, resistance, memory and manner of speech
Psychodynamic	Behaviour is motivated by both unconscious forces and interpersonal experiences	Understand and improve interpersonal skills	Interpretation of transference and modification of client's inappropriate schemata about interpersonal relationships
Humanistic and Gestalt	People are good and have innate worth	To promote personal growth and self-actualisation and to enhance clients' awareness of bodily sensations and feelings	Reduce incongruence through reflection, empathy, unconditional positive regard and techniques to enhance personal awareness and feelings of self-worth
Behaviour and cognitive behaviour	Behaviour is controlled largely by environmental contingencies, people's perception of them, or their combination	To change maladaptive behaviour and thinking patterns	Manipulate environmental variables, restructure thinking patterns and correct faulty thinking or irrational beliefs
Family/couples	Problems in relationships entail everybody involved in them	To discover how interactions influence problems in individual functioning	Analysis of patterns of family/couples' interaction and how others reinforce maladaptive and adaptive thinking and behaving

Yet another problem with scientific evaluation of psychotherapy is the question of an appropriate control group. The effects of therapeutic drugs must be determined through comparison with the effects of placebos (innocuous pills that have no effects on people's thoughts and behaviour) to be sure that the improvement has not occurred merely because the patient thinks that a pill has done some good. Placebo effects can also occur in psychotherapy: people know that they are being treated and get better because they believe that the treatment should lead to improvement. Given these problems, what can we say about the efficacy of psychotherapy?

The evidence

In a pioneering paper on psychotherapeutic evaluation, Eysenck (1952) examined nineteen studies assessing the effectiveness of psychotherapy. He reported that of the people who remained in psychoanalysis as long as their therapists thought they should, 66 per cent showed improvement. Similarly, 64 per cent of patients treated eclectically showed an improvement. However, 72 per cent of patients who were treated only custodially (receiving no psychotherapy) in institutions showed improvement. In other words, people got better just as fast by themselves as they did in therapy.

Subsequent studies were not much more optimistic. Some investigators, including Eysenck, concluded that it is unethical to charge a person for psychotherapy because there is little scientific evidence that it is effective. Others said that the problems involved in performing scientific research are so great that we must abandon the attempt to evaluate therapies: validation of the effectiveness of therapy must rely on the therapist's clinical judgement. Many forms of therapy have never been evaluated objectively because their practitioners are convinced that the method works and deem objective confirmation unnecessary.

Figure 17.4 summarises Smith *et al.* (1980) well known meta-analysis of 475 studies comparing the outcome effectiveness of psychodynamic, Gestalt, client-centred, systematic desensitisation, behaviour modification and cognitive behaviour therapies. A meta-analysis is a statistical procedure for estimating the magnitude of experimental effects reported by published studies. Relative to no therapy, each of these therapies was shown to be superior in helping people with their problems. As you can see, behavioural and cognitive therapies tended to exceed others in effectiveness, although these differences were often small. More recent research has confirmed these results, indicating that almost all people who enter behaviour or cognitive behaviour therapy tend to improve with regard to the reason that brought them to therapy (Robinson *et al.*, 1990).

Several studies have suggested that the ability to form understanding, warm and empathetic relationships is one of the most important traits that distinguish an effective therapist from an ineffective one (Beutler *et al.*, 1994). For example, Strupp and Hadley (1979) enlisted a group of lecturers on the basis of their reputation as warm, trustworthy, empathetic individuals. The lecturers (from the departments of English, history, mathematics and philosophy) were asked to hold

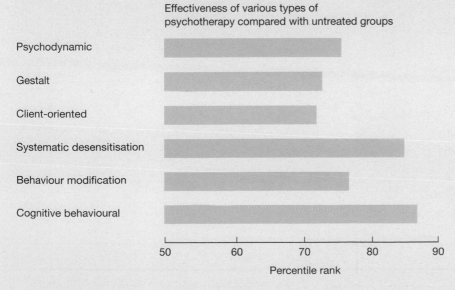

Effectiveness of various types of psychotherapy compared with untreated groups

Percentile rank

Figure 17.4

Effectiveness of psychotherapy. The results of Smith *et al.*'s meta-analysis comparing the effectiveness of different therapies.

Continued overleaf

weekly counselling sessions for students with psychological difficulties. Another group of students was assigned to professional psychotherapists, both psychologists and psychiatrists, and a third group received no treatment at all. Most of the students showed moderate depression or anxiety.

Although there was much variability, with some individual students showing substantial improvement, students who met with the lecturers did as well as those who met with the professional therapists. Both groups did significantly better than the control subjects who received no treatment. These results suggest that sympathy and understanding are the most important ingredients in the psychotherapeutic process, at least for treatment of mild anxiety or depression. In such cases, the therapists' theories of how mental disorders should be treated may be less important than their ability to establish warm, understanding relationships with their clients.

Conclusion

The results of psychotherapy (which includes cognitive behaviour therapy as well as the other, humanistic therapies) are quite positive. There are some negative outcomes: an estimated 9–13 per cent of clients worsen after psychotherapy (Beutler and Clarkin, 1990). Application of psychotherapy to schizophrenia has been associated with client deterioration (Lambert and Bergin, 1994). Also, some problems may be inappropriate for psychotherapy: criminal or antisocial behaviour, for example. For some other problems, however, such as depression, psychotherapy may be quite effective.

There are several problems with ECT treatments. An excessive number of ECT treatments has been associated with permanent memory loss (Squire *et al.*, 1981) with little enduring effect on cognitive performance (Calev *et al.*, 1995; Barnes *et al.*, 1997). Nowadays, ECT is usually administered only to the right hemisphere, in order to minimise damage to people's verbal memories, and is used only when the patient's symptoms justify it. Because ECT undoubtedly achieves its effects through the biochemical consequences of the seizure, pharmacologists may discover new drugs that can produce rapid therapeutic effects without ECT's deleterious ones. Once this breakthrough occurs, ECT can be abandoned.

One other biological treatment for mental disorders is even more controversial than electroconvulsive therapy: psychosurgery or neurosurgery (Fenton, 1998). Psychosurgery

Table 17.3 Drugs commonly used to treat mental disorders

Therapeutic function	Class of drugs	Generic name	Tradename
Antipsychotic	Soporific	Chlorpromazine	Thorazine
	Non-soporific	Acetophenazine	Tindal
	Phenothiazines	Thioridazine	Mellaril
		Fluphenazine	Permitil
		Trifluoperazine	Stelazine
		Perphenazine	Trilafon
	Butyrophenones	Haloperidol	Haldol
Antidepressant	Tricyclics	Imipramine	Tofranil
	Monoamine oxidase	Amitryptiline	Elavil
	inhibitors	Phenelzine	Nardil
	Serotonin reuptake	Fluoxetine	Prozac
	inhibitors		Miltown
Anti-anxiety	Propanediols	Meprobamate	Librium
	Benzodiazepines	Chlordiazepoxide	Valium
		Diazepam	
Antimanic	Lithium salts	Lithium carbonate	Eskalith

involves the treatment of a mental disorder, in the absence of obvious organic damage, through brain surgery. In contrast, brain surgery to remove a tumour or diseased neural tissue or to repair a damaged blood vessel is not psychosurgery, and there is no controversy about these procedures.

Psychosurgery has its origins in the late 1930s when, at a conference at University College London, the results of frontal lobectomies on two chimpanzees, Becky and Lucy, were presented. The surgery resulted in an increase in calmness and passivity in the chimps. Egas Moniz, a 59 year old Portuguese professor of neurology, one of the audience at the meeting, suggested that this technique might also be appropriate for humans. Late in 1935, the first frontal lobotomy operations were performed. While treating some symptoms, such as those in chronic schizophrenia, the prefrontal lobotomies were found to have serious side effects, such as apathy and severe blunting of emotions, intellectual impairments, and deficits in judgement and planning ability. Nevertheless, the procedure was used for a variety of conditions, most of which were not improved by the surgery. Approximately forty thousand prefrontal lobotomies were performed in the United States alone, most of them from 1935 to 1955. A simple procedure, called 'ice pick' prefrontal lobotomy by its critics, was even performed on an outpatient basis, as seen in Figure 17.5. The development of antipsychotic drugs and the increasing attention paid to the serious side effects of prefrontal lobotomy led to a sharp decline in the use of this procedure during the 1950s. Today it is no longer performed.

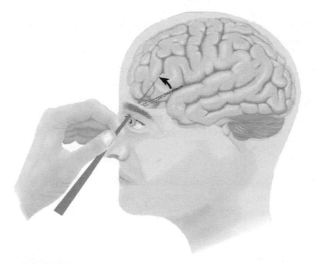

Figure 17.5

'Ice pick' prefrontal lobotomy. The sharp metal rod is inserted under the eyelid and just above the eye so that it pierces the skull and enters the base of the frontal lobe.

Source: Adapted with permission from Freeman, W., *Proceedings of the Royal Society of Medicine,* 1949, 42 (suppl.), 8–12.

A few surgeons have continued to refine the technique of psychosurgery and now perform a procedure called a **cingulotomy**, which involves cutting the cingulum bundle, a small band of nerve fibres that connects the prefrontal cortex with parts of the limbic system (Ballantine *et al.*, 1987). Cingulotomies have been shown to be effective in helping some people who suffer from severe compulsions (Tippin and Henn, 1982). In a recent study, Baer and his colleagues (1995) conducted a long-term follow-up study of eighteen people who underwent cingulotomy for severe obsessive-compulsive disorder. For each of these people, other forms of therapy – drug therapy and behaviour therapy – had been unsuccessful in treating their symptoms. However, after their surgeries, the people in Baer's study showed marked improvements in their functioning, decreased symptoms of depression and anxiety, and few negative side effects.

Evaluation

Drug therapy is the preferred biological treatment for mental disorders although it represents only a possible treatment, not a cure. Usually, the drugs are effective only to the extent that the people for whom they are prescribed actually use them. In some cases, people forget to take their drugs, only to have the disordered symptoms return. In other cases, people take their drugs, get better, and stop taking the drugs because they feel that they are no longer 'sick'. In this case, too, the symptoms soon return. For some people, this cycle repeats itself endlessly.

Questions to think about

Treatment of mental disorders

- What are the objections to psychodynamic therapy as a treatment? Why are they valid?

- Why should cognitive behaviour therapies work?

- Does the description of mental disorder as an illness increase the likelihood that a treatment should be biologically based?

- Are there some mental disorders which suggest a more behavioural than biological treatment approach, and vice versa? Would group therapy be effective for serious mental disorders, for example?

- How would you set up a study to investigate the efficacy of different treatments on one mental disorder? What factors would you need to control for?

MENTAL DISORDERS

This section describes some of the major mental disorders, their possible causes and some of the more successful treatments. It begins with the anxiety disorders.

Anxiety, somatoform and dissociative mental disorders

Anxiety, somatoform and dissociative mental disorders are often referred to as neuroses. Most neuroses are strategies of perception and behaviour that have become distorted or exaggerate. They are characterised by pathological increases in anxiety or by defence mechanisms applied too rigidly, resulting in mental processes that are maladaptive. Neurotic people are anxious, fearful, depressed and generally unhappy. However, unlike people who are afflicted with psychoses, they do not suffer from delusions or severely disordered thought processes. Furthermore, they almost universally realise that they have a problem. Most neurotics are only too aware that their strategies for coping with the world are not working. Neurotic behaviour is usually characterised by avoidance rather than confrontation of problems. People with neuroses turn to imaginary illnesses, oversleeping or convenient forgetfulness to avoid having to confront stressful situations.

Anxiety disorders

Several important types of mental disorders are classified as anxiety disorders, which have fear and anxiety as their most prominent symptoms. Anxiety is a sense of apprehension or doom that is accompanied by certain physiological reactions, such as accelerated heart rate, sweaty palms and tightness in the stomach (Gray, 1982; DSM-IV, 1994). Anxiety disorders are the most common psychological disorders and the reported rate of anxiety disorder is twice as high in European women than in men (Weiller *et al.*, 1998). Five of the most important anxiety disorders are generalised anxiety disorder, panic disorder, phobic disorders, obsessive compulsive disorder and post-traumatic stress disorder.

The most common of these are agoraphobia, panic disorder and generalised anxiety disorder, all of which are described next, together with possible aetiology. There seems to be national variation in the prevalence of these disorders. Generalised anxiety disorder is more frequent in cities such as Paris and Berlin, for example, whereas it is low in Manchester and Groningen. Panic disorder appears to be more common in Manchester and agoraphobia in Groningen (Weiller *et al.*, 1998).

Generalised anxiety disorder (GAD)

Description

The principal characteristic of generalised anxiety disorder (GAD) is excessive worry about all matters relating to the individual's life: health, money, work, relationships and so on. According to DSM-IV, these worries must be present on most days and will have occurred over a period of at least six months. The anxious individual finds it difficult to control the worry and shows at least three symptoms out of the following: restlessness, being easily fatigued, difficulty concentrating, irritability, muscle tension and sleep disturbance. Around 12 per cent of anxiety disorders are GAD (DSM-IV, 1994) and most individuals with GAD also experience depression which sometimes makes a clear-cut diagnosis of GAD difficult.

Anxious individuals spend considerably longer making decisions. For example, Tallis *et al.* (1991) asked a group of controls and clinically anxious individuals to respond if a target was present on a computer monitor. Although there was no difference between controls and anxious individuals when the target was present, the anxious group took significantly longer to make a decision when the target was absent. This finding demonstrates that anxious individuals seem to attend more to tasks that require them to make absolutely correct decisions.

Aetiology

Several models exist which try to explain GAD; some of these also apply to other mental disorders but this section limits itself to those which account for GAD explicitly. (A fuller account of these models can be found in Power and Dalgleish's (1997) excellent book, listed in the suggested reading section.)

Borkovec's model   According to Borkovec (1994), GAD arises from the individual's drive to set and anticipate a set of goals that are desirable. In this context, the anxiety arises when a past history of a frustrated failure to achieve affects the perception of cues associated with these goals. Anxiety is reflected in the individual's need to anticipate all possible outcomes, for fear of failing or not achieving.

Eysenck's model   Eysenck (1992) has argued that although Borkovec's model might explain pathological worry, it does not explain normal worry. Eysenck's model attempts to explain both by suggesting that worry or anxiety serves as an 'alarm function' which brings information concerning threat-related stimuli into awareness. In a sense, worry acts as a behaviour that will prepare an individual for future behaviour; it prompts the individual to anticipate future situations and their solutions.

Gray's model   Although older that Eysenck's, Gray's (1982) model suggests a similar mechanism but ties it to neurophysiology and certain brain systems. According to Gray, anxiety is evoked by signals of punishment, lack of reward, novel stimuli and innate fear stimuli. The individual detects such threats by means of a behavioural inhibition system (BIS) which also generates the anxiety. An important function of the BIS is that it helps the organism (Gray's theory applies to humans and other animals) to evaluate the threat-content of a stimulus or event. The neurophysiology of the system is vast and complicated, involving neuroanatomical and neurochemical interaction between a number of brain regions. The BIS, however, is thought to be represented by the septum and hippocampal formation.

Two-factor model   The two-factor model of anxiety suggests that individuals exhibit a vulnerability to anxiety owing to high trait anxiety and poor coping skills. There is a strong correlation between neuroticism and almost all major anxiety disorders (Andrews, 1991; Andrews *et al.*, 1989).

There also seems to be a loss of control exhibited by anxious individuals and anxiety is often preceded by stressful life events (Last *et al.*, 1984), as Borkovec's model also suggests. Individuals with panic disorder and GAD have been found to rate their parents as less caring and overprotective (Silove *et al.*, 1991), indicating perhaps one cause of the perceived lack of control. High trait anxiety individuals have been found to be very similar to clinically anxious patients in terms of their perception that events are out of their control and in terms of parental overprotection (Bennett and Stirling, 1998).

Information-processing models   A number of studies have suggested that individuals high in trait anxiety and those suffering GAD exhibit attentional biases. That is, they are significantly biased towards responding to threat- or anxiety-related material. There are various ways of measuring this attentional bias and three of the most common measures are the dot probe, the emotional Stroop and the interpretation of ambiguous sentences (Eysenck *et al.*, 1991; Wells and Mathews, 1994).

The dot probe task involves the presentation of two words, one above the other, on a computer monitor. Individuals are asked to read aloud the word at the top; this word is either neutral or is an anxiety- or threat-related word. After a short pause, the individual is presented with either another pair of words or a dot where the top or bottom word appeared. The individual has to press a key when such a dot appears. MacLeod and his colleagues (MacLeod *et al.*, 1986; Mathews *et al.*, 1990) have reported that latencies are shorter for anxiety-related words in GAD patients. Similar biases are reported for the emotional Stroop task in which individuals have to read the colour in which a word is written. These words are either neutral or anxiety-related. GAD patients and individuals high in trait anxiety exhibit as bias towards the anxiety-related words, although the effects found with the Stroop are not as robust as those seen in the dot probe (Williams *et al.*, 1996). Finally, anxious individuals have a tendency to interpret ambiguous sentence such as 'The two men watched as the chest was opened' as threatening, that is, they interpret the chest as being a person's torso rather than a large box (Eysenck *et al.*, 1991).

Each model of GAD has something to merit it; that Eysenck's and Gray's model flag anxiety as indicating an alarm system that prepares an individual for future action suggests that anxiety results from excessive monitoring for and detection of threat. The findings from attentional bias studies support this view. Why the anxiety should be produced by this appraisal in some individuals and not others, however, is still unclear. Borkovec's model is useful in that it specifies previous non-reward and frustration as a cause of being unable to achieve goals. Gray's model is useful because it ties this appraisal down to one neuropsychological system.

Treatment

The most common form of treatment for GAD is psychopharmacological. The drugs used to combat anxiety disorder are called anti-anxiety drugs or anxiolytics, and a list of the most common appear in Table 17.4.

Table 17.4   Some of the drugs used to treat anxiety

Substance	Generic name	Example
Benzodiazepines	Alprazolam	Xanax
	Chlordiazepoxide	Librium
	Clonazepam	Klonopin
	Clorazepate	Tranxene
	Diazepam	Valium
	Halazepam	Paxipam
	Lorazepam	Ativan
	Oxazepam	Serax, Zaxopam
	Prazepam	Centrax
Atypical agent	Buspirone	Buspar

Source: Baldessarini, 1996b. Copyright © 1996 The McGraw-Hill Companies.

The anxiolytics include barbiturates, benzodiazepines and antidepressants. Barbiturates are sedatives and include drugs such as Phenobarbital. However, because they are highly toxic and foster dependence, they are not widely used. Benzodiazepines are anticonvulsant and sedative drugs and are the most widely prescribed. Two common benzodiazepines are chlordiazepoxide (Librium) and diazepam (Valium), both of which are low in toxicity.

Panic disorder

Description

Panic has been described as a fear of fear (Foa *et al.*, 1984). Individuals who experience panic are threatened by the presence of the potential presence of fear-related physical states. People with panic disorder suffer from episodic attacks of acute anxiety – periods of acute and unremitting terror that grip them for lengths of time lasting from a few seconds to a few hours. The lifetime prevalence rate for panic disorder is estimated to be about 4 per cent (Katerndahl and Realini, 1993). Panic attacks (without agoraphobia, which is the anxiety disorder we discuss next) are equally likely to appear in men and women (Clarke, 1992). The disorder usually has its onset in young adulthood; it rarely begins after age 35 (Woodruff *et al.*, 1972).

Panic attacks include many physical symptoms, such as shortness of breath, sweating, racing heartbeat (trachycardia), physical tension, cognitive disorganisation, dizziness and fear of loss of support (jelly legs). The individual feels as if he or she is about to collapse and is on the point of death. Such catastrophic thoughts and feelings only exacerbate the physical symptoms and so the individual becomes involved in a self-fulfilling prophecy.

Between panic attacks, people with panic disorder tend to suffer from anticipatory anxiety – a fear of having a panic attack (Ottavani and Beck, 1987). Because attacks can occur without apparent cause, these people anxiously worry about when the next one might strike them. Sometimes, a panic attack that occurs in a particular situation can cause the person to fear that situation. The anxiety we all feel from time to time is significantly different from the intense fear and terror experienced by a person gripped by a panic attack, as the case study below illustrates.

Anxiety: a case study

Juliana B was a 37 year old married woman with two children when she first contacted the psychiatric clinic. Sixteen years previously she had moved from Amsterdam to Australia and now lived in the western suburb of Sydney. At that time, she had strong misgivings about moving because it meant having to leave her mother. The move was quite traumatic and on the ship voyage to Australia, she experienced chronic anxiety.

Shortly after moving, she felt deeply unhappy, especially when thinking about her life changes and leaving her mother. Eighteen months later, she gave birth to her first child. Shortly after that, she received a visit from her mother. A day before her mother's departure, however, she suffered a full-blown panic attack on the way to work. This was intense and unexpected and took the typical form of a panic attack: severe tightness of the chest and rapid heart beat (in fact, she stopped to take her own pulse and counted 30 heart beats in 15 seconds).

One year after the birth of her child, she learned that her mother had suffered a mild heart attack. This triggered of a series of panic attacks in her lasting a week. She would find leaving the house a frightening experience and would travel only 100 yards at most; if her husband was with her, she would travel 500 yards but no more. However, if she drove a car, she could travel longer distances because this gave her a feeling of control.

From this point on her agoraphobia with panic attacks became commonplace, and she experienced two to four attacks per week. These were always unexpected and she began to worry for her own physical safety. In the following year, she took a friend's advice and sought psychiatric help. Initially her therapy was psychodynamic although not Freudian. She would free-associate or would recall her dreams, but whenever she requested information as to the cause of her attacks, her therapist was not forthcoming. When pressed, he suggested that she was experiencing a fear of her sexual urges getting out of control in public. Because these explanations troubled her, she gave up this therapy after ten sessions.

A year later, she consulted another clinician who prescribed an antidepressant and explained her disorder to her in psychopharmacological terms. After a week, she became so intolerant of the drug that she discontinued its use. She then obtained a prescription for a minor tranquilliser from her local GP and has been using it daily since.

Source: Clarke, 1992

Aetiology

Genetic models   There seems to be a hereditary component to panic disorders: the concordance rate for the disorder is higher between identical twins than between fraternal twins (Torgerson, 1983). Almost 30 per cent of the first-degree relatives (parents, children and siblings) of a person with panic disorder also have panic disorder (Crowe *et al.*, 1983). According to Crowe *et al.*, the pattern of panic disorder within a family tree suggests that the disorder is caused by a single, dominant gene.

Panic attacks can be triggered in people with histories of panic disorder by giving them injections of lactic acid (a byproduct of muscular activity) or by having them breathe air containing an elevated amount of carbon dioxide (Woods *et al.*, 1988; Cowley and Arana, 1990). People with family histories of panic attack are more likely to react to sodium lactate, even if they have never had a panic attack previously (Balon *et al.*, 1989). Some researchers believe that what is inherited is a tendency to react with alarm to bodily sensations that would not disturb most other people.

Clark's model　The most comprehensive (and cognitive) model of panic disorder is that proposed by David Clark. Clark (1986, 1988) argues that panic attacks are produced by the catastrophic misinterpretation of bodily events. Slight changes in bodily sensation are interpreted as symptomatic of a physical threat which makes the individual anxious. The more anxious the individual becomes, the more intense the bodily sensations become (the self-fulfilling prophecy referred to above). According to Clark's model, two processes contribute to the maintenance of this misinterpretation. The first is *hypervigilance*: the individual repeatedly checks for changes in bodily sensations; the second is *avoidance strategies*: the individual avoids those behaviours he or she feels will exacerbate the bodily sensations. For example, a person who is afraid that he is about to have a heart attack will avoid exercise (although this prevents the individual from discovering that exercise will not cause a heart attack).

Seligman (1988), however, has argued that the catastrophic misinterpretation theory is questionable on the grounds that the realisation that death will not accompany panic attacks will eventually dawn on these patients. Seligman suggests an alternative suggestion based on evolutionary preparedness, the notion that we are evolutionarily predisposed to respond in a specific way to some stimuli because it is to our advantage to do so (Seligman, 1971). Panic, in this context, is the individual's response to biologically prepared bodily sensations.

However, as Power and Dalgleish (1997) argue, the failure to realise that death does not follow bodily sensations arises because individuals avoid situations and stimuli that would induce such bodily sensations in the first place. Seligman's formulation may not, therefore, be necessary (for the reason he suggests).

Interestingly, some patients maintain that they do not misinterpret their bodily sensations catastrophically and some are more difficult to convince that these sensations will not lead to death (McNally, 1990). These findings point to a degree of variation in panic disorder patients. The anxiety sensitivity hypothesis (Reiss and McNally, 1985), for example, suggests that some individuals are more anxiety-sensitive than others. The degree of sensitivity depends on pre-existing beliefs about the harmfulness of bodily sensations. These pre-existing beliefs predispose the individual to interpret bodily events negatively and erroneously. This leads to panic.

Treatment

Treatment for panic disorder can be both cognitive behavioural or pharmacological. Cognitive behaviour therapy, for example, is effective at reducing panic attacks. Such therapy would involve breathing and relaxation techniques, cognitive restructuring (altering misconceptions about the consequences of bodily sensations) and eliciting bodily sensations in the individual to demonstrate the non-harmful nature of such changes (Craske *et al.*, 1997).

Antidepressants and anxiolytics are sometimes used to treat panic attacks with some success. Some individuals react badly to the drugs, however, and while they treat the anxiety generated during panic, they do not address the core problem of catastrophic misinterpretation.

Phobic disorders

Phobias – named after the Greek god Phobos, who frightened his enemies – are irrational fears of specific objects or situations. Because phobias can be highly specific, clinicians have coined a variety of inventive names, some of which are summarised in Table 17.5.

Table 17.5　Name and descriptions of some common phobias

Name	Object or situation feared
Acrophobia	Heights
Agoraphobia	Open spaces
Ailurophobia	Cats
Algophobia	Pain
Astraphobia	Storms, thunder, lightning
Belonophobia	Needles
Claustrophobia	Enclosed spaces
Hematophobia	Blood
Monophobia	Being alone
Mysophobia	Contamination or germs
Nyctophobia	Darkness
Ochlophobia	Crowds
Pathophobia	Disease
Pyrophobia	Fire
Siderophobia	Railways
Syphilophobia	Syphilis
Taphophobia	Being buried alive
Triskaidekaphobia	Thirteen
Zoophobia	Animals, or a specific animal

Most individuals have one or more irrational fears of specific objects or situations, and it is difficult to draw a line between these fears and phobic disorders. If someone is afraid of spiders but manages to lead a normal life by avoiding them, it would seem inappropriate to say that the person has a mental disorder. Similarly, many otherwise normal people are afraid of speaking in public. The term phobic disorder should be reserved for people whose fear makes their life difficult. The DSM-IV recognises three types of phobic disorder: agoraphobia, social phobia and simple phobia.

Agoraphobia

Agoraphobia (*agora* means 'marketplace' in Ancient Greek) is a fear of open spaces and is the most serious and common of the phobic disorders. It occurs in between 50 and 80 per cent of phobic disorders (Mathews *et al.*, 1981). It is reported three times as often in women as in men. Onset is sudden and individuals are usually in their early twenties (Clarke, 1992). The term was coined by Westphal in 1871 to describe four (male) cases who feared open spaces.

Most cases of agoraphobia are considered to be caused by panic attacks and are classified with them. Agoraphobia associated with panic attacks is defined as a fear of 'being in places or situations from which escape might be difficult (or embarrassing) or in which help might not be available in the event of a panic attack. … As a result of this fear, the person either restricts travel or needs a companion when away from home' (DSM-IV, 1994). Agoraphobia can be severely disabling. Some people with this disorder have stayed inside their house for years, afraid to venture outside. Supermarkets and queuing are especially anxiety-provoking for agoraphobics. Features of supermarket layout such as stairways and diminished access, for example, are regarded as anxiety-provoking by agoraphobic individuals (Jones *et al.*, 1996).

Social phobia

Social phobia is an exaggerated 'fear of one or more situations … in which the person is exposed to possible scrutiny by others and fears that he or she may do something or act in a way that will be humiliating or embarrassing' (DSM-IV). Most people with social phobia are only mildly impaired, but the situations in which they can operate may be severely curtailed. Social phobics, like patients with GAD, seem to bias their attention towards threat-related stimuli (Rapee and Heimberg, 1997). At the core of the disorder seems to be conflict regarding the internal representation of their appearance and external indicators which evaluate them negatively. Rapee and Heimberg, therefore, proposed that socially phobic individuals allocate excessive attentional resources towards mental representations of

how they are perceived by their audience. In a study in which high and low anxious social phobic individuals gave a five minute speech in front of an audience that was behaving positively (smiling) or negatively (frowning), Veljaca and Rapee (1998) found that highly anxious individuals were better at detecting negative audience behaviours whereas the low anxiety individuals were better at detecting the positive behaviours.

Specific phobia

Specific phobia includes all other phobias, such as fear of snakes, darkness or heights. These phobias are often caused by a specific traumatic experience and are the easiest of all types of phobia to treat. The Epidemiological Catchment Area (ECA) Study found that insects, mice, snakes and bats were the more frequently cited feared/disgust-provoking stimuli (Robins and Regier, 1994). Animals are a common phobia. Davey (1992), for example, reported that one-third of women and one-quarter of men reported having a spider phobia.

The lifetime prevalence rate for simple phobia is estimated to be about 14 per cent for women and about 8 per cent for men (Robins and Regier, 1991), but approximately one-third of the population sometimes exhibit phobic symptoms (Goodwin and Guze, 1984).

Aetiology

Animal phobias are sometimes surprising because in Europe, for example, there are no indigenous lethally poisonous spiders, although spider phobias are common. One explanation for this anomaly is that we fear animals that have potentially lethal consequences; we are, therefore, predisposed to fear them. This is the preparedness hypothesis (Seligman, 1971) which we encountered in the section on panic disorder. Evidence for this hypothesis comes in the form of the deliberate conditioning of fear of spiders. These conditioning experiences are the most difficult to extinguish – more difficult than non-threatening stimuli (Ohman *et al.*, 1985; McNally, 1987).

However, Seligman's theory has its problems. For example, if we are adaptively predisposed to fear the stimuli producing simple phobia, what adaptive purpose does a fear of snails, moths and slugs serve? As McNally (1995) points out, we can ascribe adaptive significance to a fear of any object if we are creative enough. One theory suggests that phobia develops from a pairing of a phobic object with an aversive stimulus so that phobic stimuli become phobic by association. However, only 40–50 per cent of animal phobias appear to be accounted for in this way. Davey (1992) also reported that only 8 out of 118 spider phobics recalls having a traumatic experience with spiders.

Matchett and Davey (1991) suggest an alternative explanation: that some stimuli become the object of phobia because of our inherent fear of contamination or disease. Animals (such as spiders, slugs, cockroaches) become feared because they are disgusting and we would reject them as food on the basis of this disgust (although some individuals would be immune to such disgust responses; snails are considered a delicacy in certain parts of Europe). In fact, sensitivity to disgust may be an important determinant of the level of fear (Webb and Davey, 1993).

To investigate whether some animal phobias were disgust- or fear-related, Davey *et al.* (1998) conducted a cross-cultural study of phobia in seven countries. An analysis of the data suggested that phobic stimuli could be divided into one of three categories: fear-irrelevant (for example, chicken, hamster, cow), fear-relevant (for example, lion, bear, alligator) and disgust-relevant (for example, cockroach, spider, maggot, worm). Disgust was consistent across cultures (although there were some cross-cultural differences with Indian respondents reporting lower levels of fear to the disgust stimuli and Japanese respondents showing higher levels of fear). This finding suggests that not all stimuli may be feared for the same reasons (perhaps the term 'simple phobia' is too simplistic, as Curtis *et al.*, 1998 suggest).

Treatment

Phobias are sometimes treated by systematic desensitisation (described in the general section on treatment) or modelling. Bandura (1971), for example, has described a modelling session with people who had a phobic fear of snakes. The therapist himself performed the fearless behaviour at each step and gradually led participants into touching, stroking and then holding the snake's body with gloved and bare hands while the experimenter held the snake securely by head and tail. If a participant was unable to touch the snake following ample demonstration, she was asked to place her hand on the experimenter's and to move her hand down gradually until it touched the snake's body. After participants no longer felt any apprehension about touching the snake under these secure conditions, anxieties about contact with the snake's head area and entwining tail were extinguished. The therapist again performed the tasks fearlessly, and then he and the participant performed the responses jointly. As participants became less fearful, the experimenter gradually reduced his participation and control over the snake, until eventually participants were able to hold the snake in their lap without assistance, to let the snake loose in the room and retrieve it, and to let it crawl freely over their body. Progress through the graded approach tasks was paced according to the participants' apprehensiveness. When they reported being able to perform one activity with little or no fear, they were eased into a more difficult interaction.

This treatment eliminated fear of snakes in 92 per cent of those who participated. Modelling is successful for several

reasons. Participants learn to make new responses by imitating those of the therapist and their behaviour in doing so is reinforced. When they observe a confident person approaching and touching a feared object without showing any signs of emotional distress, they probably experience a vicarious extinction of their own emotional responses. In fact, Bandura (1971) reports that 'having successfully overcome a phobia that had plagued them for most of their lives, subjects reported increased confidence that they could cope effectively with other fear-provoking events' (p. 684), including encounters with other people.

Cognitive behaviour therapy has also been applied to agoraphobia (Ost *et al.*, 1993). In an experiment in which the effect of exposure (graded exposure to the phobic stimuli) was compared with exposure and CBT (combating negative thoughts and dysfunctional attitudes), Burke *et al.* (1997) found no difference in the effectiveness of the two therapies at six months following the therapy: both were equally effective. Similar combinations have also been found to be effective for social phobia (Scholing and Emmelkamp, 1996).

Post-traumatic stress disorder (PTSD)

Description

Post-traumatic stress disorder (PTSD) is a relatively new anxiety disorder (it made its first appearance in DSM-III in 1980) and refers to anxiety that follows a traumatic event. This event poses a threat to the individual's life or lives of others. Symptoms of the disorder include the re-experiencing of feelings related to the event (such as intrusive memories, thoughts and images related to the event), avoidant behaviour (such as denial and emotional numbing) and arousal (such as hypervigilance for trauma-related information). Sadness, guilt and anger are also associated with the disorder (Shore *et al.*, 1989). These latter symptoms are important because PTSD seldom appears alone but with other disorders or additional diagnoses (McFarlane, 1992; Bleich *et al.*, 1997).

The prevalence rate is around 25–30 per cent in the general population and rape is associated with the greatest prevalence (Green, 1994). Other events which can produce PTSD are traffic accidents in children (Stallard *et al.*, 1998), bank robberies (Kamphuis and Emmelkamp, 1998), war (Fontana and Rosenheck, 1993) and natural or human-made disasters (Freedy *et al.*, 1994). Onset of the disorder may be delayed by many years (Blank, 1993). As with GAD and panic disorder, there is a greater Stroop interference for words related to the trauma (Thrasher *et al.*, 1994).

One relatively recent, famous example of PTSD was that provoked by the *Herald of Free Enterprise* disaster. In March 1987, the roll-on, roll-off ferry, the *Herald of Free Enterprise* capsised on its way from Zeebrugge harbour in Belgium. Of the 600 passengers on board, almost 200 died in the disaster (Joseph *et al.*, 1997). Joseph and his colleagues have made a detailed study of the reactions of the survivors and have monitored closely any PTSD reaction to the disaster. For example, an early study (Joseph *et al.*, 1994) found that although crisis support was a good predictor of psychological well-being of survivors after the disaster, feelings of helplessness during the disaster, and bereavement, predicted the frequency of intrusive thoughts about the disaster. A recently reported study used survivors' attitudes towards emotional expression three years after the accident to predict symptoms of PTSD five years after the disaster (Joseph *et al.*, 1997). The researchers found that more negative attitudes towards expressing emotion (for example, agreeing with statements such as, 'I think getting emotional is a sign of weakness') were associated with increased number of PTSD symptoms.

Aetiology

Horowitz's model   Horowitz's (1979, 1986) model suggests that trauma-related information is processed because of a mechanism called *completion tendency*. Completion tendency refers to the need for new information to be integrated into existing patterns of thought and memory. Power and Dalgleish (1997) describe how there is first a stunned reaction to the traumatic event and then the experience of information overload as the individual realises the enormity of the trauma as it 'sinks in'. Such information cannot be accommodated by existing mental schemata, and defence mechanisms such as denial and numbing are a means of coping with this lack of accommodation. Completion tendency, however, insists on keeping the memory of the event alive (in fact, Horowitz calls this 'active memory') through flashbacks and nightmares. The anxiety results from the vacillation between these two processes: defence mechanisms and completion tendency.

Although an honourable attempt at explaining PTSD, Power and Dalgleish (1997) query whether the model explains some features of the disorder. Why do only some individuals develop PTSD, for example? And why is PTSD delayed in some individuals?

Janoff-Bulman's cognitive appraisal theory   An alternative model suggests that in PTSD the individual's beliefs about the world have been shattered. According to the model, the individual is assumed to view him or herself as personally invulnerable, that the world is meaningful and comprehensible and that he or she views him or herself positively (Janoff-Bulman, 1989, 1992). These assumptions provide the bedrock of our life and give it structure. This structure is shattered after the traumatic event which gives rise to PTSD. The process by which this structure breakdown occurs, however, is not explained by the model.

Treatment

Various forms of treatment have been attempted with PTSD with varying success (Shalev *et al.*, 1996; Foa and Meadows, 1997). Debriefing appears to be ineffective (Deahl *et al.*, 1994) but drug treatment meets with mixed success (O'Brien and Nutt, 1998). Treatment based on exposure seems to be effective (Foa and Meadows, 1997).

Obsessive-compulsive disorder

Description

Individuals with obsessive-compulsive disorder (OCD) suffer from obsessions – thoughts that will not leave them – and compulsions – behaviours that they cannot keep from performing. In one study, impaired control of mental activities, checking, urges involving loss of motor control, and feeling contaminated were found to be the major classes of obsession and compulsion among a large sample of American college students (Sternberger and Burns, 1990). The lifetime prevalence rate is estimated to be about 2.5 per cent (Robins and Regier, 1991; Bebbington, 1998). OCD sufferers seem to show deficits in memory, especially in recognition memory (Tallis *et al.*, 1999).

Unlike people with panic disorder, people with obsessive-compulsive disorder have a defence against anxiety – their compulsive behaviour. Unfortunately, the need to perform this compulsive behaviour often becomes more and more demanding of their time until it interferes with their career and daily life. Obsessions are seen in many mental disorders, including schizophrenia. However, unlike persons with schizophrenia, people with obsessive-compulsive disorder recognise that their thoughts and behaviours are senseless and wish that they would go away. The types of obsession and compulsion seen in these individuals are summarised in Table 17.6.

Consider the case of Sergei, a 17 year old ex-student:

'Only a year ago, Sergei seemed to be a normal adolescent with many talents and interests. Then, almost overnight he was transformed into a lonely outsider, excluded from social life by his psychological disabilities. Specifically, he was unable to stop washing. Haunted by the notion that he was dirty – in spite of the contrary evidence of the senses – he began to spend more and more of his time cleansing himself of imaginary dirt. At first his ritual ablutions were confined to weekends and evenings and he was able to stay in school while keeping them up, but soon they began to consume all his time, forcing him to drop out of school, a victim of his inability to feel clean enough.' (Rapoport, 1989, p. 63)

Women are slightly more likely than men to have this diagnosis. Like panic disorder, obsessive-compulsive disorder most commonly begins in young adulthood (Robbins *et al.*, 1984). People with this disorder are unlikely to

Table 17.6   The number and percentage of obsessive and compulsive symptoms reported by 70 children and adolescents diagnosed with obsessive-compulsive disorder

	Reported symptom at initial interview	
Obsessions	*Number*	*%*
Concern with dirt, germs or environmental toxins	28	40
Something terrible happening (fire, death or illness of self or loved one)	17	24
Symmetry, order or exactness	12	17
Scrupulosity (religious obsessions)	9	13
Concern or disgust with bodily wastes or secretions (urine, stool, saliva)	6	8
Luck or unlucky numbers	6	8
Forbidden, aggressive or perverse sexual thoughts, images or impulses	3	4
Fear might harm others or oneself	3	4
Concern with household items	2	3
Intrusive nonsense sounds, words or music	1	1
Compulsions	*Number*	*%*
Excessive or ritualised handwashing, showering, bathing, toothbrushing or grooming	60	85
Repeating rituals (going in or out of a door, up or down from a chair)	36	51
Checking (doors, locks, cooker, appliances, emergency brake on car, homework)	32	46
Rituals to remove contact with contaminants	16	23
Touching	14	20
Measures to prevent harm to self or others	11	16
Ordering or arranging	12	17
Counting	13	18
Hoarding or collecting rituals	8	11
Rituals of cleaning household or inanimate objects	4	6
Miscellaneous rituals (such as writing, moving, speaking)	18	26

Source: From 'The Biology of Obsessions and Compulsions' by Judith L. Rapoport, *Scientific American*, March 1989, international edition, p. 63. Reprinted with permission. Copyright © 1989 by Scientific American, Inc. All rights reserved.

marry, perhaps because of the common obsessional fear of dirt and contamination or because the shame associated with the rituals they are compelled to perform causes them to avoid social contact (Turner *et al.*, 1985).

There are two principal kinds of obsession: obsessive doubt or uncertainty, and obsessive fear of doing something prohibited (Salkovskis *et al.*, 1998). Uncertainties, both trivial and important, preoccupy some people with obsessive-compulsive disorder almost completely. Others are plagued with the fear that they will do something

terrible – swear aloud in church, urinate in someone's living room, kill themselves or a loved one, or jump off a bridge – although they seldom actually do anything antisocial. And even though they are often obsessed with thoughts of killing themselves, fewer than 1 per cent of them actually attempt suicide.

Most compulsions fall into one of four categories: counting, checking, cleaning and avoidance. For example, people might repeatedly check burners on the stove to see that they are off and windows and doors to be sure that they are locked. Some people wash their hands hundreds of times a day, even when they become covered with painful sores. Other people meticulously clean their homes or endlessly wash, dry and fold their clothes. Some become afraid to leave home because they fear contamination and refuse to touch other members of their families. If they do accidentally become 'contaminated', they usually have lengthy purification rituals.

Aetiology

Several possible causes have been suggested for obsessive-compulsive disorder. Unlike simple anxiety states, this disorder can be understood in terms of defence mechanisms. Some cognitive investigators have suggested that obsessions serve as devices to occupy the mind and displace painful thoughts.

Infallibility model   Cognitive researchers also point out that persons with obsessive-compulsive disorder believe that they should be competent at all times, avoid any kind of criticism at all costs, and worry about being punished by others for behaviour that is less than perfect (Sarason and Sarason, 1993). Thus, one reason people who have obsessive-compulsive disorder may engage in checking behaviour is to reduce the anxiety caused by fear of being perceived by others as incompetent or to avoid others' criticism that they have done something less than perfectly.

If painful, anxiety-producing thoughts become frequent, and if turning to alternative patterns of thought reduces anxiety, then the principle of reinforcement predicts that the person will turn to these patterns more frequently. Just as an animal learns to jump a hurdle to escape a painful foot shock, a person can learn to think about a 'safe topic' in order to avoid painful thoughts. If the habit becomes firmly established, the obsessive thoughts may persist even when the original reason for turning to them – the situation that produced the anxiety-arousing thoughts – no longer exists. A habit can thus outlast its original causes.

Genetic model   Family studies have found that OCD is associated with a neurological disorder called Gilles de la Tourette's syndrome, which appears during childhood (Janowic, 1993). Gilles de la Tourette's syndrome is characterised by muscular and vocal tics, including making facial grimaces, squatting, pacing, twirling, barking, sniffing, coughing, grunting or repeating specific words (especially vulgarities). It is not clear why some people with the faulty gene develop Gilles de la Tourette's syndrome early in childhood and others develop obsessive-compulsive disorder later in life.

Not all cases of obsessive-compulsive disorder have a genetic origin. The disorder sometimes occurs after brain damage caused by various means, such as birth trauma, encephalitis and head trauma (Hollander *et al.*, 1990).

Treatment

There are usually two forms of treatment employed in OCD. The first is behaviour therapy in which the individual may be exposed to the object, situation or event that provokes the ritualistic behaviour (Emmelkamp, 1993). One example may be to deliberately dirty the hands of an individual who ritualistically washes his or her hands twenty or thirty times a day and not allow him or her to wash them (Rapoport, 1989). This type of therapy has met with some success in serious cases of OCD. However, behavioural treatment appears to be more successful at eliminating compulsive than obsessive behaviour (Emmelkamp, 1993).

The second type of treatment, psychopharmacology, appears to eliminate both successfully. These drugs are two serotonin-specific reuptake inhibitors (which are described in more detail in the section on depression below) and act by increasing the amount of the neurotransmitter, serotonin, in the brain.

Somatoform disorders

The primary symptoms of somatoform disorder are a bodily or physical (*soma* means 'body') problem for which there is no physiological basis. The two most important somatoform disorders are somatisation disorder and conversion disorder.

Somatisation disorder

Description

Somatisation disorder occurs mostly among women and involves complaints of wide-ranging physical ailments for which there is no apparent biological basis. This disorder used to be called hysteria. The older term derives from the Greek word *hysteria*, meaning 'uterus', because of the ancient belief that various emotional and physical ailments in women could be caused by the uterus wandering around inside the body, searching for a baby.

It is true that somatisation disorder is seen almost exclusively in women; however, modern use of the term 'hysteria' does not imply any gynaecological problems. Moreover, this disorder is rare even among women: Regier *et al.* (1988) found that the incidence of somatisation disorder in a sample of over 18,000 people was less than 1 per cent in women and non-existent in men. Somatisation disorder is often chronic, lasting for decades.

Somatisation disorder is characterised by complaints of symptoms for which no physiological cause can be found. Obviously, a proper diagnosis can be made only after medical examination and laboratory tests indicate the lack of disease. DSM-IV requires that the person have a history of complaining of physical symptoms for several years. The complaints must include at least thirteen symptoms from a list of thirty-five, which fall into the following categories: gastrointestinal symptoms, pain symptoms, cardiopulmonary symptoms, pseudoneurological symptoms, sexual symptoms, and female reproductive symptoms. These symptoms must also have led the person to take medication, see a physician, or substantially alter her life. Almost every woman who receives the diagnosis of somatisation disorder reports that she does not experience pleasure from sexual intercourse. Obviously, everyone has one or more physical symptoms from time to time that cannot be explained through a medical examination, but few people chronically complain of at least thirteen of them. Although people with somatisation disorder often attempt suicide, they rarely kill themselves.

Somatisation disorder resembles another somatoform disorder, **hypochondriasis** (*hypochondria* means 'under the cartilage'; the ancients believed that the disorder occurred when black bile collected in the upper abdomen, under the cartilage of the breastbone), the persistent and excessive worry about developing a serious illness. Unlike people with somatisation disorder, who complain of specific physical symptoms, hypochondriacs demonstrate an excessive fear of illness. They interpret minor physical sensations as indications that they may have a serious disease. They spend a lot of time in doctors' surgeries and in hospitals.

Aetiology

Somatisation disorder is most common in poorly educated women of low socioeconomic status (Guze *et al.*, 1971). The disorder also runs in families. Coryell (1980) found that approximately 20 per cent of first-degree female relatives of people with somatisation disorder also had the disorder. In addition, many studies have shown that somatisation disorder is closely associated with antisocial personality disorder. First-degree male relatives of women with somatisation disorder have an increased incidence of alcoholism or antisocial behaviour, and first-degree female relatives of convicted male criminals have an increased incidence of somatisation disorder (Guze *et al.*, 1967; Woerner and Guze, 1968). These findings suggest that a particular environmental or genetic history leads to different pathological manifestations in men and women.

Conversion disorder

Description

Conversion disorder is characterised by physical complaints that resemble neurological disorders but have no underlying organic pathological basis. The symptoms include blindness, deafness, loss of feeling, and paralysis. According to the DSM-IV, a conversion disorder must have some apparent psychological reason for the symptoms; the symptoms must occur in response to an environmental stimulus that produces a psychological conflict, or they must permit the person to avoid an unpleasant activity or to receive support and sympathy. Unlike somatisation disorder, conversion disorder can afflict both men and women.

The term 'conversion', when applied to a mental disorder, derives from psychoanalytical theory, which states that the energy of an unresolved intrapsychic conflict is converted into a physical symptom. Hofling (1963) described one such case:

'The patient had taken the day off from work to be at home with his wife and [newborn] baby. During the afternoon, he had felt somewhat nervous and tense, but had passed off these feelings as normal for a new father. …

… The baby awoke and cried. Mrs. L. said that she would nurse him. … As she put the baby to her breast, the patient became aware of a smarting sensation in his eyes. He had been smoking heavily and attributed the irritation to the room's being filled with smoke. He got up and opened a window. When the smarting sensation became worse he went to the washstand and applied a cold cloth to his eyes. On removing the cloth, he found that he was completely blind. … Psychotherapy was instituted. … The visual symptoms disappeared rather promptly, with only very mild and fleeting exacerbations during the next several months. …

… He had been jealous of the baby – this was a difficult admission to make – and jealous on two distinct counts. One feeling was, in essence, a sexual jealousy, accentuated by his own sexual deprivation during the last weeks of the pregnancy. The other was … a jealousy of the maternal solicitude shown the infant by its mother.' (pp. 315–16)

Although the sensory deficits or paralyses of people with conversion disorders are not caused by damage to the nervous system, these people are not faking their illnesses. People who deliberately pretend they are sick in order to gain some advantage (such as avoiding work) are said to be malingering. Malingering is not defined as a mental disorder by the DSM-IV. Although it is not always easy to distinguish malingering from a conversion disorder, two criteria are useful. First, people with conversion disorders are usually delighted to talk about their symptoms in great detail, whereas malingerers are reluctant to do so for fear of having their deception discovered. Second, people with conversion disorders usually describe the symptoms with great drama and flair but do not appear to be upset about them.

Somatisation disorder consists of complaints of medical problems, but the examining physician is unable to see any signs that would indicate physical illness. In contrast, a patient with conversion disorder gives the appearance of having a neurological disorder such as blindness or paralysis. Psychophysiological disorders (also called psychosomatic disorders) are not the result of fictitious or imaginary symptoms; they are real, organic illnesses caused or made worse by psychological factors. For example, stress can cause gastric ulcers, asthma or other physical symptoms; ulcers caused by stress are real, not imaginary. Successful therapy would thus require reduction of the person's level of stress as well as surgical or medical treatment of the lesions in the stomach.

John Marshall and his colleagues recently reported the results of the first brain imaging study of a patient with conversion disorder (Marshall *et al.*, 1997). The female patient reported left-sided paralysis, with no organic or structural cause. Marshall and his colleagues found that when the patient prepared to move her 'paralysed' leg and her good leg, the typical motor areas of the cortex were activated. However, when the patient was required to move her 'paralysed' leg, the expected activation of the right motor cortex did not occur. Instead, areas including the right orbitofrontal cortex and anterior cingulate were activated, suggesting to the researchers that these regions were associated with inhibition of the movement in the left leg.

Aetiology

Psychoanalytical theory suggests that the psychic energy of unresolved conflicts (especially those involving sexual desires the patient is unwilling or unable to admit to having) becomes displaced into physical symptoms. In other words, psychoanalysts regard conversion disorders as primarily sexual in origin.

In contrast, behaviour analysts have suggested that conversion disorders can be learned for many reasons. This assertion gains support from the finding that people with these disorders usually suffer from physical symptoms of diseases with which they are already familiar (Ullman and Krasner, 1969). A patient often mimics the symptoms of a friend. Furthermore, the patient must receive some kind of reinforcement for having the disability; he or she must derive some benefit from it.

Treatment

Early treatment of somatoform disorders had concentrated on allowing the patient to explore past or previous traumas, although there was no evidence that this helped to treat the disorder. A method that seems to meet with some success is behaviour therapy. This may be especially relevant to those experiencing pain or sickness. The treatment involves not rewarding those behaviours which reinforce expressions of illness and pain, and rewarding ways of adapting to life and coping with it.

Dissociative disorders

In somatoform disorders, anxiety is avoided by the appearance of the symptoms of serious physical disorders. In dissociative disorders, anxiety is reduced by a sudden disruption in consciousness, which in turn produces changes in one's sense of identity.

Description

Like conversion disorder, the term 'dissociative disorder' comes from Freud. According to psychoanalytical theory, a person develops a dissociative disorder when a massive repression fails to keep a strong sexual desire from consciousness. As a result, the person resorts to dissociating one part of his or her mind from the rest.

The most common dissociative disorder is psychogenic amnesia, in which a person 'forgets' all his or her past life, along with the conflicts that were present, and begins a new one. The term 'psychogenic' means 'produced by the mind'. Because amnesia can also be produced by physical means – such as epilepsy, drug or alcohol intoxication, and brain damage – clinicians must be careful to distinguish between amnesias of organic and psychogenic origin.

A psychogenic fugue is a special form of amnesia in which a person deliberately leaves home and starts a new life elsewhere (fugue means 'flight'). Consider the following example:

'Burt Tate was questioned by the police following an argument he had had with a customer in the diner where he worked as a short order cook. He had no identification, could not recall where he had lived prior to his arrival in town several weeks earlier, and could not describe his previous job. However, he did know the name of the town in which he now lived and the date. The police later identified Burt Tate as Gene Smith, who had been reported as a missing person in a city 200 miles away about a month earlier. He was identified positively by his wife, although he did not recognise her. His wife explained that he had been experiencing problems at work (as a manager in a manufacturing company), including being overlooked for a promotion, and that 2 days before his disappearance he had an argument with his son who referred to him as a "failure."' (Spitzer *et al.*, 1981, pp. 100-1)

Dissociative identity disorder is a very rare, but very striking, dissociative disorder that is marked by the presence of two or more separate personalities within the individual, either of which may be dominant at any given time. Only about one hundred cases of dissociative identity disorder have been documented, and some investigators believe that many, if not most of them, are simulations, not actual mental disorders.

An interesting example of dissociative identity disorder is the case of Billy Milligan as told in the book *The Minds of Billy Milligan* (Keyes, 1981). Milligan was accused of rape and kidnapping but was deemed not guilty by reason of insanity. His psychiatric examination showed him to have twenty-four different personalities. Two were women and one was a young girl. There was a Briton, an Australian and a Yugoslavian. One woman, a lesbian, was a poet, while the Yugoslav was an expert on weapons and munitions and the Briton and Australian were minor criminals.

Dissociative identity disorder has received much attention; people find it fascinating to contemplate several different personalities, most of whom are unaware of each other, existing within the same individual. Bliss (1980) suggests that dissociative identity disorder is a form of self-hypnosis, established early in life that is motivated by painful experiences. In fact, the overwhelming majority of people diagnosed as having multiple personality disorder report having been physically abused when they were a child (Kluft, 1984).

As we saw in Chapter 9, some psychologists believe that hypnosis is not a state but, rather, a form of social role playing. The same has been said for dissociative identity disorder. Spanos *et al.* (1985) found that when normal subjects were given appropriate instructions, they could easily simulate two different personalities. They adopted a new name for the new personality, and they gave different patterns of answers on a personality test when the second personality was 'in control'. Although people are often impressed by the remarkable differences between the various personalities of someone with dissociative identity disorder, the acting required for this task is within the ability of most people. That is not to say that everyone with multiple personality disorder is faking, but the results of research do suggest that such patients be approached with scepticism.

Aetiology

Dissociative disorders are usually explained as responses to severe conflicts resulting from intolerable impulses or as responses to guilt stemming from an actual misdeed. Partly because they are rare, dissociative disorders are among the least understood of the mental disorders. In general, the dissociation is advantageous to the person. Amnesia enables the person to forget about a painful or unpleasant life. A person with fugue not only forgets but also leaves the area to start a new existence. And a dissociative identity disorder allow a person to do things that he or she would really like to do but cannot because of the strong guilt feelings that would ensue. The alternative personality can be one with a very weak conscience.

Treatment

Like early treatment for the somatoform disorders, early treatment for the dissociative disorders involved the patient recounting past and present traumas. It is assumed that the disorder arises from a failure to accept these traumas and the pain they caused. Acknowledging and expressing the trauma, therefore, is a means of accepting it and avoiding the need to dissociate (Oltmans and Emery, 1998). There is little evidence to suggest that the treatment is successful. Anti-anxiety drugs may also be prescribed to alleviate the patients' distress.

Questions to think about

Anxiety, somatoform disorders and dissociative disorders

- What separates anxiety disorders from general worrying?
- Are anxiety disorders best viewed as a continuum from 'not anxious' to 'clinically anxious' or is normal anxiety completely different from clinical anxiety?
- Clark's model suggests that individuals with panic disorder catastrophically misinterpret bodily symptoms. Is there evidence for this?
- Some disorders co-exist with other disorders. How can clinicians make the appropriate diagnosis? Is this possible?
- Why are cognitive behavioural treatments for obsessive-compulsive disorder effective at tackling compulsions but not obsessions?
- Is post-traumatic stress disorder a distinct disorder or a label given to a disorder that represents anxiety provoked by events or stimuli?
- What evidence is there to suggest that phobias are the result of biological predispositions to avoid certain stimuli?

Personality disorders

The DSM-IV classifies abnormalities in behaviour that impair social or occupational functioning as personality disorders. There are several types of personality disorders which DSM-IV has grouped into three clusters. Cluster A, for example, refers to the 'eccentric cluster' of schizotypal and paranoid personality disorder; Cluster B (the dramatic cluster) includes the narcissistic and antisocial personality disorders; and Cluster C (the anxious cluster) includes avoidant and dependent personality disorders (Van Velzen and Emmelkamp, 1996). Another general cluster accounts for other personality disorders not covered by these clusters. Because there are so many personality disorders, this chapter will focus on just one in depth: antisocial personality disorder. Table 17.7 provides a description of the several other personality disorders.

Antisocial personality disorder

Antisocial personality disorder refers to a failure to conform to standards of decency, repeated lying and stealing, a failure to sustain long-lasting and loving relationships, low tolerance of boredom and a complete lack of guilt. Prichard (1835) used the term moral insanity to describe people whose intellect was normal but in whom the 'moral and active principles of the mind are strongly perverted and depraved … and the individual is found to be

Table 17.7   Descriptions of various personality disorders

Personality disorder	Description
Paranoid	Suspiciousness and extreme mistrust of others; enhanced perception of being under attack by others
Schizoid	Difficulty in social functioning – poor ability and little desire to become attached to others
Schizotypal	Unusual thought patterns and perceptions; poor communication and social skills
Histrionic	Attention-seeking; preoccupation with personal attractiveness; prone to anger when attempts at attracting attention fail
Narcissistic	Self-promoting; lack of empathy for others; attention seeking; grandiosity
Borderline	Lack of impulse control; drastic mood swings; inappropriate anger; becomes bored easily and for prolonged periods; suicidal
Avoidant	Oversensitivity to rejection; little confidence in initiating or maintaining social relationships
Dependent	Uncomfortable being alone or in terminating relationships; places others' needs above one's own in order to preserve the relationship; indecisive
Obsessive-compulsive	Preoccupation with rules and order; tendency towards perfectionism; difficulty relaxing or enjoying life
Passive-aggressive	Negative attitudes; negativity is expressed through passive means: complaining, expressing envy and resentment towards others who are more fortunate
Depressive	Pervasive depressive cognitions and self-criticism; persistent unhappiness; feelings of guilt and inadequacy

Note: The antisocial personality disorder, not listed here, is described in detail in the text.

Source: adapted from Carson *et al.*, 1996, p. 317

incapable ... of conducting himself with decency and propriety.' Koch (1889) introduced the term 'psychopathic inferiority', which soon became simply psychopathy; a person who displayed the disorder was called a psychopath. The first version of the DSM (the DSM-I) used the term 'sociopathic personality disturbance', which was subsequently replaced by the present term, 'antisocial personality disorder'. Most clinicians still refer to such people as psychopaths or sociopaths.

Description

People with antisocial personality disorder cause a considerable amount of distress in society. Many criminals can be diagnosed as psychopaths, and most psychopaths have a record of criminal behaviour. The offending psychopath commits more offences than the average criminal (Hare, 1981; Kosson *et al.*, 1990) and is significantly more violent. Hare and McPherson (1984) report that psychopaths are convicted of three and a half times more violent crime than are non-psychopathic criminals. Because of data such as these, psychologists have made attempts to identify the chronic psychopathic offender early on in life. However, these studies have met with mixed success (Lynam, 1996; Raine *et al.*, 1996).

The diagnostic criteria of the DSM-IV include evidence of at least three types of antisocial behaviour before age 15 and at least four after age 18. The adult forms of antisocial behaviour include inability to sustain consistent work behaviour; lack of ability to function as a responsible parent; repeated criminal activity, such as theft, pimping or prostitution; inability to maintain enduring attachment to a sexual partner; irritability and aggressiveness, including fights or assault; failure to honour financial obligations; impulsiveness and failure to plan ahead; habitual lying or use of aliases; and consistently reckless or drunken driving. In addition to meeting at least four of these criteria, the person must have displayed a 'pattern of continuous antisocial behaviour in which the rights of others are violated, with no intervening period of at least five years without antisocial behaviour'. The lifetime prevalence rate for antisocial personality disorder is estimated to be about 3.5 per cent (Robins and Regier, 1994), although estimates of prevalence reported in the DSM-IV are lower: about 3 per cent for men and less than 1 per cent for women.

Cleckley (1976), one of the most prominent experts on psychopathy, has listed sixteen characteristics of antisocial personality disorder, seen in Table 17.8. Cleckley's list of features provides a good picture of what most psychopaths

Table 17.8 Cleckley's primary characteristics of antisocial personality disorder

1. Superficial charm and good 'intelligence'

2. Absence of delusions and other signs of irrational thinking

3. Absence of 'nervousness'

4. Unreliability

5. Untruthfulness and insincerity

6. Lack of remorse or shame

7. Inadequately motivated antisocial behaviour

8. Poor judgement and failure to learn by experience

9. Pathological egocentricity and incapacity for love

10. General poverty in major affective reactions

11. Specific loss of insight

12. Unresponsiveness in general interpersonal relations

13. Fantastic and uninviting behaviour …

14. Suicide rarely carried out

15. Sex life impersonal, trivial and poorly integrated

16. Failure to follow any life plan

Source: Cleckley, 1976, pp. 337–338. Reprinted with permission.

are like. They are unconcerned for other people's feelings and suffer no remorse or guilt if their actions hurt others. Although they may be superficially charming, they do not form real friendships; thus, they often become swindlers or confidence artists. Both male and female psychopaths are sexually promiscuous from an early age, but these encounters do not seem to mean much to them. Female psychopaths tend to marry early, to be unfaithful to their husbands, and to soon become separated or divorced. They tend to marry other psychopaths, so their husbands' behaviour is often similar to their own. Psychopaths habitually tell lies, even when there is no apparent reason for doing so and even when the lie is likely to be discovered. They steal things they do not need or even appear to want. When confronted with evidence of having lied or cheated, psychopaths do not act ashamed or embarrassed and usually shrug the incident off as a joke.

Psychopaths do not easily learn from experience; they tend to continue committing behaviours that get them into trouble. They also do not appear to be driven to perform their antisocial behaviours; instead, they usually give the impression that they are acting on whims. When someone commits

a heinous crime such as a brutal murder, normal people expect that the criminal had a reason for doing so. However, criminal psychopaths are typically unable to supply a reason more compelling than 'I just felt like it'. They do not show much excitement or enthusiasm about what they are doing and do not appear to derive much pleasure from life.

Aetiology

Cleckley (1976) suggested that the psychopath's defect 'consists of an unawareness and a persistent lack of ability to become aware of what the most important experiences of life mean to others. … The major emotional accompaniments are absent or so attenuated as to count for little' (p. 371). Some investigators have hypothesised that this lack of involvement is caused by an unresponsive autonomic nervous system. If a person feels no anticipatory fear of punishment, he or she is perhaps more likely to commit acts that normal people would be afraid to commit. Similarly, if a person feels little or no emotional response to other people and to their joys and sorrows, he or she is unlikely to establish close relationships with them.

Many experiments have found that psychopaths do show less reactivity in situations involving punishment. For example, Hare (1965) demonstrated that psychopaths show fewer signs of anticipatory fear. All subjects in Hare's study watched the numerals 1 through 12 appear in sequential order in the window of a device used to present visual stimuli. They were told that they would receive a very painful shock when the numeral 8 appeared. Psychopathic subjects showed much less anticipatory responsiveness than did normal control subjects or non-psychopathic criminals.

Psychopaths appear to be selectively aroused by some emotions. When viewing slides of facial expression of distress or threat, psychopaths are less responsive than a control group to the distress faces but are no different from controls when responding to the threatening faces (Blair *et al.*, 1997). Psychopaths also appear to respond differently to emotional words when these are presented to the left (analytical) or right (emotional) hemisphere. Psychopaths do not show the right-hemisphere advantage for recognising emotion (Day and Wong, 1996).

Psychopaths often (but not always) come from grossly disturbed families that contain alcoholics and other psychopaths. Christiansen (1970) found that the concordance rate for psychopathy was 36 per cent for identical twins and only 12 per cent for fraternal twins, which suggests a heritability of nearly 50 per cent. Mednick *et al.* (1983) examined the criminal records of men who had been adopted early in life and found that the likelihood of their being convicted of a crime was directly related to the number of convictions of their biological fathers.

The quality of parenting is strongly related to the development of antisocial personality disorder. In particular, children whose parents ignore them or who leave them unsupervised for prolonged periods, often develop patterns of misconduct and delinquency (Lynam, 1996). When the parents do pay attention to their children, it tends to be in the form of harsh punishment or verbal abuse in response to their misdeeds. Thus, the children of these parents live in an environment that ranges from no attention at all to attention in the form of physical punishment and tongue lashings. In response, the children develop a pattern of behaviour that is characterised by increased aggression, distrust of others, concern only for themselves, and virtually no sense of right and wrong.

Children who have conduct problems tend to view their environments differently from well behaved children. They perceive the world as being hostile and interpret others' actions, even those of other children, as being aggressive and threatening. They may then strike out at someone else, not the object of their misperception, in order to avoid being attacked first. Their attack leads to a retaliation, either in the form of punishment by a parent or a teacher or in the form of a counterattack by other children. These children soon develop reputations for being aggressive and unlikeable, which further contributes to the strengthening of their antisocial attitudes and behaviours.

Treatment

There is no standard, effective treatment for antisocial personality disorder and the treatments that are attempted have normally been designed for other purposes such as anger management or reducing deviant sexual behaviour (Oltmans and Emery, 1998). While evidence suggests that there is some temporary effect on the behaviour, the effect does not generalise to other settings in the long-term.

Questions to think about

Personality disorders

- Are individuals born psychopathic? What does 'born psychopathic' mean?

- One theory of personality suggests that criminals may be born with a gene predisposing them to crime. How likely do you think this is?

- The frontal lobes appear to be dysfunctional in psychopaths. Does this mean that psychopathy is neurobiologically based?

- Is antisocial personality associated with particular types of home environment?

- Is there a relationship between antisocial behaviour and alcohol abuse?

Psychoactive substance use disorders

Description

Psychoactive substance use disorders are closely related to personality disorders. Individuals who abuse alcohol and other drugs often also have personality disorders (Morgenstern *et al.*, 1997). According to the DSM-IV, psychoactive substance use disorders include psychoactive substance dependence, or what is usually called 'addiction', and psychoactive substance abuse, which is less severe but which still causes social, occupational or medical problems.

The lifetime prevalence rate for substance abuse disorder is estimated to be about 26.6 per cent (Kessler *et al.*, 1994). The lifetime prevalence rate for alcoholism is estimated to be about 13.8 per cent (Carson *et al.*, 1996).

Aetiology

People abuse certain drugs because the drugs activate the reinforcement system of the brain, which is normally activated only by natural reinforcers such as food, warmth and sexual contact. Dopamine-secreting neurons are an important component of this system. Some drugs, such as crack cocaine, activate the reinforcement system rapidly and intensely, providing immediate and potent reinforcement. For many people, the immediate effects of drug use outweigh the prospect of dangers that lie in the future.

Genetic and physiological causes

Most of the research on the effects of heredity on addiction have focused on alcoholism. We discussed most of the evidence for a genetic and physiological role in alcohol abuse in Chapter 3.

In a review of the literature on alcohol abuse, Cloninger (1987) notes that there appear to be two principal types of alcoholic: those who have antisocial and pleasure-seeking tendencies – people who cannot abstain but drink consistently – and those who are anxiety-ridden – people who are able to go without drinking for long periods of time but are unable to control themselves once they start. Binge drinking is also associated with emotional dependence, behavioural rigidity, perfectionism, introversion and guilt feelings about one's drinking behaviour. Steady drinkers usually begin their alcohol consumption early in life, whereas binge drinkers begin much later, as seen in Table 17.9.

An adoption study carried out in Sweden (Cloninger *et al.*, 1985) found that men with fathers who were steady drinkers were almost seven times more likely to become steady drinkers themselves than were men whose fathers did not abuse alcohol. Family environment had no measurable effect; the boys began drinking whether or not the

Table 17.9 Characteristic features of two types of alcoholism

Feature	Types of alcoholism	
	Steady	*Binge*
Usual age of onset (years)	Before 25	After 25
Spontaneous alcohol seeking (inability to abstain)	Frequent	Infrequent
Fighting and arrests when drinking	Frequent	Infrequent
Psychological dependence (loss of control)	Infrequent	Frequent
Guilt and fear about alcohol dependence	Infrequent	Frequent
Novelty seeking	High	Low
Harm avoidance	Low	High
Reward dependence	Low	High

Source: Cloninger, 1987. Copyright 1987 by the American Association for the Advancement of Science.

members of their adoptive families drank heavily. Very few women become steady drinkers; the daughters of steady-drinking fathers instead tend to develop somatisation disorder. Thus, genes that predispose a man to become a steady-drinking alcoholic (antisocial type) appear to predispose a woman to develop somatisation disorder. The reason for this interaction with gender is not known.

Binge drinking is influenced both by heredity and by environment. The Swedish adoption study found that having a biological parent who was a binge drinker had little effect on the development of binge drinking unless the child was exposed to a family environment in which there was heavy drinking. The effect was seen in both males and females.

Most investigators believe that differences in brain physiology are more likely to play a role than are other biological symptoms. Cloninger (1987) notes that many studies have shown that people with antisocial tendencies, which includes steady drinkers, show a strong tendency to seek novelty and excitement. These people are disorderly and distractible (many have a history of hyperactivity as children) and show little restraint in their behaviour. They tend not to fear dangerous situations or social disapproval and they are easily bored. On the other hand, binge drinkers tend to be anxious, emotionally dependent, sentimental, sensitive to social cues, cautious and apprehensive, fearful of novelty or change, rigid and attentive to details. Their EEGs show little slow alpha activity, which suggests that they are aroused and anxious (Propping *et al.*, 1981). When they take alcohol, they report a pleasant relief of tension (Propping *et al.*, 1980).

The brains of steady drinkers may contain an undersensitive punishment mechanism, which makes them unresponsive to danger and to social disapproval. They may also have an undersensitive reinforcement system, which leads them to seek more intense thrills (including those provided by alcohol) in order to experience pleasurable sensations. Thus, they seek the euphoric effects of alcohol. On the other hand, binge drinkers may have an oversensitive punishment system. Normally, they avoid drinking because of the guilt they experience afterwards; but once they begin, and once the sedative effect begins, the alcohol-induced suppression of the punishment system makes it impossible for them to stop.

Cognitive causes

Cooper *et al.* (1988) have argued that people develop patterns of heavy drug use because of what they believe about the personal benefits of using drugs. For example, people who believe that alcohol will help them to cope with negative emotions and who also expect that alcohol will make them more likeable, sociable or attractive may use alcohol to obtain these perceived positive effects. In this view, drug abuse or dependence is seen as a way of coping with what are perceived to be personal shortcomings – having negative emotions, not being outgoing enough, feeling uncomfortable around others, and so on. Under the influence of alcohol or other drugs, these feelings are replaced with a false sense that these perceived shortcomings no longer exist. Thus, the use of drugs is negatively reinforced by the escape it provides from negative feelings. But the effect is temporary. The negative feelings return when the person is sober, which leads to further drug use. Soon, the person is intoxicated or high most or all of the time.

Treatment

The treatment for psychoactive substance use disorders depends on the aims of the clinician: the patient may be instructed to stop using the substances altogether or moderate his or her use. Treatment of the disorder usually involves undergoing stages of therapy. The first stage is detoxification in which the drug is removed from the patient. This can take up to six weeks. The next stages involve making the patient less reliant on the drug. Alcoholics Anonymous (AA), for example, the self-help group founded in 1935 to help beat alcoholism, first requires abusers to acknowledge that they have lost control over their alcohol intake and that alcohol has taken over their life. This expression of powerlessness is seen as an important first step in acknowledging the grip of the alcohol. The next of the 12 steps in the AA's programme involve various thought-changing strategies such as compensating for the effects of the alcohol on others, realising the detrimental effect the drinking had on others and acknowledging the user's personal weakness. Because the

AA's assumption is that alcoholics cannot recover on their own, they are encouraged to attend frequent meetings (sometimes, every day for the first 90 days) (Oltmans and Emery, 1998). Attendance at meetings appears to be a good predictor of future abstinence. Evidence for the success of the AA's approach is, however, primarily anecdotal because conducting a well-controlled randomised experiment is almost impossible.

Questions to think about

Psychoactive substance use disorders

■ What personality characteristics do you think would pre-dispose an individual to substance use disorder?

■ Why should such personality characteristics lead to this disorder?

■ Would the same characteristics be seen in alcoholics and heroin or cocaine addicts?

■ How would you define dependence? We are dependent on water for living. If an alcoholic needs alcohol in order to function, is this need a substance disorder?

Schizophrenic disorders

Schizophrenia, the most common psychosis, includes several types, each with a distinctive set of symptoms. There is some controversy over whether schizophrenia is a unitary disorder with various subtypes or whether each subtype constitutes a distinct disorder. Because the prognosis differs for the various subtypes of schizophrenia, they appear to differ at least in severity. An individual may, at different times, meet the criteria for different subtypes, although the diagnosis of schizophrenia seems valid and reliable (Mason *et al.*, 1997).

Description

Schizophrenia refers to a group of psychological disorders involving distortions of thought, perception and emotion; bizarre behaviour; and social withdrawal. It appears to affect 1 per cent of the world population and appears to recognise no cultural or international boundaries. The illness seems to show sex differences, in that onset is usually earlier in men, and women tend to show a better outcome. However, the sex difference is not robust, with some studies showing no strong sex difference (Jablensky and Cole, 1997). Schizophrenia is probably the most serious of the mental disorders.

Descriptions of symptoms in ancient writings indicate that the disorder has been around for thousands of years (Jeste *et al.*, 1985). The word 'schizophrenia' literally means 'split mind', although it is commonly misinterpreted as 'split personality'. The schizophrenic does not suffer from split personality or multiple personality (those are other mental disorders) but from disordered thought and affect. The man who invented the term, Eugen Bleuler (in 1911), intended it to refer to a break with reality caused by such disorganisation of the various functions of the mind that thoughts and feelings no longer worked together normally.

Bleuler divided the disorder into reactive and process forms. Patients with a general history of good mental health were designated as having reactive schizophrenia, on the assumption that their disorder was a reaction to stressful life situations. Typically, these patients soon recovered, and few experienced another episode. Patients with indications of mental illness early in life were designated as having process schizophrenia and were considered to have a chronic disorder.

If process schizophrenia does have its roots in early life, an important task is to determine what the early predictors are. The ability to identify people with a high risk of schizophrenia while they are still young will allow clinicians to institute some form of therapy before the disorder becomes advanced. The early signs may also indicate whether the causes of schizophrenia are biological, environmental, or both.

Many studies of people who become schizophrenics in adulthood have found that they were different from others even in childhood. One study obtained home movies of people with adult-onset schizophrenia that showed them and their siblings when they were children (Walker and Lewine, 1990). Although the schizophrenia did not manifest itself until adulthood, viewers of the films (six graduate students and one professional clinical psychologist) did an excellent job of identifying the children who were to become schizophrenic. The viewers commented on the children's poor eye contact, relative lack of responsiveness and positive affect, and generally poor motor co-ordination.

There are also degrees of cognitive impairment seen in schizophrenia. Verbal fluency – the ability to name as many objects beginning with a particular letter or belonging to the same category – appears to be impaired in schizophrenic individuals (Gruzelier *et al.*, 1988; Crawford *et al.*, 1993), although the category version of this test appears to be better performed (Joyce *et al.*, 1996). Semantic memory and performance on 'frontal lobe' tasks is also impaired in schizophrenic individuals (Shallice *et al.*, 1991; Tamlyn *et al.*, 1992).

The prognosis for schizophrenia is described by the 'law of thirds'. Approximately one-third of the people who are diagnosed as having it will require institutionalisation for the rest of their lives. About one-third show remission of symptoms and may be said to be cured of the disorder. The final third are occasionally symptom-free (sometimes for many years) only to have the symptoms return, requiring more treatment and perhaps even institutionalisation.

Schizophrenia is characterised by two categories of symptoms: positive and negative. Positive symptoms include thought disorders, hallucinations and delusions. A thought disorder – a pattern of disorganised, irrational thinking – is probably the most pronounced symptom of schizophrenia. People with schizophrenia have great difficulty arranging their thoughts logically and sorting out plausible conclusions from absurd ones. In conversation, they jump from one topic to another as new associations come up. Sometimes, they utter meaningless words or choose words for their rhyme rather than for their meaning. Delusions are beliefs that are obviously contrary to fact. Delusions of persecution are false beliefs that others are plotting and conspiring against oneself. Delusions of grandeur are false beliefs in one's power and importance, such as a conviction that one has godlike powers or has special knowledge that no one else possesses. Delusions of control are related to delusions of persecution; the person believes, for example, that he or she is being controlled by others through such means as radar or tiny radio receivers implanted in his or her brain.

The third positive symptom of schizophrenia is hallucinations, which are perceptions of stimuli that are not actually present. The most common schizophrenic hallucinations are auditory, but such hallucinations can also involve any of the other senses. The typical schizophrenic hallucination consists of voices talking to the person. Sometimes, they order the person to act; sometimes, they scold the person for his or her unworthiness; sometimes, they just utter meaningless phrases. Sometimes, those with schizophrenia may also hear a voice that keeps a running commentary on their behaviour, or they hear two or more voices.

In contrast to the positive symptoms, the negative symptoms of schizophrenia are known by the absence of normal behaviours: flattened emotional response, poverty of speech, lack of initiative and persistence, inability to experience pleasure, and social withdrawal (Crow, 1980; Frith, 1987). Negative symptoms are not specific to schizophrenia; they are seen in many neurological disorders that involve brain damage, especially the frontal lobes which may, in fact, be dysfunctional in schizophrenia (Selemon et al., 1995).

Types of schizophrenia

DSM-IV identifies four types of schizophrenia: undifferentiated, catatonic, paranoid and disorganised. Most cases of schizophrenia, however, do not fit exactly into one of these categories. Many individuals are diagnosed as undifferentiated schizophrenia; that is, the patients have delusions, hallucinations and disorganised behaviour but do not meet the criteria for catatonic, paranoid or disorganised schizophrenia. In addition, some patients' symptoms change after an initial diagnosis, and their classification changes accordingly.

Catatonic schizophrenia (from the Greek katateinein, meaning 'to stretch or draw tight') is characterised by various motor disturbances, including catatonic postures – bizarre, stationary poses maintained for many hours – and waxy flexibility, in which the person's limbs can be moulded into new positions, which are then maintained. Catatonic schizophrenics are often aware of all that goes on about them and will talk about what happened after the episode of catatonia subsides.

The pre-eminent symptoms of paranoid schizophrenia are delusions of persecution, grandeur or control. The word 'paranoid' has become so widely used in ordinary language that it has come to mean 'suspicious'. However, not all paranoid schizophrenics believe that they are being persecuted. Some believe that they hold special powers that can save the world or that they are Christ, or Napoleon or the president of the United States.

Paranoid schizophrenics are among the most intelligent of psychotic patients, so, not surprisingly, they often build up delusional structures incorporating a wealth of detail. Even the most trivial event is interpreted in terms of a grand scheme, whether it is a delusion of persecution or one of grandeur. The way a person walks, a particular facial expression or movement, or even the shapes of clouds can acquire special significance. An example of a case study of paranoid schizophrenia appears in the 'Psychology in action' section below.

Disorganised schizophrenia is a serious progressive and irreversible disorder characterised primarily by disturbances of thought. People with disorganised schizophrenia often display signs of emotion, especially silly laughter, that are inappropriate to the circumstances. Also, their speech tends to be a jumble of words: 'I came to the hospital to play, gay, way, lay, day, bray, donkey, monkey' (Snyder, 1974, p. 132). This sort of speech is often referred to as a word salad.

Psychology in action

Treating paranoid schizophrenia

Bill McClary, a 25 year old unemployed man, did not go to the therapist willingly. His sister Coleen, with whom he had been living for 18 months, suggested that Bill receive professional help for behaviour that had become increasingly unusual. He would spend most of his time in social isolation, daydreaming, talking to himself and saying things that did not make sense. Although most people engage in such behaviour at some time, Bill's was constant and this is what worried his sister.

Psychology in action continued

On seeking professional help, Bill appeared quiet and hesitant. During therapy, he was friendly but shy and ill-at-ease. It was only later that his therapist learned of even stranger and unusual behaviour reported by Bill's brother Roger.

It transpired that Bill had had occasional but not long-lasting heterosexual and homosexual relationships. After moving in with his sister, he became convinced that people were talking about him, especially about his sexuality. He came to believe that a group of conspirators had implanted microphones and cameras in the house to spy on his sexual encounters with men. These recordings were released as a film which Bill believed had grossed $50 million at the box office; this money was used to fund the activity of the Irish Republican Army in Northern Ireland and he would often feel deeply guilty and responsible for the deaths there because his money was used to buy arms and ammunition.

Bill also heard voices discussing his sexual behaviour in unpleasant terms. Often, these discussions would involve an element of punishment, such as 'He's a faggot; we've got to kill him'. The successfully released film was called *Honour Thy Father* and Bill's name in the film was Gay Talese. Although Bill did not acknowledge the fact, this name actually belonged to a real novelist who wrote about organised crime. He maintained that his photograph had appeared on the cover of *Time* magazine in the previous year with the name Gay Talese printed clearly on it.

Bill was the youngest of four children born to Irish-American parents. He was very close to his mother and his father blamed him for the break-up of his marriage; he was often excluded from his father's activities. At the age of 12, Bill's father fell ill and Bill remembered wanting to see him dead. His schoolwork was good and he eventually became a bank clerk – a stop-gap job while he thought of which career to pursue. He was quiet and polite but eccentric; he resigned after two years to become a lift operator, a job which afforded even more thinking time, but he was sacked after a year for being disorganised. He moved in with his mother shortly after this but because each made the other anxious, he moved out and moved in with his sister, her husband and their three children. It was at this point that Bill's unusual behaviour became noticeable.

Bill did not seem to enjoy life very much – he did not like interacting with others, was ambivalent about relationships and described sex in very impersonal terms. Initial therapy sessions targeted Bill's indifference and time-keeping and his sister was advised to ignore inappropriate behaviour. If he missed breakfast, then he would not have a snack cooked for him at eleven, as had previously happened. This strategy and others like it resulted in Bill keeping time and domestic appointments. He enjoyed helping his niece with her homework and so this pleasant activity was encouraged. Eventually, his schedule approached those of the house and he began to help more with domestic chores. Mumbling and lack of social contact was tackled next. The therapist advised Bill to move to one area of the house whenever he felt the need to mumble and talk to himself. This was partly but not totally successful. His shyness with other people was tackled by asking Bill to rehearse mentally conversations that might occur with other people.

When the 'film fantasy' was made aware to the therapist, however, Bill was prescribed thioridazine, a standard antipsychotic medication. This was successful in reducing the self-talk but his delusions remained. To try and eliminate these delusions, Bill was told to visit a local library and find the cover of *Time* with his photograph on. This he did and obviously did not find such a cover. However, he believed that the covers had been switched by conspirators. He was told to go to two more libraries but he was still convinced that the covers had been switched. Over the next few weeks, he began to believe that he might just have imagined the *Time* incident and his delusions managed to recede a little.

Source: Oltmans *et al.*, 1995

Aetiology

Research into the causes of all kinds and forms of schizophrenia throughout this century reflects the challenge that psychologists face in attempting to understand how psychological and biological factors interact to influence behaviour. The diathesis–stress model of mental disorders, discussed earlier in the chapter, appears to describe accurately the causes of schizophrenia: schizophrenia appears to result from one or more inherited, biological predispositions that are activated by environmental stress. In fact, this is currently the predominant view of schizophrenia.

Genetic causes

The heritability of schizophrenia, or more precisely the heritability of a tendency towards schizophrenia, has now been firmly established by both twin studies and adoption studies. Identical twins are much more likely to be concordant for schizophrenia than are fraternal twins, and the children of parents with schizophrenia are more likely themselves to become schizophrenic, even if they were adopted and raised by non-schizophrenic parents (Kety *et al.*, 1968; Farmer *et al.*, 1987). Twin studies of schizophrenia compare the concordance rates of MZ twins with the concordance rates of siblings of different genetic relatedness who were reared either together or apart. According to Gottesman and Shields (1982) and Gottesman (1991), concordance rates for MZ twins are about 50 per cent, but they are less than about 20 per cent for DZ twins.

If a person has been diagnosed with schizophrenia, there exists the possibility that other family members have the disorder, too. It is important to note that although the likelihood of developing schizophrenia increases if a person has schizophrenic relatives, this disorder is not a simple trait, like eye colour, that is inherited. Even if both parents are schizophrenic, the probability that their child will develop schizophrenia is 30 per cent or less.

Gottesman and Bertelsen (1989) found that the percentage of schizophrenic children was nearly identical for schizophrenic and non-schizophrenic parents: 16.8 per cent for the schizophrenic parents and 17.4 per cent for the non-schizophrenic parents. For the dizygotic twins, the percentages were 17.4 and 2.1, respectively. These results provide strong evidence that schizophrenia is heritable, and they also support the conclusion that carrying a 'schizophrenia gene' does not mean that a person will necessarily become schizophrenic (see Figure 17.6). These figures suggest that the environment may be an important trigger for the activation of the biological predisposition.

Neurochemical causes

Two classes of drugs have been found to affect the symptoms of schizophrenia. Cocaine and amphetamine can cause symptoms of schizophrenia, both in schizophrenics and in non-schizophrenics; antipsychotic drugs, on the other hand, can reduce them. Because both types of drug affect neural communication in which dopamine serves as a transmitter substance, investigators have hypothesised that abnormal activity of these neurons is the primary cause of schizophrenia. That is, the dopamine hypothesis states that the positive symptoms of schizophrenia are produced by overactivity of synapses that use dopamine as a transmitter substance.

Amphetamine and related substances also make all kinds of naturally occurring schizophrenia worse: paranoids become more suspicious, disorganised schizophrenics become sillier, and catatonics become more rigid or hyperactive. Davis (1974) injected an amphetamine-like

drug into schizophrenic patients whose symptoms had abated. Within one minute, each patient's condition changed 'from a mild schizophrenia into a wild and very florid schizophrenia'.

Chlorpromazine and other antipsychotic drugs are remarkably effective in alleviating the positive symptoms of schizophrenia. Hallucinations diminish or disappear, delusions become less striking or cease altogether, and the patient's thought processes become more coherent. These drugs are not merely tranquillisers; for example, they cause a patient with catatonic immobility to begin moving again as well as cause an excited patient to quieten down. In contrast, true tranquillisers such as Librium or Valium only make a schizophrenic patient slow moving and lethargic.

Amphetamine, cocaine and the antipsychotic drugs act on synapses – the junctions between nerve cells – in the brain. One neuron passes on excitatory or inhibitory messages to another by releasing a small amount of transmitter substance from its terminal button into the synaptic cleft. The chemical activates receptors on the surface of the receiving neuron, and the activated receptors either excite or inhibit the receiving neuron. Drugs such as amphetamine and cocaine cause the stimulation of receptors for dopamine. In contrast, antipsychotic drugs block dopamine receptors and prevent them from becoming stimulated.

Neurological causes

Ventricular enlargement   Antipsychotic drugs alleviate positive, but not negative, symptoms of schizophrenia (Angrist et al., 1980). Negative symptoms appeared to be associated with brain damage in patients exhibiting these symptoms. Weinberger and Wyatt (1982) found that the ventricles in the brains of schizophrenic patients were, on average, twice as large as those of normal subjects. Similarly, Pfefferbaum et al. (1988) found evidence that the sulci (the wrinkles in the brain) were wider in the brains of schizophrenic patients. Enlargement of the hollow ventricles of the brain and widening of the sulci indicates the loss of brain tissue – thus, the evidence implied the existence of some kind of neurological disease.

This enlargement in the ventricles has been confirmed in fifty studies (Lewis, 1990); MRI studies further indicate that the medial temporal lobes may be affected (Chua and

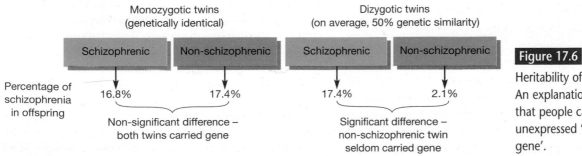

Figure 17.6

Heritability of schizophrenia. An explanation for evidence that people can have an unexpressed 'schizophrenia gene'.

McKenna, 1995), although there appears to be a reduction in whole brain size together with an increase in the occipital areas of the ventricles (Lawrie and Abukmeil, 1998).

Loss of brain tissue, as assessed by CT scans, appears to be related to negative symptoms of schizophrenia but not to positive ones (Johnstone *et al.*, 1978). In addition, patients with loss of brain tissue respond poorly to antipsychotic drugs (Weinberger *et al.*, 1980). These studies suggest that positive and negative symptoms of schizophrenia have different causes: positive symptoms are a result of overactivity of dopamine synapses, whereas negative symptoms are produced by actual loss of brain tissue.

The prefrontal cortex   There is considerable evidence that some form of frontal lobe dysfunction is characteristic of schizophrenia (Weinberger *et al.*, 1992). This dysfunction usually occurs in the form of hypofrontality, that is, a decrease in activity in the frontal cortex. Some researchers have suggested that this pattern of reduced activity is not that consistent, however, and suggest that the drugs taken by schizophrenics may have been responsible for the reduction (Gur and Gur, 1995). To test the drug-induced-reduction hypothesis, Andreasen *et al.* (1997) neuro-imaged 17 neuroleptically naive (that is, 'drug-free') patients during the early stages of the illness. They reported that there were decreases in the lateral, orbital and medial areas of the frontal cortex and the regions connected to those regions. The evidence for a reduction in activation, therefore, is persuasive. How are the frontal lobes implicated in schizophrenia?

PET studies of schizophrenic patients suggest that there is a decrease in dopamine receptors in the prefrontal cortex (Okubo *et al.*, 1997). There is also evidence that the neuronal density in the prefrontal cortex is 17 per cent higher compared with patients with Huntington's chorea and patients with schizophrenia-related disorders (Selemon *et al.*, 1995). These researchers suggested that this 'squashing' of neurons results from abnormal brain development and may account for the frontal lobe deficits. The role of the frontal lobe is also suggested by studies of working memory in schizophrenics. It appears as if the prefrontal cortex is especially important for the functioning of working memory. Keefe *et al.* (1995) have found that schizophrenic patients perform poorly at keeping information in working memory over 30-second and 60-second delay periods.

Others, however, have suggested that the important brain abnormality is the connection between the temporal and frontal regions (Frith, 1992). These conclusions are based on evidence such as that obtained from 29 schizophrenic patients who completed a battery of neuropsychological tests (Bilder *et al.*, 1995). In this study, those tests thought to tap frontal or motor function were only correlated with activity in the anterior hippocampal region only.

Neuroimaging work by Frith and his colleagues has also implicated limbic and sublimbic activation in schizophrenics during auditory verbal hallucination (Silbersweig *et al.*, 1995; McGuire *et al.*, 1996, 1998). The evidence, therefore, indicates some role for the frontal and temporal cortices in schizophrenia but the relevance of the structures is currently unclear. Crow (1998), for example, has controversially suggested that a deficit in the functional lateralisation of the brain, especially the lateralisation of language, may be the cause of schizophrenia, although the evidence for this is mixed.

Finally, Gray and colleagues have proposed that schizophrenia may be the result of abnormal connections between the limbic forebrain (especially the hippocampal formation) and the basal ganglia, the region of the brain implicated in the regulation of movement (Gray *et al.*, 1991; Gray, 1995). These neuroanatomical abnormalities correspond to increases in dopamine in a part of the basal ganglia called the nucleus accumbens. A disruption in these connections mean that steps in a motor programme are not confirmed by the brain, leading to the expected outcome of each step being perceived as novel or unexpected. Gray's model is consistent with that of Frith's and Weinberger's although it has not been widely tested.

Neurodevelopmental impairment   Another possible neurological cause of schizophrenia is interference with normal prenatal brain development (Weinberger, 1996; Hultman *et al.*, 1997). Several studies have shown that people born during the winter months are more likely to develop schizophrenia later in life. Torrey *et al.* (1977) suggest that the causal factor could be seasonal variations in nutritional factors, or, more likely, variations in toxins or infectious agents in air, water or food. Several diseases known to be caused by viruses, such as measles, German measles and chicken pox, show a similar seasonality effect. The seasonality effect is seen most strongly in poor, urban locations, where people are at greater risk for viral infections (Machon *et al.*, 1983).

A seasonally related virus could affect either a pregnant woman or her newborn infant. Two pieces of evidence suggest that the damage is done prenatally. First, brain development is more susceptible to disruption prenatally than postnatally. Second, a study of the offspring of women who were pregnant during an epidemic of type A2 influenza in Finland occurring in 1957 showed an elevated incidence of schizophrenia (Mednick *et al.*, 1990). The increased incidence was seen only in the children of women who were in the second term of their pregnancy when the epidemic occurred. Presumably, the viral infection produced toxins that interfered with the brain development of some of the foetuses, resulting in the development of schizophrenia later in life.

Weinberger (1996) has explicitly stated the neurodevelopmental hypothesis as follows: 'Schizophrenia is related to a defect in brain development. This defect predisposes to a characteristic pattern of brain malfunction in early adult life and to symptoms that respond to antidopaminergic drugs.' In a review of the evidence to suggest that this malfunction does occur and does have the consequences the hypothesis states, he suggests that the hypothesis is broadly supported although it has provoked more questions than answers.

Related to the viral hypotheses of schizophrenia are obstetric complications. Evidence suggests that complications at birth are associated with later development of schizophrenia (Hultman et al., 1999). It has been reported that infants who experience these complications are twice as likely to develop schizophrenia as is a control group (Geddes and Lawrie, 1995). Hultman et al.'s Swedish study of birth records of schizophrenic and control group infants report the same pattern: increased risk of schizophrenia is associated with complications during pregnancy and birth, especially in boys (Hultman et al., 1997). Why these complications should be a risk factor, however, is unclear.

Cognitive and environmental causes

Family and expressed emotion   A study carried out in Finland has suggested that being raised by a 'mentally healthy' family helps to protect against the development of schizophrenia (Tienari et al., 1987). The researchers examined the children of schizophrenic mothers who had been adopted away early in life. Following interviews and psychological tests, the families who adopted the children were classified as well adjusted, moderately maladjusted or severely maladjusted. The children adopted by the well adjusted families were least likely to show signs of mental disturbance, including schizophrenia. These findings suggest that the environment may be either an important cause or mediator of schizophrenia.

The personality and communicative abilities of either or both parents appear to play an influential role in the development of schizophrenic symptoms in children. Several studies have shown that children raised by parents who are dominating, overprotective, rigid and insensitive to the needs of others later develop schizophrenia (Roff and Knight, 1981). In many cases, a parent may be verbally accepting of the child yet in other ways reject him or her, which establishes a conflict for the child called a **double-bind**. For example, a mother may encourage her son to become emotionally dependent on her yet continually reject him when he tries to hug her or sit on her lap or play with her.

Schizophrenia also seems to occur at a higher than average rate among children who were reared in families characterised by verbal violence and disharmony. In a study of fourteen schizophrenic individuals, Lidz and his colleagues (1965) found that each of these individuals had a family that underwent either chronic discord in which the integrity of the parents' marriage was perpetually threatened or marital problems in which the bizarre behaviour of one family member was tolerated by the other members. Children in families in which parents treat them with hostility or in which parents present confusing communication to them are at risk of developing schizophrenia. However, it is unclear whether marital discord, family hostility, and confusing communications are a cause or an effect of children's schizophrenia.

Another environmental factor which could account for the development of schizophrenia is **expressed emotion** or EE (Hooley et al., 1996). Brown and his colleagues (Brown et al., 1966; Brown, 1985) identified a category of behaviours of families of individuals recovering from schizophrenia that seemed to be related to the patients' rates of recovery. They labelled this variable expressed emotion, which consists of expressions of criticism, hostility and emotional overinvolvement by the family members towards the patient. Patients living in a family environment in which the level of expressed emotion was low were more likely to recover, whereas those in families in which it was high were likely to continue to exhibit schizophrenic symptoms. The finding that low EE is associated with better outcome has since been replicated (Strachan et al., 1989). Perceived criticism also appears to be important: in depressed patients perceived criticism predicted a relapse in the mental disorder more reliably than did actual criticism (Hooley and Teasdale, 1989); mood disorder patients with high-EE families appear to be more non-verbally negative than patients from low-EE families (Simoneau et al., 1998).

A factor related to expressed emotion is communication deviance (Docherty, 1995). That is, the schizophrenic individual exhibits linguistic disturbances which may arise from the poor communication within families. This is an interesting hypothesis because of the consistently reported language impairment in schizophrenia. However, given that there are biological explanations for this (Crow, 1998), the role of the environment is unclear. It is possible that such poor communicative environments exacerbate the language development already hindered by poor lateralisation in schizophrenic individuals.

Jenkins and Karno (1992) report that in the past decade, over one hundred studies investigating expressed emotion in families have appeared. They found studies from North America, England, Denmark, Italy, France, Spain, Germany, Taiwan, India, Egypt and Australia. Despite differences in the ways that people of different cultures perceive mental illness and express themselves, expressed emotion does not seem to be culture-bound. Two elements appear to be common to all cultures: critical comments and emotional overinvolvement. If these elements are present in families of schizophrenics at low levels, patients are likely to recover quickly; if they are present at high levels, patients are less likely to recover quickly.

Jenkins and Karno also found that expressed emotion tends to be higher in industrialised cultures than in non-industrialised cultures. In other words, people in non-industrialised countries are more supportive of family members with schizophrenia than are people in industrialised countries. The reasons for this difference are many and appear to focus on the role that individuals play in the two environments.

Treatment

The commonest form of treatment for schizophrenia is psychopharmacological. Antipsychotic drugs help to reduce the effects of schizophrenia apparently by blocking dopamine receptors in the brain. Presumably, overactivity of dopamine synapses is responsible for the positive symptoms of schizophrenia. Although dopamine-secreting neurons are located in several parts of the brain, most researchers believe that the ones involved in the symptoms of schizophrenia are located in the cerebral cortex and parts of the limbic system near the front of the brain.

A different system of dopamine-secreting neurons in the brain is involved in the control of movement. Occasionally, this system of neurons degenerates in older people, producing Parkinson's disease. Symptoms of this disorder include tremors, muscular rigidity, loss of balance, difficulty in initiating movement, and impaired breathing that makes speech indistinct. In severe cases the person is bedridden.

The major problem with antipsychotic drugs is that they do not discriminate between these two systems of dopamine-secreting neurons. The drugs interfere with the activity of both the circuits involved in the symptoms of schizophrenia and the circuits involved in the control of movements. Consequently, when a person with schizophrenia begins taking an antipsychotic drug, he or she often exhibits a movement disorder. Fortunately, the disorder is usually temporary and soon disappears.

However, after taking the antipsychotic drug for several years, some people develop a different, more serious, movement disorder known as tardive dyskinesia (tardive means late developing; dyskinesia refers to a disturbance in movement), an often irreversible and untreatable syndrome characterised by continual involuntary lip smacking, grimacing and drooling (Cummings and Wirshing, 1989). Severely affected people have difficulty talking, and occasionally the movements interfere with breathing. The risk of developing this syndrome increases with age, dose and duration of use (Hughes and Pierattini, 1992). For example, approximately 20 per cent of older people develop tardive dyskinesia. The symptoms can be alleviated temporarily by increasing the dose of the antipsychotic drug, but doing so only serves to increase and perpetuate the person's dependence on the medication (Baldessarini and Tarsy, 1980).

Clozapine, an antischizophrenic drug, is more effective than other antipsychotic drugs in helping cases of almost untreatable schizophrenia (Kane *et al.*, 1988). It improves the symptoms of about 30–50 per cent of those people who have not responded to traditional antipsychotic drugs. Because about 2 per cent of those taking clozapine suffer an inhibition of white blood cell production, which can be fatal, weekly blood tests have to be conducted. People with schizophrenia have not yet received clozapine for a long enough time for researchers to be sure that the drug will not eventually produce tardive dyskinesia.

Questions to think about

Schizophrenic disorders

- Based on the evidence you have read so far, would you regard schizophrenia as a unitary disorder or a collection of different disorders? What evidence would support your hypothesis?

- Does the 'universality' of schizophrenia suggest that it has a neurobiological basis?

- Does the fact that some schizophrenics respond to antipsychotic medication suggest that (1) these drugs are generally ineffective, or (2) there are different types of schizophrenia with different neurobiological characteristics?

- Do you think that environment is a cause or a trigger of schizophrenic disorder? Is expressed emotion seen only in families with schizophrenic individuals or is it more common? What does this say about the notion of expressed emotion as a cause of schizophrenic symptoms?

Mood disorders

Everyone experiences moods varying from sadness to happiness to elation. We are excited when our team wins a game, saddened to learn that a friend's father has had a heart attack, thrilled at news of a higher-than-expected grade in an exam, and devastated by the death of a loved one. Some people, though, experience more dramatic mood changes than these. Significant shifts or disturbances in mood that affect normal perception, thought and behaviour are called mood disorders. They may be characterised by a deep, foreboding depression or by a combination of depression and euphoria.

Mood disorders are primarily disorders of emotion. The most severe mood disorders are bipolar disorder and major depression. Bipolar disorder is characterised by alternating periods of mania (wild excitement) and depression. Major depression involves persistent and severe feelings of sadness and worthlessness accompanied by changes in appetite, sleeping and behaviour. The lifetime prevalence rates for major depression are about 13 per cent for males and about 21 per cent for females (Kessler *et al.*, 1994).

A less severe form of depression is called dysthymic disorder. The term comes from the Greek words *dus*, 'bad' and *thymos*, 'spirit'. The primary difference between this disorder and major depression is its relatively low severity. Similarly, cyclothymic disorder resembles bipolar disorder but is much less severe.

Mania

Mania (the Greek word for madness) is characterised by wild, exuberant, unrealistic activity unprecipitated by environmental events. During manic episodes, people are usually elated and self-confident; however, contradiction or interference tends to make them very angry. Their speech (and, presumably, their thought processes) becomes very rapid. They tend to flit from topic to topic and are full of grandiose plans, but their thoughts are not as disorganised as those of people with schizophrenia. Manic patients also tend to be restless and hyperactive, often pacing around ceaselessly. They often have delusions and hallucinations, typically of a nature that fits their exuberant mood.

The usual response that manic speech and behaviour evokes in another person is one of sympathetic amusement. In fact, when an experienced clinician finds himself or herself becoming amused by a patient, the clinician begins to suspect the presence of mania. Because very few patients exhibit only mania, the DSM-IV classifies all cases in which mania occurs as bipolar disorder. Patients with bipolar disorder usually experience alternate periods of mania and depression. Each of these periods lasts from a few days to a few weeks, usually with several days of relatively normal behaviour between. Many therapists have observed that there is often something brittle and unnatural about the happiness during the manic phase, as though the patient is making himself or herself be happy to ward off an attack of depression. Indeed, some manic patients are simply hyperactive and irritable rather than euphoric.

Depression
Description

Depressed people are extremely sad and are usually full of self-directed guilt, but not because of any particular environmental event. Depressed people cannot always state why they are depressed. Beck (1967) identified five cardinal symptoms of depression: (1) a sad and apathetic mood, (2) feelings of worthlessness and hopelessness, (3) a desire to withdraw from other people, (4) sleeplessness and loss of appetite and sexual desire, and (5) change in activity level, to either lethargy or agitation. Major depression must be distinguished from grief, such as that caused by the death of a loved one. People who are grieving feel sad and depressed but do not fear losing their minds or have thoughts of self-harm. Because many people who do suffer from major depression or the depressed phase of bipolar disorder commit suicide, these disorders are potentially fatal. The fatality rate by suicide for major depression is estimated at 15 per cent (Guze and Robins, 1970).

People with severe depression often have delusions, especially that their brains or internal organs are rotting away. Sometimes, they believe that they are being punished for unspeakable and unforgivable sins, as in the following statement, reported by Coleman (1976):

> 'My brain is being eaten away. ... If I had any willpower I would kill myself. ... I don't deserve to live. ... I have ruined everything ... and it's all my fault. ... I have been unfaithful to my wife and now I am being punished ... my health is ruined ... there's no use going on ... (sigh). ... I have ruined everything ... my family ... and now myself. ... I bring misfortune to everyone. ... I am a moral leper ... a serpent in the Garden of Eden.' (p. 346)

Aetiology
Cognitive causes

People with mood disorders do not have the same outlook on life as others. Specifically, they make negative statements about themselves and their abilities: 'Nobody likes me', 'I'm not good at anything', 'What's the point in even trying, I'll just mess it up anyway'. Because they are so negative about themselves, depressed people are particularly unpleasant to be around. The problem is that the depressed individual is caught in a vicious circle: negative statements strain interpersonal relationships, which result in others withdrawing or failing to initiate social support, which, in turn, reinforces the depressed individual's negative statements (Klerman and Weissman, 1986).

Beck (1967, 1991) suggested that the changes in affect seen in depression are not primary but instead are secondary to changes in cognition. That is, the primary disturbance is a distortion in the person's view of reality. For example, a depressed person may see a scratch on the surface of his or her car and conclude that the car is ruined. Or a person whose recipe fails may see the unappetising dish as proof of his or her unworthiness. Or a nasty letter from a creditor is seen as a serious and personal condemnation. According to Beck, depressed people's thinking is characterised by self-blame (things that go wrong are always their fault), overemphasis on the negative aspects of life (even small problems are blown out of proportion), and failure to appreciate positive experiences (pessimism). This kind of pessimistic thinking involves negative thoughts about the self, about the present and about the future, which Beck collectively referred to as the cognitive triad. In short, depressed people blame their present miserable situation on their inadequacies and a lack of hope for improving the situation in the future.

The negative view of the self and events, however, seems to be time-specific. Depressed individuals who are asked to describe themselves 'right now' use negative terms, but use less negative terms when they describe how they usually feel (Brewin *et al.*, 1992). Depressed patients are also likely to be negative when discussing things globally but not when discussing specific issues (Wycherley, 1995).

Beck's model original argued that cognition caused the emotional disorder but his later reformulation of the theory suggested that cognition is part of a set of interacting mechanisms that include biological, psychological and social factors (Kovacs and Beck, 1978). Beck also distinguished between two types of depression: sociotropic depression in which the abnormal belief derived from a dependency on others, and autonomous depression in which the individual was goal-oriented and relied little on others. The evidence for these two types as distinct varieties of depression, however, is mixed (Power and Dalgleish, 1997).

Another causal factor in depression appears to involve the attributional style of the depressed person (Abramson *et al.*, 1978, 1989). According to this idea, it is not merely experiencing negative events that causes people to become depressed. What is actually more important are the attributions people make about why those events occur. People who are most likely to become depressed are those who attribute negative events and experiences to their own shortcomings and who believe that their life situations are never going to get any better. A person's attributional style, then, serves as a predisposition or diathesis for depression. In other words, people prone to depression tend to have a hopeless outlook on their life: 'I am not good at anything I try to do and it will never get any better. I am always going to be a useless person.' According to this view, depression is most likely when people with pessimistic attributional styles encounter significant or frequent life stressors (Abramson *et al.*, 1989). The pessimistic attributions are then generalised to other, perhaps smaller, stressors, and eventually a deep sense of hopelessness and despair sets in. Thus, the original formulation of the theory was called the helplessness theory whereas the later reformulation became know as the hopelessness theory.

Such people also appear to suffer a double dose of hopelessness. Not only do they perceive negative outcomes as being their own fault, they also perceive positive outcomes as being due to circumstance or to luck. In addition, they apply pessimistic attributions to a wide range of events and experiences and apply positive attributions only to a very narrow range of events and experiences, if any.

However, there is mixed evidence for a strong version of the hopelessness attribution theory. Swendsen (1998) reported that attributional style did not predict immediate depressed or anxious mood in a group of 91 individuals who were asked to report negative events, cognitions, anxiety and depression five times a day for one week. However, attributional style did predict 'individual' specific causal attributions made to negative events. Similar findings have been reported in other studies (Kapci, 1998). Lynd-Stevenson (1996, 1997) reports that hopelessness does not mediate the relationship between attributional style and depression but that there is a mediating effect when measures of hopelessness are relevant to the individual's ongoing life (in Lynd-Stevenson's sample's case, hopelessness related to unemployment). Attributional style, therefore, seems to apply only in certain, relevant contexts.

Genetic causes

Like schizophrenia, the mood disorders appear to have a genetic component. People who have first-degree relatives with a serious mood disorder are ten times more likely to develop these disorders than are people without afflicted relatives (Rosenthal, 1970). Furthermore, the concordance rate for bipolar disorder is 72 per cent for monozygotic twins, compared with 14 per cent for dizygotic twins. For major depression, the figures are 40 per cent and 11 per cent, respectively (Allen, 1976). Thus, bipolar disorder appears to be more heritable than major depression, and the two disorders appear to have different genetic causes. Recent studies, however, have cast doubt on the heritability of major depressive disorder (Andrew *et al.*, 1998).

Neurochemical causes

Drug treatments for depression (which are described in detail below) have shed some light on the biochemical causes of schizophrenia. Antidepressants such as imipramine, for example, stimulate synapses that use two transmitter substances, norepinephrine and serotonin. Other drugs such as reserpine, which is used to treat high blood pressure, can cause episodes of depression. Reserpine lowers blood pressure by blocking the release of norepinephrine in muscles in the walls of blood vessels, thus causing the muscles to relax. However, because the drug also blocks the release of norepinephrine and serotonin in the brain, a common side effect is depression. This side effect strengthens the argument that biochemical factors in the brain play an important role in depression.

Such data have suggested a biological amine theory of depression: depression results from a depletion in the monoamines, dopamine, noradrenaline or serotonin. The serotonin hypothesis is a variant of this general theory. The serotonin hypothesis suggests that this neurotransmitter (the lack of it) may be more involved in depression because blocking reuptake of serotonin is more effective than blocking norepinephrine. Given that most antidepressants augment serotonin (perhaps by different mechanisms), perhaps the involvement of other neurotransmitters is peripheral.

Neuropathological causes

There is some evidence of brain abnormality in the chronically depressed. Reduced metabolism in the left frontal and basal ganglia (Austin *et al.*, 1992) and reduced left frontal EEG activation in depressed individuals (Henriques and Davidson, 1991). There is also reported postmortem cell loss in temporal and frontal regions in suicides (Bowen *et al.*, 1989). There is recent evidence of decreased activity in the prefrontal cortex near the top of the corpus callosum (Drevets *et al.*, 1997).

Treatment

There are two principal treatments for clinical depression: cognitive therapy and antidepressant medication.

Cognitive therapy

Beck's cognitive therapy begins by arguing that the negative beliefs held by depressed individuals are seen as conclusions based on faulty logic (Beck, 1967). A depressed person concludes that he or she is 'deprived, frustrated, humiliated, rejected or punished (Beck *et al.*, 1979, p. 120). Beck views the cognitions of the depressed individual in terms of a cognitive triad: a negative view of the self ('I am worthless'), of the outside world ('The world makes impossible demands on me') and of the future ('Things are never going to get better').

Even when confronted with evidence that contradicts their negative beliefs, depressed individuals often find an illogical means of interpreting good news as bad news (Lewinsohn *et al.*, 1980). For example, a student who receives an A grade on an exam might attribute the high grade to an easy, unchallenging exam rather than to his or her own mastery of the material. The fact that few others in the class received a high grade does little to convince the depressed person that he or she deserves congratulations for having done well. The depressed student goes on believing, against contrary evidence, that the good grade was not really deserved.

Once the faulty logic is recognised for what it is, therapy entails exploring means for correcting the distortions. The following example is from an actual therapy session.

'A woman who complained of severe headaches and other somatic disturbances was found to be very depressed. When asked about the cognitions that seemed to make her unhappy, she said, "My family doesn't appreciate me"; "Nobody appreciates me, they take me for granted"; "I am worthless." As an example, she stated that her adolescent children no longer wanted to do things with her. Although this particular statement could very well have been accurate, the therapist decided to determine whether it was true. He pursued the "evidence" for the statement in the following interchange:

Patient: *My son doesn't like to go to the theatre or to the movies with me anymore.*
Therapist: *How do you know he doesn't want to go with you?*

P: *Teenagers don't actually like to do things with their parents.*
T: *Have you actually asked him to go with you?*
P: *No, as a matter of fact, he did ask me a few times if I wanted him to take me … but I didn't think he really wanted to go.*
T: *How about testing it out by asking him to give you a straight answer?*
P: *I guess so.*
T: *The important thing is not whether or not he goes with you but whether you are deciding for him what he thinks instead of letting him tell you.*
P: *I guess you are right but he does seem to be inconsiderate. For example, he is always late for dinner.*
T: *How often has that happened?*
P: *Oh, once or twice … I guess that's really not all that often.*
T: *Is he coming late for dinner due to his being inconsiderate?*
P: *Well, come to think of it, he did say that he had been working late those two nights. Also, he has been considerate in a lot of other ways.* (Beck et al., 1979, pp. 155–6)

Actually, as the patient later found, her son was willing to go to the movies with her.

This example shows that the therapist does not accept the client's conclusions and inferences at their face value. Instead, those conclusions resulting from faulty logic are discussed so that the client may understand them from another perspective, changing his or her behaviour as a result.

Antidepressant drugs

Tricyclic antidepressants   Antidepressant drugs are a class of drugs used to treat the symptoms of major depression and the most common of these are listed in Table 17.10. Antimanic drugs are used to treat the symptoms of bipolar disorder and mania. The earliest used antidepressant drugs were derived from the family of chemicals known as tricyclics, which refers to their 'three-ring' chemical structure (Lickey and Gordon, 1983).

Although the biology of depression is not well understood, the most widely accepted theory is that depression may result from a deficiency of the catecholamine neurotransmitters, norepinephrine and serotonin. Each of these neurotransmitters may be involved in different types of depression, although researchers are not sure how. Antidepressant drugs seem to slow down the reuptake of these neurotransmitters by presynaptic axons. Although tricyclic antidepressants do not work for all people, about 60–80 per cent of those whose depression has brought despair to their lives gradually return to normal after having been placed on tricyclics for 2–6 weeks (Hughes and Pierattini, 1992). Unfortunately, tricyclics have many side effects, including dizziness, sweating, weight gain, constipation, increased pulse, poor concentration and dry mouth.

Table 17.10 Some of the drugs used to treat depression

Substance	Generic name	Example
Norepinephrine-reuptake inhibitors (Tertiary amine tricyclics)	Amitriptyline Clomipramine Doxepin Imipramine Trimipramine	Elavil Anafranil Adapin, Sinequa Tofranil Surmontil
Norepinephrine-reuptake inhibitors (Secondary amine tricyclics)	Amoxapine Desipramine Maprotiline Nortriptyline Protriptyline	Asendin Norpramin, Pertofrane Ludiomil Pamelor Vivactil
Serotonin-reuptake inhibitors	Fluoxetine Fluvoxamine Paroxetine Sertraline Venlafaxine	Prozac Luvox Paxil Zoloft Effexor
Atypical antidepressants	Bupropion Nefazodone Trazodone	Wellbutrin Serzone Desyrel
Monoamine oxidase inhibitors	Phenelzine Tranylcypromine Selegiline	Nardil Parnate Eldepryl

Source: Baldessarini, 1996a. Copyright © The McGraw-Hill Companies. Reproduced with permission.

Monoamine oxidase inhibitors (MAOIs) Another class of antidepressants, introduced in the late 1950s, is the monoamine oxidase inhibitors (MAOIs), which take 1–3 weeks to begin alleviating depression. MAOIs prevent enzymes in the synaptic gap from destroying dopamine, norepinephrine and serotonin that have been released by presynaptic neurons. These drugs can have many side effects, many of them fatal. The tyramine cheese reaction, for example, arises from the eating of foods containing tyramine such as some wines, milk products, coffee and chocolate. Because the monoamine oxidase does not oxidise tyramine, tyramine displaces adrenaline at adrenaline receptors. This produces severe hypertension and blurred vision, impotence, insomnia and nausea. It can also be fatal if leading to a haemorrhage. MAOIs also have been shown to be more effective in treating atypical depressions such as those involving hypersomnia (too much sleep) or mood swings (Hughes and Pierattini, 1992).

Serotonin-specific reuptake inhibitors (SSRIs) A relatively new class of drugs is serotonin-specific reuptake inhibitors (SSRIs), which, as their name suggests, block the reuptake of serotonin in nerve cells. As a result, the common feature of all SSRIs is that they enhance the transmission of serotonin. Perhaps the most common SSRI is

fluoxetine (Prozac), first authorised for medical use in 1988. Fluoxetine inhibits the reuptake of serotonin, leaving more of that neurotransmitter in the synaptic cleft to stimulate postsynaptic receptors, and is the first drug of choice when tricyclic drug treatment has failed. SSRIs produce fewer negative side effects than do tricyclics and the MAOIs, although some individuals do experience headache, gastrointestinal discomfort, insomnia, tremor and sexual dysfunction.

Recent pharmacological treatments Two recent developments in the psychopharmacology of depression have been second generation (atypical) depressants which block either norepinephrine reuptake or dopamine reuptake, and dual-action antidepressants which block certain serotonin receptors while inhibiting its reuptake. An example of the former, nefazdone, was released in 1995; an example of the latter, mirtazapine, was released in 1997. Neither type of drug has been authorised in all European countries and, because of their youth, little research is available evaluating their long-term efficacy.

Lithium carbonate

Lithium carbonate is most effective in the treatment of bipolar disorders or simple mania. People's manic symptoms usually decrease as soon as their blood level of lithium reaches a sufficiently high level (Gerbino *et al.*, 1978). In bipolar disorder, once the manic phase is eliminated, the depressed phase does not return. People with bipolar disorder have remained free of their symptoms for years as long as they have continued taking lithium carbonate. This drug can have some side effects, such as a fine tremor or excessive urine production; but in general, the benefits far outweigh the adverse symptoms. However, an overdose of lithium is toxic, which means that the person's blood level of lithium must be monitored regularly.

The major difficulty with treating bipolar disorder is that people with this disorder often miss their 'high'. When medication is effective, the mania subsides along with the depression. But most people enjoy at least the initial phase of their manic periods, and some believe that they are more creative at that time. In addition, many of these people say that they resent having to depend on a chemical 'crutch'. As a consequence, many people suffering from bipolar disorder stop taking their medication. Not taking their medication endangers the lives of these people because the risk of death by suicide is particularly high during the depressive phase of bipolar disorder.

Seasonal affective disorder (SAD)

Some people become depressed during the winter season, when days are short and nights are long. The symptoms of this form of depression, called seasonal affective disorder, are slightly different from those of major depression (Rosenthal *et al.*, 1984). Both forms include lowered mood, lethargy and sleep disturbances, but seasonal depression includes a craving for carbohydrates and an accompanying weight gain.

The original study of SAD found a pattern of depression during winter and hypomania during the spring/summer in 29 individuals (Rosenthal *et al.*, 1984). A high percentage of these individuals exhibited bipolar disorder (92 per cent). Similar percentages have been reported elsewhere (Thompson, 1989). Although various mechanisms have been advanced, the most interesting has been the proposal that the light-sensitive hormone, melatonin, is dysfunctional in individuals with SAD. Seasonal affective disorder can be treated by exposing people to bright light for several hours a day, for example, or early in the morning (Rosenthal *et al.*, 1985; Thompson *et al.*, 1997). The direct evidence for the role of melatonin, however, appears to be inconclusive (Rosenthal and Wehr, 1992; Dalgleish *et al.*, 1996).

Questions to think about

Mood disorders

- What separates major depression and mania from a general low mood or 'high spirits'?
- The work on the cognitive biases seen in depressed patients suggest that individuals are negative about their global outlook but are less negative about specific events and situations. Why do you think this is?
- Do depressed individuals have an attributional style which promotes depression?
- What distinguishes bipolar disorder from depression?
- There has been a suggestion that depression can be described as reactive or endogenous. That is, the former results from responses to environmental events whereas the latter results from biochemical factors. How valid do you think such a distinction is? Would this explain why some depressed individuals are not responsive to antidepressants but others are?

Sexual dysfunctions

DSM-IV lists a number of sex-related disorders which have severe psychological consequences and causes. Male sexual dysfunction, for example, refers to the man's inability of achieve an erection, in the absence of impaired sexual desire – the desire is there, but the erection is not. Some authors have argued that this failure to achieve erection is due to some form of performance anxiety and that combating this anxiety will eliminate the problem; there is some evidence for this view (Munjack *et al.*, 1984). Female sexual dysfunction – the inability of the woman to achieve orgasm although the desire for orgasm is present – is sometimes treated by systematic desensitisation or masturbation training and both have been successful (Emmelkamp, 1994). Other disorders classified as sexual dysfunctions are the paraphilias.

Paraphilia

According to DSM-IV, paraphilia constitutes a mental or behavioural disorder that has a sexual content. The individuals must be distressed by the urges or behaviour they exhibit and social or occupational functioning must be impaired. The paraphilias include: fetishism (the use of non-living objects for sexual excitement), transvestic fetishism (cross-dressing), paedophilia (sex with pre-pubescent children), voyeurism (looking at people without their knowledge while they are undressing/having sex), sexual masochism (the individual derives sexual gratification from being made to suffer), **sexual sadism** (the individual derives sexual gratification from inflicting suffering), **exhibitionism** (exposure of genitalia in public), **frotterism** (rubbing against a person in public) and para-philias not otherwise specified. The case study below highlights just one of these paraphilias and shows how clinical psychologists can help treat such paraphilias.

Psychology in action

Treating exhibitionism

'Steve', a 34 year old married man, was arrested for sexual assault after attempting to help a woman whose car had broken down. After fixing the woman's fan belt, he pulled her to him and began fondling her buttocks. She pushed him away, but he exposed himself and began masturbating. After the woman contacted the police, Steve was arrested and charged.

Psychiatric assessment determined that Steve had a history of exhibitionism and frottage. As an adolescent, he would rub up against women in crowded places and, when he obtained his driver's licence, he used to park in car parks, watch women and covertly masturbate. When he was 16 years old, Steve remembered watching football in a park while sitting next to a female acquaintance. As he sat next to her, he began masturbating, eventually ejaculating. At the age of 13, he remembered playing with three young women and had an orgasm while wrestling with one of them when rubbing against her buttocks. He would repeat the behaviour with his 8-year-old sister, rubbing her buttocks until he orgasmed. When his sister threatened to tell their mother, he would masturbate to fantasies of buttock rubbing. After this, he would expose himself about 15 to 20 times a year, especially during times of stress. His sexual fantasy involved a woman catching him masturbating; the woman would be aroused by his erect state. This, however, never happened in real life. At the age of 24, he married Helen, a secretary. She gave birth to a son, who was five years old at the time of his father's arrest.

Steve's family history is a complex affair. His father changed jobs often and so the family moved frequently. Such frequent movement meant that Steve formed very few lasting relationships or friendships. He felt rejected by his father and clung to his mother, who was smothering and overprotective. She bathed him up until the age of 15. She would clean his penis by stroking it with a wet bar of soap and would enjoy seeing the erections this produced.

After the arrest, his wife complained of his lack of affection and of their poor sexual relations, but she knew nothing of his deviance. He did minimal parenting or household duties and his wife had little respect for him.

Steve's treatment was initially aimed at stopping public masturbation and frotting. These behaviours were linked to car parks, shopping centres and subways; he was, therefore, told to avoid these places. He abstained for two months, but he still experienced urges to exhibit. To combat these urges, he was instructed to distract himself whenever he felt them – by imagining himself on a beach, feeling drowsy and soaking up the sun.

To change his fantasies and improve sexual relations with his wife, Steve was instructed to masturbate only while fantasising about intercourse. When he could not do this, he was told to masturbate while fantasising about frottage but at the point of orgasm, he should switch his fantasy to intercourse. This fantasy was then encouraged to appear earlier on during masturbation. By the fourth week of therapy, he could masturbate without having deviant fantasies. He was still turned on by seeing women's buttocks in tight jeans, however, and so was asked to imagine a non-sexual fantasy when seeing these, such as thinking about the woman's occupation or looking at her face instead.

During marital therapy, he was shocked that his wife viewed him so negatively. So shocked was he that he began to help more around the house and got a new job as a camera salesman. The usual foreplay (rubbing his wife's buttocks) was replaced with manual or oral stimulation and his sexual relations with his wife improved. Although his deviant behaviour had not been 'cured', it had been contained.

Source: Oltmans *et al.*, 1995

Key terms

medical model *p.*591

culture-bound syndrome *p.*591

diathesis–stress model *p.*591

*Diagnostic and Statistical Manual (of Mental Disorders) IV (DSM-IV) p.*593

axes *p.*593

eclectic approach *p.*598

psychoanalysis *p.*598

free association *p.*599

resistance *p.*600

transference *p.*600

countertransference *p.*600

psychodynamic therapy *p.*600

humanistic therapy *p.*601

client-centred therapy *p.*601

incongruence *p.*601

unconditional positive regard *p.*601

Gestalt therapy *p.*602

systematic desensitisation *p.*603

flooding *p.*603

implosion therapy *p.*603

aversion therapy *p.*603

covert sensitisation *p.*604

behaviour modification *p.*604

token economies *p.*604

modelling *p.*604

assertiveness training *p.*604

role-playing *p.*604

cognitive behaviour therapy (CBT) *p.*605

rational-emotive therapy *p.*605

symptom substitution *p.*605

group psychotherapy *p.*606

family therapy *p.*606

electro-convulsive therapy (ECT) *p.*607

meta-analysis *p.*609

psychosurgery *p.*610

cingulotomy *p.*611

anxiety *p.*612

generalised anxiety disorder (GAD) *p.*612

behavioural inhibition system (BIS) *p.*613

attentional biases *p.*613

anti-anxiety (anxiolytic) drugs *p.*613

panic *p.*614

panic disorder *p.*614

anticipatory anxiety *p.*614

catastrophic misinterpretation *p.*615

evolutionary preparedness *p.*615

cognitive restructuring *p.*615

phobias *p.*615

agoraphobia *p.*616

social phobia *p.*616

specific phobia *p.*616

post-traumatic stress disorder (PTSD) *p.*617

obsessive-compulsive disorder *p.*618

obsessions *p.*618

compulsions *p.*618

Gilles de la Tourette's syndrome *p.*620

somatoform disorder *p.*620

somatisation disorder *p.*620

hypochondriasis *p.*621

conversion disorder *p.*621

dissociative disorders *p.*622

psychogenic amnesia *p.*622

psychogenic fugue *p.*622

dissociative identity disorder *p.*622

personality disorders *p.*623

antisocial personality disorder *p.*623

psychoactive substance use disorders *p.*626

schizophrenia *p.*628

reactive schizophrenia *p.*628

process schizophrenia *p.*628

positive symptoms *p.*628

thought disorder *p.*629

delusions *p.*629

delusions of persecution *p.*629

delusions of grandeur *p.*629

delusions of control *p.*629

hallucinations *p.*629

negative symptoms *p.*629

undifferentiated schizophrenia *p.*629

catatonic schizophrenia *p.*629

paranoid schizophrenia *p.*629

disorganised schizophrenia *p.*629

dopamine hypothesis *p.*631

double-bind *p.*633

expressed emotion *p.*633

mood disorders *p.*634

bipolar disorder *p.*634

major depression *p.*634

dysthymic disorder *p.*635

cyclothymic disorder *p.*635

mania *p.*635

cognitive triad *p.*635

tricyclic antidepressants *p.*637

monoamine oxidase inhibitors (MAOIs) *p.*638

tyramine cheese reaction *p.*638

serotonin-specific reuptake inhibitors (SSRIs) *p.*638

dual-action antidepressants *p.*638

lithium carbonate *p.*638

seasonal affective disorder *p.*639

male sexual dysfunction *p.*639

female sexual dysfunction *p.*639

paraphilia *p.*639

fetishism *p.*639

transvestic fetishism *p.*639

paedophilia *p.*639

voyeurism *p.*639

sexual masochism *p.*639

sexual sadism *p.*640

exhibitionism *p.*640

frotterism *p.*640

CHAPTER REVIEW

Classification and diagnosis of mental disorders

- Psychologists and other mental health professionals view the causes of mental disorders from several different perspectives:

  - The psychodynamic perspective argues that mental disorders arise from intrapsychic conflict that overwhelms the mind's defence mechanisms.

  - The medical perspective asserts that mental disorders have an organic basis, as physical illnesses do.

  - The cognitive behavioural perspective maintains that mental disorders are learned patterns of maladaptive thinking and behaving.

  - The humanistic perspective suggests that mental disorders arise from an oversensitivity to the demands of others and because positive regard from others is conditional on meeting those demands.

  - The sociocultural perspective focuses on how cultural variables influence the development of mental disorders and people's subjective reactions to them.

- Many elements of these perspectives are integrated into the diathesis–stress model of mental disorders which suggests that biological inheritance and early learning experiences predispose us to develop mental disorders; these disorders are expressed only if we encounter stressors that overwhelm our capacity to cope with them.

- The two major manuals for diagnostic mental disorder are the *Diagnostic and Statistical Manual of Mental Disorders IV* (American Psychiatric Association, 1994) and the *International Classification of Diseases 10* (World Health Organisation, 1992).

- There is strong cross-cultural agreement for the diagnosis of disorder such as schizophrenia, although anxiety and social phobia are not as uniformly diagnosed; there are also culture-bound disorders which are not universal.

Treatment of mental disorders

- Historically, people suffering from emotional or behavioural problems were believed to be possessed by demons or were accused of being witches. They were often subjected to torture, including trephining, in which a small hole was punctured in the skull of the afflicted person to allow demonic spirits to escape. Mental patients in sixteenth- and seventeenth-century asylums encountered abject humiliation. Philippe Pinel, a French physician, is often credited with changing the asylum environment in the late eighteenth century.

- Modern therapy adopts an eclectic approach – the borrowing of methods from different treatments and blending them in a way that will work best in treating the patient's problem. There are, however, different types of treatment approaches that have specific characteristics.

- Insight psychotherapy is based primarily on conversation between therapist and client. The oldest form of insight psychotherapy, psychoanalysis, was devised by Freud.

- Psychoanalysis attempts to discover the forces that are warring in the client's psyche and to resolve these inner conflicts by bringing to consciousness his or her unconscious drives and the defences that have been established against them. Insight is believed to be the primary source of healing.

- Humanistic therapy emphasises conscious, deliberate mental processes.

- Client-centred therapy is based on the premise that people are healthy and good and that their problems result from faulty thinking. Instead of evaluating themselves in terms of their own self-concepts, they judge themselves by other people's standards. This tendency is rectified by providing an environment of unconditional positive regard in which clients can find their own way to good mental health.

- Gestalt therapy focuses on convincing clients that they must deal honestly with their present feelings in order to become more mentally healthy. According to Gestalt therapists, the key to becoming happier is to confront one's fears and guilt and to keep one's emotions in proper perspective.

- The range of people that may benefit by undergoing insight therapy is limited and narrow. In general, those most likely to benefit from insight psychotherapy are those who are intelligent and able to articulate their problems. Insight psychotherapies are not effective with persons with serious mental disorders such as schizophrenia. There are also difficulties with evaluating their effectiveness.

- Behaviour therapists attempt to use the principles of classical and operant conditioning to modify behaviour – fears are eliminated or maladaptive behaviours are replaced with adaptive ones.

- Systematic desensitisation uses classical conditioning procedures to condition relaxation to stimuli that were previously producing fear. In contrast, implosion therapy attempts to extinguish fear and avoidance responses. Aversion therapy attempts to condition an unpleasant response to a stimulus with which the client is preoccupied, such as a fetish.

- The most formal system of therapy based on operant condition involves token economies, which arrange contingencies in the environment of people who reside in institutions.

- Some operant treatment is vicarious – people can imagine their own behaviour with its consequent reinforcement or punishment.

- Modelling involves using others as role models for behaviour.

- The major problem with behaviour therapy is the failure of patients to transfer behaviour outside the therapy setting. Techniques to promote generalisation include the use of intermittent reinforcement and recruitment of family and friends as adjunct therapists.

- Cognitive behaviour therapies attempt to change overt behaviour and unobservable cognitive processes.

- Rational-emotive therapy is based on the assumption that people's psychological problems stem from faulty cognitions. Its practitioners use many forms of persuasion, including confrontation, to encourage people to abandon faulty cognitions in favour of logical and healthy ones.

- Beck has developed ways to help depressed people correct errors of cognition that perpetuate self-defeating thoughts.

- Group therapy is based on the belief that certain problems can be treated more efficiently and more effectively in group settings.

- Practitioners of family therapy, couples therapy and some forms of group behaviour therapy observe people's interactions with others and attempt to help them learn how to establish more effective patterns of behaviour. Treatment of groups, including families and couples, permits the therapist to observe clients' social behaviours, and it uses social pressures to help convince clients of the necessity for behavioural change. It permits clients to learn from the mistakes of others and to observe that other people have similar problems, which often provides reassurance.

- The effectiveness of psychotherapeutic methods is difficult to assess: outcomes are difficult to measure objectively, ethical considerations make it hard to establish control groups for some types of disorder, and self-selection and dropouts make it impossible to compare randomly selected groups of participants. Research suggests that behaviour therapy and cognitive behaviour therapy are effective.

- Biological treatments for mental disorders include drugs, electroconvulsive therapy and psychosurgery.

- Research has shown that treatment of the positive symptoms of schizophrenia with antipsychotic drugs, of major depression with antidepressant drugs, and of bipolar disorder with lithium carbonate are the most effective ways to alleviate the symptoms of these disorders.

- Tricyclic antidepressant drugs can also alleviate severe anxiety that occurs during panic attacks and agoraphobia and can reduce the severity of obsessive-compulsive disorder.

- The anti-anxiety drugs help to reduce anticipatory anxiety that occurs between panic attacks.

- Although electroconvulsive therapy is an effective treatment for depression, its use is reserved for cases in which rapid relief is critical because the seizures may produce brain damage.

- The most controversial treatment, psychosurgery, is rarely performed today. Its only currently accepted use, in the form of cingulotomy, is for treatment of crippling compulsions that cannot be reduced by more conventional means.

Mental disorders

Anxiety, somatoform and dissociative mental disorders

- Anxiety disorders refer to mental disorders which are characterised by excessive worry or fear and include generalised anxiety disorder panic disorder, simple phobia, obsessive-compulsive disorder and post-traumatic stress disorder.

- Generalised anxiety disorder is characterised by excessive worry about all aspects of life; the most explanatory models suggest that anxiety serves as an alarm function preparing an organism for future action. It is best treated by anxiolytic (anti-anxiety) drugs.

- Panic disorder results from a fear of fear. A patient misinterprets bodily sensations catastrophically. Cognitive behaviour therapy and anti-anxiety drugs are effective treatments.

- Social phobia refers to an excessive pathological fear of speaking or performing in public. Agoraphobia, the most common phobia, is the fear of open spaces. Simple phobia is a fear of specific stimuli such as spiders and snakes.

- Post-traumatic stress disorder refers to anxiety generated by an astonishing event or trauma (such as natural catastrophe, war or rape).

- Somatoform disorders include somatisation disorder and conversion disorder.

- Somatisation disorder refers to complaints of symptoms of illness without underlying physiological causes. Almost all people with this disorder are women.

- Conversion disorder involves specific neurological symptoms, such as paralysis or sensory disturbance, that are not produced by a physiological disorder.

- Dissociative disorders include psychogenic amnesia (with or without fugue) – a withdrawal from a painful situation or from intolerable guilt; multiple personalities – the adoption of several distinct and complete personalities.

Personality disorders

- Antisocial personality disorder refers to a pathological impairment in social and personal behaviour. It is also known as psychopathy or sociopathy. Psychopaths are indifferent to the effects of their behaviour on other people, are impulsive, fail to learn from experience, are sexually promiscuous, lack commitment to a partner and are habitual liars. Some psychopaths are superficially charming and psychopathy tends to run in families.

- There is a significant association between psychopathy and alcohol abuse.

Psychoactive substance abuse disorders

- All substances that produce addiction do so by activating the reinforcement system of the brain, which involves the release of dopamine. Most people who are exposed to addictive drugs, even those with high abuse potentials, do not become addicts. Evidence suggests that the likelihood of addiction, especially to alcohol, is strongly affected by heredity.

- There may be two types of alcoholism: one related to an antisocial, pleasure-seeking personality (steady drinkers), and another related to a repressed, anxiety-ridden personality (binge drinkers).

Schizophrenic disorders

- The main positive symptoms of schizophrenia include thought disorders; delusions of persecution, grandeur and control; and hallucinations. The main negative symptoms include withdrawal, apathy and poverty of speech.

- DSM-IV classifies schizophrenia into several subtypes, including undifferentiated, catatonic, paranoid and disorganised. But the distinctions between process and reactive schizophrenia and between positive and negative symptoms also seem to be important.

- The diathesis–stress model suggests that some people seem to inherit a predisposition for the disorder, which is expressed when environmental stressors outweigh their attempts to cope with them.

- Recent research suggests that a low level of expressed emotion (including critical comments and emotional overinvolvement) on the part of family members facilitates the recovery of a patient with schizophrenia.

- Positive symptoms of schizophrenia can be produced in normal people or made worse in schizophrenic patients by drugs that stimulate dopamine synapses (cocaine and amphetamine) and can be reduced or eliminated by drugs that block dopamine receptors (antipsychotic drugs).

- These findings have led to the dopamine hypothesis, which states that schizophrenia is caused by an inherited biochemical defect that causes dopamine neurons to be overactive.

- Enlargement of the ventricles is a consistent finding in schizophrenic patients and is unrelated to drug use; there is also evidence of reduced frontal lobe activation.

- More recent studies indicate that schizophrenia can best be conceived of as two different disorders. The positive symptoms are produced by overactivity of dopamine neurons and can be treated with antipsychotic drugs. These positive symptoms are associated with limbic and sublimbic neural activation during verbal hallucination and verbal disorganisation.

- The negative symptoms, which do not respond to these drugs, are caused by brain abnormality. Investigators have found direct evidence of brain damage by inspecting CT scans of living patients' brains.

- Researchers have suggested three possible causes of the brain abnormality: a virus that triggers an autoimmune disease, which causes brain damage later in life; a virus that damages the brain early in life; and obstetric complications.

Mood disorders

- Mood disorders refer to a severe disturbance in emotion.

- Bipolar disorder consists of alternating periods of mania and depression, whereas major depression consists of depression alone.

- Beck has noted that although mood disorders involve emotional reactions, these reactions may be, at least in part, based on faulty and negative cognition. Others such as Abramson and co-workers suggest that

- depressed individuals are characterised by a negative attributional style which promotes helplessness and hopelessness.
- Heritability studies strongly suggest a biological component to mood disorders. This possibility receives support from the finding that biological treatments effectively reduce the symptoms of these disorders, while reserpine, a drug used to treat hypertension, can cause depression.

- Biological treatments include lithium carbonate for bipolar disorder and electroconvulsive therapy and antidepressant drugs (including monoamine oxidase inhibitors and tricyclic antidepressants) for depression.
- Recently developed drugs for depression, called serotonin-specific reuptake inhibitors, act by preventing reuptake of serotonin and blocking serotonin receptors.

Suggestions for further reading

Carson, R.C., Butcher, J.N. and Mineka, S. (1997). *Abnormal Psychology and Modern Life* (10th edition). New York: HarperCollins.

Davison, G.C. (1997). *Abnormal Psychology* (7th edition). Chichester: Wiley.

Oltmans, T.F. and Emery, R.E. (1998). *Abnormal Psychology* (2nd edition). Upper Saddle River, NJ: Prentice Hall.
Abnormal psychology is one of the most popular areas of study in the psychology profession and on degree courses. As a result, there are many good textbooks which are in their fifth or sixth editions (and beyond). The three books mentioned here are very good introductions to the general area of mental disorder and are recommended for more information on topics covered in this chapter.

Power, M. and Dalgleish, T. (1997). *Cognition and Emotion.* Hove, UK: The Psychology Press.

Williams, J.M.G., Watts, F.N., Macleod, C. and Mathews, A. (1997). *Cognitive Psychology and Emotional Disorders* (2nd edition). Chichester: Wiley.
More specific material on mood disorders can be found in Power and Dalgleish and Williams et al.'s excellent texts. Cognition and Emotion reviews not only theories of abnormal emotion but also normal emotion and discusses each of the major emotions in some detail. It is evaluative and up to date. Williams et al.'s book focuses more on mood disorders and evaluates the contribution of cognitive psychology to the understanding of mood disorders. It is a well-written and balanced account of cognitive input into emotional disorder.

Eysenck, M. (1997). *Anxiety and Cognition – A Unified Theory.* Hove, UK: The Psychology Press.

Frith, C.D. (1995). *The Cognitive Neuropsychology of Schizophrenia.* Hove, UK: The Psychology Press.

Hammen, C. (1997). *Depression.* Hove, UK: The Psychology Press.

McKenna, P.J. (1997). *Schizophrenia and Related Syndromes.* Hove, UK: The Psychology Press.

Rachman, S. (1997). *Anxiety.* Hove, UK: The Psychology Press.
A number of books treat mental disorders separately, and these five texts are some of the best covering anxiety, depression and schizophrenia. Each is recommended if you want to pursue an interest in a specific disorder.

Halligan, P.W. and Marshall, J.C. (1996). *Method in Madness.* Hove, UK: The Psychology Press.

Oltmans, T.F., Neale, J.M. and Davison, G. (1995). *Case Studies in Abnormal Psychology* (4th edition). Chichester: Wiley.

Sutherland, S. (1987). *Breakdown.* London: Weidenfeld.

The impact of mental disorder (on the individual and on the people around the individual) is seen vividly in personal accounts of mental illness. These three books present case studies of mental disorder but from slightly different perspectives. Halligan and Marshall's book is a collection of chapters on various disorders that straddle neuropsychology and psychiatry; Oltmans et al.'s book complements DSM-IV and presents case studies of each of the major disorders listed in the manual. Sutherland's book is remarkable. It is an account of bipolar disorder suffered by the late Stewart Sutherland and recounts the various treatments and therapies he underwent in a search for a cure. He describes the events surrounding the disorder with often painful honesty and the account is made all the more provocative by the fact that Sutherland himself was professor of psychology at the University of Sussex.

Aponte, J.F., Rivers, R.Y. and Wohl, J. (1995). *Psychological Interventions and Cultural Diversity.* Boston: Allyn and Bacon.

Kazdin, A.E. (1994). *Behaviour Modification in Applied Settings.* Pacific Grove, CA: Brooks/Cole.

Vervaeke, G.A.C. and Emmelkamp, P.M.G. (1998). Treatment selection: What do we know? *European Journal of Psychological Assessment*, 14, 1, 50–9.
The two books provide an account of some of the treatment strategies employed in alleviating mental disorder. Most books on mental disorder will have a section on treatment, these two provide a description of the application of certain types of intervention on mental disorder. Vervaeke and Emmelkamp's article gives a brief overview of the elements of psychotherapy that contribute to a successful outcome.

Journals to consult

American Journal of Psychiatry
Annals of Psychiatry
Archives of General Psychiatry
Behaviour Research and Therapy
British Journal of Clinical Psychology
British Journal of Psychiatry
Clinical Psychology and Psychotherapy
Cognitive Neuropsychiatry
Current Opinion in Psychiatry
Journal of Abnormal Psychology
Journal of Clinical Psychology
Journal of Consulting and Clinical Psychology
Journal of Psychotherapy Practice and Research
Psychotherapy

GLOSSARY

absolute threshold The minimum value of a stimulus that can be detected.

accommodation (1) Changes in the thickness of the lens of the eye that focus images of near or distant objects on the retina. (2) In developmental psychology, the process by which existing schemata are modified or changed by new experiences.

acquired dyslexia Reading impairment which results from brain injury.

acquisition In classical conditioning, the time during which a conditioned stimulus first appears and increases in frequency.

action potential A brief electrochemical event that is carried by an axon from the soma of the neuron to its terminal buttons; causes the release of a transmitter substance.

activational effect The effect of a hormone on a physiological system that has already developed. If the effect involves the brain, it can influence behaviour. An example is facilitation of sexual arousal and performance.

actor–observer effect The tendency to attribute one's own behaviour to situational factors but others' behaviour to dispositional factors.

adaptation The ability of generations of species to adapt effectively to changes in the environment

adaptive significance The effectiveness of behaviour in aiding organisms to adjust to changing environmental conditions.

adjacency principle A Gestalt principle of organisation; elements located closest to each other are perceived as belonging to the same figure. Also called proximity principle.

aerobic exercise Physical activity that expends considerable energy, increases blood flow and respiration and thereby stimulates and strengthens the heart and lungs and increases the body's efficient use of oxygen.

affix A sound or group of letters added to the beginning of a word (prefix) or its end (suffix).

affordances Features of the perceptual environment which give it its meaning or signify its use.

aggression The intent to inflict harm on others.

agoraphobia A mental disorder characterised by fear of and avoidance of being alone in public places; this disorder is often accompanied by panic attacks.

agrammatism A language disturbance; difficulty in the production and comprehension of grammatical features, such as proper use of function words, word endings and word order. Often seen in cases of Broca's aphasia.

alcoholism An addiction to ethanol, the psychoactive agent in alcoholic beverages.

algorithm A procedure that consists of a series of steps that will solve a specific type of problem.

alien hand After split-brain operation, the feeling that patients report of one hand not belonging to them.

alleles Alternative forms of the same gene.

allesthesia In spatial neglect, where patients transfer features of the right-hand side of an object/environment to the left when drawing. Also called allochiria.

allochiria *See* allesthesia.

alpha activity Rhythmical, medium-frequency activity of the electroencephalogram, usually indicating a state of quiet relaxation.

altruism The unselfish concern of one individual for the welfare of another.

Alzheimer's disease A degenerative brain disorder characterised by neuronal abnormalities which leads to confusional states and cognitive impairment.

amygdala A part of the limbic system of the brain located deep in the temporal lobe; damage causes changes in emotional and aggressive behaviour.

anal stage The second of Freud's psychosexual stages, during which the primary erogenous zone is the anal region. Freud argued that during this time, children take pleasure in retaining or expelling faeces.

anatomical coding A means by which the nervous system represents information; different features are coded by the activity of different neurons.

androgen insensitivity syndrome An inherited condition caused by a lack of functioning androgen receptors. Because androgens cannot exert their effects, a person with XY sex chromosomes develops as a female, with female external genitalia.

androgens The primary class of sex hormones in males. The most important androgen is testosterone.

androstenone A chemical secreted by wild boars and thought to be a pheromone.

animism The belief that all animals and all moving objects possess spirits providing their motive force.

anorexia nervosa An eating disorder characterised by attempts to lose weight, sometimes to the point of starvation.

anterior Towards the front.

anterograde amnesia A disorder caused by brain damage that disrupts a person's ability to form new long-term memories of events that occur after the time of the brain damage.

anti-anxiety (anxiolytic) drug A 'tranquilliser', which reduces anxiety. The most common include chlordiazepoxide (Librium) and diazepam (Valium).

antibodies Proteins in the immune system that recognise antigens and help kill invading microorganisms.

anticipatory anxiety A fear of having a panic attack; may lead to the development of agoraphobia.

antidepressant drugs Drugs used to treat depression.

antigen The unique proteins found on the surface of bacteria; these proteins are what enable the immune system to recognise the bacteria as foreign substances.

antimanic drugs Drugs used to treat bipolar disorder and mania.

antipsychotic drugs The pharmacological agents used to treat severe mental illness such as schizophrenia.

antisocial personality disorder A disorder characterised by a failure to conform to standards of decency; repeated lying and stealing; a failure to sustain lasting, loving relationships; low tolerance of boredom; and a complete lack of guilt.

anxiety A sense of apprehension or doom that is accompanied by many physiological reactions, such as accelerated heart rate, sweaty palms and tightness in the stomach.

aphasia Language impairment seen after brain damage and usually involves an inability to produce or comprehend speech.

appeasement gesture A stereotyped gesture made by a submissive animal in response to a threat gesture by a dominant animal; tends to inhibit an attack.

apperceptive agnosia An inability to recognise objects visually.

archetypes Universal thought forms and patterns that Jung believed resided in the collective unconscious.

archromatopsia A form of colour blindness in which the world is seen in shades of grey.

articulatory loop The component of working memory which stores verbal/auditory information. Also called phonological loop.

artificial intelligence The construction of computer programs that simulate mental function.

Asperger's syndrome A disorder similar to autism but characterised by a narrow and obsessional range of interests.

assertiveness training A technique which trains an individual to be more direct about his/her feelings.

assimilation The process by which new information about the world is modified to fit existing schemata.

associative agnosia An inability to make meaningful associations to visually presented objects.

attachment A social and emotional bond between infant and carer that spans both time and space.

attention deficit hyperactivity disorder (ADHD) A conduct disorder characterised by poor sustained attention, impulsiveness and hyperactivity in children.

attentional bias A tendency to attend to certain stimuli more than others.

attitude A relatively enduring set of beliefs, feelings and intentions towards an object, person, event or symbol.

attribution The process by which people infer the causes of other people's behaviour.

auditory hair cell The sensory neuron of the auditory system; located on the basilar membrane.

autobiographical memory *See* episodic memory.

autism Developmental disorder characterised by abnormal social behaviour, language abnormalities and stereotypical and repetitive patterns of behaviour.

automatic processing The formation of memories of events and experiences with little or no attention or effort.

autonomic nervous system (ANS) The portion of the peripheral nervous system that controls the functions of the glands and internal organs.

autotopagnosia An inability to name body parts following damage to the left parietal association cortex.

availability heuristic A general rule for social judgement by which a person judges the likelihood or importance of an event by the ease with which examples of that event come to mind.

aversion therapy A form of treatment in which the client is trained to respond negatively to a neutral stimulus that has been paired with an aversive stimulus.

avoidance response An operant response acquired through negative reinforcement that prevents an aversive stimulus from occurring.

avoidant attachment A kind of attachment in which infants avoid or ignore their mothers and often do not cuddle when held.

axes The criteria used in DSM-IV for classifying mental disorder.

axon A long, thin part of a neuron attached to the soma; divides into a few or many branches, ending in terminal buttons.

B lymphocytes Cells that develop in bone marrow and release immunoglobulins to defend the body against antigens.

backward masking The ability of a stimulus to interfere with the perception of a stimulus presented just before it.

barbiturate A drug that causes sedation; one of several derivatives of barbituric acid.

Barnum effect Individuals' acceptance that vague and generalised descriptions of personality that apply to almost all individuals are an accurate reflection of their own personality.

base-rate fallacy The failure to consider the likelihood that a person, place or thing is a member of a particular category – some categories are simply larger than others.

basic-level concept A concept that makes important distinctions between different categories.

basic orientations Karen Horney's sets of personality characteristics that correspond to the strategies of moving towards others, moving against others and moving away from others.

basic rest–activity cycle (BRAC) The suggestion that our behaviour patterns for drinking, feeding, sleeping and so on follow 90 minute cycles of rest and activity. The cycle is controlled by a biological clock in the pons; during sleep, it controls cycles of REM sleep and slow-wave sleep.

basilar membrane A membrane that divides the cochlea of the inner ear into two compartments. The receptive organ for audition resides here.

behaviour genetics The branch of psychology that studies the role of genetics in behaviour.

behaviour modification Behaviour therapy based on the principles of operant conditioning.

behavioural inhibition system (BIS) The brain system which allows the organism to evaluate how threatening the environment is.

behaviourism A movement in psychology that asserts that the only proper subject matter for scientific study in psychology is observable behaviour.

belief in a just world The belief that people get what they deserve in life – good things happen to good people and bad things happen to bad people.

benzodiazepine A class of drug having anxiolytic ('tranquillising') effects.

beta activity The irregular, high-frequency activity of the electroencephalogram, usually indicating a state of alertness or arousal.

between-groups design *See* independent groups design.

bilingualism The ability to communicate in two or more languages.

Binet–Simon Scale An intelligence test developed by Binet and Simon in 1905; the precursor of the Stanford–Binet Scale.

biological evolution Changes that take place in the genetic and physical characteristics of a population or group of organisms over time.

biological reductionism The belief that behaviour can be explained and described primarily by biological processes.

bipedalism The ability to move about the environment on two feet.

bipolar cell A neuron in the retina that receives information from photoreceptors and passes it on to the ganglion cells, from which axons proceed through the optic nerves to the brain.

bipolar disorder Alternating states of depression and mania separated by periods of relatively normal affect.

blending After segmenting a word, the putting together of these segments to pronounce a word.

blindsight A disorder resulting from occipital cortex damage in which patients seem to show awareness of objects but declare being consciously unaware of them.

bottom-up processing A perception based on successive analyses of the details of the stimuli that are present.

brain stem The 'stem' of the brain, including the medulla, pons and midbrain.

brightness A perceptual dimension of colour, most closely related to the intensity or degree of radiant energy emitted by a visual stimulus.

brightness constancy The tendency to perceive objects as having constant brightness even when they are observed under varying levels of illumination.

bulimia nervosa A loss of control over food intake characterised by gorging binges followed by self-induced vomiting or use of laxatives; also accompanied by feelings of guilt and depression.

bystander intervention The intervention of a person in a situation that appears to require his or her aid.

c The features which families share in common and can contribute to intelligence.

callosal syndrome The behavioural consequences of lesioning the largest bundle of nerve fibres connecting the two hemispheres, the corpus callosum.

case study Observation of the behaviour of individuals having special characteristics, such as psychological or neurological disorders.

cataplexy A neurological disorder in which the person collapses, becoming temporarily paralysed but not unconscious; usually triggered by anger or excitement; apparently related to the paralysis that normally accompanies REM sleep.

catastrophic misinterpretation The interpretation of bodily sensations as physical threat.

catatonic schizophrenia A form of schizophrenia characterised primarily by various motor disturbances, including catatonic postures and waxy flexibility.

causal event or determinant An event that causes another event to occur.

central executive The component of working memory that co-ordinates the other elements of working memory such as the phonological loop and the visuospatial scratchpad.

central nervous system The brain and the spinal cord.

central traits Descriptive traits that are significantly more important than other traits in organising information about a person into an impression.

cerebellum A pair of hemispheres resembling the cerebral hemispheres but much smaller and lying beneath and at the back of them; controls posture and movements, especially rapid ones.

cerebral cortex The outer layer of the cerebral hemispheres of the brain, approximately 3 mm thick.

cerebral hemisphere The largest part of the brain; covered by the cerebral cortex and containing parts of the brain that evolved most recently.

cerebrospinal fluid (CSF) The liquid in which the brain and spinal cord float; provides a shock-absorbing cushion.

chemosensation The process of sensing chemical stimuli by the chemosenses (olfaction and gustation).

chemosense One of the two sense modalities (gustation and olfaction) that detect the presence of chemical molecules present in the environment.

child-directed speech The speech of an adult directed towards a child; differs in important features from adult-directed speech and tends to facilitate learning of language by children.

chromosomal aberration The rearrangement of genes within chromosomes or a change in the total number of chromosomes.

chromosomes Rod-like structures in the nuclei of living cells; contain genes.

chunking A process by which information is simplified by rules which make it easily remembered once the rules are learned. For example, the string of letters TWAIBMBBC is easier to remember if a person learns the rule that organises them into smaller 'chunks': TWA, IBM and BBC.

cilia Hairlike appendages of a cell; involved in movement or in transducing sensory information. Cilia are found on the receptors in the auditory and vestibular systems.

cingulotomy The surgical destruction of the cingulum bundle, which connects the prefrontal cortex with the limbic system; helps to reduce intense anxiety and the symptoms of obsessive-compulsive disorder.

circadian rhythm A daily rhythmical change in behaviour or physiological process.

classical conditioning The process by which a response normally elicited by one stimulus (the UCS) comes to be controlled by another stimulus (the CS) as well.

client-centred therapy A form of therapy in which the client is allowed to decide what to talk about without strong direction and judgement from the therapist.

clinical judgements Diagnoses of mental disorders or predictions of future behaviour based largely on experts' experience and knowledge.

clinical neuropsychology The branch of psychology concerned with the identification and treatment of the behavioural consequences of nervous system disorders and injuries.

clinical psychology The branch of psychology concerned with the investigation and treatment of abnormal behaviour and mental disorders.

cochlea A snail-shaped chamber set in bone in the inner ear, where audition takes place.

cocktail-party phenomenon The ability to attend selectively to auditory material against a background of competing auditory stimuli.

cognitive behaviour therapy A treatment method that focuses on altering the client's maladaptive thoughts, beliefs and perceptions.

cognitive dissonance theory The theory that changes in attitude can be motivated by an unpleasant state of tension caused by a disparity between a person's beliefs or attitudes and their behaviour, especially beliefs or attitudes that are related to the person's self-esteem.

cognitive interview Technique of applying the principles of cognitive psychology to the purpose of enhancing memory retrieval in real life settings (such as witnessing and reporting a crime).

cognitive neuroscience The branch of neuroscience which seeks to localise cognitive functions (such as memory, attention, language etc) in the brain.

cognitive psychology The branch of psychology that studies complex behaviours and mental processes, such as perception, attention, learning and memory, verbal behaviour, concept formation and problem solving.

cognitive reappraisal Any coping strategy in which one alters one's perception of the threat posed by a stressor to reduce stress.

cognitive rehabilitation Specific form of rehabilitation in which patients are encouraged to recover functions such as memory and language which have been impaired by the brain injury.

cognitive restructuring Altering misconceptions about the consequences of bodily sensation.

cognitive science The branch of psychology which seeks to understand human cognitive function by using artificial intelligence and computer models.

cognitive structures According to Piaget, mental representations or rules, such as schemata or concepts, that are used for understanding and dealing with the world and for thinking about and solving problems.

cognitive triad Pessimistic thinking about the self, the present and the future.

collective unconscious According to Jung, the part of the unconscious that contains memories and ideas inherited from our ancestors over the course of evolution.

colour mixing The perception of two or more lights of different wavelengths seen together as light of an intermediate wavelength.

companionate love Love that is characterised by a deep, enduring affection and caring for another person, accompanied by a strong desire to maintain the relationship.

comparative psychology The branch of psychology that studies the behaviours of a variety of organisms in an attempt to understand the adaptive and functional significance of the behaviours and their relation to evolution.

competition A striving or vying with others who share the same ecological niche for food, mates and territory.

complementary medicine An alternative, unorthodox approach to treatment of illness that is not based on conventional medicine.

compliance Engaging in a particular behaviour at another person's request, not because you have an underlying attitude that favours the behaviour.

componential intelligence According to Sternberg, the mental mechanisms people use to plan and execute tasks; includes metacomponents, performance components, and knowledge acquisition components.

compulsion An irresistible impulse to repeat some action over and over even though it serves no useful purpose.

computerised tomography (CT) Technique that uses a special X-ray machine and a computer to produce images of the brain that appear as slices taken parallel to the top of the skull.

concept A category of objects or situations that share some common attributes.

concordance research Research that studies the degree of similarity between twins in traits expressed. Twins are said to be concordant for a trait if either both or neither twin expresses it and discordant if only one twin expresses it.

conditional response (CR) In classical conditioning, the response elicited by the CS.

conditional stimulus (CS) In classical conditioning, a stimulus which, because of its repeated association with the UCS, eventually elicits a conditional response (CR).

conditioned reinforcer (or punisher) A stimulus that acquires its reinforcing (or punishing) properties through association with a primary reinforcer (or punisher). Sometimes referred to as a secondary reinforcer (or punisher).

conditioned emotional response A classically conditioned response produced by a stimulus that evokes an emotional response, in most cases including behavioural and physiological components.

conditioned flavour-aversion learning A type of learning in which a substance is avoided because its flavour has been associated with illness.

conditions of worth Conditions that others place on us for receiving their positive regard.

conduct disorder Impairment in the child's ability to inhibit its own anti-social and deviant behaviour.

cone A photoreceptor that is responsible for acute daytime vision and for colour perception.

confidentiality Privacy of participants and non-disclosure of their participation in a research project.

confirmation bias A tendency to seek evidence that might confirm a hypothesis rather than evidence that might disconfirm it; a logical error.

conformity The adoption of attitudes and behaviours shared by a particular group of people – the internalisation of a group norm as a standard for one's own behaviour.

confounding of variables An inadvertent alteration of more than one variable during an experiment. The results of an experiment involving confounded variables permit no valid conclusions about cause and effect.

conjugate movement The co-operative movement of the eyes, which ensures that the image of an object falls on identical portions of both retinas.

connectionism The modelling of human cognitive function based on computer simulation.

conscience The internalisation of the rules and restrictions of society; it determines which behaviours are permissible and punishes wrongdoing with feelings of guilt.

consensual behaviour Behaviour that is shared by many people; behaviour that is similar from one person to the next. To the extent that different people engage in the same behaviour, their behaviour is consensual.

conservation Understanding that specific properties of objects (height, weight, volume, length) remain the same despite apparent changes in the shape or arrangement of those objects.

consistency The extent to which a person behaves the same way every time he or she is in the same situation.

consolidation The process by which information in short-term memory is transferred to long-term memory, presumably because of physical changes that occur in neurons in the brain.

consumer psychology The branch of psychology which studies the factors which influence consumer decision making and preference.

contact hypothesis The view that prejudice will disappear if you bring people from different races together to interact with one another.

content word A noun, verb, adjective or adverb that conveys meaning.

contextual intelligence According to Sternberg, intelligence that reflects the behaviours that were subject to natural selection: adaptation – fitting oneself into one's environment by developing useful skills and behaviours; selection – finding one's own niche in the environment; and shaping – changing the environment.

contralateral Residing in the side of the body opposite the reference point.

control group A comparison group used in an experiment, the members of which are exposed to the naturally occurring or zero value of the independent variable.

conventional level Kohlberg's second level of moral development, in which people realise that society has instituted moral rules to maintain order and to serve the best interests of its citizenry.

convergence The result of conjugate eye movements whereby the fixation point for each eye is identical; feedback from these movements provides information about the distance of objects from the viewer.

conversion A defence mechanism that involves converting an intrapsychic conflict into a physical form, such as blindness, deafness, paralysis or numbness.

conversion disorder A somatoform disorder involving the actual loss of bodily function, such as blindness, paralysis and numbness, due to excessive anxiety.

coping strategy A plan of action that a person follows to reduce the perceived level of stress, either in anticipation of encountering a stressor or in response to its occurrence.

cornea The transparent tissue covering the front of the eye.

coronary heart disease (CHD) The narrowing of blood vessels that supply nutrients to the heart.

corpus callosum A large bundle of axons ('white matter') that connects the cortex of the two cerebral hemispheres.

correctional mechanism In a regulatory process, the mechanism that is capable of restoring the system variable to the set point.

correlation coefficient A measurement of the degree to which two variables are related.

correlational study The observation of two or more variables in the behaviour or other characteristics of people or other animals.

counterbalancing A systematic variation of conditions in an experiment, such as the order of presentation of stimuli, so that different participants encounter them in different orders; prevents confounding of independent variables with time-dependent processes such as habituation or fatigue.

countertransference The process by which the therapist projects his or her emotions onto the client.

covert sensitisation A method used by behaviour therapists in which a client imagines the aversive consequences of his or her inappropriate behaviour.

cranial nerve A bundle of nerve fibres attached to the base of the brain; conveys sensory information from the face and head and carries messages to muscles and glands.

cri-du-chat syndrome A genetic disorder arising from partial deletion of chromosome 5 which is associated with mental retardation and mewing sounds (hence cri-du-chat).

critical period A specific time in development during which certain experiences must occur for normal development to occur.

cross-cultural psychology The branch of psychology that studies and compares the effects of culture on behaviour.

CS pre-exposure effect The name given to the effect seen in latent inhibition – the phenomenon whereby a novel object is more successfully paired with a familiar one in conditioning.

cultural evolution The adaptive changes of cultures in response to environmental changes over time.

cultural psychology The branch of psychology which studies variations in behaviour within, but not necessarily across, cultures.

culture-bound syndrome Highly unusual mental disorders, similar in nature to non-psychotic mental disorders, that appear to be specific to only one or a few cultures.

cumulative recorder A mechanical device connected to an operant chamber for the purpose of recording operant responses as they occur in time.

cyclothymic disorder A less severe form of bipolar disorder.

cytoskeleton The skeletal structure of neurons.

dark adaptation The process by which the eye becomes capable of distinguishing dimly illuminated objects after going from a bright area to a dark one.

debriefing Full disclosure to research participants of the true nature and purpose of a research project after its completion.

deductive reasoning Inferring specific instances from general principles or rules.

deep dyslexia A severe inability to read; common words are sometimes read but are often replaced by semantically similar words.

deep processing The analysis of the complex characteristics of a stimulus, such as its meaning or its relationship to other stimuli.

defence mechanisms Mental systems that become active whenever unconscious instinctual drives of the id come into conflict with internalised prohibitions of the superego.

deferred imitation A child's ability to imitate the actions he or she has observed others perform. Piaget believed deferred imitation to result from the child's increasing ability to form mental representations of behaviour performed by others.

deferred imitation paradigm A child is exposed to an adult who is performing actions with a set of novel stimuli; after a delay, the child is then allowed to manipulate objects used by the experimenter. Identical use indicates a degree of imitation and learning.

deindividuation The loss of one's individuality and sense of personal responsibility in collective events.

delta activity The rhythmical activity of the electroencephalogram, having a frequency of less than 3.5 Hz, indicating deep (slow-wave) sleep.

delusions Beliefs that are obviously contrary to fact.

delusions of control The false belief that one's thoughts and actions are being controlled by other people or forces.

delusions of grandeur The false belief that one is famous, powerful or important.

delusions of persecution The false belief that other people are plotting against one.

dementia Cognitive deterioration associated with degenerative brain disorders.

dementia of the Alzheimer type (DAT) Cognitive impairment that arises from Alzheimer's disease.

dendrite A tree-like part of a neuron on which the terminal buttons of other neurons form synapses.

dependent variable The event whose value is measured in an experiment. Manipulation of independent variables demonstrates whether they affect the value of dependent variables.

descriptive statistics Mathematical procedures for organising collections of data, such as determining the mean, the median, the range, the variance and the correlation coefficient.

detector In a regulatory process, a mechanism that signals when the system variable deviates from its set point.

deuteranopia A form of hereditary anomalous colour vision; caused by defective 'green' cones in the retina.

developmental dyslexia A difficulty in learning to read despite adequate intelligence and appropriate educational opportunity.

developmental psychology The branch of psychology that studies the changes in behavioural, perceptual and cognitive capacities of organisms as a function of age and experience.

deviation IQ A procedure for computing the intelligence quotient; compares a child's score with those received by other children of the same chronological age.

Diagnostic and Statistical Manual IV (DSM-IV) A widely used manual for classifying psychological disorders.

diathesis model The notion that asymmetrical frontal cortex activation may predispose individuals to react negatively or positively to emotional stimuli.

diathesis–stress model A causal account of mental disorders based on the idea that mental disorders develop when a person possesses a predisposition for a disorder and faces stressors that exceed his or her abilities to cope with them.

dichotic listening A task that requires a person to listen to one of two different messages being presented simultaneously, one to each ear, through headphones.

difference threshold An alternative name for just-noticeable difference (jnd).

diffusion of responsibility An explanation of the failure of bystander intervention stating that, when several bystanders are present, no one person assumes responsibility for helping.

discourse analysis Qualitative method of analysis which involves the identification of themes, thoughts and ideas from transcripts of conversations or discussions.

discrimination (1) In operant conditioning, responding only when a specific discriminative stimulus is present but not when similar stimuli are present. (2) The differential treatment of people based on their membership in a particular group – discrimination is typically 'against' an outgroup and in favour of the ingroup. (3) In classical conditioning, the appearance of a conditioned response (CR) when one stimulus is presented (the CS+) but not another (the CS–).

discriminative stimulus In operant conditioning, the stimulus that sets the occasion for responding because, in the past, a behaviour has produced certain consequences in the presence of that stimulus.

disorganised schizophrenia A type of schizophrenia characterised primarily by disturbances of thought and a flattened or silly affect.

display rule A culturally determined rule that prescribes the expression of emotions in particular situations.

dispositional factors Individual personality characteristics that affect a person's behaviour.

dissociative disorders A class of disorders in which anxiety is reduced by a sudden disruption in consciousness, which in turn produces changes in one's sense of identity.

dissociative identity disorder A rarely seen dissociative disorder in which two or more distinct personalities exist within the same person; each personality dominates in turn.

distinctive feature A physical characteristic of an object that helps distinguish it from other objects.

distinctiveness The extent to which a person engages in a particular behaviour in one situation but not in other situations.

divided attention Attention which is divided amongst two or more tasks.

dizygotic (DZ) twins Twins that are fertilised from different ova (and are, therefore, genetically different).

DNA Deoxyribonucleic acid. The DNA structure resembles that of a twisted ladder. Strands of sugar and phosphates are connected by rungs made from adenine and thymine and guanine and cytosine.

doctrine of apperception The belief that we do not see objects as separate elements but as wholes.

doctrine of the association of ideas The belief that various associations are made between events and ideas, which allow meaningful thought to occur.

doctrine of specific nerve energies Johannes Müller's observation that different nerve fibres convey specific information from one part of the body to the brain or from the brain to one part of the body.

dominant allele The form of the gene that controls the expression of a trait. When a gene pair contains two dominant alleles or when it contains both a dominant and a recessive allele, the trait regulated by the dominant gene will be expressed.

dopamine hypothesis The hypothesis that the positive symptoms of schizophrenia are caused by overactivity of synapses in the brain that use dopamine.

double-aspect theory The belief that mental and physical events are characteristics of the same underlying entity.

double-bind The conflict caused for a child when he or she is given inconsistent messages or cues from a parent.

double-blind study An experiment in which neither the subject nor the experimenter knows the value of the independent variable.

Down syndrome A genetic disorder caused by a chromosomal aberration resulting in an extra twenty-first chromosome. People having Down syndrome are generally short, have broad skulls and round faces, and suffer impairments in physical, psychomotor and cognitive development.

drive A condition, often caused by physiological changes or homeostatic disequilibrium, that energises an organism's behaviour.

drive reduction hypothesis The hypothesis that a drive (resulting from physiological need or deprivation) produces an unpleasant state that causes an organism to engage in motivated behaviours. Reduction of drive is assumed to be reinforcing.

DSM-IV *See Diagnostic and Statistical Manual IV.*

dual-action antidepressants Antidepressants which block certain serotonin receptors and inhibit its reuptake.

dual-route model of reading A model which proposes that there are two, non-semantic routes that take the reader from spelling to sound. The lexical route retrieves words from the mental lexicon; the sublexical route converts letters into sound using GPC rules.

dual-task methodology A protocol in attention research whereby the participant undertakes two tasks simultaneously in order to determine the degree to which the performance of one interferes with the other.

dualism/Cartesian dualism The philosophical belief that reality consists of mind and matter.

Duchenne smile The genuine smile of joy characterised by the activation of specific facial muscles.

dyslexia A disorder impaired reading ability.

dysthymic disorder A less severe form of depression.

echoic memory A form of sensory memory for sounds that have just been perceived.

eclectic approach A form of therapy in which the therapist uses whatever method he or she feels will work best for a particular client at a particular time.

educational psychology The branch of psychology which applies psychological principles to our understanding of the educational process and children's learning and adjustment in education.

effortful processing Practising or rehearsing information through either shallow or deep processing.

ego The self. The ego also serves as the general manager of personality, making decisions regarding the pleasures that will be pursued at the id's request and the moral dictates of the superego that will be followed.

ego-ideal The internalisation of what a person would like to be.

egocentrism Self-centredness; preoperational children can see the world only from their own perspective.

elaboration likelihood model A model that explains the effectiveness of persuasion. The central route requires the person to think critically about an argument, and the peripheral route entails the association of the argument with something positive.

elaborative rehearsal The processing of information on a meaningful level, such as forming associations, attending to the meaning of the material, thinking about it and so on.

electra complex In Freudian thinking, a girl's attachment to her father; named after the mythical Electra who killed her mother and mother's lover in order to avenge her father's death.

electro-oculogram (EOG) The measurement and graphical presentation of the electrical activity caused by movements of the eye, recorded by means of electrodes attached to the skin adjacent to the eye.

electrocardiogram (EKG) The measurement and graphical presentation of the electrical activity of the heart, recorded by means of electrodes attached to the skin.

electroconvulsive therapy (ECT) Treatment of severe depression that involves passing small amounts of electric current through the brain to produce seizure activity.

electroencephalogram (EEG) The measurement and graphical presentation of the electrical activity of the brain, recorded by means of electrodes attached to the scalp.

electroencephalography (EEG) A technique which measures the electrical activity of the brain using electrodes.

electromyogram (EMG) The measurement and graphical presentation of the electrical activity of muscles, recorded by means of electrodes attached to the skin above them.

elevation A monocular cue of depth perception; objects nearer the horizon are seen as farther from the viewer.

embryo stage The second stage of prenatal development, beginning two weeks and ending about eight weeks after conception, during which the heart begins to beat, the brain starts to function and most of the major body structures begin to form.

emotion A relatively brief display of a feeling made in response to environmental events having motivational significance or to memories of such events.

emotion-focused coping Any coping behaviour that is directed towards changing one's own emotional reaction to a stressor.

emotional stability The tendency to be relaxed and at peace with oneself.

empiricism The philosophical view that all knowledge is obtained through the senses.

encephalisation Increased brain size.

encoding The process by which sensory information is converted into a form that can be used by the brain's memory system.

encoding specificity The principle that how we encode information determines our ability to retrieve it later.

endocrine gland A gland that secretes a hormone.

enuresis Bed-wetting; a slow-wave sleep disorder.

enzymes Proteins that regulate the structure of bodily cells and the processes occurring within those cells.

epilepsy A seizure disorder which involves excessive and uncontrollable firing of neurons.

episodic memory A type of long-term memory that serves as a record of our life's experiences. Also called autobiographical memory.

ergonomics/human factors psychology The branch of psychology which studies the ways that people and machines work together and helps design machines that are safer and easier to operate.

escape response An operant response acquired through negative reinforcement that terminates an aversive stimulus.

ethology The branch of comparative psychology which studies the behaviour of animals and uses this information to draw conclusions about humn behaviour and evolution.

event-related potential (ERP) A technique which records the brain's electrical activity across several presentations of the same stimuli.

evolutionary preparedness The notion that we are predisposed to fear certain objects and contexts.

evolutionary psychology The branch of psychology that studies the ways in which an organism's evolutionary history contributes to the development of behavioural patterns and cognitive strategies related to reproduction and survival during its lifetime.

exemplar A memory of particular examples of objects or situations that are used as the basis of classifying objects or situations into concepts.

exhibitionism Exposure of genitals in public for sexual gratification.

expectancy The belief that a certain consequence will follow a certain action.

experiential intelligence According to Sternberg, the ability to deal effectively with novel situations and to solve automatically problems that have been encountered previously.

experiment A study in which the experimenter changes the value of an independent variable and observes whether this manipulation affects the value of a dependent variable. Only experiments can confirm the existence of cause-and-effect relations among variables.

experimental brain lesion Deliberate damage to a particular region of the brain.

experimental group A group of participants in an experiment, the members of which are exposed to a particular value of the independent variable, which has been manipulated by the experimenter.

explicit memory Memory that can be described verbally and of which a person is therefore aware.

expressed emotion Expressions of criticism, hostility and emotional overinvolvement by family members towards a person with schizophrenia.

externality effect In infancy, the idea that the child is more concerned with the contours of visual stimuli and rarely attends to internal features.

extinction In classical conditioning, the elimination of a response that occurs when the CS is repeatedly presented without being followed by the UCS.

extinction A decrease in the frequency of a previously reinforced response because it is no longer followed by a reinforcer.

extroversion The tendency to seek the company of other people, to be lively, and to engage in conversation and other social behaviours with them.

facial feedback hypothesis The notion that our awareness of facial expression influences the way we feel.

factor analysis A statistical procedure that identifies common factors among groups of data.

false consensus The tendency for a person to perceive his or her own behaviour as representative of general consensus of how other people behave.

family therapy A form of family therapy in which the maladaptive relationships among family members is inferred from their behaviour and attempts are made to restructure these behaviours into more adaptive ones.

fast mapping The quick learning of new, content words by children.

female sexual dysfunction The inability to achieve orgasm.

foetal stage The third and final stage of prenatal development, which lasts for about seven months, beginning with the appearance of bone tissue and ending with birth.

fetish Unusual sexual attachment to objects such as articles of clothing, learned through classical conditioning.

fetishism The use of non-living things for sexual excitement.

field experiment An experiment that is conducted in a realistic environment and over which the experimenter has little experimental control.

fight or flight response Physiological reactions that help ready us to fight or to flee a dangerous situation.

figure A visual stimulus that is perceived as a self-contained object.

fissures Grooves between the bulges (gyri) of the cortex.

five-factor model A theory stating that personality is composed of five primary dimensions: neuroticism, extroversion, openness, agreeableness and conscientiousness. This theory was developed using factor analyses of ratings of the words that people use to describe personality characteristics.

fixation (1) A brief interval between saccadic eye movements during which the eye does not move; visual information is gathered during this time. (2) An unconscious obsession with an erogenous zone resulting from failure to resolve the crisis associated with the corresponding stage of psychosexual development.

fixation point The area in space where a gaze is fixed.

fixed-interval schedule A schedule of reinforcement in which the first response that is made after a fixed interval of time since the previous reinforcement (or the start of the session) is reinforced.

fixed-ratio schedule A schedule of reinforcement in which reinforcement occurs only after a fixed number of responses have been made since the previous reinforcement (or the start of the session).

flashbulb memory A lucid memory for an event or experience that occurred during a particularly emotional experience.

flooding The intense arousal of anxious patients, usually through exposure to the anxiety-provoking stimulus or context, which is intended to demonstrate that no harm comes from such exposure.

foetal alcohol syndrome A disorder that adversely affects an offspring's brain development that is caused by the mother's alcohol intake during pregnancy.

foetal learning The notion that the foetus is capable of rudimentary learning while in the womb.

foetal stage Third and final stage of prenatal development which lasts for about seven months, beginning with the appearance of bone tissue and ending with birth.

forensic/criminological psychology The branch of psychology which uses psychological principles to study and assist in the legal and criminal process.

form constancy The tendency to perceive objects as having a constant form, even when they are rotated or their distance from the observer changes.

formal concept A category of objects or situations defined by listing their common essential characteristics, as dictionary definitions do.

fovea A small pit near the centre of the retina containing densely packed cones; responsible for the most acute and detailed vision.

fragile X A genetic disorder which leads to mental retardation. The X chromosome is fragile and easily broken.

free association A method of Freudian analysis in which an individual is asked to relax, clear his or her mind of current thoughts, and then report all thoughts, images, perceptions and feelings that come to mind.

free nerve ending An unencapsulated (naked) dendrite of somatosensory neurons.

frontal lobe The front portion of the cerebral cortex, including Broca's speech area and the motor cortex; damage impairs movement, planning and flexibility in behavioural strategies.

frotterism Rubbing against a person in public for sexual gratification.

function word A preposition, article or other word that conveys little of the meaning of a sentence but is important in specifying its grammatical structure.

functional hemisphere asymmetry The idea that a function is located in one cerebral hemisphere.

functional magnetic resonance imaging (fMRI) A development of MRI which allows the observation of brain function and not just structure.

functionalism The strategy of understanding a species' structural or behavioural features by attempting to establish their usefulness with respect to survival and reproductive success.

fundamental attribution error The tendency to overestimate the significance of dispositional factors and underestimate the significance of situational factors in explaining other people's behaviour.

fundamental frequency The lowest, and usually most intense, frequency of a complex sound; most often perceived as the sound's basic pitch.

g factor According to Spearman, a factor of intelligence that is common to all intellectual tasks; includes apprehension of experience, eduction of relations and eduction of correlates.

ganglion cell A neuron in the retina that receives information from photoreceptors by means of bipolar cells and from which axons proceed through the optic nerves to the brain.

general adaptation syndrome (GAS) The model proposed by Selye to describe the body's adaptation to chronic exposure to severe stressors. The body passes through an orderly sequence of three physiological stages: alarm, resistance and exhaustion.

general language discrimination hypothesis The notion that children can discriminate sentences from two languages based on extracting linguistic properties from these languages.

generalisation (1) The conclusion that the results obtained from a sample apply also to the population from which the sample was taken. (2) In classical conditioning, CRs elicited by stimuli that resemble the CS used in training. (3) In operant conditioning, the occurrence of responding when a stimulus similar (but not identical) to the discriminative stimulus is present.

generalised anxiety disorder (GAD) Excessive worry about all matters relating to the individual's life.

genes Small units of chromosomes that direct the synthesis of proteins and enzymes.

genetic counselling A form of counselling in which people receive information regarding their family history of genetic disorders.

genetic disorders Inherited disorders of behaviour that arise from faulty genetic material.

genetic epistemology The study of the origin of knowledge in the development of the child.

genetics The study of the genetic make-up of organisms and how it influences physical and behavioural characteristics.

genital stage The final of Freud's psychosexual stages (from puberty through adolescence). During this stage, the adolescent develops adult sexual desires.

genotype An organism's genetic make-up.

geon According to Biederman, an elementary shape that can serve as a prototype in recognising objects; a given object can consist of one or more individual geons.

gerontology The study of the process of ageing.

Gestalt psychology A school of psychology that asserts that the perception of objects is produced by particular configurations of the elements of stimuli; that cognitive processes can be understood by studying their organisation, not their elements.

Gestalt therapy A form of therapy emphasising the unity of mind and body by teaching the client to 'get in touch' with unconscious bodily sensations and emotional feelings.

Gilles de la Tourette's syndrome A neurological disorder characterised by tics and involuntary utterances, some of which may involve obscenities and the repetition of others' utterances.

glia/glial cell A cell of the central nervous system that provides support for neurons and supplies them with some essential chemicals.

glucocorticoid A chemical, such as cortisol, that influences the metabolism of glucose, the main energy source of the body.

glucose A sugar which is the primary source of fuel for the body's cells.

glucostatic hypothesis The hypothesis that hunger is caused by a low level or availability of glucose, a condition that is monitored by specialised sensory neurons.

glucostats Hypothetical entity which detects decreases in blood sugar.

glycogen An insoluble carbohydrate that can be synthesised from glucose or converted to it; used to store nutrients.

good continuation A Gestalt law of organisation; given two or more interpretations of elements that form the outline of the figure, the simplest interpretation will be preferred.

grapheme–phoneme correspondence (GPC) rules The rules used to convert written words into spoken sounds.

graphemes The smallest units of written words.

grey matter The portions of the central nervous system that are abundant in cell bodies of neurons rather than axons.

ground A visual stimulus that is perceived as a formless background against which objects are seen.

grounded theory A form of qualitative analysis which deliberately constructs theories on the basis of information derived from transcripts of conversations and discussions.

group A collection of individuals who have a shared definition of who they are and what they should think, feel and do – people in the same group generally have common interests and goals.

group polarisation The tendency for a group decision to be more extreme than the mean of its members positions, in the direction favoured by the mean.

group psychotherapy Therapy in which two or more clients meet simultaneously with a therapist, discussing problems within a supportive and understanding environment.

groupthink The tendency to avoid dissent in the attempt to achieve group consensus in the course of decision making.

gustation The sense of taste.

gyri Bulges in the surfaces of the cortex.

h The proportion of variance associated with genetic differences among individuals.

habituation The simplest form of learning; learning not to respond to an unimportant event that occurs repeatedly.

hallucinations Perceptual experiences that occur in the absence of external stimulation of the corresponding sensory organ.

handedness The degree to which an individual preferentially uses one hand for most activities.

haze A monocular cue of depth perception; objects that are less distinct in their outline and texture are seen as farther from the viewer.

health psychology The branch of psychology which applies psychological principles to health behaviour and illness prevention.

heredity The sum of the traits and tendencies inherited from a person's parents and other biological ancestors.

heritability The degree to which the variability of a particular trait in a particular population of organisms is a result of genetic differences among those organisms.

hertz (Hz) The primary measure of the frequency of vibration of sound waves; cycles per second.

'hidden observer' phenomenon The phenomenon whereby the hypnotist places a hand on the shoulder of the hypnotised and appears to be able to talk to a hidden part of the hypnotised's body.

hippocampus A structure in the limbic system, located deep in the temporal lobe, which plays an important role in memory and learning.

homeostasis The process by which important physiological characteristics (such as body temperature and blood pressure) are regulated so that they remain at their optimum level.

hormone A chemical substance secreted by an endocrine gland that has physiological effects on target cells in other organs.

hue A perceptual dimension of colour, most closely related to the wavelength of a pure light.

humanistic approach An approach to the study of personality in which the emphasis is placed on the positive, fulfilling aspects of life.

humanistic psychology An approach to the study of human behaviour that emphasises human experience, choice and creativity, self-realisation, and positive growth.

humanistic therapy A form of therapy focusing on the person's unique potential for personal growth and self-actualisation.

Huntington's chorea A genetic disorder caused by a dominant lethal gene in which a person experiences slow but progressive mental and physical deterioration.

hypnosis The process whereby verbal instructions can be acted on by another without conscious awareness of these instructions.

hypnotic analgesia The use of hypnosis to alleviate pain.

hypochondriasis A somatoform disorder involving persistent and excessive worry about developing a serious illness. People with this disorder often misinterpret the appearance of normal physical aches and pains.

hypothalamus A region of the brain located just above the pituitary gland; controls the autonomic nervous system and many behaviours related to regulation and survival, such as eating, drinking, fighting, shivering and sweating.

hypothesis A statement, usually designed to be tested by an experiment, that tentatively expresses a cause-and-effect relationship between variables.

hypothetico-deductive A methodological approach which sets hypotheses and then constructs experiments to test them.

iconic memory A form of sensory memory that holds a brief visual image of a scene that has just been perceived.

id The unconscious reservoir of libido, the psychic energy that fuels instincts and psychic processes.

idealism The belief that all ideas ultimately come from information from the senses.

idiot savants Autistic individuals who excel in specific abilities such as mental arithmetic, drawing, painting or music.

illusion of outgroup homogeneity A belief that members of groups to which one does not belong are more similar to one another than are members of one's own group.

illusory correlation The perception of an apparent relation between two distinctive elements that does not actually exist or is enormously exaggerated.

immune system A network of organs and cells that protects the body from invading bacteria, viruses and other foreign substances.

immunoglobulins The antibodies that are released by B lymphocytes.

implicit memory Memory that cannot be described verbally and of which a person is therefore not aware.

implosion therapy A form of therapy that attempts to rid people of fears by arousing them intensely until their responses diminish through habituation and they learn that nothing bad happens.

impression formation The way in which we form impressions of others and attribute specific characteristics and traits to them.

incest The mating of close relatives who share many of the same genes.

inclusive fitness The reproductive success of those who share common genes.

incongruence A discrepancy between a client's real and ideal selves.

independent variable The variable that is manipulated in an experiment as a means of determining cause-and-effect relations. Manipulation of an independent variable demonstrates whether it affects the value of the dependent variable.

independent groups design A design whereby each group in an experiment contains different participants. Also called between-groups design.

individual differences The branch of psychology concerned with the individual factors that make us different (such as personality, sex, race etc).

inductive reasoning Inferring general principles or rules from specific facts.

infantile amnesia Loss of memory for events that occur in infancy.

inferential statistics Mathematical procedures for determining whether relations or differences between samples are statistically significant.

inflection A change in the form of a word (usually by adding a suffix) to denote a grammatical feature such as tense or number.

information processing An approach used by cognitive psychologists to explain the workings of the brain; information received through the senses is processed by systems of neurons in the brain.

informed consent Agreement to participate as a subject in an experiment after being informed about the nature of the research and any possible adverse effects.

insomnia Chronic and relentless inability to fall asleep at the appropriate times.

intelligence A person's ability to learn and remember information, to recognise concepts and their relations, and to apply the information to their own behaviour in an adaptive way.

intelligence quotient (IQ) A simplified single measure of general intelligence; by definition, the ratio of a person's mental age to his or her chronological age, multiplied by 100; often derived by other formulas.

interactionism The view that the mind and body are separate physical entities which interact.

intermanual conflict The effect sometimes seen after split-brain surgery whereby one hand appears to behave in a contradictory way to the other.

intermittent reinforcement The occasional reinforcement of a particular behaviour; produces responding that is more resistant to extinction.

International Classification of Disorders-10 (ICD-10) A manual similar to DSM.

interneuron A neuron located entirely within the central nervous system.

interpersonal attraction People's tendency to approach each other and to evaluate each other positively.

interposition A monocular cue of depth perception; an object that partially occludes another object is perceived as closer.

interrater reliability The degree to which two or more independent observers agree in their ratings of another organism's behaviour.

intraspecific aggression The attack by one animal upon another member of its species.

introspection Literally, 'looking within', in an attempt to describe one's own memories, perceptions, cognitive processes or motivations.

introversion The tendency to avoid the company of other people, especially large groups of people; shyness.

ion A positively or negatively charged particle; produced when many substances dissolve in water.

ion channel A special protein molecule located in the membrane of a cell; controls the entry or exit of particular ions.

ion transporter A special protein molecule located in the membrane of a cell; actively transports ions into or out of the cell.

iris The pigmented muscle of the eye that controls the size of the pupil.

isolation aphasia A language disturbance that includes an inability to comprehend speech or to produce meaningful speech accompanied by the ability to repeat speech and to learn new sequences of words; caused by brain damage to the left temporal/parietal cortex that spares Wernicke's area.

James–Lange theory A theory of emotion that suggests that behaviours and physiological responses are directly elicited by situations and that feelings of emotions are produced by feedback from these behaviours and responses.

just-noticeable difference (jnd) The smallest difference between two similar stimuli that can be distinguished. Also called difference threshold.

kin selection A type of selection that favours altruistic acts aimed at individuals who share some of the altruist's genes, such as parents, siblings, grandparents, grandchildren and, under certain conditions, distant relatives.

language acquisition device A hypothetical brain function which all children are said to have and which embodies the rules of universal grammar.

latency period The period between the phallic stage and the genital stage during which there are no unconscious sexual urges or intrapsychic conflicts.

latent content The hidden message of a dream, produced by the unconscious.

latent inhibition The phenomenon whereby a novel object is more successfully paired with a familiar one in conditioning.

lateralisation Phenomenon whereby a function is the predominant responsibility of one side or part of the body or brain (e.g. speech production is lateralised in the left hemisphere).

law of closure A Gestalt law of organisation; elements missing from the outline of a figure are 'filled in' by the visual system.

law of common fate A Gestalt law of organisation; elements that move together give rise to the perception of a particular figure.

law of effect Thorndike's observation that stimuli that occur as a consequence of a response can increase or decrease the likelihood of making that response again.

leakage A sign of expression of an emotion that is being masked.

learned helplessness A response to exposure to an inescapable aversive stimulus, characterised by reduced ability to learn a solvable avoidance task; thought to play a role in the development of some psychological disturbances.

learning An adaptive process in which the tendency to perform a particular behaviour is changed by experience.

lens The transparent organ situated behind the iris of the eye; helps to focus an image on the retina.

leptin Protein which is secreted by fat cells that have absorbed a large amount of triglyceride.

lexical awareness The ability to understand that speech and writing are composed of different, distinct elements called words.

libido An insistent, instinctual force that is unresponsive to the demands of reality; the primary source of motivation.

liking A feeling of personal regard, intimacy and esteem towards another person.

limbic cortex The cerebral cortex located around the edge of the cerebral hemispheres where they join with the brain stem; part of the limbic system.

limbic system A set of interconnected structures of the brain important in emotional and species-typical behaviour; includes the amygdala, hippocampus and limbic cortex.

linear perspective A monocular cue of depth perception; the arrangement or drawing of objects on a flat surface such that parallel lines receding from the viewer are seen to converge at a point on the horizon.

linguistic relativity The hypothesis that the language a person speaks is related to his or her thoughts and perceptions.

linguistics The study of the rules of language and the nature and meaning of written and spoken language.

lithium carbonate Drug used to treat bipolar disorder.

localisation of function The notion that functions may be localised in the brain at the neural, chemical or anatomical level.

locus of control An individual's beliefs that the consequences of his or her actions are controlled by internal person variables or by external environmental variables.

long-term memory Memory in which information is represented on a permanent or near-permanent basis.

loving A combination of liking and a deep sense of attachment to, intimacy with, and caring for another person.

magnetic resonance imaging (MRI) Neuroimaging technique which allows neuropsychologists to observe the structure of the living brain by measuring the reverberation of hydrogen molecules in the brain as a magnetic field is passed over the head.

maintenance rehearsal The rote repetition of information; repeating a given item over and over again.

major depression Persistent and severe feelings of sadness and worthlessness accompanied by changes in appetite, sleeping and behaviour.

male sexual dysfunction The inability to achieve an erection.

mania Excessive emotional arousal and wild, exuberant, unrealistic activity.

manifest content The apparent storyline of a dream.

masking Attempting to hide the expression of an emotion.

matching A systematic selection of participants in groups in an experiment or (more often) a correlational study to ensure that the mean values of important subject variables of the groups are similar.

materialism A philosophical belief that reality can be known only through an understanding of the physical world, of which the mind is a part.

maturation Any relatively stable change in thought, behaviour or physical growth that is due to the ageing process and not to experience.

mean A measure of central tendency; the sum of a group of values divided by their number; the arithmetical average.

measure of central tendency A statistical measure used to characterise the value of items in a sample of numbers.

measure of variability A statistical measure used to characterise the dispersion in values of items in a sample of numbers.

median A measure of central tendency; the midpoint of a group of values arranged numerically.

medical model A perspective on mental illness which regards mental disorder as caused by specific abnormalities of the brain and nervous system.

medulla The part of the brain stem closest to the spinal cord; controls vital functions such as heart rate and blood pressure.

meiosis The form of cell division by which new sperm and ova are formed. The chromosomes within the cell are randomly rearranged so that new sperm and ova contain twenty-three individual chromosomes, or half of that found in other bodily cells.

memory The cognitive processes of encoding, storing and retrieving information.

meninges The three-layered set of membranes that enclose the brain and spinal cord.

menstrual synchrony The phenomenon whereby menstrual cycles of more than one female become synchronous.

mental age A measure of a person's intellectual development; the level of intellectual development that could be expected for an average child of a particular age.

mental lexicon Hypothetical cognitive store of words and their meanings.

mental model A mental construction based on physical reality that is used to solve problems of logical deduction.

mental space (M-space) A hypothetical construct in Case's model of cognitive development similar to working memory, whose primary function is to process information from the external world.

mere exposure effect The formation of a positive attitude towards a person, place or thing, based solely on repeated exposure to that person, place or thing.

mesmerism Another word for hypnosis, named after Franz Anton Mesmer, an Austrian physician.

meta-analysis A statistical procedure by which the results of many studies are combined to estimate the magnitude of a particular effect.

metamemory Knowledge of the knowledge acquisition process.

method of loci A mnemonic system in which items to be remembered are mentally associated with specific physical locations or landmarks.

microtubules Parts of the neuron which perform specific functions.

midbrain The part of the brain stem just anterior to the pons; involved in control of fighting and sexual behaviour and in decreased sensitivity to pain during these behaviours.

Minnesota Multiphasic Personality Inventory (MMPI) An objective test designed originally to distinguish individuals with different psychological problems from normal individuals. It has since become popular as a means of attempting to identify personality characteristics of people in many everyday settings.

mnemonic system A special technique or strategy consciously employed in an attempt to improve memory.

mode The most frequently occurring number in a series of numbers.

model A relatively simple system that works on known principles and is able to do at least one of the things that a more complex system can do.

modelling A technique which has individuals modelling their behaviour on that of another.

modularity The notion that the functions of the brain are organised by means of semi-independent and self-contained modules, each of which performs a specific function.

modulation An attempt to exaggerate or minimise the expression of an emotion.

monoamine oxidase inhibitors (MAOIs) Antidepressants which prevent enzymes at the synaptic gap from destroying amines.

monogamy The mating of one female and one male.

monozygotic (MZ) twins Twins that are fertilised from the same ovum (and are, therefore, genetically identical).

mood disorder A disorder characterised by significant shifts or disturbances in mood that affect normal perception, thought and behaviour. Mood disorders may be characterised by deep, foreboding depression, or a combination of the depression and euphoria.

moral realism The first stage of Piaget's model of moral development, which includes egocentrism and blind adherence to rules.

morality of co-operation The second stage of Piaget's model of moral development, which involves the recognition of rules as social conventions.

motion parallax A cue of depth perception. As we pass by a scene, objects closer to us pass in front of objects farther away.

motivation A general term for a group of phenomena that affect the nature, strength or persistence of an individual's behaviour.

motor association cortex Those regions of the cerebral cortex that control the primary motor cortex; involved in planning and executing behaviours.

motor neuron A neuron whose terminal buttons form synapses with muscle fibres. When an action potential travels down its axon, the associated muscle fibres will twitch.

muscle spindle A muscle fibre that functions as a stretch receptor; arranged parallel to the muscle fibres responsible for contraction of the muscle, it detects muscle length.

mutations Accidental alterations in the DNA code within a single gene. Mutations can either be spontaneous and occur naturally or be the result of environmental factors, such as exposure to high-energy radiation.

myelin sheath The insulating material that encases most large axons.

narrative A mnemonic system in which items to be remembered are linked together by a story.

native language recognition hypothesis The notion than infants have the ability to identify words in their native language.

natural concept A category of objects or situations based on people's perceptions and interactions with things in the world; based on exemplars.

natural selection The consequence of the fact that organisms reproduce differentially, which is caused by behavioural differences among them. Within any given population, some animals – the survivors – will produce more offspring than will other animals.

naturalistic observation Observation of the behaviour of people or other animals in their natural environments.

negative after-image The image seen after a portion of the retina is exposed to an intense visual stimulus; a negative after-image consists of colours complementary to those of the physical stimulus.

negative alliesthesia A decrease in the linking of food which is determined by internal, physiological signals.

negative feedback A process whereby the effect produced by an action serves to diminish or terminate that action. Regulatory systems are characterised by negative feedback loops.

negative reinforcement An increase in the frequency of a response that is regularly and reliably followed by the termination of an aversive stimulus.

negative symptoms Symptoms of schizophrenia that may include the absence of normal behaviour, flattened emotion, poverty of speech, lack of initiative and persistence, and social withdrawal.

neobehaviourism/radical behaviourism The strand of behaviourism developed by Skinner and others which described behaviour in terms of instrumental (or operant) learning.

nerve A bundle of nerve fibres that transmit information between the central nervous system and the body's sense organs, muscles and glands.

neural networks Computer models which hope to simulate the way in which the brain works.

neuroimaging Technique used to measure the anatomical structure and neural activity of the living human brain.

neuromodulator A substance secreted in the brain that modulates the activity of neurons that contain the appropriate receptor molecules.

neuron A nerve cell; consists of a cell body with dendrites and an axon whose branches end in terminal buttons that synapse with muscle fibres, gland cells or other neurons.

neuropsychological assessment Procedure whereby the effect of brain damage on cognitive, perceptual and emotional performance is evaluated by means of a single test or a collection of tests.

neuropsychological rehabilitation Process whereby brain-damaged individuals are trained to retrieve some of the functions lost through injury.

neuropsychology/neuroscience The study of central nervous system function.

neuroticism The tendency to be anxious, worried and full of guilt.

neurotransmitter A chemical released by the terminal buttons that causes the postsynaptic neuron to be excited or inhibited.

night terrors A children's disorder in which the child wakes up in absolute terror, usually after suddenly waking from stage 4 sleep; distinguishable from nightmares which are frightening dreams.

nominal fallacy The false belief that one has explained the causes of a phenomenon by identifying and naming it; for example, believing that one has explained lazy behaviour by attributing it to 'laziness'.

non-fluent (Broca's) aphasia Severe difficulty in articulating words, especially function words, caused by damage that includes Broca's area, a region of the frontal cortex on the left (speech-dominant) side of the brain.

norm Data concerning comparison groups that permit the score of an individual to be assessed relative to his or her peers.

object permanence The idea that objects do not disappear when they are out of sight.

objective personality tests Tests for measuring personality that can be scored objectively, such as a multiple-choice or true/false test.

observational learning Learning through observing the kinds of consequence that others (called models) experience as a result of their behaviour.

obsession An involuntary recurring thought, idea or image.

obsessive-compulsive disorder Recurrent, unwanted thoughts or ideas and compelling urges to engage in repetitive ritual-like behaviour.

occipital lobe The rearmost portion of the cerebral cortex; contains the primary visual cortex.

Oedipus complex In Freudian thinking, a boy's attachment to his mother; named after the mythical Greek king who unwittingly killed his father and married his mother.

oestrous cycle The ovulatory cycle in mammals other than primates; the sequence of physical and hormonal changes that accompany the ripening and disintegration of ova.

offender profiling A technique used by criminological psychologists which uses information about a criminal's behaviour to draw inferences about his or her personality.

olfaction The sense of smell.

olfactory bulbs Stalk-like structures located at the base of the brain that contain neural circuits that perform the first analysis of olfactory information.

olfactory mucosa The mucous membrane lining the top of the nasal sinuses; contains the cilia of the olfactory receptors.

operant chamber An apparatus in which an animal's behaviour can be easily observed, manipulated and automatically recorded.

operant conditioning A form of learning in which behaviour is affected by its consequences. Favourable consequences strengthen the behaviour and unfavourable consequences weaken the behaviour.

operational definition The definition of a variable in terms of the operations the experimenter performs to measure or manipulate it.

opioid A neuromodulator whose action is mimicked by a natural or synthetic opiate, such as opium, morphine or heroin.

opponent process The representation of colours by the rate of firing of two types of neurons: red/green and yellow/blue.

optic disk A circular structure located at the exit point from the retina of the axons of the ganglion cells that form the optic nerve.

optimal level of skill performance According to Fischer's skill model, the brain's maximal capacity for information processing.

optimum-level hypothesis The hypothesis that organisms will perform behaviour that restores the level of arousal to an optimum level.

oral stage The first of Freud's psychosexual stages, during which the mouth is the major erogenous zone – the major source of physical pleasure. Early in this stage, the mouth is used for sucking; later in the stage it is used for biting and chewing.

orbitofrontal cortex A region of the prefrontal cortex that plays an important role in recognition of situations that produce emotional responses.

organisational effect An effect of a hormone that usually occurs during prenatal development and produces permanent changes that alter the subsequent development of the organism. An example is androgenisation.

organisational/occupational psychology The branch of psychology concerned with the efficiency and effectiveness of organisation.

orienting response Any response by which an organism directs appropriate sensory organs (eyes, ears, nose) towards the source of a novel stimulus.

orthographic awareness The ability to recognise that writing systems have sets of rules that must be followed.

ossicle One of the three bones of the middle ear (the hammer, anvil and stirrup) that transmit acoustic vibrations from the eardrum to the membrane behind the oval window of the cochlea.

oval window An opening in the bone surrounding the cochlea. The stirrup presses against a membrane behind the oval window and transmits sound vibrations into the fluid within the cochlea.

overextension The use of a word to denote a larger class of items than is appropriate, for example, referring to the moon as a ball.

overtone A component of a complex tone; one of a series of tones whose frequency is a multiple of the fundamental frequency.

Pacinian corpuscle A specialised, encapsulated somatosensory nerve ending, which detects mechanical stimuli, especially vibrations.

paedophilia Sex with prepubescent children.

paleoanthropology The study of human evolution through interpreting fossil remains.

panic A feeling of fear mixed with hopelessness or helplessness.

panic disorder Unpredictable attacks of acute anxiety that are accompanied by high levels of physiological arousal and that last from a few seconds to a few hours.

papilla A small bump on the tongue that contains a group of taste buds.

parallel processor The notion that the brain is composed of different modules which allow us to work simultaneously on more than one task.

parallel distributed processing A connectionist model devised by Seidenberg and McClelland to read regular, exception and non-words.

paranoid schizophrenia A form of schizophrenia in which the person suffers from delusions of persecution, grandeur or control.

paraphilia Mental or behavioural disorder that has a sexual content.

parasympathetic branch The portion of the autonomic nervous system that activates functions that occur during a relaxed state.

parental investment The resources, including time, physical effort and risks to life that a parent spends in procreation and in the feeding, nurturing and protecting of offspring.

parietal lobe The region of the cerebral cortex behind the frontal lobe and above the temporal lobe; contains the somatosensory cortex; is involved in spatial perception and memory.

passionate love An emotional, intense desire for sexual union with another person. Also called romantic love.

Pavlovian conditioning Similar to classical conditioning – the process by which a response normally elicited by one stimulus (the UCS) comes to be controlled by another stimulus (the CS) as well.

peg-word method A mnemonic system in which items to be remembered are associated with a set of mental pegs that one already has in memory, such as key words of a rhyme.

perception (1) A rapid, automatic, unconscious process by which we recognise what is represented by the information provided by our sense organs. (2) The detection of the more complex properties of a stimulus, including its location and nature; involves learning.

perceptual disorders Disorders in perception that tend to leave elementary sensation unimpaired.

period of concrete operations The third period in Piaget's theory of cognitive development during which children come to understand the conservation principle and other concepts, such as categorisation.

period of formal operations The fourth period in Piaget's theory of cognitive development during which individuals first become capable of more formal kinds of abstract thinking and hypothetical reasoning.

peripheral nervous system The cranial and spinal nerves; that part of the nervous system peripheral to the brain and spinal cord.

perseverance The tendency to continue to perform a behaviour even when it is not being reinforced.

perseveration Responding in a manner that was previously correct but is now inappropriate.

person variables Individual differences in cognition, which, according to Mischel, include competencies, encoding strategies and personal constructs, expectancies, subjective values, and self-regulatory systems and plans.

personal constructs Idiosyncratic and personal ways of characterising other people.

personality A particular pattern of behaviour and thinking prevailing across time and situations that differentiates one person from another.

personality disorders Abnormalities in behaviour which impair social or occupational function.

personality trait An enduring personal characteristic that reveals itself in a particular pattern of behaviour in a variety of situations.

personality types Different categories into which personality characteristics can be assigned based on factors such as developmental experiences or physical characteristics.

phallic stage The third psychosexual stage. During this stage, the primary erogenous zone is the genital area. At this time, children not only wish to stimulate their genitalia but also become attached to the opposite-sex parent.

phantom limb Sensations that appear to originate in a limb that has been amputated.

phenotype The outward expression of an organism's genotype; an organism's physical appearance and behaviour.

phenylketonuria (PKU) A genetic disorder caused by a particular pair of homozygous recessive genes and characterised by the inability to break down phenylalanine, an amino acid found in many high protein foods. The resulting high blood levels of phenylalanine cause mental retardation.

pheromone A chemical secreted by the body which induces stereotypical behaviour in the perceiving organism.

phi phenomenon The perception of movement caused by the turning on of two or more lights, one at a time, in sequence; often used on theatre marquees; responsible for the apparent movement of images in movies and television.

phobia Unreasonable fear of specific objects or situations, such as insects, animals or enclosed spaces, learned through classical conditioning.

phoneme The minimum unit of sound that conveys meaning in a particular language, such as /p/.

phonetic reading Reading by decoding the phonetic significance of letter strings; 'sound reading'.

phonological awareness The capacity to appreciate the sounds of words and be able to identify letters with sounds.

phonological dyslexia A reading disorder in which people can read familiar words but have difficulty reading unfamiliar words or pronounceable non-words because they cannot sound out words.

phonological loop *See* articulatory loop.

photopigment A complex molecule found in photoreceptors; when struck by light, it splits apart and stimulates the membrane of the photoreceptor in which it resides.

photoreceptor A receptive cell for vision in the retina; a rod or a cone.

physiological psychology The branch of psychology that studies the physiological basis of behaviour.

pituitary gland An endocrine gland attached to the hypothalamus at the base of the brain.

place-dependent memory Description of greater success in retrieval of material when acquisition and retrieval of information occur in the same location.

placebo An inert substance that cannot be distinguished from a real medication by the patient or subject; used as the control substance in a single-blind or double-blind experiment.

planum temporale Structure found in the primary auditory cortex which seems to be larger in the left than right hemisphere.

pleasure principle The rule that the id obeys: obtain immediate gratification, whatever form it may take.

polyandry The mating of one female with more than one male.

polygynandry The mating of several females with several males.

polygyny The mating of one male with more than one female.

pons The part of the brain stem just anterior to the medulla; involved in control of sleep.

positive reinforcement An increase in the frequency of a response that is regularly and reliably followed by an appetitive stimulus.

positive symptoms Symptoms of schizophrenia that may include thought disorder, hallucinations or delusions.

positivism The school of thought which states that all meaningful ideas can be reduced to observable material.

positron emission tomography (PET) Technique used to measure the degree of blood flow or oxygen consumption in the living brain as it engages in activity.

postconventional level Kohlberg's third and final level of moral development, in which people come to understand that moral rules include principles that apply across all situations and societies.

posterior Towards the back.

posterior part of the parietal cortex (PPC) Part of the brain responsible for the ability to locate objects in space.

posthypnotic amnesia A failure to remember what occurred during hypnosis; induced by suggestions made during hypnosis.

posthypnotic suggestibility The tendency of a person to perform a behaviour suggested by the hypnotist some time after the person has left the hypnotic state.

postsynaptic neuron A neuron with which the terminal buttons of another neuron form synapses and that is excited or inhibited by that neuron.

post-traumatic stress disorder (PTSD) Anxiety which follows a traumatic event.

preconventional level Kohlberg's first level of moral development, which bases moral behaviour on external sanctions, such as authority and punishment.

prefrontal cortex The anterior part of the frontal lobe; contains the motor association cortex.

prejudice An attitude or evaluation, usually negative, towards a group of people defined by their racial, ethnic or religious heritage or by their gender, occupation, sexual orientation, level of education, place of residence or membership of a particular group.

prenatal period The nine months between conception and birth. This period is divided into three developmental stages: the zygote, the embryo and the foetal stages.

preoperational period The second of Piaget's periods, which represents a 4–5 year transitional period between first being able to think symbolically and then being able to think logically. During this stage, children become increasingly capable of speaking meaningful sentences.

preoptic area A region at the base of the brain just in front of the hypothalamus; contains neurons that appear to control the occurrence of slow-wave sleep.

presynaptic neuron A neuron whose terminal buttons form synapses with and excite or inhibit another neuron.

primacy effect (1) The tendency to remember initial information. In the memorisation of a list of words, the primacy effect is evidenced by better recall of the words early in the list. (2) The tendency to form impressions of people based on the first information we receive about them.

primary appraisal In anxiety research, the initial evaluation of the environment as neutral, positive or negative.

primary auditory cortex The region of the cerebral cortex that receives information directly from the auditory system; located in the temporal lobes.

primary motor cortex The region of the cerebral cortex that directly controls the movements of the body; located in the back part of the frontal lobes.

primary punisher A biologically significant aversive stimuli, such as pain.

primary reinforcer A biologically significant appetitive stimulus, such as food or water.

primary somatosensory cortex The region of the cerebral cortex that receives information directly from the somatosensory system (touch, pressure, vibration, pain and temperature); located in the front part of the parietal lobes.

primary visual cortex V1. The region of the cerebral cortex that receives information directly from the visual system; located in the occipital lobes.

proactive interference Interference in recall that occurs when previously learned information disrupts our ability to remember newer information.

problem-focused coping Any coping behaviour that is directed at reducing or eliminating a stressor.

process schizophrenia According to Bleuler, a form of schizophrenia characterised by a gradual onset and a poor prognosis.

progressive relaxation technique A relaxation technique involving three steps: (i) recognising the body's signals that indicate the presence of stress; (ii) using those signals as a cue to begin relaxing; and (iii) relaxing groups of muscles, beginning with those in the head and neck and then those in the arms and legs.

projection A defence mechanism in which one's unacceptable behaviours or thoughts are attributed to someone else.

projective tests Unstructured personality measures in which a person is shown a series of ambiguous stimuli, such as pictures, inkblots or incomplete drawings. The person is asked to describe what he or she 'sees' in each stimulus or to create stories that reflect the theme of the drawing or picture.

prosody The use of changes in intonation and emphasis to convey meaning in speech besides that specified by the particular words; an important means of communication of emotion.

prosopagnosia A form of visual agnosia characterised by difficulty in the recognition of people's faces; caused by damage to the visual association cortex.

prospective memory Remembering to perform an activity planned in the future.

protanopia A form of hereditary anomalous colour vision; caused by defective 'red' cones in the retina.

protective factor A factor – psychological or physiological – which can assist in the prevention of disease.

prototype A hypothetical idealised pattern that resides in the nervous system and is used to perceive objects or shapes by a process of comparison; recognition can occur even when an exact match is not found.

protoword A unique string of phonemes that an infant invents and uses as a word.

proximate causes Immediate environmental events and conditions that affect behaviour.

proximity principle *See* adjacency principle.

pseudohomophone A word which is legally spelled, is not a real word but sounds like a real word (e.g. 'phicks' sounds like 'fix').

pseudoword A word that is legally spelled but is not a real word.

psychiatry A branch of medicine concerned with the diagnosis and treatment of mental illness.

psychoactive substance use disorders Mental disorders that are characterised by addiction to drugs or by abuse of drugs.

psychoanalysis A form of therapy aimed at giving the client insight into his or her unconscious motivations and impulses; a branch of thinking which argues that behaviour can be explained by unconscious desires and impulses.

psychobiology *See* physiological psychology.

psychodynamic A term used to describe the Freudian notion that the mind is in a state of conflict among instincts, reasons and conscience.

psychodynamic therapy Therapy based on the understanding that unconscious drives, desires and impulses manifest themselves in behaviour.

psychogenic amnesia A dissociative disorder characterised by the inability to remember important events or personal information.

psychogenic fugue Amnesia with no apparent organic cause accompanied by a flight away from home.

psycholinguistics A branch of psychology devoted to the study of verbal behaviour.

psychology The scientific study of the causes of behaviour; also, the applications of the findings of psychological research to the solution of problems.

psychoneuroimmunology Study of the interactions between the immune system and behaviour as mediated by the nervous system.

psychophysics A branch of psychology that measures the quantitative relation between physical stimuli and perceptual experience.

psychophysiology The measurement of physiological responses, such as blood pressure and heart rate, to infer changes in internal states, such as emotions.

psychosurgery Unalterable brain surgery used to relieve the symptoms of psychological disorders.

psychoticism The tendency to be aggressive, egocentric and antisocial.

puberty The period during which people's reproductive systems mature, marking the beginning of the transition from childhood to adulthood.

punishment A decrease in the frequency of a response that is regularly and reliably followed by an aversive stimulus.

pure word deafness The ability to hear, to speak and (usually) to write, without being able to comprehend the meaning of speech; caused by bilateral temporal lobe damage.

purposive behaviourism A variation on behaviourism proposed by Tolman which argued that variables intervening between stimulus and response were important and gave behaviour its purpose.

pursuit movement The movement that the eyes make to maintain an image of a moving image upon the fovea.

qualitative analysis An approach to research which focuses on the ways in which people use words, express feelings and arguments. Themes and ideas can be interpreted from transcripts of these discussions.

quantitative research The methodological approach which regards human behaviour as measurable and subject to statistical analysis.

random assignment An assignment of participants to the various groups of an experiment by random means, thereby ensuring comparable groups.

range The difference between the highest score and the lowest score of a sample.

rapid eye movement (REM) sleep A period of sleep during which dreaming, rapid eye movements, and muscular paralysis occur and the EEG shows beta activity.

ratio IQ A formula for computing the intelligence quotient; mental age divided by chronological age, multiplied by 100.

rational-emotive therapy Therapy based on the belief that psychological problems are caused not by upsetting events but by how people think about them.

rationalisation A defence mechanism that justifies an unacceptable action with a more acceptable, but false, excuse.

reaction formation A defence mechanism that involves behaving in a way that is the opposite of how one really feels because the true feelings produce anxiety.

reactive schizophrenia According to Bleuler, a form of schizophrenia characterised by rapid onset and brief duration; he assumed the cause was stressful life situations.

reality principle The tendency to satisfy the id's demands realistically, which almost always involves compromising the demands of the id and superego.

receiver operating characteristic curve (ROC curve) A graph of hits and false alarms of subjects under different motivational conditions; indicates people's ability to detect a particular stimulus.

recency effect The tendency to recall later information. In the memorisation of a list of words, the recency effect is evidenced by better recall of the last words in the list.

receptive field That portion of the visual field in which the presentation of visual stimuli will produce an alteration in the firing rate of a particular neuron.

receptor cell A neuron that directly responds to a physical stimulus, such as light, vibrations or aromatic molecules.

receptor molecule A special protein molecule located in the membrane of the postsynaptic neuron that responds to molecules of the transmitter substance. Receptors such as those that respond to opiates are sometimes found elsewhere on the surface of neurons.

recessive allele The form of the gene that does not influence the expression of a trait unless it is paired with another recessive allele.

reciprocal altruism Altruism in which people behave altruistically towards one another because they are confident that such acts will be reciprocated towards either them or their kin.

reciprocal determinism The idea that behaviour, environment and personal variables, such as perception, interact to determine personality.

reciprocity The tendency to return, in kind, favours that others have done for us.

recovered memories Memories (usually negative) that are thought to be repressed in very early childhood and which access consciousness during therapy.

reflex An automatic response to a stimulus, such as the blink reflex to the sudden approach of an object toward the eyes.

regulatory behaviour A behaviour that tends to bring physiological conditions back to normal, thus restoring the condition of homeostasis.

reification Assuming that your subject matter is real and concrete and actually exists in substance.

reliability The repeatability of a measurement; the likelihood that if the measurement was made again it would yield the same value.

REM sleep behaviour disorder A neurological disorder characterised by absence of the paralysis that normally occurs during REM sleep; the patient acts out his or her dreams.

remember-to-know shift Period when remembered information is transferred into long-term memory and becomes permament knowledge.

repeated measures design A design whereby the same participants take part in each condition of an experiment. Also called within-groups design.

replication Repetition of an experiment or observational study to see whether previous results will be obtained.

representativeness heuristic A general rule for social judgement by which people classify a person, place or thing into the category to which it appears to be the most similar.

repression The mental force responsible for actively keeping memories, most of which are potentially threatening or anxiety provoking, from being consciously discovered.

reproductive strategies Different systems of mating and rearing offspring. These include monogamy, polygyny, polyandry and polygynandry.

reproductive success The number of viable offspring an individual produces relative to the number of viable offspring produced by other members of the same species.

resistance A development during therapy in which the client becomes defensive, unconsciously attempting to halt further insight by censoring his or her true feelings.

resistant attachment A kind of attachment in which infants show mixed reactions to their mothers. They may approach their mothers upon their return but, at the same time, continue to cry or even push their mothers away.

response bias Tendency to say 'yes' or 'no' when unsure whether a stimulus was detected.

response cost A decrease in the frequency of a response that is regularly and reliably followed by the termination of an appetitive stimulus.

retention interval Period between the acquisition and retrieval of material.

retina The tissue at the back inside surface of the eye that contains the photoreceptors and associated neurons.

retinal disparity The fact that points on objects located at different distances from the observer will fall on slightly different locations on the two retinas; provides the basis for stereopsis, one of the forms of depth perception.

retrieval The active processes of locating and using stored information.

retrieval cues Contextual variables, including physical objects or verbal stimuli, that improve the ability to recall information from memory.

retroactive interference Interference in recall that occurs when recently learned information disrupts our ability to remember older information.

retrograde amnesia The loss of the ability to retrieve memories of one's past, particularly memories of episodic or auto-biographical events.

retrospective study A research technique that requires participants to report what happened in the past.

reuptake The process by which a terminal button retrieves the molecules of transmitter substance that it has just released; terminates the effect of the transmitter substance on the receptors of the postsynaptic neuron.

rhodopsin The photopigment contained by rods.

right shift theory The theory which suggests that a single gene shifts dominance to one hand (usually the right).

rod A photoreceptor that is very sensitive to light but cannot detect changes in hue.

role-playing A technique which requires an individual to act out or rehearse skills by adopting the identity of another.

Rorschach Inkblot Test A projective test in which a person is shown a series of symmetrical inkblots and asked to describe what he or she thinks they represent.

round window An opening in the bone surrounding the cochlea. Movements of the membrane behind this opening permit vibrations to be transmitted through the oval window into the cochlea.

s factor According to Spearman, a factor of intelligence that is specific to a particular task.

saccadic movement The rapid movement of the eyes that is used in scanning a visual scene, as opposed to the smooth pursuit movements used to follow a moving object.

sample A selection of items from a larger population, for example a group of participants selected to participate in an experiment.

Sapir–Whorf hypothesis The idea that language can determine thought.

saturation A perceptual dimension of colour, most closely associated with purity of a colour.

scatterplot A graph of items that have two values; one value is plotted against the horizontal axis and the other against the vertical axis.

schema A mental framework or body of knowledge that organises and synthesises information about a person, place or thing.

schemata Mental representations or sets of rules that define a particular category of behaviour. Schemata include rules that help us to understand current and future experiences.

schizophrenia A serious mental disorder characterised by thought disturbances, hallucinations, anxiety, emotional withdrawal and delusions.

scientific method A set of rules that govern the collection and analysis of data gained through observational studies or experiments.

sclera The tough outer layer of the eye; the 'white' of the eye.

script The characteristics (events, rules and so on) that are typical of a particular situation; assists the comprehension of verbal discourse.

seasonal affective disorder A mood disorder characterised by depression, lethargy, sleep disturbances and craving for carbohydrates. This disorder generally occurs during the winter, when the amount of daylight, relative to the other seasons, is low. This disorder can be treated with exposure to bright lights.

secondary appraisal In anxiety research, the individual's ability to evaluate how best to cope with an environment and what strategies can facilitate coping.

secondary reinforcer (or punisher) *See* conditioned reinforcer (or punisher).

secretory immunoglobulin A (sIgA) A type of antibody which is secreted by and covers the mucosal surfaces.

secure attachment A kind of attachment in which infants use their mothers as a base for exploring a new environment. They will venture out from their mothers to explore a strange situation but return periodically.

segmentation The breaking up of words in order to make them more pronounceable.

selective attention The process that controls our awareness of, and readiness to respond to, particular categories of stimuli or stimuli in a particular location.

self-actualisation The realisation of one's true intellectual and emotional potential.

self-concept One's knowledge, feelings and ideas about oneself.

self-control The tendency to be kind, considerate and obedient of laws and rules.

self-efficacy The expectations of success; the belief in one's own competencies.

self-fulfilling prophecy A stereotype that causes a person to act in a manner consistent with that stereotype.

self-perception theory The theory that we come to understand our attitudes and emotions by observing our own behaviour and the circumstances under which it occurs.

self-schema A mental framework that represents and synthesises information about oneself; a cognitive structure that organises the knowledge, feelings and ideas that constitute the self-concept.

self-serving bias The tendency to make attributions that protect or enhance our self-esteem and self-image.

semantic memory A type of long-term memory that contains data, facts and other information, including vocabulary.

semantic priming A facilitating effect on the recognition of words having meanings related to a word that was presented previously.

semantics The meanings and the study of the meanings represented by words.

semi-structured interview A flexible form of the structured interview which requests responses to specific preset questions but allows the interviewer the scope to ask participants' to develop their answers further.

semicircular canal One of a set of three organs in the inner ear that responds to rotational movements of the head.

sensation The detection of the elementary properties of a stimulus.

sensorimotor period This first period in Piaget's theory of cognitive development, lasting from birth to two years. It is marked by an orderly progression of increasingly complex cognitive development: reflexes, permanence, a rough approximation of causality, imitation and symbolic thinking.

sensory association cortex Those regions of cerebral cortex that receive information from the primary sensory areas.

sensory memory Memory in which representations of the physical features of a stimulus are stored for very brief durations.

sensory neuron A neuron that detects changes in the external or internal environment and sends information about these changes to the central nervous system.

sensory-specific satiety The decrease in the pleasantness and consumption of food after eating it to satiety.

separation anxiety A set of fearful responses, such as crying, arousal and clinging to the carer, that the infant exhibits when the carer attempts to leave the infant.

serotonin-specific reuptake inhibitors (SSRIs) Antidepressants which block the reuptake of serotonin in nerve cells.

serum cholesterol A fat-like chemical found in the blood. One form (LDL) promotes the formation of atherosclerotic plaques. Another form (HDL) may protect against coronary heart disease.

set point The optimum value of the system variable in a regulatory mechanism. The set point for human body temperature, recorded orally, is approximately 98.6°F.

sex chromosomes The chromosomes that contain the instructional code for the development of male or female sex characteristics.

sex role Cultural expectations about the ways in which men and women should think and behave.

sex stereotypes Beliefs about differences in the behaviours, abilities and personality traits of males and females.

sex-influenced gene A gene which can occur in both sexes but the phenotype is more common in one sex.

sex-linked gene A gene that resides only on the sex chromosome.

sexual identity One's private sense of being male or female.

sexual masochism Sexual gratification from being made to suffer.

sexual sadism Sexual gratification from inflicting suffering.

sexual selection Selection for traits specific to sex, such as body size or particular patterns of behaviour.

shading A monocular cue of depth perception; determines whether portions of the surface of an object are perceived as concave or convex.

shadowing The act of continuously repeating verbal material as soon as it is heard.

shallow processing The analysis of the superficial characteristics of a stimulus, such as its size or shape.

shaping The reinforcement of behaviour that successively approximates the desired response until that response is fully acquired.

short-term memory An immediate memory for stimuli that have just been perceived. It is limited in terms of both capacity (7 ± 2 chunks of information) and duration (less than 20 seconds).

signal detection theory A mathematical theory of the detection of stimuli, which involves discriminating a signal from the noise in which it is embedded and which takes into account subjects' willingness to report detecting the signal.

similarity principle A Gestalt principle of organisation; similar elements are perceived as belonging to the same figure.

simulation An attempt to express an emotion that one does not actually feel.

single-blind study An experiment in which the experimenter but not the subject knows the value of the independent variable.

single-subject research An experiment or correlational study concerning the behaviour of individual participants rather than comparisons of the average performance of groups of participants.

situational factors Environmental stimuli that affect a person's behaviour.

sleep apnoea The inability to sleep and breathe at the same time.

sleeptalking Literally, talking in one's sleep.

sleepwalking Literally, walking while asleep.

slow-wave sleep Sleep other than REM sleep, characterised by regular, slow waves on the electroencephalograph.

social cognition The processes involved in perceiving, interpreting, storing and acting on social information.

social desirability The desire to be seen as competent, co-operative and sociable by the experimenter.

social facilitation The enhancement of task performance caused by the mere presence of others.

social identity That part of the self-concept that derives from membership of social groups and is associated with group, as opposed to interpersonal, behaviours.

social judgeability Perception of whether it is socially acceptable to judge a specific person.

social learning theory The idea that both consequences of behaviour and an individual's beliefs about those consequences determine personality.

social loafing A reduction in effort when people perform a task collectively with other people.

social norms Informal rules defining the expected and appropriate behaviour in specific situations.

social phobia A mental disorder characterised by an excessive and irrational fear of situations in which the person is observed by others.

social psychology The branch of psychology that studies our social behaviour – how the actual, imagined or implied presence of other people influences our thoughts, feelings and behaviours.

social representations Collectively elaborated explanations of unfamiliar and complex phenomena that transform them into a familiar and simple form.

social psychology The branch of psychology devoted to the study of the effects people have on each other's behaviour.

sociobiology The study of the genetic bases of social behaviour; the branch of biology which seeks to explain behaviour in terms of adaptation and evolution.

soma A cell body; the largest part of a neuron.

somatic marker hypothesis The idea that the ability to make decisions leading to positive or potentially negative consequences depends on the activation of somatic (bodily) states.

somatisation disorder A class of somatoform disorder, occurring mostly among women, that involves complaints of wide-ranging physical ailments for which there is no apparent biological cause.

somatoform disorder A mental disorder involving a bodily or physical problem for which there is no physiological basis.

somatosense Bodily sensations; sensitivity to such stimuli as touch, pain and temperature.

spatial neglect A perceptual disorder in which the patient neglects (or fails to attend to) one side of the body, usually the left.

species-typical behaviour A behaviour seen in all or most members of a species, such as nest building, special food-getting behaviours or reproductive behaviours.

specific language impairment Difficulty in producing or understanding spoken language in the absence of known brain injury.

specific phobia An excessive and irrational fear of specific things, such as snakes, darkness or heights.

spinal cord A long, thin collection of nerve cells attached to the base of the brain and running the length of the spinal column.

split-brain The consequence of surgical excision of the fibres connecting the two cerebral hemispheres of the brain.

split-brain surgery A surgical procedure that severs the corpus callosum, thus abolishing the direct connections between the cortex of the two cerebral hemispheres.

split-half reliability The degree to which two halves or portions of the same measure correlate.

spontaneous recovery After an interval of time, the reappearance of a response that had previously been extinguished.

sport and exercise psychology The branch of psychology concerned with studying the effect of sport and exercise on behaviour and with applying psychological principles to our understanding of sport-related behaviour.

standard deviation A statistic that expresses the variability of a measurement; square root of the sum of the squared deviations from the mean.

Stanford–Binet Scale An intelligence test that consists of various tasks grouped according to mental age; provides the standard measure of the intelligence quotient.

state-dependent memory The tendency to recall information better when our mental or emotional state at retrieval matches that during encoding.

statistical significance The likelihood that an observed relation or difference between two variables is not due to chance factors.

stereopsis A form of depth perception based on retinal disparity.

stereotaxic apparatus A device used to insert an electrode into a particular part of the brain for the purpose of recording electrical activity, stimulating the brain electrically, or producing localised damage.

stereotype A shared, often unfavourable, generalisation held by members of one group about members of another group.

stimulus equivalence A type of learning in which stimuli become equivalent even though the organism has never observed a relation between them; may be involved in learning how to read and manipulate symbols.

storage The process of maintaining information in memory.

Strange Situation A test of attachment in which an infant is exposed to different stimuli that may be distressful.

stranger anxiety The wariness and fearful responses, such as crying and clinging to their carers, that the infant exhibits in the presence of strangers.

stress A pattern of physiological, behavioural and cognitive responses to stimuli (real or imagined) that are perceived as endangering one's well-being.

stress inoculation training The stress management programme developed by Meichenbaum for teaching people to develop coping skills that increase their resistance to the negative effects of stress.

stressors Stimuli that are perceived as endangering one's well-being.

striving for superiority The motivation to seek superiority. Adler argued that striving for superiority is born out of our need to compensate for our inferiorities.

stroke A cerebrovascular accident; damage to the brain caused by a blood clot in a cerebral artery or rupture of a cerebral blood vessel.

structuralism Wundt's system of experimental psychology; it emphasised introspective analysis of sensation and perception.

structured interview Predefined format for interviewing participants in research which allows little deviation from the questions set.

sublimation A defence mechanism that involves redirecting pleasure-seeking or aggressive instincts towards socially acceptable goals.

subliminal perception The perception of a stimulus, as indicated by a change in behaviour, at an intensity insufficient to produce a conscious sensation.

subordinate concept A concept that refers to types of items within a basic-level category.

subvocal articulation Uttering words inaudibly.

superego The repository of an individual's moral values, divided into the conscience – the internalisation of a society's rules and regulations – and the ego-ideal – the internalisation of one's goals.

superordinate concept A concept that refers to collections of basic-level concepts.

superstitious behaviour A behaviour that occurs in response to the non-contingent occurrence of an appetitive stimulus; appears to cause a certain event but in reality does not.

supervisory attentional system (SAS) A cognitive system, proposed by Norman and Shallice, which is responsible for the conscious attentional control needed to regulate behaviour.

suprachiasmatic nucleus (SCN) Structures located in the posterior of the hypothalamus which are thought to regulate circadian rhythms.

surface dyslexia A reading disorder in which people can read words phonetically but have difficulty reading irregularly spelled words by the whole-word method.

sympathetic branch The portion of the autonomic nervous system that activates functions that accompany arousal and expenditure of energy.

symptom substitution The Freudian notion that the removal of one symptom will lead to its replacement by another.

synaesthesia Phenomenon where the stimulus in one sensory modality evokes a sensation in another.

synaesthete A person who experiences synaesthesia.

synapse The junction between the terminal button of one neuron and the membrane of a muscle fibre, a gland or another neuron.

synaptic cleft A fluid-filled gap between the presynaptic and postsynaptic membranes; the terminal button releases transmitter substance into this space.

syntax Grammatical rules for combining words to form phrases, clauses and sentences.

system variable The variable controlled by a regulatory mechanism; for example, temperature in a heating system.

systematic desensitisation A method of treatment in which the client is trained to relax in the presence of increasingly fearful stimuli.

T lymphocytes Cells that develop in the thymus gland that produce antibodies which defend the body against fungi, viruses and multicellular parasites.

taboo A societal rule prohibiting the members of a given culture from engaging in specific behaviours.

tachistoscope A device that can present visual stimuli for controlled (usually very brief) durations of time.

tardive dyskinesia A serious movement disorder that can occur when a person has been treated with antipsychotic drugs for an extended period.

target cell A cell whose physiological processes are affected by a particular hormone; contains special receptor molecules that respond to the presence of the hormone.

taste bud A small organ on the tongue that contains a group of gustatory receptor cells.

tectorial membrane A membrane located above the basilar membrane; serves as a shelf against which the cilia of the auditory hair cells move.

template A hypothetical pattern that resides in the nervous system and is used to perceive objects or shapes by a process of comparison.

temporal coding A means by which the nervous system represents information; different features are coded by the pattern of activity of neurons.

temporal lobe The portion of the cerebral cortex below the frontal and parietal lobes and containing the auditory cortex.

teratogens Drugs or other substances that can cause birth defects.

terminal button The rounded swelling at the end of the axon of a neuron; releases transmitter substance.

test–retest reliability The degree to which scores on one test correlate with the same test undertaken on another occasion.

texture A monocular cue of depth perception; the fineness of detail present in the surfaces of objects or in the ground or floor of a scene.

thalamus A region of the brain near the centre of the cerebral hemispheres. All sensory information except smell is sent to the thalamus and then relayed to the cerebral cortex.

Thematic Apperception Test (TAT) A projective test in which a person is shown a series of ambiguous pictures that involve people. The person is asked to make up a story about what the people are doing or thinking. The person's responses are believed to reflect aspects of his or her personality.

theory A set of statements designed to explain a set of phenomena; more encompassing than a hypothesis.

theory of mind The understanding of others' mental events.

theory of reasoned action The notion that behaviour follows from an intention to act and that these intentions are based on beliefs, feelings and attitudes.

theta activity EEG activity of 3.5–7.5 Hz; occurs during the transition between sleep and wakefulness.

thought disorder A pattern of disorganised, illogical and irrational thought that often accompanies schizophrenia.

threat gesture A stereotyped gesture that signifies that one animal is likely to attack another member of the species.

three-term contingency The relation among discriminative stimuli, behaviour and the consequences of that behaviour. A motivated organism emits a specific response in the presence of a discriminative stimulus because, in the past, that response has been reinforced only when the discriminative stimulus is present.

threshold The point at which a stimulus, or a change in the value of a stimulus, can just be detected.

timbre A perceptual dimension of sound, determined by the complexity of the sound, for example as shown by a mathematical analysis of the sound wave.

tip-of-the-tongue phenomenon An occasional problem with retrieval of information that we are sure we know but cannot immediately remember.

token economy A programme often used in institutions in which a person's adaptive behaviour is reinforced with tokens that are exchangeable for desirable goods or special privileges.

tolerance The decreased sensitivity to a drug resulting from its continued use.

top-down processing A perception based on information provided by the context in which a particular stimulus is encountered.

transduction The conversion of physical stimuli into changes in the activity of receptor cells of sensory organs.

transference The process by which a client begins to project powerful attitudes and emotions onto the therapist.

transvestic fetishism Dressing in the clothes normally associated with the opposite sex.

triarchic theory A theory of intelligence which posits that intelligence is made of componential, experiential and contextual elements.

trichromatic theory The theory that colour vision is accomplished by three types of photoreceptor, each of which is maximally sensitive to a different wavelength of light.

tricyclic antidepressants The earliest known antidepressants, so-called because of their chemical three-ring structure.

tritanopia A form of hereditary anomalous colour vision; caused by a lack of 'blue' cones in the retina.

Turner's syndrome Genetic disorder in which all or a part of the X chromosome is missing; intelligence is within the normal range but individuals have problems with social adjustment.

two-point discrimination threshold The minimum distance between two small points that can be detected as separate stimuli when pressed against a particular region of the skin.

type A pattern A behaviour pattern characterised by high levels of competitiveness and hostility, impatience and an intense disposition; supposedly associated with an increased risk of coronary heart disease.

type B pattern A behaviour pattern characterised by lower levels of competitiveness and hostility, patience and an easy-going disposition; supposedly associated with a decreased risk of coronary heart disease.

type C (cancer-prone) personality A behaviour pattern marked by co-operativeness, unassertiveness, patience, suppression of negative emotions, and acceptance of external authority; supposedly associated with an increased likelihood of cancer.

tyramine cheese reaction A potentially fatal reaction to eating certain foods in individuals taking MAOIs.

UCR *See* unconditional response.

UCS *See* unconditional stimulus.

UCS pre-exposure effect A phenomenon in which conditioning is weak because the organism has already been exposed to a novel UCS before it is used in the conditioning experiment.

ultimate attribution error The tendency to attribute ingroup failures and outgroup successes externally, and ingroup successes and outgroup failures internally.

ultimate causes Evolutionary conditions that have slowly shaped the behaviour of a species over generations.

unconditional positive regard According to Rogers, the therapeutic expression that a client's worth as a human being is not dependent on anything that he or she does, says, feels or thinks.

unconditional response (UCR) In classical conditioning, a response, such as salivation, that is naturally elicited by the UCS.

unconditional stimulus (UCS) In classical conditioning, a stimulus, such as food, that naturally elicits a reflexive response, such as salivation.

unconscious The inaccessible part of the mind.

unconscious inference A mental computation of which we are unaware that plays a role in perception.

underextension The use of a word to denote a smaller class of items than is appropriate, for example referring only to one particular animal as a dog.

undifferentiated schizophrenia A type of schizophrenia characterised by fragments of the symptoms of different types of schizophrenia.

validity The degree to which the operational definition of a variable accurately reflects the variable it is designed to measure or manipulate.

variable A measure capable of assuming any of several values.

variable error An error caused by random differences in experimental conditions, such as the subject's mood or changes in the environment.

variable-interval schedule A schedule of reinforcement similar to a fixed-interval schedule but characterised by a variable time requirement having a particular mean.

variable-ratio schedule A schedule of reinforcement similar to a fixed-ratio schedule but characterised by a variable response requirement having a particular mean.

variance The square of the standard deviation.

variation The differences found across individuals of any given species in terms of their genetic, biological (size, strength, physiology) and psychological (intelligence, sociability, behaviour) characteristics.

vertebrae Bones that encase the spinal cord and constitute the vertebral column.

vestibular apparatus The receptive organs of the inner ear that contribute to balance and perception of head movement.

vestibular sac One of a set of two receptor organs in each inner ear that detect changes in the tilt of the head.

visual agnosia The inability of a person who is not blind to recognise the identity or use of an object by means of vision; usually caused by damage to the brain.

visuospatial scratchpad The component of working memory that stores visuospatial information.

voice-onset time The delay between the initial sound of a voiced consonant (such as the puffing sound of the phoneme /p/) and the onset of vibration of the vocal cords.

voyeurism Looking at people while they are undressing or having sex, without their knowledge.

wavelength The distance between adjacent waves of radiant energy; in vision, most closely associated with the perceptual dimension of hue.

Weber fraction The ratio between a just-noticeable difference and the magnitude of a stimulus; reasonably constant over the middle range of most stimulus intensities.

Wechsler Adult Intelligence Scale (WAIS) An intelligence test for adults devised by David Wechsler; contains eleven subtests divided into the categories of verbal and performance.

Wechsler Intelligence Scale for Children (WISC) An intelligence test for children devised by David Wechsler; similar in form to the Wechsler Adult Intelligence Scale.

Wernicke's aphasia A disorder caused by damage to the left temporal and parietal cortex, including Wernicke's area; characterised by deficits in the perception of speech and by the production of fluent but rather meaningless speech.

Wernicke's area A region of auditory association cortex located in the upper part of the left temporal lobe; involved in the recognition of spoken words.

white matter The portions of the central nervous system that are abundant in axons rather than cell bodies of neurons. The colour derives from the presence of the axons' myelin sheaths.

whole-word reading Reading by recognising a word as a whole; 'sight reading'.

withdrawal symptom An effect produced by discontinuance of use of a drug after a period of continued use; generally opposite to the drug's primary effects.

within-groups design *See* repeated measures design.

working memory A short-term memory system which allows the retention and processing of information concurrently.

zygote stage The first stage of prenatal development, during which the zygote divides many times and the internal organs begin to form.

REFERENCES

Aboud, F.E. (1988). *Children and Prejudice*. Oxford, UK: Blackwell.

Abraham, C., Sheeran, P. and Orbel, S. (1998). Can social cognitive models contribute to the effectiveness of HIV-preventive behavioural interventions? A brief review of the literature and a reply to Joffe (1996; 1997) and Fife-Shaw (1997). *British Journal of Medical Psychology*, 71.

Abrams, D., Wetherell, M., Cochrane, S., Hogg, M.A. and Turner, J.C. (1990). Knowing what to think by knowing who you are: Self-categorisation and the nature of norm formation, conformity and group polarisation. *British Journal of Social Psychology*, 29, 97–119.

Abrams, D., Ando, K. and Hinkle, S. (1998). Psychological attachment to the group: Cross-cultural differences in organizational identification and subjective norms as predictors of workers' turnover intentions. *Personality and Social Psychology Bulletin*, 24, 1027–1039.

Abramson, L.Y., Metalsky, G.I. and Alloy, L.B. (1989). Hopelessness depression: A theory-based subtype. *Psychological Review*, 96, 358–372.

Abramson, L.Y., Seligman, M.E.P. and Teasdale, J.D. (1978). Learned helplessness in humans: Critique and reformulation. *Journal of Abnormal Psychology*, 87, 49–74.

Acierno, R.E., Hersen, M. and Van Hasselt, V.B. (1993). Interventions for panic disorder: A critical review of the literature. *Clinical Psychology Review*, 18, 561–578.

Adamec, R.E. and Stark-Adamec, C. (1986). Limbic hyperfunction, limbic epilepsy, and interictal behavior: Models and methods of detection. In B.K. Doane and K.E. Livingston (eds), *The Limbic System*. New York: Raven Press.

Adams, D.B., Gold, A.R. and Burt, A.D. (1978). Rise in female-initiated sexual activity at ovulation and its suppression by oral contraceptives. *New England Journal of Medicine*, 299, 1145–1150.

Adey, P. and Shayer, M. (1994) Really raising standards: cognitive intervention and academic achievement. New York: Routledge.

Adey, W.R., Bors, E. and Porter, R.W. (1968). EEG sleep patterns after high cervical lesions in man. *Archives of Neurology*, 19, 377–383.

Adler, A. (1939). *Social Interest: A challenge to mankind*. New York: Putnam.

Adolphs, R., Russell, J.A. and Tranel, D. (1999). A role for the human amygdala in recognizing emotional arousal from unpleasant stimuli. *Psychological Science*, 10, 2, 167–171.

Adolphs, R., Tranel, D., Bechara, A., Damasio, H. and Damasio, A.R. (1996). Neuropsychological approaches to reasoning and decision-making. In A.R. Damasio *et al.* (eds), *Neurobiology of Decision-making*. Berlin: Springer-Verlag.

Adolphs, R., Tranel, D., Damasio, H. and Damasio, A.R. (1994). Impaired recognition of emotion in facial expressions following bilateral damage to the human amygdala. *Nature*, 372, 669–672.

Adolphs, R., Tranel, D., Damasio, H. and Damasio, A.R. (1995). Fear and the human amygdala. *Journal of Neuroscience*, 15, 5879–5891.

Aggleton, J.P. and Mishkin, M. (1986). The amygdala: Sensory gateway to the emotions. In R. Plutchik and H. Kellerman (eds), *Biological Foundation of Emotions*. New York: Academic Press.

Aguilar-Alonso, A. (1996). Personality and creativity. *Personality and Individual Differences*, 21, 6, 959–969.

Aiken, L.R. (1994). *Dying, Death and Bereavement*. Boston: Allyn and Bacon.

Ainslie, G. (1975). Species reward: A behavioral theory of impulsiveness and impulse control. *Psychological Bulletin*, 82, 463–496.

Ainsworth, M.D.S. (1967). *Infancy in Uganda: Infant care and the growth of love*. Baltimore: Johns Hopkins University Press.

Ainsworth, M.D.S. and Bowlby, J. (1991). An ethological approach to personality development. *American Psychologist*, 46, 333–341.

Ainsworth, M.D.S., Blehar, M.C., Waters, E. and Wall, S. (1978*). Patterns of Attachment*. Hillsdale, NJ: Lawrence Erlbaum Associates.

Ajzen, I. (1985). From intentions to actions: A theory of planned behaviour. In J. Kuhl and J. Beckmann (eds), *Action Control: From cognition of behaviour*. Berlin: Springer-Verlag.

Ajzen, I. (1989). Attitude structure and behaviour. In A. R. Pratkanis, S. J. Breckler, and A. G. Greenwald (eds), *Attitude Structure and Function*. Hillsdale, NJ: Lawrence Erlbaum Associates, pp. 241–274.

Ajzen, I. (1991). The theory of planned behaviour. *Organizational Behaviour and Human Decision Processes*, 50, 179–211.

Akelaitis, A.J. (1944/45). Studies on the corpus callosum IV: Diagnostic dyspraxia in epileptics following partial and complete section of the corpus callosum. *American Journal of Psychiatry*, 101, 594–599.

Albert, R.S. (1990). Indentity, experiences and career choice among the exceptionally gifted and talented. In M.A. Runco and R.S. Albert (eds), *Theories of creativity*. Newbury Park, CA: Sage.

Albright, L., Kenny, D. A. and Malloy, T. E. (1988). Consensus in personality judgments at zero acquaintance. *Journal of Personality and Social Psychology*, 55, 387–395.

Alexander, G.M., Sherwin, B.B., Bancroft, J. and Davidson, D.W. (1990). Testosterone and sexual behavior in oral contraceptive users and nonusers: A prospective study. *Hormones and Behavior*, 24, 388–402.

Alexander, R.D. (1979). *Darwinism and Human Affairs*. Seattle: University of Washington Press.

Allen, L.S. and Gorski, R.A. (1992). Sexual orientation and the size of the anterior commissure in the human brain. *Proceedings of the National Academy of Sciences*, 89, 7199–7202.

Allen, M.G. (1976). Twin studies of affective illness. *Archives of General Psychiatry*, 33, 1476–1478.

Allport, A. (1988). What concept is consciousness? In A. Marcel and E. Bisiach (eds), *Consciousness in Contemporary Science*. Oxford: Oxford University Press.

Allport, G.W. (1954). *The Nature of Prejudice*. Reading, MA: Addison-Wesley.

Allport, G.W. (1968). The historical background of modern social psychology. In G. Lindzey and E. Aronson (eds), *The Handbook of Social Psychology*, Vol. 1. Reading, MA: Addison-Wesley.

Allport, G.W. and Odbert, H.S. (1936). Trait-names: A psycholexical study. *Psychological Monographs*, 47 (1, Whole No. 211).

Alsaker, F.D. (1992). Pubertal timing, overweight and psychological adjustment. *Journal of Early Adolescence*, 12, 396–419.

Alsaker, F.D. (1996). Annotation: The impact of puberty. *Journal of Child Psychology and Psychiatry*, 37, 3, 249–258.

Ambrosio, A.L. and Sheehan, E.P. (1991). The just world belief and the AIDS epidemic. *Journal of Social Behavior and Personality*, 6, 163–170.

Amelang, M., Schmidt-Rathjens, C. and Matthews, G. (1996). Personality, cancer and coronary heart disease: Further evidence on a controversial issue. *British Journal of Health Psychology*, 1, 191–205.

American Psychiatric Association (1994). *Diagnostic and statistical manual of mental disorders* (4th edition). Washington, DC: ABA.

Amos, A., Bostock, C. and Bostock, Y. (1998). Women's magazines and tobacco in Europe. *The Lancet*, 352, 786–787.

Anderson, D.R. and Collins, P.A. (1988). *The Impact on Children's Education: Television's influence on cognitive development*. Washington, DC: US Department of Education.

Anderson, D.R. and Field, D. (1983). Children's attention to television: Implications for production. In M. Meyer (ed.), *Children and the Formal Features of Television*. Munich: Saur.

Anderson, D.R. and Lorch, E. (1983). Looking at television: Action or reaction? In J. Bryant and D. R. Anderson (eds), *Children's Understanding of Television: Research on attention and comprehension*. New York: Academic Press.

Anderson, D.R., Field, D., Collins, P., Lorch, E. and Nathan, J. (1985). Estimates of young children's time with television: A methodological comparison of parent reports with time-lapse video home observation. *Child Development*, 56, 1345–1357.

Anderson, R.H., Fleming, D.E., Rhees, R.W. and Kinghorn, E. (1986). Relationships between sexual activity, plasma testosterone, and the volume of the sexually dimorphic nucleus of the preoptic area in prenatally stressed and non-stressed rats. *Brain Research*, 370, 1–10.

Anderson, S.W., Damasio, H., Jones, R.D. and Tranel, D. (1991). Wisconsin Card Sorting Test performance as a measure of frontal lobe damage. *Journal of Clinical and Experimental Neuropsychology*, 13, 909–922.

Andrade, J. (1995). Learning during anaesthesia: A review. *British Journal of Psychology*, 86, 479–506.

Andreasen, N.C. (1987). Creativity and mental illness: Prevalence rates in writers and first degree relatives. *American Journal of Psychiatry*, 144, 1288–1292.

Andreasen, N.C., O'Leary, D.S., Flaum, M., Nopoulos, P., Watkins, G.L. and Ponto, L.L.B. (1997). Hypofrontality in schizophrenia: distributed dysfunctional circuits in neuroleptically naive patients. *The Lancet*, 349, 1730–1734.

Andreassi, J.L. (1996). *Psychophysiology* (3rd edition). Hillsdale, NJ: Lawrence Erlbaum Associates.

Andrew, M., McGuffin, P. and Katz, R. (1998). Genetic and non-genetic subtypes of major depressive disorder. *British Journal of Psychiatry*, 173, 523–526.

Andrews, G. (1991). Anxiety, personality and anxiety disorders. *International Review of Psychiatry*, 3, 293–302.

Andrews, G., Craig, A., Feyer, A.M., Hoddinott, S., Howie, P. and Neilson, M. (1983). Stuttering: A review of research findings and theories circa 1982. *Journal of Speech and Hearing Disorders*, 48, 226–246.

Andrews, G., Pollock, C. and Stewart, G. (1989). The determination of defense style by questionnaire. *Archives of General Psychiatry*, 46, 455–460.

Andrews, G., Slade, T. and Peters, L. (1999). Classification in psychiatry: ICD 10 versus DSM-IV. *British Journal of Psychiatry*, 174, 3–5.

Angrist, B.J., Rotrosen, J. and Gershon, S. (1980). Positive and negative symptoms in schizophrenia – Differential response to amphetamine and neuroleptics. *Psychopharmacology*, 72, 17–19.

Annau, Z. and Kamin, L.J. (1961). The conditioned emotional response as a function of intensity of the UCS. *Journal of Comparative and Physiological Psychology*, 54, 428–432.

Annett, M. (1985). *Left, Right, Hand and Brain: The right shift theory*. Hove, UK: Lawrence Erlbaum Associates.

Annett, M. (1992). Spatial ability in sub-groups of left and right handers. *British Journal of Psychology*, 83, 493–515.

Annett, M. (1993). Handedness and educational success: The hypothesis of a genetic balanced polymorphism with heterozygote advantage for laterality and ability. *British Journal of Developmental Psychology*, 11, 359–370.

Annett, M. and Manning, M. (1989). The disadvantages of dextrality for intelligence. *British Journal of Psychology*, 80, 213–226.

Annett, M. and Manning, M. (1990). Reading and a balanced polymorphism for laterity and ability. *Journal of Child Psychology and Psychiatry*, 31, 4, 511–529.

Appollonio, I.M., Grafman, J., Schwartz, V., Massaquoi, S. and Hallett, M. (1993). Memory in patients with cerebellar degeneration. *Neurology*, 43, 1536–1544.

Arcelin, R., Delignieres, D. and Brisswalter, J. (1998). Selective effects of physical exercise on choice reaction processes. *Perceptual and Motor Skills*, 87, 175–185.

Areni, C.S. and Kim, D. (1993).The influence of background music on shopping behaviour: Classical versus top-forty music in a wine store. *Advances in Consumer Research*, 20, 336–340.

Arnett, J. (1995). The young and the reckless: Adolescent reckless behavior. *Current Directions in Psychological Science*, 4, 67–71.

Aronson, E. and Mills, J. (1959). The effects of severity of initiation on liking for a group. *Journal of Abnormal and Social Psychology*, 59, 177–181.

Artmann, H., Grau, H., Adelman, M. and Schleiffer, R. (1985). Reversible and non-reversible enlargement of cerebrospinal fluid spaces in anorexia nervosa. *Neuroradiology*, 27, 103–112.

Asch, S.E. (1946). Forming impressions of personality. *Journal of Abnormal and Social Psychology*, 41, 258–290.

Asch, S.E. (1951). Effects of group pressure upon the modification and distortion of judgment. In H. Guetzkow (ed.), *Groups, Leadership, and Men*. Pittsburgh: Carnegie.

Asch, S.E. (1952). *Social Psychology*. New York: Prentice-Hall.

Asch, S.E. (1955). Opinions and social pressure. *Scientific American*, 193, 31–35.

Asperger, H. (1944). Die autistischen Psychopathen im Kindesalter. *Archiv für Psychiatrie und Nervenkrankheiten*, 117, 76–136.

Aspinwall, L.G. and Taylor, S.E. (1992). Individual differences, coping, and psychological adjustment: A longitudinal study of college adjustment and performance. *Journal of Personality and Social Psychology*, 63, 989–1003.

Astley, S.J., Clarren, S.K., Little, R.E., Sampson, P.D. and Daling, J.R. (1992). Analysis of facial shape in children gestationally exposed to marijuana, alcohol, or cocaine. *Pediatrics*, 89, 67–77.

Atkinson, R.C. and Shiffrin, R.M. (1968). Human memory: A proposed system and its control processes. In K.W. Spence and J.T. Spence (eds), *The Psychology of Learning and Motivation: Advances in Research and Theory*, Vol. 2. New York: Academic Press.

Augoustinos, M. and Walker, I. (1995). *Social Cognition: An integrated introduction*. London: Sage.

Austin, M.P., Dougall, N., Ross, M., Murray, C., O'Carroll, R.E., Moffoot, A., Ebmeier, K.P. and Goodwin, G.M. (1992). Single photon emission tomography with 99m

Tc-exametazime in major depression and the pattern of brain activity underlying the psychotic/neurotic continuum. *Journal of Affective Disorder*, 26, 31–43.

Axel, R. (1995). The molecular logic of smell. *Scientific American*, 273, 154–159.

Axelrod, R. and Hamilton, W.D. (1981). The evolution of cooperation. *Science*, 211, 1390–1396.

Ayllon, T. and Azrin, N. H. (1968). *The Token Economy: A motivational system for therapy and rehabilitation*. New York: Appleton-Century-Crofts.

Baars B.J. (1988). A cognitive theory of consciousness. Cambridge: Cambridge University Press.

Baars, B.J., Newman, J. and Taylor, J.G. (1998). Neuronal mechanisms of consciousness: A relational global-workspace framework. In S.R. Hameroff, A.W. Kaszniak and A.C. Scott (eds), *Towards a Science of Consciousness II*. Cambridge, MA: MIT Press.

Babkin, B. P. (1949). *Pavlov: A biography*. Chicago: University of Chicago Press.

Badcock, C. (1991). *Evolution and Individual Behavior: An introduction to human sociobiology*. Cambridge, MA: Blackwell.

Baddeley, A.D. (1982). Domains of recollection. *Psychological Review*, 89, 708–729.

Baddeley, A.D. (1986). *Working Memory*. Oxford: Clarendon Press.

Baddeley, A.D. (1992a). Implicit memory and errorless learning : A link between cognitive theory and neuropsychological rehabilitation. In L.R. Squire and N. Butters (eds), *Neuropscyhology of Memory* (2nd edition). New York: Guilford.

Baddeley, A.D. (1996). *Human Memory: Theory and practice* (2nd edition). Hove, UK: The Psychology Press.

Baddeley, A.D. and Hitch, G.J. (1974). Working memory. In G.H. Bower (ed.), *The Psychology of Learning and Motivation: Advances in research and theory*, Vol. 8. New York: Academic Press.

Baddeley, A.D. and Logie, R.H. (1992). Auditory imagery and working memory. In R.S. Nickerson (ed.), *Attention and performance VIII*. Hillsdale, NJ: Lawrence Erlbaum Associates.

Baddeley, A.D., Thomson, N. and Buchanan, M. (1975). Word length and the structure of short-term memory. *Journal of Verbal Learning and Verbal Behaviour*, 14, 575–589.

Baenninger, M.A., Baenninger, R. and Houle, D. (1993). Attractiveness, attentiveness, and perceived male shortage: Their influence on the perceptions of other females. *Ethology and Sociobiology*, 14, 293–304.

Baer, D.M., Peterson, R.F. and Sherman, J.A. (1967). Development of imitation by reinforcing behavioral similarity to a model. *Journal of the Experimental Analysis of Behavior*, 10, 405–416.

Bagwell, C.L., Newcomb, A.F. and Bukowski, W.M. (1998). Preadolescent friendship and peer rejection as predictors of adult adjustment. *Child Development*, 69, 1, 140–153.

Bahrick, H.P. (1984a). Semantic memory content in permastore: Fifty years of memory for Spanish learned in school. *Journal of Experimental Psychology: General*, 113, 1–29.

Bahrick, H.P. (1992). Stabilized memory of unrehearsed knowledge. *Journal of Experimental Psychology: General*, 121, 1, 112–113.

Bahrick, H.P., Bahrick, P.O. and Wittlinger, R.P. (1975). Fifty years of memories for names and faces: A cross-sectional approach. *Journal of Experimental Psychology: General*, 104, 54–75.

Bailey, A., Lecouteur, A., Gottesman, I., Bolton, P., Simonoff, E., Yuzda, E. and Rutter, M. (1995). Autism as a strongly genetic disorder: Evidence from a British twin study. *Psychological Medicine*, 25, 63–78.

Bailey, A., Phillips, W. and Rutter, M. (1996). Autism: Towards an integration of clinical, genetic, neuropsychological and neurobiological perspectives. *Journal of Child Psychology and Psychiatry*, 37, 1, 89–126.

Bailey, J.M. and Pillard, R.C. (1991). A genetic study of male sexual orientation. *Archives of General Psychiatry*, 48, 1089–1096.

Bailey, J.M., Pillard, R.C., Neale, M.C. and Agyei, Y. (1993). Heritable factors influence sexual orientation in women. *Archives of General Psychiatry*, 50, 217–223.

Bain, J. (1987). Hormones and sexual aggression in the male. *Integrative Psychiatry*, 5, 82–89.

Bain, J., Langevin, R., Dickey, R. and Ben-Aron, M. (1987). Sex hormones in murderers and assaulters. *Behavioural Science and the Law*, 5, 95–101.

Baker, B.L. (1969). Symptom treatment and symptom substitution in enuresis. *Journal of Abnormal Psychology*, 74, 42–49.

Baker, S.C., Rogers, R.D., Owen, A.M., Frith, C.D., Dolan, R.J., Frackowiak, R.S.J. and Robbins, T.W. (1996). Neural systems engaged by planning: A PET study of the Tower of London task. *Neuropsychologia*, 34, 6, 515–526.

Bakker, D.J. (1992). Neuropsychological classification and treatment of dyslexia. *Journal of Learning Disabilities*, 25, 2, 102–109.

Baldessarini, R.J. (1996a). Drugs and the treatment of psychiatric disorders: depression and mania. In J.G. Hardman and L.E. Limbird (eds), *Goodman and Gilman's The Pharmacological Basis of Therapeutics* (9th edition). New York: McGraw-Hill.

Baldessarini, R.J. (1996b) Drugs and the treatment of psychiatric disorders: psychosis and anxiety. In J.G. Hardman and L.E. Limbird (eds), *Goodman and Gilman's The Pharmacological Basis of Therapeutics* (9th edition). New York: McGraw-Hill.

Baldessarini, R.J. and Tarsy, D. (1980). Dopamine and the pathophysiology of dyskinesias induced by antipsychotic drugs. *Annual Review of Neuroscience*, 3, 23–41.

Ball, K. and Sekuler, R. (1982). A specific and enduring improvement in visual motion discrimination. *Science*, 218, 697–698.

Ballantine, H. T., Bouckoms, A. J., Thomas, E. K. and Giriunas, I. E. (1987). Treatment of psychiatric illness by stereotactic cingulotomy. *Biological Psychiatry*, 22, 807–819.

Balon, R., Jordan, M., Pohl, R. and Yeragani, V. K. (1989). Family history of anxiety disorders in control subjects with lactate-induced panic attacks. *American Journal of Psychiatry*, 146, 1304–1306.

Baluch, B. and Kaur, B. (1995). Attitude change toward animal experimentation in an academic setting. *The Journal of Psychology*, 129, 4, 477–479.

Banbury, S. and Berry, D.C. (1998). Disruption of office-related tasks by speech and office noise. *British Journal of Psychology*, 89, 499–517.

Bandura, A. (1971). Psychotherapy based upon modeling principles. In A.E. Bergin and S.L. Garfield (eds), *Handbook of Psychotherapy and Behavior Change*. New York: Wiley.

Bandura, A. (1973). *Aggression: A social learning analysis*. Englewood Cliffs, NJ: Prentice Hall.

Bandura, A. (1977). *Social Learning Theory*. Upper Saddle River, NJ: Prentice-Hall.

Bandura, A. (1978). The self system in reciprocal determinism. *American Psychologist*, 33, 344–358.

Bandura, A. (1982). Self-efficacy mechanism in human agency. *American Psychologist*, 37, 122–147.

Bandura, A. (1986). *Social Foundations of Thought and Action: A social-cognitive theory*. Englewood Cliffs, NJ: Prentice Hall.

Bandura, A. and Menlove, F.L. (1968). Factors determining vicarious extinction of avoidance behavior through symbolic modeling. *Journal of Personality and Social Psychology*, 8, 99–108.

Banich, M.T. (1995). Interhemispheric processing: Theoretical considerations and empirical approaches. In R.J. Davidson and K. Hugdahl (eds), *Brain Asymmetry*. Cambridge, MA: MIT Press.

Banks, M.S., Aslin, R.N. and Letson, R.D. (1975). Sensitive period for the development of human binocular vision. *Science*, 190, 675–677.

Barash, D. (1982). *Sociobiology and Behavior*. London: Hodder & Stoughton.

Barber, J. (1996). *Hypnosis and Suggestion in the Treatment of Pain: A clinical guide.* New York: W.W. Norton.

Barber, J. (1998). The mysterious persistence of hypnotic analgesia. *The International Journal of Clinical and Experimental Hypnosis*, XLVI, 1, 28–43.

Barber, T.X. (1979). Suggested ('hypnotic') behavior: The trance paradigm versus an alternative paradigm. In E. Fromm and R.E. Shor (eds), *Hypnosis: Developments in research and new perspectives*. Chicago: Aldine Press.

Barber, T.X., Spanos, N.P. and Chaves, J.F. (1974). *Hypnotism, Imagination and Human Potentialities*. New York: Pergamon.

Barbur, J.L., Watson, J.D., Frackowiak, R.S. and Zeki, S. (1983). Conscious visual perception without V1. *Brain*, 116, 1293–1302.

Barclay, C. D., Cutting, J. E. and Kozlowski, L. T. (1978). Temporal and spatial factors in gait perception that influence gender recognition. *Perception and Psychophysics*, 23, 145–152.

Bargh, J.A. (1989). Conditional automaticity: Varieties of automatic influence in social perception and cognition. In J.S. Uleman and J.A. Bargh (eds), *Unintended Thought*. New York: Guilford Press, pp. 3–51.

Bargh, J.A., Chen, M. and Burrows, L. (1996). The automaticity of social behavior: Direct effects of trait concept and stereotype activation on action. *Journal of Personality and Social Psychology*, 71, 230–244.

Barkley, R.A. (1997). Behavioural inhibition, sustained attention and executive function: Constructing a unifying theory of ADHD. *Psychological Bulletin*, 121, 1, 65–94.

Barkley, R.A. (1998). Attention-deficit hyperactivity disorder. *Scientific American*, September, 44–49.

Barnes, R.C., Hussein, A., Anderson, D.N. and Powell, D. (1997). Maintenance electroconvulsive therapy. *British Journal of Psychiatry*, 170, 285–287.

Barnett, M.A. (1986). Commonsense and research findings in personality. *Teaching of Psychology*, 13, 62–64.

Barnier, A.J. and McConkey, K.M. (1996). Action and desire in posthypnotic responding. *International Journal of Clinical and Experimental Hypnosis*, 44, 120–139.

Baron, A. and Galizio, M. (1983). Instructional control of human operant behavior. *Psychological Record*, 33, 495–520.

Baron, A., Perone, M. and Galizio, M. (1991). Analyzing the reinforcement process at the human level: Can application and behavioristic interpretation replace laboratory research? *The Behavior Analyst*, 14, 79–117.

Baron, R.A. and Byrne, D. (1994). *Social Psychology: Understanding human interaction*. Boston: Allyn & Bacon.

Baron, R.A. and Richardson, D.R. (1994). *Human Aggression* (2nd edition). New York: Plenum.

Baron-Cohen, S. (1995). *Mindblindness: An essay on autism and theory of mind*. Cambridge, MA: MIT Press.

Baron-Cohen, S. (1997). *The Maladapted Mind: Classic readings in evolutionary psychopathology*. Hove, UK: The Psychology Press.

Baron-Cohen, S., Leslie, A.M. and Frith, U. (1985). Does the autistic child have a 'theory of mind'? *Cognition*, 21, 37–46.

Baron-Cohen, S., Wyke, M. and Binnie, C. (1987). Hearing words and seeing colours: An experimental investigation of a case of synaesthesia. *Perception*, 16, 761–767.

Baron-Cohen, S., Allen, J. and Gillberg, C. (1992). Can autism be detected at 18 months? The needle, the haystack and the CHAT. *British Journal of Psychiatry*, 161, 839–843.

Baron-Cohen, S., Harrison, J., Goldstein, L.H. and Wyke, M. (1993). Coloured speech perception: Is synaesthesia what happens when modularity breaks down? *Perception*, 22, 419–426.

Barraclough, B. (1988). International variation in the suicide rate of 15–24 year olds. *Social Psychiatry and Psychiatric Epidemiology*, 23, 75–84.

Bartlett, F. C. (1932). *Remembering: An experimental and social study*. Cambridge: Cambridge University Press.

Bartol, C.R. and Bartol, A.M. (1987). History of forensic psychology. In I.B. Weiner and A.K. Hess (eds), *Handbook of Forensic Psychology*. New York: Wiley.

Bastiaans, J. (1985). Psychological factors in the development of cancer. In E. Grundemann (ed.), *Cancer Campaign. Vol. 19: The Cancer Patient – Illness and recovery*. Stuttgart: Gustav Fischer Verlag.

Bauer, P.J. (1997). Development of memory in early childhood. In N. Cowan and C. Hulme (eds), *The Development of Memory in Childhood*. Hove, UK: The Psychology Press.

Bauer, P.J. and Dow, G.A.A. (1994). Episodic memory in 16- and 20-month old children: Specifics are generalised, but not forgotten. *Developmental Psychology*, 30, 403–417.

Bauer, P.J. and Mandler, J.M. (1992). Putting the horse before the cart: the use of temporal order in recall of events by one-year-old children. *Developmental Psychology*, 28, 441–452.

Bauer, P.J. and Travis, L.L. (1993). The fabric of an event: Different sources of temporal invariance differentially affect 24-month-olds' recall. *Cognitive Development*, 8, 319–341.

Bauer, P.J. and Wewerka, S.S. (1995). One- to two-year-olds' recall of events: The more expressed, the more impressed. *Journal of Experimental Child Psychology*, 59, 475–496.

Bauer, P.J., Hertsgaard, L.A. and Wewerka, S.S. (1995). Effects of experience and reminding on long-term recall in infancy: Remembering not to forget. *Journal of Experimental Child Psychology*, 59, 260–298.

Baum, M. (1989). Rationalism versus irrationalism in the care of the sick: Science versus the absurd. *Medical Journal of Australia*, 151, 607–608.

Bauman, M.L. and Kemper, T.L. (1994). *Neurobiology of Autism*. Baltimore: Johns Hopkins University Press.

Bausell, R.B. (1993). *Conducting meaningful experiments: 40 steps to becoming a scientist*. London: Sage.

Bayley, N. and Oden, M.H. (1955). The maintenance of intellectual ability in gifted adults. *Journal of Gerontology*, 10, 91–107.

Beardsall, L. (1998). Development of the Cambridge Contextual Reading Test for improving the estimation of premorbid verbal intelligence in older persons with dementia, *British Journal of Clinical Psychology*, 37, 2, 229–240.

Beaton, A.A. (1997). The relation of planum temporale asymmetry and morphology of the corpus callosum to handedness, gender and dyslexia: A review of the evidence. *Brain and Language*, 60, 2, 255–322.

Beatty, J. (1995). *Principles of Behavioral Neuroscience*. Madison: Wm.C. Brown Communications, Inc.

Beaumont, J.G. (1994). Expert witness. *The Psychologist*, November, 511–512.

Bebbington, P.E. (1988). Epidemiology of obsessive–compulsive disorder. *British Journal of Psychiatry*, 173, supplement, 35, 2–6.

Bechara, A., Tranel, D., Damasio, H. and Damasio, A.R. (1996). Failure to respond automatically to anticipated future outcomes following damage to prefrontal cortex. *Cerebral Cortex*, 6, 215.

Bechara, A., Damasio, H., Tranel, D. and Damasio, A.R. (1997). Deciding advantageously before knowing the advantageous strategy. *Science*, 275, 1293–1295.

Beck, A.T. (1967). *Depression: Clinical, experimental and theoretical aspects*. New York: Harper & Row.

Beck, A.T. (1976). *Cognitive therapy and the emotional disorders*. New York: International Universities Press.

Beck, A.T. (1991). Cognitive therapy: A thirty-year retrospective. *American Psychologist*, 46, 368–375.

Beck, A.T. and Emery, G. (1985). *Anxiety Disorders and Phobias: A cognitive perspective*. New York: Basic Books.

Beck, A. T., Rush, A. J., Shaw, B. F. and Emery, G. (1979). *Cognitive Therapy of Depression*. New York: Guilford Press.

Becker, M.H. and Maiman, L.A. (1980). Strategies for enhancing patient compliance. *Journal of Community Health*, 6, 113–115.

Beckerian, D.A. and Dennett, J.L. (1993). The cognitive interview technique: Reviving the issues. *Applied Cognitive Psychology*, 7, 275–297.

Beck–Jorgensen, B. (1991). What are they doing when they seem to do nothing? In J. Ehnrooth and L. Sivrala (eds), *Construction of youth*. Helsinki: Helsinki Finnish Youth Research Society.

Begleiter, H. and Kissin, B. (1995). *The Genetics of Alcoholism*. New York: Oxford University Press.

Beilin, H. (1990). Piaget's theory: Alive and more vigorous than ever. *Human Development*, 33, 362–365.

Bell, A. P. and Weinberg, M. S. (1978). *Homosexualities: A study of diversity among men and women*. New York: Simon & Schuster.

Bell, A.P., Weinberg, M.S. and Hammersmith, S.K. (1981). *Sexual Preference: Its Development in Men and Women*. Bloomington: Indiana University Press.

Bellugi, U. and Klima, E.S. (1972). The roots of language in the sign talk of the deaf. *Psychology Today*, pp. 61–76

Beloff, H. (1992). Mother, father and me: Our IQ. *The Psychologist*, 5, 309–311.

Bem, D.J. (1972). Self-perception theory. In L. Berkowitz (ed.), *Advances in Experimental Social Psychology*, Vol. 6. New York: Academic Press.

Bem, D. and Allen, A. (1974). On predicting some of the people some of the time: The search for cross-situational consistencies in behavior. *Psychological Review*, 81, 506–520.

Benn, R.K. (1986). Factors promoting secure attachment relationships between employed mothers and their sons. *Child Development*, 57, 1224–1231.

Bennett, A. and Stirling, J. (1998). Vulnerability factors in the anxiety disorders. *British Journal of Medical Psychology*, 71, 3, 311–322.

Benson, D. F. and Geschwind, N. (1969). The alexias. In P. Vinken and G. Bruyn (eds), *Handbook of Clinical Neurology*, Vol. 4. Amsterdam: North-Holland.

Benton, D. (1982). The influence of androstenol – a putative human pheromone – on mood throughout the menstrual cycle. *Biological Psychology*, 15, 249–256.

Benton, D. (1992). Vitamin and mineral intake and human behaviour. In *Handbook of Human Performance*, Vol 2. New York: Academic Press.

Benton, D. and Buts, J-P. (1990). Vitamin/mineral supplementation and intelligence. *Lancet*, 335, 1158–1160.

Benton, D. and Cook, R. (1991). Vitamin and mineral supplements improve the intelli-gence scores and concentration of six year old children. *Personality and Individual Difference*, 12, 1151–1158.

Benton, D. and Roberts, G. (1988). Effect of vitamin and mineral supplementation on intelligence of a sample of schoolchildren. *Lancet*, 1, 140–143.

Bergem, A.L., Engedal, K. and Kringlen, E. (1997). The role of heredity in late-onset Alzheimer disease and vascular dementia. A twin study. *Archives of General Psychiatry*, 54, 264–270.

Bergqvist, T.F. and Malec, J.F. (1997). Psychology: Current practice and training issues in treatment of cognitive dysfunction. *Neurorehabilitation*, 8, 49–56.

Berk, L.E. (1997). *Child Development* (4th edition). Boston: Allyn & Bacon.

Berko Gleason, J. (1993). *The Development of Language*. New York: Macmillan.

Berkowitz, L. (1964). Aggressive cues in aggressive behavior and hostility catharsis. *Psychological Review*, 71, 104–122.

Berlin, B. and Kay, P. (1969). *Basic Color Terms: Their universality and evolution*. Berkeley: University of California Press.

Berlyne, D.E. (1966). Motivational problems raised by exploratory and epistemic behavior. In S. Koch (ed.), *Psychology: A study of a science*, Vol. 5. New York: McGraw-Hill.

Bermant, G. and Davidson, J. M. (1974). *Biological Bases of Sexual Behavior*. New York: Harper & Row.

Berndt, R.S. and Mitchum, R.S. (1995). *Cognitive Neuropsychological Approaches to the Treatment of Language Disorders*. Hove, UK: Lawrence Erlbaum Associates.

Bernstein, I.L. (1978). Learned taste aversion in children receiving chemotherapy. *Science*, 200, 1302–1303.

Bernstein, I.L. (1991). Aversion conditioning in response to cancer and cancer treatment. *Clinical Psychology Review*, 11, 183–191.

Bernstein, I.L., Webster, M.M. and Bernstein, I.D. (1982). Food aversions in children receiving chemotherapy for cancer. *Cancer*, 50, 2961–2963.

Bernstein, R.N. and Berko, G.J. (1993). *Psycholinguistics*. Fort Worth: Holt, Rinehart & Winston.

Bernstein, W.M., Stephenson, B.O., Snyder, M.L. and Wicklund, R.A. (1983). Causal ambiguity and heterosexual affiliation. *Journal of Experimental Social Psychology*, 19, 78–92.

Besner, D., Twilley, L., McCann, R.S. and Seergobin, K. (1990). On the connection between connnectionism and data: Are a few words necessary? *Psychological Review*, 97, 432–446.

Bettencourt, B.A. and Miller, N. (1996). Gender differences in aggression as a function of provocation: A meta-analysis. *Psychological Bulletin*, 119, 3, 422–447.

Beutler, L.E. and Clarkin, J.F. (1990). *Systematic Treatment Selection: Toward tar-geted therapeutic interventions*. New York: Brunner/Mazel.

Beutler, L.E., Machado, P.P.P. and Allstetter Neufeldt, S. (1994). Therapist variables. In A.E. Bergin and S.L. Garfield (eds), *Handbook of Psychotherapy and Behaviour Change*. New York: Wiley.

Biddle, S. (1995). Exercise and psychosocial health. *Research Quarterly for Exercise and Sport*, 66, 4, 292–297.

Biederman, I. (1987). Recognition-by-components: A theory of human image interpretation. *Psychological Review*, 94, 115–147.

Biederman, I. (1990). Higher-level vision. In D.N. Osherson, S.M. Kosslyn and J. Hollerbach (eds), *An Invitation to Cognitive Science. Vol. 2: Visual Cognition and Action*. Cambridge, MA: MIT Press.

Biernat, M. and Wortman, C. B. (1991). Sharing of home responsibilities between professionally employed women and their husbands. *Journal of Personality and Social Psychology*, 60, 844–860.

Biglan, A., Duncan, T.E., Ary, D.V. and Smolkowski, K. (1995). Peer and parental influences on adolescent tobacco use. *Journal of Behavioural Medicine*, 18, 4, 315–330.

Bilder, R.M., Bogerts, B., Ashtari, M. (1995). Anterior hippocampal volume reductions predict frontal dysfunction in first episode schizophrenia. *Schizophrenia Research*, 17, 47–58.

Billig, M. (1992). *Talking of the Royal Family*. London: Routledge.

Billig, M. (1997). Rhetorical and discursive analysis. In N. Hayes (ed.), *Doing Qualitative Analysis in Psychology*. Hove, UK: Psychology Press.

Binder, J.R., Frost, J.A., Hammeke, T.A., Cox, R.W., Rao, S.M. and Prieto, T. (1997). Human brain language areas identified by functional magnetic resonance imaging. *Journal of Neuroscience*, 17, 1, 353–362.

Binet, A. and Henri, V. (1896). La psychologie individuelle. *Année Psychologique*, 2, 411–465.

Biondi, M., Parise, P., Venturi, P., Riccio, L., Brunetti, G. and Pancheri, P. (1993). Frontal hemisphere lateralization and depressive personality traits. *Perceptual and Motor Skills*, 77, 1035–1042.

Bird, G., Bird, G. and Scruggs, M. (1984). Determinants of family task sharing: A study of husbands and wives. *Journal of Marriage and Family Therapy*, 46, 345–355.

Birkhill, W.R. and Schaie, K.W. (1975). The effect of differential reinforcement of cautiousness in intellectual performance among the elderly. *Journal of Gerontology*, 30, 578–583.

Birren, J.E. and Morrison, D.F. (1961). Analysis of the WISC subtests in relation to age and education. *Journal of Gerontology*, 16, 363–369.

Bishop, D.V.M. (1990). *Handedness and Developmental Disorders*. Hove, UK: LEA.

Bishop, D.V.M. (1997). Listening out for subtle deficits. *Nature*, 387, 129–130.

Bishop, G.D. (1991a). Lay disease representations and responses to victims of disease. *Basic and Applied Social Psychology*, 12, 115–132.

Bishop, G.D. (1991b). Understanding the understanding of illness. In J.A. Skelton and R.T. Croyle (eds), *Mental Representation in Health and Illness*. New York: Springer-Verlag.

Bishop, G.D. (1994). *Health Psychology: Integrating mind and body*. Boston: Allyn & Bacon.

Bishop, G.D., Madey, S., Salinas, J., Massey, J. and Tudyk, D. (1992). The role of the availability heuristic in disease perception. *International Journal of Psychology*, 27, 637.

Black, S.L. and Biron, C. (1982). Androstenol as a human pheromone: No effect on perceived sexual attractiveness. *Behavioural and Neural Biology*, 34, 326–330.

Blackburn, R. (1996). What is forensic psychology? *Legal and Criminological Psychology*, 1, 3–16.

Blair, R.J.R., Jones, L., Clark, F. and Smith, M. (1997). The psychopathic individual: A lack of responsiveness to distress cues? *Psychophysiology*, 34, 192–652.

Blair, R.J.R., Morris, J.S., Frith, C.D., Perrett, D.I. and Dolan, R.J. (1999). Dissociable neural responses to facial expressions of sadness and anger. *Brain*, 122, 883–893.

Blakemore, C. and Mitchell, D.E. (1973). Environmental modification of the visual cortex and the neural basis of learning and memory. *Nature*, 241, 467–468.

Blank, A.S. (1993). The longitudinal course of post-traumatic stress disorder. In J.R.T. Davidson and E.B. Foa (eds), *Posttraumatic Stress Disorder: DSM-IV and beyond*. Washington, DC: Amercian Psychiatric Press.

Bleich, A., Koslowsky, M., Dolev, A. and Lerer, B. (1997). Post-traumatic stress disorder and depression. *British Journal of Psychiatry*, 170, 479–482.

Bliss, E.L. (1980). Multiple personalities: A report of 14 cases with implications for schizophrenia and hysteria. *Archives of General Psychiatry*, 37, 1388–1397.

Block, N., Flanagan, O. and Guzeldere, G. (1997). *The Nature of Consciousness*. Cambridge, MA: MIT Press.

Bloom, L. (1970). *Language Development: Form and function in emerging grammars*. Cambridge, MA: MIT Press.

Blum, K., Noble, E. P., Sheridan, P. J., Montgomery, A. and Ritchie, T. (1990). Allelic association of human dopamine D2 receptor gene in alchoholism. *Journal of the American Medical Association*, 263, 2055–2060.

Blum, S.H. and Blum, L.H. (1974). Do's and don'ts : An informal study of some prevailing superstitions. *Psychological Reports*, 35, 567–571.

Boaz, N. T. (1993). Origins of Hominidae. In A.J. Manyak and A. Manyak (eds), *Milestones in Human Evolution*. Prospect Heights, IL: Waveland Press.

Bogatz, G. and Ball, S. (1972). *The Second Year of Sesame Street: A Continuing Evaluation*. Princeton, NJ: Educational Testing Service.

Bogen, J.E. (1993). The callosal syndromes. In K.M. Heilman and E. Valenstein (eds), *Clinical Neuropsychology*. New York: Academic Press.

Bohannon, J.N. (1988). Flashbulb memories for the space shuttle disaster : A tale of two theories. *Cognition*, 29, 179–196.

Bohannon, J.N. (1993). Theoretical approaches to language acquisition. In J.B. Gleason (ed.), *The Development of Language*. New York: Macmillan.

Bohannon, J. N. and Stanowicz, L. (1988). The issue of negative evidence: Adult responses to children's language errors. *Developmental Psychology*, 24, 684–689.

Bohman, M., Cloninger, C.R. and Sigvardsson, S. (1981). Maternal inheritance of alcohol abuse: Cross-fostering analysis of adoptive women. *Archives of General Psychiatry*, 38, 965–969.

Bohner, G., Moskowitz, G.B. and Chaiken, S. (1995). The interplay of heuristic and systematic processing of social information. *European Review of Social Psychology*, 6, 33–68.

Boller, F. and Dennis, M. (1979). *Auditory Comprehension: Clinical and experimental studies with the token test*. New York: Academic Press.

Bolles, R.C. (1970). Species-specific defense reactions and avoidance learning. *Psychological Review*, 77, 32–48.

Bolles, R.C. (1979). *Learning Theory*. New York: Holt, Rinehart & Winston.

Bonvillian, J., Nelson, K.E. and Charrow, V. (1976). Languages and language-related skills in deaf and hearing children. *Sign Language Studies*, 12, 211–250.

Borgida, E. and Nisbett, R.E. (1977). The differential viewpoint of abstract vs. concrete information on decisions. *Journal of Applied Social Psychology*, 7, 258–271.

Boring, E.G. (1923). Intelligence as the tests test it. *The New Republic*, June, 35–37.

Boring, E.G. (1953). A history of introspection. *Psychological Bulletin*, 50, 169–189.

Borkovec, T.D. (1994). The nature, function and origins of worry. In G. Davey and F. Tallis (eds), *Worrying: Perspectives on theory, assessment and treatment*. Chichester, UK: Wiley.

Borovsky, D. and Rovee-Collier, C. (1989). Contextual restraints on memory retrieval at 6 months. *Child Development*, 61, 1569–1583.

Borysenko, J.Z. (1982). Behavioural–physiological factors in the development and management of cancer. *General Hospital Psychiatry*, 3, 69–74.

Bottini, G., Corcoran, R., Sterzi, R., Paulesu, E., Schenone, P., Scarpa, P., Frackowiak, R.S.J. and Frith, C.D. (1994). The role of the right hemisphere in the integration of figurative aspects of language. *Brain*, 117, 1241–1253.

Bouchard, T.J. (1997). IQ similarity in twins reared apart: Findings and responses to critics. In R.I. Sternberg and E. Grigorenko (eds), *Intelligence, heredity and environment*. New York: Cambridge University Press.

Bouchard, T. J. and Propping, P. (1993). *Twins as a Tool of Behavior Genetics*. Chichester: Wiley.

Bowen, D.M., Najlerahaim, A., Procter, A.W., Francis, P.T. and Murphy, E. (1989). Circumscribed changes in the cerebral cortex in neuropsychiatric disorders of later life. *Proceedings of the National Academy of Sciences of the USA*, 86, 9504–9508.

Bower, G.H. (1981). Mood and memory. *American Psychologist*, 36, 129–148.

Bower, G.H. (1987). Commentary on mood and memory. *Behaviour Research and Therapy*, 25, 443–456.

Bower, G.H. and Clark, M.C. (1969). Narrative stories as mediators for serial learning. *Psychonomic Science*, 14, 181–182.

Bower, G.H. and Cohen, P.R. (1982). Emotional influences on memory and thinking: Data and theory. In S. Fiske and M. Clark (eds), *Affect and Cognition*. Hillsdale, NJ: Lawrence Erlbaum.

Bower, G.H. and Mayer, J.D. (1989). In search of mood-dependent retrieval. *Journal of Social Behaviour and Personality*, 4, 133–168.

Bower, T.G.R. (1972). *Perception in Infancy* (2nd edition). San Francisco: W.H. Freeman.

Bowlby, J. (1969). *Attachment*. New York: Basic Books.

Bowlby, J. (1973). *Separation: Anxiety and Anger*. New York: Basic Books.

Bowles, N.L. and Poon, L.W. (1985). Aging and retrieval of words in semantic memory. *Journal of Gerontology*, 40, 71–77.

Boynton, R.M. (1979). *Human Color Vision*. New York: Holt, Rinehart & Winston.

Boysson-Bardies, B., Sagart, L. and Durand, C. (1984). Discernible differences in the babbling of infants according to target language. *Journal of Child Language*, 11, 1–15.

Bradley, L. and Bryant, P. (1983). Categorising sounds and learning to read – a causal connection. *Nature*, 301, 419–421.

Brain, P. (1984). Biological explanations of human aggression and the resulting therapies offered by such approaches: A critical evaluation. In R. Blanchard and D. Blanchard (eds), *Advances in the study of aggression*. New York: Academic Press.

Brain, P. (1994). Hormonal aspects of aggression and violence. In A. Reiss, K. Micek and J. Roth (eds), *Understanding and Preventing Violence*: Volume 2. New York: National Academic Press.

Bransford, J. D. and Johnson, M. K. (1972). Contextual prerequisites for understanding: Some investigations of comprehension and recall. *Journal of Verbal Learning and Verbal Behavior*, 11, 717–726.

Braun, A.R., Varga, M., Stager, S., Schultz, G., Selbiw, S., Maisog, J.M., Carson, R.E. and Ludlow, C.L. (1997). Altered patterns of cerebral activity during speech and language production in developmental stuttering. *Brain*, 120, 761–784.

Brazzelli, M., Colombo, N., Della Salla, S. and Spinnler, H. (1994). Spared and impaired cognitive abilities after bilateral frontal damage. *Cortex*, 30, 27–51.

Breitmeyer, B.G. (1980). *Visual Masking: An Integrative Approach*. New York: Oxford University Press.

Brewer, J.B., Zhao, Z., Desmond, J.E., Glover, G.H. and Gabrieli, J.D.E. (1998). Making memories: Brain activity that predicts how well visual experience will be remembered. *Science*, 281, 1185–1187.

Brewer, M.B. and Caporael, L.R. (1990). Selfish genes versus selfish people: Sociobiology as origin myth. *Motivation and Emotion*, 14, 237–243.

Brewer, M.B. and Miller, N. (1984). Beyond the contact hypothesis: Theoretical perspectives on desegregation. In N. Miller and M.B. Brewer (eds), *Groups in Contact: The psychology of desegregation*. New York: Academic Press, pp. 281–302.

Brewin, C.R., Smith, A.J., Power, M.J. and Furnham, A. (1992). State and trait differences in the depressive self-schema. *Behaviour Research and Therapy*, 30, 555–557.

Bridges, A.M. and Jones, D.M. (1996). Word-dose in the disruption of serial recall by irrelevant speech: Phonological confusions or changing state? *Quarterly Journal of Experimental Psychology*, 49A, 919–939.

Briggs, S.R. (1988). Shyness: Introversion or Neuroticism? *Journal of Research in Personality*, 22, 290–307.

British Psychological Society (1991). *Code of Conduct: Ethical principles and guidelines*. Leicester: British Psychological Society.

Britton, P. (1997). *The Jigsaw Man*. London: Bantam.

Broadbent, D.E. (1958). *Perception and Communication*. London: Pergamon Press.

Broberg, D.J. and Bernstein, I.L. (1987). Candy as a scapegoat in the prevention of food aversions in children receiving chemotherapy. *Cancer*, 60, 2344–2347.

Brodal, P. (1992). *The Central Nervous System: Structure and function*. Oxford: Oxford University Press.

Brooks, L. (1977). Visual pattern in fluent word identification. In A.S. Reber and D.L. Scarborough (eds), *Toward a Psychology of Reading*. Hillsdale, NJ: Lawrence Erlbaum Associates.

Brooks, P., Young, A.W., Maratos, E.J., Coffey, P.J., Calder, A.I., Isaac, C.L., Mays, A.R., Hodges, J.R., Montaldi, D., Cezayirli, E., Roberts N. and Hadley, D. (1998). Face processing impairments after encephalitis: Amygdala damage and recognition of fear. *Neuropsychologia*, 36, 1, 59–70.

Brooksbank, B.W.L., Brown, R. and Gustafsson, J.A. (1974). The detection of 5-alpha-androst-16-en-3alpha-ol in human male auxillary sweat. *Experientia*, 30, 864–865.

Brooks-Gunn, J. (1988). Antecedents and consequences of variations in girls' maturational timing. *Journal of Adolescent Health Care*, 9, 365–373.

Brooks-Gunn, J. and Furstenberg, F.F. (1989). Adolescent sexual behavior. *American Psychologist*, 44, 249–257.

Broverman, I.K., Vogel, S.R., Broverman, D.M., Clarkson, F.E. and Rosenkrantz, P.S. (1972). Sex role stereotypes: A current appraisal. *Journal of Social Issues*, 28, 59–78.

Brown, A.S. (1991). A review of the tip-of-the-tongue experience. *Psychological Bulletin*, 109, 204–223.

Brown, E. and Perrett, D.I. (1993). What gives a face its gender? *Perception*, 22, 829–840.

Brown, G.W. (1985). The discovery of expressed emotion: Induction or deduction? In J. Leff and C. Vaughn (eds), *Expressed Emotion in Families*. New York: Guilford Press.

Brown, G.W., Bone, M., Dalison, B. and Wing, J.K. (1966). *Schizophrenia and Social Care*. London: Oxford University Press.

Brown, J. (1998). Helping police with their inquiries. *The Psychologist*, November, 539–542.

Brown, J.D. (1991). Staying fit and staying well: Physical fitness as a moderator of life stress. *Personality Processes and Individual Differences*, 60, 455–461.

Brown, J.D. and Rogers, R.J. (1991). Self-serving attributions: The role of physiological arousal. *Personality and Social Psychology Bulletin*, 17, 501–506.

Brown, J.L. and Pollitt, E. (1996). Malnutrition, poverty and intellectual development. *Scientific American*, February, 26–31.

Brown, P. and Fraser, C. (1979). Speech as a marker of situation. In K.R. Scherer and H. Giles (eds), *Social Markers in Speech*. Cambridge: Cambridge University Press.

Brown, R. and Bellugi, U. (1964). Three processes in the child's acquisition of syntax. *Harvard Education Review*, 34, 133–151.

Brown, R. and Hanlon, C. (1970). Derivational complexity and order of acquisition in child speech. In J. R. Hayes (ed.), *Cognition and the Development of Language*. New York: Wiley.

Brown, R. and McNeill, D. (1966). The 'tip-of-the-tongue' phenomenon. *Journal of Verbal Learning and Verbal Behavior*, 5, 325–337.

Brown, R.J. (1988). *Group Processes: Dynamics within and between groups*. Oxford, UK: Blackwell.

Brown, R.J. (1995). *Prejudice: Its social psychology*. Oxford, UK: Blackwell.

Brown, R.T. (1989). Creativity: What are we to measure? In J.A. Glover, R.R. Ronning and C.R. Reynolds (eds), *Handbook of Creativity*. New York: Plenum.

Brown, R.W. and Kulik, J. (1977). Flashbulb memories. *Cognition*, 5, 73–99.

Brownell, K.D., Greenwood, M.R.C., Stellar, E. and Shrager, E.E. (1986). The effects of repeated cycles of weight loss and regain in rats. *Physiology and Behavior*, 38, 459–464.

Bruce, V. (1994). Stability from variation: The case of face recognition. The M.D. Vernon memorial lecture. *Quarterly Journal of Experimental Psychology*, 47A, 5–28.

Bruce, V. (1998). Fleeting images of shade: Identifying people caught on video. *The Psychologist*, 331–337.

Bruce, V. and Young, A.W. (1986). Understanding face recognition. *British Journal of Psychology*, 77, 305–327.

Bruce, V., Valentine, T. and Baddeley, A.D. (1987). The basis of the 3/4 view effect in face recognition. *Applied Cognitive Psychology*, 1, 109–120.

Bruce, V., Burton, A.M., Hanna, E., Healey, P., Mason, O., Coombes, A., Fright, R. and Linney, A. (1993). Sex discrimination: How do we tell the difference between male and female faces? *Perception*, 22, 131–152.

Bruce, V., Burton, A.M. and Dench, N. (1994). What's distinctive about a distinctive face? *Quarterly Journal of Experimental Psychology*, 47A, 1, 119–141.

Bruck, M. and Ceci, S.J. (1995) *Jeopardy in the courtroom: a scientific analysis of children's testimony*. Washington, DC: American Psychological Association.

Brunswick, N. (1998). The neuropsychology of language and language disorders. In Martin, G.N., *Human Neuropsychology*. Hemel Hempstead: Prentice Hall.

Brunswick, N., McCory, E., Price, C., Frith, C. and Frith, U. (1999). Explicit and implicit processing of words and pseudowords by adult developmental dyslexics: A search for Wernicke's Wortschatz? *Brain*, in press.

Brunswick, N. and Rippon, G. (1994). Auditory event-related potentials, dichotic listening performance and handedness as indices of lateralisation in dyslexic and normal readers. *International Journal of Psychophysiology*, 18, 265–275.

Bryant, P.E. and Bradley, L. (1985). *Children's Reading Problems: Psychology and education*. Oxford: Blackwell.

Bryden, M.P., McManus, I.C. and Bulman-Fleming, M.B. (1994). Evaluating the empirical support for the Geschwind–Behan–Galaburda model of cerebral lateralization. *Brain and Cognition*, 26, 103–167.

Bryson, S.E., Clark, B.S. and Smith, I.M. (1988). First report of a Canadian epidemiological study of autistic syndromes. *Journal of Child Psychology and Psychiatry*, 29, 433–445.

Buchanan, D. and Huczynski, H. (1997). *Organizational Behaviour: An introductory text* (3rd edition). Hemel Hempstead: Prentice Hall Europe.

Buck, L. and Axel, R. (1991). A novel multigene family may encode odorant receptors: A molecular basis for odor recognition. *Cell*, 65, 175–187.

Buck, R.W. (1975). Nonverbal communication of affect in children. *Journal of Personality and Social Psychology*, 31, 644–653.

Buck, R.W. (1977). Nonverbal communication accuracy in preschool children: Relationships with personality and skin conductance. *Journal of Personality and Social Psychology*, 33, 225–236.

Burgess, A.P. and Gruzelier, J.H. (1997). Localization of word and face recognition memory using topographical EEG. *Psychophysiology*, 34, 7–16.

Burke, D.M., MacKay, D.G., Worthley, J.S. and Wade, E. (1991). On the tip-of-the-tongue: What causes word finding failures in young and older adults? *Journal of Memory and Language*, 30, 542–579.

Burke, M., Drummond, L.M. and Johnston, D.W. (1997). Treatment choice for agoraphobic women: Exposure or cognitive-behaviour therapy? *British Journal of Clinical Psychology*, 36, 409–420.

Burt, C. (1962). The concept of consciousness. *British Journal of Psychology*, 53, 229–242.

Burton, A.M., Bruce, V. and Dench, N. (1993). What's the difference between men and women? Evidence from facial measurement. *Perception*, 22, 153–176.

Bushman, B.J. and Cooper, H.M. (1990). Effects of alcohol on human aggression: an integrative research review. *Psychological Bulletin*, 107, 341–354.

Bushnell, I.W.R. (1979). Modification of the externality effect in young infants. *Journal of Experimental Child Psychology*, 28, 211–225.

Buskist, W. and Miller, H. L. (1986). Interaction between rules and contingencies in the control of human fixed-interval performance. *Psychological Record*, 36, 109–116.

Buss, A. H. (1995). *Personality: Temperament, social behavior, and the self*. Boston: Allyn & Bacon.

Buss, D.M. (1991). Evolutionary personality psychology. *Annual Review of Psychology*, 45, 459–491.

Buss, D.M. (1995). Evolutionary psychology: A new paradigm for psychological science. *Psychological Inquiry*, 6, 1, 1–30.

Buss, D.M., Haselton, M.G., Shackelford, T.K., Bleske, A.L. and Wakefield, J.C. (1998). Adaptations, exaptations and spandrels. *Amercian Psychologist*, 53, 5, 533–548.

Buunk, B.P., de Jonge, J., Ybema, J.F. and de Wolff, C.J. (1998). Psychological aspects of occupational stress. In P.J. Denth, H. Thierry and C.J. de Wolff (eds), *The Handbook of Work and Organisational Psychology* (2nd edition). Hove: The Psychology Press.

Byrd, M. and Stacey, B. (1993). Bias in IQ perception. *The Psychologist*, 6, 16.

Byrne, R. (1995). *The Thinking Ape*. Oxford: Oxford University Press.

Cabanac, M. (1971). *Physiological role of pleasure*. Science, 173, 1103–1107.

Cabeza, R., Grady, C.L., Nyberg, L., McIntosh, A.R., Tulving, E., Kapur, S., Jennings, J.M., Houle, S. and Craik, F.I.M. (1997). Age-related differences in neural activity during memory encoding and retrieval: A positron emission tomography study. *Journal of Neuroscience*, 17, 1, 391–400.

Calder, A.J., Young, A.W., Rowland, D., Perrett, D.I., Hodges, J.R. and Etcoff, N.L. (1996). Facial emotion recognition after bilateral amygdala damage: Differentially severe impairment of fear. *Cognitive Neuropsychology*, 13, 699–745.

Calev, A., Gaudino, E.A., Squires, N.K. *et al.* (1995). ECT and non-memory cognition: A review. *British Journal of Clinical Psychology*, 34, 505–516.

Calvin, W.H. and Ojemann, G.A. (1994). *Conversations with Neil's Brain*. New York: Addison-Wesley.

Campfield, L.A., Smith, F.J., Guisez, Y., Devos, R. and Burn, P. (1995). Recombinant mouse OB protein: evidence for a peripheral signal linking adiposity and central neural networks. *Science*, 269, 546–549.

Cannon, W.B. (1927). The James-Lange theory of emotions: A critical examination and an alternative theory. *American Journal of Psychology*, 39, 106-124.

Cannon, W.B. (1931). Again the James-Lange and the thalamic theories of emotion. *Psychological Review*, 38, 281–295.

Cannon, W.B. and Washburn, A.L. (1912). An explanation of hunger. *American Journal of Physiology*, 29, 444–454.

Canter, D. (1989). Offender profiles. *The Psychologist*, 2, 12–16.

Canter, D. (1994). *Criminal Shadows: Inside the mind of a serial killer*. London: HarperCollins.

Caprara, G.V. and Perugini, M. (1994) Personality described by adjectives: Generalizability of the Big Five to the Italian lexical context. *European Journal of Personality*, 8, 357–369.

Carlson, E.A. (1998). A prospective longitudinal study of attachment disorganization/disorientation. *Child Development*, 69, 4, 1107–1128.

Carlson, N.R. (1995). *Foundations of Physical Psychology*. Boston: Allyn & Bacon.

Carlson, N.R. (1998). *Physiology of Behaviour* (6th edition). Boston: Allyn & Bacon.

Carpenter, P.A. and Just, M.A. (1983). What your eyes do while your mind is reading. In K. Rayner (ed.), *Eye Movements in Reading: Perceptual and Language Processes*. New York: Academic Press.

Carpenter, P.A., Miyake, A. and Just, M.A. (1995). Language comprehension: Sentence and discourse processing. *Annual Review of Psychology*, 46, 91–120.

Carr, E.G. and Lovaas, O.J.C. (1983). Contingent electric shock as a treatment for severe behavior problems. In S. Axelrod and J. Apsche (eds), *The Effect of Punishment on Human Behavior*. New York: Academic Press.

Carson, R.C., Butcher, J.N. and Mineka, S. (1996). *Abnormal Psychology and Modern Life* (10th edition). New York: HarperCollins.

Carstens, C.B., Huskins, E. and Hounshell, G.W. (1995). Listening to Mozart may not enhance performance on the Revised Minnesota Paper Form Board Test. *Psychological Reports*, 77, 111–114.

Carver, C. S. and Scheier, M. F. (1992). *Perspectives on Personality* (2nd edition). Boston: Allyn & Bacon.

Case, R. (1985). *Intellectual Development: A systematic reinterpretation*. New York: Academic Press.

Case, R. (1992). *The Mind's Staircase*. Hillsdale, NJ: Lawrence Erlbaum Associates.

Casey, B.J., Cohen, J.D., O'Craven, K., Davidson, R.J., Irwin, W., Nelson, C.A., Noll, D.C., Hu, X., Lowe, M.J., Rosen, B.R., Truwitt, C.L. and Turski, P.A. (1998). Reproducibility of fMRI results across four institutions using a spatial working memory task. *Neuroimage*, 8, 249–261.

Castro-Caldas, A., Petersson, K.M., Reis, A., Stone-Elander, S. and Ingvar, M. (1998). The illiterate brain: Learning to read and write during childhood influences the functional organization of the adult brain. *Brain*, 121, 1053–1063.

Catania, J.A., Kegeles, S.M. and Coates, T.J. (1990). Towards an understanding of risk behaviour: An AIDS Risk Reduction Model (ARRM). *Health Education Quarterly*, 17, 53–72.

Cavanaugh, J. C. (1990). *Adult Development and Aging*. Belmont, CA: Wadsworth.

Cerruti, D. (1990). Discrimination theory of rule-governed behavior. *Journal of the Experimental Analysis of Behavior*, 54, 129–153.

Chaiken, S. (1979). Communicator's physical attractiveness and persuasion. *Journal of Personality and Social Psychology*, 37, 1387–1397.

Chalmers, D.J. (1995). Facing up to the problems of consciousness. *Journal of Consciousness Studies*, 2, 3, 200–219.

Chalmers, D.J. (1998). On the search for the neural correlate of consciousness. In S.R. Hameroff, A.W. Kaszniak and A.C. Scott (eds), *Towards a Science of Consciousness II*. Cambridge, MA: MIT Press.

Chapin, F.S. (1938). Design for social experiments. *American Sociological Review*, 3, 786–800.

Chapman, A.J. and Perry, D.J. (1995). Applying the cognitive interview procedure to child and adult eyewitnesses of road accidents. *Applied Psychology: An International Review*, 44, 283–294.

Chapman, K. L., Leonard, L. B. and Mervis, C. B. (1986). The effect of feedback on young children's inappropriate word usage. *Journal of Child Language*, 13, 101–117.

Charmaz, C. (1990). Discovering chronic illness: Using grounded theory. *Social Science and Medicine*, 30, 11, 1161–1172.

Chasdi, E.H. (1994). *Culture and Human Development: The selected papers of John Whiting*. New York: Cambridge University Press.

Chassin, L., Presson, CC., Rose, J.S. and Sherman, S.J. (1996). The natural history of cigarette smoking from adolescence to adulthood: Demographic predictors of continuity and change. *Health Psychology*, 15, 6, 478–484.

Chaves, J.F. (1989). Hypnotic control of clinical pain. In N.P. Spanos and J.F. Chaves (eds), *Hypnosis: The cognitive-behavioural perspective*. Buffalo, NY: Prometheus.

Cherny, S.S., Fulker, D.W., Emde, R.N., Robinson, J., Corley, R.P., Reznick, J.S., Plomin, R. and DeFries, J.C. (1994). A developmental–genetic analysis of continuity and change in the Bayley Mental Development Index from 14 to 24 months: The MacArthur Longitudinal Twin Study. *Psychological Science*, 5, 354–360.

Cherry, E.C. (1953). Some experiments on the recognition of speech, with one and with two ears. *Journal of the Acoustical Society of America*, 25, 975–979.

Chincotta, D. and Underwood, G. (1996). Mother tongue, language of schooling and bilingual digit span. *British Journal of Psychology*, 87, 193–208.

Chipuer, H.M., Rovine, M.J. and Plomin, R. (1990). LISREL modelling: Genetic and environmental influences on IQ revisited. *Intelligence*, 14, 1–29.

Chomsky, N. (1957). *Syntactic Structure*. The Hague: Mouton Publishers.

Chomsky, N. (1965). *Aspects of the Theory of Syntax*. Cambridge, MA: MIT Press.

Chorney, M.J., Chorney, K., Seese, N., Owen, M.J., Daniels, J., McGriffin, P., Thompson, L.A., Detterman, D.K., Benbow, C., Lubinski, D., Eley, T. and Plomin, R. (1998). A quantitative trait locus associated with cognitive ability in children. *Psychological Science*, 9, 3, 159–166.

Christensen, H., Henderson, A.S., Griffiths, K. and Levings, C. (1997). Does ageing inevitably lead to declines in cognitive performance? A longitudinal study of elite academics. *Personality and Individual Differences*, 23, 1, 67–78.

Christianson, S.A. (1989). Flash-bulb memories: Special, but not so special. *Memory and Cognition*, 17, 435–443.

Christianson, S.A. and Loftus, E.F. (1991). Remembering emotional events: The fate of detailed information. *Cognition and Emotion*, 5, 81–108.

Christie, F. and Bruce, V. (1998). The role of movement in the recognition of unfamiliar faces. *Memory and Cognition*, 26, 4, 780–790.

Chua, S.E. and McKenna, P.J. (1995). Schizophrenia – a brain disease? A critical review of structural and functional cerebral abnormality in the disorder. *British Journal of Psychiatry*, 166, 563–582.

Churchland, P.S. (1998). Brainshy: Nonneural theories of conscious experience. In S.R. Hameroff, A.W. Kaszniak and A.C. Scott (eds), *Towards a Science of Consciousness II*. Cambridge, MA: MIT Press.

Cialdini, R.B. (1993). *Influence: Science and Practice* (3rd edition). New York: HarperCollins.

Cialdini, R.B., Borden, R.J., Thorne, A., Walker, M. R., Freeman, S. and Sloan, L.R. (1976). Basking in reflected glory: Three (football) field studies. *Journal of Personality and Social Psychology*, 34, 366–375.

Cialdini, R.B, Petty, R.E. and Cacioppo, J.T. (1981). Attitude and attitude change. *Annual Review of Psychology*, 32, 357–404.

Cicerone, K.D. and Tanenbaum, L.N. (1997). Disturbance of social cognition after traumatic arbitofrontal brain injury. *Archives of Clinical Neuropsychology*, 12, 2, 173–188.

Cioffi, D. and Holloway, J. (1993). Delayed costs of suppressed pain. *Journal of Personality and Social Psychology*, 64, 274–282.

Cipolotti, L. and Warrington, E.K. (1995). Neuropsychological assessment. *Journal of Neurology, Neurosurgery, and Psychiatry*, 58, 655–664.

Clark, D.M. (1986). A cognitive approach to panic. *Behaviour Research and Therapy*, 24, 461–470.

Clark, D.M. (1988). A cognitive model of panic attacks. In S. Rachman and J.D. Maser (eds), *Panic: Psychological perspectives*. Hillsdale, NJ: Lawrence Erlbaum Associates.

Clark, H.H. and Clark, E.V. (1977). *Psychology and Language: An introduction to psycholinguistics*. New York: Harcourt Brace Jovanovich.

Clarke, J.C. (1992). The nature and treatment of panic anxiety and agoraphobia. In S. Schwartz (ed.), *Case Studies in Abnormal Psychology*. New York: Wiley.

Clark, J.D. (1993). The African tinderbox: The spark that ignited our cultural heritage. In A.J. Almquist and A. Manyak (eds), *Milestones in Human Evolution*. Prospect Heights, IL: Waveland Press.

Clark, J.E., Lanphear, A.K. and Riddick, C.C. (1987). The effects of videogame playing on the response selection processing of elderly adults. *Journal of Gerontology*, 42, 82–85.

Cleckley, H. (1976). *The Mask of Sanity*. St Louis: C.V. Mosby.

Cleermans, A. (1993). *Mechanisms of Implicit Learning*. Cambridge, MA: MIT Press.

Cloninger, C.R. (1987). Neurogenetic adaptive mechanisms in alcoholism. *Science*, 236, 410–416.

Cloninger, C.R., Bohman, M. and Sigvardsson, S. (1981). Inheritance of alcohol abuse: Cross-fostering analysis of adoptive men. *Archives of General Psychiatry*, 38, 861–868.

Cloninger, C. R., Bohman, M., Sigvardsson, S. and von Knorring, A-L. (1985). Psychopathology in adopted-out children of alcoholics. The Stockholm Adoption Study. *Recent Developments in Alcoholism*, 7, 235.

Code, C., Wallesch, C.-W., Joanette, Y. and Roch, A. (1996) *Classic Cases in Neuropsychology*. Hillsdale, NJ: Lawrence Erlbaum Associates.

Codori, A.M., Slaveney, P.R., Young, C., Miglioretti, D.L. and Brandt, J. (1997). Predictors of psychological adjustment to genetic testing in Huntington's disease. *Health Psychology*, 16, 36–50.

Coe, W.C. and Sarbin, T.R. (1991). Role theory: Hypnosis from a dramaturgical and narrational perspectives. In S.J. Lynn and J.H. Rhue (eds), *Theories of Hypnosis: Current models and perspectives*. New York: Guilford.

Cogan, B., Cogan, D., Waltz, W. and McCue, M. (1987). Effects of laughter and relaxation on discomfort thresholds. *Journal of Behavioural Medicine*, 10, 2, 139–144.

Cohen, D.J. and Volkmar, F.R. (1997). *Autism and Pervasive Developmental Disorders: A handbook*. New York: John Wiley.

Cohen, G. (1990). Why is it difficult to put names to faces? *British Journal of Psychology*, 81, 287–297.

Cohen, G., Stanhope, N. and Conway, M.A. (1992). Age differences in the retention of knowledge by young and elderly students. *British Journal of Developmental Psychology*, 10, 153–164.

Cohen, J. and Breslin, P.W. (1984). Visual evoked-responses in dyslexic children. *Annals of the New York Academy of Sciences*, 425, 338–343.

Cohen, J.D., Peristein, W.M., Braver, T.S., Nystrom, L.E., Noll, D.C., Jonides, J. and Smith, E.E. (1997). Temporal dynamics of brain activation during a working memory task. *Nature*, 386, 604–607.

Cohen, L.A. (1987). Diet and cancer. *Scientific American*, 102, 42–48.

Cohen, M. and Davis, N. (1981). *Medication Errors: Causes and prevention*. Philadelphia: G.F. Stickley.

Cohen, S., Frank, E., Doyle, W.J., Skoner, D.P., Rabin, B.S. and Gwaltney, J.M. (1998). Types of stressors that increase susceptibility to the common cold in healthy adults. *Health Psychology*, 17, 3, 214–223.

Cohn, B.A. (1994). In search of human skin pheromones. *Archives of Dermatology*, 130, 1048–1051.

Cok, F. (1990). Body image satisfaction in Turkish adolescents. *Adolescence*, 25, 409–413.

Coleman, J. C. (1996). *Abnormal Psychology and Modern Life* (5th edition). Glenview, IL: Scott, Foresman.

Coles, C. D., Platzman, K. A., Smith, I., James, M. E. and Falek, A. (1992). Effects of cocaine and alcohol use in pregnancy on neonatal growth and neurobehavioral status. *Neurotoxicology and Teratology*, 14, 23–33.

Collaer, M.L. and Hines, M. (1995). Human behavioural sex differences: A role for gonadal hormones during early development. *Psychological Bulletin*, 118, 55–107.

Collins, A. M. and Quillian, M. R. (1969). Retrieval time from semantic memory. *Journal of Verbal Learning and Verbal Behavior*, 8, 240–248.

Colman, A.M. (1995). Testifying in court as an expert witness. *Professional Psychology Handbook*. Leicester: BPS Books.

Coltheart, M. (1978). Lexical access in simple reading tasks. In G. Underwood (ed.), *Strategies of Information Processing*. London: Academic Press.

Coltheart, M., Curtis, B., Atkins, P. and Haller, M. (1993). Models of reading aloud: Dual-route and parallel-distributed-processing approaches. *Psychological Review*, 100, 589–608.

Compton, W.M., Helzer, J.E., Hwu, H.G., Yeh, E.K., McEnvoy, L., Topp, J.E. and Spitznagel, E.L. (1991). New methods in cross-cultural psychiatry in Taiwan and the United States. *American Journal of Psychiatry*, 148, 1697–1704.

Conner, M. and Sparks, P. (1996). The theory of planned behaviour and health behaviours. In M. Conner and P. Norman (eds), *Predicting Health Behaviours: Research and practice with social cognition models*. Buckingham, UK: Open University Press.

Connors, E., Lundregan, T., Miller, N. and McEwen, T. (1996). *Convicted by juries, exonerated by science: Case studies in the use of DNA evidence to establish innocence after trial*. Washington DC: US Department of Justice.

Conway, M.A., Cohen, G. and Stanhope, N. (1991). On the very long-term retention of knowledge acquired through formal education: Twelve years of cognitive psychology. *Journal of Experimental Psychology: General*, 120, 1–22.

Conway, M.A., Cohen, G. and Stanhope, N. (1992). Why is it that university grades do not predict very-long-term retention? *Journal of Experimental Psychology: General*, 121, 3, 382–384.

Conway, M.A., Anderson, S.J., Larsen, S.F., Donnelly, C.M., McDaniel, M.A., McClelland, A.G.R., Rawles, R.E. and Logie, R.H. (1994). The formation of flashbulb memories. *Memory and Cognition*, 22, 326–343.

Conway, M.A., Gardiner, J.M., Perfect, T.J., Anderson, S.J. and Cohen, G.M. (1997). Changes in memory awareness during learning: The acquisition of knowledge by psychology undergraduates. *Journal of Experimental Psychology: General*, 126, 393–413.

Conway, S.C. and O'Carroll, R.E. (1997). An evaluation of the Cambridge Contextual Reading Test in Alzheimer's Disease, *British Journal of Clinical Psychology*, 36, 4, 623–625.

Cooper, J. and Fazio, R.H. (1984). A new look at dissonance theory. In L. Berkowitz (ed.), *Advances in Experimental Social Psychology*, Vol. 17. New York: Academic Press, pp. 229–265.

Cooper, K. (1985). Running without risk. *Runner's World*, 20, 61–64.

Cooper, M.L., Russell, M. and George, W.H. (1988). Coping, expectancies, and alcohol abuse: A test of social learning foundations. *Journal of Abnormal Psychology*, 97, 218–230.

Cooper, R.M. and Zubek, J.P. (1958). Effects of enriched and restricted early environments on the learning ability of bright and dull rats. *Canadian Journal of Psychology*, 12, 159–164.

Coover, G.D., Murison, R. and Jellestad, F.K. (1992). Subtotal lesions of the amygdala: The rostral central nucleus in passive avoidance and ulceration. *Physiology and Behavior*, 51, 795–803.

Corballis, M.C. (1997). The genetics and evolution of handedness. *Psychological Review*, 104, 4, 714–727.

Corbett, G.C. and Davies, I.R.L. (1997). Establishing basic color terms: Measures and techniques. In C.L. Hardin and L. Maffi (eds), *Color Categories in Thought and Language*. New York: Cambridge University Press.

Corbetta, M., Miezin, F.M., Doobmeyer, S., Shulman, G.L. and Petersen, S.E. (1991). Selective and divided attention during visual discriminations of shape, color, and speed: Functional anatomy by positron emission tomography. *Journal of Neuroscience*, 11, 2383–2402.

Corkin, S., Sullivan, E.V., Twitchell, T.E. and Grove, E. (1981). The amnesic patient H.M.: Clinical observations and test performance 28 years after operation. *Society for Neuroscience Abstracts*, 7, 235.

Corteen, R. and Williams, T. (1986). Television and reading skills. In T.M. Williams (ed.), *The Impact of Television: A natural experiment in three communities*. New York: Academic Press.

Coryell, W. (1980). A blind family history study of Briquet's syndrome. Further validation of the diagnosis. *Archives of General Psychiatry*, 37, 1266–1269.

Costa, P.T. and McCrae, R.R. (1980). Still stable after all these years: Personality as a key to some issues in adulthood and old age. In P.B. Baltes (ed.), *Life-span Development and Behavior*. New York: Academic Press.

Costall, A. (1995). Socialising affordances. *Theory and Psychology*, 5, 4, 467–481.

Cotton, N.S. (1979). The familial incidence of alcoholism. A review. *Journal of Studies in Alcohol*, 40, 89–116.

Courchesne, E., Hesselink, J.R., Jernigan, T.L. and Yeung-Courchesne, R. (1987). Abnormal neuroanatomy in a nonretarded person with autism. *Archives of Neurology*, 44, 335–341.

Courchesne, E., Press, G.A. and Yeung-Courchesne, R. (1993). Parietal lobe abnormalities detected with MR in patients with infantile autism. *American Journal of Roentgenology*, 160, 387–393.

Courtney, S.M., Ungerleider, L.G., Kell, K. and Haxby, J.V. (1997). Transient and sustained activity in a distributed neurla system for human working memory. *Nature*, 386, 608–611.

Cowley, D. S. and Arana, G. W. (1990). The diagnostic utility of lactate sensitivity in panic disorder. *Archives of General Psychiatry*, 47, 277–284.

Cowley, J.J. and Brooksbank, B.W.L. (1991). Human exposure to putative pheromones and changes in aspects of social behaviour. *Journal of Steroid Biochemistry and Molecular Biology*, 39, 647–659.

Cowley, J.J., Harvey, F., Johnson, A.T. and Brooksbank, B.W.L. (1980). Irritability and depression during the menstrual cycle – possible role for an exogenous pheromone? *Irish Journal of Psychology*, 3, 143–156.

Cox, R.H. (1991). *Intervention Strategies. Stress and coping: An Anthology*, A. Monat and R. S. Lazarus (eds). New York: Columbia University Press.

Craik, F.I.M. and Lockhart, R.S. (1972). Levels of processing: A framework for memory research. *Journal of Verbal Learning and Verbal Behavior*, 11, 671–684.

Craik, F.I.M. and Tulving, E. (1975). Depth of processing and the retention of words in episodic memory. *Journal of Experimental Psychology: General*, 104, 268–294.

Craske, M.G., Rowe, M., Lewin, M. and Noriega-Dimitri, R. (1997). Interoceptive exposure versus breathing retraining within cognitive-behavioural therapy for panic disorder with agoraphobia. *British Journal of Clinical Psychology*, 36, 85–99.

Crawford, H.J. (1994). Brain systems involved in attention and disattention (hypnotic analgesia) to pain. In K. Pribram (ed.), *Origins: Brain and self-organisation*. Hillsdale, NJ: Lawrence Erlbaum Associates.

Crawford, H.J., Brown, A. and Moon, C. (1993). Sustained attentional and disattentional abilities: Differences between low and highly hypnotisable persons. *Journal of Abnormal Psychology*, 102, 534–543.

Crawford, H.J., Knebel, T., Kaplan, L., Vendemia, J.M.C., Xie, M., Jamison, S. and Pribram, K.H. (1998). 1. Somatosensory event-related potential changes to noxious stimuli and 2. Transfer learning to reduce chronic low back pain. *International Journal of Clinical and Experimental Hypnosis*, XLVI, 1, 92–132.

Crawford, J.R. (1992). Current and premorbid intelligence measures in neuropsychological assessment. In J.R. Crawford, D.M. Parker and M.M. McKinlay (eds), *A Handbook of Neuropsychological Assessment*. Hove, UK: The Psychology Press.

Crick, F. (1994). *The Astonishing Hypothesis*. London: Simon & Schuster.

Crick, F. and Koch, C. (1995). Are we aware of neural activity in primary visual cortex? *Nature*, 121–6.

Crick, F. and Mitchison, G. (1983). The function of dream sleep. *Nature*, 304, 111–114.

Critchley, H.D. and Rolls, E.T. (1996). Hunger and satiety modify the responses of olfactory and visual neurons in the primate orbitofrontal cortex. *Journal of Neurophysiology*, 75, 1673–1686.

Critchley, M. (1973). *The Dyslexic Child* (2nd edition). London: Heinemann.

Critchlow, S. (1998). False memory sydrome – balancing the evidence for and against. *Irish Journal of Psychological Medicine*, 15, 2, 64–67.

Crocker, J. and Luhtanen, R. (1990). Collective self-esteem and ingroup bias. *Journal of Personality and Social Psychology*, 58, 60–67.

Crombag, H.F.M., Wagenaar, W.A. and Van Koppen, P.J. (1996). Crashing memories and the problem of 'source monitoring'. *Applied Cognitive Psychology*, 10, 95–104.

Crombie, I.K., Todman, J., McNeill, G., Florey, C.Du V., Menzies, I. and Kennedy, R.A. (1990). Effect of vitamin and mineral supplementation on verbal and non-verbal reasoning of schoolchildren. *Lancet*, 335, 744–747.

Crosby, F.J. (1991). *Juggling: The unexpected advantages of balancing career and home for women and their families*. New York: The Free Press.

Crow, T.J. (1980). Molecular pathology of schizophrenia: More than one disease process? *British Medical Journal*, 280, 66–68.

Crow, T.J. (1998). Nuclear schizophrenic symptoms as a window on the relationship between thought and speech. *British Journal of Psychiatry*, 173, 303–309.

Crowe, R.R., Noyes, R., Pauls, D.L. and Slymen, D. (1983). A family study of panic disorder. *Archives of General Psychiatry*, 40, 1065–1069.

Crowne, D. and Marlowe, D. (1964). *The Approval Motive*. New York: Wiley.

Croyle, R.T. and Cooper, J. (1983). Dissonance arousal: Physiological evidence. *Journal of Personality and Social Psychology*, 45, 782–791.

Csikszentmihalyi, M. and Larson, R. (1984). *Being Adolescent: Conflict and growth in the teenage years*. New York: Basic Books.

Culebras, A. and Moore, J. T. (1989). Magnetic resonance findings in REM sleep behavior disorder. *Neurology*, 39, 1519–1523.

Cummings, J.L. and Benson, D.F. (1992). *Dementia: A clinical approach*. Boston: Butterworth.

Cummings, J.L. and Wirshing, W.C. (1989). Recognition and differential diagnosis of tardive dyskinesia. *International Journal of Psychiatry in Medicine*, 19, 133–144.

Cummins, J. (1984). *Bilingualism and Special Education: Issues in assessment and pedagogy*. Clevedon: Multilingual Matters.

Curtis, G.C., Magee, W.J., Eaton, W.W., Wittchen, H-U. and Kessler, R.C. (1998). Specific fears and phobias. *British Journal of Psychiatry*, 173, 212–217.

Curtiss, S. (1977). *Genie: A psycholinguistic study of a modern day 'wild child'*. New York: Academic Press.

Cytowic, R. (1993). *The man who tasted shapes*. London: Abacus.

Dabbs, J.M. (1990). Salivary testosterone measurements: Reliability across hours, days and weeks. *Physiology and Behaviour*, 48, 83–86.

Dabbs, J.M., Frady, R.L., Carr, T.S. and Besch, N.F. (1987). Saliva testosterone and criminal violence in young adult prison inmates. *Psychosomatic Medicine*, 49, 174–182.

Dabbs, J.M., Jurkovic, G and Frady, R. (1991). Salivary testosterone and cortisol among late adolescent male offenders. *Journal of Abnormal Child Psychology*, 19, 469–478.

Dabbs, J.M., Ruback, J.M., Frady, R.L. and Hopper, C.H. (1988). Saliva testosterone and criminal violence among women. *Personality and Individual Differences*, 9, 269–275.

Dacey, J.S. (1989). *Fundamentals of Creative Thinking*. Lexington, MA: Lexington.

Da Costa Pinto, A. (1991). Reading rates and digit span in bilinguals: The superiority of mother tongue. *International Journal of Psychology*, 26, 471–483.

Dalgleish, T., Rosen, K. and Marks, M. (1996). Rhythm and blues: The assessment and treatment of seasonal affective disorder. *British Journal of Clinical Psychology*, 35, 163–182.

Daly, M. and Wilson, M. (1978). *Sex, Evolution, and Behavior*. North Scituate, MA: Duxbury Press.

Daly, M. and Wilson, M. (1988). *Homicide*. New York: Aldine de Gruyter.

Daly, M. and Wilson, M. (1996). Violence against stepchildren. *Current Directions in Psychological Science*, 5, 77–81.

Damasio, A.R. (1995). Toward a neurobiology of emotion and feeling: Operational concepts and hypotheses. *The Neuroscientist*, 1, 19–25.

Damasio, A.R., Yamada, T., Damasio, H., Corbett, J. and McKee, J. (1980). Central achromatopsia: Behavioural, autonomic and physiologic aspects. *Neurology*, 30, 1064–1071.

Damasio, H. (1989). Neuroimaging contributions to the understanding of aphasia. In F. Boller and J. Grafman (eds), *Handbook of Neuropsychology*, Vol. 2. Amsterdam: Elsevier.

Damasio, H., Grabowski, T., Frank, R., Galaburda, A.M. and Damasio, A.R. (1994). The return of Phineas Gage: Clues about the brain from the skull of a famous patient. *Science*, 264, 1102–1105.

Damasio, H., Grabowski, T.J., Tranel, D., Hichwa, R.D. and Damasio, A.R. (1996). A neural basis for lexical retrieval. *Nature*, 380, 499–505.

Daniels, P. and Weingarten, K. (1982). *Sooner or Later: The timing of parenthood in adult lives*. New York: W.W. Norton.

Daoussis, L. and McKelvie, S.J. (1986). Musical preferences and effects of music on a reading comprehension test for extraverts and introverts. *Perceptual and Motor Skills*, 62, 283–289.

Darley, J.M. and Latané, B. (1968). Bystander intervention in emergencies: Diffusion of responsibility. *Journal of Personality and Social Psychology*, 8, 377–383.

Darwin, C. (1872). *The Expression of the Emotions in Man and Animals*. Reprinted in 1965 by Chicago: University of Chicago Press, Chicago.

Darwin, C.J., Turvey, M.T. and Crowder, R.G. (1972). An auditory analogue of the Sperling partial report procedure: Evidence for brief auditory storage. *Cognitive Psychology*, 3, 255–267.

Darwin, F. (1887). *Charles Darwin's Autobiography*. Reprinted in 1950 by Henry Schuman, New York.

Dashiell, J.F. (1935). Experimental studies of the influence of social situations on the behavior of individual human adults. In C. Murcheson (ed.), *A Handbook of Social Psychology*. Worcester, MA: Clark University Press.

Dautrich, B.R. (1993). Visual perceptual differences in the dyslexic reader: Evidence of greater visual peripheral sensitivity to colour and letter stimuli. *Perceptual and Motor Skills*, 76, 755–764.

Davey, G.C.L. (1992). Characteristics of individuals with fear of spiders. *Anxiety Research*, 4, 299–314.

Davey, G.C.L., McDonald, A.S., Hirisave, U., Prabhu, C.G., Iwawaki, S., Jim, C.I., Mercklebach, H., de Jong, P.J., Leung, P.W.L. and Reimann, B.C. (1998). A crosscultural study of animal fears. *Behaviour Research and Therapy*, 36, 735–750.

Davidhizar, R. and Bowen, M. (1992). The dynamics of laughter. *Archives of Psychiatric Nursing*, 6, 132–137.

Davidoff, J. (1997). The neuropsychology of color. In C.L. Hardin and L. Maffi (eds), *Color Categories in Thought and Language*. New York: Cambridge University Press.

Davidson, J.E. and Sternberg, R.J. (1984). The role of insight in intellectual giftedness. *Gifted Child Quarterly*, 28, 58–64.

Davidson, J.M., Camargo, C.A. and Smith, E.R. (1979). Effects of androgen on sexual behavior in hypogonadal men. *Journal of Clinical Endocrinology and Metabolism*, 48, 955–958.

Davidson, R.J. (1992). Anterior cerebral asymmetry and the nature of emotion. *Brain and Cognition*, 20, 125–151.

Davidson, R.J. (1998). Anterior electrophysiological asymmetries, emotion and depression: Conceptual and methodological conundrums. *Psychophysiology*, 35, 607–614.

Davidson, R.J. and Fox, N.A. (1989). Frontal brain asymmetry predicts infants' response to maternal separation. *Journal of Abnormal Psychology*, 98, 2, 127–131.

Davidson, R.J. and Hugdahl, K. (1995). *Brain Asymmetry*. Cambridge, MA: MIT Press.

Davidson, R.J. and Sutton, S.K. (1995). Affective neuroscience: The emergence of a discipline. *Current Opinion in Neurobiology*, 5, 2, 217–224.

Davidson, R.J., Schwartz, G.E., Saron, C., Bennett, J. and Goleman, D.J. (1979). Frontal vs parietal EEG asymmetry during positive and negative affect. *Psychophysiology*, 16, 2, 202–203.

Davies, I.R.L., Laws, G., Corbett, G.G. and Jerrett, D.J. (1998). Cross-cultural differences in colour vision: Acquired 'colour blindness' in Africa. *Personality and Individual Differences*, 25, 1153–1162.

Davis, J.D. and Campbell, C.S. (1973). Peripheral control of meal size in the rat: Effect of sham feeding on meal size and drinking rats. *Journal of Comparative and Physiological Psychology*, 83, 379–387.

Davis, J.M. (1974). A two-factor theory of schizophrenia. *Journal of Psychiatric Research*, 11, 25–30.

Davis, K.D., Wood, M.L., Crawley, A.P. and Mikulis, D.J. (1995). fMRI of human somatosensory and cingulate cortex during painful electrical nerve stimulation. *Neuroreport*, 7, 321–325.

Davis, W.L. and Phares, E.J. (1967). Internal-external control as a determinant of information-seeking in a social influence situation. *Journal of Personality*, 35, 547–561.

Davison, G.C. and Neale, J.M. (1997). *Abnormal Psychology* (20th edition). New York: Wiley.

Davitz, J.R. (1970). A dictionary and grammar of emotion. In M. Arnold (ed.), *Feelings and Emotions: The Loyola Symposium*. New York: Academic Press.

Dawkins, R. (1986). *The Blind Watchmaker*. New York: W.W. Norton.

Dawkins, R. (1996). *Climbing Mount Improbable*. New York: W.W. Norton.

Dawson, G., Frey, K., Panagiotides, H., Osterling, J. and Hessl, D. (1997). Infants of depressed mothers exhibit atypical frontal brain activity: A replication and extension of previous findings. *Journal of Child Psychology and Psychiatry*, 38, 2, 179–186.

Day, R. and Wong, S. (1996). Anomalous perceptual asymmetries for negative emotional stimuli in the psychopath. *Journal of Abnormal Psychology*, 105, 648–652.

Deahl, M.P., Gillham, A.B., Thomas, J. *et al.* (1994). Psychological sequelae following the Gulf War. Factors associated with subsequent morbidity and the effectiveness of psychological debriefing. *British Journal of Psychiatry*, 165, 60–65.

Deb, S. and Thompson, B. (1998). Neuroimaging in autism. *British Journal of Psychiatry*, 173, 299–302.

DeCasper, A.J. and Fifer, W.P. (1980). Of human bonding: Newborns prefer their mothers' voices. *Science*, 208, 1175–1176.

DeCasper, A.J. and Spence, M. (1986). Prenatal maternal speech influences newborns' perception of speech sounds. *Infant Behavior and Development*, 9, 133–150.

DeCasper, A.J., Lecanuet, J-P., Bunsel, M-C., Granier-Deferre, C. and Maugeais, R. (1994). Fetal reactions to recurrent maternal speech. *Infant Behaviour and Development*, 17, 159–164.

Decety, J., Grezes, J., Costes, N., Perani, D., Jeannerod, M., Procyk, E., Grassi, F. and Fazio, F. (1997). Brain activity during observation of actions. *Brain*, 120, 1763–1777.

DeGrouchy, J. and Turleau, C. (1990). Autosomal disorders. In A.E.H. Emery and D.L. Rimoin (eds), *Principles and Practice in Medical Genetics*. Edinburgh: Churchill Livingstone.

Dekaban, A. (1970). *Neurology of Early Childhood*. Baltimore: Williams & Wilkins.

Delahanty, D.L., Dougall, A.L., Hawkes, L., Trakowski, J.H., Schmitz, J.B., Jenkins, F.J. and Baum, A. (1996). Time course of natural killer cell activity and lymphocyte proliferation in response to two acute stressors in healthy men. *Health Psychology*, 15, 48–55.

Deldin, P.J. and Levin, I.P. (1986). The effect of mood induction in a risky decision task. *Bulletin of the Psychonomic Society*, 24, 4–6.

Dell, G.S., Burger, L.K. and Svec, W.R. (1997). Language production and serial order: A functional analysis and a model. *Psychological Review*, 104, 1, 123–147.

DeLoache, J.S. (1984). Oh where, oh where: memory-based searching by very young children. In C. Sophian (ed.), *Origins of Cognitive Skills*. Hillsdale, NJ: Lawrence Erlbaum Associates.

DeLongis, A., Folkman, S. and Lazarus, R. S. (1988). The impact of daily stress on health and mood: Psychological and social resources as mediators. *Journal of Personality and Social Psychology*, 54, 486–495.

Dement, W.C. (1974). *Some Must Watch While Some Must Sleep*. San Francisco: W.H. Freeman.

Demonet, J.F., Fiez, J.A., Paulesu, E., Petersen, S.E. and Zatorre, R.J. (1996). PET studies of phonological processing: A critical reply to Poeppel. *Brain and Language*, 55, 352–379.

Dennett, D.D. (1991). *Consciousness Explained*. London: Penguin.

DePue, R.A. and Monroe, S.M. (1986). Conceptualization and measurement of human disorder in life-stress research: The problem of chronic disturbance. *Psychological Bulletin*, 99, 36–51.

DeRaad, B. (1998). Five big, Big Five issues: rationale, content, structure, status and crosscultural assessment. *European Psychologist*, 3, 2, 113–124.

Deregowski, J.B., Muldrow, E.S. and Muldrow, W.F. (1972). Pictorial recognition in a remote Ethiopian village. *Perception*, 1, 417–425.

DeRenzi, E. (1986). Prosopagnosia in two patients with CT scan evidence of damage confined to the right hemisphere. *Neuropsychologia*, 24, 385–389.

DeRenzi, E. and Lucchelli, F. (1993). The fuzzy boundaries of apperceptive agnosia. *Cortex*, 29, 187–215.

Desimone, R. and Duncan, J. (1995). Neural mechanisms of selective visual attention. *Annual Review of Neuroscience*, 18, 193–222.

Deutsch, J. A., Young, W. G. and Kalogeris, T. J. (1978). The stomach signals satiety. *Science*, 201, 165–167.

Deutscher, I. (1968). The quality of post-parental life. In B. L. Neugarten (ed.), *Middle Age and Aging*. Chicago: University of Chicago Press.

Devane, W.A., Hanus, L., Breuer, A., Pertwee, R.G., Stevenson, L.A., Griffin, G., Gibson, D., Mandelbaum, A., Etinger, A. and Mechoulam, R. (1992). Isolation and structure of a brain constituent that binds to the cannabinoid receptor. *Science*, 258, 1946–1949.

deVilliers, J.G. and deVilliers, P.A. (1978). *Language Acquisition*. Cambridge, MA: Harvard University Press.

De Wolff, M.S. and van Ijzendoorn, M.H. (1997). Sensitivity and attachment: A meta-analysis on parental antecedents of infant attachment. *Child Development*, 68, 4, 571–591.

Diener, F. (1980). Deindividuation: The absence of self-awareness and self-regulation in group members. In P. B. Paulus (ed.), *Psychology of Group Influence*. Hillsdale, NJ: Lawrence Erlbaum Associates.

Dijkerman, H.C. and Milner, A.D. (1997). Copying without perceiving motor imagery in visual form agnosia. *NeuroReport*, 8, 720–732.

Dijksterhuis, A., Spears, R.., Postmes, T., Stapel, D.A., Koomen, W., van Knippenberg, A. and Scheepers, D. (1999). Seeing one thing and doing another: Contrast effects in automatic behavior. *Journal of Personality and Social Psychology*, in press.

Dimsdale, J. E. (1988). A perspective on type A behavior and coronary disease. *New England Journal of Medicine*, 318, 110–112.

Dinh, K.T., Sarason, I.G., Peterson, A.V. and Onstad, L.E. (1995). Children's perceptions of smokers and non-smokers: A longitudinal study. *Health Psychology*, 14, 32–40.

Dion, K., Berscheid, E. and Walster, E. (1972). What is beautiful is good. *Journal of Personality and Social Psychology*, 24, 285–290.

Docherty, N.M. (1995). Expressed emotion and language disturbances in parents of stable schizophrenic patients. *Schizophenia Bulletin*, 21, 411–418.

Doherty, W.J. and Needle, R.H. (1991). Psychological adjustment and substance use among adolescents before and after parental divorce. *Child Development*, 62, 328–337.

Doise, W. (1986). *Levels of Explanation in Social Psychology*. Cambridge: Cambridge University Press.

Dominowski, E.L. and Dallob, P. (1996). Insight and problem solving. In R.J. Sternberg and J. Davidson (eds), *The Nature of Insight*. Cambridge, MA: MIT Press.

Donenberg, G.R. and Hoffman, L.W. (1988). Gender differences in moral development. *Sex Roles*, 18, 701–717.

Donovan, A. and Oddy, M. (1982). Psychological aspect of unemployment: An investigation into the emotional and social adjustment of school leavers. *Journal of Adolescence*, 5, 15–30.

Doty, N.D. (1998). The influence of nationality on the accuracy of face and voice recognition. *American Journal of Psychology*, 111, 2, 191–214.

Dovidio, J.F., Gaertner, S.L., Validzic, A., Matoka, K., Johnson, B. and Frazier, S., (1997). Extending the benefits of recategorization: Evaluations, self-disclosure, and helping. *Journal of Experimental Social Psychology*, 33, 401–420.

Dowling, J.E. and Boycott, B.B. (1966). *Proceedings of the Royal Society (London)*, Series B, 166, 80–111.

Drago, R. and Wooden, M. (1992). The determinants of labor absence: Economic factors and workgroup norms across cultures. *Industrial Labor Relations Review*, 45, 764–778.

Drevets, W.C., Price, J.L., Simpson, J.R., Todd, R.D., Reich, T., Vannier, M. and Raichle, M.E. (1997). Subgenual prefrontal cortex abnormalities in mood disorders. *Nature*, 386, 824–827.

Druckman, D. and Bjork, R.A. (1991). *In the Mind's Eye: Enhancing human performance*. Washington, DC: National Academy Press.

Duck, S. (1992). *Human Relationships* (2nd edition). London: Sage.

Duncan, J. (1995). Attention, intelligence and the frontal lobes. In M.S. Gazzaniga (ed.), *The Cognitive Neurosciences*. Cambridge, MA: MIT Press.

Duncan, J., Burgess, P. and Emslie, H. (1995). Fluid intelligence after frontal lobe lesions. *Neuropsychologia*, 33, 3, 261–268.

Dunn, J., Bretherton, I. and Munn, P. (1987). Conversations about feeling states between mothers and their young children. *Developmental Psychology*, 23, 132–139.

Dziurawiec, S. and Deregowski, J.B. (1992). 'Twisted perspective' in young children's drawings. *British Journal of Developmental Psychology*, 10, 35–49.

D'Zurilla, T. (1965). Recall efficiency and mediating cognitive events in 'experimental repression'. *Journal of Personality and Social Psychology*, 1, 253–257.

Eacott, M.J. and Crawley, R.A. (1998). The offset of childhood amnesia: memory for events that occurred before age 3. *Journal of Experimental Psychology: General*, 12, 22–33.

Eagly, A.H. (1978). Sex differences in influenceability. *Psychological Bulletin*, 85, 86–116.

Eagly, A.H. (1995). The science and politics of comparing women and men. *American Psychologist*, 50, 145–158.

Eagly, A.H. and Chaiken, S. (1993). *The Psychology of Attitudes*. San Diego, CA: Harcourt Brace Jovanovich.

Eagly, A.H. and Karau, S.J. (1991). Gender and the emergence of leaders: A meta-analysis. *Journal of Personality and Social Psychology*, 60, 685–710.

Eals, M. and Silverman, I. (1994). The hunter–gatherer theory of spatial sex differences: Proximate factors mediating the female advantage in recall of object arrays. *Ethology and Sociobiology*, 15, 2, 95–105.

Eastwood, J.D., Gaskovski, P. and Bowers, K.S. (1998). The folly of effort: Ironic effects in the mental control of pain. *International Journal of Clinical and Experimental Hypnosis*, 46, 1, 77–91.

Ebbinghaus, H. (1885). *Memory: A contribution to experimental psychology*. (H.A. Ruger and C.E. Busserius, trans.). Reprinted 1913, Teacher's College, Columbia University, New York.

Eccles, J.C. (1989). *Evolution of the Brain: Creation of the self*. London: Routledge.

Echebarria-Echabe, A., Fernandez-Guede, E. and Gonzalez-Castro, J.L. (1994). Social representations and intergroup conflicts: Who's smoking here? *European Journal of Social Psychology*, 24, 339–355.

Eddy, N. B., Halbach, H., Isbell, H. and Seevers, M. H. (1965). Drug dependence: Its significance and characteristics. *Bulletin of the World Health Organization*, 32, 721–733.

Eden, G.F., Stein, J.F., Wood, H.M. and Wood, F.B. (1994). Differences in eye movements and reading problems in dyslexic and normal children. *Vision Research*, 34, 10, 1345–1358.

Eden, G.F., VanMeter, J.W., Rumsey, J.M., Maisog, J.M., Woods, R.P. and Zeffiro, T.A. (1996). Abnormal processing of visual motion in dyslexia revealed by functional brain imaging. *Nature*, 382, 66–69.

Edwards, D. and Potter, J. (1992). *Discursive Psychology*. London: Sage.

Ehlers, S., Nyden, A., Gillberg, C., Sandberg, A.D., Dahlgren, S-O., Hjelmquist, E. and Oden, A. (1997). Asperger syndrome, autism and attention disorders: A comparative study of the cognitive profiles of 120 children. *Journal of Child Psychology and Psychiatry*, 38, 2, 207–217.

Ehlrichman, H. (1987). Hemispheric asymmetry and positive-negative affect. In D. Ottoson (ed.), *Duality and Unity of the Brain*. London: Macmillan.

Ehrlichman, H. and Halpern, J.N. (1988). Affect and memory: Effects of pleasant and unpleasant odours on retrieval of happy and unhappy memories. *Journal of Personality and Social Psychology*, 55, 5, 769–779.

Eibl-Eibesfeldt, I. (1989). *Human Ethnology*. New York: Aldine de Gruyter.

Eich, E. (1995). Mood as a mediator of place dependent memory. *Journal of Experimental Psychology: General*, 124, 3, 293–308.

Eich, E., Macaulay, D. and Lam, R.W. (1997). Mania, depression and mood dependent memory. *Cognition and Emotion*, 11, 5/6, 607–618.

Eich, E., Macaulay, D. and Ryan, L. (1994). Mood dependent memory for events of the personal past. *Journal of Experimental Psychology: General*, 123, 201–215.

Eich, J., Weingartner, H., Stillman, R. and Gillin, J. (1975). State-dependent accessibility of retrieval cues and retention of a categorized list. *Journal of Verbal Learning and Verbal Behavior*, 14, 408–417.

Eimas, P.D., Siqueland, E.R., Jusczyk, P. and Vigorito, J. (1971). Speech perception in infants. *Science*, 171, 303–306.

Einstein, G.O., McDaniel, M.A., Richardson, S.L., Guynn, M.J. and Cinfer, A.R. (1995). Aging and prospective memory: Examining the influences of self-initiated retrieval processes. *Journal of Experimental Psychology: Learning, Memory and Cognition*, 21, 996–1007.

Einstein, G.O., McDaniel, M.A., Smith, R.E. and Shaw, P. (1998). Habitual prospective memory and aging. *Psychological Science*, 9, 4, 284–288.

Eisenberg. D., Kessler, R.C. and Foster, C. (1993). Unconventional medicine in the United States. *New England Journal of Medicine*, 328, 246–252.

Eisenberg, N., Fabes, R. A., Schaller, M., Miller, P., Carlo, G., Poulin, R., Shea, C. and Shell, R. (1991). Personality and socialization: Correlates of vicarious emotional responding. *Journal of Personality and Social Psychology*, 61, 459 470.

Ekman, P. (1973). Cross cultural studies of facial expression. In P. Ekman (ed.), *Darwin and Facial Expression: A century of research in review*. New York: Academic Press.

Ekman, P. (1980). *The Face of Man: Expressions of universal emotions in a New Guinea Village*. New York: Garland STPM Press.

Ekman, P. (1984). Expression and the nature of emotion. In K. Scherer and P. Ekman (eds), *Approaches to Emotion*. Hillsdale, NJ: Lawrence Erlbaum.

Ekman, P. (1992). Are there basic emotions? *Psychological Review*, 99, 550–553.

Ekman, P. (1994). Strong evidence for universals in facial expressions: A reply to Russell's mistaken critique. *Psychological Bulletin*, 115, 2, 268–287.

Ekman, P. and Friesen, W.V. (1969). Nonverbal leakage and clues to deception. *Psychiatry*, 32, 88–105.

Ekman, P. and Friesen, W.V. (1974). Detecting deception from body or face. *Journal of Personality and Social Psychology*, 29, 288–298.

Ekman, P. and Friesen, W.V. (1975). *Unmasking the Face*. Englewood Cliffs, NJ: Prentice Hall.

Ekman, P., Friesen, W.V. and Ellsworth, P. (1972). *Emotion in the Human Face: Guidelines for research and a review of findings*. New York: Pergamon Press.

Ekman, P., Davidson, R.J. and Friesen, W.V. (1990). The Duchenne smile: Emotional expression and brain physiology II. *Journal of Personality and Social Psychology*, 58, 2, 542–553.

Elias, M. (1981). Serum cortisol, testosterone and testosterone binding globulin responses to competitive fighting in human males. *Aggressive Behavior*, 7, 215–224.

Ellenberger, H.F. (1972). The story of 'Anna O': A critical review with new data. *Journal of the History of the Behavioral Sciences*, 8, 267–279.

Ellis, A. (1973). Rational-emotive therapy. In R. Corsini (ed.), *Current Psychotherapies*. Itasca, IL: Peacock.

Ellis, A.W. (1992). *Reading, Writing and Dyslexia: A cognitive analysis* (2nd edition). Hove, UK: The Psychology Press.

Ellis, H.C., Ottaway, S.A., Varner, L.J., Becker, A.S. and Moore, B.A. (1997). Emotion, motivation and text comprehension: The detection of contradictions in passages. *Journal of Experimental Psychology: General*, 126, 2, 131–146.

Ellis, N.C. and Hennelly, R.A. (1980). A bilingual word-length effect. Implications for intelligence testing and the relative ease of mental calculation in Welsh and English. *British Journal of Psychology*, 71, 43–51.

Elms, A.C. (1975). The crisis of confidence in social psychology. *American Psychologist*, 30, 967–976.

Elms, A.C. (1995). Obedience in retrospect. *Journal of Social Issues*, 51, 21–32.

Elster, A.D., DiPersio, D.A. and Moody, D.M. (1990). Sexual dimorphism of the human corpus callosum studied by magnetic resonance imaging: Fact, fallacy and statistical confidence. *Brain and Development*, 12, 321–325.

Emde, R. N., Plomin, R., Robinson, J., DeFries, J., Reznick, J. S., Campos, J., Kagan, J. and Zahn-Waxler, C. (1992). Temperament, emotion, and cognition at fourteen months: The MacArthur longitudinal twin study. *Child Development*, 63, 1437–1455.

Emmelkamp, P.M.G. (1993). Technical advances in behavioral psychotherapy of obsessive-compulsive disorders. *Psychotherapeutic Psychosomatics*, 60, 57–61.

Emmelkamp, P.M.G. (1994). Behaviour therapy with adults. In A.E. Bergin and S.L. Garfield (eds), *Handbook of Psychotherapy and Behaviour Change*. New York: Wiley.

Emmelkamp, P.M.G. (1996). Psychosocial factors in HIV-AIDS. *Psychotherapy and Psychosomatics*, 65, 225–228.

Emmons, R.A., Diener, E. and Larsen, R.J. (1986). Choice and avoidance of everyday situations and affect congruence: Two models of reciprocal interactionism. *Journal of Personality and Social Psychology*, 51, 815–826.

Engen, T. (1987). Remembering odours and their names. *American Scientist*, 497–503.

England, M.A. and Wakely, J. (1991). *A Colour Atlas of the Brain and Spinal Cord*. Aylesbury: Wolfe.

Enlow, D.H. (1982). *Handbook of Facial Growth*. Philadelphia: Saunders.

Entwisle, D. (1972). To dispel fantasies about fantasy-based measures of achievement motivation. *Psychological Bulletin*, 77, 377–391.

Epstein, R. (1985). The spontaneous interconnection of three repertoires. *Psychological Record*, 35, 131–141.

Epstein, R. (1987). The spontaneous interconnection of four repertoires of behavior in a pigeon (Columba livia). *Journal of Comparative Psychology*, 101, 197–201.

Epstein, R., Kirshnit, C., Lanza, R. P. and Rubin, L. (1984). Insight in the pigeon: Antecedents and determinants of an intelligent performance. *Nature*, 308, 61–62.

Epstein, S. (1979). The stability of behavior. I. On predicting most of the people much of the time. *Journal of Personality and Social Psychology*, 37, 1097–1126.

Epstein, W. (1961). The influence of syntactical structure on learning. *American Journal of Psychology*, 74, 80–85.

Erdelyi, M.H. (1985). *Psychoanalysis: Freud's cognitive psychology*. San Francisco: W.H. Freeman.

Erickson, M.F., Sroufe, L.A. and Egeland, B. (1985). The relationship between quality of attachment and behavior problems in preschool in a high-risk sample. *Monographs of the Society for Research in Child Development*, 50 (1–2, Serial No. 209).

Ernst, M., Zametkin, A.J., Matochik, J.A., Pascualvaca, D. and Cohen, R.M. (1997). Low medial prefrontal dopaminergic activity in autistic children. *Lancet*, 350, 638.

Ernulf, K.E., Innala, S.M. and Whitam, F.L. (1989). Biological explanation, psychological explanation, and tolerance of homosexuals: A cross-national analysis of beliefs and attitudes. *Psychological Reports*, 248, 183–188.

Eron, L.D. (1950). A normative study of the thematic apperception test. *Psychological Monographs*, 64, Whole No. 315.

Erting, C.J., Johnson, R.C., Smith, D.L. and Snider, B.D. (1989). *The Deaf Way: Perspectives from the International Conference on Deaf Culture*. Washington, DC: Gallaudet University Press.

Eslinger, P.J. and Damasio, A.R. (1985). Severe disturbance of higher cognition after bilateral frontal lobe ablation: Patient EVR. *Neurology*, 35, 1731–1741.

Eslinger, P.J. and Grattan, L.M. (1993). Frontal lobe and frontal-striatal substrates for different forms of human cognitive flexibility. *Neuropsychologia*, 31, 1, 17–28.

Etnier, J.L., Salazar, W., Landers, D.M., Petruzzello, S.J., Han, M. and Nowell, P. (1997). The influence of physical fitness and exercise upon cognitive functioning: A meta-analysis. *Journal of Sport and Exercise Psychology*, 19, 249–277.

Evans, D.A., Hebert, L.E., Beckett, L.A., Scherr, P.A., Albert, M.S., Chown, M.J. *et al.* (1997). Education and other measures of socioeconomic status and risk of incident Alzheimer disease in a defined population of older persons. *Archives of Neurology*, 54, 1399–1405.

Evans, G.E., Palsane, M.N. and Carrere, S. (1987). Type A behaviour and occupational stress: A cross-cultural study of blue collar workers. *Journal of Personality and Social Psychology*, 52, 1002–1007.

Evans, P., Bristow, M., Hucklebridge, F., Clow, A. and Walters, N. (1993). The relationship between secretory immunity, mood and life events. *British Journal of Clinical Psychology*, 32, 227–236.

Evans, P., Bristow, M., Hucklebridge, F., Clow, A. and Pang, E-Y. (1994). Stress, arousal, cortisol and secretory immunoglobin A in students undergoing assessment. *British Journal of Clinical Psychology*, 33, 575–576.

Evans, P., Clow, A. and Hucklebridge, F. (1997). Stress and the immune system. *The Psychologist*, July, 303–307.

Evans, R.I., Raines, B.E. and Hanselka, L. (1984). Developing data-based communications in social psychological research: Adolescent smoking prevention. *Journal of Applied Social Psychology*, 14, 289–295.

Eysenck, H.J. (1952).The effects of psychotherapy: An evaluation. *Journal of Consulting Psychology*, 16, 319–324.

Eysenck, H.J. (1957). *Sense and Nonsense in Psychology*. London: Pelican.

Eysenck, H.J. (1970). *The Structure of Human Personality* (3rd edition). London: Methuen.

Eysenck, H.J. (1973). *The Inequality of Man*. London: Temple Smith.

Eysenck, H.J. (1985). *Decline and Fall of the Freudian Empire*. London: Pelican.

Eysenck, H.J. (1988). Personality, stress and cancer: Prediction and prophylaxis. *British Journal of Medical Psychology*, 61, 57–75.

Eysenck, H.J. (1991). Dimensions of personality: 16, 5, or 3? Criteria for a taxonomic paradigm. *Personality and Individual Differences*, 12, 773–790.

Eysenck, H.J. (1995). *Genius – A natural history of creativity*. Cambridge: Cambridge University Press.

Eysenck, H.J. and Eysenck, M.W. (1985). *Personality and Individual Differences: A natural science approach*. New York: Plenum Press.

Eysenck, H.J. and Schoenthaler, S.J. (1997). Raising IQ level by vitamin and mineral supplementation. In R.J. Sternberg and E. Grigorenko (eds), *Intelligence, Heredity and Environments*. New York: Cambridge University Press.

Eysenck, M.W. (1992). *Anxiety: The cognitive perspective*. Hove, UK: The Psychology Press.

Eysenck, M.W. and Keane, M.T. (1995). *Cognitive Psychology: A student's handbook*. Hove, UK: The Psychology Press.

Eysenck, M.W., Mogg, K., May, J., Richards, A. and Mathews, A. (1991). Bias in interpretation of ambiguous sentences related to threat in anxiety. *Journal of Abnormal Psychology*, 100, 144–150.

Fabes, R.A. and Eisenberg, N. (1992). Young children's coping with interpersonal anger. *Child Development*, 63, 116–128.

Fagot, B.I. and Hagan, R.I. (1991). Observations of parent reactions to sex-stereotyped behaviors: Age and sex differences. *Child Development*, 62, 617–628.

Faigman, D.L. (1995). The evidentiary status of social science under Daubert. *Psychology, Public Policy and Law*, 1, 4, 960–979.

Fairburn, C.G., Shafran, R. and Cooper, Z. (1999). A cognitive behavioural theory of anorexia nervosa. *Behaviour Research and Therapy*, 37, 1–13.

Fantz, R.L. (1958). Pattern vision in young infants. *Psychological Record*, 8, 43–47.

Fantz, R.L. (1961). The origin of form perception. *Scientific American*, 204, 66–72.

Farah, M.J. (1990). *Visual Agnosia: Disorders of object vision and what they tell us about normal vision*. Cambridge, MA: MIT Press.

Farah, M.J. and Radcliff, G. (1994). *The Neuropsychology of High-level Vision*. Hove, UK: The Psychology Press.

Farah, M.J., Wilson, K.D., Drain, M. and Tanaka, J.N. (1998). What is 'special' about face perception? *Psychological Review*, 105, 482–498.

Faraone, S.V., Biederman, J., Jetton, J.G. and Tsuang, M.T. (1997). Attention deficit disorder and conduct disorder: Longitudinal evidence for a familial subtype. *Psychological Medicine*, 27, 291–300.

Farmer, A., McGuffin, P. and Gottesman, I. (1987). Twin concordance in DSM-III schizophrenia. *Archives of General Psychiatry*, 44, 634–641.

Farrar, M.J. and Gordman, G.S. (1992). Developmental changes in event memory. *Child Development*, 63, 173–187.

Farrer, L.A., Cuppies, A., Haines, J.L., Hyman, B., Kukull, W.A., Mayeux, R. *et al.* (1997). Effects of age, sex and ethnicity on the association between apolipoprotein E genotype and Alzheimer Disease. *Journal of the American Medical Association*, 278, 1349–1356.

Fazio, R.H., Zanna, M.P. and Cooper, J. (1977). Dissonance and self-perception: An integrative view of each theory's proper domain of application. *Journal of Experimental Social Psychology*, 13, 464–479.

Feigenbaum, S.L., Masi, A.T. and Kaplan, S.B. (1979). Prognosis in rheumatoid arthritis: A longitudinal study of newly diagnosed younger adult patients. *American Journal of Medicine*, 66, 377–384.

Feldhusen, J.F. (1993). A conception of creative thinking and creativity training. In S.G. Isaksen, M.C. Murdoch, R.L. Firestien and D.J. Treffinger (eds), *Nurturing and Developing Creativity: The emergence of a discipline*. Norwood, NJ: Ablex.

Feldhusen, J.F. and Goh, B.E. (1995). Assessing and accessing creativity: An integrative review of theory, research and development. *Creativity Research Journal*, 8, 3, 231–247.

Feldman, D.H. and Goldsmith, L.T. (1991). *Nature's Gambit: Child prodigies and the development of human potential*. New York: Teachers College Press.

Fellows, B.J. (1990). Current theories of hypnosis: A critical review. *British Journal of Experimental and Clinical Hypnosis*, 7, 81–92.

Fenigstein, A. and Abrams, D. (1993). Self-attention and the egocentric assumption of shared perspectives. *Journal of Experimental Social Psychology*, 29, 287–303.

Fenton, G.W. (1998). Neurosurgery for mental disorder. *Irish Journal of Psychiatric Medicine*, 15, 2, 45–48.

Fergusson, D.M., Horwood, L.J. and Lynskey, M.T. (1996). Childhood sexual abuse and psychiatric disorder in young adulthood II: Psychiatric outcomes of childhood sexual abuse. *Journal of the American Academy of Child Adolescent Psychiatry*, 34, 1365–1374.

Feshbach, S. and Singer, R.D. (1971). *Television and Aggression*. San Francisco: Jossey-Bass.

Festinger, L. (1957). *A Theory of Cognitive Dissonance*. Stanford: Stanford University Press.

Festinger, L. and Carlsmith, J. M. (1959). Cognitive consequences of forced compliance. *Journal of Abnormal and Social Psychology*, 58, 203–210.

Festinger, L., Schachter, S. and Back, K. (1950). *Social Pressures in Informal Groups: A study of a housing community*. New York: Harper & Row.

Feynman, R.P. (1985). *Surely You're Joking, Mr. Feynman!* New York: Bantam Books.

Field, T. (1982). Individual differences in the expressivity of neonates and young infants. In R.S. Feldman (ed.), *Development of Nonverbal Behavior in Children*. New York: Springer-Verlag.

Field, T. (1992). Infants of depressed mothers. *Development and Psychopathology*, 4, 49–66.

Fields, L. (1993). Foreword in special issue on stimulus equivalence. *The Psychological Record*, 43, 543–546.

Fields, L., Landon-Jimenez, V., Buffington, D.M. and Adams, B.J. (1995). Maintained nodal-distance effects in equivalence classes. *Journal of the Experimental Analysis of Behavior*, 64, 129–146.

Fiez, J.A., Raichle, M.E., Miezin, F.M., Petersen, S.E., Tallal, P. and Katz, W.F. (1995). PET studies of auditory and phonological processing: Effects of stimulus characteristics and task demands. *Journal of Cognitive Neuroscience*, 7,3, 357–375.

Fife-Shaw, C. (1997). Commentary on Joffe (1996) AIDS research and prevention: A social representational approach. *British Journal of Medical Psychology*, 70, 65–73.

Filsinger, E.E. and Monte, W.C. (1986). Sex history, menstrual cycle and psychophysical ratings of alpha androstenone: A possible human sex pheromone. *The Journal of Sex Research*, 22, 2, 243–248.

Filsinger, E.E., Braun, J.J., Monte, W.C. and Linder, D.E. (1984). Human (*homo sapiens*) responses to the pig (sus scrofa) sex pheromone 5 alpha-androst-16-en-3-one. *Journal of Comparative Psychology*, 98, 2, 219–222.

Fincham, F.D. (1998). Child development and marital relations. *Child Development*, 69, 2, 543–574.

Fingerhut, L.A., Kleinman, J.C. and Kendrick, J.S. (1990). Smoking before, during, and after pregnancy. *American Journal of Public Health*, 80, 541–544.

Fink, G.R., Halligan, P.W., Marshall, J.C., Frith, C.D., Frackowiak, R.S.J. and Dolan, R.J. (1996). Where in the brain does visual attention select the forest and the trees? *Nature*, 382, 626–628.

Finkel, D., Pedersen, N.L., McGue, M. and McClearn, G.E. (1995). Heritability of cognitive abilities in adult twins: Comparison and Minnesota and Swedish data. *Behaviour Genetics*, 25, 421–432.

Finkenauer, C., Luminet, O., Gisle, L., El-Ahmadi, A., van der Linden, M. and Philppot, P. (1998). Flashbulb memories of the underlying mechanisms of their formation: Toward an emotional-integrative model. *Memory and Cognition*, 26, 3, 516–531.

Fischer, H., Wik, G. and Fredrikson, M. (1997). Extraversion, neuroticism and brain function: A PET study of personality. *Personality and Individual Differences*, 23, 345–352.

Fischer, K.W. and Farrar, M.J. (1987). Generalizations about generalizations: How a theory of skill development explains both generality and specificity. *International Journal of Psychology*, 22, 643–677.

Fischer, K.W. and Pipp, S.L. (1984). Processes of cognitive development: Optimal level and skill development. In R. Sternberg (ed.), *Mechanisms of Cognitive Development*. New York: Freeman.

Fisher, J.D. and Fisher, W.A. (1992). Changing AIDS risk behaviour. *Psychological Bulletin*, 111, 455–474.

Fisher, R.P. and Geiselman, R.E. (1992). *Memory-enhancing Techniques for Investigative Interviewing*. Springfield, Il: Charles C. Thomas.

Fisher, R.P., Geiselman, R.E., Raymond, D.S., Jurkevich, L.M. and Warhaftig, M.L. (1987). Enhancing enhanced eyewitness testimony: Refining the cognitive interview. *Journal of Police Science and Administration*, 15, 291–297.

Fiske, S.T. (1993). Controlling other people: The impact of power on stereotyping. *American Psychologist*, 48, 621–628.

Fiske, S.T. and Taylor, S.E. (1991). *Social Cognition* (2nd edition). New York: McGraw-Hill.

Fitzgerald, T.E., Tennen, H., Affleck, G. and Pransky, G.S. (1993). The relative importance of dispositional optimism and control appraisals in quality of life after coronary bypass surgery. *Journal of Behavioural Medicine*, 16, 25–43.

Fivush, R. (1984). Learning about school: The development of kindergartens' school scripts. *Child Development*, 55, 1697–1709.

Fivush, R., Gray, J.T. and Fromhoff, F.A. (1987). Two-year-olds talk about the past. *Cognitive Development*, 2, 393–410.

Flavell, J.H., Everett, B.H., Croft, K. and Flavell, E.R. (1981). Young children's knowledge about visual perception: Further evidence for the level 1–level 2 distinction. *Developmental Psychology*, 17, 99–103.

Flay, B.R., Ryan, K.B., Best, J.A., Brown, K.S., Kersell, M.W., d'Avernas, J.R. and Zanna, M.P. (1978). Are social-psychological smoking prevention programs effective? The Waterloo Study. *Journal of Behavioral Medicine*, 1985, 8, 37–59.

Fletcher, P.C., Shallice, T. and Dolan, R.J. (1998a). The functional roles of prefrontal cortex in episodic memory. I. Encoding. *Brain*, 121, 1239–1248.

Fletcher, P.C., Shallice, T. and Dolan, R.J. (1998b). The functional roles of prefrontal cortex in episodic memory. II. Retrieval. *Brain*, 121, 1249–1256.

Fletcher, R. and Voke, J. (1985). Defective Colour Vision: Fundamentals, diagnosis and management. Bristol: Adam Hilger Ltd.

Flexser, A.J. and Tulving, E. (1978). Retrieval independence in recognition and recall. *Psychological Review*, 85, 153–171.

Flin, R. (1995). Children's testimony: Psychology on trial. In M. Zaragoza, I.

Graham, G. Hall, R. Hirschman and Y. BenPorath (eds), *Memory and Testimony in the Child Witness*. Newbury Park, CA: Sage.

Flynn, J.R. (1987). Massive IQ gains in 14 nations: What IQ tests really measure, *Psychological Bulletin*, 101, 171–191.

Flynn, J.M. and Rahbar, M.H. (1994). Prevalence of reading failure in boys compared with girls. *Psychological Sch*, 31, 66–71.

Foa, E.B. and Meadows, E.A. (1997). Psychosocial treatments for post-traumatic stress disorder: A critical review. *Annual Review of Psychology*, 48, 449–480.

Foa, E.B., Steketee, G. and Young, M.C. (1984). Agoraphobia: Phenomenologic aspects, associated characteristics, and theoretical considerations. *Clinical Psychology Review*, 4, 431–457.

Fodor, E.M. (1994). Subclinical manifestations of psychosis-proneness, ego strength, and creativity. *Personality and Individual Differences*, 18, 5, 635–643.

Fodor, J. (1983). *The Modularity of Mind*. Cambridge, MA: MIT Press.

Folkman, S. and Lazarus, R.S. (1991). Coping and emotion. In A. Monat and R. S. Lazarus (eds), *Stress and Coping: An anthology*. New York: Columbia University Press.

Fontana, A. and Rosenheck, R. (1993). A causal model of the etiology of war-related PTSD. *Journal of Traumatic Stress*, 6, 475–499.

Forsyth, D.R. (1990). *Group Dynamics*. Pacific Grove, CA: Brooks/Cole.

Foster, J.J. and Parker, I. (1997). *Carrying out Investigations in Psychology*. Leicester: BPS Books.

Foster, J.K., Black, S.E., Buck, B.H. and Bronskill, M.J. (1997). Ageing and executive functions: A neuroimaging perspective. In P. Rabbitt (ed.), *Methodology of Frontal and Executive Function*. Hove, UK: The Psychology Press.

Fouts, R.S. (1983). Chimpanzee language and elephant tails: A theoretical synthesis. In J. de Luce and H.T. Wilder (eds), *Language in Primates: Perspectives and implications*. New York: Springer-Verlag.

Fouts, R.S., Hirsch, A. and Fouts, D. (1983). Cultural transmission of a human language in a chimpanzee mother/infant relationship. In H.E. Fitzgerald, J.A. Mullins and P. Page (eds), *Psychological Perspectives: Child Nurturance Series*, Vol. 3. New York: Plenum Press.

Fox, N.A. Rubin, K.H., Calkins, S.D., Marshall, T.R., Coplan, R.J., Porges, S.W., Long, J.M. and Stewart, S. (1995). Frontal activation asymmetry and social competence at four years of age. *Child Development*, 66, 1770–1784.

Fox, P.T., Ingham, R.J., Ingham, J.C., Hirsch, T.B., Downs, J.H., Martin, C., Jerabek, P., Glass, T. and Lancaster, J.L. (1996). A PET study of the neural systems of stuttering. *Nature*, 382, 158–162.

Frackowiak, R.J.S., Friston, K.J., Frith, C.D., Dolan, R.J. and Mazziotta, J.C. (1997). *Human Brain Function*. Oxford: Academic Press.

Franklin, S., Howard, D. and Patterson, K. (1994). Abstract word meaning deafness. *Cognitive Neuropsychology*, 11, 1–34.

Franks, N.P. and Lieb, W.R. (1998). The molecular basis of general anesthesia: Current Ideas. In S.R. Hameroff, A.W. Kaszniak and A.C. Scott (eds), *Towards a Science of Consciousness II*. Cambridge, MA: MIT Press.

Freedman, J.L. and Fraser, S.C. (1966). Compliance without pressure: The foot-in-the-door technique. *Journal of Personality and Social Psychology*, 4, 195–203.

Freedy, J.R., Saladin, M.E., Kilpatrick, D.G., Resnick, H.S. and Saunders, B.E. (1994). Understanding acute psychological distress following natural disaster. *Journal of Traumatic Stress*, 7, 257–273.

Freeman, R.C., Rodriguez, G.M. and French, J.F. (1996). Compliance with AZT treatment regimen of HIV-seropositive injection drug users: A neglected issue. *AIDS Education and Prevention*, 8, 58–71.

Freeman, W. (1949). *Proceedings of the Royal Society of Medicine*, 42 (suppl.), 8–12.

French, S.A., Hennrikus, D.J. and Jeffrey, R.W. (1996). Smoking status, dietary intake, and physical activity in a sample of working adults. *Health Psychology*, 15, 6, 448–454.

Freud, S. (1900). *The Interpretation of Dreams*. London: George Allen & Unwin.

Freud, S. (1933). *New Introductory Lectures on Psychoanalysis* (J. Strachey, trans.). New York: W.W. Norton.

Fridlund, A.J. (1992). The behavioural ecology and sociality of human faces. In M.S. Clark (ed.), *Emotion: Review of personality and social psychology*, Vol. 13. Newbury Park, CA: Sage.

Fridlund, A.J. (1994). *Human Facial Expression: An evolutionary view*. San Diego: Academic Press.

Fried, I., Tanguay, P.E., Boer, E., Doubleday, C. and Greensite, M. (1981). Developmental dyslexia: Electrophysiological evidence of clinical subgroups. *Brain and Language*, 12, 14–22.

Friedman, M. and Rosenman, R.H. (1959). Association of specific overt behavior patterns with blood and cardiovascular findings – Blood cholesterol level, blood clotting time, incidence of arcus senilis, and clinical coronary artery disease. *Journal of the American Medical Association*, 162, 1286–1296.

Friedman, M.I., Tordoff, M.G. and Ramirez, I. (1986). Integrated metabolic control of food intake. *Brain Research Bulletin*, 17, 855–859.

Friedman, M.I., Tordoff, M.G. and Kare, M.R. (1991). *Chemical Senses. Vol. 4: Appetite and Nutrition*. New York: Dekker.

Friesen, W.V. (1972). Cultural differences in facial expression in a social situation: an experimental test of the concept of display rules. Doctoral dissertation, University of California, San Francisco.

Frijda, N.H. (1988). The laws of emotion. *American Psychologist*, 43, 349–358.

Frijda, N.H., Kuipers, O. and Ter Schure, E. (1989). Relations among emotion, appraisal and emotional action readiness. *Journal of Personality and Social Psychology*, 57, 212–228.

Frith, C.D. (1987). The positive and negative symptoms of schizophrenia reflect impairments in the perception and initiation of action. *Psychological Medicine*, 17, 631–648.

Frith, C.D. (1992). *The cognitive neuropsychology of schizophrenia*. Hove, UK: Erlbaum.

Frith, U. (1989). *Autism: Explaining the enigma*. Oxford: Blackwell.

Frith, U. and Happé, F. (1994). Autism: Beyond 'theory of mind'. *Cognition*, 50, 115–132.

Frodi, A., Grolnick, W. and Bridges, L. (1985). Maternal correlates of stability and change in infant-mother attachment. *Infant Mental Health Journal*, 6, 60–67.

Fromkin, V. (1988). The grammatical aspects of speech errors. In F.J. Newmeyer (ed.), *Linguistics: The Cambridge survey*, Vol. 11. Cambridge: Cambridge University Press.

Frost, J.A., Binder, J.R., Springer, J.A., Hammeke, T.A., Bellgowan, P.S.F., Rao, S.M. and Cox, R.W. (1999). Language processing is strongly left lateralised in both sexes. *Brain*, 122, 199–208.

Fulder, S.J. and Munro, R.E. (1985). Complementary medicine in the United Kingdom: Patients, practitioners and consultations. *The Lancet*, ii, 542–545.

Furnham, A. (1990). The Type A behaviour pattern and the perception of self. *Personality and Individual Differences*, 11, 841–851.

Furnham, A. (1993). A comparison between psychology and non-psychology students' misperceptions of the subject. *Journal of Social Behaviour and Personality*, 8, 2, 311–322.

Furnham, A. (1994). The Barnum effect in medicine. *Complementary Therapies in Medicine*, 2, 1–4.

Furnham, A. (1996). *All in the Mind: The essence of mind*. London: Whurr.

Furnham, A. and Bhagrath, B. (1993). A comparison of health and behaviours of clients of orthodox and complementary medicine. *British Journal of Clinical Psychology*, 32, 237–246.

Furnham, A., Fong, G. and Martin, G.N. (1999). Sex and cross-cultural differences in the estimated multi-faceted intelligence quotient score for self, parents and siblings. *Personality and Individual Differences*, 26, 1025–1034.

Furnham, A. and Forey, J. (1994). The attitudes, behaviours and beliefs of patients of conventional vs alternative (complementary) medicine. *Journal of Clinical Psychology*, 50, 458–469.

Furnham, A. and Gasson, L. (in press). Sex differences in parental estimates of their children's intelligence. *Sex Roles*.

Furnham, A. and Heyes, C. (1993). Psychology students' beliefs about animals and animal experimentation. *Personality and Individual Differences*, 15, 1, 1–10.

Furnham, A. and Kirkcaldy, B. (1996). The health beliefs and behaviours of orthodox and complementary medicine clients. *British Journal of Clinical Psychology*, 35, 49–61.

Furnham, A. and Rawles, R. (1995). Sex differences in the estimation of intelligence. *Journal of Social Behaviour and Personality*, 10, 741–745.

Furnham, A. and Schofield, S. (1987). Accepting personality test feedback: A review of the Barnum effect. *Current Psychological Research and Reviews*, 6, 2, 162–178.

Furnham, A. and Smith, C. (1988). Choosing alternative medicine: A comparison of the beliefs of patients visiting a GP and a homeopath. *Social Science and Medicine*, 26, 685–687.

Furrow, D. and Nelson, K. (1986). A further look at the motherese hypothesis: A reply to Gleitman, Newport and Gleitman. *Journal of Child Language*, 13, 163–176.

Furrow, D., Nelson, K. and Benedict, H. (1979). Mothers' speech to children and syntactic development: Some simple relationships. *Journal of Child Language*, 6, 423–442.

Furry, C.A. and Baltes, P.B. (1973). The effect of age differences in ability extraneous performance variables on the assessment of intelligence in children, adults and the elderly. *Journal of Gerontology*, 28, 73–80.

Fuster, J.M. (1995). *Memory in the Cerebral Cortex: An empirical approach to neural networks in the human and nonhuman primate*. Cambridge, MA: MIT Press.

Gabrieli, J.D.E., Cohen, N.J. and Corkin, S. (1988). The impaired learning of semantic knowledge following bilateral medial temporal-lobe resection. *Brain and Cognition*, 7, 157–177.

Gaertner, S.L., Dovidio, J.F., Anastasio, P.A., Bachman, B.A. and Rust, M.C. (1993). The common ingroup identity model: recategorization and the reduction of intergroup bias. *European Review of Social Psychology*, 4, 1–26.

Galaburda, A. (1995). Anatomic basis of cerebral dominance. In R.J. Davidson and K. Hugdahl (eds), *Brain Asymmetry*. Cambridge, MA: MIT Press.

Galaburda, A.M., Sherman, G.F., Rosen, G.D., Aboitiz, F. and Geschwind, N. (1985). Developmental dyslexia: Four consecutive patients with cortical anomalies. *Annals of Neurology*, 18, 222–233.

Galaburda, A.M., Menard, M.T. and Rosen, G.D. (1994). Evidence for aberrant auditory anatomy in developmental dyslexia. *Proceedings of the National Academy of Sciences*, 91, 8010–8013.

Galizio, M. (1979). Contingency-shaped and rule-governed behavior: Instructional control of human loss avoidance. *Journal of the Experimental Analysis of Behavior*, 31, 53–70.

Galton, F. (1883). *Inquiries into Human Faculty and its Development*. London: Macmillan.

Galton, F. (1869). *Hereditary Genius: An inquiry into its laws and consequences*. Cleveland, OH: World Publishing.

Galton, F. (1878). Composite portraits. *Nature*, 18, 97–100.

Ganong, W.F. (1980). Phonetic categorization in auditory word perception. *Journal of Experimental Psychology: Human Perception and Performance*, 6, 110–125.

Garcia, J. and Koelling, R. (1966). Relation of cue to consequence in avoidance learning. *Psychonomic Science*, 4, 123–124.

Gardner, H. (1983). *Frames of Mind*. New York: Basic Books.

Gardner, R.A. and Gardner, B.T. (1969). Teaching sign language to a chimpanzee. *Science*, 165, 664–672.

Gardner, R.A. and Gardner, B.T. (1975). Early signs of language in child and chimpanzee. *Science*, 187, 752–753.

Gardner, R.A. and Gardner, B.T. (1978). Comparative psychology and language acquisition. *Annals of the New York Academy of Sciences*, 309, 37–76.

Gardner, R.M. and Dalsing, S. (1986). Misconceptions about psychology among college students. *Teaching of Psychology*, 13, 1, 32–34.

Garfield, S.L. and Bergin, A.E. (1994). Introduction and historical overview. In A.E. Bergin and S.L. Garfield (eds), *Handbook of Psychotherapy and Behaviour Change*. New York: Wiley.

Garrett, V., Brantly, P., Jones, G. and McNight, G. (1991). The relation between daily stress and Crohn's disease. *Journal of Behavioral Medicine*, 34, 187–196.

Garrity, L.I. (1977). Electromyography: A review of the current status of subvocal speech research. *Memory and Cognition*, 5, 615–622.

Garry, M., Manning, C.G., Lofus, E.F. and Sherman, S.J. (1996). Imagination inflation: Imagining a childhood event inflates the confidence that it occurred. *Psychonomic Bulletin and Review*, 3, 2, 208–214.

Gatchel, R. J., Baum, A. and Krantz, D. S. (1989). *An Introduction to Health Psychology* (2nd edition). New York: Newbery Award Records.

Gathercole, S.E. and Baddeley, A.D. (1990). The role of phonological memory in vocabulary acquisition – a study of young children learning new names. *British Journal of Psychology*, 81, 439–454.

Gathercole, S.E., Willis, C., Emslie, H. and Baddeley, A.D. (1992). Phonological memory and vocabulary development during the early school years: A longitudinal study. *Developmental Psychology*, 28, 887–898.

Gatz, M., Pedersen, N.L., Berg. S., Johansson, B., Johansson, K., Mortimer, J.A. *et al.* (1997). Heritability for Alzheimer's disease: The study of dementia in Swedish twins. *Journal of Generontology and Medical Science*, 52, 1117–1125.

Gazzaniga, M.S. (1970). *The Bisected Brain*. New York: Appleton-Century-Crofts.

Gazzaniga, M.S. (1995). *The Cognitive Neurosciences*. Cambridge, MA: MIT Press.

Gazzaniga, M.S. (1998). The split-brain revisited. *Scientific American*, July, 35–39.

Gazzaniga, M.S., Eliassen, J.C., Nisenson, L., Wessinger, C.M., Fendrich, R. and Baynes, K. (1996). Collaboration between the hemispheres of a callosotomy patient. *Brain*, 119, 1255–1262.

Geddes, J.R. and Lawrie, S.M. (1995). Obstetric complications and schizophrenia: A meta-analysis. *British Journal of Psychiatry*, 167, 786–793.

Geiselman, R.E. and Padilla, J. (1988). Cognitive interviewing with child witnesses: *Journal of Police Science and Administration*, 16, 236–242.

Geiselman, R.E., Fisher, R.P., Firstenberg, I., Hutton, L.A., Sullivan, S., Avetissian, L. and Prosk, A. (1984). Enhancement of eyewitness memory: An empirical evaluation of the cognitive interview. *Journal of Police Science and Administration*, 12, 74–80.

Geiselman, R.E., Fisher, R.P., MacKinnon, D.P. and Holland, H.L. (1985). Eyewitness memory enhancement in the police interview: Cognitive retrieval mnemonics versus hypnosis. *Journal of Applied Psychology*, 70, 401–412.

Geletko, S.M., Ballard, C.R. and Matthews, W.C. (1995). Health beliefs and discontinuation of zidovudine therapy. *American Journal of Health System Pharmacy*, 52, 505–507.

Gellaty, A. (1997). Why the young child has neither a theory of mind nor a theory of anything else. *Human Development*, 40, 32–50.

Geller, D.M., Goodstein, L., Silver, M. and Sternberg, W.C. (1974). On being ignored: The effects of the violation of implicit rules of social interaction. *Sociometry*, 37, 541–556.

Gelman, R. (1972). Logical capacity of very young children: Number invariance rules. *Child Development*, 43, 75–90.

Gerbino, L., Oleshansky, M. and Gershon, S. (1978). Clinical use and mode of action of lithium. In M.A. Lipton, A. DiMascio and K.F. Killam (eds), *Psychopharmacology: A generation of progress*. New York: Raven Press.

Gerrard, M. (1986). Are men and women really different? In K. Kelley (ed.), *Females, Males, and Sexuality*. Albany, NY: SUNY Press.

Gerschberg, F.B. and Shimamura, A.P. (1995). Impaired use of organizational strategies in free recall following frontal lobe damage. *Neuropsychologia*, 33, 1305–1333.

Geschwind, N. and Behan, P.O. (1984). Laterality, hormones, and immunity. In N. Geschwind and A.M. Galaburda (eds), *Cerebral Dominance: The biological foundations*. Cambridge, MA: Harvard University Press.

Geschwind, N. and Galaburda, A.M. (1987). *Cerebral lateralization*. Cambridge, MA; MIT Press.

Gibbons, F.X. and Eggleston, T.J. (1996). Smoker networks and the 'typical smoker': A prospective analysis of smoking cessation. *Health Psychology*, 15, 6, 469–477.

Gibbons, F.X. and Gerrard, M. (1995). Predicting young adults' health risk behaviour. *Journal of Personality and Social Psychology*, 69, 505–517.

Gibson, E.J. and Walk, R.R. (1960). The 'visual cliff'. *Scientific American*, 202, 2–9.

Gibson, J.J. (1950). *The Perception of the Visual World*. Boston, MA: Houghton Mifflin.

Gibson, J.J. (1966). *The Senses Considered as Perceptual Systems*. Boston, MA: Houghton Mifflin.

Gibson, J.J. (1979). *The Ecological Approach to Visual Perception*. Boston, MA: Houghton Mifflin.

Gibson, J.J. (1982). Affordances and behaviour. In E.S. Reed and R.K. Jones (eds), *Reasons for Realism: Selected papers of J.J. Gibson*. Hillsdale, NJ: Lawrence Erlbaum Associates.

Gil, T.E. (1989). Psychological etiology to cancer: Truth or myth? *Israel Journal of Psychiatry and Related Sciences*, 26, 164–185.

Gilbert, D.T., Fiske, S.T. and Lindzey, G. (eds) (1998). *The Handbook of Social Psychology* (4th edition). New York: McGraw-Hill.

Gilbert, P. (1998). Evolutionary psychopathology: Why isn't the mind designed better than it is? *British Journal of Medical Psychology*, 71, 353–373.

Gillberg, C. (1991). Outcome in autism and autistic-like conditions. *Journal of the American Academy of Child and Adolescent Psychiatry*, 30, 375–382.

Gillberg, C. and Coleman, M. (1992). *The Biology of Autistic Syndromes* (2nd edition). London: MacKeith Press.

Gilligan, C.F. (1977). In a different voice: Women's conceptions of self and morality. *Harvard Educational Review*, 47, 481–517.

Gilligan, C.F. (1982). *In a Different Voice.* Cambridge, MA: Harvard University Press.

Gironell, A., de la Calzada, M.D., Sagales, T. and Barraquer-Bordas, L. (1995). Absence of REM sleep and altered non-REM sleep caused by a haematoma in the pontine tegmentum. *Journal of Neurology, Neurosurgery and Psychiatry*, 59, 195–196.

Glaser, B.G. and Strauss, A.L. (1967). *The Discovery of Grounded Theory: Strategies for qualitative research.* Chicago: Aldine.

Glaser, R., Rice, J., Sheridan, J., Post, A., Fertel, R., Stout, J., Speicher, C. E., Kotur, M. and Kiecolt-Glaser, J. K. (1987). Stress-related immune suppression: Health implications. *Brain, Behavior, and Immunity*, 1, 7–20.

Glisky, E.L. (1997). Rehabilitation of memory disorders: Tapping into preserved mechanisms, *Brain and Cognition*, 35, 3, 291–292.

Glosser, G. and Deser, T. (1992). A comparison of changes in macrolinguistic and microlinguistic aspects of discourse production in normal aging. *Journal of Gerontology*, 47, 266–227.

Gluck, M.A. and Myers, C.E. (1995). Representation and association in memory: A neurocomputational view of hippocampal function. *Current Directions in Psychological Science*, 4, 23–29.

Godden, D.R. and Baddeley, A.D. (1975). Context-dependent memory in two natural environments: On land and under water. *British Journal of Psychology*, 66, 325–331.

Goel, V., Gold, B., Kapur, S. and Houle, S. (1997). The seats of reason? An imaging study of deductive and inductive reasoning. *NeuroReport*, 8, 1305–1310.

Goel, V., Gold, B., Kapur, S. and Houle, S. (1998). Neuroanatomical correlates of human reasoning. *Journal of Cognitive Neuroscience*, 10, 3, 293–302.

Goldberg, L.R. (1993). The structure of phenotypic personality traits. *American Psychologist*, 48, 26–34.

Goldin-Meadow, S. and Feldman, H. (1977). The development of language-like communication without a language model. *Science*, 197, 401–403.

Goldman-Rakic, P.S. (1995). Cellular basis of working memory. *Neuron*, 14, 477–485.

Goldsmith, H.H. and Alansky, J.A. (1987). Maternal and infant predictors of attachment: A meta-analytic review. *Journal of Consulting and Clinical Psychology*, 55, 805–816.

Goldstein, D., Haldane, D. and Mitchell, C. (1990). Sex differences in visuo-spatial ability: The role of performance factors. *Memory and cognition*, 18, 546–550.

Goldstone, R. L., Medink, D. L. and Gentner, D. (1991). Relational similarity and the nonindependence of features in similarity judgments. *Cognitive Psychology*, 23, 222–262.

Goodale, M.A. and Milner, A.D. (1992). Separate visual pathways for perception and action. *Trends in Neurosciences*, 15, 2–25.

Goodale, M.A., Milner, A.D., Jakobson, L.S. and Carey, D.P. (1991). Perceiving the world and grasping it: A neurological dissociation. *Nature*, 349, 154–156.

Goodglass, H. (1976). Agrammatism. In H. Whitaker and H. A. Whitaker (eds), *Studies in Neurolinguistics*. New York: Academic Press.

Goodwin, D.W. and Guze, S.B. (1984). *Psychiatric Diagnosis* (3rd edition). New York: Oxford University Press.

Goodwin, F.K. and Jamison, K.R. (1990). *Manic-depressive Illness*. New York: Oxford University Press.

Goodyear-Smith, F.A., Laidlaw, T.M. and Large, R.G. (1997). Surveying families accused of childhood sexual abuse: A comparison of British and New Zeland families. *Applied Cognitive Psychology*, 11, 31–34.

Gopnik, M. (1997). Language deficits and genetic factors. *Trends in Cognitive Neurosciences*, 1, 1, 5–9.

Gordon, H.W. and Sperry, R.W. (1969). Lateralization of olfactory perception in the surgically separated hemispheres of man. *Neuropsychologia*, 7, 111–120.

Gottesman, I.I. (1991). *Schizophrenia Genesis. The origins of madness*. New York: Freeman.

Gottesman, I.I. and Bertelsen, A. (1989). Confirming unexpressed genotypes for schizophrenia. *Archives of General Psychiatry*, 46, 867–872.

Gottesman, I.I. and Shields, J. (1982). *Schizophrenia: The epigenetic puzzle*. Cambridge: Cambridge University Press.

Gould, S.J. (1985). *The Flamingo's Smile*. New York: W.W. Norton.

Graf, P. and Mandler, G. (1984). Activation makes words more accessible, but not necessarily more retrievable. *Journal of Verbal Learning and Verbal Behavior*, 23, 553–568.

Graf, P., Squire, L.R. and Mandler, G. (1984). The information that amnesic patients do not forget. *Journal of Experimental Psychology: Learning, Memory, and Cognition*, 10, 164–178.

Grafman, J., Livan, I., Massaquoi, S., Stewart, M., Sirigu, A. and Hallett, M. (1992). Cognitive planning deficit in patients with cerebellar atrophy. *Neurology*, 42, 1493–1496.

Grafton, S.T., Fadiga, L., Arbib, M.A. and Rizzolatti, G. (1997). Premotor cortex activation during observation and naming of familiar tools. *Neuroimage*, 6, 231–236.

Graham, J.E., Rockwood, K., Beattie, B.L., Eastwood, R., Gauthier, S., Tuokko, H. and McDowell, I. (1997). Prevalence and severity of cognitive impairment with and without dementia in an elderly population. *Lancet*, 349, 1793–1796.

Graham, J.R. (1990). *MMPI-2: Assessing Personality and Psychopathology*. New York: Oxford University Press.

Grant, I., Marcotte, T.D., Heaton, R.K. and The HNRC Group (1999). Neurocognitive complications of HIV disease. *Psychological Science*, 10(3), 191–195.

Grant, P.R. (1986). *Ecology and Evolution of Darwin's Finches*. Princeton, NJ: Princeton University Press.

Gray, J.A. (1971). The mind-brain identity theory as a scientific hypothesis. *Philosophical Quarterly*, 21, 247–254.

Gray, J.A. (1982). *The Neuropsychology of Anxiety*. Oxford: Oxford University Press.

Gray, J.A. (1987). *The Psychology of Fear and Stress* (2nd edition). Cambridge: Cambridge University Press.

Gray, J.A. (1995). A model of the limbic system and basal ganglia: Applications to anxiety and schizophrenia. In M.S. Gazzaniga (ed.), *The Cognitive Neurosciences*. Cambridge, MA: MIT Press.

Gray, J.A. (1998). Creeping up on the hard question of consciousness. In S.R. Hameroff, A.W. Kaszniak and A.C. Scott (eds), *Towards a science of consciousness II*. Cambridge, MA: MIT Press.

Gray, J.A., Feldon, J., Rawlins, J.N.P., Hemsley, D.R. and Smith, A.D. (1991). The neuropsychology of schizophrenia. *Behavioural and Brain Science*, 14, 1–84.

Green, B.L. (1994). Psychosicla research in traumatic stress: An update. *Journal of Traumatic Stress*, 7, 341–362.

Green, D.M. and Swets, J.A. (1974). *Signal Detection Theory and Psychophysics*. New York: Krieger.

Greenberg, R. and Pearlman, C.A. (1974). Cutting the REM nerve: An approach to the adaptive role of REM sleep. *Perspectives in Biology and Medicine*, 17, 513–521.

Greene, J.D.W. and Hodges, J.R. (1996a). Identification of famous faces and famous names in early Alzheimer's disease. *Brain*, 119, 111–128.

Greene, J.D.W. and Hodges, J.R. (1996b). Identification of remote memory: Evidence from a longitudinal study of dementia of the Alzheimer type. *Brain*, 119, 129–142.

Greenough, W.T. and Volkmar, F.R. (1973). Pattern of dendritic branching in occipital cortex of rats reared in complex environments. *Experimental Neurology*, 40, 491–504.

Greenwald, D.F. (1991). An external construct validity study of Rorschach personality variables. *Journal of Personality Assessment*, 55, 768–780.

Gregory, R.L. (1998). Mythical mechanisms (2): Is the brain a computer? *Perception*, 27, 127–128.

Griffiths, M. and Payne, P. R. (1976). Energy expenditure in small children of obese and non-obese mothers. *Nature*, 260, 698–700.

Griffiths, R.R., Bigelow, G.E. and Henningfield, J.E. (1980). Similarities in animal and human drug-taking behavior. In N. K. Mello (ed.), *Advances in Substance Abuse*, Vol. 1. Greenwich, CT: JAI Press.

Griggs, R.A. and Cox, J.R. (1982). The elusive thematic-materials effect in Wason's selection task. *British Journal of Psychology*, 73, 407–420.

Grigorenko, E.L., Wood, F.B., Meyer, M.S. *et al.* (1997). Susceptibility loci for distinct components of developmental dyslexia on chromosomes 6 and 15. *American Journal of Human Genetics*, 60, 27–39.

Gross, M.U.M. (1993). *Exceptionally Gifted Children*. London: Routledge.

Grossarth-Maticek, R., Bastiaans, J. and Kanazir, D. T. (1985). Psychosocial factors as strong predictors of mortality from cancer, ischaemic heart disease and stroke: The Yugoslav prospective study. *Journal of Psychosomatic Research*, 29, 167–176.

Grossarth-Maticek, R. and Eysenck, H. J. (1990). Personality, stress and disease: Description and validation of a new inventory. *Psychological Reports*, 66, 355–373.

Groth-Marnat, G. (1997). *Handbook of Psychological Assessment* (3rd edition). New York: Wiley.

Gruzelier, J., Seymour, K., Wilson, L., Idley, A. and Hirsch, S. (1988). Impairments on neuropsychological tests of temporohippocampal and frontohippocampal function and word fluency in remitting schizophrenia and affective disorders. *Archives of General Psychiatry*, 45, 623–629.

Guariglia, C., Padovani, A., Pantano, P. and Pizzamiglio, L. (1993). Unilateral neglect restricted to visual imagery. *Nature*, 364, 235–237.

Gudjonsson, G.H. (1994). Psychological evidence in court. In G.E. Lindzey and G.H. Powell (eds), *The Handbook of Adult Clinical Psychology*. London: Routledge.

Gudjonsson, G.H. (1996a). Forensic psychology in England: One practitioner's experience and viewpoint. *Legal and Criminological Psychology*, 1, 131–142.

Gudjonsson, G.H. (1996b). Psychological evidence in court. *The Psychologist*, May, 213–217.

Gudjonsson, G.H. (1997). The members of the BFMS, the accusers and their siblings. *The Psychologist*, March, 111–115.

Gur, R.C. and Gur, R.E. (1995). Hypofrontality in schizophrenia: RIP. *The Lancet*, 345, 1383–1385.

Gustafson, G.E. and Harris, K.L. (1990). Women's responses to young infants' cries. *Developmental Psychology*, 26, 144–152.

Gustavson, A.R., Dawson, M.E. and Bennett, D.G. (1987). Androstenol, a putative human pheromone, affects human (homosapiens) male choice performance. *Journal of Comparative Psychology*, Vol. 2, 210–212.

Gustavson, C.R. and Gustavson, J.C. (1985). Predation control using conditioned food aversion methodology: Theory, practice, and implications. *Annals of the New York Academy of Sciences*, 443, 348–356.

Guze, S.B. and Robins, E. (1970). Suicide and primary affective disorders. *British Journal of Psychiatry*, 117, 437–438.

Guze, S.B., Wolfgram, E.D., McKinney, J.K. and Cantwell, D.P. (1967). Psychiatric illness in the families of convicted criminals. A study of 519 first-degree relatives. *Disorders of the Nervous System*, 28, 651–659.

Guze, S.B., Woodruff, R.A. and Clayton, P.J. (1971). Secondary affective disorder: A study of 95 cases. *Psychological Medicine*, 1, 426–428.

Gwyer, P. and Clifford, B.R. (1997). The effects of the cognitive interview on recall. Identification, confidence and the confidence/accuracy relationship. *Applied Cognitive Psychology*, 11, 121–145.

Haaga, D.A. and Davison, G.C. (1989). Cognitive change methods. In A.P. Goldstein and F.H. Kanfer (eds), *Helping People Change* (3rd edition). New York: Pergamon Press.

Haaland, K.Y. and Harrington, D.H. (1989). *Neuropsychologia*, 27, 961.

Haber, R.N. and Hershenson, M. (1973). *The Psychology of Visual Perception*. New York: Holt, Rinehart & Winston.

Haenny, P.E., Maunsell, J.H. and Schiller, P.H. (1988). State dependent activity in monkey visual cortex. II: Retinal and extraretinal factors in V4. *Experimental Brain Research*, 69, 245–259.

Hagemann, D., Naumann, E., Becker, G., Maier, S. and Bartussek, D. (1998). Frontal brain asymmetry and affective style: A conceptual replication. *Psychophysiology*, 35, 372–388.

Haier, R.J., Neuchterlein, K.H., Hazlett, E., Wu, J.C., Pack, J., Browning, H.L. and Buchsbaum, M.S. (1988). Cortical glucose metabolic rate correlates of abstract reasoning and attention studied with positron emission tomography. *Intelligence*, 12, 199–217.

Haier, R.J., Siegel, B., Tang, C., Abel, L. and Buchsbaum, M.S. (1992). Intelligence and changes in regional cerebral glucose metabolic rate following learning. *Intelligence*, 16, 415–426.

Hakim, A.A., Petrovitch, H., Burchfiel, C.M., Webster-Ross, G., Rodriguez, B.L., White, L.R., Yano, K., Curb, J.D. and Abbott, R.D. (1998). Effects of walking on mortality among non-smoking retired men. *New England Journal of Medicine*, 338, 94–99.

Halaas, J.L., Gajiwala, K.S., Maffei, M. and Cohen, S.L. (1995). Weight-reducing effects of the plasma protein encoded by the obese gene. *Science*, 269, 543–546.

Halford, G.S. (1990). Is children's reasoning logical or analytical? *Human Development*, 33, 356–361.

Hall, C.S. and Nordby, V.J. (1973). *A Primer of Jungian Psychology*. New York: New American Library.

Hall, E.T. (1966). *The Hidden Dimension*. New York: Doubleday.

Hall, J.W. and Jerger, J. (1978). Central auditory function in stutterers. *Journal of Speech and Hearing Research*, 21, 324–337.

Haller, J. (1995). The actions of vitamins and other nutrients on psychological parameters. In I. Hindmarch and P.D. Stonier (eds), *Human Psychopharmacology*, Vol 5. Chichester: Wiley.

Halligan, P.W. and Cockburn, J.M. (1993). Cognitive sequelae of stroke: Visuospatial and memory disorders. *Critical Reviews in Physical and Rehabilitation Medicine*, 5, 1, 57 81.

Halligan, P.W. and Marshall, J.C. (1994). *Spatial Neglect: Position papers on theory and practice*. London: Macmillan.

Halligan, P.W. and Marshall, J.C. (1997). The art of visual neglect. *Lancet*, 350, 139–140.

Halmi, K. A. (1978). Anorexia nervosa: Recent investigations. *Annual Review of Medicine*, 29, 137–148.

Halpern, D.F. (1992). *Sex Differences in Cognitive Abilities*. Hillsdale, NJ: Lawrence Erlbaum Associates.

Halpern, D.F. (1997). Sex differences in intelligence. *American Psychologist*, 52, 10, 1091–1102.

Hambleton, R.K. (1994). Guidelines for adapting educational and psychological tests: A progress report. *European Journal of Psychological Assessment*, 10, 229–244.

Hameroff, S.R. (1998). More neural than thou. In S.R. Hameroff, A.W. Kaszniak, and A.C. Scott (eds), *Towards a Science of Consciousness II*. Cambridge, MA: MIT Press

Hameroff, S.R. and Penrose, R. (1996). Orchestrated reduction of quantum coherence in brain microtubules: A model for consciousness. In Hameroff, S.R., Kaszniak, A.W. and Scott, A.C. (1996), *Towards a Science of Consciousness*. Cambridge, MA: MIT Press.

Hameroff, S.R., Kaszniak, A.W. and Scott, A.C. (1998). *Towards a Science of Consciousness II*. Cambridge, MA: MIT Press.

Hamilton, W.D. (1964). The genetical evolution of social behaviour: I and II. *Journal of Theoretical Biology*, 7, 1–52.

Hamilton, W.D. (1970). Selfish and spiteful behavior in an evolutionary model. *Nature*, 228, 1218–1220.

Hammarstrom, A. and Janlert, U. (1997). Nervous and depressive symptoms in a longitudinal study of youth unemployment- selection or exposure? *Journal of Adolescence*, 20, 293–305.

Hammersley, M. (1992). *What's Wrong with Ethnography*? London: Routledge.

Hamond, N.R. and Fivush, R. (1991). Memories of Mickey Mouse: Young children recount their trip to Disneyworld. *Cognitive Development*, 6, 433–648.

Hampson, E. (1990). Estogen-related variations in human spatial and articulatory–motor skills. *Psychoneuroendocrinology*, 15, 97–111.

Hanson, J.W., Jones, K.L., and Smith, D.W. (1976). Fetal alcohol syndrome: Experience with 41 patients. *Journal of the American Medical Association*, 235, 1458–1466.

Happé, F.G.E. (1993). Communicative competence and theory of mind in autism: A test of relevance theory. *Cognition*, 48, 101–119.

Happé, F.G.E. (1994). *Autism: An introduction to psychological theory*. London: UCL Press.

Hare, R.D. (1965). Temporal gradient of fear arousal in psychopaths. *Journal of Abnormal Psychology*, 70, 442–445.

Hare, R.D. (1981). Psychopathy and violence. In J.R. Hayes, T.K. Roberts and K.S. Solway (eds), *Violence and the Violent Individual*. Jamaica, NY: Spectrum.

Hare, R.D. and McPherson, L.M. (1984). Violent and aggressive behaviour by criminal psychopaths. *International Journal of Law and Psychiatry*, 7, 329–337.

Harkins, S.G. and Petty, R.E. (1982). Effects of task difficulty and task uniqueness on social loafing. *Journal of Personality and Social Psychology*, 43, 1214–1229.

Harley, T.A. (1995). *The Psychology of Language*. Hove, UK: The Psychology Press.

Harlow, H. (1974). *Learning to Love*. New York: J. Aronson.

Harlow, J.M. (1848). Passage of an iron rod through the head. *Boston Medicine and Surgery Journal*, 39, 389–393.

Harlow, J.M. (1868). Recovery from the passage of an iron bar through the head. *Massachusetts Medical Society Publications*, 2, 327–346.

Harmon-Jones, E. and Allen, J.J.B. (1998). Anger and frontal brain activity: EEG asymmetry consistent with approach motivation despite negative affective valence. *Journal of Personality and Social Psychology*, 74, 5, 1310–1316.

Harré, R. and Secord, P. (1972). *The Explanation of Social Behaviour*. Oxford: Blackwell.

Harris, B. (1979). Whatever happened to Little Albert. *American Psychologist*, 34, 2, 151–160.

Harris, J.R. (1995). Where is the child's environment? A group socialization theory of development. *Psychological Review*, 102, 458–489.

Harris, M. (1991). *Cultural Anthropology* (3rd edition). New York: HarperCollins.

Harrison, J. and Baron–Cohen, S. (1990). Acquired and inherited forms of cross-modal correspondence. *Neurocase*, 2, 3, 245–249.

Harrison, J. and Baron-Cohen, S. (eds) (1996). *Synaesthesia: classic and contemporary readings*. Oxford: Blackwell.

Hartmann, E. (1967). *The Biology of Dreaming*. Springfield, IL: Charles C. Thomas.

Hartshorne, H. and May, M.A. (1928). *Studies in Deceit*. New York: Macmillan.

Hatfield, E. (1988). Passionate and compassionate love. In R.J. Sternberg and M.L. Barnes (eds), *The Psychology of Love*. New Haven, CT: Yale University Press.

Hatfield, E. and Sprecher, S. (1986). *Mirror, Mirror … The Importance of Looks in Everyday Life*. Albany, NY: SUNY Press.

Hathaway, S.R. and McKinley, J.C. (1983). *Minnesota Multiphasic Personality Inventory: Manual for administration and scoring*. New York: Psychological Corporation.

Haward, L.R.C. (1979). The psychologist as expert witness. In D.P. Farrington, K. Hawkins and S.M.A. Lloyd-Bostock (eds), *Psychology, Law and Legal Processes*. London: Macmillan.

Haward, L.R.C. (1981). *Forensic Psychology*. London: Batsford.

Haxby, J.V., Ungerleider, L.G., Horowitz, B., Miasog, J.M., Rapoport, S.I. and Grady, C.L. (1996). Face encoding and recognition in the human brain. *Proceedings of the National Academy of Sciences USA*, 93, 922–927.

Hayes, B.K. and Delamothe, K. (1997). Cognitive interviewing procedures and suggestibility in children's recall. *Journal of Applied Psychology*, 82, 4, 562–577.

Hayes, C. (1952). *The Ape in Our House*. London: Gollancz.

Hayes, N. (1997). *Doing Qualitative Analysis in Psychology*. Hove, UK: The Psychology Press.

Hayes, S.C. (1989). *Rule-governed Behavior: Cognition, contingencies, and instructional control*. New York: Plenum.

Health Education Authority (1991). *The Smoking Epidemic*. London: HEA.

Heap, M. and Dryden, W. (1991). *Hypnotherapy: A handbook*. Milton Keyes: Open University.

Heath, A.C., Meyer, J.M. and Martin, N.G. (1989). Inheritance of alcohol consumption patterns in the Australian twin survey. In C.R. Cloninger and H. Begleiter (eds), *Genetics and Biology of Alcoholism*. Plainview, NY: Cold Spring Harbor Laboratory Press.

Heather, N. and Robertson, I. (1997). *Problem Drinking* (3rd edition). Oxford: Oxford University Press.

Hebb, D.O. (1949). *The Organization of Behaviour*. New York: Wiley/Interscience.

Hebb, D.O. (1955). Drives and the CNS (conceptual nervous system). *Psychological Review*, 62, 243–254.

Hebb, D.O., Lambert, W.E. and Tucker, G.R. (1973). A DMZ in the language war. *Psychology Today*, April, 55–62.

Heider, E.R. (1971). 'Focal' color areas and the development of color names. *Developmental Psychology*, 4, 447–455.

Heider, E.R. (1972).Universals in color naming and memory. *Journal of Experimental Psychology*, 93, 10–20.

Heider, F. (1958). *The Psychology of Interpersonal Relations*. New York: Wiley.

Heim, N. and Hursch, C. (1979). Castration for sex offenders: Treatment or punishment? *Archives of Sexual Behaviour*, 8, 281–304.

Helzer, J.E. and Canino, G.J. (1992). *Alcoholism in North America, Europe, and Asia*. New York: Oxford University Press.

Hemmasi, M., Graf, L.A. and Russ, G.S. (1994). Gender-related jokes in the workplace: Sexual humor or sexual harassment? *Journal of Applied Social Psychology*, 24, 1114–1128.

Henderson, B.J. and Maguire, B. (1998). Lay representations of genetic disease and predictive testing. *Journal of Health Psychology*, 3, 2, 233–241.

Henke, P.G. (1982). The telencephalic limbic system and experimental gastric pathology: A review. *Neuroscience and Biobehavioral Reviews*, 6, 381–390.

Henriques, J.B. and Davidson, R.J. (1991). Left frontal hypoactivation in depression. *Journal of Abnormal Psychology*, 100, 535–545.

Hepper, P.G. (1994). Auditory learning in the human fetus. *Infant Behaviour and Development*, 17, 96.

Hepper, P.G. (1995). Human fetal 'olfactory' learning. *International Journal of Prenatal, Perinatal and Psychological Medicine*, 7, 147–151.

Herdt, G. and Lindenbaum, S. (eds) (1992). *Social Analyses in the Time of AIDS*. Newbury Park, CA: Sage.

Hermans, D., Pieters, G. and Eelen, P. (1998). Implicit and explicit memory for shape, body weight, and food-related words in patients with anorexia nervosa and nondieting controls. *Journal of Abnormal Psychology*, 107, 2, 193–202.

Herrenkohl, R.C., Egolf, B.P. and Herrenkohl, E.C. (1997). Pre-school antecedents of adolescent assaultive behaviour: A longitudinal study. *American Journal of Orthopsychiatry*, 67, 422–433.

Herrnstein, R.J. and Murray, C. (1994). *The Bell Curve*. New York: Free Press.

Herrnstein, R.J., Nickerson, R.S., Sanchez, M. and Swets, J.A. (1986). Teaching thinking skills. *American Psychologist*, 41, 1279–1289.

Hertz, R.S. and Cupchik, G.C. (1992). An experimental characterization of odor-evoked memories in humans. *Chemical Senses*, 17, 5, 519–528.

Herz, R.S. and Engen, T. (1996). Odor memory: Review and analysis. *Psychonomic Bulletin Review*, 3, 3, 300–313.

Hewstone, M. (1989). *Causal Attribution: From cognitive processes to collective beliefs*. Oxford: Blackwell.

Hewstone, M. and Brown, R.J. (1986) *Causal Attribution: From cognitive processes to collective beliefs*. Oxford: Blackwell.

Higgins, E.T., Rholes, W.S. and Jones, C.R. (1977). Category accessibility and impression formation. *Journal of Experimental Social Psychology*, 13, 141–154.

Higgins, S.T., Hughes, J.R. and Bickel, W.K. (1989). Effects of d-amphetamine on choice in social versus monetary reinforcement: A discrete trial test. *Pharmacology, Biochemistry, and Behavior*, 34, 297–301.

Higgins, S.T., Budney, A.J. and Bickel, W.K. (1994). Applying behavioral concepts and principles to the treatment of cocaine dependence. *Drug and Alcohol Dependence*, 7, 19–38.

Hilgard, E.R. (1978). States of consciousness in hypnosis: Divisions or levels? In F.H. Frankel and H.S. Zamansky (eds), *Hypnosis at its Bicentennial: Selected papers*. New York: Plenum

Hilgard, E.R. (1979). Divided consciousness in hypnosis: The implications of the hidden observer. In E. Fromm and R.E. Shor (eds), *Hypnosis: Developments in research and new perspectives*. Chicago: Aldine Press.

Hilgard, E.R. (1986). *Divided Consciousness: Multiple controls in human thought and action*. New York: Wiley.

Hilgard, E.R. (1991). A neodissociation interpretation of hypnosis. In S.J. Lynn and J.H. Rhue (eds), *Theories of Hypnosis: Current models and perspectives*. New York: Guilford.

Hilgard, E.R. and Hilgard, J.R. (1994). *Hypnosis in the Relief of Pain*. New York: Brunner/Mazel.

Hill, H. and Bruce, V. (1996). Effects of lighting on the perception of facial surfaces. *Journal of Experimental Psychology: Human Perception and Performance*, 22, 4, 986–1004.

Hinton, L. and Kleinman, A. (1993). Cultural issues and international psychiatric diagnosis. *International Review of Psychiatry*, 1, 111–134.

Ho, M.R. and Bennett, T.L. (1997). *Archives of Clinical Neuropsychology*, 12, 1, 1–11.

Hobson, J.A. (1988). *The Dreaming Brain*. New York: Basic Books.

Hockett, C.F. (1960a). Logical considerations in the study of animal communication. In W.E. Lanyon and W.N. Tavolga (eds), *Animal sounds and communication*. Washington DC: American Institute of Biological Sciences.

Hockett, C.F. (1960b). The origin of speech. *Scientific American*, 203, 89–96.

Hofling, C.K. (1963). *Textbook of Psychiatry for Medical Practice*. Philadelphia: Lippincott.

Hogg, M.A. and Abrams, D. (1988). *Social Identifications: A social psychology of intergroup relations and group processes*. London: Routledge.

Hogg, M.A. and Vaughan, G.M. (1998). *Social psychology* (2nd edition). Hemel Hempstead: Prentice Hall Europe.

Holden, R. (1993). Laughter – The best medicine. London: Thorsons.

Holland, C.A. and Rabbitt, P. (1991). The course and causes of cognitive change with advancing age. *Reviews in Clinical Gerontology*, 1, 81–96.

Hollander, E., Schiffman, E., Cohen, B., Rivera-Stein, M. A., Rosen, W., Gorman, J. M., Fyer, A. J., Papp, L. and Liebowitz, M. R. (1990). Signs of central nervous system dysfunction in obsessive-compulsive disorder. *Archives of General Psychiatry*, 47, 27–32.

Hollenbeck, A.R. (1978). Television viewing patterns of families with young infants. *Journal of Social Psychology*, 105, 259–264.

Holloway, R.L., Anderson, P.J., Defendini, R. and Harper, C. (1993). Sexual dimorphism of the human corpus callosum from three independent samples: Relative size of the corpus callosum. *American Journal of Physical Anthropology*, 92, 481–498.

Holmes, T. H. and Rahe, R. H. (1967). The social readjustment rating scale. *Journal of Psychosomatic Research*, 11, 213, 218.

Holyoak, K.J. (1990). Problem solving. In D.N. Osherson and E.E. Smith (eds), *An Invitation to Cognitive Science. Vol. 3: Thinking*. Cambridge, MA: MIT Press.

Holyoak, K.J. and Spellman, B.A. (1993). Thinking. *Annual Review of Psychology*, 44, 265–315.

Hooley, J.M. and Teasdale, J.D. (1989). Predictors of relapse in unipolar depressives: Expressed emotion, marital distress and perceived criticism. *Journal of Abnormal Psychology*, 98, 229–235.

Hooley, J.M., Rosen, L.R. and Richters, J.E. (1996). Expressed emotion: Toward clarification of a critical construct. In G. Miller (ed.), *The Behavioural High-risk Paradigm in Psychopathology*. New York: Springer-Verlag.

Hoorens, V. (1993). Self-enhancement and superiority biases in social comparison. *European Review of Social Psychology*, 4, 113–139.

Hoorens, V. and Nuttin, J.M. (1993). Overvaluation of own attributes: Mere ownership or subjective frequency? *Social Cognition*, 11, 177–200.

Hoosain, R. (1984). Experiments on digit spans in the English and Chinese languages. In H.R.R. Kao and R. Hoosain (eds), *Psychological Studies of the Chinese Language*. Hong Kong: Chinese Language Society of Hong Kong.

Hoptman, M.J. and Davidson, R.J. (1994). How and why do the two cerebral hemispheres interact? *Psychological Bulletin*, 116, 2, 195–219.

Horn, G. (1998). Visual imprinting and the neural mechanisms of recognition memory. *Trends in Neurosciences*, 21, 7, 300–305.

Horn, J.L. (1968). Organization of abilities and the development of intelligence, *Psychological Review*, 75, 249.

Horn, J.L. and Cattell, R.B. (1966). Refinement and test of the theory of fluid and crystallized ability intelligences. *Journal of Educational Psychology*, 57, 253–270.

Hornak, J., Rolls, E.T. and Wade, D. (1996). Face and voice expression identification in patients with emotional and behavioural changes following ventral frontal lobe damage. *Neuropsychologia*, 34, 4, 247–261.

Horne, J.A. (1978). A review of the biological effects of total sleep deprivation in man. *Biological Psychology*, 7, 55–102.

Horne, J.A. (1988). *Why We Sleep: The functions of sleep in humans and other mammals*. Oxford: Oxford University Press.

Horne, J.A. and Minard, A. (1985). Sleep and sleepiness following a behaviourally 'active' day. *Ergonomics*, 28, 567–575.

Horney, K. (1950). *Neurosis and Human Growth*. New York: W.W. Norton.

Hornik, R. (1981). Out-of-school television and schooling: Hypothesis and methods. *Review of Educational Research*, 51, 199–214.

Horowitz, M.J. (1979). Psychological response to serious life events. In V. Hamilton and D.M. Warburton (eds), *Human Stress and Cognition*. New York: Wiley.

Horowitz, M.J. (1986). *Stress Response Syndromes* (2nd edition). Northvale, NJ: Jason Aronson.

Houston, D.M. (1994). Gloomy but smarter: The academic consequences of attributional style. *British Journal of Social Psychology*, 33, 433–441.

Houston, D.M., McKee, K.J, Carrol, L. and Marsh, H. (1998). Using humour to promote psychological wellbeing in residential homes for older people. *Aging and Mental Health*, 2, 328–332.

Houston, J.P. (1983). Psychology: A closed system of self-evident information? *Psychological Reports*, 52, 203–208.

Hovland, C. I. and Weiss, W. (1951). The influence of source credibility on communication effectiveness. *Public Opinion Quarterly*, 15, 635–650.

Howard, R.W. (1995). *Learning and Memory: Major ideas, principles, issues, and applications*. Westport, CT: Praeger.

Howlett, A.C. (1990). Reverse pharmacology applied to the cannabinoid receptor. *Trends in Pharmacological Sciences*, 11, 395–397.

Hubel, D.H. and Wiesel, T.N. (1977). Functional architecture of macaque monkey visual cortex. *Proceedings of the Royal Society of London*, Series B, 198, 1–59.

Hubel, D.H. and Wiesel, T.N. (1979). Brain mechanisms of vision. *Scientific American*, 241, 150–162.

Hugdahl, K. (1996). Brain laterality – beyond the basics. *European Psychologist*, 1, 3, 206–220.

Hughes, C., Russell, J. and Robbins, T.W. (1994). Evidence for executive dysfunction in autism. *Neuropsychologia*, 32, 477–492.

Hughes, C., Dunn, J. and White, A. (1998). Trick or treat? Uneven understanding of mind and emotion and executive dysfunction in 'hard-to-manage' preschoolers. *Journal of Child Psychology and Psychiatry*, 39, 7, 981–994.

Hughes, J.R. and Pierattini, R. (1992). An introduction to pharmacotherapy. In J. Grabowski and G.R. Vandenbos (eds), *Psychopharmacology: Basic mechanisms and applied interventions.* Master Lectures in Psychology. Washington, DC: American Psychological Association.

Hulit, L.M. and Howard, M.R. (1993). *Born to Talk: An introduction to speech and language development.* New York: Merrill/Macmillan.

Hull, C.L. (1943). *Principles of Behavior.* New Haven: Yale University Press.

Hulme, C. and Roodenrys, S. (1995). Practitioner review: Verbal working memory development and its disorders. *Journal of Child Psychology and Psychiatry*, 36, 3, 373–398.

Hultman, C.M., Ohman, A., Cnattingius, S., Wieselgren, I-M. and Lindstrom, L.H. (1997). Prenatal and neonatal risk factors for schizophrenia. *British Journal of Psychiatry*, 170, 128–133.

Hultman, C.M., Sparen, P., Takei, N., Murray, R.M. and Cnattingius, S. (1999). Prenatal and perinatal risk factors for schizophrenia, affective psychosis and reactive psychosis of early onset: Case-control study. BMJ, 318, 421–426.

Humphreys, G.W. and Riddoch, M.J. (1987a). *To See or Not To See: A case study of visual object processing.* Hove, UK: The Psychology Press.

Humphreys, G.W. and Riddoch, M.J. (1987b). The fractionation of visual agnosia. In G.W. Humphreys and M.J. Riddoch (eds), *Visual Object Agnosia: A cognitive neuropsychological approach.* Hove, UK: The Psychology Press.

Hunt, E. (1985). Verbal ability. In R.J. Sternberg (ed.), *Human Abilities: An information-processing approach.* New York: Freeman.

Hunt, M. (1974). *Sexual Behavior in the 1970s.* Chicago: Playboy.

Hunter, J.A., Platow, M.J., Howard, M.L. and Stringer M. (1996). Social identity and intergroup evaluative bias: Realistic categories and domain specific self-esteem in a conflict setting. *European Journal of Social Psychology*, 26, 631–647.

Huston, A.C. (1983). Sex-typing. In E.M. Hetherington (ed.), *Handbook of Child Psychology: Vol. 4. Socialization, Personality, and Social Development.* New York: Wiley.

Huston, A.C., Watkins, B.A. and Kunkel, D. (1989). Public policy and children's television. *American Psychologist*, 44, 424–433.

Huston, A.C., Wright, J.C., Rice, M.L., Kerkman, D. and St Peters, M. (1990). Development of television viewing patterns in early childhood: A longitudinal investigation. *Developmental Psychology*, 26, 409–420.

Hyde, T.S. and Jenkins, J.J. (1969). The differential effects of incidental tasks on the organization of recall of a list of highly associated words. *Journal of Experimental Psychology*, 82, 472–481.

Ickovics, J.R., Druley, J.A., Grigorenko, E.L., Morrill, A.C., Beren, S.E. and Rodin, J. (1998). Long-term effects of HIV counselling and testing for women: Behavioural and psychological consequences are limited at 18 months posttest. *Health Psychology*, 17, 5, 395–402.

Inglefinger, F.J. (1944). The late effects of total and subtotal gastrectomy. *New England Journal of Medicine*, 231, 321–327.

Inoue, M., Koyanagi, T., Nakahara, H., Hara, K., Hori, E. and Nakano, H. (1986). Functional development of human eye movement in utero assessed quantitatively with real time ultrasound. *American Journal of Obstetrics and Gynecology*, 155, 170–174.

Isabella, R.A. and Belsky, J. (1991). Interactional synchrony and the origins of infant-mother attachment: A replication study. *Child Development*, 62, 373–384.

Isen, A.M. and Geva, N. (1987). The influence of positive affect on acceptable levels of risk and thoughts about losing: The person with a large canoe has a large worry. *Organizational Behaviour and Human Decision Processes*, 39, 145–154.

Isen, A.M. and Partick, R. (1983). The effects of positive feelings on risk taking: When the chips are down. *Organizational Behaviour and Human Performance*, 31, 194–202.

Isen, A.M., Daubman, K.A. and Nowicki, G.P. (1987). Positive affect facilitates creative problem solving. *Journal of Personality and Social Psychology*, 52, 1122–1131.

Isen, A.M., Nygren, T.E. and Ashby, F.G. (1988). Influence of positive affect on the subjective expected utility of gains and losses: It's just not worth the risk. *Journal of Personality and Social Psychology*, 55, 710–717.

Isenberg, D.J. (1986). Group polarization: A critical review and meta-analysis. *Psychological Bulletin*, 50, 1141–1151.

Izard, C.E. (1971). *The Face of Emotion.* New York: Appleton-Century-Crofts.

Izard, C.E. (1977). *Human Emotions.* New York: Plenum Press.

Izard, C.E. (1992). Basic emotions, relations among emotions, and emotion-cognition relations. *Psychological Review*, 99, 561–565.

Jablensky, A. (1989). Epidemiology and cross-cultural aspects of schizophrenia. *Psychiatric Annals*, 19, 516–524.

Jablensky, A. and Cole, S.W. (1997). Is the earlier age at onset of schizophrenia in males a confounded finding? *British Journal of Psychiatry*, 170, 234–240.

Jablensky, A., Sartorius, N., Ernberg, G., Anker, M., Korten, A., Cooper, J.E., Day, R. and Bertelsen, A. (1992). Schizophrenia: Manifestations, incidence and course in different cultures. A WHO ten country study. *Psychological Medicine Monograph Supplement 20.* Cambridge: Cambridge University Press.

Jacklin, C.N. and Maccoby, E.E. (1983). Issues of gender differentiation in normal development. In M.D. Levine, W.B. Carey, A.C. Crocker and R.T. Gross (eds), *Developmental-Behavioral Pediatrics.* Philadelphia: Saunders.

Jackson, N. and Butterfield, E. (1986). A conception of giftedness designed to promote research. In R.J. Sternberg and J.E. Davidson (eds), *Conceptions of Giftedness.* New York: Cambridge University Press.

Jacob, F. (1977). Evolution and tinkering. *Science*, 196, 1161–1166.

Jaffe, J.H. (1985). Drug addiction and drug abuse. In L.S. Goodman and A. Gilman (eds), *The Pharmacological Basis of Therapeutics*, Vol. 7. New York: Macmillan.

James, W. (1884). What is an emotion? *Mind*, 9, 188–205.

James, W. (1890). *Principles of Psychology.* New York: Henry Holt.

James, W. (1893). *The Principles of Psychology*, Vol. 1. New York: Holt.

James, W.P.T. and Trayhurn, P. (1981). Thermogenesis and obesity. *British Medical Bulletin*, 37, 43–48.

Jamison, K.R. (1989). Mood disorders and patterns of creativity in British writers and artists. *Psychiatry*, 52, 125–134.

Jamison, K.R. (1997). Manic-depressive illness and creativity. *In Mysteries of the Mind.* New York: Scientific American.

Jang, K.L., McCrae, R.R., Angleitner, A., Riemann, R. and Livesley, W.J. (1998). Heritability of facet-level traits in a cross-cultural twin sample: Support for a hierarchical model of personality. *Journal of Personality and Social Psychology*, 74, 1556–1565.

Janis, I.L. (1967). Effects of fear arousal on attitude change: Recent developments in theory and experimental research. In L. Berkowitz (ed.), *Advances in Experimental Social Psychology*, Vol. 3. New York: Academic Press, pp. 167–224.

Janis, I.L. (1972). *Victims of Groupthink.* Boston: Houghton Mifflin.

Janis, I.L. (1982). *Groupthink: Psychological studies of policy decisions and fiascoes.* Boston: Houghton Mifflin.

Jancke, L. and Steinmetz, H. (1994). *Biological Bases of Individual Behaviour.* New York: Academic Press.

Janoff-Bulman, R. (1989). Assumptive worlds and the stress of traumatic events: Applications of the schema construct. *Social Cognition*, 7, 113–136.

Janoff-Bulman, R. (1992). *Shattered Assumptions: Towards a new psychology of trauma.* New York: Free Press.

Janowic, J. (1993). Tourette's syndrome: Phenomenology, pathophysiology, genetics, epidemiology and treatment. In S.H. Appel (ed.), *Current Neurology*, Vol. 13. Chicago: Mosby Yearbook.

Janowsky, J.S., Oviatt, S.K. and Orwoll, E.S. (1994). Testosterone influences spatial cognition in older men. *Behavioural Neuroscience*, 108, 325–332.

Janz, N. and Becker, M.H. (1984). The health belief mode: A decade later. *Health Education Quarterly*, 11, 1–47.

Jausovec, N. (1996). Differences in EEG alpha activity related to giftedness. *Intelligence*, 23, 159–173.

Jausovec, N. (1998). Are gifted individuals less chaotic thinkers? *Personality and Individual Differences*, 25, 253–267.

Jaynes, J. (1970). The problem of animate motion in the seventeenth century. *Journal of the History of Ideas*, 6, 219–234.

Jayoram, M. (1984). Distribution of stuttering in sentences: relationship to sentence length and clause position. *Journal of Speech and Hearing Research*, 27, 338–341.

Jeannerod, M. (1997). *The Cognitive Neuroscience of Action*. Oxford: Blackwell.

Jeannerod, M., Decety, J. and Michel, F. (1994). Impairment of grasping movements following a bilateral posterior parietal lesion. *Neuropsychologia*, 32, 369–380.

Jeffcoate, W.J., Lincoln, N.B., Selby, C. and Herbert, M. (1986). Correlations between anxiety and serum prolactin in humans. *Journal of Psychosomatic Research*, 30, 217–222.

Jemmott, J.B. and Magloire, K. (1988). Academic stress, social support and secretory immunoglobin A. *Journal of Personality and Social Psychology*, 55, 803–810.

Jenkins, J.G. and Dallenbach, K.M. (1924). Oblivescence during sleep and waking. *American Journal of Psychology*, 35, 605–612.

Jenkins, J.H. and Karno, M. (1992). The meaning of expressed emotion: Theoretical issues raised by cross-cultural research. *American Journal of Psychiatry*, 149, 9–21.

Jensen, A.R. (1980). *Bias in mental testing*. New York: Free Press.

Jensen, A.R. (1985). The nature of the black-white difference on various psychometric tests: Spearman's hypothesis. *Behavioral and Brain Sciences*, 8, 193–263.

Jeste, D.V., Del Carmen, R., Lohr, J.B. and Wyatt, R. J. (1985). Did schizophrenia exist before the eighteenth century? *Comprehensive Psychiatry*, 26, 493–503.

Jilek-Aal, L. (1988). Suicidal behaviour among youth: A cross-cultural comparison. *Transcultural Psychiatric Research Review*, 25, 87–106.

Jodelet, D. (1991) *Madness and Social Representations*. Hemel Hempstead: Harvester Wheatsheaf.

Joffe, H. (1996). AIDS research and prevention: A social representational approach. *British Journal of Medical Psychology*, 69, 169–190.

Joffe, H. (1997). Juxtaposing positivist and non-positivist approaches to social scientific AIDS research: Reply to Fife-Shaw's commentary. *British Journal of Medical Psychology*, 70, 75–83.

Johansson, G. (1973). Visual perception of biological motion and a model for its analysis. *Perception and Psychophysics*, 14, 201–211.

Johnson, J.H., Butcher, J.N., Null, C. and Johnson, K.N. (1984). Replicated item level factor analysis of the full MMPI. *Journal of Personality and Social Psychology*, 47, 105–114.

Johnson, J.S. and Newport, E.L. (1989). Critical period effects in second language learning: The influence of maturational state on the acquisition of English as a second language. *Cognitive Psychology*, 21, 60–99.

Johnson, M.H. and Morton, J. (1991). *Biology and Cognitive Development: The case of face recognition*. Oxford: Blackwell.

Johnson-Laird, P.N. (1983). *Mental Models*. Cambridge, MA: Harvard University Press.

Johnson-Laird, P.N. (1985). Deductive reasoning ability. In R.J. Sternberg (ed.), *Human Abilities: An information-processing approach*. New York: Freeman.

Johnson-Laird, P.N. and Byrnc, R.M.J. (1991). *Deduction*. Hillsdale, NJ: Lawrence Erlbaum Associates.

Johnson-Laird, P.N., Byrne, R.M.J. and Schaeken, W. (1992). Propositional reasoning by model. *Psychological Review*, 99, 418–439.

Johnston, W.A. and Dark, V.J. (1986). Selective attention. *Annual Review of Psychology*, 37, 43–76.

Johnston, W.A. and Heinz, S.P. (1978). Flexibility and capacity demands of attention. *Journal of Experimental Psychology (General)*, 107, 420–435.

Johnstone, E.C., Crow, T.J., Frith, C.D., Stevens, M., Kreel, L. and Husband, J. (1978). The dementia of dementia praecox. *Acta Psychiatrica Scandinavica*, 57, 305–324.

Jones, D.C. (1991). Friendship satisfaction and gender: An examination of sex differences in contributors to friendship satisfaction. *Journal of Social and Personal Relationships*, 8, 167–185.

Jones, D.M. (1995). The fate of the unattended stimulus. Irrelevant speech and cognition. *Applied Cognitive Psychology*, 9, 23–38.

Jones, D.M., Madden, C. and Miles, C. (1992). Privileged access by irrelevant speech to short-term memory: The role of changing state. *Quarterly Journal of Experimental Psychology*, 44A, 645–659.

Jones, D.T. and Reed, R.R. (1989). Golf: An olfactory neuron specific-G protein involved in odorant signal transduction. *Science*, 244, 790–795.

Jones, E.E. (1990). *Interpersonal Perception*. New York: W. H. Freeman.

Jones, E.E. and Harris, V.A. (1967). The attribution of attitudes. *Journal of Experimental Social Psychology*, 3, 1–24.

Jones, E.E. and Nisbett, R.E. (1971). The actor and observer: Divergent perceptions of the causes of behavior. In E.E. Jones, D.E. Kamouse, H.H. Kelley, R.E. Nisbett, S. Valins and B. Weiner (eds), *Attribution: Perceiving the causes of behavior*. Morristown, NJ: General Learning Press.

Jones, G.V. (1989). Back to Woodworth – Role of interlopers in the tip-of-the-tongue phenomenon. *Memory and Cognition*, 17, 1, 69–76.

Jones, G.V. and Martin, M. (1992). Conjunction in the language of emotions. *Cognition and Emotion*, 6, 369–386.

Jones, H.E. (1959). Intelligence and problem-solving. In J.E. Birren (ed.), *Handbook of aging and the individual*. Chicago: University of Chicago Press.

Jones, R.B., Humphris, G. and Lewis, T. (1996). Do agoraphobics interpret the environment in large shops and supermarkets differently? *British Journal of Clinical Psychology*, 35, 635–637.

Joseph, S., Dalgleish, T., Williams, R., Yule, W., Thrasher, S. and Hodgkinson, P. (1997). Attitudes towards emotional expression and post-traumatic stress in survivors of the *Herald of Free Enterprise* disaster. *British Journal of Clinical Psychology*, 36, 133–138.

Joseph, S., Yule, W., Williams, R. and Hodgkinson, P. (1994). Correlates of post-traumatic stress at 30 months: the *Herald of Free Enterprise* disaster. *Behaviour Research and Therapy*, 32, 5, 521–524.

Jouvet, M. (1972). The role of monoamines and acetylcholine-containing neurons in the regulation of the sleep-waking cycle. *Ergebnisse der Physiologie*, 64, 166–307.

Joyce, E.M., Collinson, S.L. and Crichton, P. (1996). Verbal fluency in schizophrenia: Relationship with executive function, semantic memory and clinical alogia. *Psychological Medicine*, 26, 39–49.

Julesz, B. (1965). Texture and visual perception. *Scientific American*, 212, 38–48.

Jusczyk, P.W. and Hohne, E.A. (1997). Infants' memory for spoken words. *Science*, 277, 1984–1986.

Just, M.A. and Carpenter, P.A. (1980). A theory of reading: From eye fixations to comprehension. *Psychological Review*, 87, 329–354.

Just, M.A. and Carpenter, P.A. (1987). *The Psychology of Reading and Language Comprehension*. Boston: Allyn & Bacon.

Just, M.A., Carpenter, P.A. and Wu, R. (1983). *Eye Fixations in the Reading of Chinese Technical Text*, Technical Report. Pittsburgh: Carnegie-Mellon University.

Justice, A. (1985). Review of the effects of stress on cancer in laboratory animals: Importance of time of stress application and type of tumor. *Psychological Bulletin*, 98, 108–138.

Kagan, J., Kearsley, R.B. and Zelazo, P.R. (1978). *Infancy: Its place in human development*. Cambridge, MA: Harvard University Press.

Kagan, J., Reznick, J. S. and Snidman, N. (1988). Biological bases of childhood shyness. *Science*, 240, 167–171.

Kageyama, T., Nishikido, N., Kobayashi, T., Kurokawa, Y. and Kabuto, M. (1997). Commuting, overtime, and cardiac autonomic activity in Tokyo. *Lancet*, 350, 639.

Kahkonen, M., Alitalo, T., Airaksinen, E., Matilamen, R., Laumiala, K., Auno, S. and Leisti, J. (1987). Prevalence of fragile X syndrome in four birth cohorts of children of school age. *Human Genetics*, 30, 234–238.

Kahneman, D. (1973). *Attention and Effort*. Englewood Cliffs, NJ: Prentice Hall.

Kail, R. (1990). *The Development of Memory in Children*. New York: Freeman.

Kales, A., Scharf, M.B., Kales, J.D. and Soldatos, C.R. (1979). Rebound insomnia: A potential hazard following withdrawal of certain benzodiazepines. *Journal of the American Medical Association*, 241, 1692–1695.

Kalichman, S.C., Carey, M.P. and Johnson, B.T. (1996). Prevention of sexually transmitted HIV infection: A meta-analytic review of the behavioural outcome literature. *American Behavioural Medicine*, 18, 6–15.

Kalish, R.A. (1976). Death and dying in a social context. In R.H. Binstock and E. Shanas (eds), *Handbook of Aging and the Social Sciences*. New York: Van Nostrand Reinhold.

Kamphuis, J.H. and Emmelkamp, P.M.G. (1998). Crime-related trauma: Psychological distress in victims of bankrobbery. *Journal of Anxiety Disorders*, 12, 3, 199–208.

Kandel, E.R., Schwartz, J.H. and Jessell, T.M. (1995). *Essentials of Neural Science and Behaviour*. Englewood Cliffs, NJ: Prentice Hall.

Kane, J., Honigfeld, G., Singer, J., Meltzer, H., and the Clozaril Collaborative Study Group. (1988). Clozapine for the treatment-resistant schizophrenic: A double-blind comparison with chlorpromazine. *Archives of General Psychiatry*, 45, 789–796.

Kapci, E.G. (1998). Test of the hopelessness theory of depression drawing negative inference from negative life events. *Psychological Reports*, 82, 355–363.

Kaplan, E.L. and Kaplan, G.A. (1970). The prelinguistic child. In J. Eliot (ed.), *Human Development and Cognitive Processes*. New York: Holt, Rinehart and Winston.

Kapp, B.S., Gallagher, M., Applegate, C.D. and Frysinger, R. C. (1982). The amygdala central nucleus: Contributions to conditioned cardiovascular responding during aversive Pavlovian conditioning in the rabbit. In C. D. Woody (ed.), *Conditioning: Representation of Involved Neural Functions*. New York: Plenum.

Karau, S.J. and Williams, K.D. (1995). Social loafing: Research findings, implications, and future directions. *Current Directions in Psychological Science*, 4, 134–139.

Karbe, H., Herholz, K., Weber-Luxenburger, G., Ghaemi, M. and Heiss, W-D. (1998). Cerebral networks and functional brain asymmetry: Evidence from regional metabolic changes during word repetition. *Brain and Language*, 63, 108–121.

Karmiloff-Smith, A. (1988). The child is a theoretician, not an inductivist. *Mind and Language*, 3, 183–197.

Karmiloff-Smith, A. (1992). *Beyond Modularity: A developmental perspective on cognitive science*. Cambridge, MA: MIT Press.

Kassin, S.M. and Kiechel, K.L. (1996). The social psychology of false confessions: Compliance, internalization and confabulation. *Psychological Science*, 7, 3, 125–128.

Katerndahl, D.A. and Realini, J.P. (1993). Lifetime prevalence rates of panic states. *American Journal of Psychiatry*, 150, 246–249.

Katz, D. (1935). *The World of Colour*. London: Kegan Paul, Trench, Trubner.

Kay, P. (1975). Synchronic variability and diachronic changes in basic color terms. *Language in Society*, 4, 257–270.

Kay, P. and Kempton, W. (1984). What is the Sapir–Whorf hypothesis? *American Anthropologist*, 86, 1, 65–79.

Kay, P., Berlin, B. and Merrifield, W. (1991). Biocultural implications of systems of color naming. *Journal of Linguistic Anthropology*, 1, 1, 12–25.

Kay, P., Berlin, B., Maffi, L. and Merrifield, W. (1997). Color naming across languages. In C.L. Hardin and L. Maffi (eds), *Color Categories in Thought and Language*. New York: Cambridge University Press.

Kazdin, A.E. (1994). *Behavior Modification in Applied Settings*. Pacific Grove, CA: Brooks/Cole.

Keane, M.M., Gabrieli, J.D.E., Mapstone, H.C., Johnson, K.A. and Corkin, S. (1995). Double dissociation of memory capacities after bilateral occipital-lobe or medial tempotal-lobe lesions. *Brain*, 118, 1129–1148.

Keefe, R.S.E., Roitman, S.E.C., Harvey, P.D. (1995). A pen-and-paper human analogue of a monkey prefrontal cortex activation task: spatial working memory in patients with schizophenia. *Schizophenia Research*, 17, 25–33.

Keller, S.E., Weiss, J.M., Schleifer, S.J., Miller, N.E. and Stein, M. (1983). Stress-induced suppression of immunity in adrenalectomized rats. *Science*, 221, 1301–1304.

Kelley, H.H. (1967). Attribution theory in social psychology. In D. Levine (ed.), *Nebraska Symposium on Motivation*, Vol. 15. Lincoln: University of Nebraska Press.

Kelley, H.H. and Michela, J.L. (1980). Attribution theory and research. *Annual Review of Psychology*, 31, 457–501.

Kelly, G.A. (1955). *The Psychology of Personal Constructs*. New York: W.W. Norton.

Kelly, J.A. and Kalichman, S.C. (1998). Reinforcement value of unsafe sex as a predictor of condom use and continued HIV/AIDS risk behaviour among gay and bisexual men. *Health Psychology*, 17, 4, 328–335.

Kelly, J.A., St Lawrence, J., Brasfield, T., Lemke, A., Amidei, T., Roffman, R., Hood, H., Smith, J., Kilgore, H. and McNeill, C. (1990). Psychological factors that predict AIDS high-risk versus AIDS precautionary behaviour. *Journal of Consulting and Clinical Psychology*, 58, 117–120.

Kelly, J.A., Otto-Salaj, L.L., Sikkema, K.J., Pinkerton, S.D. and Bloom, F.R. (1998). Implications of HIV treatment advances for behavioural research on AIDS: Protease inhibitors and new challenges in HIV secondary prevention. *Health Psychology*, 17, 4, 310–319.

Kemper, S. (1992). Language and aging. In F.I.M. Craik and T. Salthouse (eds), *The Handbook of Aging and Cognition*. Hillsdale, NJ: Lawrence Erlbaum Associates.

Kerns, K.A. and Barth, J.M. (1995). Attachment and play: Convergence across components of parent–child relationships and their relations to peer competence. *Journal of Social and Personal Relationships*, 12, 243–260.

Kerr, J.H. and van den Wollenberg, A.E. High and low intensity exercise and psychological mood states. *Psychology and Health*, 12, 603–618.

Kertesz, A. (1981). Anatomy of jargon. In J. Brown (ed.), *Jargonaphasia*. New York: Academic Press.

Kessel, R.G. and Kardon, R.H. (1979). *Tissues and Organs: A text-atlas of scanning electron microscopy*. San Francisco: W.H. Freeman.

Kessler, R.C., McGonagle, K.A., Zhao, S., Nelson, C., Hughes, M., Eshleman, S., Wittchen, H. and Kendler, K. (1994). Lifetime and 12-month prevalence of DSM-III-R psychiatric disorders in the United States. *Archives of General Psychiatry*, 51, 8–19.

Kety, S.S., Rosenthal, D., Wender, P.H. and Schulsinger, F. (1968).The types and prevalence of mental illness in the biological and adoptive families of adopted schizophrenics. In D. Rosenthal and S.S. Kety (eds), *The Transmission of Schizophrenia*. Elmsford, NY: Pergamon Press.

Keyes, D. (1981). *The Minds of Billy Milligan*. New York: Bantam.

Khachaturian, Z.S. and Blass, J.P. (1992). *Alzheimer's Disease: New treatment strategies*. New York: Dekker.

Kiang, N. Y-S. (1965). *Discharge Patterns of Single Nerve Fibers in the Cat's Auditory Nerve*. Cambridge, MA: MIT Press.

Kiecolt-Glaser, J.K., Malarkey, W.B., Chee, M., Newton, T., Caccioppo, J.T., Mao, H-Y. and Glaser, R. (1993). Negative behaviour during marital conflict is associated with immunological down-regulation. *Psychosomatic Medicine*, 55, 395–409.

Kiecolt-Glaser, J.K., Marucha, P.T., Malarkey, W.B., Mercado, A.M. and Glaser, R. (1995). Slowing of wound healing by psychological stress. *Lancet*, 346, 1194–1196.

Kiger, D.M. (1989). Effects of music information load on a reading-comprehension task. *Perceptual and Motor Skills*, 69, 531–534.

Kim, K.H.S., Relkin, N.R., Lee, K-M. and Hirsch, J. (1997). Distinct cortical areas associated with native and second languages. *Nature*, 388, 171–174.

Kim, S-M., Asche, J., Hendrich, K., Ellermann, J.M., Merkle, H., Ugurbil, K. and Georgopoulos, A.P. (1993). Functional magnetic resonance imaging of motor cortex: Hemispheric asymmetry and handedness. *Science*, 261, 615–617.

Kimura, D. (1987). Are men's and women's brains really different? *Canadian Psychology*, 28, 133–147.

Kingma, A., Mooji, J.J., Metzemaekers, J.D. and Leeuw, J.A. (1994). Transient mutism and speech disorders after posterior fossa surgery in children with brain tumours. *Acta Neurochir (Wien)*, 131, 74–79.

Kinomura, S., Kawashima, R., Yamada, K., Ono, S., Itoh, M., Yoshioka, S. *et al.* (1994). Functional anatomy of taste perception in the human brain studied with positron emission tomography. *Brain Research*, 659, 263–266.

Kinsey, A., Pomeroy, W.B. and Martin, C.E. (1948). *Sexual Behavior in the Human Male*. Philadelphia: Saunders.

Kinsey, A., Pomeroy, W.B., Martin, C.E. and Gebhard, P.H. (1953). *Sexual Behavior in the Human Female*. Philadelphia: Saunders.

Kirk-Smith, M. and Booth, D.A. (1977). Effects of androstenol as sexual and other social attitudes. In Z. le Magnen and P. Macleod (eds), *Olfaction and taste*. Vol. 6. London: IRL Press.

Kirk-Smith, M. and Booth, D.A. (1980). Effects of androstenone on choice of location in others' presence. In H. Van Der Starre (ed.), *Olfaction and Taste*, Vol. 2. London: IRL Press.

Kirk-Smith, M., Booth, D.A., Carroll, D. and Davies, P. (1978). Human social attitudes affected by androstenol. *Research and Communication in Psychology, Psychiatry and Behaviour*, 3, 379–384.

Kisilevsky, B.S. (1995). The influence of stimulus and subject variables on human fetal responses to sound and vibration. In J-P. Lecanuet, W.P. Fifer, N.A. Krasnegor and W.P. Smotherman (eds), *Fetal Development: A psychobiological perspective*. Hillsdale, NJ: Lawrence Erlbaum Associates.

Kisilevsky, B.S. and Low, J.A. (1998). Human fetal behavior: 100 years of study. *Developmental Review*, 18, 1–29.

Kissen, D.M. (1963). Personality characteristics in males conducive to lung cancer. *British Journal of Medical Psychology*, 36, 27–36.

Kitayama, S. and Markus, H.R. (1992). Construal of self as cultural frame: Implications for internalizing psychology. Paper presented to Symposium on Internalization and Higher Education, Ann Arbor, MI, May 1992.

Kleiner, K. (1993). Specific versus non-specific face of cognition device? In B. de Boysson–Bardies, S-de Schonen, P. Jusczyk, P. McNeilage and J. Morton (eds), *Developmental Neuro Cognition: Speech and face processing in the first year of life*. New York: Academic Press.

Kleitman, N. (1961). The nature of dreaming. In G.E.W. Wolstenholme and M. O'Connor (eds), *The Nature of Sleep*. London: Churchill.

Kleitman, N. (1982). Basic rest–activity cycle – 22 years later. *Sleep*, 4, 311–317.

Klerman, G.L. and Weissman, M.M. (1986). The interpersonal approach to understanding depression. In T. Millon and G. L. Klerman (eds), *Contemporary Directions in Psychopathology: Toward the DSM-IV*. New York: Guilford Press.

Klimesch, W, Doppelmayr, M., Schimke, H. and Ripper, B. (1997). Theta synchronization and alpha desynchronization in a memory task. *Psychophysiology*, 34, 169–176.

Klin, A., Volkmar, F.R. and Sparrow, S.S. (1992). Autistic social dysfunction: Some limitations of the theory of mind hypothesis. *Journal of Child Psychology and Psychiatry*, 33, 861–876.

Kline, P. (1993). *Personality – The psychometric view*. London: Routledge.

Klitzman, S. and Stellman, J.M. (1989). The impact of the physical environment on the psychological well-being of office workers. *Social Science and Medicine*, 29, 733–742.

Klug, W.S. and Cummings, M.R. (1986). *Concepts of Genetics* (2nd edition). Glenview, IL: Scott, Foresman.

Kluft, R.P. (1984). An introduction to multiple personality disorder. *Psychiatric Annals*, 7, 9–29.

Knight, B. and Johnston, A. (1997). The role of movement in face recognition. *Visual Cognition*, 4, 265–273.

Knight, G.P., Fabes, R.A. and Higgins, D.A. (1996). Concerns about drawing causal inferences from meta-analyses: An example in the study of gender differences in aggression. *Psychological Bulletin*, 119, 3, 410–421.

Knowlton, B.J., Ramus, S. and Squire, L.R. (1991). Normal acquisition of an artificial grammar by amnesic patients. *Society for Neuroscience Abstracts*, 17, 4.

Knox, J.V., Morgan, A.H. and Hilgard, E.R. (1974). Pain and suffering in ischemia: The paradox of hypnotically suggested anesthesia as contradicted by reports from the 'hidden observer'. *Archives of General Psychiatry*, 30, 840–847.

Knox, R.E. and Inkster, J.A. (1968). Postdecision dissonance at post time. *Journal of Personality and Social Psychology*, 8, 310–323.

Knutsson, A. and Goine, H. (1998). Occupation and unemployment rates by predictors of long term sickness absence in two Swedish counties. *Social Science and Medicine*, 47, 1, 25–31.

Kobasa, S.C. (1979). Stress life events, personality, and health: An inquiry into hardiness. *Journal of Personality and Social Psychology*, 42, 168–177.

Koch, J.L.A. (1889). *Leitfaden der Psychiatrie* (2nd edition). Ravensburg, Austria: Dorn.

Köhler, W. (1927). *The Mentality of Apes* (2nd edition). New York: Liveright. Reprinted 1973.

Konner, M. J. (1972). Aspects of the developmental ethology of a foraging people. In N. Blurton Jones (ed.), *Ethological Studies of Child Behaviour*. Cambridge: Cambridge University Press.

Kosslyn, S.M. (1973). Scanning visual images: Some structural implications. *Perception and Psychophysics*, 14, 90–94.

Kosson, D.S., Smith, S.S. and Newman, J.P. (1990). Evaluating the construct validity of psychopathy on Black and White male inmates: Three preliminary studies. *Journal of Abnormal Psychology*, 99, 250–259.

Kovacs, M. and Beck, A.T. (1978). Maladaptive cognitive structures in depression. *American Journal of Psychiatry*, 135, 525–533.

Kozlowski, L. T. and Cutting, J. E. (1977). Recognizing the sex of a walker from a dynamic point-light display. *Perception and Psychophysics*, 21, 575–580.

Krack, P., Pollak, P., Limousin, P., Hoffmann, D., Xie, J., Benazzouz, A. and Benabid, A.L. (1998). Subthalamic nucleus or internal pallidal stimulation in young onset Parkinson's disease. *Brain*, 121, 451–457.

Kraehenbuhl, J-P. and Neutra, M.R. (1992). Molecular and cellular basis of immune protection of mucosal surfaces. *Physiological Review*, 72, 853–879.

Kraeplin, E. (1921). *Manic–Depressive Insanity and Paranoia.* London: Churchill Livingstone.

Kral, J.G. (1989). Surgical treatment of obesity. *Medical Clinics of North America,* 73, 251–264.

Kramer, F.M., Jeffery, R.W., Forster, J.L. and Snell, M.K. (1989). Long-term follow-up of behavioral treatment for obesity: Patterns of weight regain among men and women. *International Journal of Obesity,* 13, 123–136.

Kreuger, J. and Clement, R.W. (1997). Estimates of social consensus by majorities and minorities: The case for social projection. *Personality and Social Psychology Review,* 1, 299–313.

Krueger, J., Ham, J.J. and Linford, K.M. (1996). Perceptions of behavioral consistency: Are people aware of the actor–observer effect? *Psychological Science,* 7, 259–264.

Krueger, T.H. (1976). *Visual Imagery in Problem Solving and Scientific Creativity.* Derby, CT: Seal Press.

Kris, E. (1952). *Psychoanalytic Explorations in Art.* New York: International Universities Press.

Krull, D. S. and Erickson, D. J. (1995). Inferential hopscotch: How people draw social inferences from behavior. *Current Directions in Psychological Science,* 4, 35–38.

Kubitz, K. A. and Landers, D. M. (1993). The effects of aerobic exercise on cardiovascular responses to mental stress: An examination of underlying mechanisms. *Journal of Sport and Exercise Physiology,* 15, 326–337.

Kübler-Ross, E. (1969). *On Death and Dying.* New York: Macmillan.

Kübler-Ross, E. (1981). *Living with Death and Dying.* New York: Macmillan.

Kuhl, P. K., Williams, K. A., Lacerda, F., Stevens, K. N. and Lindblom, B. (1992). Linguistic experience alters phonetic perception in infants by 6 months of age. *Science,* 255, 606–608.

Kulka, R.A. and Kessler, J.R. (1978). Is justice really blind? The effect of litigant physical attractiveness on judicial judgment. *Journal of Applied Social Psychology,* 4, 336–381.

Kunst-Wilson, W.R. and Zajonc, R.B. (1980). Affective discrimination of stimuli that cannot be recognized. *Science,* 207, 557–558.

LaFrance, M. and Woodzicka, J.A. (1998). No laughing matter: Women's verbal and nonverbal reactions to sexist humor. In J.K. Swim and C. Stangor (eds), *Prejudice: The target's perspective.* San Diego, CA: Academic Press, pp. 61–80.

Laird, J.D. (1974). Self-attribution of emotion: The effects of expressive behaviour on the quality of emotional experience. *Journal of Personality and Social Psychology,* 29, 475–486.

Lakoff, G. and Turner, M. (1989). *More Than Cool Reason: The power of poetic metaphor.* Chicago: University of Chicago Press.

Lambert, M.J. and Bergin, A.E. (1994). The effectiveness of psychotherapy. In A.E. Bergin and S.L. Garfield (eds), *Handbook of Psychotherapy and Behaviour Change.* New York: Wiley.

Lambert, W.E. (1977). The effect of bilingualism on the individual: Cognitive and sociocultural consequences. In P.A. Hornby (ed.), *Bilingualism: Psychological, social and educational implications.* New York: Academic Press.

Lang, P.J. (1979). A bio-informational theory of emotional imagery. *Psychophysiology,* 16, 495–512.

Lang, P.J. (1984). Cognition in emotion: Concept and action. In C.E. Izard, J. Kagan and R.B. Zajonc (eds), *Emotions, Cognition and Behaviour.* New York: Cambridge University Press.

Lange, C.G. (1887). *Über Gemüthsbewegungen.* Leipzig: T. Thomas.

Langer, E.J. and Abelson, R.P. (1974). A patient by any other name … Clinician group difference in labeling bias. *Journal of Consulting and Clinical Psychology,* 42, 4–9.

Langer, E.J., Bashner, R.S. and Chanowitz, B. (1985). Decreasing prejudice by increasing discrimination. *Journal of Personality and Social Psychology,* 49, 113–120.

Lankenau, H., Swigar, M.E., Bhimani, S., Luchins, S. and Quinlon, D.M. (1985). Cranial CT scans in eating disorder patients and controls. *Comprehensive Psychiatry,* 26, 136–147.

Lanzetta, J.T., Cartwright-Smith, J. and Kleck, R.E. (1976). Effects of nonverbal dissimulation on emotional experience and autonomic arousal. *Journal of Personality and Social Psychology,* 33, 354–370.

LaPiere, R.T. (1934). Attitudes and actions. *Social Forces,* 13, 230–237.

LaRue, A. (1992). *Aging and Neuropsychological Assessment.* New York: Plenum.

Last, C.G., Barlow, D.H. and O'Brien, G.T. (1984). Precipitants of agoraphobia: Role of stressful life events. *Psychological Reports,* 54, 173–180.

Latané, B. and Darley, J.M. (1970). *The Unresponsive Bystander: Why doesn't he help?* New York: Appleton-Century-Crofts.

Lauer, R.H. (1989). *Social Problems and the Quality of Life.* Dubuque, IA: W.C. Brown.

Lavie, P., Pratt, H., Scharf, B., Peled, R. and Brown, J. (1984). Localized pontine lesion: Nearly total absence of REM sleep. *Neurology,* 34, 1118–1120.

Law, M.R. and Tang, J.L. (1995). An analysis of the effectiveness of intervention intended to help people stop smoking. *Archives of Internal Medicine,* 155, 1933–1941.

Lawrie, S.M. and Abukmeil, S.S. (1998). Brain abnormality in schizophrenia. *British Journal of Psychiatry,* 172, 110–120.

Lazarus, A.A. (1971). *Behavior Therapy and Beyond.* New York: McGraw-Hill.

Lazarus, R.S. (1966). *Psychological Stress and the Coping Process.* New York: McGraw-Hill.

Lazarus, R.S. (1984). Thoughts on the relations between emotion and cognition. In K.R. Scherer and P. Ekman (eds), *Approaches to Emotion.* Hillsdale, NJ: Lawrence Erlbaum Associates.

Lazarus, R.S. (1991). *Emotion and Adaptation.* New York: Oxford University Press.

Lazarus, R. S. and Folkman, S. (1984). *Stress, Appraisal, and Coping.* New York: Springer-Verlag.

Leahey, T.H. (1997). *A History of Psychology* (5th edition). Englewood Cliffs, NJ: Prentice Hall.

Lecanuet, J-P., Granier-Deferre, C. and Busnel, M-C. (1989). Differential fetal auditory reactiveness as a function of stimulus characteristics and state. *Seminars in Perinatology,* 13, 421–429.

Lecanuet, J-P., Granier-Deferre, C., Jacquet, A-Y. and Busnel, M-C. (1992). Decelerative cardiac responsiveness to acoustical stimulation in the near term fetus. *Quarterly Journal of Experimental Psychology,* 44, 279–303.

LeCompte, D.C., Neely, C.B. and Wilson, J.R. (1997). Irrelevant speech and irrelevant tones. *Journal of Experimental Psychology: Learning, Memory and Cognition,* 23, 472–483.

LeDoux, J.E. (1992). Brain mechanisms of emotion and emotional learning. *Current Opinion in Neurobiology,* 2, 191–197.

LeDoux, J.E. (1995a). Emotion: Clues from the brain. *Annual Review of Psychology,* 46, 209–235.

LeDoux, J.E. (1995b). In search of an emotional system in the brain: Leaping from fear to emotion and consciousness. In M.S. Gazzaniga (ed.), *The Cognitive Neurosciences.* Cambridge, MA: MIT Press.

LeDoux, J. (1996). *The Emotional Brain.* Englewood Cliffs, NJ: Simon & Schuster.

Lee, S. (1995). Self-starvation in context: Towards a culturally sensitive understanding of anorexia nervosa. *Social Science and Medicine,* 41, 25–36.

Lee, Y.T. (1993). Ingroup preference and homogeneity among African American and Chinese American students. *Journal of Social Psychology,* 133, 225–235.

Lefcourt, H.M. and Martin, R.A. (1986). *Humor and Life Stress.* New York: Springer-Verlag.

Lefcourt, H.M., Davidson, K., Prkachin, K.M. and Mills, D.E. (1997). Humor as a stress moderator in the prediction of blood pressure obtained during five stressful tasks. *Journal of Research in Personality,* 31, 523–542.

Lefkowitz, M.M., Eron, L.D., Walder, L.O. and Huesmann, L.R. (1977). *Growing Up to Be Violent: A longitudinal study of the development of aggression.* New York: Pergamon Press.

Lefrancois, G.R. (1983). *Of Children, An Introduction to Child Development* (4th edition). Belmont, Calif.: Wadsworth.

Leger, D.W. (1991). *Biological Foundations of Behavior*. New York: HarperCollins.

Leibovici, D., Ritchie, K., Ledesert, B. *et al.* (1996). Does education level determine the course of cognitive decline? *Age and Ageing*, 25, 392–397.

Lennenberg, E. (1967). *Biological Foundations of Language*. New York: Wiley.

Lerner, M.J. (1977). The justice motive: Some hypotheses as to its origins and forms. *Journal of Personality*, 45, 1–52.

LeShan, L.L. and Worthington, R.E. (1956). Personality as a factor in the pathogenesis of cancer: A review of literature. *British Journal of Medical Psychology*, 29, 49–56.

Leslie, A.M. (1987). Pretense and representation: The origins of 'theory of mind'. *Psychological Review*, 94, 412–426.

LeVay, S. (1991). A difference in hypothalamic structure between heterosexual and homosexual men. *Science*, 253, 1034–1037.

Levelt, W. (1989). *Speaking: From intention to articulation*. Cambridge, MA: MIT Press.

Levenstein, S. (1998). Stress and peptic ulcer: Life beyond heliobacter. *British Medical Journal*, 316, 538–541.

Leventhal, H. and Scherer, K. (1987). The relationship of emotion to cognition: A functional approach to a semantic controversy. *Cognition and Emotion*, 1, 3–28.

Leventhal, H., Watts, J.C. and Pagano, R. (1967). Effects of fear and instructions on how to cope with danger. *Journal of Personality and Social Psychology*, 6, 313–321.

Levinson, D.J., Darrow, C.N., Klein, E.B., Levinson, M.H. and McKee, B. (1978). *The Seasons of a Man's Life*. New York: Alfred A. Knopf.

Lewin, R. (1984). *Human Evolution: An illustrated introduction*. Cambridge, MA: Blackwell Scientific.

Lewinsohn, P.M., Mischel, W., Chaplin, W. and Barton, R. (1980). Social competence and depression: The role of illusory self-perceptions. *Journal of Abnormal Psychology*, 89, 194–202.

Lewis, S.W. (1990). Computerised tomography in schizophrenia: 15 years on. *British Journal of Psychiatry*, 157 (suppl. 9), 16–24.

Lewis, V. and Boucher, J. (1988). Spontaneous, instructed and elicited play in relatively able autistic children. *British Journal of Developmental Psychology*, 6, 315–324.

Lewith, G.T. and Aldridge, D.A. (1991). *Complementary Medicine and the European Community*. Saffron Walden: C.W. Daniel.

Leyens, J-P., Yzerbyt, V.Y. and Schadron, G. (1992). Stereotypes and social judgeability. *European Review of Social Psychology*, 3, 91–120.

Leyens, J-P., Yzerbyt, V.Y. and Schadron, G. (1994). *Stereotypes and Social Cognition*. London: Sage.

Lezak, M.D. (1995). *Neuropsychological assessment*. New York: Oxford University Press.

Liberman, A.M., Cooper, F.S., Shankweiler, D.P. and Studdert-Kennedy, M. (1967). Perception of the speech code. *Psychological Review*, 74, 431–461.

Lickey, M.E. and Gordon, B. (1983). *Drugs for Mental Illness*. New York: Freeman.

Lidz, T., Fleck, S. and Cornelison, A.R. (1965). *Schizophrenia and the Family*. New York: International Universities Press.

Lieberman, I.Y., Mann, V.A., Shankweiler, D. and Werfelman, M. (1982). Children's memory for recurring linguistic and non-linguistic material in relation to reading ability. *Cortex*, 18, 367–375.

Liggett, J. (1974). *The Human Face*. London: Constable.

Light, K.A. and Girdler, S.S. (1993). Cardiovascular health and women. In C.A Niven and D. Carroll (eds), *The Health Psychology of Women*. Chur, Switzerland: Harwood Press.

Lindsay, D.S. and Read, J.D. (1994). Psychotherapy and memories of childhood sexual abuse: A cognitive perspective. *Applied Cognitive Psychology*, 8, 281–338.

Lindsley, O.R. (1956). Operant conditioning methods applied to research in chronic schizophrenia. *Psychiatric Research Reports*, 24, 289–291.

Lindsay, G.E. and Powell, G.H. (1994). *The Handbook of Adult Clinical Psychology*. London: Routledge.

Linn, M.C. and Petersen, A.C. (1985). Emergence and characterization of sex differences in spatial ability: A meta-analysis. *Child Development*, 56, 1479–1498.

Linsky, A.S., Bachman, R. and Straus, M.A. (1995). *Stress, Culture, and Aggression*. New Haven, CT: Yale University Press.

Linville, P.W. (1982). The complexity–extremity effect and age-based stereotyping. *Journal of Personality and Social Psychology*, 42, 183–211.

Linville, P.W., Fischer, G.W. and Salovey, P. (1989). Perceived distributions of the characteristics of in-group and out-group members: Empirical evidence and a computer simulation. *Journal of Personality and Social Psychology*, 57, 165–188.

Lipman, M., Sharp, A.M. and Oscanyan, F. (1980). *Philosophy in the Classroom*. Philadelphia: Temple University Press.

Lipsitz, A., Brake, G., Vincent, E. J. and Winters, M. (1993). Another round for the brewers: Television ads and children's alcohol expectancies. *Journal of Applied Social Psychology*, 23, 439–450.

Lisker, L. and Abramson, A. (1970). The voicing dimension: Some experiments in comparative phonetics. In *Proceedings of Sixth International Congress of Phonetic Sciences, Prague, 1967*. Prague: Academia.

Lloyd-Bostock, S.M.A. (1988). *Law in Practice: Applications of psychology to legal decision making and legal skills*. Leicester: BPS Books.

Locke, J.L. (1993). *The Child's Path to Spoken Language*. Cambridge, MA: Harvard University Press.

Loeber, R. and Dishion, T.J. (1983). Early predictors of male delinquency: A review. *Psychological Bulletin*, 94, 68–99.

Loehlin, J.C. (1992). *Genes and Environment in Personality Development*. London: Sage Publications.

Loehlin, J.C. and Nichols, R.C. (1976). *Heredity, Environment, and Personality*. Austin: University of Texas Press.

Loehlin, J.C., Lindzey, G. and Spuhler, J.N. (1975). *Race Differences in Intelligence*. San Fransisco: W.H. Freeman.

Loehlin, J.C., McCrae, R.R., Costa, P.T. and John, O.P. (1998). Heritabilities of common and measure-specific components of the Big Five personality factors. *Journal of Research in Personality*, 32, 431–453.

Loewen, L.J. and Sudefeld, P. (1992). Cognitive and arousal effects of masking office noise. *Environment and Behaviour*, 24, 381–395.

Loftus, E.F. (1986). Ten years in the life of an expert witness. *Law and Human Behaviour*, 10, 241–263.

Loftus, E.F. (1997). Creating false memories. *Scientific American*, September, 50–55.

Loftus, E.F., Miller, D.G. and Burns, H.J. (1978). Semantic integration of verbal information into a visual memory. *Journal of Experimental Psychology: Human Learning and Memory*, 4, 19–31.

Loftus, E.F. and Palmer, J. C. (1974). Reconstruction of automobile destruction: An example of the interaction between language and memory. *Journal of Verbal Learning and Verbal Behavior*, 13, 585–589.

Loftus, E. F. and Zanni, G. (1975). Eyewitness testimony: The influence of the wording of a question. *Bulletin of the Psychonomic Society*, 5, 86–88.

Logie, R.H. (1995). *Visuo-spatial Working Memory*. Hove, UK: The Psychology Press.

Logie, R.H. (1996). The seven ages of working memory. In J.T.E. Richardson, R.W. Engle, L. Hasher, R.H. Logie, E.R. Stoltzfus, and R.T. Zacks (eds), *Working Memory and Human Cognition*. Oxford: Oxford University Press.

Logie, R.H., Zucco, G. and Baddeley, A.D. (1990). Interference with short-term memory. *Acta Psychologia*, 75, 55–74.

LoPiccolo, J. and Friedman, J.M. (1985). Sex therapy: An integrated model. In S.J. Lynn and J.P. Garskee (eds), *Contemporary Psychotherapies: Models and methods*. New York: Merrill.

Lorenz, K. (1966). *On Aggression*. New York: Harcourt Brace Jovanovich.

Lorig, T.S. (1989). Human EEG and odor response. *Progress in Neurobiology*, 33, 387–398.

Lovell, D.M., Williams, J.M.G. and Hill, A.B. (1997). Selective processing of shape-related words in women with eating disorders, and those who have recovered. *British Journal of Clinical Psychology*, 36.

Lowe, C. and Rabbitt, P. (1997). Cognitive models of ageing and frontal lobe deficits. In P. Rabbitt (ed.), *Methodology of Frontal and Executive Function*. Hove, UK: The Psychology Press.

Lowe, C.F. (1979). Determinants of human operant behavior. In M.D. Zeiler and P. Harzem (eds), *Advances in the Analysis of Behavior: Vol. 1: Reinforcement and the Organization of Behaviour*. Chichester: Wiley.

Lowe, C.F., Beasty, A. and Bentall, R.P. (1983). The role of verbal behavior in human learning: Infant performance on fixed-interval schedules. *Journal of the Experimental Analysis of Behavior*, 39, 157–164.

Lubow, R.E. (1989). *Latent Inhibition and Conditioned Attention Theory*. Cambridge: Cambridge University Press.

Luck, S., Chelazzi, L., Hillyard, S. and Desimone, R. (1993). Effects of spatial attention on responses of V4 neurons in the macaque. *Society for Neuroscience Abstracts*, 69, 27.

Ludwig, A.M. (1994). Mental illness and creative activity in female writers. *American Journal of Psychiatry*, 151, 1650–1656.

Lumeng, L., Murphy, J. M., McBride, W. J. and Li, T. (1995). Genetic influences on alcohol preferences in animals. In H. Begleiter and B. Kissin (eds), *The Genetics of Alcoholism*. New York: Oxford University Press.

Lundy, A.C. (1985). The reliability of the Thematic Apperception Test. *Journal of Personality Assessment*, 49, 141–145.

Lundy, A.C. (1988). Instructional set and thematic apperception test validity. *Journal of Personality Assessment*, 52, 309–320.

Lupfer, M.B., Clark, L.F. and Hutcherson, H.W. (1990). Impact of context on spontaneous trait and situational attributions. *Journal of Personality and Social Psychology*, 58, 239–249.

Luria, A.R. (1968) *The Mind of the Mnemonist*. London: Penguin.

Lutsky, N. (1995). When is 'obedience' obedience? Conceptual and historical commentary. *Journal of Social Issues*, 51, 55–66.

Lynam, D.R. (1996). Early identification of chronic offenders: Who is the fledgling psychopath? *Psychological Bulletin*, 120, 2, 209–234.

Lynd-Stevenson, R.M. (1996). A test of the hopelessness theory of depression in unemployed young adults. *British Journal of Clinical Psychology*, 35, 117–132.

Lynd-Stevenson, R.M. (1997). Generalized and event-specific hopelessness: Salvaging the mediation hypothesis of the hopelessness theory. *British Journal of Clinical Psychology*, 36, 73–83.

Lynn, R. (1991). Race differences in intelligence: A global perspective. *Mankind Quarterly*, 31, 255–296.

Lynn, R. (1993). Oriental Americans: Their IQ, educational attainment and socioeconomic status. *Personality and Individual Differences*, 15, 237–242.

Lynn, R. (1996). Racial and ethnic differences in intelligence in the United States on the Differential Ability Scale. *Personality and Individual Differences*, 20, 271–273.

Lynn, R. (1998). New data on black infant precocity. *Personality and Individual Differences*, 25, 801–804.

Lynn, R. and Harland, E.P. (1998). A positive effect of iron supplementation on the IQS of iron deficient children. *Personality and Individual Differences*, 24, 6, 883–885.

Lynn, S.J. and Rhue, J.W. (1991). *Theories of Hypnosis: Current models and perspectives*. New York: Guilford.

Lynskey, M.T., Fergusson, D.M. and Horwood, L.J. (1998). The origins of the correlations between tobacco, alcohol, and cannabis use during adolescence. *Journal of Child Psychology and Psychiatry*, 39, 7, 995–1005.

Lyons-Ruth, K., Connell, D., Grunebaum, H. and Botein, S. (1990). Infants at social risk: Maternal depression and family support services as mediators of infant development and security of attachment. *Child Development*, 61, 85–98.

Lytton, H. and Romney, D.M. (1991). Parents' sex-related differential socialization of boys and girls: A meta-analysis. *Psychological Bulletin*, 109, 267–296.

Maccoby, E.E. (1980). *Social Development: Psychological growth and the parent–child relationship*. New York: Harcourt Brace Jovanovich.

Mace, F.C., Lalli, J.S., Shea, M.C., Lalli, E.P., West, B.J., Roberts, M. and Nevin, J.A. (1990). The momentum of behavior in a natural setting. *Journal of the Experimental Analysis of Behavior*, 54, 163–172.

Machon, R.A., Mednick, S.A. and Schulsinger, F. (1983). The interaction of seasonality, place of birth, genetic risk and subsequent schizophrenia in a high risk sample. *British Journal of Psychiatry*, 143, 383–388.

MacKay, D.G., Stewart, R. and Burke, D.M. (1998). HM revisited: relations between language comprehension, memory and the hippocampal system. *Journal of Cognitive Neuroscience*, 10, 3, 377–394.

MacLeod, C.M. (1992). The Stroop task: The 'gold standard' of attentional measures. *Journal of Experimental Psychology: General*, 38, 421–439.

MacLeod, C.M., Matthews, A. and Tata, P. (1986). Attentional biases in emotional disorders. *Journal of Abnormal Psychology*, 95, 15–20.

Macrae, C.N., Bodenhausen, G.V., Milne, A.B. and Jetten, J. (1994). Out of mind but back in sight: Stereotypes on the rebound. *Journal of Personality and Social Psychology*, 67, 808–817.

Maffei, M., Halaas, J., Ravussin, E., Pratley, R. E., Lee, G. H., Zhang, Y., Fei, H., Kim, S., Lallone, R. and Ranganathan, S. (1995). Leptin levels in human and rodent: Measurement of plasma leptin and ob RNA in obese and weight-reduced subjects. *Nature Medicine*, 11, 1155–1161.

Magai, C. and McFadden, S. H. (1995). *The Role of Emotions in Social and Personality Development*. New York: Plenum.

Magnavita, N., Narda, R., Sani, L., Carbone, A., DeLorenzo, G. and Sacco, A. (1997). Type A behaviour pattern and traffic accidents. *British Journal of Medical Psychology*, 70, 103–107.

Magnus, H. (1880). Untersuchungen über den Farbensinn der Naturvölker. *Physiologische Abhandlungen*, Ser. 2, no. 7.

Magnusson, D., Stattin, H. and Allen, V.L. (1986). Differential maturation among girls and its relevance to social adjustment: A longitudinal perspective. In D.L. Featherman and R.M. Learner (eds), *Lifespan Development and Behaviour*. New York: Academic Press.

Maguire, E.A., Frackowiak, R.S.J. and Frith, C.D. (1997). Recalling routes around London: Activation of the right hippocampus in taxi drivers. *Journal of Neuroscience*, 17, 7103.

Maguire, E.A., Burgess, N., Donnett, J.G., Frackowiak, R.S.J., Frith, C.D. and O'Keefe, J. (1998). Knowing where and getting there: A human navigation network. *Science*, 280, 921–924.

Maier, S.F. and Seligman, M.E. (1976). Learned helplessness: Theory and evidence. *Journal of Experimental Psychology (General)*, 105, 3–46.

Main, M. and Solomon, J. (1990). Procedures for identifying infants as disorganised/disoriented during the Ainsworth Strange Situation. In M.T. Greenberg, D. Cichetti and E.M. Cummings (eds), *Attachment in the Preschool Years*. Chicago: University of Chicago Press.

Maio, G.R., Olson, J.M. and Bush, J.E. (1997). Telling jokes that disparage social groups: Effects on the joke teller's stereotypes. *Journal of Applied Social Psychology*, 27, 1986–2000.

Mandler, J.M. and McDonough, L. (1995). Long-term recall of sequences in infancy. *Journal of Experimental Child Psychology*, 59, 457–474.

Marangolo, P., DeRenzi, E., Di Pace, E., Ciurli, P. and Castriota-Skandenberg, A. (1998). Let not thy left hand know what thy right hand knoweth. *Brain*, 121, 1459–1467.

Marcel, A.J. (1983). Conscious and unconscious perception: Experiments on visual masking and word recognition. *Cognitive Psychology*, 15, 197–237.

Markman, E.M. (1989). *Categorization and Naming in Children*. Cambridge, MA: MIT Press.

Marks, G. and Miller, N. (1987). Ten years of research on the false-consensus effect: An empirical and theoretical review. *Psychological Bulletin*, 102, 72–90.

Marks, G.A., Shaffery, J.P., Oksenberg, A., Speciale, S.G. and Roffward, H.P. (1995). A functional role for REM sleep in brain maturation. *Behavioural Brain Research*, 69, 1–11.

Markson, L. and Bloom, P. (1997). Evidence against a dedicated system for word learning in children. *Nature*, 385, 813–815.

Markus, H. (1978). The effect of mere presence on social facilitation: An unobtrusive test. *Journal of Experimental Social Psychology*, 14, 389–397.

Markus, H.R. and Kitayama, S. (1991). Culture and the self: Implications for cognition, emotion, and motivation. *Psychological Review*, 98, 224–253.

Markus, H.R. and Nurius, P. (1986). Possible selves. *American Psychologist*, 41, 954–969.

Marlatt, G.A., Baer, J.S., Donovan, D.M. and Kivlahan, D.R. (1986). Addictive behaviors: Etiology and treatment. *Annual Review of Psychology*, 39, 223–252.

Marler, P. (1961). The filtering of external stimuli during instinctive behaviour. In W.H. Thorpe and O.L. Zangwill (eds), *Current Problems in Animal Behaviour*. Cambridge: Cambridge University Press.

Marmot, M.G., Bosma, H., Hemingway, H., Brunner, E. and Stansfeld, S. (1997). Contribution of job control and other risk factors to social variations in coronary heart disease incidence. *Lancet*, 350, 235–239.

Marsh, A. and MaKay, S. (1994). *Poor Smokers*. London: Policy Studies Institute.

Marsh, G., Desberg, P. and Cooper, J. (1977). Developing strategies in reading. *Journal of Reading Behaviour*, 9, 391–394.

Marsh, P., Rosser, E. and Harré, R. (1978). *The Rules of Disorder*. Milton Keynes, UK: Open University Press.

Marshall, J.C., Halligan, P.W., Fink, G.R., Wade, D.T. and Frackowiak, R.S.J. (1997). The functional anatomy of a hysterical paralysis. *Cognition*, 64, 1, B1–B8.

Marshall, W.L., Eccles, A. and Barbaree, H.E. (1991). The treatment of exhibitionists: A focus on sexual deviance versus cognitive and relationship features. *Behaviour Research and Therapy*, 29, 129–136.

Marshark, M., Richman, C.L., Yuille, J.C. and Hunt, R.R. (1987). The role of imagery in memory: on shared and distinctive information. *Psychological Bulletin*, 102, 28–41.

Marteau, T.M., Dundas, R. and Axworthy, D. (1997). Long-term emotional and cognitive impact of genetic testing for carriers of cystic fibrosis: The effect of test result and gender. *Health Psychology*, 16, 51–62.

Martens, R. (1969). Palmar sweating and the presence of an audience. *Journal of Experimental Social Psychology*, 5, 371–374.

Martin, A., Wiggs, C.L., Ungerleider, G. and Haxby, V. (1996). Neural correlates of category-specific knowledge. *Nature*, 379, 649–652.

Martin, G.N. (1996). Olfactory remediation: Current evidence and possible applications. *Social Science and Medicine*, 43, 1, 63–70.

Martin, G.N. (1998a). *Human Neuropsychology*. Hemel Hempstead: Prentice Hall Europe.

Martin, G.N. (1998b). Human electroencephalographic (EEG) response to olfactory stimulation: Two experiments using the aroma of food. *International Journal of Psychophysiology*, 30, 287–302.

Martin, G.N. and Gray, C.D. (1996). The effects of audience laughter on men's and women's responses to humour. *Journal of Social Psychology*, 136, 2, 221–231.

Martin, G.N., Sadler, S.J. and Baluch, B. (1997). Individual group differences in the perception and knowledge of psychological research. *Personality and Individual Differences*, 22, 5, 771–774.

Martin, R.A. and Lefcourt, H.M. (1983). Sense of humor as a moderator of the relation between stressors and moods. *Journal of Personality and Social Psychology*, 45, 1313–1324.

Martindale, C. and Dailey, A. (1996). Creativity, primary process cognition and personality. *Personality and Individual Differences*, 20, 4, 409–414.

Martinsen, E. (1995). Exercise and mental health in clinical populations. In S.J.H. Biddle (ed.), *European Perspectives on Exercise and Sport Psychology*. Champaign, IL: Human Kinetics.

Martinsen, E. and Stephens, T. (1994). Exercise and mental health in clinical and free-living populations. In R.K. Dishman (ed.), *Advances in Exercise Adherence*. Champaign, IL: Human Kinetics.

Masling, J. (1960). The influence of situational and interpersonal variables in projective testing. *Psychological Bulletin*, 57, 65–85.

Maslow, A.H. (1964). *Religions, Values, and Peak-experiences*. New York: Viking Press.

Maslow, A.H. (1970). *Motivation and Personality* (2nd edition). New York: Harper & Row.

Mason, P., Harrison, G., Croudace, T., Glazebrook, C. and Medley, I. (1997). The predictive validity of a diagnosis of schizophrenia. *British Journal of Psychiatry*, 170, 321–327.

Masters, M.S. (1998). The gender difference on the Mental Rotation test is not due to performance factors. *Memory and Cognition*, 26, 3, 444–448.

Masters, M.S. and Sanders, B. (1993). Is the gender difference in mental rotation disappearing? *Behaviour Genetics*, 23, 337–341.

Masters, W.H. and Johnson, V.E. (1970). *Human Sexual Inadequacy*. Boston: Little, Brown.

Matchett, G. and Davey, G.C.L. (1991). A test of a disease-avoidance model of animal phobias. *Behaviour Research and Therapy*, 29, 91–94.

Matlin, M. (1988). *Sensation and Perception* (2nd edition). Boston: Allyn & Bacon.

Matlin, M.W. and Foley, H.J. (1992). *Sensation and Perception* (3rd edition). Boston: Allyn & Bacon.

Mattes, R.D., Arnold, C. and Boraas, M. (1987). Learned food aversions among cancer chemotherapy patients: Incidence, nature and clinical implications. *Cancer*, 60, 2576–2580.

Matthews, A., May, J., Mogg, K. and Eysenck, M.W. (1990). Attentional bias in anxiety: Selective search or defective filtering? *Journal of Abnormal Psychology*, 99, 166–173.

Matthews, A.M., Gedler, M.G. and Johnston, D.W. (1981). *Agoraphobia: Nature and treatment*. New York: Guilford.

Matthews, K.A. and Brunson, B.I. (1979). Allocation of attention and physiological responsivity in the Type A coronary-prone individual. *Perceptual and Motor Skills*, 37, 2081–2090.

Mawson, A.R. (1974). Anorexia nervosa and the regulation of intake: A review. *Psychological Medicine*, 4, 289–308.

Mayer, J. (1955). Regulation of energy intake and the body weight: The glucostatic theory and the lipostatic hypothesis. *Annals of the New York Academy of Science*, 63, 15–43.

Mayfield, C. and Moss, S. (1989). Effect of music tempo on task performance. *Psychological Reports*, 65, 1283–1290.

Maylor, E.A. (1990). Age and prospective memory. *Quarterly Journal of Experimental Psychology*, 42A, 471–493.

Maylor, E.A. (1996). Older people's memory for the past and the future. *The Psychologist*, October, 456–459.

Maynard Smith, J. (1964). Group selection and kin selection. *Nature*, 210, 1145–1147.

Mazmaninan, P.E., Martin, K.O. and Kreutzer, J.S. (1991). Professional development and educational program planning in cognitive rehabilitation. In J.S. Kreutzer and P.H. Wehman (eds), *Cognitive Rehabilitation for Persons with Traumatic Brain Injury*. Baltimore: Brookes.

Mazur, A. and Booth, A. (1998). Testosterone and dominance in men. *Behavioural and Brain Sciences*, 21, 353–397.

Mazur, A. and Michalek, J. (1998). Marriage, divorce and male testosterone. *Social Forces*, 77, 315–330.

Mazur, A., Booth, A. and Dabbs, J. (1992). Testosterone and chess competition. *Social Psychology Quarterly*, 55, 70–77.

Mazur, A. and Lamb, T. (1980). Testosterone, status, and mood in human males. *Hormones and Behavior*, 14, 236–246.

Mazur, J.E. (1994). *Learning and Behavior*. Englewood Cliffs, NJ: Prentice Hall.

McAlister, A., Perry, C., Killen, L.A., Slinkard, L.A. and Maccoby, N. (1980). Pilot study of smoking, alcohol, and drug abuse prevention. *American Journal of Public Health*, 70, 719–721.

McBride, D.M. and Dosher, B.A. (1997). A comparison of forgetting in an implicit and explicit memory task. *Journal of Experimental Psychology: General*, 126, 4, 371–392.

McCann, J.T. (1992). Criminal personality profiling in the investigation of violent crime: Advances and future directions. *Behavioral Sciences and the Law*, 10, 475–481.

McClelland, J.L. and Rumelhart, D.E. (1981). An interactive activation model of context effects in letter perception: Part 1. An account of basic findings. *Psychological Review*, 88, 375–407.

McClelland, J.L., Rumelhart, D.E. and Hinton, G.E. (1986). The appeal of parallel distributed processing. In D.E. Rumelhart, J.L. McClelland and the PDP Research Group, *Parallel Distributed Processing. Vol. 1: Foundations*. Cambridge, MA: MIT Press.

McClintock, M.K. (1971). Menstrual synchrony and suppression. *Nature*, 229, 244–245.

McClintock, M.K. and Adler, N.T. (1978). The role of the female during copulation in wild and domestic Norway rats *(Rattus norvegicus)*. *Behaviour*, 67, 67–96.

McCloskey, M., Wible, C. and Cohen, N. (1988). Is there a special flashbulb-memory mechanism? *Journal of Experimental Psychology: General*, 117, 171–181.

McCloy, T.M. and Koonce, J.M. (1982). Sex as a moderator variable in the selection and training of persons for a skilled task. *Aviation, Space and Environmental Medicine*, 53, 1170–1172.

McCrae, R.R. and Costa, P.T. (1985). Updating Norman's 'adequate taxonomy': Intelligence and personality dimensions in natural language and in questionnaires. *Journal of Personality and Social Psychology*, 49, 710–712.

McCrae, R.R. and Costa, P.T. (1987). Validation of the five-factor model of personality across instruments and observers. *Journal of Personality and Social Psychology*, 52, 81–90.

McCrae, R.R. and Costa, P.T. (1990). *Personality in Adulthood*. New York: Guilford.

McCrae, R.R., Costa, P.T. and Busch, C.M. (1986). Evaluating comprehensiveness in personality systems: The California Q-Set and the five-factor model. *Journal of Personality*, 54, 430–446.

McCutcheon, L.E., Furnham, A. and Davis, G. (1993). A cross-national comparison of students' misconceptions about psychology. *Psychological Reports*, 72, 243–247.

McDaniel, M.A., Anderson, D.C., Einstein, G.O. and O'Halloran, C.M. (1989). Modulation of environmental reinstatement effects through encoding strategies. *American Journal of Psychology*, 102, 523–548.

McFarlane, A.C. (1992). Avoidance and intrusion in post-traumatic stress disorder. *Journal of Nervous and Mental Disease*, 180, 439–445.

McGinn, C. (1989). Can we solve the mind-body problem? *Mind*, 98, 349–366.

McGinty, D.J. and Sterman, M.B. (1968). Sleep suppression after basal forebrain lesions in the cat. *Science*, 160, 1253–1255.

McGivern, R.F., Mutter, K.L., Anderson, J., Wideman, G., Bodnar, M. and Huston, P.J. (1998). Gender differences in incidental learning and visual recognition memory: Support for a sex difference in unconscious environmental awareness. *Personality and Individual Differences*, 25, 223–232.

McGue, M., Pickens, R. W. and Svikis, D.S. (1992). Sex and age effects on the inheritance of alcohol problems: A twin study. *Journal of Abnormal Psychology*, 101, 3–17.

McGue, M., Bacon, S. and Lykken, D.T. (1993b). Personality stability and change in early adulthood: A behavior genetic analysis. *Developmental Psychology*, 29, 96–109.

McGuiness, D. and Morley, C. (1991). Sex differences in the development of visuo-spatial ability in pre-school children. *Journal of Mental Imagery*, 15, 143–150.

McGuire, P.K., Silbersweig, D.A., Wright, I., Murray, R.M., Frackowiak, R.S.J. and Frith, C.D. (1996). The neural correlates of inner speech and auditory verbal imagery in schizophrenia: relationship to auditory verbal hallucinations. *British Journal of Psychiatry*, 169, 148–159.

McGuire, P.K., Quested, D.J., Spence, S.A., Murray, R.M., Frith, C.D. and Liddle, P.F. (1998). Pathophysiology of 'positive' thought disorder in schizoprenia. *British Journal of Psychiatry*, 173, 231–235.

McKay, D.C. (1973). Aspects of the theory of comprehension, memory and attention. *Quarterly Journal of Experimental Psychology*, 25, 22–40.

McKeefry, D.J. and Zeki, S. (1997). The position and topography of the human colour centre as revealed by functional magnetic resonance imaging. *Brain*, 120, 2229–2242.

McLellan, D.L. (1991). Functional recovery and the principles of disability medicine. In M. Swash and J. Oxbury (eds), *Clinical Neurology*. Edinburgh: Churchill Livingstone.

McManus, I.C. (1985). Handedness, language dominance and aphasia: A genetic model. *Psychological Medicine*, 8, 1–40.

McManus, I.C., Shergill, S. and Bryden, M.P. (1993). Annett's theory that individuals heterozygous for the right shift gene are intellectually advantaged: Theoretical and empirical problems. *British Journal of Psychology*, 84, 517–537.

McNally, R.J. (1987). Preparedness and phobias. *Psychological Bulletin*, 101, 283–303.

McNally, R.J. (1990). Psychological approaches to panic disorder: A review. *Psychological Bulletin*, 108, 403–419.

McNally, R.J. (1995). Preparedness, phobias, and the Panglossian paradigm. *Behavioural and Brain Sciences*, 18, 303–304.

McNeal, J. (1990). Children as customers. *American Demographics*, 12, 9, 36–39.

McNeil, E.B. (1967). *The Quiet Furies: Man and disorder*. Englewood Cliffs, NJ: Prentice Hall.

McNeill, D. (1970). *The Acquisition of Language: The study of developmental psycholinguistics*. New York: Harper & Row.

McReynolds, W.T. (1980). Learned helplessness as a schedule-shift effect. *Journal of Research in Personality*, 14, 139–157.

Meador, K.J., Allen, M.E., Adams, R.J. and Loring, D.W. (1991). Allochiria vs allesthesia. Is there a misrepresentation? *Archives of Neurology*, 48, 546–549.

Mednick, S.A., Gabrielli, W.F. and Hutchings, B. (1983). Genetic influences in criminal behavior: Some evidence from an adoption cohort. In K. T. VanDusen and S. A. Mednick (eds), *Prospective Studies of Crime and Delinquency*. Hingham, MA: Martinus Nijhoff.

Mednick, S.A., Machon, R.A. and Huttunen, M.O. (1990). An update on the Helsinki influenza project. *Archives of General Psychiatry*, 47, 292.

Meehl, P.E. (1956). Wanted- a good cookbook. *American Psychologist*, 11, 262–272.

Meehl, P.E. (1986). Causes and effects of my disturbing little book. *Journal of Personality Assessment*, 50, 370–375.

Mehler, J., Jusczyk, P., Lambertz, G., Halsted, N., Bertoncini, J. and Amiel-Tison, C. (1988). A precursor of language acquisition in young infants. *Cognition*, 29, 143–178.

Meichenbaum, D. (1985). *Stress Innoculation Training*. New York: Pergamon Press.

Meichenbaum, D.H. (1977). *Cognitive-behavior modification: An integrative approach*. New York: Plenum.

Meindl, J.R. and Lerner, M.J. (1985). Exacerbation of extreme responses to an out-group. *Journal of Personality and Social Psychology*, 47, 71–84.

Melzak, R. (1992). Phantom limbs. *Scientific American*, 266, 4, 120–126.

Meltzoff, A.N. (1988). Infant imitation and memory: Nine-month-olds in immediate and deferred tests. *Child Development*, 59, 217–225.

Meltzoff, A.N. (1995). What infant memory tells us about infantile amnesia: Long-term recall and deferred imitation. *Journal of Experimental Child Psychology*, 59, 497–515.

Memon, A., Cronin, O., Eaves, R. and Bull, R. (1983) The cognitive interview and child witnesses. In N. Clark and G.M. Stephenson (eds), *Children, Evidence and Procedure*. Leicester: British Psychological Society.

Menn, L. and Stoel-Gammon, C. (1993). Phonological development: Learning sounds and sound patterns. In J.B. Gleason (ed.), *The Development of Language*. New York: Macmillan.

Merikle, P.M. (1988). Subliminal auditory messages: An evaluation. *Psychology and Marketing*, 5, 355–372.

Merrens, M.R. and Richards, W.S. (1970). Acceptance of generalized bona fide personality interpretations. *Psychological Reports*, 27, 691–694.

Mervis, C.B. and Rosch, E. (1981). Categorization of natural objects. *Annual Review of Psychology*, 32, 89–116.

Metalsky, G.I, Halberstadt, L.J. and Alloy, L.Y. (1987). Vulnerability to depressive mood reactions: Toward a more powerful test of the diathesis–stress and causal mediation components of the reformulated theory of depression. *Journal of Personality and Social Psychology*, 62, 386–393.

Meyer, P.A., Garrison, C.Z., Jackson, K.L. and Addy, C.L. (1993). Undesirable life events and depression in young adolescents. *Journal of Child and Family Studies*, 2, 47–60.

Meyer-Bahlburg, H.F.L., Ehrhardt, A.A., Bell, J.J., Cohen, S.F., Healey, J.M., Feldman, J.F., Morishima, A., Baker, S.W. and New, M.I. (1985). Idiopathic precocious puberty in girls. Psychosexual development. *Journal of Youth and Adolescence*, 14, 339–353.

Miles, H.L. (1983). Apes and language: The search for communicative competence. In J. de Luce and H.T. Wilder (eds), *Language in Primates: Perspectives and implications*. New York: Springer-Verlag.

Miles, M.B. and Huberman, A.M. (1994). *Qualitative Data Analysis: A sourcebook of new methods* (2nd edition). London: Sage.

Milgram, S. (1963). Behavioral study of obedience. *Journal of Abnormal and Social Psychology*, 67, 371–378.

Milgram, S. (1974). *Obedience to Authority*. New York: Harper & Row.

Miller, D.T. and McFarland, C. (1987). Pluralistic ignorance: When similarity is interpreted as dissimilarity. *Journal of Personality and Social Psychology*, 53, 298–305.

Miller, D.T. and Porter, C.A. (1983). Self-blame in victims of violence. *Journal of Social Issues*, 39, 139–152.

Miller, G.A. (1956). The magical number seven plus or minus two: Some limits on our capacity for processing information. *Psychological Review*, 63, 81–97.

Miller, G.A., Galanter, E. and Pribram, K. (1960). *Plans and the Structure of Behavior*. New York: Holt, Rinehart & Winston.

Miller, G.A., Heise, G. A. and Lichten, W. (1951). The intelligibility of speech as a function of the context of the test materials. *Journal of Experimental Psychology*, 41, 329–335.

Miller, G.A. and Taylor, W.G. (1948).The perception of repeated bursts of noise. *Journal of the Acoustical Society of America*, 20, 171–182.

Miller, J.G. (1997). Theoretical issues in cultural psychology. In J.W.Berry, Y.H. Poortinga and J. Pandey (eds), *Handbook of Cross-Cultural Psychology: Theory and method*, Vol. 1. Boston: Allyn & Bacon.

Miller, J.N. and Ozonoff, S. (1997). Did Asperger's cases have Asperger disorder? A research note. *Journal of Child Psychology and Psychiatry*, 38, 2, 247–251.

Miller, N.E. (1983). Behavioral medicine: Symbiosis between laboratory and clinic. *Annual Review of Psychology*, 34, 1–31.

Miller, R.J., Hennessy, R.T. and Leibowitz, H.W. (1973). The effect of hypnotic ablation of the background on the magnitude of the Ponzo perspective illusion. *International Journal of Clinical and Experimental Hypnosis*, 21, 180–191.

Milliman, R.E. (1982). Using background music to affect the behaviour of supermarket shoppers. *Journal of Marketing*, 46, 86–91.

Millne, D. and Common, A. (1998). Delivering and evaluating a psychological skills training for athletes and coaches. In H. Steinberg, I. Cockerill and A. Dewey (eds), *What Sport Psychologists Do*. Leicester: The British Psychological Society.

Milner, A.D. (1998). Streams of consciousness: Visual awareness and the brain. *Trends in Cognitive Sciences*, 2, 1, 25–30.

Milner, A.D. and Goodale, M.A. (1995). *The Visual Brain in Action*. Oxford: Oxford University Press.

Milner, A.D., Perrett, D.I., Johnston, R.S., Benson, P.I., Jordan, T.R. and Healey, D.W. (1991). Perception and action in 'visual form agnosia'. *Brain*, 114, 405–428.

Milner, B. (1964). Some effects of frontal lobotomy in man. In J.W. Warren and G. Akert (eds), *The frontal granular cortex and behaviour*. New York: McGraw-Hill.

Milner, B. (1970). Memory and the temporal regions of the brain. In K.H. Pribram and D.E. Broadbent (eds), *Biology of Memory*. New York: Academic Press.

Milner, B., Corkin, S. and Teuber, H-L. (1968). Further analysis of the hippocampal amnesic syndrome: 14 year follow-up study of HM. *Neuropsychologia*, 6, 217–224.

Mirmiran, M. (1995). The function of fetal/neonatal rapid eye movement sleep. *Behavioural Brain Research*, 69, 13–22.

Mischel, W. (1968). *Personality and Assessment*. New York: Wiley.

Mischel, W. (1976). *Introduction to Personality* (2nd edition). New York: Holt, Rinehart & Winston.

Mischel, W. (1977). The interaction of person and situation. In D. Magnusson and N.S. Endler (eds), *Personality at the Crossroads: Current issues in interactional psychology*. Hillsdale, NJ: Lawrence Erlbaum Associates.

Mischel, W. (1979). On the interface of cognition and personality: Beyond the person-situation debate. *American Psychologist*, 34, 740–754.

Mischel, W. (1984). Convergences and challenges in the search for consistency. *American Psychologist*, 39, 351–364.

Mistry, W.J. and Rogoff, B. (1994). Remembering in a cultural context. In W.J. Lonner and R.S. Malpass (eds), *Psychology and Culture*. Boston: Allyn & Bacon.

Mittenberg, W., Seidenberg, M., O'Leary, D.S. and DiGiulio, D. (1989). Changes in cerebral functioning associated with normal ageing. *Journal of Clinical and Experimental Neuropsychology*, 11, 6, 918–932.

Moffat, S.D. and Hampson, E. (1996). A curvilinear relationship between testosterone and spatial cognition in humans: Possible influence of hand preference. *Psychoneuroendocrinology*, 21, 323–337.

Mohanty, A.K. (1982a). Cognitive and linguistic development of tribal children from unilingual and bilingual environment. In R. Rath, H.S. Asthana, D. Sinha and J.B.P. Sinha (eds), *Diversity and Unity in Cross-cultural Psychology*. Lisse: Swets & Zeitlinger.

Mohanty, A.K. (1982b). Bilingualism among Kond tribals in Orissa (India): Consequences, issues and implications. *Indian Psychologist*, 1, 22–44.

Mohanty, A.K. (1990). Psychological consequences of mother tongue maintenance and multilingualism in India. *Psychology and Developing Societies*, 2, 31–51.

Mohanty, A.K. and Das, S.P. (1987). Cognitive and metalinguistic ability of unschooled bilingual and unilingual tribal children. *Psychological Studies*, 32, 5–8.

Mohanty, A.K. and Perregaux, C. (1997). Language acquisition and bilingualism. In J.W. Berry, P.R. Dasen and T.S. Sarawathi (eds), *Handbook of Cross-cultural Psychology. Vol. 2: basic processes and human development*. Boston: Allyn & Bacon.

Mondin, G.W., Morgan, W.P., Piering, P.N., Stegner, A.J., Stotesbery, C.L., Trine, M.R. and Wu, M-Y. (1996). Psychological consequences of exercise deprivation in habitual exercisers. *Medicine and Science in Sports and Exercise*, 28, 9, 1199–1203.

Money, J. and Ehrhardt, A. (1972). *Man and Woman, Boy and Girl*. Baltimore: Johns Hopkins University Press.

Money, J., Schwartz, M. and Lewis, V. G. (1984). Adult erotosexual status and fetal hormonal masculinization and demasculinization: 46,XX congenital virilizing adrenal hyperplasia and 46,XY androgen-insensitivity syndrome compared. *Psychoneuroendocrinology*, 9, 405–414.

Monroe, S., Thase, M. and Simons, A. (1992). Social factors and psychobiology of depression: Relations between life stress and rapid eye movement sleep latency. *Journal of Abnormal Psychology*, 101, 528–537.

Montagu, A. (1980). *Sociobiology Examined*. New York: Oxford University Press.

Monteith, M.J. (1993). Self-regulation of prejudiced responses: Implications for progress in prejudice-reduction efforts. *Journal of Personality and Social Psychology*, 65, 469–485.

Montemayor, R. (1974). Children's performance in a game and their attraction to it as a function of sex-typed labels. *Child Development*, 45, 152–156.

Moody, K. (1980). *Growing Up on Television: The TV effect*. New York: Time Books.

Moon, C., Panneton-Cooper, R. and Fifer, W.P. (1993). Two day-olds prefer their native language. *Infant Behaviour and Development*, 16, 495–500.

Morabia, A. and Wynder, E.L. (1990). Dietary habits of smokers, people who never smoked, and ex-smokers. *American Journal of Clinical Nutrition*, 52, 933–937.

Moran, D.T., Monti-Block, L., Stenaas, L.J. and Berliner, D.L. (1995). Structure and function of human vomeronasal organ. In R.L. Doty (ed.), *Handbook of Olfaction and Gustation*. New York: Dekker.

Moray, N. (1959). Attention in dichotic listening: Affective cues and the influence of instructions. *Quarterly Journal of Experimental Psychology*, 11, 56–60.

Morgenstern, J., Langenbucher, J., Labouvie, E. and Miller, K.J. (1997). The comorbidity of alcoholism and personality disorders in a clinical population: Prevalence rates and relation to alcohol typology variables. *Journal of Abnormal Psychology*, 106, 1, 74–84.

Morris, J.S., Frith C.D., Perrett, D.L., Rowland, D., Young, A.W., Calder, A.J. and Dolan, R.J. (1996). A differential neural response in the human amygdala to fearful and happy facial expressions. *Nature*, 383, 812–815.

Morris, J.S., Friston, K.J., Buchel, C., Frith, C.D., Young, A.W., Calder, A.J. and Dolan, R.J. (1998). A neuromodulatory role for the human amygdala in processing emotional facial expressions. *Brain*, 121, 47–57.

Morris, M.W. and Peng, K.P. (1994). Culture and cause: American and Chinese attributions for social and physical events. *Journal of Personality and Social Psychology*, 67, 949–971.

Morris, N.M., Udry, J.R., Khan-Dawood, F. and Dawood, M.Y. (1987). Marital sex frequency and midcycle female testosterone. *Archives of Sexual Behavior*, 16, 27–37.

Morris, R.G.M., Garrud, P., Rawlins, J.N.P. and O'Keefe, J. (1982). Place navigation impaired in rats with hippocampal lesions. *Nature*, 182, 297, 681–683.

Morris, T.A. (1980). 'Type C' for cancer? Low trait anxiety in the pathogenesis of breast cancer. *Cancer Detection and Prevention*, 3, 102.

Morrison, D.F. (1967). *Multivariate Statistical Methods*. New York: McGraw-Hill.

Morton, J. (1979). Word recognition. In *Psycholinguistics 2: Structures and Processes*. Cambridge, MA: MIT Press.

Morton, J. and Patterson, K.E. (1980). A new attempt at an interpretation, or, an attempt at a new interpretation. In M. Coltheart, K.E. Patterson and J.C. Marshall (eds), *Deep Dyslexia*. London: Routledge & Kegan Paul.

Morton, J., Andrews, B., Bekerian, D., Brewin, C., Davies, G. and Mollon, P. (1995). *Recovered memories*. Report of the working party of the British Psychological Society. Leicester: British Psychological Society.

Moscovici, S. (1976). *Social Influence and Social Change*. London: Academic Press.

Moscovici, S. (1983). The phenomenon of social representations. In R.M. Farr and S. Moscovici (eds), *Social Representations*. Cambridge: Cambridge University Press, pp. 3–69.

Moscovici, S. and Personnaz, B. (1980). Studies in social influence V: Minority influence and conversion behavior in a perceptual task. *Journal of Experimental Social Psychology*, 16, 270–282.

Moss, A.R. and Bacchetti, P. (1989). Natural history of HIV infection. *AIDS*, 3, 55–61.

Moss, C.S. (1965). *Hypnosis in Perspective*. New York: Macmillan.

Moss, J.P., Linney, A.D., Grindrod, S.R. Arridge, S.R. and Clifton, J.S. (1987). Three-dimensional visualisation of the face and skull using computerised tomography and laser scanning techniques. *European Journal of Orthodontics*, 9, 247–253.

Mozer, M.C., Halligan, P.W. and Marshall, J.C. (1997). The end of the line for a brain-damaged model of unilateral neglect. *Journal of Cognitive Neuroscience*, 9, 2, 171–190.

Mugny, G. (1982). *The Power of Minorities*. London: Academic Press.

Mundy, P., Sigman, M., Ungerer, J. and Sherman, T. (1986). Defining the social deficits in autism: The contribution of nonverbal communication measures. *Journal of Child Psychology and Psychiatry*, 27, 657–669.

Munjack, D.J., Schlaks, A., Sanchez, V.C., Usigli, R., Zulueta, A. and Leonard, M. (1984). Rational emotive therapy in the treatment of erectile failure: An initial study. *Journal of Sex and Marital Therapy*, 10, 170–175.

Muntwyler, J., Hennekens, C.H., Buring, J.E. and Gaziano, J.M. (1998). Mortality and light to moderate alcohol consumption after myocardial infarction. *Lancet*, 352, 1882–1885.

Murphy, K.J., Pacicot, C.I. and Goodale, M.A. (1996). The use of visuomotor cues as a strategy for making perceptual judgements in a patient with visual form agnosia. *Neuropsychology*, 10, 396–401.

Murphy, P., Williams, J. and Dunning, E. (1990). *Football on Trial: Spectator violence and development in the football world*. London: Routledge.

Murray, D.M., Pirie, P., Luepker, R.V. and Pallonen, U. (1989). Five- and six-year follow-up results from four seventh-grade smoking prevention strategies. *Journal of Behavioral Medicine*, 12, 207–218.

Mutrie, N. and Biddle, S.J.H. (1995). The effects of exercise on mental health in nonclinical populations. In S.J.H. Biddle (ed.), *European Perspectives on Exercise and Sport Psychology*. Champaign, IL: Human Kinetics.

Myers, D. G. and Bishop, G. D. (1970). Discussion effects on racial attitudes. *Science*, 169, 778–789.

Myers, S.A., Ropog, B.L. and Rodgers, R.P. (1997). Sex differences in humor. *Psychological Reports*, 81, 221–222.

Nafe, J.P. and Wagoner, K.S. (1941). The nature of pressure adaptation. *Journal of General Psychology*, 25, 323–351.

Nagahama, Y., Fukuyama, H., Yamauchi, H., Matsuzaki, S., Konishi, J., Shibasaki, H. and Kimure, J. (1996). Cerebral activation during performance of a card sorting test. *Brain*, 119, 1667–1675.

Nagel, T. (1974). What is it like to be a bat? *Philosophical Review*, 4, 435–450.

Naveh-Benjamin, M. and Ayres, T.J. (1986). Digit span, reading rate and linguistic relativity. *Quarterly Journal of Experimental Psychology*, 38A, 739–751.

Nazzi, R., Bertoncini, J. and Mehler, J. (1998). Language discrimination by newborns: Toward an understanding of the role of rhythm. *Journal of Experimental Psychology: Human Perception and Performance*, 24, 3, 756–766.

Neighbors, B.D., Forehand, R. and Bau, J-J. (1997). Interparental conflict and relations with parents as predictors of young adult functioning. *Development and Psychopathology*, 9, 169–187.

Neisser, U. (1964). Visual search. *Scientific American*, 210, 94–102.

Neisser, U. (1969). Selective reading: A method for the study of visual attention. *Journal of Experimental Psychology (General)*, 113, 1, 32–35.

Neisser, U. (1984). Interpreting Harry Bahrick's discovery: What confers immunity against forgetting? *Journal of Experimental Psychology: General*, 113, 32–35.

Neisser, U. and Becklen, R. (1975). Selective looking: Attending to visually significant events. *Cognitive Psychology*, 7, 480–494.

Neisser, U., Boodoo, G., Bouchard, T.J., Boykin, W.A., Brody, N., Ceci, S., Halpern, D.F., Loehlin, J.C., Perloff, R., Sternberg, R.J. and Urbina, S. (1996a). Intelligence: Knowns and unknowns. *American Psychologist*, 51, 2, 77–101.

Neisser, U., Winograd, E., Bergman, E.T., Schreiber, C.A., Palmer, S.E. and Weldon, M.S. (1996b). Remembering the earthquake: Direct experience vs hearing the news. *Memory*, 4, 337–357.

Neisworth, J.T. and Madle, R.A. (1982). Retardation. In A.S. Bellack, M. Hersen and A.E. Kazdin (eds), *International Handbook of Behavior Modification and Therapy*. New York: Plenum Press.

Nelson, K. (1986). *Event Knowledge: Structure and function in development*. Hillsdale, NJ: Lawrence Erlbaum Associates.

Nelson, K. (1993). Events, narratives, memory: What develops? In M.E. Lamb and A.L. Brown (eds), *Memory and Affect in Development*. Hillsdale, NJ: Lawrence Erlbaum Associates.

Nelson, M., Naismith, D.J., Burley, V., Gatenby, S. and Geddes, N. (1990). Nutrient intake vitamin/mineral supplementation and intelligence in British schoolchildren. *British Journal of Nutrition*, 64, 13–22.

Neubauer, V., Freudenthaler, H.H. and Pfurtscheller, G. (1995). Intelligence and spatiotemporal patterns of event-related desynchronization. *Intelligence*, 3, 249–266.

Neugarten, B.L. (1974). The roles we play. In *American Medical Association, Quality of Life: The Middle Years*. Acton, MA: Publishing Sciences Group.

Nevid, J.S., Art, R.J. and Moulton, J.L. (1996). Factors predicting participant attrition in a community-based, culturally specific smoking cessation program for Hispanic smokers. *Health Psychology*, 15, 3, 226–229.

Neville, H.J., Bavelier, D., Corina, D., Rauschecker, J., Kami, A., Lalwani, A., Braun, A., Clark, V., Jezzard, P. and Turner, R. (1998). Cerebral organization for language in deaf and effects of experience. *Proceedings of the National Academy of Sciences of the USA*, 95, 3, 922–929.

Nevin, J.A. (1988). Behavioral momentum and the partial reinforcement effect. *Psychological Bulletin*, 103, 44–56.

Newcomb, A.F. and Bagwell, C.L. (1995). Children's friendship relations: A meta-analytic review. *Psychological Bulletin*, 117, 306–347.

Newcombe, F., Mehta Z. and Deflaan, E.H.F. (1994). Category specificity in visual recognition. In M.J. Farah and G. Ratcliff (eds), *The neuropsychology of high-level vision*. Hove, UK: LEA.

Newell, A. and Simon, H.A. (1972). *Human Problem Solving*. Englewood Cliffs, NJ: Prentice Hall.

Newman, J., Rosenbach, J.H., Burns, K.L., Latimer, B.C., Matocha, H.R. and Vogt, E.R. (1995). An experimental test of 'the Mozart effect' : Does listening to his music improve spatial ability? *Perceptual and Motor Skills*, 81, 1379–1387.

Newport, E.L. (1975). *Motherese: The speech of mothers to young children*. San Diego: University of California, Center for Human Information Processing.

Newport, E.L. Gleitman, H.R. and Gleitman, L. (1977). Mother I'd rather do it myself: Some effects and noneffects of maternal speech style. In C.E. Snow and C.A. Ferguson (eds), *Talking to Children: Language input and acquisition*. Cambridge: Cambridge University Press.

Newport, E.L. and Supalla, R. (1989). A critical period effect in the acquisition of a primary language. Unpublished manuscript cited by J.S. Johnson and E.L. Newport. Critical period effects in second language learning: The influence of maturational state on the acquisition of English as a second language. *Cognitive Psychology*, 21, 60–99.

Nezu, A.M., Nezu, C.M. and Blissett, S.E. (1988). Sense of humor as a moderator of the relation between stressful life events and psychological distress: A prospective analysis. *Journal of Personality and Social Psychology*, 54, 699–714.

Nicholl, C.S. and Russell, R.M. (1990). Analysis of animal rights literature reveals the underlying motives of the movement: Ammunition for counter-offensive by scientists. *Endocrinology*, 127, 985–989.

Nicol, R. (1998). Conduct disorder. *Current Opinion in Psychiatry*, 11, 385–388.

Nicolaus, L.K. and Nellis, D.W. (1987). The first evaluation of the use of conditioned taste aversion to control predation by mongooses upon eggs. *Applied Animal Behaviour Science*, 17, 329–346.

Nicolaus, L.K., Hoffman, T.E. and Gustavson, C.R. (1982). Taste aversion conditioning in free ranging raccoons (Procyon lotor). *Northwest Science*, 56, 165–169.

Nielsen, A.C. (1990). *Annual Nielsen Report on Television*: 1990. New York: Nielsen Media Research.

Nielsen, L.L. and Sarason, I.G. (1981). Emotion, personality, and selective attention. *Journal of Personality and Social Psychology*, 41, 945–960.

Nisbett, R.E. and Schachter, S. (1966) Cognitive manipulation of pain. *Journal of Experimental Social Psychology*, 2, 227–236.

Nisbett, R.E. and Wilson, T.D. (1977). Telling more than we can know: Verbal reports on mental processes. *Psychological Review*, 84, 231–259.

Noble, E.P., Blum, K., Ritchie, T. *et al.* (1991). Allelic association of the D2 dopamine receptor gene with receptor binding characteristics in alcoholics. *Archives of General Psychiatry*, 48, 655–663.

Nobre, A.C., Allison, T. and McCarthy, G. (1994). Word recognition in the human inferior temporal lobe. *Nature*, 372, 260–263.

Noland, M.P., Kryscio, R.J., Riggs, R.S., Linville, L.H., Perritt, L.J. and Tucker, T.C. (1990). Use of snuff, chewing tobacco, and cigarettes among adolescents in a tobacco-producing area. *Addictive Behaviors*, 15, 517–530.

Norheim, A.J. and Fonnebo, V. (1998). Doctors' attitudes to acupuncture – a Norwegian study. *Social Science and Medicine*, 47, 4, 519–523.

Norman, D. and Shallice, T. (1986). Attention to action: Willed and automatic control of behaviour. In R.J. Davidson, G.E. Schwartz and D. Shapiro (eds), *Consciousness and Self-regulation*, Vol 4. New York: Plenum.

Norman, W.T. (1963). Toward an adequate taxonomy of personality attributes: Replicated factor structure in peer nomination personality ratings. *Journal of Abnormal and Social Psychology*, 66, 574–583.

North, A.C. and Hargreaves, D.J. (1997). The musical milieu: Studies of listening in everyday life. *The Psychologist*, July, 309–312.

North A.C., Hargreaves, D.J. and McKendrick, J. (1997). In store music affects product choice. *Nature*, 26, 390, 132.

North, T.C., McCullagh, P. and Tran, V. (1990). Effects of exercise on depression. *Exercise and Sport Sciences Reviews*, 18, 379–415.

Nowak, M.A. and Sigmund, K. (1998). Evolution of indirect reciprocity by image scoring. *Nature*, 393, 573–577.

Nyberg, L., McIntosh, A.R., Cabeza, R., Habib, R., Houle, S. and Tulving, E. (1996). General and specific brain regions involved in encoding and retrieval of events: What, where and when. *Proceedings of the National Academy of Sciences, USA*, 93, 11280–11285.

Oakhill, J. and Garnham, A. (1988). *Becoming a Skilled Reader*. Oxford: Blackwell.

Oaksford, M., Morris, F., Grainger, B. and Williams, J.M.G. (1996). Mood, reasoning, and central executive processes. *Journal of Experimental Psychology: Learning, Memory and Cognition*, 22, 2, 476–492.

Oatley, K. (1992). *Best Laid Schemes: The psychology of emotion*. Cambridge: Cambridge University Press.

Oatley, K. and Jenkins, J.M. (1996). *Understanding Emotion*. Oxford: Blackwell.

Oatley, K. and Johnson-Laird, P.N. (1987). Towards a cognitive theory of emotions. *Cognition and Emotion*, 1, 29–50.

O'Brien, M. and Nutt, D. (1998). Loss of consciousness and post-traumatic stress disorder. *British Journal of Psychiatry*, 173, 102–104.

O'Carroll, R.E. (1995). The assessment of premorbid ability: A critical review. *Neurocase*, 1, 83–89.

O'Connor, N. and Hermelin, B. (1988). Low intelligence and special abilities. *Journal of Child Psychology and Psychiatry*, 29, 391–396.

Offer, D. and Sabshin, M. (1984). *Normality and the Life Cycle: A critical integration*. New York: Basic Books.

O'Haire, H. (1994). AIDS and population: Think again. *Populi*, 20/21, 8–10.

Ohman, A., Dimberg, U. and Ost, L-G. (1985). Animal and social phobias: Biological constraints on learned fear responses. In S. Reiss and R. Bootzin (eds), *Theoretical Issues in Behaviour Therapy*. New York: Academic Press.

Okubo, Y., Suhara, T., Suzuki, K., Kobayashi, K., Inoue, O., Terasaki, O., Someya, Y., Sassa, T., Sudo, Y., Matsushima, E., Iyo, M., Tateno, Y. and Toru, M. (1997). Decreased prefrontal dopamine D1 receptors in schizophrenia revealed by PET. *Nature*, 385, 634–636.

Olds, J. and Milner, P.M. (1954). Positive reinforcement produced by electrical stimulation of septal area and other regions of the rat brain. *Journal of Comparative and Physiological Psychology*, 47, 419–427.

Oltmans, T.F. and Emery, R.E. (1998). *Abnormal Psychology* (2nd edition). New Jersey: Prentice Hall.

Oltmans, T.F., Neale, J.M. and Davison, G.C. (1995). *Case Studies in Abnormal Psychology*. New York: Wiley.

Omi, M. and Winant, H. (1994). *Racial Formation in the United States: From the 1960s to the 1980s*. New York: Routledge & Kegan Paul.

Orne, M.T. (1959). The nature of hypnosis: Artifact and essence. *Journal of Abnormal and Social Psychology*, 58, 277–299.

Orne, M.T. and Evans, F.J. (1965). Social control in the psychological experiment: Antisocial behavior and hypnosis. *Journal of Personality and Social Psychology*, 1, 189–200.

Ortony, A. and Turner, T.J. (1990). What's basic about basic emotions? *Psychological Review*, 97, 315–331.

Orvis, B.R., Kelley, H.H. and Butler, D. (1976). Attributional conflict in young couples. In J.H. Harvey, W.J. Ickes and R.F. Kidd (eds), *New Directions in Attribution Research*, Vol. 1. Hillsdale, NJ: Lawrence Erlbaum Associates.

Ost, L-G., Westling, B.E. and Hellstrom, K. (1993). Applied relaxation, exposure in-vivo and cognitive methods in the treatment of panic disorder with agoraphobia. *Behaviour Research and Therapy*, 31, 383–394.

Ottaviani, R. and Beck, A.T. (1987). Cognitive aspects of panic disorder. *Journal of Anxiety Disorders*, 1, 15–28.

Ouellette, J.A. and Wood, W. (1998). Habit and intention in everyday life: The multiple processes by which past behaviour predicts future behaviour. *Psychological Bulletin*, 124, 1, 54–74.

Overmeier, J.B. and Seligman, M.E.P. (1967). Effects of inescapable shock upon subsequent escape and avoidance responding. *Journal of Comparative and Physiological Psychology*, 63, 28–33.

Owens, R.E. (1992). *Language Development: An introduction*. New York: Merrill/ Macmillan.

Ozer, D.J. (1985). Correlation and the coefficient of determination. *Psychological Bulletin*, 97, 307–315.

Paffenbarger, R.S., Hyde, J.T., Wing, A. L. and Hsieh, C.C. (1986). Physical activity, all-cause mortality, and longevity of college alumni. *New England Journal of Medicine*, 314, 605–612.

Paikoff, R. L. and Brooks-Gunn, J. (1991). Do parent-child relationships change during puberty? *Psychological Bulletin*, 110, 47–66.

Palfai, T. and Jankiewicz, H. (1991). *Drugs and Human Behavior*. Dubuque, IA: Wm C. Brown.

Palmer, R.E. and Corballis, M.C. (1996). Predicting reading ability from handedness measures. *British Journal of Psychology*, 87, 609–620.

Palmer, S.E. (1975a). In D.A. Norman, D.E. Rumelhart and the LNR Research Group (eds), *Explorations in Cognition*. San Francisco: W.H. Freeman.

Palmer, S.E. (1975b). The effects of contextual scenes on the identification of objects. *Memory and Cognition*, 3, 519–526.

Parasuraman, R. (1985). Detection and identification of abnormalities in chest x-rays: Effects of reader skill, disease prevalence, and reporting standards. In R.E. Eberts and C.G. Eberts (eds), *Trends in ergonomics/human factors II*. Amsterdam: North-Holland.

Parente, R. and Stapleton, M. (1997). History and systems of cognitive rehabilitation. *Neurorehabilitation*, 8, 3–11.

Paris, J. (1991). Personality disorders, para-suicide, and culture. *Transcultural Psychiatric Research*, 28, 25–39.

Park, B. and Rothbart, M. (1982). Perception of out-group homogeneity and levels of social categorization: Memory for the subordinate attributes of in-group and out-group members. *Journal of Personality and Social Psychology*, 42, 1051–1068.

Park, D.C. and Kidder, D.P. (1996). Prospective memory and medication adherence. In M. Brandimonte, G.O. Einstein and M.A. McDaniel (eds), *Prospective Memory: Theory and applications*. Mahwah, NJ: Lawrence Erlbaum Associates.

Parke, R.D. and Collmer, C.W. (1975). Child abuse: An interdisciplinary analysis. In E.M. Hetherington (ed.), *Review of Child Development Research*, Vol. 5. Chicago: University of Chicago Press.

Parker, D., Manstead, A.S.R. and Stradling, S.G. (1995). Extending the theory of planned behaviour: the role of personal norm. *British Journal of Social Psychology*, 34, 127–137.

Parker, I. (1992). *Discourse Dynamics: Critical analysis for social and individual psychology*. London: Routledge.

Parker, J.G., Rubin, K.H., Price, J. and De Rosier, M.E. (1995). Peer relationships, child development, and adjustment: A developmental psychopathology perspective. In D. Cicchetti and D. Cohen (eds), *Developmental Psychopathology. Vol. 2: Risk, Disorder and Adaptation*. New York: Wiley.

Parkin, A.J. (1996). *Memory and Amnesia: An introduction*. Oxford: Blackwell.

Parkin, A.J., Blunden, J., Rees, J.E. and Hunkin, N.M. (1991). Wernicke–Korsakoff syndrome of nonalcoholic origin. *Brain and Cognition*, 15, 69–82.

Parkin, A.J. and Stewart, F. (1993). Category-specific impairments? No. A critique of Sartori *et al*. *Quarterly Journal of Experimental Psychology*, 46A, 505–509.

Passingham, R.E. (1995). *The Frontal Lobes and Voluntary Action*. Oxford: Oxford University Press.

Patterson, F.G. and Linden, E. (1981). *The Education of Koko*. New York: Holt, Rinehart & Winston.

Patterson, K.E. (1994). Reading, writing and rehabilitation: A reckoning. In M.J. Riddoch and G. Humphreys (eds), *Cognitive Neuropsychology and Cognitive Rehabilitation*. Hove, UK: The Psychology Press.

Patton, J., Stinard, T. and Routh, D. (1983). Where do children study? *Journal of Educational Research*, 76, 280–286.

Paul, C.L. and Sanson-Fisher, R.W. (1996). Experts' agreement on the relative effectiveness of 29 smoking reduction strategies. *Preventive Medicine*, 25, 517–526.

Paulesu, E., Frith, U., Snowling, M., Gallagher, A., Morton, J., Frackowiak, R.S.J. and Frith, C.D. (1996). Is developmental dyslexia a disconnection syndrome? Evidence from PET scanning. *Brain*, 119, 1, 143–157.

Paulesu, E. and Mehler, J. (1998). Right on in sign language. *Nature*, 392, 233–234.

Pearson, J.C., Turner, L.H. and Todd-Mancillas, W. (1991*)*. *Gender and Communication*. Dubuque, IA: Brown.

Pease, D.M., Gleason, J.B. and Pan, B. (1993). A. Learning the meaning of words: Semantic development and beyond. In J. B. Gleason (ed.), *The Development of*

Language. New York: Macmillan.

Pelaez-Nogueras, M., Field, T., Cigales, M., Gonzales, A. and Clasky, S. (1994). Infants of depressed mothers show less 'depressed' behaviour with their nursery teacher. *Infant Mental Health Journal*, 15, 358–367.

Pell, M.D. and Baum, S.R. (1997). The ability to perceive and comprehend intonation in linguistic and affective contexts by brain-damaged adults. *Brain and Language*, 57, 80–99.

Pelleymounter, M. A., Cullen, M. J., Baker, M. B., Hecht, R. *et al.* (1995). Effects of the obese gene product on body weight regulation in ob/ob mice. *Science*, 269, 540–543.

Penfield, W. and Jasper, H. (1954). *Epilepsy and the Functional Anatomy of the Human Brain.* Boston: Little, Brown.

Penrose, R. (1989). *The Emperor's New Mind.* Oxford: Oxford University Press.

Penrose, R. (1994). *Shadows of the Mind.* Oxford: Oxford University Press.

Perani, D., Dehaene, S., Grassi, F., Cohen, L., Cappa, S.F., Dupoux, E. *et al.* (1996). Brain processing of native and foreign languages. *Neuroreport*, 7, 2439–2444.

Perani, D., Paulesu, E., Galles, N.S., Dupoux, E., Dehaene, S., Bettinardi, V., Cappa, S.F., Fazio, F. and Mehler, J. (1998). The bilingual brain: Proficiency and age of acquisition of the second language. *Brain*, 121, 1841–1852.

Perelson, A.S., Neumann, A.V., Markowitz, M., Leonard, J.M. and Ho, D.D. (1996). HIV-1 dynamics in-vivo: Virion clearance rate, infected cell life-span and viral generation time. *Science*, 271, 1582–1586.

Perkins, D.N. and Grotzer, T.A. (1997). Teaching intelligence. *American Psychologist*, 52, 10, 1125–1133.

Perls, F.S. (1967). Group vs. individual therapy. *ETC: A Review of General Semantics*, 34, 306–312.

Perls, F.S. (1969). *Gestalt Therapy Verbatim.* Lafayette, CA: Real People Press.

Perregaux, C. (1994). *Les enfants a deux vois – Des effets du bilinguisme sur l'apprentissage de la lecture.* Berne: Lang.

Perrett, D.I., May, K.A. and Yoshikawa, S. (1994). Facial shape and judgements of female attractiveness. *Nature*, 368, 239–242.

Persky, H., Lief, H.I., Strauss, D., Miller, W.R. and O'Brien, C.P. (1978). Plasma testosterone level and sexual behavior of couples. *Archives of Sexual Behavior*, 7, 157–173.

Pert, C.B., Snowman, A.M. and Snyder, S. H. (1974). Localization of opiate receptor binding in presynaptic membranes of rat brain. *Brain Research*, 70, 184–188.

Pervin, L.A. (1975). *Personality: Theory, Assessment, and Research.* New York: Wiley.

Peskin, J. (1982). Measuring houschold production for the GNP. *Family Economics Review*, 3, 16–25.

Peters, R.K., Cady, L.D., Bischoff, D.P., Bernstein, L. and Pile, M.C. (1983). Physical fitness and subsequent myocardial infarction in healthy workers. *Journal of the American Medical Association*, 249, 3052–3056.

Petersen, S.E., Fox, P.T., Posner, M.I., Mintin, M. and Raichle, M.E. (1988). Positron emission tomographic studies of the cortical anatomy of single-word processing. *Nature*, 331, 585–589.

Petersen, S.E., Fox, P.T., Snyder, A.Z. and Raichle, M.E. (1990). Activation of extrastriate and frontal cortical areas by visual words and word-like stimuli. *Science*, 249, 1041–1044.

Peterson, A.C. and Ebata, A.T. (1987). Developmental transitions and adolescent problem behavior: Implications for prevention and intervention. In K. Herrelmann (ed.), *Social Prevention and Intervention.* New York: De Gruyter.

Peterson, C.C. and Siegal, M. (1995). Deafness, conversation and theory of mind. *Journal of Child Psychology and Psychiatry*, 36, 459–474.

Peterson, L.R. and Peterson, M.J. (1959). Short-term retention of individual verbal items. *Journal of Experimental Psychology*, 58, 193–198.

Peto, R. (1994). Smoking and death: The past 40 years and the next 40. *British Medical Journal*, 309, 937–939.

Peto, R. (1998). *Update to 1995 of Analyses of Mortality from Smoking in 15 European Countries.* Oxford: University of Oxford.

Petre-Quadens, O. and De Lee, C. (1974). Eye movement frequencies and related paradoxical sleep cycles: Developmental changes. *Chronobiologia*, 1, 347–355.

Petrill, S.A., Plomin, R., Berg, S., Johansson, B., Pedersen, N.L., Ahern, F. and McClearn, G.E. (1998). The genetic and environmental relationship between general and specific cognitive abilities in twins age 80 and older. *Psychological Science*, 9, 3, 183–189.

Petruzzello, S.J., Jones, A.C. and Tate, A.K. (1997). Affective responses to acute exercise: A test of opponent-process theory. *Journal of Sports Medicine and Physical Fitness*, 37, 3, 205–212.

Pettigrew, T.F. (1979). The ultimate attribution error: Extending Allport's cognitive analysis of prejudice. *Personality and Social Psychology Bulletin*, 5, 461–476.

Petty, R.E. and Cacioppo, J.T. (1986). The elaboration likelihood model of persuasion. *Advances in Experimental Social Psychology*, 19, 123–205.

Pfefferbaum, A., Zipursky, R.B., Lim, K.O., Zatz, L.M., Stahl, S.M. and Jernigan, T.L. (1988). Computed tomographic evidence for generalized sulcal and ventricular enlargement in schizophrenia. *Archives of General Psychiatry*, 45, 633–640.

Phares, E.J. (1979). *Clinical Psychology: Concepts, methods, and profession.* Homewood, IL: Dorsey Press.

Phares, E.J. (1984). *Introduction to Personality.* Columbus, OH: Merrill.

Phares, E.J. and Chaplin, W.F. (1997). *Introduction to personality* (4th edition). New York: Longman.

Phillips, D.P. (1986). Natural experiments on the effects of mass media violence on fatal aggression: Strengths and weaknesses of a new approach. In L. Berkowitz (ed.), *Advances in Experimental Social Psychology*, Vol. 19. New York: Academic Press, pp. 207–250.

Phillips, M.L., Senior, C., Fahy, T. and David, A.S. (1998). Disgust – the forgotten emotion of psychiatry. *British Journal of Psychiatry*, 172, 373–375.

Phillips, M.L., Young, A.W., Senior, C., Brammer, M., Andrew, C., Calder, A.J., Bullmore, E.T., Perrett, D.I., Rowland, D., Williams, S.C.R. and David, A.S. (1997). A specific neural substrate for perceiving facial expressions of disgust. *Nature*, 389, 495–498.

Piaget, J. (1952). *The Origins of Intelligence in Children* (M. Cook, trans.). New York: International Universities Press.

Piaget, J. (1972). Intellectual evolution from adolescence to adulthood. *Human Development*, 15, 1–12.

Picariello, M.L., Greenberg, D.N. and Pillemer, D.B. (1990). Children's sex-related stereotyping of colors. *Child Development*, 61, 1453–1460.

Pickens, R.W., Svikis, D.S., McGue, M., Lykken, D.T., Heston, L.L. and Clayton, P.J. (1991). Heterogeneity in the inheritance of alcoholism: A study of male and female twins. *Archives of General Psychiatry*, 48, 19–28.

Pike, A., Reiss, D., Hetherington, E.M. and Plomin, R. (1996). Using MZ differences in the search for nonshared environmental effects. *Journal of Child Psychology and Psychiatry*, 37, 6, 695–704.

Pike, G.E., Kemp, R.I., Towell, N.A. and Phillips, K.C. (1997). Recognizing moving faces: The relative contribution of motion and perspective view information. *Visual Cognition*, 4, 409–438.

Pilleri, G. (1979). The blind Indus dolphin, *Platanista indi. Endeavours*, 3, 48–56.

Pinel, J.P.J. (1997). *Biopsychology* (3rd edition). Boston: Allyn & Bacon.

Pinizzotto, A.J. and Finkel, N.J. (1990). Criminal personality profiling. *Law and Human Behaviour*, 14, 3, 215–233.

Pinker, S. (1984). *Language learnability and language development.* Cambridge, MA: Harvard University Press.

Pinker, S. (1990). Language acquisition. In D.N. Osherson and H. Lasnik (eds), *An Invitation to Cognitive Science. Vol. 1: Language.* Cambridge, MA: MIT Press.

Pinker, S. (1994). *The language instinct.* New York: HarperCollins.

Pinker, S. (1997). *How the Mind Works.* New York: W.W. Norton.

Piven, J., Arndt, S. and Bailey, B.S. (1995). An MRI study of brain size in autism. *American Journal of Psychiatry*, 152, 1145–1149.

Plaisted, K., O'Riordan, M. and Baron-Cohen, S. (1998). Enhanced discrimination of novel, highly similar stimuli by adults with autism during a perceptual learning task. *Journal of Child Psychology and Psychiatry*, 39, 5, 765–775.

Plaut, D.C. and McClelland, J.L. (1993). Generalization with componential attractors: Word and nonword reading in an attractor network. In *Proceedings of the 15th Annual Conference of the Cognitive Science Society*. Hillsdale, NJ: Lawrence Erlbaum Associates.

Plaut, D.C., McClelland, J.L., Seidenberg, M.S. and Patterson, K.E. (1996). Understanding normal and impaired word reading: Computational principles in quasi-regular domain. *Psychological Review*, 103, 56–115.

Plomin, R. (1988). The nature and nurture of cognitive abilities. In R. Sternberg (ed.), *Advances in the Psychology of Human Intelligence*. Hillsdale, NJ: Lawrence Erlbaum Associates.

Plomin, R. (1990). *Nature and Nurture: An introduction to behavioral genetics*. Pacific Grove, CA: Brooks/Cole.

Plomin, R. (1997). Identifying genes for cognitive abilities and disabilities. In R.J. Sternberg and E. Grigorenko (eds), *Intelligence, Heredity and Environments*. New York: Cambridge University Press.

Plomin, R. and Bergeman, C. S. (1991). The nature of nurture: Genetic influence on 'environmental' measures. *Behavioral and Brain Sciences*, 14, 373–427.

Plomin, R. and DeFries, J.C. (1998). The genetics of cognitive abilities and disabilities. *Scientific American*, 278, 5, 40–47.

Plomin, R., McClearn, G.E., Smith, D.L., Vignetti, S., Chorney, M.J., Chorney, K., Venditti, C.P., Kasarda, S., Thompson, L.A., Detterman, D.K., Daniels, J., Owen, M.J. and McGuffin, P. (1994a). DNA markers associated with high versus low IQ: the IQ QTL project. *Behavioural Genetics*, 24, 107–118.

Plomin, R., Owen, M.J. and McGuffin, P. (1994b). Genetics and complex human behaviours. *Science*, 264, 1733–1739.

Plomin, R., McClearn, G.E., Smith, D.L., Skuder, P., Vignetti, S., Chorney, M.J., Chorney, K., Kasarda, S., Thompson, L.A., Detterman, D.K., Petrill, S.A., Daniels, J., Owen, M.J. and McGuffin, P. (1995). Allelic associations between 100 DNA markers and high versus low IQ. *Intelligence*, 21, 31–48.

Plomin, R., DeFries, J.C., McClearn, G.E. and Rutter, M. (1997). *Behavioural Genetics* (3rd edition). New York: WH Freeman.

Plutchik, R. (1980). *Emotion: A psychoevolutionary synthesis*. New York: Harper & Row.

Plutchik, R. (1984). Emotions: A general psychoevolutionary theory. In K.R. Scherer and P. Ekman (eds), *Approaches to emotion*. Hillsdale, NJ: Erlbaum.

Poeppel, D. (1996). A critical review of PET studies of phonological processing. *Brain and Language*, 55, 351.

Poggio, G. F. and Poggio, T. (1984). The analysis of stereopsis. *Annual Review of Neuroscience*, 7, 379–412.

Polich, J. and Kok, A. (1995). Cognitive and biological determinants of P300: An integrative overview. *Biological Psychology*, 41, 103–146.

Pollack, I. and Pickett, J.M. (1964). Intelligibility of excerpts from fluent speech: Auditory vs. structural context. *Journal of Verbal Learning and Verbal Behavior*, 3, 79–84.

Pollack, I.F., Polinko, P., Albright, A.L., Towbin, R. and Fitz, C. (1995). Mutism and pseudobulbar symptoms after resection of posterior fossa tumours in children: Incidence and pathophysiology. *Neurosurgery*, 37, 885–893.

Poole, D.A., Lindsay, D.S., Memon, A. and Bull, R. (1995). Psychotherapy and the recovery of memories of childhood sexual abuse: US and British practitioners' opinions, practices and experiences. *Journal of Consulting and Clinical Psychology*, 63, 3, 426–437.

Poole, M.E., Langan-Fox, J. and Omodei, M. (1991). Sex differences in perceived career success. *Genetic, Social and General Psychology Monographs*, 117, 155–174.

Porter, C., Markus, H. and Nurius, P.S. (1984). *Conceptions of possibility among people in crisis*. Unpublished manuscript. University of Michigan, Ann Arbor, 1984.

Posner, M.I. and Raichle, M. (1994). *Images of Mind*. New York: Scientific American Library.

Posner, M.I., Snyder, C.R.R. and Davidson, B.J. (1980). Attention and the detection of signals. *Journal of Experimental Psychology: General*, 109, 160–174.

Possl, J. and von Cramon, Y. (1996). Clients' view of neuropsychological rehabilitation. *Brain Injury*, 10, 2, 125–132.

Post, F. (1994). Creativity and psychopathology: A study of 291 world-famous men. *British Journal of Psychiatry*, 165, 22–34.

Post, F. (1996). Verbal creativity, depression and alcoholism. *British Journal of Psychiatry*, 168, 545–555.

Potter, J. and Wetherell, M. (1995). Discourse analysis. In J.A. Smith, R. Harre and L. vanLangenhove (eds), *Rethinking research methods in psychology*. London: Sage.

Potter, J. and Wetherell, M. (1987). *Discourse and Social Psychology*. London: Sage.

Potts, G.R. (1972). Information processing strategies used in the encoding of linear orderings. *Journal of Verbal Learning and Verbal Behavior*, 11, 727–740.

Powell, G.E. and Lindsay, S.J.E. (1994). An introduction to treatment. In S.J.E. Lindsay and G.E. Powell (eds), *The Handbook of Clinical Adult Psychology*. London: Routledge.

Powell, K.E., Thompson, P.D., Caspersen, C.J. and Kendrick, J.S. (1987). Physical activity and the incidence of coronary heart disease. *Annual Review of Public Health*, 8, 253–287.

Power, M. and Dalgleish, T. (1997). *Cognition and Emotion*. Hove, UK: The Psychology Press.

Pratkanis, A.R., Breckler, S.H. and Greenwald, A.G. (1989). *Attitude Structure and Function*. Hillsdale, NJ: Lawrence Erlbaum Associates.

Pratkanis, A.R., Eskenazi, J. and Greenwald, A.G. (1990). What you expect is what you believe, but not necessarily what you get: On the effectiveness of subliminal self-help audiotapes. Paper presented at the annual convention of the Western Psychological Association, Los Angeles, 1990. (Cited by Druckman and Bjork, 1990).

Premack, D. (1976). Language and intelligence in ape and man. *American Scientist*, 64, 674–683.

Price, C.J. (1997). Functional anatomy of reading. In R.S.J. Frachowiak, K.J. Friston, C.D. Frith, R.J. Dolan and J.C. Mazziotta (eds), *Human Brain Function*. New York: Academic Press.

Price, C.J., Wise, R.J.S., Watson, J.D.G., Patterson, K., Howard, D. and Frackowiak, R.S.J. (1994). Brain activity during reading: The effects of exposure duration and task. *Brain*, 117, 1255–1269.

Prichard, J. C. (1835). *A Treatise on Insanity and Other Disorders Affecting the Mind*. London: Sherwood, Gilbert, & Piper.

Prigatano, G.P. (1992). Personality disturbances associated with traumatic brain injury. *Journal of Consulting and Clinical Psychology*, 60, 3, 360–368.

Prior, M. (1992). Childhood autism. In S. Schwartz (ed.), *Case Studies in Abnormal Psychology*. New York: Wiley.

Propping, P., Kruger, J. and Janah, A. (1980). Effect of alcohol on genetically determined variants of the normal electroencephalogram. *Psychiatry Research*, 2, 85–98.

Propping, P., Kruger, J. and Mark, N. (1981). Genetic disposition to alcoholism: An EEG study in alcoholics and their relatives. *Human Genetics*, 59, 51–59.

Proudfoot, J., Guest, D., Carson, J., Dunn, G. and Gray, J. (1997). Effect of cognitive-behavioural training on job-find among long-term unemployed people. *Lancet*, 350, 96–100.

Provins, K.A. (1997). Handedness and speech: A critical reappraisal of the role of genetic and environmental factors in the cerebral lateralization of function. *Psychological Review*, 104, 3, 554–571.

Pugh, K.R., Shaywitz, B.A., Shaywitz, S.E., Shankweiler, D.P., Katz, L., Fletcher, J.M., Skudlarski, P., Fulbright, R.K., Constable, R.T., Bronen, R.A., Lacadie, C. and Gore, J.C. (1997). Predicting reading performance from neuroimaging profiles: The cerebral basis of phonological effects in printed word identification. *Journal of Experimental Psychology: Human Perception and Performance*, 23, 2, 299–318.

Qin, J., Quas, J.A., Redlich, A.D. and Goodman, G.S. (1997). Children's eyewitness testimony: Memory development in the legal context. In N. Cowan and C. Hulme (eds), *The Development of Memory in Childhood*. Hove, UK: The Psychology Press.

Quinn, J.F. (1996). Entitlements and the federal budget: A summary. *Gerontology News*, August, 2–3.

Rabbitt, P., Maylor, E., McInnes, L., Bent, N. and Moore, B. (1995). What goods can self-assessment questionnaires deliver for cognitive gerontology? *Applied Cognitive Psychology*, 9, S127–S152.

Rachman, S. and Hodgson, R.J. (1968). Experimentally-induced 'sexual fetishism': Replication and development. *Psychological Record*, 18, 25–27.

Rachman, S.J. and Wilson, G.T. (1980). Using direct and indirect measures to study perception without awareness. *Perception and Psychophysics*, 44, 563–575.

Rae, C., Lee, M.A., Dixon, R.M., Blamire, A.M., Thompson, C.H., Styles, P., Talcott, J., Richardson, A.J. and Stein, J.F. (1998). Metabolic anomalies in developmental dyslexia detected by 1H magnetic resonance spectroscopy. *Lancet*, 351, 1849–1852.

Ragland, D.R. and Brand, R.J. (1988). Type A behavior and mortality from coronary heart disease. *New England Journal of Medicine*, 318, 65–69.

Rahe, R.H. and Arthur, R.J. (1978). Life changes and illness reports. In K.E. Gunderson and R.H. Rahe (eds), *Life Stress and Illness*. Springfield, IL: Thomas.

Raine, A., Venables, P.H. and Williams, M. (1996). Better autonomic conditioning and faster electrodermal half-recovery time at age 15 years as possible protective factors against crime at age 29 years. *Developmental Psychology*, 32, 4, 624–630.

Rajecki, D.J. (1989). *Attitudes* (2nd edition). Sunderland, MA: Sinauer Associates.

Randich, A. and LoLordo, V.M. (1979). Preconditioning exposure to the unconditioned stimulus affects the acquisition of the conditioned emotional response. *Learning and Motivation*, 10, 245–275.

Rang, H.P., Dale, M.M. and Ritter, J.M. (1995). *Pharmacology*. New York: Churchill Livingstone.

Rapee, R.M. and Heimberg, R.G. (1997). A cognitive-behavioural model of anxiety in social phobia. *Behaviour Research and Therapy*, 35, 741–756.

Rapin, I. (1997). Autism. *New England Journal of Medicine*, 337, 2, 97–104.

Rapoport, J.L. (1989). The biology of obsessions and compulsions. *Scientific American*, March, 62–69.

Rasmussen, T. and Milner, B. (1977). The role of early left brain injury in determining lateralization of cerebral speech functions. *Annals of the New York Academy of Sciences*, 299, 355–369.

Rattner, A. (1988). Convicted but innocent: Wrongful conviction and the criminal justice system. *Law and Human Behaviour*, 12, 283–293.

Rauscher, F.H., Shaw, G.L. and Hy, K. (1993). Music and spatial task performance. *Nature*, 365, 611.

Rauscher, F.H., Shaw, G.L. and Hy, K. (1995). Listening to Mozart enhances spatial–temporal reasoning: Towards a neurophysiological basis. *Neuroscience Letters*, 185, 44–47.

Rawlings, D. (1985). Psychoticism, creativity and dichotic shadowing. *Personality and Individual Differences*, 6, 737–742.

Ray, O. and Ksir, C. (1990). *Drugs, Society, and Human Behavior* (5th edition). St Louis: Times Mirror.

Raybin, J.B. and Detre, T.P. (1969). Sleep disorder and symptomatology among medical and nursing students. *Comprehensive Psychiatry*, 10, 452–467.

Rayner, K. and Pollatsek, A. (1989). *The Psychology of Reading*. Englewood Cliffs, NJ: Prentice Hall.

Reber, A.A. and Allen, R. (1978). Analogical and abstraction strategies in synthetic grammar learning: A functionalist interpretation. *Cognition*, 6, 189–221.

Reber, A.S. (1989). Implicit learning and tacit knowledge. *Journal of Experimental Psychology: General*, 118, 219–235.

Reber, A.S. (1992). The cognitive unconscious: An evolutionary perspective. *Consciousness and Cognition*, 1, 93–133.

Redding, G.M. and Hawley, E. (1993). Length illusion in fractional Muller-Lyer stimuli: an object–perception approach. *Perception*, 22, 819–828.

Regan, D.T. (1971). Effects of a favor and liking on compliance. *Journal of Experimental Social Psychology*, 7, 627–639.

Regier, D.A., Boyd, J.H., Burke, J.D., Rae, D.S., Myers, J.K., Kramer, M., Robins, L.N., George, L.K., Karno, M. and Locke, B.Z. (1988). One-month prevalence of mental disorders in the United States. *Archives of General Psychiatry*, 45, 977–986.

Rehm, J.T., Bondy, S.J., Sempos, C.T. and Vuong, C.V. (1997). Alcohol consumption and coronary heart disease morbidity and mortality. *American Journal of Epidemiology*, 146, 495–501.

Reicher, S.D. (1987). Crowd behaviour as social action. In J.C. Turner, M.A. Hogg, P.J. Oakes, S.D. Reicher and M. S. Wetherell, *Rediscovering the Social Group: A self-categorization theory*. Oxford: Blackwell, pp. 171–202.

Reid, A.K. and Staddon, J.E.R. (1998). A dynamic route finder for the cognitive map. *Psychological Review*, 105, 3, 585–601.

Reilly, D.T. (1983). Young doctors' views on alternative medicine. *British Medical Journal*, 287, 337–339.

Reilly, J. and Mulhern, G. (1995). Gender differences in self-estimated IQ: The need for care in interpreting group data. *Personality and Individual Differences*, 18, 189–192.

Reinke, B.J., Holmes, D.S. and Harris, R.L. (1985). The timing of psychosocial changes in women's lives: The years 25 to 45. *Journal of Personality and Social Psychology*, 48, 1353–1364.

Reiss, S. and McNally, R.J. (1985). Expectancy mode of fear. In S. Reiss and R. Bootzin (eds), *Theoretical Issues in Behaviour Therapy*. San Diego: Academic Press.

Resch, E., Haffner, J., Parzer, P., Pfueller, U., Strehlow, U. and Zerahn-Hartung, C. (1997). Testing the hypothesis of the relationships between laterality and ability according to Annett's right-shift theory: Findings in an epidemiological sample of young adults. *British Journal of Psychology*, 88, 621–636.

Rescorla, R.A. (1991). Associative relations in associative learning. The Eighteenth Bartlett Memorial Lecture. *Quarterly Journal of Experimental Psychology*, 43, 1–23.

Rest, J.R. (1979). *Development in Judging Moral Issues*. Minneapolis: University of Minnesota Press.

Review Panel (1981). Coronary-prone and behavior and coronary heart disease: A critical review. *Circulation*, 673, 1199–1215.

Rheingold, H.L. and Eckerman, C.O. (1973). Fear of the stranger: A critical examination. In H.W. Reese (ed.), *Advances in Child Development and Behavior*, Vol. 8. New York: Academic Press.

Rice, M.L., Huston, A.C., Truglio, R. and Wright, J. (1990). Words from 'Sesame Street': Learning vocabulary while viewing. *Developmental Psychology*, 26, 421–428.

Richards, M.H., Crowe, P.A., Larson, R. and Swarr, A. (1998). Developmental patterns and gender differences in the experience of peer companionship during adolescence. *Child Development*, 69, 1, 154–163.

Riddoch, G. (1917). Dissociation of visual perceptions due to occipital injuries, with special reference to appreciation of movement. *Brain*, 40, 15–47.

Rideout, B.E., Dougherty, S. and Wernert, L. (1998). Effect of music on spatial performance: A test of generality. *Perceptual and Motor Skills*, 86, 512–514.

Rideout, B.E. and Laubach, C.M. (1996). EEG correlates of enhanced spatial performance following exposure to music. *Perceptual and Motor Skills*, 82, 427–432.

Riggs, L.A., Ratliff, F., Cornsweet, J.C. and Cornsweet, T.N. (1953). The disappearance of steadily fixated visual test objects. *Journal of the Optical Society of America*, 43, 495–501.

Rippon, G. and Brunswick, N. (1998). EEG correlates of phonological processing in dyslexic children. *Journal of Psychophysiology*, 12, 261–274.

Rips, L.J., Shoben, E.J. and Smith, E.E. (1973). Semantic distance and the verification of semantic relations. *Journal of Verbal Learning and Verbal Behavior*, 12, 1–20.

Rispers, J. and van Yperen, T.A. (1997). How specific are 'specific developmental disorders'? The relevance of the concept of specific developmental disorders for the classification of childhood developmental disorders. *Journal of Child Psychology and Psychiatry*, 38, 3, 351–363.

Ris-Stalpers, C., Kuiper, G.G.J.M., Faber, P.W., Schweikert, H.U., Van Rooij, H.C.J., Zegers, N.D., Hodgins, M.B., Degenhart, H.J., Trapman, J. and Brinkmann, A.O. (1990). Aberrant splicing of androgen receptor mRNA results in synthesis of a nonfunctional receptor protein in a patient with androgen insensitivity. *Proceedings of the National Academy of Sciences*, 87, 7866–7870.

Ritchie, K. (1997). Establishing the limits of normal cerebal aging and senile dementia. *British Journal of Psychiatry*, 173, 97–101.

Ritchie, K., Leibovici, D., Ledesert, B. *et al.* (1996). A typology of sub-clinical senescent cognitive disorder. *British Journal of Psychiatry*, 168, 470–476.

Ritter, R.C., Brenner, L. and Yox, D.P. (1992). Participation of vagal sensory neurons in putative satiety signals from the upper gastrointestinal tract. In S. Ritter, R.C. Ritter and C.D. Barnes (eds), *Neuroanatomy and Physiology of Abdominal Vagal Afferents*. Boca Raton, FL: CRC Press.

Ritter, S. and Taylor, J. S. (1989). Capsaicin abolishes lipoprivic but not glucoprivic feeding in rats. *American Journal of Physiology*, 256, R1232–R1239.

Rittle, R.H. (1981). Changes in helping behavior: Self-versus situational perceptions as mediators of the foot-in-the-door effect. *Personality and Social Psychology Bulletin*, 7, 431–437.

Robbins, L.N., Helzer, J.E., Weissman, M.M., Orvaschel, H., Gruenberg, E., Burke, J.D. and Regier, D.A. (1984). Lifetime prevalence of specific psychiatric disorders in three sites. *Archives of General Psychiatry*, 41, 949–958.

Roberts, G. and Sherratt, T.N. (1998). Development of cooperative relationships through increasing investment. *Nature*, 394, 175–179.

Roberts, T. and Bruce, V. (1988). Feature saliency in judging the sex and familiarity of faces. *Perception*, 17, 475–481.

Robertson, I.H. (1990). Does computerised cognitive rehabilitation work? A review. *Aphasiology*, 4, 381–405.

Robertson, I.H., Halligan, P.W. and Marshall, J.C. (1993). Prospects for the rehabilitation of unilateral neglect. In I.H. Robertson and J.C. Marshall (eds), *Unilateral Neglect: Clinical and experimental studies*. Hove, UK: Lawrence Erlbaum Associates.

Robins, L.N. and Regier, D.A. (1994). *Psychiatric Disorders in America*. New York: Free Press.

Robinson, L.A., Berman, J.S. and Neimeyer, R.A. (1990). Psychotherapy for the treatment of depression: A comprehensive review of controlled outcome research. *Psychological Bulletin*, 108, 30–49.

Rocca, W.A., Amaducci, L.A. and Schoenberg, B.S. (1986). Epidemiology of clinically diagnosed Alzheimer's disease. *Annals of Neurology*, 19, 415–424.

Rock, I. and Gutman, D. (1981). The effect of inattention on form perception. *Journal of Experimental Psychology (Human Perception and Performance)*, 7, 275–285.

Rodin, J., Schank, D. and Striegel-Moore, R. (1989). Psychological features of obesity. *Medical Clinics of North America*, 73, 47–66.

Roff, J.D. and Knight, R. (1981). Family characteristics, childhood symptoms, and adult outcome in schizophrenia. *Journal of Abnormal Psychology*, 90, 510–520.

Roffwarg, H.P., Muzio, J.N. and Dement, W.C. (1966). Ontogenetic development of human sleep-dream cycle. *Science*, 152, 604–619.

Rogers, C.R. (1961). *On Becoming a Person*. Boston: Houghton Mifflin.

Rogers, C.T. (1951). *Client-centered Therapy*. Boston: Houghton Mifflin.

Rogers, K.B. (1986). Do the gifted think and learn differently? A review of recent research and its implications for instruction. *Journal for the Education of the Gifted*, 10, 17–39.

Rogoff, B. (1990). *Apprenticeship in Thinking: Cognitive Development in Social Context*. New York: Oxford University Press.

Rogoff, B. and Chavajay, P. (1995). What's become of research on the cultural basis of cognitive development. *American Psychologist*, 50, 859–877.

Rolls, B.J., Rowe, E.A., Rolls, E.T., Kingston, B. and Megson, A. (1981). Variety in the meal enhances food intake in man. *Physiology and Behaviour*, 26, 215–221.

Rolls, B.J., Rolls, E.T. and Rowe, E.A. (1982b). How sensory properties of foods affect human feeding behaviour. *Physiology and Behaviour*, 29, 409–417.

Rolls, B.J., van Duijenvoorde, P.M. and Rolls, E.T. (1984). Pleasantness changes and food intake in a varied four course meal. *Appetitie*, 5, 337–348.

Rolls, E.T. (1997). Brain mechanisms of vision, memory and consciousness. In M. Ito, Y. Miyashita and E.T. Rolls (eds), *Cognition, Computation and Consciousness*. Oxford: Oxford University Press.

Rolls, E.T. and Baylis, L.L. (1994). Gustatory, olfactory and visual convergence within the primate orbitofrontal cortex. *Journal of Neuroscience*, 14, 5437–5452.

Rolls, E.T. and Rolls, J.H. (1997). Olfactory sensory-specific satiety in humans. *Physiology and Behaviour*, 61, 3, 461–473.

Rolls, E.T., Murzi, E., Yaxley, S., Thorpe, S.J. and Simpson, S.J. (1986). Sensory-specific satiety: Food-specific reduction in responsiveness of ventral forebrain neurons after feeding in the monkey. *Brain Research*, 368, 79–86.

Romaine, S. (1989). *Bilingualism*. Oxford: Blackwell.

Rosal, M.C., Ockene, J.K., Ma, Y., Hebert, J.R., Ockene, I.S., Merriam, P. and Hurley, T.G. (1998). Coronary artery smoking intervention study (CASIS): 5 year follow up. *Health Psychology*, 17, 5, 476–478.

Rosch, E.H. (1975). Cognitive representations of semantic categories. *Journal of Experimental Psychology (General)*, 104, 192–233.

Rosch, E.H., Mervis, C.B., Gray, W.D., Johnson, D.M. and Boyes-Braem, P. (1976). Basic objects in natural categories. *Cognitive Psychology*, 8, 382–439.

Rose, G.A. and Williams, R.T. (1961). Metabolic studies of large and small eaters. *British Journal of Nutrition*, 15, 1–9.

Rose, J.S., Chassin, L., Presson, C.C. and Sherman, S.J. (1996). Prospective predictors of quit attempts and smoking cessation in young adults. *Health Psychology*, 15, 4, 261–268.

Rose, R.J. (1988). Genetic and environmental variance in content dimensions of the MMPI. *Journal of Personality and Social Psychology*, 55, 302–311.

Rose, R.J. (1995). Genes and human behavior. *Annual Review of Psychology*, 46, 625–654.

Rose, S.P.R. (1992). *The Making of Memory*. New York: Bantam.

Rosenblatt, F. (1962). *Principles of Neurodynamics*. New York: Spartan.

Rosenblatt, J.S. and Aronson, L.R. (1958). The decline of sexual behavior in male cats after castration with special reference to the role of prior sexual experience. *Behaviour*, 12, 285–338.

Rosenman, R.H., Brand, R.J., Jenkins, C.D., Friedman, M., Straus, R. and Wurm, M. (1975). Coronary heart disease in the Western Collaborative Group Study: Final follow-up experience of $8^{1}/_{2}$ years. *Journal of the American Medical Association*, 233, 872–877.

Rosenthal, D. (1970). *Genetic Theory and Abnormal Behavior*. New York: McGraw-Hill.

Rosenthal, N.E. and Wehr, T.A. (1992). Towards understanding the mechanism of action of light in seasonal affective disorder. *Pharmacopsychiatry*, 25, 56–60.

Rosenthal, N.E., Sack, D.A., Gillin, J.C. *et al.* (1984). Seasonal affective disorder: A description of the syndrome and preliminary findings with light therapy. *Archives of General Psychiatry*, 41, 72–80.

Rosenthal, N.E., Sack, D.A., James, S.P., Parry, B.L., Mendelson, W.B., Tamarkin, L. and Wehr, T.A. (1985). Seasonal affective disorder and phototherapy. *Annals of the New York Academy of Sciences*, 453, 260–269.

Rosenthal, R. and Fode, K.L. (1963). The effect of experimental bias on the performance of the albino rat. *Behavioral Science*, 8, 183–187.

Rosenzweig, M.R. (1984). Experience, memory, and the brain. *American Psychologist*, 39, 365–376.

Ross, G., Nelson, K., Wetstone, H. and Tanouye, E. (1986). Acquisition and generalization of novel object concepts by young language learners. *Journal of Child Language*, 13, 67–83.

Ross, L. (1977). The intuitive psychologist and his shortcomings: Distortions in the attribution process. In L. Berkowitz (ed.), *Advances in Experimental Social Psychology*. New York: Academic Press.

Rosser, R. (1994). *Cognitive Development: Psychological and biological perspectives*. Boston: Allyn & Bacon.

Roth, E.M. and Mervis, C.B. (1983). Fuzzy set theory and class inclusion relations in semantic categories. *Journal of Verbal Learning and Verbal Behavior*, 22, 509–525.

Rotter, J.B. (1954). *Social Learning and Clinical Psychology*. Englewood Cliffs, NJ: Prentice Hall.

Rotter, J.B. (1966). Generalized expectancies for internal versus external control of reinforcement. *Psychological Monographs*, 80 (1, Whole No. 609).

Rotton, J. (1992). Trait humor and longevity: Do comics have the last laugh? *Health Psychology*, 11, 4, 262–266.

Rovee, C. and Rovee, D.T. (1969). Conjugate reinforcement of infant exploratory behaviour. *Journal of Experimental Child Psychology*, 8, 33–39.

Rovee-Collier, C. and Hayne, H. (1987). Reactivation of infant memory: Implications for cognitive development. In H.W. Reese (ed.), *Advances in Child Development and Behaviour*, Vol. 20. New York: Academic Press.

Rozin, P., Bressman, B. and Taft, M. (1974). Do children understand the basic relationship between speech and writing? The Mow-Motorcycle test. *Journal of Reading Behaviour*, 6, 327–334.

Rubenstein, H., Lewsi, S.S. and Rubenstein, M.A. (1971). Evidence for phonemic recoding in visual word recognition. *Journal of Verbal Learning and Verbal Behaviour*, 10, 645–657.

Rubin, D.C. (1982). On the retention function for autobiographical memory. *Journal of Verbal Learning and Verbal Behaviour*, 21, 21–38.

Rudolph, D.L. and Kim, J.G. (1996). Mood responses to recreational sport and exercise in a Korean sample. *Journal of Social Behaviour and Personality*, 11, 4, 841–849.

Ruff, C.B., Trinkhaus, E. and Holliday, T.W. (1997). Body mass and encephalization in Pleistocene Homo. *Nature*, 387, 173–176.

Rugg, M.D. (1997). *Cognitive Neuroscience*. Hove, UK: The Psychology Press.

Rumelhart, D.E., McClelland, J.L. and the PDP Research Group. (1986). *Parallel Distributed Processing: Explorations in the microstructure of cognition*. Cambridge, MA: MIT Press.

Rumsey, J.M., Horwitz, B., Donohue, B.C., Nace, K., Maisog, J.M. and Andreason, P. (1997). Phonological and orthographic components of word recognition. *Brain*, 739–759.

Rushing, W.A. (1995). *The AIDS Epidemic: Social dimensions of an infectious disease*. Boulder, CO: Westview Press.

Rushton, J.P. (1995). *Race, Evolution and Behaviour: A life history perspective*. New Brunswick, NJ: Transaction.

Rushton, J.P. (1997). Race, intelligence and the brain: The errors and omissions of the 'revised' edition of S.J. Gould's The Mismeasure of Man (1996). *Personality and Individual Differences*, 23, 1, 169–180.

Russell, D. (1988). The incidence and prevalence of intrafamilial and extrafamilial sexual abuse of female children. In L.E.A. Walker (ed.), *Handbook of Sexual Abuse in Children*. New York: Springer-Verlag.

Russell, G.F.M. and Treasure, J. (1989). The modern history of anorexia nervosa: An interpretation of why the illness has changed. *Annals of the New York Academy of Sciences*, 575, 13–30.

Russell, J.A. (1991). Culture and categorization of emotion. *Psychological Bulletin*, 110, 426–450.

Russell, J.A. (1994). Is there universal recognition of emotion from facial expression? A review of the cross-cultural studies. *Psychological Bulletin*, 115, 1, 102–141.

Russell, M.I., Suritz, G.M. and Thompson, K. (1980). Olfactory influences on the human menstrual cycle. *Pharmacology, Biochemenstrual Behaviour*, 13, 737–738.

Russell, P.A., Deregowski, J.B. and Kinnear, P.R. (1997). Perception and aesthetics. In J.W. Berry, P.R. Dasen and T.S. Sarawathi (eds), *Handbook of Cross-Cultural Psychology. Vol. 2: Basic processes and human development*. Boston: Allyn & Bacon.

Russell, P.A., Hosie, J.A., Gray, C.D., Scott, C., Hunter, N., Banks, J.S. and Macaulay, M.C. (1998). The development of theory of mind in deaf children. *Journal of Child Psychology and Psychiatry*, 39, 6, 903–910.

Russell, P.J. (1992). *Genetics*. New York: HarperCollins.

Ryback, R.S. and Lewis, O.F. (1971). Effects of prolonged bed rest on EEG sleep patterns in young, healthy volunteers. *Electroencephalography and Clinical Neurophysiology*, 31, 395–399.

Rutter, M. (1979). Language, cognition and autism. In R. Katzman (ed.), *Congenital and Acquired Cognitive Disorders*. New York: Raven Press.

Rutter, M. (1987). The 'what' and 'how' of language development: A note on some outstanding issues and questions. In W. Yule and M. Rutter (eds), *Language Development and Disorders*. London: MacKeith Press.

Rutter, M. (1994). Psychiatric genetics: Research challenges and pathways forward. *American Journal of Medical Genetics*, 54, 185–198.

Rutter, M. and English and Romanian Adoptees Study Team (1998). Developmental catch-up and deficit following adoption after global early deprivation. *Journal of Child Psychology and Psychiatry*, 39, 465–476.

Ryan, E.B., McNamara, S.R. and Kenney, M. (1977). Lexical awareness and reading performance among beginning readers. *Journal of Reading Behaviour*, 9, 399–400.

Ryan, K.M. and Kanjorksi, J. (1998). The enjoyment of sexist humor, rape attitudes, and relationship aggression in college students. *Sex Roles*, 38, 743–756.

Ryle, G. (1949). *The Concept of Mind*. New York: Barnes & Noble.

Rymer, R. (1993). *Genie: Escape from a silent childhood*. London: Michael Joseph.

Saari, S, Lindeman, M., Verkasalo, M. and Prytz, M. (1996). The Estonia Disaster: A description of the crisis intervention in Finland. *European Psychologist*, 1, 2, 135–139.

Sachs, J. (1993). The emergence of intentional communication. In J. Berko Gleason (ed.), *The Development of Language*. New York: Macmillan.

Sachs, O. (1989). *Seeing Voices: A journey into the world of the deaf*. Berkeley, CA: University of California Press.

Saegert, S.C., Swap, W. and Zajonc, R.B. (1973). Exposure, context, and interpersonal attraction. *Journal of Personality and Social Psychology*, 25, 234–242.

Saffran, E.M., Marin, O.S.M. and Yeni-Komshian, G.H. (1976). An analysis of speech perception in word deafness. *Brain and Language*, 3, 209–228.

Saffran, E.M., Schwartz, M.F. and Marin, O.S.M. (1980). Evidence from aphasia: Isolating the components of a production model. In B. Butterworth (ed.), *Language Production*. London: Academic Press.

Sakai, F., Meyer, J. S., Karacan, I., Derman, S. and Yamamoto, M. (1979). Normal human sleep: Regional cerebral haemodynamics. *Annals of Neurology*, 7, 471–478.

Sakata, H. (1997). Parietal visual neurons coding three-dimensional characteristics of objects and their relation to hand action. In P. Thier and H-O. Karnath (eds), *Parietal Lobe Contributions to Orientation in 3D Space*. Berlin: Springer-Verlag.

Salame, P. and Baddeley, A.D. (1982). Disruption of short-term memory by unattended speech: Implications for the structure of working memory. *Journal of Verbal Learning and Verbal Behaviour*, 21, 150–164.

Salame, P. and Baddeley, A.D. (1990). The effects of irrelevant speech on immediate free recall. *Bulletin of the Psychonomic Society*, 28, 540–542.

Salapatek, P. (1975). Pattern perception in early infancy. In L.B. Cohen and P. Salapatek (eds), *Infant Perception: From Sensation to Cognition*, Vol. 1. New York: Academic Press.

Salkovskis, P.M., Forrester, E. and Richards, C. (1998). Cognitive-behavioural approach to understanding obsessional thinking. *British Journal of Psychiatry*, 173 (suppl. 35), 53–63.

Salthouse, T.A. (1984). Effects of age and skill in typing. *Journal of Gerontology*, 113, 345–371.

Salthouse, T.A. (1988). Cognitive aspects of motor functioning. In J.A. Joseph (ed.), *Central Determinants of Age-related Declines in Motor Function*. New York: New York Academy of Sciences.

Salthouse, T.A. (1992). What do adult age differences in the Digit Symbol Substitution Test reflect? *Journal of Gerontology*, 47, 3, 121–128.

Salthouse, T.A. (1993). Speed mediation of adult age differences in cognition. *Developmental Psychology*, 29, 4, 722–738.

Salthouse, T.A. and Babcock, R.L. (1991). Decomposing adult age differences in working memory. *Developmental Psychology*, 27, 5, 763–776.

Samuel, M., Caputo, E., Brooks, D.J., Schrag, A., Scaravilli, T., Branston, N.M., Rothwell, J.C., Marsden, C.D., Thomas, D.G.T., Lees, A.J. and Quinn, N.P. (1998). A study of medial pallidotomy for Parkinson's disease: Clinical outcome, MRI location and complications. *Brain*, 121, 59–75.

Sande, G.N., Goethals, G.R. and Radloff, C.E. (1988). Perceiving one's own traits and others: The multifaceted self. *Journal of Personality and Social Psychology*, 54, 13–20.

Sanna, L.J. and Shotland, R.L. (1990). Valence of anticipated evaluation and social facilitation. *Journal of Experimental Social Psychology*, 26, 82–92.

Santos, M.D., Leve, C. and Pratkanis, A.R. (1994). Hey buddy, can you spare seventeen cents? Mindful persuasion and the pique technique. *Journal of Applied Social Psychology*, 24, 755–764.

Sapolsky, R. (1986). Glucocorticoid toxicity in the hippocampus: Reversal by supplementation with brain fuels. *Journal of Neuroscience*, 6, 2240–2244.

Sapolsky, R.M., Krey, L.C. and McEwen, B.S. (1986). The neuroendocrinology of stress and aging: The glucocorticoid cascade hypothesis. *Endocrine Reviews*, 7, 284–301.

Sarafino, E.P. (1998). *Health Psychology: Biopsychosocial interactions* (3rd edition). Chichester: Wiley.

Sarason, I. and Sarason, B. (1993). *Abnormal Psychology: The problem of maladaptive behavior* (7th edition). Englewood Cliffs, NJ: Prentice Hall.

Savage-Rumbaugh, E.S. (1990). Language acquisition in a nonhuman species: Implications for the innateness debate. *Development Psychobiology*, 23, 599–620.

Savage-Rumbaugh, S., Shanker, S.G. and Taylor, T.J. (1998). *Apes, Language and the Human Mind*. Oxford: Oxford University Press.

Saywitz, K.J., Geiselman, R.E. and Bornstein, G.K. (1992). Effects of cognitive interviewing and practice on children's recall performance. *Journal of Applied Psychology*, 77, 744–756.

Scarr, S. (1997). Behaviour-genetic and socialization theories of intelligence: Truce and reconciliation. In R.J. Sternberg and E. Grigorenko (eds), *Intelligence, Heredity and Environments*. New York: Cambridge University Press.

Scarr, S. and Weinberg, R.A. (1976). IQ Performance of black children adopted by white families. *American Psychologist*, 31, 726–739.

Scarr, S. and Weinberg, R. A. (1978). The influence of 'family background' on intellectual attainment. *American Sociological Review*, 43, 674–679.

Scarr, S., Webber, P.L., Weinberg, A. and Wittig, M.A. (1981). Personality resemblance among adolescents and their parents in biologically related and adoptive families. *Journal of Personality and Social Psychology*, 40, 885–898.

Schaal, B., Marlier, L. and Soussignan, R. (1995). Responsiveness to the odour of amniotic fluid in the human neonate. *Biological Neonate*, 67, 397–406.

Schaalma, H.P., Kok, G., Bosker, R.J., Parcel, G.S., Peters, L., Poelman, J. and Reinders, J. (1996). Planned development and evaluation of AIDS/STD education for secondary-school students in the Netherlands: Short-term effects. *Health Education Quarterly*, 23, 469–487.

Schachter, S. (1964). The interaction of cognitive and physiological determinants of emotional state. In P.H. Liederman and D. Shapiro (eds), *Psychobiological Approaches to Social Behavior*. Stanford, CA: Stanford University Press.

Schachter, S. and Singer, J. E. (1962). Cognitive, social and physiological determinants of emotional state. *Psychological Review*, 69, 379–399.

Schacter, D.L., Rich, S.A. and Stamp, M.S. (1985). Remediation of memory disorders: Experimental evaluation of the spaced-retrieval technique. *Journal of Clinical and Experimental Neuropsychology*, 7, 79–96.

Schaffer, C.E., Davidson, R.J. and Saron, C. (1983). Frontal and parietal electroencephalographic asymmetry in depressed and non-depressed subjects. *Biological Psychiatry*, 18, 753–762.

Schaie, K.W. (1990). Intellectual development in adulthood. In J.E. Birren and K.W. Schaie (eds), *Handbook of the Psychology of Aging* (3rd edition). San Diego: Academic Press.

Schaie, K.W. and Willis, S.L. (1992). *Adult Development and Learning* (3rd edition). New York: HarperCollins.

Schank, R. and Abelson, R.P. (1977). *Scripts, Plans, Goals, and Understanding*. Hillsdale, NJ: Lawrence Erlbaum Associates.

Schein, J.D. (1989). *At Home Among Strangers*. Washington, DC: Gallaudet University Press.

Scheier, M.F. and Carver, C.S. (1992). Effects of optimism on psychological and physical well-being: Theoretical overview and empirical update. *Cognitive Therapy and Research*, 16, 201–228.

Schenck, C.H., Bundlie, S.R., Ettinger, M.G. and Mahowald, M.W. (1986). Chronic behavioral disorders of human REM sleep: A new category of parasomnia. *Sleep*, 9, 293–308.

Schiff, B.B. and Lamon, M. (1989). Inducing emotion by unilateral contraction of facial muscles: A new look at hemispheric lateralization in emotion. *Cortex*, 30, 255–267.

Schiff, B.B. and Lamon, M. (1994). Inducing emotion by unilateral contraction of hand muscles. *Cortex*, 30, 247–254.

Schiffman, S. (1982). Relapse following smoking cessation: A situational analysis. *Journal of Consulting and Clinical Psychology*, 50, 71–96.

Schiffman, S., Gnys, M., Richards, T.J., Paty, J.A., Hickox, M. and Kassel, J.D. (1996). Temptations to smoke after quitting: A comparison of lapsers and maintainers. *Health Psychology*, 15, 6, 455–461.

Schleifer, S.J., Keller, S.E., Camerino, M., Thornton, J.C. and Stein, M. (1983). Suppression of lymphocyte stimulation following bereavement. *Journal of the American Medical Association*, 15, 374–377.

Schmahmann, J.D. and Sherman, J.C. (1998). The cerebellar cognitive affective syndrome. *Brain*, 121, 561–579.

Schmand, B., Smit, J.H., Lideboom, J., Smits, C., Hooijer, C., Jonker, C. and Deelman, B. (1997). Low education is a genuine risk factor for accelerated memory decline and dementia. *Journal of Clinical Epidemiology*, 50, 1025–1033.

Schmid, J. and Fiedler, K. (1998). The backbone of closing speeches: The impact of prosecution versus defense language on judicial attributions. *Journal of Applied Social Psychology*, 28, 1140–1172.

Schmidt, W., Boos, R., Gnirs, J., Auer, L. and Schulze, S. (1985). Fetal behavioural states and controlled sound stimulation. *Early Human Development*, 12, 145–153.

Schneider, G.E. (1969). Two visual systems. *Science*, 163, 895–902.

Schoenthaler, S. (1991). *Improve Your Child's IQ and Behaviour*. London: BBC Books.

Schoenthaler, S., Amos, S.P., Doraz, W.E., Kelly, M.A. and Wakefield, J. (1991a). Controlled trial of vitamin-mineral supplementation: Effects on intelligence and brain function. *Personality and Individual Differences*, 12, 343–350.

Schoenthaler, S., Amos, S.P., Eysenck, H.J., Peritz, E. and Yudkin, J. (1991b). Controlled trial of vitamin-mineral supplementation: Effects on intelligence and performance. *Personality and Individual Differences*, 12, 351–362.

Scholing, A. and Emmelkamp, P.M.G. (1996). Treatment of generalized social phobia: Results at long-term follow-up. *Behaviour Research and Therapy*, 34, 5/6, 447 452.

Schopler, E. (1996). Are autism and Asperger syndrome different labels or different disabilities? *Journal of Autism and Developmental Disorders*, 26, 109–110.

Schwartz, M.F., Saffran, E.M. and Marin, O.S.M. (1980). The word order problem in agrammatism. I. Comprehension. *Brain and Language*, 10, 249–262.

Schwartz, R. and Schwartz, L.J. (1980). *Becoming a Couple*. Englewood Cliffs, NJ: Prentice-Hall.

Scott, S.K., Young, A.W., Calder, A.J., Hellawell, D.J., Aggleton, J.P. and Johnson, M. (1997). Impaired auditory recognition of fear and anger following bilateral amygdala lesions. *Nature*, 385, 254–257.

Scoville, W.B. and Milner, B. (1957). Loss of recent memory after bilateral hippocampal lesions. *Journal of Neurology, Neurosurgery and Psychiatry*, 20, 11–21.

Scribner, S. (1977). Modes of thinking and ways of speaking: Culture and logic reconsidered. In P.N. Johnson-Laird and P.C. Wason (eds), *Thinking: Readings in cognitive science*. Cambridge: Cambridge University Press.

Scully, D., Kremer, J., Meade, M.M., Graham, R. and Dudgeon, K. (1998). Physical exercise and psychological well-being: A critical review. *British Journal of Sports Medicine*, 32, 111–120.

Segall, M.H., Campbell, D.T. and Herskovits, M.J. (1966). *The Influence of Culture on Visual Perception*. Indianapolis, IN: Bobbs-Merrill.

Segall, M.H., Lonner, W.J. and Berry, J.W. (1998). Cross-cultural psychology as a scholarly discipline. *Amercian Psychologist*, 53, 10, 1101–1110.

Segalowitz, S.J. and Bryden, M.P. (1983). Individual differences in hemispheric representation of language. In S.J. Segalowitz (ed.), *Language Functions and Brain Organization*. New York: Academic Press.

Segerstrom, S.C., Tayor, S.E., Kemeny, M.E. and Fahey, J.L. (1998). Optimism is associated with mood, coping and immune change in response to stress. *Journal of Personality and Social Psychology*, 74, 6, 1646–1655.

Seidenberg, M.S. and McClelland, J.L. (1989). A distributed, developmental model of word recognition and naming. *Psychological Review*, 96, 523–568.

Selemon, L.D., Rajkowska, G. and Goldman-Rakic, P.S. (1995). Abnormally high neuronal density in the schizophrenic cortex. A morphometric analysis of prefrontal area 9 and occipital area 17. *Archives of General Psychiatry*, 52, 805–818.

Selfridge, O.G. (1959). Pandemonium: A paradigm for learning. *In the mechanisation of thought process*. London: HMSO.

Selfridge, O.G. and Neisser, U. (1960). Pattern recognition by machine. *Scientific American*, 203, 60–68.

Seligman, M.E.P. (1971). Phobias and preparedness. *Behavior Therapy*, 2, 307–320.

Seligman, M.E.P. (1975). *Helplessness*. San Francisco: W.H. Freeman.

Seligman, M.E.P. (1988). Competing theories of panic. In S. Rachman and J.D. Maser (eds), *Panic: Psychological perspectives*. Hillsdale, NJ: Lawrence Erlbaum Associates.

Seligman, M.E.P. and Schulman, P. (1986). Explanatory style as a predictor of productivity and quitting among life insurance sales agents. *Journal of Personality and Social Psychology*, 50, 832–838.

Selye, H. (1956). *The Stress of Life*. New York: McGraw-Hill.

Selye, H. (1974). *Stress without Distress*. New York: Harper & Row.

Selye, H. (1991). History and present status of the stress concept. In A. Monat and R.S. Lazarus (eds), *Stress and Coping*. New York: Columbia University Press.

Selye, H. and Tuchweber, B. (1976). Stress in relation to aging and disease. In A. Everitt and J. Burgess (eds), *Hypothalamus, Pituitary and Aging*. Springfield, IL: Charles C. Thomas.

Sergent, J. (1987). A new look at the human split brain. *Brain*, 110, 1375–1392.

Sergent, J. (1990). Furtive incursions into bicameral minds: Integrative and co-ordinating role of the subcortical structures. *Brain*, 113, 537–568.

Sergent, J. (1991). Processing of spatial relations within and between the disconnected cerebral hemispheres. *Brain*, 114, 1025–1043.

Sergent, J., Ohta, S. and Macdonald, B. (1992). Functional neuroanatomy of face and object processing: A PET study. *Brain*, 115, 15–36.

Seymour, S.E., Reuter-Lorenz, P.A. and Gazzaniga, M.S. (1994). The disconnection syndrome: Basic findings reaffirmed. *Brain*, 117, 105–115.

Shackel, B. (1996). Ergonomics: Scope, contribution and future possibilities. *The Psychologist*, July, 304–308.

Shaffer, L.H. (1975). Multiple attention in continuous verbal tasks. In S. Dornic (ed.), *Attention and Performance*, Vol. 5. New York: Academic Press.

Shah, M., French, S.A., Jeffrey, R.W., McGovern, P.G., Forster, J.L. and Lando, H.A. (1993). Correlates of high fat/calorie food intake in a worksite population: The Healthy Worker Project. *Addictive Behaviours*, 18, 583–594.

Shahidullah, S. and Hepper, P. (1993). The developmental origins of fetal responsiveness to an acoustic stimulus. *Journal of Reproductive and Infant Psychology*, 11, 135–142.

Shakin, E.J. and Holland, J. (1988). Depression and pancreatic cancer. *Journal of Pain and Symptom Management*, 3, 194–198.

Shalev, A.Y., Bonne, O. and Eth, S. (1996). Treatment of the post-traumatic stress disorder. *Psychosomatic Medicine*, 58, 165–182.

Shallice, T. (1988). *From Neuropsychology to Mental Structure*. Cambridge: Cambridge University Press.

Shallice, T. and Burgess, P.W. (1991). Deficits in strategy application following frontal lobe damage in man. *Brain*, 114, 727–741.

Shallice, T., Burgess, P.W. and Frith, C.D. (1991). Can the neuropsychological case study approach be applied to schizophrenia? *Psychological Medicine*, 21, 661–673.

Shallice, T., Fletcher, P., Frith, C.D., Grasby, P., Frackowiak, R.S.J. and Dolan, R.J. (1994). Brain regions associated with acquisition and retrieval of verbal episodic memory. *Nature*, 368, 633–635.

Shanon, B. (1990). Consciousness. *Journal of Mind and Behaviour*, 11, 137–152.

Shanon, B. (1998). What is the function of consciousness? *Journal of Consciousness Studies*, 5, 3, 295–308.

Sharma, U. (1992). *Complementary Medicine Today: Practitioners and patients*. London: Routledge.

Shatz, M. and Gelman, R. (1973). The development of communication skills: Modifications in the speech of young children as a function of listener. *Monographs of the Society for Research in Child Development*, 38 (Serial no. 152).

Shaver, P.R., Shaver, W.S. and Schwartz, J.C. (1992). Cross-cultural similarities and differences in emotion and its representation: A prototype approach. In M.S. Clark (ed), *Review of Personality and Social Psychology*, vol. 13. Newbury Clark, CA: Sage.

Shavit, Y., Lewis, J.W., Terman, G.W., Gale, R.P. and Liebeskind, J.C. (1984). Opioid peptides mediate the suppressive effect of stress on natural killer cell cytotoxicity. *Science*, 223, 188–190.

Shavit, Y., Depaulis, A., Martin, F.C., Terman, G W., Pechnick, R.N., Zane, C.J., Gale, R.P. and Liebeskind, J.C. (1986). Involvement of brain opiate receptors in the immune-suppressive effect of morphine. *Proceedings of the National Academy of Sciences, USA*, 83, 7114–7117.

Shaywitz, B.A., Shaywitz, S.E., Pugh, K.R., Constable, R.T., Skudlarski, P., Fulbright, R.K., Bronen, R.A., Fletcher, J.M., Shankweiler, D.P., Katz, L. and Gore, J.C. (1995). Sex differences in the functional organization of the brain for language. *Nature*, 373, 607–609.

Sheeran, P. and Abraham, C. (1996). The health belief model. In M. Conner and P. Norman (eds), *Predicting Health Behaviour: Research and practice with social cognition models*. Buckingham, UK: Open University Press.

Shepard, R.N. and Metzler, J. (1971). Mental rotation of three-dimensional objects. *Science*, 171, 701–703.

Shepherd, J. (1983). *Incest: The biosocial view*. Cambridge, MA: Harvard University Press.

Shepherd, J. (1989). The face and social attribution. In A.W. Young and H. D. Ellis (eds), *Handbook of Research on Face Processing*. Amsterdam: North Holland.

Sheridan, J. and Humphreys, G.W. (1993). A verbal-semantic category-specific recognition impairment. *Cognitive Neuropsychology*, 10, 143–184.

Sherif, M. (1936). *The Psychology of Social Norms*. New York: Harper.

Sherif, M., Harvey, O. J., White, B. J., Hood, W. E. and Sherif, C. W. (1961). *Intergroup Conflict and Cooperation: The Robber's Cave Experiment*. Norman, OK: Institute of Group Relations.

Sherman, S.J., Presson, C.C. and Chassin, L. (1984). Mechanisms underlying the false consensus effect: The special role of threats to the self. *Personality and Social Psychology Bulletin*, 10, 127–138.

Shibley Hyde, J. and Plant, E. A. (1995). Magnitude of psychological gender differences: Another side to the story. *American Psychologist*, 50, 159–161.

Shields, D.L.L. and Bredemeier, B.J.L. (1995). *Character Development and Physical Activity*. Champaign, Il: Human Kinetics.

Shipley, E. F., Smith, C. S. and Gleitman, L. R. (1969). A study in the acquisition of language: Free responses to commands. *Language*, 45, 322–342.

Shirley, M.M. (1933). *The First Two Years. Vol. 2: Intellectual Development*. Minneapolis: University of Minnesota Press.

Shock, N. (1977). Systems integration. In C. Finch and L. Hayflick (eds), *Handbook of Biology of Ageing*. New York: Van Nostrand Reinhold.

Shore, J.H., Vollmer, W.M. and Tatum, E.L. (1989). Community patterns of posttraumatic stress disorder. *Journal of Nervous and Mental Disease*, 177, 681–685.

Shotland, R. L. and Heinold, W. D. (1985). Bystander response to arterial bleeding: Helping skills, the decision-making process, and differentiating the helping response. *Journal of Personality and Social Psychology*, 49, 347–356.

Shweder, R.A. and Sullivan, M.A. (1993). Cultural psychology: Who needs it? *Annual Review of Psychology*, 44, 497–527.

Sidman, M. and Tailby, W. (1982). Conditional discrimination versus matching to sample: An expansion of the testing paradigm. *Journal of the Experimental Analysis of Behavior*, 37, 5–22.

Sigman, M. (1995). Behavioural research in childhood autism. In M. Lenzenweger and J. Haugaard (eds), *Frontiers of Developmental Psychopathology*. New York: Springer-Verlag.

Silbersweig, D.A., Stern, E., Frith, C., Cahill, C., Holmes, A., Grootnoonk, S., Seaward, J., McKenna, P., Chua, S.E., Schnorr, L., Jones, T. and Frackowiak, R.S.J. (1995). A functional neuroanatomy of hallucinations in schizophrenia. *Nature*, 378, 176–179.

Silove, D., Parker, G., Hadzi-Pavlovic, D., Manicavasagar, V. and Blaszcynski, A. (1991). *British Journal of Psychiatry*, 159, 835–841.

Silveri, M.C., Gainotti, G., Perani, D., Cappelletti, J.Y., Carbone, G. and Fazio, F. (1997). Naming deficit for non-living items: Neuropsychological and PET study. *Neuropsychologia*, 35, 3, 359–367.

Simion, F., Valenza, E., Umilta, C. and Dalla Barba, B. (1998). Preferential orienting to faces in newborns: A temporal–nasal asymmetry. *Journal of Experimental Psychology (Human Perception and Performance)*, 24, 5, 1399–1405.

Simon, B. and Brown, R.J. (1987). Perceived intragroup homogeneity in minority–majority contexts. *Journal of Personality and Social Psychology*, 53, 703–711.

Simoneau, T.L., Miklowitz, D.J. and Saleem, R. (1998). Expressed emotion and interactional patterns in the families of bipolar patients. *Journal of Abnormal Psychology*, 107, 3, 497–507.

Simonoff, E., Bolton, P. and Rutter, M. (1996). Mental retardation: Genetic findings, clinical implications and research agenda. *Journal of Child Psychology and Psychiatry*, 37, 3, 259–280.

Simons, R.C. and Hughes, C.C. (1985). *The Culture-bound Syndromes: Folk illnesses of psychiatric and anthropological interest*. Boston: D. Reidel/Kluwer.

Simons, R.C. and Hughes, C.C. (1993). Culture-bound syndromes. In A.C. Gaw (ed.), *Culture, Ethnicity, and Mental Illness*. Washington, DC: American Psychiatric Press.

Simpson, J.A., Gangestad, S.W., Christensen, P.N. and Leck, K. (1999). Fluctuating asymmetry, sociosexuality and intrasexual competitive tactics. *Journal of Personality and Social Psychology*, 76, 159–172.

Sinden, J.D., Hodges, H. and Gray, J.A. (1995). Neural transplantation and recovery of cognitive function. *Behavioural and Brain Sciences*, 18, 10–35.

Singer, D.G. and Singer, J.L. (1990). *The House of Make-believe*. Cambridge, MA: Harvard University Press.

Singh, D.J. (1995). *Human Nature*, 6, 51–68.

Sirevaag, A. M., Black, J. E., Shafron, D. and Greenough, W. T. (1988). Direct evidence that complex experience increases capillary branching and surface area in visual cortex of young rats. *Developmental Brain Research*, 43, 299–304.

Sirigu, A., Zalla, T., Pillon, B., Grafman, J., Agid, Y. and Dubois, B. (1995). Selective impairments in managerial knowledge following pre-frontal cortex damage. *Cortex*, 31, 301–6.

Skarin, K. (1977). Cognitive and contextual determinants of stranger fear in six- and eleven-month-old infants. *Child Development*, 48, 537–544.

Skeels, H.M. (1966). Adult status of children with contrasting early life experiences. *Monographs of the Society for Research in Child Development*, 31, 1–65.

Skevington, S.M. and White, A. (1998). Is laughter the best medicine? *Psychology and Health*, 13, 157–169.

Skinner, B.F. (1948). *Walden Two*. New York: Macmillan.

Skinner, B.F. (1953). *Science and Human Behavior*. New York: Macmillan.

Skinner, B.F. (1971). *Beyond Freedom and Dignity*. New York: Vantage.

Skinner, B.F. (1986). The evolution of verbal behavior. *Journal of the Experimental Analysis of Behavior*, 45, 115–122.

Skinner, B.F. (1987). *Upon Further Reflection*. Englewood Cliffs, NJ: Prentice Hall.

Skowronski, J.J. and Carlston, D.E. (1989). Negativity and extremity biases in impression formation: A review of explanations. *Psychological Bulletin*, 105, 131–142.

Skuse, D.H., James, R.S., Bishop, D.V.M., Coppin, B., Dalton, P., Aamodt-Leeper, G., Bacarese-Hamilton, M., Creswell, C., McGurk, R. and Jacobs, P.A. (1997). Evidence from Turner's syndrome of an imprinted X-linked locus affecting cognitive function. *Nature*, 387, 705–708.

Slooter, A.J.C., Tang, M-X., van Duijn, C.M., Stern, Y., Off, A., Bell, K. *et al.* (1997). Apolipoprotein E4 and the risk of dementia with stroke: A population-based investigation. *Journal of the American Medical Association*, 277, 818–821.

Small, D.M., Jones-Gotman, M., Zatorre, R.J., Petrides, M. and Evans, A.C. (1997). Flavor processing: More than the sum of its parts. *Neuroreport*, 8, 3913–3917.

Smeets, M.A.M., Smit, F., Panhuysen, G.E.M. and Ingleby, J.D. (1997). The influence of methodological differences on the outcome of body size estimation studies in anorexia nervosa. *British Journal of Clinical Psychology*, 36, 263–277.

Smith, G.H. and Engel, R. (1968). Influence of a female model on perceived characteristics of an automobile. *Proceedings of the 76th Annual Convention of the American Psychological Association*, 3, 681–682.

Smith, L. (1996). *Critical Readings on Piaget*. London: Routledge.

Smith, L., Dockerell, J. and Tomlinson, P. (1997). *Piaget, Vygotsky and beyond*. London: Routledge.

Smith, M.L., Glass, G.V. and Miller, T.I. (1980). *Benefits of Psychotherapy*. Baltimore: Johns Hopkins University Press.

Smith, S.M. (1979). Remembering in and out of context. *Journal of Experimental Psychology: Human Learning and Memory*, 5, 460–471.

Smith, S.M. (1988). Environmental context dependent memory. In G.M. Davies and D.M. Thomson (eds), *Memory in context: context in memory*. Chichester: Wiley.

Smith, S.M. (1995). Mood is a component of mental context: Comment on Eich (1995). *Journal of Experimental Psychology: General*, 124, 3, 309–310.

Smith, T. (1983). Alternative medicine. *British Medical Journal*, 287, 307–308.

Smith, T.W. and Brehm, S. (1981). Cognitive correlates of the Type A coronary-prone behaviour pattern. *Journal of Personality and Social Psychology*, 40, 1137–1149.

Snow, C.E. (1972a). Mothers' speech to children learning language. *Child Development*, 43, 549–565.

Snow, C.E. (1972b). Young children's responses to adult sentences of varying complexity. Paper presented at the Third International Congress of Applied Linguistics, Copenhagen.

Snow, C.E. (1977). Mothers' speech research: From input to interaction. In C.E. Snow and C. Ferguson (eds), *Talking to Children: Language Input and Acquisition*. Cambridge: Cambridge University Press.

Snow, C.E. (1986). Conversations with children. In P. Fletcher and M. Garman (eds), *Language Acquisition* (2nd edition). Cambridge: Cambridge University Press.

Snow, C.E. and Goldfield, B.A. (1982). Building stories: The emergence of information structures from conversation. In D. Tannen (ed.), *Analyzing Discourse: Text and talk*. Washington, DC: Georgetown University Press.

Snow, C.E., Arlman-Rupp, A., Hassing, Y., Jobse, J., Joosten, J. and Vorster, J. (1976). Mothers' speech in three social classes. *Journal of Psycholinguistic Research*, 5, 1–20.

Snow, W.G. and Weinstock, J. (1990). Sex differences among non-brain-damaged adults on the Wechsler Adult Intelligence Scales: A review of the literature. *Journal of Clinical and Experimental Neuropsychology*, 12, 873–886.

Snowden, W. (1997). Evidence from an analysis of 2000 errors and omissions made in IQ tests by a small sample of schoolchildren, undergoing vitamin and mineral supplementation, that speed of processing is an important factor in IQ performance. *Personality and Individual Differences*, 22, 1, 131–134.

Snyder, L.H., Batista, A.P. and Andersen, R.A. (1997). Coding of intention in the posterior parietal cortex. *Nature*, 386, 167–170.

Snyder, M., Tanke, E.D. and Berscheid, E. (1977). Social perception and interpersonal behavior: On the self-fulfilling nature of social stereotypes. *Journal of Personality and Social Psychology*, 35, 656–666.

Snyder, S.H. (1974). *Madness and the Brain*. New York: McGraw-Hill.

Sobesky, W.E. (1983). The effects of situational factors on moral judgments. *Child Development*, 54, 575–584.

Sogin, D.W. (1988). Effect of three different musical styles of background music on coding by college-age students. *Perceptual and Motor Skills*, 67, 275–280.

Sohlberg, M.M. and Mateer, C. (1989). Training use of compensatory memory books: A three-stage behavioural approach. *Journal of Clinical and Experimental Neuropsychology*, 11, 871–891.

Sokejima, S. and Kagamimori, S. (1998). Working hours as a risk for acute myocardial infarction in Japan: Case-control study. *British Medical Journal*, 317, 775–780.

Solomon, G.F. (1987). Psychoneuro-immunology: Interactions between central nervous system and immune system. *Journal of Neuroscience Research*, 18, 1–9.

Solso, R.L. (1988). *Cognitive Psychology* (2nd edition). Boston: Allyn & Bacon.

Spanos, N.P. (1991). A sociocognitive approach to hypnosis. In S.J. Lynn and J.H. Rhue (eds), *Theories of Hypnosis: Current models and perspectives*. New York: Guilford.

Spanos, N.P. (1992). Compliance and reinterpretation in hypnotic responding. *Contemporary Hypnosis*, 9, 7–14.

Spanos, N.P., Weekes, J.R. and Bertrand, L.D. (1985). Multiple personality: A social psychological perspective. *Journal of Abnormal Psychology*, 94, 362–376.

Sparks, K., Cooper, C., Fried, Y. and Shirom, A. (1997). The effects of hours of work on health: A meta-analysis. *Journal of Occupational and Organizational Psychology*, 70, 4, 391–408.

Spearman, C. (1927). *The Abilities of Man*. London: Macmillan.

Spears, R. and Manstead, A.S.R. (1990). Consensus estimation in social context. *European Review of Social Psychology*, 1, 81–110.

Spears, R., van der Pligt, J. and Eiser, J.R. (1985). Illusory correlation in the perception of group attitudes. *Journal of Personality and Social Psychology*, 48, 863–875.

Speedie, L.J., Rothi, L.J. and Heilman, K.M. (1982). Spelling dyslexia: a form of cross-cueing. *Brain and Language*, 15, 340–352.

Sperling, G.A. (1960). The information available in brief visual presentation. *Psychological Monographs*, 74, 498.

Sperry, R.W. (1966). Brain bisection and consciousness. In J. Eccles (ed.), *Brain and Conscious Experience*. New York: Springer-Verlag.

Sperry, R.W., Gazzaniga, M.S. and Bogen, J.E. (1969). Interhemispheric relationships: The neocortical commissures and syndromes of hemisphere disconnection. In P.J. Vinken and G.W. Bruyn (eds), *Handbook of Clinical Neurology*, Vol. 4. Hillsdale, NJ: North-Holland.

Spirduso, W.W. and MacRae, P.G. (1990). Motor performance and aging. In J.E. Birren and K.W. Schaie (eds), *Handbook of the Psychology of Aging* (3rd edition). San Diego: Academic Press.

Spiro, R.J. (1977). Remembering information from text: The 'state of schema' approach. In R.C. Anderson, R.J. Spiro and W.E. Montague (eds), *Schooling and the Acquisition of Knowledge*. Hillsdale, NJ: Lawrence Erlbaum Associates.

Spiro, R.J. (1980). Accommodative reconstruction in prose recall. *Journal of Verbal Learning and Verbal Behavior*, 19, 84–95.

Spitzer, R.L., Skodol, A.E., Gibbon, M. and Williams, J.B.W. (1981). *Diagnostic and Statistical Manual of Mental Disorders Case Book*. Washington, DC: American Psychiatric Association.

Sprengelmeyer, R., Young, A.W., Calder, A.J., Karnat, A., Lange, H.W., Homberg, V., Perrett, D. and Rowland, D. (1996). Loss of disgust: Perception of faces and emotions in Huntington's disease. *Brain*, 119, 1647–1665.

Sprengelmeyer, R., Young, A.W., Sprengelmeyer, A., Calder, A.J., Rowland,

D., Perrett, D., Homberg, V. and Lange, H. (1997). Recognition of facial expressions: Selective impairment of specific emotions in Huntington's disease. *Cognitive Neuropsychology*, 14, 6, 839–879.

Squire, L.R. (1987). *Memory and Brain*. Oxford: Oxford University Press.

Squire, L.R., Slater, P.C. and Miller, P.L. (1981). Retrograde amnesia following ECT: Long-term follow-up studies. *Archives of General Psychiatry*, 38, 89–95.

Staats, A.W. and Staats, C.K. (1958). Attitudes established by classical conditioning. *Journal of Abnormal and Social Psychology*, 57, 37–40.

Staats, C.K. and Staats, A.W. (1957). Meaning established by classical conditioning. *Journal of Experimental Psychology*, 54, 74–80.

Stager, C.L. and Werker, J.F. (1997). Infants listen for more phonetic detail in speech perception than in word-learning tasks. *Nature*, 388, 381–382.

Stagner, R. (1958). The gullibility of personnel managers. *Personnel Psychology*, 11, 347–352.

Stahl, S.A. and Murray, B.A. (1994). Defining phonological awareness and its relationship to early reading. *Journal of Educational Psychology*, 86, 2, 221–234.

Stallard, P., Velleman, R. and Baldwin, S. (1998). Prospective study of post-traumatic stress disorder in children involved in road traffic accidents. *British Medical Journal*, 317, 1619–1623.

Standing, L. (1973). Learning 10,000 pictures. *Quarterly Journal of Experimental Psychology*, 25, 207–222.

Stanhope, N., Cohen, G. and Conway, M. (1993). Very long-term retention of a novel. *Applied Cognitive Psychology*, 7, 239–256.

Stanton, A.L. and Snider, P.R. (1993). Coping with breast cancer diagnosis: A prospective study. *Health Psychology*, 12, 16–23.

Stanton, N. (1996). Engineering psychology: Another science of common sense? *The Psychologist*, July, 300–303.

Stattin, H. and Magnusson, D. (1990). *Pubertal Maturation in Female Development*. Hillsdale, NJ: Erlbaum.

Stavridou, A. and Furnham, A. (1996). The relationship between psychoticism, trait-creativity and the attentional mechanism of cognitive inhibition. *Personality and Individual Differences*, 21, 1, 143–153.

Stebbins, W.C., Miller, J.M., Johnsson, L-G. and Hawkins, J.E. (1969). Ototoxic hearing loss and cochlear pathology in the monkey. *Annals of Otology, Rhinology, and Laryngology*, 78, 1007–1026.

Steen, S.N., Oppliger, R.A. and Brownell, K.D. (1988). Metabolic effects of repeated weight loss and regain in adolescent wrestlers. *Journal of the American Medical Association*, 260, 47–50.

Steers, R.M. and Rhodes, S.R. (1984). Knowledge and speculation about absen-

teeism. In P. Goodman and R. Atkin (eds), *Absenteeism*. San Fransisco: Jossey-Bass.

Steffenburg, S., Gillberg, C., Helgren, L., Anderson, L., Gillberg, L., Jakobsson, G. and Bohman, M. (1989). A twin study of autism in Denmark, Finland, Iceland, Norway and Sweden. *Journal of Child Psychology and Psychiatry*, 30, 405–416.

Stein, J.F. and Walsh, V. (1997). To see but not to read; the magnocellular theory of dyslexia. *Trends in Neurosciences*, 20, 4, 147–152.

Steinberg, H., Cockerill, I. and Dewey, A. (1998). *What Sports Pyschologists Do*. Leicester: The British Psychological Society.

Steinberg, H., Sykes, E.A., Moss, T., Lowery, S., LeBoutillier, N. and Dewey, A. (1997). Exercise enhances creativity independently of mood. *British Journal of Sports Medicine*, 31, 240–245.

Sterman, M.B. and Clemente, C.D. (1962a). Forebrain inhibitory mechanisms: Cortical synchronization induced by basal forebrain stimulation. *Experimental Neurology*, 6, 91–102.

Sterman, M.B. and Clemente, C.D. (1962b). Forebrain inhibitory mechanisms: Sleep patterns induced by basal forebrain stimulation in the behaving cat. *Experimental Neurology*, 6, 103–117.

Stern, J.A., Brown, M., Ulett, G.A. and Sletten, I. (1977). A comparison of hypnosis, acupuncture, morphine, Valium, aspirin, and placebo in the management of experimentally induced pain. In *Hypnosis and Relaxation: Modern Verification of an Old Equation*. New York: Wiley/Interscience.

Stern, K. and McClintock, M.K. (1998). Regulation of ovulation by human pheromones. *Nature*, 392, 177–179.

Stern, W. (1914). *The Psychological Methods of Testing Intelligence*. Baltimore: Warwick & York.

Sternberg, R.J. (1985). *Beyond IQ: A triarchic theory of human intelligence*. Cambridge: Cambridge University Press.

Sternberg, R.J. (1988a). *The Psychologist's Companion*. Leicester: BPS.

Sternberg, R.J. (1988b). Triangulating love. In R.J. Sternberg and M.L. Barnes (eds), *The Psychology of Love*. New Haven, CT: Yale University Press.

Sternberg, R.J. (1997). Intelligence and lifelong learning. *American Psychologist*, 52, 10, 1134–1139.

Sternberg, R.J. and Davidson, J. (1996). *The Nature of Insight*. Cambridge, MA: MIT Press.

Sternberg, R.J. and Detterman, D.K. (1986). *What Is Intelligence? Contemporary viewpoints on its nature and definition*. New Jersey: Norwood.

Sternberg, R.J. and Grigorenko, E. (1997). *Intelligence, Heredity and Environment*. New York: Cambridge University Press.

Sternberg, R.J. and Wagner, R.K. (1986). *Practical Intelligence: Nature and origins of*

competence in the everyday world. New York: Cambridge University Press.

Sternberger, L.G. and Burns, G.L. (1990). Obsessions and compulsions: Psychometric properties of the Padua inventory with an American college population. *Behavior Research and Therapy*, 28, 341–345.

Stevenson, R.E., Schroer, R.J., Skinner, C., Fender, D. and Simensen, R.J. (1997). Autism and macroencephaly. *Lancet*, 349, 1744–1745.

Stewart, F., Parkin, A.J. and Hunkin, N.M. (1992). Naming Impairments following from herpes simplex encephalitis: category-specific? *The Quarterly Journal of Experimental Psychology*, 44A, 261–284.

Stich, S.P. (1990). Rationality. In D.N. Osherson and E.E. Smith (eds), *An Invitation to Cognitive Science. Vol. 3: Thinking*. Cambridge, MA: MIT Press.

Stine, E.L. and Bohannon, J.N. (1983). Imitations, interactions, and language acquisition. *Journal of Child Language*, 10, 589–603.

Stoddard, J.T. (1886). Composite portraiture. *Science*, 8, 89–91.

Stoerig, P. and Cowey, A. (1997). Blindsight in man and monkey. *Brain*, 120, 535–559.

Stokoe, W.C. (1983). Apes who sign and critics who don't. In J. de Luce and H.T. Wilder (eds), *Language in Primates: Perspectives and implications*. New York: Springer-Verlag.

Stone, A.A., Cox, D.S., Valdimarsdottir, H., Jandorf, L. and Neale, J.M. (1987). Evidence that secretory IgA antibody is associated with daily mood. *Journal of Personality and Social Psychology*, 52, 988–993.

Stone, V.E., Baron-Cohen, S. and Knight, R.T. (1998). Frontal lobe contributions to theory of mind. *Journal of Cognitive Neuroscience*, 10, 5, 640–656.

Stough, C., Kerkin, B., Bates, T. and Mangan, G. (1994). Music and spatial IQ. *Personality and Individual Differences*, 17, 695.

Strachan, A.M., Feingold, D., Goldstein, M.J., Miklowitz, D.J. and Nuechterlein, K.H. (1989). Is expressed emotion an index of transactional process? II. Patient's coping style. *Family Process*, 28, 169–181.

Strack, F., Stepper, S. and Martin, L.L. (1988). Inhibiting and facilitating conditions of the human smile: A nonobtrusive test of the facial feedback hypothesis. *Journal of Personality and Social Psychology*, 54, 768–777.

Strauss, A.L. and Corbin, J. (1990). *Basics of Qualitative Research: Grounded theory procedures and techniques*. Newbury Park, CA: Sage.

Strickland, B.R. (1979). Internal–external expectancies and cardiovascular functioning. In L.C. Perlmutter and R.A. Monty (eds), *Choice and Perceived Control*. Hillsdale, NJ: Lawrence Erlbaum Associates.

Stritzke, W.G.K., Lang, A.R. and Patrick, C.J. (1996). Beyond stress and arousal: A reconceptualization of alcohol–emotion relations with reference to psychophysiological methods. *Psychological Bulletin*, 120, 3, 376–395.

Stroop, J.R. (1935). Studies of interference in serial verbal reactions. *Journal of Experimental Psychology*, 18, 743–762.

Strupp, H.H. (1993). The Vanderbilt psychotherapy studies: Synopsis. *Journal of Consulting and Clinical Psychology*, 61, 431–433.

Strupp, H.H. and Hadley, S.W. (1979). Specific vs. nonspecific factors in psychotherapy. *Archives of General Psychiatry*, 36, 1125–1136.

Stunkard, A.J., Sørenson, T.I., Harris, C., Teasdale, T.W., Chakraborty, R., Schull, W.J. and Schulsinger, F. (1986). An adoption study of human obesity. *New England Journal of Medicine*, 314, 193–198.

Sturr, J.F., Zhang, L., Taub, H.A., Hannon, D.J. and Jackowski, M.M. (1997). Psychophysical evidence for losses in rod sensitivity in the aging visual system. *Vision Research*, 37, 4, 475–481.

Stuss, D.T. and Levine, B. (1996). The dementias: Nosological and clinical factors related to diagnosis. *Brain and Cognition*, 31, 99–113.

Stuss, D.T., Gow, C.A. and Hetherington, C.R. (1992). 'No longer Gage': Frontal lobe dysfunction and emotional changes. *Journal of Consulting and Clinical Psychology*, 60, 3, 349–359.

Sugiyama, T., Takei, Y. and Abe, T. (1992). The prevalence of autism at Nagoya, Japan. In H. Naruse and E.M. Ornitz (eds), *Neurobiology of Infantile Autism*. Amsterdam: Excerpta Medica.

Sullivan, M.W., Rovee-Collier, C. and Tynes, D.M. (1979). A conditioning analysis of infant long-term memory. *Child Development*, 50, 152–162.

Sullivan, R.M., Taborsky-Barba, S., Mendoza, R., Itano, A., Leon, M., Cotman, C.W., Payne, T.F. and Lott, I. (1991). Olfactory classical conditioning in neonates. *Pediatrics*, 87, 511–518.

Sundstrom, E., Town, J.P. and Rice, R.W. (1994). Office noise, satisfaction and performance. *Environment and Behaviour*, 26, 195–222.

Sutherland, S. (1993). *Breakdown*. London: Wiedenfeld & Nicholson.

Suzdak, P.D., Glowa, J.R., Crawley, J.N., Schwartz, R.D., Skolnick, P. and Paul, S.M. (1986). A selective imidazobenzodiazepine antagonist of ethanol in the rat. *Science*, 234, 1243–1247.

Suzuki, L.A. and Valencia, R.R. (1997). Race-ethnicity and measured intelligence. *American Psychologist*, 52, 10, 1103–1114.

Swaab, D.F. and Hofman, M.A. (1990). An enlarged suprachiasmatic nucleus in homo-

sexual men. *Brain Research*, 537, 141–148.

Swendsen, J.D. (1998). The helplessness–hopelessness theory and daily mood experience: An idiographic and cross-situational perspective. *Journal of Personality and Social Psychology*, 74, 5, 1398–1408.

Swettenham, J., Baron-Cohen, S., Charman, T., Cox, A., Baird, G., Drew, A., Rees, L. and Wheelwright, S. (1998). The frequency and distribution of spontaneous attention shifts between social and nonsocial stimuli in autistic, typically developing, and nonautistic developmentally delayed infants. *Journal of Child Psychology and Psychiatry*, 39, 5, 747–753.

Symons, D. (1979). *The Evolution of Human Sexuality*. New York: Oxford University Press.

Szasz, T.S. (1960). The myth of mental illness. *American Psychologist*, 15, 113–118.

Szasz, T.S. (1987). *Insanity: The idea and its consequences*. New York: Wiley.

Szymusiak, R. and McGinty, D. (1986). Sleep-related neuronal discharge in the basal forebrain of cats. *Brain Research*, 370, 82–92.

Tajfel, H. (1981). Social stereotypes and social groups. In J.C. Turner and H. Giles (eds), *Intergroup Behaviour*. Oxford, UK: Blackwell, pp. 144–167.

Tajfel, H. (ed.) (1984). *The Social Dimension: European developments in social psychology*. Cambridge: Cambridge University Press.

Tajfel, H., Billig, M., Bundy, R.P. and Flament, C. (1971). Social categorization and intergroup behaviour. *European Journal of Social Psychology*, 1, 149–177.

Tajfel, H. and Turner, J.C. (1986). The social identity theory of intergroup behaviour. In S.G. Worchel and W. Austin (eds), *Psychology of Intergroup Relations* (2nd edition). Chicago: Nelson–Hall, pp. 7–24.

Tallis, F., Eysenck, M.W. and Matthews, A. (1991). Elevated evidence requirements and worry. *Personality and Individual Differences*, 12, 21–108.

Tamlyn, D., McKenna, P., Mortimer, A., Lund, C., Hammond, S. and Baddeley, A. (1992). Memory impairment in schizophrenia: Its extent, affiliations and neuropsychological character. *Psychological Medicine*, 22, 101–115.

Tanaka-Matsumi, J. (1979). Taijin Kyofusho: Diagnostic and cultural issues in Japanese psychiatry. *Culture, Medicine and Psychiatry*, 3, 231–245.

Tanaka-Matsumi, J. and Draguns, J.G. (1997). Culture and psychopathology. In J.W. Berry, P.R. Dasen and T.S. Sarawathi (eds), *Handbook of Cross-cultural Psychology. Vol 2: Basic Processes and Human Development*. Boston: Allyn & Bacon.

Tanenhaus, M.K. (1988). *Psycholinguistics: An overview*. Cambridge: Cambridge University Press.

Taras, H.L., Sallis, J.F., Patterson, T.L., Nader, P.R. and Nelson, J.A. (1989). Television's influence on children's diet and physical activity. *Journal of Developmental and Behavioral Pediatrics*, 10, 176–180.

Tartaglia, L.A., Dembski, M., Weng, X., Deng, N.H., Culpepper, J., Devos, R., Richards, G.J., Campfield, L.A., Clark, F.T., Deeds, J., Muir, C., Sanker, S., Moriarty, A., Moore, K.J., Smutko, J.S., Mays, G.G., Woolf, E.A., Monroe, C.A. and Tepper, R.I. (1995). Identification and expression cloning of a leptin receptor, OB-R. *Cell*, 83, 1263–1271.

Taylor, S.E. (1983). Adjustment to threatening events. *American Psychologist*, 38, 1161–1173.

Taylor, S.E., Peplau, L.A. and Sears, D.O. (1994). *Social Psychology*. Englewood Cliffs, NJ: Prentice Hall.

Temoshok, L. (1987). Personality, coping style, emotion and cancer: Towards an integrative model. *Cancer Surveys*, 6, 545–567.

Temoshok, L., Heller, B.W., Sagebiel, R.W., Blois, M.S., Sweet, D.M., DiClemente, R.J. and Gold, M.L. (1985). The relationship of psychosocial factors to prognostic indicators in cutaneous malignant melanoma. *Journal of Psychosomatic Research*, 29, 139–153.

Temple, C.M. and Marshall, J.C. (1983). A case study of developmental phonological dyslexia. *British Journal of Psychology*, 74, 517–533.

Terenius, L. and Wahlström, A. (1975). Morphine-like ligand for opiate receptors in human CSF. *Life Sciences*, 16, 1759–1764.

Terman, L.M. and Merrill, M.A. (1960). *Stanford–Binet Intelligence Scale*. Boston: Houghton Mifflin.

Terrace, H.S., Petitto, L.A., Sanders, R.J. and Bever, T.G. (1979). Can an ape create a sentence? *Science*, 206, 891–902.

Terry, R.D. and Davies, P. (1980). Dementia of the Alzheimer type. *Annual Review of Neuroscience*, 3, 77–96.

Thal, L.J. (1992). Cholinomimetic therapy in Alzheimer's disease. In L.R. Squire and N. Butters (eds), *Neuropsychology of Memory*. New York: Guilford.

Thelen, E. (1995). Motor development: A new synthesis. *American Psychologist*, 50, 79–95.

Thibadeau, R., Just, M.A. and Carpenter, P.A. (1982). A model of the time course and content of reading. *Cognitive Science*, 6, 157–203.

Thompson, C. (1989). The syndrome of seasonal affective disorder. In C. Thompson and T. Silverstone (eds), *Seasonal Affective Disorder*. London: CNS Publishers.

Thompson, C., Childs, P.A., Martin, N.J., Rodin, I. and Smythe, P.J. (1997). Effects of morning phototherapy on circadian markers in seasonal affective disorder. *British Journal of Psychiatry*, 170, 431–435.

Thompson, T. and Schuster, C.R. (1968). *Behavioral Pharmacology*. Englewood Cliffs, NJ: Prentice Hall.

Thorndike, E.L. (1905). *The Elements of Psychology*. New York: Seiler.

Thrasher, S.M., Dalgleish, T. and Yule, W. (1994). Information processing in post-traumatic stress disorder. *Behaviour Research and Therapy*, 32, 247–254.

Thun, J.T., Peto, R., Lopez, A.D. *et al.* (1997). Alcohol consumption and mortality among middle-aged and elderly US adults. *New England Journal of Medicine*, 337, 1705–1714.

Thurstone, L.L. (1938). *Primary Mental Abilities*. Chicago: University of Chicago Press.

Tibben, A., Tomman, R., Bannink, E.C. and Duivenvoorden, H.J. (1997). Three-year follow-up after presymptomatic testing for Huntington's disease in tested individuals and partners. *Health Psychology*, 16, 20–35.

Tice, D.M. and Baumeister, R.F. (1997). Longitudinal study of procrastination, performance, stress and health: The costs and benefits of dawdling. *Psychological Science*, 8, 6, 454–458.

Tienari, P., Sorri, A., Lahti, I., Naarala, M., Wahlberg, K- E., Moring, J., Pohjola, J. and Wynne, L.C. (1987). Genetic and psychosocial factors in schizophrenia: The Finnish adoptive family study. *Schizophrenia Bulletin*, 13, 476–483.

Tippin, J. and Henn, F.A. (1982). Modified leukotomy in the treatment of intractable obsessional neurosis. *American Journal of Psychiatry*, 139, 1601–1603.

Tobin, S.A. (1991). A comparison of psychoanalytic self-psychology and Carl Rogers's person-centered therapy. *Journal of Humanistic Psychology*, 31, 9–33.

Tomarken, A.J., Davidson, R.J. and Henriques, J.B. (1990). Resting frontal brain asymmetry predicts affective responses to films. *Journal of Personality and Social Psychology*, 59, 4, 791–801.

Tomasello, M. and Farrar, J. (1986). Joint attention and early language. *Child Development*, 57, 1454–1463.

Tooby, J. and Cosmides, L. (1989). Evolutionary psychology and the generation of culture. Part I: Theoretical considerations. *Ethology and Sociobiology*, 10, 39–49.

Tooby, J. and Cosmides, L. (1990). On the universality of human nature and the uniqueness of the individual: The role of genetics and adaptation. *Journal of Personality*, 58, 17–67.

Tooby, J. and DeVore, I. (1987). The reconstruction of hominid behavioural evolution through strategic modelling. In G.W. Kinzey (ed.), *The Evolution of Human Behaviour: Primate models*. New York: SUNY Press.

Tootell, R.B., Reppas, J.B., Dale, A.M. and Look, R.B. (1995). Visual motion aftereffect in human cortical area MT revealed by functional magnetic resonance imaging. *Nature*, 375, 139–141.

Torgerson, S. (1983). Genetic factors in anxiety disorders. *Archives of General Psychiatry*, 40, 1085–1089.

Torrance, E.P. (1975). Creativity research in education: Still alive. In I.A. Taylor and J.W. Getzels (eds), *Perspectives in Creativity*. Chicago: Aldine.

Torrey, E.F., Torrey, B.B. and Peterson, M.R. (1977). Seasonality of schizophrenic births in the United States. *Archives of General Psychiatry*, 34, 1065–1070.

Tourangeau, R. and Ellsworth, P.C. (1979). The role of facial response in the experience of emotion. *Journal of Personality and Social Psychology*, 37, 1519–1531.

Tourney, G. (1980). Hormones and homosexuality. In J. Marmor (ed.), *Homosexual Behavior*. New York: Basic Books.

Tranel, D., Damasio, A.R. and Damasio, H. (1988). Intact recognition of facial expression, gender and age in patients with impaired recognition of face identity. *Neurology*, 38, 690–696.

Trapold, M.A. and Spence, K.W. (1960). Performance changes in eyelid conditioning as related to the motivational and reinforcing properties of the UCS. *Journal of Experimental Psychology*, 59, 212.

Travis, F. (1998). Cortical and cognitive development in 4th, 8th and 12th grade students. *Biological Psychology*, 48, 37–56.

Treffinger, D.J., Feldhusen, J.F. and Isaksen, S.G. (1990). Organization and structure of productive thinking. *Creative Learning Today*, 4, 2, 6–8.

Treisman, A.M. (1960). Contextual cues in selective listening. *Quarterly Journal of Experimental Psychology*, 12, 242–248.

Treisman, A.M. (1964). Verbal cues, language, and meaning in selective attention. *American Journal of Psychology*, 77, 206–219.

Triplett, N. (1897). The dynamogenic factors in pacemaking and competition. *American Journal of Psychology*, 9, 507–533.

Trivers, R.L. (1971). The biology of reciprocal altruism. *Quarterly Review of Biology*, 46, 35–57.

Trivers, R L. (1972). Parental investment and sexual selection. In B. Campbell (ed.), *Sexual Selection and the Descent of Man*. Chicago: Aldine.

Tronick, E., Als, H., Adamson, L., Wise, S. and Brazelton, T.B. (1978). The infant's response to entrapment between contradictory messages in face-to-face interaction. *Journal of the American Academy of Child Psychiatry*, 17, 1–13.

Truax, C.B. (1966). Reinforcement and non-reinforcement in Rogerian psychotherapy. *Journal of Abnormal Psychology*, 71, 1–9.

Tryon, R. (1940). Genetic differences in maze-learning ability in rats. *Yearbook of the National Society for the Study of Education*, 39, 111–119.

Tseng, W-S., Xu, N., Ebata, K., Hsu, J. and Cui, Y. (1986). Diagnostic pattern of neurosis among China, Japan and America. *American Journal of Psychiatry*, 143, 1010–1014.

Tseng, W-S., Asai, M., Jiequi, L., Wibulswasd, P., Suryani, L.K., Wen, L-K., Brennan, J. and Hieby, E. (1990). Multicultural study of minor psychiatric disorders in Asia: Symptom manifestations. *International Journal of Social Psychiatry*, 36, 252–264.

Tseng, W-S., Asai, M., Kitanishi, K., McLaughlin, D. and Kyomen, H. (1992). Diagnostic patterns of social phobia: Comparison in Tokyo and Hawaii. *Journal of Nervous and Mental Diseases*, 180, 380–385.

Tseng, W-S., Lin, T.Y. and Yee, E. (1995). Concluding comments. In T.Y. Lin, W-S. Tseng and E. Yee (eds), *Mental health in Chinese societies*. Hong Kong: Oxford University Press.

Tulving, E. (1972). Episodic and semantic memory. In E. Tulving and W. Donaldson (eds), *Organization of Memory*. New York: Academic Press.

Tulving, E. (1983). *Elements of Episodic Memory*. Oxford: Oxford University Press.

Tulving, E. (1984). Precis of 'Elements of Episodic Memory'. *The Behavioral and Brain Sciences*, 7, 223–268.

Tulving, E., Kapur, S., Markowitsch, H.J., Craik, F.I., Habib, R. and Houle, S. (1994). Neuroanatomical correlates of retrieval in episodic memory: Auditory sentence recognition. *Proceedings of the National Academy of Sciences, USA*, 91, 2012–1225.

Tupes, E.C. and Christal, R.E. (1961). *Recurrent personality factors based on trait ratings*. USAF ASD Technical Report, 61–97.

Turner, A.M. and Greenough, W.T. (1985). Differential rearing effects on rat visual cortex synapses. I. Synaptic and neuronal density and synapses per neuron. *Brain Research*, 329, 195–203.

Turner, J.C. (1991). *Social Influence*. Milton Keynes, UK: Open University Press.

Turner, J.C., Hogg, M.A., Oakes, P.J., Reicher, S.D. and Wetherell, M.S. (1987). *Rediscovering the Social Group: A self-categorization theory*. Oxford, UK: Blackwell.

Turner, J.C., Wetherell, M.S. and Hogg, M.A. (1989). Referent informational influence and group polarization. *British Journal of Social Psychology*, 28, 135–147.

Turner, S.M., Beidel, D.C. and Nathan, R.S. (1985). Biological factors in obsessive-compulsive disorders. *Psychological Bulletin*, 97, 430–450.

Tversky, A. and Kahneman, D. (1974). Judgment under uncertainty: Heuristics and biases. *Science*, 185, 1124–1131.

Tversky, A. and Kahneman, D. (1982). Judgment under uncertainty: Heuristics and biases. In D. Kahneman, P. Slovic and A. Tversky (eds), *Judgment Under Uncertainty*. New York: Cambridge University Press.

Tyler, C.W. (1998). Painters centre one eye in portraits. *Nature*, 392, 877–878.

Udolf, R. (1983). *Forensic Hypnosis: Psychological and legal aspects*. Lexington, MA: Lexington Books.

Ullman, L.P. and Krasner, L. (1969). *Psychological Approach to Abnormal Behavior*. Englewood Cliffs, NJ: Prentice Hall.

Ulusahin, A., Basoglu, M. and Paykel, E.S. (1994). A cross-cultural comparative study of depressive symptoms in British and Turkish clinical samples. *Social Psychiatry and Psychiatric Epidemiology*, 29, 31–39.

Umilta, C., Simion, F. and Valeuza, E. (1996). Newborn's preference for faces. *European Psychologist*, 1, 3, 200–205.

Ungerleider, L.G. and Mishkin, M. (1982). Two cortical visual systems. In D.J. Ingle, M.A. Goodale and R.J.W. Mansfield (eds), *Analysis of Visual Behavior*. Cambridge, MA: MIT Press.

Valenza, E., Simion, F., Cassia, V.M. and Umilta, C. (1996). Face preference at birth. *Journal of Experimental Psychology: Human Perception and Performance*, 27, 4, 892–903.

Vallar, G. (1998). Spatial hemineglect in humans. *Trends in Cognitive Sciences*, 2, 3, 87–97.

Van de Vijver, F. and Hambleton, R.K. (1996). *Translating Tests: Some practical guidelines*, 1, 2, 89–99.

Van den Broek, M.D., Schady, W. and Coyne, H.J. (1995). *Living with Head Injury*. Manchester: Manchester University Press.

Van Goozen, S.H.M., Cohen-Kettenis, P.T., Gooren, L.J.G., Frijda, N.A. and Van De Poll, N.E. (1995). Gender differences in behaviour: Activating effects of cross-sex hormones. *Psychoneuroendocrinology*, 20, 343–363.

Van Velzen, C.J.M. and Emmelkamp, P.M.G. (1996). The assessment of personality disorders: Implications for cognitive and behavior therapy. *Behaviour Research and Therapy*, 34, 8, 655–668.

Vaughan, E. (1977). Misconceptions about psychology among psychology students. *Teaching of Psychology*, 4, 138–141.

Vecera, S.P. and Farah, M.J. (1994). Does visual attention select objects or locations? *Journal of Experimental Psychology*, 123, 146–160.

Veljaca, V-A. and Rapee, R.M. (1998). Detection of negative and positive audience behaviours by socially anxious subjects. *Behaviour Research and Therapy*, 36, 311–321.

Venter, A., Lord, C. and Schopler, E. (1992). A follow-up study of high-functioning autistic children. *Journal of Child and Adolescent Psychiatry*, 33, 646–649.

Vernon, P.E. (1989). The nature–nurture problem in creativity. In J.A. Glover, R.R. Ronning and C.R. Reynolds (eds), *Handbook of Creativity*. New York: Plenum.

Vervaeke, G.A.C. and Emmelkamp, P.M.G. (1998). Treatment selection: What do we know? *European Journal of Psychological Assessment*, 14, 1, 50–59.

Vincent, C. and Furnham, A. (1996). Why do patients turn to complementary medicine? An empirical study. *British Journal of Clinical Psychology*, 35, 37–48.

von Békésy, G. (1960). *Experiments in Hearing*. New York: McGraw-Hill.

von Cramon, D. and Kerkhoff, G. (1993). On the cerebral organization of elementary visuospatial perception. In B. Gulyas, D. Ottoson and P.E. Roland (eds), *Functional Organisation of the Human Visual Cortex*. Oxford: Pergamon.

Von Wright, J. M., Anderson, K. and Stenman, U. (1975). Generalization of conditioned GSRs in dichotic listening. In P.M.A. Rabbitt and S. Dornic (eds), *Attention and Performance*, Vol. 5. London: Academic Press.

Vygotsky, L. S. (1987). Thinking and speech. In R.W. Rieber and A.S. Carton (eds), *The Collected Works of L. S. Vygotsky. Vol. 1: Problems of General Psychology* (N. Minick, trans.). New York: Plenum. Original work published in 1934.

Wade, C. and Tavris, C. (1994). The longest war: Gender and culture. In W.J. Lonner and R. Malpass (eds), *Psychology and Culture*. Boston: Allyn & Bacon.

Wade, G.N. and Gray, J.M. (1979). Gonadal effects on food intake and adiposity: A metabolic hypothesis. *Physiology and Behavior*, 22, 583–593.

Wagner, A.D., Schacter, D.L., Rotte, M., Koutsaal, W., Maril, A., Dale, A.M., Rosen, B.R. and Buckner, R.L. (1998). Building memories: Remembering and forgetting of verbal experiences as predicted by brain activity. *Science*, 281, 1188–1191.

Wagner, A.R., Siegal, S., Thomas, E. and Ellison, G.D. (1964). Reinforcement history and the extinction of a conditioned salivary response. *Journal of Comparative and Physiological Psychology*, 58, 354–358.

Wagner, R.K. and Sternberg, R.J. (1985). Executive control of reading, 1983. Cited by Sternberg, R.J. *Beyond IQ: A Triarchic Theory of Human Intelligence*. Cambridge: Cambridge University Press.

Wagstaff, G.F. (1987). Hypnotic induction, hypnotherapy and the placebo effect. *British Journal of Experimental and Clinical Hypnosis*, 4, 168–170.

Wagstaff, G.F. (1991). Compliance, belief and semantics in hypnosis: A nonstate, sociocognitive perspective. In S.J. Lynn and J.H. Rhue (eds), *Theories of Hypnosis: Current models and perspectives*. New York: Guilford.

Wagstaff, G.F. (1993). What expert witnesses can tell courts about hypnosis: A review of the association between hypnosis and the law. *Expert Evidence: The International Digest of Human Behaviour Science and Law*, 2, 60–70.

Wagstaff, G.F. (1996). Methodological issues in hypnosis. In J. Haworth (ed.), *Psychological Research*. London: Routledge.

Wagstaff, G.F. and Royce, C. (1994). Hypnosis and the treatment of nailbiting: A preliminary trial. *Contemporary Hypnosis*, 11, 9–13.

Wakefield, H. and Underwager, R. (1992). Recovered memories of alleged sexual abuse: Lawsuits against parents. *Behavioral Sciences and the Law*, 10, 483–507.

Walker, E. and Lewine, R.J. (1990). Prediction of adult-onset schizophrenia from childhood home movies of the patients. *American Journal of Psychiatry*, 147, 1052–1056.

Walker, L.J. (1989). A longitudinal study of moral reasoning. *Child Development*, 60, 157–166.

Wallach, M. and Kogan, N. (1965). *Modes of Thinking in Young Children*. New York: Holt, Rinehart & Winston.

Wallen, K. (1990). Desire and ability: Hormones and the regulation of female sexual behavior. *Neuroscience and Biobehavioral Reviews*, 14, 233–241.

Wallen, K., Mann, D.R., Davis-DaSilva, M., Gaventa, S., Lovejoy, J.C. and Collins, D. C. (1986). Chronic gonadotropin-releasing hormone agonist treatment suppresses ovulation and sexual behavior in group-living female rhesus monkeys (macaca mulatta). *Animal Behaviour*, 36, 369–375.

Walster, E., Aronson, V., Abrahams, D. and Rottman, L. (1966). Importance of physical attractiveness in dating behavior. *Journal of Personality and Social Psychology*, 4, 508–516.

Wann, D.L. and Dolan, T.J. (1994). Spectators' evaluations of rival and fellow fans. *The Psychological Record*, 44, 351–358.

Ward, I. (1972). Prenatal stress feminizes and demasculinizes the behavior of males. *Science*, 175, 82–84.

Warr, P. (1987). Work, unemployment and mental health. Oxford: Clarendon Press.

Warr, P. (1990). Job control, job demands and employee well being. *Work and Stress*, 4, 285–294.

Warrington, E.K. and James, M. (1967). An experimental investigation of facial recognition in patients with unilateral cerebral lesions. *Cortex*, 3, 317–326.

Warrington, E.K. and Shallice, T. (1980). Word form dyslexia. *Brain*, 103, 99–112.

Warrington, E.K. and Shallice, T. (1984). Category specific semantic impairments. *Brain*, 107, 829–853.

Wason, P. (1968). Reasoning about a rule. *Quarterly Journal of Experimental Psychology*, 20, 273–281.

Wason, P.C. and Johnson-Laird, P.N. (1972). *Psychology of Reasoning: Structure and content*. Cambridge, MA: Harvard University Press.

Waters, E., Wippman, J. and Sroufe, L.A. (1979). Attachment, positive affect, and competence in the peer group: Two studies in construct validation. *Child Development*, 50, 821–829.

Watkins, C.E. (1991). What have surveys taught us about the teaching and practice of psychological assessment? *Journal of Personality Assessment*, 56, 426–437.

Watson, J.B. (1913). Psychology as the behaviorist views it. *Psychological Review*, 20, 158–177.

Watson, J.B. (1919). *Psychology from the Standpoint of a Behaviorist*. Philadelphia: Lippincott.

Watson, J.B. (1930). *Behaviorism*. New York: W.W. Norton.

Watson, J.B. and Rayner, R. (1920). Conditioned emotional reactions. *Journal of Experimental Psychology*, 3, 1–14.

Watson, J.D. (1976). *Molecular Biology of the Gene*. Menlo Park, CA: Benjamin.

Watson, J.S. and Ramey, C.T. (1972). Reactions to responsive contingent stimulation in early infancy. *Merrill–Palmer Quarterly*, 18, 219–227.

Watten, R.G. (1997). Gender and consumption of alcohol: The impact of body composition, sensation seeking and coping styles. *British Journal of Health Psychology*, 2, 15–25.

Waugh, N.C. and Norman, D.A. (1965). Primary memory. *Psychological Review*, 72, 89–104.

Weaver, C.A. (1993). Do you need a 'flash' to form a flashbulb memory? *Journal of Experimental Psychology: General*, 122, 39–46.

Webb, K. and Davey, G.C.L. (1993). Disgust sensitivity and fear of animals: Effect of exposure to violent or revulsive material. *Anxiety, Stress and Coping*, 5, 329–335.

Weeks, S.J. and Hobson, R.P. (1987). The salience of facial expression for autistic children. *Journal of Child Psychology and Psychiatry*, 28, 137–152.

Wegner, D.M. (1989). *White Bears and Other Unwanted Thoughts*. New York: Viking.

Wegner, D.M. (1994). Ironic process of mental control. *Psychological Review*, 101, 34–52.

Wegner, D.M., Schneider, D.J., Carter, S. and White, L. (1987). Paradoxical effects of thought suppression. *Journal of Personality and Social Psychology*, 53, 5–13.

Weigel, R.H., Vernon, D.T.A. and Tognacci, L.N. (1974). Specificity of the attitude as a determinant of attitude–behavior congruence. *Journal of Personality and Social Psychology*, 30, 724–728.

Weiller, E., Bisserbe, J-C., Maier, W. and Lecrubier, Y. (1998). Prevalence and recognition of anxiety syndromes in five European primary care settings. *British Journal of Psychiatry*, 174 (suppl. 34), 18–23.

Weinberger, D.R. (1996). On the plausibility of 'the neurodevelopmental hypothesis' of schizophrenia. *Neuropsychopharmacology*, 14, 1S–11S.

Weinberger, D.R. and Wyatt, J.R. (1982). Brain morphology in schizophrenia: In vivo studies. In F.A. Henn and G.A. Nasrallah (eds), *Schizophrenia as a Brain Disease*. New York: Oxford University Press.

Weinberger, D.R., Bigelow, L.B., Kleinman, J.E., Klein, S.T., Rosenblatt, J.E. and Wyatt, R.J. (1980). Cerebral ventricular enlargement in chronic schizophrenia: An association with poor response to treatment. *Archives of General Psychiatry*, 37, 11–13.

Weinberger, D.R., Berman, K.F., Suddath, R. and Torrey, E.F. (1992). Evidence for dysfunction of a prefrontal-limbic network in schizophrenia: An MRI and rCBF study of discordant monozygotic twins. *American Journal of Psychiatry*, 149, 890–897.

Weiner, B. (1985). An attributional theory of achievement motivation and emotion. *Psychological Review*, 92, 548–573.

Weir, W. (1984). Another look at subliminal 'facts'. *Advertising Age*, 55, 46.

Weisberg, R.W. (1994). Genius and madness? A quasi-experimental test of the hypothesis that manic–depression increases creativity. *Psychological Science*, 5, 6, 361–367.

Weiskrantz, L. (1986). *Blindsight: A case study and implications*. Oxford: Oxford University Press.

Weiskrantz, L. (1997). *Consciousness Lost and Found: A neuropsychological exploration*. Oxford: Oxford University Press.

Weisner, T.S. and Wilson-Mitchell, J.E. (1990). Nonconventional family life-styles and sex typing in six-year-olds. *Child Development*, 61, 1915–1933.

Weiss, J.M. (1968). Effects of coping responses on stress. *Journal of Comparative and Physiological Psychology*, 65, 251–260.

Weitzman, E.D. (1981). Sleep and its disorders. *Annual Review of Neuroscience*, 4, 381–418.

Wells, A. and Matthews, G. (1994). *Attention and Emotion: A clinical perspective*. Hove, UK: Lawrence Erlbaum Associates.

Wells, G.L. and Seelau, E.P. (1995). Eyewitness identification: Psychological research and legal policy on line-ups. *Psychology, Public Policy and Law*, 1, 4, 765–791.

Weltzin, T.E., Hsu, L.K.G., Pollice, C. and Kaye, W.H. (1991). Feeding patterns in bulimia nervosa. *Biological Psychiatry*, 30, 1093–1110.

Werner, H. (1935). Studies on contour. *American Journal of Psychology*, 37, 40–64.

Wernicke, K. (1874). *Der Aphasische Symptomenkomplex*. Breslau, Poland: Cohn and Weigert.

Wertheimer, M. (1912). Experimentelle Studien uber das Sehen von Bewegung. *Zeitschrift der Psychologie*, 61, 161–265.

Wertheimer, M. (1961). Psychomotor co-ordination of auditory–visual space at birth. *Science*, 134, 1692.

West, R., French, D., Kemp, R. and Elander, J. (1993). Direct observation of driving, self-reports of driver behaviour, and accident involvement. *Ergonomics*, 36, 557–567.

West, R.L. (1996). An application of prefrontal cortex function theory to cognitive aging. *Psychological Bulletin*, 120, 272–292.

Westberg, K.L, Archambault, F.X., Dobyns, S.M. and Salvin, T. (1993). The Classroom Practices Observational Study. *Journal for the Education of the Gifted*, 16, 120–146.

Wheeler, R.W., Davidson, R.J. and Tomarken, A.J. (1993). Frontal brain asymmetry and emotional reactivity: A biological substrate of affective style. *Psychophysiology*, 30, 82–89.

White, G.L. (1980). Physical attractiveness and courtship progress. *Journal of Personality and Social Psychology*, 39, 660–668.

White, S., Evans, P., Milhill, C. and Tysoe, M. (1993). *Hitting the headlines: A practical guide to the media*. Leicester: BPS.

Whitehead, R.G., Rowland, M.G.M., Hutton, M., Prentice, A.M., Müller, E. and Paul, A. (1978). Factors influencing lactation performance in rural Gambian mothers. *Lancet*, 2, 178–181.

Whiteman, M.C., Deary, I.J., Lee, A.J. and Fowkes, F.G.R. (1997). Submissiveness and protection from coronary heart disease in the general population: Edinburgh Artery Study. *Lancet*, 350, 541–545.

Whitfield, P. and Stoddart, M. (1985). *Hearing, Taste and Smell: Pathways of perception*. New York: Torstar Books.

Whorf, B. L. (1956). Science and linguistics. In J.B. Carroll (ed.), *Language, Thought and Reality: Selected Writings of Benjamin Lee Whorf*. Cambridge, MA: MIT Press.

Wilcoxon, H.C., Dragoin, W.B. and Kral, P.A. (1971). Illness-induced aversions in rat and quail: Relative salience of visual and gustatory cues. *Science*, 171, 826–828.

Wilhile, S.C. (1991). Evidence of a negative environmental reinstatement effect. *British Journal of Psychology*, 82, 325–342.

Wilkes, K.V. (1988). Information, physics, quantum: The search for links. In W. Zurek (ed.), *Complexity, Entropy and the Physics of Information*. Redwood City, CA: Addison-Wesley.

Williams, J.D., Rippon, G., Stone, B.M. and Annett, J. (1995). Psychophysiological correlates of dynamic imagery. *British Journal of Psychology*, 86, 12, 283–300.

Williams, J.M.G., Watts, F.N., MacLeod, C. and Matthews, A. (1996). *Cognitive Psychology and Emotional Disorders* (2nd edition). Chichester: Wiley.

Williams, K., Harkins, S. and Latané, B. (1981). Identifiability as a deterrent to social loafing: Two cheering experiments. *Journal of Personality and Social Psychology*, 40, 303–311.

Williams, R.B., Hanel, T.L., Lee, K.L. and Kong, Y.H. (1980). Type A behavior, hostility, and coronary atherosclerosis. *Psychosomatic Medicine*, 42, 539–549.

Williams, W., Blythe, T., White, N., Li, J., Sternberg, R.J. and Gardner, H. (1996). *Practical Intelligence for School Handbook*. New York: HarperCollins.

Wilson, B.A. (1991). Long-term prognosis of patients with severe memory disorders. *Neuropsychological Rehabilitation*, 1, 117–134.

Wilson, B.A. and Moffat, N. (1992). *Clinical Management of Memory Problems* (2nd edition). London: Chapman & Hall.

Wilson, B.A. and Powell, G.E. (1994). Neurological problems: Treatment and rehabilitation. In S.J.E. Lindsey and G.E. Powell (eds), *Handbook of Clinical Adult Psychology*. London: Routledge.

Wilson, E.O. (1975). *Sociobiology: The new synthesis*. Cambridge, MA: Harvard University Press.

Wilson, E.O. (1978). *On Human Nature*. Cambridge, MA: Harvard University Press.

Wilson, M. and Daly, M. (1996). Male sexual proprietariness and violence against wives. *Current Directions in Psychological Science*, 5, 2–7.

Winberg, J. and Porter, R.H. (1998). Olfaction and human neonatal behaviour: Clinical implications. *Acta Paediatrica*, 87, 6–10.

Winchester, A.M. (1972). *Genetics: A survey of the principles of heredity*. Boston: Houghton-Mifflin.

Windholz, G. (1997). Ivan P. Pavlov. *American Psychologist*, 52, 9, 941–946.

Winefield, A.H. and Tiggemann, M. (1994). Affective reactions to employment and unemployment as a function of prior expectations and motivation. *Psychological Reports*, 75, 243–247.

Winner, E. (1996). *Gifted Children: Myths and realities*. New York: Basic Books.

Winner, E. (1997). Exceptionally high intelligence and schooling. *American Psychologist*, 52, 10, 1070–1081.

Winograd, E. and Killinger, W.A. (1983). Relating age at encoding in early childhood to adult recall: Development of flashbulb memories. *Journal of Experimental Psychology: General*, 112, 413–422.

Witelson, S.F., Glezer, I.I. and Kigar, D.L. (1985). Women have greater density of neurons in posterior temporal cortex. *Journal of Neuroscience*, 15, 5, 1, 3418–3428.

Woerner, P.L. and Guze, S.B. (1968). A family and marital study of hysteria. *British Journal of Psychiatry*, 114, 161–168.

Wolfe, D.E. (1983). Effects of music loudness on task performance and self-report of college-aged students. *Journal of Research in Music Education*, 31, 191–201.

Wolff, P.H. (1969). Crying and vocalization in early infancy. In B.M. Foss (ed.), *Determinants of Infant Behaviour*, Vol. 4. London: Methuen.

Wolpe, J. (1958). *Psychotherapy by Reciprocal Inhibition*. Stanford, CA: Stanford University Press.

Wood, C. and Cowan, N. (1995). The cocktail party phenomenon revisited: How frequent are attention shifts to one's name in an irrelevant auditory channel? *Journal of Experimental Psychology: Learning, Memory and Cognition*, 21, 255–260.

Woodall, K.L. and Matthews, K.A. (1993). Changes in and stability of hostile characteristics: Results from a 4-year longitudinal study of children. *Journal of Personality and Social Psychology*, 63, 491–499.

Woodman, R.W. and Schoenfeldt, L.F. (1989). Individual differences in creativity: An interactionist perspective. In J.A. Glover, R.R. Ronning and C.R. Reynolds (eds), *Handbook of Creativity*. New York: Plenum.

Woodruff, R.A., Guze, S.B. and Clayton, P.J. (1972). Anxiety neurosis among psychiatric outpatients. *Comprehensive Psychiatry*, 13, 165–170.

Woodruff-Pak, D.S. (1997). *The Neuropsychology of Aging*. Oxford: Blackwell.

Woods, R.T. (1994). Problems in the elderly. In S.J.E. Lindsey and G.E. Powell (eds), *Handbook of Clinical Adult Psychology*. London: Routledge.

Woods, S.W., Charney, D.S., Goodman, W.K. and Heninger, G.R. (1988). Carbon dioxide-induced anxiety. *Archives of General Psychiatry*, 45, 43–52.

Woolley, J.D. (1997). Thinking about fantasy: Are children fundamentally different thinkers and believers from adults? *Child Development*, 68, 6, 991–1011.

Worchel, F.F., Aaron, L.L. and Yates, D.F. (1990). Gender bias on the Thematic Apperception Test. *Journal of Personality Assessment*, 55, 593–602.

World Health Organisation (1979). *Schizophrenia: An international follow-up study*. Geneva: WHO.

World Health Organisation (1983). *Depressive disorders in different cultures: Report of the WHO collaborative study of standardised assessment of depressive disorders*. Geneva: WHO.

World Health Organisation (1992). *The ICD-10 Classification of Mental and Behavioural Disorders- Clinical descriptions and diagnostic guidelines*. Geneva: WHO.

Wright, B.A., Lombardino, L.J., King, W.M., Puranik, C.S., Leonard, C.M. and Merzenich, M.M. (1997). Deficits in auditory temporal and spectral resolution in language-impaired children. *Nature*, 387, 176–178.

Wright, D.B. (1993). Recall of the Hillsborough disaster over time: Systematic biases of 'flashbulb' memories. *Applied Cognitive Psychology*, 7, 129–138.

Wright, D.B., Gaskell, G.D. and O'Muircheartaigh, C.A. (1998). Flashbulb memory assumptions: Using national surveys to explore cognitive phenomena. *British Journal of Psychology*, 89.

Wycherley, R.J. (1995). Self-evaluation and self-reinforcement in depressed patients. *Clinical Psychology and Psychotherapy*, 2, 98–107.

Wynn, V.E. and Logie, R.H. (1998). The veracity of long-term memory: Did Bartlett get it right? *Applied Cognitive Psychology*, 12, 1–20.

Yates, W. R., Perry, P. and Murray, S. (1992). Aggression and hostility in anabolic steroid users. *Biological Psychiatry*, 31, 1232–1234.

Yehuda, S. and Youdim, M.B.H. (1989). Brain iron: a lesson for animal models. *American Journal of Clinical Nutrition*, 50, 618–629.

Young, A., Stokes, M. and Crowe, M. (1984). Size and strength of the quadriceps muscles of old and young women. *European Journal of Clinical Investigation*, 14, 282–287.

Young. A.W., Newcombe, F., deHaan, E.H.F., Small, M. and Hau, D.C. (1993). Face perception after brain injury. *Brain*, 116, 941–959.

Youniss, J. and Smollar, J. (1985). *Adolescent Relations with Mothers, Fathers, and Friends*. Chicago: University of Chicago Press.

Yu, D.W. and Shepard, G.H. (1998). Is beauty in the eye of the beholder? *Nature*, 396, 321–322.

Zaragoza, M.S. and Mitchell, K.J. (1996). Repeated suggestion and the creation of false memories. *Psychological Science*, 7, 294–300.

Zajonc, R.B. (1965). Social facilitation, *Science*, 149, 269–274.

Zajonc, R.B. (1968). Attitudinal effects of mere exposure. *Journal of Personality and Social Psychology*, Monograph Supplement, 9, 1–27.

Zajonc, R.B. (1984). On primacy of affect. In K.R. Scherer and P. Ekman (eds), *Approaches to Emotion*. Hillsdale, NJ: Lawrence Erlbaum Associates.

Zajonc, R.B. (1985). Emotion and facial efference: A theory reclaimed. *Science*, 228, 15–21.

Zatorre, R.J., Evans, A.C., Meyer, E. and Gjedde, A. (1992). Lateralization of phonetic and pitch discrimination in speech processing. *Science*, 256, 846–849.

Zatorre, R.J., Meyer, E., Gjedde, A. and Evans, A.C. (1996). PET studies of phonetic processing of speech – review, replication and reanalysis. *Cerebral Cortex*, 6, 1, 21–30.

Zeanah, C.H., Boris, N.W. and Scheeringa, M.S. (1997). Psychopathology in infancy. *Journal of Child Psychology and Psychiatry*, 38, 1, 81–99.

Zeier, H., Brauchli, P. and Joller-Jemelka, H.I. (1996). Effects of work demands on immunoglobin A and cortisol in air-traffic controllers. *Biological Psychology*, 42, 413–423.

Zeki, S. (1991). *La Recherche*, 21, 712–721.

Zeki, S. (1993). *A Vision of the Brain*. Oxford: Blackwell Scientific.

Zeki, S. (1998). Art and the brain. *Daedalus*, 127, 2, 71–103.

Zeki, S. and ffytche, D.H. (1998). The Riddoch syndrome: Insights into the neurobiology of conscious vision. *Brain*, 121, 25–45.

Zimbardo, P.G. (1970). The human choice: Individuation, reason, and order versus deindividuation, impulse, and chaos. In W.J. Arnold and D. Levine (eds), *Nebraska Symposium on Motivation*. Lincoln: University of Nebraska Press.

Zisook, S., Schuchter, S.R., Irwin, M., Darko, D.F., Sledge, P. and Resovsky, K. (1994). Bereavement, depression and immune function. *Psychiatry Research*, 52, 1–10.

Zola, D. (1984). Redundancy and word perception during reading. *Perception and Psychophysics*, 36, 277–284.

Zorzi, M., Houghton, G. and Butterworth, B. (1998). Two routes or one in reading aloud? A connectionist dual-process model. *Journal of Experimental Psychology: Human Perception and Performance*, 24, 4, 1131–1161.

Zuckerman, M. (1991). *Psychobiology of Personality*. Cambridge: Cambridge University Press.

Zukier, H. and Pepitone, A. (1984). Social roles and strategies in prediction: Some determinants of the use of base-rate information, *Journal of Personality and Social Psychology*, 47, 349–360.

NAME INDEX

SUBJECT INDEX

Note: Page numbers in *italic* type indicate figures; those in **bold** type indicate key concepts